JUDGES
Canada
J	Justice
JA	Justice of Appeal
JJ	Justices
CJ	Chief Justice

United Kingdom
LJ	Lord Justice
MR	Master of the Rolls

CASELAW REPORTERS
Canada
AR	Alberta Reports
BCDLA	British Columbia Decisions, Labour Arbitration
BCLR	British Columbia Law Reports
BLR	Business Law Reports
CBR	Canadian Bankruptcy Reports
CCC	Canadian Criminal Cases
CCEL	Canadian Cases on Employment Law
CCLT	Canadian Cases on the Law of Torts
CELR	Canadian Environmental Law Reports
CPR	Canadian Patent Reporter
CTC	Canada Tax Cases
DLR	Dominion Law Reports
DTC	Dominion Tax Cases
Ex CR	Canada Law Reports: Exchequer Court of Canada
FC	Federal Court Reports
FTR	Federal Trial Reports
LAC	Labour Arbitration Cases
NBR	New Brunswick Reports
Nfld & PEIR	Newfoundland and Prince Edward Island Reports
NSR	Nova Scotia Reports
OLR	Ontario Law Reports
OLRB Rep	Ontario Labour Relations Board Reports
OR	Ontario Reports
OTC	Ontario Trial Cases
OWN	Ontario Weekly Notes
PPSAC	Personal Property Security Act Cases
Sask R	Saskatchewan Reports
SCR	Supreme Court Reports
WWR	Western Weekly Reports

United Kingdom
AC	Appeal Cases
All ER	All England Reports
App Cas	Appeal Cases
Ch D	Chancery Division
ER	English Reports
HL Cas	House of Lords Cases

D1272561

KB	King's Bench
LR	Law Reports
Lloyds Rep	Lloyd's Law Reports
QB	Queen's Bench
WLR	Weekly Law Reports

United States
F	Federal Reporter
F Supp	Federal Supplement
NE	Northeastern Reporter
NY	New York Reports
P	Pacific Reporter
So	Southern Reporter
WL	Westlaw

Quicklaw Databases
BCJ	British Columbia Judgments
OJ	Ontario Judgments
YJ	Yukon Judgments

Australia and New Zealand
CLR	Commonwealth Law Reports
SR (NSW)	State Reports (New South Wales)
Qd R	Queensland Reports

STATUTES
Canada
RRO	Revised Regulations of Ontario
RSC	Revised Statutes of Canada
RSA	Revised Statutes of Alberta
RSBC	Revised Statutes of British Columbia
RSM	Revised Statutes of Manitoba
RSN	Revised Statutes of Newfoundland
RSNB	Revised Statutes of New Brunswick
RSNWT	Revised Statutes Northwest Territories
RSNS	Revised Statutes of Nova Scotia
RSO	Revised Statutes of Ontario
RSPEI	Revised Statutes of Prince Edward Island
RSQ	Revised Statutes of Quebec
RSS	Revised Statutes of Saskatchewan
RSY	Revised Statutes of Yukon
SOR	Statutory Orders and Regulations

United Kingdom
Vict	Victoria
Cha	Charles

United States
USC	United States Code

PERIODICALS
Berkeley Tech LJ	Berkeley Technology Law Journal
Can Bar Rev	Canadian Bar Review
Cornell LQ	Cornell Law Quarterly
Osgoode Hall LJ	Osgoode Hall Law Journal

Managing THE LAW

The Legal Aspects of Doing Business

Second Edition

MITCHELL McINNES
Faculty of Law
University of Alberta

IAN R. KERR
Faculty of Law, Common Law Section
University of Ottawa

J. ANTHONY VanDUZER
Faculty of Law, Common Law Section
University of Ottawa

CHI CARMODY
Faculty of Law
The University of Western Ontario

PEARSON
Prentice
Hall

Toronto

Library and Archives Canada Cataloguing in Publication

Managing the law : the legal aspects of doing business / Mitchell McInnes ... [et al.]. — 2nd ed.

Includes index.

ISBN 0-13-191846-X

1. Commercial law—Canada—Textbooks. I. McInnes, Mitchell

KE919.M35 2007   346.7107   C2005-905726-2   KF889.M35 2007

ISBN 0-13-191846-X

Vice-President, Editorial Director: Michael J. Young
Editor-in-Chief: Gary Bennett
Acquisitions Editor: Laura Paterson Forbes
Marketing Manager: Cas Shields
Developmental Editor: Maurice Esses
Production Editor: Cheryl Jackson
Copy Editor: Ann McInnis
Proofreader: Trish O'Reilly/Gilda Mekler
Production Coordinator: Patricia Ciardullo
Page Layout: Christine Velakis/Gerry Dunn
Art Director: Julia Hall
Cover Image: Getty Images

1 2 3 4 5   11 10 09 08 07

Printed and bound in United States of America.

Alison—for more than words can express; Kate—for her keen legal insights during table talk; Ben—for always using the force; and Sam—for being Sammy.

Erin—"Out of the night/Into the water/We push the boat from the shore/Breaking the air in the stillness of the bay."

Jodie—for her continuing indulgence and support; Taylor and Eli—for their patience with their too often absent father; and Shirley—for being my most enthusiastic fan.

Daphne—with every best wish.

ABOUT THE AUTHORS

Mitchell McInnes, PhD (Cambridge), LLM (Cambridge), LLB (Alberta), BA (Alberta), of the Alberta Bar, Professor

Professor McInnes joined the Faculty of Law at the University of Alberta in 2005. He previously taught at the University of Western Ontario, the University of Melbourne, and Deakin University. He has clerked at the Supreme Court of Canada and served as a Legal Research Officer with the Alberta Court of Appeal.

Professor McInnes' research focuses on Unjust Enrichment, Restitution, Remedies, Trusts, Contract, and Tort. He has published more than 80 papers in leading journals, including the *Canadian Bar Review*, the *University of Toronto Law Journal*, the *Cambridge Law Journal*, and the *Law Quarterly Review*. He is a co-author of three casebooks: *Cases and Materials on the Law of Torts* (Carswell 2003), *Oosterhoff on Trusts: Text, Commentary and Cases on Trusts* (Carswell 2004), and *Cases and Materials on the Law of Restitution* (Emond Montgomery 2004). And he has published two collections of essays on the law of unjust enrichment: *Restitution: Developments in Unjust Enrichment* (Law Book Company 1996) and *Understanding Unjust Enrichment* (Hart 2004). His work has been relied upon by a number of courts, including the Supreme Court of Canada and the High Court of Australia.

While teaching at the University of Western Ontario, Professor McInnes received a number of teaching awards, and he has been recognized by *Maclean's* magazine as one of Canada's leading university teachers.

Ian R. Kerr, PhD (Western), MA (Western), LLB (Western), BA Hons (Alberta), BSc (Alberta), of the Bar of Ontario, Associate Professor

As Canada Research Chair in Ethics, Law, and Technology, Ian Kerr is Canada's leading authority on how legal and ethical issues intersect with electronic commerce. Ian plays a significant role in the development of national and international laws in e-commerce, privacy policy, and digital copyright reform. He has advised various Canadian agencies on legal policy for online activities, and has served as a Canadian delegate to the United Nations' Special Working Group on e-Commerce, a project of the United Nations Commission on International Trade Law. Ian teaches at the Faculty of Law, University of Ottawa, where he co-designed a new graduate program in law and technology. He holds cross-appointments to the Faculty of Medicine and the Department of Philosophy, and has won numerous awards for teaching excellence.

Ian's current research projects include On the Identity Trail, a multi-disciplinary project supported by one of the largest-ever grants from the Social Sciences and Humanities Research Council, which studies the impact of information and authentication technologies on identity and anonymity. He also co-leads An Examination of Digital Copyright, a large private sector grant from Bell Canada and the Ontario Research Network in Electronic Commerce examining the implications of copyright reform on Canadian values including privacy and freedom of expression. With his background in philosophy, technology, and private law, Ian has published numerous articles and papers and has edited and contributed to several books and journals on the legal implications of doing business online, including the *Canadian Business Law Journal* and the *Electronic Commerce Research Journal*. He has also contributed scholarly articles and chapters in several books on a range of other subjects, including cyberspace law, nanotechnology, bioethics, contract law, information ethics, and the philosophy of law, and has lectured world-wide on these topics.

J. Anthony VanDuzer, LLM (Columbia), LLB (Ottawa), BA (Queen's), of the Bar of Ontario, Associate Professor

J. Anthony VanDuzer has taught and practised extensively in the area of corporate and commercial law for more than 20 years. Following five years in private practice, he joined the Faculty of Law at the University of Ottawa. He teaches a variety of advanced business law subjects, for which he has received several teaching awards. He regularly teaches in the University of Ottawa's Executive MBA program and is an Adjunct Research Professor at the Norman Paterson School of International Affairs at Carleton University.

Tony has published over 50 articles and papers on subjects ranging from pharmaceutical patents and health care to corporate law. He has also written several significant books on business law, including *The Law of Partnerships and Corporations*, 2d ed. (Concord: Irwin, 2003); and *Merger Notification in Canada* (with Albert Gourley, Toronto: CCH Canadian, 1994).

Over the past decade, he has often been called on to advise Canadian government agencies and organizations on business and trade law issues. He completed a study for the Canadian Competition Bureau in 1999 on anti-competitive pricing practices. In 2004, a bill amending the *Competition Act* to incorporate many of his recommendations was introduced into Parliament. His study for the Department of Foreign Affairs and International Trade of the impact of the WTO General Agreement on Trade in Services on the delivery of health, education, and social services in Canada was presented to the Standing Committee on Foreign Affairs and International Trade in 2005.

Tony has worked with international development agencies around the world, such as the Canadian International Development Agency and the World Bank, delivering workshops, drafting new laws, and providing other forms of technical assistance to foreign governments on issues related to business and trade. He played a key role in the drafting of the foreign trade law and business registration law, both recently passed by the Russian Duma.

His expertise in international trade law was recognized in 2002, when he was made a member of the Academic Advisory Council to the Deputy Minister for International Trade. Tony is also the Chair of the Centre for Trade Policy and Law, an institute jointly established by the Faculty of Law and the Norman Paterson School of International Affairs and engaged in trade policy research and international technical assistance.

Chi Carmody, SJD (Georgetown), LLM (Michigan), LLB (Ottawa), BJour (California State University, Northridge), BA Hons (Toronto), of the Bars of Ontario and New York, Assistant Professor

Professor Chi Carmody joined the University of Western Ontario Faculty of Law in 1999. Prior to that time he clerked with the Ontario Court of Appeal and was in private practice in Toronto. In early 1999 he interned with the Appellate Body Secretariat of the World Trade Organization.

Chi has written articles in the fields of international law, international trade law, and international business transactions. He was a contributor to, and the general editor of, *Trilateral Perspectives on International Law* (American Society of International Law 2003) and author of a forthcoming book, *A Theory of WTO Law*. Chi has been a visiting professor at Université Montpellier I and Georgetown University Law Center, and an Emile Noël Fellow at New York University Law School. Since 2002 he has also been Canadian Director of the Canada–United States Law Institute.

A Great Way to Learn and Instruct Online

The Pearson Education Canada Companion Website is easy to navigate and is organized to correspond to the chapters in this textbook. Whether you are a student in the classroom or a distance learner you will discover helpful resources for in-depth study and research that empower you in your quest for greater knowledge and maximize your potential for success in the course.

[www.pearsoned.ca/mcinnes]

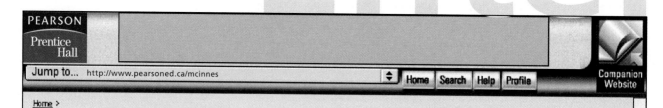

Home >

Companion Website

Managing the Law: The Legal Aspects of Doing Business, Second Edition by McInnes, Kerr, VanDuzer, and Carmody

Student Resources

For each chapter, we provide the following tools for enhancing the learning experience:
- 3 new Cases & Problems (with model answers)
- 25 Self-Test Questions (with instant feedback)
- 1 Internet Exercise
- Web Destinations
- Provincially specific material (on topics listed at the end of each chapter)

Additional Resources

- Chapter 28W: Doing Business in a Global Economy
- Additional Discussion Boxes
- The text of the *Charter of Rights and Freedoms*
- Boilerplate contractual clauses and sample mortgage documents
- Glossary
- CBC Videos

Instructor Resources

Instructors can click on a link on the opening page to visit our online catalogue to download versions of the Instructor's Manual, PowerPoint Slides, and computerized Testbank.

BRIEF CONTENTS

CONTENTS

PREFACE

Managing the Law: The Legal Aspects of Doing Business, Second Edition, aims to equip students with the conceptual tools and intellectual skills to identify, assess, and manage the legal risks that arise in the course of doing business. Students who study this text will be able to achieve the following:

- a basic understanding of the function of law
- a basic understanding of the structure of the Canadian legal system
- a basic understanding of legal sources, concepts, and principles
- a sound understanding of the specific areas of the law that are especially important to business
- the ability to identify legal problems that arise in business contexts
- the ability to formulate reasoned opinions on important socio-legal issues that affect business
- the ability to apply basic legal principles to problems that arise in business contexts
- the ability to critically evaluate legal arguments put forth by others
- the ability to devise arguments and present them persuasively

Training students "to think like lawyers" (to use a favourite phrase of law professors) has long been the main purpose of law courses, even those designed for business students. But although this book provides valuable insight into legal thought processes, we have written this text to address a different primary goal. With *Managing the Law*, we aim to help students learn how "to think like successful business people." The key concept here is **risk management**. Business people should know enough about the law to identify legal issues and arrange their affairs so as to avoid difficulties. Moreover, they should know enough about the law to recognize when it is appropriate to obtain expert advice from the legal profession. Success in the business world often depends on thoughtful delegation.

This book was written with these considerations firmly in mind. As a result, *Managing the Law* differs from other books on the market in two important ways. First, it is a book for business students, not law students. *Managing the Law* provides a thorough and current picture of the legal rules that are relevant in the business world. It does not sacrifice important information for the sake of simplicity. At the same time, however, it does not overwhelm the business student with unnecessary detail or impenetrable jargon. The text is accessible and comprehensible, regardless of the reader's background.

Second, the text's recurring theme is *risk management*. That focus is reflected in both the choice and the presentation of material. Legal topics are chosen for their relevance to the commercial context. Furthermore, they are presented in a manner that fosters the development of effective risk-management skills. Through the extensive use of discussion boxes, review exercises, cases and problems, video cases, and the like, the text draws students into the business-law world and requires them to actively resolve practical problems. Sometimes, of course, the proper resolution of a problem involves recognition of the need for a lawyer's assistance.

Business students, like Canadians in general, are an increasingly diverse group. They come from a variety of backgrounds in terms of personal characteristics, past qualifications, and professional aspirations. Some are new Canadians; others have long-established roots. Some are embarking on post-secondary education for the first time; others are engaged in advanced degrees. Some have little experience in the business world; others are retraining after successful careers. Some are seeking a generalized education; others are more focused on a particular career. This book is appropriate for them all.

Law texts are invariably dense and uninviting, not only in substance and language but also in appearance. By extension, business law texts often suffer the same flaw. In contrast, *Managing the Law* has been specifically designed with the full breadth of its target audience in mind. It is visually engaging. Its use of colour, boxes, icons, figures, and layout draws readers in and provides them with room to breathe intellectually.

Managing the Law has also been designed for use in any course that deals with legal issues in a "business context" (using that phrase broadly). Consequently, without limiting its scope, it is appropriate for students who are studying the legal aspects of any of the following areas:

- accounting
- business administration
- commerce
- finance
- management
- marketing
- office administration

ORGANIZATION

This text is divided into nine parts.

Part 1 (Introduction to Law) consists of two chapters. The first chapter, dealing with risk management and sources of law, opens with an explanation of why business people should study law. In doing so, it explains the core concept of risk management. The chapter then sketches the essential features of the Canadian legal system, including:

- the nature of law
- branches of law
- sources of law

The second chapter, dealing with litigation and alternative dispute resolution, explains various mechanisms for the resolution of legal disputes:

- the litigation process
- the court system
- alternative dispute resolution

Part 2 (Torts) is divided into four chapters. The focus throughout is on risk management in the business context. Here we introduce such key concepts as vicarious liability and liability insurance. And we examine business torts such as nuisance and defamation. The final chapter, which deals with the tort of negligence, places special emphasis on professional negligence as it arises in commercial matters.

Part 3 (Contracts) consists of 8 chapters dealing at length with the central concept of contract. Because of the significance of enforceable agreements in the commercial context, separate chapters are devoted to each of the following:

- formation of contracts
- consideration and privity

- terms and representations
- contractual defects
- discharge and breach
- remedies

The final chapters of Part 3 focus on two particularly important types of contracts:

- sales of goods
- negotiable instruments

Part 4 (Property) consists of three chapters on the law of property. The discussion, as always, places the reader at the heart of practical business-law problems. The examination of personal property, for instance, centres on the institution of bailment and the means by which various forms of insurance can be used to manage legal risks.

Part 5 (Business Law in the Digital Age), consisting of two chapters, is special. It provides an unprecedented introduction to business law in the digital age. In separate chapters, it deals with:

- knowledge-based businesses and intellectual property rights
- electronic commerce

Part 6 (Business Organizations) deals with various types of business organizations. Its opening chapter examines agency relationships, joint ventures, and franchises. The following two chapters are devoted to sole proprietorships, partnerships, and corporations. The principles of risk management are highlighted throughout.

Part 7 (Practical Business Decisions) addresses specific decisions that affect business. Its two chapters focus on issues arising from:

- secured transactions
- bankruptcy and insolvency

Part 8 (Government Regulation of Business) moves the discussion out of the purely private realm and into the world of public regulation and international relations. Its one chapter examines the various means by which Canadian governments regulate commercial conduct. It considers, for example, competition law, consumer protections laws, and environmental protection laws.

Part 9 (Employment and Labour Law) is divided into two chapters. The first focuses on individual employment. Risk management issues are highlighted at all stages of the employee/employer relationship, ranging from pre-employment matters (such as advertising and hiring) to post-employment matters (such as dismissal and severance packages). The second chapter focuses on organized labour. It includes a discussion of collective agreements, grievances, and industrial conflicts.

Taken together, these nine parts provide a thorough examination of the legal issues that generally affect Canadian businesses. At the same time, we have organized the material to offer instructors the utmost flexibility in matching the book to their course designs. We recognize that time is usually tight in business law courses. Therefore, we have adopted a modular approach in organizing the material. After covering the introductory Chapters 1 and 2, instructors can feel free to cover the remaining units and chapters in the order that best suits their needs.

FEATURES

Students will learn effectively when they are interested, enthusiastic, and engaged. Therefore, we have designed this text to encourage students to participate actively, rather than merely read passively. The following features help to make the materials accessible and stimulating.

Objectives—Each chapter opens with a list of 10 Objectives that stress key issues and highlight risk-management skills that students should aim to develop. By providing a roadmap at the beginning of each chapter, the Objectives help students to read and understand the material more efficiently and more effectively.

Key Terms—Key terms are boldfaced where they are defined in the body of the text. They are also restated with their definitions in the margins.

Discussion Boxes—The chapters include four distinct types of Discussion Boxes. These Boxes provide instructors with additional opportunities to stimulate critical thinking and engage students in classroom debate. With the exception of the *Case Briefs*, virtually every Discussion Box ends with *Questions for Discussion*. (Model answers appear in the *Instructor's Resource Manual*.) Each type of box fulfils a particular pedagogical goal.

- **Case Briefs** illustrate how the courts have formulated and applied legal rules in specific business contexts. They also introduce students to many of the leading cases in the common law system.

- **Business Decision** boxes ask students to respond as business people to common legal problems. These boxes are designed to foster the development of sound commercial judgment. Accordingly, they focus less on purely legal concepts and more on practical matters that influence decisions in the commercial world.

- **You Be the Judge** boxes ask students to respond as judges to legal problems that commonly arise in the business world. They are designed to give students insight into legal thought processes.

- **Ethical Perspective** boxes ask students to assess morally contentious business-law scenarios. They compel students to place both business considerations and legal concerns into a larger social context, and to develop an appreciation of the fact that alternative solutions often pull in different directions. The Ethical Perspective boxes are particularly effectively in generating classroom discussions.

Concept Summaries—Every chapter contains at least one Concept Summary; most contain two, three, or more. Presented in tabular form, the Concept Summaries provide succinct and easily understood reviews of difficult concepts and rules. They are often used to compare and contrast related areas of law.

Figures—Most chapters contain at least one figure. Many contain considerably more. Diagrams and drawings are used to illustrate and clarify important concepts. Aside from their inherent pedagogic value, the figures contribute to the visual appeal of the book and therefore draw students further into the material.

Chapter Summaries—Each chapter ends with a Chapter Summary that briefly reviews the important concepts of the chapter. These summaries help prepare students for the end-of-chapter exercises.

Review Questions—20 Review Questions appear at the end of each chapter. In some instances, students are required to define and explain key concepts and terms. In others, they are asked to respond to short problems. The Review

REVIEW QUESTIONS

1. Under what federal and provincial powers is business regulated in Canada?
2. How is a conflict between federal and provincial law resolved in Canada?
3. Name two business-related subjects under federal

CASES AND PROBLEMS

1. Seymour is a supplier of custodial cleaning products. While negotiating a contract to sell a crate of floor wax, Seymour makes the statements below. Categorize each statement as (i) a pre-contractual representation, (ii) a mere opinion, (iii) a contractual term, or (iv) a collateral contract. Give reasons

CANADIAN CASE STUDY FOR PART

McTort: Fast Foods and Tort Law

In many ways, Janice Foster is a typical 16-year-old Canadian. Like many people her age, she enjoys eating fast foods, especially at McDonald's restaurants. The problem is that she eats there too often. In an average week, she will eat ten meals at McDonald's—some for breakfast, some for lunch, most for dinner. Perhaps not surprisingly, Janice shares one other trait. Janice Foster certainly hopes so. McDonald's. She claims that a steady diet of made her obese. She also says that, until her for the evidence, she had no idea that fast dangerous. In one U.S. case, the judge described McNuggets as a "McFrankenstein" creation cals, and additives. The same judge also

WEBLINKS

Intellectual Capital—Industry Canada   http://strategis.ic.gc.ca/ SSG/pi00004e.html
This website provides information on current developments and intellectual capital through links to journal articles, research papers, and interviews.

ADDITIONAL RESOURCES FOR ON THE COMPANION WEBSITE

(www.pearsoned.ca/mcinnes)

In addition to self-test multiple-choice, true-false, and sh with immediate feedback), three additional Cases and gested answers), and links to useful Web destinations, t provides the following resources for Chapter 2:

- Sample Contingency Fee Agreement
- Sample Arbitration Clause
- Weblinks to information on the provincial small cla

Provincial Material

- **British Columbia:** Court Structure in British Colum

Questions can be discussed in class or assigned to students for independent study. (Model answers are provided in the *Instructor's Resource Manual*.)

Cases and Problems—Each chapter concludes with 12 Cases and Problems (with the exception of the first and second chapters, which contain six), at least three of which are new to this edition. The exercises vary in both length and difficulty. They are ideally suited to classroom discussion, but they too can be assigned to students for independent study. (Model answers are provided in the *Instructor's Resource Manual*.)

Canadian Case Studies—A special Canadian Case Study, associated with a CBC video segment, is provided at the end of each of Parts 1, 2, 5, 8, and 9. These Canadian Case Studies have been designed so that they can be completed even without viewing the accompanying videos. (The videos are available to instructors on cassettes or DVDs. They are also available online to students.) With or without the videos, these cases readily lend themselves to classroom discussion. (Model answers are provided in the *Instructor's Resource Manual*.)

Annotated Weblinks—Most chapters conclude with a list of annotated Weblinks, grouped by topic, that make it easier for students to further explore selected legal issues.

Additional Resources Online—A listing at the end of each chapter describes the additional resources for the chapter that are provided on the Companion Website. These resources include self-test questions (with immediate feedback), three additional Problems and Cases (with model answers), some additional Discussion Boxes (with model answers), sample documents, and provincially specific material. For a more complete description, please see the section below titled Supplements.

NEW TO THIS EDITION

While retaining the strengths of the first edition of *Managing the Law*, this second edition introduces several important changes. Some changes are structural; others are substantive.

Risk Management—The focus on the management of legal risks has been sharpened throughout the book.

Organization—The structure of the book has been simplified and substantially modified.

- **Levels**—To increase the possibilities for modular teaching, the levels of organization have been reduced from three (Parts, Units, and Chapters) to two (Parts and Chapters).

- **Introduction**—Part 1 (Introduction to Law) now consists of two chapters, rather than one. Chapter 1 is devoted exclusively to risk management and sources of law. Chapter 2, which is almost entirely new, examines litigation and alternative dispute resolution in depth.

- **Torts and Contracts**—Reflecting the approach of most instructors, Part 2 (Torts) and Part 3 (Contracts) have been re-ordered, so that the chapters on torts now appear before those on contracts.

- **Torts**—Part 2 (Torts) now consists of four chapters, rather than three. Introduction to Torts and Intentional Torts now comprise separate chapters (namely, Chapters 3 and 4).

- **Agency**—The material on agency has been moved to form the new Chapter 20. It now opens, rather than closes, Part 6 (Business Organizations).

- **Doing Business in a Global Economy**—The chapter on international trade (the new Chapter 28W) has been updated, removed from the book, and posted on the Companion Website.

Electronic Commerce—Chapter 19 has been substantially revised to reflect changing ways in which technology affects today's commerce.

Tax—New to this edition, the issue of taxation is addressed in Chapter 21 on Business Organizations and in Chapter 25 on Government Regulation of Business.

Concept Summaries—In response to the overwhelmingly favourable reaction to their inclusion in the first edition, the number of Concept Summaries has been increased significantly in the new edition.

Testbank—The TestGen (*i.e.,* the computerized testbank) has been increased in size by 25 percent. The total number of questions now exceeds 1900.

Companion Website—The Companion Website has been substantially revised and enlarged, as described below under Supplements.

SUPPLEMENTS

Companion Website (www.pearsoned.ca/mcinnes)
As mentioned above, we have created a new robust Companion Website for the second edition of the book. This protected website is designed for students and instructors. It includes the following material:

- **Chapter 28W: Doing Business in a Global Economy**, an earlier version of which appeared in the first edition of the book.
  - 25 **Self-Test Questions** for each chapter, consisting of
  - 15 multiple-choice questions
  - 10 true/false questions
  - 5 short essay questions.

  Students can try the questions, send the answers to the electronic grader, and receive instant feedback. The feedback consists of
  - the correct answer
  - the relevant page number in the textbook
  - a difficulty level (*i.e.,* Easy, Moderate, or Challenging)

  None of these questions duplicate those found in the Testbank.

- One **Internet Exercise** for each chapter that requires students to use their computer-research skills to analyze and resolve a business law problem.
- Three **Cases and Problems** for each chapter, of the type found at the end of each chapter in the book, along with instantly accessible model answers.
- **Provincially specific material** relating to topics in each chapter. This material is aimed at the following four regions of the country:
  - British Columbia
  - Alberta
  - Manitoba/Saskatchewan
  - Ontario
- **Additional materials** relating to the chapter, such as
  - additional Discussion Boxes
  - the text of the *Charter of Rights and Freedoms*
  - sample forms, such as boilerplate contractual clause, and mortgage documents.

Instructor's Resource CD-ROM
We have also carefully prepared an Instructor's Resource CD-ROM to aid instructors in presenting lectures, fostering class discussion, and administering examinations. It contains the following items:

- **Instructor's Resource Manual**—The Instructor's Resource Manual is designed to enhance the organization and presentation of course materials. It includes model answers for all of the questions that appear in the *Discussion Boxes*, *Review Questions*, and *Cases & Problems*. Where appropriate, the answers also explain the pedagogic purpose of their associated questions. The Manual also provides case briefs for every judicial decision that is mentioned in the text or its footnotes. In addition, the Manual includes teaching tips and suggestions that instructors might find useful in tailoring the materials in the textbook for their students.

- **Testbank (Pearson TestGen)**—As mentioned in the preceding section, we have enlarged the testbank by 25 percent so that it now provides nearly 2000 questions that can be used for tests and examinations. For each chapter, the testbank consists of
  - 40 multiple-choice questions
  - 15 true/false questions
  - 15 short essay questions

  Each question is accompanied by
  - a model answer
  - the relevant page number in the textbook
  - the skill required (*i.e.,* recall or applied)
  - a level of difficulty (*i.e.,* 1 for Easy, 2 for Moderate, and 3 for Challenging)

  The entire testbank is presented in Pearson TestGen, a special computerized program that enables instructors to view and edit the testbank questions, generate tests, and print the tests in a variety of formats. Powerful search and sort functions make it easy to locate questions and arrange them in any order desired. TestGen also enables instructors to administer tests on a local area network, have the tests graded electronically, and have the results prepared in electronic or printed reports. Pearson TestGen is compatible with IBM or Macintosh systems.

- **PowerPoint Slides** for each chapter that can be used in electronic form to present materials in class or in printed form to guide the preparation of new lecture notes.

- An electronic **Image Library** that consists of all the figures and Concept Summary boxes in the textbook.

CBC/Pearson Education Canada Video Library for Business Law

The CBC and Pearson Education Canada have combined their expertise in educational publishing and global reporting to create a special video ancillary to the text. The library consists of five video segments from the CBC programs *The National* and *Venture*. Each segment has been chosen to supplement a Canadian Case Study in the book. These videos are also available on DVDs for instructors and online for viewing by students on their own.

Instructors can also download most of these items separately from our online catalogue (http://vig.pearsoned.ca).

Course Management Systems

Pearson Education Canada supports instructors interested in using online course management systems. We provide text-related content in WebCT, Blackboard, and our own private label version of Blackboard called CourseCompass. To find out more about creating an online course using Pearson content in one of these platforms, contact your local Pearson Education Canada representative.

ACKNOWLEDGMENTS

The focus, content, and style of this book reflect the comments—often challenging and always insightful—that we received from external reviewers. We are grateful to each of the following for providing formal reviews of parts part of the manuscript:

Bruce Anderson (Saint Mary's University)
Travis K Beauchemin (University of Regina)
Craig Dyer (Red River College)
Barbara H Eccles (Lakehead University)
Ronald Gallagher (New Brunswick Community College)
R William Hooker (British Columbia Institute of Technology)
Murray Kernaghan (Assiniboine College)
Donna Koziak (Athabasca University)
Avner Levin (Ryerson University)
Joseph G Lucchetti (Sault College of Applied Arts and Technology)
Shelley McGill (Wilfrid Laurier University)
Emir A C Mohammed (University of Toronto)
Douglas H Peterson (University of Alberta)
Manfred S Schneider (University of Toronto)
Martha Spence (Confederation College)
Judith C Sidolfsky Stoffman (University of Guelph)
Brian Sugg (Douglas College)
Jerome A. Tholl (University of Regina)
Kenneth Wm Thornicroft (University of Victoria)

We owe special thanks to Brian Sugg, of Douglas College, for his remarkably thorough and insightful comments on much of the manuscript.

We also wish to thank a number of other people who were instrumental in the production of this book.

Several members of Pearson Education's team made vital contributions. Maurice Esses expertly guided the work through its various stages of development. Cheryl Jackson efficiently guided the book through production. Michael Young provided vision. And Gary Bennett brought tremendous enthusiasm to his role as Acquisitions Editor.

The Faculties of Law at the University of Western Ontario, the University of Ottawa, and the University of Alberta each provided a stimulating and supportive environment in which to work.

A number of students at these institutions served as research assistants: Goldie Bassie, Marcus Bornfreund, Robert Gazdag, Heather Gray, Vanessa Gruben, Greg Hagen, Brett Harrison, John Hoben, Nikiforos Iatrou, Carole Johnson, Cherolyn Knapp, Kathryn Kirkpatrick, Corey Levin, Todd Mandel, Trevor McGowan, Michelle McLean, Bernard Sandler, Linda Smits, Katie Warfield, and Hilary Young.

Our special thanks go to Mysty Clapton (now a Professor at the University of Western Ontario), who was integrally involved in the entire first edition and whose editorial contributions as a research assistant were truly inestimable. Special thanks as well to Alex Cameron (a doctoral candidate in the law and technology program at University of Ottawa) for his excellent work on the second edition.

And finally, special thanks for Alison Hughes for preparing the Canadian Case Studies, and for updating TestGen and the Self-Test Questions on the Companion Website.

Mitchell McInnes
Ian Kerr
Tony VanDuzer
Chi Carmody

TABLE OF STATUTES

TABLE OF CASES

1 Risk Management and Sources of Law

OBJECTIVES

After completing this chapter, you should be able to:

1. Explain why it is important for business people to study law.

2. List four basic strategies for managing risks.

3. List three strategies for risk management that businesses often use in different situations.

4. Provide a general definition of the word "law."

5. List four areas of public law and three areas of private law. Provide examples that demonstrate how each one of those areas is relevant to business people.

6. Outline one way in which tort and contract law are similar and two ways in which they are different.

7. Explain how federalism is related to the division of powers.

8. Describe the *Canadian Charter of Rights and Freedoms* and provide several examples of how it can help or hurt a business.

9. Explain two meanings of the term "civil law" and three meanings of the term "common law."

10. Explain the historical development of equity. Briefly explain the relationship between law and equity today.

Law is essential to any society. It both reflects and shapes the ways in which people interact. As we will see in this textbook, it can affect a person even before birth (can you sue someone for injuries that you suffered as a fetus?) and even after death (what happens to your property after you are gone?). It also governs the most important issues that arise in between: the freedom to choose how to live, the right to marry, the ability to care for children, the obligation to pay taxes, and so on.

The law, not surprisingly, is an enormous subject. As a whole, it cannot be studied in a single course. Indeed, as a whole, it cannot be mastered in an entire lifetime. Therefore, we have to make choices. We must examine some topics and leave others to the side. To a large extent, those choices depend upon our reason for studying law in the first place.

WHY STUDY LAW?

We therefore begin with the obvious question. Why study law? The answer depends upon who you are. As consumers, we all need to be aware of the rules that govern commercial transactions. In terms of employment, you may intend to work in the public sector. If so, you need to understand not only the nature of government organizations, but also the different types of laws that may affect you. Chances are, however, that you are a business student. And as you know, businesses exist primarily to make money. The goal is to maximize gains and minimize losses. Of course, there are many factors in that equation: hard work, natural talent, good luck, and so on. But for the most part, success and failure are the results of choices. A business must choose, for example, a product, a price, a location, and a marketing strategy. And every one of those *business* choices has *legal* consequences. Some consequences are profitable; others are financially disastrous. The difference between winning and losing in the business world often depends upon the ability to make the right choices from a legal perspective. That fact suggests, in general terms, both *why* you should study law and *which* parts of the law you should study.

It is important to realize that the law can both hurt *and* help. Many people think of laws only in terms of prohibitions and punishments. For example, if you break the rule against murder, you may be sent to jail. But the law can also allow you to do things that you could not otherwise do. Generally speaking, for instance, I am entitled to ignore my promises. I can stay home and read even if I agreed to meet you at the movies. Beyond the fear of making you angry, there is nothing that compels me to keep my word. In the business world, however, that sort of behaviour simply cannot be tolerated. If I promise to provide materials to your factory, you may act on the assumption that I will deliver. For instance, you may hire extra staff or promise to re-sell the materials to someone else. You therefore need some way of holding me to my word. Your best bet is to persuade me to enter into a *contract*. As we will see in a later chapter, a contract is a legal concept that allows people to create *enforceable* promises. In that situation, you would not have to worry (as much) that I might ignore my promise.

Risk Management

Throughout this book, we will see a number of other ways in which businesses can positively benefit from the law. Much more often, however, we will be concerned about avoiding losses. The main theme of our discussion is that legal education plays a critical role in *risk management*. **Risk management** is the process of identifying, evaluating, and responding to the possibility of harmful events. Business Decision 1.1 provides a simple example.

risk management is the process of identifying, evaluating, and responding to the possibility of harmful events

BUSINESS DECISION 1.1

Risk Management

One of your ex-employees is hoping to join another company. She has asked you to write a reference letter on her behalf. She obviously does not know that you have a very low opinion of her, largely because you believe that she stole money from your business. Furthermore, since the company that she wants to join is one of your best customers, you are tempted to write a candid letter.

Question for Discussion

1. Will you write a reference for your ex-employee? If so, what will it say?

Unless you know something about the law of torts, you are not in a position to answer those questions properly. You need to identify, evaluate, and respond to the legal risks involved.

- **Identification:** If you accuse your ex-employee of theft, she may sue you for defamation because your statement would cause a reasonable person to think less of her. You need to be concerned about *liability*, about actually being held legally responsible. But you also need to be concerned about the possibility of being sued. As we will see in the next chapter, litigation is time-consuming and expensive, even when you win.

- **Evaluation:** Having identified the risk of being sued for defamation, you may decide that a candid letter would nevertheless be legally acceptable. Your allegations may be true. Even if they are not, you may be justified in sharing your suspicions with the other company. Furthermore, you may believe that the arguments in your favour are strong enough to discourage your former employee from suing you.

- **Response:** Finally, having identified and evaluated the risks, you need to formulate a response. You have several options. You can refuse to write a letter. You can write a letter that does not mention your suspicions. Or you can write a letter that accuses your former employee of theft. The choice is still yours. Significantly, however, you are now in a position to make an informed decision. A basic understanding of the law makes you a better business person.

Notice that we are talking about risk *management*. There are potential costs associated with nearly every form of behaviour, and that includes doing nothing at all. A business probably cannot exist, and certainly cannot profit, unless it is willing to take some chances. The goal therefore is not necessarily to eliminate risks; it is to *manage* them. The appropriate strategy depends upon the circumstances.

- **Risk avoidance:** Some risks are so serious that they should be avoided altogether. An automobile that regularly explodes upon impact should be removed from the market. Aside from issues of morality, the financial costs of being held liable will probably outweigh any sales profits.[1]

- **Risk reduction:** Some risks can be reduced to an acceptable level through precautions. For example, a bank that lends $500 000 to a manufacturer realizes that the loan may not be repaid if the economy goes into recession. The bank can, however, protect itself by requiring the business to grant a *mortgage* over its factory. In that case, if the bank does not get its money, it may at least get the property.

[1.] *Grimshaw v Ford Motor Co* 119 Cal App (3d) 757 (1981).

- **Risk shifting:** Even if a risk cannot be avoided or reduced, it may be shifted onto another party. We will very shortly introduce two exceptionally important strategies for shifting risks: *insurance* and *exclusion clauses*. There are others. Suppose, for example, that a construction company requires the temporary use of a crane. It has two options. First, it may rent a crane and have it operated by one of its own employees. Second, it may rent a crane and hire an *independent contractor* to operate it.[2] An independent contractor is a person who performs services on behalf of a company, but who is not a regular employee of that company. Although it is often difficult to distinguish between an employee and an independent contractor, there is a crucial difference in terms of risk management. Suppose that the crane is carelessly operated in a way that injures a bystander. The bystander will certainly be able to sue the person who was actually in control of the equipment. Furthermore, if that person was an employee, then the bystander will also be entitled to sue the company. Even if it did not do anything wrong, a company is *vicariously liable* for the actions of its employees.[3] A company is not, however, vicariously liable for an independent contractor. In some situations, it is therefore prudent to have work done by an independent contractor, rather than an employee.

- **Risk acceptance:** It is sometimes appropriate to simply accept a risk. Imagine a golf course that operates behind a factory. It is possible that a wild shot might hit a factory window, and that the golf course could be held responsible for the resulting damage. Nevertheless, if the likelihood of such an accident is small, the club might decide to do nothing at all. It certainly would not close the course to avoid the risk altogether. It might also find that the costs of reducing the risk by erecting a large safety net, or shifting the risk by buying an insurance policy, are too high. The most sensible approach might be to hope for the best and pay for any windows that are broken.

As we have seen, it sometimes is possible to deal with individual problems as they arise. Some of the most effective forms of risk management, however, apply more broadly. We will discuss those strategies in greater detail in later chapters. At this point, it is enough to simply introduce three important concepts.

- **Insurance:** Insurance is a contract in which one party agrees, in exchange for a price, to pay a certain amount of money if another party suffers a loss. There are many types of insurance. For now, we will mention two. Liability insurance provides a benefit if the purchaser is held liable for doing something wrong.[4] Property insurance provides a benefit if the purchaser's property is damaged, lost, or destroyed.[5] In either situation, insurance shifts the risk. For instance, while millions of Canadians buy liability insurance every year, only a fraction are actually

---

[2.] We will examine the difference between employees and independent contractors in Chapters 3 and 26.

[3.] We will examine the doctrine of vicarious liability in Chapter 3.

[4.] Liability insurance also creates a *duty to defend*. That means that the insurance company is responsible for the expenses associated with the lawsuit against the insured party. We will examine liability insurance in Chapter 3.

[5.] We will examine property insurance in Chapter 17.

sued. Insurance works by spreading the cost of that liability over the entire group.

- **Exclusion clauses:** Many businesses make money by selling goods or services. Those sales are created by contracts. And those contracts very often contain exclusion clauses.[6] An exclusion clause is a contractual term that changes the usual rules of liability. For instance, a courier company may provide notice that it will not be held liable for more than $100 if a package is lost, damaged, or destroyed. Or a company that rents all-terrain vehicles may require customers to sign a contract that prevents them from suing for injuries. While exclusion clauses are subject to certain rules and restrictions, the law generally allows people to sign away their right to sue.

- **Incorporation:** There are many ways to carry on business. If an individual chooses to simply act in a personal capacity, then he or she may be held personally liable if something goes wrong. To avoid that risk, many businesses are set up as corporations or companies.[7] The most significant benefit of incorporation is limited liability. That means that if something goes wrong, it is usually only the company itself, and not the people who run it, that may be held liable. The company may be lost, but the people behind it will be safe.

Risk management does not require you to become a lawyer. It may, however, require you to hire a lawyer. As a business person, you need to know enough about the law to recognize potential problems. In some situations, you will be able to resolve those problems yourself, preferably by taking steps to avoid them in the first place. But in other situations, it makes sense to call in an expert. Although lawyers' fees can be quite high, you may end up paying much more in the long run if you do not seek professional advice at the outset. Compared to the cost of losing a lawsuit or watching a deal collapse, a lawyer's bill is often a bargain. In fact, many businesses have *in-house counsel*. Instead of hiring lawyers from time to time as the need arises, a company may create its own permanent legal department. While that option creates an additional expense, it also provides more efficient risk protection. Lawyers will be on hand not only to resolve legal problems, but also to help identify them.

AN INTRODUCTION TO THE LEGAL SYSTEM

In the chapters that follow, we will examine various areas of law, including tort, contract, and property. But first, we must discuss the Canadian legal system as a whole. We can do so quite quickly. While it is important for business people to understand the basic structure of the courts, for instance, most of the details can be left to the lawyers.

The Nature of Law

What are laws? Most people would say that they are rules. That may be true, but it is also clear that not every rule is a law. Sometimes that point is obvious.

[6.] We will examine exclusion clauses in Chapters 9 and 12.

[7.] We will examine corporations, and others ways of carrying on business, in Chapter 21.

For example, there is a rule against moving a bishop horizontally across a chess board, but there certainly is not any law to that effect. Sometimes, however, it is much more difficult to determine whether a rule is also a law. Consider Ethical Perspective 1.1.

ETHICAL PERSPECTIVE 1.1

Rules and Laws

While fishing from a lakeshore, I saw a canoeist tip his boat and fall into the water. Although he screamed for help for over 20 minutes, I did nothing at all. My motor boat was nearby, and I could have easily rescued him, but I preferred to continue fishing. Was there any rule that required me to get involved? Assuming that the canoeist drowned, can I be held legally responsible?

Most people would agree that I was required to rescue the canoeist, especially since I could have done so safely and easily. However, that rule may exist only in *morality*, and not in *law*. According to an old American case, I could not be held legally responsible even if I had rented the boat to the deceased when I knew that he was drunk.[8] A Canadian court would undoubtedly decide otherwise in the same circumstances today.[9] But if I did not have a business relationship with the canoeist, the answer would be less clear. The courts traditionally drew a distinction between moral obligations and legal obligations, and generally said that there was no duty to rescue in law. Recently, however, Canadian judges have begun to adopt a different attitude. Consequently, while we now know that there is sometimes both a moral duty *and* a legal duty to rescue, we do not know exactly when that is true.

Questions for Discussion

1. How would you, as a business person, decide when to follow a moral rule, even if you were not obligated to do so by a legal rule?

2. Does your answer depend entirely upon morality? Are there also important business consequences to acting morally or immorally?

Ethical Perspective 1.1 demonstrates that it is occasionally difficult to distinguish between moral obligations and legal obligations. However, it also points us toward a workable definition of the word "law." Although philosophers have debated the issue for thousands of years, it is sufficient for our purposes to say that a **law** is a rule that can be enforced by the courts. If I merely broke a moral obligation by refusing to rescue the canoeist, then I might be punished, but only through public opinion. Colleagues might stop talking to me, and newspapers might print unflattering articles. However, if I also broke a legal obligation, then I would have more serious things on my mind. Depending on the precise nature of the legal obligation, a court might decide to put me in jail or require me to compensate the victim's family for his death.

Of course, moral issues may arise even if a rule is identified as a law. For instance, as a clothing manufacturer, you may be legally entitled to reduce production costs by using child labour in developing nations. If so, you may be faced with a difficult choice as between your heart and your wallet. The Ethical Perspective boxes throughout this book provide many more examples.

a law is a rule that can be enforced by the courts

A Map of the Law

Even after it has been distinguished from other types of rules, the law remains an enormous topic. To make sense of it all, we need to organize it into different parts. There are many ways of doing so. In Canada, for example, it is necessary

---

[8.] *Osterlind v Hill* 160 NE 301 (Mass 1928).

[9.] *Crocker v Sundance Northwest Resorts Ltd* (1988) 51 DLR (4th) 321 (SCC). That case is discussed in Chapter 6 (Case Brief 6.5 on p. 138).

to distinguish between *civil law* and *common law*.[10] **Civil law** systems trace their history to ancient Rome. Since the Roman Empire covered almost all of Europe, the legal systems of the vast majority of countries in that continent are still *civilian*. The only civil law *jurisdiction* in Canada, however, is Quebec, which initially borrowed its law from France. (Although it has many different meanings, **jurisdiction** in this situation refers to a geographical area that uses the same set of laws.) **Common law** systems trace their history to England. Consequently, most jurisdictions that were settled by English colonists continue to use the common law. That is true of the rest of Canada, as well as jurisdictions like Australia, New Zealand, and most of the United States.[11] Since there are significant differences between civil law systems and common law systems, there are also significant differences between the laws that apply in Quebec and the laws that apply in the rest of this country.[12] It is for that reason that we will focus on Canadian laws that apply outside of Quebec. At the same time, however, it is important to recognize that some types of laws are the same across the entire country. That is true, for example, of criminal laws and constitutional laws. We will therefore occasionally look at cases from Quebec.

Within Canada's common law system, we can further organize legal rules on the basis of the topics that they address. Although it does not cover every possibility, Figure 1.1 (see p. 8) represents some of the most important areas that we will discuss in this book.

Public Law

Figure 1.1 (see p. 8) shows that the major division is between *public law* and *private law*. **Public law** is concerned with governments and the ways in which they deal with their citizens. It includes:

- constitutional law
- administrative law
- criminal law
- tax law

Constitutional law provides the basic rules of our political and legal systems. It determines who is entitled to create and enforce laws, and it establishes the fundamental rights and freedoms that Canadians enjoy. We will discuss the Constitution in more detail in a later part of this chapter.

In the past 50 years, Canadians have grown to expect more and more from their elected officials. To manage the workload, governments regularly *delegate* or *assign* responsibility to a variety of agencies, boards, commissions, and tribunals. **Administrative law** is concerned with the creation and operation of those bodies. It has a profound impact on business. For instance, a human rights tribunal may decide that a corporation discriminated against women by

----

10. There are other systems of law as well, such as Aboriginal law and Islamic law.

11. The exception in the United States is Louisiana. Like Quebec, it was settled by France and therefore uses a civil law system.

12. "Civil law" is a confusing phrase. It often refers to a legal system that can be traced to ancient Rome. We will, however, encounter another definition later in this chapter. Within a common law system, it can also refer to private law rather than public law. For example, when Canadian lawyers talk about "civil litigation," they are usually referring to cases involving contracts or torts.

"Common law" is also a confusing phrase. It often refers to a legal system that can be traced to England. However, as we will see later in this chapter, it may also refer to rules that are made by judges, rather than by legislators. And within the context of rules made by judges, it may refer to judges who sat in the courts of law, as opposed to judges who sat in the courts of equity.

Margin notes:

civil law systems trace their history to ancient Rome

a jurisdiction is a geographical area that uses the same set of laws

common law systems trace their history to England

public law is concerned with governments and the ways in which they deal with their citizens

constitutional law provides the basic rules of our political and legal systems

administrative law is concerned with the creation and operation of administrative agencies and tribunals

FIGURE 1.1 A Map of the Law

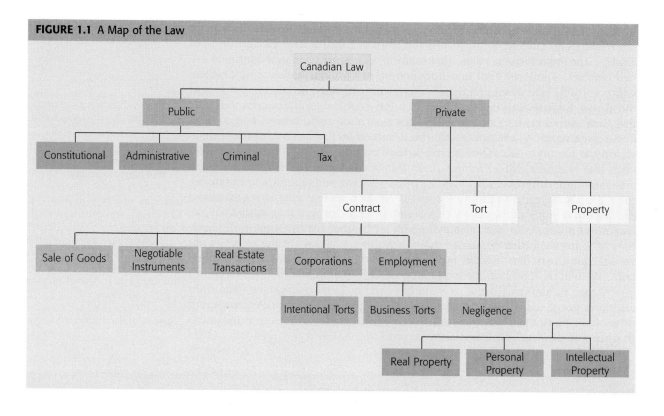

paying them less than it paid men for work of similar value. If so, the company may be ordered to pay millions of dollars in compensation.[13] Even if a particular business never becomes involved in that sort of landmark case, it probably has to deal, in the normal course of operations, with a number of administrative bodies. There are literally hundreds. Figure 1.2 (see p. 9) lists a sampling of federal, provincial (or territorial), and municipal bodies that regularly affect business.[14]

criminal law deals with offences against the state

Criminal law deals with offences against the state. In other words, it is concerned with people who break rules that are designed to protect society as a whole. For instance, if you punch me, you have committed a *tort* because (as discussed below) you have done something wrong to me personally. However, you have also committed a *crime* because you have done something wrong to the entire community. Even if I am not particularly upset about being hit, society may want to discourage and punish your behaviour. Consequently, the police and the prosecutor may bring you to court even if I would prefer to drop the matter. Although we tend to think of criminals as violent individuals, it is important to know that crime can happen in the business world as well.

- *White-collar crimes*, as the name suggests, are committed by people in suits. A manager who steals money from the petty cash drawer is a white-collar criminal.

- A crime can even be committed by a company itself. A *corporate crime* occurs, for instance, when a used car dealership adopts a policy of

---

[13.] *Bell Canada v Canadian Telephone Employees Association* (2001) 199 DLR (4th) 664 (FC CA).

[14.] This list is not exhaustive. Some bodies serve more than one function. Note that, below the federal level, the name of a particular body may vary from place to place.

FIGURE 1.2 Administrative Bodies Affecting Business

Federal	
Canadian Radio-television and Telecommunications Commission	regulates broadcasting and telecommunications systems
National Energy Board	regulates pipelines, energy development, and trade in the energy industry
Canadian International Trade Tribunal	investigates possible violations of international trade regulations
Competition Tribunal	resolves disputes under the *Competition Act*[15]
Provincial or Territorial	
Workers' Compensation Board	promotes workplace safety and rehabilitates and compensates injured workers
Labour Relations Board	assists in the resolution of labour disputes
Environmental Appeal Board	assists in the resolution of environmental disputes
Professional Society (*eg* Law Society of Alberta)	regulates and licenses the practice of a particular profession (*eg* law)
Municipal	
Zoning and Planning Board	regulates the use of land
Building and Inspections Department	regulates and licenses building projects
Licence Division	regulates and licenses business operations

rolling back the odometers on its vehicles. That company is guilty of fraud.[16]

The various branches of government, such as Parliament, administrative bodies, and courts, require a great deal of money in order to operate. **Tax law** is concerned with the rules that are used to collect money for public spending. This is an area of great interest to the business community.

tax law is concerned with the rules that are used to collect money for the purposes of public spending

Private Law

Although we will occasionally discuss public law, our focus is on *private law*. **Private law** is concerned with the rules that apply in private matters. Both parties in a private dispute are usually private *persons*, either individuals or organizations like corporations. For instance, your theatre company might sue me if I failed to perform a play as promised. However, private law can also apply to the government. First, it is possible for a private person to sue a public body.[17] Suppose that the municipal government carelessly forgot to inspect the foundations of your house while it was being built. If your basement later develops cracks, you could sue the construction company for providing shoddy work, but you could also sue the city for its failure to enforce its own building regulations.[18] The government is also subject to private law rules when it enters into

private law is concerned with the rules that apply in private matters

---

[15.] The *Competition Act* is discussed in Chapter 25.

[16.] *R v Waterloo Mercury Sales Ltd* (1974) 49 DLR (3d) 131 (Alta Dist Ct). Corporate crime is discussed in Chapter 22.

[17.] And vice versa. If you accidentally burned down city hall, the municipal government could sue you.

[18.] *Neilson v City of Kamloops* (1984) 10 DLR (4th) 641 (SCC).

private transactions, such as when a government contractually agrees to purchase paper from a store.

Private law is usually divided into three main parts:

- the law of torts
- the law of contracts
- the law of property

a tort is a private wrong

We have defined a crime as a public wrong, an offence against society as a whole. A **tort**, in contrast, is a private wrong, an offence against a particular person. The law of torts covers a great deal of territory. For the purposes of discussion, we will split the category into three: (i) *intentional torts*, such as assault and false imprisonment, (ii) *business torts*, such as deceit and conspiracy, and (iii) *negligence*, which covers most situations in which one person carelessly hurts another.

the law of contracts is concerned with the creation and enforcement of agreements

The **law of contracts** is concerned with the creation and enforcement of agreements. For business people, this is a tremendously important area of law. Business is based on transactions, and the law of contracts governs virtually every one of them. For instance, even if we limit ourselves to the headings in Figure 1.1, we can see that contracts are involved in (i) the *sale of goods*, such as cows and computers, (ii) the use of *negotiable instruments*, such as cheques, (iii) *real estate transactions*, such as the purchase of land, (iv) the operation of *corporations*, and (v) the *employment* relationship that exists between a business and its workers. We will see many more examples throughout this book.

We will have much more to say about torts and contracts in later chapters. Given the tremendous importance of those two subjects, however, you may want to turn to page 59 now for a comparison between those two areas of law.

the law of property is concerned with the acquisition, use, and disposition of property

As the name suggests, the **law of property** is concerned with the acquisition, use, and disposition of property. The discussion is once again divided into three main parts: (i) *real property*, which involves land and things that are attached to land, (ii) *personal property*, which involves things that can be moved from one place to another, and (iii) *intellectual property*, which involves things that consist of original ideas, such as patents and copyrights. All three forms of property are important in business. Every company owns personal property; the vast majority have interests in real property; and a growing number rely heavily on intellectual property. There are also several areas of law that deal with all forms of property. For instance: (i) the law of *succession* deals with the distribution of a person's property after death, and (ii) the law of *trusts* deals with a situation in which one person holds property on behalf of another.

Overlap

Before leaving this section, we must stress that different areas of law can overlap. There are at least two possibilities.

- First, a single event can trigger more than one set of rules. We have already mentioned one example. If you punch me, you may commit both a crime and a tort. Other illustrations are more common in the business world. For instance, if you hire lawyers who provide poor work and bad advice, you may have the option of suing them for both the tort of negligence (because they carelessly caused you to suffer a loss) and breach of contract (because they did not fulfill your agreement).[19]

[19.] *Central Trust Co v Rafuse* (1986) 31 DLR (4th) 481 (SCC).

- Second, some situations involve various types of laws. For example, an employment relationship is based on a contract between the employer and the employee. Nevertheless, the parties should also have some knowledge of administrative law (in case a company discriminates against ethnic minorities), criminal law (in case a boss sexually harasses an employee), and tort law (in case one worker injures another).

Sources of Law

In the last section, we organized laws according to topics. In this section, we organize them according to sources. Broadly speaking, there are three sources:

- the Constitution
- legislation
- the courts

As we will see, not all laws are created equal. Some are more important than others.

The Constitution

The most important source of law is the **Constitution**. This document creates the basic rules for Canadian society, including our political and legal systems.[20] The fact that it provides the foundation for everything else has two significant consequences.

the Constitution is the document that creates the basic rules for Canadian society, including its political and legal systems

First, every other law in the country must be compatible with it. Section 52 of the Constitution states: "The Constitution of Canada is the supreme law of Canada, and any law that is inconsistent with the provisions of the Constitution is, to the extent of the inconsistency, of no force or effect."

Second, the Constitution is *very* difficult to change. It is one thing to tinker with, say, the rules that govern the enforcement of contracts. It is a far more serious matter to alter the fundamental rules of Canadian society. Most laws can be changed by a legislature or by a court. The Constitution is different—as a general rule, it can be changed only through a special *amending formula*. This requires the consent of Parliament plus the legislatures of at least two-thirds of the provinces, where those consenting provinces represent at least 50 percent of the country's population. Not surprisingly, Constitutional amendments are rare.

Division of Powers   Many parts of the Constitution are important to business people. We will look at two. The first concerns the *division of powers*.[21] To understand that concept, it is necessary to appreciate that Canada is a **federal** country because it has two levels of government.[22]

Canada is a federal country because it has two levels of government

- **Federal:** The Parliament of Canada, which is located in Ottawa, governs the country as a whole. It is composed of two parts. The House of Commons consists of members of Parliament (MPs), who are elected from every province and territory. The Senate consists of senators, who are

---

[20.] *Constitution Act 1982*, being schedule B to the *Canada Act 1982* (UK), 1982, c 11. Although our current Constitution came into force in 1982, it is virtually identical to the *British North America Act*, which contained Canada's first Constitution in 1867: see *Constitution Act 1867*, 1867 (UK), 30 & 31 Victoria, c3. The most notable feature of the new Constitution is that it includes the *Canadian Charter of Rights and Freedoms*.

[21.] Chapter 25 examines the division of powers as it affects business regulation in Canada.

[22.] There is, in fact, a third level of government. Section 92 of the Constitution allows provinces and territories to create municipalities.

appointed to their jobs. Since Canada began life as a British colony and is still part of the British Commonwealth, the Queen of England remains our head of state.[23] In reality, however, the country is run by the political party that has the most MPs. The leader of that party is the prime minister.

- **Provincial and territorial:** In addition to electing members of Parliament to represent them nationally in Ottawa, Canadians also elect politicians to represent them within their own provinces and territories.[24] The elected body, or *legislature*, is usually called the Legislative Assembly.[25] And for the most part, each of the 13 legislatures is similar to Parliament. Once again, even though the official head of state is the Queen, power really is held by the party with the most elected members, whose leader is the premier.[26]

Wherever you live in Canada, you are subject to two sets of laws: federal and provincial (or territorial). With respect to any particular issue, however, there is generally only one law. Our system would not work very well, for instance, if Parliament required you to drive on the right side of the road at the same time that your legislature required you to drive on the left. Sections 91 and 92 of the Constitution therefore set out a **division of powers**, stating the areas in which each level of government can create laws. Concept Summary 1.1 lists some areas that are particularly important to business people. Note the last item on the left side of the chart. The federal government has the **residual power**, the power over everything that is not otherwise mentioned. Consequently, Parliament now has authority over a number of topics that did not exist when our original Constitution was written in 1867, such as telecommunications and air travel.

A government sometimes tries to create a law outside of its own area. When it does so, it acts ***ultra vires***, which literally means "beyond the power." As a

*the **division of powers** states the areas in which each level of government can create laws*

*the **residual power** gives the federal government authority over everything that is not specifically mentioned*

CONCEPT SUMMARY 1.1

Division of Powers

Federal	Provincial or Territorial
criminal law	property and civil rights (*eg.* contracts, torts)
taxation	direct taxation to raise money for provincial purposes
unemployment insurance	corporations with provincial objects
banks	the creation of municipalities
bankruptcy and insolvency	matters of a local or private nature within a province
money	
negotiable instruments (such as cheques)	
international and interprovincial trade and commerce	
navigation and shipping	
copyright	
any matter that is not exclusively given to the provinces	

[23.] The Queen is represented by the Governor General.

[24.] Provinces and territories do not have senators.

[25.] There is some variation. Newfoundland, for instance, has a House of Assembly, while Quebec has a National Assembly.

[26.] The Queen is represented by a lieutenant governor in each province and by a commissioner in each territory.

result of section 52 of the Constitution (which we quoted earlier), such laws are "of no force or effect." In other words, they are not really laws at all. In one famous case, the federal government tried to create a law that prohibited people from importing or manufacturing margarine. It did so to protect the dairy industry from competition. The Supreme Court of Canada found that that law was partially invalid.[27] The federal government was entitled to ban the *importation* of margarine because it had authority over international and interprovincial trade. It could not, however, ban the *manufacture* of margarine. Because a province has authority over "property and civil rights," it has the authority to regulate the production or sale of margarine within its own borders.

Charter of Rights and Freedoms Traditionally, as long as a government acted within the scope of its power (or *intra vires*), its laws were generally valid. The situation changed dramatically in 1982, however, when the *Canadian Charter of Rights and Freedoms* was written into the Constitution.[28] As its name indicates, the *Charter* was introduced to protect basic rights and freedoms. Case Brief 1.1 illustrates the different bases upon which a law may now be attacked.

CASE BRIEF 1.1

Irwin Toy Ltd v Quebec (Attorney General) (1989) 58 DLR (4th) 577 (SCC)

Quebec created a law that generally prohibited advertisements aimed at pre-teens. Irwin Toys wanted to promote its products on television. It argued that the law was unconstitutional because (i) it dealt with television, which is a federal matter, rather than a provincial matter, and (ii) it violated the *Charter* right to freedom of expression.

Division of powers: The Supreme Court of Canada agreed that the federal Parliament has authority over telecommunications as part of its residual power. However, the Court also said that the disputed law only affected television in an indirect or incidental way. The province's goal was not to regulate broadcasters; it was to regulate advertisers. And since

the regulation of advertisers is a provincial matter, the law was acceptable under the division of powers.

Charter of Rights and Freedoms: The Supreme Court of Canada agreed that the disputed law violated the right to freedom of expression under section 2(b) of the *Charter*. After all, it prevented the toy company from using television to tell children about its products. However, the Court also held that under Section 1, the province was justified in placing restrictions on the ability to advertise. Society has an interest in protecting young children from commercial exploitation. Furthermore, the ban was reasonable. For instance, it only applied to toys aimed at children under 13 years of age.

The *Charter* has had a profound impact on virtually every aspect of life in this country. It has, for example, led to the recognition of same-sex marriages,[29] and it may also dramatically affect the availability of health care by allowing people to receive treatment outside of the public system.[30] Indeed, it is difficult to understand Canadian law, Canadian politics, or Canadian society without some appreciation of the *Charter*. We will therefore consider it in some detail.

The *Charter* protects a large number of rights and freedoms. Some deal with democratic rights (sections 3–5), some deal with legal rights that usually arise in criminal cases (sections 8–14), some deal with official languages and minority language education (sections 16–23), and some deal with Aboriginals and multiculturalism (sections 25 and 27). For present purposes, we will focus on three sections of the *Charter* which, in addition to affecting Canadians

---

[27.]*Reference Re Validity of s 5(a) of the Dairy Industry Act (Canada)* [1949] 1 DLR 433 (SCC).

[28.]Part I of the *Constitution Act, 1982*, being Schedule B to the *Canada Act, 1982* (UK), 1982, c 11.

[29.]*Reference Re Same-Sex Marriage* (2004) 246 DLR (4th) 193 (SCC).

[30.]*Chaoulli v Quebec (Attorney General)* (2005) 254 DLR (4th) 577 (SCC).

generally, sometimes have an impact on businesses. (A complete copy of the *Charter* is available through our Companion Website.)

Fundamental Freedoms

2   Everyone has the following fundamental freedoms:
  (a) freedom of conscience and religion;
  (b) freedom of thought, belief, opinion and expression, including freedom of the press and other media of communication;
  (c) freedom of peaceful assembly; and
  (d) freedom of association.

Mobility Rights

6   (1) Every citizen of Canada has the right to enter, remain in and leave Canada.
  (2) Every citizen of Canada and every person who has the status of a permanent resident of Canada has the right
    (a) to move to and take up residence in any province; and
    (b) to pursue the gaining of a livelihood in any province . . . .

Equality Rights

15 (1) Every individual is equal before and under the law and has the right to the equal protection and equal benefit of the law without discrimination and, in particular, without discrimination based on race, national or ethnic origin, colour, religion, sex, age or mental or physical disability.
  (2) Subsection (1) does not preclude any law, program or activity that has as its object the amelioration of conditions of disadvantaged individuals or groups including those that are disadvantaged because of race, national or ethnic origin, colour, religion, sex, age or mental or physical disability.

A court may be able to choose from amongst several remedies if a *Charter* right has been violated. We will consider some of those remedies in greater detail below. For now, it is enough to appreciate that since the *Charter* is part of the Constitution, any law that is inconsistent with it is "of no force or effect." From a business perspective, the result can be quite dramatic. A few examples, based on the rights that have been quoted, demonstrate that point.

- To protect Christian beliefs, Parliament created a law that required most stores to close on Sundays. That law was declared invalid because it discriminated against non-Christians.[31] It violated their freedom of religion under section 2(a).

- Alberta created a law that prohibited law firms in that province from creating partnerships with law firms in other provinces. That law was declared invalid because it prevented lawyers from working in different parts of the country.[32] It violated their mobility rights under section 6(2).

- British Columbia passed a law that prevented people who were not Canadian citizens from practising law in that province. That law was declared invalid because it discriminated against people on the basis of their national origin.[33] It violated their right to equality under section 15(1).

---

[31] *R v Big M Drug Mart Ltd* (1985) 18 DLR (4th) 321 (SCC).

[32] *Black v Law Society of Alberta* (1989) 58 DLR (4th) 317 (SCC).

[33] *Andrews v Law Society (British Columbia)* (1989) 56 DLR (4th) 1 (SCC).

Although the *Charter* may affect business people, it is important to realize that it does not contain general rights to enjoy property or carry on business activities (**property rights** or **economic rights**). To the contrary, the people who drafted the *Charter* expressly rejected a right to "the enjoyment of property." They were concerned that such a right would, for instance, hamper the government's ability to protect the environment, regulate the use of land, control resource-based industries, or restrict foreign ownership of Canadian land. They were also concerned that economic rights would allow wealthy individuals to frustrate government plans to act in the public's best interests. The Supreme Court of Canada has therefore said that there is no right under the *Charter* to "unconstrained freedom" in economic activities, nor is there an "unconstrained right to transact business whenever one wishes."[34] That denial of economic rights has made it difficult for disadvantaged Canadians to force governments to provide social assistance.[35] The courts have not, for instance, been willing to interpret the *Charter* in a way that ensures that every person enjoys accommodation or a certain standard of living.

Leaving aside the general exclusion of property rights and economic rights, the *Charter* is also subject to a number of other important restrictions. Those restrictions reveal a great deal about the *Charter*'s role in Canadian society.

- **Government action:** The *Charter* was introduced to govern the relationship between the individual and the state. Section 32(1) states that the document applies to "Parliament" and "the legislature . . . of each province." Consequently, the *Charter*'s rights and freedoms have full effect only if a person is complaining about the government's behaviour.[36] The *Charter* does not directly apply to disputes involving private parties. For instance, the right to freedom of expression that is found in section 2(b) does not entitle a union to picket a private corporation.[37] Interestingly, however, the Supreme Court of Canada has said that private law should be developed in a way that is consistent with *Charter* values.[38] It is not yet clear exactly what that means.

- **Corporations:** The *Charter* generally does not apply *against* private corporations. It may not apply in *favour* of them either. It depends on the circumstances. For example, section 2(b) refers to "everyone," while section 15(1) refers to "every individual." A company is a kind of "person," but it is not an "individual." As a result, it enjoys freedom of expression, but not the right to equality.[39]

- **Reasonable limits:** Section 1 of the *Charter* states that the rights and freedoms are subject to "such reasonable limits prescribed by law as can

property rights are rights to enjoy property

economic rights are rights to carry on economic activities

---

[34] *Edwards Books & Art Ltd v R* (1986) 35 DLR (4th) 1 (SCC). It had been argued that economic and property rights were protected by section 7 of the *Charter*, which states that everyone "has the right to life, liberty and security of the person." The court denied that "liberty" generally includes economic liberty.

[35] *Gosselin v Quebec (Attorney General)* (2002) 221 DLR (4th) 257 (SCC).

[36] In this situation, "government" refers to Parliament, the legislatures, and other organizations that are closely controlled by the government, including the police and community colleges, but not universities and hospitals.

[37] *RWDSU Local 580 v Dolphin Delivery Ltd* (1986) 33 DLR (4th) 174 (SCC).

[38] *Dobson v Dobson* (1999) 174 DLR (4th) 1 (SCC).

[39] Although "everyone" includes both people and corporations, not all of the freedoms listed in section 2 are available to companies. For instance, while a corporation has a need to express itself, it cannot have a religious belief. Its employees can, however, hold religious beliefs, which is why Sunday closing laws can be declared invalid, as discussed above.

be demonstrably justified in a free and democratic society." The Constitution therefore recognizes that it is occasionally acceptable to violate a person's rights. In one famous case, the Supreme Court of Canada held that a shop owner's freedom of expression was infringed by a law that prevented him from selling violent pornography.[40] However, the judges also held that society was justified in banning that sort of material because it is degrading, dehumanizing, and harmful to women. The law was therefore enforceable and the shop owner was prohibited from selling the offending material.

- **Notwithstanding clause:** Section 33 may allow Parliament or a legislature to create and enforce a law "notwithstanding" the fact that it violates the *Charter*.[41] That is, of course, a serious matter. It requires the government to expressly declare that it is overriding fundamental rights and freedoms. Canadians generally oppose such a move. As a result, section 33 has been used only once in the common law provinces and territories.[42] The situation has been different in Quebec, perhaps because of the feeling that the *Charter* was introduced without sufficient regard to that province's special status. An interesting example arose in connection with Bill 101, which prohibited the use of languages other than French on outdoor signs. Although that law violated the *Charter*'s right to freedom of expression, Quebec's government used section 33 to say that its law applied notwithstanding the *Charter*.[43]

Charter **Remedies**　What happens if the *Charter* has been violated? We have already seen that any law that is inconsistent with the *Charter* is "of no force or effect." Section 24 of the *Charter* further states that a court may award "such remedy as [it] considers appropriate and just in the circumstances." The precise nature of the court's response therefore depends upon the circumstances.

We can list a few of the more important possibilities. Notice that some remedies are more active than others. Judges try to strike a balance between respecting the legislature and respecting the *Charter*. They are, nevertheless, sometimes criticized for going too far—for *making* laws rather than *applying* them.

- **Declaration:** A court may simply *declare* that the *Charter* has been violated. The legislature will then have the obligation of finding some solution to the problem.[44]

- **Injunction:** A court may take a more active role. It may impose an

---

[40.] *R v Butler* (1992) 89 DLR (4th) 449 (SCC). As we saw in Case Brief 1.1, the court also relied on section 1 in finding that a law restricting advertising to pre-teens was justified as a limitation on the right to freedom of expression.

[41.] The notwithstanding clause applies only to some of the rights and freedoms listed in the *Charter*. Parliament or a legislature can override section 2 (fundamental freedoms) or section 15 (equality rights), for instance, but not section 6 (mobility rights). Furthermore, the notwithstanding clause can be used for only five years at a time. At the end of that period, the clause must be re-applied. That rule ensures that significant constitutional rules are re-examined on a regular basis.

[42.] The province of Saskatchewan applied section 33 to protect back-to-work legislation from potential *Charter* attack. The notwithstanding clause was, however, unnecessary. The Supreme Court of Canada found that the legislation was valid in any event: *RWDSU v Saskatchewan* (1987) 38 DLR (4th) 277 (SCC).

[43.] *Ford v Quebec (Attorney General)* (1988) 54 DLR (4th) 577 (SCC). A Parti Québécois government had previously applied the notwithstanding clause to *all* of Quebec's legislation: *Alliance des professeurs de Montréal v Quebec (Attorney General)* (1985) 21 DLR (4th) 354 (Que CA).

[44.] *Eldridge v British Columbia (Attorney General)* (1997) 151 DLR (4th) 577 at 631–632 (SCC) ("there are myriad options available to the government that may rectify the unconstitutionality of the current system" and it was "not this Court's role to dictate how this is to be accomplished").

injunction that requires the government to address the problem in a certain way.[45] The choice therefore lies with the judge, rather than with the legislature.[46]

- **Striking down:** Going even further, a court may *strike down* or eliminate a statute that violates the *Charter*. The decision to do so may take effect immediately or its effect may be *temporarily suspended*.[47] A temporary suspension is appropriate where the immediate elimination of a statute would create substantial problems.[48]

- **Severance, reading down, and reading in:** Sometimes, a court may save a statute by re-writing part of it. If only one part of a statute is offensive, it may be *severed* or cut out.[49] If a statute is written too broadly, it may be *read down* so that it applies only where it can be justified.[50] Likewise, if a statute is written too narrowly, the court may *read in* a broader interpretation so that the law no longer discriminates against some people by excluding them from a certain benefit.[51]

- **Damages:** Just as a successful litigant in a private law case may be awarded damages for the loss that has been suffered,[52] so too may a person who has suffered a *Charter* violation.[53]

As we have seen, judges have a great deal of power under the *Charter*. It is

YOU BE THE JUDGE 1.1

Charter Remedies[54]

The *Family Benefits Act* provides social assistance to any "mother whose dependent child was born out of wedlock." Charles Phillips, a single father, cares for his daughter, who was born out of wedlock. Phillips applied for benefits under the statute, but was denied assistance because he is a father, rather than a mother. He has shown that the Act violates his right to equality under section 15(1) of the *Charter*. You are now required to decide the appropriate remedy.

Questions for Discussion

1. The province argues that it should have the right to determine which citizens receive social assistance, and that the only appropriate remedy is to strike down the entire statute. Do you agree? If so, what will happen to single mothers who care for children born out of wedlock?

2. Phillips argues that he should be entitled to receive benefits under the Act. Do you agree? If so, which remedy will you use? Is it possible to achieve the desired result through severance, reading down, reading in, or damages?

45. We will examine injunctions in more detail in Chapters 3 and 12.

46. *Marchand v Simcoe County Board of Education* (1986) 29 DLR (4th) 596 (Ont HCJ).

47. *R v Big M Drug Mart Ltd* (1985) 18 DLR (4th) 321 (SCC).

48. *Reference Re Manitoba Language Rights* (1985) 19 DLR (4th) 1 (SCC).

49. *Canada (Employment and Immigration Commission) v Tétreault-Gadoury* (1991) 81 DLR (4th) 358 (SCC).

50. *R v Sharpe* (2001) 194 DLR (4th) 1 (SCC).

51. *Miron v Trudel* (1995) 124 DLR (4th) 693 (SCC).

52. Chapters 3 and 12.

53. *Jane Doe v Metropolitan Toronto (Municipality) Commissioners of Police* (1998) 160 DLR (4th) 697 (Ont Gen Div).

54. *Phillips v Nova Scotia (Social Assistance Appeal Board)* (1986) 27 DLR (4th) 156 (NS SC TD), aff'd (1986) 34 DLR (4th) 633 (CA).

parliamentary supremacy means that while judges are required to interpret constitutional and statutory documents, they must also obey them

important to appreciate, however, that the *Charter* was not intended to destroy the doctrine of *parliamentary supremacy*. **Parliamentary supremacy** means that while judges are required to interpret constitutional and statutory documents, they must also obey them. For that reason, Canadian judges present their decisions as part of an ongoing *dialogue*. Even when they strike down a law, they are merely indicating that the legislature failed to follow the rules. The government is often able to respond by creating a new law that properly respects the *Charter*. Case Brief 1.2 illustrates the idea of a dialogue.

CASE BRIEF 1.2

RJR MacDonald v Canada (Attorney General) (1995) 127 DLR (4th) 1 (SCC)

The federal government introduced legislation that imposed a *complete* ban on virtually all tobacco advertisements. One of the major tobacco companies complained that the statute violated its right to freedom of expression under section 2(b) of the *Charter*. The Supreme Court of Canada agreed and struck down the legislation. However, the court also indicated that a *partial* ban on advertising would be acceptable. In effect, it invited Parliament to try again. The government accepted that invitation and enacted legislation that prohibited advertisements that were, for instance, more specifically aimed at young people.

Legislation

legislation is law that is created by Parliament or a legislature

The Constitution, including the *Charter*, is the first source of law. *Legislation* is the second. **Legislation** is law that is created by Parliament or a legislature. The most important kinds of legislation are *statutes*, or *acts*. For example, every jurisdiction in Canada has an act that allows companies to be created.[55] And the *Criminal Code*, which is a federal statute, applies across the country to determine the types of behaviour that are crimes.[56]

The Legislative Process   As a matter of risk management, it is important to understand how legislation is created. That may seem surprising. After all, when we talk about risk management, we are usually worried about laws that already exist. Sometimes, however, the best strategy is to either prevent the creation of a law or make sure that it is written in a way that causes as little trouble as possible.

We will focus on the legislative process at the federal level.[57] As we saw earlier, Parliament consists of the House of Commons and the Senate. In most cases, a *bill* is introduced into the House of Commons by an MP.[58] If the majority of MPs support it, it passes the *first reading*, usually without much discussion. Some time, it re-appears for *second reading*, when it is the subject of debate amongst the MPs. If it once again enjoys majority support, it is sent to a legislative committee for detailed study. After that, it re-appears for a *third reading*, when the MPs take a final vote. If the bill passes that stage, it is sent to

---

[55.] The usual name is the *Business Corporations Act*, the *Corporations Act*, or the *Companies Act*. Those statutes are examined in Chapter 22.

[56.] *Criminal Code*, RSC 1985, c C-46.

[57.] The process is much the same at the provincial and territorial level. The main difference is that the provinces and territories do not have senates.

[58.] A bill sometimes is introduced in the Senate, where it must pass before being sent to the House of Commons.

the Senate, where the three-stage process is repeated. If all goes well, and the bill is passed by Parliament, it simply requires one last formality. Since the head of state in Canada technically is the Queen, the bill must receive *royal assent*, which is Her Majesty's approval. That approval is given on her behalf by the Governor General.[59]

Members of Canadian society may influence the legislative process during at least three stages. First, although you cannot introduce a bill into Parliament, you may *lobby*, or encourage, an MP to do so. Because of the influence that some lobbyists have, their activities are controlled by legislation. Those rules are, however, difficult to enforce. Politicians often meet with business people, and it is difficult to know when a conversation crosses the line. Second, before a bill appears for second reading, you may contact an MP and express any concerns that you may have. The MP may then raise those concerns during debate. And finally, legislative committees often receive advice and assistance from people outside Parliament. If you are concerned about any particular aspect of a bill, you may have a chance to be heard in committee.

Subordinate Legislation and Municipalities   It is impossible for Parliament and the legislatures to constantly monitor all of their legislation to make sure that it is effective and up to date. Therefore, statutes often set up a basic structure but allow someone else (such as a government minister, a commission, or a tribunal) to create specific rules without the need to go through the entire legislative process. Those regulations are known as **subordinate legislation**.[60] For example, Parliament created the Canadian Radio-television and Telecommunications Commission (CRTC) and gave it the power to regulate broadcasting in Canada.

subordinate legislation is the term given to rules that are created with the authority of Parliament or the legislature

One of the most important types of subordinate legislation involves *municipalities*. The Constitution is concerned with only two levels of government: federal and provincial (or territorial). However, a third level is needed. For instance, neither Parliament nor the legislature will decide whether cats can roam free in a particular town. That decision must be made locally. The Constitution gives the provinces the power to create **municipalities**, which are towns and cities. And when a province creates a municipality, it gives that new body the authority to pass **by-laws**, which are a type of subordinate legislation. Although municipalities are the lowest level of government, their impact on business can be significant. Among other things, by-laws are used to license businesses, impose some sorts of taxes, plan commercial developments, and regulate parking. City hall is a powerful place.

a **municipality** is a town or city

a **by-law** is a type of subordinate legislation that is created by a municipality

The Courts

The third source of laws are the *courts*. The courts certainly play a crucial role in connection with the other two sources of law. Courts must *interpret* and apply the words that appear in the Constitution and in legislation. We are now concerned, however, with rules that judges themselves *create*.

The process that courts use to create laws is too large to fully consider in this section. We will therefore return to that topic in the next chapter. For present purposes, it will be enough to introduce two important concepts: the *common law* and *equity*.

[59.] Although provincial or territorial legislation must also receive royal assent, the Queen is represented in those places by a lieutenant governor or a commissioner.

[60.] There are various types of subordinate legislation, including regulations, by-laws, statutory instruments, ordinances, and Orders-in-Council. The appropriate one depends on the circumstances.

The Common Law   Although lawyers often refer to judge-made rules as "the common law," that phrase has at least three different meanings, depending upon whether it refers to a *system of law*, a *source of law*, or a *type of court*.

- **Systems:** We previously used the term "common law" to refer to legal systems that can be traced to England, and compared the common law system that operates throughout most of Canada to the civil law system that Quebec borrowed from France.[61]

- **Sources:** Within a common law system, the term "common law" can also be used in a more specific way to refer to rules that are created by judges rather than by legislators or the drafters of the Constitution. Most of the rules in contract law, for instance, are common law rules because they were developed by the courts. Statutes apply only to certain small areas of contract. The law of taxation, in contrast, is almost completely based on statutes. For the most part, judges simply interpret and apply the legislation.

- **Courts:** Finally, if we limit our discussion to judge-made rules, we can use the phrase "common law" in an even more specific way. England traditionally had two sets of courts: the *courts of law* and the *courts of equity*. Lawyers sometimes still talk about the "common law" when referring to rules developed in the first type of court, and about "equity" when referring to rules developed in the second type of court. We will examine that difference in greater detail in the next section.

Figure 1.3 uses a diagram to explain the various meanings of the term "common law."

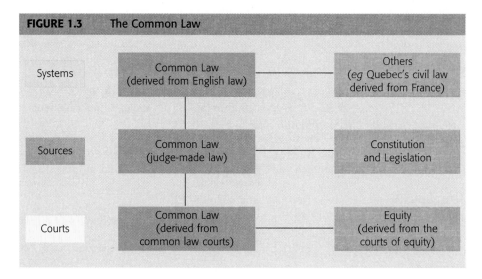

FIGURE 1.3   The Common Law

Systems	Common Law (derived from English law)	Others (*eg* Quebec's civil law derived from France)
Sources	Common Law (judge-made law)	Constitution and Legislation
Courts	Common Law (derived from common law courts)	Equity (derived from the courts of equity)

Law and Equity   The legal system that developed in England originally had only one type of court: *courts of law*. And because those courts usually insisted on applying the strict letter of the law, they were often rigid and harsh. At the same time, however, the king (or queen) was seen as the ultimate source of law.

[61.] "Civil law" is another confusing phrase. It often refers to a legal system that can be traced to ancient Rome. However, within a common law system, it can also refer to private law rather than public law. For example, when Canadian lawyers talk about "civil litigation," they are usually referring to cases involving contracts or torts.

Consequently, people who were unhappy with decisions they received in court could ask the king for relief. Not surprisingly, the king was too busy to deal with all of those *petitions* personally. He therefore asked the *chancellor*, who was his legal and religious adviser, to act on his behalf. As the number of petitions continued to increase, the chancellor asked other people to act on his behalf. The chancellor and the people under him eventually became recognized as a separate court that was known as the *court of equity* (or the *court of chancery*).

That name reflects the way in which the new court originally decided cases. The king, the chancellor, and the chancellor's men simply did what they believed was right. Unlike the courts of law, they were much less concerned with rigid rules and much more concerned with justice. In other words, their decisions were based on **equity**, which, in a general sense, means fairness.

equity is, in a general sense, fairness

Equity continues to play an important role in our legal system. However, it is much different from when it was first created. Two changes are especially significant.

- **The nature of equity:** The concept of equity no longer allows judges to decide cases simply on the basis of fairness. Like the courts of law, the courts of equity eventually developed and applied a consistent set of rules. Equity may still be slightly more flexible than law. But for the most part, those two systems are different only because they occasionally apply different rules. For instance, if I break a contract by refusing to transfer a house to you, the law says that you are only entitled to the *monetary value* of that house, not to the property itself. Equity, however, may be willing to grant *specific performance* and force me to actually transfer the house to you.

- **One set of courts:** Initially, the courts of law and the courts of equity were completely separate. They occupied different buildings, they used different judges, they heard from different lawyers. At the end of the nineteenth century, however, the two court systems were joined into one. Consequently, nearly every Canadian court is now a court of law *and* a court of equity. The same judges apply both sets of rules.[62]

Given that there has been a "fusion" of the courts of law and equity, it may seem strange that we continue to draw a distinction between them. And, in fact, in some circumstances, Canadian courts have begun to ignore the historical differences. A good example occurs in connection with the protection of secrets. If you stole secret information that I had regarding the location of a gold mine, I traditionally would go to a court of equity and sue you for breach of confidence. Recently, however, the Supreme Court of Canada has said that breach of confidence is neither equitable nor legal, but rather a unique combination of the two.[63] Nevertheless, the distinction between law and equity remains critically important for some purposes. The best example is the trust, which is briefly considered in Business Decision 1.2 (see p. 22).

---

[62] If there is any inconsistency, the equitable rules apply.

[63] *LAC Minerals Ltd v International Corona Resources* (1989) 61 DLR (4th) 14 at 74 (SCC). We will consider breach of confidence again in Chapters 4 and 18.

Law, Equity, and the Trust

You own a small airline. Like other airlines, you do most of your business through travel agents. Those agents attract passengers, issue tickets, and receive payment on your behalf. Unfortunately, a travel agent may become bankrupt. And if that happens, you may not receive all of the money that customers had paid to the agent for seats on your planes. Even if you can show that the money from the customers is still sitting in the agent's bank account, there will be many other people, just like you, who are demanding payment. The amount of money that you receive will depend upon whether your relationship with the agent exists in law or in equity.

Law: If your relationship with the agent exists only in law, you will receive little, if any, money. Although the agent sold tickets on your behalf, it received payment from the customers for *itself*. The money belonged entirely to the agent as soon as it was received. The agent merely promised that it would pay you an appropriate amount when you asked for it. Of course, the agent also promised to pay a number of other people as well. And unfortunately, there is not

enough money to go around. Each of you might receive a few cents on each dollar.

Equity: The result will be much different if you entered into an equitable relationship with the agent. If so, then when the agent sold tickets on your behalf, it received payment from the customers on *trust* for you. A trust occurs when one person holds property for the benefit of someone else. Although the common law will say that the agent owns the money, equity will say that you are the real, or *beneficial*, owner. It will also say that the agent cannot pay its debts with your money. You therefore are entitled to take everything in the bank account—perhaps leaving nothing behind for anyone else.

Question for Discussion

1. We will consider trusts again in Chapter 8. As you can already see, however, they can be very useful. Is there any reason why you would not always insist upon receiving payment by way of a trust?

CHAPTER SUMMARY

The study of law is important to business because of the need for risk management. Risk management is the process of identifying, evaluating, and responding to the possibility of harmful events. Depending on the circumstances, a business can pursue various strategies for risk management, including risk avoidance, risk reduction, risk shifting, and risk acceptance.

A law is a rule that can be enforced by the courts. It is important to distinguish laws from other types of rules, including rules of morality. With the exception of Quebec, Canada is a common law country because its legal system was adopted from England. Canadian law can be divided into public law and private law. Public law is concerned with governments and the ways in which they deal with people. Examples of public law include constitutional law, administrative law, criminal law, and tax law. Constitutional law provides the basic rules of our legal system. Administrative law is concerned with the creation and operation of administrative bodies. Criminal law deals with offences against the state. And tax law is concerned with the rules that are used to collect money for public spending. Private law is concerned with the rules that apply in private matters. Examples include tort law, contract law, and property law. The law of torts is con-

cerned with private wrongs; the law of contracts is concerned with the creation and enforcement of agreements; the law of property governs the acquisition, use, and disposition of property.

The three sources of law are the Constitution, Parliament and the legislatures, and the courts. The most important is the Constitution, which is the document that creates the basic rules for Canadian society. Section 52 of that document says that any law that is inconsistent with the Constitution is "of no force or effect." Canada is a federal country because it has two levels of government: federal and provincial or territorial. Sections 91 and 92 of the Constitution create a division of powers by stating the areas in which each level of government can create laws. A government that tries to create a law outside of its own area acts *ultra vires*. The *Canadian Charter of Rights and Freedoms* is a part of the Constitution that protects basic rights and freedoms. Although many of its provisions are quite broad, the *Charter* is also subject to several restrictions. It applies only against government behaviour; it may not apply in favour of corporations; it is subject to reasonable limits; and some of its sections can be overridden by the notwithstanding clause. If a *Charter* right or freedom has not been respected, a court may award a number of remedies, including a declaration, an injunction, striking down, severance, reading down, reading in, and damages.

Legislation is law that is created through the authority of Parliament or a legislature. As a matter of risk management, it is sometimes possible for business people to affect the creation of a law during the legislative process. Subordinate legislation, which is law that is created by someone on behalf of Parliament or the legislature, is important to municipalities.

Parliamentary supremacy requires that the courts obey the Constitution and elected officials. Nevertheless, in some areas, the courts do have the authority to create laws. Historically, there were two court systems: courts of law and courts of equity. Equity was developed in response to the harsh nature of law. Today, there is only one court system. Every Canadian judge applies both legal rules and equitable rules. While those rules are still sometimes different, the concept of equity no longer allows judges to decide cases simply on the basis of fairness.

REVIEW QUESTIONS

1. Briefly define the term "risk management." Why is risk management important in the business world and how is it related to the study of law?

2. What are the three steps that are involved in risk management? Illustrate your answer with an example.

3. "The only sensible way to manage a risk is to avoid it." Explain whether that statement is accurate.

4. What is "in-house counsel"? Identify an advantage and a disadvantage to in-house counsel.

5. Are there any moral obligations that are not also legal obligations? Prove your answer by providing an example.

6. What is the difference between public law and private law? Can the government ever be involved in a private law case?

7. What is administrative law? Explain how it is relevant to business.

8. What is the difference between white-collar crime and corporate crime?

9. Briefly outline three areas of private law. Provide an example of each that is important to business.

10. What is the significance of section 52 of the Constitution? How is that section related to the concept of *ultra vires* legislation?

11. "The Constitution provides the basic rules for Canadian society. And because it needs to continually reflect the nature of that society, the Constitution

is easy to amend or change." Explain whether or not that statement is accurate.

12. "Since Canada is a *federal country*, the Constitution provides for a *division of powers*." Explain the meaning of that statement by focusing on the italicized terms.

13. Briefly explain how the introduction of the *Canadian Charter of Rights and Freedoms* changed Canadian constitutional law. Did it increase or decrease the grounds upon which laws can be declared invalid?

14. Does the *Charter* contain general property or economic rights? Explain why the drafters of the *Charter* did or did not include such rights.

15. Describe four restrictions to the application of the *Charter*.

16. Describe five types of remedies that a court may award under the *Charter*. Explain why some remedies are more active than others.

17. Explain the "dialogue" that some people believe exists between the courts and the legislatures. Why is that dialogue thought to be important?

18. What is the difference between legislation and subordinate legislation? Explain how those concepts are related to the operation of municipalities.

19. Explain two meanings of the term "civil law" and three meanings of the term "common law."

20. Explain the historical difference between law and equity. Are law and equity still separate systems of law?

CASES AND PROBLEMS

1. The Nagatomi Corporation is Canada's largest manufacturer of farm machinery. It specializes in custom-designing equipment to meet its customers' individual needs. Inga Raimani operates a farm in the foothills of Alberta. Because the terrain in the area is quite uneven in places, she cannot use a standard harvesting machine. Unfortunately, the custom-built harvester that she has used for the past 23 years was destroyed in a fire last winter.

Immediately after the accident, she contacted Nagatomi and ordered a replacement. She stressed to the sales representative that she absolutely needed the machine by the first day of September. The parties drafted a contract, which contained the following provisions:

(5) The Nagatomi Corp shall deliver the unit by the last day of August of the current year.

(6) Inga Raimani shall pay the full price of $150 000 before delivery.

(9) In the event that payment is not received by the last day of August of the current year, Inga Raimani shall lose the right to demand possession of the machine and the Nagatomi Corp shall have the right to sell the machine to another customer. If the machine is re-sold to another customer, Inga Raimani shall compensate the Nagatomi Corp for any expenses or losses that it incurs as a result.

By the middle of August, Nagatomi contacted Inga and informed her that the machine was ready for delivery. At that point, however, she informed the company that she did not have $150 000 and that she was unable to obtain a bank loan. She explained that her financial situation had been badly damaged by a number of health problems and by a sharp increase in the cost of farm supplies. But she also further explained that her crop was particularly good and that she would easily be able to pay the full price, with interest, *after* the harvest. She therefore pleaded with the company to deliver the machine first and to accept payment later.

Nagatomi realizes that Inga cannot harvest her crop without the machine. It also realizes, in light of her recent problems, that she would probably be forced into bankruptcy if she could not bring in the harvest. At the same time, however, it knows that it is not under any legal obligation to deliver the machine before payment. Furthermore, it has received an order from a farmer in Colorado for a custom-built harvester with exactly the same specifications as Inga's. That harvester does not need to be delivered until the end of next summer.

Is Nagatomi under any obligation to deliver the machine to Inga? Does it have a legal obligation? A moral obligation? Even if it does not have any obligation, should it agree to Inga's proposal? What factors influence your answer?

2. Rabby Industries Ltd manufactures computer software. Late last year, it launched Budget Smart, a program that allows users to manage their finances from their home computers. It shipped 1 000 000 units to stores around Canada. As a result of an extensive advertising campaign and favourable reviews in the media, sales have been very good. About 600 000 units have already been sold, and the rest are moving quickly from store shelves. Recently, however, Rabby's engineers discovered a problem. After 18 months in use, the program causes damage to some types of home computers. At this point, the full extent of the problem remains unknown. For instance, it is not clear which types of systems will be affected. It is clear, however, that in at least some situations, the defect will irreversibly erase the entire hard drive, and all of the computer's information will be lost.

Rabby has not yet received any customer complaints. The company knows, however, that the situation will soon change. It is therefore concerned about a number of things. It is distressed by the thought of damaging customers' computers. It is worried that it might be forced into bankruptcy if it is held liable in a large number of cases. And it is worried that it might even be financially ruined by a small number of claims. Since it is still a relatively new company in a highly competitive field, it could be wiped out by bad publicity.

Discuss Rabby's situation from a risk management perspective. Explain the process of risk management and identify several responses that the company might consider.

3. After years of feeling politically neglected and abused by the federal government, the voters of a particular province elected a government that was committed to eventually forming a new country. Although the government of that province is not yet ready to declare its independence, it has decided to take steps in that direction. For instance, it recently enacted a statute that creates a new system of money. The premier believes that the people of her province will develop an even greater sense of pride if they have their own bills and coins to spend. Is that legislation valid? Explain your answer.

4. As a result of a number of scandals, the federal government has become extremely sensitive to criticism. Parliament therefore has recently added a section to the *Criminal Code* that makes it a crime to criticize the prime minister's behaviour. Because of concerns about freedom of speech, that section was written to ensure that the new law does *not* apply to individuals. It applies only to corporations and similar types of organizations. The company that owns *Picayune*, a political magazine, believes that the new provision is unconstitutional. Is it correct? Explain your answer.

5. You live in the city of Peterborough. City Council recently created By-law 2720, which states:

    1. No bill, poster, sign or other advertisement of any nature whatsoever shall be attached to any public property, including any pole, post or other object which is used for the purpose of carrying the transmission lines of any telephone, telegraph or electric power company within the limits of the City of Peterborough.
    2. Every person who contravenes this by-law is guilty of an offence and liable to a penalty not to exceed Two Thousand Dollars ($2,000.00) exclusive of costs for each and every such offence.

    You operate a nightclub that regularly features live musical performances. You advertise those performances by posting signs on telephone poles. You have been charged under By-law 2720. You are worried about the possibility of paying a fine, but you are more worried about the general effect that the by-law will have on your business. You simply cannot afford to buy advertising space in newspapers or on television. If you cannot attach your advertisements to city poles, you will not be able to effectively advertise at all.

Is it possible for you to successfully challenge By-law 2720 under the *Charter of Rights and Freedoms*? Explain the arguments that you would make to a court. Explain how the city would likely respond if the court agreed that the by-law violated your *Charter* rights.

6. Because skateboarding is a particularly dangerous activity, the Ontario government recently created the *Skateboarding Liability Act*. Its purpose is to force certain people to take responsibility for their own risky behaviour. The relevant sections of the statute state:

    12. No action shall be brought against the owner or operator of a licensed skateboarding park for any injuries that are suffered as a result of a skateboarding accident.
    13. This act only applies to adults and does not affect the rights of minors. A minor is any person who is under the age of 18 at the time of an accident.
    14. This act does not apply if an injury is suffered as a result of the gross negligence of the owner or operator of a skateboarding park.

    Anna Eagles recently sued the Concrete Wave Skateboarding Corporation for catastrophic injuries she suffered as a result of an accident at one of their outdoor parks. The evidence indicates that she visited the park very early one morning and slipped on a wet patch. The parties agree that the wet patch was a small puddle that was created by a light rain shower the night before. They also agree that Concrete Wave was negligent (that is, careless), but not grossly negligent (that is, extremely careless) in failing to remove the water before the park opened.

    The corporation proved that Anna was 18 at the time of the accident and therefore argued that the *Skateboarding Liability Act* prevented her from suing. Anna, on the other hand, argued that a Canadian court can ignore a statute if it would lead to an unfair result. The trial judge accepted Anna's position after being influenced by a number of factors.

    Anna is now a paraplegic with enormous medical bills.

    Concrete Wave is a large company with a great deal of money and full insurance coverage.

    If Anna had suffered the same injuries before her eighteenth birthday, she would be entitled to sue the corporation. Furthermore, Anna is somewhat immature. While she does not have any sort of mental disability, it is quite clear that she was "young for her age" at the time of the accident. Her lawyer made a compelling argument that she was in need of the same sort of protection that the statute gives to people who are, say, 17.

    Has the trial judge in this case done anything wrong?

Weblinks

Primary Resources

Canadian Legislation   www.legis.ca/en/index.html

This website provides access to online versions of statutes and regulations for every province and territory.

Canadian Constitution   http://laws.justice.gc.ca/en/const/index.html

This website contains access to the complete text of the Canadian Constitution.

Criminal Code   http://laws.justice.gc.ca/en/C-46/

This website, belonging to the Government of Canada, provides online access to the complete *Criminal Code*.

The Canadian Legal System

Supreme Court of Canada   www.scc-csc.gc.ca/Welcome/index_e.asp

This is the official website of the Supreme Court of Canada. Among other things, it provides access to biographies of the judges on that court, and links to all of the Court's judgments since 1983.

Canada's Court System   http://canada.justice.gc.ca/en/dept/pub/trib/index.html

This link to the Department of Justice website gives an overview of Canada's court system. It describes the different types of courts and their administration.

Canada's Legal Tradition   www.mta.ca/faculty/arts/canadian_studies/english/about/law/index.htm

This website, prepared by the Department of Canadian Heritage, offers information on Canada's legal tradition, including descriptions of the distinction between common law and civil law, the distinction between public law and private law, sources of law, and the division of powers.

Canadian Justice System   http://canada.justice.gc.ca/en/jus/index.html

This comprehensive website contains information on the goals, sources, and operation of the Canadian justice system. It also gives an overview of the procedure used in civil and criminal cases.

Legal Research

Access to Justice Network   www.acjnet.org/splash/default.aspx

This educational resource has a searchable database and numerous links to a variety of legal topics.

Department of Justice Canada   http://canada.justice.gc.ca

This website offers a range of information related to the Canadian justice system. Besides providing information on the department's programs and services, the site contains links to other legal resources.

Canadian Legal Information Institute   www.canlii.org

This information resource, created by the Federation of Law Societies of Canada, provides a searchable database and links to court websites and legislative materials arranged by jurisdiction.

Jurist Canada   http://jurist.law.utoronto.ca

Jurist provides links to websites developed by Canadian law teachers for courses on such topics as contracts, labour, and property law. It also offers access to a variety of national and international research resources.

Best Guide to Canadian Legal Research   http://legalresearch.org

This guide offers strategies and techniques for Canadian legal research, links to a number of online research tools, and access to statutory materials arranged by jurisdiction.

Duhaime Law: Legal Dictionary   www.duhaime.org/dictionary/diction.aspx

This website provides a free online legal dictionary.

General Interest

Duhaime Law: Law Museum   www.duhaime.org/Law_museum

This website contains links to a number of interesting documents, including *Timetable of World Legal History*, *Law Museum Archives* (contains links to pages that provide some of history's most famous laws or legal codes: the *Code of Hammurabi*, the *Ten Commandments*, the *Magna Carta*, the English *Bill of Rights*, and the American *Declaration of Independence*), *Law Hall of Fame* (containing biographical sketches of some of the most outstanding lawyers and judges in history) and *Law Hall of Horrors* (containing descriptions of some of the most infamous people and events in legal history).

ADDITIONAL RESOURCES FOR CHAPTER 1 ON THE COMPANION WEBSITE

(www.pearsoned.ca/mcinnes)

In addition to self-test multiple-choice, true-false, and short essay questions (all with immediate feedback), three additional Cases and Problems (with suggested answers), and links to useful Web destinations, the Companion Website provides the following resources for Chapter 1:

- *Constitution Act 1867*, sections 91 and 92
- *Canadian Charter of Rights and Freedoms*

Provincial Material

- **British Columbia:** British Columbia's Legislative Process, Administrative Tribunals, Judicial Review, Statutory Interpretation, Municipal Bylaws, British Columbia's Electoral System, Government Lobbyists, Self-Regulating Professionl Bodies
- **Alberta:** *Adult Interdependent Relationships Act*, *Alberta Human Rights Code*
- **Manitoba and Saskatchewan:** Division of Powers, Subordinate Legislation and Municipalities
- **Ontario:** Administrative Law, Agreements to Share Power, *Charter of Rights and Freedoms*, Exemption Clauses, Legislation, Same Sex Marriage, Jurisdiction, Public Liability Insurance

2 Litigation and Alternative Dispute Resolution

CHAPTER OVERVIEW

OBJECTIVES

After completing this chapter, you should be able to:

1. Describe class actions and explain when they can be used.

2. List the advantages and disadvantages of hiring lawyers and paralegals.

3. Define "pleadings" and list five types of pleadings.

4. Explain the difference between winning a lawsuit and enforcing a judgment.

5. Define "costs" and identify two situations in which a court may award costs that are higher than usual.

6. Describe contingency fee agreements.

7. Identify different types of trial courts and appeal courts.

8. Explain the advantages and disadvantages of small claims courts.

9. Describe the court hierarchy and explain how it is related to the doctrine of precedent and the rule of law.

10. Identify forms of alternative dispute resolution and explain how they compare to litigation.

When people think about the law, they usually think about courts—about lawyers standing up and making arguments, and about judges sitting back and making decisions. One side wins and the other side loses. And indeed, that is an important part of Canadian law. In this chapter, we will examine the *litigation* process in more detail. **Litigation** is the system of resolving disputes in court. As always, our discussion will focus on issues of risk management. We will see how a business person may reduce the risks that are associated with litigation. We will, however, also look outside of the litigation system. As successful business people realize, litigation is often a poor way to settle disputes. Among other things, it is usually expensive, often unpredictable, and frequently fatal to business relationships. We will therefore examine several types of *alternative dispute resolution* (ADR) that allow people to settle their disputes without going to court.

litigation is the system of resolving disputes in court

We need to stress one point at the outset: Very few cases actually go to trial. It is easy to overlook that fact. We seldom hear about disputes that are settled out of court. Our focus instead is on those relatively rare cases that are decided by judges. Because a judgment is a public document, it may be reproduced in a case reporter and perhaps even mentioned in a newspaper.[1] Those cases are, however, the exception. By some estimates, fewer than 1 percent of private disputes are decided by judges.

THE LITIGATION PROCESS

This section provides an introduction to litigation.[2] We will look at some of the people who are involved in that system, the steps that have to be taken in order to win a case, and the different types of courts that may be involved. As we will see, it is sometimes possible for business people to deal with lawsuits by themselves. As a general rule, however, it is a good idea to hire an expert to help out with more serious matters. For that reason, we will focus on the big picture, rather than the details.

Who Can Sue and Be Sued?

In discussing who can sue and be sued, it is helpful to draw a distinction between people and organizations. As a general rule, every adult is free to use the Canadian courts, whether or not they are Canadian citizens. It is, for example, possible for an American consumer to sue a Canadian company for delivering shoddy merchandise. An adult who is suffering from a mental incapacity, however, must use a court-appointed representative. Children similarly must be represented by a parent or *litigation guardian*.

The situation is somewhat more complicated with organizations. As a matter of law, a corporation is a type of person. A company may therefore sue or be sued.[3] In contrast, unincorporated organizations, like clubs and church groups, are not classified as legal persons. As a result, they normally cannot sue or be sued. Instead, it is necessary to sue the individual members of those organizations. In some provinces, however, there is an important exception to

---

[1] Case reporters are books containing court judgments. A list of the most important case reporters can be found on the inside cover of this text.

[2] We will focus on civil litigation. The procedures that are used for criminal cases are somewhat different.

[3] There are, however, restrictions on foreign corporations, which may need to be provincially licensed before they can use Canadian courts.

that rule. Although trade unions are unincorporated organizations, they can sue and be sued directly.

Special rules may also apply when the government is sued. The traditional rule said that "the King can do no wrong." As a result, it was impossible to sue the Crown unless the Crown agreed to be sued. That traditional rule has now been changed by legislation.[4] The statutes are, however, complicated and they often introduce unusual restrictions. They need to be read very carefully.

Class Actions

Sometimes it makes little sense for people to individually sue, even if they have clearly suffered some sort of legal wrong. If so, there is a danger that the wrongdoer may get away with millions of dollars. Consider the recent case against the Consumers' Gas Company.[5] It sold natural gas to businesses and homeowners in Ontario. As part of its pricing scheme, it imposed a penalty of 5 percent on bills that were paid late. That late payment penalty was, in fact, contrary to the *Criminal Code*. For most people, however, it was not worth a fight—it was easier to pay the small penalty (say, $25) than to start a lawsuit. But because there were as many as 500 000 of those people, Consumers' Gas was able to illegally collect as much as $150 million. The law fortunately has a way to deal with that sort of problem. A **class action** allows a single person, or a small group of people, to sue on behalf of a larger group of claimants. In the case of Consumers' Gas, that individual was Gordon Garland. Although he had paid only about $75 in late payment penalties, he was able to hold the corporation accountable through a class action.

a class action allows a single person, or a small group of people, to sue on behalf of a larger group of claimants

Class actions are becoming increasingly common in Canada. Concept Summary 2.1 (see p. 30) lists some of the situations in which they are frequently seen. The primary attraction is obvious: They allow small individuals to take on large organizations. While it is difficult to find a lawyer to fight a large corporation for $75, it is much easier to find a law firm willing to take on a case that may be worth $150 million. The threat of a class action may also prevent a wrong from occurring in the first place. A company may not worry about thousands of claims worth a few dollars each, but it may worry about a single claim worth $150 million. Finally, class actions may also save society money. If there are thousands of claims, and each one is almost identical, it is cheaper to deal with them all at once. Court time is very expensive.

Seven provinces have legislation dealing with class actions.[6] Although the details vary from place to place, the basic ideas are the same.

- **Common issues:** There must be *common issues* amongst the various members of the class. For instance, they may all be women who received

---

[4.] See *Canada Crown Liability and Proceedings Act*, RSC 1985, c C-50 (Can); *Proceedings Against the Crown Act*, RSA 2000, c P-25 (Alta); *Crown Proceeding Act*, RSBC 1996, c 89 (BC); *Proceedings Against the Crown Act*, CCSM, c P140 (Man); *Proceedings Against the Crown Act*, RSNB 1973, c P-18 (NB); *Proceedings Against the Crown Act*, RSNL 1990, c P-26 (Nfld); *Proceedings Against the Crown Act*, RSNS 1989, c 360 (NS); *Crown Proceedings Act*, RSPEI 1988, c C-32 (PEI); *Proceedings Against the Crown Act*, RSO 1990, c P.27 (Ont); and *Proceedings Against the Crown Act*, RSS 1978, c P-27 (Sask).

[5.] *Garland v Consumers Gas Co* (2004) 237 DLR (4th) 385 (SCC).

[6.] *Class Proceedings Act*, SA 2003, c C-16.5 (Alta); *Class Proceedings Act*, RSBC 1996, c 50 (BC); *Class Proceedings Act*, CCSM, c C130 (Man); *Class Actions Act*, SNL 2001, c C-18.1 (Nfld); *Class Proceedings Act, 1992*, SO 1992, c 6 (Ont); *Class Actions Act*, SS 2001, c C-12.01 (Sask); *Code of Civil Procedure*, RSQ, c C-25, ss 999–1051 (Que). Class actions are also possible in the Federal Court: *Federal Court Rules*, 1998, SOR/98-106, ss 299.1 to 299.42, as amended by *Rules Amending the Federal Court Rules*, 1998, SOR/2002-417, s 17.

CONCEPT SUMMARY 2.1

Class Action Claims

- product liability (*eg* prescription drugs that have disastrous side effects)
- mass torts (*eg* contaminated water that affects an entire town)
- workplace discrimination (*eg* a system that pays female employees less than male employees)
- clubs and churches (*eg* sexual abuse of children by clergy)
- banking law (*eg* improper service charges)
- business law (*eg* price fixing among companies that sell similar products)
- company law (*eg* misleading information that attracts investors)
- securities law (*eg* insider trading that hurts shareholders)

defective breast implants from the same manufacturer, or they may all be medical patients who received tainted blood from the same source. It is not necessary, however, for every claim to be identical. Even if the court allows a class action to occur, it may set up a process to deal with the special circumstances that affect some claimants.

- **Representative plaintiff:** The plaintiff must qualify as a *representative plaintiff*. He or she must demonstrate a workable plan for fairly representing the interests of the class members. That will not be true, for instance, if the plaintiff wants the court to rely on a rule that will help his or her claim, but that will also hurt other claimants.

- **Notification:** A representative plaintiff must also have a workable plan for *notifying* potential class members. It is not unusual, for instance, to see class action notices in newspapers or magazines. Those notices are very important. In most situations, a class action automatically includes every claimant who has not expressly *opted out* within a certain length of time.[7] And every member of that class will be bound by the decision that the court gives at the end of the trial. People who have not opted out cannot bring separate actions on their own.

- **Preferable procedure:** The court must be convinced that a class action is the *preferable procedure* for dealing with the claims. It will, for instance, consider whether a class action will become too complicated, and whether there are enough similarities between the class members.

certification represents the court's decision to allow the various claims to be joined together into a class action

- **Certification:** Assuming that the previous requirements are met, the action will be *certified*. **Certification** represents the court's decision to allow the various claims to be joined together and proceed as a class action. It is usually the most important step in the entire process. It demonstrates that the court believes that there is a serious and genuine claim to be considered. The certification of a class action is often enough to persuade the defendants in a class action lawsuit to settle.

[7.] In most provinces, *residents* of the province in which a class action is brought are automatically included in the class. Out-of-province claimants, however, must expressly *opt in* within the relevant time period. Otherwise, they are excluded. In Ontario and Quebec, however, there is no residency requirement. Both in-province and out-of-province claimants are automatically included in the class.

As we have seen, most provinces now have class action legislation. Those statutes have done a great deal to clarify the applicable rules. It is important to appreciate, however, that class actions are also possible in jurisdictions that have not yet enacted legislation. Case Brief 2.1 discusses the Supreme Court of Canada's latest thoughts on the issue.

CASE BRIEF 2.1

Western Canadian Shopping Centres v Dutton (2000) 201 DLR (4th) 385 (SCC)

Muh-Min Lin and Hoi-Wah Wu, along with 229 other individuals, invested in a company that was controlled by Joseph Dutton. Some time later, Lin and Wu became convinced that their investments were being mismanaged and that Dutton was acting improperly. They attempted to bring a class action in Alberta on behalf of themselves and the other investors.

Although Alberta now has class action legislation, the statute was not in force at the relevant time. The Supreme Court of Canada nevertheless held that the judge was entitled to allow a class action to occur under the *Rules of Court*. Chief Justice McLachlin established certain requirements:

- The class must be clearly defined.
- There must be issues of fact or law that are common to every class member.
- Success for one class member must mean success for all.
- The representative plaintiff must represent the interests of the entire class.
- The advantages to a class action must outweigh the disadvantages.

Legal Representation

Assuming that you want to sue, or that you have been sued, you need to make a decision regarding *legal representation*. Who will argue for your side? That question raises an important risk management issue.

Self-Representation

You have the right to represent yourself. You can go into court and argue your case before a judge, even if you are not a lawyer. And in some situations, it makes sense to do so. As we will see later in this chapter, for example, small claims courts have been set up to encourage people to deal with some sorts of disputes by themselves. There is, however, a great deal of truth in the old saying: if you represent yourself, you have "a fool for a lawyer and a fool for a client." Litigation is often very complicated. While it is expensive to hire a lawyer, it may be far more expensive in the long run to lose a lawsuit because of your own lack of experience.

Lawyers

If you do not want to represent yourself in court, you may hire someone to act on your behalf. The obvious choice is a lawyer.[8] There are advantages to doing so. Hiring a lawyer obviously does not guarantee success, but it does provide you with competent help and it may increase your likelihood of success.

Each province and territory has legislation to deal with the legal profession. That legislation restricts the practice of law to people who have met certain

---

[8] As we saw in Chapter 1, many large businesses have *in-house* counsel. Instead of hiring a lawyer every time that a problem occurs, permanent legal departments are part of the organization. While that approach is occasionally more expensive, it also increases the chances that potential problems will be identified before they become major difficulties.

requirements. A person cannot act as a lawyer until he or she has graduated from law school, completed an apprentice period known as a *period of articles*, and *passed the bar* by successfully writing a number of examinations. The legislation also establishes a body, usually called the Law Society, that regulates the profession.[9] The Law Society imposes codes of conduct and punishes members who act improperly. For instance, a lawyer who misleads a client or steals the client's money may be fined, suspended, or disbarred.

Law societies also require every lawyer to hold *professional liability insurance*. If your lawyer acts carelessly, and you suffer a loss as a result, you may sue your lawyer for professional negligence.[10] The lawyer may not, however, have enough money to pay for that loss. **Professional liability insurance** allows you to receive compensation from the lawyer's insurance company. Law societies also create **assurance funds**, which provide compensation to people who have been hurt by dishonest lawyers.

There are a number of other advantages to hiring a lawyer. For instance, conversations with your lawyer are generally *confidential* and *privileged*. That means that your lawyer cannot share your information with anyone without your consent and that your discussions cannot be used against you in court.

professional liability insurance allows a client to receive compensation from the lawyer's insurance company if the lawyer has acted carelessly

*an **assurance fund** provides compensation to people who are hurt by dishonest lawyers*

Paralegals

Depending upon your particular circumstances, you may hire a *paralegal* instead of a lawyer. A **paralegal** is a person who is not a lawyer, but who provides legal advice and services. Paralegals are an important part of the Canadian legal system. It is occasionally difficult to find a lawyer to work in a certain area or at an affordable price. Consequently, paralegals are particularly common in small claims courts and landlord and tenant tribunals.

*a **paralegal** is a person who is not a lawyer, but who provides legal advice and services*

Although the vast majority of paralegals are knowledgeable, professional, and honest, paralegals remain somewhat controversial. In contrast to lawyers, paralegals (i) do not always have formal legal education (though many have completed training programs), (ii) are not regulated and controlled by a governing body, like a law society, (iii) are not subject to mandatory codes of conduct, (iv) are not required to carry liability insurance, (v) cannot have their bills reviewed by a courthouse official, and (vi) are not covered by the blanket privilege that applies between lawyers and clients.

CONCEPT SUMMARY 2.2

Lawyers and Paralegals

	Affordability	Expertise	Accessibility	Mandatory Training	Regulated Profession	Mandatory Codes of Conduct	Privilege
Lawyers	✗	✓	✗	✓	✓	✓	✓
Paralegals	✓	✓	✓	✗	✗	✗	✗

Concept Summary 2.2 may be somewhat misleading. It might seem to suggest that you should *never* hire a paralegal. That is not true. There is, however,

---

[9.] There are exceptions. In Nova Scotia, the body is called the Barristers' Society.

[10.] We will consider the tort of professional negligence in Chapter 6.

a widespread belief that paralegals should be carefully controlled.[11]

Governments, law societies, paralegals, and other concerned organizations are therefore working together to find a solution to those concerns. It seems likely that paralegals will eventually be regulated in much the same way as lawyers. They will, for instance, be required to undergo formal training, pass standardized tests, carry liability insurance, and obey general codes of conduct. In addition to protecting the public, those changes will enhance the reputation of paralegals.

Pleadings

Whether you act for yourself or hire someone to help, a great deal must be done before your case can appear in court. In this section, we will look at *pleadings*. **Pleadings** are the documents that are used to identify the issues and clarify the nature of a dispute. Some are prepared by the *plaintiff*, while others come from the *defendant*.[12] The **plaintiff** is the person who is making the complaint. The **defendant** is the person about whom the complaint is being made.

It is important to start the pleadings process promptly. Most types of claim are subject to *limitation periods*. A **limitation period** is a period of time within which an action must be started. The details vary depending upon the nature of the claim and the jurisdiction in which the claim is brought. We will discuss limitation periods at several places in this book. For now, we can offer a few general observations.

- Canadian limitation statutes traditionally drew a distinction between claims in contract (which had to be commenced within six years) and claims in tort (which had to be commenced within two years). That remains true in some jurisdictions.[13] Recently, however, there has been a move toward a simplified system in which most claims must be started within two years from the day on which the plaintiff discovered, or should have discovered, the cause of action.[14]

- Outside of the general limitation provisions, periods vary considerably. Depending upon the circumstances, the relevant period may vary from days to decades.[15] For instance, it is usually necessary to act *very* quickly if you intend to sue a municipality or the Crown.[16] But you may have twenty years to sue someone who has been improperly occupying your land.[17]

- The consequences of missing a deadline may also vary. The general rule in contract is that while the debt still exists, it is *unenforceable*. The

pleadings are the documents that are used to identify the issues and clarify the nature of a dispute

the **plaintiff** is the person who makes the complaint

the **defendant** is the person about whom the complaint is being made

a **limitation period** is a period of time within which an action must be started

---

11. *R v Romanowicz* (1999) 178 DLR (4th) 466 at 495 (Ont CA).

12. In a criminal case, the *Crown* (or government) makes the complaint against the *accused*.

13. *Limitation of Actions Act*, CCSM, c L150 (Man); *Limitation of Actions Act*, RSNB 1973, c L-8 (NB); *Limitation of Actions Act*, RSNWT 1988, c L-8 (NWT); *Limitation of Actions Act*, RSNS 1989, c 258 (NS); *Statute of Limitations*, RSPEI 1988, c S-7 (PEI); *Limitation of Actions Act*, RSY 2002, c 139 (Yuk).

14. *Limitations Act*, RSA 2000, c L-12 (Alta); *Limitations Act*, RSBC 1996, c 266 (BC); *Limitation of Actions Act*, CCSM, c L150 (Man); *Limitations Act*, SNL 1995, c L-16.1 (Nfld); *Limitations Act, 2002*, SO 2002, c 24, Sched B (Ont); *Limitations Act*, SS 2004, c. L-16.1 (Sask).

15. Limitation periods are contained in a number of statutes. Claims that are not caught by statutory limitation periods may be caught by the equitable *doctrine of laches*. A court may refuse to award a remedy if you waited for an unreasonable length of time and if the other party would be hurt by the delay.

16. For instance, if you want to sue a municipality in Ontario for an injury that was caused by a road that was in poor repair, you may need to give notice within seven days and start your action within three months: *Municipal Act, 2001*, SO 2001, c 25, s 44(10) (Ont).

17. See *eg Real Property Limitations Act*, RSO 1990, c L15 (Ont).

money should still be paid, but the courts are not willing to do anything about it. In other circumstances, however, the plaintiff's rights may die along with the limitation period. That may be true, for instance, if you let me occupy your property for thirty years. After the period closes, I may become the owner of that land.

- It may seem harsh that a limitation period could prevent a plaintiff from pursuing an otherwise valid claim against the defendant.[18] Limitation periods are, however, necessary for at least two reasons. First, after a time, memories fade and evidence is lost. The courts do not want to resolve disputes on the basis of unreliable information. Second, it is unfair to have a claim permanently hanging over a person's head. At some point, it should be possible to get on with life.

In most jurisdictions, a lawsuit starts with a *statement of claim*.[19] A **statement of claim** is a document in which the plaintiff outlines the nature of the complaint. It states the facts that the plaintiff intends to rely upon and the remedy that it wants to receive. Like all pleadings, it must be *issued* by the court and *served* on the other party.[20]

Once a party is served with a statement of claim, it must react quickly. If it does nothing within the relevant period (usually less than one month), the plaintiff may go to court alone and receive a *default judgment*. In other words, the defendant may lose by default, without having said a word.[21] Assuming that the defendant intends to deny liability, it should therefore prepare a **statement of defence**, which is a document in which the defendant sets out its version of the facts and indicates how it intends to deny the claim. Depending upon the circumstances, the defendant may also include a *counterclaim* along with the statement of defence. A **counterclaim** is a claim that the defendant makes against the plaintiff. For instance, if the plaintiff makes a claim for the price of goods that it delivered to the defendant, the defendant may make a counterclaim if it believes that it was injured as a result of a defect in that merchandise.

The plaintiff is entitled to respond to the defendant's pleadings. It may use a **reply** if it wants to dispute anything in the statement of defence. And if it received a counterclaim, it may use a *statement of defence to the counterclaim*. After receiving the basic pleadings, the parties may still not be entirely sure what the other side has in mind. They may therefore use a **demand for particulars**.

Pre-Trial Activity

A case does not normally go to court immediately after the pleadings have closed. The parties will first conduct *examinations for discovery*. **Examination for discovery** is a process in which the parties ask each other questions in order to obtain information about their case. For instance, if the dispute involves a claim against a car company for a vehicle that exploded on impact, the plaintiff's lawyer might ask the defendant's chief engineer about the

---

a statement of claim is a document in which the plaintiff outlines the nature of the complaint

a statement of defence is a document in which the defendant sets out its version of the facts and indicates how it intends to deny the claim

a counterclaim is a claim that the defendant makes against the plaintiff

a reply is a document in which a party responds to a statement of defence

a demand for particulars is a document that requires the other side to provide additional information

an examination for discovery is a process in which the parties ask each other questions in order to obtain information about their case

---

[18.] The rules regarding limitation periods are sometimes softened. For instance, a period may not start until the plaintiff could have reasonably discovered that it had a cause of action.

[19.] In some jurisdictions, a *writ* comes before the statement of the claim. A writ simply notifies the defendant that the plaintiff intends to sue.

[20.] Although the pleadings are written by the parties, they must be stamped and recorded by a court official before being put to use.

[21.] It may be possible to have default judgment later set aside, but it is obviously better to do things right in the first place.

company's product safety studies. Although discoveries occur outside of court, they are conducted under *oath* and the answers that they generate may be used as evidence during the trial.

While discoveries may be time-consuming, that time is better spent outside of court than in front of a judge. Court time is remarkably expensive and difficult to schedule. Discoveries, in comparison, are cheaper and more flexible. Discoveries may also serve another important function. By revealing the strengths and weaknesses of a claim, they may indicate which side is likely to lose if the case goes to trial. If so, it may be foolish for that party to press on. Further proceedings will simply add to the eventual cost. Discoveries therefore encourage *settlement*. A **settlement** occurs when the parties agree to resolve their dispute out of court. In the earlier example, for instance, the chief engineer might have been forced to reveal that the car company knew about the risk of explosion. If so, the company might agree to pay for the plaintiff's injuries in exchange for her promise to drop her claim.[22]

> a settlement occurs when the parties agree to resolve their dispute out of court

The vast majority of claims (more than 95 percent) are settled out of court. That is not surprising. The rules are designed to encourage settlements. Every jurisdiction has a system for *pre-trial conferences*. A **pre-trial conference** is a meeting that occurs between the parties and a judge. After the parties outline their positions, the judge may indicate which of them is likely to lose if the case goes to trial. If so, the likely loser may be persuaded to settle. Depending upon the jurisdiction, a pre-trial conference may be required, or it may be initiated by the parties or by the judge. Ontario has gone even further. Since 1999, it has had a Mandatory Mediation Program (MMP). **Mediation** is a process in which a neutral person—called a *mediator*—helps the parties reach an agreement.[23] That program currently applies to most claims that are brought in large centres, and it may expand province-wide in the future. Under the MPP, the parties are required to meet with a mediator within 90 days after the defence has been filed. The parties cannot go to trial until they have gone through mediation, and a party who refuses to cooperate may, for instance, be required to pay costs. Even when that process does not produce a settlement, it is intended to speed up the litigation process considerably.[24]

> a pre-trial conference is a meeting that occurs between the parties and a judge

> mediation is a process in which a neutral person—called a *mediator*—helps the parties reach an agreement

The Trial

If a lawsuit does go to trial, it will normally be decided by a judge. While a person who is accused of a crime generally has the option of appearing before a jury, civil litigation is almost always decided by a judge alone. If there is a jury, the judge is responsible for finding the law, and the jury is responsible for finding the facts and applying the law.

The court will hear first from the plaintiff and then from the defendant. Each side will present arguments and *evidence*. **Evidence** consists of the information that is provided in support of the arguments. In order to get that evidence in front of the court, each side will call *witnesses*. *Ordinary witnesses* testify about facts that they know first-hand (eg a pedestrian may describe a car accident that she saw happen). *Expert witnesses* provide information and opinions based on the

> evidence consists of the information that is provided in support of an argument

---

22. The company will also want the plaintiff to promise that she will keep quiet about the case. Negative publicity is bad for business.

23. We will discuss mediation in greater detail at the end of this chapter.

24. Unfortunately, the program has not been entirely successful. It may be modified or even terminated: J Jaffey "Memo Suggests Axing Case Management, Mandatory Mediation" *The Lawyers Weekly* (1 October 2004) 3.

evidence (*eg* a physician may suggest how the defendant's ability to drive was affected by the alcohol that he was drinking). The party who calls a particular witness will ask questions and receive answers during a process known as *examination-in-chief*. The other party will then have an opportunity to vigorously *cross-examine* the same witness. Canadian law is based on the belief that an *adversarial system* is the best way to get to the truth. Each side is encouraged to present its own version of events and to attack the other side's story. The truth of the matter usually lies somewhere in between.

There are strict—and often complicated—rules that determine which types of evidence are *admissible*. For instance, the courts generally insist upon *direct evidence*. They normally will not listen to *hearsay evidence*. **Hearsay evidence** is information that a witness heard from someone else, rather than directly from the source. Going back to an example in the previous paragraph, the court is not interested, for instance, in what the pedestrian's father heard about the accident from his daughter. The main problem with hearsay evidence is that it cannot be tested in court. The pedestrian's father does not have direct knowledge of the facts. He cannot explain precisely where the pedestrian was standing, what she saw, what she heard, and so on.

On the basis of its arguments and evidence, the plaintiff has to prove its claim on a *balance of probabilities*. That means that every important part of its claim must be *probably* true. While it is impossible to accurately measure these things, it may help to think of a set of scales. At the end of the trial, the defendant will be held *liable* only if the scales are tipped in the plaintiff's favour. If the scales are either evenly balanced or tipped in the defendant's favour, then the defendant will be *not liable*. In criminal cases, the standard of proof is much higher. The Crown has to prove the accused's guilt *beyond a reasonable doubt*. If that standard is met, then the accused will be found *guilty*. If not, the verdict will be *not guilty*.

> hearsay evidence is information that a witness heard from someone else, rather than directly from the source

The Remedy

Various punishments may be available if a person is convicted of a crime. The court may, for instance, impose a *fine* or a *prison sentence*. Canadian courts also frequently use *conditional sentences*, which allow criminals to serve time in their own houses, rather than in prisons. A different variety of remedies is available if the plaintiff wins a civil lawsuit. We will look at some of those remedies in more detail in later chapters. For now, Concept Summary 2.3 (see p. 37) will introduce a few of the more important possibilities.

Enforcement

There is a difference—sometimes a very disappointing difference—between winning a lawsuit and enforcing a judgment. A defendant who has been found liable and ordered to pay money to the plaintiff is called a **judgment debtor**. Unfortunately, even if the court has said that the plaintiff is entitled to a remedy, the judgment debtor simply may not have any assets available. For instance, it may be a company that is bankrupt. And even if the judgment debtor does have enough money to pay its debt, it may be reluctant to do so. There are, fortunately, several ways to deal with that second sort of problem.[25]

> a judgment debtor is a defendant who has been found liable and ordered to pay money to the plaintiff

---

[25.] In some circumstances, at least, there may also be ways of dealing with the problem of the defendant's bankruptcy. As we saw in Business Decision 1.2 (see page 22), it may be possible to use a *trust* in order to avoid the unfortunate consequences of the defendant's bankruptcy. We will see several other possibilities in Chapter 23 when we look at secured transactions.

CONCEPT SUMMARY 2.3

Remedies in Civil Litigation

Name of Remedy	Purpose	Example
Compensatory damages	provides the plaintiff with compensation for a loss	compensate an employee who lost income after being wrongfully fired
Punitive damages	punishes the defendant for acting very badly	punish an insurance company that fabricated an allegation of arson in an attempt to avoid paying a benefit under an insurance policy
Nominal damages	symbolically recognizes that the defendant acted wrongfully, even though the plaintiff did not suffer any loss	recognize the right of a store that sued for trespass, even though the unwanted customer did no harm
Specific performance	requires the defendant to fulfill a promise	compel performance by a vendor who contractually agreed to sell a piece of land to a purchaser
Injunction	requires the defendant to act in a particular way	compel a construction company to remove its equipment from a neighbour's property
Rescission	terminates a contract	eliminate a contract that a con artist tricked an elderly couple into signing

For instance, it may be possible to *garnishee* a judgment debtor's income by forcing his or her employer to pay money to the plaintiff. Or it may be possible to *seize and sell* some of the judgment debtor's assets, such as computers, vehicles, and land. (There are, however, limits to that type of remedy. The judgment debtor cannot be stripped bare or left without any way to earn an income.) Court officials and other types of public authorities, such as the sheriff, are available to help with those enforcement procedures.

Business Decision 2.1 demonstrates that it is important to know, even before starting a lawsuit, whether the judgment that you hope to receive will be enforceable.

BUSINESS DECISION 2.1

Judgment Debts and the Decision to Sue

Your company sells books and CDs over the Internet. It was recently brought to a standstill for three days as a result of a computer virus that infected your system. The overall cost of that incident, including the loss of sales and the expense involved in repairing your equipment, is about $750 000. After some investigation, you discovered that the virus was sent to you by a hacker in Whitehorse. As is common in this type of situation, that hacker is a high-school student who lives with his parents.

Further investigations and a brief discussion with your lawyer revealed additional information.

- The precedents consistently state that a hacker in this type of situation is legally responsible for the damage that has been caused.

- Experience suggests that this type of litigation tends to be quite expensive because of the technical nature of

the evidence. Furthermore, your investigations indicate that while the boy is remarkably lazy and unlikely to ever make much of his life, he is also very knowledgeable about computers. He has threatened to "create as much trouble as possible" if he is sued.

- Parents are generally not liable for their children's behaviour. Consequently, although the hacker was living at home when he sent the virus, he is the only person who could be sued. You could not bring an action against his mother or father.

Questions for Discussion

1. Should you sue the boy?
2. From a risk management perspective, what is the major argument against doing so?

Appeals

A lawsuit does not necessarily end after a trial. The losing party is often entitled to *appeal* to a higher court. An **appeal court** (or appellate court) decides whether a mistake was made in the court below. The party who attacks the decision of the lower court is called the **appellant** and the party who defends that decision is called the **respondent**. An appeal must be started promptly, normally within 30 days after the trial court gave its decision.

There are a number of significant differences between trials and appeals. First, while there is only one judge at trial, most appeals are heard by three judges (and sometimes more). Second, appellate courts do not listen to witnesses or receive evidence. Instead, they simply hear arguments from the parties or their lawyers. Third, appellate courts will normally deal with the law, but not with the facts. They will correct *any* mistakes that the trial judge made regarding the law. But they will overturn a finding of fact only if the trial judge made a *palpable and overriding error*.

The majority rules in an appellate court. For that reason, appeals are almost always heard by an odd number of judges, in order to avoid tie votes. If the majority believes that the decision in the court below was correct, it will *affirm* the lower court's decision. If it believes that the lower court decision was wrong, it may have a number of options depending upon the circumstances. It may *reverse* the lower court decision (for instance, by saying that the defendant was liable rather than not liable), *vary* some part of it (for instance, by saying that the defendant was liable, but for $15 000 rather than $10 000), or send the case back for a *re-trial* (if it does not have enough information to make the right decision itself). A judge who disagrees with the majority is entitled to write a separate judgment called a *dissent*. A dissent often serves a useful purpose by calling attention to some weakness in the majority's decision. And because the law is continually evolving, today's dissent may become tomorrow's law.

As we will see below, it is sometimes possible to appeal the decision of an appellate court. The most obvious example occurs when a case goes from a trial court, to a Court of Appeal in a particular province or territory, to the Supreme Court of Canada.

Costs

Litigation is an expensive exercise and somebody has to pay for it. To a large extent, the government supports the court system (including judges' salaries and the construction of courthouses) through the collection of taxes. Litigants are also charged fees for filing court documents and other services. For most litigants, however, the most obvious expenses are associated with lawyers. It is not unusual for lawyers to charge hundreds of dollars per hour. On top of that, lawyers often charge substantial amounts of money for *disbursements* (such as the cost of mailing letters and hiring expert witnesses).

Depending upon the outcome of a case, a litigant may get some relief from the court. Judges have a discretion to order one party to pay *costs* to the other. **Costs** are the expenses that a party incurred during litigation. As a general rule, they are awarded to whichever side wins the lawsuit. As a result, losing a case usually hurts twice. If the plaintiff loses, then it will be denied the remedy that it wanted *and* it will have to pay the defendant's costs. If the defendant loses, then it will have to pay for both the judgment *and* the plaintiff's costs.

It is important to realize, however, that there is often a substantial difference between court costs and actual costs. A judge will normally order the

an appeal court decides whether a mistake was made in the court below

the appellant is the party who attacks the decision of the lower court

the respondent is the party who defends the decision of the lower court

costs are the expenses that a party incurred during litigation

losing party to pay costs on a *party-and-party* basis. That amount is determined by regulations. And those regulations almost always set court costs at a lower amount than what the lawyer actually charged to the client. Suppose, for example, that I wrongfully cause you to suffer a loss of $10 000. You win your lawsuit. The court orders me to pay $10 000, plus costs of (say) $2000. Your lawyer, however, actually charges you $4000. While you will be better off than if you did not sue me, you will not be put back into your original position—as if the accident never happened. At the end of the day, your experience with the court system will still cost you $2000.

The courts do, however, sometimes apply a different rule. A judge may award costs on a *solicitor-and-client* basis. If so, the loser will have to pay for a much greater share of the winner's *actual* costs. Solicitor-and-client costs are, however, awarded only in exceptional circumstances. That might be true if the lawsuit was *frivolous and vexatious* (for example, if the plaintiff knew that it did not have a good claim, but sued the defendant anyway as a form of harassment).[26]

Costs may also be affected by an offer to settle. Although the specific rules vary from place to place, the rules are generally designed to encourage litigants to accept reasonable offers to settle out of court. Suppose, for instance, that you sue me for $20 000. Before the trial actually begins, you offer to settle your claim in exchange for $15 000. I refuse. If you win the case and the court finds that I am liable for *more* than $15 000, I may be ordered to pay solicitor-and-client costs, rather than party-and-party costs.[27] The same rules may also work in the other direction. You sue me for $20 000. I immediately offer to settle the case for $15 000. You refuse. Even if you eventually win the case, you may be ordered to pay my costs on a party-and-party basis if the court finds that I am liable for *less* than $15 000.[28]

Contingency Fees

The fear of losing a case and paying for one set—and quite possibly *both* sets—of lawyers may discourage people from suing. In some circumstances, however, that problem may be overcome through the use of *contingency fee agreements*. **A contingency fee agreement** requires a client to pay its lawyer only if the lawsuit is successful. Contingency fees are allowed in almost every province and

a contingency fee agreement requires a client to pay its lawyer only if the lawsuit is successful

---

[26] Ontario adopted a different system in 2002. Instead of party-and-party costs and solicitor-and-client costs, it now offers *partial indemnity* and *substantial indemnity*. Partial indemnity usually provides the winning party with about 40 to 50 percent of its actual costs; substantial indemnity usually covers about 70 to 80 percent. A second change involves the calculation of costs. Ontario has abandoned its old tariff for a new system in which costs are based on the number of years that the lawyer has been in practice, the number of hours that he or she spent on the case, and the type of proceedings that were involved (such as a discovery or a trial).

[27] The rules that apply in the Federal Court are even harsher. A judge may award *double* party-and-party costs (excluding disbursements) from the time that the offer was made if the defendant is held liable for at least the amount contained in the plaintiff's offer: *Federal Rules of Court*, SOR 98-106, Rule 420(1).

[28] The rules in the Federal Court are again even harsher. If the defendant is held liable for less than the amount contained in its offer, then the plaintiff may be entitled to party-and-party costs up until the time of the offer, but the defendant may be entitled to *double* party-and-party costs from the time of the offer. And if the court finds that the defendant is not liable at all, then the plaintiff may be ordered to pay party-and-party costs from the time that the case started, plus *double* party-and-party costs from the time that the offer was made: *Federal Rules of Court*, SOR 98-106, Rule 420(1).

territory.[29] The only exception is Ontario, and it appears to be close to accepting contingency fees as well.[30]

Contingency fee agreements undoubtedly serve a useful purpose. Many people cannot generally afford to litigate. Consider the situation of a small business that has been wrongfully injured by a much larger corporation. The small business certainly does not have enough money to pay a monthly lawyer's bill as the case (slowly) makes its way through the system. And even if the law firm is prepared to *defer* collection of its bill until after the case is finished, the small business may not be willing to accept the risk of losing the case and eventually being required to pay a massive bill. A contingency fee agreement would help. Assuming that the lawyer is willing to work on such a basis, the small business would be able to sue without the fear of being financially ruined.

Contingency fee agreements are not, however, necessarily as attractive as they may seem. They cut both ways. While the client may not be required to pay anything if the case is lost, it will be required to pay much more than usual if the case is won. Lawyers are, after all, in the business of making money. If they lose money in some cases, they want to make it up in others. As a result, it is not unusual for a contingency fee agreement to allow a lawyer to keep 25–40 percent of everything that is won.[31] The precise amount will depend upon the circumstances.[32] A contingency fee agreement may also encourage a lawyer to settle a claim quickly and cheaply. Both of those concerns can be seen in Ethical Perspective 2.1.

ETHICAL PERSPECTIVE 2.1

Contingency Fee Agreement

You have become seriously ill. You believe that the problem was caused by toxic waste that a company illegally dumped into a lake near your home. You require expensive prescription drugs and you will probably never be able to return to a full-time job. The evidence indicates that your damages amount to $1 000 000. Because you have little money, and because toxic waste claims are difficult to prove (especially against wealthy corporations with teams of high-priced lawyers), it is difficult to find someone to take your case. You did, however, recently meet a lawyer who is willing to work for a contingency fee of 40 percent. Unfortunately, he also appears to be down on his luck and a bit desperate.

Questions for Discussion

1. Should you accept the lawyer's offer? Even if you win your case and the judge orders the defendant to pay $1 000 000, you will only receive $600 000 after the lawyer has taken his share. Will you only buy 60 percent of the medication that you require? How will you live?

2. Assume that you signed the contingency fee agreement. Early in the case, the defendant's lawyers offers to pay $200 000 if you will drop the claim and keep quiet (the company is worried about bad publicity that may encourage other people to sue). You ask your lawyer for his advice. He strongly suggests that you should accept the offer. You are not sure that you can trust him. Is he perhaps subconsciously motivated by a desire to earn an easy $80 000, rather than face the risk of being paid nothing?

---

[29] The governing rules often prohibit contingency fee agreements in certain types of cases, such as criminal prosecutions and family matters.

[30] Ontario already allows contingency fees agreements to be used in class action proceedings.

[31] In most jurisdictions, there is no set limit. British Columbia is an exception. In that province, a contingency fee generally cannot exceed 33 percent in a case of personal injury or death arising from a motor vehicle accident, or 40 percent for other causes of personal injury or death: *British Columbia Law Society Rules*, Rule 8-2. There are no limits for other types of claims.

[32] For instance, contingency fee agreements often apply only to the lawyer's fee, so that the client is required to pay for disbursements (expenses) in any event.

THE COURT SYSTEM

We have already seen the general structure of the Canadian court system: there are trial courts, appeal courts, and the Supreme Court of Canada. We can now describe some of those courts in more detail.

The Supreme Court of Canada

The Supreme Court of Canada is the highest court in the country. It has nine members: the Chief Justice and eight others (called *puisne* judges).[33] They are all appointed by the federal government,[34] and like most Canadian judges, they are entitled to keep those jobs until they turn 75.[35] In recent years, that appointment process has become increasingly controversial. As we saw in the last chapter, the Supreme Court of Canada's interpretation of the *Charter of Rights and Freedoms* significantly affects Canadian society. At the same time, however, the appointment process remains highly secretive. Although there have been minor reforms, the prime minister still effectively has the power to select judges by him or herself. In contrast to the United States, that process is not open to the public and the opposition parties in Parliament do not have an opportunity to question candidates. Should the public have more say in selecting the people who may fundamentally change the way that the country operates?

The Supreme Court of Canada is not a trial court. With rare exceptions, it only hears appeals from other appellate courts.[36] Furthermore, it is generally entitled to choose which appeals it will hear.[37] If you want to take your case to the Supreme Court, you must successfully apply for *leave*, or permission, to appeal. That is not easy to do. Most leave applications are *denied*. The Supreme Court of Canada will generally not *grant* leave to appeal simply because the lower courts made a mistake. It normally agrees to hear an appeal only if a case raises an issue of national importance. Appeals are almost always heard by five, seven, or nine *justices* (as the judges are properly called). As previously explained, an odd number is required in case some of the justices *dissent*, or disagree, on the outcome. In that situation, the majority opinion prevails.

Court of Appeal

Every province and territory has a court of appeal. Although each one is concerned with the law in its own jurisdiction, its members are appointed by the federal government, not by the provincial or territorial government. Appeals at

---

[33]. Pronounced "puny." The term is derived from a Latin word meaning "later born" or "younger." The Chief Justice is not, however, necessarily the oldest (or largest) person on the court, or the one who has been on the court the longest. The Chief Justice is selected by the federal government (or, more specifically, the prime minister).

[34]. Some types of American judges are elected. Canadian judges are never elected—they are always appointed by the government.

[35]. Judges "hold office during good behaviour." That means that they may be removed for serious misconduct. The removal process is, however, very cumbersome (it must pass through the House of Commons, the Senate, and the Governor General) and it has never been used to remove a member of the Supreme Court of Canada.

[36]. It occasionally hears *references*, which occur when the government asks for an opinion as to whether a statute is constitutionally valid.

[37]. Some exceptions exist for criminal cases.

this level are usually heard by three justices, but the number is sometimes higher. The name of the court varies between jurisdictions, as Concept Summary 2.4 shows.

CONCEPT SUMMARY 2.4

Court Names

Province or Territory	Superior Court	Appeal Court
Alberta	Queen's Bench	Court of Appeal
British Columbia	Supreme Court	Court of Appeal
Manitoba	Queen's Bench	Court of Appeal
New Brunswick	Queen's Bench	Court of Appeal
Newfoundland and Labrador	Supreme Court, Trial Division	Supreme Court, Court of Appeal
Northwest Territories	Supreme Court	Court of Appeal
Nova Scotia	Supreme Court	Court of Appeal
Nunavut	Court of Justice	Court of Appeal
Ontario[38]	Superior Court	Court of Appeal
Prince Edward Island	Supreme Court, Trial Division	Supreme Court, Appeal Division
Quebec	Superior Court	Court of Appeal
Saskatchewan	Queen's Bench	Court of Appeal
Yukon	Supreme Court	Court of Appeal

Superior Court

The federal government also appoints judges to the superior court in each province and territory. The main job of the superior courts is to hear trials. However, they also occasionally hear appeals from lower courts. The names vary across the country, as Concept Summary 2.4 shows.

Federal Court

Finally, the federal government appoints the members of three specialized courts that deal only with cases that affect the federal government.[39] The Tax Court allows a person to dispute the government's demand for the payment of a tax. The Trial Division of the Federal Court hears trials concerning issues that the Constitution assigns to the federal government, such as copyright, bills of exchange, and telecommunications.[40] And the Appeal Division of the Federal Court hears appeals from its own Trial Division and from the Tax Court.

---

[38] In addition to the Superior Court and the Court of Appeal, Ontario has a Divisional Court. It consists of the Chief Justice of the Superior Court and other Superior Court judges. It acts as a court of appeal for provincial courts and administrative tribunals.

[39] The Federal Court's role in the government's regulation of business is discussed in Chapter 25.

[40] Concept Summary 1.1 (see p. 13), which appeared in the last chapter, listed some of the subjects that are federal matters.

Provincial Court

The provincial governments appoint the members of the provincial courts. These are trial courts. Although the details vary from place to place, they generally deal with four types of cases: (i) small claims, which are private disputes involving small amounts of money (we will discuss small claims courts in more detail below), (ii) family matters, such as support payments, (iii) youth matters, such as young offenders and neglected children, and (iv) most criminal cases. More serious trials are usually moved up to a superior court. That is true, for instance, of private claims involving large amounts of money and criminal cases involving crimes like murder. Decisions in the provincial courts can be appealed to the superior court or, in some circumstances, directly to the court of appeal.

Small Claims Courts

It will be useful to say something more about small claims courts. A **small claims court** is a type of provincial court that deals with disputes involving limited amounts of money. Although the basic ideas are the same everywhere, some of the details vary from one jurisdiction to the next. You should therefore check the rules before suing. Fortunately, because these courts are designed for easy access, basic information is often readily available on the Internet. A list of websites appears at the end of this chapter.[41]

a small claims court is a type of provincial court that deals with disputes involving limited amounts of money

Small claims courts are very popular with business people because they are faster, simpler, and less expensive than regular courts.[42] Since the rules and procedures are less complicated than usual, many parties act on their own behalf (though they are entitled to use lawyers or paralegals). Although the parties must pay court fees, the amounts are fairly modest.[43] Furthermore, small claims courts are, by their very nature, well-suited to deal with a variety of situations that frequently arise in the business context. Concept Summary 2.5 (see p. 44) lists a few examples of claims that are brought to small claims courts.

There are, however, certain drawbacks to small claims courts.

- **Geographical limits:** Small claims courts exist in many cities and towns across Canada. As a general rule, the plaintiff must sue either where the relevant event happened (for example, in the town where she slipped on the defendant's icy sidewalk) or where the defendant lives or carries on business. If the claim is started in the wrong location, it may be transferred to another court, which will involve additional expenses.

- **Types of claims:** Small claims courts can deal with most cases in which the plaintiff is suing for either a limited amount of money or the return

---

[41.] There are also several "how-to" manuals that are aimed at non-lawyers. See *eg* M Celap & P Larmondin *Small Claims Court for the Everyday Canadian* (2000).

[42.] In 2000, approximately 132 000 new civil claims (excluding divorces) were started in Ontario. Over 62 percent of those claims (82 000) appeared in small claims courts. See JF Kenkel & WS Chalmers *Small Claims and Simplified Procedure Litigation* 4th ed (2002) 1.

[43.] Although the amounts change from time to time, it is helpful to note, as an example, the fees that were charged in the Ontario small claims court when this book was written. It generally cost $75 to file a claim. The amount rose to $145, however, for "frequent" claimants (that is, claimants who had filed more than 10 claims in the preceding 12 months). That category included home renovators who regularly sued for the value of their work, and lending agencies who regularly sued for repayment of loans.

CONCEPT SUMMARY 2.5

Small Claims Courts—Common Business Disputes

Disputes Dealing with Money Owed	Disputes Dealing with Wrongful Losses
• repayment of loans	• losses arising from a breach of contract
• payment for goods delivered	• losses due to poor workmanship
• payment for services provided	• delivery of shoddy merchandise
• payment of rent	• damage to goods being moved or stored
• payment of wages	• personal injuries caused by defective products
• charges associated with NSF cheques	• losses occurring under a *Parental Responsibility Act*[44]

of property that it already owns. There are, however, several restrictions. The precise rules vary from place to place. In some provinces, for instance, a dispute arising from a defamatory statement or a false imprisonment must be taken to a superior court. Small claims courts are also incapable of dealing with federal statutes, including the *Income Tax Act* and the *Copyright Act*. Nor can they evict tenants or grant divorces.

- **Types of remedies:** Small claims courts cannot award equitable relief, such as specific performance and injunctions.[45] You therefore must go to a different court if, for instance, you want to force someone to perform a contractual obligation or you want to stop a neighbouring factory from polluting your water. As a general rule, small claims courts are limited to ordering the payment of money. As an exception, however, a judge may order a defendant to hand over property that already belongs to the plaintiff.

- **Monetary limits:** The most significant drawback to suing in a small claims court is that the court can only hear *small claims*. The size of the claim is determined by the amount of money at stake. The limit varies, sometimes quite widely, between jurisdictions. Concept Summary 2.6 states the limit that applied in each province and territory at the time that this chapter was written.[46] While a claim that is worth more than the limit may be brought in a small claims court, the excess amount has to be abandoned. It is not possible to split a single large claim into two smaller ones. For instance, if you live in Ontario and are owed $15 000 on a contract, you cannot sue twice in the small claims court, once for $9000 and again for $6000. Nor can you sue for part of the money in a small claims court and the rest in a superior court.

---

44. As we will see in Chapter 6, several provinces have enacted statutes that allow a person who has suffered a loss as a result of a child's wrongful behaviour to use a special procedure in order to sue that child's parents.

45. We introduced the remedies of specific performance and injunctions in Concept Summary 2.3 (see page 37). We will consider them in more detail in Chapter 3 and Chapter 12.

46. The limits change from time to time. Before suing, you should double check the rules.

CONCEPT SUMMARY 2.6

Small Claims Courts—Monetary Limits

Province or Territory	Maximum Amount
Alberta	$25 000
British Columbia	$25 000
Manitoba	$7500
New Brunswick	$6000
Newfoundland and Labrador	$5000
Northwest Territories	$10 000
Nova Scotia	$15 000
Nunavut	no separate small claims court
Ontario[47]	$10 000
Prince Edward Island	$8000
Saskatchewan	$5000
Yukon	$5000

Court Hierarchy

As we have already suggested, Canadian courts are arranged in a **hierarchy** according to their importance. We need to look at that concept in greater detail. The court hierarchy does not merely determine where a party needs to go for the purposes of a trial or an appeal. It also determines which rules each court must apply.

Figure 2.1 (see p. 46) illustrates the concept of a court hierarchy. The first thing to notice is that we should be talking about court *hierarchies*, rather than just a single court *hierarchy*. There is a separate hierarchy for each province and territory, and another for the federal courts. To simplify matters, however, we have limited Figure 2.1 to the systems that exist in two provinces (Province A and Province B) and the Federal Court.[48] The second thing to notice is that even though there are 14 separate court systems in this country, each one ends in the same place: the Supreme Court of Canada.

To fully understand the importance of that scheme, we need to introduce a second concept: the *doctrine of precedent*. The **doctrine of precedent** requires a court to follow any other court that is above it in a hierarchy.[49] We can demonstrate that idea by taking a few examples from Figure 2.1.

courts are arranged in a hierarchy according to their importance

the doctrine of precedent requires a court to follow any other court that is above it in a hierarchy

---

[47.] In Ontario, claims valued between $10 001 and $50 000 are resolved *outside* of the small claims court, but on the basis of a special set of simplified rules. The goal, again, is to make it easier and less expensive to deal with disputes involving limited amounts of money.

[48.] Figure 2.1 is simplified in another way as well. It does not list *every* court that may exist. As we previously noted, for example, Ontario has a separate level of court called the Divisional Court. Furthermore, some courts are divided into different divisions. The provincial courts, for example, contain small claims courts, youth courts, and so on.

[49.] Lawyers sometimes refer to that doctrine by the Latin *stare decisis*, which means "to stand by decided matters."

FIGURE 2.1 The Court Hierarchy

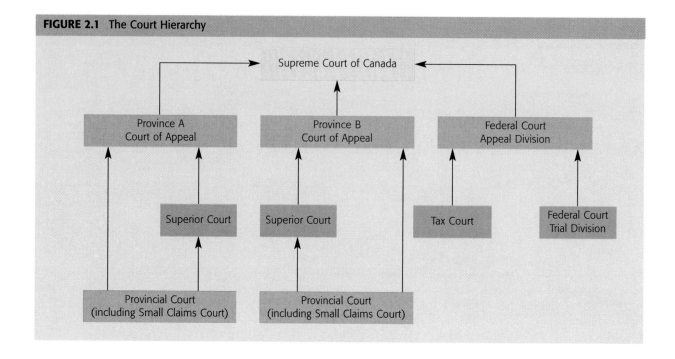

- Since it is at the top of the entire court structure, the Supreme Court of Canada is not required to obey any other court.[50] (It is, however, required to obey the Constitution and legislation.)

- The Superior Court of Province A must obey both the Court of Appeal of Province A and the Supreme Court of Canada. Those courts stand above it in the *same* court hierarchy. They are connected by the *same* set of lines.

- However, the Superior Court in Province A does *not* have to obey the Court of Appeal in Province B or the Appeal Division of the Federal Court. Figure 2.1 illustrates that these courts are not connected by the *same* set of lines. That means that they belong to different judicial hierarchies. That does not mean, however, that judges *never* rely on decisions from other jurisdictions. Suppose that a trial judge in Province A has a difficult case. Neither the Court of Appeal for Province A, nor the Supreme Court of Canada, has decided one like it. That judge is allowed to look elsewhere. Help may be found in the Court of Appeal for Province B or in the Appeal Division of the Federal Court. Decisions from those courts are not *binding*, but they may be *persuasive*.

- A decision may also be persuasive even though it comes from a *lower* court. Suppose, for instance, that the Court of Appeal for Province B is presented with a question that the Supreme Court of Canada has not yet answered. It may, for instance, look for help in a trial judgment from Province B or Nova Scotia. (It may even look to a judgment from outside of Canada.)

- A court does not have to obey a court that is below it, but it does have to obey one that is above it. There is one more possibility. Does a court have

---

[50] Until 1949, it was possible for Canadians to send their appeals to the Judicial Committee of the Privy Council in England, which the Supreme Court of Canada was therefore required to obey.

to follow its *own* decisions?[51] The answer is surprisingly unclear. While courts traditionally considered themselves bound by their own decisions, there is an obvious problem with that rule.[52] If a mistake occurs, there may be no way to correct it. And even if the old rule was appropriate when it was created, changes in society may call for a different rule today. The courts therefore appear to be moving in a new direction. The Supreme Court of Canada will now overrule itself in the right circumstances,[53] and lower courts sometimes do the same.[54]

Having looked at the court hierarchy and the doctrine of precedent, we can now introduce a third concept. The **rule of law** states that disputes should be settled on the basis of laws, rather than personal opinions. The concept of a hierarchy and the doctrine of precedent support the rule of law by requiring judges to follow the courts above them. That system has a number of benefits. One of the most important is consistency. For instance, the Supreme Court of Canada has decided that a mother cannot be sued for carelessly injuring her child before birth.[55] If that issue arises again in British Columbia, Saskatchewan, or the Yukon, it must be resolved in the same way. And that sort of consistency creates another important benefit: respect for the legal system. Even if you disagree with the trial judge's decision in one of those jurisdictions, you can be confident that it was based on law, not the judge's personal preference.

As a review of this section, consider how you would answer the questions in You Be the Judge 2.1 (see p. 48).

the rule of law states that disputes should be settled on the basis of laws, rather than personal opinions

ALTERNATIVE DISPUTE RESOLUTION

Courts are essential to a civilized society. Judges provide a way of peacefully resolving disputes when all else fails. As most lawyers will tell you, however, you should go to court only as a last resort. The litigation process has a number of drawbacks. Because it is usually necessary to hire a lawyer to work through the various stages of a lawsuit, litigation is time-consuming and expensive.[56] Because of the number of factors that go into a trial, the result may be difficult to predict.[57] Because the process is adversarial—with both sides attacking each other—it tends to be harmful to ongoing business relationships. And because the courts are open to the public, litigation may generate bad publicity.

[51.] The question is interesting largely because each court has many judges. Consequently, for example, although two very similar cases may be heard in the Court of Appeal for Province A, they may be heard by entirely different *panels*. In other words, each case may be heard by different judges. Of course, that will certainly be true if the second case is heard years after the first one.

[52.] In England, the Court of Appeal is still bound by its own decisions. Since 1966, however, the House of Lords has been entitled to overrule itself: Practice Note (Judicial Precedent) [1966] 1 WLR 1234.

[53.] *Harrison v Carswell* (1975) 62 DLR (3d) 68 at 71–72 (SCC).

[54.] There may be less need for the courts of appeal to correct their own mistakes. The Supreme Court of Canada can do that job for them. Nevertheless, the modern view tends to be that lower courts are entitled to correct their own mistakes. That view reflects the fact that the Supreme Court of Canada grants leave to appeal to very few cases.

[55.] *Dobson v Dobson* (1999) 174 DLR (4th) 1 (SCC).

[56.] It is not at all unusual for a case to wait two years before getting to trial. In 2003, lawyers' fees for a two-day trial were, on average, $10 200 per party. And the average cost of an appeal was $8310: "The Going Rate 2004" *The Canadian Lawyer* (September 2004) 48.

[57.] Litigation has even been likened to a lottery: T Ison *The Forensic Lottery* (1968); P Atiyah *The Damages Lottery* (1997).

YOU BE THE JUDGE 2.1

Court Structure

Oscar Reynes has sued the company that owns the Alberta Fire, a professional soccer team. Due to an administrative error, the team sold 20 000 tickets to a game even though its stadium contains only 10 000 seats. A riot erupted in the stands as fans fought with each other and with the police. Twelve people were killed, and many more were severely injured. Although Oscar did not attend the game and did not personally know anyone who did, he watched the entire spectacle on television. He claims that he has suffered psychological distress as a result of the incident.

As a member of the Court of Queen's Bench in Alberta, you heard Oscar's trial in Edmonton. You are convinced that he has, in fact, suffered emotional harm as a result of watching the riot. You are also convinced that the soccer club acted carelessly by selling too many tickets. However, you are not sure if the defendant is legally responsible for the plaintiff's injury. On the one hand, neither the Supreme Court of

Canada nor the Alberta Court of Appeal has discussed that precise issue. On the other hand, several other courts in the country have dealt with very similar cases. Both the Supreme Court of British Columbia and the Saskatchewan Court of Appeal *have* imposed liability. In contrast, both the Superior Court in Quebec and the Ontario Court of Appeal *have refused* to impose liability.

Questions for Discussion

1. Are any of those precedents binding on you? If not, are any of them relevant?

2. Given that consistency is one of the goals of our legal system, what can be done to make the law the same across the country?

---

alternative dispute resolution (ADR) is any process that allows the parties to resolve their dispute without going to court

For all of those reasons, many Canadians—especially business people—are turning to *alternative dispute resolution (ADR)*. **Alternative dispute resolution (ADR)** is any process that allows the parties to resolve their dispute without going to court. We have already seen that ADR is *required* in some situations. In Ontario, for example, litigants usually have to pass through the Mandatory Mediation Program before they are even allowed to go to court. For the most part, however, ADR is *voluntary*. The parties choose it because they want to avoid a trial. ADR may be used in almost any type of case. It is very common in family matters (because of the damage that the adversarial process may do to the parties' relationship), and it may even be used in criminal cases (as when criminals of Aboriginal heritage opt for *sentencing circles*). Our focus, of course, is on the use of ADR in business disputes. There are many examples:

- *international sales*—a manufacturer claims that the buyer failed to make suitable shipping arrangements
- *franchises*—local outlets in a chain of fast-food restaurants claim that they are entitled to control their own advertising campaigns
- *employment*—an employee claims discrimination on the grounds of a disability
- *consumer protection*—a group of customers claim that they were hurt by a defective product
- *leases*—a department store claims that it is entitled to renew its lease without an increase in rent
- *professional fees*—a client claims that its lawyer has charged too much for services
- *intellectual property*—a musician claims that her songs were sold without permission
- *sports*—an Olympic athlete claims that he was wrongly tested for performance-enhancing drugs

There are three major types of ADR:

- negotiation
- mediation
- arbitration

We will look at each of those possibilities in more detail. By way of introduction, however, Concept Summary 2.7 suggests how they compare to litigation.

CONCEPT SUMMARY 2.7

Alternative Dispute Resolution—A Comparison

	Quick and Inexpensive	Parties Select Decision-Maker	Parties Control Outcome	Likely to Maintain Ongoing Relationship	Confidential	Conclusive
Litigation	✗	✗	✗	✗	✗	✓
Negotiation	✓	✓	✓	✓	✓	✗
Mediation	✓	✓	✓	✓	✓	✗
Arbitration	✓	✓	✗	✓	✓	✓

Negotiation

A **negotiation** is a discussion aimed at settling a dispute. It is the most common form of ADR. Business people routinely settle their differences by doing what they do best—they make deals. It happens all the time, usually without much fanfare. For instance, if a purchaser is unhappy with the quality of the merchandise, the vendor may simply agree to reduce the price. If the situation is more complicated, the parties may negotiate through their lawyers or representatives.[58]

negotiation is a discussion aimed at settling a dispute

Like the other forms of ADR, negotiation often has several advantages over litigation.

- It tends to be quicker, less complicated, and less expensive.
- It allows the parties to control the process and decide the outcome themselves.
- It often helps the parties to remain on good terms with each other.
- Since it is a private procedure, it can be used to avoid bad publicity.

It is important to realize, however, that negotiation may also have disadvantages.

- Since negotiation requires co-operation, it may not be possible if a dispute has already turned ugly.
- One party may take the opportunity to simply drag the matter out—possibly in the hope that the other side will eventually lose interest or run out of resources.

[58.] Earlier in this chapter, we saw that costs may be awarded against a party who rejected a *formal* offer to settle that was filed with the court. That rule does not apply, however, to an *informal* offer made during negotiations.

- If the parties do not have equal bargaining power—perhaps because one side is represented by a team of lawyers, while the other side is small and inexperienced—then negotiations may not result in a fair settlement.
- Confidentiality may be undesirable—a consumer who has been hurt by a defective product may want to go to trial in order to publicize the manufacturer's poor safety standards.
- There is no guarantee of success—negotiations may collapse after years of effort, and the parties may have to go to court after all.
- If a dispute is covered by an insurance policy, the insured party may lose the benefit of the policy unless it immediately hands the matter over to the insurance company.

Mediation

mediation is a process in which a neutral party, called a mediator, helps the parties reach an agreement

Mediation is a process in which a neutral party, called a *mediator*, helps the parties reach an agreement. Mediation is different from negotiation because it involves an outsider. In other respects, however, the two processes are quite similar. The parties still control the process because they select the mediator. And they still control the outcome because mediation is *non-binding*. The mediator brings the parties together, listens to their arguments, outlines the issues, comments on each side's strengths and weaknesses, and suggests possible solutions. But the mediator does *not* give a decision, and the parties are *not* required to obey any orders.

Arbitration

arbitration is a process in which a neutral third person, called an arbitrator, imposes a decision on the parties

Arbitration is a process in which a neutral third person, called an *arbitrator*, imposes a decision on the parties.[59] As Concept Summary 2.7 suggests, it sits somewhere between mediation and litigation. It is faster and cheaper than going to trial. It allows the parties to control the process by selecting their own arbitrator. It helps them to maintain an ongoing relationship. And it is confidential. At the same time, however, it shares two important features with court proceedings. The parties do *not* control the outcome and they *are* (usually) required to obey someone else's decision.

The parties may decide to go to arbitration after a dispute has already erupted. It is, however, very common for business people to agree to arbitration in advance. A fruit producer in Honolulu promises to deliver pineapples to a beverage manufacturer in Vancouver. A Russian hockey star signs a long-term deal to play with a Canadian team. A construction company agrees to erect an office tower for a building mogul. The parties hope that things will go smoothly, but they are sophisticated enough to realize that problems may occur. If so, the parties want to have easy access to definite results. They therefore insert an *arbitration clause* into their contract. In a typical case, that clause will require the parties to *submit to binding arbitration* (perhaps after an attempt at mediation). It will also set out as much information as possible regarding the actual arbitration process. It may, for instance, set out a process for selecting the arbitrators and it may state that the arbitrator's decision is final. If necessary, it is usually possible to take the arbitrator's decision to court and enforce it in much the same way as a judgment.

[59.] It is not unusual for the parties to select more than one arbitrator. For instance, arbitrators often sit in panels of three.

The actual arbitration process will vary with the circumstances. It may occur anywhere in the world that is convenient for the parties. It may be fairly informal or it may closely resemble court proceedings. The arbitrator may, for instance, hear arguments from lawyers and receive evidence from witnesses who are under oath. But even when an arbitration looks a great deal like a trial, there will often be one important difference. The arbitrator will usually have greater expertise than the judge. The government selects people to become judges for a variety of reasons. And once those people are *on the bench*, they generally hear every type of case. Sometimes they have considerable experience in an area; sometimes they have none at all. After working as a criminal defence lawyer for many years, a person may become a judge and be assigned to a case involving a complicated international sales contract. In contrast, the parties will select an arbitrator on the basis of experience and expertise. Arbitrators are often lawyers or professors who have spent decades dealing exclusively in specific areas of law. They earn their reputations by consistently delivering decisions that are fair and well-informed.

Business Decision 2.2 examines the operation of an arbitration clause.

BUSINESS DECISION 2.2

Arbitration Clause

Frozen Pond Inc, a Canadian company, operates a wide range of manufacturing businesses around the world. One of those businesses is a car manufacturing plant in South Korea. Frozen Pond recently entered into a contract with Deutsch GmbH, a German company that produces steel. The contract will run for a period of ten years and it may, depending upon the circumstances, involve over $50 000 000.

The parties have agreed to use arbitration for any disputes that may arise. They have included the following clause in their contract: "All disputes arising out of, or in connection with, this contract shall be settled by arbitration."

Question for Discussion

1. The primary purpose of an arbitration clause is to set up a procedure that will allow disputes to be resolved quickly and easily. Have the parties selected an appropriate clause? What additional information should the clause include? What questions might arise if the parties eventually have to go to arbitration?

CHAPTER SUMMARY

Legal disputes may be resolved either through litigation or through alternative dispute resolution. Litigation is the system of resolving disputes in court. As a general rule, any adult can sue or be sued. Certain restrictions do apply, however, to children and people with intellectual disabilities. Corporations are treated like human beings, but other types of organizations are not. Special rules may apply when the government is sued. A class action may allow a single person, or a small group of people, to sue on behalf of a larger group of claimants. Parties to a legal dispute may represent themselves, or they may hire lawyers or paralegals.

Pleadings are the documents that are used in a lawsuit. They identify the issues and clarify the nature of the dispute. There are various types of pleadings, including statements of claim, statements of defence, counterclaims, replies, and demands for particulars. Pleadings

must be filed within certain time periods. The plaintiff's rights may be lost or unenforceable if the claim is not made within the limitation period. The plaintiff may receive a default judgment if the defendant does not react quickly to a statement of claim. The plaintiff is the person who makes the complaint. The defendant is the person about whom the complaint is made.

Before the parties go to trial, they will usually conduct examinations for discovery. They may also go through a pre-trial conference or a Mandatory Mediation Program. Most lawsuits are heard by a judge alone, but some are heard by a judge and a jury. Each side will present evidence. There may be ordinary witnesses or expert witnesses, who go through examinations-in-chief and cross-examinations. The court normally will not allow hearsay evidence. The litigation process is adversarial. In a civil trial, the plaintiff must prove the claim on a balance of probabilities. (In a criminal trial the Crown must prove the accused's guilt beyond a reasonable doubt.) In a civil trial, the judge will find that the defendant is either liable or not liable. (In a criminal trial, the court will normally find that the defendant is either guilty or not guilty.) If the plaintiff wins a lawsuit, the court may award compensatory damages, punitive damages, nominal damages, specific performance, injunctions, or rescission. A defendant who has been found liable and ordered to pay money to the plaintiff is called a judgment debtor. It is, however, sometimes more difficult to enforce a judgment than to win a case.

A party who is unhappy with a trial judgment may appeal. Appellate courts usually have at least three judges. The party who attacks the decision of the lower court is called the appellant and the party who defends that decision is called the respondent. An appellate court will correct any mistakes of law, but they will correct mistakes of fact only if the trial judge made a palpable and overriding error. The appellate court may affirm, vary, or reverse a trial judgment, or it may send the case back for a re-trial. An appellate judge who disagrees with the majority's decision may dissent.

Costs are the expenses that a party incurs during litigation. As a general rule, costs are awarded to whichever side wins the lawsuit. Costs may be awarded on a party-and-party basis or a solicitor-and-client basis. A judge may award costs either to punish a party for acting improperly, or for rejecting a settlement offer. A party who is concerned about the costs of litigation may find a lawyer to work on a contingency fee basis. A contingency fee agreement requires a client to pay its lawyer's fees only if the lawsuit is successful.

There are several types of courts in Canada, including the Supreme Court of Canada, courts of appeal, superior courts, federal courts, and provincial courts. A small claims court is a type of provincial court that uses simplified procedures for claims involving limited amounts of money. Canadian courts are arranged in a hierarchy according to their importance. The doctrine of precedent requires a court to follow any other court that is above it in the same hierarchy. The concept of a court hierarchy and the doctrine of precedent support the rule of law.

Alternative dispute resolution (ADR) is any process that allows the parties to resolve their dispute without going to court. Although ADR often has significant advantages over litigation, it may be inappropriate or undesirable in some circumstances. The parties usually choose to use ADR, but they are sometimes required to use it. There are three major types of ADR: negotiation, mediation, and arbitration. Negotiation is a discussion that leads to the settlement of a dispute. Mediation is a process in which a neutral party, called a mediator, helps the parties reach an agreement. Arbitration is a process in which a neutral third person, called an arbitrator, imposes a decision on the parties. Business contracts often contain arbitration clauses that set out the procedure that will be used if a dispute occurs. Arbitration is generally binding on the parties and the arbitrator's decision often cannot be appealed.

REVIEW QUESTIONS

1. "An organization can always be sued in the same way as a person." Is that statement true? Explain your answer.
2. List five requirements for a class action.
3. "Class actions are possible only in those jurisdictions that have class action legislation." Is that statement true? Explain your answer.
4. What is a paralegal?
5. List reasons why it may be preferable to hire a lawyer or a paralegal.
6. What is a limitation period? What happens if the plaintiff misses a limitation period?
7. What may happen if a defendant does not react quickly to a statement of claim?
8. What is the difference between a statement of claim and a counterclaim?
9. What is an examination for discovery? What purposes do examinations for discovery serve?
10. Explain the purpose of a pre-trial conference.
11. Explain the meaning of these two phrases: "the balance of probabilities" and "beyond a reasonable doubt." In what type of case will each phrase be used?

12. Define the following terms: "plaintiff," "defendant," "appellant," and "respondent."
13. Describe four different results that an appellate court may reach.
14. "Winning in court is often the easy part—enforcing the judgment may be much more difficult." Discuss that statement.
15. Explain how the courts use the concept of "costs" to encourage the parties to behave appropriately.
16. Assuming that you are a client, describe the advantages and disadvantages of a contingency fee agreement.
17. Explain the advantages and disadvantages to suing in a small claims court.
18. Describe the doctrine of precedent. Explain how it is related to the court hierarchy and to the rule of law.
19. List four disadvantages to resolving a legal dispute through court proceedings.
20. Define the term "alternative dispute resolution." Name three forms of ADR and identify some of the advantages and disadvantages of each.

CASES AND PROBLEMS

1. Hupton Motors Inc, an automobile manufacturer, produces several types of vehicles, including the Sprite. Although the Sprite is generally well regarded by consumers, there are several problems with the 2004 model. The colour on the dashboard fades rather quickly in sunlight, the upholstery is unusually difficult to clean, and the glue that holds the carpeting in place sometimes stinks in warm weather. Those problems do not affect the operation of the vehicles or create any safety hazards. They do, however, annoy the 6000 people who had purchased 2004 Sprites.

   Hupton has reacted quickly. It has changed its manufacturing process to prevent the same problems from happening again. And it is confident that a new advertising campaign will overcome the effect of any bad publicity that may be created by customer complaints. The only remaining question concerns the unhappy customers. The evidence indicates three things. First, because of the problems, the re-sale value of each car is about $500 less than usual. Second, it would cost about $1500 per car to fix the problems. And third, because the Sprite is aimed at the low end of the market, most of the purchasers would be unwilling or unable to spend a great deal on litigation. Hupton has therefore decided that there is little danger of being held liable and that the unhappy customers will simply have to get used to being unhappy.

   Identify and explain two concepts that may help the purchasers hold Hupton responsible for the problems that are associated with the 2004 Sprite.

2. Nomi owns a travel agency. Although her place of business is small, it is highly visible because of a custom-designed plate glass window at the front of the office. That window was shattered some time ago as a result of a careless accident. Nomi now wants to start a lawsuit. Will she face any particular complications? What if the accident was caused by the careless actions of (i) a corporation, (ii) a rowdy chess club, (iii) the government?

3. Windsor Construction Company built an office tower for the Bank of Regina four years ago. The building unfortunately has now begun to sink and lean to one side. The source of that problem is not entirely clear. The Bank of Regina blames Windsor Construction, which it claims did a poor job. Windsor Construction, however, claims that the problem is caused by the fact that the soil underneath the building is too soft. The company also says that it relied on a soil report that it received from the bank.

   Because the parties have become very hostile to each other, there is no hope for an out-of-court settlement. Furthermore, neither one is willing to go to arbitration. It is therefore clear that the case, which may be worth as much as $100 000 000, will eventu-ally go to trial. There are two main sets of issues. First, there are questions of law. For instance, the court will have to decide whether or not Windsor Construction owed a duty of care to the Bank of Regina even though the bank provided the soil report. Second, there are questions of fact. For instance, the court will have to decide whether or not the problem with the building was caused by poor workmanship or by weak soil.

   Windsor Construction recently met with its lawyer. The lawyer said that the case will certainly end up in the Supreme Court of Canada. "The Supremes have to hear a case that involves this much money—they've got no choice in the matter." The lawyer also said that since the case will eventu-ally go the Supreme Court of Canada, there is no need to make much of an effort in the trial court. "We can count on the Chief Justice of Canada to straighten out the facts and the law." Has Windsor Construction received good advice?

4. Roberto Norris owns a resort complex in Kananaskis. He was delighted to receive a call last summer from Carol Chambers, the president of the National Association of Authors (the NAA). Chambers indicated that her organization wanted to hold a month-long series of conferences, retreats, and workshops in February. Norris agreed to rent his entire complex to the NAA for a four-week period. That contract contained a number of provi-sions. One provision stated that the NAA would incur a substantial penalty unless it provided two weeks' notice that it wished to cancel.

   Chambers called Norris on January 29. She explained that the members of the NAA had decided in November to go to the Bahamas instead, and that they therefore would not be coming to Kananaskis after all. Chambers was able to re-rent some of the chalets in his complex, but he eventually lost a great deal of money on the deal.

   Norris would like to sue the NAA. He is, how-ever, worried about lawyers' bills and the costs of lit-igation. What can you tell him about the issue of costs? How would costs be calculated if he (i) won the case, or (ii) lost the case?

5. Glenn Brendel is a classical musician. Although he is now internationally famous for his work with sym-phony orchestras, he began his career by recording piano pieces by Bach and Beethoven. Those record-ings sat unnoticed for many years in the basement of the Vancouver studio where they were made. Recently, however, Trilby Svengali, the owner of that studio, rediscovered the recordings and realized that they had economic value. She quickly released them on a series of CDs, which have since topped the charts.

   While he is delighted with the public's reaction to his early work, Glenn Brendel is quite upset that the recordings were released without his knowledge, and he is very upset that he has not been paid for them. Svengali has responded by pointing to a contract that Brendel signed in 1971. Svengali believes that that contract gave her ownership of the recordings.

Brendel sued Svengali in the Federal Court for breach of copyright. While each party was confident that he or she would win, neither was anxious to go to court. Consequently, at the beginning of the dispute, Brendel formally offered to settle his claim for $400 000. Svengali immediately responded by formally offering to settle the claim for $200 000. Unfortunately, the parties were unable to reach an agreement and the case has now gone to trial. Both sides have run up very large lawyers' bills.

Consider the issue of costs. What will the result likely be if the judge finds that (i) Svengali is liable for $500 000, (ii) Svengali is liable for $100 000, or (iii) Svengali is not liable at all?

6. You operate a small lawn-care business. You have a staff of eight workers, which you employ from the beginning of April to the end of October of each year. You own several pieces of equipment, which you store in a large shed at the back of your property. Although that equipment is vital to your business, it is not insured. As a result of several incidents in the past, insurance companies have classified you as high risk. Therefore, you cannot afford insurance. As an alternative form of protection, however, you bought a combination burglar alarm/fire detector from the Sentinel Corporation, Canada's largest security company. In mid-October, the security system was smashed, your storage shed was vandalized, and all of your equipment was stolen. The police have indicated that there is virtually no chance of recovering the goods. You have explained to Sentinel that you believe that the theft would not have occurred if the intruder alarm had worked properly. Although the evidence quite clearly points in that direction, Sentinel has taken the position that the device did not prevent the theft because you did not use it properly.

The dispute is complicated by several factors.

- Since winter is approaching, you do not need to replace your equipment immediately. However, if you are unable to do so by the beginning of the next season, your business will be in serious jeopardy and might even be wiped out altogether. Due to a backlog of cases, court officials have told you that you probably could not get a trial date before June.

- If you won your case at trial, you would probably receive compensation for all of your losses. On the other hand, if you lost, you would not receive any compensation. As usual, litigation offers an all-or-nothing solution. At the same time, you realize that you could operate your business with less equipment. Consequently, you might be satisfied if Sentinel agreed to provide compensation for at least 70 percent of your losses.

- Your primary goal is to receive money from Sentinel. However, you also believe that an important principle is involved. After the theft, you discovered that Sentinel has a reputation for (i) occasionally selling shoddy equipment, and (ii) using its size to force dissatisfied customers into accepting small and confidential payments. Ideally, you would like to defeat Sentinel in court as a way of publicizing its unethical tactics.

- And finally, assuming that you are able to save your business, you will once again need security equipment. As a result of the theft, insurance coverage will be even more expensive than before. Furthermore, although there are a number of local security companies, their prices tend to be higher than Sentinel's because they deal in smaller volumes. Consequently, despite your current problems, you would probably want to do business with Sentinel again.

What type of dispute resolution techniques will you use to resolve your dispute with Sentinel? What are the advantages and disadvantages to each of the various options?

WEBLINKS

General

Duhaime Law: Discovery and Trial   www.duhaime.org/Civil/cabcsup2.aspx#discovery

This page explains the basic processes of pre-trial discovery and trial.

Duhaime Law: Alternative Dispute Resolution   www.duhaime.org/Civil/adr1.aspx

This website contains a general discussion of the various forms of alternative dispute resolution.

Department of Justice Canada: Paralegals   http://canada.justice.gc.ca/en/dept/ri/paralegals/about.html

This website examines the nature and significance of paralegals in Canada.

Paralegal Society of Ontario   www.paralegalsociety.on.ca

This website provides information regarding Canada's largest paralegal organization.

ADDITIONAL RESOURCES FOR CHAPTER 2 ON THE COMPANION WEBSITE

(www.pearsoned.ca/mcinnes)

In addition to self-test multiple-choice, true-false, and short essay questions (all with immediate feedback), three additional Cases and Problems (with suggested answers), and links to useful Web destinations, the Companion Website provides the following resources for Chapter 2:

- Sample Contingency Fee Agreement
- Sample Arbitration Clause
- Weblinks to information on the provincial small claims courts

Provincial Material

- **British Columbia:** Court Structure in British Columbia (Provincial Court, Supreme Court, Court of Appeal, Small Claims Court, Federal Court, Lawyers Fees, Law Society of British Columbia, Notaries, Paralegals, Sheriffs and Bailiffs, Class Action Lawsuits, Limitation Periods, Litigation Guardian, Enforcement of Judgments, Garnishment, Seizure and Sale, Mediation and Arbitration, Contingent Fee Agreements—See Lawyers' Fees, *Creditor Assistance Act*, International Arbitration, Juries for Civil Actions, Practice of Law, Proceedings Against the Crown, Writ of Execution

- **Alberta:** Civil Enforcement, Class Actions, Contingency Fees, Costs, Jurisdiction, Reciprocal Enforcement, Small Claims Court, ADR, Judgment Interest

- **Manitoba and Saskatchewan:** Garnishment & Remedies Before Judgment, Costs, Trial Courts, Lawyers' Fees

- **Ontario:** ADR, Administrative Law, Arbitration, Case Management, Class Actions, Contingency Fees, Costs, Court System, Judgment Debtor, Legal Aid, Legal Profession, Paralegals, Professional Liability Insurance, Mandatory Mediation, Simplified Procedure, Small Claims Court, Solicitor Client Privilege, Trial Process

You Have E-Mail—And a Lot of Evidence

Jamaycah Venne owns Good for Life, a business that sells vitamins and dietary supplements. Like many new ventures, Good for Life operates entirely through the Internet. Customers place their orders on a website, pay with credit cards, and receive their products through the mail. Business has boomed and Good for Life has grown considerably from its humble beginnings. Jamaycah has therefore hired a dozen sales representatives over the past three years. Those employees work from their own homes, which are scattered around the country. Aside from an annual meeting, when everyone in the company gets together for a few days, all of Good for Life's communications occur through e-mail.

Good for Life buys its stock from a number of suppliers. Until recently, that list of suppliers included Vivavex Inc, a diet pill manufacturer. While Good for Life has not yet received any complaints from its own customers, Jamaycah unfortunately became violently sick after using some of Vivavex's pills. She does not know for certain that Vivavex's pills caused her illness. She became deeply suspicious, however, after overhearing a conversation between two of Vivavex's scientists during an industry conference. Those scientists seemed to be discussing a secret company e-mail in which Vivavex's president told his employees to do whatever was necessary to cover up certain health risks associated with the diet pills. Not surprisingly, when Jamaycah stepped into the conversation and began asking questions, Vivavex's scientists stopped talking and walked away.

Jamaycah no longer wants anything to do with Vivavex. However, when she tried to return the diet pills that Good for Life still had in stock, Vivavex insisted that its products were perfectly safe and it refused to take them back. And when Jamaycah threatened that Good for Life would sue for breach of contract (because the pills that it received from Vivavex were defective), Vivavex's president simply laughed. "Good luck!" he chortled. "We pay our people very well and there's no way any of them would ever say anything that would hurt the company. And we're very careful to make sure that our official documents are all above board. You'll never get the evidence you would need to win your case."

Jamaycah is feeling a bit discouraged. Vivavex is a large company with a reputation for "playing hardball" when it comes to lawsuits. Jamaycah therefore seriously doubts that, regardless of the truth, any of Vivavex's people would ever voluntarily provide useful information. At the same time, however, she is deeply concerned about the risks associated with Vivavex's diet pills. She is worried that those pills may have long-term health affects on people who have used them—including herself. She is also worried that Good for Life may be sued if one of its customers becomes sick after taking the Vivavex pills.

Questions to Consider

1. As a general rule, is it ever possible for a plaintiff to force a defendant to hand over incriminating evidence? Explain your answer.

2. Assume that Vivavex's president was right about two things. All of the company's official documents indicate that the diet pills are perfectly safe, and none of the company's people are willing to say anything helpful. Where else should Good for Life look for incriminating evidence? In answering that question, think about the ways in which people communicate within modern organizations.

3. Although the topic is not discussed in the text, suggest several ways in which the legal system might respond if a party, like Vivavex, hides or destroys evidence that might be useful to the other side in a lawsuit.

4. Given her dealings with Vivavex, Jamaycah has begun to recognize some of the dangers that are created by interoffice communications. She also knows from personal experience that people often say things in e-mails that they would never write in regular letters or formal memos. What steps should she take to effectively manage the legal risks associated with the e-mails that Good for Life's people routinely send to each other?

Video Resource: "Email Alert" *Venture* 851, 27 October 2002.

Additional Resources

Bennett Jones *Document Retention Policies* **www.bennettjones.ca/ Publications/documentretention-2004.pdf**
This website contains a useful discussion of the potential consequences of eliminating or concealing evidence. It also provides a set of policies for organizing, maintaining, and destroying records within a company.

R Sommers & A Siebert "Intentional Destruction of Evidence" (1998) 78 *Canadian Bar Review* 38 **www.sommersandroth.com/ Intentional_Destruction_of_Evidence.pdf**
This website contains an article discussing the various ways in which a court may respond to a party that has destroyed or concealed documentary evidence.

E-Mail Policy www.emailcash.com/email-policy.html
This American website outlines the legal risks facing a business that does not devise and implement a comprehensive e-mail policy.

JISC Records Management http://195.10.246.65/legal_2.asp
This website contains pages that explain the importance of managing e-mails and outline the legal rules regarding the retention and destruction of documents (including e-mail). Although the website is British, its observations and recommendations are generally relevant in Canada as well.

3 Introduction to Torts

OBJECTIVES

After completing this chapter, you should be able to:

1. Define the word "tort."
2. Explain the similarities and differences between torts and crimes.
3. Explain the similarities and differences between torts and contracts.
4. Distinguish between intentional torts, negligence torts, and strict liability torts.
5. Explain the circumstances in which tort law will adopt a rule of strict liability.
6. Describe the nature of liability insurance and explain why it is important to business people.
7. Describe the concept of vicarious liability and explain how it affects business people.
8. Use the concept of risk management to explain how the difference between employees and independent contractors is important to the doctrine of vicarious liability.
9. Outline the types of remedies that are generally available in tort law.
10. Describe two important types of alternative compensation schemes and explain why they have been created.

There are two main sources of obligations in private law: contract and tort. Part 3 of this book is devoted to contract. We begin in this Part, however, with tort. Our discussion is split into four sections. The current chapter provides a general introduction to tort law. Chapter 4 considers intentional torts; Chapter 5 considers a variety of torts that affect business people; and Chapter 6 considers the most important tort of all—negligence.

INTRODUCTION TO TORT LAW

"Tort" is not a word that people often use outside of the law. It is derived from the French word *"tort"* (meaning "wrong") which came from the Latin word *"tortus"* (meaning "twisted or crooked"). While it is difficult to precisely define the term, we can say that a **tort** generally consists of a failure to fulfill a private obligation that was imposed by law.

a **tort** generally consists of a failure to fulfill a private obligation that was imposed by law

Torts and Crimes

That definition of "tort" contains a number of important ideas. Notice, for instance, that it refers to the breach of a *private* obligation.[1] An obligation in tort law is owed to a person.[2] For instance, I owe an obligation to you personally to not make defamatory statements about your past.[3] That obligation will be broken if I falsely tell your employer that you were once convicted of murder. I will be a **tortfeasor**—a person who has committed a tort. You will then be entitled to sue me.[4] If you win that lawsuit, the court will hold me liable and it will probably order me to pay damages to you.

a **tortfeasor** is a person who has committed a tort

A tort can be compared with a crime. Whereas a tort occurs when a person breaks a *private* obligation, a crime occurs if a person breaks a *public* obligation. A public obligation is owed to society as a whole, rather than to any particular person. Consequently, if something goes wrong, the government will prosecute the accused on behalf of the whole community. That is true even if the crime was one (such as theft) that affected a specific person. Finally, if the court agrees with the government, then the accused will be found guilty and may be subject to some form of punishment (such as a fine or imprisonment).[5]

Concept Summary 3.1 (see p. 59) summarizes the differences between torts and crimes.

Although it is important to distinguish between torts and crimes, it is also important to appreciate that the two concepts often arise from the same facts. If I hit you, I will commit the tort of battery and the crime of assault; if I take your car without permission, I will commit the tort of conversion and the crime of theft; if I sneak into your house, I commit the tort of trespass to land and the crime of break and enter; and so on.

---

[1] The definition also refers to a private obligation that was "imposed by law." As discussed below, a contract also contains private obligations that must not be broken. Contractual obligations are different from tort obligations, however, because they are created by the parties, rather than imposed by law.

[2] As we will see in Chapter 21, the legal definition of a "person" generally includes a corporation.

[3] The tort of defamation is discussed in Chapter 5.

[4] As we saw in the last chapter, you have to prove your tort claim on a *balance of probabilities*—the judge has to be satisfied that your version of events is *probably* true.

[5] As we saw in the last chapter, the government in a criminal prosecution has to prove its case *beyond a reasonable doubt*—the judge has to be satisfied that the accused almost certainly committed the crime.

CONCEPT SUMMARY 3.1

Tort Law and Criminal Law

	Private law or public law?	Which parties are involved in the obligation?	Who are the parties to the action if that obligation is broken?	What is the usual remedy?
Tort Law	private law	the defendant owes an obligation to the plaintiff	the plaintiff sues the defendant	compensatory damages
Criminal Law	public law	the accused owes an obligation to society	the government prosecutes the accused	punishment (such as a fine or imprisonment)

That overlap between tort and crime is not surprising. Those two areas of law share a common history. Every society has to respond to misconduct. Those responses tend to become more sophisticated over time. For instance, the common law long ago abolished the rule of *blood feud*, which allowed the family of a murder victim to take revenge by killing the murderer or someone in his family. In place of that rule, local communities began the practice of requiring a murderer to pay money to the victim's family. The same process also applied to other types of wrongs (such as breaking a person's arm or killing his horse). Over time, those basic ideas branched off in two directions. The idea of allowing a victim to demand compensation from a wrongdoer developed into the system of private tort law. And the idea of allowing the community to punish a wrongdoer developed into the public system of criminal law.[6]

Torts and Contracts

Just as torts may be confused with crimes, they may also be confused with contracts. We will look at contracts in much more detail in Part 3. For now, it will be enough to outline one similarity and four differences between torts and contracts.

- **Structure:** Both tort and contract involve *primary* and *secondary* obligations. Primary obligations tell people how they ought to act. For instance, the tort of battery says, "Do not touch another person in an offensive way."[7] The law of contract says, "Keep your promises." Secondary obligations are remedial. They tell people how they must act *after* primary obligations have been broken. In most cases, the defendant is told, "Pay money to the plaintiff as compensation for the losses that you caused." That is true whether the case involves a tort or a contract.

- **Source of Primary Obligations:** There are, however, some fundamental differences between tort and contract. The first is concerned with the source of primary obligations. Obligations in tort are simply imposed by law.[8] Even though you never promised to behave yourself, even though

---

[6] For an excellent summary of tort law's historical connection to criminal law, see M Kerr, J Kurtz & L Olivo *Canadian Tort Law in a Nutshell* (1997) 1–11.

[7] Battery is discussed in more detail later in the next chapter.

[8] The same is true of public obligations in criminal law.

we are complete strangers, and even if (remarkably) you never heard of such a law, the law says that you must not commit a battery against me. Obligations in contract, on the other hand, are created by the parties. If you have an obligation to deliver a car to me, it is only because you voluntarily agreed to do so.

- **Privity:** When two people enter into a contract, they create a special relationship for themselves. Consequently, as we will see in Chapter 8, the doctrine of *privity* states that the only people who can sue, or be sued, on a contract are the parties themselves. In contrast, because obligations in tort are simply imposed by law, there is no need for the parties to create a special relationship for themselves. I can sue you for battery, for instance, even if you never promised to not hit me.

- **Compensation:** Compensation is available in both tort and contract. As a general rule, however, it is calculated differently in each. The purpose of imposing obligations in tort law is to prevent harm. The tort of battery prohibits you from harming me with punches and kicks. Consequently, if you have breached your primary obligation, then you will have a secondary obligation to put me back into the position that I enjoyed at the outset. If I had to spend $5000 on medical treatment, I am entitled to recover that amount from you. In contrast, the purpose of creating obligations in contract is usually to provide benefits. I paid $10 000 to you because I wanted your car. If you breach your primary obligation, then you will once again be required to compensate me. This time, however, the goal is to put me into the position that I expected to enjoy once you fulfilled your promise. Consequently, if the car was really worth $13 000, then you will have to pay that amount to me. We therefore can say that while tort looks *backwards*, contract looks *forwards*.

- **Risk Management:** The fact that primary obligations in tort and contract arise for different reasons also has a significant impact on the issue of risk management. Because tort obligations are imposed by law, they are more likely to take a person by surprise, and they may require more than a person is actually able to give.[9] In contrast, because obligations in contract are created voluntarily, they should never take the parties by surprise, and they should never require more than the parties believe they can actually provide.

Concept Summary 3.2 (see p. 61) summarizes our discussion of tort and contract.

Types of Torts

So far, we have distinguished between tort law and other types of law. It is, however, also important to distinguish between different types of torts. As we will discover in the next three chapters, tort law covers a great deal of territory. It includes almost every sort of private law wrong outside of breach of contract.[10]

---

[9] For instance, as we will see in Chapter 6, the tort of negligence requires people to act with "reasonable care." That is true even if a particular person suffers from a mental incapacity and therefore cannot possibly meet the legal expectation.

[10] As we saw in Chapter 1, our legal system was divided into courts of law and courts of equity until the end of the nineteenth century. Torts were developed in the courts of law. Courts of equity also developed a small number of private law wrongs, including breach of confidence and breach of fiduciary duty. Although those equitable wrongs look a great deal like common law wrongs, they are usually excluded from the category of "tort" on entirely historical grounds.

CONCEPT SUMMARY 3.2

Comparing Tort and Contract

	Source of Obligation	Privity	Compensatory Damages	Risk Management
Tort	imposed by law	enforceable regardless of any agreement between the parties	place the plaintiff as if the tort did not occur	• may take a person by surprise • may require more than a person is able to give
Contract	voluntarily created by the parties	enforceable only by or against a party to the contract	place the plaintiff as if contract performed	• always possible to know the obligations in advance • always possible to limit the obligations to promises that can be fulfilled

Not surprisingly, different situations call for different rules. Tort law has to strike a balance between competing interests. While it wants to respect freedom of choice, it also wants to discourage dangerous behaviour. While it wants to allow businesses to be innovative and efficient, it also wants to compensate consumers who are hurt by manufactured goods. While it wants to tightly control activities that threaten physical safety, it also wants to adopt a more lenient approach where the only risk is to financial well-being. And so on.

Tort law responds to those challenges in a variety of ways. One of its most important strategies focuses on *mental culpability*. Because tort law needs to strike a different balance in different circumstances, some torts require proof that the defendant acted with a *guilty mind*, while others do not. There are three possibilities.

- *Intentional torts* occur when a person intentionally acts in a certain way. As we will see in the next two chapters, however, the law sometimes uses a rather odd definition of "intention." Some torts require proof that the defendant intended to hurt the plaintiff. Others are satisfied by proof that the defendant merely intended to do the act, even if they did not realize that they would hurt the plaintiff.
- *Negligence torts* occur when a person acts carelessly.
- *Strict liability torts* occur when a person does something wrong without intending to do so and without acting carelessly. It is enough that the defendant was responsible for the situation that resulted in the plaintiff's injury.

Concept Summary 3.3 (see p. 62) classifies the intentional torts, negligence torts, and strict liability torts that we will examine in this book.

Strict Liability

We will discuss intentional torts and negligence torts in considerable detail over the next three chapters. At this point, however, it is important to say something about strict liability torts, which are unusual and often misunderstood.

Strict liability torts create special problems for risk management. As previously explained, the courts do not require proof of any sort of intentional or careless wrongdoing. It may be enough that the defendant was innocently responsible for the situation that resulted in the plaintiff's injury. Consequently,

CONCEPT SUMMARY 3.3

Forms of Tortious Wrongdoing

Intentional torts	• assault
	• battery
	• false imprisonment
	• trespass to land
	• interference with chattels
	• conspiracy
	• intimidation
	• interference with contractual relations
	• unlawful interference with economic relations
	• deceit
Negligence torts	• occupiers' liability
	• nuisance[11]
	• negligence
	• professional negligence
	• product liability
Strict liability torts	• animals
	• *Rylands v Fletcher*[12]

the only way for the defendant to effectively manage the risk of liability is to entirely avoid such situations.

Strict liability torts therefore have the potential to substantially affect the way that people act. It would, however, be wrong to overestimate that possibility. As indicated in Concept Summary 3.3, tort law is dominated by intentional torts and negligence torts. Strict liability torts are rare.[13] The reason is clear. In most situations, it would be unfair to impose liability on a person who did not intentionally or carelessly cause the plaintiff's injury. Strict liability is therefore limited to situations in which the defendant is involved in some extraordinarily dangerous activity. Tort law strikes a balance. It allows the defendant to engage in that activity, but it also requires the defendant to pay for any damage that occurs. That is the idea behind the rule that holds the owner of livestock strictly liable for any damage that the ani-

---

[11.] As we will see in Chapter 5, nuisance and occupiers' liability are not always classified as negligence torts.

[12.] Some people also consider *vicarious liability* to be a form of strict liability. As we will see later in this chapter, however, an employer who is held vicariously liable has not really committed a tort. Instead, the employer is held liable for a tort that its employee committed. In contrast, as we will see in Chapter 5, the rule in *Rylands v Fletcher* (1868) LR 3 HL 330 is true strict liability. The defendant is held liable for doing something wrong even though it did not act intentionally or carelessly.

[13.] The only one that we will discuss in detail is the rule in *Rylands v Fletcher*, which appears in Chapter 5.

CASE BRIEF 3.1

Cowles v Balac (2005) 29 CCLT (3d) 284 (Ont SCJ)

David Balac and Jennifer Cowles began dating in 1996. He worked as an accordion player and studied at Sheridan College; she worked as an "exotic dancer." On a warm spring day, they visited African Lion Safari (ALS). ALS offers a unique wildlife experience. In a typical zoo, the animals are enclosed and the customers roam freely from one exhibit to the next. But at ALS, the roles are reversed. The animals roam freely within their reserves and it is the customers who are enclosed (in their own vehicles) as they drive through the park. Not surprisingly, ALS has become very popular with people who want a close encounter with wildlife. Where else can a family sit in safety while their van is swarmed by monkeys!

Jennifer and David's wildlife encounter was, tragically, *too* close. Shortly after they had entered the tiger reserve, their car was attacked by the big cats. Although the facts were rather sketchy, the judge found that the initial attack startled David, who accidentally hit a button that rolled down Jennifer's window. A Siberian tiger named Paca then lunged through the window and mauled the pair. The injuries were severe. Because of permanent scarring to her scalp and hip, Jennifer was unable to work as a "featured dancer." David fared even worse. In addition to physical injuries that prevented him from playing the accordion, he suffered psychological injuries that further limited his employment prospects.

The court awarded $1 701 032 to David and $813 169 to Jennifer. It offered two explanations for holding ALS liable.

- **Negligence:** The trial judge held that an ALS employee had carelessly created the accident by driving through the area with a young tiger cub in the cab of her truck. The employee should have realized that by doing so, she would cause Paca to become excited and aggressive.

- **Strict Liability:** The trial also held that ALS would have been responsible for the accident even if its employee had taken every conceivable precaution. A special rule applies to certain types of extraordinary risks. As Justice MacFarland explained, a business that displays "dangerous, unpredictable, wild predators. . . in out of control settings. . . should be strictly liable for any damage" that occurs. Consequently, a person who is hurt by a wild animal is not required to prove that the animal's owner intentionally or carelessly did something wrong. It is enough for the victim to show that his or her injury was caused by the danger in question.

The threat of strict liability obviously creates a tremendous problem for zoos and wildlife parks. That is not to say, however, that they will be held liable to *every* customer who is injured by one of their animals. They may have a defence. Most importantly from a business perspective, the trial judge suggested that Jennifer and David would have lost their case if they had been sufficiently warned about the risk of attack and if they had consented to that danger. It was not enough, however, for ALS to simply post warning signs. It should have taken steps to ensure that Jennifer and David were fully aware of those warnings.[14]

mals cause by trespassing on someone else's property.[15] As Case Brief 3.1 illustrates, a similar rule applies to the owner of a wild creature.[16]

[14.] The defence of voluntary assumption of risk is discussed in Chapter 6.

[15.] The same explanation applies to the rule in *Rylands v Fletcher*, which we will examine in Chapter 5.

[16.] Tort law draws a distinction between wild animals (such as tigers) and tame animals (such as dogs). As a general rule, the owner of a wild animal is liable for any damage that it causes. In contrast, the owner of a tame animal is usually liable only if they knew that the animal in question was unusually dangerous. In other words, tame animals are entitled to "one free bite." Recently, however, some governments have enacted legislation that allows the victim of a dog bite to recover damages without proving that the owner knew that the animal was especially dangerous: see *eg Stray Animals Act*, RSNS 1989, c 448, s 12 (NS); *Dog Owner's Liability Act*, RSO 1990, c D.16, s 2 (Ont).

GENERAL PRINCIPLES OF TORT LAW

Having identified different types of torts, we can now begin to look at several general principles that apply throughout tort law. In this section, we will concentrate on three concepts:

- liability insurance
- vicarious liability
- remedies

Liability Insurance

liability insurance is a contract in which an insurance company agrees, in exchange for a price, to pay damages on behalf of a person who incurs liability

a **duty to defend** requires the insurance company to pay the expenses that are associated with lawsuits brought against the insured party

Because torts can occur unexpectedly, risk management is especially important. Business people should know enough about tort law to predict potential problems and to develop strategies for avoiding liability. They should also protect themselves with *liability insurance*.[17] **Liability insurance** is a contract in which an insurance company agrees, in exchange for a price, to pay damages on behalf of a person who incurs liability. Figure 3.1 provides an illustration. Liability insurance also includes a *duty to defend*. A **duty to defend** requires the insurance company to pay the expenses that are associated with lawsuits brought against the insured party.[18] That is significant. As we saw in the last chapter, litigation costs can be very high, even if you win your case.

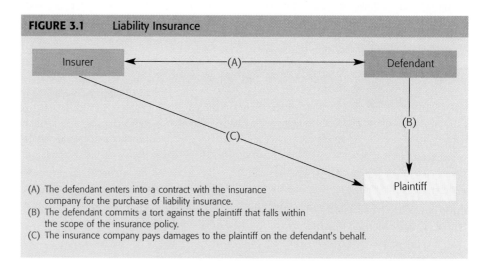

FIGURE 3.1   Liability Insurance

(A) The defendant enters into a contract with the insurance company for the purchase of liability insurance.
(B) The defendant commits a tort against the plaintiff that falls within the scope of the insurance policy.
(C) The insurance company pays damages to the plaintiff on the defendant's behalf.

Liability insurance creates an interesting tension between two of tort law's most important functions.

compensatory function aims to fully compensate people who are wrongfully injured

- On the one hand, it contributes to the *compensatory function* of torts. The **compensatory function** aims to fully compensate people who are wrongfully injured. The tortfeasor may not personally have enough money to pay damages. If so, the victim will not receive complete compensation unless the tortfeasor has insurance.

[17.] There are also other types of insurance, which are considered in Chapter 17.
[18.] *Scott v Wawanesa Mutual Insurance Co* (1989) 59 DLR (4th) 660 (SCC).

- On the other hand, liability insurance undermines the *deterrence function* of tort law. The **deterrence function** discourages people from committing torts by threatening to hold them liable for the losses that they cause. People have little reason to be afraid, however, if they know that their insurance companies will pay if something goes wrong. That is one reason why tort law has surprisingly little deterrent effect.[19]

deterrence function discourages people from committing torts by threatening to hold them liable for the losses they cause

Liability insurance plays an important role in tort law.[20] It is important to understand, however, that liability insurance policies do not usually cover *all* torts. Case Brief 3.2 provides a recent illustration.

CASE BRIEF 3.2

Non-Marine Underwriters, Lloyd's of London v Scalera (2000) 185 DLR (4th) 1 (SCC)

The plaintiff, a young teenager, worked in a corner store that was located at the end of a city bus line. The defendant, a bus driver, sexually abused her on a number of occasions. She later sued him for battery. He claimed coverage under his liability insurance policy. His insurance company rejected his claim, however, by pointing to a clause in that contract that excluded coverage for injuries inflicted through "intentional or criminal acts."

The Supreme Court of Canada held that the defendant was not protected by his insurance policy because he had committed the tort of battery with the intention of injuring the plaintiff. As a result, the plaintiff's chances of recovering full damages were reduced. While the insurance company was wealthy, the defendant was not.

Vicarious Liability

Liability insurance is always a good idea, especially for businesses that have employees. That additional need for insurance arises from the doctrine of *vicarious liability*. **Vicarious liability** occurs when an employer is held liable for a tort that was committed by an employee. As Ethical Perspective 3.1 (see p. 66) shows, the idea of holding one person responsible for another person's actions raises difficult ethical issues.

vicarious liability occurs when an employer is held liable for a tort that was committed by an employee

The doctrine of vicarious liability may be justified on a number of grounds.

- It serves the compensatory function of tort law because it allows the plaintiff to claim damages from both an employee (who may not have any money) and an employer (which is more likely to have money or, at least, liability insurance).

- Vicarious liability may serve the deterrence function of tort law by providing employers with an incentive to avoid unusually hazardous activities and to hire the best people available.

- As a matter of fairness, it may be appropriate to require a business to take responsibility for the losses that its activities create, even if those losses are caused by employees who misbehave.

---

[19] M Trebilcock & D Dewees "The Efficacy of the Tort System and Its Alternatives: A Review of Empirical Evidence" (1992) *30 Osgoode Hall LJ* 57.

[20] It is also possible to purchase insurance for liabilities arising outside of tort. For example, a company may obtain coverage for liabilities arising through breach of contract.

Bazley v Curry (1999) 174 DLR (4th) 45 (SCC)

The defendant was a charitable organization that operated a residential care facility for emotionally troubled children. It employed a number of people, including a man named Curry, to act as substitute parents (for example, by bathing children and putting them to bed at night). Although the defendant conducted a reasonably thorough investigation before hiring Curry, it failed to discover that he was a pedophile. Sadly, Curry sexually assaulted a number of children, including the plaintiff, within the defendant's facilities. The plaintiff sued the defendant organization on the basis that it was vicariously liable for Curry's actions.

The Supreme Court of Canada held that an employer is vicariously liable for both (i) acts that it authorized an employee to do, and (ii) other closely connected acts. On the facts of the case, the Court found that Curry's actions fell within the second category.[21] While recognizing that the employer certainly did not want its employees to sexually abuse the children, the Court held that the nature of the employer's operation significantly increased the risk of wrong-doing.

Questions for Discussion

1. Is it fair to impose liability on an employer that acted reasonably?

2. Why should an innocent person be responsible for someone else's wrongs?

It is important to note several other points about vicarious liability. First, an employer is not liable *every time* an employee does something wrong. As the Supreme Court of Canada stressed in *Bazley v Curry*, an employer is not vicariously liable if an employee's tort occurred completely outside of the employment relationship.

independent contractor is a worker who is not as closely connected to the employer's business as is an employee

Second, an employer may be held vicariously liable for employees, but not for *independent contractors*. An **independent contractor** is a worker who is not as closely connected to the employer's business as is an employee. Consequently, as a matter of risk management, it is sometimes preferable for a business to have work performed by an independent contractor rather than by an employee.[22] While it is often difficult to distinguish between those two types of workers, the courts are more inclined to find that a person is an employee if (i) the employer generally controls what is done, how it is done, when it is done, and where it is done, (ii) the worker uses the employer's equipment and premises, (iii) the worker is paid a regular wage or salary rather than a lump sum at the end of each project, and (iv) the worker is integrated into the employer's business and is not in their own business.

Third, vicarious liability does not relieve the employee of responsibility. Rather, it allows the plaintiff to sue both the employer *and* the employee, and to recover all or some of its damages from either defendant. Furthermore, if the employer actually pays damages to the plaintiff, it is usually entitled to claim that amount from the employee. In practice, however, employers seldom do so. Aside from the fact that an employee is unlikely to have much money, employers usually realize that morale would drop if employees were worried about being held liable.

[21.] It is often difficult to determine whether an employee's tort falls within the second branch of the test. On the same day that it held the employer responsible in *Bazley v Curry*, the Supreme Court of Canada refused to impose vicarious liability in a similar case: *Jacobi v Griffiths* (1999) 174 DLR (4th) 71.

[22.] We introduced the distinction between employees and independent contractors in Chapter 1. The issue is considered in more detail in Chapter 26.

Fourth, an employer may be both *vicariously liable* and *personally liable* in the *same situation*. Vicarious liability occurs if the employer is responsible for an *employee's tort*. Personal liability occurs if the employer is responsible for its *own tort*. Business Decision 3.1 provides an illustration.

BUSINESS DECISION 3.1

Vicarious Liability and Personal Liability

You suffer a serious injury after falling out of a chairlift at a ski resort. The evidence indicates that the accident was caused by the fact that the lift was carelessly operated by Alberto, an employee of the resort. The evidence also indicates that the resort failed to properly train Alberto.

Liability could arise in three ways. First, Alberto might be *personally* liable, under the tort of negligence, because he carelessly operated the chairlift. Second, the resort might be *vicariously* liable because it was Alberto's employer. Third, the

resort might also be *personally* liable, under the tort of negligence, because it carelessly failed to train its employee.

Questions for Discussion

1. Why should you sue both Alberto and the resort?

2. Who would pay for your injuries if (i) Alberto alone was held liable, (ii) both Alberto and the resort were held liable, and (iii) the resort alone was held liable?

Figure 3.2 summarizes our discussion of vicarious liability. It assumes that the only tort was committed by the employee.

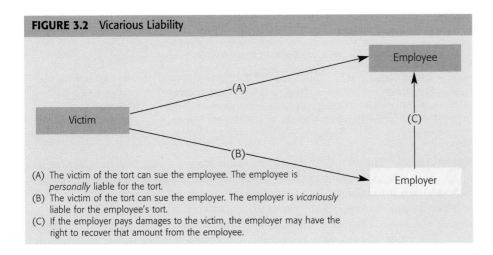

FIGURE 3.2   Vicarious Liability

(A) The victim of the tort can sue the employee. The employee is *personally* liable for the tort.
(B) The victim of the tort can sue the employer. The employer is *vicariously* liable for the employee's tort.
(C) If the employer pays damages to the victim, the employer may have the right to recover that amount from the employee.

Remedies

A variety of remedies are available in tort, depending upon the circumstances. We will see several examples in the next three chapters. This section simply provides an introduction to the most important possibilities:

- compensatory damages
- punitive damages
- nominal damages
- injunctions

Compensatory Damages

As previously mentioned, most private law obligations arise in either tort or contract. Compensatory damages are the standard remedy in both. In either situation, the defendant is required to pay the monetary value of the losses that it caused the plaintiff to suffer. As we also saw, however, there is a significant difference between contract and tort. While compensation in tort is designed to put the plaintiff back into the position that that party enjoyed *before* the tort occurred, compensation in contract is usually designed to put the plaintiff *forward* into the position that that party expected to enjoy after the contract was performed.

The distinction that exists between compensation in contract and tort is important because it is sometimes possible for the plaintiff to sue in both tort *and* contract. The plaintiff can recover damages for only one of those actions, even if both are successful. It will, of course, choose whichever option provides the most money.[23] To better understand these issues, consider You Be the Judge 3.1.

YOU BE THE JUDGE 3.1

Compensation in Tort and Contract[24]

Pippa agreed to buy a pizzeria from David. During the negotiations that led up to that contract, David said a number of things about the restaurant's profitability. If those statements had been true, Pippa would have received a net profit of $80 000 on her investment. In fact, as David knew, the business was actually far less profitable than he had said. As a result of relying on David's statement, Pippa lost $65 000 on the purchase.

David admits that he is guilty of both (i) a breach of contract (because his promises were untrue), and (ii) the tort of deceit (because he lied to Pippa). The parties simply want you, as the judge, to determine how much money Pippa is entitled to receive in damages.

Questions for Discussion

1. How much money would be required to place Pippa in the position that she would have enjoyed if the contract had turned out as expected?

2. How much money would be required to place Pippa in the position that she would have enjoyed if she had not entered into the contract?

3. Given that the plaintiff ultimately can recover compensation for either breach of contract or tort, but not both, how much will she receive?

Remoteness   Compensation is not available for *every* loss that the plaintiff suffered. First, the defendant is only responsible for losses that it in fact *caused*. Second, even if the defendant's tort caused the plaintiff to suffer a loss, the court will not award damages if the connection between the tort and the loss is too *remote*.[25] A loss is **remote** if it would be unfair to hold the defendant responsible for it. The judge will ask whether a reasonable person in the defendant's position would have realized that a particular activity might cause the sort of harm that the plaintiff suffered.[26] Suppose that one of your employees develops a rare disease after coming into contact with rat urine. You might not be liable even if you carelessly allowed rats to run loose in your warehouse. A judge once held that a reasonable person would recognize the danger of *rat bites*, but not *rat urine*.[27]

a loss is remote if it would be unfair to hold the defendant responsible for it

[23.] *Central Trust Co v Rafuse* (1986) 31 DLR (4th) 481 (SCC).

[24.] *Goldstar Management Ltd v Varvis* (1995) 175 AR 321 (QB).

[25.] Compensatory damages in contract are also limited by a principle of remoteness. We will look at the special rules that apply in contract in Chapter 12.

[26.] *Overseas Tankship (UK) Ltd v Morts Dock and Engineering Co Ltd, The Wagon Mound (No 1)* [1961] AC 388 (PC).

[27.] *Tremain v Pike* [1969] 3 All ER 1303.

There is an important limitation on the remoteness principle. The concept of remoteness applies to most types of torts, but not to intentional torts.[28] People who intentionally do wrong do not deserve any leniency in tort law.[29]

Mitigation Compensatory damages are also limited by the principle of *mitigation*.[30] Compensation is not available for a loss that the plaintiff unreasonably failed to mitigate. **Mitigation** occurs when the plaintiff takes steps to minimize the losses that result from the defendant's tort. Suppose that a customer was bitten by a rat that you negligently allowed to run around your warehouse. You advised her to get a tetanus shot, but she refused. As a result, she developed lockjaw and was unable to work for eight months. If she had received a tetanus shot, she would have missed only three days of work. We can use that example to illustrate four aspects of mitigation.

mitigation occurs when the plaintiff takes steps to minimize the losses that result from the defendant's tort

- First, the plaintiff is only responsible for taking *reasonable* steps to mitigate a loss. For instance, the court would not expect her to receive a tetanus shot if she would be at risk of developing serious side effects.
- Second, lawyers sometimes say that there is a "duty to mitigate." In fact, there is not really a *duty*. The plaintiff is not *required* to mitigate. She will, however, be denied compensation for losses that she could have reasonably avoided. Mitigation is a question of risk management.
- Third, damages are denied *only to the extent that* the plaintiff unreasonably failed to mitigate. Even if the plaintiff had received a tetanus shot, she still would have missed work for three days. She is entitled to compensation for that loss.[31]
- Finally, the plaintiff can recover the costs associated with mitigation. For example, if she had received a tetanus shot, and if she had been billed $100 for it, she would be entitled to compensation for that amount.

Punitive Damages

Damages are usually intended to compensate the plaintiff for a loss. *Punitive damages*, however, have a different purpose. **Punitive damages** are intended to punish the defendant. If the defendant has done something particularly outrageous or reprehensible, the court may impose both compensatory damages *and* punitive damages.

punitive damages are intended to punish the defendant

It is, however, important to appreciate that punitive damages are unusual. There is a popular perception, based on American movies and news programs, that they are awarded very often and in very large amounts. In fact, Canadian courts take a much narrower view of the matter. In this country, punitive damages are available only in exceptional circumstances. The Supreme Court of Canada has said that, in addition to committing a tort, the defendant must have acted in a "harsh, vindictive, reprehensible and malicious" manner. For example, punitive damages have been awarded against an elderly doctor who committed the tort of battery on a young woman by refusing to give her drugs unless she had sex with him, against a reform school that committed the tort of negligence by failing to fire a predatory employee who sexually abused a young inmate, and against a land developer who committed the tort of trespass to land

---

[28.] We will examine intentional torts in the next chapter.

[29.] *Bettel v Yim* (1978) 88 DLR (3d) 543 (Ont Co Ct).

[30.] As we will see in Chapter 12, the principle of mitigation also applies in contract.

[31.] *McAuley v London Transport Executive* [1957] 2 Lloyds Rep 500 (CA).

by cutting down trees on a neighbouring lot to enhance the view from its own property.[32] In the leading case of *Whiten v Pilot Insurance Co*, the Supreme Court of Canada confirmed a jury's decision to award $1 000 000 in punitive damages against an insurance company that deliberately concocted a false allegation of arson after a family home burned down.[33]

Nominal Damages

Nominal damages can be awarded for *some* torts. **Nominal damages** symbolically recognize that the defendant committed a tort, even though the plaintiff did not suffer any loss. Since nominal damages are merely symbolic, they are awarded in very small sums, say $10. Furthermore, because they are usually awarded only if the plaintiff did not suffer any loss, they are generally restricted to torts that are actionable *per se*. Most torts (such as negligence) occur only if the defendant inflicted a loss upon the plaintiff. However, some torts (such as the intentional torts) occur as long as the defendant acted wrongfully. They are therefore actionable *per se*, that is, in themselves, rather than being actionable upon proof of a loss.

nominal damages symbolically recognize that the defendant committed a tort even though the plaintiff did not suffer any loss

Injunctions

Compensatory damages provide a substitute for the thing that the plaintiff has lost. For instance, they may allow the plaintiff to replace a car that has been destroyed, or they may provide the equivalent of an income that has been lost. In some situations, however, damages do not provide an adequate remedy. No amount of money can provide a substitute for the thing that the plaintiff has lost. In that situation, the court may award an *injunction*. An **injunction** is a court order that requires the defendant to do something or to refrain from doing something. For instance, the defendant may be told to close a foul-smelling pig farm that is operating in a residential area, or it may be told to tear down a billboard that it wrongfully erected on the plaintiff's property. Of course, it is often too late to impose an injunction. If the defendant carelessly kills the plaintiff's horse, the court cannot bring the animal back to life.

an injunction is a court order that requires the defendant to do something or to refrain from doing something

Alternative Compensation Schemes

Tort law is not the only source of compensation. In fact, in recent years, the number of *alternative compensation schemes* has increased considerably. An **alternative compensation scheme** is a system that allows a person who has suffered an injury to receive compensation without bringing an action in tort. Two such systems are especially important:

an alternative compensation scheme is a system that allows a person who has suffered an injury to receive compensation without bringing an action in tort

- workers' compensation
- no-fault insurance

[32.] *Norberg v Wynrib* (1992) 92 DLR (4th) 449 (SCC) ($10 000 in punitive damages); *Roose v Hollett* (1996) 139 DLR (4th) 260 (NS CA) ($35 000 in punitive damages); *Horseshoe Bay Retirement Society v SIF Development Corp* (1990) 66 DLR (4th) 42 (BC SC) ($100 000 in punitive damages).

[33.] *Whiten v Pilot Insurance Co* (2002) 209 DLR (4th) 257 (SCC). The case was actually concerned with a claim for breach of contract. The court nevertheless discussed punitive damages in tort as well.

Because job-related injuries are so common, workers' compensation schemes exist across the country. While the details vary among jurisdictions, the basic ideas are always the same. A fund is established with compulsory contributions from employers. Workers who are injured on the job are usually prevented from suing in tort. They are, however, entitled to receive compensation from the fund without having to prove that anyone has wrongfully caused their injuries. That system is much quicker and much easier than tort law.

The second major type of alternative compensation scheme applies to injuries that are caused by automobile accidents. Several provinces have adopted some form of no-fault system.[34] In Manitoba and Quebec, for example, victims of traffic accidents cannot sue in tort, but they are entitled to receive compensation from the scheme without having to prove that another driver was at fault. Other provinces have enacted less extensive schemes. In British Columbia, the right to no-fault benefits exists alongside the right to sue in tort. In Saskatchewan, people can choose between tort and no-fault insurance coverage. And in Ontario, the no-fault system prevents an action in tort unless the victim's losses are especially serious.

There are two main reasons for the rise of alternative compensation schemes.

- First, tort law provides compensation only if a person is injured as a result of a *wrongful* act. From the victim's perspective, however, the physical and financial consequences of being injured are the same, even if an injury occurs *innocently*. Consequently, it is sometimes desirable to allow that person to collect compensation regardless of fault.

- Second, tort law is inefficient. Since it is based on an adversarial system in which lawyers compete on behalf of clients, it requires a great deal of time and expense. Studies suggest that less than one-third of all the money involved in the tort system is actually used for compensating injuries.[35] Because alternative compensation schemes operate on a no-fault basis, there is far less need for costly investigations and lengthy disputes.

While alternative compensation schemes have many advantages, they also have a major disadvantage. They provide compensation more often, but they also provide less of it. In tort law, the plaintiff is usually entitled to recover the full value of a loss. In alternative compensation schemes, however, the level of compensation is almost always capped. Because such schemes include many more claimants, they would quickly go broke if they provided full compensation for every loss.

---

[34] For a useful summary of automobile accident compensation schemes, see AM Linden & LN Klar *Canadian Tort Law* 11th ed (1999) at 754–7.

[35] Ontario Ministry of Financial Institutions *Ontario Task Force on Insurance, Final Report* (1986) at 66. Part of the remaining money is paid to lawyers; part is paid to simply operate the system.

CHAPTER SUMMARY

A tort generally consists of a failure to fulfill a private obligation that was imposed by law. It is important to distinguish between torts, and crimes. Torts involve private obligations; crimes involve public obligations. It also is important to distinguish between torts and contracts. Torts generally involve obligations imposed by law; contracts generally involve obligations that the parties voluntarily create for themselves.

Tort law needs to strike a balance between competing interests in a variety of situations. It therefore includes three types of torts: intentional torts, negligence torts, and strict liability torts. Strict liability torts are unusual. The defendant may be held liable even though it did not act intentionally or carelessly. Strict liability torts are limited to situations in which the defendant was involved in an extraordinarily dangerous activity.

Liability insurance is a contract in which an insurance company agrees, in exchange for a price, to pay damages on behalf of a person who incurs liability. It is critically important in tort law, especially in the business context. Liability insurance furthers tort law's compensatory function, but undermines its deterrence function.

Even if an employer did nothing wrong, it may be held vicariously liable for a tort committed by its employee.

The victim of a tort usually receives compensatory damages. Compensation in tort looks backward. It is intended to place the plaintiff in the position that that party enjoyed before the tort occurred. It is not available for losses that are remote, or for losses that the plaintiff failed to mitigate. In unusual situations, a court may award punitive damages or nominal damages, or impose an injunction.

The tort system does not provide compensation to people whose injuries are innocently caused. It is also expensive and inefficient. Therefore, alternative compensation schemes have been introduced in some jurisdictions for some purposes.

REVIEW QUESTIONS

1. What is a tort?
2. How does a tort differ from a crime?
3. Is it ever possible for the same set of events to be both a tort and a crime? Explain your answer.
4. Compare torts and contracts in terms of primary obligations and secondary obligations.
5. Describe three types of torts and explain how they differ in terms of the defendant's mental culpability.
6. Explain why strict liability torts create special problems for risk management.
7. How is liability insurance related to the concept of risk management?
8. When does a "duty to defend" arise? Why is it important?
9. "Liability insurance creates an interesting tension between two of tort law's most important functions." Explain the meaning of that statement.
10. "Liability insurance provides protection for *every* type of tort liability." Explain whether or not that statement is true.
11. What is the difference between "vicarious liability" and "personal liability"?
12. On what grounds can vicarious liability be justified?
13. When will an employer be held vicariously liable for torts committed by its employees? When will an employer be held vicariously liable for torts committed by its independent contractors?
14. How does the vicarious liability of an employer affect the personal liability of an employee?
15. Are compensatory damages calculated in the same way in both tort and contract? Explain your answer.
16. Explain the relationship between compensatory damages and the concept of remoteness.
17. Explain the relationship between compensatory damages and the concept of mitigation.
18. "Because they are very large and very common, punitive damages create a significant risk management problem for Canadian businesses." Explain whether or not that statement is true.
19. What is the difference between damages and an injunction?
20. What are "alternative compensation schemes"? From the perspective of an injured person, how are such schemes more favourable than tort law? How are they less favourable?

CASES AND PROBLEMS

1. Francesca owns and operates a small stereo store. That store was robbed last night after Francesca had locked up and gone home. The thief broke a window, entered the premises, and stole a dozen portable disc players. Francesca fortunately had installed a security camera several weeks ago. After discovering the theft in the morning, she reviewed the tape and recognized that the thief was her neighbour, Ned. Francesca now has several concerns. She believes that Ned should be responsible to her personally, but she also believes that he owes a debt to society. Briefly describe two types of proceedings that may be brought against Ned.

2. Kwik Office Supplies hired Jackson to act as its manager. The employment contract spelled out, in substantial detail, the various rights and obligations that the parties assumed under the agreement. Two years later, Jackson was fired after the company received an angry letter from a dissatisfied company that had been defrauded by Jackson. In order to protect its reputation, and in recognition of the validity of the allegation, Kwik Office Supply is prepared to settle the customer's tort claim. As part of that same process, however, it believes that once it has compensated the customer, it is entitled to receive reimbursement from Jackson. Jackson rejects that claim. He insists that his only relationship with the company is contractual and he correctly notes that the employment contract did not deal with the situation that has actually occurred. Will Jackson be required to reimburse the company for the money that it pays to the customer? How can he be held liable for an obligation that he never accepted as part of his contract?

3. Rochard owns and operates a video rental store. Because business is often slow during the day, and because he worries about robberies, Rochard regularly brings his dog, Sid, to work with him. Sid has been a bit of a mixed blessing over the years. He has provided good companionship and his aggressive nature has discouraged teenagers from hanging around the store. At the same time, Sid has occasionally frightened customers and on a couple of occasions he has tried to bite small children. Rochard's luck recently ran out when Sid did, in fact, attack and severely injure Sarah, a young girl who was visiting the store with her father. Although Rochard feels very sorry for Sarah, he denies that he is responsible for her medical bills. As he correctly points out, he did not intentionally cause Sid to attack Sarah. To the contrary, he took every reasonable precaution to prevent the incident from occurring. Rochard therefore insists that he cannot be held liable in tort. Is he correct? Explain your answer.

4. Toronto's SkyDome was owned and operated by Sportsco. The Toronto Blue Jays rented the building for their home games. One of those games, against the Kansas City Royals, was cancelled after portions of SkyDome's retractable roof broke off and fell to the ground. The Blue Jays sued Sportsco in tort for its loss of profits. Sportsco was worried that the lawsuit might become very expensive, not only because of the need to hire lawyers, but also because of the need to hire expert witnesses to explain why the roof fell apart. Sportsco did, however, have an insurance policy that it had purchased from ING Insurance Company of Canada. Explain the significance of that policy.

5. SuperMart, a large grocery store, was recently held liable to Doris Spracko as a result of an injury that she suffered while shopping. Doris slipped and fell on some ketchup that had spilled onto the floor. The judge found that SuperMart was negligent because it did not have any system for routinely checking its floors and removing dangerous substances. During the trial, Doris told the judge that she was concerned about two things: (i) she wanted to be compensated for the income that she lost while she was off work and recuperating from her injury, and (ii) she wanted to make sure that SuperMart never let the same type of accident happen again. On each of those points, explain the significance of the fact that SuperMart has liability insurance that covers Doris's case.

6. Dave Woodstock was hired to clean and deliver vehicles for EconoCar, a car rental agency. Although Dave drives very safely in his own vehicle, he tends to be rather careless when he is behind the wheel of one of his employer's vehicles. Not surprisingly, then, he was recently involved in an accident while driving a truck owned by EconoCar. Although that truck did not suffer any serious damage, the car that Dave crashed into requires $10 000 in repairs. Dave has admitted that he was at fault, but as he explained to his girlfriend, he was not worried. "What's the worst that could happen? I've already quit my job and found a new one. And obviously, EconoCar is on the hook for repairing the other guy's vehicle. I'm totally out of the picture." Is Dave correct? Explain your answer.

7. Sonata Assurance is in the life and health insurance business. It employed Vic Arpeggio as a sales agent. Under the terms of that agency relationship, Arpeggio was not permitted to personally receive any money from the customers who purchased insurance. He was instead required to direct customers to make their cheques payable to "Sonata Assurance." During his first (and only) month on the job, Arpeggio sold a number of policies at a total price of approximately $57 000. In each instance, he broke his obligation to Sonata Assurance by asking the customers either for cash or for cheques payable

to "Victor Arpeggio." He also broke his employment contract by failing to forward the customers' insurance applications to the insurance company. And finally, at the end of the month, Arpeggio disappeared from the scene, taking all of the money with him. The customers have now sued Sonata Assurance in tort for compensation. Sonata is sympathetic to those claims, but insists that it cannot be held responsible for Arpeggio's actions, especially since he did precisely what he was not supposed to do. Are the customers entitled to relief? Explain your answer.

8. SoftSeat Inc manufactures synthetic sheepskin car seat covers. It sold its product to Canadian Tire for over thirty years. Until recently, sales to Canadian Tire accounted for more than half of SoftSeat's annual business. Sedemolle Inc also manufactured car seat covers. It hired AIM Inc, a marketing company, in an effort to obtain Canadian Tire's business. AIM achieved that goal by bribing the head of Canadian Tire's automotive division. The loss of Canadian Tire's business devastated SoftSeat. SoftSeat claims that AIM committed a number of torts, and that Sedemolle is vicariously liable for AIM's wrongdoing. Is that correct? How will a judge decide whether or not Sedemolle is vicariously liable for AIM?

9. One-for-One Pizza operates a fleet of four vehicles for the purpose of making pizza deliveries. One of those vehicles was very badly damaged as a result of a tort that Selena committed. In order to keep its business running smoothly, the owners of One-for-One Pizza have temporarily rented a car at a cost of $750 per week. They also realize that they have two long-term options. They could either (i) buy a replacement vehicle from a used car lot for $10 000, or (ii) repair their damaged vehicle at a cost of $9000. A replacement vehicle could be obtained by the end of the first week. The repairs, in contrast, will take at least four weeks to complete. Assuming that Selena is liable in tort, how much will she have to pay to One-for-One Pizza?

10. Dominion Tankship owned a large tanker ship called *The Erie Mistake* that it operated on the Great Lakes. The ship arrived at the Port of Toronto carrying a cargo of Flamonol, a synthetic lubricant used by manufacturers. As a result of the captain's carelessness, *The Erie Mistake* rammed into a dock that Mortimer Docking owned. In addition to causing some structural damage to the dock, the accident punctured a hole in the side of the ship, which caused several thousand litres of Flamonol to leak into the water. The manager for Mortimer Docking asked if there was any danger that the Flamonol might catch fire. The captain of *The Erie Mistake* gave his assurance that Flamonol was entirely non-flammable. Mortimer Docking therefore began repair work on its dock. During the course of those repairs, sparks from a welding gun fell onto the Flamonol, which was still floating on top of the water. The Flamonol almost immediately burst into flames and the ensuing fire completely destroyed the dock. Mortimer Docking has sued Dominion Tankship. The company admits that the captain of *The Erie Mistake* committed a tort when he rammed into the dock, and it is willing to pay for that original damage. However, Dominion Tankship has also established that, at the time of the accident, there was no scientific evidence that Flamonol could be set on fire. It therefore refuses to pay for the additional damage that the fire caused. Is Dominion Tankship liable for destruction of the dock or merely for the damage caused by the original ramming accident? Explain your answer.

11. Jessica worked as a courier for Pony Express Deliveries. Although Pony Express had no way of knowing it when they hired her, Jessica has a pathological hatred for Simone. The source of that hatred is not clear, but it seems to stem from a dispute between the two women dating back to high school. Three months ago, Pony Express asked Jessica to deliver a package to an office in the Dominion Tower. After making that delivery, Jessica went to the cafeteria in the basement of the building, where she knew Simone worked as the manager of a fast food restaurant. Jessica jumped Simone from behind and administered a severe beating. The unprovoked attack has left Simone in constant pain and unable to work. Simone therefore intends to sue in tort. She wants compensation for her losses, but she also wants to see Jessica punished for her actions. Although she realizes that Jessica has very little money, Simone believes that she should be entitled to payment from Pony Express or from Western Insurance (which sold a general liability insurance policy to Jessica). Explain the remedies that Simone may be entitled to receive, and identify the party or parties who are most likely to pay for those remedies.

12. Bickle's Cab Company owns and operates a fleet of taxis. Last autumn, one of its cars was involved in an unfortunate incident. The driver almost ran into Jody DeNiro, a bike courier, as she emerged from an alleyway. Although DeNiro was entirely at fault for that near-accident, she was the one who became furious. She kicked the taxi's door repeatedly before being restrained by a passerby. The damage to the car consisted of a large dent and scraped paint. Bickle's Cab Co then parked the damaged vehicle in an outdoor lot for the winter. When it re-examined the car in the spring, it found extensive rust damage. That damage would not have occurred if the car had been promptly repaired. It is clear that DeNiro intentionally interfered with the car. There is, however, a disagreement regarding the amount of compensation that she will have to pay. The evidence indicates a number of things. Immediately before the accident, the car was worth $7000. Immediately after the accident, the car was worth $5000. The cost of repairs at that time would have been $3000. Because of the rust damage, the car is now worth $2000. It would now cost $6000 to fully repair. A new car of the same model can be purchased for $15 000. How much is the Bickle Cab Co entitled to receive?

WEBLINKS

Duhaime Law: Tort Law—An Introduction   www.duhaime.org/Tort/ tort1.aspx

This page on Duhaime Law provides an overview of tort law.

CanadaLegal.com   www.canadalegal.com/search.asp?a=36&n=100

This website provides links, arranged by jurisdiction, to tort and negligence articles and newsletters prepared by Canadian law firms.

Legal Information Institute—Tort Law
www.law.cornell.edu/ topics/torts.html

This site provides an overview of tort law from an American perspective and links to federal and state legislative materials and case law.

Economica Ltd   www.economica.ca/articles.htm

Economica Ltd is a consulting firm that provides litigation support in personal injury and fatal accident actions. Its website features articles on the economics of personal injury and damage assessment.

So Sue Me!   www.legal-info-legale.nb.ca/showpub.asp?id=2&langid=1

This website provides a general introduction to tort law.

ADDITIONAL RESOURCES FOR CHAPTER 3 ON THE COMPANION WEBSITE

(www.pearsoned.ca/mcinnes)

In addition to self-test multiple-choice, true-false, and short essay questions (all with immediate feedback), three additional Cases and Problems (with suggested answers), and links to useful Web destinations, the Companion Website provides the following resources for Chapter 3:

Provincial Material

- **British Columbia:** Insurance Corporation of British Columbia (ICBC), Motor Vehicle Insurance, Parental Liability, Workers' Compensation, Workers' Compensation Board of British Columbia—refers to WorkSafeBC, WorkSafeBC, No-Fault Insurance
- **Alberta:** Automobile Insurance, *Maternal Tort Liability Act*, *Charitable Donation of Food Act*
- **Manitoba and Saskatchewan:** No-Fault Automobile Insurance
- **Ontario:** No-Fault Liability Insurance, Strict Liability, Vicarious Liability, Workers' Compensation

4 Intentional Torts

OBJECTIVES

After completing this chapter, you should be able to:

1. Explain the general nature of intentional torts, and define "intention" as it applies to those torts.

2. Describe and distinguish the torts of assault and battery.

3. Identify a situation in which battery presents a particular danger for business people who occasionally attract undesirable customers.

4. Explain why the concept of "reasonable force" is important to the tort of battery.

5. List four reasons why tort law does not yet contain a separate tort of invasion of privacy.

6. List five ways in which tort law may indirectly protect privacy interests.

7. Explain the tort of false imprisonment, and describe how a business can protect itself against liability.

8. Describe the tort of malicious prosecution.

9. Describe the tort of trespass to land, and explain when a business is entitled to prohibit people from coming onto its premises.

10. Outline the torts that protect the possession of chattels and explain the dangers that arise when stolen goods are bought by mistake.

A number of torts require proof of the defendant's intention. We will see several examples in the next chapter. In this chapter, however, we will focus on the torts that traditionally have been labelled the "intentional torts":

- assault
- battery
- invasion of privacy
- false imprisonment
- trespass to land
- interference with chattels

Intentional torts involve intentional, rather than merely careless, conduct.[1] For instance, the defendant may be held liable for battery if he deliberately punched the plaintiff. Somewhat surprisingly, however, tort law actually defines "intention" in a much broader way. It is enough if the defendant knew that a particular act would have particular consequences. The plaintiff does *not* have to prove that the defendant intended to either cause harm or commit a tort. For example, if you build a fence on my property, you commit the intentional tort of trespass to land, even if you think that the land belongs to you. It is enough that you know that your actions will result in a fence being constructed on *that* piece of ground. The courts have adopted that broad definition of "intention" because they want to protect the interests that I have in myself and in my property. From a risk management perspective, the lesson is clear. Before acting in a particular way, you should know as much as possible about the consequences of doing so.

intentional torts involve intentional, rather than merely careless, conduct

ASSAULT AND BATTERY

It is easy to confuse the ideas of assault and battery. People often use those terms interchangeably. And even lawyers use the word "assault" to describe the crime of physically attacking a person. In tort, however, "assault" and "battery" have very different meanings. An **assault** occurs when the defendant intentionally causes the plaintiff to reasonably believe that offensive bodily contact is imminent. There are several important points in that definition.

the tort of **assault** occurs when the defendant intentionally causes the plaintiff to reasonably believe that offensive bodily contact is imminent

- First, the tort is not based on physical contact. It is based on a reasonable belief that such contact will occur. The tort is designed to keep the peace by discouraging people from alarming others. As a result, you may commit an assault by swinging your fist at me, even if you do not actually make contact. But if you punch me from behind, you do not commit the tort of assault if I did not know that the blow was coming (although you do commit the tort of battery).
- Second, it is enough if the plaintiff *reasonably believed* that bodily contact would occur. As a result, you may commit an assault by pointing a gun in my direction, even if the gun is not really loaded. I would only

---

[1.] Confusingly, Canadian courts occasionally say that an intentional tort can consist of either intentional *or* careless conduct: *Cook v Lewis* [1952] 1 DLR 1 (SCC). Our discussion, however, can be limited to intentional acts. The intentional torts are also characterized by a requirement of *directness*—the plaintiff's injury must flow naturally from the defendant's conduct and must not depend upon the intervention of some outside factor. That requirement is complicated, but it seldom creates problems in practice. There is no need to explore it in this book.

have to prove that a reasonable person would have thought that a gunshot was possible.

■ Third, the plaintiff must have believed that bodily contact was *imminent*. Although that requirement is rather vague, you probably would not commit an assault if you threatened to kick me two weeks from today. Something more immediate is necessary.

■ Fourth, an assault can occur even if the plaintiff was not frightened. It is enough that the defendant threatened some form of *offensive contact*. For example, you may commit an assault by swinging your fist at me, even if I know that you are far too small to do any harm.

People seldom sue for assault alone. It normally is not worth the trouble and expense of litigation. A claim for assault is usually joined with a claim for *battery*. A **battery** consists of offensive bodily contact.[2] There are several points to note about this definition.

the tort of **battery** consists of offensive bodily contact

■ First, the requirement of "bodily contact" is not strictly applied. It is enough if the defendant causes something, such as a knife or a bullet, to touch the plaintiff. It is also enough if the defendant makes contact with the plaintiff's clothing or with something that the plaintiff is holding.

■ Second, not every form of contact is offensive. Normal social interaction is allowed. Consequently, you do not commit a battery if you gently brush past me in a crowded elevator or if you tap my shoulder to get my attention. At the same time, however, contact may be offensive even if it is not harmful. Consequently, you will commit a battery if you kiss me despite my objections. You may even commit a tort if your actions are highly beneficial (as when a physician performs a life-saving blood transfusion against a patient's wishes).[3]

Understanding the tort of battery is especially important for businesses that control crowds or remove rowdy customers. Bouncers and security personnel often injure patrons whom they eject from taverns, concerts, and sporting events. Given the doctrine of vicarious liability and the need for risk management, such employees should be carefully trained. Case Brief 4.1 serves as a warning.

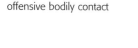

CASE BRIEF 4.1

Vasey v Wosk's Ltd [1988] BCJ No 2089 (SC)

The plaintiff was escorted out of a bar after becoming drunk and belligerent. Once outside, he struck one of the bouncers from behind. In retaliation, that bouncer knocked him to the ground with a kick to the head. Another bouncer then climbed on top of the plaintiff and punched him in the face for about five minutes. The plaintiff suffered a number of injuries and consequently sued the company that owned the bar.

The court held that the bar's employees were entitled to use reasonable force to remove the obnoxious customer from the premises. It further held that the plaintiff was partially to blame for the disturbance because he had struck one of the bouncers from behind. However, it also held that the employees used excessive force. It therefore allowed the plaintiff to recover compensation for the losses that he suffered, minus a reduction of 30 percent to reflect the fact that he had provoked the attack. The bouncers were held personally liable and the company that owned the bar was held vicariously liable.

[2.] A person who commits the tort of battery often commits a crime at the same time.

[3.] *Malette v Shulman* (1990) 67 DLR (4th) 321 (Ont CA). But see *Hobbs v Robertson* (2004) 243 DLR (4th) 700 (BC SC).

As we shall see, the concept of reasonable force is important in other situations as well. While you may be entitled to make a citizen's arrest, or remove a trespasser from your property, or recover your goods from a thief, you can never use anything more than reasonable force. You cannot, for instance, set a deadly trap to catch a burglar or viciously beat a bike thief. If you go overboard, you may be sued in tort or prosecuted for a crime.

INVASION OF PRIVACY

Torts like assault and battery traditionally focused on the risk of physical injury. As new technologies continue to emerge, however, people are becoming more concerned with their privacy interests. A telephoto lens can capture a photograph from far away; a camera-equipped cellular telephone can secretly record images from inside a public restroom. Tort law has not yet caught up with those technological advances. There is no general tort of *invasion of privacy*. Consequently, a business that owns land next to a race track is entitled to erect a high platform, watch the races, and broadcast the events over the radio.[4] As the court explained in that case, people are not required to look away or to keep quiet about what they see.

There are several reasons why the courts traditionally have been reluctant to recognize a tort of invasion of privacy. They want to support freedom of expression and freedom of information. They are concerned about defining the concept of privacy in a way that strikes a fair balance between the parties.[5] They are reluctant to award damages in favour of celebrities who seek out publicity, but then complain when they are shown in a bad light. And they find it difficult to calculate compensatory damages for the kinds of harm, such as embarrassment, that an invasion of privacy usually causes.

That is not to say that tort law does not provide any protection at all. Privacy is *indirectly* protected by several torts.

- A photographer who sneaks onto someone's property to obtain candid pictures commits the tort of *trespass to land*.[6]
- Employees who publish embarrassing details about their employer's private life may be held liable for *breach of confidence*.[7] That action also allowed an English court to award damages against a magazine that published unauthorized photographs taken by a guest at a private wedding between two Hollywood heavyweights, Michael Douglas and Catherine Zeta-Jones.[8]
- Despite rejecting a tort of invasion of privacy, English courts have recognized a tort of *abuse of private information*. Consequently, supermodel Naomi Campbell was able to sue a newspaper that published a photograph of her coming out of a Narcotics Anonymous meeting.[9]

[4.] *Victoria Park Racing and Recreation Grounds Co Ltd v Taylor* (1937) 58 CLR 459 (HCA).

[5.] *Wainwright v Home Office* [2004] 2 AC 406 (HL).

[6.] The tort of trespass to land is considered later in this chapter.

[7.] *Stephens v Avery* [1988] Ch 449. The action for breach of confidence is examined in Chapter 18.

[8.] *Douglas v Hello! Ltd* [2001] QB 969 (CA).

[9.] *Campbell v Mirror News Group* [2004] 2 AC 457 (HL). Interestingly, the court relied upon the action for breach of confidence even though the photograph was taken of the plaintiff while she was emerging from a public building. The element of secrecy was provided by the fact that the newspaper added a caption explaining that Ms Campbell was leaving a substance abuse meeting.

- A company that makes unauthorized use of a celebrity's image to sell its own products may commit the tort of *misappropriation of personality*.[10]

- A newspaper that ignores a judge's instructions and publishes the name of a police officer who had been sexually assaulted during an undercover investigation may commit the tort of *negligence*.[11]

While those torts provide some protection, many people still believe that there is room for a separate tort of invasion of privacy. New Zealand's highest court recently accepted that argument,[12] and Australia's highest court seems inclined to follow suit.[13] Canadian courts may not be far behind. An Ontario judge imposed liability upon a couple who, as part of a petty feud, installed a surveillance camera that continuously monitored their neighbours' backyard. While recognizing that the law generally does not prohibit one person from watching another, the judge held that an intentional invasion of privacy will not be permitted.[14] Similarly, although the decision in Case Brief 4.2 was decided under Quebec's civil law and therefore is not directly applicable in Canada's other jurisdictions, it may also signal a new direction in the protection of privacy interests. If so, it will mean that certain types of businesses will have to change the way they operate.

CASE BRIEF 4.2

Aubry v Éditions Vice-Versa Inc (1998) 157 DLR (4th) 577 (SCC)

A photographer took a picture of a young woman sitting on the steps of a building in Montreal. When the photograph was published in an arts magazine, the young woman was teased by her school friends. She then brought an action against the photographer and the magazine for invasion of privacy.

A majority of the Supreme Court of Canada awarded $2000 to the young woman. It said that a balance must be struck, in light of the circumstances of each case, between the right to privacy and the right to freedom of expression. On the facts, the plaintiff's right was more worthy of protection, partially because she was identifiable and therefore should have been asked for her consent. The court was also influenced by the fact that the plaintiff was the primary subject of the photograph. She was not simply part of a larger image of a building or a crowd.

Because the courts are moving slowly in this area, legislators are becoming more involved. At the time of writing, Parliament was considering Bill C-2, which would create a crime of "voyeurism" in order to punish people who make or sell images that violate the subjects' "reasonable expectation of privacy." That law could, for instance, catch the sort of unscrupulous paparazzi who earned millions of dollars by secretly photographing supermodel Claudia Schiffer as she sunbathed topless in her parents' garden in Majorca, and the Duchess of York Sarah Ferguson as she lounged topless beside a private pool in St Tropez.

In addition, several provinces already have legislation to protect privacy interests.[15] While those statutes vary from jurisdiction to jurisdiction, they generally impose liability if a person "wilfully" violates another's privacy by

---

[10.] *Athans v Canadian Adventure Camps Ltd* (1977) 80 DLR (3d) 583 (Ont HCJ).

[11.] In *LR v Nyp* (1995) 25 CCLT (2d) 309 (Ont Gen Div), the court was anxious to protect sexual assault victims from embarrassment by preserving their privacy. The tort of negligence is considered in Chapter 6.

[12.] *Hosking v Runting* [2005] 1 NZLR 1 (CA).

[13.] *ABC v Lenah Game Meats* (2001) 208 CLR 199 (HCA).

[14.] *Lipiec v Borsa* (1996) 31 CCLT (2d) 294 (Ont Gen Div).

[15.] *Privacy Act*, RSBC 1996, c 373 (BC); *Privacy Act*, CCSM, c P125 (Man); *Privacy Act*, RSNL 1990, c P-22 (Nfld); *Privacy Act*, RSS 1978, c P-24 (Sask).

doing something that they know to be wrong. The definition of "privacy" has been left open so that the courts can flexibly respond to different types of situations. Case Brief 4.3 illustrates the statutory action.

CASE BRIEF 4.3

Hollinsworth v BCTV [1999] 6 WWR 54 (BC CA)

The plaintiff entered into a contract with the defendant, Look International Enterprises (LIS), to have a hairpiece surgically attached to his scalp. Under the terms of that contract, LIS was allowed to videotape the procedure for instructional purposes only. Seven years later, without the plaintiff's knowledge, LIS allowed a television station to use the videotape during a news feature on hair grafts. When the station's reporter asked if the patient had consented to such use, LIS wrongly said, "Yes." The plaintiff suffered great embarrass-

ment as a result of the broadcast. He sued both LIS and the television station under British Columbia's *Privacy Act*.

The court awarded damages of $15 000 against LIS for its "wilful" invasion of privacy. The plaintiff's claim against the television station failed, however, because the station had not acted "wilfully." Given the information that its reporter had received from LIS, the station believed that the plaintiff had consented to the use of the videotape.

FALSE IMPRISONMENT

False imprisonment occurs when a person is confined within a fixed area without justification. That would clearly be true if the plaintiff was physically dragged to an actual prison and thrown into a locked cell. The scope of the tort is, however, considerably wider than that.

the tort of false imprisonment occurs when a person is confined within a fixed area without justification

- An actual prison is not necessary. The tort can be committed if a person is trapped in a car, locked in a room, or set adrift in a boat. But in any event, the confinement must be practically complete. The defendant does not commit a false imprisonment by obstructing one path while leaving a reasonable alternative open. Nor is the tort committed if the plaintiff can easily escape.

- Perhaps surprisingly, physical force is *not* necessary. The detention may be *psychological*. A tort may be committed, for example, if a shopper accompanies a security guard to a back room in order to avoid public embarrassment.[16] Confronted by a person in uniform who is making a serious demand, many people feel that they have no choice but to do as they are told. In that type of case, the judge has to decide whether the plaintiff voluntarily chose to go to the back room (no liability) or whether the plaintiff believed that there really was no other option (liability).

- Because a police officer has a wider power of arrest than a private citizen, a business person may *reduce* the risk of liability by calling a police officer, instead of directly arresting a suspect. That tactic will not, however, *eliminate* the risk. The business may still be held liable if it *directed* the officer to make the arrest, rather than merely state the facts and allow the officer to draw a conclusion.[17]

[16.] *Chaytor v London, New York & Paris Assoc of Fashion Ltd* (1961) 30 DLR (2d) 527 (Nfld SC TD).

[17.] *Valderhaug v Libin* (1954) 13 WWR 383 (Alta CA); *Lebrun v High-Low Foods Ltd* (1968) 69 DLR (2d) 433 (BC SC).

- Even if the business did not direct a police officer to make an arrest (and therefore cannot be held liable for false imprisonment), it may be liable for the tort of *malicious prosecution*.[18] **Malicious prosecution** occurs when the defendant improperly causes the plaintiff to be prosecuted. The focus is not on the plaintiff's detention or imprisonment, but rather on the fact that he or she was subject to criminal proceedings. That might be true, for instance, if a business concocted a story about shoplifting and persuaded the government to lay charges against the plaintiff. Malicious prosecution is, however, difficult to prove. The court has to be satisfied that (i) the defendant started the proceedings, (ii) out of malice, or for some improper purpose, and (iii) without honestly believing on reasonable grounds that a crime had been committed, and that (iv) the plaintiff was eventually acquitted of the alleged crime.[19]

Although the tort of false imprisonment is quite wide, the defendant will not be held liable if the plaintiff agreed to be confined. *Consent* is a complete defence to all intentional torts. Consequently, bus passengers cannot complain if the driver refuses to make an unscheduled stop.[20] A company that operates a mine is generally entitled to leave a worker underground until the end of a shift.[21] And a traveller at an airport may be detained for the purpose of a search. The same rule may apply to a customer in a store, at least if the store gave advance warning. Likewise, although a false imprisonment can be committed by wrongfully detaining someone's valuable property, the tort does not arise if the plaintiff agreed to that arrangement. Consequently, a person cannot remove a vehicle from a car park without paying the appropriate fee.

An imprisonment is false only if it is done *without authority*. That statement raises an important question for business people. When is there authority to make an arrest? Unfortunately, the law is complicated and somewhat unsettled. The basic rules are found in the *Criminal Code*.

- A *police officer* may arrest anyone who is reasonably suspected of (i) being in the act of committing a crime, or (ii) having committed a *serious* crime in the past.[22] If that test is satisfied, the police officer cannot be held liable, even if the person who was arrested was actually innocent.

- The rules are much narrower, however, for *private citizens*—including *security guards*. A private citizen is entitled to make an arrest only if a crime is *actually being committed* by the suspect.[23] If, in fact, no crime was being committed, the arrest is unjustified. And whoever made the arrest may be held liable in tort, even if they acted honestly and reasonably. The law generally favours a customer's freedom of movement over a store's desire to protect its property.

The rules that apply to private citizens often create difficulties for business people. For instance, a person who objects to the price of a meal and tries to leave the restaurant without fully paying the bill usually commits a breach of

---

[18] *Roberts v Buster's Auto Towing Service Ltd* (1976) 70 DLR (3d) 716 (BC SC).

[19] *Nelles v Ontario* (1989) 60 DLR (4th) 609 (SCC).

[20] *Martin v Berends* [1989] OJ No 2644 (Ont Prov Ct).

[21] *Herd v Weardale Steel, Coal & Coke Co Ltd* [1915] AC 67 (HL).

[22] *Criminal Code*, RSC 1985, c C-46, s 495 (Can).

[23] *Criminal Code*, RSC 1985, c C-46, s 494 (Can); *Hayward v FW Woolworth Co Ltd* (1979) 98 DLR (3d) 345 (Nfld SC TD). A private citizen may also arrest a person who is reasonably believed to have committed a crime *and* who is being chased by a police officer. If that test is satisfied, the citizen will not be liable in tort, even if no crime had actually been committed.

contract, but not a crime.[24] In that situation, the law is faced with a difficult choice.[25] It could allow the business to detain the customer (or the customer's property) until it receives payment. That approach would, however, violate the customer's freedom of movement. Alternatively, the law could merely allow the business to sue the customer for breach of contract. Quite often, however, the amount in question will be too small to justify the expense of a lawsuit. Although neither solution is perfect, the law prefers the latter. Consequently, while the restaurant is entitled to take down the patron's name and sue for breach of contract, it may be liable for false imprisonment if it tries to detain the customer.[26] Business Decision 4.1 illustrates another common dilemma.

BUSINESS DECISION 4.1

False Imprisonment and Detention by Security Guards

Terrence works as a security guard in your music store. He notices that Martin, who has been caught shoplifting in the past, is clutching his jacket closed. While Terrence strongly suspects that Martin is attempting to steal a CD, he also knows that the young man's father is a lawyer who specializes in tort law. He asks for advice.

You have several options.

■ You could tell Terrence to let Martin walk away, possibly with a stolen CD.

■ You could tell Terrence to ask Martin to follow him into a back room for the purposes of questioning. If Martin was shoplifting, you have no need to worry. But if he was not, he may sue you and Terrence for false imprisonment.

■ You could tell Terrence to contact the police. If the investigating officers believed that Martin was committing a crime, they could arrest him. If Martin was not actually shoplifting, the police would be protected as long as they acted on reasonable grounds. Furthermore, Martin probably could not sue you or Terrence because you did not personally detain him.

Questions for Discussion

1. Which option will you adopt?

2. If you adopt the third option, do you believe that Martin will still be in the store when the police arrive?

As we previously suggested, even if a business is authorized to make an arrest, it should not use more force than is necessary. In most situations, the customer should be given an opportunity to surrender peacefully. And in any event, the arrested person should be turned over to the police as soon as possible.

TRESPASS TO LAND

A **trespass to land** occurs when the defendant improperly interferes with the plaintiff's land. Interference can take several forms. A trespass is obviously committed if a vandal sneaks onto someone's property. However, the tort can also arise quite innocently. That is true, for instance, if I kick a ball into your yard (even if I do not walk onto your property to retrieve the ball), or if a lawn

the tort of **trespass to land** occurs when the defendant improperly interferes with the plaintiff's land

---

[24] A crime of fraud or false pretences will be committed only if, for instance, the customer intended to refuse payment from the outset, tried to sneak out of the restaurant, gave a false name, or provided a worthless cheque: *Criminal Code*, RSC 1985, c C-46, ss 362, 364, 380. A crime is also committed if, for instance, a shopper switches price tags, or puts a more expensive item into the carton of a less expensive item, in order to obtain a "discount."

[25] One solution is for the business to require payment *before* providing service. Aside from gas stations, however, most businesses find that approach to be inconvenient and off-putting to the customer.

[26] *Bahner v Marwest Hotel Ltd* (1969) 6 DLR (3d) 322 (BC SC); *Perry v Fried* (1972) 32 DLR (3d) 589 (NS SC TD).

care company mistakenly cuts your grass instead of your neighbour's. If that seems surprising, remember our earlier discussion of "intention." It is enough if I intended to do the act, even if I did not intend to do wrong or to cause damage. The law wants to protect property interests. As the old saying goes, "A man's home is his castle."

The tort of trespass is not committed, however, by a person who has legal authority to be on a property. For example, police officers are entitled to enter premises under a search warrant. Likewise, a number of other public officials, such as building inspectors and meter readers, may do whatever is reasonably necessary to carry out their duties.

More significantly for our purposes, a trespass does not occur merely because a customer walks into a place of business during regular hours. Under normal circumstances, it is assumed that the business *consented* to the intrusion—indeed, it implicitly *invited* the customer onto the property. However, a business can usually revoke its consent, as long as it does not violate human rights legislation (for example, by excluding a person on racial grounds).[27] Consequently, the owner of a shopping mall is not required to allow mall employees to set up a picket line on its premises as part of a labour dispute.[28] Similarly, the owner of a racetrack may exclude a highly successful gambler.[29] And once a business has revoked its consent, a customer who remains on its property becomes a trespasser. If the customer still refuses to leave, the business may use reasonable force to eject them. However, as we discussed under the tort of battery, it should be very careful when doing so.

Quite often, a business will deal with an unwelcome visitor by simply removing the trespasser. In some situations, however, the business may want to do more—it may want to arrest the trespasser. There is legislation in most jurisdictions that allows an occupier to arrest a trespasser.[30] And indeed, Intelligarde, one of Ontario's largest security guard companies, has made over 30 000 arrests during the past 20 years. Nevertheless, it only recently became clear that an occupier is entitled to use *reasonable force* in making such an arrest. In *R v Asante-Mensah*, Binnie J explained that since the legislature granted the special power of arrest, it must have intended to protect people who exercise that power in a reasonable way. However, he also stressed the need for private citizens to use caution.

> Many trespasses are of trivial importance. . . They are best handled by means short of arrest. . . . An arrest is a grave imposition on another person's liberty and should only be attempted if other options prove ineffective. Further, an arrest may lead to a confrontation that is more serious than the initial offence of trespass. . . . Excessive force, or

27. The business will not always be able to revoke its consent. For example, a customer who has paid to attend a baseball game and has not broken any of the conditions attached to his ticket cannot be ejected merely because he refuses to show his ticket to an attendant during the game: *Davidson v Toronto Blue Jays Baseball Ltd* (1999) 170 DLR (4th) 559 (Ont Gen Div).

28. *Harrison v Carswell* (1975) 62 DLR (3d) 68 (SCC). In some provinces, legislation now allows picketing in such circumstances: *eg* see *Petty Trespasses Act*, CCSM, c P150 (Man).

29. *Russo v Ontario Jockey Club* (1987) 46 DLR (4th) 359 (Ont HCJ).

30. *Trespass to Premises Act*, RSA 2000, c T-7, s 5 (Alta); *Trespass Act*, RSBC 1996, c 462, s 10 (BC); *Petty Trespasses Act*, CCSM, c P50, s 2 [rep and am 1992, c 21, s 3] (Man); *Trespass Act*, SNB 1983, c T-11.2, s 7 [am 1985, c 70, s 5; 1989, c 42, s 5; 1990; c 22, s 51] (NB); *Petty Trespass Act*, RSNL 1990, c P-11, s 4 (Nfld); *Protection of Property Act*, RSNS 1989, c 363, s 6 (NS); *Trespass To Property Act*, RSO 1990, c T.21, s 9 (Ont); *Trespass To Property Act*, RSPEI 1988, T-6, s 5 (PEI). The wording of those statutes sometimes varies. In British Columbia, Nova Scotia, and Prince Edward Island, for instance, the legislation gives a power of arrest to police officers, but not to occupiers.

improper use of the arrest power, may leave the occupier . . . open to both criminal charges and civil liability.[31]

The usual remedy for a trespass to land is compensation for the harm that it caused. However, a court may also award nominal damages if there was no loss, or punitive damages if the defendant's conduct was shockingly bad. Furthermore, if the defendant's wrong is ongoing, the plaintiff may be entitled to an injunction to stop the trespass. For example, if a company constructs a billboard on a person's land without permission, the judge will likely demand that it be torn down. In some circumstances, however, the courts are faced with a difficult choice between protecting the plaintiff's property interests and avoiding economic waste. In deciding whether to grant an injunction, a judge will consider a number of factors, including the defendant's motivation for committing the wrong, the extent to which monetary damages would adequately protect the plaintiff, and the costs associated with removing the trespass. How would you decide the case in You Be the Judge 4.1?

YOU BE THE JUDGE 4.1

Trespass to Land and Injunctions

Vista Inc, a real estate developer, built a 20-storey apartment complex. Unfortunately, as a result of an innocent error, a corner of the building extends two metres onto the neighbouring lot, which is owned by Paolo. Vista admits that it committed the tort of trespass and it is willing to either pay compensatory damages or buy the affected land from Paolo. Paolo, however, insists that he should be able to exercise complete control over his property. He therefore wants an injunction to prevent Vista's ongoing trespass. To do so, Vista would have to tear down a substantial part of its building.

Questions for Discussion

1. Would you grant the injunction?

2. Would your answer be different if the cost of removing the trespassing portion of the apartment complex was $50 000? What if it was $5 000 000?

3. Would your answer be different if Paolo suffered no financial loss as a result of the trespass? What if, for some reason, he suffered a substantial loss of $50 000 or $5 000 000? What if he was simply very upset that his rights had been infringed?

4. Would your answer be different if Vista had committed the trespass on purpose? What if Vista knew at the outset that it was committing a tort but was confident that, even if Paolo noticed the trespass, a court would award only nominal damages for the minor infringement?

INTERFERENCE WITH CHATTELS

Tort law protects not only land, but also *chattels*. **Chattels** are moveable forms of property, such as horses, books, and cars. The rules are quite complicated, largely because the courts have developed a number of torts to protect chattels. We will outline the most important of those torts:

- trespass to chattels
- conversion
- detinue

Concept Summary 4.1 lists the essential features of those torts (see p. 86).

chattels are moveable forms of property

[31.] *R v Asante-Mensah* (2003) 227 DLR (4th) 75 (SCC). Although the Supreme Court of Canada's decision technically applies only to the Ontario statute, the court's reasoning will apply in some other jurisdictions as well.

Intentional Interference with Chattels

Tort	Basis of the Tort	General Remedy
Trespass to chattels	defendant's interference with chattels in plaintiff's possession	compensation for loss
Conversion	defendant's interference with chattels in plaintiff's possession—serious enough to justify forced sale	forced sale of chattel from plaintiff to defendant
Detinue	defendant's failure to return chattels that plaintiff has right to possess	compensation for loss or return of chattels

the tort of **trespass to chattels** occurs when the defendant interferes with chattels in the plaintiff's possession

Trespass to chattels occurs when the defendant interferes with chattels in the plaintiff's possession. The element of interference is satisfied if the defendant damages, destroys, takes, or uses the plaintiff's goods. There may even be a trespass if the defendant merely touches the plaintiff's property, at least if that property is, for example, a priceless painting that requires protection.[32] As a general rule, the remedy for trespass to chattels is compensatory damages.[33] Consequently, if you completely destroyed my car, you would be required to pay the vehicle's market value. In contrast, if you merely damaged my car, you would be required to pay either for the value that it lost or for its repairs, whichever is less.

the tort of **conversion** occurs when the defendant interferes with the plaintiff's chattels in a way that is serious enough to justify a forced sale

The tort of **conversion** occurs when the defendant interferes with the plaintiff's chattels in a way that is serious enough to justify a forced sale. That may be true if the defendant takes, detains, uses, buys, sells, damages, or destroys the plaintiff's property. If so, the defendant will be required to buy the item by paying the market value that the chattel had at the time of the tort. In exchange for that payment, the defendant acquires the property.

The main difficulty with the tort of conversion is that it is often difficult to know whether the defendant's actions are serious enough to justify a forced sale. The courts consider all of the facts, including:

- the extent to which the defendant exercised ownership or control over the chattel
- the extent to which the defendant intended to assert a right that was inconsistent with the plaintiff's right to the property
- the duration of the defendant's interference
- the expense and inconvenience caused to the plaintiff[34]

Conversion is clearly committed if a thief steals my property or if a vandal destroys it. The tort may also occur if you habitually use my umbrella without my permission, but not if you use it only once because you were caught in a downpour.[35]

Once again, the tort may be committed even if the defendant did not intend to do anything wrong. It is enough, for instance, that you intended to exercise

---

[32.] JG Fleming *The Law of Torts* 9th ed (1998) at 59.

[33.] In exceptional cases, the plaintiff may receive nominal damages or punitive damages.

[34.] W Prosser "The Nature of Conversion" (1957) 42 *Cornell LQ* 168 at 174.

[35.] *Canadian Orchestrophone Ltd v British Canadian Trust Co* [1932] 2 WWR 618 (Alta CA).

control over my property, even if you thought that you were entitled to do so. That rule presents a particular danger for business people. As a matter of risk management, it means that you should use every reasonable effort to ensure that you buy goods from people who are actually entitled to sell them. And even that may not be enough to protect you from liability. Ethical Perspective 4.1 illustrates the rules.

? ETHICAL PERSPECTIVE 4.1

Conversion and Innocent Purchasers[36]

John stole a herd of cattle from Katherine and sold the animals to you for $50 000. Before you paid, you checked the cattle and noticed that they were not branded. You also asked John about the herd and were convinced that he owned the animals. Unfortunately, he has disappeared, and Katherine has sued you for conversion. You protest that you had acted honestly.

While an unsuspecting buyer or seller of goods is sometimes protected by a special defence, a court would probably hold you liable for conversion. In buying the cattle and treating them as your own, you seriously interfered with

Katherine's rights. Consequently, you would have to pay her $50 000, which was the market value of the animals. Note that while you will be entitled to keep the herd, you have now paid $100 000 for it. You could try to recover $50 000 from John, but he has disappeared, as rogues often do.

Questions for Discussion

1. Are the rules for conversion fair?

2. Why do you think that the law of conversion is so strict?

The tort of **detinue** occurs when the defendant fails to return a chattel that the plaintiff is entitled to possess. The word "detinue" is derived from the old French word "*detenue*," which means detention. Because the tort is based on a wrongful detention, the plaintiff is normally required to demand possession of the property before bringing an action. That requirement is removed, however, if the demand would obviously be refused. The fact that detinue consists of a wrongful detention also affects the remedies that may be available to a plaintiff.

> *the tort of* detinue *occurs when the defendant fails to return a chattel that the plaintiff is entitled to possess*

- First, the tort comes to an end as soon as the defendant returns the property to the plaintiff. At that point, the plaintiff is normally limited to compensation for losses that it suffered during the detention, as well as for any harm done to the item.

- Second, if the property has not been returned by the time of trial, the plaintiff can ask the court to compel the defendant to do so.[37] The court usually gives the defendant the option of either giving the property back or paying damages. However, the judge may require the property to be returned if it is special or if damages would not satisfy the plaintiff.

Detinue is the only tort that generally allows a court to order the defendant to return a chattel to the plaintiff. In some situations, however, the plaintiff may not need the court's help. The right of **recaption** allows a person to take their own property back. For instance, a shopkeeper may be entitled to grab a watch away from a shoplifter who is trying to leave the store. That right should, however, be exercised very carefully. The owner is only entitled to use reasonable force while recovering the property. Anything more will expose the owner to the risk of liability for battery.

> *the right of* recaption *allows a person to take their own property back*

[36.] *Nilsson Bros Inc v McNamara Estate* [1992] 3 WWR 761 (Alta CA).

[37.] That option does not exist under trespass to chattels or conversion. Those torts generally only support monetary damages.

Chapter Summary

Intentional torts involve intentional conduct. It is enough if the defendant knew that particular conduct would have particular consequences. The plaintiff does not have to prove that the defendant intended either to cause harm or commit a tort.

Several types of intentional torts may be committed against a person. An assault occurs when the defendant intentionally causes the plaintiff to reasonably believe that offensive bodily contact is imminent. A battery consists of offensive bodily contact. False imprisonment occurs when a person is confined within a fixed area without justification. Malicious prosecution occurs when the defendant improperly causes the plaintiff to be prosecuted.

Although there traditionally has not been a separate tort of invasion of privacy, Canadian courts may be in the process of developing one. In the meantime, certain aspects of privacy are protected by other torts, including breach of confidence, abuse of private information, trespass to land, misappropriation of personality, and negligence. Some provinces have introduced statutory actions for invasion of privacy.

There are several types of intentional torts that may be committed against a person's property. Trespass to land occurs when the defendant improperly interferes with land that the plaintiff possesses. An occupier may use reasonable force when removing or arresting a trespasser. Trespass to chattels occurs when the defendant interferes with chattels that the plaintiff possesses. Conversion occurs when the defendant interferes with the plaintiff's chattels in a way that is serious enough to justify a forced sale. Detinue occurs when the defendant fails to return goods that the plaintiff has the right to possess. In some circumstances, a person may be entitled to recover property by recaption.

Review Questions

1. In what sense do the intentional torts require intentional conduct? Is tort law's definition of "intention" fair? Explain your answer.

2. Explain the difference between assault and battery. Describe a situation in which there is an assault but not a battery. Describe a situation in which there is a battery but not an assault.

3. Identify and explain a situation in which the concept of "reasonable force" is important to the removal of a person who is trespassing on business property.

4. "The tort of battery exists to protect people from injury. If the defendant's actions did not actually cause any physical harm, the plaintiff's claim must fail." Is that statement correct? Explain your answer.

5. Does tort law recognize a special claim for invasion of privacy? Explain your answer.

6. Describe how privacy statutes generally operate.

7. List four ways in which tort law indirectly protects privacy.

8. "A business person is at liberty to use any amount of force to remove or arrest an undesirable customer." Is that statement true? As a business person, what factors would you consider before making an arrest or removing a customer from your place of business?

9. Does a false imprisonment occur every time that a person is detained against his or her wishes? If not, list situations in which the tort is not committed despite a detention.

10. Describe the tort of malicious prosecution and explain how it is related to the tort of false imprisonment.

11. Do police officers, security guards, and private citizens have the same rights when it comes to arresting criminals and suspected criminals? Explain the special dangers that arise when a business person arrests a suspected shoplifter.

12. Is it generally possible for a restaurant owner to arrest a person who refuses to pay the full amount of a bill? Explain your answer.

13. Briefly summarize the situations in which a person *will* commit a crime by refusing to pay for a meal in a restaurant.

14. "The tort of trespass to land requires proof that the defendant knew or ought to have known, that the property belonged to the plaintiff." Is that statement true? Explain your answer.

15. Does a person commit a trespass to land by walking into a store if the owner of the store actually did not want any visitors? Explain your answer.

16. Explain the extent to which a business may use force to arrest a person who is suspected of trespassing on land.

17. When will a court impose an injunction to stop a continuing trespass to land?

18. Explain the special dangers that the tort of conversion presents when a business person buys chattels.

19. Describe the special remedy that is available for detinue but not for trespass to chattels or conversion?

20. What is a "right of recaption"?

Cases and Problems

1. During an office party, Sonny saw his friend Fredo standing near the railing of a stairwell. Wanting to scare Fredo as a joke, Sonny sneaked up and gave him a gentle push from behind. Unfortunately, while Sonny had intended to grab his friend to prevent him from falling over the railing, he lost his grip on Fredo's jacket. Fredo fell forward, tumbled over the railing, and suffered severe injuries when he hit the landing below. Angry over the incident, Fredo has ended the friendship and insists that Sonny should have to pay his medical bills. Sonny feels badly about the situation but insists that since he never intended to do any harm, he should not be held responsible. Can Sonny be held liable to Fredo for an intentional tort? Explain your answer.

2. The Oxbridge Rowing Association (ORA) arranged to hold a race on the river running through the city of Camford. It received the city's permission to use a section of the riverbank to erect a grandstand and charge an admission fee to the public. On the day of the race, the ORA, with the city's permission, used a barricade to block off a section of the footpath that normally allowed the public to stroll along the riverbank. Shortly before the race was to start, Regina, a member of the ORA, noticed that Henley, who was in the regular habit of strolling along the river in the morning, was climbing over the barricade. Regina explained the situation to Henley and informed him that a detour had been set up that would allow members of the public to walk along another portion of the riverbank. Henley objected, saying that he wanted to follow his usual route. When he tried to press forward, Regina politely but firmly stood her ground. At that point, Henley declared, "You have no right to hold me here. I will stand here all day if you force me to do so, but mark my words, I will get through eventually." Regina responded by saying, "You can stand there if you want to, or you can use the detour if you want to, but I will not let you through until the race is over." True to her word, Regina continued to block Henley's way until the race finished. At that point, she stepped aside and allowed him to proceed along his usual route. Henley has now sued Regina for false imprisonment. He insists that she detained him when she would not allow him to walk where he wanted to walk. Is he correct? Explain your answer.

3. Although Jasmine Bhasin usually rode the bus to work, a one-day transit strike required her to drive instead. Not surprisingly, she was unable to find a parking space when she arrived at her office tower. She therefore simply parked in front of a fire hydrant and hoped for the best. At the end of the day, she was disappointed, but not particularly surprised, to find that her car had been towed away. After a few phone calls, she determined that her vehicle was being held in a compound that belonged to Buster's Towing Service. She went to the com-

pound, paid the towing charge, and collected her car. As she approached the exit gate, she rolled down her window and expressed her displeasure to the attendant—in rather colourful and abusive language. The attendant tried to close the gate in order to prevent Jasmine from leaving, but he was too late. Jasmine slipped past him without difficulty. She thought nothing more of the incident until the police appeared at her office the next day and charged her with a crime. In the criminal case that followed, the attendant accused Jasmine of trying to run over him after collecting her car from Buster's compound. The judge rejected that evidence, however, and found that the attendant had concocted the whole story out of anger. Jasmine was therefore acquitted on all charges. She now believes that she should be entitled to sue the attendant in tort. Is she correct? Explain your answer.

4. Richard wanted to buy a portable stereo, but was not keen on paying the full price. He therefore came up with a plan to get a discount. He went to the Stereo Shed and switched price tags on two models of portable stereos. He then took the more expensive item (with the less expensive price tag) up to the cashier, paid the "discount price," and headed for the exit. Just as he was about to leave the store, however, Maude, Stereo Shed's manager, stopped him and said that she wanted to see the contents of his bag. Richard insisted that she had no right to detain him and he pushed his way toward the door. At that point, Maude asked Stefan, a security guard, to hold on to Richard until she called the police. The police eventually arrived and charged Richard with a crime. The criminal charge has not yet been heard in court. Richard nevertheless wants to know whether Maude and Stefan were entitled to "arrest" him. What opinion would you give to Richard?

5. As part of a promotional campaign, the Blacksox Baseball Club ran an advertisement in a local newspaper that featured a picture of about three dozen fans who were cheering wildly at a recent home game. In one corner of the picture, a man and a woman were hugging and kissing, apparently delighted with their team's success. The man's wife, however, knew better. When she saw the photo, she realized that her husband had resumed an affair with a woman he had promised to never see again. Angry that the Blacksox had exposed his infidelity, the man wants to sue the organization for invasion of privacy. Assuming that no relevant conditions were attached to the ticket that the man had purchased, and assuming that the relevant events occurred in Alberta, can he successfully bring an action against the team on the basis of an intentional tort? Explain your answer.

6. Indira, an employee of Speedit Delivery Service, left a package at the front door of 57 Rollingwood Drive. In fact, she was supposed to leave it at the front door

of 75 Rollingwood Drive. Late that night, when Anton arrived home at 57 Rollingwood Drive, he tripped over the box and suffered serious injuries. Is he entitled to sue for an intentional tort? If so, whom should he sue? Explain your answer.

7. Elaine and Latka each operate a stall in a market. During a particularly busy day, Elaine noticed that she had nearly run out of coins. She normally walked to a nearby bank to obtain change. However, since business was so brisk, she did not want to leave her stall unattended for long. She went to Latka's stand to ask if she could borrow his vehicle. He was out for lunch, but she noticed that he had left his car keys under his counter. While she did not really know Latka very well, Elaine assumed that he would not mind if she borrowed his car for a few minutes. When she returned, however, Latka was furious to learn that she had taken his car without permission. Has Elaine committed an intentional tort? If so, which one? Explain the remedy that Latka may receive.

8. Basil, who operated a small hotel in Banff, was excited to learn that the town had been chosen to host a major conference of environmentalists during the off-season. At that time of year, most of his rooms were usually vacant. The event's organizers announced that they would visit hotels on a particular day to decide where to lodge delegates during the conference. Basil consequently spent a great deal of time and money improving his facilities. Unfortunately, his neighbour, Sybil, noticed his preparations. Shortly before the organizers were scheduled to arrive in town, and while Basil was temporarily away on business, Sybil constructed a shed out of biologically hazardous and non-recyclable materials. She acted purely out of spite. She wanted to upset the environmentalists and ensure that Basil's hotel was not chosen for the conference. Her ploy worked. The organizers were thoroughly offended by the sight of the structure. Consequently, while they were otherwise impressed with Basil's facilities, they refused to award a contract to him. Basil is very upset with Sybil, especially since he discovered that she intentionally had constructed much of the building on his property. Has Sybil committed an intentional tort? If so, what remedies are available to Basil?

9. Felicity and Oscar formerly operated a travel agency together. As a result of an unpleasant disagreement over the future of the business, however, Oscar brought the relationship to an end. While he was willing to leave the shop premises to Felicity, he took a number of items, including a tank full of goldfish. Although Felicity is happy to get along without most of those items, she is very upset about the goldfish because she loves them dearly. Oscar agrees that the fish belong to Felicity, but he refuses to return them to her. Has Oscar committed any intentional torts? Which tort should Felicity use? Explain your answer.

10. Madeleine sees Hugh stealing her car. Because she does not know who he is or where he lives, she realizes that she would have little chance of successfully suing him in tort. She also realizes that if she does not act immediately, she may lose her car permanently. What can Madeleine do?

11. Mary operates a convenience store. Much to her dismay, it has become a hangout for teenagers. She hired Frank to act as a security guard between the hours of 3:00 and 5:00 pm, when the store is at its busiest. Mary noticed that a young woman named Shelley, whom she had previously suspected of shoplifting, was acting suspiciously. She notified Frank, who approached Shelley and said in a loud voice and an accusing tone, "Come here. I've got a few questions to ask you." Shelley realized that Frank was acting on instructions from his employer and shouted over his shoulder at Mary, "If you've got a problem, come over here and speak to me yourself! I'll smack you silly!" At that point, Frank lunged at Shelley in an attempt to determine whether she was concealing stolen goods in her jacket. He grabbed her arm, but she managed to wrestle free and run out of the store. A number of Shelley's classmates saw the fracas and later teased her about it. Angry that Frank and Mary had humiliated her, Shelley returned to the street outside the store later that night and threw a garbage can through the shop window. Discuss the intentional torts that the parties may have committed.

12. Hannah's Holiday Foods Inc (HHF) operated a slaughterhouse where it killed, butchered, and packaged "exotic" animals, including rabbits and possums. HHF's business was fully licensed and entirely legal. An unknown animal rights group nevertheless believed that the public would be horrified to learn about the conditions under which the animals were killed. It therefore sneaked onto the premises one night and installed video surveillance cameras. The end product was a film showing rabbits in great distress before being slaughtered. That film was then delivered to a national television station, which announced its intention to broadcast the footage during its nightly news program. HHF has now gone to court and asked a judge to grant an injunction prohibiting the broadcast. While admitting that the television station acquired the film innocently, HHF insists that the film violates its right to privacy and almost certainly will hurt its business. Assuming that an injunction will be available if HHF can persuade the judge that there is, or should be, a right to privacy in private law, explain how you expect the case will be decided.

WEBLINKS

Bill C-2: Protection of Children and Other Vulnerable Persons   www.parl.gc.ca/38/1/parlbus/chambus/house/bills/government/C-2/C-2_1/C-2.html

This page contains the complete text of Bill C-2, a set of proposed amendments to the *Criminal Code* aimed at better protecting privacy rights.

McConchie Law: Invasion of Privacy   www.libelandprivacy.com/areasofpractice_privacy.html

This site discusses various laws dealing with the protection of privacy.

Recent Litigation in the Law of Malicious Prosecution
www.cacole.ca/conference%202003/conf_presentations/Recent%20Developments%20-%20Malicious%20Prosecution%20-%20P%20Knoll.pdf

This paper discusses recent Canadian cases dealing with false arrest and malicious prosecution.

Inc.com: Tort Claims Business Owners Should Watch Out For   www.inc.com/articles/1999/11/15379.html

This American website explains why businesses should be concerned about intentional torts like false imprisonment and battery.

ADDITIONAL RESOURCES FOR CHAPTER 4 ON THE COMPANION WEBSITE

(www.pearsoned.ca/mcinnes)

In addition to self-test multiple-choice, true-false, and short essay questions (all with immediate feedback), three additional Cases and Problems (with suggested answers), and links to useful Web destinations, the Companion Website provides the following resources for Chapter 4:

- Weblinks to provincial privacy legislation

Provincial Material

- **British Columbia:** Privacy Rights, Trespass to Land, Freedom of Information
- **Alberta:** Trespass
- **Manitoba and Saskatchewan:** Privacy Legislation, Trespass to Land
- **Ontario:** Private Investigators and Security Guards, Trespass

5 Miscellaneous Torts Affecting Business

OBJECTIVES

After completing this chapter, you should be able to:

1. Describe the tort of conspiracy and explain the risks that arise when two or more companies plot together against another business.

2. Explain the two ways in which a business can commit the tort of intimidation.

3. Distinguish between direct inducement to breach of contract and indirect inducement to breach of contract.

4. Describe the tort of unlawful interference with economic relations.

5. Outline the elements of the tort of deceit.

6. Explain the rules that apply to occupiers' liability in your province or territory.

7. Outline the range of situations in which the courts may impose liability on a business for committing the tort of nuisance.

8. Describe the elements of the rule in *Rylands v Fletcher* and explain how that tort involves strict liability.

9. Explain why businesses are frequently in danger of committing the tort of defamation.

10. Describe the tort of injurious falsehood.

In Chapter 4, we began our consideration of specific torts by examining several intentional torts that commonly affect business people. In this chapter, we continue our discussion by looking at a number of other torts that are important in the business context.

- conspiracy
- intimidation
- interference with contractual relations
- unlawful interference with economic relations
- deceit
- occupiers' liability
- nuisance
- the rule in *Rylands v Fletcher*
- defamation
- injurious falsehood

As you will have gathered by now, tort law is something of a grab bag. With a few exceptions,[1] it covers every type of private wrongdoing (as opposed to criminal wrongdoing) that is not a breach of contract. Consequently, while some of the torts that are included in this chapter overlap with one another, many of them have very little in common.

CONSPIRACY

One person is generally entitled to use lawful actions to economically hurt another.[2] Curiously, however, those same lawful actions may be tortious if they are performed by *several people*. The tort of **conspiracy** usually occurs when two or more defendants agree to act together with the primary purpose of causing a financial loss to the plaintiff. The lesson is clear. While the law generally condones aggressive competition between individuals, its sense of fair play may be offended if several people conspire against another.

The tort of conspiracy is hard to prove.[3] The courts are reluctant to find that the defendants co-operated for the *primary purpose* of hurting the plaintiff. For example, in one recent case, a number of people organized a consumer boycott of a paper company's products to draw attention to Aboriginal land claims.[4] Although the company lost a lot of money when many of its customers were persuaded to buy elsewhere, its tort action against the boycott organizers failed. The court held that the protestors' main purpose was not to hurt the company, but rather to raise public awareness of a political issue.

the tort of conspiracy usually occurs when two or more people agree to act together with the primary purpose of causing the plaintiff to suffer a financial loss

---

[1] Those exceptions include breach of confidence and breach of fiduciary duty, which we examine in other chapters.

[2] *Allen v Flood* [1898] AC 1 (HL). In Chapter 25, we will look at statutes that control unfair business practices that improperly affect competition.

[3] In some jurisdictions, the tort of conspiracy has been statutorily restricted or abolished with respect to actions performed by members of trade unions during trade disputes: see *eg Labour Relations Code*, RSBC 1996, c 244, s 69 (BC); *Rights of Labour Act*, RSO 1990, c R.33, s 3(1) (Ont); *Trade Union Act*, RSS 1978, c T-17, s 28 (Sask); but see *Labour Relations Act*, RSNL 1990, c L-1, s 103 (Nfld).

[4] *Daishowa Inc v Friends of the Lubicon* (1998) 158 DLR (4th) 699 (Ont Gen Div).

The tort of conspiracy raises difficult issues, both legally and ethically. Consider Ethical Perspective 5.1.

ETHICAL PERSPECTIVE 5.1

Conspiracy to Injure a Plaintiff by Lawful Means

Do the rules governing the tort of conspiracy make sense from an ethical or legal point of view?

Questions for Discussion

1. Should a single person, acting alone, be entitled to intentionally hurt another person's business interests, as long as lawful means are used? What arguments can be made for and against the current law?

2. If it is ethically permissible for one person, acting alone, to intentionally harm another person's economic interests, why should the situation be any different merely because several people act together to achieve the same result? Is the plaintiff more vulnerable if it is targeted by a single, but enormous, multinational corporation, rather than two small local businesses?

We have seen that conspiracy is hard to prove if the defendants injured the plaintiff by acting in an otherwise *lawful* way. The rules are different if the defendants injured the plaintiff by conspiring to perform an *unlawful* act. For instance, they might agree to commit a tort, or to violate the *Criminal Code*, labour relations legislation, or licensing regulations.[5] In that situation, the court does not have to be satisfied that the defendants' *primary purpose* was to hurt the plaintiff. It is enough if the defendants *should have known* that their actions might have that result.[6]

INTIMIDATION

the tort of **intimidation** occurs when the plaintiff suffers a loss as a result of the defendant's threat to commit an unlawful act against either the plaintiff or a third party

two-party intimidation occurs when the plaintiff is directly coerced into suffering a loss

three-party intimidation occurs when the defendant coerces a third party into acting in a way that hurts the plaintiff

The tort of *intimidation* is concerned with unethical business practices. **Intimidation** occurs when the plaintiff suffers a loss as a result of the defendant's threat to commit an unlawful act against either the plaintiff or a third party. As that definition suggests, the tort of intimidation has two branches, which are represented in Figure 5.1 (see p. 95).

- **Two-party intimidation** occurs when the defendant directly coerces the plaintiff into suffering a loss. For example, the manager of a supermarket might use threats of physical violence to frighten the owner of a small convenience store into closing down.

- **Three-party intimidation** occurs when the defendant coerces a third party into acting in a way that hurts the plaintiff. In the leading case of *Rookes v Barnard*, the plaintiff was an employee of an airline.[7] The defendant, a trade union, was angry with him as a result of a labour dispute. The union threatened the airline with an illegal strike unless it

---

[5] If the unlawful act also constitutes a separate tort, such as deceit, the plaintiff can bring an action in that tort, without relying on the tort of conspiracy.

[6] *Canada Cement LaFarge Ltd v BC Lightweight Aggregate Ltd* (1983) 145 DLR (3d) 385 (SCC).

[7] *Rookes v Barnard* [1964] AC 1129 (HL).

fired the plaintiff. The plaintiff successfully sued the defendant after the airline gave in to that pressure and fired him.

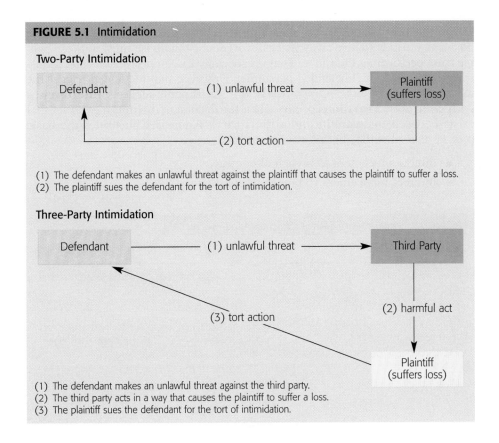

FIGURE 5.1 Intimidation

Two-Party Intimidation

Defendant ——————— (1) unlawful threat ——————→ Plaintiff (suffers loss)

——————————— (2) tort action ———————————

(1) The defendant makes an unlawful threat against the plaintiff that causes the plaintiff to suffer a loss.
(2) The plaintiff sues the defendant for the tort of intimidation.

Three-Party Intimidation

Defendant ——————— (1) unlawful threat ——————→ Third Party

(3) tort action

(2) harmful act

Plaintiff (suffers loss)

(1) The defendant makes an unlawful threat against the third party.
(2) The third party acts in a way that causes the plaintiff to suffer a loss.
(3) The plaintiff sues the defendant for the tort of intimidation.

Whether intimidation involves two or three parties, the basic rules remain the same.

- First, the plaintiff must prove that the defendant threatened to commit an unlawful act, such as a crime, a tort, or even a breach of contract.[8]

- Second, the tort does not occur unless the threatened party gave in to the intimidation. For example, the plaintiff would not have won in *Rookes v Barnard* if the airline had ignored the union's threat.

- Third, as long as the other elements of the tort are established, there is no need to prove that the defendant intended to hurt the plaintiff. For instance, intimidation may occur even if the tortfeasor was motivated by a desire to benefit itself, rather than injure the plaintiff.

[8.] It is not clear if two-party intimidation can ever be based on the defendant's threat to break a contract with the plaintiff. The courts have sometimes said that the plaintiff should resist that sort of pressure by simply suing for breach of contract. That tactic is not possible in a three-party situation, however, because the plaintiff cannot sue on a contract that exists between the defendant and the third party. Furthermore, the Supreme Court of Canada has indicated that a threat to break a contract is not intimidation in either a two-party or a three-party situation if the defendant reasonably believed that such a threat was lawful: *Central Canada Potash Co v Saskatchewan* (1978) 88 DLR (3d) 609 (SCC).

INTERFERENCE WITH CONTRACTUAL RELATIONS

the tort of **interference with contractual relations** occurs when the defendant disrupts a contract that the plaintiff has with another party

One of the most effective ways of gaining an advantage over a competitor in the business world is to hire away its best workers or otherwise prevent those people from performing their jobs. That is especially true in professions and industries that employ highly skilled personnel. However, that tactic can trigger the tort of *interference with contractual relations*. As its name suggests, **interference with contractual relations** occurs when the defendant disrupts a contract that exists between the plaintiff and a third party. Figure 5.2 illustrates the basic process that underlies both forms of the tort:

- direct inducement to breach of contract
- indirect inducement to breach of contract

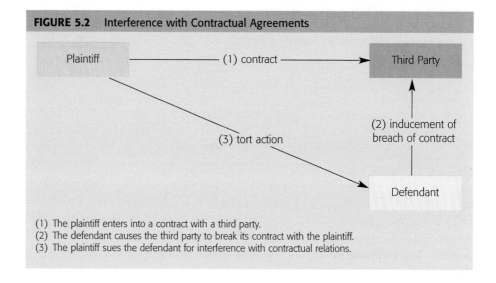

FIGURE 5.2   Interference with Contractual Agreements

(1) The plaintiff enters into a contract with a third party.
(2) The defendant causes the third party to break its contract with the plaintiff.
(3) The plaintiff sues the defendant for interference with contractual relations.

a **direct inducement to breach of contract** occurs when the defendant directly persuades a third party to break its contract with the plaintiff

A **direct inducement to breach of contract** occurs when the defendant directly persuades a third party to break its contract with the plaintiff. Liability requires four factors.

- First, the defendant must *know about the contract* that exists between the third party and the plaintiff. The defendant does not, however, have to know all the details of that contract.
- Second, the defendant must *intend to cause* the third party to breach that contract. However, the defendant does not have to intend to hurt the plaintiff. The tort may be committed even if the defendant is motivated by a desire to benefit itself.
- Third, the defendant must *actually cause* the third party to break its contract with the plaintiff. For instance, the defendant might hire the third party in a way that makes it impossible for that person to work for the plaintiff. The issue is much more difficult, however, if the defendant simply *informs* the third party about the advantages and disadvantages of working for the plaintiff. In that situation, the judge will ask whether the defendant actually *encouraged* the third party to commit a breach of contract.

■ Fourth, the plaintiff must suffer a *loss* as a result of the defendant's conduct. In most cases, that requirement is satisfied by the fact that the third party does not perform its contract with the plaintiff.

Note that in addition to suing the defendant in *tort* for inducing breach of contract, the plaintiff can also sue the third party in *contract* for the actual breach. However, the plaintiff cannot recover full damages under both actions.[9] Finally, if the defendant's conduct is particularly outrageous, the plaintiff may be entitled to recover punitive damages, as well as compensatory damages, under the tort.

Case Brief 5.1 illustrates the rules for inducing breach of contract.

CASE BRIEF 5.1

Lumley v Gye (1853) 118 ER 749 (QB)

An opera singer named Johanna Wagner agreed to sing for one season with the plaintiff's company, Her Majesty's Theatre. Ms Wagner broke that promise after being offered a higher fee to sing with the defendant's company, the Royal Italian Opera. The plaintiff suffered a financial loss as a result of losing Miss Wagner's services. He sued the defendant for inducing breach of contract.

The plaintiff was able to satisfy most of the requirements of that tort: (1) the defendant knew of Ms Wagner's contract with the plaintiff, (2) the defendant persuaded Ms Wagner to break her contract with the plaintiff, and (3) the plaintiff suffered a loss as a result of the defendant's intervention. The court nevertheless rejected the claim on the ground that the defendant had acted in *good faith*. He honestly believed that Ms Wagner had not been paid by the plaintiff and therefore was entitled to terminate her contract to sing at Her Majesty's Theatre.

In another case arising from the same facts, however, the court awarded an injunction to prevent Ms Wagner from singing for the defendant's company.[10]

As we have seen, a tort may be committed if the defendant *directly* interferes with a contract that exists between the plaintiff and a third party. A tort can also be committed through *indirect* interference. An **indirect inducement to breach of contract** occurs when the defendant indirectly persuades a third party to break its contract with the plaintiff.[11] For example, the defendant may physically prevent the third party from going to work, or steal tools that the third party needs to perform the contract with the plaintiff. Liability depends upon the same four factors that we have discussed *plus* proof that the defendant's actions were themselves *unlawful*.[12] Consequently, the tort may be committed if the defendant illegally detains the third party or steals that person's tools. But the tort is not committed if, for instance, a union (the defendant) calls a *legal* strike that causes a company (the third party) to breach its contract with a customer (the plaintiff).

an indirect inducement to breach of contract occurs when the defendant indirectly persuades a third party to break its contract with the plaintiff

---

9. We will discuss the possibility of concurrent actions in tort and contract in Chapter 6.

10. *Lumley v Wagner* (1852) 42 ER 687 (Ch D).

11. *DC Thompson & Co Ltd v Deakin* [1952] Ch 646 (CA).

12. Note that the defendant must have intended to induce a breach of contract, even if it did not intend to hurt the plaintiff.

UNLAWFUL INTERFERENCE WITH ECONOMIC RELATIONS

We have already seen several torts that the defendant may commit by doing something *unlawful* that causes the plaintiff to suffer a loss: intimidation, interference with contractual relations, and conspiracy.[13] The existence of those torts leads to a larger question. Even if it is impossible to satisfy the requirements for those torts, can the defendant still be held liable for hurting the plaintiff by doing something unlawful? Although that possibility was traditionally overlooked, Canadian courts have begun to recognize a general tort of *unlawful interference with economic relations*. The tort of **unlawful interference with economic relations** may occur if the defendant commits an unlawful act for the purpose of causing the plaintiff to suffer an economic loss. The leading case is discussed in Case Brief 5.2. Notice that the Ontario Court of Appeal adopted a very broad approach to two of the tort's three elements.

the tort of unlawful interference with economic relations *may occur if the defendant commits an unlawful act for the purpose of causing the plaintiff to suffer an economic loss*

CASE BRIEF 5.2

Reach MD Inc v Pharmaceutical Manufacturers Association of Canada (2003) 227 DLR (4th) 458 (Ont CA)

The plaintiff sold calendars to health care professionals. The calendar in question was called "Herman MD" because it featured the cartoon character named "Herman" in various medical settings. The venture was remarkably successful, largely because the calendars also contained advertisements that had been purchased by drug companies.

The plaintiff's business suffered a devastating blow, however, when its calendars caught the defendant's attention. The defendant is an organization of companies that are involved in the drug industry. It told its members that the advertisements contravened its Code of Conduct. In fact, that was not true. While the defendant could have prohibited its members from purchasing advertising space in the plaintiff's calendars, its Code of Conduct did not actually do so.

The Ontario Court of Appeal held that the defendant was liable for the tort of unlawfully interfering with the plaintiff's economic relations. The court set three requirements.

■ First, there must be *intent to injure*. The defendant argued that liability should depend upon proof that its primary purpose was to hurt the plaintiff. Significantly, however,

the court said that it was enough that the defendant's unlawful act was in some way directed against the plaintiff.

■ Second, there must be an *unlawful or illegal act*. The defendant argued for a narrow reading of this requirement. It suggested that it should be held liable only if it perpetrated a crime, broke a contract, or committed some other tort. The court disagreed. It was enough that the defendant had done something that it was not entitled to do. Since the Code of Conduct did not actually prohibit the purchase of advertising space on the calendars, the defendant did not have the authority to tell its members to stop advertising.

■ Third, the plaintiff must suffer an *economic loss*. That requirement was met because the plaintiff lost the revenue that it otherwise would have earned from advertisements on "Herman MD."

The court awarded damages equal to the value of the lost revenue. However, it limited liability to a one-year period to reflect the fact that the defendant was entitled to change its Code of Conduct to prohibit the advertisements.

Before going on to the next section, it will be useful to briefly summarize the torts that we have already considered. Conspiracy, intimidation, interference with contractual relations, and interference with economic relations are commonly referred to as "the business torts." They all deal with situations in

---

[13] Liability may also be imposed, in limited circumstances, if the defendant hurt the plaintiff by doing something that was otherwise *lawful*. That is true if the defendant *directly* induced a breach of contract, or if the defendant was part of a conspiracy that had the *primary purpose* of hurting the plaintiff.

which one business may try to gain an advantage over another. Because they overlap, however, they are easily confused. Concept Summary 5.1 therefore compares how those torts deal with two important questions:

- whether the tort must involve behaviour that is otherwise unlawful
- whether the defendant must intend to harm the plaintiff

CONCEPT SUMMARY 5.1

Business Torts—A Summary

Name of Tort	Unlawfulness	Intent to Harm
Conspiracy	defendant's act may be lawful or unlawful	*lawful act*—hurting plaintiff must be defendant's primary purpose
		unlawful act—hurting plaintiff must be foreseeable
Intimidation	defendant must threaten unlawful act	defendant's act must be directed at plaintiff—but hurting plaintiff need not be defendant's primary purpose
Interference with contractual relations	*indirect* inducement to breach of contract—defendant's act must be unlawful	defendant's act must be directed at plaintiff—but hurting plaintiff need not be defendant's primary purpose
	direct inducement to breach of contract—defendant's act may be lawful or unlawful	
Interference with economic relations	defendant's act must be unlawful or unauthorized	defendant's act must be directed at plaintiff—but hurting plaintiff need not be defendant's primary purpose

DECEIT

The law encourages ethical behaviour in the business world through the tort of *deceit*.[14] **Deceit** occurs if the defendant makes a false statement, which it knows to be untrue, with which it intends to mislead the plaintiff, and which causes the plaintiff to suffer a loss.[15] There are four parts to that definition.

First, the defendant must make a *false statement*. That requirement is easily met if the defendant says or writes something that is positively untrue. However, it may also be satisfied in other ways.

- The defendant may be held liable for a *half-truth*. For example, if I am selling my business to you, I may present figures representing gross profits as if they reflect net profits.
- The defendant may be held liable for *failing to update information*. For example, if I am selling my business to you, I may provide information that is accurate when I give it, but that later becomes inaccurate because of a dramatic change in the market. If that change happens before our deal closes, I may have to tell you about it. If I do not, my silence may amount to a representation that the circumstances have stayed the same.

the tort of **deceit** occurs if the defendant makes a false statement, which it knows to be untrue, with which it intends to mislead the plaintiff, and which causes the plaintiff to suffer a loss

---

[14.] As we will see in Chapter 9, the concept of fraud or deceit is also important in the law of contract. For example, it may allow one party to rescind an agreement.

[15.] *Derry v Peek* (1889) 14 App Cas 337 (HL).

■ The general rule in the commercial world is *caveat emptor*: "let the buyer beware." Consequently, the seller is usually not obligated to volunteer information. The buyer is responsible for asking questions and making investigations. There are, however, exceptions to that rule. For instance, if I am selling a house to you, I am required to warn you about hidden defects that make the building dangerous or unfit for habitation. If I fail to do so, I may be held liable for silently deceiving you. And if I am buying an insurance policy from you, I have a duty to disclose important information. If I fail to do so, I may be unable to claim a benefit under the policy.

The lesson is clear. As a matter of risk management, business people must not only avoid lying; they must also avoid creating the wrong perception.

Second, the defendant must *know*, at the time of making a statement, that it is false. It is enough if the defendant acted recklessly, without regard to the truth. But it is not enough if the defendant was merely careless.[16]

Third, the defendant must make the statement with the *intention of misleading* the plaintiff. The statement does not have to be made directly to the plaintiff. However, the court must be satisfied that the defendant intended to deceive the plaintiff, or at least was substantially certain that the plaintiff would be misled. Suppose that you and I are involved in complex commercial negotiations. I may be liable for deceit if I make a false statement to your banker with the intention of tricking you into signing a contract.

Fourth, the plaintiff must suffer a *loss* as a result of *reasonably relying* upon the defendant's statement. The plaintiff's reliance is "reasonable" if a reasonable person might have reacted to the defendant's statement in the same way. That rule has several consequences.

■ The defendant's statement normally has to refer to a *past or present fact*. Liability is usually not possible if the defendant offered an opinion, predicted the future, or made the sort of boastful claim (called a "puff") that salespeople often make. Reasonable people do not rely on those kinds of statements.

■ Occasionally, however, a statement of fact may be *implied* by an opinion, a prediction, or a puff. Suppose that I persuade you to buy my car by lying: "This little miser will go 300 kilometres between fill-ups." A court might find that my prediction includes a statement of existing fact regarding the vehicle's current rate of gas consumption.

In terms of remedies, it is important to remember that we are dealing with a tort, rather than a contract. As we saw in You Be the Judge 3.1, that means that compensatory damages look backward, rather than forward. The plaintiff is entitled to be put into the position that it would have enjoyed if the defendant had not lied—not into the position that it would have enjoyed if the defendant's statement had been true. Suppose that I tricked you into buying an apartment complex from me for $600 000. The building is actually worth $500 000. But if my deceitful statement had been true, it would have been worth $750 000. In tort, you are entitled to $100 000—not $250 000.[17]

[16.] The next chapter discusses how the plaintiff may be held liable under the tort of negligence as a result of carelessly making a false statement.

[17.] We will look at the calculation of compensatory damages for breach of contract in Chapter 12.

OCCUPIERS' LIABILITY

The tort of **occupiers' liability** requires an occupier of premises to protect visitors from harm.

- An **occupier** is any person who has substantial control over premises. Note that the critical element is *control*, not *ownership*. A tenant, for instance, can control an apartment without owning it.

- A **visitor** is any person who enters onto premises. We will discuss different types of visitors later.

- **Premises** include more than land. Apartments and offices certainly count, but occasionally, so do elevators, vehicles, ships, trains, and airplanes. The scope of occupiers' liability is therefore quite wide and potentially very dangerous for business people.[18] Although there has been a sharp rise in electronic commerce, most businesses still occupy premises that are visited by customers, suppliers, sales representatives, cleaners, government officials, trespassers, and so on. If one of those visitors trips over a step, slips on spilled food, falls through a decrepit floorboard, crashes into a plate-glass window, or is beaten by another visitor, the business may be held liable as result of being the occupier.

The law of occupiers' liability is complicated, partly because it differs between jurisdictions. Legislation has been enacted in every jurisdiction *except* Newfoundland, Saskatchewan, and the three territories. We will therefore separately consider:

- the common law rules (which were made by judges)
- the statutory rules (which were made by legislators)

Even if you live in a jurisdiction that now has a statute, it is useful to understand the traditional common law rules in order to appreciate why legislation has been introduced.

Common Law Rules

The traditional common law rules recognized four categories of visitors. Each type of visitor was owed a different type of obligation. Concept Summary 5.2 (see p. 102) summarizes the traditional approach. As we will see, however, that approach is now being changed.

There are a number of problems with the traditional system of occupiers' liability.

- First, it can lump together different types of people. For example, a person who breaks into an office is a trespasser, but so is a child who curiously wanders onto a construction site. It seems unfair that the occupier should not have to do more for the child than for the criminal.

- Second, it is often difficult to distinguish between the different categories. That is especially true for licensees and invitees. For example, does a visitor to a municipal library or a provincial park provide an economic benefit to the occupier?[19] Should the visitor's ability to recover compensation for a loss depend upon the answer to that narrow question?

the tort of occupiers' liability requires an occupier of premises to protect visitors from harm

an occupier is any person who has substantial control over premises

a visitor is any person who enters onto premises

premises include more than land

---

[18] The law of occupiers' liability is not restricted to the business world. Any person who controls premises (including residential premises) falls within the tort.

[19] *Nickell v City of Windsor* (1926) 59 OLR 618 (CA); *Coffyne v Silver Lake Regional Park Authority* (1977) 75 DLR (3d) 300 (Sask QB).

- Third, a visitor's status may change from one moment to the next. For example, a customer who refuses a request to leave a store is transformed from an invitee into a trespasser.
- Fourth, it often is difficult to decide whether a danger is *hidden* or *unusual*. Does an icy parking lot during a Canadian winter satisfy either requirement?[20]

CONCEPT SUMMARY 5.2

Traditional Rules for Occupiers' Liability

Type of Visitor	Description of Visitor	Occupier's Obligation
trespasser	a person who does not have permission to enter the premises (for example, a burglar)	not to *intentionally or recklessly injure* a trespasser (for example, by setting a trap for a burglar)
licensee	a person who has permission to enter the premises, but who does not further the occupier's economic interest (for example, a social guest)	to protect a licensee from *hidden dangers* that were *actually known* to the occupier
invitee	a person who has permission to enter the premises and who furthers the occupier's economic interests (for example, a business customer)	to take reasonable care to protect an invitee from *unusual dangers* that the occupier *knew or should have known* about
contractual entrant	a person who enters into a contract to use the premises, rather than to receive services that are offered on the premises (for example, a hotel guest, but not a restaurant diner)	a contractual obligation to make sure that the premises were as *safe as reasonably possible*

Business Decision 5.1 illustrates some of the difficulties associated with the traditional rules.

BUSINESS DECISION 5.1

Common Law Categories of Occupiers' Liability[21]

In the course of describing the law of occupiers' liability, a judge once posed this question.

> A canvasser who comes onto your premises without your consent is a trespasser. Once he has your consent, he is a licensee. Not until you do business with him is he an invitee. Even when you have done business with him, it seems rather strange that your duty towards him should be different when he comes to your front door than when he goes away. Does he change his colour in the middle of the conversation?

Questions for Discussion

1. Does the judge believe that it is possible to determine the precise moment when a person changes from a trespasser into a licensee and then into an invitee?

2. If your answer to the last question was "no," then how do courts actually decide cases? Might they intuitively decide an appropriate result and then characterize the plaintiff in a way that achieves that result?

---

[20] *cf Francis v IPCF Properties Inc* (1993) 136 NBR (2d) 215 (QB) and *Waldick v Malcolm* (1991) 83 DLR (4th) 114 (SCC).

[21] *Dunster v Abbott* [1953] 2 All ER 1572 at 1574 (CA) *per* Lord Denning.

Because of those difficulties, the jurisdictions that still use the common law rules have modified them.[22] They have generally moved away from categorizing visitors and toward increasing the occupier's obligations.

- First, an occupier must do more than simply refrain from intentionally or recklessly hurting a trespasser. The law now uses a duty of *common humanity* that strikes a balance between the parties.[23] The occupier's obligations are determined by a number of factors, including:

  - the age of the trespasser
  - the reason for the trespass
  - the nature of the danger that caused the injury
  - the occupier's knowledge of that danger
  - the occupier's cost of removing that danger

- Second, licensees and invitees are now generally treated the same. An occupier must protect them both from *unusual* dangers. Previously, a licensee was only protected from *hidden* dangers.[24]

- Third, the courts in Newfoundland have gone even further. An occupier in that province is required to use *reasonable care* toward all *lawful* visitors.[25]

Statutory Rules

Because of the problems associated with the common law rules, six provinces have enacted legislation to govern occupiers' liability.[26] Although the statutes vary somewhat between jurisdictions, the basic principles are the same. We can note the most important differences between the common law and the legislation.

- First, the common law generally applies only to dangers that are created by the *condition* of the premises. The legislation also applies to *activities* that occur on the premises. For example, under a statute, the occupier of a campsite can be held liable not only for failing to remove a rotten tree that collapsed on a visitor, but also for failing to prevent one drunken guest from attacking another.

- Second, as a general rule, the standard of care no longer depends upon a visitor's classification. Nor are special distinctions drawn between, say, hidden or unusual dangers. An occupier must use *reasonable care*, which depends upon a number of factors, including:

---

22. Newfoundland, the Northwest Territories, Nunavut, Saskatchewan, and the Yukon.

23. *Veinot v Kerr-Addison Mines Ltd* (1974) 51 DLR (3d) 533 (SCC).

24. There may still be a slight difference. It may be that a licensee can only sue for a danger that the occupier *knew* about, while an invitee can also sue for a danger that the occupier *should have known* about: *Yelic v Gimli (Town)* (1986) 33 DLR (4th) 248 (Man CA).

25. *Stacey v Anglican Church of Canada (Diocesan Synod of Eastern Newfoundland and Labrador)* (1999) 182 Nfld & PEIR 1 (Nfld CA).

26. *Occupiers' Liability Act*, RSA 2000, c O-4 (Alta); *Occupiers' Liability Act*, RSBC 1996, c 337 (BC); *Occupiers' Liability Act*, CCSM, c O8 (Man); *Occupiers' Liability Act*, SNS 1996, c 27 (NS); *Occupiers' Liability Act*, RSO 1990, c O.2 (Ont); *Occupiers' Liability Act*, RSPEI 1988, c O-2 (PEI). New Brunswick has gone even further by doing away with a separate tort of occupiers' liability altogether: *Law Reform Act*, SNB 1993, c L-1.2, s 2. In that province, the courts simply use the general tort of negligence, which is discussed in Chapter 6.

- the potential danger to the visitor
- the occupier's cost of removing the danger
- the purpose of the visit
- the nature of the premises

There are special exceptions to that general rule in some provinces.

- In Alberta, occupiers are not required to protect adult trespassers from danger. They are merely prohibited from wilfully or recklessly hurting them. In contrast, reasonable care must be taken to protect child trespassers that the occupier knows, or ought to know, are on the property.

- Likewise, an occupier in Ontario or Prince Edward Island does not have to use reasonable care to protect some types of trespassers. It is enough to simply refrain from intentionally hurting them. A similar rule applies in Manitoba, but only to trespassing snowmobilers.

- Third, the statutes generally allow an occupier to avoid liability by issuing a warning. For example, the occupier of a ski resort might conspicuously post signs that state:

> AS A CONDITION OF USING THESE FACILITIES, YOU
> ASSUME ALL RISK OF PERSONAL INJURY, DEATH OR
> PROPERTY LOSS RESULTING FROM ANY CAUSE WHATSOEVER.[27]

An occupier's liability may also be affected by other statutes.[28]

- Fourth, under the common law, a landlord generally cannot be held liable for injuries that a person suffers while visiting a tenant. The primary reason is that a landlord has ownership, but not control, over the premises and therefore is not an occupier. A different rule applies under the legislation. A landlord may be liable to a visitor if it fails to make repairs under its lease with the tenant. For example, a landlord may be held responsible if a tenant's guest falls in a stairwell due to the absence of a handrail.[29]

NUISANCE

the tort of **nuisance** occurs when the defendant unreasonably interferes with the plaintiff's use and enjoyment of its own land

The tort of *nuisance*, like the tort of occupiers' liability, involves land. Generally, a **nuisance** occurs when the defendant unreasonably interferes with the plaintiff's use and enjoyment of its own land.[30] There is a tension between the way in which the defendant wants to use *its* property and the way in which the

---

[27.] Exclusion clauses will be discussed in Chapter 9.

[28.] For example, innkeepers in Ontario need to take less care than usual: *Innkeepers Act*, RSO 1990, c I.7.

[29.] *Zavaglia v MAQ Holdings Ltd* (1986) 6 BCLR (2d) 286 (CA).

[30.] Our discussion is limited to the tort of *private nuisance*. There is also a less important tort of *public nuisance*. A public nuisance occurs when the defendant commits the crime of common nuisance against the public, but creates a special loss for the plaintiff: *Criminal Code*, RSC 1985, c C-46, s 180(2) (Can). That tort can arise, for instance, if the defendant creates a hazard on a street that not only interferes with the general public's right to use that roadway, but also causes the plaintiff to be injured in a traffic accident: *Ryan v Victoria (City)* (1999) 168 DLR (4th) 513 (SCC).

plaintiff wants to use *its* property. The courts have a great deal of flexibility in resolving a dispute between neighbours.[31]

A nuisance occurs if the defendant *interferes* with the plaintiff's use of its land. Interference can happen in a variety of ways. Simple cases involve *physical damage* to the plaintiff or its property. For instance:

- the defendant's factory may emit chemical particles that drift with the wind and destroy the paint on the plaintiff's building, or
- the defendant's construction project may create a heavy vibration that cracks the foundations of the plaintiff's store.

A nuisance can also occur if the defendant creates a smell or a sound that *impairs the enjoyment* of the plaintiff's property. For instance:

- the defendant may operate a pig farm that causes a stench to waft over the plaintiff's outdoor café, or
- the blaring music from the defendant's nightclub may keep nearby residents awake at night.

It may even be possible to commit a *non-intrusive* nuisance, without causing anything to travel onto the plaintiff's property. For instance:

- the defendant may install a sewer system on its own property that drains water *from* the plaintiff's land in a way that damages the foundations of the plaintiff's building, or
- the defendant may operate a brothel that brings traffic and criminals close to the plaintiff's home.

Note, however, that certain types of activities generally will *not* support a claim in nuisance. For instance, it is unlikely that a tort is committed if:

- the defendant builds something on its own property that ruins the plaintiff's view of a lake or reduces the amount of sunshine that enters the plaintiff's house, or
- the defendant paints its building a colour that reduces the market value of the plaintiff's house.[32]

A nuisance occurs only if the defendant's interference is *unreasonable*. In deciding that issue, the courts look at a number of factors. The most important is the nature of the interference. The defendant's conduct is almost always considered unreasonable if it causes substantial *physical damage*. In contrast, the courts are less likely to hold the defendant liable if it merely *impairs the enjoyment* of the plaintiff's property, especially if the defendant's interference is *non-intrusive*. Beyond that, the courts also consider:

- the *nature of the neighbourhood* (for example, the smell of livestock may be reasonable in the country but not in the city)
- the *time and day* of the interference (for example, construction sounds that are reasonable at noon on a weekday may be unreasonable late at night or on the weekend)
- the *intensity and duration* of the interference (for example, a barking dog or a foul odour may have to be tolerated if it occurs occasionally, but not if it is nearly constant)

[31.] Strictly speaking, it is not necessary for *both* parties to have an interest in land. While the plaintiff can sue only if its land is affected, the defendant does not have to commit the nuisance from its own property. In practice, however, most nuisance cases arise between neighbours.

[32.] It may be different if the defendant *intentionally* annoys or hurts the plaintiff.

- the *social utility* of the defendant's conduct (for example, the late night sound of screeching tires may be reasonable if it is caused by an ambulance, but not if it is caused by drag racing)

- the defendant's *motivation* (for example, the sound of a gun may be reasonable if it occurs in the course of normal activities, but not if it is made to terrify the plaintiff's foxes and ruin his breeding business)[33]

Defences to Nuisance

There are several defences to the tort of nuisance, but they are generally interpreted very narrowly.[34] The courts are reluctant to allow the defendant to escape liability despite unreasonably interfering with the plaintiff's property. The defence of *statutory authority* provides a good example. **Statutory authority** means that the defendant caused a nuisance while acting under legislation. Significantly, that defence applies only if the defendant's nuisance was an *inevitable result* of the statutorily authorized activity. Business Decision 5.2 illustrates that rule.

statutory authority means that the defendant caused a nuisance while acting under legislation

BUSINESS DECISION 5.2

Nuisance and the Defence of Statutory Authority[35]

Legislation allowed the Town of Sepsis to build a sewage system that conformed with industry standards. Such systems usually use pipes that are between 1 metre and 1.5 metres in diameter. In the course of construction, the mayor of Sepsis decided, for financial reasons, to use 1-metre pipes. Several months after the project was completed, the town received a lot of rain. While the system generally performed quite well, it backed up in one neighbourhood and pumped raw sewage into your restaurant. As a result, you were required to replace all of your kitchen equipment, which had been ruined by the mess. The evidence indicates that the problem was caused by the fact that the pipes were too narrow to accommodate the rainfall. It also indicates that the problem would not have occurred if 1.5-metre pipes had been used.

Since litigation is expensive, you do not want to sue the Town of Sepsis unless there is a good chance that you will win your case. How would you make that decision?

Questions for Discussion

1. Did Sepsis commit the tort of nuisance?

2. If Sepsis did commit the tort, could it nevertheless avoid liability by pleading the defence of statutory authority? Given the legislation and the evidence, was a nuisance inevitable?

Before leaving the issue of defences, it is important to note that the defendant is not relieved of liability merely because the nuisance already existed when the plaintiff arrived in the neighbourhood. For instance, a physician can complain that the noise from a factory disrupts his practice, even though the person who previously occupied his building was not affected by that sound.[36]

[33.] *Hollywood Silver Fox Farm v Emmett* [1936] 2 KB 468 (QB).

[34.] For example, the plaintiff cannot complain if it *consented* to the defendant's activity. However, consent usually requires proof that the plaintiff encouraged the defendant's activity, not that it merely failed to complain.

[35.] *Tock v St John's (City) Metropolitan Area Board* (1989) 64 DLR (4th) 620 (SCC); *Ryan v Victoria (City)* (1999) 168 DLR (4th) 513 (SCC).

[36.] *Sturges v Bridgman* (1879) 11 Ch D 852.

Remedies for Nuisance

The most common remedies for nuisance are compensatory damages and injunctions. The usual rules regarding compensation apply and do not have to be repeated here. Injunctions are more complicated. A judge will usually grant one to stop a nuisance. For example, the defendant may be required to close a chemical plant that is emitting noxious fumes, or it may be ordered to refrain from dumping toxic material into a river. Occasionally, however, the court may exercise its discretion to refuse an injunction. That is clearly true if the nuisance causes relatively little damage to the plaintiff and if damages can provide an adequate remedy. It may also be true if an injunction would create an intolerable hardship for the defendant or, more importantly, for the community as a whole. Consequently, if a town's entire economy revolves around a single factory, a judge would be reluctant to grant an injunction that would have the effect of closing that factory. Finally, the courts sometimes award both compensatory damages and an injunction. The damages take care of past losses, and the injunction prevents harm in the future.

THE RULE IN *RYLANDS V FLETCHER*

The rule in *Rylands v Fletcher* is a third tort that deals with land.[37] The **rule in Rylands v Fletcher** states that the defendant can be held strictly liable for its non-natural use of land if something escapes from its property and injures the plaintiff.[38] We need to examine three aspects of that rule.

the rule in *Rylands v Fletcher* states that the defendant can be held strictly liable for a non-natural use of land if something escapes from its property and injures the plaintiff

First, the defendant must have made a *non-natural use* of its land. Courts have interpreted this in two ways. Some courts say that it refers to any use of land that creates a *special* danger; others say that the defendant must create a *special and unusual* danger. Judges have recently preferred the second interpretation.[39] As a result, the defendant cannot be held liable simply because it installs a gas appliance in its building, or deliberately starts a fire to burn away scrub grass in the normal course of its farming operations. While those activities are non-natural, they are not unusual. It is therefore irrelevant that they endangered the plaintiff. However, the tort may be committed if the defendant collects an unusual amount of water in a reservoir, or stacks fireworks in a store display. Those activities are not only especially dangerous; they are also unusual.

Second, something associated with a non-natural use must *escape* from the defendant's land and cause the plaintiff to suffer a loss. For instance, water may break through a reservoir and flood a neighbour's house, or explosives may ignite in a store, shoot onto the sidewalk, and injure a pedestrian. The need for an escape may create problems if the plaintiff suffers an injury *on the defendant's property*. A spectator who is hit by flying debris at a racetrack may not be able to use *Rylands v Fletcher* since nothing *left* the defendant's premises. It would not be surprising, however, if a judge ignored the requirement of an escape in order to avoid an unfair result.

[37.] *Rylands v Fletcher* (1868) LR 3 HL 330.

[38.] We discussed the idea of *strict liability* in Chapter 3.

[39.] *Tock v St John's (City) Metropolitan Area Board* (1989) 64 DLR (4th) 620 (SCC).

Third, most torts are based on some form of *fault*. The defendant is usually liable only if it intentionally, or at least carelessly, caused the plaintiff's injury. The rule in *Rylands v Fletcher*, in contrast, is *strict*. The defendant may be held liable even though it acted as carefully as possible. Strict liability does not, however, mean that liability is imposed *every time* there is a non-natural use, an escape, and an injury. A defence may be available in exceptional circumstances. For example:

- the plaintiff may have *consented* to the defendant's non-natural use of its land
- the escape may have been caused by a *third party* or a *natural force* (such as a tornado or an earthquake) that the defendant could not have guarded against
- the plaintiff's injury may have been the *inevitable result* of an activity that the defendant was *statutorily authorized* to do

Those defences, however, are difficult to prove. Consequently, business people should learn an important lesson from the rule in *Rylands v Fletcher*. They should take special precautions whenever they use land in a non-natural way.

We have seen four torts that involve the use of land. We discussed trespass to land in Chapter 4 and occupiers' liability, nuisance, and the rule in *Rylands v Fletcher* in this chapter. Concept Summary 5.3 shows the most important features of those torts.

CONCEPT SUMMARY 5.3

Torts Involving the Use of Land

Tort	Basis of Liability
Occupiers' liability	The defendant, who is the occupier of premises, fails to take adequate precautions to protect the plaintiff, who is visiting those premises.
Nuisance	The defendant unreasonably interferes with the plaintiff's use and enjoyment of its own land.
Rule in *Rylands v Fletcher*	The defendant uses its land in a non-natural way with the result that something escapes and injures the plaintiff.
Trespass to land	The defendant intentionally interferes with the plaintiff's land.

DEFAMATION

the tort of **defamation** occurs when the defendant makes a false statement that could lead a reasonable person to have a lower opinion of the plaintiff

Communication is essential to the success of any business. However, it also creates the risk of *defamation*. **Defamation** occurs when the defendant makes a false statement that could lead a reasonable person to have a lower opinion of the plaintiff.[40]

The defendant's statement is defamatory only if a reasonable person would have thought that it referred to the plaintiff. That requirement is quite broad.

- First, it can be satisfied even if the defendant did not *intend* to refer to the plaintiff. The purpose of the tort is to protect reputations. It is

---

[40.] Some parts of defamation have been modified by legislation. Nevertheless, the most important issues are governed by the common law rules that are discussed below.

therefore enough if a reasonable person would have *thought* that the defendant was referring to the plaintiff. Reputations are often hurt by mistake.

- Second, a claim for defamation can be made by any sort of *living person*. As we will see in Chapter 21, the term "person" refers not only to human beings, but also to things like corporations.

- Third, defamation may be difficult to prove if the defendant made a statement about a *group of individuals*. Each person must prove that the statement can be reasonably interpreted as referring to them *personally*. That is unlikely if the group is large and if the statement is a generalization. Consequently, I probably could not sue you for saying "All lawyers are crooks!"

Lawyers sometimes draw a distinction between *slander* and *libel*. **Slander** is a defamatory statement that is spoken; **libel** is a defamatory statement that is written.[41] While that distinction is important for technical reasons in some parts of Canada, the general rule is that defamation can occur through any sort of communication, including spoken words, written documents, gestures, photographs, and puppet shows.

slander is a defamatory statement that is spoken

libel is a defamatory statement that is written

Almost any uncomplimentary statement can be defamatory, as long as it could hurt a person's reputation. You will defame me if you suggest, for example, that I am incompetent, racist, lazy, dishonest, infected with a communicable disease, or involved in criminal activity. Furthermore, even a seemingly harmless statement may be defamatory once it is considered in context. For example, although I would not normally be defamed if you said that I sold pork chops, it might be different if I own a kosher deli.

There cannot be defamation without *publication*. **Publication** occurs when a statement is communicated to a third party. Remember that the tort is concerned with the protection of reputations. If I say something uncomplimentary to you in private, I may hurt your feelings or upset you, but I cannot damage your reputation, which is based on what *other people* think of you. The rule about publication can, however, work in your favour. A new tort may occur every time that a statement is *repeated*. Consequently, if I write a defamatory book about you, I commit a tort when I deliver the manuscript to my publisher. But my publisher may also commit a tort against you when it sells the book to the public.

publication occurs when a statement is communicated to a third party

Defences to Defamation

The tort of defamation is broadly interpreted. In some situations, however, the defendant will not be held liable even though it published a statement that hurt the plaintiff's reputation. We will briefly look at three important defences to the tort of defamation:

[41.] The distinction between libel and slander has been abolished in several provinces, including Alberta, Manitoba, New Brunswick, Nova Scotia, and Prince Edward Island. Where it has not been abolished, the difference is important mainly because the plaintiff in a slander action (though not in a libel action) is usually required to prove *special damages*. That distinction is based on the belief that libel is usually more serious than slander. Written words normally last longer and reach more people. Special damages for the purpose of a slander action may include a financial loss, but not mere embarrassment. However, even in a slander action, there is no need to prove special damages if the defendant made a false statement that (i) the plaintiff had committed a crime serious enough to result in imprisonment, (ii) the plaintiff was an "unchaste" woman, (iii) the plaintiff suffers from a contagious disease that people would want to avoid, or (iv) the plaintiff is unfit to carry on his or her profession or business.

- justification
- privilege
- fair comment

justification occurs if the defendant's statement is true

Justification occurs if the defendant's statement is true. Note that the statement must *actually* be true. The defendant will not avoid liability simply because it *honestly believed* that the statement was true. Note also that the defendant has the burden of proof. Once the plaintiff satisfies the requirements that we discussed, a judge will assume that the defendant's uncomplimentary statement was false. The defendant must prove otherwise.

The courts want people to speak freely on important issues. Consequently, they sometimes grant a *privilege*. A **privilege** is an immunity from liability. It takes two forms. First, an *absolute privilege* provides a complete immunity. It applies even if the defendant knowingly made a false statement for a malicious purpose. That defence is available only when the law needs to encourage people to communicate without *any* fear of being sued. It is therefore usually limited to statements made:

privilege is an immunity from liability

- during parliamentary proceedings
- between high government officials who are dealing with government business
- by a judge, lawyer, litigant, or witness in the context of legal proceedings
- between spouses

The second form of the defence is a *qualified privilege*. Rather than being limited to specific situations, it may apply whenever (i) the defendant has a legal, moral, or social obligation to make a statement, and (ii) the statement is made to someone who had a similar duty or interest in receiving it. Both of those elements must be satisfied. Consequently, a qualified privilege may be recognized if:

- a manager makes an unfair statement about a former employee to the personnel director of a company that is considering hiring that individual—but not if the manager makes the same statement to a friend during idle gossip, or
- a department store discreetly posts a notice instructing its employees not to accept cheques from a customer who is wrongly suspected of fraud—but not if the notice is large enough to be noticed by other customers, who have no interest in the matter.[42]

The defence of qualified privilege is also limited to statements that the defendant made in good faith. It is not available if the defendant knew that its statement was untrue or if the defendant was motivated by some malicious purpose.

The defence of *fair comment* is intended to encourage useful debate on significant social issues. A **fair comment** is an honest expression of an opinion regarding a matter of public importance. That defence has several requirements.

a fair comment is an honest expression of an opinion regarding a matter of public importance

- First, it is intended to protect *informed opinions*. The defendant has to prove that a reasonable person would have interpreted the statement as an opinion based on fact, rather than as a fact. Consequently, the defence

---

[42.] *Pleau v Simpson-Sears Ltd* (1977) 75 DLR (3d) 747 (Ont CA).

may apply if a newspaper columnist accurately describes a politician's behaviour and suggests that "the leadership of this country is morally corrupt"—but not if that statement is made without the support of any background information.[43]

■ Second, the defendant's opinion must concern an issue of *public interest*, such as a cultural, religious, or political matter. Consequently, while it is possible to criticize the public activities of poets, priests, and politicians, the defence does not allow personal attacks on their private lives.

■ Third, a comment is not "fair" unless it was *honestly held*.[44] But as long as that requirement is met, the defendant may be protected even if its statement was highly critical and very damaging.

■ Finally, the defence of fair comment is not available if the defendant acted *maliciously*.

Remedies for Defamation

The usual remedy for defamation is compensation. Punitive damages may also be awarded if the defendant's conduct was particularly outrageous.[45] And in truly exceptional circumstances, a court may impose an injunction to prevent a person from even making a statement—but only if it is clear that the statement would be defamatory. In most situations, judges are reluctant to restrict freedom of speech in that way.

INJURIOUS FALSEHOOD

Our legal system protects personal reputations through the tort of defamation.[46] The tort of **injurious falsehood** occurs when the defendant makes a false statement about the plaintiff's business that causes the plaintiff to suffer a loss.[47] That tort may take a variety of forms.

the tort of **injurious falsehood** occurs when the defendant makes a false statement about the plaintiff's business that causes the plaintiff to suffer a loss

■ **Slander of Title:** The defendant may falsely say that the plaintiff does not own a particular piece of land, therefore making it difficult for the plaintiff to sell that property for its full value.

---

43. The background information may be expressed or implied.

44. That requirement creates difficulties for letters to the editor that are printed in newspapers. The Supreme Court of Canada has held that a newspaper is entitled to use the defence of fair comment only if the publisher honestly shares the opinion that is contained in such a letter: *Cherneskey v Armadale Publishers Ltd* (1978) 90 DLR (3d) 321 (SCC). That is a very narrow rule. As a result, several provinces have legislation that allows a newspaper to use the defence as long as an honest person could have held the opinion in question, even if the publisher did not: *Defamation Act*, RSA 2000, c D-7, s 9 (Alta); *Defamation Act*, CCSM, c D20, s 9 (Man); *Defamation Act*, RSNB 1973, c 58, s 8.1(1), as amended by *An Act to Amend the Defamation Act*, SNB 1980, c 16, s 1 (NB); *Libel and Slander Act*, RSO 1990, c L.12, s 24 (Ont).

45. *Hill v Church of Scientology of Toronto* (1995) 126 DLR (4th) 129 (SCC).

46. The tort of injurious falsehood is easily confused with the tort of defamation. It may also be confused with the tort of deceit, which we considered earlier in this chapter. There is, however, a critical difference between those two torts. Injurious falsehood occurs when the defendant makes a false statement that misleads the plaintiff's *customers*; deceit occurs when the defendant makes a false statement that misleads the *plaintiff*.

47. Another related tort is *passing off*. As we will see in Chapter 18, that tort occurs when the defendant makes it seem as if its own goods were manufactured by the plaintiff.

- **Slander of Quality:** The defendant may falsely disparage the plaintiff's products in a way that causes potential customers to take their business elsewhere. The tort is not committed, however, if the defendant merely suggests that its products are better than the plaintiff's. Nor if the defendant's statement about the plaintiff's business is true. Nor if the defendant tries to gain an advantage by making a false statement about the high quality of its *own* products.[48]

- **Other Situations:** Even if there is no slander of title or slander of quality, the defendant may be held liable for making some *other* type of false statement about the plaintiff's business. For example, in *Manitoba Free Press v Nagy*, the defendant newspaper said that the plaintiff's house was haunted, and therefore made it difficult for the plaintiff to sell that property.[49]

Regardless of the precise form of the injurious falsehood, the plaintiff must prove three elements.

- **False Statement:** The defendant must make a *false* statement about the plaintiff's business or property. Because the tort is concerned with reputations, that statement must be made to a third party.

- **Malice:** The defendant must have acted out of *malice*. The meaning of that requirement is, however, somewhat unclear. The defendant certainly may be held liable if it made the false statement for the purpose of hurting the plaintiff. However, it also appears to be enough if the defendant either knew that the statement was false or was reckless as to the truth of the assertion, and if the defendant either intended to hurt the plaintiff or knew that the plaintiff was likely to be injured.

- **Loss:** The defendant's false statement must have caused the plaintiff to suffer a loss. The plaintiff may prove, for example, that a customer broke a contract to purchase the plaintiff's goods, or that a customer took its business elsewhere, or that a customer was only willing to pay a reduced price. It is not enough, however, for the plaintiff to merely show that its profits began to decline *after* the defendant uttered the false statement. A business may fall on hard times for a variety of reasons. A court will therefore insist upon persuasive evidence that the defendant's injurious falsehood actually *caused* the plaintiff's loss.

The ten torts discussed above cover a great deal of territory. It is, however, important to repeat a point that we made at the beginning of this chapter. Unless the defendant's conduct is specifically caught by one of those torts, the plaintiff will not be entitled to compensation even if it suffers a significant loss. By way of review, consider how you would decide the case that appears in You Be the Judge 5.1.

[48.] In that situation, however, the defendant may be held liable for misleading advertising.

[49.] *Manitoba Free Press v Nagy* (1907) 39 DLR 340 (SCC).

YOU BE THE JUDGE 5.1

Secondary Picketing[50]

The employees of Pepsi-Cola were legally on strike. In an attempt to put pressure on their employer, they set up *secondary pickets*. As well as picketing their employer's premises, the employees also picketed (i) stores that sold Pepsi-Cola, in an effort to disrupt the delivery of the employer's products and to discourage people from buying those products, (ii) a hotel where replacement workers were staying, and (iii) houses belonging to the employer's managers, where they chanted slogans, screamed insults, and threatened bodily harm.

Questions for Discussion

1. Have the employees committed any of the torts that we examined in this chapter (or in the last chapter)?

2. Should the courts allow secondary picketing? By setting up a picket in front of a store, for instance, the employees may have discouraged customers from going into that store. Why should the store have to suffer simply because the employees have a dispute with their employer?

---

50. *Pepsi-Cola Canada Beverages (West) Ltd v RWDSU, Local 558* (2002) 208 DLR (4th) 385 (SCC).

CHAPTER SUMMARY

In this chapter, we examined ten torts that are particularly important for business people.

Conspiracy usually occurs when two or more defendants agree to act together with the primary purpose of causing a financial loss to the plaintiff. The conspiring parties can be held liable even if their actions are otherwise lawful. However, the courts are more willing to impose liability if the defendants acted in an otherwise unlawful way.

Intimidation occurs when the plaintiff suffers a loss as a result of the defendant's threat to commit an unlawful act against either the plaintiff or a third party. Two-party intimidation occurs when the defendant directly coerces the plaintiff into suffering a loss. Three-party intimidation occurs when the defendant coerces a third party into acting in a way that hurts the plaintiff.

Interference with contractual relations occurs when the defendant disrupts a contract that exists between the plaintiff and a third party. A direct inducement to breach of contract occurs when the defendant directly persuades a third party to break its contract with the plaintiff. An indirect inducement to breach of contract occurs when the defendant indirectly persuades a third party to break its contract with the plaintiff.

Unlawful interference with economic relations occurs when one person intentionally does an unlawful (or unauthorized) act that causes the plaintiff to suffer a loss.

Deceit occurs if the defendant makes a false statement, which it knows to be untrue, with which it intends to mislead the plaintiff, and which causes the plaintiff to suffer a loss.

The law of occupiers' liability requires an occupier of premises to protect visitors from harm. Some provinces and territories rely on the traditional common law rules. Others rely upon occupiers' liability statutes.

Nuisance occurs when the defendant unreasonably interferes with the plaintiff's ability to use and enjoy its own land. The defence of statutory authority may protect a defendant from liability, but it has been narrowly interpreted by the courts. The courts often award injunctions to stop or prevent nuisances.

The rule in *Rylands v Fletcher* states that the defendant may be held strictly liable for its non-natural use of land if something escapes from its property and injures the plaintiff.

Defamation occurs when the defendant makes a false statement that could lead a reasonable person to have a lower opinion of the plaintiff. Liability may be avoided through the defences of justification, privilege, and fair comment.

Injurious falsehood occurs when the defendant makes a false statement to a third party about the plaintiff's business in a way that causes the plaintiff to suffer a loss.

REVIEW QUESTIONS

1. Why is it usually difficult to prove the tort of conspiracy if the defendants' actions were otherwise *lawful*? Is the situation different if the defendants' actions are otherwise *unlawful*? Explain your answer.

2. The courts sometimes say that the tort of intimidation cannot be based on a threat to commit a breach of contract. Why does that apparent rule apply to two-party intimidation, but not to three-party intimidation?

3. "It is not enough for the plaintiff to prove that the defendant acted in an intimidating way. The plaintiff also has to show that the defendant's intimidation was effective." Explain the extent to which that statement is true.

4. "A company is in danger of committing a tort every time it hires a person away from a rival company." Explain the extent to which that statement is true.

5. Which tort is easier to prove: direct inducement to breach of contract or indirect inducement to breach of contract? Explain your answer.

6. "There is really no difference between interference with contractual relations and unlawful interference with economic relations." Explain the extent to which that statement is true.

7. It is sometimes said that the tort of deceit requires a statement of fact. How is a statement of fact different from an opinion, a prediction, or a puff? Why is a statement of fact necessary?

8. Why are almost all businesses potentially in danger of committing the tort of occupiers' liability?

9. Describe the main problems created by the common law's traditional approach to occupiers' liability. How have Canadian courts improved that tort?

10. Explain the general approach of occupiers' liability legislation. In what ways are the statutory rules significantly different from the common law rules?

11. What factors do the courts consider in deciding whether the defendant has committed the tort of nuisance? What is the most important factor?

12. Explain why the defence of statutory authority seldom applies in an action for nuisance.

13. What remedies are available for the tort of nuisance? How does a judge decide which remedy to award in any particular case?

14. What do the courts mean when they say that a person can be held liable under the rule in *Rylands v Fletcher* only if there has been a "non-natural use" of land? Why is the meaning of that term important?

15. Why is the rule in *Rylands v Fletcher* considered a strict liability tort?

16. Explain three defences that may be available against the rule in *Rylands v Fletcher*.

17. Why is publication critically important to the tort of defamation? Why do I not commit the tort of defamation if, in the course of a private conversation, I wrongly accuse you of some horrible crime?

18. Explain the defences of absolute privilege and qualified privilege. Outline the situations in which those defences will apply.

19. Describe the defence of fair comment. Why is that defence especially important to businesses like newspapers, magazines, and television broadcasters?

20. Briefly describe the remedies that may be available for the tort of defamation.

CASES AND PROBLEMS

1. The federal government operated a program under which it leased land to Aboriginal Canadians. It entered into one such lease with David Cardinal, a member of the River Valley Band. Shortly afterwards, however, several other members of that band began to harass Cardinal by using their trucks to block access to that property, allowing their cattle to stray onto the land, and, despite his repeated objections, hunting on his land. Cardinal believes that they did so to frighten him into terminating his lease with the government. If that happened, the other members of the band would be able to lease the land for themselves. When he confronted them with that allegation, one of their group replied, "We haven't done anything wrong. But if you can't stand the heat, maybe you should just get out of the kitchen!"

Does Cardinal have a cause of action in intimidation? Do you have enough information to answer that question?

2. DeJohnette Developments was in the process of building a recording studio. It agreed to purchase about $5 000 000 worth of sound equipment from Peacock Electronics Inc. Jarrett Koln, who custombuilds sound equipment, heard that DeJohnette was planning a new recording studio. Koln did not know that DeJohnette had already entered into a contract with Peacock. He sent a letter to DeJohnette that said:

> You should not, under any circumstances, buy equipment from Peacock. Although that company has been around for years, the quality of its merchandise is vastly inferior compared to mine.

DeJohnette knew that Koln was correct. Recent studies had shown that Peacock's equipment was second rate. DeJohnette nevertheless honoured its contract with Peacock and refused to buy from Koln. Peacock, however, is upset that Koln jeopardized its agreement with DeJohnette. Can Peacock successfully sue Koln for inducing breach of contract? Provide several reasons for your answer.

3. The cement-manufacturing business is a cut-throat industry. For many years, a small number of large companies, including Ash Inc and Izzy Supplies Ltd, have enjoyed a virtual monopoly. They have strongly resisted the emergence of new competitors. Two years ago, Roxel Corp attempted to break into the business. Because of certain technological advances that it had developed, Roxel was able to produce a much better product than was currently available in the market. Although Roxel's product was initially available only in the Atlantic provinces, Ash and Izzy were worried that their profits might drop sharply if Roxel became successful and expanded across the country. They therefore agreed to sell their own cement in the Maritimes at a drastically reduced price. That agreement had two effects: (i) It allowed Ash and Izzy to maintain their traditional share of the market across the country, and (ii) it incidentally drove Roxel out of the cement business. The agreement between Ash and Izzy was unlawful under the *Competition Act* because it involved regional price discrimination. Can Roxel successfully sue Ash and Izzy for the tort of conspiracy? Explain your answer.

4. The directors of Sol-Go Inc publicly declared that their company intended to develop a high-speed commuter rail system between Ottawa and Toronto that would operate on solar power. Wei Chang, who was interested in investing in solar-powered modes of transportation, contacted the company and asked whether government approval for the plan had been granted. She received a letter that stated, "Although government approval has not yet been received, we can assure you that it is forthcoming. Our application has met all government requirements." Satisfied with that answer, Wei bought $50 000 worth of shares in Sol-Go. She was very disappointed several weeks later when she read in a newspaper that the government had rejected the company's application on the grounds that the proposed project failed to extend beyond Ottawa to Montreal. When Wei contacted the directors of Sol-Go, they honestly assured her that, at the time of writing their previous letter, they believed that government approval would be granted. They also pointed out to her that while the proposed commuter project had fallen through, several other projects had done unexpectedly well, and that the value of her shares consequently was still $50 000. Is Sol-Go liable to Wei Chang for the tort of deceit? Provide several reasons for your answer.

5. The Alkabe Corporation owned a large piece of land on which it planned to develop a shopping mall. When the starting date of that project was delayed, the company erected a one-metre-high fence around the site and posted a notice: "ABSOLUTELY NO TRESPASSING." The site nevertheless became a very popular play area for local children. A number of young teens created a large ramp that they used for jumping their bikes. Alkabe learned of that fact, but it took no steps to stop the children from playing on the site. Some time later, Jyoti, a 13-year-old, was seriously injured when she flipped her bike while racing over the ramp. Would Alkabe be held liable for the tort of occupiers' liability under the traditional common law rules? Assuming that the accident occurred in the jurisdiction in which you live, will the Alkabe Corporation be held liable for the tort of occupiers' liability? Explain your answer.

6. Big Nickel Metals Inc has operated a steel plant in Sudbury for a number of years and employs 5000 residents of that town (out of a total workforce of about 65 000). One of the main pieces of equipment in the plant is a 720-tonne press that is used to produce sheet metal. Denari Inc recently purchased an unused building across the street from the plant and converted it into a condominium complex for senior citizens. Immediately after opening that complex, however, Denari was flooded with complaints from its tenants because of the noise that was produced by Big Nickel's press. The manager of Big Nickel is sympathetic to that complaint, and has offered to refrain from using the press between midnight and dawn. However, he has also indicated that the press is essential to the operation of the plant and that without it, his company would have to lay off almost all of its employees. The manager of Denari, in response, has said that the seniors living in his complex are very upset by the noise from the press, regardless of when it is operated. He has also shown that a number of units in the condominium complex remain empty, even though there is generally a great demand for such accommodation in Sudbury. Those vacancies are caused by the noise produced by Big Nickel. The resulting loss of revenue to Denari is estimated to be $50 000, and that amount is expected to rise by $10 000 for every month that the press continues in operation. Can Denari Inc successfully sue Big Nickel Metals Inc for nuisance? If so, what remedy will the plaintiff receive? Explain your answer.

7. The Putrescible Food Company operates a plant that processes and packages a wide variety of foods, including meats and vegetables. In the course of doing so, it generates a large amount of waste product. It has long been in the habit of burying that waste in a ravine that is located just inside the boundary of its property. (A residential district is situated on the other side of the ravine.) The company knew that the buried waste might generate methane gas, but did nothing to prevent that from happening. Consequently, an invisible cloud of that gas recently drifted out of the ravine, across the company's property, and into the nearby residential district. Alonzo suffered terrible injuries after striking a match to

light a cigar. The flame from the match ignited the cloud of gas and caused a fireball that engulfed him. At the time of the accident, Alonzo was standing on a public street in front of his house. Which of the torts, if any, that we have discussed in this chapter provides him with the best possibility of successfully suing the Putrescible Food Company? Explain your answer.

8. A new runway was added to the Vancouver International Airport. As usually occurs with large infrastructure projects, the development was governed by statutes and regulations. That legislation determined, among other things, the loction and direction of the new runway. The final result has been a mixed blessing. The new runway has created hundreds of jobs and further added to the city's reputation as a desirable holiday destination. Unfortunately, it has also "ruined" several neighbourhoods. Until recently, for example, Bridgeport had been a peaceful community in which residents spent a great deal of time enjoying the outdoors. As a result of air traffic associated with the new runway, however, life has become unpleasant, if not intolerable. It is impossible to conduct a conversation outdoors if a jet is passing overhead, and in some situations, it is even difficult to hear a television or radio while indoors. The noise regularly keeps some residents awake at night. Those problems have caused property values to plummet. It is very difficult to find a buyer for a home in Bridgeport. Has a tort been committed? If so, what remedy will the residents of Bridgeport likely receive?

9. *World Truth* is a weekly newspaper that appears across the country. It recently published two articles. The first article appeared under the headline "Radical Groups Advocate World Destruction." One of the groups that it discussed was the Falun Gong. That article said, among other things, that Falun Gong's "anti-science and anti-society" beliefs had caused over 1700 deaths in Mainland China, and that the movement's ultimate purpose was to destroy civilization. Although Falun Gong is based in China, it has over 100 million adherents worldwide. Jian Bai, a Canadian citizen living in Vancouver, is one of those people. The second article appeared under the headline "Corruption Runs High with Union Bosses." That article was concerned with a labour dispute that had gripped British Columbia for several weeks. Although it did not mention any names, the article said that "the union bosses" had used the occasion to steal money from their members. That allegation is completely false. Paul Harris is one of three elected leaders of the union. Bai and Harris have sued *World Truth* for defamation. Is there any chance that their claims will succeed?

10. Tony Twist was a professional hockey player with the Quebec Nordiques and the St Louis Blues. During his career, he was known as an enforcer—while playing in the NHL for a decade, he amassed only 10 goals, but over 1100 minutes in penalties. Todd McFarlane is the publisher of a number of comic books. One of those publications, *Spawn*, features a vicious gangster named Antonio Twistelli, who also goes by the nickname of "Tony Twist." The real Tony Twist's mother became very upset when she discovered that such a character shared her son's name. She was worried that *Spawn* would lead people to think badly of her boy. McFarlane insists that he did not base his comic book villain on any real person and argues that if he wanted to borrow a hockey player's name, he would have called the gangster Wayneatelli Gretzkytello. Can the real-life Tony Twist successfully sue McFarlane for defamation? What test would a court apply in these circumstances?

11. Mary Tran graduated with a business degree three years ago. She began working almost immediately as a financial analyst for Marshall James Inc, an investment-consulting company. After starting that job, she contacted the bank that had carried her student loan to settle the details of her debt and arrange a repayment schedule. The bank informed her that her debt had been assigned to Financial Debt Recovery Ltd (FDR). When she contacted FDR, she was told that she would be required to make monthly payments of $1000. She was also told that she would be required to pay "a substantial amount" of interest. She asked for details about the outstanding amount, but FDR refused to provide that information. Tran therefore said that she would not begin making payments until she knew how much she owed in total. Under the terms of the loan contract that she had originally signed with the bank, she was entitled to do so.

Tran heard nothing more from FDR for several weeks. She then began to receive telephone messages that threatened her with serious violence unless she immediately paid a $2000 "loan transfer fee." Although her loan contract did not require the payment of such a fee, she complied with FDR's demand out of fear for her life. FDR also called John Molloy, the managing partner of Marshall James, and said (i) that Tran was actively seeking employment elsewhere, and (ii) that Tran had a criminal record for fraud. Both of those statements were entirely untrue, but they were told in such a convincing way that Molloy believed them. As a result, Molloy followed FDR's advice and terminated Tran's employment with Marshall James Inc. If FDR's allegations had been true, Molloy's actions would have been justified. On the true facts, however, they amounted to a breach of contract. Tran found a position with another firm some time later, but at a much lower rate of pay. She has suffered a $50 000 loss as result of changing jobs.

Tran bears no ill will toward Molloy or Marshall James Inc because she realizes that they were tricked by FDR. She does, however, want to sue FDR. Describe three torts that we discussed in this chapter that Tran could use against FDR.

12. Canaural Inc was a small Canadian company that manufactured audio components. Until recently, the brains behind the operation were two key employees: Jurgen Ballack and Karl Heinz. DeutscheSonic

GmbH is a large German company that trades around the world. Its success is due in part to its tactic of ruthlessly "squeezing out" its competitors. A year ago, it set its sights on Canaural. DeutscheSonic realized that Ballack and Heinz were the key players in Canaural. It therefore secretly approached them with lucrative job offers. Ballack and Heinz initially resisted. They explained that their contracts required them to give six months notice to quit, and that Canaural was a small operation that was unlikely to ever challenge DeutscheSonic. DeutscheSonic, however, was not to be denied. Its president explained the situation to Ballack and Heinz. "Wake up boys! Canaural is going to die. You can either be my assassins, or you can be buried along with the rest of your little company. Get rich or get dead!" It turned out to be an easy choice. Ballack and Heinz quickly experienced a change of heart, abruptly quit their jobs with Canaural, and joined DeutscheSonic. Without Ballack and Heinz, Canaural soon crumbled beneath DeutscheSonic. The Canadian company has, in effect, been wiped out. Explain the causes of action and the remedies that are available to Canaural.

WEBLINKS

Nuisance

Duhaime Law: Nuisance   www.duhaime.org/Tort/nuis.aspx

This website contains a discussion of the tort of nuisance, as well as defences and remedies.

Secondary Picketing Is Legal Unless Wrongful Conduct Is Involved   www.emond-harnden.com/apr02/rwdsu.html

This document discusses the Supreme Court of Canada's decision in *Pepsi-Cola Canada Beverages (West) Ltd v RWDSU, Local 558*, which deals with the legality of secondary picketing.

Pepsi-Cola Canada Beverages (West) Ltd v RWDSU, Local 558   www.lexum.umontreal.ca/csc-scc/en/pub/2002/vol1/html/2002scr1_0156.html

This document contains the Supreme Court of Canada's decision in *Pepsi-Cola Canada Beverages (West) Ltd v RWDSU, Local 558*, which deals with the legality of secondary picketing.

Defamation

Canadian Internet Law Resource Page   http://aix1.uottawa.ca/~geist/torts.html

This page contains links to materials that discuss the tort of defamation in the context of the Internet.

Canadian Law Site.com   www.canadianlawsite.com/libel-slander-defamation-of-%20character.htm

This website contains information and links on the tort of defamation.

Duhaime Law: Defamation   www.duhaime.org/Tort/ca-defam.aspx

This website contains an overview of the tort of defamation.

ADDITIONAL RESOURCES FOR CHAPTER 5 ON THE COMPANION WEBSITE

(www.pearsoned.ca/mcinnes)

In addition to self-test multiple-choice, true-false, and short essay questions (all with immediate feedback), three additional Cases and Problems (with suggested answers), and links to useful Web destinations, the Companion Website provides the following resources for Chapter 5:

- Weblinks to *Occupiers' Liability Acts* for each province and territory

Provincial Material

- **British Columbia:** Occupiers' Liability, Defamation
- **Alberta:** Defamation, Occupiers' Liability, Privacy
- **Manitoba and Saskatchewan:** Occupiers' Liability (Invitees & Licensees), Defamation
- **Ontario:** Defamation, Occupiers' Liability

6 Negligence

OBJECTIVES

After completing this chapter, you should be able to:

1. Describe the nature and function of the concept of a duty of care.

2. Explain the term "reasonable foreseeability" and explain the ways in which that concept is relevant to the tort of negligence.

3. Explain why the concept of proximity is important to the duty of care, especially in the context of claims for negligent statements.

4. Explain the role of policy under the duty of care concept, especially as it applies to the regulation of professions.

5. Describe the reasonable person and explain how that person is relevant to the standard of care.

6. Outline the special considerations that arise when a court decides whether a professional has acted carelessly.

7. Outline the nature and function of the but-for test.

8. Briefly describe the defence of contributory negligence.

9. Explain why and how the courts have limited the defence of voluntary assumption of risk.

10. Outline the scope of the defence of illegality.

In this chapter, we finish our discussion of torts by examining the most important tort of all: negligence. In non-legal terms, that word usually means "carelessness." Its legal meaning is much the same. The **tort of negligence** determines whether the defendant can be held liable for carelessly causing the plaintiff to suffer a loss or injury. That issue can arise in numerous ways: a manufacturer may produce a beverage that makes a consumer sick; an investment counsellor may provide bad advice that leads a client to purchase worthless stocks; a golfer may hit an errant shot that cracks a spectator's skull; a builder may construct a defective bridge that collapses on a motorist's vehicle; an employer may write an inaccurate report that prevents an employee from receiving a promotion; and so on.

the tort of negligence determines whether the defendant can be held liable for carelessly causing injury to the plaintiff

The tort of negligence requires the plaintiff to prove that the defendant:

- owed a *duty of care*, in that it was required to act carefully toward the plaintiff
- *breached the standard of care* by acting carelessly
- *caused harm* to the plaintiff

Even if the plaintiff proves those three elements, the defendant may be able to avoid liability by proving a defence. Three possibilities are especially important. The defendant may show that at least one of these defences existed:

- The plaintiff's injury was caused by its own *contributory negligence*.
- The plaintiff *voluntarily assumed the risk* of being injured by the defendant.
- The plaintiff was injured while engaged in some form of *illegal behaviour*.

Those elements are represented in Figure 6.1.

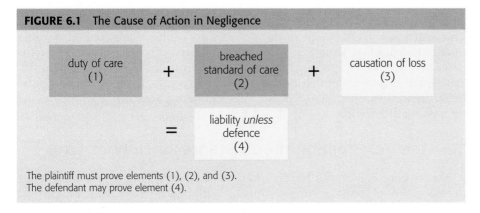

FIGURE 6.1   The Cause of Action in Negligence

The plaintiff must prove elements (1), (2), and (3).
The defendant may prove element (4).

Before examining those elements, we must discuss two preliminary matters. First, people sometimes talk about *professional negligence*. That phrase is misleading because it suggests that there is a separate tort by that name. In fact, the term "professional negligence" simply refers to negligence that is committed by a professional person, such as a banker, a lawyer, or an accountant.[1] However, it *is* true that the cause of action in negligence is flexible enough to reflect different types of situations. For example, the standard of care always requires the defendant to act as a reasonable person would act *in similar*

[1.] Chapter 22 explains how a professional may also be held liable on other grounds, such as breach of contract and breach of fiduciary duty.

circumstances. The precise content of that requirement therefore depends upon the circumstances. An architect who is drafting plans for an office tower must act much more carefully than a gas station attendant who is washing a car. And in that way, the idea of "professional negligence" makes sense. It refers to the special considerations that shape the general cause of action in negligence when it is applied to professional people. The topic of professional negligence is discussed later in this chapter.

Second, the law of negligence contains a tension between two important values. On the one hand, the courts want a wide scope of liability in order to compensate people who suffer injuries. On the other hand, the courts recognize that the imposition of liability sometimes actually hurts society. If a business had to fully compensate every person whom it injured, it might not be able to afford to carry on. Admittedly, in some situations, that would be a good thing. An especially hazardous industry that produces few social benefits perhaps should be shut down. In other situations, however, it may be in society's best interests to protect certain types of activities from liability. For example, it is quite difficult to successfully sue a physician, largely because judges do not want to discourage doctors from practising in risky areas, such as obstetrics.[2] The tension between the desire to provide compensation and the desire to encourage socially useful activities appears in all areas of tort law. It is particularly noticeable in negligence, however, because that cause of action is so flexible. It is not much of an exaggeration to say that a judge, with a bit of ingenuity, can often reasonably find for either the plaintiff or the defendant. The actual decision frequently depends on which interests the judge finds more compelling. As we discuss the action in negligence, note how the courts view the societal role of different types of business activities.

DUTY OF CARE

The courts use the concept of *duty of care* to control the scope of liability under the cause of action in negligence. A **duty of care** occurs when the defendant is required to use reasonable care to avoid injuring the plaintiff. Without a duty of care, there cannot be liability, even if the defendant carelessly injured the plaintiff. Ethical Perspective 6.1 (see p. 121) provides an interesting illustration.

a **duty of care** occurs when the defendant is required to use reasonable care to avoid injuring the plaintiff

Test for Determining the Existence of Duty of Care

A duty of care is required for an action in negligence. But how does a judge decide when to impose such a duty? Traditionally, there was no general answer—a duty of care was restricted to certain types of relationships, such as innkeeper and traveller, lawyer and client, railway company and passenger, and surgeon and patient. A plaintiff could win only if it fell within one of those relationships. Eventually, however, the courts replaced those individual categories with a single test. A duty of care can now be recognized any time that certain conditions are met. Case Brief 6.1 (see p. 121) discusses one of the most famous cases in our legal system.

[2.] *Reibl v Hughes* (1980) 114 DLR (3d) 1 (SCC); *ter Neuzen v Korn* (1995) 127 DLR (4th) 577 (SCC).

ETHICAL PERSPECTIVE 6.1

Duty of Care[3]

The Supreme Court of Canada has held that a pregnant woman does not owe a duty of care to her unborn child. Consequently, if a pregnant woman carelessly causes a traffic accident that results in damage to her unborn child, that child cannot sue in negligence even if born later with a disability.

Interestingly, the same rule does *not* apply between an unborn child and other people. Anyone, except a mother, can owe a duty of care. For example, if a father carelessly causes a child to suffer an injury before birth, he can be held liable if that child is later born with a disability. Furthermore, everyone, including a mother, can be held liable for carelessly causing an injury to a child *after* it is born.

The rule that denies the existence of a duty of care between a pregnant woman and her unborn child reflects the Court's attempt to strike a balance between the desirability of providing compensation for the injured child and the desirability of protecting the woman's freedom of action. Because nearly everything that a woman does can affect her unborn child, it has been argued that a duty of care would unfairly require her to be on guard for nine months.

Questions for Discussion

1. Has the Supreme Court of Canada struck a fair balance?

2. From a legal and moral perspective, should a pregnant woman be entitled to carelessly injure her unborn child?

When answering those questions, consider that the mother would usually want to be held liable to her injured child. More precisely, she would want her child to be able to recover compensatory damages from her insurance company.

CASE BRIEF 6.1

Donoghue v Stevenson [1932] AC 562 (HL)

The plaintiff, Mrs Donoghue, visited a café with a friend. Her friend bought her a bottle of ginger beer that the defendant had manufactured. After drinking some of the beverage, the plaintiff poured the remainder into her glass. She then noticed that the bottle contained, along with ginger beer, a decomposed snail. The event made her sick, and she sued the defendant for carelessly allowing a snail to get into the drink.

The issue before the court was whether a manufacturer owes a duty of care to a person who consumes, but did not personally buy, a particular product. Lord Atkin said "yes."

> You must take reasonable care to avoid acts or omissions which you can reasonably foresee would be likely to injure your neighbour. Who, then, in law is my neighbour? The answer seems to be—persons who are so closely and directly affected by my act that I ought reasonably to have them in contemplation as being so affected when I am directing my mind to the acts or omissions which are called in question.

That decision is important to business people for two reasons.

- First, it created a general test for determining the existence of a duty of care. It is no longer necessary to bring a case within one of the traditional categories.

- Second, it established that a manufacturer can be held liable to any consumer. Manufacturers therefore have to worry not only about the people who buy their products, but also about the people who use their products. We will discuss the second point later.

Based on *Donoghue v Stevenson*, the Canadian courts have developed a unique test for the creation of a duty of care.[4]

- The judge will first ask whether or not the duty of care question has already been answered for the particular type of case that she is hearing. We already know, for instance, that the bottler of a beverage owes a duty

---

3. *Dobson v Dobson* (1999) 174 DLR (4th) 1 (SCC).

4. *Nielsen v Kamloops (City)* (1984) 10 DLR (4th) 641 (SCC); *Cooper v Hobart* (2001) 206 DLR (4th) 193 (SCC).

of care to a consumer, and that a mother does not owe a duty of care to an unborn child.

■ If the duty of care question has not already been answered for the particular type of case that the judge is hearing, then it will be necessary to ask three questions in order to determine whether or not a duty of care *should* exist.

    ■ Was it *reasonably foreseeable* that the plaintiff could be injured by the defendant's carelessness?

    ■ Did the parties share a relationship of sufficient *proximity*?

    ■ If an injury was reasonably foreseeable, and if the parties shared a relationship of sufficient proximity, then a duty of care will presumably exist. The judge might still deny a duty of care, however, on the basis of *policy* reasons.

We will look at those three requirements in more detail.

Reasonable Foreseeability

The reasonable foreseeability test is *objective*. The issue is not whether the defendant *personally knew* that its activities might injure the plaintiff. It is whether a *reasonable person* in the defendant's position would have recognized that possibility. That test is intended to strike a balance between the parties. It would be unfair to deny compensation simply because the defendant was unaware of a danger. The plaintiff should not have to suffer simply because the defendant was not paying attention. But at the same time, it would be unfair to hold the defendant liable for *every* injury that it creates, even those that were unforeseeable. A person cannot take precautions against a hidden danger. Similarly, it is difficult to arrange liability insurance for an unpredictable event. To better understand the reasonable foreseeability test, consider Business Decision 6.1.

 ## BUSINESS DECISION 6.1

Reasonable Foreseeability and Risk Management[5]

Hermes Holdings Ltd sold a piece of land to Mercury Developments Inc for $500 000. Mercury intended to build a shopping mall on that property. To do so, however, it needed certain documents to be delivered to a government office by December 31. If it failed to do so, it would not be able to proceed with its project and it would suffer a loss of $1 000 000. Hermes still had possession of those documents. Mercury therefore told it to send them to the government office by courier.

Hermes contacted your courier company. You agreed to deliver an envelope to the government office by December 31 in exchange for $10. Hermes did not, however, tell you what the envelope contained, nor that Mercury would suffer an enormous loss if delivery was late. Unfortunately, because you were very busy, you did not actually deliver the envelope until January 3.

Hermes is not particularly concerned about the late delivery. Mercury, however, is very upset. Your carelessness cost it $1 000 000. Nevertheless, you probably would not be held liable. A reasonable person in your position might not have appreciated the consequences of late delivery.

Questions for Discussion

1. Why would it be unfair to hold you liable if Mercury's loss was not reasonably foreseeable?

2. If the situation had been fully explained to you at the outset, would you still have charged only $10? Would it make good business sense to expose yourself to the risk of $1 000 000 in damages in exchange for such a small price?

[5.] *BDC Ltd v Hofstrand Farms Ltd* (1986) 26 DLR (4th) 1 (SCC).

Proximity

Reasonable foreseeability is only a start. A duty of care will not be recognized unless there was also a relationship of *proximity*. The concept of proximity is hard to define. The basic idea is that there must somehow be a close and direct connection between the parties. In simple situations, the court will focus on *physical* proximity (as when the defendant carelessly swings a baseball bat while standing next to the plaintiff). In more complicated situations, however, the court will look at the issue of proximity from a variety of perspectives. Depending upon the circumstances, it may ask:

- whether the parties shared a *social relationship* (for example, a parent is required to look after a child, but a stranger is not)

- whether the parties shared a *commercial relationship* (for example, a tavern may be responsible if a drunken customer later causes a traffic accident, but the host of a house party may not be responsible if a drunken guest injures a pedestrian on the way home)[6]

- whether there was a *direct causal connection* between the defendant's carelessness and the plaintiff's injury (for example, a motorist who rams into a bridge will be liable for the damage to the bridge, but probably not for the profits that were lost when customers could not reach a store that was located on the other side of the bridge)[7]

- whether the plaintiff *relied* on the fact that the defendant *represented* that it would act in a certain way (for example, a railway company may have a duty to continue operating a safety gate that it voluntarily installed and that pedestrians have come to rely upon)[8]

As you can see, the concept of proximity is very broad and very open-ended. It allows the court to look at all of the circumstances before deciding whether or not it would be appropriate to recognize a new duty of care.

Duty of Care for Professional Statements   Although it is difficult to define, the concept of proximity often plays a crucial role in determining whether or not a duty of care exists. In the business context, the best example concerns *negligent statements*. The Canadian economy is increasingly based on the supply of information and advice, rather than on the production of physical goods. Inevitably, some of the statements that are made by professionals (such as financial advisers, business consultants, lawyers, stockbrokers, and bankers) will be inaccurate. And inevitably, consumers and clients will suffer as a result. The law of negligence must strike a balance between the need to compensate people who are hurt by negligent statements and the need to protect businesses from the potentially disastrous consequences of being held liable.

Special rules are needed because *careless statements* are different from *careless actions* in at least three ways.

- Since the dangers associated with physical conduct are usually obvious, the need for precaution is normally clear as well. You know that if you swing a baseball bat in a crowded room, you may hurt someone. In contrast, because the risks associated with statements are often hidden, the

---

[6.] *Jordan House Ltd v Menow & Honsberger* (1973) 38 DLR (3d) 105 (SCC); *Childs v Desormeaux* (2004) 239 DLR (4th) 61 (Ont CA).

[7.] *Star Village Tavern v Nield* (1976) 71 DLR (3d) 439 (Man QB).

[8.] *Soulsby v Toronto* (1907) 15 OLR 13 (Ont HCJ).

need for care is usually less apparent. Consequently, people tend to speak loosely, especially in social settings.

- "Words are more volatile than deeds."[9] In most situations, the risk created by a careless action is limited in time and space. Drunk drivers pose a real threat, but generally only for the motorists and pedestrians in their path. Furthermore, they will likely be stopped once the first accident occurs. In contrast, if a duty of care exists for a careless statement, there is a possibility of "liability in an indeterminate amount for an indeterminate time to an indeterminate class."[10] Suppose that a financial report that was created for personal purposes is mistakenly distributed to the public. If it contains inaccurate information, many people may later rely upon it and suffer financial loses when they make bad investments.

- Careless actions usually result in property damage or personal injuries. A negligent driver may crash through your fence or run you down. Careless statements, however, usually result in *pure economic losses*, financial losses that are not tied to any property damage or personal injuries. For example, if you follow your stockbroker's negligent advice and make a poor investment, you will simply lose money. And significantly, the law is more reluctant to provide compensation for pure economic losses than for property damage or personal injuries.[11] Some things are more important than others.

For those reasons, Canadian courts apply special rules when deciding whether to recognize a duty of care if the defendant's *careless statement* caused the plaintiff to suffer a *pure economic loss*.[12] Case Brief 6.2 discusses a simplified version of a leading case.

CASE BRIEF 6.2

Hercules Managements Ltd v Ernst & Young (1997) 146 DLR (4th) 577 (SCC)

The defendant was an accounting firm that prepared audited financial statements for a company. Those statements were required by statute and were intended to allow shareholders to supervise the management of the company. The plaintiff, who was one of the shareholders in the company, claimed that the defendant carelessly prepared those statements. He also claimed that he suffered pure economic losses after relying on inaccurate information that they contained. More specifically, he argued that the statements caused him to continue his investment in the company, which later went broke.

The Supreme Court of Canada first asked whether it was *reasonably foreseeable* that the plaintiff would suffer a loss by relying upon the defendant's statement. A duty of care is more likely to be imposed with respect to a statement if:

- the defendant possessed, or claimed to possess, *special knowledge*—it is often reasonable to rely upon information that is provided by an apparent expert
- the statement was communicated on a *serious occasion*—it is often reasonable to rely upon information

continued

[9.] *Hedley Byrne & Co v Heller & Partners Ltd* [1963] 2 All ER 575 at 602 (HL).

[10.] *Ultramares Corp v Touche* 255 NY 170 (CA 1931).

[11.] That is true whether a pure economic loss is caused by careless words or by careless conduct. In contrast, the courts generally do not feel the need to apply special rules if the defendant's careless statement causes the plaintiff to suffer property damage or physical injury. In one case, a model suffered physical injuries as a result of falling off a stage while following a director's instructions: *Robson v Chrysler Corp (Canada)* (1962) 32 DLR (2d) 49 (Alta CA). The director clearly owed a duty of care.

[12.] The courts are more willing to impose liability if the defendant's inaccurate statement was intentional rather than merely careless. In this section, we are discussing the law of *negligent statements*. However, as Chapter 5 explained, liability can also be imposed under the tort of *deceit* if the defendant intentionally misled the plaintiff.

continued

that is provided during a business meeting, but not during an informal party

- the defendant's statement was made in response to *an inquiry*—a person who is specifically asked for information should realize that the answer may be relied upon
- the defendant received a *financial benefit* in exchange for the statement—reasonable people do not usually pay for information unless they intend to rely upon it
- the defendant communicated a *statement of fact*, or an *opinion or prediction based on fact*, rather than a purely personal opinion—it is often reasonable to rely upon a professional evaluation of certain stocks, but not upon a prediction as to the outcome of a horse race

However, a duty of care is less likely to be imposed if:

- the defendant issued a *disclaimer* along with its statement—a reasonable person does not generally rely upon a statement if the speaker was unwilling to assume responsibility for it

Given the facts of the case, including the lack of a disclaimer, the Court held that it was reasonably foreseeable that the plaintiff would reasonably rely upon the defendant's statement.

At the second stage of the duty of care analysis, however, the Court was worried about "indeterminate liability." The defendant prepared the statements for a specific purpose—to allow shareholders to monitor the management of the company. It did not intend for those statements to be used as investment advice by people like the plaintiff.[13] The Court was also worried that the fear of widespread liability would cause businesses in the defendant's position to substantially increase their prices to offset the risk of being held responsible. The Court therefore held that a duty of care will be recognized only if:

- the defendant knew that the plaintiff, either individually or as a member of a defined group, might rely upon the statement, and
- the plaintiff relied upon that statement for its intended purpose

Because he was a shareholder, the plaintiff was a member of an identifiable class. He did not, however, use the statement for its intended purpose. He used it as investment advice, rather than for management of the company.

The defendant therefore did not owe a duty of care to the plaintiff.

As a business person, you should learn three important lessons from Case Brief 6.2. First, you should be very careful about providing information and advice. Second, if you do not wish to be held liable for your statements, you should clearly disclaim responsibility. Third, you should be careful about relying on statements made by others. While you may be entitled to compensation, your claim may also be rejected for lack of proximity.

Policy

A duty of care will not necessarily exist even if there was reasonable foreseeability and proximity. The court will also ask whether liability should be precluded on *policy* grounds. It is often difficult to distinguish the issues of proximity and policy.[14] Broadly speaking, however, proximity deals with the relationship that exists between the parties, whereas policy is concerned with the effect that a duty of care would have on the legal system and on society generally. For example, depending upon the circumstances, a court may ask whether the recognition of a duty of care would:

[13.] Financial statements may be relied upon for many reasons by many types of people, including creditors, customers, competitors, and employees.

[14.] Canadian courts previously used a *two-part* test to determine the existence of a duty of care. If they were satisfied that harm was reasonably foreseeable, they asked whether there were any policy factors that prevented a duty of care from arising. Those policy factors included the idea of proximity. As previously explained, the new *three-part* test deals separately with proximity and policy (as well as reasonable foreseeability). It is, however, often difficult to draw that distinction in practice. In Case Brief 6.2 (see page 124), was a duty of care rejected in *Hercules Managements Ltd v Ernst & Young* because the connection between the parties was not close and direct enough (proximity) or because the court was worried about indeterminate liability (policy)? Does it really matter?

- "open the floodgates" by encouraging a very large number of people to swamp the courts with lawsuits (that is one reason why the courts are reluctant to recognize a duty of care for negligent statements)[15]

- interfere with political decisions (that is why a government may be able to escape responsibility for deciding that it could not afford to frequently check a stretch of road for fallen trees)[16]

- hurt a valuable type of relationship (that is one reason why a mother does not owe a duty of care to her unborn child)[17]

Duty of Care and Policy: Regulation of Professions An excellent example of the importance of policy appears in cases dealing with the *regulation of professions*. Many professions are governed by regulatory bodies. As we saw in Chapter 2, for instance, every jurisdiction in Canada has a Law Society that sets standards, imposes a code of conduct, and punishes members who misbehave. The same is true for accountants, mortgage brokers, stockbrokers, physicians, psychiatrists, dentists, architects, and so on. A difficult question may arise, however, if a person is hurt by a professional's incompetence or dishonesty. It is usually obvious that the professional will be held personally liable. But what if the plaintiff also wants to sue the regulatory body? She may argue that if that body had done its job properly (for example, by rigorously enforcing its code of conduct and imposing a suspension), the professional would not have been in a position to commit the tort. Case Brief 6.3 illustrates how the courts decide whether or not the regulatory body owes a duty of care.

CASE BRIEF 6.3

Cooper v Hobart (2001) 206 DLR (4th) 193 (SCC)[18]

Like thousands of other people, Mary Cooper invested money in Eron Mortgage Corporation. And like the rest of them, she lost her money as a result of crimes committed by Eron's managers. Cooper sued the Registrar of Mortgages, who was responsible for investigating complaints, freezing funds, and suspending delinquent brokers. She claims that the Registrar negligently allowed Eron to carry on business, even after he knew that Eron was in serious violation of the *Mortgage Brokers Act*. The question for the courts was whether the Registrar owed a duty of care to Mary Cooper.

The Supreme Court of Canada said "no." It was willing to accept that the plaintiff's loss was reasonably foreseeable. However, it denied that there was proximity between the parties. The Registrar's job was to serve the general public—not individual investors. His function was to promote integrity and efficiency within the profession—not to protect Mary Cooper's money.

The Court further held that even if there had been a close and direct connection between the parties, policy considerations would have prevented a duty of care from arising. It mentioned several concerns:

- The Registrar fills a largely political and judicial role by creating policies and deciding when to suspend brokers—and the courts are generally reluctant to interfere with political or judicial decisions.

- Recognition of a duty of care could open the floodgates—aside from Mary Cooper, thousands of other people who lost money on Eron would also sue the Registrar.

- The Registrar is a public official, and if he was held liable, the judgment would actually have to be paid with tax dollars—in effect, taxpayers would have to insure Mary Cooper's investment.

---

15. As we saw in Case Brief 6.2 (on p. 124).

16. *Swinamer v Nova Scotia (Attorney General)* (1994) 112 DLR (4th) 18 (SCC).

17. As we saw in Ethical Perspective 6.1 (on p. 121).

18. See also *Edwards v Law Society of Upper Canada* (2001) 206 DLR (4th) 211 (SCC).

BREACH OF THE STANDARD OF CARE

The first element of the cause of action in negligence requires the plaintiff to prove that the defendant owed a duty of care. The second element requires the plaintiff to prove that the defendant breached the standard of care. The **standard of care** tells the defendant how it should act. It is **breached** when the defendant acts less carefully.

The standard of care is based on the **reasonable person test**—the defendant must act in the same way that a reasonable person would act in similar circumstances. The reasonable person is a *fictional character*. One judge provided this description.

> I shall not attempt to formulate a comprehensive definition of "a reasonable man.". . . I simply say that he is a mythical creature of the law whose conduct is the standard by which the Courts measure the conduct of all other persons. . . . He is not an extraordinary or unusual creature; he is not superhuman; he is not required to display the highest skill of which anyone is capable; he is not a genius who can perform uncommon feats, nor is he possessed of unusual powers of foresight. He is a person of normal intelligence who makes prudence a guide to his conduct. He does nothing that a prudent man would not do and he does not omit to do anything that a prudent man would do. He acts in accord with general and approved practice. His conduct is guided by considerations which ordinarily regulate the conduct of human affairs.[19]

The reasonable person test gives the courts a great deal of flexibility in deciding whether the defendant acted carelessly. Although it is impossible to list all of the relevant factors, we can identify some important ones.

- The reasonable person test is said to be *objective*.[20] It does not make allowances for the defendant's *subjective*, or personal, characteristics. For example, I cannot avoid liability by simply proving that I did my best. I may be held liable even though my carelessness was caused by the fact that I suffer from a mental disability.[21] The courts are more concerned with providing compensation to my victims than with showing sympathy for my shortcomings. Nevertheless, judges do lower the standard of care somewhat for children. A child is generally not required

the standard of care tells the defendant how it should act

the standard of care is breached when the defendant acts less carefully

the reasonable person test requires the defendant to act in the same way that a reasonable person would act in similar circumstances

[19] *Arland v Taylor* [1955] 3 DLR 358 (Ont CA) *per* Laidlaw JA.

[20] By applying an "objective" test, the courts create the appearance of approaching tort law without making value judgments. A judge who is criticized in a particular case might respond by insisting that his decision simply reflected the views of the "reasonable person," rather than his own political perspective. Feminist scholars, in contrast, have long argued that the "reasonable person" usually bears a striking resemblance to the judges themselves, most of whom continue to be white males from wealthy backgrounds. They further argue that tort law consequently tends to unfairly favour white, affluent males: L Bender "A Lawyer's Primer on Feminist Theory and Tort" (1988) 38 *J of Legal Education* 3. On a deeper level, however, it might be asked whether it is really possible to create an objective reasonable person, or whether judges will always decide disputes according to their own views of right and wrong, reasonable and unreasonable.

[21] I might be able to avoid liability, however, if my mental disability was so severe that I effectively had no control over my actions: *Buckley v Smith Transport Ltd* [1946] 4 DLR 721 (Ont CA) (the defendant caused a traffic accident because he believed that his vehicle was being operated by remote control). Likewise, I might be able to avoid liability if I suffer from a severe physical disability. The law does not expect me to see if I am blind. It does, however, require me to recognize my limitations and to avoid dangerous activities, such as driving.

to act like a reasonable adult.[22] It is enough to act like a reasonable child of similar age, intelligence, and experience.[23]

- The reasonable person takes precautions against *reasonably foreseeable risks*. Notice that the test does not refer to "probable" or "likely" risks. As long as it is not fanciful, something may be reasonably foreseeable even if it is unlikely to occur. A 1-in-100 or 1-in-1000 chance may be sufficient. At the same time, however, there is no need to take precautions against unforeseeable risks. The reasonable person does not guard against every conceivable danger.

- The reasonable person is influenced by both the *likelihood of harm* and the *potential severity of harm*. Greater care is required if the chance of injury is 90 percent rather than 10 percent. Likewise, greater care is required if the relevant injury is death rather than a light bruise.

- The reasonable person is more likely to adopt *affordable precautions*. For example, a taxi company that regularly carries children should certainly pay $50 for tamper-proof door locks. But it does not have to spend an enormous sum by purchasing the safest vehicles on the market.

- The reasonable person may act in a way that has great *social utility*, even though it creates a risk. For instance, it is sometimes appropriate for an ambulance driver to speed through a red light to save a dying patient.

- The standard of care requires the defendant to act as the reasonable person would act "in similar circumstances." Consequently, less care is required during emergencies. The *sudden peril doctrine* states that even a reasonable person may make a mistake under difficult circumstances.

The Standard of Care for Professionals: Professional Negligence

We previously discussed the rules that determine when a *duty of care* will be imposed on a professional. We stressed two particularly important factors: first, the existence of a close *relationship* between the parties, and second, the extent to which the client *relied* upon the professional. We now need to consider the *standard of care* that professionals are expected to meet. The basic rule is the same as always: A professional must act as a reasonable person would act in similar circumstances. The courts do, however, pay special attention to four factors when they are dealing with professionals.

First, it is not enough for a professional person, while engaged in a professional activity, to meet the standard that would be applied if a layperson performed the same task. A professional must act as the *reasonable professional* would act in similar circumstances.

- Professional people must live up to the training that they received or claim to have received. The last part of that sentence is important: If people claim to have special expertise, they cannot avoid liability by later confessing that they lied about their qualifications.

[22.] The rule is different if a child participates in an adult activity, like driving a boat.

[23.] *McEllistrum v Etches* (1956) 6 DLR (2d) 1 (SCC). There are relatively few cases in this area, largely because there is seldom anything to be gained from suing a child. Furthermore, parents are not *vicariously liable* for their children's torts. That is true even under "parental responsibility" legislation: *Parental Responsibility Act*, CCSM, c P-8 (Man); *Parental Responsibility Act 2000*, SO 2000, c 4 (Ont); *Parental Responsibility* Act, SBC 2001, c 45 (BC). Parents may, however, be held personally liable for failing to properly supervise their children.

- Even within the same profession, more may be expected of a specialist than of a generalist. For example, an accountant who specializes in a particular type of transaction must perform to a higher level when acting within that area than an accountant who does not claim to have the same expertise.

- Special allowances are *not* made for beginners. Even an inexperienced professional must conform to the standard of a reasonably competent and experienced professional.

Those rules are based on the reasonable expectations that people have about professionals.

Second, by the time a case gets to trial, it is often easy to say what the defendant could have done to avoid injuring the plaintiff. It would be unfair, however, to judge the defendant's actions in *hindsight*. That is especially significant in scientific or technical fields, where knowledge often develops very quickly. The standard of care is therefore based on information that was reasonably available to the defendant at the time of the accident.[24]

Third, a professional who follows an *approved practice* generally cannot be held liable. Consequently, the standard of care is usually met if the defendant either complies with requirements established by a professional organization or follows the same procedures that are used by other members of the profession. But sometimes, an approved practice is itself careless. A court will reach that conclusion, however, only if the relevant activity can be judged by common sense and does not involve technical or complex matters. As the Supreme Court of Canada explained:

> [C]ourts do not ordinarily have the expertise to tell professionals that they are not behaving appropriately in their field. . . . As a general rule, where a procedure involves difficult or uncertain questions of medical treatment or complex, scientific or highly technical matters that are beyond the ordinary experience and understanding of a judge or jury, it will not be open to find a standard medical practice negligent. On the other hand, as an exception to the general rule, if a standard practice fails to adopt obvious and reasonable precautions which are readily apparent to the ordinary finder of fact, then it is no excuse for a practitioner to claim that he or she was merely conforming to such a negligent common practice.[25]

Fourth, carelessness is different from mere *errors of judgment*. The former can result in liability; the latter cannot. A professional does not have to be perfect. As long as the defendant's mistake is one that a reasonable professional might make, the standard of care is not breached. For example, a surgeon will not be held liable for incorrectly choosing one procedure over another if a reasonable physician might have done the same.

The Standard of Care for Manufactured Products: Product Liability

Like professional negligence, the topic of *product liability* falls within the general action in negligence. However, it also requires special attention. **Product liability** may occur if a person is injured by a product. As we will see

product liability can occur when a person is injured by a product

---

[24.] *Walker Estate v York Finch General Hospital* (2001) 198 DLR (4th) 193 (SCC).

[25.] *ter Neuzen v Korn* (1995) 127 DLR (4th) 577 (SCC).

in Chapter 11, it may be possible to sue for breach of contract if the victim was the person who actually bought the item. (And as we will see in Chapter 13, that action for breach of contract may be made even easier by the *Sale of Goods Act*.) Liability for breach of contract is *strict*. The plaintiff does not have to prove that the defendant *carelessly* provided a defective product. It is enough that the contract was defective in a way that caused harm.

Sometimes, however, the parties are not linked together by a contract. In *Donoghue v Stevenson* (Case Brief 6.1), for example, the defective bottle of ginger beer was purchased for the plaintiff by her friend. Mrs Donoghue therefore had to sue for the tort of negligence. And, as always, that tort required Mrs Donoghue to prove that her injury was caused by the manufacturer's *carelessness*. That rule continues to apply in Canada: Tortious liability for defective products is *not* strict.[26] The situation is different in the United States. The American law of product liability *is* strict. The plaintiff does not have to prove that the defendant was careless. It is enough to show that a defective product caused an injury. Some people believe that Canadian law should similarly adopt strict liability. Such a rule would (i) better ensure that consumers are compensated for injuries that are caused by defective products, (ii) encourage manufacturers to develop safer products, and (iii) require manufacturers to pay for the losses that they cause as a result of selling their products and earning their profits. On the other hand, there are concerns that a rule of strict liability would (i) unfairly require a manufacturer to pay for an injury even though it had used reasonable care, (ii) increase the number of lawsuits against manufacturers, (iii) increase the cost of liability insurance for manufacturers, and (iv) eventually increase the cost of products. Which approach do you prefer?

Under current Canadian law, a person who wants to sue in tort for product liability must use the action in negligence. The courts almost always find that a duty of care was owed to a person who was injured by a defective product, whether that person was the purchaser, a consumer, or simply a bystander. It is reasonably foreseeable that a defective product may hurt someone; there is sufficiently close proximity between the manufacturer and the victim; and there are no policy reasons for generally denying relief. Liability therefore usually turns on the standard of care. We divide that discussion into three parts:

- manufacture
- design
- failure to warn

Manufacture

The courts usually impose liability if the defendant carelessly *manufactured* a product that injured the plaintiff. *Donoghue v Stevenson*, which we discussed in Case Brief 6.1, is the classic case. Mr Stevenson was required to compensate Mrs Donoghue because he negligently allowed a snail to crawl into a bottle of ginger beer that he manufactured.

---

[26] SM Waddams *Product Liability* (2001) c 11. Several Canadian statutes introduce elements of strict liability, but do not create a general rule that allows a person who is injured by a defective product to claim damages without proving negligence: *Consumer Protection Act*, SS 1996, c C-30.1, s 64 (Sask); *Consumer Product Warranty and Liability Act*, SNB 1978, c C-18.1, s 27 (NB). As we will see in Chapter 13, consumers are also protected by the *Sale of Goods Act*.

Design

The courts are more cautious if the plaintiff's injury was caused by the *design*, rather than the *manufacture*, of a product. A manufacturing defect usually affects only a few items. Not every bottle of Mr Stevenson's ginger beer contained a decomposed snail. A design defect, in contrast, usually affects every item that is produced. For instance, if a system of headlights is poorly designed, *every* vehicle that uses that system will create a danger. The courts are therefore more concerned about imposing a tremendous burden on the defendant. In the headlights case, the judge demanded proof that the product's disadvantages outweighed its advantages.[27] He carefully balanced the probability and severity of harm against the difficulty and expense of using an alternative design.

Warning

Even if a product is carefully designed and manufactured, liability may arise if consumers are not reasonably *warned* about its dangers. For instance, ladders should carry stickers that caution people against using them on slippery surfaces, just as some electrical appliances should alert people to the risk of electrocution in water. Several more points should be noted.

- The nature and extent of the warning depends upon the circumstances. Greater care is required if the danger is severe or if the consumers are unsophisticated. Less care is required if the risk is marginal or if the product is invariably sold to professionals who are specially trained to use it. And no warning at all is required if a danger is obvious. People are assumed to realize that knives cut and matches burn.

- A warning is usually needed only for a product's intended use. Sometimes, however, a warning may be required for a use that is unintended, but foreseeable. Glue is not meant to be sniffed, but manufacturers realize that their product is often abused.

- A warning may be required even though the manufacturer discovers the danger *after* the product has been sold. In that situation, it should take reasonable steps to contact consumers and, if necessary, recall the dangerous items.

- A warning may be required not only by a manufacturer, but also by someone who sells, distributes, or installs a product. The key question is whether the particular person knew, or should have known, of the danger.

- In some situations, the defendant can avoid liability if it provided a warning to a *learned intermediary*. The law in this area is complicated. For our purposes, it is enough to know that the rule may apply if a product is always sold to a professional rather than directly to the intended consumer. Breast implants, for instance, are not bought off store shelves. They are supplied to physicians, who then insert them into patients. If a manufacturer does not warn a doctor, it may be held liable if the implants later rupture inside a woman.[28]

Claims for product liability often raise difficult issues of personal responsibility. A consumer may use a product that is obviously dangerous, but then expect the manufacturer to provide compensation when something goes wrong. Ethical Perspective 6.2 raises some tough questions about tobacco litigation.

[27.] *Rentway Canada Ltd v Laidlaw Transport Ltd* (1989) 49 CCLT 150 (Ont HCJ).

[28.] *Hollis v Dow Corning Corp* (1995) 129 DLR (4th) 609 (SCC).

ETHICAL PERSPECTIVE 6.2

Tobacco Litigation

Tobacco is big business in Canada. The three major tobacco companies annually earn profits of approximately $4 billion. Few products are, however, more controversial. Although there is some disagreement on the statistics, one commonly cited figure states that tobacco products kill 45 000 Canadians every year.

Not surprisingly, the tobacco industry has increasingly become the subject of litigation. And perhaps predictably, Americans have led the way. In 1998, the major tobacco companies entered into a settlement with 46 states. In addition to accepting new advertising restrictions, the tobacco industry agreed to pay $25 billion over the course of a quarter century. That money will be used to reimburse the state governments for the financial burden that tobacco products place upon the health care system. Tobacco companies have also been sued in tort law by private individuals. In one case, non-smoking flight attendants received $300 million after contracting diseases caused by inhaling second-hand smoke during flights. And in a third line of cases, liability has stretched beyond the cigarette companies. An asthmatic corrections officer won $300 000 after his employer failed to provide a smoke-free work environment; a court declared that it was "cruel and unusual punishment" to expose a prisoner to a smoke-filled jail; and a tenant was entitled to withhold rent as long as his landlord allowed smoke to seep into his apartment from a downstairs nightclub.

That trend has begun to move north into this country. British Columbia has enacted legislation that allows the province to sue tobacco companies for the expenses that they generate for the health care system.[29] Within the context of private litigation, a court in that same province recently certified a class action against cigarette companies.[30] That class action claims that the companies fraudulently misled consumers by suggesting that "light" cigarettes were somehow less harmful than regular cigarettes. The plaintiffs are not asking to be compensated for their own losses. They are instead arguing that the tobacco companies should be required to disgorge (give up) the profits that they earned by deceiving the public.[31]

Canadian courts will eventually be required to decide whether or not tobacco companies should be held liable in tort law for manufacturing products that cause disease and death. Consider a typical case. Carey, a 45-year-old Canadian, is dying of lung cancer. The medical evidence strongly suggests that his condition was caused by smoking. He began smoking when he was 15, as a result of peer pressure and the attractive images (such as the Marlboro Man) that tobacco companies used to promote their products. Carey had heard the health warnings, but did not pay any attention to them at first. By the time he reached his early 20s, and fully appreciated the potential effects of smoking, he had become addicted and was unable to kick his habit. He now insists that the company that manufactured his brand of cigarettes should be held liable for his illness and impending death. The defendant responds with two arguments. First, it denies that there is any connection between cigarettes and poor health. And second, it says that since Carey had known about the risks allegedly associated with cigarettes when he began smoking, he must accept responsibility for his own behaviour.

Questions for Discussion

1. How should tort law strike a balance between Carey's claim that he has been injured by the company's products, and the company's claim that Carey should have to live the consequences of his own lifestyle?

2. We will consider the defences of contributory negligence and voluntary assumption of risk at the end of this chapter. Would either of those defences apply in this case? Have the Canadian courts formulated those defences too narrowly?

3. Assuming that Carey sues in the tort of negligence, how should he phrase his specific allegation? What exactly did the cigarette company do wrong? Were the cigarettes carelessly manufactured or carelessly designed? If so, is there something that the cigarette company could have done to produce a safe product? Or did the company fail to issue an adequate warning? If so, is there any reason to believe that a more explicit warning would have prevented Carey from smoking? (Indeed, given the fact that people continue to smoke despite the gruesome appearance of cigarette packages today, is it reasonable to believe that warnings are really effective?)

4. Carey has a health condition that requires treatment. Who should pay for that treatment? Should you and I, as taxpayers, be required to provide care to people who are hurt by the tobacco companies' dangerous products? Or should the legal system find a way of imposing those costs on the tobacco industry? In that respect, are cigarettes significantly different from other unhealthy products? What about alcohol, fast foods, and chocolate? What about other products that obviously create health risks, such as motorcycles and skateboards?

---

[29] *Tobacco and Health Care Costs Recovery Act*, SBC 2000, c 30. The validity of that legislation was upheld by the British Columbia Court of Appeal: *British Columbia v Imperial Tobacco Canada Ltd* (2004) 239 DLR (4th) 412 (BC CA), and the Supreme Court of Canada (2005) 257 DLR (4th) 193 (SCC).

[30] *Knight v Imperial Tobacco Canada Ltd* (2005) 250 DLR (4th) 357 (BC SC). The action is based on the *Trade Practice Act*, RSBC 1996, c 457, rather than the tort of negligence.

[31] Disgorgement is the opposite of compensation. Compensation is measured by the plaintiff's wrongful loss. Disgorgement is measured by the defendant's wrongful gain.

CAUSATION OF HARM

The third element of the claim in negligence is *causation of harm*. Even if it owed a duty of care and breached the standard of care, the defendant will not be held liable unless its carelessness caused the plaintiff to suffer a loss.[32] Although causation can be a difficult issue, we will only highlight the basic principles. The reason is simple. From a risk-management perspective, much can be done to avoid liability under the first two stages of the negligence action. But once a business has come under a duty of care and has acted carelessly, there is relatively little that it can do to avoid causing harm. As a matter of luck, its carelessness either will or will not hurt somebody.

The issue of causation is usually decided by the *but-for test*. The **but-for test** requires the plaintiff to prove that it would not have suffered a loss but for the defendant's carelessness. It is based on a simple question, "If the defendant had not acted carelessly, would the plaintiff have still suffered the same loss?" If the answer is "yes," the defendant cannot be held liable. If the answer is "no," the defendant may be held liable. To better understand that test, consider Concept Summary 6.1 and answer the questions in You Be the Judge 6.1.

the but-for test requires the plaintiff to prove that it would not have suffered a loss but for the defendant's carelessness

CONCEPT SUMMARY 6.1

The But-For Test

Question	Answer	Result
But for the defendant's carelessness, would the plaintiff have suffered the same loss?	Yes—the plaintiff would have suffered the same loss even if the efendant had not acted carelessly.	The defendant cannot be held liable.
	No—the plaintiff would not have suffered the same loss if the defendant had not acted carelessly.	The defendant may be held liable.

YOU BE THE JUDGE 6.1

The But-For Test[33]

A man went to a hospital complaining of stomach pain. The doctor on duty believed that there was nothing seriously wrong with the patient and simply told him to go home and sleep. The man later died of arsenic poisoning. His widow has shown that the doctor (i) owed a duty of care to her husband, and (ii) carelessly failed to realize that her husband's stomach pains were due to arsenic poisoning.

Questions for Discussion

1. Will the doctor be held liable if the evidence indicates that the man would have lived if he had received proper diagnosis and treatment?

2. Will the doctor be held liable if the evidence indicates that the man's arsenic poisoning was so serious that he could not have been saved even if he had been properly diagnosed?

---

32. As we have already seen, that loss may take many forms. The plaintiff may sustain a physical injury, property damage, or a pure economic loss.

33. *Barnett v Chelsea & Kensington Hospital Mgmt Committee* [1969] 1 QB 428.

There are several other things to note about causation of harm. First, as we saw in Chapter 2, the plaintiff generally has to prove all of the elements of the tort of negligence, including causation, on a *balance of probabilities*.

Second, the law generally adopts an *all-or-nothing* approach. If there is at least a 51 percent chance that the defendant's carelessness caused the plaintiff's loss, then the court will award damages for *all* of that loss. In contrast, if there is less than a 51 percent chance that the defendant's carelessness caused the plaintiff's injury, then the court will not award damages for *any* of that loss.

Third, the plaintiff has to prove only that the defendant's carelessness was *a cause*—not necessarily *the only cause*—of a loss. Suppose that my back pain was caused mostly by poor posture but partly by the fact that you pushed me off my bike. I may be entitled to receive 100 percent of my damages from you.[34]

Fourth, if *different defendants* cause the plaintiff to suffer *different injuries*, then each one is responsible accordingly. For example, if you break my arm, and Mary breaks my leg, you can be held liable only for my arm and she can be held liable only for my leg.

Fifth, the situation is more complicated if *different defendants* create a *single injury*. Suppose that you slip on my neighbour's sidewalk after leaving my party. You lost your balance and fell only because (i) I secretly drugged your drinks, *and* (ii) my neighbour, Shannon, failed to shovel her sidewalk. Shannon and I will be held *jointly and severally liable*.[35] That means that you can recover all of your damages from her, *or* all of your damages from me, *or* some of your damages from each of us. The choice is yours. As between ourselves, Shannon and I are responsible in proportion to our share of the blame. Suppose that the court said that she was 30 percent to blame and that I was 70 percent to blame. If you recovered all of your damages from Shannon, she could demand 70 percent of that money from me.

Sixth, a court may reject the but-for test if it would lead to an unfair result. Suppose that you and I went hunting with Akbar. When you made a rustling sound in a bush, he and I both turned and shot because we carelessly mistook you for a deer. You were hit by a single bullet, but you have no way of knowing whose. The but-for test seems to suggest that neither Akbar nor I will be held liable. You cannot prove on a balance of probabilities (that is, at least 51 percent) that he fired the relevant shot. Nor can you prove on a balance of probabilities (that is, at least 51 percent) that I fired the relevant shot. For each of us, there is only a 50 percent chance. A court, however, would probably hold both of us liable and allow you to recover all of your damages from either one or both.[36]

Remoteness

a loss is **remote** if it would be unfair to hold the defendant responsible for it

Even if the defendant caused the plaintiff to suffer a loss, liability will not be imposed if that loss was too *remote* from the careless conduct. A loss is **remote** if it would be unfair to hold the defendant responsible for it. We already examined that concept in connection with intentional torts in Chapter 4. We can now add a few more points.

---

[34] *Athey v Leonati* (1996) 140 DLR (4th) 235 (SCC).

[35] "Joint" liability means that all of the defendants are liable for the same tort. "Several" liability means each defendant is individually liable to the plaintiff for the entire amount. "Joint and several" liability therefore means that while all of the defendants are liable for the tort, the plaintiff is entitled to decide which of the defendants she will collect from.

[36] *Cook v Lewis* [1952] 1 DLR 1 (SCC).

In negligence, the basic issue is whether the *type of harm* that the plaintiff suffered was a *reasonably foreseeable* result of the defendant's carelessness. As always, the phrase "reasonably foreseeable" does not mean "probable" or "likely." It simply refers to a possibility that is not far-fetched. Furthermore, if the *type of harm* that the plaintiff suffered was reasonably foreseeable, it is irrelevant that the *manner in which it occurred* was not. To understand that distinction, consider Case Brief 6.4.

CASE BRIEF 6.4

Hughes v Lord Advocate [1963] AC 837 (HL)

The defendant's employees had been working in a manhole. They left the cover off the manhole when they went for lunch. They also left a paraffin lamp nearby. A young boy crawled down the manhole with the lamp. He was badly burned when the lamp fell and exploded.

The explosion occurred because vapours escaped from the lamp and were ignited by the flame. The court held that

that series of events was entirely unforeseeable. It nevertheless imposed liability because the *type* of injury that the plaintiff suffered, a burn, was reasonably foreseeable. It did not matter that the source of that burn was a bizarre accident rather than direct contact with the lamp's flame, as might have been expected.

The remoteness principle is used to resolve *thin skull* cases. **A thin skull** case occurs if the plaintiff was unusually vulnerable to injury. In a literal example, suppose that I am injury-prone because my skull is very thin. If you carelessly hit me on the head with a stick, are you responsible for all of my losses? What if a normal person would not have suffered any injury? What if a normal person would have suffered a minor injury, but not one as serious as mine? The law tries to strike a balance between its desire to compensate me and its desire to treat you fairly. You are *not* responsible at all if a normal person would not have suffered *any* harm. But you are fully responsible for *all* of my losses if it was *reasonably foreseeable* that a normal person would have suffered *some* damage.[37] For instance, if your carelessness would have bruised a normal person, I can fully recover for the fact that I also suffered brain damage.[38]

a thin skull case occurs if the plaintiff was unusually vulnerable to injury

Significantly for business people, the courts traditionally refused to apply a *thin wallet* principle. In other words, the defendant was not responsible for the fact that the plaintiff suffered to an unusual extent because the victim was poor. More recently, however, the courts have begun to suggest that the defendant may be fully liable if it was reasonably foreseeable that the plaintiff's poverty would cause it to suffer more than usual.[39] Business Decision 6.2 explores those issues.

[37.] The same principles could apply, for example, if I drive a type of vehicle that is unusually vulnerable to damage in an accident: *Oke v Weide Transport Ltd* (1963) 41 DLR (2d) 53 (Man CA).

[38.] While the thin skull doctrine may hold the defendant fully liable for the plaintiff's injury, damages are reduced if the plaintiff's skull was not only thin but also *crumbling*. In other words, the plaintiff is denied compensation to the extent that his condition was so fragile that he eventually would have suffered the same injury, even without the defendant's carelessness. In that situation, the defendant merely caused the plaintiff's injury to happen sooner than expected. Damages are therefore available only for the period leading up to the time when the plaintiff would have suffered the loss in any event.

[39.] *Alcoa Minerals of Jamaica v Broderick* [2000] 3 WLR 23 (PC). A leading Canadian textbook nevertheless still supports the rule on the basis that "a thin pocket book is less worthy of protection than a thin skull": A Linden *Canadian Tort Law* 7th ed (2001) 349.

Remoteness and Thin Wallets[40]

You had a contract with Acme Goods Ltd to carry several loads of timber between Vancouver and Halifax. Unfortunately, Darva carelessly caused an accident that destroyed your truck. You therefore needed to use another vehicle to fulfill your agreement with Acme. The purchase price for a replacement was $100 000, but you were unable to buy one because you did not have immediate access to that much money and because your credit rating is very poor. Consequently, you were forced to lease a truck. You were able to afford that option because you could periodically meet the rental charge after being paid for each delivery of timber. That option, however, eventually cost you $150 000, which is $50 000 more than the purchase price of a truck.

Assuming that Darva is liable in negligence, you are entitled to compensation for your loss. However, you might recover only $100 000, rather than $150 000. Even though the loss of your truck was reasonably foreseeable, a court might say that Darva is not responsible for the fact that you suffered to an unusual extent because of your own financial problems.

Questions for Discussion

1. Would it be fair if the court rejected the thin wallet principle in your case? Explain your answer.

2. The courts historically accepted the thin skull principle but rejected the thin wallet principle. What does that contrast say about the law's attitude toward personal injuries on the one hand and economic losses on the other? Which sort of harm is considered more important?

---

an intervening act is an event that occurs *after* the defendant's carelessness and that causes the plaintiff to suffer an additional injury

The remoteness principle is also used to deal with *intervening acts*. An **intervening act** is an event that occurs *after* the defendant's carelessness and that causes the plaintiff to suffer an additional injury. Suppose that you carelessly broke my leg. A week later, I suffered a broken arm, either because I fell while walking down stairs on crutches or because I was hit by lightning in my physician's parking lot. In either event, you are *factually responsible* for my broken arm. But for your initial negligence, I would not have been using crutches, nor would I have been visiting my physician. The crucial question, however, is whether you are *legally responsible* or whether, in light of the intervening act, my broken arm is too *remote*. A judge would ask if it was reasonably foreseeable that your initial carelessness would result in my later injury. As usual, that test may be flexible enough to allow a judge to decide my case on policy grounds. As a general rule, liability will be imposed if your original negligence increased the risk of my subsequent injury. I was more likely to fall while using crutches, but being hit by lightning is a freak accident in any event.

DEFENCES

The plaintiff is usually entitled to compensatory damages once the court is satisfied that there was (i) a duty of care, (ii) a breach of the standard of care, and (iii) a causation of harm. Occasionally, however, the defendant can avoid liability, at least in part, by proving a defence. We will briefly consider the three most important defences:

- contributory negligence
- voluntary assumption of risk
- illegality

---

40. *The Dredger Liesbosch v SS Edison* [1933] AC 449 (HL).

Contributory Negligence

The most important defence is *contributory negligence*. **Contributory negligence** occurs when a loss is caused partly by the defendant's carelessness and partly by the plaintiff's own carelessness. In deciding whether the plaintiff is guilty of contributory negligence, the courts generally use the same factors that they use when deciding whether the defendant breached the standard of care: foreseeability of harm, likelihood of injury, severity of harm, and so on. The cases tend to fall into three groups. Contributory negligence can arise if the plaintiff:

- unreasonably steps into a dangerous situation (as when a sober person accepts a ride from drunk, who then drives into a wall)
- unreasonably contributes to the creation of an accident (as when a passenger in the back of an open bed truck is thrown to the ground while carelessly standing up at the same time that the driver turns a corner too quickly)
- unreasonably contributes not to the creation of an accident, but to the damage that it causes (as when a passenger in a carelessly driven car suffers unusually severe head injuries after refusing to wear a seatbelt)

the defence of **contributory negligence** occurs when a loss is caused partly by the defendant's carelessness and partly by the plaintiff's own carelessness

Contributory negligence was traditionally a complete defence. If it applied, the plaintiff could not recover *any* damages. That rule was often unfair. The plaintiff could be denied compensation even though the defendant was mostly responsible for causing the injury. Consequently, modern legislation allows for *apportionment*.[41] A court can assign responsibility for the plaintiff's loss between the parties and award damages accordingly. Suppose that you broke your wrist and suffered $10 000 in damages after falling over a package that I carelessly dropped onto the sidewalk. The evidence indicates that you were 25 percent responsible because you did not watch where you were going. A judge could reduce your damages by 25 percent and require me to only pay $7500.

Although judges can apportion the blame between the parties in whatever way is appropriate, they usually place contributory negligence at less than 30 percent. A court is normally reluctant to further reduce the amount of compensation that is available to the plaintiff, especially since the defendant often has liability insurance.

Voluntary Assumption of Risk

The defence of **voluntary assumption of risk** applies if the plaintiff freely agreed to be exposed to a risk of injury. Unlike contributory negligence, *volenti*, as it is sometimes called, remains a complete defence. If it applies, the plaintiff cannot recover *any* damages. The courts therefore interpret it very narrowly. The defendant has to prove that the plaintiff expressly or implicitly agreed to be exposed to both the physical *and* the legal risk of injury. The last part of that test is not satisfied unless the plaintiff agreed to give up the right to sue the defendant for negligence. Consequently, that defence rarely succeeds.[42]

the defence of **voluntary assumption of risk** applies if the plaintiff freely agreed to be exposed to a risk of injury

---

[41.] *Contributory Negligence Act*, RSA 2000, c C-27 (Alta); *Negligence Act*, RSBC 1996, c 333 (BC); *Tortfeasors and Contributory Negligence Act*, CCSM, c T90 (Man); *Contributory Negligence Act*, RSNL 1990, c C-33 (Nfld); *Contributory Negligence Act*, RSNB 1973, c C-19 (NB); *Contributory Negligence Act*, RSNS 1989, c 95 (NS); *Contributory Negligence Act*, RSNWT 1988, c C-18 (NWT and Nun); *Negligence Act*, RSO 1990, c N.1 (Ont); *Contributory Negligence Act*, RSPEI 1988, c C-21 (PEI); *Contributory Negligence Act*, RSS 1978, c C-31 (Sask); *Contributory Negligence Act*, RSY 2002, c 42 (Yuk).

[42.] *Dubé v Labor* (1986) 27 DLR (4th) 653 (SCC).

Although it is quite narrow, the defence may be an important tool for risk management. The best way of proving the voluntary assumption of risk is to show that the plaintiff signed an *exclusion clause*. We will examine exclusion clauses in more detail in Chapter 9. The most important point for now is that they must be drawn to a customer's attention. Case Brief 6.5 demonstrates that fact.

CASE BRIEF 6.5

Crocker v Sundance Northwest Resorts Ltd (1988) 51 DLR (4th) 321 (SCC)

The defendant organized an event in which contestants raced down a snow-covered mountain on inner tubes. Before being allowed to compete, the plaintiff was presented with a form that released the defendant from liability for negligence. Although the plaintiff signed that document, he had not read it, nor had it been explained to him. He was later injured after being thrown from his tube during the race. He sued the defendant on the basis that it carelessly allowed him to compete even though he was obviously very drunk. The defendant responded by pleading the *volenti* defence.

The Supreme Court of Canada held that the plaintiff had not voluntarily assumed the risk of injury.

[T]he waiver provision in the entry form was not drawn to the plaintiff's attention . . . he had not read it, and, indeed, did not know of its existence. He thought he was simply signing an entry form. In these circumstances [the defendant] cannot rely upon the waiver clause in the entry form.

The Court did, however, reduce the plaintiff's damages by 25 percent to reflect his own contributory negligence.

Illegality

A court may refuse to award damages if the plaintiff suffered a loss while participating in an *illegal act*. Like voluntary assumption of risk, however, illegality is unpopular with the courts because it is a complete defence. It does not allow for the apportionment of liability. The courts have therefore interpreted it very narrowly. Case Brief 6.6 considers the leading case.

CASE BRIEF 6.6

Hall v Hebert (1993) 101 DLR (4th) 129 (SCC)

The plaintiff and the defendant went out for a night of drinking and driving. The defendant stalled his car and allowed the plaintiff to try to start it. The plaintiff lost control of the vehicle, drove it off a steep embankment, and suffered serious injuries. He claimed that the defendant was negligent in allowing him to drive while drunk. In response, the defendant argued that the plaintiff was injured while he was engaged in the illegal act of drunk driving.

While reducing the plaintiff's damages by 50 percent to reflect his own contributory negligence, the Supreme Court of

Canada rejected the defence of illegality. It held that that defence applies only when the plaintiff attempts to use the tort system in a way that would undermine the integrity of the law. And that occurs only if the plaintiff tries to either profit from his illegal act or avoid a criminal penalty. The defence does not apply if, as in *Hall v Hebert*, the plaintiff merely seeks compensation for the injuries that were caused by the defendant's negligence.

Chapter Summary

Negligence is the most important tort. It requires proof of three elements: (i) a duty of care, (ii) a breach of the standard of care, and (iii) the causation of harm.

A duty of care requires the defendant to use reasonable care to avoid injuring the plaintiff. A duty will be imposed if (i) it was reasonably foreseeable that the defendant's carelessness might hurt the plaintiff, (ii) there was proximity between the parties, and (iii) there are no compelling policy reasons for refusing to impose a duty.

The defendant cannot be held liable unless it breached the standard of care, which is based on the reasonable person test. A court must ask whether the defendant acted as a reasonable person would have acted in similar circumstances. That test is flexible and allows the courts to consider all of the circumstances of a case. Judges use special considerations in applying the standard of care in a case of professional negligence or product liability.

The defendant cannot be held liable unless its carelessness caused the plaintiff to suffer a loss. Causation is usually decided by the but-for test. Causation normally has to be established on a balance of probabilities, but once it is, the courts generally adopt an all-or-nothing approach to the issue of liability. The plaintiff merely has to prove that the defendant's carelessness was *a* cause of a loss. If two or more defendants combine to inflict a single injury on the plaintiff, they may be held jointly and severally liable. Even if the defendant caused the plaintiff to suffer a loss, liability will not be imposed if that loss was too remote from the breach of the standard of care. The remoteness principle is used to resolve cases involving thin skulls and intervening acts.

Even if the plaintiff proves duty, breach, and causation, the court may limit or deny liability if the defendant establishes a defence. Damages may be reduced if the plaintiff was guilty of contributory negligence. Damages may be denied entirely if the plaintiff either voluntarily assumed the risk of injury or was engaged in an illegal activity at the time of the accident. The last two defences, however, are interpreted very narrowly by the courts.

Review Questions

1. Although tort law is generally concerned with striking a balance between the desire to provide compensation and the desire to protect socially useful activities from liability, that issue is particularly important in the context of the tort of negligence. Why?

2. How does the element of reasonable foreseeability ensure that potential defendants are treated fairly? In the business context, how does it affect risk management?

3. How will a court decide whether or not a duty of care will exist in a particular case?

4. List the ways in which negligent actions are different from negligent statements.

5. When will a court recognize a duty of care for a negligent statement?

6. Do the courts rely upon an objective test or a subjective test when they apply the standard of care? Provide one explanation for your answer.

7. Summarize the factors that a judge considers in deciding whether the defendant breached the standard of care.

8. Will a court find that professionals breached the standard of care if they complied with an approved practice? Explain your answer.

9. "Causation is determined on a balance of probabilities in an all-or-nothing manner." What does that statement mean?

10. Explain the concept of joint and several liability. How does it arise in the context of the issue of causation?

11. Is the but-for test always applied to resolve the issue of causation? Illustrate your answer with an example.

12. "The judge in a negligence action must be satisfied that the defendant's breach was the primary cause of the plaintiff's injury or loss." Explain whether that statement is correct.

13. What is the basic test for resolving the issue of remoteness? Must the plaintiff prove that a reasonable person would have foreseen both the type of harm that occurred *and* the manner in which it occurred?

14. Describe the thin skull and thin wallet concepts. Are those concepts applied in Canadian law?

15. When will an intervening act cause a court to find that the plaintiff's loss is too remote?

16. What is the main reason why Canadian courts prefer the defence of contributory negligence to the defences of voluntary assumption of risk and illegality?

17. Outline three situations in which the defence of contributory negligence can arise.

18. What factors will a judge consider in deciding whether a plaintiff was guilty of contributory negligence?

19. Outline the steps a business should take to ensure that it will be protected by the defence of voluntary assumption of risk.

20. In general terms, when will the defence of illegality succeed?

CASES AND PROBLEMS

1. Maya, who was seven months pregnant, was involved in a snowmobiling accident with Escobar. Although he came away unscathed, his snowmobile suffered light damage. However, while Maya's snowmobile was unmarked, she suffered moderate injuries as a result of the collision. Two months later, Maya delivered Juan, who was born with a mental disability. The medical evidence suggests that Juan's condition was caused by the accident. Discuss the various actions that might be brought between the parties. What if the accident was caused by Maya's carelessness? What if it was caused by Escobar's carelessness? Your answers should focus on the issue of duty of care.

2. John Brokaw was interested in purchasing an apartment building. He was, however, very concerned about the price. Since he did not trust the revenue figures that the vendor had provided, he hired Lonnie Hauser, a property value appraiser. Brokaw explained in great detail that he needed to know, as precisely as possible, how much the apartments would generate in rent. Hauser's final report indicated that the building was worth $1 400 000. Brokaw accepted that information and purchased the property at that price. He soon discovered, however, that the building was actually worth considerably less. The tenants were all on social assistance. The basic rent that the government was willing to pay was set at $325 per month, and each apartment contained two tenants. Hauser therefore had simply assumed that each apartment would produce $650 per month. In fact, however, whenever the two tenants were related, then the government set the rent at $520 per month. A number of apartments were occupied by married couples. As a result, the actual value of the property was $1 000 000. Hauser nevertheless says that he should not be held responsible because he had reasonably assumed that the same rent would apply to every apartment. Will Brokaw be successful if he sues Hauser in negligence? Explain your answer.

3. The Blacksox Baseball Club, a professional baseball team, plays its home games at Dotcom Park, which it built 15 years ago in a predominantly residential area. Initially, the close proximity of the ballpark to neighbouring houses caused no problem, primarily because home runs were never hit out of the stadium. Recently, however, that situation has changed due to the combination of increasingly poor pitching and rampant steroid use amongst batters. The Blacksox and their opposition now hit an average of three home runs per game. Furthermore, a home run clears the stadium walls and enters a neighbouring yard about once every three games. One of those long balls, hit by a Blacksox player, recently cracked Abner's skull as he sat reading a book in his backyard. As a result of that injury, he has sustained losses of about $250 000. The Blacksox organization has admitted that it owed a duty of care to Abner, but insists that neither it nor its player breached the standard of care. Do you agree? What factors are important in resolving that issue?

4. Renata owns an importing business. She sought legal advice regarding the possibility of obtaining government approval to enter into a particular contract to purchase widgets from a company in Peru. Because her regular lawyer, a specialist in trade law, was away on vacation, she brought her file to Franz, whom she found in the telephone book. Although Renata did not know it, Franz was not really a lawyer. While he had attended two years of law school, he never graduated and he never passed the bar exam. Furthermore, although he is a distinguished-looking 50-year-old, he only recently began to hold himself out as a lawyer. Franz prepared the necessary documents but, because he failed to read the governing statute carefully, he did not instruct Renata to place her corporate seal on them. Renata's application was consequently rejected by the government, and she lost the $75 000 profit that she expected to earn under her contract with the Peruvian company. She has sued Franz, claiming that her loss was caused by his professional negligence. He has responded by arguing that since he was not really a lawyer, he was not really a professional and therefore could not be held to a professional standard of care. He also has argued that even if he can be treated as a professional, he never claimed to have special expertise in the area of trade law and therefore should not be expected to fulfill the standard that would be applied to Renata's regular lawyer. Will either of those arguments succeed?

5. In February 1983, Pia entered the hospital for a simple operation. During that procedure, she received a blood transfusion. Although the operation was entirely successful, Pia was diagnosed with HIV several years later. The blood she had received had come from Everett, a carrier of HIV. He had donated that blood to the Canadian Red Cross Society (CRCS) at a blood donor clinic in January 1982. When it became well known that HIV can be transmitted through blood, the CRCS started using a detailed questionnaire to prevent people in high-risk groups from making donations. Because of his lifestyle, Everett would have fallen into one of those groups. At the time of donation in January 1982, however, there was very little medical information available about HIV, and there was no reasonable basis for believing that it could be spread through blood transfusions. The CRCS therefore did not take any steps to screen out potentially harmful donors. Pia sued Everett and the CRCS in negligence shortly after learning that she was infected. Sadly, both Pia and Everett have since died of AIDS. Pia's widower has nevertheless continued the lawsuit against the CRCS. He claimed that the CRCS was careless in allowing a person of Everett's lifestyle to donate blood. Would that claim succeed? Explain your answer.

6. Arthur Fairchild contracted mesothelioma, an incurable and fatal disease, as a result of inhaling an asbestos fibre. He had been repeatedly exposed to asbestos fibres while working for five different employers over a period of thirty years. Each employer had breached the standard of care by failing to prevent the inhalation of asbestos fibres. Significantly, however, the medical evidence indicates that the disease was caused by the inhalation of a *single* fibre. Fairchild was not at all hurt by the countless *other* fibres that he inhaled. The evidence also indicates that it is impossible to determine precisely *which* fibre caused the disease or *when* it was inhaled. Mesothelioma may lie dormant for many decades after a harmful fibre has taken effect. Fairchild therefore cannot prove on a balance of probabilities that his condition was caused by the carelessness of one of the five employers. Does that mean that Fairchild will not be entitled to any compensation under the tort of negligence?

7. For many years, the Funch Gum Company sold a product that it called "aspargum," a low-calorie gum made from asparagus and other ingredients. Although aspargum never enjoyed great success in the market, it did prove very popular with a small number of people. Clint was one such person. He chewed aspargum almost daily for nearly two decades. Several years ago, however, aspargum was taken off the market when it was discovered to cause several forms of cancer, including mouth cancer. Clint was recently diagnosed with mouth cancer and has sued Funch. Funch admits that it owed a duty of care to Clint, and that it had carelessly sold a product that it should have known was carcinogenic. It insists, however, that Clint's cancer was not caused by the aspargum but by the cigarettes, which he smoked over the same period. In fact, the evidence indicates that there is a 60 percent chance that the cancer was caused by the aspargum and a 40 percent chance that it was caused by smoking. Assuming that Clint's damages are valued at $1 000 000, how much should he actually receive? Should Funch's liability be reduced to $600 000 to reflect the possibility that the cancer was caused by cigarettes? Explain your answer.

8. Generus Inc is a manufacturer of no-frills products. Until recently, it sold "loobster," an imitation of lobster meat made primarily out of fish entrails. Christian suffered a permanently paralyzing infection after eating a package of loobster. As a result, he no longer is able to work as one of the world's leading heart surgeons and consequently will lose $2 000 000 per year in income over the next 30 years. Generus has admitted (i) that it owed a duty of care to Christian, and (ii) that it had carelessly allowed fish entrails to sit for several days in the hot sun before tossing them into the batch of loobster that produced the package that Christian bought. However, it insists that it should not be liable for all of Christian's losses. It argues that loobster is aimed at the very low end of the market and that it was entirely unforeseeable that someone with Christian's wealth would buy such cheap food. Will Generus' argument succeed? Explain your answer.

9. Claire brought her truck to Darius's garage for repairs. In the course of the job, Darius carelessly punctured the gas tank. Fuel leaked onto the floor of his garage and was ignited when he carelessly threw a cigarette butt away. When he noticed the small blaze, he was in the process of carrying a heavy piece of equipment over to the truck. He instructed Claire, who was waiting for her vehicle, to use a nearby fire extinguisher. Unfortunately, she panicked. Instead of grabbing the fire extinguisher, she tried to douse the small, but rapidly growing, flame by throwing snow on it. Her effort was unsuccessful and within a short time, her entire truck was destroyed. Darius has admitted liability, but he insists that Claire was contributorily negligent and should shoulder part of the blame for the damage. Is he correct? Explain your answer.

10. Alcoa Vending Inc operates a fleet of hot-dog stands. Those stands allow Alcoa's employees to cook and sell hot dogs and other meals from portable carts. Although most of the carts are moved from time to time to attract the largest number of customers, one stand has been in almost continuous operation for several years on the sidewalk outside of a hockey arena. Broderick owns a house across the street from the arena. The evidence indicates that the fumes from Alcoa's hot-dog cart have corroded the paint on his house and the shingles on his roof. When he first noticed that damage four years ago, he obtained an expert opinion that suggested that the damage would cost $20 000 to repair. Broderick did not have enough money to undertake those repairs, but he did sue Alcoa immediately. The trial date for that action has finally arrived. However, due to general inflation and sharp increase in the cost of appropriate roofing shingles, it would now cost $90 000 to properly repair Broderick's house. Assuming that Broderick can establish a cause of action in negligence against Alcoa, will he be entitled to receive $20 000 or $90 000? Explain your answer.

11. Miranda, a 17-year-old student from Moose Jaw, was a thrill seeker. She had always wanted to try bungee jumping. Consequently, while vacationing in Vancouver with friends, she built up her courage by drinking six shots of vodka and went to a theme park operated by X-Treme Adventures Inc. When she arrived, she was asked to pay a fee of $20 and to sign a contract that contained the following clause.

> I am over eighteen (18) years of age and I have read this form in its entirety. I understand that bungee jumping is a dangerous sport and I am aware that by participating in this activity, I may suffer some form of physical injury.

Miranda signed the contract. As she was about to make her jump, an employee of X-Treme Adventures instructed her to hold her arms straight out to her sides while she was falling. In the excitement of the event, however, Miranda ignored that advice. Furthermore, due to the employee's carelessness, the bungee cord was a bit too long. As a result, Miranda fell too far, hit her head on a rock, and suffered a spinal injury that has left her paralyzed from the waist down. She has sued X-Treme Adventures. In response, the defendant has argued:

(i) Miranda's damages should be reduced on the ground that she was contributorily negligent because (a) she failed to hold her arms out as instructed, (b) she lied about her age, and (c) she attempted the jump while under the influence of alcohol; and

(ii) Miranda's claim should fail entirely because she had voluntarily assumed the risk of injury by signing the contract.

Will either of those defences succeed? Explain your answer.

12. Jake was stopped in his car at a red light. A pair of teenagers unexpectedly ran up to the vehicle and smashed the windshield with a baseball bat. Jake put his car into park and leapt out to chase the teenagers. Unfortunately, he did not catch them. Worse yet, upon returning to the traffic light, he found that his car had been stolen. A few minutes later, several blocks away, the thief rammed Jake's vehicle into Mysty's truck. The teenagers and the thief have never been identified. Mysty has therefore sued Jake. She claims that if Jake had not left his keys in the ignition while he chased the vandals, the thief would not have been in a position to steal his car and crash into her truck. Jake admits that he should have taken the keys with him, but m denies that he committed the tort of negligence. Who is right? Explain your answer.

WEBLINKS

General

Duhaime Law: Negligence—An Introduction www. duhaime.org/Tort/ca-negl.aspx

This website provides a general overview of the tort of negligence, as well as a brief discussion of the standard of care.

Duhaime Law: Causation www.duhaime.org/Tort/ca-caus.aspx

This website looks at the issue of causation within the tort of negligence.

Economica Ltd www.economica.ca/ew33p1.htm

This website considers the tort of negligence from an economic perspective.

ADDITIONAL RESOURCES FOR CHAPTER 6 ON THE COMPANION WEBSITE

(www.pearsoned.ca/mcinnes)

In addition to self-test multiple-choice, true-false, and short essay questions (all with immediate feedback), three additional Cases and Problems (with suggested answers), and links to useful Web destinations, the Companion Website provides the following resources for Chapter 6:

Provincial Material

- **British Columbia:** Good Samaritans, Contributory Negligence, Parental Liability

- **Alberta:** Contributory Negligence, Professional Liability, *Emergency Medical Aid Act*, Social Hosts

- **Manitoba and Saskatchewan:** Vicarious Liability of Employees, Parental Responsibility, Tobacco Litigation, Contributory Negligence

- **Ontario:** Causation, Code of Conduct, Conflict of Interest, Contributory Negligence, Disclaimer, Duty of Care, Fiduciary Duty, Lawyers, Multi-disciplinary Partnerships, Parental Responsibility, Professional Discipline, Professional Organizations, Reverse Onus

CANADIAN CASE STUDY FOR PART 2

McTort: Fast Foods and Tort Law

In many ways, Janice Foster is a typical 18-year-old Canadian. Like many people her age, she enjoys eating fast foods, especially at McDonald's restaurants. The problem is that she eats there too often. In an average week, she will eat ten meals at McDonald's—some for breakfast, some for lunch, most for dinner.

Perhaps not surprisingly, Janice shares one other trait with many Canadians: She is obese. She weighs 110 kilograms, more than twice the recommended weight for a person of her age and height. She has already been diagnosed with a number of weight-related health problems. She suffers from high blood pressure and diabetes, and her back and knees constantly ache under the strain of the additional weight. Aside from her physical ailments, Janice feels shunned by her classmates and she frequently becomes depressed. Her physician has warned her that if she does not get her weight under control, the situation will become far worse.

Janice has always known, at least in a general sense, that fast foods are not healthy. She believes, however, that she has no practical options. She lives with her family in a small apartment in a rundown section of town. Although the apartment has a kitchen, it is cramped and poorly ventilated. Furthermore, because Janice's parents both work two jobs, home-cooked meals are rare. Janice therefore eats out a lot. She prefers McDonald's because the portions are large (especially when the meals are "super-sized"), the food is tasty, and the prices are relatively inexpensive compared with prices at other restaurants.

Obesity is a problem for Janice, but it is also a problem for society. By some estimates, one-third of all Canadians are dangerously overweight and the problem is getting worse. Alarmingly, childhood obesity has tripled in the past twenty years. The societal costs are staggering. The health care system annually directs more than $2 billion to the issue of obesity. The economy loses billions of dollars more in lost productivity as people with weight-related health problems are unable to work. And worst of all, obesity is the second leading preventable cause of death—trailing only cigarette smoking.

One solution to the problem may be tort law. Twenty years ago, peopled scoffed when lawyers in the U.S. began to sue tobacco companies. As discussed in Ethical Perspective 5.2, however, tobacco litigation has become big business in the United States. In recent years, tobacco companies have been held liable for billions of dollars in compensation. And many of the same lawyers who have sued the tobacco industry are now setting their sights on fast food restaurants like McDonald's. Following the U.S. model, Canadian courts have begun to hear claims against cigarette companies. They may soon be open to claims against fast-food chains as well.

Janice Foster certainly hopes so. She has sued McDonald's. She claims that a steady diet of fast food has made her obese. She also says that, until her lawyer showed her the evidence, she had no idea that fast foods were so dangerous. In one U.S. case, the judge described Chicken McNuggets as a "McFrankenstein" creation of fats, chemicals, and additives. The same judge also found that although Chicken McNuggets are often believed to be a healthier option than hamburgers (because they are based on chicken rather than beef), they actually contain twice as much fat as the alternative.[43]

McDonald's says that Janice's lawsuit is ridiculous. It claims that there is nothing wrong with its meals. It suggests that Janice's weight problems are due to her genetic makeup and her complete lack of exercise. And finally, it insists that consumers have to accept responsibility for their own actions. After all, everyone knows that hamburgers, French fries, and milkshakes are "junk food."

Questions to Consider

1. Which tort will best serve Janice Foster's goal of holding McDonald's liable for her obesity? Precisely what will Janice have to prove in order to win her lawsuit? Are there any defences that might allow McDonald's to avoid liability even if Janice establishes all of the elements of her claim?

2. The primary goal of a tort action is to provide monetary compensation for the plaintiff's losses. Looking beyond Janice Foster, however, how might society as a whole benefit if McDonald's were held liable for the costs of health problems that result from their fast foods?

3. Obesity has been called a "Canadian health epidemic." Who should pay for that epidemic? Is it realistic to expect individual consumers to bear responsibility for their own decisions? How can Janice Foster possibly pay for her weight-related problems? Alternatively, is it fair to expect Canadian taxpayers to pay for the costs that are inevitably associated with fast foods? Or should those costs be forced back onto the companies that earn billions of dollars in profits by selling junk food?

Video Resource: "Food Lawsuits: Sue the Bastards" *Venture* 908, 1 January 2004.

Additional Resources

McDonald's Canada www.mcdonalds.ca/en/index.aspx
This website includes pages devoted to the nutritional value of McDonald's meals.

---

43. *Pelman v McDonald's Restaurants (Pelman No 2)* 2003 US Dist Lexis 15202 (SD NY 2003).

John Banzhaf—Using Legal Action to Help Fight Obesity
http://banzhaf.net/obesitylinks.html

This website belongs to John Banzhaf, the lawyer who appears in the video and who is at the forefront of fast-food litigation.

Pelman v McDonald's Restaurants **http://news.findlaw.com/cnn/docs/mcdonalds/plmnmcd12203opn.pdf**

http://caselaw.lp.findlaw.com/data2/circs/2nd/039010p.pdf

The first document is a judgment from a New York court. Although the judge dismissed the plaintiff's claim against McDonald's Restaurants, many lawyers believe that the judge was also inviting other litigants, with better claims and stronger evidence, to sue fast-food restaurants again in the future. The second document is a decision of the Second Circuit Court of Appeal that overturned part of the trial decision and allowed the plaintiff to go ahead with part of the claim.

The Observer **http://observer.guardian.co.uk/print/0,3858,4770168-108294,00.html**

This website contains an article that discusses lawsuits that have been launched in the United States by people claiming that McDonald's is responsible for their obesity.

Canadian Medical Association Journal—The Skinny on Obesity in Canada **www.cmaj.ca/misc/obesity/index.shtml**

This website contains information about obesity—and the costs of obesity—in Canada.

7 The Nature and Creation of Contracts

CHAPTER OVERVIEW

OBJECTIVES

After completing this chapter, you should be able to:

1. Identify three essential elements of most contracts.

2. Outline the situations in which people generally do or do not have an intention to create legal relations.

3. Distinguish between an offer and an invitation to treat.

4. Explain five ways by which an offer may cease to exist.

5. Explain the effect of a firm offer.

6. Outline the role of offer and acceptance in the tendering process.

7. Explain how the courts resolve a battle of the forms.

8. Distinguish between bilateral contracts and unilateral contracts, and explain the difference between acceptance by promise and acceptance by performance.

9. Explain whether an offer can ever be accepted by conduct or by silence.

10. Describe the postal rule and explain when it will apply.

Most people are unaware of the vast number of contracts they enter into every day. Consider your acquisition of this textbook. You may have found it, borrowed it, or received it as a gift; but most likely you bought it. Try to recall that transaction. At that time, did you know that you were creating a contract? Did you realize that your conduct generated a number of legal rights and obligations?

You may have had a choice in how you purchased this book. You probably bought it from your university or college bookstore, but you also may have bought it directly from the publisher via telephone, fax, or the Internet. Or you may have acquired a used copy from a former student. In any event, you probably paid with cash, a credit card, or a debit card. Those, however, were not the only possibilities. For example, if you bought this book from a former student, you may have acquired it in exchange for a set of computer disks. Or if you were industrious, you may have convinced the owner of a bookstore to give you a copy in exchange for your promise to work a weekend at the store.

Whichever option you used, you presumably became party to a **contract**. You and the other person entered into an agreement that created rights and obligations that can be enforced in law. You were able to enter into that agreement, in part, because you both experienced a **meeting of the minds**. You shared a mutual agreement to enter into an enforceable transaction on a particular basis.[1] And the most obvious feature of that contract is that it involved a mutual **exchange of value**. You both gave up something as part of the deal.[2] You provided, say, cash in return for the book, while the other person provided the book in return for cash.

It is important to realize that a contractual relationship can continue even after there has been an exchange of value. Indeed, one reason for entering into a contract may be to reserve some rights and obligations for the future. Therefore, the choices you made when entering into the transaction can be important.

For example, if you paid with a promise to work in the bookstore, you limited your options for the future. You will have to spend your weekend stocking shelves. Or consider what would happen if your book becomes unglued during the semester, and pages fall out. If you bought this book "as is" from a used book seller, you might not have any remedy. The situation would be different, however, if you purchased it from a bookseller who offered a "satisfaction or money back" guarantee. You would enjoy the right to a refund.[3] Having already given the guarantee, the bookseller no longer has a choice about returning your purchase price. The law of contract would require them to do so. As an aside, consider why some booksellers are willing to give such guarantees. While they presumably value freedom of choice as much as you do, they also recognize that guarantees generate goodwill and increase the price that customers are willing to pay. By limiting their choices in the future, booksellers hope to attract more business.

Fortunately, textbooks seldom come unglued. That fact raises an important point about the operation of contracts. Because the book that you bought almost certainly is of satisfactory quality, the seller's guarantee will probably never be enforced. As with most contracts, many rights and duties lie quietly beneath the surface while the future unfolds as the parties expected. In that sense, contract law represents the pathology of commerce. Legal issues usually arise only if a commercial relationship becomes unhealthy.

a **contract** is an agreement that creates rights and obligations that can be enforced in law

a **meeting of the minds** is a mutual agreement to enter into a legal transaction on a particular basis

an **exchange of value** occurs when the parties each give up something

---

[1] Lawyers sometimes refer to this as *consensus ad idem*, or "agreement on that previously mentioned."

[2] Lawyers sometimes refer to this as *quid pro quo*, or "something for something."

[3] As we will see in Chapter 13, the law imposes a number of obligations on a person who sells goods (such as books) even if the parties' contract does not expressly do so.

However, it would be dangerous to assume that business people do not really need to know about the law. It is true that most contracts are performed without problems. But it is also true that many of the problems that do arise stem from the parties' failure to carefully consider the legal implications of their actions. Bear this in mind as you read the chapters on contract. Most of the cases that you will encounter are unusual precisely because they went to court. People need the help of a judge only when something has gone terribly wrong. By knowing your rights and obligations, you can almost always avoid that situation.

Of course, when something does go wrong, it may be preferable from a business perspective to avoid the court system. We discussed that proposition in Chapter 2. While a clear understanding of your legal rights and obligations allows you to litigate more effectively, it may be better to resolve a dispute informally. Legal proceedings tend to signal the end of a relationship. The long-term benefits of retaining a healthy commercial relationship are often more important than winning a particular dispute.

So far, we have been discussing the creation of contracts in very general terms. As we will see, however, every contract actually requires a number of distinct steps or elements. Three are especially important:

1. The parties must have an *intention to create legal relations*.
2. They must reach a mutual agreement through the process of *offer* and *acceptance*.
3. They must enter into a bargain by each giving *consideration*.

We will discuss the first two elements in this chapter and the third in Chapter 8. As you may have noticed, our list does *not* include the *writing* of a contract. In fact, most contracts do not have to be written in order to be enforceable. In Chapter 10, we will discuss some exceptions to that rule. At the same time, we will also consider other factors that may render a contract ineffective, such as *illegality* and *lack of capacity*.

COMPARING TORTS AND CONTRACTS

Before turning to a detailed examination of the creation of contracts, it is important to consider one more introductory issue: the difference between torts and contracts. We previously addressed that issue in Chapter 1 and again in Chapter 3. You should take a moment to review that material, especially Concept Summary 3.2.

INTENTION TO CREATE LEGAL RELATIONS

A contract will not arise without an **intention to create legal relations**. The parties must have intended to create a legally enforceable agreement. To decide that issue, a court asks whether a "reasonable person" would have believed that the parties intended to enter into a contract.[4] Note that that test is *objective* rather than *subjective*. The judge is concerned with what a reasonable person would have thought, not necessarily with what the parties themselves actually

an intention to create legal relations arises if a reasonable person would believe that the parties intended to create a legally enforceable agreement

---

[4.] The concept of a "reasonable person" is discussed in detail in Chapter 6.

thought. There are two reasons for that rule. First, a test of subjective intentions would be difficult to apply because a person could easily lie at trial. Second, an important goal of the law of contracts is to protect reasonable expectations. If you and I enter into an apparent contract for the sale of certain components, I will reasonably expect to receive those components even if, during the sale negotiations, you secretly planned to keep them for yourself. Furthermore, on the basis of my reasonable expectation, I may have arranged to resell the components to someone else, who may have arranged to sell them to yet another person, and so on. The business world could not function smoothly unless people were entitled to rely on outward appearances.

The presence or absence of an intention to create legal relations is usually obvious. A reasonable person simply ignores unrealistic and exaggerated proposals. For instance, a lecturer's sarcastic promise to pay $5000 for a correct response in class cannot be taken at face value. To further simplify matters, the courts usually presume that an intention to create legal relations exists in a commercial context, but not between friends or family members.[5] However, those presumptions can be *rebutted*, or disproved. For example, a business person may be able to convince a judge that while a commercial agreement was contained in a formal document, it *was not* really intended to be legally binding.[6] Likewise, a son may be able to persuade a judge that while his mother's promise to pay his tuition at business school was given within a family setting, it really *was* intended to create contractual obligations.[7] The most difficult cases arise when social relations and commercial transactions mix. How would you decide the case in You Be the Judge 7.1?

YOU BE THE JUDGE 7.1

Fobasco Ltd v Cogan (1990) 72 OR (2d) 254 (HCJ)

When major league baseball came to Toronto in 1976, Eddie Cogan bought eight season's tickets in a prime location—field level, behind first base. At that time, he agreed to sell four of his tickets to Fobasco Ltd, a company owned by his friend and business associate, David Fingold. David, in turn, gave the tickets away to Fobasco Ltd's prospective customers to drum up business. Although that arrangement lasted for many years, Eddie decided in 1986, around the same time that the Blue Jays became contenders and shortly before they moved into SkyDome, that he would prefer to sit next to his own sons rather than Fobasco Ltd's clients. He told his old friend that their arrangement was at an end. David was upset because he could not otherwise get good seats to the games. He therefore sued for breach of contract, claiming that Eddie had contractually agreed to sell tickets to Fobasco Ltd on an annual basis.

Questions for Discussion

1. Would a reasonable person believe that the parties had entered into contractual relations? Or did they merely have a social arrangement?

2. While contracts generally do not need to be written to be effective, do you believe that the lack of writing in this case is significant? What if the parties, as businessmen, normally put all of their contracts into writing?

3. If you believe that a contract should be recognized, should Eddie be required to make tickets available to Fobasco Ltd forever?

[5.] *Balfour v Balfour* [1919] 2 KB 571 (CA).

[6.] *Rose & Frank Co v JR Crompton & Rose Ltd* [1923] 2 KB 261 (CA).

[7.] *Jones v Padavatton* [1969] 2 All ER 616 (CA).

OFFER

The Nature of an Offer

The parties must have more than an intention to create legal relations. They must also enter into a mutual agreement through the process of offer and acceptance. An **offer** is an indication of a willingness to enter into a contract on certain terms. The party who offers to enter into a contract is called the **offeror**. The party who is entitled to accept or reject the offer is called an **offeree**.

Great care must be taken in making offers because a contract comes into existence as soon as an offer is accepted. At that point, both parties become obligated to fulfill the promises contained in the agreement. And once a contract comes into existence, neither party acting alone can alter its contents or bring it to an end.

Consider the dangers that can arise from making an offer. Suppose that you sent a message to your class website offering to sell your cars. If 10 people simultaneously show up at your door wanting to buy a vehicle, are you contractually obliged to honour 10 contracts even though you have only two cars to sell? The courts recognize that it would be impractical if every proposal could be classified as an offer that is capable of being transformed into a contract. Therefore, judges have developed guidelines for deciding which types of statements qualify as offers. They have also placed limits on how long offers will last.

> an **offer** is an indication of a willingness to enter into a contract on certain terms
>
> an **offeror** is a party who is offering to enter into a contract
>
> an **offeree** is a party who is entitled to accept or reject an offer to enter into a contract

Invitation to Treat

The courts classify some statements not as offers but rather as *invitations to treat*. An **invitation to treat** is not an offer—it is an indication of a willingness to receive an offer. In other words, it is an invitation for *others* to make offers. In such circumstances, a person who responds to the invitation is an offeror, and the person who initially presented the invitation is the offeree.

The distinction between an offer and an invitation to treat depends on an objective test. A court will ask how a reasonable person would interpret a particular statement in the circumstances. Would a reasonable person believe that the person making the statement was prepared to enter into to a contract as soon as he or she received an acceptance? Or would it be more reasonable to believe that the person making the statement was simply prepared to receive and consider offers?

Those questions are often difficult to answer. Fortunately, the courts tend to apply certain presumptions. Most significantly, they usually say that the display of an item on a store shelf, even if it carries a price tag, is an invitation to treat.[8] Similarly, a statement placed in a newspaper advertisement or catalogue is usually not an offer. There is a very good reason for those presumptions. Recall our example in which 10 people see your advertisement and they each want to buy a car. If your ad is classified as an offer, you might be held liable to fulfill 10 contracts, even though you have only two cars to sell. However, if your ad is classified as an invitation to treat, each response is an offer, which you are free to accept or reject. The presumptions regarding advertisements and displays generally protect business people from overexposing themselves. There are, however, exceptions to those presumptions. An advertisement may be considered an

> an **invitation to treat** is an indication of a willingness to receive an offer

---

[8.] *Pharmaceutical Society of Great Britain v Boots Cash Chemists (Southern) Ltd* [1953] 1 QB 401 (CA).

offer if a reasonable person would read it that way. That may be true, for example, if it expressly indicates that a limited number of items are available while supplies last. Your ad therefore might be an offer if it said, "Cars for sale. $10 000 each. First come. First served." In that situation, you would not be in danger of being bound to an unmanageable number of contracts.[9]

Communication of an Offer

A statement is not an offer unless it is communicated and received *as* an offer. The issue is not as simple as it might appear. Suppose the directors of a company decide during a meeting to offer a $10 000 bonus to a long-serving secretary in exchange for her early retirement. The directors ask the secretary to type the handwritten notes of their meeting. In doing so, she learns of the proposed bonus, completes the task at hand, and promptly tenders her resignation. She is probably not entitled to the bonus payment. The minutes of the meeting were communicated to her, not as a contractual offer, but rather as a typing assignment. In those circumstances, the reasonable person would not believe that the directors intended to be bound by their communication.[10]

However, as long as a proposition is communicated and received as an offer, it usually does not have to take any particular form.[11] It may be contained in a written document. For example, if you buy a television from a department store on credit, you will probably be asked to complete a lengthy application that contains countless terms and conditions. That is your offer to the store. Alternatively, an offer may be made verbally. For example, if you go to a restaurant and say, "A cheeseburger and a milkshake, please," you are offering to enter into a contract for the purchase of a meal. An offer may even be inferred from conduct alone. For example, if you enter a barber shop, sit silently in the chair, and get a trim, you have offered, and the barber has accepted, a contract to cut your hair.[12]

The Life of an Offer

An offer does not last forever. If it is accepted, it gives way to a contract. And if it is not accepted, it may cease to exist in a variety of ways:

- revocation
- lapse of time
- death or insanity
- rejection
- counter offer

[9.] Business people occasionally try to take advantage of that rule by advertising items they do not have to sell in the hopes of attracting customers who can be persuaded, once they are in the store, to buy other items. In most jurisdictions, such practices, known as "bait and switch," are prohibited by statute: *Competition Act*, RSC 1985, c C-34, s 52 (Can); *Fair Trading Act*, RSA 2000, c F-2, s 9 (Alta); *Trade Practice Act*, RSBC 1996, c 457, s 2 (BC); *Trade Practices Inquiry Act*, CCSM, c T110, s 2 (Man); *Trade Practices Act*, RSN 1990, c T-7, s 5 (Nfld); *Consumer Services Act*, RSNS 1989, c 94, s 6(1)(c) (NS); *Business Practices Act*, RSO 1990, c B.18, s 2 (Ont); *Business Practices Act*, RSPEI 1988, c B-7, s 2 (PEI); *Competition Protection Act*, RSQ, c P-40.1, ss 224–225 (Que); *Consumer and Commercial Affairs Act*, RSS 1988, c C-29.2, s 8 (Sask).

[10.] *Blair v Western Mutual Benefit Association* [1972] 4 WWR 284 (BC CA).

[11.] In Chapter 10, we will discuss situations in which a contract must be written to be enforceable.

[12.] If the parties to a contract do not stipulate a price, the courts may require the purchaser to pay a reasonable price. Lawyers sometimes refer to that as *quantum meruit* ("as much as it is worth").

Revocation

Revocation occurs if the party who made an offer withdraws it. The offeror is the master of the offer and is generally entitled to revoke it at any time.[13] As a matter of risk management, however, there is some need for caution. Revocation is not effective unless it is reasonably communicated to the offeree. Until that occurs, the offer remains open, and the offeree can create a contract through acceptance.

revocation occurs if the offeror withdraws an offer

Firm Offers Although the basic rules regarding revocation are quite simple, two types of situations call for special attention. The first involves a **firm offer,** which occurs when the offeror promises to hold an offer open for acceptance for a certain period. Do not be misled by the terminology. A firm offer is not very firm at all. As a general rule, the offeror can revoke it at any time. The reason, as Ethical Perspective 7.1 shows, turns on the fact that a firm offer is not contained in a contract and therefore is not enforceable in law. Nevertheless, as you read that case, consider how you, as a business person, would act in such

a firm offer occurs when the offeror promises to hold an offer open for acceptance for a certain period

---

ETHICAL PERSPECTIVE 7.1

Dickinson v Dodds (1876) 2 Ch D 463 (CA)

George Dickinson was one of several people interested in buying a piece of land from John Dodds. On Wednesday, John wrote to George, offering to sell the property and promising to hold that offer open until Friday morning. While George was considering his options on Thursday, he learned that John was negotiating with another potential buyer. George immediately tried to find John to accept the offer. Although George failed to locate John that night, he did manage to leave a letter of acceptance with John's mother-in-law. Moreover, he caught up with John the next morning and expressed his desire to buy the property. By that time, however, George had learned from a third party that the land had already been sold to someone else. George sued John for failing to fulfill his promise to keep the offer open.

The lawsuit failed. The court held that John's promise was unenforceable because it was entirely *gratuitous*. He had not received anything of value in exchange for his promise to hold his offer open until Friday.

Questions for Discussion

1. Do you approve of John's behaviour? What do you think of the fact that the law allowed him to break his promise? Is the legal rule pertaining to firm offers morally acceptable?

2. Although firm offers are revocable, most successful business people honour such promises. What reasons might motivate them to do so?

---

circumstances.

Despite the general rule, a firm offer *cannot* be revoked if the offeror's promise was placed under *seal* or if the offeree paid for the right to accept within a certain period.[14] For example, if you think that you might want to buy a particular piece of land in the future, but are not prepared to commit yourself to that transaction just yet, you might try to purchase an *option* from the owner. An **option** is a contract in which the offeror receives something of value in exchange for a binding promise to hold an offer open for acceptance for a specific period. That option would accomplish two things. First, it would allow you

an option is a contract in which the offeror receives something of value in exchange for a binding promise to hold an offer open for acceptance for a specific period

---

[13] Generally, an offeror can communicate revocation in the same way that it communicated the offer. For instance, if the offer appeared in a newspaper advertisement, the revocation can appear there as well.

[14] We discuss seals in Chapter 8.

and the offeror, at some point in the future, to create a contract for the sale of land. Second, it would immediately create an entirely separate contract requiring the offeror to wait while you decided whether to buy the land. As you might expect, one must take special care in granting options. Consider the situation in Business Decision 7.1.

BUSINESS DECISION 7.1

The Granting of Options

ABC Corporation is investigating the possibility of developing a shopping mall in a certain neighbourhood. To do so, it will need to buy your land. It will also need to obtain zoning approval for its proposal. Although you have offered to sell your property for $100 000, ABC Corporation does not want to incur any obligations to you unless its zoning application is allowed. However, it also knows that other companies may offer to buy your land to develop their own projects. It therefore wants to buy an option which will require you to hold your offer open for 90 days.

Questions for Discussion

1. Will you grant the option? If so, on what terms?

2. How does the existence of other prospective buyers affect your decision?

3. How will your expectations about the future market value of your land affect your decision?

---

a tender is an offer to undertake a project on particular terms

Tenders The second special situation involving the revocation of offers is more complicated. It is also very important in the business world. Suppose that a city wants a new library built. It will probably call for *tenders*. A **tender** is an offer to undertake a project on particular terms. In calling for tenders, the city issues an invitation to treat and promises to award the project to the company that submits the best offer. If the general rule applied, each bidder would be entitled to withdraw its offer any time before acceptance. The city, however, needs some assurance that that will not happen. It needs to know that the offers will remain open while it considers them. Otherwise, the process would not work—at least not very well.

To avoid that problem, a court will probably find that the bidding process immediately creates a special contract between the city and each company that submits an offer.[15] Thus, the city's call for tenders serves two purposes.

1. It constitutes an offer to enter into a special contract, called "Contract A," to hold a fair tendering process in exchange for the submission of an irrevocable bid.

2. It also constitutes an invitation to treat to receive offers to enter into a contract, called "Contract B," for the construction of the library.

A company's tender also serves two purposes.

1. It constitutes acceptance of the city's offer to enter into a fair and irrevocable tendering process under Contract A.

2. It also constitutes an offer to enter into a contract for the construction of the library under Contract B.

[15.] *R v Ron Engineering & Construction (Eastern) Ltd* (1981) 119 DLR (3d) 267 (SCC).

There will be many Contract As—one for each company that submits a tender to the city, but only one Contract B—between the city and the company that submits the winning tender. Concept Summary 7.1 illustrates this view of the tendering process.

CONCEPT SUMMARY 7.1

The Tendering Process

Stages	Contract A (Contract to Enter Process)	Contract B (Contract to Build Library)
Call for Tender by City to Company	offer by city to hold a fair tendering process	invitation to treat issued by city
Submission of Tender by Company to City	acceptance by company of offer	offer by company to build library
Award of Project by City to Company		acceptance by city of offer

Lapse of Time

An offeror is entitled to limit the lifespan of an offer, possibly by stating that acceptance must occur by a specific date. That is almost always true with an option. But even if no time period is stated, an offer is only open for a "reasonable period." In deciding what constitutes a reasonable period, a court will look at many factors, including the subject matter of the proposed contract, the nature of the agreement, the volatility of the market, and the usual practice in the industry. An offer to sell farmland in a financially depressed region may be open for many weeks; an offer to sell shares in a wildly fluctuating market may be open for mere hours.

Death or Insanity

It is often said that an offer is automatically revoked if either the offeror or the offeree dies. A dead person does not have the capacity to enter into a contract, and there cannot be a meeting of the minds if only one person is alive. An exception may apply, however, if the proposed contract does not call upon the affected party to perform personally. For example, that may be true if the offer pertains to the sale of land rather than the performance of a concert. In that situation, the offeree may communicate acceptance to the deceased offeror's estate, or the deceased offeree's estate may communicate acceptance to the offeror.[16] The same analysis generally holds true for insanity.

Rejection

Rejection occurs when the offeree refuses an offer. An offer is terminated once it is rejected. Suppose that Bruno offers to sell his business to Helga for $100 000. If she says, "No, thank you, I'm not interested," the offer is dead. And because it is dead, Helga cannot later accept it if she changes her mind and

rejection occurs when the offeree refuses an offer

---

16. In this context, "estate" refers to the person representing the interests of the deceased.

decides that she really would like to buy the business after all. Unless Bruno repeats his initial offer, Helga must make an offer to him and hope that he accepts it.

Counter Offer

a **counter offer** occurs when an offeree responds to an offer by indicating a willingness to enter into a contract but on different terms

A similar rule applies to *counter offers*. A **counter offer** occurs when an offeree responds to an offer by indicating a willingness to enter into a contract, but on different terms. A counter offer has the effect of rejecting an existing offer and creating a new one. Consequently, as Concept Summary 7.2 shows, a counter offer causes the parties to switch roles.

CONCEPT SUMMARY 7.2

Offer and Counter Offer

Event	Party A	Party B
Offer	Offeror ⟶	Offeree
Counter Offer	Offeree ⟵	Offeror

To create a contract, an offer must be *entirely* accepted. Any attempt to accept in modified terms constitutes a counter offer. Returning to our previous example, suppose that Helga responded to Bruno's offer by saying, "You've got yourself a deal, but I can pay only $50 000." Her statement is a counter offer. It kills Bruno's offer to sell for $100 000 and replaces it with her own offer to buy at $50 000. If Bruno rejects Helga's offer, she cannot revive his initial offer by saying, "Okay, I'll pay the full $100 000." If she wants the business, she must hope that Bruno repeats his original offer. He may do so expressly or implicitly by responding to her counter offer by saying something like, "No, I won't take less than $100 000."

Because the general rule regarding counter offers may be harsh, the courts sometimes characterize an offeree's statement as a harmless inquiry rather than a counter offer. Therefore, if Helga had said, "I'd love to buy your business, but I'm just wondering if you'd take $50 000 for it," she might be able to persuade a judge that even if Bruno had said "No," his original offer would still be open for acceptance.

a **battle of the forms** occurs when each party claims to have entered into a contract on the basis of its own standard form document

Judges also try to avoid the general rule regarding counter offers in cases involving a *battle of the forms*. A **battle of the forms** occurs when each party claims to have entered into a contract on the basis of its own standard form document. A business often prepares a complicated contractual form, containing many terms, which it will insist upon using for every transaction. This only makes sense, as it would be too difficult and expensive to constantly negotiate new contracts.[17] Problems arise, however, if both parties insist upon using their *own* forms and if those forms contain *different* terms. To decide which contractual form, if either, applies, a judge will consider several factors, including the usual practice in the industry, past dealings between the parties, the precise sequence of events, and the forms, if any, that the parties actually signed. Consider the example in Business Decision 7.2.

[17] Problems can also arise if only one party uses a standard form contract. Corporations often try to use such documents to force complicated and harsh terms on their customers. That problem is addressed in Chapter 9.

BUSINESS DECISION 7.2

Battle of the Forms

For years, Vendor Inc has been selling computer chips to you without any problems. During that time, it developed a standard form document, which it uses to offer its goods for sale. That document contains a clause that allows unsatisfactory goods to be returned for a refund within 7 days. You also developed a standard form document, which you use for accepting offers of sale. That document, however, contains a clause that allows unsatisfactory goods to be returned for a refund within 21 days. In fact, most businesses that buy and sell computer chips use a 21-day return period. You and Vendor purport to create a contract for the sale of 5000 computer chips. As always, you each use your own form and, as always, neither of you realizes that those forms have different terms. If, after 10 days, the chips are found to be defective and you want your money back, are you entitled to a refund?

Strictly speaking, because it did not exactly match the terms of Vendor's offer, your document seems to be a counter offer rather than an acceptance. And if there has been no offer and acceptance, there cannot be a contract. Nevertheless, since the agreement is *executed* (already performed) rather than *executory* (not yet performed), and since you both reasonably believed that a contract existed, a judge might be persuaded to find that a contract was created. For example, if Vendor signed and returned a copy of your document before shipping the computer chips, the judge might hold that Vendor agreed to the terms contained in your counter offer, especially since those terms reflect industry practice.[18] In some situations, however, it will simply not be possible to save the transaction, and you will be without a contractual remedy for the defective goods.[19]

Questions for Discussion

1. What does this example demonstrate about the need to carefully read every document that affects your business?

2. How can you avoid the sort of difficulties that arise in this case?

ACCEPTANCE

In discussing acceptance, it is important to distinguish two situations:

- acceptance by promise
- acceptance by performance

Acceptance by Promise

Many contracts are *bilateral*. A **bilateral contract** occurs when a promise is exchanged for a promise. The offer consists of the offeror's promise to do something; the acceptance consists of the offeree's promise to do something. Therefore, when the contract comes into existence, both parties have promises to fulfill. Suppose, for example, that you offer to sell your car for $7500. To accept your promise to transfer ownership of the vehicle, I promise to pay the price. As Figure 7.1 illustrates, we have a bilateral contract. That would be true whether we expected to complete the exchange immediately or next week.

a bilateral contract occurs when a promise is exchanged for a promise

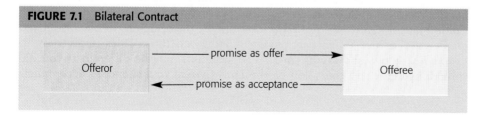

FIGURE 7.1 Bilateral Contract

Offeror — promise as offer → Offeree

Offeror ← promise as acceptance — Offeree

---

[18] *Butler Machine Tool Co v Ex-cell-O Corp* [1979] 1 All ER 695 (CA).

[19] In some situations, however, the court may rely on the cause of action in unjust enrichment if one party has conferred a benefit on the other party. That possibility is discussed in Chapter 12.

We can define the element of acceptance even more precisely. **Acceptance** occurs when an offeree agrees to enter into the contract proposed by the offeror. Acceptance generally has to be communicated to the offeror. It must be unequivocal and it must correspond precisely with the terms of the offer. If the offeree changes the terms, it does not create an acceptance but rather a counter offer, as we saw in the last section. An acceptance must also be a *response* to an offer. For that reason, no contract is formed if I send you a letter that says, "I will sell you my car for $5000," at the same time that you send me a letter that says, "I will buy your car for $5000." This situation is sometimes described as a "cross-offer"—each letter contains an offer and neither contains an acceptance. Therefore, there is no meeting of the minds.

Words

Acceptance usually occurs through written or spoken words. The offeror, as master of the offer, can dictate how those words must be communicated. It is possible to insist that acceptance be communicated to a particular location or provided in a particular form. For example, if an offeror states that "acceptance *must* be sent in writing to my office," a contract is not formed if acceptance is communicated orally or if it is sent to the offeror's home. Often, however, the offeror does not impose any restrictions, and the offeree can accept by any reasonable means. If so, it is usually best to avoid complications by responding in kind, for example, by providing written acceptance to a written offer. It may be possible, however, to use any equally effective method, for example, by responding to a faxed offer with a telephoned acceptance.

Conduct

In some circumstances, an offer may be accepted by conduct. Suppose that I offer $5000 in exchange for your promise to develop a software program for me. If you accept, you will probably say, "Yes," either orally or in writing. However, you might also nod agreeably and silently shake my hand. A reasonable person would likely interpret your conduct as acceptance.

Silence

While acceptance may occur without words if the offeree acts in a certain way, silence alone cannot be acceptance. That rule can be very important. An unscrupulous company may send goods to you along with a note that says, "Unless you inform us that you do not want to purchase these things, you will be charged for them." Generally speaking, you will not be required to pay, even if you completely ignore the offer.[20]

The courts developed that basic rule. Some jurisdictions also have statutes that discourage businesses from foisting goods on unsuspecting consumers. In Ontario, for example, the *Consumer Protection Act* allows recipients of unsolicited goods to use them without fear of being charged.[21] And in British Columbia, the *Consumer Protection Act* allows the recipient of an unsolicited credit card to use it without paying.[22] However, those rules apply only to *unsolicited* goods and credit cards. The situation may be different if you did something in the past that allows a company to treat your silence as acceptance.

---

[20] *Felthouse v Bindley* (1862) 142 ER 1037 (Ex Ch).

[21] *Consumer Protection Act*, RSO 1990, c C.31, s 36.

[22] *Consumer Protection Act*, RSBC 1996, c 69, s 47.

For example, by joining a book club, you may enter into a contract that requires you to pay for a monthly selection unless you return it within a specified time. In such circumstances, your acceptance of the book will consist of your silence *plus* your earlier promise to abide by your agreement with the company. The result may be the same if you regularly accept goods from a company and pay for them.

Acceptance at a Distance

Special problems can occur when people do not deal face to face. Practically speaking, contracts cannot always be created in person. Business people often deal with each other across vast distances. And even when they are neighbours, they may not have the time or inclination to arrange a meeting. Furthermore, individual consumers are increasingly entering into transactions and paying bills not only through the mail, but also over the telephone or by various electronic means, such as ATMs and the Internet.

Two issues arise when parties deal with each other at a distance. First, if the lines of communication break down, it is necessary to decide whether a contract was formed. Suppose that an insurance company, in exchange for a certain payment, offers to protect your business against the risk of property damage. As required by the offer, you mail your letter of acceptance and a cheque to the insurer. The letter is lost in the postal system and never arrives. If your property is later damaged by a flood, do you have insurance coverage? Is the insurer liable even though it never received your letter?

Second, even if the lines of communication work properly, it may be necessary to determine where and when a contract was formed. Returning to the previous example, suppose that your business is located in Alberta, but that the insurance company is located in Manitoba. Assume that the insurance company is required to pay a fee to the Government of Manitoba if a contract is formed there, but not if it is formed in Alberta. Where was your contract formed? Is the insurer liable for the fee?

The General Rule The law in this area is complicated, partly because the courts have not yet decided how to deal with many of the newer forms of technology, such as portable pagers and the Internet. The courts have, however, used a pair of basic rules for many years. First, the **general rule** states that acceptance by *instantaneous communication* is effective when and where it is received by the offeror. That rule was initially formulated at a time when people typically conducted business face to face. There was **instantaneous communication** because the parties' interactions involved little or no delay. Courts today hold that many modern forms of communication, including the telephone and the fax machine,[23] are also instantaneous.[24]

We can illustrate the general rule governing instantaneous communications with our previous example. Suppose that while you are in Alberta, you telephone your insurer located in Manitoba and accept its offer of coverage. Your acceptance takes effect when and where it is received. Your contract is therefore formed in Manitoba when your insurer hears you say, "I accept." However, if your statement was inaudible because you happened to be driving through a tunnel while talking on your cell phone, a contract would not be formed. Acceptance is effective only when and where the offeror *actually* receives it.

the **general rule** states that acceptance by instantaneous communication is effective when and where it is received by the offeror

an **instantaneous communication** is any form of communication in which there is little or no delay in the interaction between the parties

---

[23.] *Rolling v Willann Investments Ltd* (1989) 63 DLR (4th) 760 (Ont CA).

[24.] The rule that applies to e-mail is discussed in Chapter 19.

a non-instantaneous communication is any form of communication that involves a substantial delay between the time that it leaves one person and reaches another

The Postal Rule

The general rule works well for instantaneous communications. It can cause problems, however, for *non-instantaneous communications*. A **non-instantaneous communication** is one that involves a substantial delay between the time that it leaves one person and reaches another, such as when a letter is mailed or a package is sent by courier.[25]

The courts refuse to rigidly classify communications as instantaneous or non-instantaneous. Even if a form of communication *appears* to be instantaneous, it may be considered non-instantaneous if, in the circumstances, it involves a substantial delay between transmission and receipt. For example, although a fax is usually received without delay, not every faxed communication is considered instantaneous. A judge would consider the parties' objective intentions, usual business practices, and the fairness of placing the risk on one person rather than the other. Therefore, if an offer states that "acceptance must be conveyed by means of instantaneous communication no later than Friday," you should not fax an acceptance letter at 11:59 pm on that day. If you know that the offeror's office always closes for the weekend at 5:00 pm, and that no one will be there to receive a late-night fax, your communication is not really instantaneous. It will not be effectively received until Monday morning. Given the circumstances, the acceptance would be late, and a contract would not be formed.

Consider why the courts draw a distinction between instantaneous and non-instantaneous communications. If a non-instantaneous acceptance was effective only when and where it was actually received, the offeree would be required to frequently check with the offeror in order to know whether a contract was formed. And until the receipt of the acceptance was confirmed, the offeree would be reluctant to perform the contract. Suppose I mail a letter from Saskatoon accepting your offer to pay me $5000 to deliver a series of lectures in Charlottetown. Unless I can be sure that we have a contract as soon as I put my letter in the mailbox, I will hesitate to book a flight, even if air fare will be much more expensive if I delay. I would be afraid that if I bought a ticket today, you might revoke your offer tomorrow before receiving my acceptance. If so, I would have a ticket to Charlottetown and no real reason to go there.

the postal rule states that an acceptance that is communicated in a non-instantaneous way is effective where and when the offeree sends it

For those reasons, the general rule does not apply to non-instantaneous forms of communication. Instead, according to the **postal rule**, an acceptance that is communicated in a non-instantaneous way is effective where and when the offeree sends it.[26] Continuing with our example, a contract is formed in Saskatoon as soon as I drop my acceptance letter into the mailbox, even though you will not receive that letter in Charlottetown for several days. Figure 7.2 (see p. 159) illustrates the general rule and the postal rule.

By holding that my acceptance takes effect as soon as I send it, rather than when you receive it, the postal rule prevents you from revoking your offer while my letter is in the postal system. After all, you cannot revoke an offer that I have already accepted. In fact, the postal rule may work against you in an even stranger way. As long as the judge believes that I actually sent the letter, a contract can be formed between us even if my letter is lost in the mail and never reaches you.

Notice that the postal rule imposes certain risks upon you as the offeror. Until you actually receive a clear acceptance or rejection from me, you cannot be sure if a contract has been created. There are, however, ways around the

---

[25] *Nova Scotia v Weymouth Sea Products Ltd* (1983) 149 DLR (3d) 637, affd 4 DLR (4th) 314 (NS CA).

[26] Of course, the postal rule will not apply if the offeree's letter was not capable of being delivered. That will be true, for instance, if the offeree used the wrong address or failed to place sufficient postage on the envelope.

FIGURE 7.2 General Rule and Postal Rule

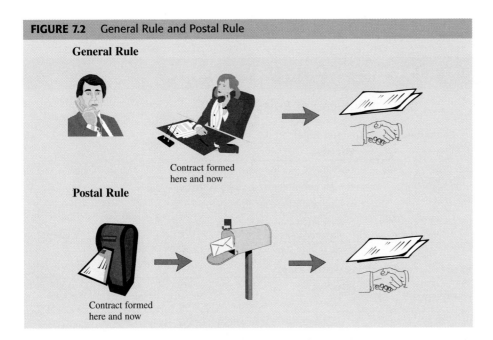

postal rule. First, you could carefully draft your business proposals to ensure that they are invitations to treat rather than offers. If so, any replies that you receive will be offers seeking your acceptance rather than acceptances of your offers. You remain in control of the process. Second, even if you make an offer and are willing to receive acceptance by mail, you are entitled, as master of the offer, to eliminate the postal rule. You could, for example, say that a letter of acceptance is effective only when and where you actually receive it. You would therefore not be bound by an acceptance letter that was lost in the mail. Third, even if you have not used your authority as master of the offer to limit the offeree's ability to accept an offer by mailing an acceptance, the postal rule will not apply where it would be unreasonable. For instance, a court might decide that in the particular circumstances of a case, no reasonable person would be willing, as an offeror, to be bound by a contract simply because the offeree dropped an acceptance letter into a mailbox.

We emphasize one more point about the postal rule. It applies only to acceptances. It does not apply to an offer, a revocation, a rejection, or a counter offer. An offer or a revocation is effective only when and where it is received by the offeree. And a rejection or counter offer is effective only when and where it is received by the offeror. Consider the situation in Business Decision 7.3.

BUSINESS DECISION 7.3

The Postal Rule

On June 1, Maria sent you a letter offering to sell her watch for $50. On June 3, she sent another letter that supposedly revoked her offer. On June 5, you received Maria's offer and immediately put an acceptance letter into a mailbox. On June 7, you received Maria's revocation letter. And on June 9, she received your acceptance letter.

Question for Discussion

1. Assuming that the usual rules apply, do you and Maria have a contract?

The rules in this area are somewhat complicated. Concept Summary 7.3 provides a review.

CONCEPT SUMMARY 7.3

Communication Rules

Rules Governing Instantaneous Communications (General Rule)

Type of Communication	Effective
• offer by offeror	• when and where received by offeree
• revocation by offeror	• when and where received by offeree
• rejection by offeree	• when and where received by offeror
• counter offer by offeree (who becomes the offeror)	• when and where received by initial offeror (who becomes the offeree)
• acceptance by offeree	• when and where received by offeror

Rules Governing Non-Instantaneous Communications (Postal Rule)

Type of Communication	Effective
• offer by offeror	• when and where received by offeree
• revocation by offeror	• when and where received by offeree
• rejection by offeree	• when and where received by offeror
• counter offer by offeree (who becomes the offeror)	• when and where received by initial offeror (who becomes the offeree)
• acceptance by offeree	• when and where sent by offeree

Acceptance by Performance

We have discussed bilateral contracts in which a promise is exchanged for a promise. One party offers to do something in the future, and the other party accepts by similarly promising to do something in the future. The rules are different for *unilateral contracts*. A **unilateral contract** occurs when an act is exchanged for a promise. In that situation, the offeror promises to pay a reward to anyone who performs a particular act. As Figure 7.3 illustrates, the offeree accepts by actually performing its part of the agreement. Note two things about unilateral contracts. First, no contract exists unless and until the offeree fully performs. Second, if the offeree performs and the contract is created, the offeror is the only one who has an outstanding obligation.

a unilateral contract occurs when an act is exchanged for a promise

FIGURE 7.3   Unilateral Contract

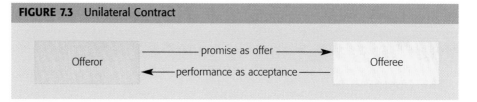

Offeror	——— promise as offer ———▶	Offeree
	◀——performance as acceptance———	

For example, suppose that I offer to pay $100 to anyone who finds and returns my lost cat. At that point, we do not have a contract, and you are not required to look for her. However, a contract may be created if and when you bring her home to me. If so, you will not be obligated to do anything more, but I will be expected to pay the reward. Note that we said that a unilateral contract *may* be created if you return my cat to me. That will be true only if you acted with the *intention of accepting* my offer. If you did not, we did not have a meeting of the minds, and there is no contract. Perhaps you had not seen my offer but returned my cat out of the goodness of your heart. Although your actions took the proper form for acceptance, they were not performed in *response* to my offer.[27] Therefore, you are not entitled to the reward.

Case Brief 7.1 provides a famous illustration of a unilateral contract.

CASE BRIEF 7.1

Carlill v Carbolic Smoke Ball Co [1893] 1 QB 256 (CA)

In the 1890s, England was plagued by two related phenomena: an influenza epidemic and quack medicine. The Carbolic Smoke Ball Co was one of many companies that tried to capitalize on the country's ill health. It produced a hand-held gadget which, when squeezed, emitted a small cloud of carbolic acid dust. The company claimed that if one inhaled the dust regularly, it would prevent a long list of ailments ranging from diphtheria and bronchitis to snoring and sore eyes. As part of its marketing ploy, it published an advertisement that offered to pay £100 to any person who contracted influenza while using the Carbolic Smoke Ball. Mrs Carlill saw the ad, bought the product, and used it as directed. When she later came down with the flu, she claimed to be entitled to £100. The company refused to pay. It said that there was no contract because she had not told them that she had accepted their offer and was using their product.

The Court, undoubtedly put off by the company's unsavoury practices, rejected that argument. It held that the contract was unilateral and that the company, as offeror, had implicitly dispensed with the usual need for the communication of acceptance. Consequently, Mrs Carlill, as offeree, effectively accepted the offer by using the product as directed. As a result, she was entitled to collect £100.

The courts generally prefer bilateral contracts over unilateral contracts.[28] Bilateral contracts provide more protection. Neither party has to worry about wasting time and expense. The offeree knows that if it performs, it will be entitled to the offeror's performance, and *vice versa*. In contrast, a unilateral contract might operate unfairly. Consider a twist on the facts of *Carbolic Smoke Ball*. The company said that it would pay £100 to anyone who caught the flu despite using the device three times a day for two weeks. What if Mrs Carlill had gone to the trouble and expense of buying and using the ball three times a day for 13 days, but just as she was about to complete the treatment, a company representative knocked on her door and said, "Sorry, the deal's off"? Acceptance of a unilateral offer is not effective until the stipulated act is completed, and, as we saw earlier, an offeror is generally free to revoke an offer any time before acceptance. Consequently, it might appear that Mrs Carlill could not collect the reward even if she became sick after continuing to use the smoke ball.

A court would struggle to avoid that result. It would want to give Mrs Carlill an opportunity to inhale the dust for one more day and claim the money if she became sick. Its approach to the problem might be quite complex. For example, a judge might hold that the company's notice actually contained offers for *two* unilateral contracts. The main contract would involve the company's promise to pay £100 to anyone who became sick despite using the smoke ball. The other contract would involve the company's promise to not revoke its offer once a customer began using the device.[29] Alternatively, the judge might simply say, as a matter of fairness, that the company was not entitled to revoke its offer while Mrs Carlill was in the process of accepting.[30]

27. *R v Clarke* (1927) 40 CLR 227 (HCA).

28. *Dawson v Helicopter Exploration Co* [1955] 5 DLR 404 (SCC).

29. *Errington v Errington* [1952] 1 KB 290 (CA).

30. *Ayerswood Development Corp v Hydro One Networks Inc* (2004) 39 CLR (3d) 288 (Ont SCJ).

Chapter Summary

A contract is an agreement that creates rights and obligations that can be enforced in law. The formation of a contract usually requires three things: an intention to create legal relations, a meeting of the minds, and an exchange of value. The first two requirements were discussed in this chapter; the third is considered in the next chapter.

The courts presume an intention to create legal relations in commercial contexts but not in family or social settings. However, these presumptions can be rebutted.

A meeting of the minds occurs through the process of offer and acceptance. Not every statement regarding a proposed transaction is an offer. The courts will not recognize a contract if a reasonable person would have interpreted the parties' communications as involving mere inquiries or invitations to treat.

Contractual offers must be communicated and received as offers. An offer may be made orally, in writing, or through conduct. The life of an offer is usually limited. To create a contract, acceptance must occur before the offer is terminated. An offer can be brought to an end through revocation, lapse of time, death or insanity, rejection, or counter offer. A counter offer creates a new offer in which the person who originally was the offeree becomes the offeror. The process of offer and acceptance requires special attention in the case of an option, a tender, or a battle of the forms.

A bilateral contract occurs when a promise is exchanged for a promise. Acceptance arises when an offeree agrees to enter into the contract proposed by the offeror. Acceptance usually occurs through words, but it may also occur through conduct. Mere silence generally cannot be acceptance, but silence may be sufficient if it is coupled with other factors. In any event, acceptance must be unequivocal and correspond precisely with the terms of the offer. Generally, it must be communicated to the offeror. With instantaneous forms of communication, acceptance is effective and a contract is formed when and where the communication is received by the offeror. The same is not true for non-instantaneous forms of communication, where acceptance occurs when and where it is sent, whether it is received or not. The general rule and the postal rule can be altered or eliminated by the offeror. The offeror, as master of the offer, can set special rules for acceptance.

A unilateral contract occurs when performance is exchanged for a promise. The offeree accepts by performing its part of the agreement. No contract exists unless and until the offeree performs. And if the offeree performs and the contract is created, the offeror is the only one who has an outstanding obligation. The courts generally prefer bilateral contracts over unilateral contracts.

Review Questions

1. What is meant by the term "meeting of the minds"? How is it significant to the formation of contracts?

2. What is meant by the term "exchange of value"? How is it significant to the formation of contracts?

3. What risks are associated with offers? Describe two techniques by which the courts reduce those risks.

4. Describe a principle that the courts often apply to commercial agreements but not to agreements between family members.

5. Why do the courts generally rely upon an objective test rather than a subjective test when deciding contractual issues?

6. In what sense is an offeror the "master of the offer"? What special powers does the master of the offer enjoy?

7. Distinguish between an offer and an invitation to treat. Give an example of each. How does the distinction help to promote commercial activity?

8. Briefly discuss the commercial and ethical implications of revoking a firm offer.

9. Explain how options operate. Why is an option enforceable, whereas a firm offer is not?

10. Describe how the tendering process works. Explain the two types of contracts that are involved.

11. Briefly discuss the factors that a court will consider to determine whether an offer has been open for a reasonable period of time. Why do you think these factors are important? Give an example of a situation where these factors come into play.

12. Explain when and why death or insanity will result in the termination of an offer.

13. What is the effect of rejecting an offer? Why do you think the rule is set up this way? If you change your mind after rejecting an offer, what can you do to revive the transaction?

14. What is a counter offer? What effect does a counter offer have on an offer?

15. Describe the problems that arise from a "battle of the forms."

16. What is the difference between a bilateral contract and a unilateral contract? How is each type of contract accepted?

17. Can an offer ever be accepted through the offeree's silence? Why or why not?

18. What is the difference between instantaneous and non-instantaneous forms of communication? How is that difference relevant to the formation of contracts?

19. What is the postal rule? Why have the courts created it? When does it apply?

20. Can an offer of a unilateral contract be revoked while the offeree is in the process of performing the stipulated act of acceptance? Why or why not?

CASES AND PROBLEMS

1. Susan and Hector, long-time friends, go to the races together. They each place a Sweep Six bet, which requires predicting the winning horse in each of six consecutive races. After the third race, Susan and Hector realize that they had both picked the first three winners, but they also realize that they had chosen different horses for the remaining races. Therefore, to maximize their individual chances of success, they each promise that, if they win, they will split the jackpot evenly with the other person. Hector's horse loses the next race, but Susan's wins. Susan's predictions for the fifth and sixth race also prove accurate, and the track awards her $500 000. Susan claims that she can avoid paying Hector because there had not been an intention to create legal relations. What arguments can you make for and against her claim?

2. On July 1st, Donna ran the following advertisement in a local newspaper:

   > **HAIR** removed safely and permanently
   > by **ELECTROLYSIS**. No Marks, No
   > Scars, Success Guaranteed. Contact
   > **DONNA SMITH**, 275 Huron Street. Call
   > 555-4212 for an appointment.

   Peter suffers from lycanthropism, a rare condition that results in a heavy growth of hair covering his entire body. He telephoned Donna on September 1st. His call was answered by a machine that quoted a price of $500 per treatment. He left a message indicating that he would be willing to pay that amount, and he made an appointment for October 1. When Peter arrived at Donna's premises on October 1, however, she refused to treat him. Having glanced at Peter, who was wearing only an undershirt and shorts, she explained that she could not possibly cure a condition as severe as his. In response, Peter pointed to the part of Donna's advertisement that "guaranteed" success. He also pointed to the case of *Carlill v Carbolic Smoke Ball*. Was Donna contractually obliged to remove Peter's unwanted hair?

3. The city of Darlington, which wants to build a new recreational centre, places an advertisement in a local newspaper requesting that contractors submit tenders. The newspaper advertisement states that tenders must be received by 4:00 pm on June 15 and that tenders are irrevocable after they have been received by the city. Ronaldo is among the contractors who submit tenders. At 4:15 on June 15, however, he realizes that he had miscalculated the expenses that would be involved in the project and that his bid consequently is grossly understated. He telephones the city and asks it to remove his tender from consideration. Even though the city has yet to select the winning tender, it rejects Ronaldo's request and informs him that it will select his bid if that bid offers to build the recreation centre for the lowest price. Explain whether Ronaldo will be able to revoke his bid.

4. Parktown Realty Inc developed an upscale condominium complex. On October 1, Miranda Wine signed an offer to purchase one of the units. Part of that document said, "This offer is irrevocable by the Purchaser until one minute before midnight on the fifteenth day after its date, after which time if not accepted, this offer shall be null and void." As both parties were aware, the real estate market was highly volatile at the time that Miranda signed her offer to purchase. In the preceding months, prices had gone up and down, quite unpredictably. On October 10, Parktown signed that document with the intention of accepting Miranda's offer. Because of an oversight, however, the company did not mail the signed document back to Miranda until October 14. Miranda eventually received the letter on October 20. By that time, the real estate market had collapsed and she was no longer interested in buying a condominium unit at the original price. She therefore insists that her offer lapsed before it had been turned into a contract by Parktown's acceptance. Is she correct?

5. Birinder was considering the purchase of a laptop computer, but he was not yet sure exactly what he needed. He visited Singh's Computer Shop and explained his situation to the saleswoman. She said that she would try to find something appropriate. The next day, she sent a laptop to Birinder's home, along with a note that said, "Take a look at this one. If it suits your needs, you can buy it. If not, just let us know and we'll come around to collect it. We have to insist, however, that you not use it until you've decided to purchase." After examining the unit, Birinder was impressed, but he decided that he would try to find the same model at a different shop for a lower price. He therefore telephoned Singh's and left a message on the answering machine: "Many thanks for the suggestion. I have, however, decided that I don't want the laptop that you sent over. You can come by to retrieve it." Immediately after hanging up, however, Birinder realized that he would need a computer to write a major assignment for his business law course. He therefore used the laptop that he had received from Singh's. Once that was done, he packed up the computer and returned it to the computer shop. The saleswoman seemed surprised to see him. "Didn't you get my message?" Birinder asked. "No," she said, "our answering machine broke. Why, don't you want the unit?" Birinder then explained the whole story, including his use of the computer. "Well, then," said the saleswoman, "it's too late. You've already bought yourself that computer." Is she right? Do the parties have a contract?

6. Ahmad owned Regent Arms, an apartment block in downtown Vancouver, which he wished to sell. He knew that Felicity, a real estate developer, was interested in such properties. Therefore, on Thursday, he faxed this offer to her: "I will sell Regent Arms to

you for $5 000 000. If you wish to accept this offer, please do so as soon as possible. I promise that I will not make a similar offer to anyone else while you are considering this proposal." Felicity was very interested in the offer but received it just as she was about to leave for a meeting in Medicine Hat. When she returned on the following Monday, she immediately faxed a letter purporting to accept Ahmad's offer. He replied that since he had not heard from her earlier, he had sold Regent Arms to another party on Saturday. Felicity now claims that because Ahmad had done nothing to communicate the revocation of his offer, his offer was still open for acceptance when she sent her fax to him. Is she correct? Has the offer lapsed or been revoked? Explain the arguments that Ahmad and Felicity might make if their dispute went to court.

7. On June 1, Elsa mails a letter to Ivan offering to buy a painting from him for $100 000. He receives that letter on June 8 and on the same day mails a letter rejecting her offer. The next day, however, he changes his mind and contacts her by telephone to accept her offer. By June 15, however, when Elsa receives Ivan's letter, she has decided that she no longer wants to go through with the deal. Applying the rules summarized in Concept Summary 7.3 to each step of these negotiations, determine if and when the parties formed a contract.

8. On October 15, Olaf mails a letter in Winnipeg offering to sell widgets to Simone. The next day, before Simone receives Olaf's offer, he sends another letter from Winnipeg revoking his offer. Simone receives Olaf's offer letter in Kelowna on October 21 and immediately sends a letter of acceptance. The next day, she receives Olaf's revocation letter in Kelowna. Applying the rules summarized in Concept Summary 7.3, determine if, when, and where the parties formed a contract.

9. Ten years ago, Edgar's daughter, Tina, married Hussein. Because the young couple could not afford to buy a house by themselves, Edgar placed a down payment of $90 000 on a home and told his daughter and son-in-law that they could live in the house and that if they paid monthly mortgage instalments of $1000 until the mortgage was satisfied, he would transfer the clear title into their name. Unfortunately, Tina and her parents recently had a falling out. Although Tina and Hussein have regularly paid the monthly mortgage instalments and wish to continue doing so until the mortgage is paid off (which they predict will occur in about seven years), Edgar has purportedly revoked his offer and stated that he intends to pay the remaining mortgage instalments and permanently live in the house himself. Did the parties act with an intention to create legal relations? Was the contract proposed by Edgar's initial offer a bilateral contract or a unilateral contract? Have Tina and Hussein fully accepted Edgar's offer? If not, can Edgar revoke his offer? If it was a unilateral contract, were Tina and Hussein obligated to pay the full mortgage once they began to make instalment payments?

10. Five years ago, Arvid and Dora were involved in an amorous relationship while they studied business together at college. Since that time, they have gone their separate ways and have moved to different cities, but they are still intimate on those rare occasions when their paths cross. Unfortunately, while Arvid's business has flourished, Dora's has foundered and she has fallen on hard times. Last month, Arvid wrote to Dora to offer her a job with his company. The relevant portion of his letter stated, "Given all that we have been through together and given the generous salary that I am offering, I just know that you'll accept. I'm considering the deal done and I'll begin setting up an office for you tomorrow." Arvid's letter did not mention that his offer was also motivated partly by a secret desire to rekindle their old romance into a permanent and stable relationship. When Dora received the letter, she decided to definitely take the job and began making arrangements to join Arvid's company. She did not, however, inform her old friend of that decision. She wanted to surprise him by simply appearing at his door the next week. However, three days later, her own company received an unexpected financial grant from the federal government. At that point, she reconsidered her earlier decision to work for Arvid and telephoned him to say that she would not be joining him after all. Because he had already spent a considerable amount of money preparing for Dora's arrival and because he was upset that she spurned his offer, Arvid reacted angrily. He insisted that a contract had been created and that she was his employee. Is he correct? Did Arvid act with an intention to create legal relations? Does it necessarily matter that both Arvid and Dora firmly believed that they had formed an enforceable agreement? Has there been valid acceptance?

11. Ekaterina owned a farm in a remote region of Saskatchewan, which she had been trying to sell for several years. In late November, Rasheed faxed her an offer to purchase the property for $50 000 and asked that she quickly reply by fax or telegram. Two weeks later, Ekaterina responded with a letter that stated that, by coincidence, another person had recently expressed interest in the farm and that, in the circumstances, she would sell for not less than $60 000. Her message stated that if that price was satisfactory, the deal "could be completed immediately," and suggested January 1 as a closing date. Ekaterina's letter also asked Rasheed to reply by telephone or e-mail to avoid delay. A week later, Ekaterina's letter was delivered to Rasheed's house. As he was abroad on business, his wife, Naima, opened it in his absence. Without Rasheed's authorization, Naima immediately sent a telegram to Ekaterina, stating that Rasheed would return in 10 days and asking that the offer be held open until that time. The telegram also indicated that Rasheed had earlier expressed interest in the property and stated that if he purchased the farm, he would not require the land until March, as it would not be possible to commence farming operations until the spring. Ekaterina did not reply to that telegram. Ten days

later, Rasheed returned from abroad and promptly e-mailed Ekaterina to accept her offer to sell the farm for $60 000. She replied that she had sold the property to a third party the previous day and that her offer consequently was no longer open. Rasheed believes that since his acceptance was communicated before he was informed of the sale to the third party, a contract was formed between himself and Ekaterina. Is he correct? Was Ekaterina's offer still open when Rasheed purported to accept it? What factors would a judge consider in deciding that issue?

12. Nostromo Corporation has its headquarters in Edmonton but operates throughout Canada. A branch office in Halifax sent a letter to Conrad, a prospective customer in Nova Scotia, offering to sell widgets. The offer stated, "Acceptance should be made by return mail." Conrad sent a fax to Nostromo Corp's head office in Edmonton purportedly accepting the offer. He then entered into a sub-

contract with a third party, under which he agreed to resell the widgets that he expected to receive from Nostromo Corp. Conrad was subsequently disappointed, however, when the company stated that it did not recognize his acceptance and refused to deliver the widgets to him. (As a result, he was forced to breach his contract with the third party.) Was a contract formed between Nostromo Corp and Conrad? Specifically, was Conrad entitled to accept by fax rather than by mail? Was he entitled to deliver his acceptance to the home office in Edmonton rather than the branch office in Halifax? How would a judge likely interpret the passage quoted from the company's offer? Was there any commercially compelling reason for the branch operation to insist upon acceptance by mail? Was there any commercially compelling reason for the branch operation to insist upon acceptance to the office in Halifax?

WEBLINKS

Duhaime Law: Contract Law   www.duhaime.org/contract
This page provides an overview of contract law and a comparison to tort law.

Duhaime Law: Offer & Acceptance   www.duhaime.org/contract/ca-con4.aspx#offer
This website reviews the general rules for offer and acceptance.

Deeth Williams Wall: Electronic Creation of Effective Contracts   www.dww.com/articles/online.htm
This website reviews the basic rules of contract creation and offers guidance on how to create effective contracts online.

The Business Link   www.cbsc.org/servlet/ContentServer?pagename=CBSC_AB/CBSC_WebPage/AB_WebPage_Template&cid=1104766632008&c=CBSC_WebPage
This website includes access (under the heading of "Legal Resources") to several types of sample contracts.

British Columbia Law Institute: Proposals for a Contract Law Reform Act   www.bcli.org/pages/projects/contractlaw/index2.html
This page proposes a new statute to deal with some of the problems that businesses occasionally encounter when trying to create or enforce a contract.

Ontario *Consumer Protection Act*   www.e-laws.gov.on.ca/DBLaws/Statutes/English/02c30_e.htm#BK14
This page contains Ontario's *Consumer Protection Act*. Section 13 of that statute protects consumers from unwanted goods by declaring that the receipt or use of unsolicited goods does not generally constitute acceptance of a contractual offer.

British Columbia *Consumer Protection Act*   www.qp.gov.bc.ca/statreg/stat/C/96069_01.htm#section47
This page contains British Columbia's *Consumer Protection Act*. Section 47 of that statute protects consumers from unwanted goods by declaring that the receipt or use of unsolicited goods does not generally constitute acceptance of a contractual offer.

ADDITIONAL RESOURCES FOR CHAPTER 7 ON THE COMPANION WEBSITE

(www.pearsoned.ca/mcinnes)

In addition to self-test multiple-choice, true-false, and short essay questions (all with immediate feedback), three additional Cases and Problems (with suggested answers), and links to useful Web destinations, the Companion Website provides the following resources for Chapter 7:

Provincial Material

- **British Columbia**: Government Procurement and Tenders, Cooling Off Period, Electronic Transactions
- **Alberta:** Exemption Clauses (Breach), Form of Contract, Consumer Protection Acts
- **Ontario:** Acceptance, Consumer Agreements, Cooling Off Periods, *Consumer Protection Act*, 2002, E-commerce Legislation, Exemption Clauses, Electronic Contracts, Standard Form Contracts, Terms Requiring Notice

8 Consideration and Privity

OBJECTIVES

After completing this chapter, you should be able to:

1. Explain the nature of consideration and the role it plays in the formation of contracts.

2. Describe past consideration and explain why it cannot support a contract.

3. Distinguish between (i) pre-existing public duties, (ii) pre-existing contractual obligations owed to a third party, and (iii) pre-existing contractual obligations owed to the same party.

4. Describe the nature and effect of a seal.

5. Define promissory estoppel and identify its four requirements.

6. Describe the concept of privity of contract and explain its relationship to the concept of consideration.

7. Distinguish between equitable assignments and statutory assignments and explain how assignments provide an exception to the privity of contract rule.

8. Explain how a trust can be used to create an apparent exception to the privity of contract rule.

9. Identify two types of statutes that provide exceptions to the privity of contract rule.

10. Explain when and why employees will be entitled to enforce exclusion clauses that are contained in contracts to which they are strangers.

In Chapter 7, we looked at some of the ingredients necessary to the formation of a contract: intention to create legal relations, offer, and acceptance. In this chapter, we examine another: *consideration*. As we will see, "consideration" refers to the thing that each party provides under a contract. This is critical—unless consideration exists on both sides of a bargain, the courts will usually not enforce the parties' agreement.

We will also examine the concept of *privity of contract*. Consideration, offer and acceptance, and intention to create contractual relations are required for the formation of a contract. "Privity of contract" refers to an individual's relationship to a contract. It identifies who can sue or be sued under an agreement.

CONSIDERATION

The main goal of contract law is to enforce bargains. And as business people know, a bargain involves more than an offer and an acceptance. It also involves a *mutual exchange of value*. Without that sort of exchange, a contract usually cannot exist. Suppose that I offer to give you a computer and you simply agree to receive it. I have made a **gratuitous promise**—I did not receive anything of legal value in exchange for it. I have promised to give you something, but you have not promised to do anything in return. Consequently, while you will be entitled to keep the computer if I actually give it to you, you cannot force me to hand it over to you in the first place. Because we did not have a bargain, we did not have a contract. And because we did not have a contract, I am entitled to change my mind.[1]

The creation of a contract therefore generally depends on an exchange of value. *Consideration* must be provided by both parties. While that term is notoriously difficult to define, we can generally say that **consideration** exists when a party either gives (or promises to give) a benefit to someone else *or* suffers (or promises to suffer) a detriment to itself.[2] Consideration must move *from* each side of a contract but not necessarily *to* the other side. For example, you and I will have a contract if I promise to give $5000 to your brother, and you promise to give a car to my sister. In that situation, it is enough that we have both promised to provide a benefit to *someone*; we did not have to promise to provide benefits to each other.[3]

Because the idea of consideration is so broad, it seldom causes problems. Difficulties do, however, occasionally arise. It is therefore important to examine the concept in some detail.

Sufficient and Adequate Consideration

A contract must be supported by *sufficient consideration*. That requirement is, however, easily met. **Sufficient consideration** may be almost anything of value. It is, for instance, sufficient if a person promises to give up smoking,

a gratuitous promise is a promise for which nothing of legal value is given in exchange

consideration exists when a party either gives (or promises to give) a benefit to someone else or suffers (or promises to suffer) a detriment to itself

sufficient consideration may be almost anything of value

[1.] An interesting application of that rule may occur if you promise to give money to a charity. Unless the charitable organization promised to do something in exchange for your promise, you are entitled to change your mind: *Dalhousie College v Boutilier Estate* [1934] 3 DLR 593 (SCC).

[2.] *Currie v Misa* (1875) LR 10 Ex 153 (HL).

[3.] As we will see, however, even though the contract is made for their benefit, your brother and my sister lack "privity of contract" and therefore may find it impossible to enforce our agreement.

drinking, or swearing.[4] There are nevertheless exceptions. "Love and affection" is not enough to support an enforceable agreement. Consequently, if an elderly gentleman promises to pay $10 000 to his wayward niece in exchange for her promise to "always be kind and caring," the parties will not have a contract. The reason for this rather surprising attitude is not entirely clear. It probably arises from the fact that during the nineteenth century, when many of the rules in law of contract were created, judges generally wanted to avoid becoming involved in intimate matters.[5]

Although consideration must be sufficient, it does not have to be *adequate*. **Adequate consideration** has essentially the same value as the consideration for which it is exchanged. For example, if I promise to give you a computer worth $5000, and you promise to give up smoking, drinking, and swearing for a year, it would seem that I have made a very bad bargain. In economic terms, I will be giving up far more than you will be providing in return. Nevertheless, we probably have a contract, and it is unlikely that a judge will save me from my own foolishness. Because the law presumes that people are able to look after their own interests, it generally allows them to decide what price they will demand under a contract.[6]

> adequate consideration has essentially the same value as the consideration for which it is exchanged

Forbearance to Sue

For business people, the difference between sufficient consideration and adequate consideration is particularly important in the context of *forbearance to sue*. **Forbearance to sue** is a promise not to pursue a lawsuit. Because lawsuits are expensive and unpredictable, very few are actually decided by judges. In the vast majority of cases, the parties settle their dispute out of court. They often enter into a contract for that purpose. The plaintiff promises not to bring the matter into court, and the defendant agrees to pay less money than it allegedly owed. If the plaintiff's action would have succeeded in court, there obviously is consideration on both sides of the contract. The plaintiff surrendered the right to claim full damages, and the defendant paid money.[7] But what if it is later discovered that the plaintiff would have lost the case if it had gone to court? In that situation, it might appear that the plaintiff did not give consideration. After all, it merely agreed not to pursue a lawsuit that it would have lost. Nevertheless, a judge would likely hold the parties to their agreement. As you read You Be the Judge 8.1 (see p. 170), consider the possible reasons for enforcing such contracts. Also consider the importance of receiving advice from a lawyer before agreeing to forbear on a possible action.

> forbearance to sue is a promise to not pursue a lawsuit

In some situations, the courts will not enforce forbearance agreements, especially if the party that threatened to sue did not honestly believe that it had a valid claim in the first place. Case Brief 8.1 (see p. 170) provides an interesting illustration.[8]

---

[4] *Hamer v Sidway* 27 NE 256 (1891 NY CA).

[5] Furthermore, as Chapter 7 explained, the courts generally assume that there is no intention to create legal relations between family members and close friends.

[6] However, as Chapter 10 will explain, when one party exercises an unfair advantage over the other, the courts may become concerned about the inadequacy of consideration. For example, if a con artist tricks a senior citizen into trading her home for his essentially worthless share certificates, a judge may strike down the parties' agreement because it is grossly unfair.

[7] The term "damages" refers to the money that the court may order the defendant to pay to the plaintiff. Chapter 12 discusses the damages that may be awarded for a breach of contract.

[8] See also *Moss v Chin* (1994) 120 DLR (4th) 406 (BC SC).

YOU BE THE JUDGE 8.1

Forbearance to Sue[9]

Igor works as a stockbroker for a company. Following procedures that he remembered reading in the company's official policy, he purchased $100 000 worth of shares on instructions from a client. Unfortunately, despite Igor's repeated demands, the client refused to pay for those shares. Worse yet, during that time, the value of the shares dropped by 60 percent. Eventually, the company took control of the account, sold the shares for $40 000, and threatened to sue Igor for $60 000. In the company's view, the whole fiasco was his fault. Igor vigorously denied liability, but he was worried that a lawsuit would damage his professional reputation. He was also unable to find the policy document that he had relied on. Consequently, he agreed to pay $50 000 in exchange for the company's promise to drop the matter. Two weeks later, however, before actually making the payment, Igor located the lost document. It proved that he could not be held liable in the circumstances.

Questions for Discussion

1. Can the company force Igor to pay the $50 000? Did he incur a contractual obligation to do so? Did the company provide consideration in exchange for his promise?

2. Even if the company did not actually have a valid claim against Igor, is it true to say that it gave nothing of value when it agreed to drop its lawsuit against him?

3. As a matter of policy, why are the courts eager to find the existence of a contract, even if the underlying claim is invalid? If they refused to do so, would it ever make sense for a party to forbear? Consider the general consequences that would follow from such an approach.

CASE BRIEF 8.1

DBC v Zellers Inc (1996) 138 DLR (4th) 309 (Man QB)

A teenager was caught allegedly stealing a number of items from a Zellers store. The store sent a letter to the boy's mother, threatening to exercise its "legal right to claim Civil Restitution" from her unless she paid $225. She promptly paid that amount, but later realized that while the store may have had a right to sue her son, it did not actually have any right to sue her. (As we discussed in Chapter 6, parents are not vicariously liable for their children. In other words, a parent cannot be sued simply because his or her child broke the law.) The woman therefore insisted that she was entitled to repayment of the $225. The store eventually agreed that it did not, in fact, have a right to sue the teenager's parent. It nevertheless argued that it was entitled to the money

because it had honestly thought otherwise when it received the payment.

The store would have been entitled to keep the money if it had truly believed that it was entitled to sue the boy's parent. In that situation, the parties would have had a binding contract. In exchange for the mother's payment of $225, the store would have given its forbearance to sue. The court held, however, that the lawyer who wrote the initial letter on behalf of the store could not have "seriously thought that this claim could succeed." Consequently, since the store had not given consideration, there was no contract. And since there was no contract, the woman was entitled to recover her money.

Past Consideration

Because the law views a contract as a bargain, consideration must be provided by both sides. There must also be **mutuality of consideration**. Each party must provide consideration *in return* for the other party's consideration.

The requirement of mutuality is important to the idea of *past consideration*. **Past consideration** consists of something that a party did *before* entering into a contract. In that situation, there is no mutuality. Past consideration is not

mutuality of consideration requires that each party provide consideration *in return* for the other party's consideration

past consideration consists of something that a party did *prior* to the contemplation of a contract

---

[9.] The facts are based on *Stott v Merit Investments Inc* (1988) 48 DLR (4th) 288 (Ont CA).

given *in exchange for* the other party's consideration. And for that reason, past consideration is not really consideration at all. It therefore cannot support a contract.

Sometimes it is difficult to determine whether something is past consideration. Consider two situations. In the first, you arrive home to find that a landscaping company has worked on your lawn. Although you had not asked the company to do so, you are delighted with the result. You therefore promise to pay $250. You are not legally obligated to keep that promise. There is no contract. One reason is that the company provided its services *before* you promised to pay the money. The company did not work *in exchange for* your promise.[10]

Now suppose that you see the landscapers working on your neighbour's lawn and ask them to work on your lawn as well. The company's manager agrees to do so, but neither of you says anything about the price. After the company finishes the job, you promise to pay $250. It might appear, once again, that there is no contract. After all, your promise to pay came *after* the company provided its services. Those services therefore might seem like past consideration. A court, however, would view the matter differently. A reasonable person would have interpreted your initial request to include promise to pay the company for its services. A judge would therefore require you to pay a "reasonable price."[11] A judge would also find that your *subsequent* promise to pay $250 merely provided evidence of a reasonable price. (If you had not subsequently promised to pay $250, the judge would determine the value of the company's services after considering all of the circumstances.) In other words, although the terms of the contract were not entirely settled at the outset, there was a sufficient meeting of the minds. And on that view, the company's actions were good consideration, rather than past consideration. They were provided *in return* for your implicit promise that you would pay.[12] They were part of a bargaining process.

The rule on past consideration may produce results that do not easily fit with basic notions of fairness and morality. Consider the situation in Ethical Perspective 8.1.

ETHICAL PERSPECTIVE 8.1

Past Consideration[13]

While strolling on a beach, you discover Heena unconscious and face down in the water. You pull her ashore, administer first aid, and bring her back to life. Shaken, but grateful, she promises to pay you $500 every year for the remainder of your life. However, when you attempt to collect the first payment, she states that she has changed her mind and refuses to pay anything.

Questions for Discussion

1. Does Heena have a moral obligation to pay any money to you? Does she have a legal obligation to do so?

2. Leaving aside the rule governing past consideration, do you believe that Heena should be required to pay anything to you?

[10.] *Eastwood v Kenyon* (1840) 113 ER 482 (CA). As we saw in Chapter 7, a court could also refuse to recognize a contract on the basis that there was no offer and acceptance. There was, rather, simply a promise to pay for work that had already been done.

[11.] Lawyers sometimes refer to the reasonable price for services as *quantum meruit*, or "as much as it is worth."

[12.] *Lampleigh v Braithwait* (1615) 80 ER 255 (KB).

[13.] The facts are based on *Webb v McGowin* 168 So 2d 196 (Ala CA 1935).

Pre-Existing Obligation

Because past consideration is no consideration at all, an act that was *actually performed* before a contract was proposed cannot provide consideration for that agreement. But can a contract be supported by a *promise* to fulfill a **pre-existing obligation**, that is, an obligation that existed, but was not actually performed, before the contract was contemplated?

a pre-existing obligation is an obligation that existed, but was not actually performed, before the contract was contemplated

We must distinguish three types of pre-existing obligations:

- a pre-existing public duty
- a pre-existing contractual obligation owed to a third party
- a pre-existing contractual obligation owed to the same party

Pre-Existing Public Duty

A person who owes a *pre-existing public duty* cannot rely upon that obligation as consideration for a new contract. For example, firefighters and police officers who are called to your office during an emergency cannot sell their services to you under a contract. One reason is that when they became public servants, they already promised to help people like you in times of need. Therefore, they do not have anything more that they can offer as part of a new agreement. An even stronger reason, which is not tied to the idea of past consideration, is that it would be against *public policy* to allow public servants to take advantage of your misfortune by charging for their services. It would also be undesirable if public servants were tempted to pass by poor citizens and enter into lucrative contracts with wealthy citizens.

However, by becoming a public servant, a person does not promise to protect citizens around the clock. For example, after police officers finish their shifts, they can generally do as they please. They are certainly not required to guard your house during their "off" hours, even if you are worried that thieves might be lurking in the area. If you want that type of protection, you have to pay for it.

Pre-Existing Contractual Obligation Owed to Third Party

We have seen that a promise to perform a pre-existing *public duty* is not good consideration for a new contract. In contrast, a promise to perform a pre-existing obligation that previously arose under a *contract with a third party* can

CASE BRIEF 8.2

Pao On v Lau Yiu Long [1980] AC 614 (PC)

The plaintiff bought 4 200 000 shares from a company called Fu Chip. Under the terms of that agreement, the plaintiff promised Fu Chip that it would not resell more than 60 percent of those shares within one year. Resale of a larger number of the shares would hurt Fu Chip's financial situation. The plaintiff later realized, however, that it might suffer a financial loss itself if, for some reason, the value of the shares dropped. It would be required to retain the shares while their value declined. The plaintiff therefore approached the defendants,

who were the majority shareholders in Fu Chip, and persuaded them to enter into a separate, *indemnification* contract.[14] Under that agreement, the plaintiff promised to honour its earlier sale contract with Fu Chip, and the defendants promised to compensate the plaintiff for any loss that it suffered as a result. The plaintiff therefore used the same consideration twice. It separately promised both the defendants and Fu Chip (which, as a stranger to the indemnification contract, was classified as a *third party* to that agreement) that it

---

14. Indemnification occurs when a party receives compensation for a loss that it suffered.

would not resell 60 percent of the shares within one year.

As feared, the value of the shares dropped, and the plaintiff claimed indemnification under its contract with the defendants. The defendants argued that the plaintiff had merely promised to fulfill the first (sale) contract and had not

provided good consideration for the second (indemnification) contract. The court, however, held that the plaintiff's promise to perform the contractual obligation that it already owed to Fu Chip (the third party) was good consideration for its later contract with the defendants.

be good consideration for a new contract. That rule is often important in business, as Case Brief 8.2 shows.

In one sense, there is an advantage to using the same consideration for two different contracts. Despite promising to do only one thing, you may be able to extract valuable promises from two different parties. However, there is also a danger in that sort of arrangement. Suppose a classical quartet agrees with a promoter to perform a concert in exchange for $15 000. The quartet subsequently persuades a music publisher, under a separate contract, to pay $20 000 for the right to record the concert. If all goes well, the quartet will receive $15 000 from the promoter *and* $20 000 from the publisher, even though it essentially did only one thing. However, if the quartet refuses to perform, it will be held liable to both the promoter *and* the publisher, even though it essentially failed to do only one thing.

Pre-Existing Contractual Obligation Owed to the Same Party

We have seen that a promise to perform a pre-existing obligation that previously arose under a contract with a *third party* can be good consideration for a new contract. But what if the pre-existing obligation arose under an earlier contract with the *same party* that is on the other side of the new contract? Perhaps surprisingly, a different rule applies in that situation. The courts usually hold that the *same* person cannot be required to pay twice for the same benefit. If a promise is merely repeated, it does not provide anything new. Furthermore, the courts want to prevent a person from threatening to breach one contract in order to get the other party to enter into a second contract at a higher price. The leading case is discussed in Case Brief 8.3.

The court's analysis may seem appropriate in *Gilbert Steel*, but it does not sit so well in other situations. Parties sometimes fail to appreciate the effort and expense that will be involved in the performance of their contract. If so, they may genuinely agree that the terms of their original contract should be revised to ensure that the deal benefits both of them, especially if they want to develop and maintain goodwill. Successful business people often recognize that a small sacrifice in the short term can lead to larger benefits in the long term. For those

CASE BRIEF 8.3

Gilbert Steel Ltd v University Construction Ltd (1976) 67 DLR (3d) 606 (Ont CA)

The plaintiff contractually agreed to sell several shipments of steel to the defendant at a set price. After that agreement was partially fulfilled, the plaintiff's own supplier raised its prices. The defendant then promised to pay the plaintiff a higher price for the remaining shipments of steel. The plaintiff delivered the rest of the steel, but the defendant refused to honour its promise to pay the extra amount. The defendant

argued that the plaintiff had already promised to deliver the steel under the initial contract and therefore did not provide anything in exchange for the later promise of the higher price.

The court agreed. It held that the defendant was not required to pay the extra price because it had not received anything new in exchange for its promise to do so.

reasons, many scholars argue that a party's promise to revise the terms of a contract should sometimes be enforceable if the revision accurately reflects an unexpected change in circumstances. That argument was accepted in England and may eventually be adopted in Canada as well.[15]

In the meantime, there are other ways in which Canadian business people can avoid the rule in *Gilbert Steel*. First, they can use the process of *novation* to discharge their initial contract and enter into a new agreement that includes a higher price.[16] Second, they can agree that something new is to be done in exchange for the extra price. For example, in *Gilbert Steel*, the plaintiff could have promised to deliver either somewhat more steel or the same amount of steel somewhat earlier. Third, as we will discuss in the next section, the defendant's promise in *Gilbert Steel* would have been binding, despite the lack of any new consideration from the plaintiff, if it had been made under *seal*. And finally, as previously suggested, business people can simply ignore the rule in *Gilbert Steel*. They may be unaware of it. And even if they are aware of it, they may realize that financial success in the long run sometimes requires short-term flexibility.

Concept Summary 8.1 lists the general rules regarding pre-existing obligations and consideration.

CONCEPT SUMMARY 8.1

Pre-Existing Obligations and Consideration

Situation	Can a Pre-Existing Obligation Generally Provide Consideration for a New Contract?
Pre-existing public duty	No
Pre-existing contractual obligation owed to third party	Yes
Pre-existing contractual obligation owed to same party	No

Promise to Forgive an Existing Debt   Before leaving this topic, it is important to discuss one more set of cases. The question in *Gilbert Steel* was whether a pre-existing obligation can be used to support the enforcement of a new promise between the same parties. Similar issues arise when a creditor promises to forgive a debt in exchange for something less than full payment.

Suppose you lend me $100 000, which I promise to repay in cash on June 1. (To keep things simple, assume that the loan is interest free.) When the repayment date arrives, however, I honestly explain that I do not have that much money. You recognize the reality of the situation and promise to discharge my entire debt in exchange for $70 000. I pay that amount, but after receiving the money, you insist that I still owe $30 000. Are you entitled to do so?

Your promise to accept the lesser amount is, as usual, enforceable only if it was supported by fresh consideration. I therefore have to prove that I provided something *new*. I will argue that even though I had previously *promised* to pay $100 000 under our original agreement, my *actual* payment of $70 000 provided you with a new benefit. If you had not accepted that amount, you would have

---

[15.] *Williams v Roffey Bros & Nicholls (Contractors) Ltd* [1990] 1 All ER 512 (CA).

[16.] *DeLuxe French Fries Ltd v McCardle* (1976) 10 Nfld & PEIR 414 (PEI CA). The concept of novation is discussed in Chapter 11.

been put to the trouble and expense of suing me. Furthermore, if my financial situation continued to deteriorate, I might have declared bankruptcy. And if that happened, you would have been required to share my assets with my other creditors and you therefore might have received far less than $70 000.[17] As a practical matter, then, it would appear that I did provide fresh consideration. As a matter of law, however, my argument will fail. A court will say that my payment of $70 000 was merely part performance of my earlier promise, and that I did not provide any fresh consideration for your promise. You are therefore entitled to demand the remaining $30 000.[18]

That analysis is often criticized as being unfair and unrealistic. Not surprisingly, the courts have developed several exceptions. First, a promise to accept a smaller sum is enforceable if it is placed under *seal*. Second, a promise to accept less money is enforceable if the debtor gives something new in exchange for it. Returning to our earlier example, I might have promised to give you $70 000 *plus* a vehicle that I own. Or I might have promised to pay $70 000 on May 31 instead of $100 000 on June 1. If you agreed to that arrangement, you effectively would have purchased one day for $30 000. Perhaps most surprisingly, your promise might even be enforceable if I promised to pay $70 000 by *cheque* instead of $100 000 in *cash*.[19]

In addition to those judicially created exceptions, an important statutory exception exists in many parts of Canada. Several jurisdictions have legislation that allows a debt to be extinguished upon payment of lesser amount.[20] Section 16 of the *Mercantile Law Amendment Act* of Ontario is typical.[21]

> Part performance of an obligation either before or after breach thereof when expressly accepted by the creditor or rendered in pursuance of an agreement for that purpose, though without any new consideration, shall be held to extinguish the obligation.

While that provision is important, it is also subject to certain restrictions. First, it requires *part performance*—part of the debt must have been paid. Therefore, it would apply if you *actually received* $70 000 from me. In contrast, if you merely received my *promise* to pay that amount, you could change your mind and insist upon full payment any time before I handed over the $70 000. Second, a court will not allow the statute to be used in an unconscionable manner.[22] Suppose, for instance, that I had enough money to pay my full debt of $100 000. However, I also knew that you were desperate for cash, and that if you did not receive at least $70 000 soon, you would be ruined. I tried to exploit the circumstances by telling you that I would either pay $70 000 or nothing at all. Even if you accepted payment of the lesser amount, you can still sue for the remainder of the original debt.[23]

---

[17] Bankruptcy is discussed in Chapter 24.

[18] *Foakes v Beer* (1884) 9 App Cas 605 (HL).

[19] *Foot v Rawlings* (1963) 37 DLR (2d) 695 (SCC). But see *D & C Builders v Rees* [1965] 3 All ER 837 (CA).

[20] *Judicature Act*, RSA 2000, c J-2, s 13(1) (Alta); *Law and Equity Act*, RSBC 1996, c 253, s 43 (BC); *Mercantile Law Amendment Act*, CCSM, c M120, s 6 (Man); *Judicature Act*, RSNWT 1988, c J-1, s 40 (NWT); *Judicature Act*, SNWT 1998, c 34, s 37 (Nun); *Queen's Bench Act, 1998*, SS 1998, c Q-1.01, s 64 (Sask); *Judicature Act*, RSY 2002, c 128, s 25 (Yuk).

[21] *Mercantile Law Amendment Act*, RSO 1990, c M.10 (Ont).

[22] The concept of unconscionability is examined in Chapter 10.

[23] *Graham v Voth Bros Construction (1974) Ltd* [1982] 6 WWR 365 (BC Co Ct).

Promises Enforceable Without Consideration

Generally speaking, a promise is enforceable only if it is contained in a contract that is supported by consideration. That rule is subject to two major exceptions:

- seals
- promissory estoppel

Seals

a seal is a mark that is put on a written contract to indicate a party's intention to be bound by the terms of that document, even though the other party may not have given consideration

A **seal** is a mark that is put on a written contract to indicate a party's intention to be bound by the terms of that document, even though the other party may not have given consideration. The essential purpose of a seal is to draw the parties' attention to the importance of the occasion and to ensure that they appreciate the seriousness of making an enforceable promise outside the usual bargaining process. Before you affix your seal to a document, you should therefore think carefully about the fact that you may be agreeing to do something for nothing.

The process of placing a seal on a document is subject to a loose rule and a strict rule. On the one hand, the seal need not take any particular form. Historically, a seal was applied by pressing an insignia (usually of a family crest or a coat of arms) into a drop of hot wax on a document. The usual practice today is to affix a red adhesive wafer to a document. However, it is also acceptable to simply write the word "seal" on the paper. On the other hand, the courts insist that the seal must be applied at the time that a party signs the document. It is not sufficient, for example, to use a form that already has the word "seal" written on it or to add the word "seal" after the fact.[24]

Promissory Estoppel

estoppel is a rule that precludes a person from disputing or retracting a statement that they made earlier

To explain the concept of *promissory estoppel*, we need to first define the term "estoppel."[25] **Estoppel** is a rule that precludes a person from disputing or retracting a statement that they made earlier. In a variety of situations, a court may hold that a person is "estopped" from unfairly denying the truth of a prior statement if the person to whom the statement was made relied on it. For example, suppose you trick me into building a house on your property by saying that the land is mine. When I complete the project, the law will not allow you to unfairly assert your ownership in the property. You will be estopped from denying the truth of your earlier statement that I owned the land. I therefore may be entitled to keep the property along with the house.[26]

promissory estoppel is a doctrine that prevents a party from retracting a promise that the other party has relied upon

Traditionally, the concept of estoppel applied only to statements regarding *past* or *present* facts.[27] More recently, however, it has been applied to statements regarding *promises* and *future* facts as well. **Promissory estoppel** is a doctrine that prevents a party from retracting a promise that another party has relied upon. That doctrine therefore creates an important exception to the general rule that only enforces promises that were acquired in exchange for consideration. Case Brief 8.4 discusses the decision that established the modern principle of promissory estoppel.

---

[24] *Royal Bank of Canada v Kiska* (1967) 63 DLR (2d) 582 (SCC).

[25] The term is derived from the Latin word meaning "to stop" or "to prevent."

[26] *Willmott v Barber* (1880) 15 Ch D 96.

[27] *Jorden v Money* (1854) 5 HL Cas 185 (HL).

CASE BRIEF 8.4

Central London Property Ltd v High Trees House Ltd [1947] KB 130 (KB)

The defendant leased an apartment block in London, England from the plaintiff. The lease began in 1937 and was to run for 99 years, at a yearly charge of £2500. The defendant intended to rent out the individual apartments to other tenants. However, it became apparent after World War II began that the defendant could not rent out enough apartments to cover its obligations under the main lease. The plaintiff was sympathetic and therefore promised that it would reduce the rent to £1250 per year. That was a gratuitous promise because the defendant did not give any consideration in exchange for it. The parties proceeded on that basis for sev-

eral years. By 1945, however, the war had ended, and the building was fully occupied. The plaintiff then brought an action to determine (i) whether it could charge the original rent of £2500 in future years, and (ii) whether it could recover as back rent the amount that it had allowed the defendant to not pay during the war.

The court held that while original rent could be reinstated in *future years*, the plaintiff was estopped from retracting its promise that it would only charge half rent during the war. In other words, for the *past years*, the plaintiff's promise was enforceable even though it was not supported by consideration.

As Case Brief 8.4 shows, the doctrine of promissory estoppel will apply only if four requirements are met.

1. The *representor* (the party making the promise) must clearly indicate that it will not enforce its legal rights against the *representee* (the party receiving the promise). Therefore, promissory estoppel will not apply if, for example, one party is simply slow in collecting money that it is owed. Accepting late payment is not the same thing as clearly saying that future payments need not be made on time or that they need not be made at all.[28]

2. The representee must *rely* upon the statement in a way that would make it unfair for the representor to retract its promise. For example, the representee might have rearranged its business plans because of the promise. However, if the promise was not relied upon in any way, then it is not enforceable.

3. The representee must not be guilty of *inequitable behaviour*. This means that the doctrine of promissory estoppel does not apply, for example, if the representee unfairly pressured the representor into making the statement.[29]

4. The representor's statement must be made in the context of an *existing legal relationship*. Although American courts use the similar doctrine of "injurious reliance" to *create* rights, Canadian courts usually hold that promissory estoppel can be used only to *vary* existing rights. (As lawyers in this country sometimes say, promissory estoppel can be used as a shield, but not as a sword.) Consequently, unless a legal relationship already exists between the parties, our courts will not enforce a gratuitous promise even if the representee has relied upon it.[30]

If these four requirements are met, the representor cannot assert its original rights with respect to the *past*. However, that party may be allowed to enforce its original rights in the *future* if it gives reasonable notice of its intention to do so. As we saw, this occurred in *High Trees*. That possibility does not exist, however, if it would result in an unfair hardship for the representee.

----

28. *John Burrows Ltd v Subsurface Surveys Ltd* (1968) 68 DLR (2d) 354 (SCC).

29. *D & C Builders Ltd v Rees* [1965] 3 All ER 837 (CA).

30. *Maracle v Travelers Indemnity Co of Canada* (1991) 80 DLR (4th) 652 (SCC); *cf Re Tudale Exploration Ltd v Bruce* (1978) 20 OR (2d) 593 (HCJ).

PRIVITY OF CONTRACT

Consideration is necessary for the *creation* of a contract. The concept of *privity of contract* is different. It identifies the people who can be involved in the *enforcement* of a contract. Nevertheless, we address it in this chapter because it is closely tied to the idea of consideration.

It is often important to ask who can enforce a contract or have a contract enforced against them. In a simple two-party situation, each party enjoys the right to enforce the agreement against the other. Suppose, for example, that you agree to sell your car to me for $5000. You can sue me if I fail to pay the money, and I can sue you if you fail to transfer the car.

a stranger is someone who did not participate in the creation of the contract

Complications can arise, however, if the facts involve a *stranger*. A **stranger** is someone who did not participate in the creation of the contract. Suppose you agreed to transfer your car to me if I paid $5000 to your sister. If I get the vehicle but refuse to pay the price, the real complaint lies with your sister. She is the one who suffers from my broken promise. Can she compel me to fulfill the contract that I made with you?

A court would probably answer "no." A contract is used to distribute benefits and burdens *amongst the parties*. The last part of that sentence is important. You and I cannot impose an obligation on someone who is not part of our agreement. Likewise, someone who is not part of our agreement generally cannot take advantage of it. Those rules are reflected in the *privity of contract* doctrine. **Privity of contract** refers to the relationship that exists between the individuals who create a contract. Only those people are *parties* to the agreement, and in most situations, only parties can sue or be sued on the contract.[31]

the privity of contract doctrine refers to the relationship that exists between the individuals who create a contract

Although the two concepts are technically distinct, the privity of contract doctrine is often expressed in terms of the consideration doctrine. That approach emphasizes the bargaining aspect of contracts and says that, generally speaking, only a person who has provided something of value can sue or be sued on the contract. Returning to our illustration, we can see why your sister cannot compel me to fulfill my promise. Although she expected to take the benefit of that promise, she did not bargain for it. She gave nothing in return for my agreement to pay $5000. If you are surprised by that result, consider what might happen if *you* tried to enforce my promise against me. You provided consideration when you promised to transfer the car to me. You therefore have the right to sue me *in theory*. But *in practice*, I might be able to persuade a court that I do not have to pay the money to you either.[32] After all, I was supposed to pay $5000 to your sister rather than to you. Why should you now be able to demand payment from me?

As our discussion suggests, the privity of contract rule sometimes seems unfair. A number of common law jurisdictions around the world, including one in Canada, have therefore abolished that doctrine.[33] In those places, a stranger who was intended to enjoy the benefit of a promise can generally enforce it. Other jurisdictions rely on narrower and less dramatic ways of occasionally avoiding the harsh consequences of the privity doctrine. We will examine a number of those exceptions and apparent exceptions:

[31.] *Dunlop Pneumatic Tyre Co Ltd v Selfridge & Co Ltd* [1915] AC 847 at 853 (HL).

[32.] *Woodar Investment Development Ltd v Wimpey Construction UK Ltd* [1980] 1 WLR 277 (HL).

[33.] *Contracts (Rights of Third Parties) Act 1999*, c 31 (UK); *Law Reform Act*, SNB 1993, c L-1.2, s 4 (NB).

- assignment
- trusts
- statutes
- employment[34]

As we do so, notice the business contexts in which these issues arise, as well as the ways in which business people can prevent problems from arising in the first place.

Assignment

A business person who wants to allow a stranger to enforce a contract will usually use an *assignment*. **Assignment** is a process in which a contractual party transfers its rights to a third party. The contractual party who assigns its rights is called the **assignor**; the stranger to whom the contractual rights are assigned is called the **assignee**; and the original contracting party against whom the assigned rights can be enforced is called the **debtor**. In effect, as Figure 8.1 illustrates, the assignee steps into the assignor's shoes to enforce the promise against the debtor.

assignment is a process in which a contractual party transfers its rights to a third party

the assignor is the contractual party who assigns its contractual rights

the assignee is the stranger to whom the contractual rights are assigned

the debtor is the original contracting party against whom the assigned right can be enforced

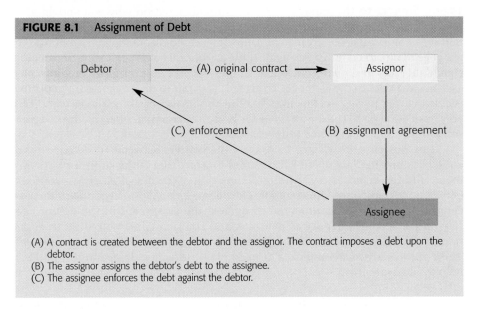

FIGURE 8.1   Assignment of Debt

(A) A contract is created between the debtor and the assignor. The contract imposes a debt upon the debtor.
(B) The assignor assigns the debtor's debt to the assignee.
(C) The assignee enforces the debt against the debtor.

Assignment often provides the best way to avoid the harsh consequences of the privity doctrine. The process is, however, quite complex. This section merely provides a basic overview of assignments. A business person who is faced with a complicated assignment issue should consult a lawyer.

Equitable Assignments

We start with the fact that the assignment can occur either as an *equitable assignment* or as a *statutory assignment*. An **equitable assignment** is an assignment that was traditionally enforced by the courts of equity, which we discussed

an equitable assignment is an assignment that was traditionally enforced by the courts of equity

---

34. Several other exceptions to the privity doctrine are examined in other chapters: promises that run with the land (Chapter 15), negotiable instruments (Chapter 14), and agency (Chapter 20).

in Chapter 1. It is usually possible to make an equitable assignment of a contractual right, although there are some exceptions. First, the parties to a contract can agree that their rights are non-assignable. Furthermore, the courts sometimes refuse to allow an assignment on policy grounds. For example, contracts for matrimonial support cannot be assigned.

In some respects, the process involved in an equitable assignment is very simple. No particular documents are required, and the assignment can even be completed orally. As a matter of risk management, however, it is best to use a written document whenever possible to avoid complications and disputes.

A valid assignment does not depend on the debtor's consent. Nevertheless, if you are an assignee, there are several reasons why you should provide *notice* of the assignment to the debtor as soon as possible. A debtor has to pay a debt only once. Consequently, if it pays the assignor before receiving notice from you, you cannot demand a second payment for yourself. (You can, however, sue the assignor.) A similar danger occurs if the assignor improperly assigns the same debt to you and then to another person. If that person is unaware of your assignment, it is entitled to payment if it provides the debtor with notice before you do. And again, since the debtor has to pay only once, you could not demand a second payment for yourself. (You could, however, sue the assignor.)

Taking Subject to the Equities   There is another reason why you should give notice as soon as possible. An assignment is **subject to the equities**, which means that the debtor can generally use the same defences and counterclaims against the assignee that it could have used against the assignor. That is a fair rule. The debtor should not be in a worse position simply because the original creditor has assigned the debt to the assignee. The rule is also fair to the assignee. If the debtor is able to avoid paying the full amount of the original debt, the assignee will probably have the right to sue the assignor for breach of contract. After all, the assignee received less than it expected to receive under the assignment.

It is, however, important to draw a distinction between (i) defences and counterclaims that arose out of the *same contract* that is the subject of assignment, and (ii) defences and counterclaims that arose out of *other transactions* between the debtor and the assignor. The debtor can *always* rely on the first category of defences and counterclaims against the assignee. But the debtor can rely on the second category of defences and counterclaims only if its transaction with the assignor occurred *before* it received notice from the assignee. These rules are rather complex. The examples in Business Decisions 8.1 and 8.2 help to illustrate them.

> **subject to the equities** means that the debtor can generally use the same defences and counterclaims against the assignee that it could have used against the assignor

---

BUSINESS DECISION 8.1

Equities Arising from the Assigned Contract

In January, Stetson Construction agreed to build a cottage in May in exchange for Ahmad's promise that he would pay $60 000 in August. Since Stetson needed money up front to buy supplies, it assigned its rights to you in March for $55 000. You immediately notified Ahmad of the assignment.

After you gave notice, Stetson broke its contract with Ahmad by using inadequate materials in the construction of the cottage. As a result, Ahmad was required to spend $40 000 to hire another contractor to repair the problem. It is now September.

Question for Discussion

1. If you bring an action against Ahmad under the equitable assignment, how much will you probably be able to collect?

BUSINESS DECISION 8.2

Equities Arising from Other Transactions

Citron Used Cars sold a vehicle to White Stationery Inc for $7000. When White failed to pay the purchase price, Citron assigned its contractual right to recover that money to you. White later delivered $5000 worth of paper products to Citron under a separate contract. Citron has not yet paid that price.

Questions for Discussion

1. How much would you be entitled to collect from White if

you gave notice *before* Citron became indebted to White for the receipt of the paper products?

2. How much would you be able to collect from White if you gave notice *after* Citron became indebted to White for the receipt of the paper products?

Although equitable assignments of contractual rights are quite flexible, they can also create problems for the assignee. Most significantly, if it wants to sue the debtor, the assignee may have to include the assignor as a party to that action.[35] That may be difficult to do, however, if the assignor is no longer available. For example, the assignor may have been a company that ceased to exist after it made the assignment.

Statutory Assignments

Because of the problems associated with equitable assignments, legislation has been introduced across Canada that creates an alternative form of assignment.[36] A **statutory assignment** is an assignment that conforms with the requirements of a statute.

While they generally follow the same principles as equitable assignments, statutory assignments are subject to three special requirements.

1. While an equitable assignment may be oral, a statutory assignment must be *written*.

2. While notice to the debtor is merely advisable under an equitable assignment, *written notice* is required for a valid statutory assignment.

3. Unlike an equitable assignment, a statutory assignment must be *absolute* at the time that it is created. An assignment is not absolute if it is *conditional*, for example, because it depends on some uncertain event in the future. That situation would arise if the assignor continues to deliver goods to the debtor on credit and therefore alters the amount of the debt. Nor is an assignment absolute if it is *incomplete*, for example, because it covers only part of a debt. That situation would arise if the assignor assigned $3000 of a $5000 debt to the assignee.

a **statutory assignment** is an assignment that conforms with the requirements of a statute

---

[35] The assignor is included in the action as a co-plaintiff if it is willing to co-operate with the assignee, or as a co-defendant if it is not.

[36] *Judicature Act*, RSA 2000, c J-2, s 20(1) (Alta); *Law and Equity Act*, RSBC 1996, c 253, s 36 (BC); *Law of Property Act*, CCSM, c L90, s 31 (Man); *Conveyancing and Law of Property Act*, RSO 1990, c C.34, s 53(1) (Ont); *Judicature Act*, RSNB 1973, c J-2, s 31 (NB); *Judicature Act*, RSNL 1990, c J-4, s 103 (Nfld); *Judicature Act*, RSNS 1989, c 240, s 43(5) (NS); *Choses in Action Act*, RSS 1978, c 11, s 2 (Sask). The legislation in Manitoba and Saskatchewan is slightly broader in scope; the discussion in the text focuses on the position in the other common law jurisdictions.

A statutory assignment is simply an alternative to an equitable assignment. Consequently, even if the requirements of the statute are not met, an assignment can still be effective in the equitable sense. In fact, equitable assignments are sometimes preferred for that very reason. For example, the assignor may intend to have ongoing transactions with the debtor, with the result that the amount of debt will vary from time to time. If so, an assignment of the right to receive payment from the debtor would be conditional. The assignment would therefore have to be equitable, rather than statutory.

Assignments by Operation of Law

Equitable and statutory assignments arise from the assignor's intention. Other types of assignment, however, occur by operation of law. The best examples involve bankruptcy and death. When a contractual party becomes bankrupt, all of its rights and liabilities are placed under the administration of a *trustee in bankruptcy*.[37] When a person dies, all of their contractual rights and liabilities are placed under the administration of a *personal representative*. In either event, the assignee has the responsibility of collecting and paying the person's debts. For reasons that are explained in the next section, however, the assignee is not required to satisfy obligations of a *personal* nature that were owed by the bankrupt or the deceased.

Vicarious Performance

So far we have discussed the assignment of contractual *rights*. We have not considered the assignment of contractual *obligations*. In fact, contractual obligations cannot be assigned. The general rule is that a party must personally perform. That is clearly true if the party's personal skills are essential to the fulfillment of the contract. For example, if a Broadway producer hires a famous actress to star in a production, she is not entitled to send her understudy to play the role. The contract is intended to secure *her* services.

In many situations, however, *vicarious performance* is allowed. **Vicarious performance** occurs when a contractual party arranges to have a stranger perform its obligations. That is possible if the contractual party's personal skills are not essential to performance. For instance, if you enter into a contract with a house builder, you cannot reasonably expect that individual to *personally* undertake the work alone. It is clear that the contractor will use employees or subcontractors. However, vicarious performance is not a form of assignment. The obligation to build the house remains on the builder. Consequently, if the house is defective because the employees or subcontractors were careless, you will still sue the builder.[38]

Trusts

An apparent exception to the privity doctrine involves the equitable concept of the *trust*. We discussed trusts in Chapter 1. As we saw, a **trust** occurs when one person holds property on behalf of another. The person who holds the property is the **trustee**, and the person for whom the property is held is the **beneficiary**. For example, suppose that an elderly couple want to provide for their grandchildren's education but are afraid that the money may be wasted. They may

vicarious performance occurs when a contractual party arranges to have a stranger perform its obligations

a **trust** occurs when one person administers property on behalf of another

the **trustee** is the person who holds the property on behalf of the other

the **beneficiary** is the person on whose behalf the property is held

---

37. The process of bankruptcy is discussed in detail in Chapter 24.

38. The builder, in turn, may have a contractual action against the workers. Moreover, as we saw in Chapter 3, you may have actions in tort against both the builder and the workers.

give the money to a trustee, who will sensibly spend it on the grandchildren's behalf. The trustee may, for example, pay for the grandchildren's tuition or accommodation while they are at school.

A trust can be used to avoid the consequences of the privity doctrine. Suppose that you and I enter into a contract. I may receive your promise as trustee for my sister. If so, I will hold that promise on trust for her, and she will be entitled to enforce the agreement even though she did not personally participate in the creation of the contract. Figure 8.2 illustrates that situation.

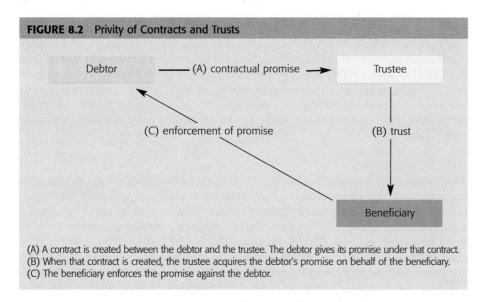

FIGURE 8.2 Privity of Contracts and Trusts

(A) A contract is created between the debtor and the trustee. The debtor gives its promise under that contract.
(B) When that contract is created, the trustee acquires the debtor's promise on behalf of the beneficiary.
(C) The beneficiary enforces the promise against the debtor.

The trust was once commonly used to avoid the privity doctrine. At times, however, the courts have demanded clear proof that the contractual promise really was intended to be held on trust. Case Brief 8.5 examines one attempt to avoid the consequences of the privity doctrine.

CASE BRIEF 8.5

Vandepitte v Preferred Accident Insurance Co [1933] AC 70 (PC)

Mr Berry purchased liability insurance coverage for his vehicle from the defendant insurance company. That insurance policy was contained in a standard form document and was said to cover not only Mr Berry but also anyone driving his car with his consent.

While driving her father's car with his consent, Jean Berry caused an accident that injured the plaintiff, Alice Vandepitte. Mrs Vandepitte sued the defendant insurance company and argued that the insurer was liable for Jean's actions under the terms of her father's policy. In response, the defendant company argued that while Jean fell within the wording of that policy, she was not a party to the insurance contract and therefore had no rights under the policy. And if that was true, then the defendant could not be compelled to compensate Mrs Vandepitte for the injuries that she sustained as a result of Jean's careless driving.

In response to that argument, Mrs Vandepitte claimed that Jean *was* made a party to the contract by way of a trust. On that view, Mr Berry purchased the insurance policy from the defendant not only for himself but also on trust for his daughter. He therefore held the defendant's promise to provide insurance coverage on behalf of himself *and* his daughter.

The Privy Council recognized the possibility of such an arrangement. The argument was, however, defeated on the evidence. The court did not believe that Mr Berry had actually intended to purchase the insurance policy on trust for both himself *and* his daughter. The court consequently said that since Jean Berry was not a party to the insurance contract, she was not entitled to the benefit of the policy. Mrs Vandepitte was certainly entitled to receive damages from Jean Berry, but Jean Berry could not shift that loss onto the insurer.

Statute

A person who wants the benefit of a trust must still show that the contractual parties really did intend to enter into such an arrangement. At the same time, however, Canadian law has increasingly recognized that the privity doctrine often creates injustice. The Supreme Court of Canada has therefore questioned the attitude of the Privy Council in *Vandepitte v Preferred Accident Insurance Co.*[39] For the same reason, the legislatures have created a number of true exceptions that allow strangers to enforce promises. The clearest illustrations arise in the context of insurance contracts. For example, *Vandepitte* would be decided differently today because legislation has been introduced throughout Canada that allows people like Jean Berry to enforce insurance contracts made for their benefit.[40] Similar provisions have been introduced for life insurance.[41] The primary purpose of a life insurance policy is to benefit someone who is not a party to that contract, usually a grieving family member. It would be grossly unfair if an insurance company could invoke the privity doctrine and refuse to make payment to that person after an insured party died.

Employment

The same reasoning has led the courts to create exceptions to the privity doctrine in other situations. Judges, however, proceed more cautiously than legislators, and the judicial exceptions are much narrower in scope. The clearest example arises in the employment context. When a company agrees to do work for a customer, it is usually obvious that the actual task will be performed by the company's employees. Furthermore, the contract that is created between the customer and the company may include an exclusion clause that expressly says that the customer cannot sue either the company *or* its employees if something goes wrong.[42] However, if the employees do perform carelessly, the customer may sue them in tort and argue that they cannot rely upon the contractual exclusion clause. After all, they were not parties to that contract. As explained in Case Brief 8.6, however, the Supreme Court of Canada has held that employees may be entitled to rely upon an exclusion clause that was created for their benefit, even though they lack privity of contract.[43]

---

[39] *Fraser River Pile & Dredge Ltd. v Can-Dive Services Ltd* (1999) 176 DLR (4th) 257 (SCC).

[40] *Insurance Act*, RSA 2000, c I-3, s 616 (Alta); *Insurance Act*, RSBC 1996, c 226, s 159 (BC); *Insurance Act*, CCSM, c I40, s 258 (Man); *Insurance Act*, RSNB 1973, c I-12, s 250 (NB); *Automobile Insurance Act*, RSNL 1990, c A-22, s 26 (Nfld); *Insurance Act*, RSNWT 1988, c I-4, s 28 (NWT); *Insurance Act*, RSNS 1989, c 231, s 133 (NS); *Insurance Act*, RSNWT 1988, c I-4, s 151 (Nun); *Insurance Act*, RSO 1990, c I.8, s 258 (Ont); *Insurance Act*, RSPEI 1988, c I-4, s 240 (PEI); *Saskatchewan Insurance Act*, RSS 1978, c S-26, s 210 (Sask); *Insurance Act*, RSY 2002, c 119, s 157 (Yuk).

[41] *Insurance Act*, RSA 2000, c I-3, s 583 (Alta); *Insurance Act*, RSBC 1996, c 226, s 53 (BC); *Insurance Act*, CCSM, c I40, s 172 (Man); *Insurance Act*, RSNB 1973, c I-2, s 156 (NB); *Life Insurance Act*, RSNL 1990, c L-14, s 26 (Nfld); *Insurance Act*, RSNWT 1988, c I-4, s 93 (NWT and Nun); *Insurance Act*, RSNS 1989, c 231, s 197 (NS); *Insurance Act*, RSO 1990, c I.8, s 195 (Ont); *Insurance Act*, RSPEI 1988, c I-4, s 143 (PEI); *Saskatchewan Insurance Act*, RSS 1978, c S-26, s 157 (Sask); *Insurance Act*, RSY 2002, c 119, s 100 (Yuk).

[42] Exclusion clauses are discussed in Chapters 9 and 12.

[43] See also *Fraser River Pile & Dredge Ltd v Can-Dive Services Ltd* (1999) 176 DLR (4th) 257 (SCC).

CASE BRIEF 8.6

London Drugs Ltd v Kuehne & Nagel International Ltd (1992) 97 DLR (4th) 261 (SCC)

The plaintiff delivered an expensive piece of machinery, called a "transformer," to the defendant for storage. The storage contract contained a clause that limited the defendant's liability to $40. The plaintiff rejected the defendant's offer to raise that limit in exchange for an additional price.

The defendant's employee damaged the plaintiff's transformer while moving it for storage purposes. The plaintiff sued the employee personally for $34 000. The employee argued that he was covered by the limitation clause contained in the storage contract. In response, the plaintiff argued that the employee was not a party to that contract and therefore could not rely upon it for protection.

The Supreme Court of Canada found in favour of the employee by creating an exception to the privity rule. That new rule states that an employee is covered by a limitation clause contained in an employer's contract with a third party if:

- the employee was expressly or implicitly contained within the clause, and
- the employee performs the work that was required by the contract.

The court based that rule on commercial reality. On the facts of the case, the plaintiff knew that its equipment would be handled not by the defendant (which was, after all, a corporation), but rather by the defendant's employees. The court also explained that the purpose of a limitation clause is to allocate the risk of damage to one of the parties, and to alert that party to the need for insurance. Consequently, the plaintiff should have either accepted the defendant's offer to raise the amount in the limitation clause, or purchased protection from an insurance company.

CHAPTER SUMMARY

Consideration is an essential element in the formation of most contracts. Because the law of contract is based on the concept of a bargain, gratuitous promises are generally not enforced. There must be an exchange of consideration between the parties. The bargain between the parties need not be a good one; as long as there is an exchange of value, a contract will be created. Consideration must be sufficient but it need not be adequate. An important application of the rules governing the sufficiency and adequacy of consideration arises in the context of forbearance to sue.

Past consideration is no consideration at all because it fails to satisfy the requirement of mutuality. Good consideration can be based on a pre-existing contractual obligation owed to a third party. However, good consideration cannot be based on a pre-existing public duty and usually cannot be based on a pre-existing contractual obligation owed to the same party.

As a general rule, a creditor's promise to accept less than full payment from a debtor is not binding. That rule is, however, subject to several exceptions.

A promise may be enforceable even if it is not sup-

ported by consideration if it was placed under seal or if it falls under the doctrine of promissory estoppel. In Canada, the doctrine of promissory estoppel is used to vary existing contractual rights but not to create new ones.

The doctrine of privity of contract is closely associated with the doctrine of consideration. A person who has not provided consideration and who is not a party to a contract generally cannot sue or be sued on the contract.

The privity of contract doctrine is subject to several exceptions and apparent exceptions. A stranger to a contract can enforce a contractual promise that has been assigned to it. An assignment of a contractual right may be either equitable or statutory and may arise either from the assignor's intention or by operation of law. A beneficiary can enforce a contractual promise acquired on its behalf by a trustee. In a number of situations, statutes allow strangers to enforce contractual rights created for their benefit. Likewise, the courts have recently allowed employees to take advantage of exclusion clauses that are contained in contracts for which they have not provided consideration and with respect to which they lack privity.

REVIEW QUESTIONS

1. What is a gratuitous promise? Can such a promise support a contract?

2. Is it possible for a person to enter into an enforceable contract without receiving any benefit from the agreement?

3. How and why do the courts distinguish between the "adequacy" and the "sufficiency" of consideration?

4. What is a forbearance agreement? Why do the courts generally uphold such agreements? Are such agreements supported by consideration?

5. What is the requirement of mutuality? How is it related to the bargain theory of contract?

6. What is past consideration? In light of the bargaining process that underlies a contract, explain why judges hold that past consideration is no consideration at all.

7. "There is a difference between past consideration on the one hand and on the other hand a promise that indicates the reasonable price for work that was previously performed under a contract." Explain the meaning of that statement. Provide an example to illustrate your answer.

8. Explain why a pre-existing public duty cannot be good consideration under a new contract. Does your explanation rely entirely on the doctrine of consideration, or does it also include other factors?

9. "Good consideration usually cannot be based on a pre-existing contractual obligation owed to the same party." Describe three ways by which business people can avoid that rule. What commercial reasons might motivate them to do so?

10. Suggest reasons why good consideration for a new contract can be based on a pre-existing contractual obligation that is owed to a third party, but cannot be based on a pre-existing contractual obligation

that is owed to the same party that is involved in the new agreement.

11. List and briefly describe the non-statutory exceptions to the general rule that payment of a lesser sum does not discharge a debt of a larger amount.

12. In your province or territory, does legislation ever allow you to discharge a debt by paying your creditor a lesser amount than you actually owe to it?

13. What is the effect of placing a seal on a contractual document?

14. Describe the doctrine of promissory estoppel. What does it mean to say that promissory estoppel can be used to vary, but not create, contractual rights? Give examples to illustrate your answer.

15. Explain the relationship between the requirement of consideration and the privity of contract doctrine.

16. "The process of assignment sidesteps the privity of contract doctrine." Discuss the extent to which that statement is true.

17. Explain why it would be undesirable if contractual parties were free to assign contractual obligations, even though contractual rights generally can be assigned. Illustrate your answer with examples. Discuss the extent to which the doctrine of vicarious performance provides an exception to the general rule precluding assignment of contractual obligations.

18. Explain how a trust can be used to avoid the consequences of the privity of contract doctrine.

19. Explain the circumstances in which an employee may be entitled to rely upon an exclusion clause contained in an employer's contract.

20. Why do you think judges allow employees to take advantage of exclusion clauses to which they are strangers? Give at least two reasons for your answer.

CASES AND PROBLEMS

1. On Maria's eighteenth birthday, her uncle Juan said to her, "I still think that you're too young to be driving, but I promise that when you turn 21, I'll buy a car for you. All I want from you in return is your love and affection." He then wrote down his words and, being something of a show-off, applied his seal using hot wax and his family insignia. Despite the fact that Maria, who was desperate for a car, was particularly adoring toward her uncle for the next three years, Juan refused to honour his promise when she turned 21. Can Maria get the car? Did she provide consideration in exchange for Juan's promise?

2. The Goldberg Conservatory, a music school, ran a notice in several newspapers to announce that it had decided to have a new organ built and installed on its premises. The notice also asked for donations to help fund the project. John Sebastien, a local businessman and patron of the arts, responded to the notice by immediately promising the Conservatory that he would donate $100 000. He explained that a cheque would be sent within a month, after he had made suitable arrangements with his accountant. Before he was able to send a cheque, however, Sebastien's finances suffered a severe setback as a result of several failed business ventures. He therefore informed the Conservatory that, with regret, he

would not be able to make a donation after all. The Conservatory insists that he no longer has a choice in the matter. While admitting that it had planned to acquire the organ in any event, it says that it would be unfair if it was deprived of the money that Sebastien had promised. It also says that Sebastien is legally obligated to fulfill his promise. Is Sebastien's promise enforceable?

3. Hardy Construction Ltd contractually agreed to build an office complex for Schtick Corp. Under the terms of that contract, Hardy Construction would incur a financial penalty if it failed to complete the project on schedule. Hardy Construction hired Laurel Electric Co as a subcontractor to install wiring in the building. The terms of that subcontract required payment of $50 000 on completion. Laurel Electric began work immediately but later discovered that it had honestly underestimated the cost of performance. Accordingly, it approached Hardy Construction and stated that unless it was promised an additional $20 000, it simply would not be able to complete the job. Hardy Construction realized (i) that it could not possibly find a replacement for Laurel Electric on such short notice, and (ii) that any delay in completion of the project would trigger the penalty provision contained in its contract with Schtick Corp. Hardy Construction consequently agreed to Laurel Electric's request. Nevertheless, although Laurel Electric subsequently completed its performance on schedule, Hardy Construction refuses to pay more than $50 000. Does it have a right to do so in law? Regardless of its legal position, why might Hardy Construction consider honouring its promise to pay an extra $20 000? Explain whether you believe that the law should more closely reflect business practice.

4. Jacques was indebted to Rumana for $5000, plus 15 percent interest per annum, which he was required to pay in cash in monthly instalments of $400. Jacques, however, was unhappy with that arrangement and asked Rumana if she would be willing to lower the interest rate to 12 percent in exchange for his promise to pay monthly instalments of $600 in a series of postdated cheques. Although she initially agreed to that proposal, Rumana later insisted that Jacques comply with the terms of their original agreement. Is she entitled to do so? Identify two arguments that Jacques could present in response to the suggestion that he provided no consideration for Rumana's promise to abide by the revised repayment schedule.

5. Mr Chin ran down Mrs Moss at a pedestrian crosswalk. Because she suffered severe brain damage, her interests were represented by the Public Trustee. The Public Trustee sued Mr Chin in the tort of negligence and claimed, among other things, compensatory damages for the cost of Mrs Moss's future medical expenses. Over time, as negotiations between the parties progressed, Mrs Moss's physical condition deteriorated, and she eventually died. The Public Trustee, however, chose not to reveal that fact to Mr Chin. Based on his belief that Mrs Moss would require ongoing medical treatment, Mr Chin eventually settled the case out of court for more than $300 000. He has now discovered the truth. He therefore demands payment. The Public Trustee, on the other hand, points to the settlement contract that it had persuaded Mr Chin to sign. It insists that the money was given in exchange for good consideration. Which party is correct?

6. The Blacksox Baseball Club and Roark Designs Corp conducted extensive negotiations concerning the development of a new ball park. During those negotiations, the owner of the Blacksox said to the owner of Roark, "Look, we both know that this stadium will eventually be built. The lawyers will have to work out the details, and of course nothing will be official until we sign a formal contract. But as far as I'm concerned, we might as well get started. I can promise you right now that if you draft the plans, we'll pay you $100 000 for your efforts." Roark spent a considerable amount of time and money preparing a blueprint for a new stadium. Unfortunately, the entire proposal collapsed when, through no fault of either the Blacksox or Roark, the local government denied zoning approval for the project. Roark nevertheless insists that the Blacksox abide by the promise made by their president. Will the doctrine of promissory estoppel assist Roark in that regard?

7. Julio Cruz and Ingrid Forsberg were married more than a year ago. On the wedding day, Julio's father, Mr Cruz, and Ingrid's mother, Mrs Forsberg, entered into a contract that was intended to provide financial support for the young couple. Mr Cruz promised to pay $5000 to the couple on their first anniversary. In exchange, Mrs Forsberg promised to pay $4000 to the couple on the same day. Nevertheless, on the couple's first anniversary, neither Mr Cruz nor Mrs Forsberg was willing to honour their promises. Does a contract exist in these circumstances? If so, who are the parties to that contract? If a contract does exist, what consideration was provided in support of it? Who provided that consideration? Are Julio and Ingrid entitled to compel their parents to pay the promised amounts?

8. Everlast Tire Co, which manufactures automobile tires, sold a shipment of tires to Automotive Wholesaler Inc. Under the terms of that contract, Automotive Wholesaler was allowed to resell the tires below the price suggested by Everlast if (i) the sub-buyer was a business in the car industry, and (ii) the sub-buyer promised not to resell below the price suggested by Everlast. Automotive Wholesaler then sold the tires to AJ's Used Cars Ltd. Under the terms of that contract, AJ's, which was engaged in the car industry as a used car dealer, promised Automotive Wholesaler that it would not resell the tires below the price suggested by Everlast. AJ's also promised Automotive Wholesaler that if it broke that promise, it would pay $100 to Everlast for each tire that was sold below the manufacturer's suggested price. In fact, AJ's did sell 10 tires to individual customers at

prices that were well below the price suggested by Everlast. Everlast now argues that it is entitled to recover $1000 from AJ's. Is that true? If not, does the result seem fair? And if not, what are the simplest means by which Everlast could have arranged the resale of its tires so that it would be able to enforce the promise that AJ's made to Automotive Wholesaler?

9. Ann agreed to provide a car to Bruno in exchange for his promise to pay $8000 to her sister, Claire. Ann actually delivered the vehicle as promised, but Bruno refuses to pay any money to Claire. Is Claire entitled to compel Bruno to honour his undertaking? If not, does Ann have the right to recover the $8000 from Bruno? Is there anything that Ann can now do that would allow Claire to enforce Bruno's promise?

10. Fraser River Inc owned a boat called *The Squamish*. Fraser River did not actually use the boat. Instead, it chartered (rented) the boat to other people. Until recently, it had chartered *The Squamish* to Can-Dive Corp. The boat unfortunately was badly damaged as a result of Can-Dive's negligence. In normal circumstances, Fraser River would have sued Can-Dive in either tort or contract for compensation. In fact, Fraser River did not need to do so. It had purchased an insurance policy from London Insurance Inc. That policy required the insurance company to pay for the repairs. As we will see in Chapter 17, an insurance company that provides compensation to a policy holder is normally "subrogated" to the rights of that policy holder. In the present situation, that would mean that London Insurance could "step into the shoes" of Fraser River and sue Can-Dive for the damage that Can-Dive created. Can-Dive, however, points to a provision that was contained in the insurance contract that Fraser River bought from London Insurance. That provision states: "It is agreed that the insurer waives any right of subrogation against any charterer." Can-Dive therefore argues that it cannot be sued by London Insurance. Is that correct?

11. Hank and Dale Gribble were twin brothers who could not have been more different. Hank was an established personal trainer who led an exceptionally healthy lifestyle, whereas Dale had never worked a day in his life, smoked cigarettes and drank alcohol constantly, and ate fast food on a daily basis. Dale's doctor recently told him that if he did not change his ways, he would have a heart attack before his thirty-fifth birthday. Needless to say, Hank was extremely worried about his brother. He begged his brother to join a gym, but Dale refused to pay the outrageous fees. Hank was so troubled that he offered to be Dale's personal trainer and nutritionist for three nights per week in exchange for Dale's promise to quit smoking, drinking, and eating poorly. Hank was so sure he could make a difference

in Dale's life that he promised to give up a week's wages to the Heart and Stroke Foundation (HSF) if Dale was not under 300 pounds by the end of the month. Dale was tired of listening to Hank nag, so he agreed to the arrangement.

True to his word, Dale met with Hank three nights a week, but by the end of the first month, Dale was still well over 300 pounds. Coincidentally, Peggy, the area co-ordinator of the local HSF, overheard the brothers' initial agreement while working out one day. Since that time, she followed Dale's progress closely, and knew when the brothers did not meet their 300-pound goal. She approached Hank and asked him to make the contribution that he promised, but he refused. Hank claims that the agreement between him and Dale is unenforceable for lack of consideration. Is he correct? Can Dale enforce the agreement between him and his brother? Can Peggy enforce the agreement between Hank and Dale? Explain your answers.

12. Busy Conference Centre (BCC) owed Delish Catering Company $5000 for a conference Delish catered two weeks before. Delish, in turn, owed $3000 to Fresh Food Suppliers Inc (FFS). The owners of FFS refused to deliver any more produce to Delish until it received payment in full. Delish offered to assign $3000 of its accounts receivable from BCC to FFS, but FFS would only agree to the assignment if it was in writing. Without consulting a lawyer, Fern, a representative from Delish, wrote up the following agreement:

> For value received, the undersigned hereby assigns and transfers to Fresh Food Suppliers the right to $3000 that shall be due the undersigned from Busy Conference Centre under a contract for services rendered. Signed under seal this 23rd day of June 2002.
>
> Fern M. Dupelle

In the week following the assignment, Delish broke a new contract with BCC by forgetting to cater an important business meeting. As a result, BBC was required to spend $5000 to hire another caterer to fill in at the last minute. In the interest of their ongoing business relationship, Delish and BCC agreed to settle the matter by balancing the $5000 accounts receivable with the $5000 liability under the catering contract. The day after reaching the settlement, BCC received notice from FFS concerning the $3000 assignment. BCC and Delish have both refused to make payment. FSS plans to use the written agreement to prove that there is a valid assignment under provincial statute. Will that argument succeed? Why or why not? How should FSS argue its case and against whom?

WEBLINKS

Canadian Law Site.com　www.canadianlawsite.com/contracts.htm#a

This website provides a general introduction to the law of contracts, as well as a summary of the doctrines of offer, acceptance, and consideration.

Duhaime Law: Consideration　www.duhaime.org/contract/ca-con3.aspx#consideration

This website reviews the general rules on consideration.

ADDITIONAL RESOURCES FOR CHAPTER 8 ON THE COMPANION WEBSITE

(www.pearsoned.ca/mcinnes)

In addition to self-test multiple-choice, true-false, and short essay questions (all with immediate feedback), three additional Cases and Problems (with suggested answers), and links to useful Web destinations, the Companion Website provides the following resources for Chapter 8:

- Weblinks to legislation allowing for the discharge of a larger debt upon receipt of a smaller amount
- Weblinks to legislation allowing for the statutory assignment of debts

Provincial Material

- **British Columbia:** Statutory Assignment, Debt Settlement
- **Alberta:** Seals, Trusts
- **Manitoba and Saskatchewan:** Promise to Forgive an Existing Debt, Statutory Assignments
- **Ontario:** Promissory Estoppel (Equitable Estoppel), Partial Payment of Debt, Seals, Death Without a Will, Executors, Statutory Assignments, Trusts, Consumer Credit

9 Representations and Terms

OBJECTIVES

After completing this chapter, you should be able to:

1. Identify pre-contractual and contractual statements.

2. Distinguish misrepresentations from other false statements made during contractual negotiations.

3. Identify the various circumstances when silence might amount to misrepresentation.

4. Explain the differences between innocent, fraudulent, and negligent misrepresentation.

5. Describe the legal effects of innocent, fraudulent, and negligent misrepresentation.

6. Outline the rules associated with proving the existence of express terms.

7. Summarize and apply the various judicial approaches to interpreting express terms.

8. Discuss when, how, and why a court might imply a term into a contract.

9. Describe the nature of ticket contracts.

10. Outline the advantages and disadvantages of standard form agreements and describe why a business should use plain language in contracts.

We have considered how a contract is formed. Now we will examine the legal effect of statements made or adopted by parties in connection with their contracts. First, we will investigate statements made by the parties during the negotiation of a contract. Second, we will consider what happens when those statements are false. Third, we will consider how terms can be incorporated into a contract. Fourth, we will consider standard form agreements in consumer transactions, including reasons to use plain language in contracts.

PRE-CONTRACTUAL AND CONTRACTUAL STATEMENTS

Because the communication of an offer and its acceptance can be accomplished in a number of ways, it is sometimes difficult to identify which of the parties' statements are part of the negotiations and which are part of the actual contract. We therefore need to distinguish between *contractual terms* and *pre-contractual representations*.

Not every statement communicated during the negotiation process is a *contractual term*. A statement becomes a **contractual term** only if it is included in the agreement as a legally enforceable obligation. A contractual term is, by its very nature, a *promissory statement*. The person who makes it voluntarily agrees to do something in the future.

> a contractual term is a provision in an agreement that creates a legally enforceable obligation

In contrast, a **pre-contractual representation** is a statement one party makes by words or conduct with the intention of inducing another party to enter into a contract. By definition, it does not impose a contractual obligation. Although a pre-contractual representation may induce the creation of a contract, it does not form part of that contract. Figure 9.1 illustrates some of the differences between contractual terms and pre-contractual representations.

> a pre-contractual representation is a statement one party makes by words or conduct with the intention of inducing another party to enter into a contract

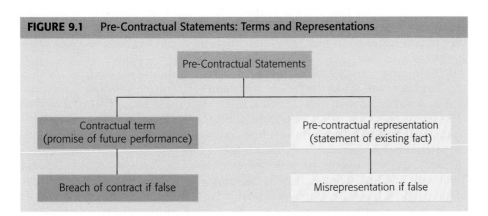

FIGURE 9.1   Pre-Contractual Statements: Terms and Representations

MISREPRESENTATION

The distinction between contractual terms and pre-contractual representations is especially important if a statement is false. If a non-contractual statement is false, we say that one of the parties has made a *misrepresentation*. When a contractual statement is not fulfilled, we say that one of the parties is in *breach of contract*. That distinction is important because misrepresentation and breach of contract have different legal effects. Pre-contractual representations may result in a form of legal liability, such as actionable misrepresentation, but not in an action for breach of contract. In this section we will focus on misrepresentation.[1]

The Nature of Misrepresentation

A **misrepresentation** is an incorrect statement of an *existing* fact. It is false when it is made. In contrast, a contractual term is not meant to describe an existing state of facts, but rather it provides a promise of *future* performance. Given its promissory nature, a contractual term cannot be false when it is given. Nor can a breach of contract occur as soon as such a promise is made. A breach occurs only when one of the parties fails to perform precisely as promised.

Misstatement of Fact

Not every misstatement during pre-contractual negotiations is a misrepresentation. A misrepresentation occurs only if the speaker claimed to state a *fact*. The difficulty with that requirement is that people often make *non-factual* statements during negotiations. For example, they sometimes state their own *opinions*. An **opinion** is the statement of a belief or judgment. For example, a person offers an opinion when they estimate the potential future revenue of an income-earning property. Opinions can range from carefree speculations to deliberate assessments based on a substantial body of evidence.

A personal opinion is not usually a misrepresentation, even if it is false. There are, however, situations in which it is risky to offer an opinion. If you state an opinion in a way that leads me to think that it *must* be true, a court may find that your statement includes not only an opinion but also an implied statement of fact that can be treated as a misrepresentation. That is true especially if you offer an opinion within your area of expertise. It is also risky to offer an opinion if you have no reason to believe that it is actually true. Suppose you are trying to persuade me to buy a particular vehicle from your used car lot. When I explain that I know nothing about gas consumption but am very concerned about fuel costs, you say, "I think that you'll find this model to be very thrifty, indeed." In fact, you know that the car in question is a notorious gas guzzler.

During pre-contractual negotiations, a person may describe how they (or someone else) will act in the future. A statement of **future conduct** is a second type of non-factual statement. Such statements are not usually treated as misrepresentations. However, a statement of future conduct *is* a misrepresentation if it is made fraudulently or if the future conduct is described in terms of a present intention. For instance, to persuade me to buy your farm, you might say, "I certainly do not intend to sell the neighbouring land to Herb's Sewage Treatment Facility." That statement contains a indication of your *present* state of mind, and if it is false, it may be classified as a fraudulent misrepresentation.

People sometimes discuss the law during pre-contractual negotiations.[2] A misrepresentation does not arise merely because you inaccurately describe a particular *law itself*. We all are presumed to know the law. However, the court may find a misrepresentation if you inaccurately describe the *consequences of a law*, because those consequences are treated as a matter of fact rather than law. Suppose you are trying persuade me to buy your land. It is not a misrepresentation if you incorrectly tell me that zoning laws do not apply to the prop-

---

[1.] We consider the remedies for breach of contract in Chapter 12.

[2.] *cf Rule v Pals* [1928] 2 WWR 123 (Sask CA) and *Graham v Legault* [1951] 3 DLR 423 (BC SC).

Margin notes:

a misrepresentation is a false statement of fact that causes the recipient to enter into a contract

an opinion is the statement of a belief or judgment

a non-promissory statement as to a party's future conduct is not usually treated as a misrepresentation

erty. That is a matter of law. However, it may be a misrepresentation if you inaccurately tell me that zoning approval has been granted and that I therefore would be able to develop the land. That is a matter of fact.[3]

Concept Summary 9.1 shows that expressions of opinion, descriptions of future conduct, and statements of law—even when they are inaccurate and induce the creation of contracts—are not normally treated as misrepresentations. To prove misrepresentation in those circumstances, a party must prove that the speaker implicitly claimed to state some fact. It is often difficult to tell when a factual statement has been made. Consider the case in Business Decision 9.1.

CONCEPT SUMMARY 9.1

Types of Pre-Contractual Statements Inducing Contracts

Non-factual statements (not actionable as misrepresentation)	Factual statements (actionable as misrepresentation)
Opinion based on speculation	Expert opinion
Description of another's future intent	Description of one's present intent
Statement of law	Statement of legal consequences

 BUSINESS DECISION 9.1

Statement of Fact or Opinion?[4]

An agent of Relax Realtors Inc is negotiating with a prospective purchaser of a strip mall. The purchaser is satisfied with the building, price, zoning restrictions, and closing date. The only unresolved issue is that one of the current tenants in the mall has a 10-year lease, which will remain in effect even if the building is sold. The purchaser is reluctant to enter into a relationship with an unknown tenant for that length of time and therefore asks the real estate agent a series of questions about the tenant. In response, the real estate agent describes the person as "a most desirable tenant" and says only good things about the tenant. Taking these statements on faith, the purchaser decides to buy the strip mall. Six months after completing the real estate transaction, the purchaser finds out that the tenant's rent has been in arrears for several months and that the tenant was often in arrears.

Question for Discussion

1. Was Relax Realtor's description of the leaseholder as "a most desirable tenant" a statement of fact or opinion? Explain your answer.

Silence as Misrepresentation

As a general rule, parties are not required to disclose material facts during pre-contractual negotiations, no matter how unethical non-disclosure may be. Suppose a company director is negotiating to buy shares from a shareholder. The director does not have to reveal that he knows certain information that will cause the value of the shares to increase within a few months.[5] There are, however, at least four occasions when the failure to speak will amount to misrepresentation:

- when silence would distort a previous assertion
- when the contract requires a duty of utmost good faith

[3.] *Hopkins v Butts* (1967) 65 DLR (2d) 711 (BC SC).

[4.] *Smith v Land & House Property Corp* (1885) 28 ChD 7 (CA).

[5.] *Prudential Insurance Co Ltd v Newman Industries Ltd* [1981] Ch 257.

- when a special relationship exists between the parties
- when a statutory provision requires disclosure

When Silence Would Distort a Previous Assertion   A party's silence some-times has the effect of falsifying a statement that was previously true. When a change in circumstances affects the accuracy of an earlier representation, the party that made that statement has a duty to disclose the change to the other party. Failure to do so amounts to a misrepresentation.

A misrepresentation may also occur if a party tells half the truth and remains silent on the other half. Despite the right to remain silent, a party cannot give a *partial* account if the unspoken words would substantially alter the meaning of the actual statement, even if the actual words are literally true. Suppose you take your cotton shirts to the dry cleaner. You are asked to sign a claim ticket, which, the cleaner tells you, "excludes liability for damage caused to silk and crushed velvet during the dry cleaning process." That is true. But the ticket *also* excludes liability for any other damage to any kind of fabric. The half-truth is a misrepresentation.[6]

When the Contract Requires a Duty of Utmost Good Faith   By their very nature, some contracts require a party to make full disclosure of the material facts. These are known as *contracts of utmost good faith*. The requirement of utmost good faith arises when one party is in a unique position to know the material facts. The best example involves insurance contracts. In order to assess the risk that a particular type of loss might occur, and to determine how much to charge for coverage, an insurance company needs to know as much as pos-sible about the situation. Of course, the only person who has that information is the customer. The law therefore imposes an obligation of good faith that requires the customer to disclose all of the relevant facts. A breach of that obli-gation is usually treated as a misrepresentation that allows the insurance com-pany to avoid the contract.

 ETHICAL PERSPECTIVE 9.1

Misrepresentation and Silence[7]

Johnny Grievor has always wanted to be a firefighter but he is functionally blind in his left eye. Knowing that the city of Ottawa would not hire him if it knew about his visual impairment, Grievor applied to be a firefighter but did not mention his dis-ability. He also remained silent about the fact that he had arranged for a friend to take the required medical examination. On the basis of his résumé and the results of his friend's med-ical examination, the city offered Grievor a position.

One day, while responding to a fire alarm, the fire truck that Grievor was driving collided with a van, killing two peo-ple. A short time later, the fire chief received an anonymous tip that Grievor was blind in his left eye. As a result, the city persuaded Grievor to resign and then had charges pressed against him under the *Criminal Code*. Although he had resigned from the fire department, Grievor relied on a clause

in his old employment contract that required the city to pay for "any and all damages or claims for damages or injuries or accidents done or caused by [him] during the performance of [his] duties." He therefore argued that, since the accident had occurred while he was working, the city was required to pay any legal fees that arose during the criminal proceedings. The city responded by arguing that Grievor had misrepresented the facts regarding his eyesight and that it consequently did not incur liability under the agreement.

The court held that the failure to disclose his visual impairment amounted to a misrepresentation that *would have* justified Grievor's dismissal. But the court also said that since the city accepted Grievor's resignation, rather than ter-minate his contract, it was obliged to pay his legal fees.

(continued)

---

6. *Curtis v Chemical Cleaning and Dyeing Co Ltd* [1951] 1 KB 805.

7. *Ottawa (City) v Ottawa Professional Fire Fighters* (1985) 52 OR (2d) 129 (Div Ct).

(continued)

Questions for Discussion

1. Do you agree that Grievor had a duty to disclose his disability? Would these facts have given rise to misrepresentation if Grievor had not used a friend to pass his medical examination? Explain your answer.

2. Do you agree that the city should be required to pay Grievor's legal fees? What if circumstances were different and money was owing to the families of the car crash victims? Should the city be required to pay the families if Grievor cannot? Explain your answer.[8]

When a Special Relationship Exists Between the Parties   When the relationship between two parties is one of trust, or when one of the parties has some other form of special influence over the other, a duty of disclosure may arise. Suppose your accountant is selling her cottage. If she sells it to a stranger, she is not obliged to disclose information about its structural defects if the purchaser does not ask the relevant questions. But she cannot remain silent if she is selling it to you. Because you would otherwise trust her on the basis of your special relationship, she has to fully disclose all material facts, whether or not you asked questions about the building's structure.

When a Statutory Provision Requires Disclosure   Some statutes require the disclosure of material facts in a contractual setting.

- Insurance legislation in many provinces contains statutory conditions that are deemed to be part of every insurance contract and must be printed on every policy. Many provinces have statutes that automatically insert certain conditions into every insurance contract. One of those conditions requires the disclosure of relevant information by those seeking insurance. If a customer does not satisfy that obligation, the contract may be unenforceable.[9]

- Some financial officers have a duty to disclose material facts. For instance, an officer or director has to speak up if they (or someone close to them) have an interest in a contract with their own company. If they fail to do so, the company may be entitled to set aside the contract.[10] The same holds true for some Crown corporations.[11] A similar disclosure requirement arises in the securities law.[12]

- Many provinces have legislation regulating the formation of domestic contracts. If a party failed to disclose significant assets or significant liabilities that existed when the domestic contract was made, the court can set aside the agreement or a provision in it.[13]

[8.] You may want to review the discussion of vicarious liability that we presented in Chapter 3.

[9.] *Securities Act*, RSO 1990, c S.5, s 75 (Ont); *Securities Act*, RSA 1981 c S-6.1, s 119 (Alta); *Securities Act*, RSBC 1996, c 418, s 85 (BC); *Securities Act*, CCSM, c S50, ss 50, 72 (Man).

[10.] *Eg Insurance Act*, RSBC 1996, c 226, s 126 (BC); *Insurance Act*, RSO 1990, c I.8, s 148 (Ont).

[11.] *Eg Bank Act*, SC 1991, c 46, s 206 (Can); *Credit Unions and Caisses Populaires Act, 1994*, SO 1994, c 11, s 148 (Ont); *Credit Union Act, 1985*, SS 1985, c C-45.1, s 74 (Sask).

[12.] *Financial Administration Act*, RSC 1985, c F-11, s 118 (Can).

[13.] *Eg Family Law Act*, RSO 1990, c F.3, s 56 (Ont); *Family Law Act*, SNWT 1997, c 18, s 8 (NWT).

Inducement

For a statement to be actionable as a misrepresentation, the deceived party must prove that the false statement induced the contract. In other words, the statement must have misled its recipient into creating the contract. The statement does not have to be the *only* inducing factor. A party can claim relief for misrepresentation even if other factors were also influential. However, a statement will not be actionable if it did not affect the recipient's decision, even if the other party made the representation with an intention to deceive. Nor will a statement be actionable if the recipient conducted an independent inquiry into the matter. In that situation, the contract is induced by the results of the party's own investigation, rather than the other party's representation.

What happens if the recipient of a false representation has an opportunity to test its accuracy, but fails to do so? Should that failure to investigate preclude a claim of misrepresentation? Consider the situation in You Be the Judge 9.1.

YOU BE THE JUDGE 9.1

Failure to Investigate a Misrepresentation[14]

Hurd saw Redgrave's advertisement for the sale of a suburban residence and a share in a local law practice. Hurd requested information about the earning potential of the practice. Redgrave indicated that the annual income of the practice was £400. In support of that claim, he produced business summaries from the previous three years indicating receipts of about £200 per year. When asked about the source of the remaining income, Redgrave produced boxes of papers and letters relating to additional business and allowed Hurd to inspect all of the accounts at his leisure. Despite the opportunity to do so, Hurd never bothered to inspect the documents. Relying instead on Redgrave's representations, Hurd agreed to buy the house and practice for £1600. Shortly after moving in, Hurd realized that the practice was utterly worthless.

Questions for Discussion

1. From a business perspective, do you think that it was reasonable for Hurd to rely on Redgrave's representations about the income earning potential of the practice?

2. If you were the judge, would you allow Hurd to claim misrepresentation even though he did not bother to inspect the documents?

3. Would your decision be any different if Redgrave intentionally deceived Hurd and buried the actual accounts in boxes of irrelevant documents?

The Legal Consequences of Misrepresentation

There are two possible consequences of an actionable misrepresentation. The deceived party may receive:

- the remedy of rescission
- the right to damages

Rescission is the only *contractual* consequence of misrepresentation.

Rescission

rescission is the cancellation of a contract by the court with the aim of restoring the parties, to the greatest extent possible, to their pre-contractual state

Rescission is the cancellation of a contract with the aim of restoring the parties, to the greatest extent possible, to their pre-contractual state. It can be done by the parties or, if necessary, through the courts. However, it is often

---

14. *Redgrave v Hurd* (1881) 20 Ch D 1 (CA).

difficult to know in advance whether a court will grant rescission because it is a *discretionary remedy*, one that is not available *as of right*. The remedy is awarded on the basis of the court's judgment about what is best according to the rules of reason and justice.[15]

The remedy of rescission is often accompanied by an order for *restitution*. **Restitution** involves a giving back and taking back on both sides.[16] Suppose you manufacture snowboards and need to order a steady supply of waterproof paints. A supplier represents that it has waterproof paints to sell but insists that you agree to purchase four shipments over the next two years to take advantage of a special rate. You agree to those conditions, requisition a cheque, and send it to the supplier. When the first shipment arrives, you discover that the paint is not waterproof and is therefore useless to you. You ask for your money back, but the supplier refuses. Assuming that the shipments of paint are worth thousands of dollars, it might be wise to seek an order of rescission from the courts rather than simply disregard the contract. Merely setting aside the contract will not be sufficient. You paid thousands of dollars that you will want back. Likewise, the supplier delivered a truckload of paint that it will want back. Restitution is therefore the appropriate remedy. The court will try to restore the pre-contractual situation by allowing you to recover the money at the same time that it allows the supplier to recover the paint.

restitution involves a giving back and taking back on both sides

The victim of a misrepresentation may be barred from rescission in certain circumstances. First, if the misled party *affirmed* the contract, then rescission is not available. **Affirmation** occurs when the misled party declares an intention to carry out the contract or otherwise acts as though it is bound by it. To continue the earlier example, suppose you discover that the first shipment of paint is not waterproof but do nothing about it. Six months pass, and the next shipment arrives. You then complain that neither shipment contained waterproof paint. The six-month *lapse of time* suggests you affirmed the contract.[17]

affirmation occurs when the misled party declares an intention to carry out the contract or otherwise acts as though it is bound by it

Second, rescission may be barred if restitution is impossible. If the parties cannot be substantially returned to their pre-contractual positions, a court is reluctant to grant rescission. The more that has been done under the contract, the less likely a court is to grant rescission. To further continue our example, if you used a substantial portion of the paint supply before discovering that it was not, in fact, waterproof, restitution is not possible in a strict sense. Since you cannot give the paint back, rescission may not be available.

Third, rescission may be unavailable if it would affect a third party. In this case, it is the rights of a third party that make restitution impossible. Suppose you buy a strip mall on the basis of certain representations about its earning potential. You lease portions of the mall to tenants but are unable to earn enough to pay down your mortgages on the building, let alone make anywhere near the profits you were promised. If you seek an order for rescission against the vendor of the mall, you would probably fail. The tenants have acquired a right to occupy the premises. Those third-party rights therefore preclude the court from forcing the vendor to give back your purchase price in exchange for an empty shopping mall.

---

15. *Wrights Canadian Ropes Ltd v Minister of National Revenue* [1946] 2 DLR 225 (SCC).

16. We will discuss restitution in more detail in Chapter 12 under the heading of "Unjust Enrichment."

17. *Leaf v International Galleries* [1950] 2 KB 86 (CA).

Damages

damages are intended to provide monetary compensation for the losses that a person suffered as a result of relying upon a misrepresentation

A court may respond to a misrepresentation by awarding *damages* against the party that made the statement. In this situation, **damages** are intended to provide monetary compensation for the losses that a person suffered as a result of relying upon a misrepresentation. It is important to understand the precise reason for those damages. As we will see in Chapter 12, damages may be awarded for a breach of contract. Nevertheless, if damages are awarded for a misrepresentation, the plaintiff's claim arises not in contract, but rather in tort. (That is true even though the plaintiff is complaining that the misrepresentation induced the creation of a contract.) As Part 2 of this book explained, tort law is based on the principle that "a person who by his or her fault causes damage to another may be held responsible."[18] There are many types of tort. The one that is relevant for present purposes depends upon the nature of the misrepresentation.

Types of Misrepresentation

The law distinguishes between three types of misrepresentation: innocent, fraudulent, and negligent. The rules are somewhat different for each.

Innocent Misrepresentation

an innocent misrepresentation is a statement a person makes carefully and without knowledge of the fact that it is false

An **innocent misrepresentation** is a statement a person makes carefully and without knowledge of the fact that it is false. If the speaker is innocent of any fraudulent or negligent conduct, the general rule is that the deceived party is not entitled to recover damages. The only legal remedy available for innocent misrepresentation is rescission, and rescission is available only when there is a substantial difference between what the deceived party had bargained for and what was, in fact, obtained.

Negligent Misrepresentation

a negligent misrepresentation is a false, inducing statement made in an unreasonable or careless manner

Even a person who acts honestly may *carelessly or unreasonably* make a statement that is inaccurate and that induces the creation of a contract. The party making the statement does not need to know that it is false in order to be liable. Such statements are known as **negligent misrepresentations**. Until recently, the law did not distinguish between innocent misrepresentations and negligent misrepresentations. In either event, the only possible remedy was rescission. However, the courts have now recognized that a negligent misrepresentation may also amount to a tort that supports an award of damages.[19]

Fraudulent Misrepresentation

a fraudulent misrepresentation occurs when a person makes a statement they know is false *or* that they have no reason to believe is true *or* that is reckless

A **fraudulent misrepresentation** occurs when a person makes a statement that they know is false *or* that they have no reason to believe is true *or* that they recklessly make without regard to the truth.[20] Liability will arise under the tort of deceit.[21] Fraud is, of course, a very serious matter, especially in the business world. A person who is held liable for fraud will find it difficult to attract investors, partners, or customers. For that reason, the courts require an

---

18. *Canadian National Railway v Norsk Pacific Steamship* (1992) 91 DLR (4th) 289 (SCC).

19. Chapter 6 covers the tort of negligent misrepresentation.

20. *Derry v Peek* (1889) 14 App Cas 337 (HL).

21. The tort of deceit was discussed in Chapter 5.

allegation of fraud to be supported by very clear evidence.[22] At the same time, however, if fraud is proven, then the courts are particularly eager to award damages.[23]

CONCEPT SUMMARY 9.2

Types of Misrepresentation and Their Legal Effect

	Elements of proof	Available remedies
Innocent misrepresentation	• false statement of fact or misleading silence • inducing contract	• rescission of contract
Negligent misrepresentation	• false statement • made in an unreasonable or careless manner • inducing a contract • causing a loss that is not always sufficiently remedied by rescission	• rescission of contract • damages in tort
Fraudulent misrepresentation	• false statement or misleading silence • made without honest belief in its truth • made with intent to induce contract • inducing contract • causing a loss not always sufficiently remedied by rescission	• rescission of contract • damages in tort

CONTRACTUAL TERMS

Having considered pre-contractual statements, we can now turn to statements that actually become part of a contract. Unlike representations and misrepresentations, contractual terms arise from statements that actually impose obligations under the contract. We will consider two types of contractual terms: terms expressed by the parties and those that are implied by a court or statute.

Express Terms

An **express term** is a statement made by one of the parties that a reasonable person would believe was intended to create an enforceable obligation.

an express term is a statement made by one of the parties that a reasonable person would believe was intended to create an enforceable obligation

Proof of Express Terms

When the contract is formed on the basis of an oral agreement, it is first necessary to determine what words were actually spoken. That is primarily a question of evidence. Written contracts produce different difficulties. For example, what if the formation of a contract involves the exchange of several conflicting documents?[24] Perhaps even more difficult is the situation that arises when a combination of written and spoken words are used during the formation of a contract. We consider each of these situations.

[22.] In order to discourage improper allegations of fraud, the courts often award costs against people who fail to prove such claims. The concept of costs was discussed in Chapter 2.

[23.] A court may award not only compensatory damages, but also punitive damages. The concept of punitive damages was discussed in Chapter 3.

[24.] In Chapter 7, we discussed the possibility of the "battle of forms."

It is often difficult to prove the terms of a contract that was created orally. When an agreement is unwritten and unwitnessed, a court is required to determine whose version of events is more believable. Still, as long as there is no formal writing requirement and all of the other conditions of contract formation have been met, oral agreements are binding. As a matter of risk management, however, it is usually a good idea for a business person to "get it in writing." Aside from issues of proof, the writing process encourages the parties to contemplate the terms more carefully.

parol evidence is evidence that is not contained within the written contract

If an agreement is written, oral evidence generally cannot be used to add to, subtract from, qualify, or vary the terms of the document.[25] That is known as the *parol evidence rule*. **Parol evidence**, in this context, refers to evidence that is not contained within the written contract. Knowledge of that rule is an important element of risk management. Business people often sign a written agreement on the assurance that some of its terms will not be enforced, or on the assurance that certain items discussed during negotiations are part of the deal even though they are not mentioned in the written document. One should be extremely suspicious of such oral assurances. The parol evidence rule generally means that they are unenforceable.

There are several exceptions to the parol evidence rule. Parol evidence is admissible:

- to rectify or fix a *mistake* in a contractual document
- to prove that a contract was *never really formed* or is somehow *defective*
- to *resolve ambiguities* in the document
- to demonstrate that a document does not contain the parties' *complete agreement*

a collateral contract is a separate undertaking one person makes to another in consideration of that other person's entry into a formal contract

There is one other way around the parol evidence rule. A statement may be characterized as a *collateral contract* that independently exists alongside the main contract. A **collateral contract** is a separate agreement one party makes in exchange for the other party's agreement to enter into the main contract. Suppose you want to buy oil of a certain quality. The seller's standard written contract contains a clause indicating that it *does not* warrant the quality of its oil.[26] You therefore offer to enter into a contract for the purchase of oil under the seller's standard form contract, but only if the seller enters into a collateral contract that *does* warrant the quality of the oil. You have avoided the parol evidence rule. The seller's promise regarding the quality of the oil is inadmissible under the main contract but it is enforceable as a separate agreement.

CONCEPT SUMMARY 9.3

Exceptions to the Parol Evidence Rule

- Parol evidence is admissible to rectify a mistaken contractual document.
- Parol evidence is admissible to prove that a contract was never formed or is defective.
- Parol evidence is admissible to resolve contractual ambiguities.
- Parol evidence is admissible to demonstrate an incomplete agreement.
- Parol evidence rule is not applicable to collateral contract.

[25.] *Goss v Lord Nugent* (1833) 110 ER 713 at 715.

[26.] *LG Thorne & Co Pty Ltd v Thomas Borthwick & Sons (A'asia) Ltd* (1956) 56 SR (NSW) 81 at 94.

Interpretation of Express Terms

Even if the parties agree on particular terms and write them into a document, they may disagree on the interpretation of those words. Consider Business Decision 9.2.

BUSINESS DECISION 9.2

Contractual Interpretation

It was Julia's twenty-fifth birthday, and she was about to be married to Robert. Just before the ceremony, Robert's wealthy mother, Fiona, handed Julia a one-page document, which contained this offer: "If you promise to go through with this today, I promise to pay you $1 000 000 on your thirty-fifth birthday, as long as the two of you do not remarry." Julia smiled and signed the document. She knew that the offer was a serious one. The marriage lasted only five years. Shortly after Julia's thirtieth birthday, Robert divorced her and went to "find himself" somewhere in the Himalayas.

Three years later, Robert found himself back in his hometown and saw a woman from across the bar and fell in love with her on the spot. It was Julia. They began dating again and decided to get remarried. Three weeks after exchanging their vows, Julia turned 35. Julia approached Fiona about her contractual promise to pay $1 000 000. Fiona refused to pay, arguing that Julia and Robert had breached the terms of the agreement.

Julia and Fiona agree that their contract contains the term "as long as the two of you do not remarry." However, they each have a different view of what that means. The term is **ambiguous**, having more than one plausible meaning. That is quite common. A great deal of contractual litigation turns on differences in interpretation. In resolving such disputes, the courts ask how a reasonable business person in the parties' position would have interpreted the relevant clause. Nevertheless, the issue can still be difficult.

> an ambiguous term has more than one plausible meaning

Fiona would likely take a **literal approach** to the words in the document and stress their *ordinary meaning*. She would argue that the contract plainly stated payment was due only if Julia and Robert did not remarry. By divorcing and then marrying each other again, they broke that condition.

> the literal approach assigns words their ordinary meaning

Julia would interpret the contract somewhat differently. She would take a *contextual approach*. The **contextual approach** goes beyond the four corners of the document by looking at the parties' intentions and their circumstances. Julia would argue that her mother-in-law wanted to make sure that she and Robert stayed married *to each other*. On that view, the term "as long as the two of you do not remarry" was meant to discourage Robert and Julia from marrying *other* people. And since they were married to each other on Julia's thirty-fifth birthday, they fell within the meaning of the contract.

> the contextual approach goes beyond the four corners of the document by looking at the parties' intentions and their circumstances

Which of those two approaches is more plausible? If you are inclined to side with Fiona, you should also consider the *golden rule* of interpretation. According to the **golden rule**, words will be given their plain, ordinary meaning unless to do so would result in absurdity.[27] If we were to adopt a strict, literal reading of the term "so long as the *two* of you do not remarry," a strange result would follow. We would be forced to conclude that Julia should be paid even if she abandoned Robert and married someone else, as long as Robert remained unmarried on Julia's thirty-fifth birthday. Given Fiona's intention at the time she made the offer, such an interpretation would seem absurd. In this case, the golden rule suggests that we avoid a strict, literal interpretation.

> the golden rule says that words will be given their plain, ordinary meaning unless to do so would result in absurdity

---

27. *Suncor Inc v Norcen Int Ltd* (1988) 89 AR 200 (QB).

Another possible reason for finding against Fiona is the *contra proferentem* rule. The **contra proferentem rule** ensures that the meaning that is least favourable to the author will prevail. That rule is justified by the fact that the author, in this case Fiona, is in the best position to create a clear and unambiguous term.

Implied Terms

Even if the parties carefully write out their agreement, that document may not contain all of the relevant terms. A contract may contain both express terms and *implied terms*. An **implied term** arises by operation of law, either through the common law or under a statute.

Terms Implied by a Court

Unlike representations and express terms, implied terms do not arise from the parties themselves. They are inserted into a contract by the law. And since people are generally entitled to create their own agreements, a court will normally not imply a term unless that term is necessary in order to implement the parties' presumed intentions. An implied term is "necessary" in this context if (i) it is an obvious consequence of the parties' agreement, or (ii) it is required for the purpose of business efficacy.

Those two criteria often overlap. Suppose you are in the business of leasing equipment. A customer returns some leased equipment to you on time but in damaged condition. What if your contract did not expressly say anything about the condition of the equipment? That sort of term was presumably intended by both parties. After all, the whole point of a rental agreement is that the thing must be returned at the end of the lease. Consequently, a court will imply a term that requires the equipment to come back in the same condition in which it went out, subject to reasonable wear and tear.[28]

Courts will not imply a term simply because it is reasonable or would improve the contract. To the contrary, a term generally will be implied only if it is reasonable, necessary, capable of exact formulation, and clearly justified having regard to the parties' intentions when they contracted. Of those considerations, the last one is the most important.[29] A contract may also contain an implied term that reflects a standard practice that has evolved within in a particular field, as long as that term would not be inconsistent with the parties' express intentions. Return to our example in which you created a lease with a company that regularly rents equipment. Even though your contract is silent on the point, it may contain a term that people in your trade habitually include in their agreements.[30]

The courts sometimes imply a term on the basis of a contract's legal characteristics. Certain kinds of agreements, by their very nature, involve certain obligations, even if the parties did not intend them. The Supreme Court of Canada, for example, has held that an employment contract contains a term that requires the employer to provide reasonable notice before dismissing the employee, even if a contract is silent on the issue or even if the agreement expressly says that the employee can be dismissed without notice.[31]

---

28. *Con-force Prods Ltd v Luscar Ltd* (1982) 27 Sask R 299 (QB).

29. *Canadian Helicopters Ltd v Interpac Forest Products Ltd*, 2001 BCCA 39.

30. *British Crane Hire Corp Ltd v Ipswich Plant Hire Ltd* [1975] QB 303.

31. *Machtinger v HOJ Industries* (1992) 91 DLR (4th) 491 (SCC). Employment contracts are discussed in Chapter 26.

Terms Implied by Statute

Terms are often implied by statute. In Chapter 13, we will see several examples that arise under the *Sale of Goods Act*. Likewise, consumer protection laws in Manitoba, the Northwest Territories, and the Yukon imply a term that the goods being sold are new and unused, unless otherwise described.[32] Whenever a statute implies a term into a contract, the term is incorporated automatically without judicial intervention. If a dispute comes before the courts, the term is treated as if the parties expressly created it. In some cases, however, a statutory term will not apply if the parties have expressly excluded it.

Standard Form Agreements

The terms of many business transactions are dictated by *standard form agreements*. **Standard form agreements** are mass-produced documents, usually drafted by the party in an economic position to offer certain terms on a "take-it-or-leave-it" basis. Standard form agreements are most often used for transactions that occur over and over again. A bank, for instance, does not want to negotiate a completely new contract every time it lends money to a customer. As a matter of risk management, it is better to avoid the risk of trouble by using a model that has been refined and tested over the years. Furthermore, it would be time consuming and expensive to allow each customer to negotiate new terms. Those additional costs would, of course, translate into higher interest rates. The same general principles apply to any business that enters into similar agreements on a repetitive basis.

There is, however, a downside to standard form agreements. Such contracts are often so long and complex that few customers actually read and understand them. Furthermore, because they tend to be offered on a take-it-or-leave-it basis, customers have no realistic opportunity to bargain for better terms. In a sense, the customer is at the mercy of the other party. If the customers refuse to accept the standard terms, they cannot purchase the goods or services in question.

One type of term that customers are often required to accept in standard form agreements is an **exclusion clause**, or *limitation clause*, or *waiver*. For example, an outdoors adventure company might try to use an exclusion clause to preclude the risk of being sued by customers who are injured during their expeditions. Such a term is perfectly legitimate if the following three things can be demonstrated:

- First, the term must have been drafted in clear, *unambiguous language*. If an exclusion clause is ambiguous, it will be interpreted as strictly and as literally as possible, and it will be given the meaning that is least favourable to its author.

- Second, the party against whom the exclusion clause is meant to operate must be given *reasonable notice* of the term and its effect.

- Third, it must be shown that the party against whom the exclusion clause is meant to operate *agreed* that the exclusion clause is part of the contract. A signature is usually the best evidence of that agreement.

An exclusion clause will not be invalidated merely because one party was in a stronger bargaining position than the other. A judge will, however, consider such an imbalance when deciding whether the weaker party truly did agree to the clause.

standard form agreements are mass-produced documents usually drafted by a party who is in an economic position to offer those terms on a "take-it-or-leave-it" basis

an exclusion clause is a contractual term that seeks to protect one party from various sorts of legal liability

---

[32] CCSM c C200, s 58 (Man); RSNWT 1988, c C-17 s 70 (NWT); RSY 2002, c 40, s 58 (Yuk).

Ticket Contracts

Standard form agreements sometimes take the form of a ticket or receipt. As a business person, you might try to incorporate certain terms, including exclusion clauses, into your contract by having them printed on the back of a ticket you issue to your customers. Whether those clauses are valid depends on how they are presented. As with exclusion clauses, the general rule is that the terms must be brought to the customer's notice either before or when the contract is made. As usual, the question is not whether the customer actually read those terms, but whether they were given *reasonable notice*. If the reasonable person would not have known about the printing on the back of the ticket, then the customer probably will not be bound by those terms. On the other hand, if the customer knew that the back of the ticket contained terms, those terms will be incorporated into the contract even if the customer chose not to read them.

BUSINESS DECISION 9.3

Standard Form Agreements

Friedrich has a small book store. He registered an Internet domain name and hired a consultant to help him set up his page for e-commerce. Because he will now be offering books for sale worldwide, Friedrich wants to be sure that his standard purchase contract includes a "no refund" policy and a requirement that all payments are to be made in Canadian currency. Friedrich's consultant has offered him a choice of three design layouts for an electronic catalogue that would be the equivalent of 19 pages in a paper document.

The first layout is a very long, one-page catalogue. Rather than having page breaks signifying the end of each paper page equivalent, the customer scrolls through the electronic catalogue by clicking on the scroll bar. The "no refund" policy and the Canadian currency requirement are found somewhere in the middle of the catalogue. At the bottom of the catalogue is an electronic order form, which allows the customer to enter the desired book titles. Once the customer has completed the form, all that is left to do is click on the "order now" button, at which point the purchase request is sent to Friedrich electronically. With this layout, the customer has the opportunity to view the "no refund" policy and the Canadian currency requirement but could, accidentally or on purpose, miss them entirely and place an order without being aware of those terms.

The second layout has a much more elegant design. It has the appearance of an all-in-one page design, but the entire catalogue is accessible from a single screen and does not require the customer to scroll through the document. Instead, access to all of the same text is available through hyperlinks. By clicking on specific icons, the customer can choose which information to view. One icon in this layout is labelled "terms & conditions." If the customer clicks on it, the "no refund" policy, the Canadian currency requirements, and the other key terms appear on the screen. Another icon is the "order now" button. Customers can order whether or not they have clicked on the terms and conditions hyperlink.

The third layout is similar to the second except that it is more cumbersome. It requires customers to click on the "terms & conditions" icon. It also requires them to answer "yes" when asked, "Have you read the terms and conditions and do you agree to them?" Once they have done so, they are then required to answer "yes" a second time when asked, "Are you sure?" That mechanism makes it virtually impossible for customers to place orders without being aware of the existence of Friedrich's terms and conditions.

Questions for Discussion

1. Which of these layouts will ensure that Friedrich's terms will be incorporated into the contract? Explain your answer.

2. From a business perspective, which layout would you recommend to Friedrich? Why?

3. Are there any other terms that Friedrich should incorporate into the standard contract to help the success of his new worldwide business venture?

Signed Forms

As a general rule, people who sign standard form agreements are bound by all of the terms expressed in them, even if they have not actually read or understood those terms. There is a rationale for this rule. By signing a document, a customer indicates a willingness to be bound by its terms, and the other party receives some assurance that the agreement is enforceable.

Many standard form agreements are, however, extremely long and complicated. A judge therefore may apply an exception to the general rule if the customer is required to quickly sign the document without enjoying a reasonable opportunity to study its terms. In such circumstances, there is an onus on the party relying on the document to prove that the customer was given reasonable notice of its relevant terms. That exception prevents a more powerful party from burying onerous or unusual terms in the small print of a difficult document.

CASE BRIEF 9.1

Tilden Rent-a-Car Co v Clendenning (1978) 83 DLR (3d) 400 (Ont CA)

While filling out a car rental application at the Vancouver airport, Mr Clendenning was asked by the rental agent whether he wanted to purchase collision insurance for an additional, modest fee. After agreeing to pay extra, Clendenning was handed a complicated rental contract. Being in a hurry, he signed the document without reading it. The rental agent neither asked him to read the contract nor mentioned that it included an unusual term that excluded insurance coverage if the driver had consumed *any* amount of alcohol.

During the rental period, Clendenning got into an accident and damaged the vehicle. He admitted to drinking a small quantity of alcohol that day, but it was unclear exactly how much he had consumed. Not having read the agreement, Clendenning was unaware of the term that excluded coverage if *any* alcohol was consumed. That term did not

appear on the face of the contract; it was found on the back in small print. Clendenning claimed he was led to believe that the insurance provided complete coverage. Tilden, on the other hand, argued that Clendenning's signature was sufficient to bind him to the terms of the contract. Tilden also claimed that Clendenning's previous dealings with Tilden provided him with ample opportunity to read the terms of the contract despite the fact that he signed it that day in a hurry.

The Court of Appeal held that Clendenning's signature did *not* represent a true acceptance of the terms in the contract. Because the relevant term was onerous and unusual, Tilden was required to provide Clendenning with reasonable notice of it as well as a reasonable opportunity to understand and appreciate what he was signing.

The clause that was contained in the standard form contract that Mr Clendenning signed is an example of a *boilerplate clause*. A **boilerplate clause** is a clause that is used repeatedly without any variation.[33] As we have seen, businesses often use boilerplate clauses to quickly and efficiently allocate contractual risks, manage exposure to liability, and highlight the need to purchase insurance (among other things). The Companion Website for this chapter contains a survey of some of the more significant types of boilerplate clauses.

a boilerplate clause is a clause that is used repeatedly without any variation

Using Plain Language in Contracts

Contracts and other legal documents can sometimes be difficult to understand, especially if they contain complex legal terminology. That is particularly a problem with standard form contracts. Fortunately, there is now a movement away from legalistic jargon and obscure Latin phrases, and toward *plain language*. By using plain language, governments and businesses can increase the likelihood that their documents will be understood by everyone, including people who do not have legal training.

[33.] The source of the phrase is not entirely clear. It may refer to sheets of metal that were used by newspapers in the first half of the twentieth century. Those sheets were very strong and very durable.

As one example, the official *Communications Policy of the Government of Canada* requires the use of plain language in all government communications, both internally within government and externally to the public.[34] The Canadian Bankers Association aims to ensure that mortgage documents are written in understandable plain language.[35] Some laws even make it mandatory to use plain language in certain circumstances.[36]

The use of plain language in contracts is clearly a consumer protection issue, as discussed in Chapter 19. However, businesses can also benefit from the use of plain language in contracts and other documents by reducing employee training (regarding the meaning of different business documents), improving communication with customers, and reducing time spent answering customer questions arising from confusion about documents. These effects can lead to tremendous cost-savings and improved customer relations.[37]

CONCEPT SUMMARY 9.4

Managing Risk in Association with Standard Form Contracts

- Use standard form contracts that have been tested and have a proven record of use, over a period of years if possible.
- Use clear, unambiguous language for onerous terms and consider using plain language throughout the contract.
- Give reasonable notice of onerous and unusual terms, and instruct staff to draw customers' attention to such terms.
- Require customers to clearly indicate their agreement to be bound by onerous or unusual terms, perhaps by requiring their initials in a box next to the term itself.

---

[34] *Communications Policy of the Government of Canada* (November 29, 2004) <www.tbs-sct.gc.ca/pubs_pol/sipubs/comm/comm1_e.asp#03>.

[35] Canadian Bankers Association, Plain Language Mortgage Documents—CBA Commitment <www.cba.ca/en/viewdocument.asp?fl=3&sl=11&tl=127&docid=296&pg=1>.

[36] See *eg* the *Bank Act*, 1991, c 46, sc459.1(4.1): "A bank shall disclose the prohibition on coercive tied selling set out in subsection (1) in a statement in plain language that is clear and concise, displayed and available to customers and the public at all of its branches . . ."

[37] C M Stephens *Plain Language Legal Writing* (1992).

Chapter Summary

Not every statement made during pre-contractual negotiations becomes a contractual term. Pre-contractual representations are assertions of fact made with the intention of inducing another party to enter into a contract, but do not form part of the contract. Contractual terms, on the other hand, are provisions in an agreement that create legally enforceable obligations. If necessary, a court will determine whether a statement is a representation or a term, based on how a reasonable person would have understood the statement and the parties' intentions.

A misrepresentation is a false pre-contractual statement that induces the recipient of the statement into a contract. Inaccurate expressions of opinion, descriptions of future conduct, and statements of law are normally not treated as misrepresentations. To prove misrepresentation in those circumstances, a party must prove that the speaker implicitly claimed to state some fact. Silence can amount to misrepresentation in certain circumstances.

For a false statement to be actionable misrepresentation, the deceived party must be able to prove that it induced the contract. The two possible consequences of an actionable misrepresentation are (i) the remedy of rescission, and (ii) the right to damages. The remedy of rescission usually coincides with restitution, requiring a giving back and taking on both sides. Its aim is to return the parties to their pre-contractual state. Rescission may be barred if (i) the misled party ultimately affirms the contract, (ii) restitution is not possible, or (iii) a third party's rights are affected. Damages are an award of money meant to compensate the loss suffered by the misled party due to the misrepresentation.

An innocent misrepresentation involves a statement made carefully and without knowledge that it is false. A negligent misrepresentation is a false statement made in an unreasonable or careless manner. A fraudulent misrepresentation is made without any belief in its truth or with reckless indifference. All three types of misrepresentation can give rise to rescission. Only fraudulent and negligent misrepresentation can give rise to tort damages.

An express term, whether oral or written, is a statement intended to create a legally enforceable obligation. When an agreement has been reduced to writing, the parol evidence rule states that oral evidence is inadmissible to vary or qualify the written contract unless it meets certain requirements. Parol evidence can also be used to demonstrate the existence of a collateral contract.

Courts use several approaches to resolve business disputes over the interpretation of contractual terms. The literal approach assigns words their ordinary meaning. The contextual approach takes into account the parties' intentions, as well as the surrounding circumstances. The golden rule suggests that words be given their plain meaning unless doing so would result in absurdity. Courts imply a term only if it is necessary to implement the parties' presumed intentions. Some statutes imply certain terms into particular types of contract.

Standard form agreements are mass-produced documents drafted by the party who is in an economic position to offer those terms on a take-it-or-leave-it basis. A person who signs a standard form agreement is generally bound by its terms, whether or not they ever read or understood those terms. Courts require that the existence of onerous or unusual terms in a standard form agreement be brought to the attention of the other party. Businesses should use plain language in their contracts with consumers. Plain language helps ensure that consumers understand contracts and can result in cost-savings and improved customer relations for businesses.

Review Questions

1. Distinguish between a pre-contractual representation and a contractual term, giving examples of each. Why is that distinction important?

2. Define "misrepresentation" in your own words. Can a statement be a misrepresentation if neither party is aware that the statement is false? What must one be able to demonstrate to prove misrepresentation?

3. What is the difference between a misrepresentation and a breach of contract?

4. Name three types of false statements that are often made during the course of negotiations that are not misrepresentations. Give an example of each.

5. Provide examples of the four circumstances in which the failure to speak will amount to misrepresentation.

6. What are two possible legal consequences of an actionable misrepresentation? Which of those possibilities provides a contractual remedy?

7. What is meant by the term "rescission"?

8. List three circumstances that may preclude the victim of a misrepresentation from seeking restitution. Why is restitution unavailable in these circumstances?

9. What is an express term? Why is it sometimes difficult to determine the meaning of an express term?

10. What is meant by the term "parol evidence"?

11. Why is it important for business people to know and understand the parol evidence rule?

12. When is a contractual term ambiguous? Describe how courts resolve disputes over ambiguous terms.

13. What is the difference between the literal approach and contextual approach to contractual interpretation?

14. State and explain the golden rule of interpretation.

15. State and explain the *contra proferentem* rule.

16. What is an implied term?

17. When will a court find that a contract contains an implied term? When will a court be reluctant to do so?

18. Briefly describe the significance of the standard form agreement in modern commercial transactions.

19. When is it irrelevant that a standard form agreement was signed?

20. When might it be appropriate for a business to design and use a ticket contract? Why should a business use plain rather than legalistic language on the ticket?

CASES AND PROBLEMS

1. Seymour is a supplier of custodial cleaning products. While negotiating a contract to sell a crate of floor wax, Seymour makes the statements below. Categorize each statement as (i) a pre-contractual representation, (ii) a mere opinion, (iii) a contractual term, or (iv) a collateral contract. Give reasons for your answer and describe the legal effect of each statement.

   a. "This floor wax is the best made anywhere in the world."

   b. "I personally truly believe this floor wax is the best made anywhere in the world."

   c. "Studies have shown that this floor wax is the best made anywhere in the world."

   d. "If, after trying this floor wax, you don't agree that it is unquestionably the best made anywhere in the world, I'll come and polish your floors myself for a month."

   e. "If, after trying this floor wax, you don't agree that it is unquestionably the best made anywhere in the world, I'll eat my hat."

2. Marc recently arrived in Vancouver to go mountain biking on Vancouver's famous North Shore mountains, the birthplace of extreme mountain biking. Up to that time, Marc had only ridden his bike in Manitoba where there were no extreme mountain bike trails. Marc thought it would be a good idea to have an experienced guide take him to the North Shore trails because he was not familiar with the level of difficulty on the different trails. The guide Marc hired had been riding the North Shore for ten years and was a very experienced biker. Before signing a contract with the guide to take him on five specific trails on the North Shore, Marc asked the guide how difficult the trails were. The guide told Marc, "I don't find them difficult myself." On the basis of this statement, Marc signed the contract to hire the guide.

   On the first trail that Marc rode with the guide, Marc found that he was in way over his head. The trail was much more difficult than Marc ever imagined and he ended up walking most of the trail because he was so scared. After the first trail, Marc decided that he didn't want to ride any of the other trails. He demanded his money back from the guide, claiming that the guide had made a misrepresentation about the difficulty of the trails in order to induce Marc to enter the contract. Do you think Marc will be successful in proving that the guide made a material misrepresentation that induced the contract?

3. Ziggy purchased some farmland and a small farmhouse with the aim of growing tobacco. After a very successful first season, he realized that he should insure his business. He contacted Farmers Choice Insurance Ltd. Simone, a broker for Farmers Choice, appraised Ziggy's farm and set up the policy. Ziggy paid for the entire year's insurance upfront. Two months after the policy took effect, a fire destroyed the entire crop. Although the cause of the fire could not be determined, Ziggy put in a claim for the damage incurred. After its investigation, Farmers Choice refused to pay Ziggy's insurance claim, stating that it was previously unaware of these facts:

   a. Ziggy had suffered a previous loss by fire.

   b. Ziggy's wife had previously been convicted of fraud and had served time in a penitentiary.

   c. A fire insurance policy issued by another insurance company had previously been cancelled prior to its expiration date.

   d. Ziggy's wife admittedly had enemies and there was therefore a danger of arson.

   e. Ziggy was a chronic alcoholic and, although never proven, it was suspected that the previous fire had been caused by a still exploding in Ziggy's basement.

   Simone admits that she did not specifically ask Ziggy any questions pertaining to those facts. Will Farmers Choice be able to avoid its contract with Ziggy altogether? Should the original contract stand even if no payment is to be made on this particular claim?

4. Navinder decided to list her summer cottage for sale at a price of $130 000. Nancy, a prospective purchaser, asked Navinder whether she knew anything about its current market value. Navinder indicated that although it had not recently been appraised, the cottage was originally built for $50 000 on land for which she paid $25 000. She indicated that a professional builder had made a number of improvements to the cottage, thereby increasing its value. These

included a second-storey loft with two bedrooms and a new bathroom. Navinder stated that the addition added $25 000 to the resale value of the cottage. She also mentioned that a professional landscaper had been hired at a cost of $2500 to finish the property and that she had purchased one acre of undeveloped land on either side of the property at a total cost of $30 000. On that basis, Navinder claimed that the cottage was worth $132 500. Although Nancy loved everything about the cottage, she was somewhat skeptical of Navinder's valuation. Nancy hired Al's Appraisals to determine the value of the property. Al provided a written appraisal at $129 750. Nancy decided to buy the cottage at the listed price. A few months later, Nancy's insurance company reappraised the house for insurance purposes at $82 000. Nancy was astounded. She hired a third appraiser, who provided a detailed report proving beyond the shadow of a doubt that the entire property was worth no more than $85 000. Can Nancy successfully sue Navinder for misrepresentation? Is there any other possible legal means for Nancy to recoup her losses?

5. Antonio and Susanna have decided to leave the big city. They arranged to purchase a large country inn from Jay Jonah Investments Inc. According to the terms of their contract, Antonio and Susanna agreed to transfer ownership of their house in the city and to pay Jay Jonah Investments an additional monthly mortgage of $2000 for 24 months in exchange for the country inn. Several months after the deal closed, Antonio and Susanna learned that the representations made about the potential earnings of the country inn were clearly false. They therefore refuse to make any further mortgage payments. In the meantime, Jay Jonah had demolished their house to build a condominium complex. Assuming that Antonio and Susanna can prove that they were induced to contract by misrepresentation, what remedy do you think that a court should grant?

6. Mac's Machines Ltd, an importer of high-tech German industrial equipment, had an ongoing shipping arrangement with Take Care Tankers Inc. According to Clause 4 of Take Care Tankers' standard form agreement:

> Subject to express instructions in writing given by the customer, Take Care Tankers reserves to itself complete freedom in respect of means, routes, and procedures to be followed in the handling and transportation of the goods.

Although the parties had done business before on several occasions, a representative from Mac's telephoned Take Care Tankers to request that a particular shipment of machines be stored below deck. Although the machines were usually transported in waterproof plastic containers that were amenable to deck transportation, the shipment in question was packaged in wooden crates and was therefore susceptible to rust if left on deck. The shipping manager

at Take Care Tankers assured the Mac's representative over the phone that the special arrangement would be no problem. Despite that promise, the shipment was inadvertently stored on deck. During the voyage, the crate fell overboard, and the machines were lost at sea. On the basis of the telephone call, Mac's claims that Take Care Tankers was not merely negligent but also in breach of contract. Relying on Clause 4 of its standard form agreement, Take Care Tankers claims that the oral assurances made over the telephone were not part of the contract. Leaving aside the issue of negligence, apply your understanding of the parol evidence rule to determine how a court would resolve the contract issue in this case.

7. Sperry Rand makes farm machinery. To promote its products, Sperry published a sales brochure that includes the following representations:

> You'll fine-chop forage to one centimetre season after season! You'll harvest over 45 tonnes per hour with ease. Under test conditions, the big New Holland harvesters have harvested well over 60 tonnes per hour. And Micro-Shear cutting action gives you a choice of crop fineness—from one to six centimetres.

Induced by the brochure, John decided to buy one of Sperry's machines from a third-party dealer. As a result of the failure of the machine to live up to its description in the brochure, John lost his entire season's crop. Aiming to recover damages for breach of contract, John attempted to sue the dealership. Unfortunately the dealership had gone bankrupt. John decided that he would try to sue Sperry Rand. Assume that his contract with the dealership excluded any possible tort liability against Sperry Rand. Does John have a contractual remedy against Sperry? Is the parol evidence rule relevant to your determination?

8. Paula's Pets has developed a standard form agreement for its employees. Having had problems in the past with employee absenteeism, Paula's Pets has included a term in its employment contracts stating that an employee shall not miss more than five work days per year subject to statutory holidays, illness, and the like. Another clause in the agreement provides for a leave of absence in the case of a death in the family:

> All full-time employees of Paula's Pets are entitled to a compassionate leave of absence for the bereavement of a loved family member.

Randall, a full-time employee, decided to take a week off work after his dog was hit and killed by a train. In response to the employer's charge of absenteeism, Randall stated that his employment contract provides for a compassionate leave for "the bereavement of a loved family member." Randall believed that this included his dog; his employer claimed that the contractual term applies only to human family members. Using the various approaches to interpretation, build the best possible argument in favour of each interpretation.[38]

9. Clinton was 14 years old when his mother entered into a written agreement with the town library on his behalf. According to the agreement, Clinton would obtain full borrowing privileges and his mother would become "responsible for any fines, loss or damage occasioned by the use of the library card." Shortly after Clinton lost his library card, a stranger used it to borrow more than 30 items. Those items were never returned. The library issued a bill to Clinton's mother for $1570, the replacement value of those items. Do you think Clinton's mother should have to pay? How might the library have better managed its affairs?

10. The Upper Crust Academy, an exclusive boarding school, has inserted the following clause into its standard form agreement:

   The parents of _____ hereby authorize the Principal to ensure that said child shall receive a proper social and academic education in accordance with the highest standards of personal conduct and that said child will be kept free from danger while in the custody of Upper Crust Academy.

Like everyone else whose child attended the academy, Manjunath's parents signed the agreement. One evening, Manjunath was returned to the academy by the local police after he was found stealing pylons off the street. In addition to the mischief he caused in the streets, Manjunath was in breach of the curfew rule at the academy. After unsuccessfully attempting to contact Manjunath's parents by phone, the principal decided to sentence Manjunath to 20 hours of peeling potatoes in the academy kitchen to dissuade him from repeating such inappropriate behaviour. When his parents found out that the potato peeling had caused Manjunath to develop unsightly calluses on his hands, they quickly removed their darling son from the academy. The principal of the academy responded by issuing a bill for the remainder of the year's tuition plus an additional fee for boarding. The academy claims that the disciplinary action taken by the principal was within its contractual rights. Manjunath's parents disagree. Given that the agreement makes no specific mention of discipline, how could the principal persuade a court to side with the academy? Explain your reasoning.

11. Don wanted to do something special for his birthday. He decided that he would rent a high-performance sports car for a day and cruise the city with his friends with the top down. When he went to rent the car from High-Performance Auto Rentals (HPAR), he was presented with HPAR's standard form rental agreement. Because it was a beautiful Friday afternoon, there was a long line of customers waiting to rent cars. The salesman who served Don was anxious to help other customers and to close the shop for the day so he could go away for the weekend. The salesman presented the standard form contract to Don and told him to sign it quickly. When Don turned over the contract to read the fine print on the back, the salesman became irritated and told Don not to bother reading all the fine print because it just dealt with what time he had to return the car and that he had to fill the tank with gas. Don signed the contract without reading it.

That afternoon, Don drove the high-performance car into a concrete wall, causing significant damage to the vehicle. When he contacted HPAR to let them know what had happened, HPAR told him that it would take 30 days to fix the car because the parts had to be imported from Italy. HPAR also told Don that he had to pay the full daily rental rate ($900 per day) for every day the car could not be rented while it was in the shop being repaired. This would total $27 000. HPAR claimed that this obligation to pay was contained in the fine print on the back of the standard form contract that Don had signed and been provided a copy of. Don disputed that he was required to pay because he never saw that clause and because the salesman told him not to read the fine print. Would a court find Don liable to pay the $27 000 pursuant to the HPAR standard form contract? How might HPAR have avoided this dispute?

12. You work at a company called CuddleTech ("CT"). CT operates a website where users can play 3-D interactive video games online. When users create an account for the CT website, they are required to agree to a standard form contract. You have been assigned the task of reviewing and rewriting this contract. Under the contract, users are required to disclose any physical disabilities or medical conditions that might cause them to react negatively in CT's online 3-D game environment. CT is concerned that users with certain medical conditions may be prone to negative reactions in the 3-D game environment. This obligation to disclose any disabilities applies continuously so long as the user continues to use their account to play games at the CT website. You have been asked to ensure that CT's standard form contract contains a term which gives CT the right to immediately terminate the account of any user who does not comply with this disclosure obligation. You have been presented with the following two options for this clause. Which option would you recommend CT use in its contracts and why?

Option 1:

   If at any time the user intentionally or unintentionally, or fraudulently, or negligently or otherwise fails in any direct or indirect manner to comply with their obligation to disclose any and all physical disabilities that might in any direct or indirect way cause them to react negatively in CT's 3-D gaming environment, then CT shall have the right and be entitled to declare that this contract is null, void and unenforceable immediately or at any time in its sole discretion.

Option 2:

CT is concerned about your health. Throughout the duration of your account with CT, you must disclose to CT any physical disability or medical condition that might cause you to react negatively in CT's 3-D game environment. If at any time you do not disclose such a condition or disability to CT, CT may immediately terminate your account.

WEBLINKS

Contract Law   www.duhaime.org/ca-con1.htm

This page provides an introduction to various areas of contract law, including offer and acceptance, privity, mistake, misrepresentation, breach, and remedies. The site also offers summaries of leading case law.

Contracts Canada   http://contractscanada.gc.ca/en/index.html

This site offers information on how the federal government conducts business with its suppliers, including government purchasing and government contracts.

Industry Canada Consumer Information   http://strategis. ic.gc.ca/sc_consu/engdoc/homepage.html?categories=e_con

This website provides information to consumers on such matters as recalls, consumer law, and awareness.

The Plain Language Association International (PLAIN) www.plainlanguagenetwork.org

This site provides information about international plain language initiatives, including those in Canada. This site also provides detailed information about ways to effectively write legal and other documents in plain language.

ADDITIONAL RESOURCES FOR CHAPTER 9 ON THE COMPANION WEBSITE

(www.pearsoned.ca/mcinnes)

In addition to self-test multiple-choice, true-false, and short essay questions (all with immediate feedback), three additional Cases and Problems (with suggested answers), and links to useful Web destinations, the Companion Website provides the following resources for Chapter 9:

■ Boilerplate Terms

Provincial Material

■ **British Columbia:** Terms Implied by Statute, *Sale of Goods Act*
■ **Alberta:** Legislation Interpretation
■ **Ontario:** *Consumer Protection Act 2002*, Exemption Clauses—Exclusion Clauses, Implied Terms, *Interpretation Act*, *Sale of Goods Act*, Standard Form Contracts, Terms Requiring Notice

10 Contractual Defects

OBJECTIVES

After completing this chapter, you should be able to:

1. Identify six types of parties that lack capacity or have limited capacity to contract.

2. Distinguish between voidable and enforceable contracts with a minor.

3. Explain what it means for a corporation to act beyond its capacity.

4. Outline the types of contracts that must be evidenced in writing, state the basic writing requirements that must be proved, and summarize the legal effect of non-compliance.

5. Explain how writing requirements protect consumers.

6. Explain the doctrine of frustration and its effect.

7. Determine when a contract is or is not frustrated.

8. Summarize the traditional factors that courts take into account in determining whether an agreement is illegal. Discuss the doctrine of public policy and its effect.

9. Define duress of goods and economic duress.

10. Distinguish between undue influence and unconscionable transactions, and identify when a presumption is created in each case.

Contractual defects are particularly significant because they often provide one of the parties with a defence when the other party commences a lawsuit. In this chapter we survey six different contractual defects and their legal consequences: incapacity, absence of writing, mistake, frustration, illegality, and unfairness during bargaining.

INCAPACITY TO CONTRACT

A person cannot enter into a contract unless they have the legal power to give consent. For example, although a 10-year-old may be able to read, understand, and sign a contractual document, he may not be legally bound by it. The same is true for adults who, for some other reason, lack the ability to consent. To protect specific groups of people, the law has drawn a distinction between those who have the *capacity* to contract and those who do not. **Capacity** is the legal power to give consent. Sometimes the question of capacity depends on a person's ability to understand the nature and consequences of their acts. At other times it does not.

capacity is the legal power to give consent

We will consider six groups of persons who may have no capacity or only limited capacity to create a contract:

- minors
- mentally disabled persons
- intoxicated persons
- corporations
- associations
- Indian bands and Aboriginal persons
- public authorities

Personal Incapacity

Minors

The law distinguishes between *minors* and those who have reached *the age of majority*. The **age of majority** is the age at which a person is held fully accountable in law. Those who have not reached the age of majority are **minors**. The law simply says that everyone under the age of majority lacks capacity. In some jurisdictions, including Alberta, Saskatchewan, and Ontario, the age of majority is 18 years.[1] In other provinces, including Newfoundland, New Brunswick, and British Columbia, it is 19 years.[2] Though perhaps overprotective in some instances, the law's approach shields minors from exploitation and the consequences of their own inexperience. It is therefore important for businesses that transact with minors to understand how the law operates.

the **age of majority** is the age at which a person is held fully accountable in law

minors are people who have not reached the age of majority

Some contracts are *voidable* at the minor's option. A contract is **voidable** if the minor is entitled to avoid the legal obligations that it created. Note an important legal subtlety here. *Some* contracts with minors are voidable; not *every* contract with a minor is *void* at the outset. If a contract is voidable, the

a contract is **voidable** if a minor is entitled to avoid the legal obligations that it created

---

[1] *Age of Majority Act*, RSA 2000, c A-6, s 3 (Alta); *Age of Majority Act*, RSS 1978, c A-6, s 2 (Sask); *Age of Majority and Accountability Act*, RSO 1990, c A.7, s 3 (Ont).

[2] *Age of Majority Act*, RSNB 1973, c A-4, s 2 (NB); *Age of Majority Act*, RSBC 1996, c 7, s 1 (BC).

minor may elect to avoid contractual liability. If so, they are relieved of all future liabilities under the contract. However, the minor may also choose to carry out the contract, making the obligations binding.

A minor who wants to avoid contractual liability should do so as soon as possible. Suppose a 15-year-old boy rents stereo equipment for a year. If he elects to avoid the contract after two months, he cannot be sued for the other ten. He can, however, be sued for the rent that accumulated before he avoided the agreement. Furthermore, if there is a substantial delay, a court may say that the boy *affirmed* the contract and therefore lost the right to avoid it. Finally, once a person reaches the age of majority, they must decide, within a reasonable time, whether they want to void a contract that they created as a minor.

The ability to avoid certain contracts does not mean that a minor can take the benefit of a contract and then cancel it with impunity. Minors who elect to avoid contracts must give back any benefits that they received under them.

These rules regarding contracts with minors have been modified by statute in some cases. In British Columbia, for example, the *Infants Act* states that a contract with a minor is unenforceable unless certain prescribed circumstances are met.[3] There are some contracts that minors cannot avoid—contracts for necessary goods and services like food, clothing, education, medical treatment, and legal advice, which are to their benefit.[4] Minors cannot avoid contracts of employment that are to their benefit.

Mental Incapacity

Regardless of age, a person may also lack capacity because of a deficient intellect. We need to distinguish two situations. First, if a court has declared a person to lack mental capacity, their contracts are *void* and cannot be enforced at all. Second, even if there is no court declaration, a person may still be considered mentally incompetent. If so, their contracts are *voidable*, just as in the case of a minor. They can avoid the agreement within a reasonable time of becoming competent. There is, however, an important difference between mental incapacity and minority. A minor's contract is voidable even if the other party was unaware of the age issue. In contrast, the contract of a person with a mental incapacity is voidable only if the other party should have recognized the problem.

It is sometimes difficult to tell if a person is incapacitated. A person may obviously lack capacity because of extreme age or because of some kind of impairment in mental function. Often, however, it requires a careful examination of the circumstances, which may be further complicated by the fact that an incapacitated adult may later regain capacity. As a matter of risk management, employees should be trained to identify potential problems.

Intoxication

The rules for drunkenness are similar to those for mental incapacity. An otherwise capable person may enter into a contract while intoxicated. That agreement is voidable if two conditions are met. First, the person must have been so drunk that they could not know or appreciate what they were doing. Second, the other contractual party must have been alerted to that fact. Often, the courts are as much concerned with the possibility of fraud or unfairness as they

---

[3.] *Infants Act*, RSBC 1996, c 223.

[4.] This rule aims at ensuring that people are willing to sell such goods and services to minors. Goods that are considered "necessaries" are usually enumerated by statute. See *Sale of Goods Act*, RSPEI 1988, c S-1, s 4 (PEI); *Sale of Goods Act*, CCSM, c S10, s 4 (Man).

are with the issue of incapacity. To set aside a contract, the intoxicated party must make a prompt election to avoid it once sober. A failure to do so will be taken as affirmation of the agreement. Case Brief 10.1 illustrates one court decision regarding the effect of intoxication on the ability to contract.

CASE BRIEF 10.1

McLaren v McMillan (1907) 5 WLR 336 (Man KB)

John McLaren had been drinking heavily throughout the day. Shortly after sundown, he was approached by a horse trader named McMillan, who offered him a share in a pony called Silver Coin. After stumbling outside the bar to examine the horse, McLaren expressed satisfaction and signed the relevant documents. When he became sober the next morning, he tried to get out of the deal. Although he vaguely remembered having signed something and also remembered a different transaction that he made with some other cowboy, McLaren tried to

withdraw from the bargain with McMillan. McMillan refused.

The court recognized that intoxication could give rise to a contractual defect. However, it held that drunkenness is not a ground for setting the contract aside if it merely "causes excitement" without producing an excessive state of inebriation. Since McLaren's state of intoxication only darkened his ability to reason without actually depriving him of the ability to reason altogether, he was not entitled to avoid the contract.

Business Corporations

Corporations are treated as legal persons.[5] The law distinguishes between *chartered corporations* and *statutory corporations*. In the context of contractual capacity, **chartered corporations** are treated the same as individuals who have reached the age of majority. If a chartered corporation enters into contracts in breach of its charter, its charter may be forfeited, but the contracts made in breach of the corporate charter will still be binding. **Statutory corporations**, on the other hand, have a more limited contractual capacity. Because they are statutory creations, their capacity to contract is limited by the powers given to them through legislation. If a statutory corporation attempts to contract in a manner that exceeds its statutory powers, it acts *ultra vires*, literally "beyond the authority." When a corporation acts *ultra vires*, it lacks the capacity to contract. Those agreements are consequently unenforceable. Generally, the question is whether the purported transaction is in line with the legal objects and purposes of the corporation. To understand the importance of this, read Business Decision 10.1 (see p. 216).

chartered corporations are treated the same as individuals who have reached the age of majority

statutory corporations have limited contractual capacity

Associations

Capacity issues arise more frequently with another type of business structure—*associations*. **Associations** are usually unincorporated business organizations, including private clubs, charities, and religious societies. Although they share some features with corporations, most associations do not enjoy independent legal existence and are thus incapable of contracting. Therefore, some provinces have legislation that gives contractual capacity to associations involved in such activities as education, religion, and charity. Trade unions may also be given capacity.[6] Those statutes define an association's capacity in much

associations are usually unincorporated business organizations that lack contractual capacity

---

[5.] Corporations and other types of business organizations are considered in detail in Chapters 21 and 22.

[6.] Trade unions are examined in Chapter 27.

BUSINESS DECISION 10.1

Drafting Articles of Incorporation

Reva is named a director of a statutory corporation. While drafting the constitutional documents of the corporation, she and the other directors enter into a discussion about how best to characterize its objects. According to its current business plan, the corporation will focus exclusively on the business of constructing the exterior of buildings. For this reason, one of the directors, Ling, recommends the following characterization: "To carry on in the business of pouring concrete foundations and erecting building exteriors." Reva expresses concerns about Ling's characterization and counters with the suggestion of a much broader description: "To carry on in the business of construction."

Questions for Discussion

1. Assume that you are also on the board of directors. In what sense is the capacity issue relevant to your decision about whether to adopt the recommendation made by Reva or Ling?

2. What are the advantages and disadvantages of Reva's broader statement of the objects of the corporation?

the same way as a statutory corporation's constitution. If an association attempts to contract outside of those limits, it lacks capacity, and its agreement is ineffective.

Because an association generally lacks capacity, one of its members may enter into a contract for its benefit. Significantly, it is that individual member who becomes liable under the agreement. Unlike corporate officers and directors, individuals cannot escape liability by pleading that they were merely contracting on the association's behalf. On the other side of the bargain, if your business intends to contract with someone who claims to act on behalf of an association, you can manage the risk by ensuring that the association has capacity or that the individual personally has the resources to perform the obligations.

Indian Bands and Aboriginal Persons

an **Indian band** is a body of Aboriginal people whose land and money are held by the Crown

One kind of unincorporated association that *does* have legal capacity is an *Indian band*. According to the *Indian Act*, an **Indian band** is a body of Aboriginal people whose land and money are held by the Crown.[7] Nevertheless, despite the Crown's role, Indian bands have contractual capacity in much the same way as corporations.[8] They can sue or be sued.

The same is not always true, however, of individual Aboriginal persons who qualify as "Indians" under the *Act*. There are some restrictions on their capacity to contract, principally in relation to reserve land. For instance, property on a reserve cannot be used as security for a credit transaction, nor can it be transferred to another member of the band without the Crown's consent.[9] Under section 28 of the *Indian Act*, any deed, lease, contract, instrument, document, or agreement purporting to permit a person other than a member of a band to occupy or use a reserve, or to reside or otherwise exercise any rights on a reserve, is void, unless approved by the Crown. Other than these special restrictions in the *Indian Act*, Aboriginal persons generally have capacity and are free to contract just like any other person.

[7.] *Indian Act*, RSC 1985, c I-5, s 2 (Can).

[8.] *Wewayakum Indian Band v Canada and Wawayakai Indian Band* [1992] 42 FTR 40 (FC TD).

[9.] *Indian Act*, RSC 1985, c I-5, s 24 (Can).

Public Authorities

Many contracts are created on a daily basis by public authorities at the federal, provincial, and municipal levels. Generally speaking, a public authority acting on behalf of a governmental body has the capacity to contract, independent of any specific statutory authority to do so.[10] The only limit on a particular official's capacity to contract is the division of powers section of the *Constitution Act 1867*—in order to have capacity, the action must be consistent with that division of powers.

CONCEPT SUMMARY 10.1

Managing Risk in Association with Incapacity

- Train employees to identify potential capacity problems in the contracts that your business enters into.
- Be aware of the rules governing contracts with minors, particularly if your business is likely to enter into contracts with minors.
- In potential cases of contracts involving minors, mental incapacity, or intoxication, take steps that will help to show that the other party has affirmed the contract. For example, you might attempt to have the other party commence performance of their obligations under the contract or pay them money under the contract. If they begin performance or accept the payment, then these may be taken as signs of affirmation of the contract. These steps should be taken at a time when you know they are no longer a minor, mentally incapacitated, or intoxicated.
- Be aware of whether your company may contract with statutory corporations, associations, Indian bands, individual First Nations' people, and public authorities, and act accordingly.
- Where you are not certain about the other party's capacity, you might consider requiring a written representation from the other party in the contract which states that they have the capacity to enter and fulfill the contract. If it later turns out that they did not have capacity, then you may have an action against them in tort for misrepresentation.

ABSENCE OF WRITING

For most contracts, there are no formal requirements. However, certain types of contracts must be *evidenced* in writing. That requirement first arose as a result of an old piece of English legislation—the *Statute of Frauds*.[11] More recently, consumer protection legislation has required certain types of contracts to be made in writing. Both are discussed below.

Statute of Frauds

The *Statute of Frauds* required some contracts to be evidenced in writing as a way of reducing the risk of perjury, or lying in legal proceedings. The requirement was intended to discourage people from falsely claiming the existence of oral contracts. That rationale is less persuasive today. Electronic and paper documents can now be produced, altered, and reproduced with a few clicks of a mouse. For that reason and others, many jurisdictions have amended their legislation.[12] And some jurisdictions, like British Columbia and Manitoba, have

---

[10.] PW Hogg *Liability of the Crown* 2d ed (1989) at 161–62.

[11.] *Statute of Frauds*, 1677 (29 Cha 2), c 3.

[12.] Law reform has been recommended in other provinces, including Ontario and Newfoundland. See Ontario Law Reform Commission *Report on the Amendment of the Law of Contract* (1987) c 5; M Bridge "The *Statute of Frauds* and the Sale of Land Contracts" (1986) 64 *Can Bar Rev* 58.

repealed the Statute altogether. As electronic commerce continues to expand, it can be assumed that the issue will be examined even more broadly.

Despite such law reform, risk management still requires understanding the *Statute of Frauds*, even for businesses in British Columbia and Manitoba. After all, a company in Kamloops or Brandon may enter into a contract with a party in another jurisdiction where the Statute is still in force. We will therefore discuss the types of contracts that must be evidenced in writing, the basic writing requirements that must be proved, and the legal effect of non-compliance.

Types of Contracts That Must Be Evidenced in Writing

Only certain types of contracts fall under the *Statute of Frauds*. In Chapter 13, we will examine the circumstances in which an agreement for the *sale of goods* must be evidenced in writing. For now, we can look at three other types of contracts: guarantees, contracts for the sale of an interest in land, and contracts not to be performed within a year.[13]

a guarantee is a contractual promise by a third party, called a *guarantor*, to satisfy a debtor's obligation if that debtor fails to do so

Guarantees The Statute applies to *guarantees*. A **guarantee** is a contractual promise by a third party, called a *guarantor*, to satisfy a debtor's obligation if that debtor fails to do so.[14] For example, you may apply for overdraft protection that allows you to withdraw more than your bank account actually contains, which is, in effect, a bank loan. The bank may refuse that arrangement unless you find a third party (such as your parent or your spouse) to guarantee repayment.

The guarantor gives a *conditional* promise, and is required to discharge the debt only if you fail to do so. A guarantee can be distinguished from an *indemnity*. An **indemnity** is an *unconditional* promise to assume another's debt completely. To continue with our example, if your spouse promises to indemnify the bank for your overdraft, the bank is entitled to collect payment from your spouse as soon as the overdraft amount becomes due, even if the bank has not bothered to ask you for payment first. An indemnity is therefore not a promise to answer for another's debt. It is a promise to assume another's debt altogether.

an indemnity is an unconditional promise to assume another's debt completely

In many provinces, the *Statute of Frauds* applies to contracts of guarantee but not to contracts of indemnity. Consequently, the bank will not be able to demand payment from the guarantor unless that agreement was evidenced in writing. However, a bank may be able to enforce an indemnity even if the agreement was entirely oral. In British Columbia, the judicial distinction between guarantee and indemnity has been abolished.

Contracts for the Sale of an Interest in Land Contracts for the sale of an interest in land are unenforceable unless they are evidenced in writing.[15] It is sometimes difficult to distinguish contracts that concern an interest in land from those that do not. Consider the example in You Be the Judge 10.1 (see p. 219).

Other cases are more clear-cut. For example, a contract to repair a building need not be evidenced in writing, nor must an agreement for room and board. On the other hand, a long-term lease of land clearly must be evidenced in writing.

---

13. Most provincial statutes require writing in other circumstances, including (i) ratifications of contracts made by minors upon reaching age of majority, (ii) promises by executors or administrators to be personally liable for the debts of a testator or intestate, (iii) contracts made upon consideration of marriage, (iv) assignment of express trusts, (v) creation of trusts of land, and (vi) leases or agreements to lease land for a term exceeding three years.

14. Guarantees are examined in Chapter 23.

15. The sale of interests in land is discussed in Chapter 16.

YOU BE THE JUDGE 10.1

Van Berkel v De Foort [1933] 1 WWR 125 (Man CA)

Van Berkel entered into an oral agreement that permitted De Foort to cut and remove a crop of wild hay from his land in exchange for a promise to pay $500 upon removal of the crop. De Foort had intended to use the hay to feed his dairy cattle. In the early part of the autumn that year, De Foort decided to give up the dairy business altogether. No longer having any need for wild hay, De Foort simply left the crop on the land to spoil. Van Berkel sued for breach of contract. De Foort attempted to escape liability by pleading the *Statute of Frauds*. He claimed that the contract concerned the sale of an interest in land and was therefore unenforceable since it was not evidenced in writing.

Questions for Discussion

1. Do you think that the contract entered into by Van Berkel and De Foort was a contract for the sale of an interest in land?

2. Should De Foort be able to walk away from his contractual obligations simply on the basis of this formal defect?

Contracts Not to Be Performed Within a Year   Contracts that are not to be performed within a year of their creation are unenforceable unless they are evidenced in writing. This extends the writing requirement to all sorts of agreements of indefinite duration regardless of their subject matter. Because the Statute applies so broadly, it can catch parties by surprise. Contrary to their expectations, they may not have an enforceable agreement. The courts therefore tend to interpret this part of the Statute quite narrowly. For instance, they usually say that a contract is not caught if it could *possibly* be performed within one year. And sometimes they go to great lengths to enforce oral agreements, notwithstanding the existence of the Statute.

Writing Requirements

If a contract falls within the Statute, the court must decide if the writing requirement was satisfied.

Form and Content of the Note or Memorandum

Either the contract must be in writing or there must be a note or memorandum that provides evidence of it. The document does not have to take any particular form, but has to (i) provide evidence of the essential elements of the contract (such as the parties' names, the subject matter of the agreement, and the price), and (ii) be signed by the party against whom the agreement is being enforced. The courts are often lenient. For instance, they sometimes allow the signature requirement to be satisfied by a name on letterhead or an invoice. Furthermore, they are sometimes satisfied by the combined effect of several documents, even if they do not expressly refer to each other.[16]

Effect of Non-Compliance   The *Statute of Frauds* renders some contracts *unenforceable* unless they are sufficiently evidenced in writing. Such contracts therefore cannot support an action for breach of contract where the defendant pleads the *Statute of Frauds* as a defence. If one party does not perform, the other cannot demand a remedy. This does not mean that their agreement is entirely irrelevant. Their contract is not void; it is merely unenforceable. It can therefore be used to pass property and may provide a defence. The difference

---

[16.] *Harvie v Gibbons* (1980) 109 DLR (3d) 559 (Alta CA).

is somewhat obscure but can be demonstrated through examples. Suppose that someone pays you $5000 as a down payment under an oral contract for the sale of land. A down payment acts as part of the purchase price, but it also provides an incentive to perform. If the payor does not go through with the deal, the payee can keep the money. Now suppose that the other party refuses to complete the transaction. Although your contract is unenforceable, it still provides a valid explanation as to why you do not have to repay the $5000. To use another example, if a party provides goods under an oral contract and the other party accepts the goods, and the contract is found unenforceable under the *Statute of Frauds*, then the doctrine of *quantum meruit* may require the party who accepted the goods to pay for the benefit it received.

Consumer Protection and Writing Requirements

Some consumer protection laws require certain types of agreements to be made in writing in order to protect consumers' interests. By requiring agreements to be in writing, and in some cases, that a copy of the agreement be provided to the consumer, these laws can help prevent exploitation of consumers and prevent disputes about the terms of the contract. Reducing disputes about the terms of an agreement is good for consumers, who are often the weaker party to the contract and who do not have the resources to fight disputes, but it is also good for business.

Under Ontario's *Consumer Protection Act 2002*, for example, all personal development services contracts must be made in writing in cases where the consumer's payment in advance is required under the contract.[17] Personal development services contracts are service contracts in the areas of health, fitness, diet, modelling, talent, martial arts, sports, and dance. If such contracts are not made in writing, then the business is not permitted to require or accept payment from the consumer. Ontario's consumer protection law also requires businesses to deliver a written copy of an Internet contract in cases where the consumer is required to pay more than a prescribed amount under the contract in advance.

CONCEPT SUMMARY 10.2

Managing Risk in Association with Writing Requirements

- Ensure that guarantees, contracts for the sale of an interest in land, and contracts not to be performed within a year are always made in writing.
- To meet the writing requirement, you should, as a minimum, (i) provide evidence of the essential elements of the contract (such as the parties' names, the subject matter of the agreement, and the price), and (ii) ensure that the party against whom the agreement is being enforced has signed the written document.
- To avoid the uncertainty and debate that oral agreements can create, all contracts should be written whenever possible.
- Businesses should ensure that they understand the requirements that may exist under provincial consumer protection laws to put certain agreements in writing and to provide consumers with a copy.

MISTAKE

We have examined incapacity and the absence of writing. A third kind of contractual defect arises from *mistakes*.

[17.] *Consumer Protection Act, 2002*, SO 2002, c 30, Sch A, s 30 (Ont).

General Principles

Contracts are based on agreements. As discussed in Chapter 7, contracts require a meeting of the minds, or *consensus ad idem*, which is a shared mutual agreement to enter into an enforceable transaction on a particular basis. However, anyone involved in business knows that people sometimes are mistaken about their agreements.

■ Some mistakes occur when an error affects the basic process of contract formation. When that happens, the mistake may negate the existence of an agreement between the parties. And without an agreement, there cannot be a contract.

■ Other mistakes make it impossible for the object of the contract to be achieved. Here, the mistake does not affect the process of contract formation but rather pertains to the very existence of the contract's subject matter. In that case, the contract may be defective.

Mistakes Preventing the Creation of Contracts

Two types of mistakes prevent the creation of a contract: mistaken identity and mistake as to subject matter.

Mistaken Identity   Many business relationships are based on trust and reliability. People are more willing to invest in institutions that are known to be reliable. Financial institutions are more willing to lend money or give credit to people who have a history of paying their debts. Therefore, a mistake about corporate or personal identity may become a contractual issue. The situation is even more difficult if a con artist obtains goods under a contract and then resells them to a third party. The person who was duped under the first transaction may try to recover the goods from the third party on the basis of the mistake.

Sometimes that approach succeeds; sometimes it does not. The courts are required to weigh the interests of the seller against those of the innocent purchaser. Mistaken identity will therefore not render a contract defective unless (i) the mistake was known to the other contractual party, and (ii) the mistake was *material*. A **material mistake** is one that matters to the mistaken party in an important way.

It is difficult to always be clear about the difference between mistakes and a lack of *consensus ad item*. The difficulty in this distinction is revealed in Business Decision 10.2 (see p. 222).

a material mistake is one that matters to the mistaken party in an important way

Mistake about Subject Matter   Some mistakes put the parties at cross-purposes and therefore prevent the formation of a contract. This often occurs when the parties are mutually mistaken about the subject matter of an agreement. Suppose you enter a contract to buy cotton that will arrive on a ship called the *Peerless*, which you believe will arrive in October. However, neither you nor the seller knows that there is actually more than one ship called *Peerless*. One is set to arrive in October and another in December. The seller, not knowing of the earlier ship, sends the cotton on the later ship. By the time the cotton arrives, you no longer have a use for it and refuse to purchase it. In the circumstances, there was a mutual mistake about a material issue—which *Peerless* the cotton was to be shipped on—which prevented a true agreement or the creation of a contract.[18]

[18.] These facts are derived from *Raffles v Wichelhaus* (1864) 159 ER 375.

BUSINESS DECISION 10.2

Shogun Finance v Hudson (2004) 1 AC 919 (HL)

A fraudster approached Shogun Finance to finance the purchase of a valuable vehicle. The fraudster claimed that his name was Mr Patel. He presented false identification which confirmed this identity. In fact, Mr Patel was a real individual with a good credit rating. Shogun performed a credit check against 'Mr Patel' and found that he had good credit. On this basis, Shogun financed the fraudster's purchase of the vehicle thinking that he was Mr Patel. The fraudster then sold the vehicle to an innocent purchaser, Mr Hudson. When the fraudster did not make his payments to Shogun, Shogun tried to repossess the vehicle.

By a 3 to 2 majority, the House of Lords held that no contract had been created between Shogun and the fraudster because no agreement was reached between them—there was no meeting of the minds. The majority held that the fraudster did not intend to contract with the finance company and that the fraudster's identity was fundamental to the transaction for the purpose of checking credit. Therefore, the court said that there was either (i) no meeting of the minds, and therefore no contract formed, or (ii) there was a contract formed between the real Mr Patel and Shogun. In neither case was a contract formed between the fraudster and Shogun. With no contract formed, the fraudster had no title to the vehicle and could not pass title to Mr Hudson, meaning that the vehicle in fact belonged to Shogun. If the contract between Shogun and the fraudster had been upheld, then Mr Hudson would have been entitled to keep the vehicle as an innocent purchaser under English legislation.

The minority held that there had been a meeting of the minds between Shogun and the fraudster despite the fact that Shogun was mistaken about the identity of the fraudster. In other words, Shogun had authorized the vehicle dealer to hand over the vehicle to the fraudster and intended to sell it to that person. The mistaken belief in the fraudster's identity did not negate the intention to contract. With the contract between the fraudster and Shogun upheld, the minority of the court held that Mr Hudson was entitled to keep the vehicle as an innocent purchaser under English law.

Questions for Discussion

1. Do you think that the decision of the majority of the court is fair to Mr Hudson?

2. Setting aside your views about the fairness of the decision to Mr Hudson, if you were working at Shogun, what measures would you implement to prevent this kind of fraud from occurring in the future?

Mistakes Rendering Impossible the Purpose of the Contract

Even if a mistake does not pertain to the process of contract formation, it may be relevant if it makes the contract impossible to perform. We will consider one possibility and another related scenario: (i) mistake about existence of the subject matter, and (ii) frustration.

Mistake about Existence of the Subject Matter

The parties' mistake may render the contract impossible to perform. In this situation, both parties make the *same* mistake, which is usually based on a false assumption. Suppose you agree to lease your beach house to me for the summer. We draft a contract, sign it, and exchange keys for money. The next day, however, we learn that the house had been completely destroyed by a fire a week earlier. Consequently, when we created our contract, we both made the same mistake— we believed that the house existed and that our agreement could be performed. The contract is therefore defective. You have to return my money, and I have to return your keys. And neither one of us can sue to enforce the deal.

However, a common mistake about the existence of the subject matter of a contract does not *always* prevent the enforcement of the agreement. A business should therefore protect itself by inserting into the contract a *force majeure*, or "irresistible force," clause, which states which party bears the hardship if the subject matter of the contract is destroyed or if some other unexpected event occurs. The affected party should then arrange insurance against the potential loss.

The Doctrine of Frustration

We have considered situations involving a mistake about an existing fact. Sometimes, however, the parties may make a mistake about the *future*. Even if they are fully informed when they create their contract, subsequent events may make it impossible for them to perform as anticipated.

Going back to our earlier example, I agree to rent your beach house for the summer. We create a contract and exchange keys for money. At that time, the building is in excellent shape. During the spring, however, it is completely destroyed by a fire. I could still occupy the empty lot for the summer, but that is not what we had in mind. The purpose of our agreement has been *frustrated* by an unexpected occurrence. A contract is **frustrated** when some event makes performance impossible or has the effect of radically undermining its very purpose.

It is important to note that a contract is not frustrated merely because it becomes more expensive or somewhat more difficult to perform. For instance, our agreement would still be effective even if, because of heavy rains, you were required to spend a considerable amount of money cleaning up the beach house to make it fit for habitation during the summer. In some cases, an agreement will still be effective where performance of the contract is still possible, but slightly delayed due to circumstances beyond the control of both parties. For example, in a contract for a six-day guided wilderness tour, a court has held that no frustration takes place when an airline cancels flights because of terrorist attacks (delaying the arrival of the guest) in circumstances where the guest can arrive two days later and the guide offers to take the guest on the tour two days later than originally planned.[19]

The doctrine of frustration, like the law of mistake, tries to strike a fair balance between the parties. Ultimately, however, it requires a decision about who will bear the risk of a loss. In some situations, the parties themselves supply the answer.

- The doctrine of frustration applies only if neither party is responsible for the relevant event. If one party is responsible, then that party bears the loss. For instance, I would not be entitled to a refund if I carelessly burned the beach house down during the first night of my stay.

- Even if neither party is at fault, they may have agreed that one of them would bear the risk of loss. For instance, as a business that is aware of potential risks, you may have inserted a *force majeure* clause into our agreement. If so, I could not demand a refund of the rent even though the house is gone.

If the parties themselves cannot settle the issue in some way, a judge must do so. First, however, we must draw a distinction between provinces that use the common law rules and those that have legislation on point.[20] Common law jurisdictions use an all-or-nothing rule. A purchaser can recover *all* of its contractual payments if it has not received *any* benefit from the seller. However, if the purchaser has received *some* benefit, it cannot recover *any* payments. In neither event can the seller actually demand payment from the purchaser, even if the seller incurred substantial expenses under the agreement.

In other jurisdictions, the effect of the legislation turns upon the existence of a contractual payment or a benefit.

a contract is frustrated when some event makes performance impossible or radically undermines the purpose behind the agreement

---

[19] *Allen v Taku Safari* [2003] BCJ No 754 (BC SC).

[20] Legislation has been enacted in Alberta, British Columbia, Manitoba, Newfoundland, New Brunswick, Ontario, and Prince Edward Island.

- If the purchaser paid an advance or a deposit under the contract, the court has discretion to divide that money between the parties as it sees fit. Consequently, if the seller incurred some expense under the contract, it may be entitled to retain an appropriate amount as compensation. In other circumstances, the purchaser may be entitled to a complete refund.

- If the purchaser received some benefit from the seller, the seller is entitled to either retain money that it has received or make a fresh claim for compensation against the purchaser. That compensation, however, cannot exceed the value of the benefit.

- If the purchaser neither paid money nor received a benefit under the contract, the entire burden of the frustrating event falls on the seller. In that situation, the seller cannot claim compensation, regardless of how much expense it incurred under the agreement.[21]

Documents Mistakenly Signed

Another type of mistake occurs when a person signs a contractual document in error. As a general rule, that sort of mistake is irrelevant. A person is usually bound by a signature, even if they did not read the document. The other party is normally entitled to assume that a signature represents an acceptance of the agreement. There are, however, exceptions to that rule. As we saw in Chapter 9, unusual or onerous terms are not binding unless they are reasonably drawn to the attention of the person who signed the contract. There is another exception—*non est factum*.

non est factum literally means "this is not my deed"

Non est factum, literally "this is not my deed," allows the mistaken party to avoid any obligations under the contract. The plea is available only if there is a *fundamental, total, or radical difference* between what a person signed and what that person thought they were signing. This is a high threshold and will rarely be met. It may happen if the document was presented as a sale of land, when it was actually a purchase of shares. However, if the issue is merely misrepresentation, then the contract may only be voidable, not void. Similarly, the doctrine does not apply if the difference is merely a matter of degree. Consequently, a signatory cannot plead *non est factum* simply because they were mistaken about the quantity of goods that were sold under the contract. Furthermore, the doctrine cannot be used by someone who, through carelessness, failed to take steps to understand the document. This means that the doctrine cannot be used by someone who could read a contract but did not because his glasses were broken at the time. It may also mean that someone who cannot understand a contract in English, but who could have asked a friend to translate, cannot rely on *non est factum*.

UNFAIRNESS DURING BARGAINING

As we saw in the discussion on incapacity, weaker parties are not always required to complete their agreements. If a disadvantaged party is pressured into an agreement or placed in an unfair position during the bargaining process, the contract may be ineffective. We conclude this chapter with a brief

---

[21.] An exception exists in British Columbia, where the seller can claim compensation for half of its expenses.

examination of three types of unfair bargaining: duress, undue influence, and unconscionable transactions.

Duress

Duress of person refers to physical violence or the threat of violence against a person or that person's loved one. If a contract is the product of duress, it is *voidable*. The innocent party may choose not to perform and recover any payments they made under the agreement. Similar rules apply to *duress of goods*. **Duress of goods** occurs when one person seizes or threatens to seize another person's goods to force that person to create a contract. The innocent party can avoid the contract if they can show that the pressure was practically irresistible.

Fortunately, the courts seldom hear cases involving duress of person or of goods. Unscrupulous business people do, however, occasionally resort to a more subtle form of pressure—*economic duress*. **Economic duress** arises when a person enters into a contractual arrangement after being threatened with financial harm. For example, a contractual party, claiming that the cost of performance is higher than expected, may indicate that it will not fulfill its obligations unless it receives additional money.

Economic duress is more difficult to determine than duress of person or duress of goods. It is always wrong to put a gun to someone's head; it is not always wrong to exert economic pressure over them. Indeed, that sort of thing regularly happens in the business world. Courts look at several factors before determining that a pressure was an illegitimate threat.

- Economic pressure is more likely to be considered illegitimate if it was made in *bad faith*. It is one thing for a party to honestly say that it cannot perform without more money; it is another to apply pressure on someone simply because they are vulnerable.
- The victim of the pressure must show that they *could not have reasonably resisted*. Sometimes, it is reasonable to resist by bringing the matter to court; sometimes the situation requires a much quicker response.
- The courts are more sympathetic if the victim started *legal proceedings promptly* after the effects of the pressure passed.
- The courts are more likely to become involved if the victim *protested* when presented with the pressure. However, a failure to protest is not necessarily fatal if that course of conduct was obviously futile in the circumstances.
- A contract is more likely to be considered voidable if the victim *succumbed to the pressure without legal advice*; otherwise, agreement to a contractual proposal tends to look more like a sound business decision.

Undue Influence

Even if the elements of common law duress cannot be established, relief may be available under the equitable principle of *undue influence*. **Undue influence** is the use of any form of oppression, persuasion, pressure, or influence—short of actual force, but stronger than mere advice—that overpowers the will of a weaker party and induces an agreement. Cases involving undue influence are usually one of two types: where the parties are in a *fiduciary relationship*, and where there is no special relationship between the parties. Figure 10.1 illustrates the differences.

duress of person refers to physical violence or the threat of violence

duress of goods occurs when one person seizes or threatens to seize another person's goods to force that person to create a contract

economic duress arises when a person enters into a contractual arrangement after being threatened with financial harm

undue influence is the use of pressure to overpower the will of a weaker party and induce an agreement

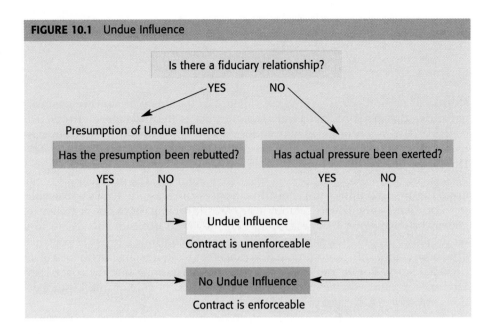

FIGURE 10.1   Undue Influence

Is there a fiduciary relationship?

YES   NO

Presumption of Undue Influence

Has the presumption been rebutted?   Has actual pressure been exerted?

YES   NO   YES   NO

Undue Influence

Contract is unenforceable

No Undue Influence

Contract is enforceable

---

a fiduciary relationship is a relationship in which one person is in a position of dominance over the other

A **fiduciary relationship** occurs when one person is in a position of dominance over the other. That power imbalance usually exists in a relationship that is based on trust or confidence. Fiduciary relationships generate a special kind of duty that requires the more powerful party to subordinate its personal interests in favour of the weaker party. Whenever parties in a fiduciary relationship enter into a business transaction, there is good reason to suspect undue influence on the part of the more powerful party. For this reason, the law imposes a *presumption of undue influence* whenever a fiduciary is involved in a transaction.

Not every transaction involving a fiduciary is defective, and the presumption of undue influence can be rebutted. If the fiduciary can prove that the transaction was fair, the contract will stand. Often, the best tactic for a fiduciary is to ensure that the other party receives independent legal advice before entering into the agreement.

The second type of undue influence scenario arises when there is no special relationship between the parties. In such a case, there will be *no presumption* of undue influence. The party seeking relief from such a contract must prove that undue pressure was applied. When a business is not in a position of domination, it will be much harder for the other party to have the transaction set aside for undue influence. As a matter of risk management, a business can avoid that possibility by refraining from using bullying tactics and, in appropriate circumstances, by suggesting independent legal advice.

Unconscionable Transactions

an unconscionable transaction is an agreement that no right-minded person would ever make and no fair-minded person would ever accept

an improvident bargain is a bargain made without regard to one's future

Equity also provides relief from *unconscionable transactions*. An **unconscionable transaction** is characterized by its one-sidedness. It is an agreement that no right-minded person would ever make and no fair-minded person would ever accept. The weaker party must prove (i) that there was an **improvident bargain**, one that was made without proper regard to the future, and (ii) that there was an inequality in the bargaining position of the two parties. (Figure 10.2 distinguishes the differences.) If those elements are satisfied, the court presumes that the transaction

FIGURE 10.2 Unconscionability

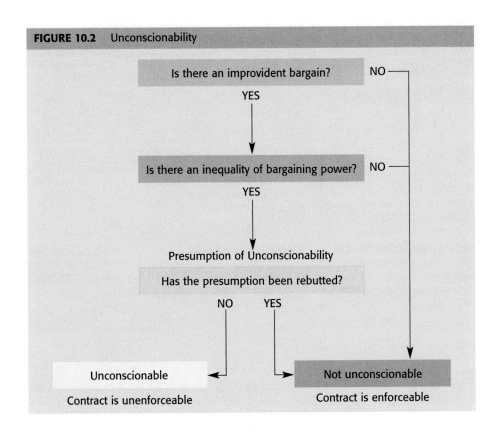

was unconscionable. The stronger party must then rebut the presumption of unconscionability. Even if the contract does not provide a benefit for the weaker party, the agreement may stand if the stronger party shows that the bargaining process was fair, right, and reasonable after all.[22] As usual, the risk can be managed, most notably by ensuring that the weaker party receives independent legal advice. Ethical Perspective 10.1 (see p. 228) illustrates the problem.

Several provinces have legislation governing unfair transactions. Some is preventive, using such devices as disclosure requirements or "cooling-off" periods to reduce the risk of a stronger party taking advantage of a weaker one.[23] Other statutes prohibit the use of particular unfair terms, such as exclusion or forfeiture clauses.[24] Still other statutes give the court a broad discretion to render harsh or unconscionable agreements ineffective, typically in legislation regulating money lending institutions and insurance companies.[25]

[22.] *Turner Estate v Bonli Estate* [1989] 5WWR 730 (Sask QB), affd [1990] 5WWR 685 (Sask CA).

[23.] *Consumer Protection Act*, RSBC 1996, c 69, s 11 (BC); *Consumer Protection Act*, CCSM c C200, s 62(1) (Man); *Consumer Protection Act*, RSO 1990, c C.31 s 21 (Ont); *Direct Sellers Act*, RSNB 1973, c D-10, s 17 (NB).

[24.] *Consumer Protection Act*, CCSM, c C200, s 58 (Man); *Consumer Protection Act*, RSO 1990, c C.31, s 34 (Ont); *Sale of Goods Act*, RSBC 1996, c 410, s 20 (BC).

[25.] *Money-lenders Act*, RSNS 1989, c 289, s 3 (NS); *Unconscionable Transactions Act*, RSA 2000, c U-2, s 2 (Alta); *Insurance Act*, RSO 1990, c I.8 (Ont); RSPEI 1988, c I-4, s 92 (PEI); RSNWT 1988, c I-4, s 46 (NWT).

ETHICAL PERSPECTIVE 10.1

Beach v Eames (1976) 82 DLR (3d) 736 (Ont Co Ct)

Mr Beach was lying on his chesterfield with his legs propped up on pillows when Mr Pyatt, an insurance adjuster, unexpectedly showed up at his house. Beach was suffering the effects of a car accident, which had occurred a month earlier. Although he had missed several weeks of work because of his injuries, Beach had not yet seen his doctor or his lawyer, nor had he consulted with his own insurance agent.

Pyatt quickly and accurately sized up the situation. He knew that Beach had limited education and modest mental abilities. He also knew that Beach trusted him. Pyatt seized the opportunity and offered to settle, for a payment of $500, any potential claims that Beach might enjoy under his insurance policy. Beach agreed and signed the document, not realizing that his injuries might be worse than he suspected but not worse than Pyatt suspected.

Beach eventually realized that his injuries were very serious and that he had agreed to a very bad deal. He therefore sued to set aside the settlement contract.

Questions for Discussion

1. Did the insurance adjuster do anything wrong or was he just doing his job? Explain.

2. If you owned the insurance company, how would you respond to this incident?

3. If you were the judge in this case, how would you respond to this incident?

ILLEGALITY

illegal agreements are expressly or implicitly prohibited by statute

A contract may be ineffective because it violates the law. There are several variations on that theme. **Illegal agreements** are expressly or implicitly prohibited by statute and are therefore void. Other agreements, though not strictly prohibited, come into conflict with a common law rule or offend public policy. They too are often unenforceable.

Agreements Prohibited by Statute

the purpose of a regulatory statute is not to punish individuals for wrongdoing but rather to regulate their conduct through an administrative regime

Most statutes that prohibit particular types of agreements are *regulatory* in nature. The purpose of a **regulatory statute** is not to punish individuals for wrongdoing, but rather to regulate their conduct through an administrative regime. For example, there are statutes that prohibit the sale of apples that have not been graded in accordance with provincial regulations.[26] Other statutes require licences to be obtained prior to engaging in certain kinds of transactions.

Common Law Illegality

Some agreements are illegal even if they do not contravene a particular statute. The common law is unwilling to recognize agreements that are contrary to public policy. For example, a mobster may hire a thug to kill a politician. If the thug decides instead to take the money and run, the mobster cannot sue for breach of contract. The same is true of any agreement that is aimed at committing a crime or a tort.

[26.] *Kingshott v Brunskill* [1953] OWN 133 (CA).

The common law will not recognize several other types of agreement, including those that are damaging to a country's safety or foreign relations, that interfere with the administration of justice, that promote corruption, or that promote sexual immorality. Each type of agreement is contrary to public policy.

The Doctrine of Public Policy

It may seem odd that a court can strike down a contract simply because it is contrary to public policy. After all, the law of contract is intended to facilitate stable and predictable business relationships by allowing people to freely enter into whatever bargains they choose. The notion of public policy, however, is notoriously vague. It may allow judges to make or unmake contracts on the basis of their own personal views as to what is best for society. Public policy, according to an old saying, becomes "an unruly horse" if it is let out of the barn.

Covenants in Restraint of Trade

An agreement may be ineffective on the grounds of public policy if it contains a *covenant in restraint of trade*. A **covenant in restraint of trade** is a contractual term that *unreasonably restricts* one party's liberty to carry on a trade, business, or profession in a particular way. Such covenants often require a person to (i) trade or *not* trade with someone in particular, or (ii) work for someone in particular or, at least, *not* work for anyone else. In its most unreasonable form, a broadly drafted restraint of trade provision comes close to slavery. In that situation, the covenant will be presumed contrary to public policy unless the party seeking to enforce it can demonstrate that the restriction is reasonable. However, even if an unacceptable provision is struck down, the rest of the contract may remain.

Many restrictive covenants are perfectly reasonable and therefore not contrary to public policy. Suppose you are thinking about buying a convenience store. You may legitimately insert a provision into the contract that prevents the current owner from opening or operating another convenience store within a six-block radius. That provision merely ensures that the current owner does not steal all of your expected customers. It would be different, however, if the contract prohibited the current owner from operating another convenience store *anywhere* in Canada. A convenience store in another neighbourhood, let alone another city, does not create a threat to your business. The contractual term would therefore be an unreasonable restraint of trade, contrary to public policy, and hence ineffective.

Restraint of trade clauses are often found in employment contracts. As a matter of risk management, employers should consider drafting such provisions as narrowly as possible to achieve the desired goals while maximizing the likelihood of enforcement. This issue is discussed in more detail in Chapter 26.

a covenant in restraint of trade is a contractual term that *unreasonably restricts* one party's liberty to carry on a trade, business, or profession in a particular way

Chapter Summary

A contract may be defective due to (i) incapacity, (ii) absence of writing, (iii) mistake, (iv) frustration, and (v) unfairness during bargaining.

A contract cannot normally be created by a person who lacks the legal power of consent. With the exception of a limited class of contracts concerning employment and the purchase of necessaries, a minor's contracts are voidable. Similarly, an agreement created by a mentally incapacitated adult may be set aside. Intoxicated persons who seek to avoid contractual liability can only do so if they can prove that they were incapable of knowing or appreciating what they were doing, and that the other party was aware of this incapacity. A statutory corporation, unlike a chartered corporation, has a limited contractual capacity. Although associations are generally incapable of contracting, some provinces have enacted legislation that enables associations involved in specific purposes to enter into contracts. Generally, a public authority acting within its powers has the capacity to contract independent of any specific statutory authority to do so.

The *Statute of Frauds* requires the party seeking to enforce contracts such as guarantees, contracts for the sale of an interest in land, and contracts not to be performed within a year, to adduce evidence in the form of a written and signed memorandum or note. Some consumer protection laws contain similar requirements that certain agreements be made in writing, with a copy provided to consumers.

A mistake can interfere with the parties' attempt to reach an agreement or make it impossible for the object of the contract to be achieved. A mistake of identity or a material mistake about the terms of a contract may preclude its formation if the mistake is known to the other party. A material mistake about the subject matter of a contract may also negate consent. A common mistake about the existence of the subject matter renders it impossible for a contract to be fulfilled and will sometimes operate as a defence. A mistaken assumption that one or both parties make about the future can result in frustrating a contract. A contract is frustrated when some event occurs that makes further performance of the contract impossible or radically undermines its very purpose.

When a party is pressured into an agreement or placed in an unfair position during the bargaining process, the agreement may be defective. Economic duress arises when a party enters into a contractual arrangement after being threatened with financial harm. Undue influence occurs when pressure is exerted by a stronger party to overpower the will of a weaker party and thereby induce an agreement. The law imposes a rebuttable presumption of undue influence whenever a fiduciary is involved in a transaction. The presumption is usually rebutted if the stronger party shows that the weaker party had the opportunity to seek independent advice. An unconscionable transaction is an agreement that no right-minded person would ever make and no fair-minded person would ever accept. Although it is generally up to the parties to make their own bargains, courts will interfere if a contract was the result of duress, undue influence, or unconscionability.

Illegal agreements are those that are expressly or implicitly prohibited by statute. Illegal agreements, along with other agreements that come into conflict with a common law rule or public policy, are often unenforceable. An example of an agreement that conflicts with public policy is a covenant in restraint of trade, which is enforceable only if it is reasonable.

Review Questions

1. What is meant by the term "contractual capacity"?
2. Why are some contracts entered into by a minor voidable? What is an election, and when must it be made?
3. Give examples of contracts that will be enforced even if a person has not attained the age of majority.
4. Compare the legal effect of a contract entered into by a mentally disabled adult and a contract entered into by a minor.
5. Describe a situation that would lead a court to allow an intoxicated person to avoid contractual liability.
6. Explain how the contractual capacity of a chartered corporation differs from that of a statutory corporation.
7. Why must a business person be particularly careful when contracting with or on behalf of an association?
8. Do Indian bands have the legal capacity to contract? Under what circumstances do Aboriginal persons have the capacity to contract? Explain.
9. What is the difference between a guarantee and an indemnity?
10. Does the *Statute of Frauds* have effect throughout Canada? Briefly explain the rationale for the writing requirement.
11. Outline the writing requirements typically stipulated by a *Statute of Frauds*.
12. If a contract does not comply with the *Statute of Frauds*, making it unenforceable, does it follow that the agreement has no legal effect? Explain your answer.
13. Outline the difference between mistakes preventing the creation of contracts and mistakes that make it

impossible for the object of a contract to be achieved. Provide examples of each.

14. How might a case of mistaken identity provide a contractual defence?

15. Explain the doctrine of frustration. What are its effects?

16. What is the difference between common law and statutory approaches to the doctrine of frustration?

17. Explain why the plea of *non est factum* is part of the law of mistake.

18. What is a restrictive covenant? How is it relevant to the doctrine of public policy?

19. Outline three bases upon which a court might set aside an unfair contract. Is there a common thread underlying the rationale in each?

20. Explain the basic characteristics of a fiduciary relationship. Give examples.

Cases and Problems

1. Erin had always been independent. Shortly before her seventeenth birthday, she moved out of her parents' house and bought a used car, which she needed for her fledgling chocolate-covered-cranberry enterprise. She agreed to pay $15 000 for the car, $5000 as a down payment and the rest in monthly instalments over one year. She used the car mostly to make deliveries and to pick up supplies. After she drove the car for three months, the bearings burnt out. Since Erin was in a position to hire a delivery person, she decided that she no longer wanted the car. Having studied the basics of contract law in high school, Erin attempted to return the vehicle to the car dealership, claiming that she had elected to avoid the contract. The dealership refused, having received an opinion from its lawyer that a contract for necessaries is enforceable against a minor. Erin replied that the car was not a necessary, and that the contract was therefore not enforceable. Do you think that Erin will be permitted to avoid her contract with the dealership? Give reasons to support your position.

2. Elwood is a pig farmer who is known to enjoy a drink or two. One day in July, after a weekend of particularly heavy drinking, he staggered into the office of Pork Bellies of America and offered to sell all of his piglets. He promised to deliver them in October, as soon as they were fattened up. Hank, Pork Bellies' purchasing agent, saw that Elwood was extremely drunk, but decided to write up the contract anyway since the price was a fair one. After the deal was signed, Hank and Elwood went to the neighbourhood saloon to play darts and have lunch. The next day, after sobering up, Elwood was reminded about their agreement. In fact, over the course of the next two weeks, Hank and Elwood ran into each other on a number of occasions. Each time, Hank mentioned the deal, and Elwood acknowledged it. In September, the price of pork nearly doubled. Consequently, Elwood sent Pork Bellies of America a registered letter saying that he would not be delivering the pigs. He had decided to sell them to someone else at a higher price. Pork Bellies has sued Elwood. Will the court allow Elwood to avoid contractual liability? Give reasons to support your position.

3. Michel is a 22-year-old man who has been declared mentally incompetent. He can barely read or write and has an IQ of 41. Nevertheless, he executed a deed of conveyance transferring his proprietary interest in his late father's farm to his stepmother, Paula, in exchange for a small annual payment. Without providing much in the way of detail, Michel told his legal guardian about signing the papers and giving them to Paula. Michel's guardian quickly made an application to the court to set aside the deed and the agreement. The guardian freely admits that the price agreed to is fair and that Paula was not intent on fraud. Is the agreement between Paula and Michel enforceable? Would your answer be different if Paula were not related to Michel and did not know about his condition?

4. The general manager of Nunzio's Kosher Pizzeria has hired you to wash dishes in the evening. On your third shift, you are finally introduced to Nunzio. He seems like a nice guy as he welcomes you aboard. You are paid weekly by a cheque drawn from the account of a numbered company called 551999 Alberta Ltd. Nunzio's name is one of the two signatures on the cheques. Things go well for the first two months. Then you are not paid for three weeks in a row. The following week, the pizzeria is shut down. After finding out that the numbered company has gone bankrupt, you see your lawyer about suing Nunzio personally. After reviewing the corporate records, your lawyer tells you that there has been a mistake of identity—your employment contract was with the numbered company, but Nunzio is neither an officer or shareholder in that company. What does your lawyer mean by mistaken identity, and how will it apply in your case?

5. Fedor's law firm represents the Hole-In-One Mini Donuts Co. While doing some legal work for the company, Fedor discovers that the Hole-In-One no longer owns any assets. Rodya and Philka, the two corporate shareholders, verbally assure Fedor that they will not only answer for the legal fees already incurred by the corporation but will also take responsibility for any and all future charges. Although Fedor accepts this proposal, he does not require it to be put into writing.

On the faith of their promise, the law firm continues to do work for the corporation. Fedor sends another bill to Hole-In-One, knowing full well that the corporation is unable to pay. Shortly thereafter, Fedor commences an action against Rodya and Philka. The defendants claim that their promise is unenforceable because it was not in writing. How would you respond to that argument?

6. In January 2001, Allen entered into a contract with Taku Safari and paid a deposit of $3000. Under the contract, Taku was to take Allen on a six day back-country adventure in Alaska between September 15 and 21, 2001. Allen was to fly to Juneau, Alaska on September 14 where Taku's float plane would take him to the backcountry. On September 14, Allen learned that his flight had been cancelled and rescheduled for September 16 in the wake of the terrorist events of September 11, 2001. Taku told Allen that it could not guarantee that its float plane would be available on September 16 but that Allen should get to Juneau as soon as possible. Taku told Allen that he would get a full six-day tour even if he arrived on September 16, or afterwards. Thus, Taku indicated that it could perform the contract, although performance would be delayed due to Allen's late arrival. Allen was not willing to fly to Juneau on September 16 without a guarantee that the float plane would be available on that date. He told Taku that he was cancelling the trip and that he wanted his deposit back. Allen claimed that the doctrine of frustration applied because the terrorist events of September 11, 2001 led to the rescheduling of his flight to Juneau and prevented performance of the contract for a tour from September 15–21, 2001. The contract was silent about who bore the risk of loss in this kind of situation and did not contain a *force majeure* clause. If you were the judge deciding this case, would Allen be successful in invoking the doctrine of frustration? Why or why not?

7. Several years back, Golden Joe's Geology bought a 1000-acre package of land in the Northwest Territories. When he purchased the property, Joe was sure to purchase the mineral rights as well. For years, Joe spent his summers panning for gold on the property. Recently, quite by accident, Joe discovered that his land is at the heart of a potentially lucrative diamond stash. Joe is overjoyed and has decided to sell his property so that he can retire to a tropical locale. He has agreed to sell the property and mineral rights to Prospectus Prospecting, which will invest the money needed to mine and process the diamonds. The agreement is drawn up and signed by both parties, and everyone is satisfied. However, when the actual land transfer is about to take place, it is discovered that the Crown grant of property to Joe has been substantially revoked. As a result, the land available for sale is in fact reduced by 90 percent. Is Joe still entitled to performance of the contract with Prospectus? Explain why or why not. As a prudent business manager, could Joe have better protected himself against such a possibility? Explain how.

8. Edmond is the first mate on an old fishing trawler in Nova Scotia. Go Fish Inc has just purchased and outfitted a new vessel and wants to hire Edmond as its captain. The president of Go Fish Inc offers Edmond the job and, as an inducement, gives him a $10 000 loan. According to the terms of their arrangement, $3000 of the loan will be forgiven once Edmond completes the new vessel's maiden voyage as captain. Two days after the maiden voyage, Edmond suffers a long-term disability and is told that he might not be able to sail ever again. He phones his boss to tell her that he cannot continue to fulfill his part of the bargain. The ship continues to sail without him. Go Fish Inc wonders whether it can recover the $10 000 loan and an additional sum from Edmond for breach of contract. Your business consulting firm is contacted by Go Fish Inc to provide advice. What advice will you give? How might the business manager at Go Fish Inc have avoided having to seek your advice?

9. Mr Stone has no formal education. He speaks English and has worked as a labourer and a truck driver in Canada for 20 years. Mr Stone recently decided that he wanted to start a business of his own. He sought a loan for his business from $peedy Financial $ervices (SFS). SFS lent Mr Stone's business $80 000 and required Mr Stone to sign a personal guarantee for all of the business's future obligations to SFS. SFS's loan officer explained the significance of the personal guarantee to Mr Stone. The loan officer spoke Punjabi and English with Mr Stone when arranging for the loan and the personal guarantee. However, all of the documentation was written in English. Mr Stone's company later became indebted to SFS and SFS sought to collect the debt from Mr Stone based on the personal guarantee. Mr Stone has raised the defence of *non est factum*. He admits that he knew that he was signing documents to facilitate a loan to his company, but he claims that he was not aware that he was signing a personal guarantee for the debts of his company, thereby creating a personal liability to SFS. He claims that no one at SFS told him to read the documents, and that even if he had read them, he would not have understood most of them because he could not read English well. Mr Stone made no inquires of anyone and asked no questions to determine what he was signing when he signed the personal guarantee. SFS is concerned that it may not be able to collect the debt from Mr Stone given that he did not read the document and can't read English well. You work at SFS and have been asked to assess whether Mr Stone's *non est factum* defence might be upheld by a court, including the reasons why or why not.

10. Mind Games Inc hires CompuNerd to overhaul its entire computer network for a flat fee of $350 000. Marinka, Mind Games Inc's general manager, stresses that the computer upgrades must be finished by the end of July so that there is enough time for Mind Games Inc to complete a large consulting project before its fall deadline. Marinka explains to CompuNerd that a failure to meet these deadlines would cause Mind Games Inc severe financial hard-

ship. From the start, the computer overhaul seems jinxed. Due to several delays, the software upgrades are not quite half finished by the beginning of August. Bernie, the nerd in charge of the upgrades, meets with Marinka that afternoon. He claims that the delays were unavoidable and that CompuNerd is incurring unexpected costs. He insists on renegotiating their agreement to include additional payment for "time and materials." He threatens Marinka by saying that, unless she agrees to the new terms, he will reduce his staff by half. Marinka realizes that such a reduction would mean that the computer upgrades would not be completed for two additional months. Finding herself in a serious bind, Marinka reluctantly agrees to alter the terms of the original flat-fee contract to include additional payment for time and materials. But after the job is finished, Mind Games Inc pays only the originally agreed upon amount. CompuNerd sues to recover the amount owing under the renegotiated terms. Marinka asks you to determine whether Mind Games Inc is obligated to pay the additional amount. How did you arrive at your conclusion?

11. Coby and Maya immigrate to Canada. Unlike her doctor husband, Maya speaks no English and misses her friends and family terribly. She becomes depressed. Her husband, Coby, prescribes an antidepressant in ever-increasing dosages. Eventually, the couple separates. Maya continues to take her medication. They enter into a separation agreement whereby Coby pays Maya support, but the monthly sum barely covers her rent and living expenses. During divorce proceedings, Maya claims that she was forced into the separation agreement by her overbearing husband and that she was heavily sedated at the time. What is the legal basis of her claim? What must her husband prove to

ensure that the separation agreement contract is enforceable?

12. In 1995, Oli Bonli was 88 years old. He owned some land which he agreed to lease to Mr Turner for five years with an option to purchase the land when the lease expired. The purchase price for the land at the end of the five-year lease term was set at $100 000, payable over 20 years at $5000 per year. No interest was payable under the agreement. In fact, the value of the land in 1995 was $167 000, much higher than the purchase price. Land prices in the area were skyrocketing at this time and Mr Turner knew it. At that time, Mr Turner was 47 years old and he personally drafted a written contract on the terms agreed to. He had Mr Bonli come to his office to sign the contract at 7:00 a.m. when no one was likely to be around. Mr Bonli did not obtain independent legal advice before entering into the contract. Despite being a longtime farmer on the same piece of land, Mr Bonli made two errors in the legal description of his land on the contract. At that time, age was catching up to Mr Bonli—he had good days and bad days when he was very confused. Very shortly after signing the contract, Mr Bonli denied that he had sold his land and told someone that he thought he had actually *bought* land from Mr Turner. In 1996, Mr Bonli was taken to a nursing home as he could no longer care for himself properly. By the end of the lease term in 2000, the value of Mr Bonli's land had risen to $418 000. Mr Turner then sought to exercise his option to purchase the land for $100 000 pursuant to the payment terms of the contract. Mr Bonli's estate refused to sell the land to Mr Turner, claiming that the contract was unconscionable. If you were the judge deciding this case, would you find the contract to be unconscionable? Why or why not?

WEBLINKS

Contract Law   www.duhaime.org/ca-con1.htm

This page provides an introduction to various areas of contract law, including offer and acceptance, privity, mistake, misrepresentation, breach, and remedies. The site also offers summaries of leading case law.

Contracts Canada   http://contractscanada.gc.ca/en/index.html

This site offers information on how the federal government conducts business with its suppliers, including government purchasing and government contacts.

Ontario *Statute of Frauds* RSO 1990, c S-19
www.e-laws.gov.on.ca/DBLaws/Statutes/English/90s19_e.htm

This Statute is representative of provincial legislation that sets out the types of contracts that must be evidenced in writing.

British Columbia *Frustrated Contract Act*, RSBC 1996, c 166   www.qp.gov.bc.ca/statreg/stat/F/96166_01.htm

This Act applies to contracts that are discharged by reason of the application of the doctrine of frustration.

ADDITIONAL RESOURCES FOR CHAPTER 10 ON THE COMPANION WEBSITE

(www.pearsoned.ca/mcinnes)

In addition to self-test multiple-choice, true-false, and short essay questions (all with immediate feedback), three additional Cases and Problems (with suggested answers), and links to useful Web destinations, the Companion Website provides the following resources for Chapter 10:

Provincial Material

- **British Columbia:** Minors, Mentally Incompetent Persons, Committee, Public Guardian and Trustee, Business Corporations, Societies and Associations, Form of Contract, Frustrated Contracts, Consumer Protection Legislation, Adult Guardianship, Litigation Guardian, Representation Agreement
- **Alberta:** Dishonest Trade Practices, Insurance, Legality, Limitation of Actions, Limited Capacity, Minors/Infants, Statute of Frauds, Unconscionable Transactions, Undue Influence, Deposits v. Downpayments, Fair Trading Act
- **Manitoba and Saskatchewan:** Minors, Statute of Frauds, Frustration in Statute, Unconscionable Transactions—Legislation
- **Ontario:** Age of Majority, Confidentiality Agreements, *Consumer Protection Act 2002*, Effect of Frustration, Identity Theft, Independent Legal Advice, Insurance Legislation, Incompetence, Limitation Periods, Lotteries, Necessaries, Non-competition Clauses, Option to Terminate, Powers of Attorney, *Sale of Goods Act*, Statute of Frauds, Unconscionable Transactions, Undue Influence, Unfair Business Practices

11 Discharge and Breach

OBJECTIVES

After completing this chapter, you should be able to:

1. Explain the nature and effect of a discharged contract.

2. Discuss the manner in which a contract may be discharged by performance.

3. Describe the circumstances in which a contract can be discharged if a party has not performed in a timely manner.

4. Explain the difference between a condition subsequent, a true condition precedent, and a condition precedent.

5. Explain the difference between rescission, accord and satisfaction, and release.

6. Explain the difference between a variation and a novation.

7. Describe the circumstances under which a contractual right is waived.

8. Discuss three situations in which a contract may be discharged by operation of law.

9. Describe the differences between conditions, warranties, and intermediate terms. Explain the situations in which a contract may be discharged for breach.

10. Describe three different types of breach.

We have considered the formation of contracts, the contents of contracts, and the ways in which contracts may be defective. We will now finish our general discussion of contracts by examining the end of the contractual process. In this chapter, we will examine the ways in which a contract may be brought to an end. In the next, we will examine the remedies that may be available to the innocent party if a contract is wrongfully brought to an end.

A business person is often keenly interested in knowing whether a contract has been brought to an end. Suppose a manufacturer contractually agrees to deliver 500 computers to a business. Do the manufacturer's obligations come to an end after it delivers the 500th item? If the purchaser wants more computers, does the manufacturer have to supply them? What if some of the computers that have been delivered are defective? Is the manufacturer obligated to repair or replace them? To answer those questions, we must examine the discharge of contracts.

As we saw in Chapters 9 and 10, some contracts come to an end when they are voided or rescinded. Most contracts, however, are brought to an end through discharge. A contract is **discharged** when the parties are relieved of the need to do anything more under the contract. We will look at a number of ways in which a contract can be discharged. (See Figure 11.1 on p. 237.) Some involve performance; others reflect the parties' agreements or intentions; still others arise by operation of law; and one particularly important type of discharge occurs when one party fails to perform as expected.

a contract is discharged when the parties are relieved of the need to do anything more

DISCHARGE BY PERFORMANCE

When parties enter into a contract, they generally assume that everything will go well. And, in fact, the most common method of discharge is *performance*. **Performance** occurs when the parties fulfill all of the obligations contained in the contract. In some situations, however, it may be difficult to determine whether proper performance has occurred. As a general rule, the parties must perform *exactly* as the contract requires. Any deviation from the terms of the contract, however small, is considered a breach, rather than performance, and will entitle the innocent party to a remedy.

performance occurs when the parties fulfill all of the obligations contained in the contract

Time of Performance

Although the parties generally have to perform exactly as the contract says, the courts usually hold that **time is not of the essence**. In other words, even if a contract states that performance must occur by a particular date, a party may be entitled to perform late. However, if it does so, it can be held liable for losses that the other party suffers as a result of the delay. Suppose that I contractually agree to deliver a vehicle to you by June 1. Although our agreement stipulated that date, I may be allowed to discharge our contract by delivering on June 8. But if I do so, I may be required to compensate you for the fact that you had to rent a car for a week.

time is not of the essence in most situations

In some situations, however, time *is* of the essence. If so, late performance can be refused, and if that happens, the contract will not be discharged by performance. For example, time is of the essence if the parties agree to that fact, either expressly or impliedly. Furthermore, even if time is not initially of the essence, a party can insist upon timely performance by giving reasonable notice that performance must occur by a specific date. Finally, even if the parties do not agree on a specific time or date, the courts will find that performance must

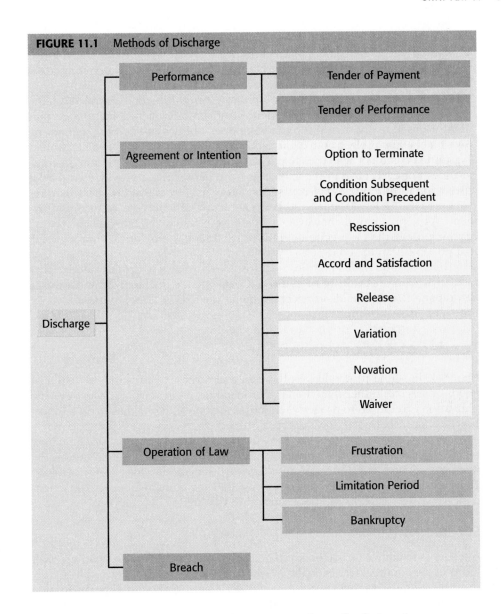

FIGURE 11.1 Methods of Discharge

occur within a reasonable time, having regard to all of the circumstances, including the subject matter of the contract. A contract dealing with perishable goods or a volatile market may therefore require the parties to act promptly.

Tender of Payment

Most contracts require a payment of money by at least one of the parties. We have all satisfied that sort of obligation on many occasions, usually without giving it much thought. Business people should, however, be aware of some very specific rules that govern payments.

First, the debtor has the primary obligation of locating the creditor and *tendering* (offering) payment, even if the creditor has not asked for it. The method of tendering payment must be reasonable. It cannot occur at an inconvenient time or under inconvenient circumstances. However, a reasonable tender has to be made only once. If such a tender is rejected, the debtor still has to pay the debt, but it can wait for the creditor to come by. Furthermore, interest does not accrue on a payment once a reasonable tender has been made, even if that tender is improperly rejected. Likewise, if the case eventually goes to trial, a judge may punish a creditor who improperly rejected a reasonable tender by holding that party liable for the debtor's costs of litigation.[1]

Second, unless a contract says otherwise, a creditor can insist on receiving *legal tender*. **Legal tender** is a payment of notes (bills) and coins to a certain value.[2] Consequently, a creditor generally does not have to accept payment by way of a cheque or electronic debit. Nor does it have to accept payment from a disgruntled customer who tries to pay with an enormous bag of pennies. A creditor does not even have to make change—the debtor must provide exactly the correct amount of money. Of course, creditors usually waive the strict requirements regarding legal tender and happily receive any acceptable form of payment. As a precaution, however, a business person who intends to pay by anything other than a precise amount of legal tender may want to provide for that possibility in the contract.

Third, despite the usual rule, a debtor does not have to actually tender payment if it would obviously be refused. Consequently, if the creditor indicates beforehand that it intends to reject payment, the debtor does not have to waste time on a useless gesture.

Tender of Performance

Many of the same principles apply when a contract requires the provision of goods or services rather than money. For instance, while the party who owes the obligation is required to properly tender performance, it only has to do so once. Furthermore, that party is discharged of its duty to perform if the other party renders performance impossible. For example, the owner of a piece of land may refuse to allow a building contractor onto the work site. In that situation, the innocent party is entitled to begin a lawsuit immediately to recover *damages*. **Damages**, which is the amount of money that the court may order the defendant to pay to the plaintiff, are discussed in Chapter 12.

damages is the amount of money that the court may order the defendant to pay to the plaintiff

Substantial Performance

A tender is usually effective only if the goods or services conform precisely with terms of the contract. Occasionally, however, a party may be discharged from further obligations if it provides *substantial performance*.[3] **Substantial performance** generally satisfies the contract but is defective or incomplete in some minor way.

substantial performance generally satisfies the contract but is defective or incomplete in some minor way

In deciding whether substantial performance has occurred, a court will consider a number of factors, including the nature of the defect, and the difference between the contract price and the cost of curing the defect. For example, many building contracts state that payment is due only once construction is completed. Nevertheless, if a builder leaves a work site without having installed, say, several door knobs, it will likely be discharged from its obligations and entitled to payment.

Of course, if a contract is discharged by substantial performance, the innocent party is not required to pay for work that was not done. Continuing on

---

[1] We examined the issue of costs in Chapter 2.

[2] *Currency Act*, RSC 1985, c C-52, s 8 (Can). In terms of coinage, legal tender consists of up to $40 in two-dollar coins, $25 in one-dollar coins, $10 in quarters, $10 in dimes, $5 in nickels, and 25¢ in pennies.

[3] *H Dakin & Co Ltd v Lee* [1916] 1 KB 566 (CA).

with our example, while the builder might not be required to install the door knobs, it obviously will not be entitled to be paid for that task. To the contrary, the contract price will be reduced by the amount that the innocent party had to pay a third party to install the knobs. That is true even if, for example, the third party charged $250 for work that the builder could have performed for $100.

A difficult issue may arise if a builder leaves a work site *without* providing at least substantial performance. There are two possibilities. First, the parties may have used a single contract to deal with a series of tasks. In that situation, part of the overall price is earned each time that a task is performed. For instance, if the defendant agreed to cut the plaintiff's lawn ten times in exchange for $100, but only performed twice, a court will likely say that it is entitled to $20.[4]

The second situation is more difficult. Even if their agreement requires a number of tasks to be performed, the parties may create an *entire contract*. An **entire contract** says that *no* part of the price is payable unless *all* of the work is done. The results of that rule are sometimes surprising.[5] Assume, for instance, that a builder agreed to construct a house in exchange for $100 000. After doing half of the job, he ran out of money and stopped work. The landowners then used materials (such as lumber and nails) that the builder had left behind and finished the house themselves. The builder now wants to be paid for both the materials that he left behind and the work that he performed. He will probably be disappointed. According to the traditional rule, the landowners are liable only for those benefits that they *chose* to accept after the builder breached the contract. Since the landowners *chose* to use the discarded materials, they will have to pay for them. But they probably will *not* be liable for the work that the builder performed.[6] The landowners had agreed to pay for a whole house—not half of one. And when the builder abandoned the work site, the landowners were not in a position to accept or reject the work that had been done. As one judge explained, "What is an owner to do? He cannot keep the buildings on his land in an unfinished state forever."[7]

> an entire contract says that *no* part of the price is payable unless *all* of the work is done

DISCHARGE BY AGREEMENT

In some situations, one or both parties can discharge a contract even though it was not fully performed. That type of discharge can occur in several ways.

Option to Terminate

When creating a contract, the parties can insert an **option to terminate**, which allows one or both of them to discharge the contract without the agreement of the other. That sort of provision is often found in employment con-

> an option to terminate is a contractual provision that allows one or both parties to discharge a contract without the agreement of the other

---

4. *Kemp v McWilliams* (1978) 87 DLR (3d) 544 (Sask CA). Of course, the innocent party will be entitled to counterclaim for breach of contract. Consequently, if the innocent party had to spend $15 in order to find another lawn care company to work on the same terms, it will be entitled to damages of $15. By offsetting the price and the damages, the innocent party will therefore pay the difference of $5.

5. Not surprisingly, the courts sometimes try to avoid finding that the parties' agreement is an entire contract. They often prefer to find that a party earned part of the overall price each time that he performed part of the contract.

6. *Sumpter v Hedges* [1898] 1 QB 673 (CA). The builder's right to payment for the materials did not arise under the contract. Instead, it arose under the cause of action in unjust enrichment, which we will briefly consider in Chapter 12.

7. *Sumpter v Hedges* [1898] 1 QB 673 at 676 (CA).

tracts. Each party may be permitted to end the relationship on, say, two months' notice.[8] In principle, however, an option to terminate can be inserted into any type of contract.

Options to terminate are frequently subject to restrictions. For example, a party may be entitled to terminate only after giving reasonable notice that it intends to do so. Similarly, the contract may require the party that exercises the option to compensate the other party for the losses that it suffered as a result of the early termination.

Condition Subsequent and Condition Precedent

a **condition subsequent** is a contractual term that states that the agreement will be terminated if a certain event occurs

When creating a contract, the parties can also insert a **condition subsequent**, a contractual term that states that the agreement will be terminated if a certain event occurs. A condition subsequent is different from an option to terminate because it does not have to be exercised by either party to be effective. Under a condition subsequent, a contract may be automatically discharged as soon as the relevant event happens. For example, the contract represented by a ticket to an open-air concert may state that the musicians' obligation to perform is discharged in the event of rain. If so, the contract will probably also entitle the disappointed ticket holder to either a refund or a ticket to another event.

a **true condition precedent** is a contractual term that states that an agreement will come into existence only if and when a certain event occurs

A contract that is subject to a condition subsequent exists until the relevant event occurs. It is also possible, however, to make a contract subject to a true condition precedent. A **true condition precedent** is a contractual term that states that an agreement will come into existence only if and when a certain event occurs.[9] Suppose that you and I want to deal in a specific type of weapon, but we are concerned that such a contract may be illegal. We can settle the terms of the agreement but state that our contract will actually be created only if it receives government approval. In that situation, we would not have a contract, and therefore would not break the law, if government approval was refused.

Strictly speaking, a condition subsequent is a contractual term that causes an existing contract to come to an end if a certain event occurs, whereas a true condition precedent is a contractual term that allows a contract to come into existence only if a certain event occurs. Unfortunately, Canadian courts also use the term "condition precedent" to refer to a contract that is *formed* immediately, but that does not have to be *performed* until later or perhaps not at all. As we will see in Chapter 16, that type of condition precedent is very common in contracts for the sale of land. Consider the example in Business Decision 11.1 (on p. 241).

Note two more things about the type of condition precedent discussed in this exercise. First, because a contract exists from the outset, Yuri is not entitled to sell his house to another person during the 30-day period. If he does, he will be in breach of his contract with you. After all, he has only one house to sell and he has already agreed to sell it to you. To avoid that problem, Yuri probably insisted on having another term inserted into your contract. That term will be activated if Yuri receives an offer from another potential purchaser. In that situation, you will have a limited amount of time (say, three days) to either find a buyer for your cottage or somehow come up with the money to buy Yuri's house. If you fail to do so, your contract with Yuri will be discharged and he will be free to sell his house to the other purchaser.

[8.] As discussed in Chapter 26, if an employment contract does not contain such a provision, the courts will allow the contract to be terminated on "reasonable notice."

[9.] *Pym v Campbell* (1856) 119 ER 903 (KB).

Condition Precedent[10]

Yuri offers to sell his house to you for $250 000. You are eager to accept that offer, but you do not want to completely commit yourself to the purchase until you are sure that you can sell your own cottage for at least $200 000. You and Yuri therefore agree on the terms for the sale of Yuri's house, but state that the performance of that contract is conditional on your ability to find a buyer for your cottage within 30 days.

Although the relevant term of your agreement will be called a "condition precedent," it will not affect the *existence* of the contract between you and Yuri. It will merely *suspend* your obligations to perform. In other words, your contract occurs immediately, but unless and until you are able to find a buyer for your cottage, you do not have to pay $250 000 to Yuri and he does not have to transfer his house to you. Furthermore, if you cannot find a buyer for your cottage within 30 days, your contract with Yuri will be discharged.

Questions for Discussion

1. Why would you want to enter into such an agreement?

2. Why would Yuri agree to such an agreement?

Second, while a condition precedent may suspend the *primary* obligations under an existing contract, one or both parties may have *subsidiary* obligations that they are required to perform right away. For example, while you would not have to pay the purchase price for Yuri's house immediately, you probably would have to make a reasonable effort to satisfy the condition precedent by finding a purchaser for your cottage. If you failed to do so, you could be held liable for the losses that you cause by breaching that subsidiary obligation.[11]

Concept Summary 11.1 shows the differences between conditions subsequent, true conditions precedent, and conditions precedent.

CONCEPT SUMMARY 11.1

Conditions Subsequent, True Conditions Precedent, and Conditions Precedent

Type of Condition	Time of Creation of Contract	Effect of Condition
Condition subsequent	Immediate	Discharge of existing contract
True condition precedent	If and when condition is satisfied	Creation of contract
Condition precedent	Immediate	Suspension of primary obligations

Rescission

Options to terminate, conditions subsequent, and conditions precedent are ways in which the parties can agree, *when initially creating a contract*, that their obligations will be discharged in certain circumstances. The same sort of agreement can also be reached *after a contract has been created*.

First, we must distinguish between *executory contracts* and *executed contracts*. A contract is **executory** if a party has not fully performed its obligations. A contract is **executed** if a party has fully performed its obligations.

a contract is **executory** if a party has not fully performed its obligations

a contract is **executed** if a party has fully performed its obligations

---

10. *Wiebe v Bobsein* [1986] 1 WWR 270 (BC CA).

11. *Dynamic Transport Ltd v OK Detailing Ltd* (1978) 85 DLR (3d) 19 (SCC).

rescission occurs when the parties agree to bring a contract to an end

If a contract is executory on both sides, it can be discharged through *rescission*. **Rescission** occurs when the parties agree to bring their contract to an end.[12] That agreement may be express or implied. For example, if neither party performs under a contract for a very long time, a court may infer that they agreed to abandon it. Similarly, the parties can enter into a new contract that necessarily implies the discharge of an earlier one. Suppose I agree to sell my car to you for $5000. If, before executing that agreement, we enter into another contract that calls upon me to deliver my car and my boat to you in exchange for $7500, the second contract necessarily implies the rescission of the first. After all, we both know that I have only one car to sell.

As Chapter 8 explained, an agreement is usually enforceable only if it is supported by *consideration*. Each party must provide a benefit or suffer a detriment. If an executory contract is rescinded, that requirement is easily satisfied. Each party suffers a detriment by giving up the right to insist upon performance of the original contract.

Accord and Satisfaction

The situation is more difficult if one party has fully performed, or *executed*, the contract. In that case, a mere agreement to discharge a contract may be unenforceable for lack of consideration. The party that has not performed cannot suffer a detriment by giving up the right to insist upon performance. After all, the other party has already performed. Consider the case in You Be the Judge 11.1.

YOU BE THE JUDGE 11.1

Accord and Satisfaction

Miles and Sudevi entered into a contract. He agreed to repair her roof and she promised to drill a water well on his farm. Miles immediately fulfilled his obligation by repairing Sudevi's roof. Sudevi later discovered, however, that contrary to her initial assumption, Miles's farm is situated on rock rather than sand. She also realized that she did not have the type of equipment required to drill a well through rock. Miles took pity on her and generously agreed to simply discharge their contract.

Questions for Discussion

1. Did Sudevi provide consideration in exchange for Miles's agreement to discharge the contract? Could she provide consideration by releasing Miles from his obligation to repair her roof?

2. Is Miles required to honour his promise to discharge the contract?

accord and satisfaction occurs when a party gives up its right to demand contractual performance in return for some new benefit

The agreement to discharge the original contract in the last exercise would have been enforceable if there had been accord and satisfaction. **Accord and satisfaction** occurs when a party gives up its right to demand contractual performance in return for some new benefit. "Accord" refers to the parties' new agreement; "satisfaction" to the new consideration provided by the party that is relieved of the need to perform the original contract. Suppose that Miles's second agreement with Sudevi (the accord) required her promise to build a

---

[12.] This use of the term "rescission" must be distinguished from the way in which "rescission" was discussed in Chapter 9. In this context, the word refers to a *bilateral*, or two-party, agreement to discharge a contract. In the context of contracts induced by fraud, misrepresentation, or mistake, the same word refers to a *unilateral*, or one-party, decision by the innocent party to terminate a contract.

water tank on his property (the satisfaction). If so, he could not require Sudevi to perform the original contract. In effect, by promising to build a water tank, she bought the right to not drill the well.

Accord and satisfaction requires fresh consideration. It is, however, sometimes difficult to determine whether or not a party has given anything new. In that regard, we must remember some of the rules that we saw in Chapter 8. It is especially important to appreciate that, as a general rule, a promise to pay a smaller sum cannot discharge an obligation to pay a larger amount. For example, if I am contractually obliged to pay $5000 to you, but do not have that much on hand, I might ask if you would agree to take $4000 in satisfaction of my entire debt. Even if you agree to that proposal, you probably are still entitled to sue for the remaining $1000. There are, however, exceptions to that rule.

Release

The parties can agree to discharge a contract without fresh consideration if they enter into a *release*. A **release** is an agreement under seal to discharge a contract. As we saw in Chapter 8, a seal serves as a substitute for consideration. As a result, an agreement can be enforceable even if it is not supported by an exchange of value.

a release is an agreement under seal to discharge a contract

Variation

Parties usually use an accord and satisfaction or a release when they want to terminate a contractual relationship. In some situations, however, they may want to retain their agreement, but in a modified form. **Variation** involves an agreement to alter the terms of an existing contract.

variation involves an agreement to vary the terms of an existing contract

A variation requires fresh consideration on both sides of the agreement. A party usually provides consideration either by giving up rights that it held under the original terms of the contract, or by accepting new obligations under the modified terms of the contract.

Suppose that Stefan and Nicole enter into a contract. He promises to cut her lawn 20 times during the summer, and she agrees to pay a lump sum of $2000 at the end of the season. However, spring arrives unusually late, and Nicole's lawn will not require as much attention as expected. The parties might agree to vary their contract by requiring Stefan to perform only 15 times and by requiring Nicole to pay only $1500. If so, Stefan provides consideration by giving up the right to $500 and Nicole provides consideration by giving up the right to lawn care on five occasions.

Novation

Variation can be used to introduce small changes to an existing contract. However, if the parties want to introduce substantial changes that go to the root of their agreement, they can use *novation*. Broadly speaking, **novation** is a process in which one contract is discharged and replaced with another.

novation is a process in which one contract is discharged and replaced with another

The new contract may differ from the old one because it imposes significantly different obligations on the same parties. Suppose Lucy initially agrees to sell an apartment building to Ricardo. If she later discovers that she is unable to perform that contract, she might offer to sell a condominium complex instead. If Ricardo agrees to that proposal, the parties could discharge their original agreement for the apartment building and replace it with a new agreement for the condominium complex.

Usually, however, novation involves a substitution of parties rather than obligations. The Supreme Court of Canada has defined novation as "a *trilateral* agreement by which an existing contract is extinguished and a new contract is brought into being in its place."[13] In that situation, the parties under the new contract essentially adopt the rights and liabilities that existed under the old contract. For instance, in order to purchase a piece of land, you might have borrowed money from a bank and given it a mortgage over your new property. If you later decided to sell the land to me, and if I also required a mortgage in order to afford the property, the bank might agree to a novation. In effect, I would step into your shoes. I would acquire the land, but I would also assume the debt under the mortgage.

There are several things to notice about novations. First, a novation cannot occur unless all of the affected parties consent to the new arrangement. Second, whether new obligations or new parties are introduced, the agreement to discharge the old contract is supported by consideration. The parties to the original contract agree to give up their rights under that agreement. Third, although novation can be achieved either expressly or impliedly, as a matter of risk management, the agreement should always be clearly written.

Waiver

We have seen a number of situations in which the parties agree to discharge their contractual obligations. In each instance, the agreement is enforceable only if it is supported by consideration or a seal. However, a promise to discharge or suspend a contractual obligation may be enforceable even without consideration or a seal.

waiver occurs when a party abandons a right to insist on contractual performance

Waiver occurs when a party abandons a right to insist on contractual performance.[14] There are several points to notice. First, waiver does *not* require consideration or a seal. It operates as an exception to the general rule that the courts will not enforce gratuitous promises. Second, waiver does not have to take any particular form. It can be either written or oral, express or implied. Third, because waiver allows a contractual party to obtain a benefit without providing anything in return, the courts require clear evidence that the other party intended to waive its rights. Fourth, although the cases are somewhat inconsistent, the better view is that waiver is effective only if the party who received the waiver relied upon it. And finally, a party can retract its own waiver if it gives reasonable notice of its intention to do so *and* if retraction is not unfair to the other party. Case Brief 11.1 (see p. 245) illustrates these rules.

We have considered a number of ways in which a contract may be discharged before it is fully completely. Concept Summary 11.2 (see p. 245) reviews two essential features of those various possibilities.

---

[13] *National Trust Co v Mead* (1990) 71 DLR (4th) 488 at 500 (SCC).

[14] Waiver is similar to the concept of promissory estoppel, which we examined in Chapter 8. Some commentators suggest that the main difference between the two is simply jurisdictional. Waiver was developed by the courts of law, and promissory estoppel was developed by the courts of equity. The distinction between law and equity was discussed in Chapter 1.

CASE BRIEF 11.1

Maritime Life Assurance Company v Saskatchewan River Bungalows Ltd (1994) 115 DLR (4th) 478 (SCC)

Maritime Life Assurance (MLA) sold an insurance policy to Saskatchewan River Bungalows (SRB) on the life of Mr Fikowski. The contract required the premium (that is, the price) to be received at the insurer's head office in Halifax by July 26 of each year. In 1984, SRB sent a cheque for the premium on July 24, but that letter was lost in the mail. At that point, MLA was entitled to terminate the policy for non-payment. Nevertheless, it sent a number of notices that offered to accept late payment. By February 1985, however, it ran out of patience and sent a letter stating that the policy had been cancelled. In April, SRB collected its mail for the first time in many months and finally became aware that MLA had not received the cheque for the premium. It then waited another three months before delivering a replacement cheque. Unfortunately, by that time, Mr Fikowski had fallen ill

and died soon after. SRB then claimed a benefit under the life insurance policy and argued that MLA had waived its right to timely payment because it had not insisted on strict performance under the contract.

The Supreme Court of Canada held that MLA had implicitly waived its right to timely payment when it offered to accept late payment. However, the Court also held that MLA was entitled to retract its waiver. Furthermore, because SRB received notice that the policy was cancelled at the same time that it received the insurer's earlier offer to accept late payment (April 1985), it had not relied upon that offer. Consequently, MLA was not required to give reasonable notice of its intention to retract its waiver. The result was that SRB could not collect a benefit under the life insurance policy when Mr Fikowski died.

CONCEPT SUMMARY 11.2

Discharge by Agreement

	Consideration	Usual Effect on Contract
Rescission	each party gives up rights under contract	contract terminated
Accord and Satisfaction	one party gives up old right—other party provides new consideration	contract varied
Release	seal	contract terminated
Variation	each party either gives up old rights or provides new consideration	contract varied
Novation	each party gives up rights under old contract	contract varied or replaced
Waiver	none	contract varied

DISCHARGE BY OPERATION OF LAW

We have examined contracts that are discharged by performance or by agreement of the parties. However, a contract may also be discharged by operation of law. In this section, we will briefly consider three situations in which that frequently happens:

- frustration
- lapse of limitation period
- bankruptcy

Frustration

As Chapter 10 explained, a contract is *frustrated* when it becomes impossible to perform or when the circumstances change so much that performance would be something much different than the parties initially expected. One result of frustration is that the parties are, as a matter of law, discharged from performing any remaining obligations.

Lapse of Limitation Period

statutes of limitation require a party who has suffered a breach of contract to sue within a certain period

The need to perform a contractual obligation can also be displaced by the passage of time. **Statutes of limitation** require a party who has suffered a breach of contract to sue within a certain period (usually either two or six years, depending upon the jurisdiction).[15] There are two main reasons for that legislation. First, the courts do not want to deal with claims if the evidence is old and unreliable. Second, it is unfair to hold the threat of a lawsuit over a person's head for a very long time.

Technically speaking, a contract is not usually discharged if a person fails to sue within the required time. That person is simply prevented from starting legal proceedings. There are, however, exceptions to that rule. Most significantly, the right to sue may be revived, even after the lapse of the limitation period, if the party that broke the contract acknowledges that it is still liable. It might do so by paying part of its outstanding debt. Consider Ethical Perspective 11.1.

 ETHICAL PERSPECTIVE 11.1

Limitation Periods

Twelve years ago, you entered into a contract with Estevan Flooring Inc for the installation of a hardwood dance floor in your tavern. Estevan Flooring completed the work and delivered a bill for $7500. Unfortunately, your tavern had fallen on hard times and you were able to pay only $2500. In the circumstances, the owner of Estevan Flooring saw little point in suing you for the rest of the money. In the past two years, however, your tavern has become very popular and prosperous. Estevan Flooring therefore has asked you for the remaining $5000, plus interest. It has done so despite being informed by its lawyer that the statutory limitation period has expired.

Questions for Discussion

1. Will you pay the remainder of the bill that you initially received from Estevan Flooring?

2. Is your decision based strictly on legal considerations? Is it influenced by commercial considerations? By moral considerations? To what extent do those different considerations overlap?

Bankruptcy

Bankruptcy is discussed at length in Chapter 24. Here, it is enough to note that a bankrupt debtor is discharged from outstanding contractual obligations *if* the bankruptcy was caused by misfortune rather than by misconduct.[16]

[15.] Information concerning limitation periods in each province and territory was provided in Chapter 2.

[16.] *Bankruptcy and Insolvency Act*, RSC 1985, c B-3, s 175 (Can).

DISCHARGE BY BREACH OF CONDITION

Finally, a contract may be discharged if one of the *terms*, or promises, that it contains is broken. As we saw in the discussion on discharge by performance, a contract must be strictly performed. Consequently, a **breach** occurs whenever a party does not perform precisely as promised. However, not every breach will result in the discharge of a contract.

a **breach** occurs whenever a party does not perform precisely as promised

Types of Terms

According to the traditional approach, the law distinguishes between two types of contractual terms. First, a term is a **condition** if the innocent party would be substantially deprived of the expected benefit of the contract if a breach occurred.[17] For example, if a rental company delivers a minivan, instead of a large moving truck as it promised, the customer receives something much different than it expected. Furthermore, given the serious consequences of the company's breach, it would be unfair to require the customer to carry on with the contract by accepting the vehicle and paying for it, even at a reduced price. Since the customer is deprived of the essence of what it expected to receive, it should not be required to uphold its end of the bargain. Consequently, the customer enjoys an option. It can choose to continue on with the contract and merely claim damages for the losses that it suffered because it received a minivan instead of a large moving truck. Or it can choose to discharge the contract and claim damages for the losses that it suffered as a result of the breach. Notice, then, that the breach of a condition does not automatically discharge a contract. Nor can a party generally bring a contract to an end simply by breaching a condition. The right of discharge lies with the innocent party.

a term is a **condition** if the innocent party would be substantially deprived of the expected benefit of the contract if a breach occurred

Second, a term is a **warranty** if the innocent party would *not* be substantially deprived of the expected benefit of the contract if a breach occurred. Suppose that a rental company properly delivers a large moving truck but, contrary to its promise, the vehicle has not been fully cleaned. Given the relatively insignificant nature of that breach, it is fair to require the customer to carry on with the contract. It is, after all, still receiving the essence of what it expected to receive. Consequently, a breach of warranty does *not* provide the innocent party with the option of discharging the contract. Although that party can claim damages for any losses that it suffered as a result of the breach (for example, by cleaning the truck before using it), it must continue on with the contract.

a term is a **warranty** if the innocent party would *not* be substantially deprived of the expected benefit of the contract if a breach occurred

While the courts generally continue to follow the traditional approach, they have recently recognized that some contractual terms cannot be treated so simply. Historically, it was thought that every term could be classified, as soon as a contract was formed, as either (i) a condition, which would support the right of discharge if breached, or (ii) a warranty, which would not. That view can lead to unfair or inconvenient results. It is sometimes clear that the breach of a particular term will, or will not, substantially deprive the innocent party of the expected benefit of a contract. But often, a seemingly important term may be

---

[17.] We must carefully distinguish "condition" as it is used in this context from the same word as it was used in the context of "conditions subsequent" and "conditions precedent."

breached in a trivial way, or a seemingly unimportant term may be breached in a significant way. For example, the courts have occasionally held that the date of shipment is a condition of a contract, and that if goods are shipped one day earlier or later than agreed, the innocent party is entitled to discharge the contract, even if it did not suffer a loss as a result of the breach.[18] That result may be difficult to justify, especially if the innocent party discharges the contract only because it wanted a way out of a contract that it realized was unprofitable.

To avoid that sort of situation, the courts now recognize a third type of term that applies when the consequences of a breach are not obvious at the outset. A term is **intermediate** if, depending upon the circumstances, the innocent party may or may not be substantially deprived of the expected benefit of the contract in the event of breach.[19] As you would expect, the innocent party may or may not have the right to discharge the contract if an intermediate term is breached. The existence of that right depends upon whether the breach *in fact* substantially deprived that party of the expected benefit of the agreement. In that sense, intermediate terms are "wait-and-see" terms. Case Brief 11.2 provides an excellent example.

a term is intermediate if, depending upon the circumstances, the innocent party may or may not be substantially deprived of the expected benefit of the contract in the event of breach

CASE BRIEF 11.2

Hong Kong Fir Shipping Co v Kawasaki Kisen Kaisha Ltd [1962] 2 QB 26 (CA)

The plaintiff owned a ship that it chartered (rented) to the defendant for two years. A term of that contract required the plaintiff to provide a "seaworthy" vessel. The contract also stated that if the ship was out of service for repairs during the life of the agreement, the defendant would be entitled to extend the duration of the contract accordingly. In fact, the ship was out of commission for most of the first seven months of the contract because its engines required extensive repairs. The defendant therefore attempted to discharge the agreement on the basis of the plaintiff's breach of condition. The plaintiff, however, denied that it had breached a condition. Indeed, it claimed that the defendant had breached a condition of the contract when it tried to discharge the agreement.

The English Court of Appeal held for the plaintiff. It said that the seaworthiness term could be breached in a variety of ways, some serious and others trivial. For example, a ship might be unseaworthy either because its hull is irreparably pierced or because its toilets do not work quite right. The disputed term therefore was classified as an intermediate term, which would support a right of discharge only if its breach substantially deprived the defendant of the expected benefit of the agreement. And in the circumstances, the court held that the defendant could still enjoy the essence of the agreement even though the vessel required extensive repairs during the initial part of the contract. As a result, the defendant became liable for a breach of contract when it wrongfully claimed to discharge the agreement.

Concept Summary 11.3 shows the basic differences between conditions, warranties, and intermediate terms.

[18.] *Bowes v Shand* (1877) 2 App Cas 455 (HL).

[19.] Lawyers sometimes use the phrase "innominate term" instead. That type of term is innominate, or unnamed, because it is not named either a "condition" or a "warranty."

CONCEPT SUMMARY 11.3

Conditions, Warranties, and Intermediate Terms

Type of Term	Effect of Breach on Innocent Party	Rights of Innocent Party
Condition	substantially deprived of benefit of contract	discharge contract and claim damages *or* continue with contract and claim damages
Warranty	not substantially deprived of benefit of contract	continue with contract and claim damages
Intermediate	depending upon circumstances—may or may not be substantially deprived of benefit of contract	depending upon seriousness of breach— discharge contract and claim damages *or* continue with contract and claim damages

It is often difficult to distinguish between conditions, warranties, and intermediate terms. The parties can expressly state that the breach of a certain term will or will not support a right of discharge. A statute may also classify a term as either a condition or a warranty.[20] Usually, however, a judge must decide the issue by examining all of the circumstances. In essence, the court asks whether the parties, as reasonable people, would have intended to allow the innocent party to bring the contract to an end in the particular situation. In doing so, the judge may be influenced by the portion of the total performance that is defective, the likelihood that the breach will be repeated in the future if the contract calls for performance by instalments, and the seriousness of the breach to the innocent party.

As a matter of risk management, note that uncertainty regarding the classification of terms often creates the sort of dilemma that arose in *Hong Kong Fir Shipping*. You may believe that the other party breached the contract in a way that allows you to discharge the agreement and sue for damages. But if you are wrong about that, *you* may commit a breach that allows the other party to discharge the contract and sue *you* for damages. Consequently, in a doubtful case, you should seek legal advice before attempting to discharge a contract for breach. You should also be aware, however, that even your lawyer may not be able to predict how a judge will interpret the situation. Business Decision 11.2 (see p. 250) illustrates that difficulty.

Types of Breach[21]

Whether it applies to a condition, a warranty, or an intermediate term, a breach can occur in three ways:

- defective performance
- anticipatory breach
- self-induced impossibility

---

20. That is true under the *Sale of Goods Act*, which is discussed in Chapter 13.

21. We will consider the issue of "fundamental breach" in the next chapter when we discuss exclusion clauses.

BUSINESS DECISION 11.2

Discharging for Breach

You wanted to operate a live-bait kiosk during a week-long fishing competition at Lake Katenben. Although you expected to sell some of the worms to recreational anglers, you assumed that most of your sales would be to the competitors. You entered into a contract with LJ, a local farmer, which required him to deliver 10 kilograms of worms to you each morning at 3:00 am for the seven days that the fishing competition was scheduled to run. LJ properly performed on the first day, but he did not deliver the second day's box of worms until 9:30 am. Although you were able to sell a small portion of the second day's shipment to recreational anglers, you sold nothing to the competitive anglers, who had all left the dock before sunrise.

You are in a dilemma. One the one hand, you know that if you miss another day of trade with the competitive anglers, you will probably not earn a profit during the week-long competition. You also know that if you discharge your contract

with LJ, you can arrange an alternative supply of worms without difficulty. On the other hand, you are worried that if LJ's single late delivery does not really justify discharge, you will be liable to him in breach of contract.

Questions for Discussion

1. Should you attempt to discharge your contract with LJ?

2. Would it be relevant that LJ's breach was caused by his difficulty in finding 10 kilograms of worms on the second night? What if his breach was caused by the fact that he was involved in an automobile accident at 2:00 am while driving to deliver the load of worms to you?

3. Would it be relevant if the competition lasted one month rather than one week?

Defective Performance

defective performance occurs when a party fails to properly perform an obligation due under a contract

Most breaches take the form of *defective performance*. **Defective performance** occurs when a party fails to properly perform an obligation due under a contract. That idea is quite broad. It includes a complete lack of performance. For example, a photographer may entirely fail to attend a wedding that he was expected to film. It also includes a relatively trivial departure from the terms of a contract. For example, a wedding photographer may use 49 rolls of film, rather than 50 as promised.

Anticipatory Breach

anticipatory breach occurs when a party indicates in advance, by words or conduct, that it does not intend to fulfill an obligation when it falls due under a contract

Defective performance applies to an obligation that is already due. An *anticipatory breach* occurs before an obligation is scheduled to be performed. **Anticipatory breach** occurs when a party indicates in advance, by words or conduct, that it does not intend to fulfill an obligation when it falls due. Generally, the same rules apply to an anticipatory breach as to other types of breach. For example, depending upon the seriousness of the situation, the breach may or may not entitle the innocent party to discharge the contract. And even if an anticipatory breach is serious enough to support discharge, a contract will not actually be brought to an end unless the innocent party chooses to do so. As an English judge poetically said, "An unaccepted repudiation is like a thing writ in water and of no value to anybody."[22]

The innocent party is entitled to seek relief *immediately* if there is an anticipatory breach. There is no need to wait until the time when the obligation was to be performed. Suppose you enter into a contract to rent a cottage for the summer months. If the landlord contacts you in February and states that the premises will not be available, you do not have to wait until June before suing.

[22.] *Howard v Pickford Tool Co* [1951] 1 KB 417 at 421 (CA) *per* Asquith LJ.

If an anticipatory breach is serious enough to support discharge, the innocent party must make a decision. It may reject the breach, claim damages, and carry on with the contract. Or it may accept the breach, claim damages, and discharge the other party from future performance. In either event, however, the innocent party will be held to the choice that it makes. Suppose that you agreed to carry my cattle on your truck at the beginning of September. In July, I called to say that the animals would not be ready on time. You rejected my breach and insisted that we perform as planned. We each receive a surprise at the end of August. I am delighted to discover that my cattle are ready after all, but you are saddened to discover that your truck requires repairs and will not be available until October. Now *you* are liable to *me* for breach of contract.

Self-Induced Impossibility

As we saw in Chapter 10, a contract is discharged for frustration if, through no fault of either party, it becomes impossible to perform. However, if the impossibility is caused by one of the parties, then that party will be held liable for breach. Suppose that I agree to deliver a specific cord of firewood to you by January 1. If I burn that wood in my own fireplace during December, I have made the contract impossible to perform. Consequently, you will be entitled to discharge our contract and claim damages from me.

The Effect of Discharge

It is important to understand the consequences of discharge. In Chapters 9 and 10, we examined contracts that were rescinded or voided. In those situations, the contracts are wiped out altogether, as if they never existed. The effect of discharging a contract for breach is quite different. The parties are merely relieved of the need to perform their primary obligations in the future. For example, once the contract in *Hong Kong Fir Shipping* was discharged, the owner no longer had to provide a seaworthy ship, and the charterer no longer had to pay for the use of the ship. Discharge does not, however, wipe out the contract altogether. The agreement survives for the purposes of contractual liability. Returning to *Hong Kong Fir Shipping*, the owner would have to rely on the contract to sue the charterer for damages. Similarly, if the contract contained an exclusion clause that limited the charterer's liability, that clause would have effect because the contract would still be alive for that purpose.[23]

Factors Affecting the Right to Discharge

Even if a contract is breached in a way that would normally support a right of discharge, that right may be lost if, for example, the innocent party chooses to continue on with the agreement. Discharge may also be impossible if the party in breach provided a benefit that the innocent party cannot return. In that situation, the innocent party must perform its own obligations under the contract and be content with a claim for damages. Suppose that a lawn-care company breaches a contract by spreading an inferior grade of fertilizer on your lawn. Because the fertilizer cannot be returned, you do not have the option of discharging the contract. You can, however, claim damages for the fact that you received an inferior product.

[23.] Exclusion clauses were examined in Chapter 9. We will consider them again in Chapter 12.

CHAPTER SUMMARY

A contract may be discharged by performance if both parties completely or substantially fulfill their obligations. Time is usually not of the essence, but it may be in some circumstances. A tender of payment or performance must be reasonable, but once done, it need not be repeated. Payment and performance do not have to be tendered if a tender would clearly be rejected. In some situations, a contract may be discharged if one party has provided substantial performance.

A contract may be discharged by agreement in a number of ways.

1. A contract may contain an option to terminate that allows one or both parties to bring that contract to an end without the agreement of the other.

2. A contract may be discharged on the basis of a condition subsequent. Moreover, a contract that is subject to a "condition precedent" does not exist unless and until the specified event occurs.

3. An executory contract can be rescinded if both parties agree to do so. Each party provides consideration by releasing the other from the obligation to perform the original contract.

4. A partially executed contract may be discharged by accord and satisfaction. If so, the party that has yet to fully perform must provide new consideration.

5. A contract may be discharged by a release if the parties make an agreement under seal to terminate the contract.

6. The terms of a contract may be subject to variation if each party provides consideration for the alterations.

7. A contract may be discharged and replaced with a new contract under the process of novation. If so, consideration for the new contract consists of the parties' agreement not to enforce the terms of the original contract.

8. Performance of a contractual obligation may be waived by the party that was not required to perform the obligation.

A contract can be discharged by law if it is frustrated or if a contractual party becomes bankrupt. Similarly, although the passage of time does not technically discharge a contract, it may prevent a party from suing for breach of contract.

A contract may be discharged for breach of a condition, a warranty, or an intermediate term. Classification of a term generally depends on whether a breach substantially deprives the innocent party of the expected benefit of the contract. The innocent party is entitled to discharge a contract only if the breached term is a condition or an intermediate term that has resulted in a substantial deprivation. A term may be breached through (i) defective performance of an obligation that has fallen due, (ii) anticipatory breach of an obligation that has yet to fall due, or (iii) self-induced impossibility.

REVIEW QUESTIONS

1. Briefly explain the effect of discharging a contract.

2. Explain the meaning of the term "time is of the essence." Is time of the essence under most contracts? If time is of the essence under a particular contract, what happens if performance does not occur on schedule?

3. Will a contractual party ever be relieved of the obligation to tender performance? Explain.

4. What is legal tender? How is the concept of legal tender relevant to the issue of discharge by performance?

5. Explain the term "substantial performance." Can a contract be discharged on the basis of substantial performance? If so, does the failure to tender complete performance give rise to any consequences?

6. Explain the operation of a condition subsequent.

7. Explain the operation of a condition precedent.

8. Explain the operation of a condition precedent that merely suspends the performance, rather than the creation, of a contract.

9. Explain the difference between rescission, accord and satisfaction, and release. Why does the issue of consideration cause problems for accord and satisfaction but not for rescission or release?

10. Explain the difference between variation and novation. Why does the issue of consideration cause problems for variation but not for novation?

11. Does the process of waiver require consideration?

12. If a contract is discharged by operation of law as a consequence of the lapse of a limitation period, can the right to sue for breach of contract ever be revived? Explain your answer.

13. What test do the courts use to distinguish between conditions, warranties, and intermediate terms?

14. Why does the breach of a condition support the right to discharge?

15. Why does the breach of a warranty not support the right to discharge?

16. When will the breach of an intermediate term support the right to discharge?

17. What is an anticipatory breach? How does it differ from a normal breach?

18. Describe the circumstances in which a breach will arise from self-induced impossibility. How do those circumstances differ from circumstances involving frustration?

19. If a contract is discharged for breach of a condition, does that contract completely cease to exist? Explain your answer.

20. Under what circumstances will the right to discharge be lost even if there has been a breach of a condition?

CASES AND PROBLEMS

1. Elda entered into an employment contract with the Blacksox Baseball Club to sell food at a concession stand during the team's home games. One term of the contract stated: "The employer agrees to pay to the employee $200 per game plus a 10 percent commission on food sales." Another term of the contract stated: "This agreement shall not be binding if, for whatever reason, fan attendance is so low as to render the employee's services unnecessary." After a promising start to the season, the Blacksox team went into a prolonged losing streak, during which attendance dropped by 60 percent. At that point, the team asked Elda to hand in her uniform and told her that her contract was terminated. She is very upset because she was relying on that job to pay for this year's school tuition. Did the Blacksox organization have the right to terminate the contract? Explain your answer.

2. Tadpole Inc wanted to sell a warehouse that it owned. It therefore entered into a contract with Bentley Properties Inc, a real estate agent. That contract contained a number of important terms. First, it gave Bentley the exclusive right to list and advertise the warehouse for 90 days. Second, it stated that Bentley would be entitled to receive a sales commission of 10 percent on "any successful sale contract created within the exclusive listing period." Eighty days into the listing period, Bentley showed the property to Janhelene Inc. Janhelene was seriously interested in the warehouse, but since it thought that it could get a better price by dealing directly with the owner, it sent an offer to Tadpole rather than to Bentley. After further communications, Tadpole and Janhelene signed a document, according to which Janhelene agreed to buy the warehouse "subject to the availability of suitable financing." That document was created on the 88th day of the listing period. A week later, Janhelene informed Tadpole that it had arranged financing, and the sale was completed two days later. When Bentley eventually discovered the details of the sale, it demanded the payment of a commission from Tadpole. Is Tadpole obligated to pay? What should Bentley have done to better protect itself in its contract with Tadpole?

3. Dennis and Carmen entered into a contract under which he agreed that, in one week's time, he would pay $10 000 in exchange for her motorcycle. Three days later, however, he contacted her and said, "Look, as it turns out, my financial situation isn't as strong as I thought it was. I wonder if you'd be willing to just call off our agreement?" She replied, "Fine. You keep the money and I'll keep the motorcycle." After considering the matter further, however, Carmen called him back and said that she wanted the contract to be performed as initially planned. Dennis refuses to comply. In fact, he insists that the contract no longer exists. Is he correct? If the parties' contract did come to an end, explain the process that was used to achieve that result.

4. Rabby Computer Inc agreed to design a networking system for Pendulum Publishing Ltd. The contract called for Pendulum to pay $50 000 after Rabby completed its performance. However, when Rabby finished designing the system, Pendulum stated that it could not afford to pay that amount of money in cash. Pendulum therefore asked Rabby if it would agree to discharge the contract upon receipt of $35 000. Although Rabby initially agreed to the proposal, it later insisted upon full payment. It did so before it actually received any money from Pendulum. Is Pendulum entitled to have the contract discharged if it pays $35 000? Would your answer be different if Rabby had promised under seal that he would discharge the contract upon receipt of $35 000? Would your answer be different if Rabby had initially agreed to discharge the contract in exchange for $35 000 plus a set of encyclopedias from Pendulum? Explain your answers.

5. On May 21, the Bremen Bread Co agreed to purchase flour from Lausanne Granary Inc. The contract called for Lausanne to deliver a tonne of flour to Bremen every Monday for a year. The contract also stated that time was of the essence with respect to the delivery dates. From the outset, however, there were problems. During the first two months of the contract, Lausanne delivered the flour twice on a Monday, four times on a Tuesday, once on a Wednesday, and once on a Thursday. After the eighth week, Bremen informed Lausanne that it was discharging the contract for breach of a condition. In response, Lausanne argued that Bremen was precluded from doing so because it had already accepted late delivery on six occasions without a word of complaint. Did Lausanne breach the contract? If so, was Bremen entitled to rely upon that breach? If Bremen cannot complain of the defective nature of Lausanne's past performance, must it also accept late deliveries in the future? Explain your answers.

6. Ten years ago, Stanislav purchased a car from his co-worker Kerri for $10 000. The full purchase price was supposed to be paid on delivery. However, Stanislav paid only $2000 when Kerri delivered the car to him, and he has not paid anything since. For many years, Kerri did not mention the matter because she did not want to create an unpleasant situation in her workplace. Recently, however, when she retired from her job, she notified Stanislav that she wanted to be paid the remaining part of the purchase price plus interest. He replied, "I know that I still owe at least $8000 to you, but I also know that there is some law that prevents you from claiming it anymore." Is he correct? Is Kerri now entitled to receive any money? Explain your answers.

7. Debbie Krawchuk wanted to buy a horse for her eleven year old daughter to ride around their ranch. She agreed to purchase an eight year old Anglo-Arabian gelding, named Omar, from Eva Ulrychova. The contract was conditional upon Eva's ability to provide a veterinarian's certificate of good health. Eva therefore had the horse checked by Dr Rach, who issued a clean bill of health. Debbie then paid $3000 and took Omar home to her daughter. A short time later, however, she noticed that Omar was "cribbing." Cribbing occurs when a horse bites onto a fence rail and breathes deeply. The effect is to give the animal a sort of "high." Depending upon the severity of the condition, a horse may suffer a number of side effects, including a loss of appetite, weight loss, and colic. When Debbie complained about the situation, Eva provided her with a "cribbing collar," which effectively prevented Omar from continuing on with his bad habit. Debbie nevertheless wants to return Omar to Eva for a full refund. Eva refuses to comply. She believes that Debbie actually wants get rid of Omar because he has an occasional tendency to "buck." Eva also says, quite correctly, that while cribbing is a condition that affects a horse's health, bucking is not. The fact that Omar bucks therefore cannot possibly constitute a breach of contract. Is Debbie entitled to get her money back? If not, is there any other remedy that she may receive?

8. Bettini entered into a contract with the Vancouver Opera Company under which he agreed to perform for the company twice a month for one year. A term in the contract required Bettini to arrive in Vancouver at least three days before each performance to attend rehearsals. As a seasoned professional, however, he believed that he did not need that much rehearsal and he therefore arrived only one day before his first scheduled performance. The director of the opera company was furious and tried to discharge the agreement on the basis that Bettini had committed a serious breach of the contract. Was the director entitled to do so? Would your answer be the same if Bettini had arrived as scheduled for the first 10 performances, but had arrived only one day before the eleventh? Would your answer be different if Bettini was not a seasoned professional, but rather a novice? Explain your answers.

9. Ivan entered into a contract with Poe Paperback Inc, a small publishing company, to write a mystery novel in exchange for $5000. Under the terms of the contract, Ivan was to deliver a manuscript to Poe within 18 months. However, after three weeks of staring hopelessly at a blank computer screen, Ivan reached the conclusion that he had developed an irreparable writer's block and that he would not be able to produce the promised novel. He sent a letter to Poe that said, "I am terribly sorry, but I will have to withdraw from our contract. Since you have not made any payments to me yet, I cannot imagine that you have any objections and I will assume that my proposal is acceptable to you." Ivan received no response from Poe. After another 12 months, however, he suddenly found the inspiration to write a brilliant mystery novel in the space of two weeks. He then entered into negotiations with Christie Mysteries Ltd, a large publishing company, to sell the completed manuscript for $100 000. At that point, Poe contacted Ivan and insisted that the book belonged to them. Ivan, however, insists that he was relieved of his contractual obligations to Poe. Did Ivan breach his contract with Poe? If so, describe the nature of the breach. If there was a breach of contract, is Poe entitled to rely upon it and to seek legal relief from Ivan? Explain.

10. Anatal Developments Ltd agreed to sell 150 plots of land to Eastwalsh Homes Ltd. Eastwalsh intended to use the plots as part of a new subdivision. In order to do so, however, it would be necessary to receive planning approval from the city. The parties' agreement therefore contained the following terms: "This sale will close 90 days after this agreement is signed. . . . Anatal will use its best efforts to secure planning approval before the date of closing. . . . If planning approval is not obtained before the date of closing, this agreement will automatically terminate." Although the agreement was signed by both parties, Anatal made little effort and consequently failed to secure planning approval. The agreement therefore terminated after 90 days. Eastwalsh claims that it is entitled to compensation for the loss of its ability to develop the subdivision. Anatal disagrees. It argues that since the agreement contained a condition, it never really was a contract. It also points out that even if it had used its best efforts, the city still might have denied planning approval. In fact, the evidence indicates that there had only been a 50 percent chance that the city could have been persuaded to grant approval. Is Anatal liable to Eastwalsh for breach of contract?

11. Gerry and Harlan both have lawn-care businesses. For a number of years, they agreed to take care of each other's clients for a two-week period while the other took a family vacation. Seven years ago, while Harlan was away, Gerry fully performed his part of the agreement. That same summer, just as Gerry was about to leave for his vacation, Harlan fell off his riding lawn mower and broke his leg. Harlan was no longer able to perform under their arrangement and,

although Gerry was upset to miss his vacation, he agreed to discharge their contract and do his own maintenance. Harlan was uncomfortable about being indebted to Gerry, so he proposed a number of solutions to clear the debt:

- He offered to have his young son, Jeb, complete the work. Gerry, however, was not confident that the quality of Jeb's work would meet his high standards. Gerry thanked Harlan for his offer, but told him that he would do the work himself.
- Harlan offered to pay Gerry market value for his earlier work, but Gerry told him not to give it another thought.
- Harlan also tried to give Gerry three bags of top-of-the-line fertilizer, but it was not the brand Gerry liked to use, so he politely declined the offer.

Harlan decided he had done what he could to fulfill his obligations, so he gave up trying.

For many years, Gerry and Harlan maintained the same arrangement. This past summer, the day before leaving for his vacation, Gerry told Harlan that he intended to take an extended four-week holiday, but expected that Harlan would not charge anything more under their agreement on account of the incident that had happened seven years earlier. Harlan acknowledged his indebtedness to Gerry and agreed to work one extra week, but simply refused to do Gerry's lawn maintenance for two additional weeks on such short notice. Gerry is furious at Harlan's refusal and insists that he will sue Harlan if Harlan does not perform. Is Harlan legally obligated to perform under the seven-year-old agreement? Would Gerry succeed in court? Give reasons for your answer.

12. Dolores Van de Laer and her husband, Harry, recently had an in-ground pool constructed in their backyard. To protect their seven children, they hired Ruth, a certified lifeguard, to teach the family proper swimming techniques and basic rescue procedures. From the beginning, Ruth had difficulty keeping the older children in line while she assisted the younger ones. She complained to Dolores and Harry, and even though they spoke to the children, the situation did not improve. After a few lessons, Ruth told the Van de Laers that she could not take it anymore and that she had arranged to have her friend Kirk, also a certified lifeguard, replace her as their swimming instructor. Dolores and Harry grudgingly agreed to the new arrangement. They soon discovered that Kirk was great with all of the children and that he was also experienced at pool maintenance. Neither Dolores nor Harry had much luck keeping the pool's pH balanced, so they instructed Kirk to take over that responsibility as well.

Later that summer, Kirk bumped into Ruth at a friend's pool party. When she asked how the job was going, Ruth was surprised to learn that Kirk was disappointed with the pay. Ruth had thought the pay was quite good, but apparently the Van de Laers were paying Kirk $50 less per week than they had promised Ruth. When Kirk learned this, he was outraged that the Van de Laers had taken advantage of him. The next day, before beginning the lesson, Kirk spoke with Dolores and demanded to receive the money she owed him under the original agreement with Ruth. Additionally, he asked for an extra $25 dollars per week as payment for the pool maintenance. Dolores refused to pay Kirk any extra money. She claims that the original agreement with Ruth was discharged by agreement and that a new one with different rights and obligations was created with Kirk. Kirk, however, argues that there was a novation and that he adopted the same rights and obligations that existed under the old contract. Analyze each party's argument. Do you think Kirk is entitled to more money? Explain your answer.

Weblinks

Duhaime Law: Restraint of Trade Contracts
www.duhaime.org/contract/ca-con6.aspx#assign
This website contains a discussion of assignment, novation, and frustration.

Currency Act, s 8   www.canlii.org/ca/sta/c-52
This page contains the federal legislation that determines the amount of coins that a creditor must accept in payment of a debt.

Bankruptcy and Insolvency Act, s 175   www.canlii.org/ca/sta/b-3
This page contains the federal legislation that states when a contractual obligation is discharged by bankruptcy.

ADDITIONAL RESOURCES FOR CHAPTER 11 ON THE COMPANION WEBSITE

(www.pearsoned.ca/mcinnes)

In addition to self-test multiple-choice, true-false, and short essay questions (all with immediate feedback), three additional Cases and Problems (with suggested answers), and links to useful Web destinations, the Companion Website provides the following resources for Chapter 11:

Provincial Material

- **British Columbia:** Tender of Payment, Tender of Performance, Frustrated Contracts, Limitation Periods
- **Alberta:** Frustration, Fundamental Breach, Substantial Performance
- **Manitoba and Saskatchewan:** Promise to Forgive an Existing Debt, Lapse of Limitation Period
- **Ontario:** Effect of Frustration, Exemption Clauses, Fundamental Breach, Limitation Periods, Options to Terminate, Substantial Performance

12 Contractual Remedies

OBJECTIVES

After completing this chapter, you should be able to:

1. Define the term "damages" and explain why the courts will generally award only damages for a breach of contract.

2. Describe expectation damages and explain how they are calculated.

3. Explain two important limitations on the availability of expectation damages.

4. Explain the nature of reliance damages and distinguish them from expectation damages.

5. Explain the concept of "account of profits" and suggest when that sort of remedy may be available for a breach of contract.

6. Describe nominal damages and punitive damages and explain how they are calculated.

7. Distinguish liquidated damages from penalties.

8. Describe specific performance and injunctions and explain when they are awarded.

9. Explain how exclusion clauses apply under contracts that are discharged for breach.

10. Describe the cause of action in unjust enrichment and the remedy of restitution, and explain when those concepts are applicable in a contractual context.

One or more remedies may be available if a contract is breached. As we saw in Chapter 11, if the breach substantially deprives the innocent party of the benefit that it expected to receive under the agreement, that party is usually entitled to discharge the contract. Other remedies may also be available, whether or not a contract is discharged for breach. Figure 12.1 outlines the possibilities that we will discuss.

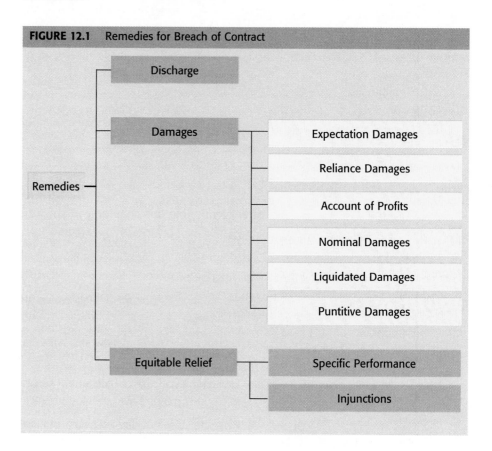

FIGURE 12.1   Remedies for Breach of Contract

Remedies
- Discharge
- Damages
  - Expectation Damages
  - Reliance Damages
  - Account of Profits
  - Nominal Damages
  - Liquidated Damages
  - Puntitive Damages
- Equitable Relief
  - Specific Performance
  - Injunctions

DAMAGES

In the vast majority of cases, the remedy for a breach of contract is *damages*. **Damages** is an award of money that is intended to cure a wrongful event, such as a breach of contract. The nature of that remedy needs to be stressed. Except in rare cases, the plaintiff is *not* entitled to receive the *exact thing* that it expected to get under the agreement. It is only entitled to the *monetary value* of that thing. For example, if I agree to sell my car to you, but later break my promise after you have paid the price, you are probably not entitled to get the car itself. Instead, you are entitled to the monetary value of that car.

There are several reasons why courts usually award only monetary damages for a breach of contract. First, the courts of law historically did not have the power to compel a defendant to do anything other than pay money.[1]

damages is an award of money that is intended to cure a wrongful event, such as a breach of contract

---

[1] In contrast, the courts of equity did have the authority to compel a defendant to do other things. As we discuss below, courts can still award *specific performance* and *injunctions* instead of monetary damages when they use their equitable powers. The difference between law and equity was explained in Chapter 1.

Second, contracts traditionally were seen as commercial arrangements between business people. And even today, money is usually the only thing that matters in the commercial world. Consequently, there is no need to award any other sort of remedy. Third, especially in the business world, it would often be inconvenient to award something other than monetary damages. Returning to our earlier example, suppose that I am a used car dealer and that I agreed to sell a specific car to you. What would happen if, as a result of my breach, you could sue me and demand the delivery of that particular vehicle? It could be several years before our dispute was resolved. And in the meantime, I would not be able to deal with the car. I would have to set it aside in case you won the case. An efficient economy, however, requires the free flow of goods and value.

Expectation Damages

Within the broad category of damages, there are many different *measures of relief*, or ways in which the courts can calculate the amount of money that the plaintiff is entitled to recover from the defendant. The most common measure of relief in contract law is *expectation damages*. **Expectation damages** represent the monetary value of the benefit that the plaintiff expected to receive under the contract.

That definition contains an important idea. Expectation damages are *forward-looking* because they are intended to place the plaintiff in the position that it expected to be in *after* the contract was properly performed. In contrast, as discussed in Chapter 3, compensatory damages in tort law are *backward-looking* because they are intended to place the plaintiff in the position that it was in *before* the defendant acted wrongfully. Consider the difference.

- Backward-looking damages are easily justified. They allow the plaintiff to recover the value of something, such as a favourable reputation or an unbroken leg, that it previously enjoyed, but lost as a result of the defendant's wrongful act.

- Forward-looking damages go further. They allow the plaintiff to recover the value of something that it never previously enjoyed, but merely expected to receive under its contract with the defendant. Nevertheless, forward-looking damages can be justified in contract law. The business world operates largely on the basis of credit, which is a promise to do something in the future. Such a promise is valuable only if the person who receives it can be confident that it will be fulfilled. Expectation damages therefore provide an assurance that if a promise is not actually fulfilled, the innocent party will at least be able to recover the monetary value of that promise.

As Figure 12.2 shows, expectation damages are equal to the value of the benefit that the plaintiff expected to receive under the contract *minus* the value of the costs that it expected to incur. Suppose that you agree to pay $5000 for a computer that is really worth $7000. You expect to make a profit of $2000.

> **expectation damages** represent the monetary value of the benefit that the plaintiff expected to receive under the contract

FIGURE 12.2   Calculation of Expectation Damages

Expectation Damages	=	expected benefits under the contract	−	costs under the contract

Consequently, if the vendor breaches the contract by refusing to deliver the computer, and if you have not yet paid the price, you will be entitled to receive $2000 in cash. And if you paid the entire price before the breach occurs, you will be entitled to $7000 in cash. In either event, you are entitled to enjoy the profit of $2000.

The examples in You Be the Judge 12.1 and 12.2 will help you understand how expectation damages are calculated. As you work through them, ask yourself these two questions. How much did the plaintiff *expect* to have at the end of the contract? How much does the plaintiff *actually* have after the defendant's breach? Expectation damages should be equal to the difference between those two numbers.

YOU BE THE JUDGE 12.1

Calculation of Expectation Damages

José agreed to sell a car to Maria for $5000. Although she made a down payment of $4000, he refused to deliver the vehicle because he discovered that it was really worth $7500. Assuming that José has breached the contract, Maria will be entitled to recover expectation damages of $6500.

Questions for Discussion

1. As a judge, how would you arrive at that conclusion?
2. Does that conclusion seem fair?

YOU BE THE JUDGE 12.2

Calculation of Expectation Damages

José agreed to sell a car to Maria for $5000. Although she made a down payment of $4000, he refused to deliver the vehicle. He did so despite the fact that the car was really worth only $1000. Assuming that José has breached the contract, Maria will not be entitled to recover any expectation damages. (However, she may be entitled to restitution, as explained at the end of this chapter.)

Questions for Discussion

1. As a judge, how would you arrive at that conclusion?
2. Does that conclusion seem fair?

As we have seen, it is usually fairly easy to calculate expectation damages. In some situations, however, the exercise is much more difficult. We will consider five issues:

- difficulty of calculation
- cost of cure or loss of value
- intangible losses
- remoteness
- mitigation of damages

Difficulty of Calculation

Expectation damages are usually available even if they are very difficult to calculate. The courts will do the best they can. In one famous case, the defendant breached a contract by depriving the plaintiff of an opportunity to win a beauty contest.[2] While the plaintiff's actual chance of winning the contest was highly speculative, the court awarded expectation damages based on its best guess as to how she would have fared in the competition. In contrast, if the calculation of the plaintiff's loss is not merely difficult, but entirely speculative, a court will not award damages. A court of law is not a proper place for wild guesses.[3]

Cost of Cure or Loss of Value

Sometimes, it is difficult to decide exactly what the plaintiff expected to receive from the defendant. For example, there may be a question as to whether the plaintiff expected to receive a *service* or the *value of the end-product* of that service. Consider the illustration in Case Brief 12.1.

CASE BRIEF 12.1

Groves v John Wunder Co (1939) 286 NW 235 (Minn CA)

The plaintiff rented a piece of land to the defendant for $105 000. The defendant was entitled to operate a sand and gravel mine on that property, but it was also required to level the ground at the end of the lease. After removing a great deal of sand and gravel, the defendant left huge craters on the property. It did so for economic reasons. It would have cost $60 000 to level the land. But even if the land was level, it would have been worth only $12 000.

The plaintiff claimed that expectation damages should be measured by the *cost of cure*. It argued that it expected to receive a level piece of land at the end of the lease and that it was therefore entitled to receive the amount of money that would be required to put the land into that condition. In response, the defendant claimed that expectation damages should be measured by the *loss of value*. It argued that what the plaintiff really expected to receive under the contract was land worth $12 000.

The court agreed with the plaintiff and awarded $60 000 in expectation damages.

That result may seem surprising, especially when you learn that the plaintiff did not actually use the damages that it received from the defendant to level the land.[4] Nevertheless, the court's decision may be justifiable. The defendant's promise to level the land was part of the price that it agreed to pay in exchange for the right to mine sand and gravel from the property. If the plaintiff had known that the land would be left with huge craters, it probably would have insisted on a different deal. For instance, instead of asking for $105 000 plus level land, it might have asked for $165 000.

The courts often follow the approach taken in *Groves v John Wunder Co*. They are most likely to do so if the plaintiff has a legitimate interest in having the work done or if the plaintiff has actually already spent money curing the defendant's defective performance.[5] However, judges usually refuse to award damages on a "cost of cure" basis if the difference between the cost of cure and the benefits of the cure is unreasonably large. For example, in a recent English case, the defendant breached a contract by building a swimming pool to a depth of six feet six inches (198 centimetres), rather than seven feet six inches (228 centimetres). The cost of curing that defect was £22 000. The value of the

---

[2.] *Chaplin v Hicks* [1911] 2 KB 786 (CA).

[3.] *McRae v Commonwealth Disposals Commissioners* (1951) 84 CLR 377 (HCA).

[4.] The plaintiff is generally entitled to spend its damages as it chooses.

[5.] *Nu-West Homes Ltd v Thunderbird Petroleum Ltd* (1975) 59 DLR (3d) 292 (Alta CA).

swimming pool, however, was the same in either event. The evidence also indicated that the defendant's breach did not make the pool any more dangerous for diving. The court therefore refused to award expectation damages on a "cost of cure" basis.[6]

Intangible Losses

an intangible loss is a loss that does not have any apparent economic value

Expectation damages are also difficult to calculate when the plaintiff suffers an intangible loss as a result of the defendant's breach. An **intangible loss** is a loss that does not have any apparent economic value. Examples include the anger, frustration, sadness, or disappointment that may occur when a promise is broken.

Historically, the courts generally refused to award damages for intangible losses. As we discussed earlier, contracts were seen as commercial arrangements between business people who were concerned with financial matters rather than hurt feelings. Furthermore, the courts did not traditionally feel comfortable assigning dollar figures to personal emotions. What is the monetary value of your sense of disappointment if a car rental company delivers a mini-van instead of the sporty convertible that it had promised?

Recently, however, the courts have started to recognize that "peace of mind" is one of the things that a person may expect to receive under a contract. Accordingly, while the cases remain somewhat inconsistent, damages may be available if, contrary to the plaintiff's expectation, the defendant performed the contract in a way that caused distress.[7] For example, expectation damages have been awarded for the disappointment that was caused when a holiday was ruined and for the grief that was caused when a beloved pet dog was suffocated to death during air travel.[8] However, the courts still refuse to compensate a person for the humiliation or dejection they may feel as a result of being unfairly fired from a job.[9]

Remoteness

The plaintiff cannot recover expectation damages for *every* loss that it suffers after the defendant's breach. The loss must, as a matter of fact, have been *caused* by the breach. Furthermore, the loss must not be *remote* from the breach. A loss is **remote** if it would be unfair to hold the defendant legally responsible for it.

a loss is remote if it would be unfair to hold the defendant legally responsible

A loss is *not* remote if the defendant either *should have known* or *actually did know* that it was the sort of loss that might occur if the contract was breached. That test has two parts.

- First, liability may be imposed if *a reasonable person would have known* that the plaintiff's loss might result from a breach. That is true even if the plaintiff did not draw the defendant's attention to that possibility.

[6.] *Ruxley Electronics & Construction Ltd v Forsyth* [1996] 1 AC 344 (HL). The court did, however, award £2500 for "loss of amenity" or "intangible loss."

[7.] *Farley v Skinner* [2002] 2 AC 732 (HL); *Turczinski v Dupont Heating & Air Conditioning Ltd* (2004) 246 DLR (4th) 95 (Ont CA).

[8.] *Jarvis v Swan Tours Ltd* [1973] QB 233 (CA); *Newell v Canadian Pacific Airlines Ltd* (1976) 74 DLR (3d) 574 (Ont Co Ct).

[9.] *Wallace v United Grain Growers Ltd* (1997) 152 DLR (4th) 1 (SCC). As we will see in Chapter 26, however, the same case said that if an employer acts in bad faith and fires an employee in a humiliating way, damages may be calculated on the basis of an artificially enlarged "notice period." Furthermore, an ex-employee may also recover "punitive damages" in exceptional circumstances. We will consider that possibility later.

■ Second, liability may be imposed if the *defendant actually knew* that the plaintiff's loss might result from the breach. That is true even if a reasonable person would not have normally expected such a loss.

Case Brief 12.2 illustrates the two parts of the remoteness test.

CASE BRIEF 12.2

Victoria Laundry (Windsor) Ltd v Newman Industries Ltd [1949] 2 KB 528 (CA)

The defendant agreed to deliver a boiler to the plaintiff on June 5. When the contract was created, the defendant knew in a general sense that the plaintiff operated a laundry, but it did not know the specific details of the plaintiff's business. The defendant broke the contract by delivering the boiler 20 weeks late. As a result of that breach, the plaintiff suffered two types of losses. First, it lost £16 per week because it was unable to perform ordinary laundry operations, such as cleaning and pressing shirts. Second, it lost £262 per week because it was unable to obtain a highly lucrative and highly unusual dyeing contract from the government.

As a matter of fact, the defendant's breach caused both types of losses. Liability therefore turned on the issue of remoteness. Even though the plaintiff had not specifically mentioned the possibility of the first type of loss when the contract was created, the defendant was liable for £16 per week in expectation damages. The court held that any reasonable person, even without being told, would have known that that type of loss might occur. In contrast, the court held that the second type of loss was remote. Because the government contract was highly unusual, a reasonable person would not have known about it without being told. And furthermore, the plaintiff had not told the defendant about it. The plaintiff therefore could not recover the additional £262 per week.

Remoteness is a principle of fairness. It is applied to the time when the parties created their contract, not to the time when the defendant committed the breach or when the judge hears the case. Before entering into a contract, a party will consider all of the costs potentially associated with the agreement, including the risk of being held liable as a result of committing a breach. As that risk increases, the party will ask for a higher price. And at some point, the risk will become too much and the party will refuse to enter into the contract altogether. The party can only be expected to perform that calculation on the basis of information that it *should know* or that it *does know*. It would be unfair to impose liability for a loss that a party could not have predicted.

Victoria Laundry provides a good example of this. It was fair to impose liability for £16 per week because the defendant must have realized that if it broke its promise, the plaintiff would be unable to conduct its ordinary laundry business. However, the defendant had no way of knowing that its breach might cause the plaintiff to lose the government contract. And if it had known of the possibility of being held liable for £262 per week, it almost certainly would have demanded a higher price from the plaintiff.

As a matter of risk management, the lesson is clear. Before entering into a contract, you should make sure that the other party is aware of any unusual losses that you might suffer as a result of its breach. The other party may demand a higher price or even refuse to enter into the agreement.[10] But if you do not draw attention to the possibility of an unusual loss, you will not be able to recover expectation damages if that loss occurs.

[10.] The other party could also enter into the contract at a lower price, but insist on the insertion of an "exclusion clause." Exclusion clauses are discussed later in this chapter.

Mitigation of Damages

mitigation occurs when the plaintiff takes steps to minimize the losses flowing from the defendant's breach

Even if remoteness is not a problem, the plaintiff cannot recover damages for a loss that it unreasonably failed to *mitigate*.[11] **Mitigation** occurs when the plaintiff takes steps to minimize the losses flowing from the defendant's breach. Consider the example in Business Decision 12.1.

BUSINESS DECISION 12.1

Mitigation of Damages

Manfred agreed to deliver a shipment of potato chips to you each week for a year. If he had fulfilled that promise, you would have been able to earn a net profit of $1000 per week by reselling the chips in your convenience store. Unfortunately, Manfred breached the contract at the outset and refused to make any deliveries. Instead of ordering the same number of chips from someone else, you simply complained for the next 52 weeks. At the end of the year, you brought a claim against Manfred for $52 000 in expectation damages.

Questions for Discussion

1. Assuming that your loss is not remote, is Manfred liable for all of your loss?

2. Assuming that you could have arranged an alternative supply of chips within three weeks of the breach, how much will you receive in damages?

Business Decision 12.1 illustrates four more points about mitigation.

- First, lawyers sometimes say that there is a "duty to mitigate." In fact, there is not really a *duty* in the sense of something that *must* be done. The plaintiff is not required to mitigate. Failing to do so is, however, a poor business decision. As we saw, you are unable to recover damages for losses that you could have mitigated.

- Second, the plaintiff is responsible only for taking *reasonable* steps to mitigate a loss. The plaintiff is not denied expectation damages simply because it failed to adopt an unreasonably difficult, inconvenient, or risky way of minimizing the loss that resulted from the defendant's breach.

- Third, damages are denied *only to the extent that* the plaintiff unreasonably failed to mitigate. Although you did not take any steps toward mitigation, you are still entitled to $3000 in damages. You would have suffered that loss even if you had acted reasonably.

- Fourth, the plaintiff can recover the costs associated with mitigation. For example, if you had spent $500 arranging the alternative supply of chips within three weeks, you would have been entitled to $3000 in lost profits, plus $500 as the cost of mitigation.

Reliance Damages

reliance damages represent the monetary value of the expenses that the plaintiff wasted under a contract

Expectation damages are the usual remedy for a breach of contract. In some situations, however, other types of damages may be awarded. *Reliance damages* are the most common alternative. **Reliance damages** represent the monetary value of the expenses that the plaintiff wasted under a contract.

[11.] *Asamera Oil Corp v Sea Oil & General Corp* (1978) 89 DLR (3d) 1 (SCC).

In one sense, reliance damages are the opposite of expectation damages. If you ask for expectation damages, you are saying, "Give me what I expected to get. Put me in the position that I would have been in if the contract had been properly performed." If you ask for reliance damages, you are saying, "Give me what I lost. Put me in the position that I would have been in if I had not wasted resources under this contract." Expectation damages look *forward* in an attempt to fulfill a contract; reliance damages look *backward* in an attempt to undo the effects of a contract.[12]

The plaintiff is generally entitled to recover either expectation damages or reliance damages, but not both. Expectation damages represent the benefit that the plaintiff expected to receive under the contract; reliance damages represent the costs that it incurred. If the plaintiff wants the benefit, it must be willing to pay the cost. As a result, the plaintiff should sometimes carefully consider which measure of damages is preferable.[13] Business Decision 12.2 provides an illustration.

 BUSINESS DECISION 12.2

Expectation Damages and Reliance Damages

As a music promoter, you hired Ursula to perform a piano concert in exchange for $5000. Based on your experience in the music business, you expected to personally receive a net profit of $7000 from the concert. Ursula received full payment when she signed the contract, but told you a week later that she was not willing to perform. You reluctantly cancelled the concert. You are now doubly unhappy. Not only did you pay $5000 for a piano recital that never occurred, you were also deprived of your expected revenue.

Question for Discussion

1. Assuming that Ursula has breached the contract, will you claim expectation damages or reliance damages?

Reliance damages are subject to an important limitation. They can be awarded only to the extent that a contract is *not unprofitable*.[14] The plaintiff therefore cannot claim reliance damages in order to escape the consequences of having entered into a bad bargain. It must bear responsibility for having made a poor deal. While that rule may seem complicated, it can be easily illustrated. Consider Ethical Perspective 12.1 (on p. 266).

[12.] In that sense, reliance damages in contract are similar to the damages that are awarded in tort. Tort damages were explained in Chapter 3.

[13.] The plaintiff is entitled to sue for both expectation damages and reliance damages. However, if it successfully proves that the defendant committed a breach of contract, the plaintiff must tell the trial judge which measure of relief it wants to receive.

[14.] *Bowlay Logging Ltd v Domtar Ltd* (1982) 135 DLR (3d) 179 (BC CA).

Reliance Damages and Bad Bargains[15]

You agreed to pay $14 000 to Anwar in exchange for a shipment of steel. Although you provided $5000 as a down payment, he refused to deliver the goods. You sue for breach of contract. At trial, the evidence indicates that you had entered into a bad bargain. Although you agreed to pay $14 000, the steel was really worth only $11 000. If the contract had been fully performed, you would have suffered a net loss of $3000.

Because you did not expect to earn a profit under the contract, you cannot recover any expectation damages. Moreover, although you paid $5000 under the contract, you can recover reliance damages only to the *extent* that your contract was *not unprofitable*. Since you would have suffered a net loss of $3000 if the contract had been performed, you can recover only $2000 in reliance damages. In effect, you are responsible for the $3000 that you expected to lose as a result of entering into a bad bargain.[16]

Questions for Discussion

1. Does that result seem fair to you?

2. Suggest a reason why the courts have adopted that rule.

Account of Profits

The usual remedy for breach of contract is compensation. Damages are measured by the plaintiff's loss. Occasionally, however, the plaintiff may prefer to complain about the defendant's gain. As a result of breaking a promise, the defendant may have received a substantial benefit for itself. It may seem unfair to allow a party to profit from its own wrongdoing. Nevertheless, the courts traditionally rejected such claims: "The question is not one of making the defendant disgorge what he has [received] by committing the wrong, but one of compensating the plaintiff."[17] As seen in Case Brief 12.3, however, the British House of Lords recently created a new rule.

Attorney General v Blake [2001] 1 AC 268 (HL)

George Blake was a double agent during the Cold War. While pretending to be a spy for the British, he actually worked for the Soviets. After his treachery had cost countless lives, he was caught, tried in a British court, and sentenced to 42 years in Wormwood Scrubs Prison in London. Five years later, however, he made a daring escape and fled to Moscow. While still in Russia, he entered into a contract with an English publisher for the release of his memoirs, *No Other Choice*. The publisher agreed to pay him an advance of £150 000. It had already paid £60 000 of that amount when the British government began legal proceedings.

The government sued for breach of contract. When Blake initially joined the British secret service in 1944, he signed an agreement that contained a promise "not to divulge any official information gained by me as a result of my employment." He clearly broke that promise by writing his memoirs. On the question of remedies, however, the government could not prove that it had suffered any loss. It is

(continued)

[15.] *Bush v Canfield* 2 Conn 485 (1818).

[16.] We will examine the cause of action in unjust enrichment later in this chapter. When we do so, return to Ethical Perspective 12.1 and calculate the amount of money that you would be entitled to receive as restitution rather than as expectation damages or reliance damages.

[17.] *Tito v Waddell* [1977] Ch 106.

(continued)

impossible to put a monetary value on the protection of state secrets. Furthermore, by the time of publication, the Berlin Wall had fallen and the Cold War was over. Consequently, much of the information contained in Blake's book had become public knowledge.

The House of Lords nevertheless held in favour of the government. While recognizing that contractual remedies usually focus on the plaintiff's loss, Lord Nicholls insisted that they may, "in exceptional circumstances," focus on the defendant's gain. Consequently, instead of awarding damages, he applied the equitable remedy of *account of profits*.[18] The government was entitled to the profits that George Blake received as a result of breaking his contract.

Attorney General v Blake is a landmark decision. It means that the remedy for breach of contract may now reflect the defendant's gain, rather than the plaintiff's loss.[19] The scope of the decision is, however, unclear. Lord Nicholls said that it was impossible to establish "fixed rules." By way of guidance, he merely suggested that a judge must consider all of the circumstances before asking "whether the plaintiff had a legitimate interest in preventing the defendant's profit-making activity and, hence, in depriving him of his profit." More precise rules will have to be "hammered out on the anvil of concrete cases." Consequently, it will be many years before we are able to confidently predict when an account of profits will be given for a breach of contract.[20]

Nominal Damages

If the plaintiff proves that a contract was broken, but cannot prove that it suffered any loss as a result of the breach, the court may award *nominal damages*. **Nominal damages** symbolize the fact that the plaintiff suffered a wrong when the defendant broke a promise. Because they are merely symbolic, nominal damages are awarded in very small amounts, such as $10.

It is usually a bad idea to bring an action to recover nominal damages. Judges do not like to waste time on trivial matters. If a court believes that the plaintiff did not have a legitimate reason for suing the defendant, it may require the plaintiff to pay the costs associated with the trial. And as we saw in Chapter 2, the value of those costs will be much greater than the value of the nominal damages that the plaintiff is entitled to receive from the defendant.

nominal damages symbolize the fact that the plaintiff suffered a wrong when the defendant broke a promise

Liquidated Damages

At the time of creating a contract, the parties may want to avoid the risk of becoming involved in a complicated and expensive lawsuit in the future. They

---

[18] The concept of equity was discussed in Chapter 1. We will look at other equitable remedies later in this chapter.

[19] The Supreme Court of Canada has accepted the application of this approach in Canada: *Bank of America Canada v Mutual Trust Co* (2002) 211 DLR (4th) 385 (SCC).

[20] Although the House of Lords referred to an "account of profits," a variety of labels have been applied to the same remedy. Gain-based relief is sometimes called "disgorgement" or "restitution." That second possibility should, however, be avoided. As we will see at the end of this chapter, "restitution" is the name of the remedy that is triggered by the cause of action in unjust enrichment. It would be confusing to use the same label to describe two different remedies. In this situation, the question is whether the defendant received a benefit *from anyone* as a result of committing a breach of contract against the plaintiff. Under the action for unjust enrichment, the defendant is liable only for those benefits that he received *from the plaintiff*.

may also want to provide each other with an incentive to properly perform. If so, they may include a *liquidated damages* clause in their agreement. **Liquidated damages** represent a genuine attempt to estimate the value of the loss that may occur as a result of a breach. If the contract is in fact broken, the innocent party is entitled to recover the liquidated amount, even if that amount turns out to be more than the loss that it actually suffered. Liquidated damages also work the other way. The innocent party is usually entitled to recover only the liquidated amount, even if it suffered a larger loss as a result of the breach.

Liquidated damages must be distinguished from *penalties*. A **penalty** requires a party to pay an exorbitant amount if it breaches the contract. Unlike liquidated damages, a penalty is not a genuine attempt to estimate the loss that may be caused by a broken promise. It is merely an attempt to coerce performance of an agreement. While the courts enforce liquidated damages, they do not enforce penalties. If a contract contains a penalty clause, the court will ignore it and calculate damages in the usual way.

liquidated damages represent a genuine attempt to estimate the value of the loss that may occur as a result of a breach

a penalty requires a party to pay an exorbitant amount if it breaches the contract

Punitive Damages

Damages are usually intended to compensate the plaintiff for a loss. *Punitive damages*, however, have a different purpose. **Punitive damages** are intended to punish the defendant. Consequently, if the defendant has done something that the court thinks deserves punishment, the plaintiff may be entitled to recover both compensatory damages (either expectation damages or reliance damages) *and* punitive damages.

punitive damages are intended to punish the defendant

Because of the influence of American media, it is important to appreciate that punitive damages are quite different in this country. In comparison to American courts, Canadian courts award punitive damages far less often and in far smaller amounts. That is especially true if the plaintiff is relying upon a breach of contract, rather than a tort. The Supreme Court of Canada has said that two conditions generally must be met.[21] First, the defendant must not only commit a breach of contract, but also act in a "harsh, vindictive, reprehensible and malicious" manner. Second, in committing that breach of contract, the defendant must have also committed another independently actionable wrong, such as a tort or another breach of contract. Those requirements can be satisfied only in very unusual circumstances. In one famous example, a professional hockey team broke its contract with a player by refusing to allow him to visit a physician for treatment of an injury.[22] In that situation, the team (i) breached its contract, (ii) in a morally reprehensible way, and (iii) in a way that also created the tort of negligence. The player was therefore entitled to both compensatory damages and punitive damages.

Concept Summary 12.1 reviews the different remedies that we have discussed.

---

[21] *Whiten v Pilot Insurance Co* (2002) 209 DLR (4th) 257 (SCC); *cf Royal Bank of Canada v W Got & Associates Electric Ltd* (1999) 178 DLR (4th) 385 (SCC).

[22] *Robitaille v Vancouver Hockey Club Ltd* (1981) 124 DLR (3d) 228 (BC CA).

Monetary Relief

Type	Purpose
Expectation damages	place the plaintiff in the position that it would have enjoyed if the contract had been performed
Reliance damages	compensate the plaintiff for the costs that it incurred in reliance upon the contract
Account of profits	strip the defendant of a benefit that he received as a result of breaking a contract
Nominal damages	symbolically demonstrate that the defendant breached its promise to the plaintiff
Liquidated damages	enforce the parties' estimate of the loss that the plaintiff would suffer if the defendant breached the contract
Punitive damages	punish the defendant for breaching the contract in an outrageous way

EQUITABLE RELIEF

As we discussed earlier, a person who suffers a breach of contract usually receives monetary damages. In most situations, that sort of remedy is adequate. Suppose that a car dealer breaks a promise by refusing to deliver a particular vehicle to you. If you are limited to monetary damages, you will not receive that specific car. But with the money that you recover from the defendant, you can buy another car that is virtually identical. Furthermore, by limiting you to monetary relief, the law allows the car dealer to carry on with business as usual. He does not have to hold onto the disputed vehicle while your lawsuit slowly works its way through the court system. In some situations, however, money is not enough. The courts of equity therefore developed other types of remedies.[23]

Specific Performance

The most common type of equitable relief is *specific performance*. **Specific performance** occurs when the court orders the defendant to fulfill a contractual obligation to do something.[24] Notice that the plaintiff does not just receive the monetary value of the defendant's promise; it receives the actual performance of that promise.

It is sometimes said that specific performance, like other equitable remedies, is *discretionary*. The plaintiff does not have a *right* to receive it simply because the defendant breached the contract. The court has to be convinced that specific performance would be *appropriate* in the circumstances. That discretion is, however, exercised on the basis of settled rules. For example, a judge will not order the defendant to specifically perform a promise unless the plaintiff came to court with "clean hands." The plaintiff has dirty hands if, for instance, it somehow took advantage of the defendant. Specific performance will also be refused if it would create a hardship for the defendant, or if the plaintiff unreasonably delayed before starting the lawsuit.

specific performance occurs when the court orders the defendant to fulfill a contractual obligation to do something

---

[23.] The courts of equity were explained in Chapter 1.

[24.] If the defendant refuses to obey the court's order, it can be held in *contempt of court*, and therefore be subject to a fine or imprisonment.

Specific performance depends on four other factors:

- adequacy of damages
- mutuality
- judicial supervision
- personal services

The first limitation is the most important. Specific performance is awarded only if monetary damages would provide an *inadequate* remedy. In our earlier example, you could not get specific performance against the car dealer because monetary damages were sufficient for your purposes. You could use those damages to buy a virtually identical vehicle from someone else. The situation would be different, however, if the specific car that the dealer promised to deliver was unique, and if you had a legitimate reason for wanting to receive that car in particular. For instance, you might be entitled to specific performance if your contract with the dealer concerned John Lennon's infamous psychedelic Rolls Royce.

Specific performance is rarely awarded for contracts that deal with goods, such as cars. In contrast, equity is almost always willing to award specific performance against a person who agreed to sell land. Every piece of land is thought to be unique. And if that is true, then monetary damages will not allow the plaintiff to buy an adequate substitute from someone other than the defendant. That traditional approach was, however, recently modified. The Supreme Court of Canada said that, in the modern world, "[r]esidential, business and industrial properties are all mass produced much in the same way as other consumer goods."[25] Consequently, if the plaintiff wants specific performance of a promise to transfer land, it now has to prove that it really does have a substantial interest in receiving that property.

The concept of *mutuality* provides a second important limitation on the availability of specific performance. **Mutuality** means that specific performance can be awarded *to* a party only if it could also be awarded *against* that same party. It would be unfair to award specific performance to one person, but only monetary damages to the other. For example, the courts generally will not award specific performance *against* a child. Consequently, they also generally will not award specific performance *to* a child. If a person who enters into a contract with a child cannot be assured of getting anything more than monetary damages, it should not be compelled to give anything more in return.

Third, specific performance generally will not be awarded if it would require ongoing *judicial supervision*. Judges want to resolve disputes once and for all. They do not want the parties repeatedly coming to court. Furthermore, they are not willing to constantly monitor a situation to ensure that the defendant is behaving properly. For those reasons, a court may refuse to order specific performance of a promise to keep a grocery store in operation.[26]

Finally, the courts generally will not order specific performance of a promise to perform a *personal service*. For example, an actress will not be compelled to appear in a movie even if she promised to do so. Aside from the fact that specific performance would require ongoing judicial supervision, it would require the actress to work for the movie studio against her will.

The factors that determine the availability of specific performance are reviewed in Concept Summary 12.2.

mutuality means that specific performance can be awarded to a party only if it could also be awarded against that same party

----

[25] *Semelhago v Paramadevan* (1996) 136 DLR (4th) 1 (SCC).
[26] *Co-operative Insurance v Argyll Stores Ltd* [1998] AC 1 (HL).

CONCEPT SUMMARY 12.2

Criteria for Specific Performance

Inadequacy of damages	Specific performance will not be ordered if monetary damages will adequately protect the plaintiff's expectations.
Mutuality	Specific performance will not be ordered in *favour* of someone unless it could also be ordered *against* that same person.
Judicial supervision	Specific performance must not require ongoing judicial supervision to ensure compliance.
Personal services	Specific performance must not require the provision of services of a personal nature.

Injunctions

Specific performance compels a person to fulfill a contractual obligation to *do something*. An *injunction* usually operates in the opposite direction. That term is used in a variety of ways. For now, we will say that an **injunction** occurs when the court orders the defendant to *not do something* that is prohibited by the contract. Suppose that you enter into an agreement with a manufacturer that allows you to sell its product in only one province. If you try to sell in another province, the manufacturer may obtain an injunction to prevent you from doing so.

The same rules generally govern specific performance and injunctions. For example, neither type of remedy is available if monetary damages are sufficient to protect the plaintiff's interests. There are, however, some differences. The courts are much more willing to award injunctions than specific performance. That rule is based on the courts' desire to restrict freedom of action as little as possible. Specific performance requires a party to *do* something. And while they are doing that thing, they cannot do anything else. In contrast, an injunction usually requires a party to *not do* something. And while they are not doing that thing, they remain free to do anything else.

That difference between the two types of equitable remedies creates an interesting tension in some situations. As we saw, the courts generally refuse to order specific performance of a promise to provide personal services. For example, a court will not compel an actress to appear in a movie. However, it may impose an injunction to prevent her from breaching a contractual promise to *not* perform for anyone else. Consider the decision in Case Brief 12.4 (see p. 272).

Although the court awarded an injunction in *Warner Bros Pictures Ltd v Nelson*, it also stressed that that injunctive relief is subject to an important restriction. An injunction will not be granted if it would compel the defendant to choose between working for the plaintiff and not working at all. That rule is seen in Case Brief 12.5 (see p. 272).

an **injunction** occurs when the court orders the defendant to not do something that is prohibited by the contract

CASE BRIEF 12.4

Warner Bros Pictures Inc v Nelson [1937] 1 KB 209

Early in her career, Bette Davis signed a contract with Warner Bros movie studio.[27] That agreement contained positive *and* negative undertakings. Positively, Davis promised to act in the studio's films. Negatively, she promised not to act for anyone else. By 1937, however, she had enjoyed great success in *Of Human Bondage* with Leslie Howard, *The Petrified Forest* with Humphrey Bogart, and *Dangerous*, for which she won an Academy Award. She therefore decided that her contract with Warner Bros did not pay enough for someone of her stature. She wanted to work elsewhere for more money.

Warner Bros did not seek specific performance of Davis's positive promise to perform in its movies. And, indeed, the court said that such an order would not have been granted. The studio did, however, obtain an injunction with respect to the actress's negative promise not to appear in anyone else's movies. The court held that if Davis wanted to appear on film during the life of her contract with Warner Bros, she had to work for that studio. The court also held, however, that she was free to earn a living in other ways if she chose.

CASE BRIEF 12.5

Page One Records Ltd v Britton [1968] 1 WLR 157 (Ch D)

The defendants, four young English musicians who played as *The Troggs*, had a hit song in 1966 with "Wild Thing." Several years earlier, they had signed a contract with the plaintiff. Under the terms of that agreement, the defendants gave a positive promise to employ the plaintiff as their manager and a negative promise to not employ anyone else in that capacity. Unfortunately, the relationship between the parties deteriorated, and the group decided that it could no longer work with the plaintiff. The plaintiff sought an injunction preventing *The Troggs* from hiring anyone else to act as their manager.

The court refused to grant an injunction for several reasons. Most significantly, the judge recognized that an injunction would have effectively prevented the defendants from earning a living. Bette Davis could have made money by doing things other than acting in film. *The Troggs*, in contrast, had no skills outside of music. And they could work as musicians only if they had a manager. It therefore would have been unfair to make them choose between unemployment and working with the plaintiff.

EXCLUSION CLAUSES

Before completing our discussion of contractual remedies, it is important to stress that the parties are generally entitled to create whatever contract they want. Consequently, they are free to reject or modify the remedies that are usually available for breach of contract. We have already seen that they can agree to *liquidated damages* (but not *penalties*). They can also insert an *exclusion clause* into their contract. An **exclusion clause** excludes or limits liability for breach of contract. The clause may apply to certain types of breach. For example, the parties may agree that liability will arise if a promise is intentionally broken, but not if it is carelessly broken. Or the clause may limit the amount of damages that are available. For example, the parties may agree that an action cannot be brought for more than $500. In either event, the exclusion clause will apply even if the parties' contract has been discharged for breach.

an exclusion clause excludes or limits liability for breach of contract

---

[27.] The style of cause refers to "Nelson" because Bette Davis was married to Harmon Nelson at the time of the case.

Exclusion clauses play a important role in the commercial world. Because they allow a business to limit its liability, they create a crucial form of risk management. They also allow for the efficient allocation of risks. If the parties know who will be responsible for a certain type of loss, they also know which of them should arrange insurance.[28] In some situations, however, exclusion clauses may produce unfair results, especially when they are contained in *standard form contracts*. Consequently, as we saw in Chapter 9, they are subject to certain rules and restrictions.

- An exclusion clause will be strictly enforced against the party that drafted it. For instance, a sign in a restaurant that excludes liability for "lost and stolen clothes" may not protect the restaurateur if a diner's briefcase is stolen. Similarly, an exclusion clause that limits liability in contract may not be effective against a claim in tort.[29] Exclusion clauses should therefore be written in clear, *unambiguous language*.

- A business that wants to limit its liability must provide *reasonable notice* of its exclusion clause. The effect of that requirement depends upon the circumstances. In some situations, a court may simply assume that the clause in question is so common that the customer must have known about it. Often, however, the business must actually draw the customer's attention to the clause *before* entering into the contract. For instance, a large, easily-read sign may need to be posted at the entrance of a parking lot. Or a car rental agent may be required to specifically identify and explain an unusually onerous clause in a rental contract.[30]

- If a business wants to rely upon an exclusion clause, it must prove that the other party *agreed* to it. Although that agreement may take any form, the best evidence is usually a signature.

- Finally, even if all of those requirements have been met, an exclusion clause will not apply to a *fundamental breach* if the effect of enforcing the clause would be unfair. Although the law remains somewhat unclear, a **fundamental breach** essentially consists of a breach that goes to the very "core" of the contract. If a breach of that sort was protected by an exclusion clause, then the contract would become radically different than what the parties had initially agreed upon. Assume, for example, that the plaintiff paid to store his car in the defendant's garage. The defendant required the plaintiff to sign a contract that excluded liability "for any loss or damage, however caused, either intentionally or by accident." That clause would not protect the defendant if he deliberately destroyed the plaintiff's vehicle.

a fundamental breach consists of a breach that goes to the very "core" of the contract

UNJUST ENRICHMENT

If an agreement is broken, the innocent party usually complains about the breach of contract and asks for damages, specific performance, or an injunction. In some situations, however, that party may bring an action in *unjust enrichment* and ask for *restitution*. The rules for unjust enrichment and restitution are quite complex. We will consider them briefly.

---

[28] *Fraser Jewellers (1982) Ltd v Dominion Electric Protection Co* (1997) 148 DLR (4th, 496 (Ont CA).

[29] As we saw in Chapter 3, the same set of facts may support claims in both contract and tort.

[30] *Tilden Rent-a-Car Co v Clendenning* (1978) 83 DLR (3d) 400 (Ont CA).

Unjust enrichment is a cause of action that requires proof of three elements:

- an enrichment to the defendant
- a corresponding deprivation to the plaintiff
- the absence of any juristic reason for the defendant's enrichment[31]

The remedy for unjust enrichment is always *restitution*. **Restitution** requires the defendant to give back the enrichment that it received from the plaintiff. We earlier said that expectation damages allow the plaintiff to demand, "Give me what I expected to get," and that reliance damages allow the plaintiff to demand, "Give me what I lost." Following the same pattern, we can now say that restitution allows the plaintiff to demand, "Give me what you received from me."

We must stress one point about the relationship between the law of contract and the law of unjust enrichment. Unjust enrichment can be claimed only if the parties' transaction is *not* governed by an enforceable contract. Unjust enrichment therefore can be used if there *never was* a contract between the parties. For example, if I mistakenly pay $1500 in rent to you, rather than to my landlord, there is no contract between us and I can demand restitution from you. Unjust enrichment can also be used if an apparent contract between the parties is either *void* because its terms are uncertain, or *unenforceable* because it is not in writing.[32] Finally, unjust enrichment can be used if a valid contract has been *discharged* on the basis of a breach.

Since the law of unjust enrichment is very complicated, a business person should consult a lawyer whenever a problem arises in that area. As Case Brief 12.6 demonstrates, however, an action for unjust enrichment is sometimes much more effective than an action for breach of contract.

CASE BRIEF 12.6

Boomer v Muir (1933) 24 P 2d 570 (Cal DC)[33]

The plaintiff agreed to build a dam for the defendant in exchange for a price that it later realized was well below market value. The plaintiff worked on the project and received a number of payments during the first 18 months of the contract. However, as the project neared completion, the defendant refused to honour its obligation to supply materials. The plaintiff therefore discharged the contract on the basis of that breach.

At that point, the plaintiff had an option. It could have claimed expectation damages under the cause of action in breach of contract. However, because it had entered into a bad bargain, that choice was not very appealing. In light of the payments that the defendant had already made, the plaintiff would have only received an additional $20 000.

The plaintiff therefore claimed restitution in unjust enrichment for the value of the construction services that it had rendered:

- the defendant was *enriched* because it had received the value of the plaintiff's services,
- the plaintiff suffered a *corresponding deprivation* because it had supplied the services, and
- and since the defendant was unwilling to perform its own obligations under the contract, there was *no juristic reason* why it should be able to retain the value of the plaintiff's services.

Significantly, once the plaintiff established the cause of action in unjust enrichment, it was entitled to restitution of the *actual value* of its services. Because the plaintiff's claim was not breach of contract, its remedy was not limited by the terms of its contract with the defendant. Consequently, after taking into account the payments that the defendant had already made, the court awarded $257 000 to the plaintiff. That was $237 000 more than it expected to receive under the contract.

31. *Pettkus v Becker* (1980) 117 DLR (3d) 257 (SCC); *Garland v Consumers' Gas Co* (2004) 237 DLR (4th) 385 (SCC).

32. *Clarke v Moir* (1987) 82 NSR (2d) 183 (CA); *Deglman v Guaranty Trust Co of Canada* [1954] 3 DLR 785 (SCC). As we saw in Chapter 10, most contracts do not have to be written.

33. See also *Lodder v Slowey* [1904] AC 442 (PC); *Komorowski v Van Weel* (1993) 12 OR (3d) 444 (Gen Div).

CHAPTER SUMMARY

If a contract is breached, the innocent party may be entitled to a variety of remedies. If the breach is serious, the innocent party may be allowed to discharge the contract. Whether or not a contract is discharged for breach, the innocent party may be entitled to damages.

Expectation damages allow the innocent party to recover the monetary value of the benefit that it expected to receive under the contract. The calculation of expectation damages is complicated if the plaintiff claims the cost of cure or the value of intangible losses. Expectation damages are subject to two important restrictions: remoteness and mitigation. Instead of expectation damages, the innocent party may be entitled to reliance damages, which allow it to recover the monetary value of expenses that it wasted in reliance upon the contract. Reliance damages are available only to the extent that the contract was not unprofitable. In exceptional circumstances, a court may impose an account of profits in order to compel the defendant to disgorge a benefit that it acquired in breach of contract. The courts will enforce a contractual term regarding liquidated damages, but they will not enforce a penalty. If the innocent party did not suffer any loss as a result of a breach, the court may award nominal damages. Punitive damages are occasionally awarded to punish the defendant.

Equitable remedies are sometimes available for a breach of contract. Specific performance occurs when the court orders the defendant to fulfill a contractual obligation to do something. An injunction occurs when the court orders the defendant to refrain from doing something that is prohibited by the contract. Specific performance and injunctions are subject to special limitations.

Even if a contract has been discharged for breach, an exclusion clause contained in that contract may continue to limit the defendant's liability.

In some situations, it may be possible to sue for unjust enrichment rather than breach of contract. The cause of action in unjust enrichment requires proof that (i) the defendant received an enrichment, (ii) the plaintiff suffered a corresponding deprivation, and (iii) there was an absence of any juristic reason for the defendant's enrichment. The remedy for unjust enrichment is always restitution.

REVIEW QUESTIONS

1. What are "damages"?

2. How are expectation damages calculated?

3. In what sense do expectation damages compensate the plaintiff? Why is it desirable to award damages based on expectations?

4. What is the difference between "loss of value" and "cost of cure" damages? Present arguments for and against cost of cure damages.

5. What problems are associated with the calculation of damages for intangible losses?

6. How does the concept of remoteness relate to the general theory of expectation damages?

7. Under what circumstances will damages be considered remote and therefore unavailable?

8. Briefly outline the rules regarding mitigation of loss.

9. Do the rules governing mitigation seem fair to you? Is there any justification for requiring the plaintiff to minimize the losses that are caused by the defendant's breach?

10. How do reliance damages differ from expectation damages?

11. Can a party escape the consequences of a bad bargain by claiming reliance damages rather than expectation damages?

12. What are nominal damages? How are they calculated? What purpose do they serve?

13. "The recovery of nominal damages does not always mean that the plaintiff comes out ahead." Discuss the accuracy of that statement.

14. What are liquidated damages? How do they differ from penalties? Are liquidated damages recoverable? Are penalties recoverable?

15. What are punitive damages? How are they calculated? Under what circumstances are they available? What purpose do they serve?

16. Explain the main reason why the courts prefer to award monetary damages rather than specific performance.

17. Under what circumstances will a court order specific performance?

18. Why are the courts more willing to grant injunctions than specific performance?

19. When will the courts allow a party to bring a claim in unjust enrichment?

20. Define the term "restitution." How does restitution differ from expectation damages and reliance damages?

CASES AND PROBLEMS

1. Redwood Inc, which owned a parcel of land that contained dense forests, entered into a contract with Bunyon Corp. Bunyon was required to cut and remove the trees from a 40-hectare area. In exchange, Redwood was required to pay $150 000 and provide trucks to Bunyon to transport the cut logs from the work site. After Bunyon had cleared about 20 hectares, Redwood breached a condition of the contract by failing to provide a sufficient number of trucks. Bunyon therefore discharged the contract for breach and claimed damages. At trial, the evidence indicated that Bunyon had entered into a bad bargain. It had cleared about half of the designated area and had received $75 000 in payment from Redwood. In doing so, however, Bunyon had actually incurred $300 000 in expenses. That amount represented the true market value of the services rendered and was not at all attributable to incompetence or mismanagement. If Bunyon claims expectations damages, what amount of money should it receive? If Bunyon claims reliance damages, what amount of money should it receive? Is there any other basis upon which Bunyon could claim relief? If so, what amount of money would it receive?

2. Pacific Guano Ltd wanted to mine phosphate on Ocean Island in the South Pacific. The small population of that island formed the Ocean Island Residents Co (OIRC) and entered into an agreement with Pacific Guano. Under the terms of that contract, Pacific Guano received the right to extract unlimited quantities of phosphate from the island for 20 years in exchange for its promises to pay $20 000 000 and to undertake an extensive reforestation project at the end of the 20-year term. Shortly after signing the contract, the members of the OIRC, which consisted of all the residents of Ocean Island, permanently resettled to another nearby island. Pacific Guano carried out its mining operations and paid $20 000 000. However, at the end of the lease, it refused to replant the property and left the island resembling a lunar landscape. The reforestation project that the contract required would have cost about $3 000 000, but it would have improved the value of the land by only $600 000. Is the OIRC entitled to recover $3 000 000 as cost of cure damages? Leaving aside the legal rules, do you think that the OIRC *should* be able to recover $3 000 000 as cost of cure damages? If, at the time of forming the contract, the OIRC had known that Pacific Guano would not reforest the land as promised, would the OIRC have entered into the same contract? Explain your answers.

3. Classique Cars Ltd rents out limousines for $200 per day, almost invariably to people arranging wedding parties. It is one of several companies to do so. On one occasion, Classique found that it was overbooked and did not have enough limousines to meet its rental obligations. It therefore called Adam, with whom it had entered into a rental contract a week earlier, and informed him that he would not be provided with a vehicle. Adam responded by informing Classique for the first time that he did not want a limousine for a wedding party. He needed the car to film a scene in a movie that he was directing. Adam also told Classique that if he did not receive a limousine, the filming schedule for his movie would be set back one day at a cost of $50 000. If Adam sues Classique, identify two reasons why he may not be entitled to recover $50 000 in expectation damages.

4. For the return flight home to Halifax from a prestigious European dog show, Connie wanted her prizewinning Scottish terrier, Thistle, to travel with her in the first-class section of the plane. As she explained to the airline representatives, in addition to Thistle's value as a show dog, he was the only family she had and he meant the world to her. Safeway Airlines, however, had a strict policy against carrying animals in the passenger section. Connie, who was terribly concerned about the welfare of Thistle, offered to purchase the entire first class section of the airplane so that the dog could travel with her. Much to her disappointment, the airline representatives refused her offer, but assured her that Thistle would arrive safely in Halifax. Sadly, upon arriving at the Halifax airport, it was discovered that Thistle had suffocated to death in the cargo compartment of the Safeway Airlines plane.

   Connie had purchased Thistle two years earlier for $750. She had originally purchased the dog as a companion, but soon discovered that Thistle's delightful disposition was perfect for showing. By all accounts, Thistle was expected to earn a considerable amount in prize money. Connie is deeply distressed about the loss of her beloved pet and feels that she should be compensated for the loss of Thistle's companionship. Is she entitled to recover damages? If so, how would you characterize and calculate those damages?

5. Paolo owns an apartment complex in a poor area of town. The building contains a large number of identical apartments. Because demand is low, there are always several empty apartments. Paolo leased an apartment to Dhalia for one year at a rent of $1000 per month. After two months, however, Dhalia broke the lease, moved out, and refused to pay the remaining rent. The next day, Paolo convinced Xavier to live in the apartment that Dhalia had occupied. In doing so, did Paolo mitigate the loss that resulted from Dhalia's breach? Would your answer be the same if Dhalia had introduced Xavier to Paolo? What if Dhalia had introduced Xavier to Paolo only because she was moving out? In answering those questions, place yourself in Paolo's position and ask whether Xavier's contract really made up for the loss that Dhalia caused when she broke her lease.

6. Cornwall Gravel wanted to submit a tender (offer) for a government contract. It contacted Purolator Courier to arrange delivery of the offer to the government office. Purolator collected the envelope at 6:00 pm on October 1. At that time, Cornwall Gravel told Purolator's employee that the envelope contained a "tender" and stressed that it had to be delivered by 3:00 pm on October 2. It then signed a bill of lading, which was presented by Purolator's employee, and which created a contract between Cornwall and Purolator. That contract contained a paragraph that said: "Purolator's liability for any loss or damage to the package shall be limited to $1.50 per kg based on the weight of the envelope." Due to the employee's carelessness, Cornwall's envelope was not delivered to the government office until 3:17 pm on October 2. As a result, the government refused to consider Cornwall's offer. The evidence indicates that if the envelope had been delivered on time, Cornwall would have received the government contract and would have earned a net profit of $700 000. Cornwall has therefore sued Purolator for breach of contract. In defence, Purolator says (i) that since the package weighed only 1 kilogram, damages must be limited to $1.50, and (ii) that even if the exclusion clause does not apply, it should not be held liable for $700 000 because it did not know all of the details concerning the contract that Cornwall hoped to receive from the government. What will the court decide?

7. In 1975, Wayne Gretzky was a 15-year-old phenomenon. Although he was from the town of Brantford, his desire to compete at a higher level of competition led him to sign with the Toronto Nationals, an elite club in Toronto. The Ontario Minor Hockey Association (OMHA), however, refused to grant him permission to do so. It insisted that it was unhealthy for children to move away from home simply to play hockey. Gretzky's lawyer therefore brought the matter to court. He relied on the fact that, as a minor hockey player, Gretzky had a contractual relationship with the OMHA. He then asked for an injunction that would force the OMHA to allow his client to play for the Nationals. Did the judge accept that argument? On what bases might the court have refused to grant an injunction? (Before answering that question, you may want to review the discussion in Chapter 10 dealing with a minor's capacity to contract.)

8. CanPro, a Canadian film company, hired Alan Smithee, a relatively unknown actor, to star in a biographical movie about Pierre Trudeau. Although the contract called for payment of only $15 000 in exchange for four months of work, Smithee accepted the role because he believed that the film would be widely publicized in Canada and consequently would give his career an invaluable boost. The evidence supports that belief. In similar circumstances, other actors have seen their annual income rise to an average $100 000 in the year following the release of a major motion picture. Given the other factors involved in the movie industry, however, it is almost impossible to predict the longer-term effects of starring in a major motion picture. Unfortunately, Smithee never actually tasted glory. Just days before filming was scheduled to begin, CanPro decided to replace Smithee with another actor. The movie has now been made and Smithee is unhappy. CanPro has not given any reason for its decision to replace him, but it insists that its breach of contract did not really cause him to suffer much of a loss. Although Smithee is trained as an actor, he has spent the last four years working as a waiter for $2000 per month. Out of "generosity," CanPro is willing to pay $2000 to Smithee on the assumption that he stopped working a month before filming was scheduled to begin in order to rehearse his part. Would a court agree with that conclusion? Explain your answer.

9. In September, Marcy's Department Store placed an order with Fuego Toys Inc for the upcoming holiday season. While it is difficult to predict which toys will be popular with children, both parties expected that the Squiggles line of giggling squirrels would be among the market leaders. Marcy's therefore agreed to buy 50 000 Squiggles at $20 each. From that stock, the department store expected to earn a gross profit of $1 000 000 by charging $40 per item. Marcy's was concerned, however, because it knew that Fuego's overseas manufacturing operations were experiencing labour difficulties. Marcy's therefore persuaded Fuego to insert the following clause into the contract.

> Fuego Toys Inc promises to deliver 50 000 Squiggles to Marcy's Department Store by 15 December. If Fuego is unable to meet that obligation, it will pay liquidated damages of $40 for each Squiggle that it is unable to deliver on schedule.

As the holiday season drew closer, the Squiggles fad grew much more dramatically than the parties had anticipated. By mid-December, their market value reached $100 per item. Unfortunately, Fuego's overseas labour problems also grew unexpectedly. As a result, it was unable to deliver any Squiggles to Marcy's. Furthermore, it was impossible for Marcy's to obtain an alternative source of Squiggles so close to the holidays. Assuming that Marcy's paid the purchase price at the time of signing the contract, how much can it recover in damages? Explain your answer.

10. Five years ago, Vladimir Ulyanov, a professional hockey player, signed a contract with the Rebels Hockey Club, which contained these terms:

   (a) Vladimir Ulyanov agrees to perform for the Rebels Hockey Club and not to perform for any other hockey club for the duration of this contract.

   (b) This contract shall run for 10 years from the date of signing.

(c) The Rebels Hockey Club agrees to pay Vladimir Ulyanov a base salary of $6 000 000 per year for the duration of this contract.

Last year, the Rebels hired a new coach, who changed the club's style of play by focusing far more on intimidation and far less on skill. Vladimir, a highly talented, but slightly built, player, wants no part of the new approach and has signed a contract to play with a rival team. The Rebels have brought an action against him for breach of contract. The team argues that monetary damages would not be an adequate remedy because (i) no amount of money would allow them to hire another player of Vladimir's calibre, (ii) it is impossible to accurately predict the loss of merchandising and ticket revenue that would be caused by Vladimir's defection to a rival team. In response, Vladimir says that his only employment prospects outside of professional hockey lie in the food service industry, and that if he is required to take a job in a restaurant, his annual income would drop from $6 000 000 to $25 000. Will a court order specific performance against Vladimir? Will a court order an injunction against Vladimir? What do you believe would be a fair result in this case?

11. Daphne purchased fire insurance for her home from Pontius Insurance Co. Several years later, her house was destroyed by fire, and she asked Pontius to pay $250 000, which was the value of her home. After a brief investigation, Pontius realized that the claim was legitimate and that Daphne was legally entitled to that money. However, it also realized that she was in a psychologically vulnerable state and that if she was threatened, she might withdraw her claim. Pontius therefore contacted Daphne and falsely told her that its investigators had found evidence that strongly suggested that she had committed arson to collect money under her insurance policy. Pontius's tactic backfired. Daphne did not retract her claim. Instead, she instructed her lawyer to sue Pontius for as much money as possible. Is there any chance that she is entitled to collect more than $250 000? Why or why not?

12. Tele-planet Inc entered into a contract with the government of Ruvutu, an island nation in the South Atlantic, to construct a telecommunications centre. The project was to be completed by Tele-planet in Canada and then shipped in segments to Ruvutu by June 1. As Tele-planet was told at the time of entering into the agreement, the government of Ruvutu intended to use the centre for, amongst other things, broadcasting commercial television signals to neighbouring countries. Tele-planet, however, breached its contractual obligations by failing to deliver on schedule. In fact, it did not ship the components until late November. After the government of Ruvutu received the components, it brought an action against Tele-planet for expectation damages of $1 000 000, the amount of money it initially expected to earn between June and November by using the telecommunications centre to broadcast commercial television signals. In response, Tele-planet insisted that Ruvutu suffered no loss as a result of the breach. That argument was based on the fact that, during June, Ruvutu was engaged in a brief, but destructive, war with a neighbouring island. During the skirmish, the enemy destroyed almost all of Ruvutu's existing telecommunication devices. Accordingly, Tele-planet claims that Ruvutu actually benefited from the late delivery because the telecommunications centre would have been destroyed during the war if it had been delivered on schedule. How would you expect a judge to resolve those arguments?

WEBLINKS

Duhaime Law: Time Limits, Breach and Remedies
www. duhaime.org/contract/ca-con8.aspx#time

This page contains a discussion of statutes of limitations, breach of contract, and contractual remedies.

Remedies for the Breach of Contract www.law.unb.ca/cpwala/First103.htm

This website considers various issues concerning remedies for breach of contract.

Damages in Lieu of Specific Performance www.law.unb.ca/Siebrasse/Download/Semelhago.PDF

This page consists of an academic paper written by Professor Norman Siebrasse regarding the availability of specific performance and damages for breach of contract.

Limiting Liability Under Contract www.torys.com/publications/pdf/ARTech-8T.pdf

This page consists of a paper that explores the use of limitation and exclusion clauses in business contracts.

Restitution and Unjust Enrichment www.ucc.ie/law restitution/restitution.htm

This website is devoted to the concepts of unjust enrichment and restitution, which are often applicable in contractual contexts.

ADDITIONAL RESOURCES FOR CHAPTER 12 ON THE COMPANION WEBSITE

(www.pearsoned.ca/mcinnes)

In addition to self-test multiple-choice, true-false, and short essay questions (all with immediate feedback), three additional Cases and Problems (with suggested answers), and links to useful Web destinations, the Companion Website provides the following resources for Chapter 12:

Provincial Material

- **British Columbia:** Specific Performance, Injunction
- **Ontario:** Debt Collection Process, Equitable Remedies, Execution, Garnishment, Judgment Debtor Examination

13 Special Contracts: Sale of Goods

OBJECTIVES

After completing this chapter, you should be able to:

1. Explain why a knowledge of the *Sale of Goods Act* is important for risk management.

2. Define the term "sale of goods" and explain when it applies.

3. Outline the rules that determine when property and risk pass under a sale of goods.

4. Summarize the rules that the Act implies with respect to the seller's title to sell.

5. Summarize the rules that apply when goods are sold on the basis of a sample.

6. Explain the extent to which the Act requires goods to match their description. Explain the difference between "merchantability" and "fitness for an intended purpose."

7. Describe the rules that the Act implies with respect to delivery and payment.

8. Outline the situations in which an action for the price is available and explain how that sort of action is different from a claim for damages under a breach of contract.

9. Explain the difference between a lien and a stoppage in transit, and describe the situations in which each can apply.

10. Explain when the seller can exercise a right of repossession.

We have completed our basic examination of contracts. Before leaving the topic, however, we will look at several types of contracts that are subject to special rules. We will discuss a number of these in other chapters, including leases, mortgages, insurance, agency, electronic commerce, and employment. In this chapter and the next, we will briefly consider two types of special contracts that are especially important in the business context: *sales of goods* and *negotiable instruments*.

THE *SALE OF GOODS ACT*

The Canadian economy was traditionally based on the sale of tangible (physical) goods, like beaver pelts, timber, oil, and grain. Recently, that situation has started to change. We are beginning to depend much more on intangible things, like information and services. The sale of goods nevertheless remains vitally important. First, as individual consumers, we will always need to buy things like food and clothing. Second, many businesses in this country continue to deal primarily in goods, either buying or selling things like bicycles, apples, and cows. Third, even those businesses that do focus on information occasionally find it necessary to participate in the sale of goods. For example, although accountants are paid to provide analysis and advice, they cannot do so without first buying calculators, computers, and pens.

Because sale of goods contracts are so significant, they are governed by a special statute, the *Sale of Goods Act*. Interestingly, that statute was initially introduced as a *codification*. Over several hundred years, judges had developed a large number of rules that applied when goods were sold. They did this to ensure the smooth flow of commerce. Business people do not want to spend time or money in court. They want clear and comprehensive laws that allow them to quickly deal with potential problems and get on with the job of making money. With that same goal in mind, the British Parliament transferred, or *codified*, the judge-made rules into the *Sale of Goods Act* in 1893. Since then, all of the common law jurisdictions in Canada have adopted virtually identical legislation.[1]

The history of the Act continues to be significant. Judges never intended to force contractual parties into certain types of agreements. They merely wanted to provide *default rules* that would apply if the parties did not deal with particular issues themselves. The general concept of freedom of contract meant the parties were usually free to make up different rules if they wished. That generally remains true today. While some exceptions do exist, the *Sale of Goods Act* is typically intended to fill in gaps. Goods can be bought and sold quickly because the parties do not have to negotiate and agree on a long list of terms. The Act does much of that work for them. At the same time, however, the Act also gives parties the freedom to create contracts with different terms, which better serve their purposes.

[1.] *Sale of Goods Act*, RSA 2000, c S-2 (Alta); *Sale of Goods Act*, RSBC 1996, c 410 (BC); *Sale of Goods Act*, CCSM, c S10 (Man); *Sale of Goods Act*, RSNB 1973, c S-1 (NB); *Sale of Goods Act*, RSNL 1990, c S-6 (Nfld); *Sale of Goods Act*, RSNWT 1988, c S-6 (NWT); *Sale of Goods Act*, RSNS 1989, c 408 (NS); *Sale of Goods Act*, RSO 1990, c S.1 (Ont); *Sale of Goods Act*, RSPEI 1988, c S-1 (PEI); *Sale of Goods Act*, RSS 1978, c S-1 (Sask); *Sale of Goods Act*, RSY 2002, c 198 (Yuk). Because the statutes are almost identical, references in this text will be made to the Ontario legislation. A table of concordance, which provides a comparative listing of section numbers for all of the statutes, can be found in GHL Fridman *Sale of Goods in Canada* 4th ed (1997) at 3–5.

It is important to understand how the *Sale of Goods Act* affects risk management. Because the Act provides default rules, a contract may include terms that the parties did not even discuss. Suppose you sell a conveyor belt to a mining company that is involved in a large and expensive project. If the belt is defective and causes the mining operation to shut down for several weeks, you may be held responsible for an enormous loss. Whether or not you were aware of the fact, your contract with the mining company may have included a condition that the conveyor belt was of *merchantable quality* or *fit for its intended purpose*. And if one of those conditions was breached, you might be liable for, say, $500 000 even though you only charged $500 for the belt. Knowledge of the *Sale of Goods Act* is therefore critically important. You cannot effectively manage a risk unless you are at least aware of it. If you are buying or selling goods, you should know the rights and obligations that the statute implies. And if you are unwilling to accept those rights and obligations, you should either walk away from the deal or persuade the other party to adopt different terms. If you do enter into a contract, you should use your knowledge of the Act to ensure that you are properly covered by insurance.

A SALE OF GOODS

a **sale of goods** is a contract whereby the seller transfers or agrees to transfer the property in goods to the buyer for a money consideration called the price

The *Sale of Goods Act* applies only to a *sale of goods*. It defines a **sale of goods** as "a contract whereby the seller transfers or agrees to transfer the property in goods to the buyer for a money consideration, called the price."[2] We stress four points.

- The Act applies only to a *sale*.
- The Act applies only to a sale of *goods*.
- The Act applies only to a sale of goods for *money*.
- The Act is sometimes enforceable only if the contract is *evidenced in writing*.

a **sale** occurs if the buyer obtains ownership in the goods as soon as the contract is created

an **agreement to sell** occurs if the buyer does not obtain ownership of the goods until some time after the contract is created

First, the Act usually applies only to a *sale*.[3] That term covers two situations: *sale* and *agreement to sell*. A **sale** occurs if the buyer obtains ownership in the goods as soon as the contract is created. An **agreement to sell** occurs if the buyer does not obtain ownership of the goods until some time after the contract is created. For example, the buyer may agree to purchase a car that has not yet been manufactured or a bicycle that has not yet been separated out from an inventory of several dozen bikes. However, a sale of goods does *not* occur if the buyer is not intended to eventually obtain ownership. Consequently, the Act does not apply, for instance, if goods are leased (because ownership is not transferred), if they are given as a gift (because there is no contract), or if they are provided as security for a loan (because ownership is not transferred for the purpose of a sale).[4] And, as usual, a court will be guided by the substance,

---

[2] *Sale of Goods Act* s 2(1) (Ont).

[3] The situation is different in British Columbia, where the *Sale of Goods Act* has been amended to include contracts in which goods are leased primarily for personal, family, or household purposes.

[4] The Act is not excluded merely because goods are sold on credit. For instance, when goods are sold under a *conditional sales contract*, the buyer obtains possession immediately, but the seller retains ownership until the full price is paid. The Act nevertheless applies because the ultimate purpose of that transaction is to transfer ownership in exchange for money.

rather than the form, of a transaction. Consequently, the parties cannot turn a lease into a sale simply by calling it "an agreement to sell."[5]

Second, the Act applies only to a sale of *goods*. Goods are tangible (physical) things that can be moved.[6] These include cars, books, pigs, and crops that will be harvested from the land. It does not include land or things that have already been attached to land, such as houses and fences, as those things are not moveable. Nor does the definition of "goods" include things that are not tangible. For that reason, the Act does not apply to the sale of trademarks, shares, debts, or negotiable instruments.[7] And finally, services are not caught by the legislation. A difficult question often arises, however, when goods are sold together with services. In such circumstances, a judge must determine whether the essence of the contract was the performance of a service on the one hand or the transfer of property on the other.[8] Although the courts are not always consistent in their approach, Case Brief 13.1 provides a common illustration.

 ## C A S E   B R I E F   1 3 . 1

Gee v White Spot Ltd (1987) 32 DLR (4th) 238 (BC SC)

Mr Gee developed botulism after eating a meal at the defendant's restaurant. Claiming that the food he had purchased fell within the definition of "goods," he sued for damages under the *Sale of Goods Act*. The restaurant responded by arguing that the contract was really based on services, that is, the preparation of the meal.

The judge stressed that a contract does not have to deal exclusively with goods to fall within the Act. He then found in favour of Mr Gee for two main reasons. First, he held that a customer's primary purpose in ordering a meal in a restaurant usually is not to receive the services of a cook and a waiter, but rather to receive the food itself. Second, the judge was influenced by the fact that consumers like Mr Gee are better protected from defective goods if they are allowed to sue under the *Sale of Goods Act*.

Third, the Act applies only if the buyer provides consideration in the form of money. It does not apply if the parties simply trade goods, say, a car for a boat. However, the buyer does not have to pay entirely with cash. "Money" includes both cash and other forms of payment, such as cheques and credit cards, that allow the seller to receive cash. Furthermore, the Act may apply even if the buyer pays with money and goods. For example, you may purchase a new bicycle by paying $200 and trading in your old bike. That transaction would be considered a sale of goods.

Finally, a sale of goods is sometimes enforceable only if it is *evidenced in writing*. That requirement is limited in several ways. First, it applies only in

---

[5.] *Helby v Matthews* [1895] AC 471 (HL).

[6.] *Sale of Goods Act* s 1(1) (Ont).

[7.] Those things are intangible even though they can be *represented* by something tangible, such as a share certificate.

[8.] As we will see, one of the Act's most important functions is that it implies a number of terms regarding quality. Even if a contract involves services rather than goods (so that the Act does not apply), the courts may imply similar terms. For example, in *Maple Leaf Construction (1978) Ltd v Maloney* (1987) 34 BLR 93 (Man QB), a contract to build a tennis court was not a sale of goods, but it did contain an implied condition as to quality.

some jurisdictions and only if the price is over a specific amount.[9] Second, a lack of writing does not mean that a contract is invalid, but rather that a court will not enforce it. And third, the rule does not apply if the buyer (i) accepts part of the goods, (ii) pays part of the price, or (iii) provides something "in earnest." The first two exceptions are straightforward. The third occurs when the buyer gives something valuable, other than part of the purchase price, to make the agreement binding. That is an ancient idea that is seldom used today.

PASSING OF PROPERTY

If a contract involves a sale of goods, the Act implies a number of terms. A particularly important one is concerned with the *passing of property*. **Property passes** when the ownership or title in goods is transferred from the seller to the buyer. At that point, the property stops belonging to the seller and starts belonging to the buyer. Significantly, however, there is often a difference between *property* and *possession*. The seller may still possess the goods, in the sense of having physical control over them, even though the buyer has become the owner. Likewise, the buyer may obtain possession of the goods even though the seller is still the owner. As we will see, that separation of ownership and possession can cause considerable problems.

The passing of property is important for several reasons. It may affect the remedies that are available if a contract is breached.[10] It may also be important if one party becomes bankrupt. Suppose you pay for goods that the seller promises to deliver in a week. If the seller declares bankruptcy before having a chance to deliver, you will want to prove that you already acquired ownership in the goods. Otherwise, they may form part of the seller's bankrupt estate, and you will have to share them with the other creditors.[11] The passing of property is most important, however, because the Act states that *risk* passes with property unless the parties otherwise agree.[12] **Risk** is any loss or damage that may occur to the goods. Consequently, the party who bears the risk suffers the loss if, for example, goods are destroyed in a fire or stolen by a thief. From a risk management perspective, the lesson is clear. If you are buying valuable goods, you should make sure that you have an insurance policy that protects your investment from the moment that the risk passes to you.

The Act provides rules for determining when property and risk pass under five situations.[13] We will quote each rule and follow it with a brief illustration.

property passes when the ownership or title in goods is transferred from the seller to the buyer

risk is any loss or damage that may occur to the goods

[9.] The dollar value varies: $50 (Alberta, Newfoundland and Labrador, Northwest Territories, Nunavut, and Saskatchewan), $40 (Nova Scotia), $30 (Prince Edward Island), and $1000 (Yukon). There is no writing requirement in Manitoba, New Brunswick, or Ontario. And in British Columbia, executory (unperformed) contracts for more than $20 are unenforceable unless they are evidenced in writing, according to the *Consumer Protection Act*, RSBC 1996, c 65, s 12.

[10.] In particular, the seller may bring an action for the price if property has passed.

[11.] As we will discuss under the heading of "Repossession," different rules may apply if a buyer becomes bankrupt after receiving title, but before paying the price. The seller may be protected from the buyer's bankruptcy.

[12.] *Sale of Goods Act* s 21 (Ont). Business people often use certain types of contracts that allocate property and risk in different ways. As discussed in the special Companion Website Chapter 28W, *Doing Business in a Global Economy*, that is true for bills of lading, as well as CIF and FOB contracts.

[13.] *Sale of Goods Act* s 19 (Ont).

RULE 1 Where there is an unconditional contract for the sale of specific goods in a deliverable state, the property in the goods passes to the buyer when the contract is made and it is immaterial whether the time of payment or the time of delivery or both is postponed.

BUSINESS DECISION 13.1

Passing of Property—RULE 1

After closing a major deal and earning your first $1 000 000 in business, you decide to reward yourself by buying something special. You therefore visit Clouseau's Jewellery store, pick out a diamond, and agree to buy it for $50 000. However, because you want to go straight to the gym afterwards, you persuade Clouseau to place the diamond in his safe. You promise that you will pick it up the next morning when you bring in the purchase price. Unfortunately, Clouseau's store is burglarized that night, and the thief makes off with the diamond.

Because there was an unconditional sale of a specific item that was already in a deliverable state, the property and the risk passed to you as soon as the contract was made. It is irrelevant that Clouseau still had possession of the diamond and that you had not yet paid the price. Consequently, the theft is your problem. You are still required to pay $50 000 to Clouseau, even though he no longer has the diamond. To protect yourself, you should have bought an insurance policy from an insurer at the same time that you bought that diamond from the jeweller.

RULE 2 Where there is a contract for the sale of specific goods and the seller is bound to do something to the goods for the purpose of putting them into a deliverable state, the property does not pass until such thing is done and the buyer has notice thereof.

BUSINESS DECISION 13.2

Passing of Property—RULE 2

Assume the same facts as before, except that you agree to pay $50 000 for a particular diamond on the condition that Clouseau recut it. He agrees, estimates that the job will take between one and two weeks, and says that he will call you when he is finished. Eight days later, Clouseau recuts the diamond, places it in his safe, and leaves a reminder for himself to call you the next day. However, before he can call you, his store is burglarized, and the thief makes off with the diamond.

There was a sale of goods that required Clouseau to do something to put the diamond into a "deliverable state," that is, to put it into a condition that would require you to accept it under the contract. Consequently, property did not pass to you. While Clouseau had recut the diamond, he had not yet notified you. The theft is therefore his problem. You do not have to pay the purchase price, and unless he had insurance, he will suffer the loss.[14]

RULE 3 Where there is a contract for the sale of specific goods in a deliverable state but the seller is bound to weigh, measure, test or do some other act or thing with reference to the goods for the purpose of ascertaining the price, the property does not pass until such act or thing is done and the buyer has notice thereof.

[14.] If you already paid the purchase price, you would be able to recover it from Clouseau either under the contract or under an action for unjust enrichment, as explained in Chapter 12.

BUSINESS DECISION 13.3

Passing of Property—RULE 3

Assume the same facts, except that you leave the diamond with Clouseau so that he can weigh it to determine its exact price. After doing so, he calls and tells you that the diamond is ready to be collected. Before you can get to his store, however, it is burglarized, and a thief makes off with the diamond.

There was a sale of goods that required Clouseau to do something to determine the price of the diamond.

Consequently, property did not pass to you immediately. It did, however, pass as soon as Clouseau weighed the diamond *and* notified you of that fact. The theft is therefore your problem. Unless you bought insurance for the diamond, you will have to pay $50 000 to Clouseau for nothing.

RULE 4 When goods are delivered to the buyer on approval or "on sale or return" or other similar terms, the property therein passes to the buyer,

(i) when the buyer signifies approval or acceptance to the seller or does any other act adopting the transaction;
(ii) if the buyer does not signify approval or acceptance to the seller but retains the goods without giving notice of rejection, then if a time has been fixed for the return of the goods, on the expiration of such time, and, if no time has been fixed, on the expiration of a reasonable time; what is a reasonable time is a question of fact.

BUSINESS DECISION 13.4

Passing of Property—RULE 4

Assume the same basic facts, except that Clouseau allows you to take the diamond away on a trial basis because you are not sure that you really want to buy it. He is hoping that you will be persuaded to finalize the sale once your friends see the item and express their envy. Ten days later, a thief breaks into your house and steals the diamond.

More information is required to determine who will bear the loss of the diamond. Property would have passed if you

had told Clouseau that you had chosen to keep the diamond or if you had done something that was inconsistent with his ownership of it (such as having it set into your own ring). Property also would have passed if you had agreed to return the diamond within three days, or if ten days was more than a reasonable length of time.

RULE 5
(i) Where there is a contract for the sale of unascertained or future goods by description and goods of that description and in a deliverable state are unconditionally appropriated to the contract, either by the seller with the assent of the buyer, or by the buyer with the assent of the seller, the property in the goods thereupon passes to the buyer, and such assent may be expressed or implied and may be given either before or after the appropriation is made.
(ii) Where in pursuance of the contract the seller delivers the goods to the buyer or to a carrier or other bailee (whether named by the buyer or not) for the purpose of transmission to the buyer and does not reserve the right of disposal, the seller shall be deemed to have unconditionally appropriated the goods to the contract.[15]

[15.] Bailees are discussed in Chapter 17.

BUSINESS DECISION 13.5

Passing of Property—RULE 5

Assume the same basic facts, except that Clouseau does not have an appropriate diamond in stock. You therefore pay $50 000, and he agrees to obtain a diamond from his dealer, which he will then deliver to you within a month. A week later, Clouseau receives an appropriate diamond from his supplier. He places it in his safe with the intention of delivering it to your office the next day. Unfortunately, his store is burglarized that night, and the thief makes off with the diamond.

Because there was a sale of unascertained goods, property would pass to you only after Clouseau obtained *and* unconditionally appropriated a particular diamond to your contract. The courts have interpreted that requirement narrowly. Unconditional appropriation occurs only if the seller has lost the ability to use the goods for any purpose other than fulfilling the buyer's contract. Very often, that happens only when the goods are actually delivered to the buyer. Consequently, although the courts are somewhat inconsistent, the stolen diamond was probably *not* unconditionally appropriated to your contract.[16] After all, Clouseau could have changed his mind overnight and ordered another diamond for you. If so, property did not pass and the theft is his problem, not yours.

Concept Summary 13.1 reviews the rules regarding the passing of property.

CONCEPT SUMMARY 13.1

Passing of Property—Default Rules

Type of Contract	Property Passes
RULE 1: an unconditional contract for the sale of specific goods that are already in a deliverable state	• at the time of the contract, even if delivery and payment occur later
RULE 2: a contract for specified goods that requires the seller to do something to put the goods into a deliverable state	• when the seller has done that thing *and* the buyer has been notified
RULE 3: a contract for specified goods that requires the seller to do something to the goods (such as weigh, measure, or test them) in order to determine the price	• when the seller has done that thing *and* the buyer has been notified
RULE 4: a delivery of goods "on sale or return"	• when the buyer has signified approval *or* adopted the transaction *or* retained the goods beyond a reasonable time
RULE 5: a contract for unascertained or future goods by description	• when goods of that description, that are in a deliverable state, are unconditionally appropriated to the contract by one party with the other party's assent

Before leaving the issue of property passing, note two more points.

- First, it bears repeating that the Act merely provides default rules. The parties are generally entitled to override the Act and adopt other rules for the passing of property and risk.[17] Suppose that you take possession of a specific diamond after promising to pay $50 000 to Clouseau. According to RULE 1, property has passed to you even though he has not yet received any money. However, if Clouseau is worried about your ability to pay, he might insert a *retention of title* clause into your contract

---

[16.] If Clouseau's actions *do* amount to unconditional appropriation, the court would probably find that you had given your "assent" (agreement) beforehand when you asked him to obtain an appropriate diamond.

[17.] *Sale of Goods Act* s 18 (Ont).

that specifically says that he will continue to own the diamond until you have paid the full price. Otherwise, if you became bankrupt, he might lose the jewel *and* he might not be paid in full.

- Second, even if property has passed to the buyer, the risk is still on the seller if that party creates a loss by improperly delaying delivery.[18] Suppose that Clouseau agrees to deliver a specific diamond to you on Monday. He carelessly forgets to do so and the diamond is stolen early Tuesday morning. Although property passed to you under RULE 1 when the contract was made, he bears the risk of the loss. The theft is his problem.

TERMS IN CONTRACTS OF SALE

The *Sale of Goods Act* implies a number of terms in addition to the rules that determine the passing of property. We will look at three types:

- terms regarding the seller's title to sell
- terms regarding the nature of the goods themselves
- terms regarding delivery and payment

Before we do so, we will repeat several points that we made in Chapter 11. There are generally two categories of contractual terms: *conditions* and *warranties*. Conditions are more important than warranties. If a condition is breached, the innocent party substantially loses the expected benefit of the contract. That party therefore usually has the option of either continuing on with the contract and suing for damages *or* discharging the contract and suing for damages. That choice has to be made promptly, and once it is made, it cannot be changed. In contrast, the benefit of a contract is not substantially lost if there is merely a breach of a warranty. Consequently, the innocent party never has the option of discharging the contract. The only remedy is to carry on with the agreement and sue for damages. The *Sale of Goods Act* adopts those rules. Some of the implied terms under the Act are classified as conditions, while others are classified as warranties.

Title to Sell

When you are buying goods, you want some assurance that the seller actually has *title to sell*. A person who does not actually own the goods cannot normally transfer ownership to you.[19] You may end up paying for nothing; or worse, you may commit a tort by attempting to buy property that belongs to someone else.[20] The Act therefore implies a condition that the seller either has the right to sell the goods or will have the right to do so when the time comes to pass property.[21]

[18.] *Sale of Goods Act* s 21 (Ont). Likewise, a party who possesses goods that are owned by someone else can be held responsible as a "bailee" for wrongfully causing those goods to be damaged or lost. We will examine bailees and bailors in Chapter 17.

[19.] Lawyers often use the Latin phrase *"nemo dat quod non habet,"* which means "no one can give what they do not have." There are some exceptions to that rule. For example, the *Sale of Goods Act* says that a buyer who possesses goods, but who has not yet obtained ownership from the seller, can sell the property to an innocent person who was unaware of the seller's rights. The same basic rule applies to a seller who has possession of goods but no longer owns them. Those rules are intended to protect innocent people who honestly believe that they dealing with property owners.

[20.] The tort of conversion was examined in Chapter 4.

[21.] *Sale of Goods Act* s 13 (Ont).

Similarly, you normally want some assurance that the seller is the *only* person who has an interest in the goods. Even if the seller is the owner, you do not want to buy property that is, for instance, the subject of a mortgage in favour of a third party. The Act therefore implies warranties that the buyer will receive clear title.

Nature of the Goods

The Act implies a number of conditions dealing with the goods themselves.

- Goods sold by description must match that description.
- Goods sold by sample must correspond with the sample.
- Goods must be of merchantable quality.
- Goods must be fit for their intended purpose.

Description

The Act implies a condition that goods sold by description will match that description.[22] Suppose you want to buy a stereo that can hold six CDs. You see such a product advertised on a website and place an order. When the equipment arrives, however, you discover that it can hold only three CDs. The seller has breached a condition, and you are entitled to reject the goods and discharge the contract.

Note that the term "description" refers to the *identity* of goods rather than to their *quality*. Consequently, there would not be a breach of contract (at least not under this heading) if the stereo you received could hold six CDs but was not as loud as you had hoped. You still received an item that matched its description: a six-CD stereo.

Note also that goods can be sold by "description" even if a sale occurs in person. Suppose you bought a stereo from a store rather than over the Internet. There were 20 identical boxes on a shelf and you picked one. You could still discharge the contract for breach of a condition if you got home and discovered that the stereo did not really hold six CDs as the box had promised. You relied on the description of the goods even though you also selected one particular box for yourself.

Sample

A special set of conditions applies if goods are sold by *sample*. A **sale by sample** occurs when the parties agree to deal in goods that correspond to a particular specimen. Suppose after seeing a circular saw being demonstrated in a hardware store, you read a brochure about that tool and tell the salesperson that you want to buy 10 units for your construction company. Four rules will apply to the sale.[23]

- First, if you bought by description as well as by sample, the store is required to deliver goods that correspond to both the description *and* the sample. Consequently, the saws must be the same kind that was demonstrated *and* they must have the features that were listed in the brochure.
- Second, the store must deliver saws that are of the same *quality* as the sample. Consequently, you would be able to discharge the contract if

a **sale by sample** occurs when the parties agree to deal in goods that match a particular specimen

---

[22.] *Sale of Goods Act* s 14 (Ont).
[23.] *Sale of Goods Act* ss 14, 16(2) (Ont).

they did not cut as quickly or as accurately as the saw that was used in the demonstration.

- Third, the store must give you a *reasonable opportunity to compare* the saws to the one that was used during the demonstration.

- Fourth, the saws would have to be free from any defect that would make them *unmerchantable* and could not have been discovered by a *reasonable examination*. Consequently, you will have a strong incentive to inspect the saws when they are delivered. If they later turn out to be defective, you will not be able to complain if you could have discovered those defects at the outset. However, you are only expected to conduct a *reasonable* inspection. You would not have to take the saws apart or perform complicated tests on them.

Merchantable Quality

the general rule in sales is *caveat emptor*: Let the buyer beware

The general rule in sales is ***caveat emptor***: "let the buyer beware." Therefore, unless the seller made specific promises, you cannot complain if you are disappointed by the goods that you bought. The law expects you to be responsible for yourself. If you want to be protected from defective goods, you should either inspect them before you enter into a contract or pay the seller to guarantee their quality. At the same time, however, the law recognizes that those options are unrealistic in many circumstances. Suppose you visit a major electronics store to buy a new computer for your office. You will probably not have much opportunity to actually inspect or test a specific unit before taking it away. Furthermore, the store will probably be reluctant to draft a new contract that reflects your particular needs or concerns. It will want to use the standard document that it uses for all of its sales. For those reasons, to protect buyers like you, the *Sale of Goods Act* creates certain exceptions to the general rule of *caveat emptor*.[24]

First, the Act implies a condition that goods are of a *merchantable quality* if they are purchased by description from someone who normally deals in those sorts of goods. That rule requires four comments.

goods are **merchantable** if a reasonable person would buy them without a reduction in price despite knowing their imperfections

- First, goods are **merchantable** if a reasonable person would buy them without a reduction in price despite knowing their imperfections. Goods do not have to be perfect to be merchantable. Returning to our example, a reasonable person might pay the full price for a computer even if a couple of pads on the keyboard are a bit sticky. However, no sensible person would pay full price for a computer with a cracked hard drive. Note that the implied condition can apply to both manufactured goods (such as computers) and natural products (such as milk). It can also apply to both new and used goods, although the expected quality of used goods is often lower. And finally, the implied condition can apply to both the quality of the goods themselves and such things as their labelling and packaging.[25]

- Second, the implied condition applies only if the *seller normally deals* in those sorts of goods. Consequently, a requirement of merchantability would arise if you bought a computer from an electronics store, but not if you bought it from me. I am not in the business of selling computers.

---

24. *Sale of Goods Act* s 15.

25. *Sale of Goods Act* s 1(1) (Ont).

- Third, the implied condition of merchantability does not cover *defects that the buyer should have noticed* if they examined the goods. Although the cases are somewhat inconsistent, it appears that the buyer is not actually required to conduct an examination. But if an inspection does occur, the seller is no longer responsible for problems that the buyer should have noticed. The seller does remain liable, however, for defects that could not have been discovered even with a reasonable examination. Consequently, if you spent 40 minutes thoroughly inspecting a computer without noticing any defects, you would still be able to discharge the contract if you later discovered that the machine overheats if it is left running for more than six hours.

- Fourth, it is unclear whether the implied condition of merchantability (or fitness for purpose) includes a requirement that the goods be durable for a reasonable length of time. The answer is clearly "yes" if the lack of durability is due to some defect that existed, but was hidden, at the time of delivery. But what if the goods were merchantable when they were delivered, but soon fell apart? Buyers in that situation seldom win in court. Consequently, some provinces have amended their legislation to include an implied condition of durability. In British Columbia, section 18(c) of the *Sale of Goods Act* says that "there is an implied condition that the goods will be durable for a reasonable period of time having regard to the use to which they would normally be put and to all the surrounding circumstances." Other provinces have adopted similar rules in their consumer protection legislation.[26]

Fit for Intended Purposes

The requirement of merchantability is concerned with quality: The goods must not be defective. In some situations, the Act also implies a condition that goods must be *fit for their intended purpose*. Although those two requirements often overlap, they are different. Even if goods are not defective, they may not be suitable for the buyer's needs. For example, a computer is not defective simply because it does not have a DVD player. However, it is not fit for your purpose if you require a DVD player for use in your marketing business.

Although the implied condition of fitness is potentially very useful, it applies only in certain circumstances.

- First, the *seller must normally deal* in the sorts of goods that the buyer purchased.

- Second, the *buyer must rely on the seller's skill or judgment* in selecting goods for a particular purpose and the *seller must be aware* of that fact. The buyer does not have to expressly mention a purpose that is obvious. It can be assumed that a personal computer will be used for word processing at least part of the time. However, the buyer does have to stipulate less obvious purposes. For instance, if you are relying on the seller to select a computer that is capable of operating a small Internet business, you must say so. Indeed, as a matter of risk management, you should specify your purpose whenever there is any doubt.

- Third, the implied condition does not apply if the buyer purchases goods on the basis of a *trade name*, rather than relying on the seller's judgment.

[26.] *Eg Consumer Protection Act*, SS 1996, c C-30.1, s 48(g) (Sask). Also, *Sale of Goods Act*, RSBC 1996, c 410, s 18(c), and *Consumer Protection Act*, RSNS 1989, c 92, s 26(3)(j).

The condition is intended to protect someone who relies on a vendor's skill and experience in selecting appropriate goods. Consequently, if you simply tell a store that you want a specific model of computer, you cannot later complain if that machine does not suit your needs. You made the choice for yourself. However, the implied condition is not barred every time you mention a trade name. The court has to decide whether you were relying on your own judgment or whether you were seeking the store's advice as to the suitability of a particular product.

Exclusion Clauses

The implied conditions and warranties that we have considered impose substantial burdens. For that reason, a person who sells goods will often try to avoid those obligations by writing an *exclusion clause* into the contract.[27] Such clauses may, however, allow the seller to unfairly escape responsibility for shoddy goods. The courts and legislatures have therefore developed several techniques for controlling exclusion clauses. First, judges read exclusion clauses very narrowly. For instance, a clause that excludes "all implied *warranties*" may not affect the Act's implied *conditions*. Second, an exclusion clause will not be enforced if it would be unfair or unconscionable.[28] Perhaps most significantly, however, the *Sale of Goods Act* may itself forbid an exclusion clause. As a general rule, the Act allows the parties to exclude or vary any of the implied terms.[29] Nevertheless, in some provinces, an agreement to vary or negate a condition or warranty under the *Sales of Goods Act* will be void and of no effect.[30]

Delivery and Payment

The Act also implies a number of terms dealing with *delivery* and *payment*.

- First, unless the parties otherwise agree, *delivery and payment should occur concurrently*.[31] The buyer should take possession of the goods at the same time that the seller receives the money. Very often, however, the parties agree that delivery and payment will be separated, such as when goods are bought with a cheque. The buyer may get the property immediately, even though the seller has to wait for payment from the bank.

- Second, although the Act is rather vague, the courts usually say that the *time of delivery is a condition*, whereas the *time of payment is a warranty*.[32] Consequently, the buyer may be able to discharge the contract if delivery is late, whereas the seller may have to settle for damages if payment does not occur promptly. The parties are entitled to stipulate when payment and delivery must occur. If they fail to do so, the contract must be performed within a "reasonable time." As always, the courts determine "reasonableness" in light of all of the circumstances.[33]

---

[27] We examined exclusion clauses in Chapters 9 and 12.

[28] See Chapter 9.

[29] *Sale of Goods Act* s 53 (Ont).

[30] See *eg Sale of Goods Act*, RSBC 1996, c 410, s 20 (BC); *Consumer Product Warranty and Liability Act*, RSNB 1973, SNB 1978, c 18.1, ss 24–25 (NB); *Consumer Protection Act*, RSO 1990, c.31, s 34 (Ont); *Consumer Products Warranties Act*, RSS 1978, c C-30, s 7 (Sask).

[31] *Sale of Goods Act* s 27 (Ont).

[32] *Sale of Goods Act* s 11 (Ont).

[33] *Sale of Goods Act* s 54 (Ont).

- Third, *delivery normally occurs at the seller's place of business*, unless the parties agree to some other arrangement.
- Fourth, there is an implied condition that the *seller will deliver goods that conform with the contract*. That requirement is quite broad. For example, you are entitled to reject a shipment of peas if you ordered carrots. Similarly, if you ordered 50 cartons of peas for $500, you do not have to accept more or less. If the seller delivers 48 cartons of peas, you have the option of either rejecting them all *or* paying at the reduced price of $480. And if the seller delivers 52 cartons, you have the option of rejecting them all *or* accepting 50 at the price of $500 *or* accepting them all and paying at the contract rate of $520.

Concept Summary 13.2 reviews the terms that are implied under the Act.

CONCEPT SUMMARY 13.2

Implied Terms—Default Rules

Title to sell	• condition that the seller has title to sell • warranty that the buyer will receive clear title
Nature of the goods	• condition that goods sold by description will match that description • condition that goods sold by sample will match the sample in quality *and* that the buyer will have reasonable opportunity to compare the goods to the sample *and* that the goods are free from unmerchantable defects • condition that goods are of a merchantable quality if they are purchased by description from someone who normally deals in such goods • condition that goods will be fit for their intended purpose if the buyer relies on the skill or judgment of a seller who normally deals in such goods *and* if the seller knows of that reliance
Delivery and payment	• delivery and payment shall be concurrent • condition that delivery will occur on time and warranty that payment will occur on time • delivery will occur at the seller's place of business • condition that seller will deliver goods that conform with the contract

REMEDIES

If there is a breach of a contract for the sale of goods, several remedies may be available. The *Sale of Goods Act* provides a number of special remedies for an unpaid seller.[34] However, it also allows the parties to use the general remedies that we saw in the last two chapters. We will consider four possibilities.

General Remedies

First, the innocent party generally has the right to discharge a contract if there has been a breach of a *condition*. Suppose that you agree to pay $50 000 to Nordic Furniture for the delivery of five oak desks to your office on June 1. You

[34.] This section discusses remedies that may be available for a breach of contract. Note that a contractual party may occasionally be entitled to rely on a different cause of action. For instance, it may be possible to rescind a contract that was induced by a misrepresentation (Chapter 9), sue for damages under the torts of deceit (Chapter 5) or negligence (Chapter 6), or claim restitution for unjust enrichment (Chapter 12).

will be able to discharge the contract if, for instance, Nordic delivers desks on June 10 (late delivery), or if it delivers the wrong number of desks (wrong quantity) or pine desks (failure to correspond to description) or desks that topple over (unmerchantable and unfit for intended purpose). If you do discharge the contract, you will not have to pay the price, and if you already paid the price, you will be able to recover it. In other circumstances, the seller would have the right to discharge the agreement. For instance, Nordic would be able to bring the contract to an end if, contrary to the usual rule, the time of payment was a condition, which you breached by failing to provide $50 000 on June 1 (late payment).

Second, the innocent party always has the right to claim compensatory damages. That is normally the only remedy that is available if there is a breach of a *warranty*. However, if there is a breach of a *condition*, the innocent party usually has the ability to discharge the contract in addition to claiming damages. In other words, that party can treat the term as either a condition (discharge plus damages) or a warranty (damages alone). Sometimes, however, that option is lost.[35] The Act states that a condition *must* be treated as a warranty if:

- the contract is not severable (in other words, if delivery is not made in instalments) and if the buyer has accepted at least some of the goods, or
- property in specific goods has already passed to the buyer.

In any event, the general purpose of compensatory damages is to put the innocent party in the same financial position that it would have enjoyed if the contract had been properly performed. Consider the case in You Be the Judge 13.1.

YOU BE THE JUDGE 13.1

Compensatory Damages and the *Sale of Goods Act*

The town of Noix holds an annual, one-day Nut Festival, which attracts a large number of tourists. Helene, who operates a restaurant in Noix, contacted Ranjit, who owns a dry goods supply company, and ordered 50 kilograms of walnuts. As she explained to him, she intended to devote her entire menu during the festival to dishes prepared with walnuts. She paid $2500, and Ranjit promised to deliver the goods on May 30. Ranjit delivered on time, but the nuts were almost all mouldy. As she was entitled to do, Helene rejected them on the ground that they were unfit for their intended purpose.

They would have made her customers sick. Unfortunately, given the circumstances, Helene was unable to arrange an alternative supply of nuts and therefore was forced to remain closed during the festival. She consequently lost $10 000 in net profits from that day.

Question for Discussion

1. How much will Helene receive in damages from Ranjit? Explain how you reached that decision.

Third, as we saw in Chapter 12, the courts will enforce a contractual term for *liquidated damages*.[36] The parties are allowed to agree in advance that a certain amount will be paid if their agreement is breached. In the context of sale of goods, the most important illustration of that rule concerns *deposits*. A **deposit** is a sum of money that the buyer pays when entering into a contract and that the seller is allowed to keep if the contract is not performed. Suppose that you promise to pay within one week for a television that is worth $1000.

a **deposit** is a sum of money that the buyer pays when entering into a contract and that the seller is allowed to keep if the contract is not performed

[35] *Sale of Goods Act* s 12 (Ont).

[36] However, the courts will not enforce a *penalty*, which is an amount of money that is completely out of proportion to the consequences of a breach.

The store clerk may demand a deposit of $100. If you return within a week and pay the remaining $900, you will be allowed to take the television home. But if you fail to pay the outstanding balance, the store will be entitled to keep the television *plus* the $100.

Fourth, in exceptional circumstances, a court may award *specific performance* of a contractual promise.[37] However, as we saw in Chapter 12, that remedy is available only if monetary damages would be inadequate. As a result, a buyer will not be entitled to specific performance unless the goods in question are special or unique, such as a family heirloom or a priceless painting.

Special Remedies for the Seller

An unpaid seller has a number of special remedies under the Act. We will consider four:

- an action for the price
- a lien
- stoppage in transit
- repossession

Action for the Price

The *Sale of Goods Act* states that the seller can sometimes bring an *action for the price*.[38] An **action for the price** occurs when the seller sues the buyer for the price of the goods. To help you understand how that type of action is different from a claim for damages under a breach of contract, consider Ethical Perspective 13.1.

an **action for the price** occurs when the seller sues the buyer for the price of the goods

---

ETHICAL PERSPECTIVE 13.1

Action for the Price and Expectation Damages

You own a used car dealership. One afternoon in late September, Conchita came onto your lot. She explained that she had moved to town to study for a business degree and that she needed a small vehicle for shopping. She looked at a number of cars before settling on a particular convertible. Because you were concerned about her financial circumstances, you persuaded her to sign a contract that required her to pay the full price of $8000 on October 1, even though she would not actually take possession of the car until October 4.

On September 29, however, Conchita informed you that she had dropped out of school because she needed to return home to care for a sick relative. She also asked if you would

consider letting her out of the contract. You told her that you would think about it overnight. Later that same day, Logan wandered onto the lot and offered to pay $7000 for the same convertible.

You have three main options. First, you could simply release Conchita from the contract. She would not pay anything, and you could sell the car to Logan. Second, you could rely on the Act and bring an action for the price against Conchita. She would have to pay $8000, and you would have to deliver the car to her. Third, you could discharge your contract with Conchita and sue her for damages. Under the normal rules, you would be entitled to recover only $1000 from her. As Chapter 12 explained, if you sue for damages, you are
(continued)

---

37. *Sale of Goods Act* s 50 (Ont).
38. *Sale of Goods Act* s 47 (Ont).

(continued)

expected to mitigate (or minimize) your loss. You could do so by selling the car to Logan. And in that situation, you would lose only $1000 as a result of Conchita's breach, since you would have sold the car for $7000 instead of $8000.

2. Is it fair that you have the ability to force Conchita to pay for a car that she no longer wants? Would your answer be different if you could not find anyone else to buy that particular vehicle?

Questions for Discussion

1. Which of those three options would you choose? Why?

Although the action for the price is an important remedy, it is available in only two situations: (i) if property has already passed to the buyer, or (ii) regardless of whether or not property has passed, if the contract requires payment to be made on a certain day and the buyer fails to do so.

Lien

a lien allows a person to retain possession of something until another person fulfills an obligation

The Act allows the seller to exercise a *lien* in some circumstances.[39] A **lien** allows a person to retain possession of something until another person fulfills an obligation. In the context of sale of goods, the seller may have the right to hold the goods until the buyer pays the price. That right can arise whether or not property has already passed.[40] It can also arise even if the time of payment is a warranty rather than a condition. In that case, while the seller cannot discharge the agreement if it does not receive the price on time, it may be able to hold onto the goods until the money is paid.

The right to exercise a lien is limited in several ways. First, a lien requires possession. Consequently, once the buyer legitimately takes control of the goods, the seller loses the right to apply a lien. Second, the seller normally cannot exercise a lien if the buyer enjoys credit under the contract. Suppose that you agree to deliver furniture to Leon on February 14, even though the contract does not require him to pay until October 31. You could not enforce a lien on Valentine's Day. You would have to deliver the goods and then wait until Halloween for the money.[41] The situation would be different, however, if Leon became *insolvent* before February 14. **Insolvency** occurs when a person is unable to meet their debts as they become due.[42] In that case, the Act allows a lien to be exercised, even if goods were sold on credit. However, sometimes it is dangerous for a seller to use a lien in such circumstances, as Business Decision 13.6 shows.

insolvency occurs when a person is unable to meet their debts as they become due

---

[39.] *Sale of Goods Act* s 39 (Ont).

[40.] Technically, the seller cannot exercise a lien unless property has passed. A person cannot have a lien over their *own* goods. However, a seller can exercise a similar right to *withhold delivery* if property has not passed and if payment has not been received: *Sale of Goods Act* s 38(2) (Ont).

[41.] A lien can be exercised, however, if the time for credit has *expired*. Consequently, if you agreed to deliver some of the furniture on Valentine's Day and the rest on New Year's Eve, you would not have to make the second delivery if Leon failed to pay the price on Halloween.

[42.] The issue of insolvency will be discussed in Chapter 24.

BUSINESS DECISION 13.6

Seller's Lien and Insolvency

You agree to sell 100 dictionaries to Erykah, who operates a small bookstore. Under the terms of that agreement, you are required to deliver the dictionaries on July 31, and she is required to pay $5000 before October 15. You know that she intends to eventually resell the books for $75 each.

On July 29, you hear a rumour that Erykah has experienced severe financial difficulties and has stopped paying her debts. For the next two days, you unsuccessfully try to contact her to determine if that rumour is true.

When July 31 arrives, you find yourself in a dilemma. You do not know whether you should deliver the books as promised.

Questions for Discussion

1. Explain the dilemma. What will happen if you deliver the books and later learn that Erykah is insolvent? What will happen if you refuse to deliver the books and later learn that the rumour was false, and that Erykah was not insolvent?

2. How will you resolve the dilemma? As you continue to read through the rest of this section on remedies, consider your other options.

Stoppage in Transit

The remedy of *stoppage in transit* is similar to a lien, but it is even more remarkable.[43] It can be exercised even if the seller no longer has property *or* possession. **Stoppage in transit** occurs when an unpaid seller instructs a carrier to not deliver goods to a buyer. Suppose you agree to sell a bull to Festus. Under the terms of that contract, you are required to send the animal to him by train, and he is required to pay $7500 when it arrives. During the course of the trip, however, you learn that Festus has become insolvent. In that situation, the Act allows you to contact the train company and prevent it from delivering the bull as initially directed. You can also demand that Festus pay within a reasonable time.[44] If he does so, he will be entitled to the bull. If not, you are free to sell the animal to another buyer and claim damages from Festus for any loss that his breach caused.[45]

stoppage in transit occurs when an unpaid seller instructs a carrier to not deliver goods to a buyer

Like a lien, stoppage in transit cannot be exercised if the buyer has already acquired possession of the goods.[46] Furthermore, it can only be exercised if the buyer has actually become insolvent. Consequently, the dilemma that we saw in Business Decision 13.6 can again arise.

Repossession

Section 81.1 of the *Bankruptcy and Insolvency Act* provides the most remarkable remedy of all. A seller is sometimes entitled to *repossess* goods from a buyer. That right may be available even though the buyer has already obtained

---

[43] *Sale of Goods Act* ss 42–44 (Ont). Stoppage in transit is no longer much used. Many people believe that it unfairly favours the seller over the buyer's other creditors. Furthermore, payment today is very often made by way of bankers' confirmed credits. Consequently, there is less danger that the seller will be unpaid.

[44] If the goods are "perishable," the seller can re-sell them immediately without first demanding payment from the buyer: *Sale of Goods Act* s 46(3).

[45] The same right of re-sale arises in connection with a lien and (presumably) with a repossession.

[46] The right of stoppage in transit is also lost if a "document of title" (such as a *bill of lading*, which we consider in the special Companion Website Chapter 28W, *Doing Business in a Global Economy*) is transferred to the buyer, who then uses that document to sell the goods to a third party who is unaware of any stoppage: *Sale of Goods Act* s 45 (Ont).

property *and* possession. The remedy of repossession is, however, limited to very narrow circumstances. It can be used only if:

- the goods are purchased for use in the buyer's business (and not for personal use)
- the seller delivers the goods to the buyer without receiving full payment
- the buyer becomes bankrupt or insolvent
- the seller provides written notice to the buyer's trustee in bankruptcy, within 30 days after delivery, that the goods are being repossessed
- the goods remain in the buyer's possession, have not been resold to an innocent third party, and are in the same condition as when they were delivered

The effect of repossession is significant. Rather than being forced to bring an action and stand in line with the buyer's other creditors, the seller is allowed to recover the goods and simply walk away from the purchaser's financial problems.[47]

Concept Summary 13.3 reviews the extraordinary remedies that may be available to an unpaid seller of goods.

CONCEPT SUMMARY 13.3

Special Remedies for Unpaid Sellers

Remedy	Nature
Action for price	The seller is entitled to sue for the price of the goods, even if that price exceeds the damages arising from the buyer's breach
Lien	The seller is entitled to retain possession of the goods until payment is made, even if property has passed to the buyer
Stoppage in transit	The seller is entitled to prevent a carrier from delivering the goods to the buyer, even if property has passed to the buyer
Repossession	The seller is entitled to recover possession of the goods from the buyer, even though property and possession have passed to the buyer

---

[47.] Special remedies apply in favour of farmers, fishermen, and aquaculturists: *Bankruptcy and Insolvency Act*, RSC 1985, c B-3, s 81.2 (Can).

CHAPTER SUMMARY

Sale of goods contracts are governed by a special statute called the *Sale of Goods Act*. That Act supplies default rules that apply unless the parties have agreed otherwise. A knowledge of the Act is therefore necessary for the purposes of risk management.

The Act applies only to a sale of goods. There must be a sale that transfers property from the seller to the buyer. The contract must substantially deal with goods rather than services. The buyer must provide money as consideration. In some jurisdictions, some sale of goods contracts must be evidenced in writing.

The Act provides a number of default rules regarding the passing of property. The passing of property is important for several reasons. First, it may affect the remedies that are available to the parties. Second, it may allow one party to avoid financial complications if the other party becomes insolvent. And third, the party who has the property usually also bears the risk.

The Act implies several default terms. Some terms are conditions, and others are warranties. There is an implied condition that the seller has title to sell and an implied warranty that the buyer will receive clear title. There is an implied condition that goods sold by description must match their description. A number of conditions may apply if goods are sold by sample: (i) the goods must correspond to the sample, (ii) the buyer must be given a reasonable opportunity to inspect the bulk and compare it to the sample, and (iii) the goods must be merchantable. If goods are sold by description, there may be an implied condition that the goods are merchantable or fit for their intended purpose. Implied conditions or warranties can sometimes be avoided through exclusion clauses.

The Act implies a number of terms regarding delivery and payment. As a general rule, delivery and payment should occur at the same time. Time of delivery is normally a condition, but time of payment is normally a warranty. Delivery should usually occur at the seller's place of business. The seller must deliver goods that conform with the contract.

In addition to allowing general contractual remedies, the Act provides a number of special remedies for unpaid sellers. If property has passed, or if the buyer has not paid on a fixed date as required by the contract, the seller can bring an action for the price. A seller is generally entitled to enforce a lien to retain possession of goods until full payment is made. If the buyer is insolvent, the seller can exercise a right of stoppage in transit to recover goods that are in the possession of a third-party carrier. Even if the buyer has received possession and property, the seller can sometimes exercise a right of repossession if the buyer is insolvent or bankrupt.

REVIEW QUESTIONS

1. Briefly explain why knowledge of the *Sale of Goods Act* is important for managing risk.

2. Define a "sale" according to the Act. Does a lease qualify as a sale? Does a gift? Explain your answers.

3. Define "goods" according to the Act. Can a transaction ever fall under the Act if one party provides services? Explain your answer.

4. Can a sale of goods occur if I trade my bicycle to you for a stereo? Explain your answer.

5. When, if ever, does a sale of goods have to be evidenced in writing in your jurisdiction?

6. Briefly explain three reasons why the passing of property is important.

7. "As a general rule, the risk in specific goods that are already in a deliverable state does not pass to the buyer until the seller has received the price." Is that statement correct? Explain your answer.

8. "As a general rule, if the seller has agreed to do something (such as repair or weigh) specific goods, property does not pass to the buyer until delivery actually occurs." Is that statement correct? Explain your answer.

9. Describe a contract that is "on sale or return." When does property normally pass under that sort of contract?

10. Explain the significance of the concept of "unconditional appropriation" under a contract for unascertained goods. When does unconditional appropriation occur?

11. Outline the terms that the Act implies with respect to the seller's title to sell. Are those terms conditions or warranties? What is the practical difference between a condition and a warranty?

12. The Act implies a term that goods must correspond to their "description." Does that requirement apply to both the identity and the quality of goods? Can goods be bought by description if the buyer selects a particular item off a store shelf?

13. Define the term "sale by sample." Why should the buyer always inspect goods that are sold by sample?

14. What is meant by the phrase *caveat emptor*? Why is it important to a sale of goods contract? Does the Act entirely eliminate the need to be concerned with that phrase?

15. When are goods considered "merchantable"? Can imperfect goods be merchantable? Outline the situations in which the Act implies a term of merchantability.

16. When are goods considered "fit for their intended purpose"? Explain three limitations on the rule that goods must be fit for their intended purpose.

17. "According to the Act, delivery and payment must always occur at the same time. Furthermore, a contract can always be discharged if either delivery or payment is late." Are those statements true? Explain your answers.

18. The Act allows a court to impose a remedy that occurs under the general law of contract. Outline four possibilities.

19. When will the seller be able to bring an action for the price? How does that type of action differ from an action for damages under a breach of contract?

20. Summarize the differences between a lien, a stoppage in transit, and a repossession. Why might it be true to say that repossession is the most remarkable of those remedies?

CASES AND PROBLEMS

1. Celebrity Sports Inc (CSI) holds an annual celebrity softball game, which involves hockey players, politicians, and movie stars. Because of the nature of the event, a large part of CSI's profits come from merchandising. In particular, it has traditionally made a great deal of money from souvenir programs, which feature biographies and photographs of the people who play in the game. After its old publisher went out of business, CSI entered into an agreement with Page One Ltd (POL) to produce the programs. The relevant portion of that contract states:

> POL shall provide whatever services are necessary to produce 20 000 programs, each consisting of 44 pages. Those programs shall contain biographies and colour photographs of every player. CSI agrees to pay $15 000 for POL's services.

Although POL produced the appropriate number of programs, the pages appeared in reverse order due to a printing error. As a result, the programs were unmerchantable and unfit for their intended purpose. CIS therefore wants to bring an action under the *Sale of Goods Act*. POL, however, argues that the Act does not apply because the contract was for services. Did the parties have a contract for the sale of goods? Explain your answer.

2. Because she and her partner were unable to conceive a child naturally, Miranda Lopez visited Dr Omar Korn, a fertility expert. He suggested artificial insemination using semen collected from a donor. She agreed, and three weeks later, after Dr Korn had obtained semen from an anonymous donor, Mrs Lopez underwent an artificial insemination procedure. In exchange, she paid $1500. The procedure was unfortunately a failure. First, Mrs Lopez did not become pregnant. She does not, however, wish to sue Dr Korn on that basis. As he had explained to her at the outset, there was a chance that the semen would fail to fertilize an egg. Second, Mrs Lopez contracted HIV. The evidence indicates the man who donated the semen carried the virus, which was passed on to Mrs Lopez as a result of the procedure. Mrs Lopez wants to sue Dr Korn under the *Sale of Goods Act* because the semen that he provided was unmerchantable and unfit for its intended purpose. Did the parties enter into a contract for the sale of goods? Explain your answer.

3. Over the course of many years, Reliable Accounting Inc and Porteau Furnishings Ltd had entered into a number of contracts. Reliable had purchased desks and chairs from Porteau, and Porteau had purchased financial advice from Reliable. Recently, Reliable required new office furniture for two temporary members of staff. Unfortunately, as a result of certain financial difficulties, it did not have a great deal of money in its general account. It persuaded Porteau to grant a lease of two new desks in exchange for free accounting services during the next tax season. The desks were delivered, but they were useless. Due to poor workmanship, they collapsed whenever a computer was placed on them. Reliable wants to sue Porteau for supplying unmerchantable goods under the *Sale of Goods Act*. Did the parties enter into a sale of goods? Give two reasons for your answer.

4. Western Environmental Inc decided to close down an oil refinery, which was its only substantial asset. It therefore began to sell off the various pieces of equipment that were located within the refinery. On June 1, it sold a specific piece of pipe to Brendel Industries Co for $250 000. Under the terms of that contract, Brendel immediately paid the purchase price and promised to collect the pipe from Western's refinery within one month. Before Brendel did so, however, Western contacted another oil company, Fink Pipe Inc (Fink) with an offer to sell. Within two days, Fink had paid the purchase price and transported the pipe to its own facilities. A short time later, Brendel began to hear rumours of the deal between Western and Fink. Further investigation revealed a "worst case" scenario. Not only had Western resold the same pipe to Fink, it had also ceased operations. Western's president had fled the country with all of the company's liquid assets, leaving behind only an empty refinery and a mountain of debts. Brendel realizes that there is no point in suing Western. It has therefore sued Fink for the tort of conversion. Brendel insists that the pipe belongs to it. Furthermore, while admitting that Fink had acted honestly when it dealt with Western, Brendel also insists that its own property rights in the pipe have been violated by Fink's actions in taking possession of the pipe. Does Brendel have a good claim in tort law? How does that claim relate to the *Sale of Goods Act*?

5. Three days before Vera was scheduled to start university, she visited Paragraphs Bookshop in search of a good dictionary. Although the salesperson showed her a number of options, Vera was most intrigued by the enormous, 20-volume *Canadian Comprehensive Dictionary*. She hesitated in buying it only because it was priced at $525. The manager of Paragraphs Bookshop therefore agreed to let her take the set home for one week "on sale or return." Four days later, Vera decided to buy the volumes. She therefore stamped her name, in very small letters, on the back cover of the first volume. She intended to return to Paragraphs Bookshop the next day to pay for the set. Before she did so, however, her father unexpectedly presented her with another copy of the *Canadian Comprehensive Dictionary* as a gift. Vera was delighted at the prospect of saving $525 and therefore took the first copy of the set back to the book store. The manager, however, refused to accept it and insisted that Vera was required to pay the purchase price. Was the manager entitled to do this? Explain your answer.

6. Auric Bond was seeking a safe investment for $100 000 that he had inherited from his parents. He contacted Goldcomp Inc, a company that dealt in precious metals. Goldcomp presented a standard form contract to Auric. The relevant portion of that document said:

> Gold is one of the safest investments available, and Goldcomp makes every effort to ensure that your investment is protected as it grows. Goldcomp holds a large amount of gold bullion in its guarded vault. Once you have paid the purchase price, an appropriate percentage of that gold will be allocated to you, and you will receive a certificate verifying your ownership of that gold. You can, at any time, take physical delivery of your purchase by providing Goldcomp with seven days' notice.

Auric agreed to those terms, paid $100 000 to Goldcomp, and received a certificate stating that he was the owner of a certain amount of gold.

Goldcomp recently became bankrupt. Its debts exceed its assets by a 10:1 ratio. Furthermore, it was recently discovered that Goldcomp never actually separated its gold into separate bundles for Auric or its other customers. All of its gold sat in an undifferentiated mass in its vault. Auric has given seven days' notice under the agreement, but because of its bankruptcy, Goldcomp has not delivered any gold to him. In the circumstances, Auric can sue Goldcomp for breach of contract. However, if he does so, he will simply obtain a personal judgment and will have to share Goldcomp's meagre assets with the other creditors. He would be lucky to get $10 000 under that approach. Auric therefore wants to argue that he can take possession of $100 000 worth of gold on the basis that he already has property or ownership in it. Will that argument be successful? Explain your answer.

7. Denise Wharton visited Harris Motors, a car dealership, with a view to buying a new car. While she indicated that she was particularly interested in Cadillacs, she also sought the sales representative's advice. She explained that she was nearing retirement age and that she was looking for a car that was suitable for long, relaxing drives. She stressed that she wanted a vehicle with a good stereo and a quiet ride. The sales representative showed her several models, but focused on the Cadillac Eldorado Touring Coupe, a luxury vehicle. The sale was finalized when Denise paid $62 000 and drove the Eldorado off the lot. Unfortunately, the sound system soon developed a loud buzzing sound. That sound was almost constant, and it was loud enough to disrupt normal conversation. Not surprisingly, the noise caused Denise a great deal of frustration and disappointment. Her dream car had become something of a nightmare. Over the next two years, she returned the car a several times to Harris Motors with the aim of having the problem solved. (Since she was from out of town, those visits to the dealership involved expenses amounting to $2500.) The dealer's mechanics were, however, unable to identify the source of the noise. Denise eventually gave up hope and sold the car to a stranger for $31 000. She now intends to sue Harris Motors under the *Sale of Goods Act*. What provisions should she rely upon and what arguments should she make? If her claim is successful, how will the judge determine the remedy? What losses did Denise suffer? (You may want to re-read parts of Chapter 12, which deal with remedies for breach of contract.)

8. Kerasic Lumber Inc agreed to sell planks to Chios Home Supply Ltd. The parties' contract contained the following paragraph:

> Kerasic Lumber will deliver 1000 redwood planks to Chios Home Supply on June 1. Chios Home Supply will pay $7 per plank for a total contract price of $7000. Each plank shall be:
>
> (i) 3 centimetres thick,
> (ii) between 30 and 35 centimetres wide, and
> (iii) between 3 metres and 3.1 metres in length.

On June 1, Kerasic Lumber delivered 1020 planks to Chios Home Supply. Each plank fell within the terms of the contract with respect to width and length, but about half of the planks were between 3.2 and 3.3 centimetres thick. Chios Home Supply rejected the goods and refused to pay the purchase price. Its motivation for doing so turned on the fact that it had discovered that it could buy the goods from another supplier at a lower price. Kerasic has sued under the contract. As part of its claim, it is able to prove that the planks were free from defects and were entirely fit for Chios's purposes. Will Kerasic win? Provide two reasons for your answer.

9. Woltz Homes Ltd was building a new house. As the project neared completion, the company's manager,

Jack, realized that he needed glue to install the carpet. Jack therefore visited Khartoum Flooring and spoke to a salesperson named Tom. When Jack explained what he needed, Tom confessed that he was new to the job and admitted that he could not provide much help. In response, Jack said that he knew what he was looking for and simply asked Tom to take him to the right section of the store. Tom did so, and Jack picked up a large bucket of glue. Tom offered to open the bucket, but Jack said, "No need. This is the stuff that I'm after." Before Jack paid, Tom asked him to sign a contract, which was standard practice for all sales at Khartoum Flooring. That document contained a paragraph that said, "This sale shall not be affected by any warranties that may be implied by statute or law." When Jack got back to the work site and opened the bucket, he discovered that the glue was crystallized and therefore useless. He returned the bucket to Khartoum Flooring, but the store refused to provide a refund or a substitute. The store's owner insists that (i) Jack has to take responsibility for the fact that he declined the opportunity to inspect the glue before buying it, and (ii) the exclusion clause contained in the sale contract negates any terms that might be implied by the *Sale of Goods Act*. Is he correct? Explain your answer.

10. The University of Southern Alberta wanted to upgrade its football stadium. Rather than grass, it wanted a field made from a long-lasting, synthetic material that would not easily wear down and that would not discolour under the warm Alberta sun. It also wanted the turf to be purple, rather than green, in order to reflect the school's colours. It explained its needs to Cyber-Turf Inc, an artificial turf company that is located in Calgary. The sales representative from Cyber-Turf assured the university that it would be able to develop such a product. The parties then entered into a contract. The University agreed to pay $100 000 and Cyber-Turf agreed to manufacture the turf within six months. Approximately six months later, the company informed the university that the new turf was finished and that it was being stored on the company's back lot. The university promised to collect the purple carpet within one month and provide payment at that time. The company agreed to that arrangement. Two weeks later, however, the Calgary area was hit by a severe rain storm, followed by six days of intense sunlight and heat. The combined effect of the rain and the sun was to badly discolour portions of the new turf, from bright purple to light blue. Consequently, when the university came to collect the turf a week later, it refused to take delivery. Cyber-Turf, in contrast, insists that it is entitled to the purchase price and that the new turf, whatever its condition, is solely the university's concern. Discuss the parties' rights and liabilities.

11. After upgrading his film studio, Werner agreed to sell his old equipment to Isabelle, a young director who wanted to film a movie beginning on May 1. The equipment consisted of a number of cameras and related items that were valued at $250 000. The parties signed a contract on March 1 that contained this paragraph:

> The seller agrees to deliver the equipment to the buyer's residence on or before April 30. The buyer agrees to pay the purchase price of $250 000 on April 15. The seller will remain the owner of the equipment until full payment has been received or the equipment is delivered to the buyer, whichever is earlier.

On April 15, Isabelle explained to Werner that she would not be able to pay the price for at least two months. However, she also insisted that she required the equipment by April 30 to begin filming her own movie on May 1. Werner indicated that he was reluctant to hand the equipment over until he received full payment. On April 30, Isabelle repeated her demand. Having done some legal research, she also told Werner that time of delivery was a condition of a contract, and that he could be held liable for any losses that she suffered as a result of late delivery. She also told him that the equipment was already hers because the property in it passed as soon as they signed their agreement. Is she correct? Does the equipment already belong to her? Is Werner required to deliver the equipment before receiving the purchase price? If Werner wants to sue for the purchase price, is he entitled to do so? Explain your answers.

12. Solstar Inc manufactures cellular telephones. In July, it agreed to sell 10 000 units to Buy-Lo, a discount department store. The contract required delivery to occur on September 1 at Buy-Lo's store. It also required payment to be made in full on September 15. In late August, shortly before Solstar intended to ship the goods, its manager, Emily, heard a rumour that Buy-Lo had become insolvent and was no longer able to pay its debts. She therefore told the foreman in Solstar's warehouse to not ship the goods as planned. Due to a clerical error, however, the goods were sent to an independent trucking company for delivery to Buy-Lo. When Emily learned of that, she instructed her assistant, Jeremy, to contact the trucking company and demand that the shipment be returned to Solstar. Was she entitled to do so? What should Solstar do if Emily's request does not reach the trucking company until after the goods are delivered to Buy-Lo? What additional facts do you need to know to answer those questions? Explain your answers.

ADDITIONAL RESOURCES FOR CHAPTER 13 ON THE COMPANION WEBSITE

(www.pearsoned.ca/mcinnes)

In addition to self-test multiple-choice, true-false, and short essay questions (all with immediate feedback), three additional Cases and Problems (with suggested answers), and links to useful Web destinations, the Companion Website provides the following resources for Chapter 13:

■ Weblinks to the *Sale of Goods Act* in each province and territory

Provincial Material

■ **British Columbia:** *Sale of Goods Act*, Consumer Protection Legislation, Tender of Payment, Tender of Performance, Passing of Property, Stoppage in Transit, Lien, Terms Implied by Statute

■ **Alberta:** Sale of Goods

■ **Ontario:** *Consumer Protection Act 2002*, *Sale of Goods Act*

14 Special Contracts: Negotiable Instruments

CHAPTER OVERVIEW

OBJECTIVES

After completing this chapter, you should be able to:

1. Explain why it is often more dangerous to pay with cash than with a negotiable instrument.

2. Summarize five requirements that a document must satisfy before it will fall within the *Bills of Exchange Act.*

3. Explain how a cheque works by describing the events that occur between (i) the drawer and the payee, (ii) the drawer and the drawee, and (iii) the drawee and the payee.

4. Distinguish between overdrawn cheques and countermanded cheques.

5. Describe the process of certification, and explain how it affects the rights of the parties to a cheque.

6. Distinguish between a bill of exchange and a cheque.

7. Explain how a promissory note operates.

8. Describe the requirements for the negotiation of (i) a bearer instrument, and (ii) an order instrument.

9. Summarize seven forms of endorsement and explain how each form affects the issue of liability.

10. Distinguish between (i) immediate parties, (ii) holders, and (iii) holders in due course; and between (i) personal defences, (ii) defect in title defences, and (iii) real defences.

In Chapter 13, we saw that contracts dealing with the sale of goods are governed by special rules that are intended to make the business world operate efficiently. The same is true for contracts that take the form of *negotiable instruments*. Even if you are not familiar with that term, you certainly are familiar with the underlying concept. In fact, when you pay for something with a cheque, you are dealing with a negotiable instrument.

There are many different ways of making payments. Sometimes it is easiest to use cash.[1] The simplest way of buying a cup of coffee is to hand over, say, $1.25 in coins. Cash, however, can be inconvenient and dangerous. It is inconvenient because it is bulky. The price of a cup of coffee easily fits into your pocket, but the price of a car does not. More significantly, cash is dangerous because it is usually impossible to recover if it is lost or stolen. The essential feature of cash is that it is *currency*. A $20 bill is valuable in itself—it does not simply represent a right to acquire something else that is valuable. Furthermore, a person can become the owner of cash by honestly paying for it. Suppose that I steal $10 000 from your wallet. My dishonesty prevents me from becoming the owner of that money. However, if I use that cash to buy a stereo from a storekeeper who was unaware of the theft, you no longer own the money; the storekeeper does.[2] Consequently, you cannot retrieve it from her. You can sue me, but like many thieves, I may have disappeared or I may be so poor that I am not worth suing. As a matter of risk management, the lesson of that story is clear. Never carry more cash than you are prepared to do without.

There are other ways of making payments that are more convenient and less dangerous than cash. For instance, credit cards and debits cards can be used. In this chapter, we will discuss negotiable instruments. **A negotiable instrument** consists of a contract that contains an obligation to pay money. Suppose that you buy a car from a dealership. A contract is created—you are required to pay the price, and the dealer is required to transfer the car to you. But *how* will you pay the price? It would be foolish for you to carry $20 000 in cash from your bank to the car lot.[3] At the same time, however, the dealer wants something more than your simple promise under the sale agreement. You therefore write out a cheque for $20 000. That cheque is a *new* contract. You have promised that $20 000 will be paid to whoever presents that piece of paper to your bank. Consequently, if your bank refuses to honour the cheque, the

a negotiable instrument consists of a contract that contains an obligation to pay money

---

[1] In fact, as we saw in Chapter 11, unless the parties have otherwise agreed, a creditor is entitled to receive payment in *legal tender*, that is, cash.

[2] The law allows the storekeeper to become the owner of the $10 000 because it wants cash to flow freely. If the storekeeper were required to determine if I actually owned the $10 000 that I gave her, the business world would grind to halt. Every cash purchase would involve a long, expensive, and perhaps impossible process of proving ownership of the coins and bills that the buyer offered. Different rules apply to things other than money. As we saw in Chapter 13, the general rule is *nemo dat quod non habet*, "no one can give what they do not have." Consequently, if I stole your car and traded it to my neighbour for her boat, you would probably be entitled to recover the value of the car from her, even if she had acted honestly.

[3] It might be equally foolish for the dealership to accept cash. If that money were lost or stolen before it could be deposited in a bank, the dealership would suffer the loss. The dealership would be in a safer position if you paid by cheque. If that cheque were lost or stolen, the dealer could ask you to provide another one: *Bills of Exchange Act*, RSC 1985, c B-4, s 155 (Can). In exchange, it would have to indemnify you for any loss that might occur because of the existence of two cheques.

dealer can sue you either on the sale contract *or* on the cheque itself.[4] The second option is usually preferable. It is easier to prove the existence of a negotiable instrument than the existence of a sales contract.

Understandably, most people do not realize that a cheque is a type of contract.[5] Many of the rules that normally govern contracts do not apply in the same way to negotiable instruments. We note three important differences.

- **Consideration:** Like all contracts, a cheque is enforceable only if it is supported by *consideration*. Something of value must be given in exchange for it. However, the requirement of consideration is more easily satisfied in the case of a cheque. As Chapter 8 explained, consideration normally cannot consist of a promise to perform an obligation that is already owed to the same party. However, that rule does not apply to a cheque.[6] In our previous example, the dealership's promise to transfer a car to you acted as consideration twice: first for the sale contract and then for your cheque.

- **Privity:** Normally, a contract can be enforced only by someone with *privity*. Chapter 8 explained that a stranger, someone who did not participate in the creation of the agreement, cannot sue on it. Nevertheless, anyone who holds a cheque can sue on it. Suppose that the dealership in our earlier example coincidentally owed $20 000 to the *Daily Bugle* for a newspaper advertisement. Instead of cashing your cheque and using that money to pay its bill, the dealer might simply sell your cheque to the newspaper. The *Daily Bugle* could then sue you on the cheque, even though it was not originally a party to that contract.

- **Assignment:** Contractual obligations can generally be *assigned* to a stranger. As we saw in Chapter 8, however, assignment is a cumbersome process.[7] Furthermore, a person who receives a contractual right through an assignment takes it *subject to the equities*. The assignee cannot be in a better position than the assignor. Assume that the dealership assigned its rights under the *sales contract* to the *Daily Bugle*. If the newspaper sued you for the price, you could use any defence that you could have used against the dealership. Suppose that the dealer breached the contract by selling you a car that required $5000 in repairs. If the purchase price was $20 000, you would only have to pay $15 000 to the newspaper. The situation might be different, however, if the dealership sold your *cheque* to the *Daily Bugle*. The most remarkable thing about a negotiable instrument is that, depending on the circumstances, it can improve as it is passed from one person to the next. Consequently, the newspaper might be able to recover $20 000 from you even though your car was defective. You would have to sue the dealership for breach of contract if you wanted to be paid $5000 for the repairs.

[4.] Your obligation to pay $20 000 under the sales contract was *conditionally discharged* when you gave the cheque to the dealership. When your bank refused to honour that cheque, however, your obligation under the sales contract was revived.

[5.] Although this section refers to cheques, the same observations generally apply to other types of negotiable instruments as well.

[6.] *Bills of Exchange Act* s 52. The Act also presumes that consideration was given by every person whose signature appears on a negotiable instrument: s 57(1).

[7.] For instance, an assignee normally is required (as a matter of risk management, if not as a matter of law) to give notice of an assignment to a debtor. That requirement does not apply to a negotiable instrument.

A negotiable instrument therefore represents a compromise between a simple contract and money. A negotiable instrument is more valuable than a simple contract because, like money, it is *negotiable*. It can be easily transferred from one party to another in a way that may remove any defects. The *Daily Bugle* acquired clear title to the cheque that you had given to the car dealership, just as the storekeeper became the owner of the cash that I had stolen from you in our earlier example. At the same time, however, a negotiable instrument is not actually money. It is a contract that is intended to eventually result in the payment of money. Consequently, it carries the major risk that is associated with every contract: non-performance. While it is often much better to sue on a negotiable instrument than on a simple contract, enforcement is ultimately necessary in either event. And if a cheque is created by a person who simply does not have any assets, it may be a worthless piece of paper.[8] Coins and bills, in contrast, are never worthless. They have value in themselves.

THE *BILLS OF EXCHANGE ACT*

The subjects of this chapter and the previous one have many similarities. Negotiable instruments and sales of goods both involve contracts that are critically important in the business world. Furthermore, because of the need for commercial certainty, both have been *codified*. As you will recall, when the British Parliament introduced the *Sale of Goods Act* in 1893, it adopted the rules that judges had developed over many years. The legislature's aim was to ensure that the economy ran smoothly. The same process occurred for negotiable instruments. In 1882, the British Parliament enacted the *Bills of Exchange Act*, which formally adopted rules that judges had developed over several centuries. The legislature's intention was to increase economic efficiency by providing business people with a comprehensive set of rules regarding non-monetary payments. The Canadian Parliament once again followed the British model and introduced its own *Bills of Exchange Act* in 1890.[9] With a few exceptions, that statute has hardly changed in more than a century.

Although both statutes were motivated by similar concerns, they are quite different in some ways. The most important difference is that the *Bills of Exchange Act* is much less flexible than the *Sale of Goods Act*. The *Sale of Goods Act* is a relatively simple statute that provides default rules. The parties are generally free to pick and choose among those rules and, even if they accept some and reject others, their contract can still fall within the Act. The *Bills of Exchange Act* is a much longer and more complicated statute. Furthermore, as we will see in the next section, it contains a large number of rules that a contract *must* satisfy. If those requirements are not met, the Act does not apply. That difference arises because a sale of goods normally involves only two parties, whereas negotiable instruments are designed to be freely transferred among many people. Consequently, there is an even greater need for certainty with negotiable instruments. If I did not participate in the creation of a cheque, for instance, I may not be willing to buy it unless I can be assured, by simply looking at that piece of paper, that it is valuable.

[8.] Interestingly, as we shall see, a cheque may be valuable even if the person who wrote it is penniless. It may be possible to collect money from anyone who *endorsed* the cheque.

[9.] *Bills of Exchange Act*, 45 & 46 Vict, c 61. Sales of goods are a provincial matter, but negotiable instruments are a federal matter. Consequently, while each province and territory has its own *Sale of Goods Act*, there is only one *Bills of Exchange Act*, which applies across the country.

TYPES OF NEGOTIABLE INSTRUMENTS

There are many varieties of negotiable instruments. Share certificates, for instance, are sometimes placed into that category. The *Bills of Exchange Act*, however, applies only to three types of negotiable instruments: *cheques*, *bills of exchange*, and *promissory notes*. We will look at each of those separately. But first, we can summarize the five requirements that must always be met before the Act will apply.[10] Note how each requirement serves the goal of certainty that we just discussed. A negotiable instrument must tell a complete story. A business person cannot be expected to look behind it.

- **Signed and written:** First, although most contracts can be created orally, a negotiable instrument must be *signed* and *written*. The reason is obvious. A promise cannot be clearly passed from one person to the next unless it is in writing.

- **Parties identified:** Second, the *parties* must be clearly identified. It must be possible to immediately determine who is required to make the payment. That information is important when the time comes to "cash" the instrument. However, it is also useful in deciding whether to buy a document in the first place. A cheque that is created by a con artist who holds an account at a bank that is in the process of collapsing is probably not worth the paper it is written on.

- **Certain sum of money:** Third, the contract must involve an obligation to pay a *certain sum of money*. The obligation must deal entirely with the payment of money, not with such things as the delivery of goods or the performance of services. It also must be possible to calculate the amount of money by simply looking at the document itself. Consequently, while a negotiable instrument may involve the payment of interest, it cannot, for instance, require the payment of "a reasonable price" or "any money that may be won in a lottery."

- **Time of payment:** Fourth, the *time of payment* must be clearly stated. A person buying a negotiable instrument must be able to determine precisely when that piece of paper can be turned into cash.

- **Unconditional obligation:** Fifth, the contract must contain an *unconditional obligation*. For instance, if a person paid the price of a car with a cheque, that document could not require payment to be made "if the buyer is satisfied with the vehicle." As always, it must be possible for a person who buys a negotiable instrument to immediately know exactly what they are receiving.

Concept Summary 14.1 summarizes those requirements, and looking ahead, compares the essential concepts of a cheque, a bill of exchange, and a promissory note.

---

[10]. A document that does not meet those requirements may still be a valid contract, but it does not fall under the *Bills of Exchange Act*.

CONCEPT SUMMARY 14.1

Nature and Requirements of Negotiable Instruments

Type of Instrument	Nature	Basic Requirements
Cheque	an order by one party (drawer) that directs a bank (drawee) to provide money to someone (payee)	• signed and written • identify parties • certain sum of money • time of payment • unconditional obligation
Bill of exchange	an order by one party (drawer) that directs another party—who may or may not be a bank (drawee)—to provide money to someone (payee)	
Promissory note	a promise by one party (maker) to pay money to someone (payee)	

Cheques

The most common form of negotiable instrument is a *cheque*. A **cheque** is created when a person orders a bank to pay a specific amount of money to someone.[11] Suppose that Hank Quinlan, an accountant, bought an oak desk from Anna Schmidt for $5000. Hank did not have any money in his pocket but he did have a chequing account at the Bank of Edmonton. He gave Anna the cheque in Figure 14.1, which shows that (i) Hank is the *drawer*, (ii) the Bank of Edmonton is the *drawee*, and (iii) Anna is the *payee*. The **drawer** is the person who "draws," or creates, the cheque. The **drawee** is the bank that is ordered to pay the money. And the **payee** is the person who is entitled to receive the money from the bank.

To appreciate the effect of that cheque, you must understand the relationships that exist between the parties.

a cheque is created when a person orders a bank to pay a specific amount of money to someone

the drawer is the person who "draws," or creates, the cheque

the drawee is the bank that is ordered to pay the money

the payee is the person who is entitled to receive the money from the bank

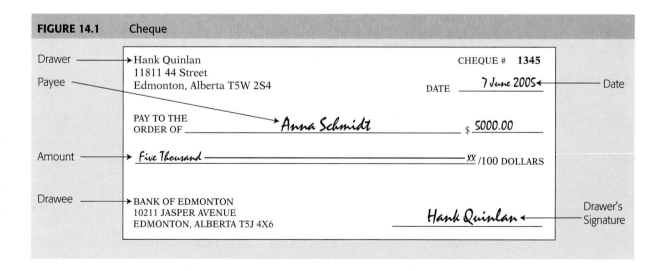

FIGURE 14.1   Cheque

Drawer — Hank Quinlan
11811 44 Street
Payee — Edmonton, Alberta T5W 2S4

CHEQUE #   **1345**

DATE   *7 June 2005* — Date

PAY TO THE
ORDER OF   *Anna Schmidt* $ *5000.00*

Amount — *Five Thousand* ———— *xx*/100 DOLLARS

Drawee — BANK OF EDMONTON
10211 JASPER AVENUE
EDMONTON, ALBERTA T5J 4X6

Hank Quinlan — Drawer's
Signature

[11.] The term "bank" includes some credit unions and trust companies: *Bills of Exchange Act* s 164.
If an instrument is not drawn on a bank, it cannot be a cheque, but it may be a bill of exchange.

- **Hank and Anna:** There are two contracts between Hank and Anna. The first is the sale of goods agreement; the second is the cheque itself. By writing that cheque, Hank tried to fulfill his obligation under the sales contract by ordering the Bank of Edmonton to pay $5000 to Anna.

- **Hank and the Bank of Edmonton:** Hank has a contractual relationship with the Bank of Edmonton. When he opened his chequing account at the bank, he exchanged a large number of promises. For example, he agreed to allow the bank to *debit* his account—withdraw money from it—whenever he wrote a cheque.[12] In exchange, the bank promised to *honour*, or pay, cheques that Hank wrote, as long as they appeared in the correct form and he had enough money in his account. Hank ordered the bank to fulfill that promise when he wrote the cheque to Anna. Assuming that everything went well, the bank honoured that cheque, paid $5000 to Anna, and deducted that same amount from Hank's account. If the bank improperly refused to pay $5000 to Anna when she presented the cheque to it, it could be held liable to Hank for breach of contract.[13]

- **Anna and the Bank of Edmonton:** Anna does *not* have a relationship with the Bank of Edmonton. She is a stranger to the agreement that exists between Hank and the bank. Consequently, she could not sue the bank if it refused to pay $5000 to her. If she wanted that money, she would have to sue Hank, either on the cheque or on the sales contract.

Most cheques operate smoothly. However, there are five possible complications:

- postdated cheques
- staledated cheques
- overdrawn cheques
- countermanded cheques
- certification

Before we look at those complications, however, it is important to remember that while the bank has a contractual relationship with the drawer, it does not normally owe any obligations to the payee. As a result, the bank may instruct its tellers to use rules that are slightly different than the ones that we are about to examine. If necessary, the bank will ensure that its contract with the drawer allows for those variations.

Postdated Cheques

Sometimes, a drawer is willing to deliver a cheque immediately, but does not want it to be cashed until later. Assume that while Hank and Anna entered into their sales contract on June 1, 2005, he *postdated* the cheque to June 7, 2005.[14] A **postdated cheque** is dated in the future. Perhaps Hank was expecting to

a postdated cheque is dated in the future

---

[12] That statement is not entirely accurate. When money is deposited into an account, the bank almost always becomes the owner of the bills and coins that it received. In exchange, it gives its contractual promise to repay a similar amount when the depositor asks for it. Consequently, in our example, the Bank of Edmonton would not actually withdraw any *money* from Hank's account after cashing his cheque. Rather, it would simply reduce the amount that it owed to him.

[13] For the sake of simplicity, we assume that Anna personally took Hank's cheque to the Bank of Edmonton for payment. She could have *endorsed* that cheque to her own bank and allowed it to collect the money on her behalf. We will discuss *endorsements* later.

[14] *Bills of Exchange Act* s 26(d).

receive payment from a client on June 3 that would ensure that his chequing account held at least $5000.[15] Anna could not receive payment from the bank until June 7. According to the contract that exists between Hank and the Bank of Edmonton, the bank is allowed to debit his account only if it acts in accordance with his instructions. And in this case, his instructions did not allow Anna to be paid before June 7.

Staledated Cheques

A postdated cheque causes problems if the payee seeks payment too soon. A *staledated* cheque, in contrast, causes problems if the payee seeks payment too late. A cheque is **staledated** when the payee does not seek payment within a reasonable time. Suppose that Anna did not present the cheque to the Bank of Edmonton until June 7, 2006, a whole year later. The bank would probably refuse payment. Banks normally will not honour a cheque that is presented more than six months after the date that appears on it. In that case, Anna would be forced to sue Hank for the $5000, either on the cheque or on the sales contract.[16]

a cheque is staledated when the payee does not seek payment within a reasonable time

Overdrawn Cheques

A cheque is **overdrawn** when the drawer's account does not hold enough money to satisfy it completely. Some people use the term "NSF," or "not sufficient funds." That would occur in our example if Hank's chequing account did not contain at least $5000 when Anna presented his cheque for payment. At that point, the Bank of Edmonton would have an option. It would almost certainly refuse to honour the cheque, in which case Anna would sue Hank for non-payment.[17] However, the bank could treat Hank's overdrawn cheque as his request for a loan, pay $5000 to Anna, and then seek repayment from Hank. Interestingly, that would be true even if the bank failed to realize that Hank's account was overdrawn and paid Anna by mistake.

a cheque is overdrawn when the drawer's account does not hold enough money to satisfy it completely

Countermanded Cheques

As a general rule, a bank can deal with a customer's money only if it has that person's authorization. That rule is important whenever there is a *countermand*. A **countermand** occurs when a customer orders a bank to refuse payment on a cheque.[18] This is also known as a *stop payment order*. Returning to our example, assume that Hank noticed that the desk was badly damaged after he took it home. If Anna had not yet cashed his cheque, he might contact the Bank of Edmonton and tell it to stop payment. After all, if he intends to return the desk to Anna, he does not want her to have his money. By countermanding the cheque, Hank would remove the bank's authority to deal with his account. And since the bank would not be willing to give its own money to Anna, it would not pay her $5000 when she presented the cheque.

a countermand occurs when a customer orders a bank to refuse payment on a cheque

---

15. Postdated cheques are often used if a contract requires instalment payments. For example, if you lease a car for six months, you may be asked for a series of postdated cheques: one for January 1, one for February 1, and so on.

16. Although a bank may not honour a cheque that is presented more than six *months* after its date, the payee usually has two or six *years* to sue the drawer. Statutes of limitation say that contracts, including cheques, become unenforceable only after that time: Chapter 11.

17. If Hank knew, when he wrote the cheque, that his account did not contain sufficient funds, he could be charged with the crime of false pretences: *Criminal Code*, RSC 1985, c C-46, s 362(4) (Can).

18. *Bills of Exchange Act* s 167.

The ability to countermand a cheque can be very useful. In practice, however, it is limited by two factors.

- First, a bank will not normally accept a countermand unless the drawer gives that order in person and unless the cheque in question is fully described (including the date, the payee, and the amount). Banks require that level of detail because they do not want to stop payment on a cheque incorrectly.

- Second, many bank contracts include a term that allows a bank to debit a customer's account if a countermanded cheque is honoured by mistake. Otherwise, the bank may have to sue the payee if it wants to recover a payment that it made by mistake.[19]

Also note that a cheque is automatically countermanded if the bank is notified that the drawer has died before the payee receives payment.[20]

Certified Cheques

certification occurs when a drawee bank promises to honour a cheque

Although a cheque is a special kind of contract, it is still a *promise* to pay. And as always, a promise may or may not be kept. Consequently, there is no guarantee that a cheque will actually be cashed. The cheque may be countermanded by the drawer or dishonoured by the drawee. The best way to avoid those problems is through *certification*.[21] **Certification** occurs when a drawee bank promises to honour a cheque.[22] It normally does so by stamping the word "certified" and the date on the front of the cheque. It then deducts the appropriate amount from the drawer's account, places those funds in a "suspense account," and uses them to honour the cheque when it is presented for payment.

A cheque can be certified by the payee (or holder). Assume that after receiving the cheque from Hank, Anna presented it to the Bank of Edmonton for certification. Perhaps she was travelling to Calgary and felt safer carrying a certified cheque rather than $5000 cash. More commonly, however, a cheque is certified by the drawer. For example, if she was concerned about Hank's ability to pay, Anna might have required him to certify his cheque before giving it to her as payment for the desk.

Whether a cheque is certified by the payee or by the drawer, the consequences are basically the same. Although the law is not entirely clear, the courts generally treat certification as "something equivalent to money."[23] We can see the effects of that rule by continuing on with our example.

- A bank normally owes an obligation only to its own customer. However, once the Bank of Edmonton certified Hank's cheque, it also owed an obligation to Anna. In effect, it promised her that it would honour the cheque. If it later broke that promise, it could be sued by Anna.

- By certifying the cheque, the Bank of Edmonton assured Anna that it would not later dishonour that instrument on the ground that Hank's account was *overdrawn*. A bank normally will not certify a cheque until

---

[19.] In that case, the bank would sue for restitution under the action in unjust enrichment: *Barclays Bank v WJ Simms, Son & Cooke (Southern) Ltd* [1980] QB 677. We discussed that cause of action in Chapter 12. The bank could not sue in contract because it does not have a contract with the payee.

[20.] *Bills of Exchange Act* s 167(b).

[21.] The *Bills of Exchange Act* does not refer to certification. That procedure is based on American banking law rather than the English statute copied by the Canadian Parliament.

[22.] Banks charge a fee for certification.

[23.] *Centrac Inc v CIBC* (1994) 120 DLR (4th) 765 at 768 (Ont CA).

after it has transferred funds from the drawer's account into a suspense account. But Anna could demand payment even if the bank certified the cheque in the mistaken belief that Hank's account held enough funds. A bank cannot hide behind its own error; it must fulfill its promise.

- Certification also assured Anna that Hank's cheque could not be *countermanded*. A drawer is normally entitled to issue a stop payment order any time before a cheque is cashed. However, since certification is treated as "something equivalent" to payment, Hank lost the right to countermand the cheque once the Bank of Edmonton certified it.[24] The bank would have to pay Anna even if Hank objected.[25]

Bills of Exchange

A **bill of exchange** is created when one person orders another person to pay a specific amount of money to a third person. Suppose that Marisa Figo, who operates a manufacturing plant in Winnipeg, bought a shipment of steel from Olaf Bregstein, an industrialist in Sweden. Although that contract was made on March 1, 2005, the parties agreed that the purchase price of $100 000 was not due until September 1, 2005. Marisa arranged for payment to be made through the Red River Trust Company, with which she held a line of credit.[26] She issued the bill of exchange shown in Figure 14.2.

a **bill of exchange** is created when one person orders another person to pay a specific amount of money to a third person

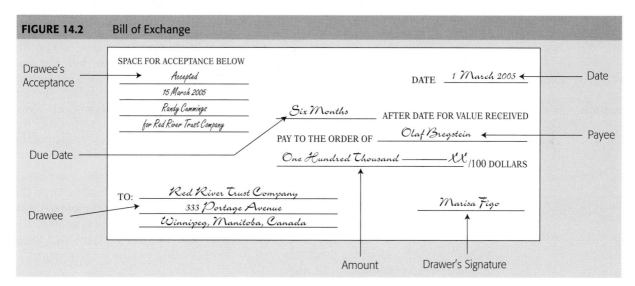

FIGURE 14.2 Bill of Exchange

That bill of exchange looks very similar to a cheque. In fact, a cheque is simply a special type of bill of exchange. The major difference between them is

---

[24.] *Maubach v Bank of Nova Scotia* (1987) 62 OR (2d) 220 (CA). Exceptionally, a bank may allow a certified cheque to be countermanded if the drawer is willing to provide *indemnification* by promising to provide compensation to the bank if it is sued by the payee.

[25.] An exception may occur when a cheque is certified by the drawer. If the drawer returns the cheque to the bank, the bank will cancel it and return the funds from the suspense account to the chequing account. However, once the drawer actually delivers the cheque to the payee, countermand is no longer possible.

[26.] A line of credit is an amount of money that an institution is willing to lend to a person from time to time.

that a cheque *must* be drawn on a bank, while a bill of exchange *may* be drawn on a bank *or* on anyone else. We can quickly describe the parties in this case. Marisa was the *drawer* because she ordered money to be paid from one person to another. The Red River Trust Company was the *drawee* because it was ordered by one person to pay money to another. And Olaf was the *payee* because he was intended to receive the money eventually.

We can understand how a bill of exchange works by examining Figure 14.2.

- Marisa used a basic pre-formatted bill of exchange and filled in the relevant blanks. In effect, she ordered the Red River Trust Company to pay $100 000 to Olaf. Marisa then gave the bill to Olaf. Olaf was not entitled to receive payment immediately, since the parties' contract said that payment for the steel was not due until September 1. Marisa therefore made sure that Olaf could not receive the money from the Red River Trust Company any earlier. Although she created the bill on March 1, she expressly stated that payment was due "*Six Months* AFTER DATE."

- Olaf could have simply kept the bill until September 1. However, he wanted some assurance that he would actually receive $100 000 on that date. He therefore presented the bill to the Red River Trust Company on March 15.

- The Red River Trust Company had two options when it received the bill from Olaf. It could have indicated that it was not prepared to pay $100 000 on September 1. It would have done so, for instance, if Marisa's line of credit was limited to $50 000. In that case, the trust company would have *dishonoured* the bill, and Olaf would have been entitled to sue Marisa for immediate payment.[27] In this case, however, it appears that Marisa's line of credit was large enough to satisfy the bill. The Red River Trust Company therefore indicated that it was willing to *honour* the bill when it came due. Randy Cummings, an authorized signing agent for the trust company, *accepted* the bill.[28] **Acceptance** occurs when the drawee promises to pay a bill. Randy did so by writing "*Accepted*," the date of acceptance, and his signature on the bill, and then returning the document to Olaf.[29] At that point, the trust company became the *acceptor* rather than simply the drawee.

- Acceptance of a bill is very similar to certification of a cheque. Once the drawee has accepted a bill, it can be sued by the payee for failing to make payment on the due date. Furthermore, once a bill is accepted, the drawer loses control of it. Consequently, after March 15, the Red River Trust Company was required to pay $100 000 to Olaf on September 1, *and* Marisa lost the ability to cancel the bill.

- Assuming that everything went as planned, Olaf presented the bill to the Red River Trust Company on September 1 and received $100 000. The trust company then required Marisa to repay that amount (undoubtedly with interest).

acceptance occurs when the drawee promises to pay a bill

---

[27] *Bills of Exchange Act* s 81. Note that Olaf could sue Marisa immediately, even though the bill was not due until September 1.

[28] Marisa also could have asked the Red River Trust Company to accept the bill before she delivered it to Olaf.

[29] *Bills of Exchange Act* s 38. Note two things about Randy's acceptance. First, he signed "*for the Red River Trust Company*." If he had not used those words, he might have been personally liable as the acceptor. Second, strictly speaking, acceptance only requires the acceptor's signature: s 35(2). However, additional information is usually added to avoid difficulties.

Note four more things about bills of exchange.

- A bill of exchange, like a cheque, is a contract. Therefore, it is not enforceable unless it is supported by consideration. In this case, Olaf gave consideration for Marisa's bill when he promised to deliver steel to her. That fact is indicated by the phrase "FOR VALUE RECEIVED" that appears on the bill.

- A cheque *must* be payable "on demand."[30] In other words, the drawer must order the drawee to make payment as soon as the payee presents the cheque.[31] A bill of exchange *may* be payable on demand, in which case it is called a *demand draft*. However, it can also be a *sight draft*. This is like a demand draft, except that the payee is not entitled to receive any money until three days after the bill has been presented to the drawee. And finally, as in our example, a bill of exchange can be a *time draft*, which is payable only on a future date. Although Marisa's bill was dated March 1, Olaf could not obtain payment until "*Six Months* AFTER DATE." The date of payment therefore would be September 1.

- A bill of exchange is usually used for one of two purposes. Both are seen in our example. First, a bill of exchange can be used, like a cheque, to safely transfer funds. Second, because a bill does not have to be payable on demand, it can be used to easily extend credit. In this case, Olaf gave Marisa credit for half of a year. He was not entitled to receive $100 000 until September 1, even though her debt under the sales contract arose on March 1.

- Bills of exchange were traditionally much more common than cheques. Today, however, the situation is reversed. Bills are usually used only in special circumstances, such as international trade between large business enterprises. In our example, Olaf agreed to deliver $100 000 worth of steel from Sweden to Winnipeg.

Promissory Notes

A cheque or a bill of exchange normally involves an *order* between *three* parties: The drawer instructs the drawee to transfer money to the payee. A *promissory note* is usually a *promise* between *two* parties. A **promissory note** is created when one person gives another person a written promise to pay a specific amount of money.[32] The person who is intended to receive the money is once again called the *payee*. The person who creates the instrument is called the *maker*.

Suppose that on May 1, 2005, Rita Perez agreed to deliver a shipment of sleds to John Chang for $50 000. Because John did not have enough cash to cover the purchase price immediately, Rita agreed to accept instalment payments. The parties assumed that John would be able to pay for the sleds as he resold them in his sporting goods store during the next winter. John therefore gave Rita the promissory note shown in Figure 14.3.[33]

a promissory note is created when one person gives another person a written promise to pay a specific amount of money

---

[30] *Bills of Exchange Act* s 165.

[31] A postdated cheque is payable on demand, but the payee cannot demand payment before the date that appears on the cheque.

[32] *Bills of Exchange Act* s 176(1).

[33] Although payment was postponed under the promissory note, Rita could have received payment immediately if she had sold the note to a third party. That third party, as the holder of the note, would have been entitled to receive $50 000, plus 10 percent interest, from John starting on November 1.

FIGURE 14.3 Promissory Note

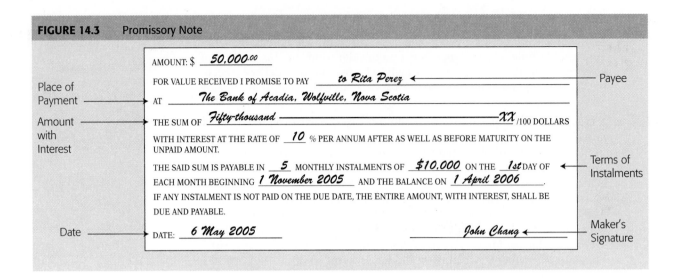

Examining Figure 14.3 will help us understand promissory notes.

- Although there is no drawee under a promissory note, the document indicated that Rita was entitled to collect the money at the Bank of Acadia in Wolfville, Nova Scotia. John presumably had an account there. If the note did not say anything about the place of payment, Rita could have collected the money at John's office.

- A promissory note is almost always used as a credit instrument. In this case, John was allowed to postpone payment for the sleds. As usually occurs with credit transactions, the promissory note required payment *with interest*. John promised to pay $50 000 *plus* 10 percent interest.

- Like a cheque or a bill of exchange, a promissory note can be payable as a lump sum. However, notes are often payable in *instalments*. That was true in our case. John promised to pay $10 000 per month beginning in November of 2005, and to pay the remaining amount on April 1, 2006. As a matter of risk management, John should have made sure that a short receipt was written on the note each time that an instalment was paid. For instance:

$10 000 received in part payment
Rita Perez (1 November 2005)

Without that sort of notation, John might have been forced to make the same payment twice. Assume that Rita received $10 000 on November 1, and then sold the note to an innocent third party. If the payment to Rita was not indicated on the note itself, the third party could probably require John to pay the November instalment again. To encourage commercial transactions, the law usually allows a third party to take a negotiable instrument at face value.

an acceleration clause states that the entire amount of the promise becomes due immediately if a single instalment is not paid on time

- An *acceleration clause* is often found in promissory notes. An **acceleration clause** states that the entire amount of a promise becomes due immediately if a single instalment is not paid on time. There is one in the last line of the pre-formatted note that John used. The explanation for an acceleration clause is quite simple. Suppose that John failed to pay the November instalment in a way that made it clear to Rita that the other instalments would fail as well. Without an acceleration clause, she could sue for only $10 000 in November, another $10 000 in December, and so on. An acceleration clause, however, would allow her to immediately claim the entire $50 000 plus interest.

NEGOTIATION

We have focused on situations in which the payee receives money under a negotiable instrument. However, we have also seen that a negotiable instrument can be *negotiated*, that is, transferred from one party to another. In this section, we examine the process of negotiation.

Methods of Negotiation

The process of negotiation depends on whether an instrument is payable to *bearer* or to *order*. A negotiable instrument is payable to **bearer** if any person who holds it is entitled to receive payment. A bearer instrument can arise in several ways. We can use the promissory note in Figure 14.3 for illustration.

a negotiable instrument is payable to bearer if any person who holds it is entitled to receive payment

- John could have made the note payable "*to Rita Perez or bearer*" or simply "*to bearer.*"
- John could have left the name of the payee blank.[34]
- John could have made the note payable to a fictitious person, such as "*to Sherlock Holmes*," or to a non-person, such as "*to cash.*"[35]
- Although the note in Figure 14.3 is an order note, it would have become a bearer note if Rita had delivered it to someone else after *endorsing* it with her signature and nothing more: "*Rita Perez.*"[36] The note would then remain a bearer instrument unless some later party turned it back into an order instrument by using a *special endorsement*. (We will examine endorsements shortly.)

The important point is that a bearer instrument can be negotiated by the simple delivery, or physical transfer, of the document. An endorsement is unnecessary.

A negotiable instrument is payable to **order** if the party that is entitled to receive payment is named. For example, the note in Figure 14.3 provides an example because the note is payable "*to Rita Perez.*"[37] An order instrument cannot be negotiated unless it is *endorsed and delivered* to a new party. Suppose that Rita wanted to negotiate the note to her sister, Carmen. She could not do so by simply giving that piece of paper to her.[38] She would also have to endorse it by at least signing her name on the back: "*Rita Perez.*"

a negotiable instrument is payable to order if the party entitled to receive payment is named

---

[34.] In that situation, Rita could have filled in her own name: *Bills of Exchange Act* ss 30, 31.

[35.] *Bills of Exchange Act* s 20(5).

[36.] *Bills of Exchange Act* s 66(5). It appears that an instrument that starts as a bearer instrument (for instance, if John made the note "*to bearer*") always remains a bearer instrument: s 20(3).

[37.] The note also would have been payable to order if John had written "*to the order of Rita Perez*" or "*to Rita Perez or order.*" Note that the cheque in Figure 14.1 and the bill of exchange in Figure 14.2 are also order instruments.

[38.] An order instrument that is delivered but not endorsed may create an equitable assignment. In that case, however, the person who receives the instrument does not receive any special benefits under the Act: *Aldercrest Developments Ltd v Hamilton Co-axial (1958) Ltd* (1973) 37 DLR (3d) 254 (SCC).

Liability

In this section, we will consider several types of endorsements. Before doing so, however, we will briefly discuss how negotiation can affect liability. Staying with Figure 14.3, we assume this series of events.

- John Chang made a promissory note payable "*to Rita Perez.*"
- Rita changed that order note into a bearer note by simply signing her name on it before delivering it to her sister, Carmen.
- Carmen sold the note to Vlad Hlinka in exchange for a car. Because the note had become a bearer instrument, Carmen was able to negotiate it to Vlad by simply giving it to him. Vlad changed the instrument back into an order note by delivering it to his business associate, Enya McCall, along with the following endorsement: *Vlad Hlinka – Pay to Enya McCall.*
- Enya asked John to make payment under the note.

Those events are represented in Figure 14.4.

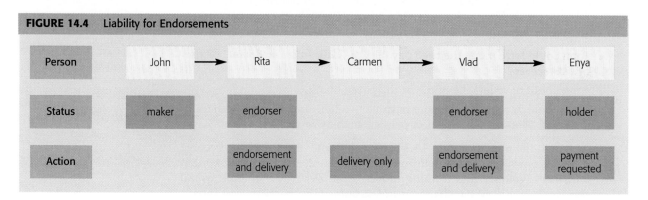

FIGURE 14.4   Liability for Endorsements

Person	John	→	Rita	→	Carmen	→	Vlad	→	Enya
Status	maker		endorser				endorser		holder
Action			endorsement and delivery		delivery only		endorsement and delivery		payment requested

The primary liability under a promissory note falls on the maker.[39] In this case, John had the initial obligation to pay Enya. One of the most interesting features of a negotiable instrument, however, is that an endorser may also be held liable. As a general rule, a person who provides an endorsement promises people who later acquire the instrument that it will be paid.[40]

- As a result of that rule, Enya might receive full payment even if John was unable to pay a cent. She could sue everyone who endorsed the note: Rita and Vlad. Rita could be held liable even though she did not have any direct contract with Enya. Her responsibility would arise entirely from the fact that she endorsed the note. However, Enya could *not* sue Carmen.[41] Although Carmen negotiated the note to Vlad, she did so when it was in bearer form. She was therefore able to transfer it to him by delivery alone. And since she did not endorse the note, she did not promise that it would be paid.

[39.] The rules discussed in this section generally apply to cheques and bills of exchange as well. Under a cheque, the drawer has the primary liability. Under a bill, the primary liability falls on the drawer at first. However, if a bill is accepted, then the drawee/acceptor has the primary liability: *Bills of Exchange Act* s 186.

[40.] *Bills of Exchange Act* s 132.

[41.] *Bills of Exchange Act* s 136(2).

- An endorser who is held liable can sometimes sue a person who negotiated the instrument at an earlier time. Assume that Enya collected payment from Vlad. He might be able to shift that loss to either Carmen or Rita.

- Unlike Enya, Vlad could sue Carmen even though she did not endorse the note. There are two possibilities. First, the Act would allow Vlad to sue Carmen if she gave him an instrument that (i) was not genuine, (ii) she had no right to transfer, or (iii) she knew was worthless.[42] On our facts, it is unlikely that any of those requirements could be met. Second, Vlad might be able to sue Carmen on the basis of their sales contract if, in exchange for his car, she had promised that she would pay the note if asked to do so.

- Vlad could sue Rita because she endorsed the note before he acquired it.

- Now, assume that Enya collected payment from Rita rather than Vlad. Rita could *not* in turn sue Vlad. Although he endorsed the note, he did so *after* she did. A person who wants payment on an instrument must look to an *earlier* party. Consequently, since John was unable to pay, Rita would probably suffer the eventual loss in this case.

The ability to demand payment from an endorser is significant. It is, however, subject to an important limitation. Liability generally cannot be imposed on an endorser unless that person received a *notice of dishonour*.[43] A **notice of dishonour** consists of a statement that the person who was primarily liable on the instrument failed to pay. Note these other things about a notice of dishonour.

a notice of dishonour consists of a statement that the person who was primarily liable on the instrument failed to pay

- Notice normally must be given very quickly—usually within one business day.[44]

- Notice does not normally have to be in writing, but it must clearly identify the instrument in question.[45]

- Notice must be given by a holder who wants payment from an endorser. Enya, for example, should have given notice to Vlad and Rita as soon as John refused to pay. Notice must also be given by one endorser who wants payment from another. Vlad, for example, should have given notice to Rita as soon as Enya asked him to pay.

- If notice is not properly given, an endorser is discharged and cannot be held liable on the instrument.

- Notice is not required, however, if (i) the endorser cannot be reached through a reasonable effort, or (ii) the endorser waived the need for notice, for instance, by writing "notice of dishonour unnecessary" beside a signature.[46]

---

[42] *Bills of Exchange Act* s 173.

[43] *Bills of Exchange Act* s 95. Since the primary liability for an *accepted* bill of exchange falls on the acceptor, the notice requirements apply to the drawer as well as the endorsers.

[44] *Bills of Exchange Act* s 96. A delay may be excused if the circumstances were beyond a person's control: s 104. Furthermore, a notice that is sent through the postal system only has to be mailed by the next day: s 102(2). And finally, notice is deemed to have been given even if it is lost in the postal system: s 103.

[45] *Bills of Exchange Act* s 97. A much more formal notice, called a protest, must be given if an instrument is drawn, payable, or accepted in Quebec or outside of Canada: ss 108–125. As a matter of risk management, one should always give notice in writing, which is easy to prove.

[46] *Bills of Exchange Act* s 105.

From a risk management perspective, the lesson is clear. If the person who is primarily liable under an instrument is unable to pay, you must give notice as soon as possible to everyone you might want to sue. If you fail to do so, your rights may be lost.

Forms of Endorsement

Several types of endorsement are allowed under the *Bills of Exchange Act*. We will consider seven:

- special endorsement
- identifying endorsement
- qualified endorsement
- conditional endorsement
- accommodation endorsement
- general endorsement
- restrictive endorsement

To better understand each of those possibilities, we return to Figure 14.1 and assume that the following parties dealt with the cheque that Hank Quinlan drew on his account at the Bank of Edmonton: (i) Anna Schmidt, (ii) Jed Leland, (iii) Michael O'Hara, (iv) Isabel Minafer, (v) Elsa Bannister, (vi) Harry Lime, and (vii) Susana Vargas. Figure 14.5 shows the endorsement that each person placed on the cheque.

FIGURE 14.5	Endorsements on a Cheque

Anna Schmidt — Pay to Mike O'Hara

Jed Leland—Anna Schmidt hereby identified

Mike O'Hara — pay to Isabel Minafer without recourse

Isabel Minafer — Pay to Harry Lime if he takes me to Vienna

Elsa Bannister— Guarantor for I. Minafer

Harry Lime

Susana Vargas—for deposit only

Special Endorsement

Hank made the cheque payable to Anna. After receiving it, she added a *special endorsement*.[47] She did so by signing her name on the back of the cheque and by indicating that the money should be paid to Mike O'Hara. Once Mike obtained the cheque from Anna, he replaced her as the only person who was entitled to receive payment.

[47.] *Bills of Exchange Act* s 66(3).

Identifying Endorsement

Before Mike received the cheque from Anna, however, Jed Leland added an *identifying endorsement*. Presumably, Mike was reluctant to buy the cheque from Anna because he did not personally know her. Jed, however, knew both parties and was willing to assure Mike that Anna was indeed the payee. Significantly, Jed could not be held liable as a normal endorser. He could only be held liable if the person who negotiated the cheque to Mike was not really Anna Schmidt.

Qualified Endorsement

After receiving the cheque from Anna, Mike transferred it to Isabel Minafer under a *qualified endorsement*.[48] By stating that his endorsement was "without recourse," Mike indicated that he was not willing to be held liable if the cheque was later dishonoured. Consequently, if Susana Vargas was eventually unable to receive payment from Hank's account at the Bank of Edmonton, she could not sue Mike.

Conditional Endorsement

A cheque must contain an unconditional obligation. Hank, for instance, could not have drafted the cheque payable to "*Anna Schmidt if she takes me to Vienna.*" That order would be conditional on the trip. An endorsement, however, can be conditional.[49] In this case, Isabel has endorsed the cheque "*to Harry Lime if he takes me to Vienna.*" Consequently, if Isabel was later sued on her endorsement, she could in turn sue Harry if he did not take her to Vienna.

Accommodation Endorsement

Before Isabel actually delivered the cheque to Harry, Elsa Bannister added an *accommodation endorsement*.[50] Presumably, Harry was concerned that if he ever tried to sue Isabel on her endorsement, she might not have enough money to pay. Elsa was therefore persuaded to sign as "*Guarantor for I. Minafer.*" That endorsement is called an "accommodation" because it accommodated, or helped, Isabel's effort to negotiate the cheque to Harry. It is also called "anomalous" because it is unusual. A person normally uses an endorsement to negotiate an instrument that they own. In this case, however, Elsa was not trying to transfer her own property. Instead, she was assisting in the transfer of Isabel's property. Elsa nevertheless could be held liable as an endorser.

General Endorsement

After Harry received the cheque from Isabel, he added his *general* (or *blank*) *endorsement*.[51] By simply writing his signature and nothing more, Harry transformed the cheque from an order instrument into a bearer instrument.

[48] *Bills of Exchange Act* s 33(a).

[49] *Bills of Exchange Act* s 65. The Act also indicates that later parties can assume that the condition was fulfilled.

[50] *Bills of Exchange Act* ss 54, 130.

[51] *Bills of Exchange Act* s 66.

Restrictive Endorsement

Finally, after Susana received the cheque from Harry, she added her *restrictive endorsement*.[52] By writing "*for deposit only*," Susana prevented the instrument from being negotiated any further. The cheque could be used only to pay funds into Susana's bank account. As a matter of risk management, that sort of endorsement provides good protection against theft.

DEFENCES

Contractual rights can generally be assigned from one party to another. For better or worse, however, the assignee simply steps into the assignor's shoes. Most significantly, the assignee acquires the contract *subject to the equities*. If sued by the assignee, the debtor can rely on any defence that it could have used against the assignor.

A negotiable instrument is a type of contract. It is, however, a special type of contract. As a result of the process of negotiation, the rights under an instrument can be easily transferred *and* they can be improved as they are transferred. Consequently, a defence that could have been used against a payee may not be available against a person who received the instrument by way of negotiation. In this section, we will consider several defences and discover when they apply. The issue of defences is quite complicated. To simplify the discussion, we will use the cheque that appears, front and back, in Figure 14.6 (on the next page). As you can see, it appears that:

- Iman Khan drew a cheque for $9000 on her account at the Island National Bank in favour of Felix Sobers
- Felix Sobers specially endorsed the cheque to Janet Botham
- Janet Botham specially endorsed the cheque to Waqar Akram
- Waqar Akram now wants payment

Types of Parties

To discuss defences, we need to identify three types of parties: (i) *immediate parties*, (ii) *holders*, and (iii) *holders in due course*.

- **Immediate parties** are parties who dealt directly with each other. In our case, there are three sets of immediate parties: Iman and Felix, Felix and Janet, and Janet and Waqar.
- A **holder** is a person who has possession of a negotiable instrument.[53] In our example, Waqar is the holder. Depending upon the circumstances, he may also be a holder in due course.
- A **holder in due course** is a person who acquired a negotiable instrument under specific conditions.[54] While those conditions are complex, we can summarize them. Note that they all relate to honesty. Only an honest person deserves the special treatment that the Act gives to a holder in due course.

immediate parties are parties who dealt directly with each other

a holder is a person who has possession of a negotiable instrument

a holder in due course is a person who acquired an instrument in special circumstances

[52.] *Bills of Exchange Act* s 67.

[53.] *Bills of Exchange Act* s 2.

[54.] *Bills of Exchange Act* s 55. Unless there is evidence to the contrary, the Act assumes that every holder is a holder in due course: s 57(2).

FIGURE 14.6   Defences

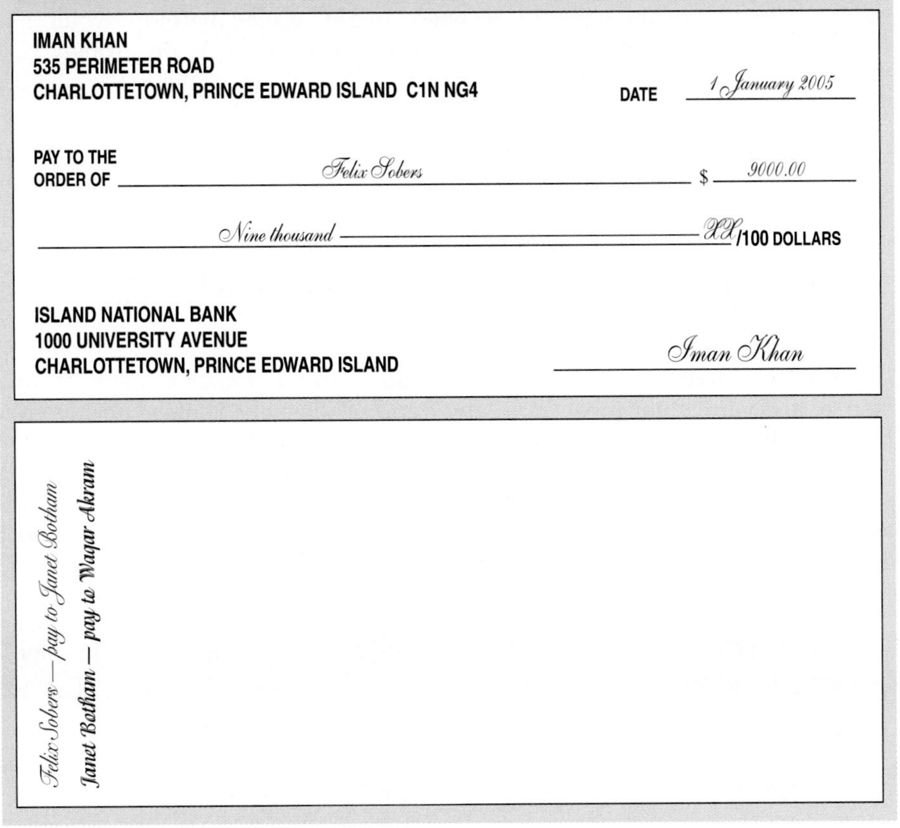

IMAN KHAN
535 PERIMETER ROAD
CHARLOTTETOWN, PRINCE EDWARD ISLAND C1N NG4   DATE   *1 January 2005*

PAY TO THE
ORDER OF ___ *Felix Sobers* ___ $ ___ *9000.00* ___

___ *Nine thousand* ___ *XX*/100 DOLLARS

ISLAND NATIONAL BANK
1000 UNIVERSITY AVENUE
CHARLOTTETOWN, PRINCE EDWARD ISLAND   ___ *Iman Khan* ___

Felix Sobers — pay to Janet Botham
Janet Botham — pay to Waqar Akram

- **Supported by value:** The instrument must be *supported by value*, that is, consideration. Interestingly, Waqar could be a holder in due course even if he did not personally give consideration. It would be enough if someone before him gave consideration for the cheque.[55]

- **Complete and regular on its face:** The holder must have taken an instrument that was *complete and regular on its face*. An instrument is not complete if an important part is left blank. That would be true if, for instance, Waqar received a cheque that did not state an amount.[56] And an instrument is not regular if it looks suspicious. That would be the case, for instance, if the cheque contained obvious erasures or alterations.

- **Without notice of dishonour:** The holder must have acquired the instrument *without notice of any previous dishonour*. Consequently, Waqar would not be a holder in due course if, for example, he knew or strongly suspected either that the Island National Bank had already refused to honour the cheque or that Iman had countermanded it.

[55.] *Bills of Exchange Act* s 53. Unless there is evidence to the contrary, the Act presumes that every person who signs an instrument gave value: s 57(1).

[56.] Interestingly, the holder of an instrument generally has the right to fill in any blanks: *Bills of Exchange Act* s 30.

- **Good faith and without notice of defect:** The holder must have taken the instrument in *good faith* and *without notice of any defect* in the title of the person who negotiated it. Waqar therefore would not be a holder in due course if, for instance, he knew or strongly suspected that Iman had been forced or tricked into drawing the cheque, or that Janet had forged Felix's endorsement.

- **Before overdue:** The holder must have acquired the instrument *before it was overdue*.[57] As we have seen, an instrument may be due at different times.[58] In our example, the cheque was drawn on January 1 and was payable on demand. As a result, Waqar might not be a holder in due course if he received the document from Janet on May 23. There is usually something suspicious about a cheque that has not been cashed for almost six months.[59]

Note that every person who acquires an instrument *after* a holder in due course, and who is not involved in any fraud or illegality, is also considered a holder in due course.[60]

There are three types of defences that are available under the Act: (i) *personal defences*, (ii) *defect in title defences*, and (iii) *real defences*. The availability of each type of defence depends on the type of party involved. Concept Summary 14.2 presents a general overview.

CONCEPT SUMMARY 14.2

Parties and Defences

	Personal Defences	Defect in Title Defences	Real Defences
Immediate party	✓	✓	✓
Holder	✗	✓	✓
Holder in due course	✗	✗	✓

Personal Defences

a personal defence is one that affects the parties themselves, rather than the instrument

If an action occurs between two immediate parties, the defendant can use any type of defence, including a *personal defence*. As the name suggests, a **personal defence** is one that affects the parties themselves rather than the instrument. Assume that Waqar presented the cheque to the Island National Bank for payment, but left empty-handed because Iman's account did not contain enough money. He could sue Janet on the cheque because she endorsed it. In response, however, she could raise any defence that arose from her dealings with him. We can consider two common examples.

---

[57] *Bills of Exchange Act* s 69.

[58] A bill of exchange or promissory note that is payable on a specific day, rather than on demand, is due on that day.

[59] A promissory note that is payable on demand is not overdue simply because a reasonable length of time has passed: *Bills of Exchange Act* s 182. That is because a promissory note, unlike a bill or cheque, is normally used to extend credit.

[60] *Bills of Exchange Act* s 56.

- **Set-off:** Janet could *set off* any debt that Waqar owed to her. Suppose that she negotiated the cheque to him because he sold her a car for $9000. A few days later, she sold him a boat for $5000, but he failed to pay. If Waqar sued Janet on the cheque, she could admit liability, set off the price of the boat, and pay only $4000.

- **Failure of consideration:** Janet could also rely on a *failure of consideration*.[61] For instance, if the car that Waqar sold to her was defective and required $3000 in repairs, she could admit liability, plead breach of contract, and pay only $6000. After all, she expected to receive a car worth $9000 but received one worth only $6000.

Defect in Title Defences

Defect in title defences are available against an immediate party *and* against a simple holder. A **defect in title defence** occurs when an instrument is obtained improperly. It is different from a personal defence because it affects the instrument itself.

Suppose that Waqar is a holder, but not a holder in due course, because he received the cheque from Janet when it was overdue.[62] Further suppose that the Island National Bank refused to honour the cheque because Iman's account was overdrawn. Waqar could sue Iman as the drawer of the cheque. If he did so, however, she could avoid liability by proving any of the following defect in title defences.

a defect in title defence occurs when an instrument is obtained improperly

- **Fraud or duress:** Iman would not have to pay Waqar if she initially drafted the cheque as a result of Felix's *fraud* or *duress*.[63] Perhaps Felix tricked her, or threatened her with a beating unless she created the instrument. In that situation, Felix did not obtain good title to the cheque. And since Waqar was not a holder in due course, he did not obtain good title either.

- **Illegal consideration:** Likewise, Iman would not have to pay Waqar if she issued the cheque to Felix in exchange for *illegal consideration*. That would be the case if, for instance, Felix promised to deliver drugs to her.

- **Drunkenness or insanity:** Felix's title also would have been defective if he knew, or should have known, that Iman was *drunk* or *insane* when she drafted the cheque.[64] Once again, that defect would affect Waqar as well.

- **Absence of delivery:** A defect in title can occur when there is an *absence of delivery*. Suppose that Iman completed the cheque as it appears in Figure 14.6, but never actually gave it to Felix. If he took it from her desk

---

[61.] If consideration was *never* given in exchange for the cheque, that instrument would be entirely unenforceable.

[62.] To simplify the situation, assume that Janet received the cheque as a gift from Felix. Since she would not be a holder in due course in the examples that follow, Waqar could not become a holder in due course by obtaining the cheque from her: *Bills of Exchange Act* s 56.

[63.] *Bills of Exchange Act* s 55(2). Fraud is usually a defect in title defence. However, it may be a real defence if it amounts to *non est factum* (literally, "this is not my deed"). As we saw in Chapter 10, that defence is available in very limited circumstances. It might work in our case, for instance, if Iman, who was illiterate, infirm, or blind, was tricked into signing the cheque because she thought she was being asked for her autograph.

[64.] Insanity normally creates a defect in title defence. However, it can also lead to a real defence if the person was legally declared to be mentally incompetent: *Bills of Exchange Act* s 46(1).

without her permission, he would obtain a defective title, as would Waqar.[65]

- **No authority:** If Iman gave the cheque to Felix with instructions to fill in $7000 as the amount, he would have obtained a defective title if he instead made the cheque out for $9000. He had *no authority* for what he actually did.

- **Discharge or renunciation:** Finally, Waqar would have received a defective title if the cheque that he acquired from Janet had been *discharged* or *renounced*.[66] Suppose, for instance, that after Iman issued the cheque to Felix, he wrote her a note that said, "You don't really owe this money to me. I therefore won't ask for payment." He nevertheless gave the cheque to Janet, who in turn sold it to Waqar. Because of Felix's renunciation, Iman would not have to pay Waqar. To be safe, of course, she should have asked Felix to return the cheque to her as soon as he renounced his rights.[67]

Real Defences

a real defence occurs when an instrument is fundamentally flawed

A holder in due course cannot be defeated by personal defences or defect in title defences. That person has to worry only about *real defences*. A **real defence** occurs when an instrument is fundamentally flawed. Such a defence is *real* in the sense that it affects the *res*—the thing—itself. It does not simply concern a personal matter between the parties or a defect in one party's title to an instrument.

Assume that Waqar is a holder in due course and that the Island National Bank has refused to honour the cheque. If Waqar sought payment from someone else, he might be met by a real defence. We have already seen that *fraud* or *duress*, *drunkenness* or *insanity*, *absence of delivery*, and *discharge or renunciation* can lead to either a defect in title defence or a real defence, depending on the circumstances. We also need to consider three more possibilities.

- **Minority:** Iman would not have to pay if she created the cheque when she was a *minor*.[68] Waqar could, however, demand payment from either Felix or Janet, on the basis of their endorsements, if they were adults.[69]

- **Material alteration:** A *material alteration* may create a real defence.[70] Suppose that Felix changed the amount of the cheque from $9000 to $29 000 after he received it from Iman. The effect of that alteration would depend on Felix's skills as a con artist.

[65.] There was a defect in title because Iman did not deliver a *completed* instrument. However, she would have a real defence if she did not deliver the cheque *and* if that instrument was *incomplete*. Perhaps Felix stole it from her desk, filled in the amount (which she had left blank), and gave it to Janet, who sold it to Waqar. In that case, Waqar could not demand payment from Iman, even if he was a holder in due course.

[66.] *Bills of Exchange Act* ss 139, 141.

[67.] As a matter of risk management, a cheque that has been honoured should have "paid" written on its face. A mere holder cannot sue on a cheque that has been discharged. However, a holder in due course *can* sue on a discharged or cancelled cheque, as long as that fact is not apparent from the instrument itself: *Bills of Exchange Act* s 141. Suppose that Felix was allowed to keep the cheque even though he had been paid. If Waqar later became a holder in due course, he could force Iman to pay again if the cheque had not been stamped "paid."

[68.] Although Iman could not be liable to anyone on the cheque, she could be held liable to Felix on the sales contract if he provided her with *necessary* goods or services, as discussed in Chapter 10.

[69.] *Bills of Exchange Act* s 47. The same rules apply if a contract is drafted by a corporation that does not have the capacity to incur liability under a negotiable instrument.

[70.] *Bills of Exchange Act* ss 144, 145.

- If the alteration *was not* apparent to the naked eye, Waqar could enforce the cheque against Iman but only for the original amount of $9000. However, he could also enforce the cheque against Felix or Janet for $29 000. Felix would be liable for that amount because he was the wrongdoer. Janet would be fully liable because she chose to add her endorsement to the cheque *after* it was altered. She therefore promised to pay $29 000.

- If the alteration *was* apparent to the naked eye, Waqar could not enforce it against Iman at all. However, for the reasons that we just discussed, he could enforce it against Felix or Janet for $29 000.

- Note one more thing about alterations. Look carefully at the cheque in Figure 14.6 and compare it to the cheque in Figure 14.1. As you can see, Iman was sloppy in a way that Hank was not. She left spaces in the cheque that allowed Felix to easily alter the amount. Assume that the Island National Bank honoured the cheque and paid $29 000 to Waqar. Normally, the bank could only debit $9000 from Iman's account because that was the only amount that she authorized. However, since the alteration in this case was caused by Iman's carelessness, the bank could take $29 000 from her account. As a matter of risk management, you should always follow Hank's lead and draft instruments in a way that prevents fraud.

■ **Forgery:** A holder in due course may also be met by a defence of *forgery*. Suppose that someone stole the cheque from Felix, forged his endorsement, and then transferred the instrument to Janet. Although the rules that would apply in that case are complex, the main points can be stated briefly.[71]

- A person whose signature is forged generally cannot be held liable. Consequently, if the bank refused to honour the cheque, Waqar could not sue Felix.

- Similarly, a person who signed an instrument *before* a forgery occurred generally cannot be held liable. Consequently, Waqar would also be unable to sue Iman.

- However, a person who signed an instrument *after* a forgery occurred generally can be held liable. Consequently, Waqar could demand payment from Janet, even if she did not know that Felix's signature had been forged. By adding her own endorsement, she promised to pay in any event.

- If the Island National Bank honoured the cheque and paid Waqar, it would have debited Iman's account for $9000. Iman could recover that money from the bank, but only if she promptly notified the bank after learning about the forgery.[72]

- If the bank honoured the cheque, it could recover the amount that it paid from either Waqar (because he received the money) or Janet (because she endorsed the cheque after the forgery), but only if it notified them within a reasonable time after it learned of the forgery.

The effect of these rules can be summarized. The person who committed the forgery should bear the loss. However, that sort of person often

---

71. *Bills of Exchange Act* ss 48, 49.

72. If an *endorser's* signature had been forged, Iman would have to give notice within one year. If her own signature, as the *drawer*, had been forged, Iman would have to notify the bank within "a reasonable time."

disappears or does not have enough money. Therefore, the loss usually falls on the first person who endorsed the instrument after the forgery, in this case, Janet.

CONSUMER BILLS AND NOTES

The *Bills of Exchange Act* has changed very little since it was enacted over 100 years ago. The only substantial alteration was introduced in 1970 to protect consumers. The problem that Parliament wanted to avoid is illustrated in Business Decision 14.1.

BUSINESS DECISION 14.1

Consumer Bills and Notes

Christine used a promissory note to buy $10 000 worth of aluminum siding for her house from Noel's Exteriors Inc. Noel, however, never delivered the goods. In fact, he disappeared altogether. Because Noel was an immediate party, Christine could have relied on his breach of contract if he had sued her on the note. Furthermore, she could have sued him on the sales contract for damages. In the circumstances, that action would have been a waste of time and money.

To make matters worse, Noel sold the note to Mastiff Financing Ltd, which was a holder in due course. When Mastiff sued Christine, she did not have any defence to its claim. Most significantly, since Mastiff was not an immediate party to her, it did not take the instrument subject to the equities. Consequently, Christine could not argue that Noel never delivered the siding. She therefore had to pay $10 000 to Mastiff, even though she received nothing in return.

In response to that problem, Parliament added a series of sections to the Act to provide some protection to consumers.[73] The new provisions apply to *consumer instruments* only. A **consumer instrument** is a bill of exchange, cheque, or promissory note that is used by a consumer to buy goods or services from a business on credit. Note three things about that definition. First, the instrument must be used for *credit* purposes. That requirement is satisfied by a promissory note, and by a bill of exchange or cheque that is postdated at least 31 days. Second, the instrument must be used to purchase goods or services from a business person. And third, the instrument must be given by a "consumer," that is, someone who intends to use the purchase for personal, rather than business, purposes.

> a consumer instrument is a bill of exchange, cheque, or promissory note that is used by a consumer to buy goods or services on credit

The front of a consumer instrument must be marked with the words "consumer purchase." The effect of those words is dramatic. Any person, including a holder in due course, who acquires a properly marked consumer instrument takes it subject to the equities. Consequently, if that person sues on the instrument, the consumer can use almost any defence that it could have used against the original seller. The situation is more complicated if an instrument is not properly marked.

- A holder in due course who acquires an instrument without notice that it was used for a consumer purchase does not take it subject to the equities. Consequently, it can be defeated only by a real defence.
- In the hands of any other sort of person, however, an unmarked consumer instrument is void.
- A seller who fails to properly mark a consumer instrument can be fined or imprisoned. The same is true for people who transfer unmarked instruments that they know were used for consumer purchases.

[73.] *Bills of Exchange Act* ss 188–192.

Chapter Summary

A negotiable instrument is a special kind of contract that contains an obligation to pay money. The process of negotiation requires the modification of several general contractual principles, including consideration, privity, and assignment. The *Bills of Exchange Act* codifies the rules for three types of negotiable instruments: cheques, bills of exchange, and promissory notes.

The Act will not apply unless an instrument satisfies five basic requirements. A negotiable instrument must (i) be written and signed, (ii) clearly identify the parties, (iii) contain an obligation to pay a specific sum of money, (iv) clearly state a time of payment, and (v) contain an unconditional obligation. Those requirements are intended to create the level of certainty that is necessary for the process of negotiation.

A cheque is created when a person orders a bank to pay a specific amount of money to someone. It has three parties: (i) the drawer is the person who "draws," or creates, the cheque, (ii) the drawee is the bank that is ordered to pay money, and (iii) the payee is the person who is entitled to receive the money from the bank. Although most cheques operate smoothly, complications can arise if a cheque is (i) postdated, (ii) staledated, (iii) overdrawn, (iv) countermanded, or (v) certified.

A bill of exchange is created when one person orders another person to pay a specific amount of money to a third person. A bill may be payable (i) on demand, (ii) on sight, or (iii) on a specific date. A bill may be accepted by the drawee before it is due. If so, the drawee becomes an acceptor and must honour the bill when it is presented for payment.

A promissory note is created when one person gives another person a written promise to pay a specific amount of money. A promissory note is generally different from a cheque or a bill because (i) it contains a promise rather than an order, and (ii) it involves two parties, rather than three. A promissory note (i) is often payable with interest, (ii) is often payable in instalments, and (iii) often contains an acceleration clause.

Negotiation involves the transfer of an instrument from one party to another. A bearer instrument is payable to whoever holds it. It can be negotiated by delivery alone. An order instrument is payable to a named person. It can be negotiated by endorsement and delivery. The primary liability for an instrument is on the drawer in the case of a cheque, the drawer or acceptor in the case of a bill, and the maker in the case of a note. However, liability can usually also be imposed on any person who endorsed the instrument. An endorsement usually creates a promise to pay. There are seven main types of endorsement: (i) special, (ii) identifying, (iii) qualified, (iv) conditional, (v) accommodation, (vi) general, and (vii) restrictive.

For the purposes of defences, there are three types of parties: (i) immediate parties, (ii) holders, and (iii) holders in due course. There are three types of defences: (i) personal defences, which are available against immediate parties, (ii) defect in title defences, which are available against immediate parties and holders, and (iii) real defences, which are available against immediate parties, holders, and holders in due course.

Review Questions

1. If a negotiable instrument is used to pay for goods, the parties usually enter into two separate contracts. Describe those contracts.

2. Briefly compare the rules that apply to negotiable instruments with the general contractual rules that govern the issues of consideration and privity.

3. What is the main advantage of receiving the negotiation of an instrument rather than the assignment of a contract?

4. Why does the *Bills of Exchange Act* require an instrument to be written and signed?

5. "A cheque becomes staledated only when the statutory limitation period lapses." Is that statement correct? Explain your answer.

6. What options does a bank have if a customer writes a cheque on an overdrawn account?

7. What is a "stop payment order"? How is such an order given?

8. "The drawee owes the payee an obligation to honour a valid cheque." Is that statement ever correct? If so, when?

9. Is a drawee bank required to honour a certified cheque if the drawer's account is overdrawn or if there has been a countermand? Explain the policy that underlies your answer.

10. Which party has the ability to accept a bill of exchange? What is the effect of acceptance from that party's perspective? What is the effect of acceptance from the perspective of the drawer and the payee?

11. Explain the difference between (i) a demand draft, (ii) a sight draft, and (iii) a time draft.

12. If you make a promissory note that is payable in instalments, what precaution should you take after you pay each instalment? What is the potential result of not adopting that precaution?

13. What is the purpose of an acceleration clause?

14. What is the danger of receiving an instrument in bearer form? Explain how you can protect yourself against that danger once you have received the instrument.

15. Explain the requirements for negotiating (i) a bearer instrument, and (ii) an order instrument.

16. What risk do you normally assume when you endorse a negotiable instrument?

17. What is a notice of dishonour? When must it be given? What are the consequences of not giving a notice of dishonour?

18. Briefly describe a holder in due course. What types of defences are available against a holder in due course? Why is a holder in due course given special treatment under the *Bills of Exchange Act*?

19. When creating a negotiable instrument, you should always ensure that you use all of the space that is available for the amount." Is that good advice? Explain your answer.

20. List and briefly explain four types of defences that may act as either defect in title defences or real defences.

CASES AND PROBLEMS

1. Every year for a decade, Chamique gave an expensive birthday gift to her friend Ahmad. Last year, she gave him a diamond ring; the year before, a stereo. This year, however, she found that she was too busy with work to actually spend time shopping for a present, so she drafted a cheque for $5000 and gave it to Ahmad. Ahmad accepted it, but later told Chamique that he was hurt that she did not make more of an effort. Chamique became very upset herself and placed a stop payment order on the cheque before Ahmad cashed it. Since the bank will not honour the cheque, Ahmad wants to sue Chamique on the instrument. Is he entitled to do so? Give the best reason for your answer.

2. Gilles, who is 16 years old but looks much older, bought a snowboard from Eva's Sporting Goods. He paid the $750 price with a promissory note that was payable in three monthly instalments of $250 each. Eva stamped the words "consumer purchase" on the note at the time of the sale. Unfortunately, the board was stolen the first time that Gilles took it to the mountains. He believes that he should no longer be required to pay for something that he no longer enjoys. Not surprisingly, Eva has a different opinion. She believes that Gilles got what he wanted and that he is liable to pay the full price. Is Gilles liable on the note? Explain your answer.

3. Bibi, a lawyer, provided legal advice to Bjorn on a small matter. When he asked her for her fee, she said, "Oh, just pay whatever you think is appropriate." Although the evidence indicates that the reasonable value of Bibi's work was $2500, Bjorn gave her a cheque on February 14 for $15 000. Bibi slipped it into her desk without even looking at the amount. The cheque sat there until December, when Bibi presented it to the drawee bank for payment. The bank refused to honour it, however, because Bjorn's account was overdrawn. Bibi then telephoned Bjorn personally and asked him for payment of $15 000. He refused, claiming that he was temporarily insane when he drafted the cheque: "You should have known that I was on the verge of a complete mental collapse and that I was madly—if irrationally—in love with you. Why else would I give you a cheque for that much money on Valentine's Day? You certainly didn't earn $15 000." And indeed, the evidence indicates that Bjorn was quite obviously insane when he drafted the cheque. Bibi wanted nothing more to do with Bjorn, but she did want the money. Therefore she sold the cheque to the Bergman Collection Agency, which was entirely unaware of Bjorn's argument when it purchased the instrument from Bibi. Bergman has since learned of Bjorn's argument, but claims that it is entitled to payment as a holder in due course. Is that correct? Explain your answer.

4. Roger, who was in the market for a computer, visited Hussein's Electronics with a view to finding a bargain. He was directed to a computer that had been used as a floor model in the store. Although the sales representative was unwilling to provide a warranty, he did assure Roger that the unit could be returned if it did not perform satisfactorily during the first month. He also assured Roger that the price could be dropped by $500 if the computer developed minor problems. Roger agreed on that basis to purchase the computer for either $2000 or $1500, depending upon how well the machine performed. By way of payment, he provided a cheque, which he modified to suit the circumstances. First, he stated the amount of the cheque to be either "$1500 or $2000." Second, although he entered the date of purchase on the cheque, Roger added a notation saying "payable six months after date." And third, he added a notation to the cheque that said, "payment conditional upon quality of computer." Roger has now used the computer for five weeks without any problems at all. Will Hussein's Electronics, as the payee of his cheque, be able to obtain payment from the drawee bank? Explain your answer.

5. On May 1, Alexa drew a bill of exchange for $25 000 on her line of credit at the People's Trust Company. The bill was payable to Svend on October 26. On June 1, Svend took the bill to the trust company. Audrey, a clerk, ensured that Alexa's credit was in good standing and wrote the following on the bill: "Accepted, October 26, Alexa Ulianov [signature]." At that point, which party was primarily liable for paying the bill on October 15?

6. Sam Jasper agreed to sell 4000 L of animal feed to Kate Hughes, who operates a wildlife park. After receiving the product, but before inspecting it, Kate told Sam that he could collect a cheque, as payment,

from on top of the desk in her office. Before Sam did so, however, Kate inspected the feed and realized that it was contrary to the terms of the sale contract. Consequently, although she had completely written out a cheque in Sam's favour, she did not leave it on top of her desk as promised. She instead put it into her desk drawer, with the intention of calling him and explaining her concerns. Before she could do so, however, Sam came by her office while she was out. When he realized that there was no cheque on top of her desk, he looked through the drawers, where he found the cheque that Kate had drawn. Sam immediately added his general endorsement to the back of that cheque and gave it to Benjamin Gigger as payment for another, unrelated contract. Kate soon discovered the facts and ordered the Bank of Alberta (the drawee) to refuse payment. Because Benjamin could not cash the cheque at the bank, he has sued both Sam and Kate for payment. Will he be successful against either party? What if the cheque that Sam took from the drawer was incomplete because Kate had not filled in the amount (although she had otherwise added all of the necessary details, including her signature)? Explain your answer.

7. Laurie is a fine art dealer, specializing in Inuit carvings. Claude agreed to purchase a large soapstone sculpture of a polar bear. By way of payment, Claude provided a cheque for the purchase price of $25 000. The cheque was drawn on Claude's account at the Bank of St Albert. Because the amount was so large, the cheque was certified by the drawee bank. Laurie subsequently presented the cheque to the bank for payment. The bank, however, refused to do so on two grounds. First, at the time of certification, it had overlooked the fact that Claude's account held far less than $25 000. That is still true. Second, after certification, but before Laurie presented the cheque for payment, Claude had gone to the bank and issued a countermand or stop order payment. In the circumstances, does Laurie have a right to receive payment from the Bank of St Albert? Does it matter whether the cheque was certified by Claude, as drawer, or by Laurie, as payee?

8. After opening up her first bank account, Chloe sat around with her friends one evening, playing with her new cheques. As a joke, she made a cheque for $10 000 payable to "Superman." At the end of the evening, Chloe simply threw that cheque into a trash can. During the evening, Simon, who works as a janitor in Chloe's apartment building, found the cheque and put it in his pocket. A few days later, he gave it to Ivan in exchange for a car engine. Ivan presented the cheque to Chloe's bank, which honoured the instrument and debited $10 000 from Chloe's account. Chloe has sued the bank on the basis that it disposed of her money without her authority. She insists that it must pay $10 000 to her. Is she correct? Explain your answer.

9. In late January, Kurtz Enterprises purchased office supplies from Kilgore Equipment. It paid with a promissory note for $25 000 that was made to the order of Kilgore Equipment and was due on September 1. In June, Kilgore specially endorsed the note and sold it to Willard Financial Inc. On September 1, Willard tried to claim $25 000 from the maker, only to discover that Kurtz Enterprises had disappeared. Over the next week, the president of Willard discussed the situation with her lawyer and accountant. On September 8, she contacted Kilgore Equipment and demanded payment. She took the position that Kilgore was liable on the basis of its endorsement. Is she correct? Explain your answer.

10. Dr Gaius, a veterinarian, bought a large shipment of medicine from George Taylor, who operated a medical supply company. Payment was made by way of a promissory note for $50 000, which was payable to Taylor in five equal monthly instalments beginning on August 15. Because Taylor doubted Dr Gaius's financial security, he required her to arrange for another signature to be added to the instrument. Dr Gaius persuaded her friend Cornelius McDowall to sign the back of the document alongside the words: "I will pay the debt if Dr Gaius cannot." The note also contained an acceleration clause. On the morning of August 15, Taylor telephoned Dr Gaius and reminded her that the first instalment of $10 000 was due. Using information that she had previously received from him, she deposited that amount into his bank account. In the early afternoon on the same day, Taylor sold the note to Kym Heston, who was unaware that Dr Gaius had already made the first payment. Not surprisingly, when Heston requested payment later that same day, Dr Gaius objected on the basis that she had already paid $10 000 to Taylor. Heston is sympathetic and points out that she had also been conned by Taylor, who had since disappeared. Nevertheless, having bought the note from Taylor, Heston wants payment. Is she entitled to any money? If so, when and from whom?

11. Earl Tetley worked as a payroll clerk for Tinwings Inc. Over the course of several months, he defrauded the company of about $250 000. His plan was simple. He drafted cheques, on behalf of the company, that were payable to people who had recently quit or been fired from Tinwings. He then forged the payees' blank endorsements and presented the cheques to the drawee, the Bank of Manitoba. The bank honoured the cheques, paid the money to Earl, and debited Tinwings's account. Tinwings eventually discovered that scheme. Although it normally would have contacted the police immediately, it hesitated to do so because Earl was the company president's nephew. Tinwings therefore agreed that it would keep the situation quiet as long as Earl repaid the money with interest within 18 months. After a year and a half, however, Earl had made only a token repayment of $5000. Earl has since been convicted and imprisoned for his fraud. Without any other option, Tinwings has now sued the Bank of Manitoba. The company argues that since the endorsements on the cheques were forged, the bank had no authority to debit its account. Is that correct? Explain your answer.

12. Marlon bought a delivery van for his business from Tanita for $20 000. Half of the purchase price was paid with cash, and the other half with a cheque that was payable to bearer. After meeting with Marlon, Tanita took the subway back to her office. Unfortunately, she forgot her purse, which contained both the cash and the cheque that she had received from Marlon, on the subway. After several days of frantic phone calls, it became clear to Tanita that the person who picked up her purse did not intend to return it. Has Tanita necessarily suffered a $20 000 loss? What should she do to minimize the damage? What should Marlon do?

WEBLINKS

Bills of Exchange Act   www.canlii.org/ca/sta/b-4

ADDITIONAL RESOURCES FOR CHAPTER 14 ON T HE COMPANION WEBSITE

(www.pearsoned.ca/mcinnes)

In addition to self-test multiple-choice, true-false, and short essay questions (all with immediate feedback), three additional Cases and Problems (with suggested answers), and links to useful Web destinations, the Companion Website provides the following resources for Chapter 14:

Provincial Material

- **Alberta:** Consumer Credit
- **Ontario:** Limitation Periods, Consumer Credit

15 Real Property: Interests and Leases

OBJECTIVES

After completing this chapter, you should be able to:

1. Name three types of estates, and explain how they differ from one another.

2. Describe the process of expropriation, and explain why it often creates ethical issues.

3. Distinguish between co-ownership and joint tenancy, and explain why one is often preferred in the business world.

4. Explain the nature of condominium ownership.

5. Define "easement," and explain how that type of interest can be created.

6. Distinguish between dominant tenements and servient tenements, and name two types of interests for which that distinction is important.

7. Outline the situations in which it is possible to enforce a restrictive covenant against a person who did not participate in its creation.

8. Distinguish between different types of leases on the basis of how long they last.

9. Outline the basic difference between an assignment and a sublease.

10. Define "quiet possession," and explain two ways in which a landlord can break that type of covenant.

real property includes land and anything attached to land

In this chapter, we begin our discussion of *real property*. Generally speaking, **real property** includes land and anything attached to land (such as fences and buildings).[1] Lawyers historically went much further and viewed real property rights in terms of the "giant carrot theory," which held that a person who owned a particular piece of land also owned the air up to the heavens and the ground down to the centre of the Earth. The modern approach, however, does not go that far. A landowner can control the airspace only to a reasonable height. While that test is rather vague, it does mean, for instance, that you can complain about a crane swinging over your property, but not about a plane flying safely overhead. Similarly, although there are few cases in the area, a landowner can control the ground only to a reasonable depth beneath the surface.

Despite those limitations, property rights remain critically important to Canadian business, even as our economy continues to move away from its traditional focus on natural products (like wheat and oil) to new forms of wealth (like ideas and information). Although a lot of commerce can now be conducted through computers from anywhere in the world, the vast majority of businesses still rely on real property. An Internet bookseller, for instance, requires a warehouse to store its products and probably at least one office for its personnel. Furthermore, just as a private residence is often a person's most valuable asset, real property often represents the largest part of a business's total wealth.

It is therefore important that you have a basic understanding of real property. However, real property is a notoriously large and complex body of law, which contains a number of specialized areas. For the purposes of risk management, many of those details can be left to the experts. A business person is not required, for instance, to know how to draft a long-term commercial lease. Lawyers are available for that purpose. From a business perspective, it is enough to appreciate the possibilities and to recognize the need for outside assistance.

This chapter is divided into two parts. The first summarizes the most important types of interests in land. The second describes the essential elements of leasing agreements. Chapter 16 continues the discussion of real property by explaining the process involved in the sale of real property. It also provides an overview of mortgages. Chapter 17 examines personal property.

INTERESTS IN LAND

an interest in land is a right that a person can enforce with respect to a particular piece of land

In this section, we consider different types of **interests in land**, that is, rights that a person can enforce with respect to a particular piece of land. Note that we are discussing rights to property *itself*. This is important. Suppose you buy a football stadium from me. Two sets of rights and obligations are created.

- First, you and I have a contract. Significantly, we are the only people affected by that agreement. It does not impose rights or obligations on anyone else in the world. Consequently, if I break my promise to transfer the land, I am the only person whom you can sue in contract. Likewise, if you fail to pay the price, I cannot demand the money from anyone other than you.

[1.] Land is called "real" property because the owner can recover the *res* (which is Latin for "thing") itself. If someone wrongfully takes your house, the law will evict them and allow you to regain possession. Other types of property are called "personal," because the courts usually will not allow you to recover the thing itself. If someone steals your cow, the law will probably only require the thief to pay you the monetary value of the animal. See Chapter 4.

- Second, once I transfer the property, the stadium belongs to you. If I continue using it for my own purposes, you can get a court order to evict me. Even more significantly, you can exercise the same rights against *anyone else* who interferes with your property rights. That is because property rights are good against the *whole world*, not just the person from whom they are acquired.[2]

Estates in Land

The most significant interests in land are called *estates*. An **estate** is an exclusive right to possess a property for a period of time. We will consider three varieties:

- the fee simple
- the life estate
- the leasehold estate

an **estate** is an exclusive right to possess land for a period of time

Fee Simple

A **fee simple** is the largest package of rights that a person can hold in land. Although it technically does not amount to absolute ownership, it comes very close.[3] Consequently, if you enjoy the fee simple in a particular property, you are entitled to possess it for an indefinite duration. You can sell it, lease it, or give it away tomorrow, or you can keep it until you die. And if you do hang on to it for the rest of your life, you are entitled to give it away upon your death. Furthermore, you can generally use or abuse the land however you want. You can maintain it in pristine condition, or you can clear it down to scorched earth.

a **fee simple** is the largest package of rights that a person can hold in land

Although your rights under a fee simple are very broad, they are subject to several important limitations. We mention three.

- First, as we saw in Chapter 5, whenever you possess land, you must avoid committing torts like occupiers' liability, nuisance, and the rule in *Rylands v Fletcher*. For instance, if you live in a residential suburb, you cannot operate a pig farm in your backyard. The stench would create a nuisance for your neighbours.
- Second, your use of the land is subject to various forms of regulation. For instance, governments are increasingly creating regulations to prevent people from using their properties in ways that hurt the *environment*.[4] Furthermore, every municipality in Canada uses *zoning and planning* regulations to control the types of activities that occur within certain areas. For example, you probably cannot build a casino on your land if a school is located next door.

[2.] That is also true for personal property, which we will discuss in Chapter 17. For instance, as Chapter 4 showed, you can use the tort of conversion against *anyone* who substantially interferes with your car. The entire world must respect your property rights in that vehicle.

[3.] Every piece of the land in Canada is ultimately owned by the Crown, that is, the government. For practical purposes, however, it is generally safe to treat the person with the fee simple as the owner. The Crown's interest is usually relevant only if that person dies without disposing of the property by will *and* without leaving behind any relatives to whom it can be given under *intestacy legislation*. Intestacy means that a person has died without a "testament," or will. In that case, the Crown will take control of the land.

[4.] Environmental regulations are discussed in Chapter 25.

expropriation occurs when the government takes property for a public purpose

■ Third, your property may be *expropriated*. **Expropriation** occurs when the government takes property for a public purpose, such as the construction of a new bridge or the widening of a highway. You will be entitled to compensation, but you cannot insist upon keeping the land. Similarly, even if the government does not expropriate a section of your land, it may exercise a right to build a sewer system underground or run telephone wires overhead. Expropriation can be particularly controversial in some situations. Consider Ethical Perspective 15.1.

ETHICAL PERSPECTIVE 15.1

Expropriation

Molly lives in a house in Come-by-Chance, Newfoundland, which her family has occupied for six generations. She was recently notified by the provincial government that her property was required for the purpose of constructing a natural gas pipeline that would substantially contribute to the region's economy. She insisted that she would never sell her ancestral home, but was told that she had no choice in the matter. While sympathetic to Molly's situation, the government noted several factors that identified her land as the only suitable place for the pipeline. For instance, her land was located near the gas well and the refinery. Furthermore, other nearby areas were especially vulnerable to environmental damage. The government also assured Molly that she would receive fair compensation. She tearfully insists that no amount of money could ever replace her home.

Question for Discussion

1. Is expropriation ethical? On what grounds do you base your answer?

Life Estate

a life estate entitles a person to exclusive possession of a property for the duration of a particular life

A *life estate* is similar to a fee simple, but it carries fewer rights. As the name suggests, a **life estate** entitles a person to exclusive possession of a property for the duration of a particular life. The life in question usually belongs to the person who holds the estate, but it can also belong to someone else. Suppose I hold the fee simple in a property and agree to sell a life estate to you. We might agree that the land is yours until you die *or* we might agree that your interest will exist only while my brother is alive. In either event, you will lose control of the property once the relevant life ends. At that time, I will regain control. In most instances, the property will simply come back to me (or to my estate if I have already died) by way of a **reversion**. Alternatively, if I transfer my reversionary interest to someone else, that person will take the property as a **remainder**.

a reversion occurs when the property returns to the person who holds the fee simple

a remainder occurs when the property goes to a third party who was selected by the person who holds the fee simple

waste occurs when a property is changed in a way that significantly affects its value

The rights under a life estate are limited in another important way. A person with a fee simple is generally free to use or abuse the property. The situation is somewhat different with a life estate. A person who holds that sort of interest is normally entitled to the profits that are generated from the land, but cannot commit an act of *waste*. **Waste** occurs when a property is changed in a way that significantly affects its value. That includes, for example, digging pits and cutting down trees. A person with a life estate who commits an act of waste can be held liable to the person who holds the reversion or remainder. The rule against waste normally applies, however, only to acts and not to omissions. Consequently, if you purchase a life estate from me, you cannot demolish a building without my permission, but you are not required to spend money to keep that building in good condition.

Life estates are often useful in family situations.[5] Suppose you hold the fee simple in a residential property that you share with your younger sister, who has a disability. While you want your younger brother to eventually inherit that house, you also want to ensure that your sister always has a place to live after you are gone. Consequently, you draft a will that leaves the fee simple to your brother, but that also carves out a life estate for your sister. Upon your death, she will enjoy the use of the property for the rest of her life (assuming that she does not predecease you) and then the land will go to your brother (or his estate if he has died by that point). In the business world, however, life estates tend to be unattractive. Because it is impossible to determine when a person will die, and when their interest will come to an end, life estates are usually too unpredictable for business people. Certainty is important in the commercial world.

Leasehold Estate

A **leasehold estate** occurs when a person has exclusive rights to a property for a specific period of time. A lease is like a fee simple or a life interest because it carries the right of exclusive possession. But a lease is also different because it is not defined by a life. A person with a fee simple can retain the property for life and then dispose of it upon death. A person with a life estate can retain the property during the relevant lifetime. A person with a lease can retain the property for only a specific block of time. That block may be long or short—a day or a century, for instance. It may be limited to a single term, or it may be automatically renewed if neither party objects. But in any event, the duration of the lease is established at the outset. It does not depend upon the length of any particular life. We will discuss leases in the last section of this chapter.

Concept Summary 15.1 reviews the main differences between a fee simple, a life estate, and a lease.

a **leasehold estate** occurs when a person has exclusive rights to a property for a specific period of time

---

CONCEPT SUMMARY 15.1

Fee Simple, Life Estate, and Lease

Type of Estate	Nature and Duration of Estate
Fee simple	right to exclusive possession during own life *and* right to dispose of property upon death
Life estate	right to exclusive possession during relevant life *but no* right to dispose of property upon death
Lease	right to exclusive possession during specified period

Shared Ownership

To this point, we have assumed that an estate—whether a fee simple, a life interest, or a lease—is owned by only one person. However, ownership can also be shared among several people. It is therefore important to distinguish

---

[5.] In the family context, life estates are sometimes imposed as a matter of law. For example, a woman was historically entitled upon her husband's death to *dower*, which was a life interest in one-third of any real property in which he held a fee simple. Because of problems associated with that rule, dower has been abolished in Canada and replaced with a variety of even more extensive statutory rights.

individual ownership and *shared ownership*. For the purposes of discussion, suppose there is a large piece of land for sale.

- If you buy the east half and I buy the west half, we *do not* share ownership. Rather, the single piece of land is divided in two, and we each become the *individual* owner of a separate piece. I can put a fence around my property to keep you out, and you can do the same to me.

- In contrast, if we act together and buy *undivided interests* in a single piece of land, we *do* share ownership. We are both owners of the *same* property. Furthermore, we both own the *whole* property. Consequently, neither one of us can put a fence around any part of the land to keep the other out.[6] One very common example of shared ownership occurs when a couple buys a home together.

There are two important types of shared ownership:

- joint ownership (or *joint tenancy*)
- co-ownership (or *co-tenancy* or *tenancy in common*)

joint ownership occurs when two or more people share exactly the same interest in a property

Joint ownership occurs when two or more people share *exactly* the same interests in a property. Consequently, if you and I are joint tenants with two other people, we each have a 25 percent interest.[7] The most significant feature of a joint tenancy is the *right of survivorship*. The **right of survivorship** means that upon death, a joint tenant's interest automatically passes to the remaining joint tenants. For instance, if I die first, my interest must pass to you and the others—I cannot give it away to anyone else. You and the other joint tenants will then each have a 33 percent interest in the property. That process can be repeated until the last surviving joint tenant takes the whole property.

the **right of survivorship** means that upon death, a joint tenant's interest automatically passes to the remaining joint tenants

co-ownership occurs when two or more people share an undivided interest in a property

Co-ownership also occurs when two or more people share an undivided interest in a property. However, there are at least two important differences between co-ownership and joint ownership.

- Co-owners do not have to have *exactly* the same interests. Assume, once again, that you and I share ownership with two other people. While our shares must be undivided, in the sense that none of us can assert individual rights over any particular piece of ground, they do not have to be equal. For instance, I may own a 70 percent interest, while you and the other co-owners each enjoy 10 percent interests.[8]

- More significantly, co-owners do not enjoy the right of survivorship. Consequently, if I die first, you and the other co-owners will not automatically acquire my interest. I can, for instance, leave my share to a friend, who would then become a co-owner along with you and the others.

The differences between co-tenancy and joint tenancy may affect the type of ownership that you choose for your business. Consider Business Decision 15.1.

[6.] You and I can use a contract to change the rule between ourselves. For instance, we may agree that, while we share ownership of the whole property, you can put a fence around the east part, and I can put a fence around the west part.

[7.] Each of us is therefore generally entitled to 25 percent of the profits from the land. That rule applies to profits that are received from a *third party* (for example, by renting the property to an outsider). It might be different, however, if one of us earns profits through our own labour (for example, by harvesting raspberries).

[8.] I am therefore entitled to 70 percent of the general profits, while you and the others each get 10 percent.

BUSINESS DECISION 15.1

Choice of Shared Ownership

You and your partner have enjoyed great success over the years in a variety of business ventures. As you both near an early retirement at age 60, you decide to enter into one last project. Together you obtain a 75-year lease over a parcel of land on the outskirts of town. You do so with the intention of developing a theme park.

Questions for Discussion

1. Should your shared ownership take the form of a co-tenancy or a joint tenancy?

2. What if the other person is your "partner" in the sense of being the person with whom you have shared an intimate, monogamous, co-habitational relationship for four decades?

3. What if the other person is your "partner" in the sense of being the person with whom, in a purely professional capacity, you have made a great deal of money? Assume that you also have a "partner" of the other sort, with whom you have produced five children.

Joint tenants can avoid the right of survivorship through the process of *severance*.[9] **Severance** occurs when a joint tenant deals with the property in a way that is inconsistent with joint ownership. Suppose you jointly owned a cottage along with my sister and me. You then sold your interest to a stranger. You are no longer an owner of any kind. Furthermore, while the stranger has become *some* kind of owner, he is *not* a joint tenant with my sister and me. He does not have *exactly* the same interest as us, since he acquired his rights after we acquired ours. Consequently, while my sister and I are still joint tenants with respect to each other, we are co-tenants with respect to the stranger.

severance occurs when a joint tenant deals with the property in a way that is inconsistent with joint ownership

The right of survivorship can be lost in other ways as well. One of the most significant is through the process of *partition*.[10] **Partition** occurs when there is a division of either the property or its sale proceeds. The parties may agree among themselves as to who gets what. But if they cannot do so, they can ask a judge to resolve the matter. The courts generally have a broad discretion in deciding whether to physically divide the land, sell the land and divide the proceeds, or refuse relief altogether.[11]

partition occurs when there is a separation of the property or its sale proceeds

Concept Summary 15.2 (see page 340) summarizes the most important features of shared ownership.

Condominiums

It is sometimes possible to have both individual ownership *and* shared ownership. The most common example involves *condominiums*. A **condominium** exists when several people share ownership of some parts of a building, while

a **condominium** exists when several people share ownership of some parts of a building, while individually owning other parts

---

[9.] The law tries to avoid the right of survivorship by assuming, in the absence of evidence to the contrary, that property held under shared ownership is subject to a tenancy in common, rather than a joint tenancy.

[10.] It is generally said that a joint tenancy may be severed in three ways. First, as suggested by the last paragraph, a new interest may be created that is different from the rest. Second, the parties may agree together to sever their joint tenancy. And third, some other event may have the effect of turning a joint tenancy into a tenancy in common. That may be true, for example, if one party becomes bankrupt, if one party's share is forcibly sold through a court process, or if one joint tenant murders another: *Schobelt v Barber* (1966) 60 DLR (2d) 519 (Ont HC).

[11.] Although the procedures vary between jurisdictions, it is usually possible to bring either form of shared ownership to an end through the process of partition.

CONCEPT SUMMARY 15.2

Shared Ownership

Type of Shared Ownership	Description	Nature of Interests	Effect Upon Death
Joint ownership	two or more people share *the same* undivided interests in a property	each person's interest must be *exactly* the same as the other's (*eg* ownership between two parties must be split 50–50)	right of survivorship: deceased's interest automatically passes to remaining joint tenant
Co-ownership	two or more people share *some* undivided interests in a property	each person may have a *different* undivided interest (*eg* ownership between two parties may be split 70–30)	no right of survivorship: deceased's interest passes to person named in will or to next-of-kin

individually owning other parts.[12] Although the legislation varies considerably across the country, the basic arrangement is always the same.[13] A building is divided into a number of separate units, plus a variety of common areas (such as hallways, stairwells, parking lots, and tennis courts). The separate units are usually residential, but they may also be used for commercial purposes, such as restaurants and shops. If you purchase a unit in a condominium, you receive three sets of rights.

- First, you receive individual ownership of that particular unit. Your rights closely resemble those of a fee simple, except that you do not have the exclusive right to possess a piece of ground, as well as a portion of the earth below and the sky above. Instead, you have a "flying fee." In other words, while you do have a large bundle of rights, they apply only to the specific unit that is held in the air by the other parts of the building.

- Second, you and the other individual unit owners share ownership of the common areas as tenants in common. As a result, subject to any more specific rules or arrangements that may be created by contract, you can all use those common areas, such as the pool.

- Third, as you can see, a condominium is a small community. And like other communities, it requires decisions to be made and enforced. For those reasons, it will have a *condominium corporation*, which is a non-profit organization that manages the complex. As the owner of a separate unit, you are entitled to vote on matters concerning the corporation, such as the creation of bylaws and the election of directors. You are also required to pay condominium fees, which are effectively the community's tax.

[12.] The word "condominium" is derived from the Latin words meaning "joint" (*com*) and "control" (*dominium*).

[13.] *Condominium Property Act*, RSA 2000, c C-22 (Alta); *Condominium Act*, RSBC 1996, c 64 (BC); *Condominium Act*, CCSM, c C170 (Man); *Condominium Property Act*, RSNB 1973, c C-16 (NB); *Condominium Act*, RSNL 1990, c C-29 (Nfld); *Condominium Act*, RSNWT 1988, c C-15 (NWT and Nun); *Condominium Act*, RSNS 1989, c 85 (NS); *Condominium Act, 1998*, SO 1998, c 19 (Ont); *Condominium Act*, RSPEI 1988, c C-16 (PEI); *Condominium Property Act*, RSS 1978, c C-26 (Sask); *Condominium Act*, RSY 2002, c 36 (Yuk).

Non-Possessory Interests in Land

We have examined several property interests that provide a right to possession. Canadian law also recognizes a number of *non-possessory* interests in land. In other words, a person may have rights in a property, without being able to actually possess that property. We will briefly discuss three important possibilities:

- easements
- restrictive covenants
- mineral leases

Easements

An **easement** is a right to use a neighbour's land. Most easements are positive. For instance, you might let me drive across your property to reach a road, or periodically drain my water reservoir onto your land. While less common, an easement can also be negative. For instance, you might be prohibited from constructing a building that would deprive my house of sunlight, or from cutting down a line of trees that protects my fields from wind erosion.

As our examples suggest, an easement can exist only between neighbours. While our properties do not necessarily have to be touching, they do have to be reasonably close together. I must be able to show that I have the **dominant tenement**—the property that benefits from the easement, and that you have the **servient tenement**—the property that accommodates the easement. As long as those requirements are met, an easement can **run with the land**. That means that it can apply even if different people acquire possession of the affected properties.

An easement can be created in several ways.

- **Express:** The simplest method is for the parties to expressly agree to create an easement. For example, before selling part of my land to you, I might insist that our contract recognize my right to swim in the pond that will be located on your part of the property.

- **Implied:** An easement can also arise by necessary implication. For instance, I might buy a section of your land without realizing that my new property is completely cut off from the highway. In that situation, the courts will presume, unless there is evidence to the contrary, that we silently agreed that I would be allowed to drive across the remaining section of your property to reach the highway.

- **Prescription:** The law traditionally allowed an easement to be acquired by *prescription*, even if there was no agreement between the parties.[14] Prescription exists in only some jurisdictions in Canada.[15] Although the rules vary from place to place, the basic idea is the same. An easement by **prescription** is created if land is used in a particular way, for a long time (usually 20 years), without secrecy, without objection, and without permission. Suppose I have openly used a portion of your backlot for a

an **easement** is a right to use a neighbour's land

a **dominant tenement** is a property that benefits from an easement

a **servient tenement** is a property that accommodates an easement

an easement can **run with the land** and therefore be enforceable by or against whoever owns the land

an easement by **prescription** is created if land is used in a particular way, for a long time, without secrecy, without objection, and without permission

---

[14.] In this context, "prescription" is derived from an old English word meaning "establishment of a claim."

[15.] Prescription is generally abolished in those jurisdictions that use a *land titles* system of registration. The aim of that system, which is discussed in Chapter 16, is to provide documents which make it clear, at all times, what interests exist in each piece of land. Interests that arise by operation of law tend to frustrate that goal because they are hidden from view.

compost heap for decades. You have done nothing about it. The law may now recognize an easement that provides me with the right to continue dumping on your property.[16]

- **Statutory:** Statutes often give utility companies and similar organizations the right to bury television cables, dig sewers, and so on. The telephone company can, for instance, run wires over your yard even if its office is not located nearby. Although such rights are often called *public easements* or *statutory easements*, they are not true easements because there is no dominant tenement.

a **licence** is permission to act in a way that would otherwise be prohibited

It is important to distinguish an easement from a mere *licence*. A **licence** is permission to act in a way that would otherwise be prohibited. For example, if your property is located close to a stadium, you might allow me to park on your lawn while I attend a football game. Unlike an easement, a licence is not an interest in land, it does not run with the property, and it can be revoked at any time (subject to any contractual rights that may exist between the parties). Furthermore, because a licence is not an easement, it does not require the existence of dominant and servient tenements.

Restrictive Covenants

a **restrictive covenant** is a promise to use piece of land in a way that benefits one property and burdens another

An easement must be distinguished from a *restrictive covenant*. A **restrictive covenant** is a promise to use a piece of land in a way that benefits one property and burdens another. It is like an easement because it requires a dominant tenement and a servient tenement. In other respects, however, it is quite different. First, while an easement can sometimes arise through prescription, a restrictive covenant can only be created by agreement. Second, a restrictive covenant never allows me to use your land. It merely limits how you can use your own property.[17]

Restrictive covenants raise difficult issues of enforcement. Suppose I own several business chains, including one that rebuilds abandoned vehicles. You own a large piece of land, which you use in part to operate a florist shop. You are willing to sell half of that property to me, but you are concerned that I might behave in a way that scares off your customers and hurts the value of your land. Consequently, when drafting the sale contract, we insert two *covenants*, which are promises that are written and placed under seal.

- Under the first, I promise that I will repaint the buildings on my part of the land every two years.
- Under the second, I promise that I will not use my premises as an autobody shop.

Are those promises enforceable? What if one or both of us later sell our properties—you to Miguel and me to Janet? The answers to those questions depend upon (i) the identity of the parties, and (ii) the nature of the covenant. We consider the three situations shown in Figure 15.1.

[16.] While less common, a *possessory interest* may be acquired through the similar process of *adverse possession*. If I openly take possession of your land and continuously treat it as my own for a long time (usually 20 years), I may become the owner of that property if you fail to assert your rights against me. Once again, that doctrine has generally been modified or abolished in those parts of the country that use the land title system of registration.

[17.] That limitation cannot be immoral or against public policy. For example, the courts will not enforce a promise that discriminates against people on the grounds of race or religion.

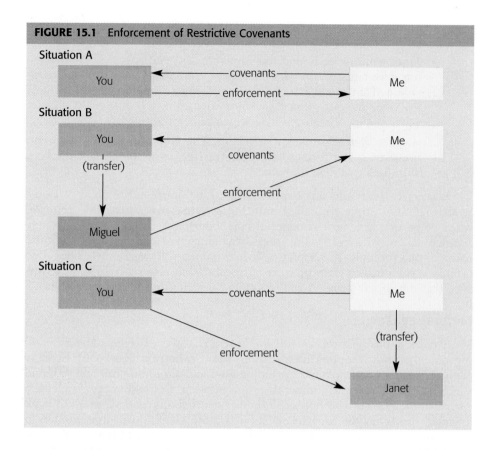

FIGURE 15.1 Enforcement of Restrictive Covenants

- **Situation A:** If we both still own the properties, you can sue me if I break either promise. You are entitled to damages if my breach creates a loss. I might also be forced, through specific performance or an injunction, to actually fulfill my promises.

- **Situation B:** Now assume that while you sold your property to Miguel, I still have mine. A potential problem arises. As we saw in Chapter 8, a contract can usually be enforced only by someone with *privity*, who was a party to the original agreement. However, as we also saw, that rule has exceptions. Perhaps most significantly, contractual *benefits* can generally be *assigned*. Consequently, as long as the original covenants were intended to run with the land, Miguel can sue me if I break either promise.

- **Situation C:** What if you held on to your property, but I sold my property to Janet? If she refused to paint the buildings or if she opened an autobody shop, could you sue her? This situation appears to be similar to the last one, but there is an additional complication. It is generally possible to assign contractual *benefits*, but not contractual *burdens*. The courts are reluctant to impose obligations upon a person simply because they bought a piece of land. Consequently, in deciding whether Janet is caught by the covenants, a judge would look at several factors.[18]

  • Janet may be bound by a *negative* covenant, but not by a *positive* one. She could be *prevented* from doing something, but she could not be *required* to do something else. Accordingly, while she could be

---

18. *Tulk v Moxhay* (1848) 41 ER 1143 (Ch).

restrained from opening an autobody shop, she could not be compelled to paint her buildings.[19]

- Janet will *not* be bound unless, as the original parties, we intended our covenants to *run with the land* so as to benefit the dominant tenement. That might be true if our agreement was intended to protect the value of your property, whoever owned it.

- Janet will *not* be bound if she bought the land without any reason to suspect that there was a covenant. The situation will be different, however, if she received the land for free, or if she bought the land with notice of the covenant.

Restrictive covenants are sometimes used to control entire areas of a city. In that situation, they are called **building scheme covenants**. For example, when constructing a new residential neighbourhood, a land developer may create a scheme that limits the range of colours that can be used for house paint, or that prohibits the display of lawn ornaments. By agreeing to obey such promises, each owner gives up a bit of freedom, but also receives some assurance that the neighbourhood will retain its character and its market value.

a **building scheme covenant** is a collection of restrictive covenants that are used to control the development of an entire area

Mineral Leases

Many types of business rely on *mineral leases*. That phrase tends to be misleading and therefore requires clarification. First, **minerals** consist of virtually every substance in the ground, including gold and aluminum, oil and gas, and sand and gravel. Second, a mineral lease is different from other types of leases. As usual, the person who holds the right is entitled to possess a piece of land. Typically, however, the area in question is quite small—just large enough to facilitate the mining operation. After all, the aim of a **mineral lease** is to allow one person to extract and retain something of value from another person's property.

minerals consist of virtually every substance contained in the ground

a **mineral lease** allows one person to extract and retain something of value from another person's property

There are two more important things to note about mineral leases.

- Most mineral leases are acquired from the government, even if the fee simple to the affected property belongs to someone else. All of the land in Canada starts with the Crown, which can then distribute it through *grants*. Grants historically included mineral rights. Since the 1880s, however, the government has *reserved* those rights by keeping them for itself. As a result, depending upon where you live in this country, you probably do not have the right to sell the valuable deposits that lie beneath your property. The government does.

- A mineral lease is similar to *profit à prendre*. A **profit à prendre** is a right to take something valuable away from another person's property.[20] That sort of right can apply not only to minerals, but also to other natural things, like blueberries and moose. Significantly, like a mineral lease, a *profit à prendre* is an interest in land, but not an automatic right to the things in question. Consequently, if you buy a *profit à prendre* with respect to the trees on my property, the timber does not belong to you until you actually harvest it from my land.

a *profit à prendre* is a right to take something valuable away from another person's property

---

[19.] Similarly, as we saw in Chapter 12, courts ar more willing to award injunctions than specific performance. An order that *prevents* a person from doing something limits their freedom of choice less than an order that *requires* them to do something.

[20.] The term "*à prendre*" is derived from French and means "a right to take."

Concept Summary 15.3 reviews various types of non-possessory interests.

CONCEPT SUMMARY 15.3

Non-Possessory Interests in Land

Type of Interest	Description	Dominant Tenement Required?
Easement	a right to use a piece of land in a way that benefits a neighbouring piece of land (for example, a right to take water from a neighbour's lake)	yes
Restrictive covenant	a restriction that is placed on one property in order to benefit a neighbouring property (for example, a promise to not construct a building that would block sunlight from entering a neighbour's garden)	yes
Mineral lease	a right to remove minerals from a piece of land (for example, a right to extract oil from beneath a property)	no
Profit à prendre	a right to take something valuable away from a piece of land (for example, a right to cut and remove timber from a property)	no

LEASES

We have already seen that a lease is an estate in land that creates an exclusive right to possession. However, given the significant role that leases play in the modern business world, it is necessary to look at them in detail.[21]

A **lease**, or a *tenancy* as it is sometimes called, is a property interest created by contract. Therefore, the usual contractual requirements must be satisfied, including intention to create legal relations, offer and acceptance, and consideration. In addition, while most contracts can be created orally, some leases must be put into print. The legislation varies from jurisdiction to jurisdiction, but the basic rule is that a lease must be evidenced in writing unless it is for three years or less.[22] Although an oral lease for a longer period is valid, it is generally unenforceable and therefore can be ignored by either party.[23] (As a general rule, to reduce the danger of uncertainty and litigation, you should put *all* of your contracts into writing.) Because a lease is created by contract, there must be a mutual agreement between two parties: the *landlord* and the *tenant*. The **landlord** is the person with an interest in land who agrees to allow someone else to take possession.[24] The **tenant** is the person who receives the right to possess the property.

> a lease is a property interest created by contract

> the landlord is the person with an interest in land who agrees to allow someone else to take possession

> the tenant is the person who receives the right to possess the property

---

[21.] In this chapter, we are only concerned with leases of land. As we will see in Chapter 17, it is also possible to lease other types of property.

[22.] *Law and Equity Act*, RSBC 1996, c 253 (BC); *Statute of Frauds*, RSNB 1973, c S-14, s 7 (NB); *Statute of Frauds*, RSNS 1989, c 442, s 3 (NS); *Statute of Frauds*, RSO 1990, c S.19, ss 1–3 (Ont); *Statute of Frauds*, 1677 (Eng), c 3, ss 1–2 (Alta, Nfld, NWT, Nun, PEI, Sask, Yuk). In Manitoba, the English *Statute of Frauds* has been repealed by RSM 1987, c F158.

[23.] An exception may be created by part performance if the tenant is actually in possession *and* has paid rent.

[24.] Although the landlord typically holds the fee simple in the property, it is also possible for a person with a life estate, or even an earlier lease, to grant a new lease. That last possibility is called a *sublease* and it is discussed below.

Duration

When a fee simple or a life estate is created, there is no way of knowing exactly how long it will last. The relevant life may continue for decades or end the next day. The maximum duration of a lease, however, must be definite. Consequently, it would not be possible to create a lease that would last "until the Maple Leafs next win the Cup."[25] There are several possibilities.

a **fixed-term tenancy** exists when it is possible at the outset to determine when the tenancy will end

- **Fixed-term tenancy:** A **fixed-term tenancy** exists when it is possible at the outset to determine when the tenancy will end. The parties may actually specify a date, such as "December 31, 2020." Alternatively, if they do not know a specific date at the outset, they may provide a formula that is capable of generating one, such as "the last day of Ramadan in 2020." Even if they initially agreed to a fixed term, the parties can enter into new lease at the end of the old one. And even if they do not create a new fixed-term lease, a *periodic tenancy* may arise if the tenant remains in possession and the landlord continues to accept rent at regular intervals.

a **periodic tenancy** is for a fixed period and is automatically renewed at the end of each term unless one of the parties provides notice of termination

- **Periodic tenancy:** A **periodic tenancy** is also for a fixed period, but it is automatically renewed at the end of each term unless one of the parties provides *notice to quit*. You are probably most familiar with that type of lease, since it is generally used for residential tenancies. The basic term of the lease can be for any length of time. A week, a month, and a year are the most common options. As a general rule, the length of the term mirrors the intervals at which the tenant pays rent. The length of the term usually also mirrors the notice period. Consequently, to terminate a monthly lease, you must provide one clear month's notice.[26] (A longer notice period is required under a residential lease.) A yearly tenancy, however, normally only requires six months' notice.[27]

a **tenancy at will** exists if there is no set term and either party can terminate the lease at any time

- **Tenancy at will:** A **tenancy at will** exists if there is no set term and either party can terminate the lease at any time. Because there is no definite duration, it is sometimes said that a tenancy at will is not really a leasehold estate. Nevertheless, there is at least an implicit agreement between the parties, and the tenant is liable to pay rent. Tenancies at will most often arise when the owner of a property allows a potential purchaser to move in before the sale is finalized, or when a tenant remains on the premises with the landlord's consent after the end of a lease.[28]

a **tenancy at sufferance** occurs when a tenant continues to possess the premises at the end of a lease without the landlord's permission

- **Tenancy at sufferance:** A **tenancy at sufferance** occurs when a tenant continues to possess the premises at the end of a lease *without* the landlord's permission. In that situation, there is not really a lease because the parties do not even have an implied agreement. Indeed, tenant who does not vacate the property within a reasonable time after being asked to do so commits the tort of trespass (as discussed in Chapter 4), and the landlord can take steps to have the tenant forcibly removed. While there is no

---

[25.] The *maximum* duration must be definite, but a tenancy may end earlier. Therefore it would be possible to have a lease "for 999 years or until the Maple Leafs next win the Cup."

[26.] Note that the period is one *clear* month's notice. For example, if you want to vacate the premises at the end of July, you must give notice by the end of June. If you wait until the first day of July, your lease will continue until the end of August.

[27.] In New Brunswick, Nova Scotia, and Prince Edward Island, the notice period is only three months.

[28.] However, if the landlord continues to receive rent from the tenant at regular intervals, a court may recognize the creation of a periodic tenancy, with the result that notice must be given in a timely manner to terminate the new lease.

obligation to pay "rent" (because there is no tenancy), the person in possession is required to pay compensation for the use and occupation of the property.[29]

Assignments and Subleases

As a tenant, you may find that you do not want to occupy the premises for the full length of your lease. Perhaps you have been transferred to another city and no longer require an apartment. Perhaps your business has fallen on hard times and you no longer can afford to rent a warehouse. You have several options.

- You might persuade your landlord to terminate the lease early. That is unlikely to happen, however, unless you also introduce the landlord to a new tenant.

- Even if you cannot escape your lease, you might be able to *assign* it. As we saw in Chapter 8, an **assignment** occurs when you transfer your contractual rights to a third party. That third party (the *assignee*) would step into your shoes (at least for some purposes) and become the tenant. That possibility is subject to four limitations.

  *an **assignment** occurs when a contractual party transfers its rights to a third party*

  - Although contractual rights can generally be assigned, your lease may either prohibit an assignment or require your landlord's consent (which, your lease may also say, cannot be withheld "unreasonably").[30] Such provisions are very common. Landlords want control over the people who occupy their premises.

  - Second, an assignment would not necessarily include all of the terms in the lease. The assignee would only be bound by the *real covenants*. **Real covenants** include promises that are directly related to the land (like the obligation to pay rent or repair the premises), but not merely personal obligations (like the landlord's promise to buy goods from the original tenant's warehouse).

    real covenants include promises that are directly related to the land, but not merely personal obligations

  - Third, an assignment would not necessarily protect you from liability. If your assignee did not fulfill the lease, the landlord could normally demand relief from you. You could ask your landlord to release you from responsibility, but the landlard would probably refuse. You should therefore ensure that your assignment requires the assignee to honour the lease *and* to compensate you for any money that you may have to pay to the landlord.

  - Fourth, an assignment must cover the entire term of a lease. If it falls short, even by one day, then it cannot be an assignment—but it may be a *sublease*.

- A **sublease** occurs when a tenant grants a lease to a third party.[31] In that case, the third party would not step into your shoes. You would continue

  *a **sublease** occurs when a tenant grants a lease to a third party*

---

29. If the landlord does accept "rental" payments, a court may recognize the implied creation of a periodic tenancy.

30. To protect tenants, some jurisdictions have legislation to that effect unless the parties expressly say otherwise: *Landlord and Tenant Act*, CCSM, c L70, s 22 (Man); *Landlord and Tenant Act*, RSNB 1973, c L-1, s 11 (NB); *Commercial Tenancies Act*, RSNWT 1988, c C-10, s 11 (NWT and Nun); *Commercial Tenancies Act*, RSO 1990, c L.7, s 23 (Ont); *Landlord and Tenant Act*, RSPEI 1988, c L-4, s 12 (PEI); *Landlord and Tenant Act*, RSS 1978, c L-6, s 13 (Sask); *Landlord and Tenant Act*, RSY 2002, c 131, s 11 (Yuk).

31. It is often difficult to distinguish between an assignment and a sublease. There is no magic in words. A court will base its decision on the substance of the transaction, rather than the language that the parties used.

to be the tenant under the original lease, but you would also be a land-lord under the sublease. Your sublease might apply to the whole property or to just one section of it. Similarly, it might contain the same terms as the original lease, but it need not do so. Once again, however, the original lease may prohibit subleasing or require you to obtain your landlord's consent.

Commercial Leases

Generally speaking, there are two types of leases: *commercial* and *residential*. We will focus on the former, and discuss the latter briefly at the end of this chapter.

Standard Covenants

a **commercial lease** occurs when premises are rented for a business purpose

A **commercial lease** occurs when premises are rented for a business purpose. Although some modifications have been introduced by statute or by the common law, the basic contractual rules apply, and the parties are generally free to set their own terms. Consequently, depending upon the circumstances, a commercial lease may consist of a book-length document (for the long-term lease of an office tower) or a few words written on the back of an envelope (for temporary use of a patch of ground as a souvenir kiosk along a parade route). Nevertheless, certain *covenants*, or promises, are standard.

Perhaps the most obvious covenant is the tenant's obligation to pay *rent*. Although that concept may seem obvious, it is important to appreciate a number of specific points.

- **Express or implied:** The parties will normally set the rent in advance. But even if they do not expressly agree on a price, the law will normally require the payment of a "reasonable" amount.
- **Calculation of rent:** In residential leases, the rent is usually set at a flat rate that reflects the type of tenancy. For instance, a periodic tenancy for an apartment may require the tenant to pay $1000 per month to the landlord. The rent provision in a commercial lease is often more complicated. For instance, the rent may be based on the size of the premises. An accountant in a business complex may pay $10 per foot for an office. If the unit has 1000 square feet, then the rent will be $10 000 per year. Alternatively, the rent may be calculated on the basis of the profits that the tenant earns on the premises. For instance, a store in a shopping mall may be required to pay 10 per cent of gross profits. If the store earns $400 000 during a particular year, then the landlord is entitled to receive $40 000.
- *Rent review:* Many commercial leases last for long periods. Very often, however, it would be unreasonable to use the same rent for the entire time. Commercial leases therefore often allow for periodic reviews. The parties may agree, for instance, that they will negotiate a new rent every five years. They may also agree that the new rate will reflect prevailing market values or some percentage of the tenant's profits. And because the parties may not be able to reach an agreement, the lease may also require disputes to be sent to an arbitrator.[32]

[32.] Arbitration was discussed in Chapter 2. A sample of a rent review arbitration clause can be found on the Companion Website for Chapter 2.

- **Independent obligation:** Perhaps surprisingly, the obligation to pay rent is generally independent of other obligations in the lease. As a result, a tenant has no right to refuse to pay rent even if (for instance) the landlord fails to honour a promise to keep the property in good repair. In that situation, the tenant is expected to pay the rent and sue the landlord for breach of contract.

A covenant for **quiet possession** prohibits the landlord from interfering with the tenant's enjoyment of the premises.[33] That covenant can be broken in a number of ways.

a covenant for quiet possession prohibits the landlord from interfering with the tenant's enjoyment of the premises

- The landlord may be unable to grant an effective lease because, for example, the property is still occupied by another tenant.
- The landlord may disturb the tenant's use of the premises by, for example, allowing carbon monoxide to seep up from a parking lot, or habitually using a jackhammer that causes an intolerable amount of noise and vibration.
- While the landlord is not responsible for another tenant's *wrongful* behaviour, it may be liable for granting a lease with an incompatible use by, for example, allowing a bowling alley to operate directly over a relaxation clinic.

Depending upon the circumstances, a court may respond to a breach of a covenant for quiet possession in various ways:

- award an injunction requiring the landlord to remedy the interference
- allow the tenant to discharge the lease and recover compensatory damages
- allow the tenant to have a reduction in rent

As a general rule, a landlord is under no obligation to *repair or maintain* the premises before or during a lease. However, if the property is in *very poor* condition, there may be a breach of the covenant for quiet possession. Nor is the tenant generally responsible for fixing or replacing things that are broken or worn as a result of normal wear and tear, such as fallen fence posts or threadbare carpets. The tenant is, however, responsible for any damage that it intentionally or negligently causes. It is also required to treat the premises in a "tenant-like manner" by doing things like unplugging blocked toilets.[34] Because neither party has extensive obligations under the common law, commercial leases almost always impose additional responsibilities concerning repair and maintenance. It is in no one's interest to allow the property to become completely run down.

Unless the parties otherwise agree, the landlord is required to pay the *taxes* associated with a property. And while neither party is generally obliged to obtain *insurance* over the premises, the landlord normally does so to protect its investment. In some cases, the lease will shift the expense of that insurance to the tenant. And as a matter of risk management, the tenant should, in any event, obtain insurance coverage for the things that it stores on the premises and for any damage that it may cause to outsiders. For instance, a fire may not only destroy the contents of the rental unit, but also spread to a neighbouring property.

[33.] A landlord is, however, entitled to inspect the premises occasionally for signs of damage and abuse.

[34.] *Warren v Keen* [1954] 1 KB 15 (CA).

Remedies

A commercial lease is created by contract and therefore supports the usual contractual remedies if there is a breach. We referred to several options in Chapter 12, including compensatory damages, injunctions, and discharge. There are also several special forms of relief that may be available to a landlord if the tenant commits a serious breach. We can mention two.

eviction or **right of re-entry** allows a landlord to resume possession of the premises

forfeiture occurs when a tenant loses its interest in a property

- **Eviction:** If the tenant commits a serious breach, such as not paying the rent, the landlord may be entitled to exercise a right of **eviction** (sometimes called a **right of re-entry**) to resume possession of the premises before the end of the lease. That remedy often creates hardship for the tenant because it results in a **forfeiture**—the tenant loses its interest in the property. Consequently, even if a tenant has committed a serious breach, a court may grant relief from forfeiture by allowing the tenant to make amends and to retain possession of the property. Each jurisdiction has detailed legislation regarding evictions.

distress occurs when the landlord seizes the tenant's belongings and sells them in order to pay the rent

- **Distress:** If a tenant is not evicted for not paying the rent, it may be subject to the remedy of *distress*. **Distress** occurs when the landlord seizes the tenant's belongings and sells them to pay the rent. Once again, each jurisdiction has detailed legislation on this point.

Finally, it is important to note that some of the rules that normally govern contractual remedies may not apply to commercial leases. As we discussed in Chapter 12, a person who suffers a breach of contract can claim *expectation damages* for the benefit it should have received under the agreement. Those damages are reduced, however, to the extent that the plaintiff unreasonably failed to *mitigate* a loss. Suppose I agree to buy a car from you for $9000. I later refuse to go through with that deal when I learn that the car is worth only $6000. It seems that your expectation damages are $3000, which was your expected profit. However, you will only be entitled to $2000 if I can prove that you could have resold the car to someone else for $7000. You are responsible for the other $1000 because you unreasonably failed to mitigate that loss by selling the car to a third party.

That same rule may not apply to commercial leases. Although the cases are inconsistent, the Supreme Court of Canada has suggested that if a tenant wrongfully vacates the premises, the landlord can sometimes let the premises sit empty and recover the value of the rent that would have been paid over the entire tenancy.[35] Does that seem fair? How would you respond to the dispute in You Be the Judge 15.1?

Residential Leases

a **residential lease** provides a place to live

Although it shares the same basic purpose as a commercial lease, a *residential lease* is different in some respects. A **residential lease** provides a place to live. The law therefore is much more willing to become involved in the landlord–tenant relationship. It may be acceptable to allow two businesses to freely negotiate the terms of their agreement. It seems unfair and unrealistic, however, to expect a residential tenant to do the same. In that situation, there is probably a great difference in bargaining power between the parties, especially when accommodation is scarce. Almost by definition, a residential tenant has limited resources. People with large amounts of money usually buy, rather than rent, so

---

[35]. *Highway Properties Ltd v Kelly Douglas & Co* (1971) 17 DLR (3d) 710 (SCC). Damages are reduced, however, to the extent that the landlord does in fact limit its loss by renting the property to a third party.

YOU BE THE JUDGE 15.1

Commercial Leases and Mitigation

Archer Holdings Ltd owns a shopping centre in a suburban area. Although a number of smaller shops rent space in the mall, the "anchor" (that is, the main tenant) is Bainsbury Foods, a grocery store. Bainsbury signed a lease with Archer for a fixed term of 15 years. Business was brisk for the first 12 months, but after a downturn in the economy, Bainsbury began to lose a lot of money as a result of operating in that particular location. Consequently, two years into the lease, it removed its stock and equipment, transferred its employees to other outlets, and closed its doors in Archer's mall.

Archer has resumed control of the vacated space, but has made no effort to find another anchor. The evidence indicates that, despite the downturn in the economy, a replacement tenant could be found if the landlord were willing to reduce the rent by 25 percent. Bainsbury admits that it breached the contract, but insists that it should not be responsible for 13 years of full rent on a property that it no longer occupies.

Question for Discussion

1. Do you agree with Bainsbury's argument? Explain your answer.

that their payments create an investment. Consequently, every jurisdiction in Canada has extensive legislation that regulates residential tenancies by requiring some terms, prohibiting others, providing mechanisms for resolving disputes, and so on.[36]

It is impossible for us to consider that legislation in detail.[37] We can, however, note several important differences between residential and commercial leases.

- **Termination:** In the commercial context, it is usually possible to terminate a periodic tenancy by giving notice equal to the length of one term. Residential notice periods, however, tend to be much longer, for example, 60 or 90 days for a monthly lease. Likewise, in the residential context, a periodic tenancy may automatically arise at the end of a fixed-term lease unless notice was given.

- **Rental rates:** Commercial parties are generally free to agree upon any price. Residential leases, in contrast, are governed by rent control mechanisms that prevent landlords from gouging tenants.

- **Distress:** A commercial landlord may be entitled to seize and sell a tenant's belongings if rent is not paid. However, that right usually is not available against a residential tenant.

- **Repair and maintenance:** Unlike a commercial landlord, a residential landlord has a statutory obligation to repair and maintain the property.

- **Mitigation:** Although a commercial landlord may be relieved of the need to mitigate when a tenant wrongfully vacates a property, a residential landlord is generally required to take reasonable steps to minimize the losses that result from a breach.

[36.] *Residential Tenancies Act*, SA 2004, c R-17.1 (Alta); *Residential Tenancy Act*, RSBC 1996, c 406 (BC); *Residential Tenancies Act*, CCSM c R119 (Man); *Residential Tenancies Act*, SNB 1975, c R-10.2 (NB); *Residential Tenancies Act, 2000*, SNL 2000, c R-14.1 (Nfld); *Residential Tenancies Act*, RSNWT 1988, c R-5 (NWT and Nun); *Residential Tenancies Act*, RSNS 1989, c 401 (NS); *Tenant Protection Act, 1997*, SO 1997, c 24 (Ont); *Rental of Residential Property Act*, SPEI 1988, c 58 (PEI); *Residential Tenancies Act*, RSS 1978, c R-22 (Sask); *Landlord and Tenant Act*, RSY 2002, c 131 (Yuk).

[37.] See C Bentley *et al* William & Rhodes *Canadian Law of Landlord and Tenant* 6th ed looseleaf (1988).

CHAPTER SUMMARY

Real property includes land and things attached to land. A defining feature of property interests is that they are generally enforceable against the whole world and not merely against the person from whom they are acquired.

An estate in land involves the right to exclusive possession. A fee simple entitles a person to exercise rights over a piece of property for life and to dispose of it after death. A life estate lasts only as long as the relevant life—upon death, the property either reverts to the person from whom it was obtained or passes as a remainder to someone else. A lease provides the right to exclusive possession and therefore qualifies as an estate in land. However, its duration is not measured by anyone's life—a lease must be for a definite duration.

Ownership in a piece of land can be shared between two or more people. With co-ownership, two or more people share an undivided interest in a property. With joint ownership, two or more people share exactly the same interests in a property. Joint ownership includes the right of survivorship. Joint ownership can be turned into co-ownership through the process of severance. Shared ownership can be brought to an end through the process of partition. In a condominium, several people share ownership of some parts of a building, while individually owning other parts.

An easement is a right to use a neighbour's land. An easement must exist between two neighbouring properties—the dominant tenement and the servient tenement. An easement may be created expressly or implicitly. In some jurisdictions, it can also be created through prescription. A statutory or public easement is not really an easement because it does not require a dominant tenement. A licence is permission to act in a way that would otherwise be prohibited, but it is neither an easement nor an interest in land.

A restrictive covenant is a promise to use property in a way that benefits the dominant tenement and burdens the servient tenement. A restrictive covenant can be created only by agreement. The enforcement of a covenant depends upon (i) the identity of the parties, and (ii) the nature of the covenant.

A mineral lease allows a person to extract and retain minerals from another person's property. It is similar to a *profit à prendre*.

A lease (or tenancy) is contractually created between the landlord and the tenant. Its maximum duration must be definite. A fixed-term tenancy exists when it is possible at the outset to determine when the tenancy will end. A periodic tenancy is also for a fixed period, but it is automatically renewed at the end of each term unless one of the parties provides notice to quit. A tenancy at will exists when there is no set term and either party can terminate the lease at any time. With a tenancy at sufferance, a tenant continues to possess the premises at the end of a lease without the landlord's permission. The parties do not really have a lease because they do not have an agreement.

Tenants can sometimes assign their rights under a lease to a third party, who then becomes the tenant. A tenant may also sublease a property. If so, that person remains a tenant under the original lease, but also becomes a landlord under the sublease. Many leases either prohibit assignments and subleases or require the landlord's consent.

With a commercial lease, premises are rented for a business purpose. The parties are generally free to negotiate the terms. Some promises or covenants, however, are standard. If a tenant breaks a commercial lease, the landlord may be entitled to use the special remedies of eviction and distress. In some situations, a landlord can claim contractual relief without the need to mitigate its losses.

A residential lease provides a place to live. Every jurisdiction in Canada has extensive legislation regulating residential tenancies. They all require some terms, prohibit others, and provide mechanisms for resolving disputes.

REVIEW QUESTIONS

1. Provide a basic definition of "real property."
2. As a general rule, against whom are property rights enforceable?
3. "A private person who owns a piece of land has complete control over that property." Is that statement true? Provide three illustrations in support of your answer.
4. Outline the difference between a reversion and a remainder.
5. Explain why life estates are generally unattractive in a commercial context.
6. Describe the right of survivorship. Explain when and how it applies. Describe two ways in which that right can be brought to an end.
7. Explain the process of partition. Provide an example of when it would be desirable to use that process.
8. What is a "flying fee"?
9. What does it mean to say that an interest "runs with the land"? Provide two examples of interests that run with the land.
10. I have been secretly dumping waste into your pond for 25 years. Provide at least one reason why I probably cannot claim that an easement has been created by prescription.

11. Explain the meaning of "adverse possession."

12. "A public easement is not really an easement." Is that statement correct? Explain your answer.

13. Describe a licence, and explain how it differs from an easement.

14. What is the difference between positive and negative covenants? Provide an example of each. In the context of restrictive covenants, why does the law draw that distinction?

15. Explain why the government may be able to grant a mineral lease with respect to oil that lies beneath your property.

16. What is a *profit à prendre*? If you have a *profit à prendre*, do you automatically own the things to which it applies?

17. Explain why a tenancy at sufferance is not really a tenancy at all, and why a tenancy at will may not really be a true lease either.

18. As a general rule, which party to a commercial lease has the obligation to repair the premises?

19. Describe two special types of remedies that may be available to a landlord under a commercial lease if the tenant fails to pay rent.

20. Explain five general differences between commercial leases and residential leases. Why have the legislatures felt the need to introduce those changes?

Cases and Problems

1. Serena and Douglas were joint tenants of a piece of land. Although Serena did not take much interest in the property, Douglas saw its potential value in the rental market. He therefore leased the property to Marcus Inc for $50 000 per year. Because Douglas did not want Serena to know about the lease, he persuaded Marcus Inc that there was no need for a written agreement. Marcus Inc occupied the property for five years, during which it paid a total of $250 000 in rent to Douglas. The land now sits empty. Serena died two months ago. Shortly before she passed away, however, she discovered the details of the rental arrangement that Douglas had created with Marcus Inc, and she demanded a share of the profits. Douglas refused. The situation became more complicated upon Serena's death due to the fact that she left a will that gave everything that she owned, including her interest in the land, to her sister, Rumana. Discuss the rights and liabilities that may affect Douglas, Serena, and Rumana.

2. Raj owned the fee simple in a piece of land known as Blackacre, which contained a small shopping mall. Although he had no children of his own, he was especially fond of his nephew, Ludwig, and his niece, Elise. Raj wanted to ensure that they enjoyed the benefit of Blackacre, especially after he died. He therefore created the following arrangement. Beginning immediately, and for the rest of Raj's life, Ludwig was entitled to enjoy a life estate in Blackacre. Upon Raj's death, Elise (who is 25 years younger than Ludwig) would become entitled to enjoy a life estate in the property. Although all of the parties were initially happy with that arrangement, difficulties arose after the economy went into a recession and the shops that had been operating in the shopping mall on Blackacre began leaving the premises. Within six months, the entire mall was empty. Despite protests from Elise, Ludwig did nothing to protect the value of the property, even though vandals were smashing windows and tres-

passers had begun to use the parking lot as a garbage dump. Has Ludwig done anything wrong? Aside from Elise, is there anyone who might be concerned about the condition of Blackacre?

3. Because of a number of problems that have arisen under the existing law, the provincial government intends to enact new legislation governing condominiums. Section 67(2) of that statute states: "Unless otherwise agreed, all common areas shall be shared among the individual unit owners as joint tenants." Explain the difficulties that this provision would create. How could those difficulties be avoided?

4. For many years, Marina DelMare operated an outdoor adventure company from a cabin on a lake in northern Ontario. As a licensed pilot, she carried herself and her customers to the cabin in an aircraft that was capable of landing on the water. After a downturn in the economy, however, she was forced to close her business and sell her cabin. She found a willing buyer in Marc Ryan, a Canadian actor who had become a television star in Hollywood. Although he spent most of the year in California, Marc wanted to keep in touch with his roots. He became very disappointed, however, the first time that he tried to visit his new property. The cabin was accessible by two land routes. The first, which followed the public highways and then cut across part of the land that Marina had sold to him, was very long and inconvenient. Marc realized that if he was forced to rely upon it, he would seldom have the opportunity to use his cabin. The second route, which passed almost exclusively through land owned by Wendy Dais, was more direct and much quicker. Marc offered to purchase the road from Wendy, but she absolutely refused. His lawyer then informed her that Marc was entitled, by reason of necessity, to an easement over that road. Will that argument succeed? Provide two reasons for your answer.

5. Lester Tulk held the fee simple to a number of connected properties in Fredericton. Moxie Case, a wealthy land developer, offered to buy one of the properties, Elm Square, for $500 000. Although Elm Square had long been used as a park, Moxie explained that she wanted to clear the land and build an apartment complex. Lester was attracted by the price, but he did not approve of the purpose. Since he intended to retain the neighbouring properties for himself, at least for a decade, he much preferred the land to remain in its present condition. Therefore he made a counter-offer to Moxie under which he would sell the land for $100 000, and she would covenant that she would not develop Elm Square for at least 25 years. Moxie accepted that offer, and the appropriate documents were carefully drafted to reflect the parties' agreement. Six months after the deal closed, however, Moxie resold Elm Square to François Cottenham, another local developer, for $400 000. Cottenham almost immediately began to clear the land in preparation for the construction of an apartment complex. Lester is outraged and has informed François that Elm Square must remain green for almost another quarter century. In response, François admits that he knew of the agreement between the original parties, but insists that he is not bound by a contract that he neither negotiated nor signed. What will happen to Elm Square? Explain your answer. Is that result fair?

6. Elias Gamel has the fee simple to a large area of land in northern Alberta. Six months ago, Choi Paper Products Inc persuaded him to enter into a contract. That agreement allowed Choi to harvest timber from Elias's land for a period of 50 years. In exchange, Choi promised to pay a fee based on the amount of timber that it removed on an annual basis, and it promised to undertake a reforestation project that would renew the source on a continuous basis. Choi intends to begin harvesting the wood within one year. The government recently announced a new tax incentive program that provides a tax credit to any individual or corporation "that owns timber that it has harvested or that it will harvest within a reasonable period." Choi has claimed a tax credit with respect to all of the trees on Elias' land. Is it entitled to do so? Explain your answer.

7. Ryan Furniture Ltd holds the fee simple in a large building that it uses for manufacturing, selling, and storing home furnishings. After a recent fire, Pol Lawn Care Inc was forced to temporarily relocate its business. It was able to quickly find a site for its manufacturing operations, but it still required storage space for its inventory. Because the owners of the two companies were old friends, Ryan and Pol signed a document that contained the following provisions.

> For as long as it requires the space, Pol is entitled to use the warehouse facilities in Ryan's building. Pol and Ryan will both be entitled to use the same storage space simultaneously.

Each party, however, shall clearly label its goods. Pol will pay $1500 to Ryan for each month, or part of a month, that it stores its goods in Ryan's building.

Although that arrangement worked well initially, tensions have developed between the parties, largely due to the fact that renovations of Pol's own property have been considerably delayed. Therefore Ryan has ordered Pol to remove all of its goods within a reasonable time and no later than one week. Pol admits that storage space is available elsewhere, but only at a significantly higher price. It wants to remain in Ryan's building until its own premises are rebuilt. The parties' lawyers agree that, in light of other provisions in the document that have not been reproduced, Pol is entitled to remain on Ryan's premises only if a lease exists. Is that the case? Provide two explanations for your answer. If the parties did not create a lease, what interest, if any, did Pol receive?

8. Solomon Holdings Ltd entered into an agreement with Kostal Sporting Goods Supplies Inc. The agreement provided a formula for calculating monthly rent based on a combination of the market value of the premises and the net profit generated by Kostal's sale of sporting goods. The document also contained the following provision.

> Kostal shall have exclusive possession of the premises for a single five-year period commencing the first day of January in the next calendar year.

The agreement proceeded as planned. At the end of the five-year period, however, Kostal remained in the premises and continued to pay rent according to the formula established in the agreement. Solomon received such payments for nearly three years without objection. Recently, however, Kostal has discovered an alternative location at a lower rental price. On the first day of July, it provided Solomon with written notice that it intended to vacate the premises by the first of August. Solomon was generally agreeable to that proposal, but it insisted that Kostal was liable to pay rent for August, as well as July. Which party is correct? Explain your answer.

9. Takahana Sushi, a Japanese restaurant, rented its premises from Gunnar Schultz. The contract signed by the parties was very brief. For our purposes, these are the relevant provisions.

(a) Schultz promises to provide Takahana with quiet possession.

(b) Takahana shall pay an annual rent of $36 000, payable monthly in equal instalments.

(c) This lease shall be for a single fixed term of 10 years.

Three months after taking possession of the premises, Takahana was informed by a public health inspector that the property was unfit for use as a restaurant because the plumbing in the toilets was defective. The cost of the necessary replacement was about $50 000. Takahana asked Schultz to make the necessary repairs. Schultz, however, refused because the lease did not require him to make repairs. He expressed some sympathy for Takahana's position, and indicated that he would not object if the tenant replaced the defective plumbing. He also insisted, however, that he was entitled to full rent for the remainder of the 10-year term. At that point, Takahana left the premises, relocated to a new building, and refused to continue paying rent to Schultz. Which party will prevail in this dispute? Explain your answer.

10. Last summer, Mysty signed up for the business program at Yonge College in downtown Toronto. Because she wanted to commute to school from her apartment in Richmond Hill (north of the city), she was worried about finding a parking space. And because she was paying for her education through student loans, she was worried about the expense. Her problems seemed to be resolved, however, after she met a young man, named Sanjeev, at a party shortly before the school year began. He explained, over drinks, that he lived in a house near Yonge College that his parents had purchased for him. He also explained that the house had parking spaces for several cars, even though he had only one vehicle. He therefore invited Mysty to park at his house, free of charge, for the upcoming year. She jumped at the offer and thanked him profusely. Furthermore, secure in the belief that her parking problems were a thing of the past, she did not bother purchasing a parking permit from either Yonge College or one of the nearby commercial parking lots. That decision unfortunately came back to haunt her. Although Mysty had assumed that Sanjeev was simply being friendly, she later discovered that he had been hoping to enter into a romantic relationship with her. When she made it clear, three weeks into the term, that she already had a boyfriend, he told her that she no longer was welcome on his property. Mysty is now very upset. All of the reasonably priced parking spots have been taken up by other students, and the only spaces still available are exceptionally expensive. She therefore wants to know if she has any right to hold Sanjeev to his promise and to park at his house for the remainder of the year. What would you advise her? In particular, does she have any interest in the property in question? (You may want to review your notes on Contracts before answering the first question.)

11. Wilson Hum leased a commercial property to Frank Mosher for use as a pizzeria. The parties' agreement contained three important provisions.

(a) The tenant shall not during the term of the lease sell, assign, or sublet or part with possession of the said premises or any part thereof without the written consent of the landlord. Such consent shall not be unreasonably withheld.

(b) During the term of this lease, the tenant shall keep the premises in good repair, both interior and exterior. Damage by fire or other circumstances beyond the tenant's control is excepted.

(c) This lease shall be for a fixed term of five years. Annual rent of $30 000 shall be paid in equal monthly instalments.

Frank operated the pizzeria for two years, but he soon tired of the business. However, his friend Janine Gallant indicated that she would be willing to take control of the business for the three years remaining under the lease. Frank wrote to Wilson to seek consent for an assignment of the lease. At the same time, he provided documentation that established that Janine had good credit and was experienced in the food sales industry. Although Wilson simply ignored the request, Frank proceeded to assign his interest under the original lease to Janine. Unfortunately, for reasons that were completely unforeseeable at the time of the assignment, Janine's personal life fell into turmoil. As a result, she totally lost interest in the pizzeria. She failed to pay the rent and she allowed the property to fall into very poor condition. By the time that Wilson discovered that state of affairs, Janine had become destitute. She had no assets and was clearly not worth suing. Wilson therefore insists that Frank is responsible for paying the overdue rent and for the cost of repairing the premises. Do paragraphs (b) and (c) of the lease still apply to Frank? Explain your answer.

12. Igor Polska, an entrepreneur with varied interests, entered into two contracts with Ishtla Singh. The first was for the sale of goods. Ishtla promised to pay $5000 for a rare book. The second contract was for the rental of a property. Ishtla agreed to take possession for a one-year term beginning on the first day of July. The total rent was to be $36 000, paid in equal monthly instalments. Ishtla moved into the premises on the first day of July and paid $3000 in rent. Within two days, however, she informed Igor that she only intended to remain until the end of that month. She also told him that she had found another copy of the same book elsewhere at a lower price, and that she therefore was unwilling to pay the $5000 as promised. Igor nevertheless insists that he is entitled to the full value of both contracts, which he calculates to be $38 000 ($5000 for the book and $33 000 for the property). Ishtla believes that Igor's position is unreasonable. She relies on the fact that she has already introduced him to one person who is willing to pay $4000 for the book, and to another who is willing to occupy the property immediately under a monthly tenancy at a rent of $2000. Is Igor correct? Explain your answer. Do you require additional information to calculate the full value of Ishtla's liability?

WEBLINKS

Duhaime Law: Fee Simple and Life Interests www.duhaime.org/Real-estate/ca-re7.aspx

This website explains different types of estates.

Duhaime Law: Joint and Common Tenancies www.duhaime.org/Real-estate/ca-re10.aspx

This website briefly considers the rules regarding two types of shared ownership.

Duhaime Law: Easements and Covenants www.duhaime.org/Real-estate/ca-re9.aspx

This website briefly considers the rules regarding easements and restrictive covenants.

Commercial Tenancies Act Brochure www.mah.gov.on.ca/userfiles/HTML/nts_1_4541_1.html

This website explains some of the more important aspects of commercial leases, including the rights and obligations of the landlord and the tenant.

Resolving Commercial Lease Disputes www.lawsonlundell.com/resources/ResolvingCommercialLeaseDisputes.pdf

This document, written by the law firm of Lawson Lundell, provides guidance on how to resolve commercial lease disputes.

Questions to Ask Before You Sign a Lease www.cbsc.org/sask/sbis/search/display.cfm?Code=5779&coll=SK_PROVBIS_E

This website, provided by the Government of Saskatchewan, explains some of the more important issues that ought to be addressed during lease negotiations.

Commercial Lease Negotiating Strategies www.rmabc.org/pdfs/commercial_lease_negotiating.pdf

This document offers advice on lease negotiations.

ADDITIONAL RESOURCES FOR CHAPTER 15 ON THE COMPANION WEBSITE

(www.pearsoned.ca/mcinnes)

In addition to self-test multiple-choice, true-false, and short essay questions (all with immediate feedback), three additional Cases and Problems (with suggested answers), and links to useful Web destinations, the Companion Website provides the following resources for Chapter 15:

Provincial Material

- **British Columbia:** Fraudulent Transfer of Property, Distress for Rent, Condominums—see Strata Title, Conveyance of Land, Strata Title, Residential Leases, Commercial Leases, Adverse Possession and Prescriptive Easements, Fixtures, Riparian Rights, Partition of Property, Expropriation, Fraudulent Conveyance—see Fraudulent Transfers of Property, Fraudulent Preference—see Fraudulent Transfers of Property, Trespass to Land, Property Taxes

- **Alberta:** Commercial Leases, Condominiums, Distress, Fixtures, Residential Tenancies, Spousal Interests in Land (Dower Rights)

- **Manitoba and Saskatchewan:** Partition, Condominiums, Subleases, Commercial Leases (Statute), Residential Lease Information

- **Ontario:** Adverse Possession, Condominiums, Dower (Family Law Legislation), Land Registration Reform, Land Titles, Matrimonial Home, Registry System, Reserve Fund, Restrictive Covenants, Title Insurance, Assignment of Tenancy, Assignment of Rents, Ontario Rental Housing Tribunal, Distress, Fixtures, Leasehold Improvements, Overholding, Tenant Protection Act, Landlord and Tenant Legislation

16 Real Property: Sales and Mortgages

OBJECTIVES

After completing this chapter, you should be able to:

1. Explain the basic differences between a registry system and a land titles system, and indicate which system operates in your jurisdiction.

2. Describe the concept of indefeasibility and its underlying principles.

3. Describe five types of unregistered interests that may be enforceable against the owner of a registered interest.

4. Explain the risk management issues that arise in the purchase of land.

5. Outline the purpose of an agreement of purchase and sale, and explain the role of the conditions that are frequently contained in that type of agreement.

6. Describe the remedies that may be available if an agreement of purchase and sale is breached.

7. Describe a mortgage, and identify the mortgagor and the mortgagee.

8. Outline the basic difference between a mortgage under a registry system and a mortgage under a land titles system, and identify three situations in which that difference has practical consequences.

9. Describe a subsequent mortgage, and explain the risk management issues that are associated with that type of arrangement.

10. Describe four types of remedies that may be available to a mortgagee if a mortgagor does not fulfill the terms of a mortgage.

In Chapter 15, we began our discussion of real property by describing a variety of interests and by examining one important type of transaction: the lease. In this chapter, we discuss another important type of transaction: the sale. We also consider a form of financing that is often used to facilitate the purchase of land: the mortgage. First, however, it is necessary to briefly explain the registration systems that operate in Canada.

REGISTRATION SYSTEMS

A variety of interests may simultaneously exist in a single piece of land: a fee simple, a life estate, a lease, an easement, a restrictive covenant, and so on. We will discover even more possibilities in this chapter. As a matter of risk management, it is necessary to keep track of all of those interests. If you intend to purchase a particular property, you will want to know exactly what you are getting for your money. You certainly would not want to pay for a fee simple and then discover that you received only a life estate. Likewise, if you enjoy the benefit of a restrictive covenant, you would want to advertise that fact to a potential buyer of the servient tenement. Otherwise, the new owner might not be bound by the covenant. In either event, you will be able to rely upon one of two *registration systems*, depending upon where you live in Canada. A **registration system** documents the existence of interests in land.

a registration system documents the existence of interests in land

Registry System

A *registry system* (or *deeds registration system*, as it is sometimes called) is used in the four Atlantic provinces, as well as parts of Manitoba and Ontario.[1] A **registry system** provides an opportunity to inspect and evaluate documents that may affect real property. Suppose you are interested in buying a cottage from me, but you are not sure that I actually own it. Before you go ahead with the purchase, you will visit the registry office, search through all of the relevant records, and try to satisfy yourself that I am at the end of a good **chain of title**—that is, a series of transactions in which ownership was validly passed from one person to the next. Theoretically, it is possible to trace that chain all the way back to the time when the government held the land. Fortunately, as a result of legislation, it is only necessary to go back a much shorter period, for example, 40 years.

a registry system provides an opportunity to inspect and evaluate documents that may affect real property

a chain of title is a series of transactions in which ownership was validly passed from one person to the next

The task of *searching title* nevertheless is often difficult and hazardous. Consequently, it is usually best left to someone with expertise in the area, such as a lawyer specializing in real estate. The records may be unclear or misleading. Mistakes may be made, and errors may be overlooked for decades, only to be later discovered after many people have relied on the appearance of a good title. Continuing with our example, suppose I thought that I had purchased the cottage 15 years ago from Alison. She in turn believed that she had inherited it from her uncle. In fact, her uncle's will actually left the property to her brother. Consequently, my chain of title is defective. Even though the records for the last 15 years seem to indicate that the property is mine, it really belongs to someone else (presumably Alison's brother). Furthermore, one of the defining features of the registry system is that the government's role is passive. It provides access to the documents, but it does not guarantee their accuracy. Therefore,

---

[1.] There is, however, a gradual shift toward land titles systems in a number of those jurisdictions.

even if you pay the price, you cannot get good title to the cottage from me. Because of that possibility, you may want to purchase *title insurance*, which provides a source of compensation if our transaction does not include everything promised.[2]

From a risk management perspective, the registry system leaves something to be desired. Although it does not happen often, a simple oversight during a title search may have disastrous consequences. You may end up paying a lot of money without actually getting any land in exchange. That is one reason for hiring a lawyer to assist in the purchase of land. It is the lawyer's job to ensure that the seller actually has a good chain of title. If the lawyer makes a mistake, you will not be able to get the land, but you will be able to sue the lawyer.

There is another point to note about risk management. If I did have a good chain of title, and if we did go through with the sale, you (or your lawyer) should return to the registry office as soon as possible to register the transfer documents. If that does not happen, you might actually lose the cottage. After selling the land to you, I might dishonestly sell it again to a third party named Tre. The general rule under a registry system is that competing claims are resolved by the *timing* of registration. If Tre did not have notice of your earlier transaction, and if he gave valuable consideration for his purchase, he gets the cottage if he registers before you. You can bring an action against me for damages, but you cannot get the property from Tre. In contrast, if you register your transfer first, you will provide Tre and the rest of the world with notice of your rights. Your claim to the land therefore cannot be defeated.

Land Titles System

To avoid many of the problems associated with the registry system, the three western-most provinces, the territories, and some parts of Manitoba and Ontario operate under a *land titles system* (or *Torrens system*, as it is sometimes called).[3] A **land titles system** does more than simply provide an opportunity to inspect and evaluate documents. It generates certificates of title that virtually guarantee the validity of the interests that are listed.

The key to a land titles system is the doctrine of *indefeasibility*. **Indefeasibility** means that, with very few exceptions, the interests that are included in a certificate of title cannot be defeated. That doctrine is based on three principles. To illustrate this, we return to our earlier example.

- **Mirror principle:** The **mirror principle** states that all of the interests listed in a certificate of title are generally valid. The certificate reflects reality. For example, when I purchased the land from Alison 15 years ago, the land titles office examined the transfer documents and issued a new certificate of title that named me as the owner. (It also would have listed any other type of interest that existed, such as an easement or a mortgage.) You are entitled to rely upon that certificate when buying the cottage from me. That is true even if my chain of title was defective because Alison never really inherited the property from her uncle.

- **Curtain principle:** The **curtain principle** states that the only valid interests in a property are generally the ones that are listed in the certificate of title. Consequently, it is unnecessary for you to "lift the

a **land titles system** generates certificates of title that virtually guarantee the validity of the interests that are listed

indefeasibility means that, with very few exceptions, the interests that are included in a certificate of title cannot be defeated

the **mirror principle** states that all of the interests listed in a certificate of title reflect valid interest

the **curtain principle** states that the only valid interests in a property are the ones listed in the certificate of title

---

[2] Insurance is considered in detail in Chapter 17.

[3] Robert Torrens was a marine customs collector in South Australia, who developed the land titles system partially on the basis of the system that was used to register ships.

curtain" and look behind the certificate of title to determine whether anyone else has rights in the property. By the same token, even though Alison's brother at one time was entitled to the cottage, his rights were lost when the land titles office issued a certificate of title naming me as the owner. The curtain fell on him.

- **Insurance principle:** The **insurance principle** states that a person who suffers a loss as a result of an error in the system is generally entitled to compensation. The land titles system includes an *assurance fund* that helps people like Alison's brother. Although he cannot get the cottage back, he is entitled to a payment of money.

> the insurance principle states that a person who suffers a loss as a result of an error in the system is entitled to compensation

Unregistered Interests

Although the land titles system was designed to avoid uncertainty, a certificate of title is not entirely indefeasible. In some circumstances, an interest in land may be effective even if it is not registered. That is also true under a registry system. Consequently, when buying the cottage from me, you should conduct more than a single search at the land titles or land registry office. There are other places to look. Furthermore, unless you have expertise in this area, you should leave those tasks to your lawyer. Consider these common examples.

- **Short-term leases:** A short-term (say, three-year) lease may be enforceable against a purchaser even if it is not registered. For that reason, you should inspect the premises for any signs of tenants.

- **Prescription and adverse possession:** As we discussed in Chapter 15, it is sometimes possible for a person to acquire an interest in land as a result of a long period of use or occupation. That is true under registry systems and even under some land titles systems. Consider that fact when you inspect the premises. Look for signs of "squatters."[4]

- **Public easements:** As we saw in Chapter 15, a utility company or similar body may have the right to bury cables beneath a property or run wires overhead. Consequently, your lawyer should look for signs of activity on the land and perhaps contact the organizations in question.[5] If an easement does exist, its exact location should be determined. A house that sits directly beneath a tangle of power lines may, for instance, be difficult to resell.

- **Unpaid taxes:** As a land owner, I am required to pay taxes on that property. If I fail to do so, the government may be entitled to seize and sell the land to raise the necessary money. Furthermore, its right to do so may continue to exist even after I have transferred the cottage to you. Before you buy, therefore, your lawyer should search the municipal and provincial records to ensure that there are no outstanding taxes.

- **Unpaid creditors:** Your lawyer should also search the records in the sheriff's office to determine whether there are any *writs of execution* (or *writs of seizure and sale*) against me. A **writ of execution** is a document that allows a court's judgment to be enforced. Suppose someone successfully sued me in tort. If they filed the writ with the sheriff, that officer might have the power to seize and sell any property registered in my

> a writ of execution is a document that allows a court's judgment to be enforced

---

[4.] A "squatter" is a person who occupies a piece of land without any right or permission to do so.

[5.] Private easements are generally enforceable only if they are registered.

name in order to pay my debt.[6] And significantly, as long as the writ was filed while I was still the owner, the seizure and sale could take place even after I transferred the property to you. To keep the property, you would have to pay my debt.[7]

Is it fair that those interests can be enforced against you, even though they were not registered, and even though you were unaware of them when you bought the land from me? Consider Ethical Perspective 16.1.

ETHICAL PERSPECTIVE 16.1

Unregistered Interests in Land

Questions for Discussion

Suggest reasons why it might be fair to subject a purchaser to unregistered interests that are based on:

1. short-term leases
2. interests acquired by way of prescription or adverse possession
3. public easements

4. municipal taxes owed by the vendor
5. writs of execution filed against the vendor

In answering those questions, consider:

- the purchaser
- the person with the unregistered interest
- society as a whole

LAND SALES

Ownership of land can be passed between people in a variety of ways. We have already mentioned several possibilities, including expropriation, gifts, and adverse possession. From a business perspective, however, the most important possibility is *sale*. A **sale** occurs when ownership is transferred in exchange for consideration.

a sale occurs when ownership is transferred in exchange for consideration

Risk Management

The sale of land is a complicated matter, involving a large number of people performing a variety of tasks. That is true for both residential and commercial properties. The explanation lies in the need for risk management. A great deal can go wrong during a real estate transaction. In the last section, we saw that people other than the apparent owner may have interests in the land. There are many other dangers. Suppose you are interested in buying a factory from me. You should enlist the help of the following people.

- **Real estate agent:** Even if my property appeals to you, there may be others that better suit your needs. Given the time and expense involved in a real estate transaction, it is highly unlikely that you would want to relocate after only a few years in my factory. A real estate agent can search the market for alternatives and help you find the right property in the first place. An agent can also put you into contact with the other people you will need to safely purchase a property.

[6.] The governing rules, which are quite complicated, vary among jurisdictions. In some instances, the power to seize and sell only arises when the writ is filed with the registry office.

[7.] You would then be allowed to sue me for the same amount, but I may not have it. If I did, I presumably would have paid the judgment myself.

- **Lawyer:** It is important that you hire a lawyer. In addition to conducting the searches that we previously discussed, a lawyer will perform a large number of other tasks, including (i) communicating with the seller or the seller's lawyer, (ii) verifying which secondary pieces of property are included in the sale (such as machines in the factory), (iii) ensuring that local bylaws will allow you to use the land for your intended purpose, (iv) obtaining insurance coverage for the property, (v) checking mortgage arrangements (if any), and (vi) preparing, filing, and registering the formal documents that are needed for the transfer. It is also very common for the lawyer to secure the services of other professionals on this list.

- **Appraiser:** It is often difficult to determine the correct price for a property. Several factors can affect the value of land, including the condition of the buildings, the value of neighbouring properties, accessibility to public transport, the uses that are permitted under zoning regulations, and the municipality's plans for future development in the area. Consequently, before agreeing to a price, you should get an opinion from a professional appraiser.

- **Surveyor:** During the course of negotiations, I will provide a *legal description* of my property, which includes its precise size and location. That description, however, may be inaccurate. For instance, it might overlook the fact that my building *encroaches* upon a neighbour's land by a few metres.[8] A survey would reveal that fact. Since you would not be willing to pay full market value for a property that could lead you into a lawsuit, you would likely refuse to go ahead with our sale unless I either obtained the neighbour's consent to the encroachment or reduced the price.

- **Inspector:** You are concerned about the physical condition of the premises, especially since the value of the property is affected by its state of repair. Furthermore, a dangerous structure could expose you to liability by causing injuries or deaths among your employees or guests.[9] And even if no one is hurt, health and safety regulations might eventually require you to spend a lot of money fixing the defects. For those reasons, you should hire an inspector to check the premises for potential problems.

- **Environmental auditor:** Depending upon the nature of my business, you might be concerned by the possibility that my factory has leaked toxic substances into the environment. Even if no one is killed or injured as a result, you may eventually be required, as the owner of the premises, to pay a substantial amount of money for a cleanup operation.[10] An environmental auditor could identify that possibility.

One final, perhaps cynical, observation is appropriate. We opened this section by discussing the need for risk management. The individuals in the preceding list could minimize the risks by identifying potential problems at the outset. However, by hiring those people, you would also create a safety net for yourself. Suppose you discover an underground pool of hazardous waste on the property shortly after our deal closed. If you sue me for the cost of the cleanup, I might honestly say that I simply do not have the money to pay damages. Therefore you will need another source of compensation. If you had hired an environmental auditing company, you might now be able to sue it for breach of

---

[8.] We discussed the tort of trespass in Chapter 4.

[9.] We discussed the torts of occupiers' liability, nuisance, and *Rylands v Fletcher* (1868) LR 3HL 330, in Chapter 5.

[10.] Environmental regulations are discussed in Chapter 25.

contract or for the tort of negligence because it failed to detect the problem. As we discussed in Chapter 6, a professional can be held liable for doing a job carelessly. And furthermore, even if the environmental auditor does not have a lot of money, it very likely has liability insurance.[11]

As we have seen, the purchase of land creates a number of risks. Concept Summary 16.1 provides a checklist of some of the dangers you should guard against. (You may either do all of the work yourself or ask your lawyer to take care of the issues.)

CONCEPT SUMMARY 16.1

Risk Management and the Purchase of Land

Danger	Precaution
• subsequent purchaser acquiring interest in same property	• registration as soon as possible to provide notice or obtain certificate of title
• short-term leases	• inspection of property to discover tenants
• rights to use or occupation of land created through prescription or adverse possession	• inspection of property to discover signs of use or occupation
• public easements	• inspection of property to discover activity • inquiries to utility companies and similar organizations
• unpaid taxes creating a right of seizure and sale	• search of municipal records
• unsatisfied writs creating a right of seizure and sale	• search of sheriff's records
• payment of excessively high price	• valuation of property by professional appraiser
• misdescription of property	• description of land and buildings by professional surveyor
• defects in building and equipment	• inspection by engineer and similar professionals
• toxic or hazardous substances	• inspection of property by environmental auditor

---

Agreement of Purchase and Sale

Transactions involving commercial properties are often complicated by the fact that the parties are dealing with several matters at the same time. For instance, if you are buying my factory, you may also want to obtain the equipment in it.[12] You may even be interested in acquiring my business as a whole, including my customer lists and the name of my company. However, we will focus on the sale of the real property itself. That sale is created by an **agreement of purchase and sale**.

An agreement of purchase and sale is a contract and therefore must satisfy all of the usual contractual elements, including an intention to create legal relations, an offer and acceptance, and consideration. Furthermore, although most types of contracts can be created orally, a contract for the sale of an interest in land must be evidenced in writing.[13] And as always, the parties must agree on all of the important terms. That does not mean, however, that the **vendor** (the

*an **agreement of purchase and sale** creates a contract for the sale of land*

*the **vendor** is the person who sells the land*

[11.] When purchasing my factory, you should also have considered buying *property insurance* that would cover the cost of an environmental clean-up. Chapter 17 explains property insurance.

[12.] Chapter 17 explains that, when you buy land, you are generally entitled to the *fixtures*, which are things that are attached to the land.

[13.] As Chapter 10 explained, although a contract for a sale of land that is not evidenced in writing is valid, it cannot be enforced by either party.

the purchaser is the person who buys the land

a condition or condition precedent is a requirement that must be satisfied before the transaction can be completed

person selling the property) and the **purchaser** (the person buying the property) must settle every point at the outset. It is very common for an agreement of purchase and sale to include *conditions*.

A **condition** (or a **condition precedent**) is a requirement that must be satisfied before the transaction can be completed.[14] It does not prevent the creation of a contract, but it does suspend the parties' obligations to complete the deal. Several possibilities might arise in our earlier example.

- If my building was partially constructed on someone else's land, you might agree to buy the property from me, but only on the condition that I obtain my neighbour's permission for the encroachment.
- If a heap of toxic waste sits at the back of my lot, you might make our agreement conditional upon my ability to remove the hazard and obtain a clean report from an environmental auditor.
- If you intend to use the property differently than I did, you might make the sale conditional upon your ability to obtain zoning permission for the proposed activity.
- If you are unsure that you can afford to buy my land, you might make our agreement conditional upon your ability to obtain financing on reasonable terms.

If any condition is not met, then our sale will not be completed.[15] Nevertheless, one of us might still be held liable. Most conditions expressly or implicitly require at least one party to act in a certain way. For instance, I might be required to use my best efforts to obtain my neighbour's consent to the encroachment or to remove the toxic substances from the land. You might be required to use your best efforts to obtain zoning permission or to arrange financing. If a condition fails due to a lack of effort, the other party may be entitled to damages. Consider how you would respond in You Be the Judge 16.1.

YOU BE THE JUDGE 16.1

Agreement of Purchase and Sale and Conditions[16]

OK Detailing Ltd owns a piece of land. Dynamic Transport Ltd wants to buy part of it. The parties therefore entered into an agreement of purchase and sale. Dynamic promised to pay $250 000 and OK Detailing promised to transfer a specific portion of its property. There is, however, a problem. At the time of entering into that agreement, both parties knew that the sale could not proceed without permission under the *Planning Act* to subdivide the property into two lots. Unfortunately, their agreement does not expressly say that the sale is conditional on that fact. Nor does it expressly impose an obligation upon either party to obtain the planning approval.

Since the parties signed their agreement, the value of the land has increased from $250 000 to $400 000. OK Detailing realizes that it entered into a very bad bargain and it is anxious to find some way out of it. It therefore argues that the sale cannot be completed because the planning authority has not approved the necessary subdivision.

In response, Dynamic notes that OK Detailing has not even applied for permission to subdivide its property. Dynamic also argues that it would be unfair if the vendor could avoid the sale by simply refusing to seek planning approval.

(continued)

---

14. As we saw in Chapter 11, there are different types of "conditions precedent."

15. In some circumstances, it is possible for the person who was intended to benefit from the condition to waive the need for satisfaction and to insist upon the completion of the sale: *Beauchamp v Beauchamp* (1972) 32 DLR (3d) 693 (Ont CA). Chapter 11 discusses the concept of waiver.

16. *Dynamic Transport Ltd v OK Detailing Ltd* (1978) 85 DLR (3d) 19 (SCC).

(continued)

The only relevant sections of the *Planning Act* state:

19(1)   A person who proposes to carry out a division of land shall apply for approval of the proposed subdivision.

19(2)   A subdivision means a division of a land by means of. . . transferring an interest in land to another person.

Questions for Discussion

1. Do the parties have a valid agreement?

2. If so, is the performance of that agreement subject to a condition?

3. If so, which party, if either, has an obligation to satisfy that condition?

4. What relief, if any, should be available if that obligation is not met?

Closing

Once all conditions attached to the sale have been satisfied, the parties' transaction can be *closed*, or completed. It is common for *adjustments* to occur at that time. For instance, if the vendor has already paid the annual property tax, the price will be increased to reflect the fact that the purchaser will enjoy the benefit of that payment for the remainder of the year. The purchaser's lawyer will also conduct one last search at the various offices to ensure that competing interests have not been filed or registered against the land at the last minute. And at that point, the vendor's lawyer will provide the purchaser's lawyer with the formal document that is needed to convey ownership in the property. In jurisdictions under a registry system, a *deed* (or *deed of conveyance*) is used. In jurisdictions under a land titles system, a document called a *transfer* is used. The purchaser's lawyer will promptly register the deed or transfer to protect the client's rights. The lawyer will generally also help with the paperwork that is needed to obtain insurance coverage on the property, and may notify the municipality, the utility companies, and so on of the change in ownership.

Remedies

In most situations, an agreement of purchase and sale ends with a successful closing. The vendor receives full payment and the purchaser receives clear title. Occasionally, however, problems arise. The parties are entitled to rely upon the usual remedies for breach of contract that were discussed in Chapter 12. For instance, the plaintiff is normally entitled to recover the value of the property that it expected to obtain. Furthermore, at least historically, the courts would order *specific performance*. In other words, instead of being restricted to the monetary value of the property, the plaintiff could obtain the property itself by forcing the defendant to go through with the sale. That remedy was justified by the belief that every piece of land was unique, with the result that money could never truly provide an adequate substitute for actual performance.[17] Recently, however, the Supreme Court of Canada has adopted a different view. Case Brief 16.1 discusses its decision.

[17.] Given that explanation, it seems strange that vendors can also demand specific performance. After all, a vendor is normally interested only in receiving the payment of money under a sale. Consequently, monetary damages should normally be an adequate remedy if the purchaser refuses to complete the sale. It might be different, however, if the vendor has a special or non-monetary reason for wanting to complete the sale: *Hoover v Mark Minor Homes Inc* (1998) 75 OTC 165 (Gen Div).

Semelhago v Paramadevan (1996) 136 DLR (4th) 1 (SCC)

The plaintiff agreed to buy a house from the defendant for $205 000. As the closing date approached, however, the defendant said that he was not willing to go through with the sale. The plaintiff sued for breach of contract. By the time of trial, the property had increased in value to $325 000. The judge held that the purchaser was entitled to choose between (i) an order for specific performance, and (ii) monetary damages that would place the plaintiff in the position that he would have enjoyed if the sale had been completed. The plaintiff chose the second option and therefore received about $120 000 from the defendant.

The defendant appealed all the way to the Supreme Court of Canada. Justice Sopinka agreed with the result reached at trial. In doing so, however, he rejected the traditional view that specific performance is almost *always* available for a contract dealing with the purchase of land.

While the common law traditionally regarded every piece of land to be unique, that is no longer true, given the nature of modern real estate developments. Residential, business, and industrial properties are all mass produced much in the same way as other consumer products. If a deal falls through for one property, another is frequently, though not always, readily available.

The Court therefore introduced a new rule that limits specific performance to situations in which the plaintiff has legitimate grounds for saying that monetary damages would not provide an adequate remedy.

On the facts before him, Justice Sopinka saw nothing special about the property in question. Nevertheless, since both parties had assumed that the property was unique, he did so as well.

We mention two more special remedies that may be available under a contract for the sale of land.

- A *purchaser's lien* is generally created whenever the purchaser pays money to the vendor. For example, before the completion of a transaction, the vendor often requires payment of a deposit or part of the price. If the deal later falls through, the purchaser will want a refund. A **purchaser's lien** allows the purchaser to have the land sold in order to satisfy the outstanding debt. In practice, however, property is seldom sold under a lien. In most instances, the vendor simply repays the money. And in other cases, the purchaser may wait until the vendor voluntarily sells or mortgages the land to someone else, and then take part of the proceeds.

a purchaser's lien allows the purchaser to have the land sold to satisfy the outstanding debt

- A *vendor's lien* is similar. Occasionally, a person may be willing to sell land on credit, without insisting upon full payment at the time of closing. In that situation, there is a danger that the purchaser will later refuse to pay the remaining amount even though it has already received ownership. The law therefore provides a **vendor's lien**, which allows the vendor to have the property sold in order to satisfy the outstanding debt.[18]

a vendor's lien allows the vendor to have the property sold to satisfy the outstanding debt

Note that a lien is a form of *security*.[19] That means that the lien holder may be entitled to priority over other types of claimants. Business Decision 16.1 illustrates this.

---

[18] A lien should be registered as an interest in the property. If it is not, it can be defeated if a person buys the land from the purchaser without notice of the vendor's claim.

[19] Chapter 23 discusses security.

BUSINESS DECISION 16.1

Vendor's Lien and Priority

Sukie Petroutsas sold a piece of land worth $90 000 to Anthony Sidhu. Anthony paid $30 000 at the time of closing and promised to pay the remaining $60 000 within two years. Unfortunately, shortly after obtaining ownership of the property, Anthony's business began to falter. He was unable to make any more payments to Sukie. And to make matters worse, he also incurred $120 000 in debts to other creditors. Anthony's only significant asset is the land that he bought from Sukie.

Questions for Discussion

1. Assume that Sukie has exercised her unpaid seller's lien and has had the property sold for $90 000. How much of that amount will she receive? How much will Anthony's other creditors receive?

2. What would likely happen if Sukie did not have the right to exercise an unpaid seller's lien? Assuming that Anthony sold the land to pay his debts, how much would Sukie receive? How much would the other creditors receive?

MORTGAGES

The purchase of land is often the largest single transaction that a person or a business will ever complete. Real property tends to be very expensive, especially if it is located in a commercially desirable area or if it contains a development, such as an apartment complex or a shopping mall. Consequently, the purchaser can seldom pay the full price from pre-existing resources. It is usually necessary to obtain a loan. A lender, however, will be reluctant to extend *credit* (that is, provide money in exchange for a mere promise of repayment) without some form of *security*. A bank, for instance, is unlikely to lend you the $500 000 that you need to buy a new factory unless you have something that the bank can take or sell if you do not repay your debt. The purchase of land is therefore usually financed through a *mortgage*. Broadly speaking, a **mortgage** is an interest in land that provides security for the repayment of a debt.[20] The person who borrows the money and gives an interest in land is the **mortgagor**. The person who lends the money and acquires an interest in land is the **mortgagee**. Take a moment to repeat those terms. They are often confused.

A mortgage can be used in several ways.

- The previous example presents a typical situation. The same property was involved in two transactions. First, you bought the factory from the vendor. Second, to pay for that purchase, you granted a mortgage over your newly acquired asset as security for a bank loan.[21]

- The two transactions can, however, be distinct. For instance, if you already own a factory, but wish to buy new equipment, you might borrow money for that purchase by allowing the lender to take a mortgage over the land. You would be using one asset (the factory) to acquire another (the equipment).

a **mortgage** is an interest in land that provides security for the repayment of a debt

the **mortgagor** is the person who borrows the money and provides the interest in land

the **mortgagee** is the person who lends the money and acquires the interest in land

---

[20.] Although less common, a mortgage can also be created by using other types of property, such as cars and boats, as security for a loan.

[21.] It is highly unlikely that the bank would give credit for the full value of the property. The reason is risk management. Suppose the bank allowed you to borrow $500 000 on the basis that your new factory was worth that much when the mortgage was created. A downturn in the economy might have two effects: (i) it might prevent you from repaying the loan, and (ii) it might cause the value of the land to collapse. Consequently, at the end of the story, the bank might be left holding a property worth only $300 000, even though it had given you $500 000. It would suffer a loss of $200 000.

■ Our examples to this point have involved three parties. You bought property from one person and borrowed money from another. But often, there are only two parties. For instance, in the first case, the vendor presumably received full payment when the sale closed. You paid with the money that you borrowed from the bank. Under a different arrangement, however, the vendor could have allowed you to take the factory on credit. And to secure your promise to pay the price in the future, the vendor itself could have taken a mortgage over the property that it just sold to you.

In any event, the basic operation of the mortgage itself remains the same. Figure 16.1 illustrates the process. (Some of the features of that diagram are discussed below.)

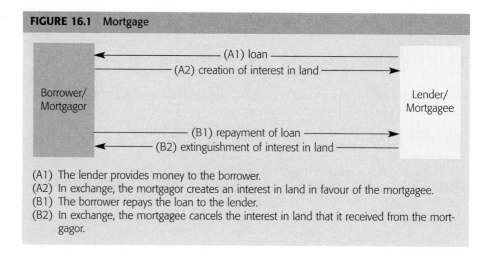

FIGURE 16.1   Mortgage

(A1) loan

(A2) creation of interest in land

Borrower/ Mortgagor

Lender/ Mortgagee

(B1) repayment of loan

(B2) extinguishment of interest in land

(A1) The lender provides money to the borrower.
(A2) In exchange, the mortgagor creates an interest in land in favour of the mortgagee.
(B1) The borrower repays the loan to the lender.
(B2) In exchange, the mortgagee cancels the interest in land that it received from the mortgagor.

Nature of Mortgages

Although we have provided a general definition of a mortgage, the specific rules are different in every jurisdiction. The most important differences depend upon whether the security is given under a land titles system or a registry system.

Registry System and Land Titles System

If the land in question is held under a land titles system, a mortgage creates a *charge* over the property. A **charge** occurs when the mortgagor agrees that the land will be available to the mortgagee if the debt is not repaid. As we will discuss, the mortgagee is required to remove that charge if the loan is repaid and if the other terms of the parties' agreement are satisfied.

However, if the land in question is held under a registry system, then a mortgage does not merely create a charge; it actually involves a *conveyance of title*. In exchange for the loan, the mortgagor transfers the property to the mortgagee, who then becomes the legal owner.[22] The mortgagor is, however, entitled to have the title reconveyed if the mortgage is fulfilled.

a **charge** occurs when the mortgagor agrees that the land will be available to the mortgagee if the debt is not repaid

---

22. In most cases, the mortgagor holds the fee simple to the property at the outset. However, it is also possible to mortgage other interests in land, such as a lease or even an easement: *Russell v Mifflin (SW) Ltd* (1991) 89 Nfld & PEIR 168 (Nfld SC TD).

Subsequent Mortgages

Under the registry system, the mortgagee acquires the *legal title* to the property. But the mortgagor is not left without anything—it receives an *equitable interest* in the land. That interest arises because the borrower enjoys the *equity of redemption*. As Chapter 1 explained, there were traditionally two types of courts: courts of law and courts of equity. The courts of law initially adopted a very harsh approach to mortgages. If the mortgagor did not repay the loan within the required time, the mortgagee could keep the property for itself *and* it could sue for the late payment. Not surprisingly, the results of that rule were often grossly unfair. A mortgagor who missed the repayment schedule by even a single day could lose its land forever and still be liable for the debt. The courts of equity therefore created the **equity of redemption**, which allows the mortgagor to recover the property by repaying the loan even after the due date.[23] The two types of court are now combined, but the distinction between legal and equitable rights remains important.

the equity of redemption entitles the mortgagor to recover legal title to the land by repaying the loan

The mortgagor therefore holds an interest in the land under either a land titles system (because it retains the legal title) or under a registry system (because it acquires an equitable interest). That is significant because it allows for the creation of subsequent mortgages. As the name suggests, a **subsequent mortgage** is one that takes effect after the initial mortgage. Suppose you own a large piece of land, called Greenfield, that is worth $500 000. To acquire a new fleet of trucks, you borrow $300 000 from the Primus Bank and give a mortgage over Greenfield as security for that loan. At that point, the bank acquires either legal title or a charge, and you enjoy the equity of redemption. Your interest in the land, or your *equity*, is worth $200 000. That is a valuable property interest in itself. Consequently, you might be able to use it if you later want to buy a new computer system for $100 000. To secure a loan in that amount from the Nether Bank, you could grant a second mortgage over your interest in Greenfield.

a subsequent mortgage is one that takes effect after the initial mortgage

As you might expect, subsequent mortgages raise a number of interesting risk management issues.

Vulnerability of Mortgagors   Although subsequent mortgages can help you to raise additional funds, they also carry an obvious danger. If you have two mortgages, you also have two outstanding loans. And if you fail to repay either one of them, you may lose your land.

Vulnerability of Subsequent Mortgagees   If a mortgagor does not repay a loan, the mortgagee may be entitled to *foreclose*, that is, permanently keep the land for itself. And in doing so, the mortgagee will extinguish not only the mortgagor's equity of redemption, but also the interest held by any subsequent mortgagee.[24] After all, if the mortgagor no longer has an interest in the property, there is nothing that the subsequent mortgagee can use as security. Consequently, in our previous example, Nether Bank is in a vulnerable position. If you fail to fulfill your first mortgage, Primus Bank could foreclose on Greenfield. And while Nether Bank could still sue you for repayment of its loan, it would probably have little chance of success. It no longer has any security, and since you were unable to repay Primus Bank, you presumably do not have

[23] Although a mortgage under a land titles system does not involve the transfer of ownership to the lender, it is still common to use the term "equity of redemption" to describe the borrower's right to re-acquire clear title to the property upon fulfillment of the mortgage.

[24] Subsequent mortgagees are also treated less favourably in other situations. For instance, if the property is sold rather than foreclosed, the first mortgagee will be paid off completely before a subsequent mortgagee can claim any part of the sale proceeds.

much money. To avoid that result, Nether Bank would be required to prevent foreclosure by paying off your outstanding debt to Primus Bank. Not surprisingly, because of that possibility, Nether Bank would almost certainly charge a higher rate of interest than Primus Bank. A subsequent mortgagee will demand additional compensation for the additional risks that it faces.

In theory, it is possible to have any number of subsequent mortgages. However, very few lenders are willing to stand worse than second, since a subsequent mortgagee faces the danger of foreclosure by any of the earlier mortgagees.

Priority of Mortgages   Mortgages generally take priority in the order that they are registered, not necessarily in the order that they are created. Suppose Primus Bank received all of the relevant documents from you on Monday, but did not take them to the land registry office until Friday. If Nether Bank received all of its documents from you on Tuesday and filed them promptly, it would take first priority as long as it did not have notice of your earlier transaction with Primus Bank. That could be important. Suppose the economy collapsed, the value of Greenfield slumped to $250 000, and the land was sold to satisfy your debts. Nether Bank would be entitled to the full amount of its loan ($100 000) and Primus Bank would only receive half of its loan ($150 000 out of $300 000). The lesson is clear. As a matter of risk management, a mortgagee should register its interest as soon as it is created, because registration provides notice to the whole world.

Disposition of Interests

Since we have been discussing the people who may be involved in a mortgage, it is appropriate to briefly mention two more possibilities.

- **Disposition by mortgagee:** A mortgagee may wish to sell its rights to a third party. Although it is entitled to do so, the parties should act carefully. A mortgage is a *property interest* that is created by *contract*. The mortgagee can use a simple *assignment* to transfer its *contractual* rights (such as the right to demand repayment).[25] But the third party will not acquire the *security* unless it also receives the mortgagee's property interest—either title (under a registry system) or a charge (under a land titles system). Furthermore, as soon as the appropriate transfer takes place, the third party should promptly register its interest.[26] It should also notify the mortgagor of the assignment.[27] Figure 16.2 illustrates the basic process (on the next page).

- **Disposition by mortgagor:** The distinction between the proprietary and contractual aspects of a mortgage is also important when a mortgagor sells its interest. Suppose a third party wants to buy a piece of land that is already subject to a mortgage. The third party might pay for the property partially by providing cash and partially by promising to pay the balance of the vendor's loan.[28] Figure 16.3 illustrates the basic process.

---

[25] Chapters 8 and 15 discuss assignments.

[26] If the third party fails to register its interest, it can be defeated if another person later buys the mortgagee's interest and registers first.

[27] The mortgagor is required to pay only once. If it pays the original mortgagee before receiving notice of the assignment, it is not required to make the same payment again to the third party assignee. (The third party can, however, sue the original mortgagee for its improper receipt of that payment.)

[28] Alternatively, the third party might arrange to discharge the existing mortgage by repaying the loan on the mortgagor's behalf. In that situation, the third party would probably finance its purchase by giving a new mortgage over the property as security for a bank loan. The choice between assuming an existing mortgage and creating a new one is usually based on whether the third party can get a new loan with better terms than are contained in the existing mortgage.

FIGURE 16.2   Disposition by Mortgagee

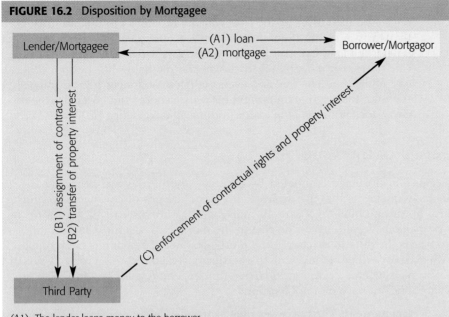

(A1)   The lender loans money to the borrower.
(A2)   The borrower creates a mortgage by giving the lender a proprietary interest in a piece of land. The borrower is the mortgagor and the lender is the mortgagee.
(B1)   The lender/mortgagee assigns to a third party the contractual right to demand repayment of the loan from the borrower/mortgagor.
(B2)   The lender/mortgagee transfers its proprietary interest to the third party.
(C)   The third party enforces the contractual rights and the proprietary interest against the borrower/mortgagor.

FIGURE 16.3   Disposition by Mortgagor

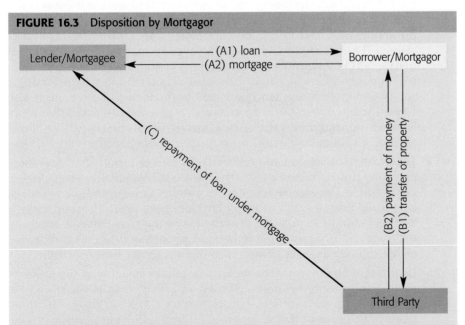

(A1)   The lender loans money to the borrower.
(A2)   The borrower creates a mortgage by giving the lender a proprietary interest in a piece of land. The borrower is the mortgagor and the lender is the mortgagee.
(B1)   The mortgagor sells its property interest to a third party. The mortgagor is now also the vendor.
(B2)   The third party satisfies part of the purchase price by paying money to the vendor/mortgagor.
(C)   The third party satisfies the rest of the purchase price by repaying the loan that the vendor/mortgagor received from the lender/mortgagee.

Note two more points about that arrangement. First, as long as the lender registered its mortgage, the land will still be subject to that security, even though it is in the third party's hands. Consequently, if the loan is not repaid, the land can still be used to satisfy the debt. Second, the general rule states that it is possible to assign contractual rights, but not contractual obligations. As a result, even though it no longer has an interest in the land, the original mortgagor (now the vendor) can be sued if the third party does not repay the loan as promised (see Figure 16.3 on p. 371.).

Terms of the Contract

Because a mortgage is created by contract, the parties are generally free to include any terms that are appropriate. Certain types of covenants (promises) are, however, standard. (Sample mortgage documents can be found on our Companion Website.) With respect to the mortgagee, the most important term concerns the duty to discharge the mortgage once the debt has been repaid. It will do so by either reconveying title to the mortgagor (under a registry system) or by registering a *cessation of charge* (under a land titles system). The mortgagor tends to have more obligations.

an acceleration clause requires the mortgagor to immediately repay the full amount of the loan if it misses a single payment

- **Repayment:** The borrower must repay the debt according to the parties' agreement. That will generally mean that payments must be made on certain days, in certain amounts, and with a certain amount of interest. Furthermore, it is very common for a mortgage to contain an **acceleration clause**, which requires the mortgagor to immediately repay the full amount of the loan if it misses a single payment. It is easy to see why a mortgagee would insist upon such a clause. Once the contract is breached, the mortgagee does not want to wait and see if it will be breached again. It wants to bring the matter to an end immediately.[29] An acceleration clause can be contrasted with a *prepayment privilege clause*. The mortgagor sometimes repays the loan earlier, or in larger instalments, than initially agreed. In most circumstances, the mortgagee will impose a financial penalty (or a *bonus*) on the mortgagor for doing so. After all, while the mortgagee wants the loan to be repaid, it also wants the interest to build up as much as possible. To avoid that problem, the mortgagor may insist upon a **prepayment privilege** that allows early or additional payments to be made without penalty.

a prepayment privilege allows early or additional payments to be made without penalty

- **Taxes:** If the mortgagee has registered its interest, its security is reasonably safe. However, even a registered interest can sometimes be defeated. For example, the government may be entitled to seize and sell a piece of land if the taxes on that property have not been paid. The mortgagor is therefore usually required to promise to pay the taxes. Indeed, to ensure that payment actually occurs, the mortgagee may insist upon receiving an appropriate amount of money so that it can pay the taxes itself.

- **Insurance:** The mortgagee's security is only as valuable as the property itself. For instance, a mortgage over an office complex that is worth $1 000 000 provides sufficient protection for a $600 000 loan. The situation will be much different, however, if the building burns to the ground and leaves the land with a market value of only $200 000. To protect itself

---

[29.] An acceleration clause can create hardship. It might be unfair, for instance, to demand full payment from a mortgagor who simply missed a single payment due to illness. The courts therefore sometimes grant relief from acceleration if the borrower puts the loan back on track.

against that danger, the mortgagee will require the mortgagor to pur-chase adequate insurance for the property.[30] Furthermore, the mort-gagee will insist upon being named as a beneficiary of that insurance policy. Therefore, if the building is destroyed, the lender will effectively receive repayment of the loan from the insurance company.

- **Waste:** For similar reasons, mortgages usually contain a clause that pro-hibits the borrower from committing an act of waste. As we saw in Chapter 15, waste occurs when a property is changed in a way that sig-nificantly affects its value.

Remedies for Default

A mortgage typically comes to an end when the borrower fulfills the terms of the parties' agreement, and the lender discharges its interest in the land. Difficulties do occasionally arise, however, especially during economic reces-sions or depressions. The most common source of problems is the mortgagor's failure to repay the loan. As we saw with respect to the equity of redemption, our legal system has struggled to find ways of fairly balancing the parties' inter-ests in that situation. The mortgagor is often vulnerable and in need of protec-tion. But at the same time, the mortgagee has a legitimate interest in recovering the debt that it is owed, by using its security if necessary. There is no obvious way to resolve that tension. Not surprisingly, the rules vary significantly between jurisdictions. Each province and territory has legislation that governs the remedies that are available in the event of default.[31] There are generally four possibilities:

- suing on the covenant
- possession of the property
- foreclosure
- sale

Suing on the Covenant

A mortgagee has both property rights and contractual rights. To enforce repay-ment of the loan, it is entitled to use the security interest that it holds in the mortgagor's land. But it is not required to do so. In most circumstances, it has the option of simply suing the mortgagor for the outstanding amount. There are, however, certain limitations on that right. Most significantly, legislation in Alberta, British Columbia, and Saskatchewan generally prevents an action from being brought against an individual or against a corporation that has not *waived* its statutory protection.

Possession of the Property

Under a registry system, the mortgagee becomes the legal owner of the prop-erty. In theory, it is therefore entitled to possession at the outset. Almost invari-ably, however, the parties' agreement states that the mortgagor is allowed to occupy the premises unless it goes into *default* by breaching the contract. In theory, the situation is somewhat different under a land titles system because

---

[30.] Chapter 17 considers insurance policies in more detail.

[31.] Given the large number of statutory provisions that are involved, citations are not provided.

the mortgagee merely acquires a charge, rather than ownership. It therefore has no natural right to possess the land. In practice, however, the situation is much the same. The parties' agreement generally states that the borrower's right to occupy the premises may be lost in the event of default.

The mortgagee's right to possession is, however, far less attractive than it might seem.

- Most mortgagees are financial institutions that have little interest in occupying land. As a general rule, banks want "the money, not the mud." They do not want the problems associated with the possession of real property.

- A mortgagee who takes possession acquires a number of responsibilities. It must keep the property in good repair and cannot commit acts of waste. It must also take reasonable steps to generate income from the property. And when it does generate income (such as rent), it is generally required to use that money to reduce the mortgagor's debt.[32]

- The mere fact that the mortgagee took possession does not prevent the mortgagor from later exercising its equity of redemption (assuming that it is still available), repaying the amount that is due under the loan, and resuming possession of the property.

For those reasons, the mortgagee normally will not take possession of the property unless the mortgagor has either abandoned it or is acting in a way that will decrease its value.

Foreclosure

To understand the remedy of *foreclosure*, we must once again look at the history of mortgages. The mortgagee was traditionally entitled to keep the land that had been transferred into its name if the mortgagor was even a single day late with a payment. Because the effects of that rule were often unfair, the Court of Chancery created the equity of redemption, which allowed the mortgagor to recover the property by repaying the loan at a later date. In time, however, that led to complaints by mortgagees. They could never be sure that they were entitled to keep the land that they had acquired. A mortgagor was often allowed to redeem a property years after the loan had become due. The Court of Chancery therefore created a new rule that allowed mortgagees to apply for orders for foreclosure. **Foreclosure** (from the Latin words meaning "to close from outside") is a procedure for extinguishing the mortgagor's equity of redemption.

Once again, the remedy tends to be more attractive in theory than in practice.[33] Although the details vary between jurisdictions, the procedure tends to be quite drawn out. And surprisingly, it often lacks finality. After the mortgagee applies for foreclosure, the court initially grants an order *nisi* (Latin for "unless") as a way of informing the mortgagor and any subsequent mortgagees that the equity of redemption may be foreclosed unless the outstanding debt is repaid.[34] If that does not occur within the required period (usually six months), the court will grant a final order of foreclosure. But even at that point the mortgagee is not necessarily entitled to the property forever. As long as the lender

foreclosure is a procedure for extinguishing the mortgagor's equity of redemption

---

[32] The mortgagee is, however, entitled to deduct a reasonable amount for repairs and expenses.

[33] The concept of foreclosure is best suited to a registry system, in which the mortgagee receives legal title at the outset. However, the same terminology, and essentially the same procedures, are used under a land titles system, in which the lender starts with only a charge.

[34] Foreclosure will extinguish both the mortgagor's equity of redemption and a subsequent mortgagee's security interest.

still holds the land, the borrower can apply to the court to have the foreclosure set aside in exchange for repayment of the loan.

There are other reasons why foreclosure is often not a satisfactory remedy.

- Mortgagees tend to be lending institutions that are not particularly interested in owning land. They want money.

- Foreclosure often seems unfair from the perspective of the mortgagor and any subsequent mortgagees. The mortgagor will lose the property and the subsequent mortgagees will lose their security. Furthermore, the mortgagee may be overcompensated. Suppose you borrow $60 000 from a bank by mortgaging a property that is worth $100 000. Some time later, you buy $20 000 worth of goods from a supplier. Because that purchase is made on credit, you are required to give a second mortgage over your land. Your business then experiences financial difficulties, and you are unable to repay either creditor. If the bank is able to foreclose, it will receive land worth $100 000, even though it was owed only $60 000 at the outset. By the same token, you will effectively pay $100 000 to discharge a debt of $60 000. And the holder of the second mortgage will lose its security. For that reason, mortgagors and subsequent mortgagees can seek a court order that requires the mortgagee to proceed by way of *sale*, rather than foreclosure. The mortgagee also has the option of requesting a sale.

Sale

The remedy of **judicial sale** occurs when the mortgaged property is sold under a judge's order. Although the rules vary from place to place, the process is carefully controlled. It is done under the authority of the court or another government official (the registrar of titles), who must approve the terms of the sale. In some jurisdictions, the court or the registrar of titles may set the minimum price for which the land can be sold.

The sale proceeds are used to repay the loan that was granted by the first mortgagee.[35] If there is money left over, it is used to satisfy the claims of subsequent mortgagees. And if any money still remains at that point, it is paid to the mortgagor.[36] However, if the sale proceeds are insufficient to cover the debts, there is a *deficiency*, and the mortgagee may be entitled to sue the mortgagor for the shortfall.[37]

The use of sale varies significantly between jurisdictions. In Nova Scotia, the courts insist upon it, rather than foreclosure. Similarly, although foreclosure is available in Alberta, Saskatchewan, and the parts of Manitoba that are under the land titles system, the courts prefer a sale to be attempted first. The mortgagee is entitled to foreclose ony if the attempted sale did not generate a reasonable offer. In the rest of the country, the lender generally has a greater choice between remedies.

As an alternative to seeking a court-ordered sale, the mortgagee can sometimes exercise a **power of sale** that is contained in the parties' agreement. Although quite common in some places (especially Ontario), that type of term

the remedy of judicial sale occurs when the mortgaged property is sold under a judge's order

a power of sale is a contractual right that allows the mortgagee to sell the land in order to obtain payment

---

[35] The mortgagee is also entitled to the payment of interest and compensation for the costs associated with enforcing its rights.

[36] If the mortgagee forecloses and later sells the property to a third party, the mortgagor and the subsequent mortgagees are usually not entitled to a share of the sale proceeds, even if those proceeds exceed the amount that was owed under the first mortgage.

[37] Some jurisdictions generally prohibit the mortgagee from suing the mortgagor on the covenant.

is severely restricted in others (especially Alberta). In any event, the mortgagee is responsible for getting a reasonable price for the property. If it fails to do so, it can be held liable for the shortfall.

Combination of Remedies

The preceding remedies can often be used in combination. For example, if the mortgagor has abandoned the property, the mortgagee may take possession of the land to prevent it from losing value, and then have it sold. As we have seen, some jurisdictions allow the mortgagee to sell the property and then sue the mortgagor on the covenant for any outstanding debt. And quite often, a financial institution will obtain a property by way of foreclosure and then sell it for its own benefit. Banks, as we have said, usually want "the money, not the mud."

CHAPTER SUMMARY

A registration system documents interests in land. Two registration systems operate in different parts of the country. A registry system provides an opportunity to inspect and evaluate documents that may affect real property. It provides access to the documents, but it does not guarantee their accuracy. A land titles system does more than simply provide an opportunity to inspect and evaluate documents. It generates certificates of title that virtually guarantee the validity of the interests that are listed on those certificates. Although both systems are based on registration, some types of unregistered interests are enforceable.

The sale of land is a complicated matter, involving a large number of people performing a variety of tasks. As a matter of risk management, the purchaser should retain various professionals. A sale occurs through an agreement of purchase and sale that is created by the vendor and the purchaser. Such agreements often contain conditions that suspend the parties' obligations to complete the deal. A sale closes when the vendor provides the purchaser with the formal document needed to actually convey ownership in the property. As a matter of risk management, the purchaser should register that document as soon as possible. If an agreement of purchase and sale is breached, the innocent party may be entitled to a variety of contractual remedies, including specific performance or a lien.

A mortgage is an interest in land that is created to provide security for the payment of a debt. The person who borrows the money and gives an interest in land is the mortgagor. The person who lends the money and acquires an interest in land is the mortgagee. Under a land titles system, a mortgage creates a charge over the property. Under a registry system, a mortgage involves a conveyance of title. In either event, the mortgagor enjoys an equity of redemption. The mortgagor can use the equity of redemption to create subsequent mortgages.

A mortgage involves both an interest in land and a contractual relationship between the parties. The contract imposes various obligations on the mortgagee and the mortgagor.

If the mortgagor defaults, the mortgagee may be entitled to a variety of remedies, including an action on the covenant, possession, foreclosure, and sale.

REVIEW QUESTIONS

1. What is the major difference between a registry system and a land titles system? Why is it necessary to trace a good chain of title under the former, but not the latter?

2. "Title to land is always safer under a land titles system." Is that statement true? Explain your answer.

3. Explain the meaning of "indefeasibility," and describe the three principles upon which it is based.

4. List five types of unregistered interests that may be enforced against a person who purchases land. In each instance, briefly explain why enforcement is allowed without registration.

5. Identify six types of people who may be hired to minimize the risks associated with the purchase of land. Briefly explain the role of each.

6. "Unless a condition is satisfied, the parties do not really have an agreement of purchase and sale." Is that true? Explain your answer.

7. "The failure of a condition may prevent the parties from closing a sale, but it cannot expose either party to liability." Is that statement true? Explain your answer.

8. Why did the Supreme Court of Canada recently decide that specific performance should not always be available under an agreement for the purchase of land?

9. What is a purchaser's lien? What is a vendor's lien? Describe situations in which each type of remedy would be available.

10. What is a mortgage? Identify the two parties that are always involved in a mortgage.

11. Can a mortgage be used to finance the purchase of something other than the land that is being mortgaged? Illustrate your answer with an example.

12. The mortgagee receives an interest in land. Is that interest the same under both a registry system and a land titles system? Explain your answer.

13. "A mortgage involves a difficult tension between the rights of the mortgagor and the rights of the mortgagee." Discuss that statement in light of the history of the equity of redemption and the remedy of foreclosure.

14. What is a subsequent mortgage? How is a subsequent mortgage related to the equity of redemption?

15. Explain the vulnerability of a subsequent mortgagee in terms of risk management.

16. "Registration is irrelevant to priorities between competing mortgagees." Is that true? Illustrate your answer with an example.

17. What is an acceleration clause? What is a prepayment privilege? Which would you prefer to insert into a mortgage agreement if you were a mortgagor? What if you were a mortgagee?

18. Is the mortgagee always required to use its security interest to enforce the repayment of the loan that it gave to the mortgagor? Does your answer depend upon where you live in Canada?

19. Explain the effect of foreclosure. How does foreclosure relate to the equity of redemption? Does foreclosure always allow the mortgagee to permanently retain the land in question?

20. Describe a situation in which the mortgagor and a subsequent mortgagee would prefer the remedy of sale to the remedy of foreclosure by the first mortgagee.

CASES AND PROBLEMS

1. Five years ago, Megarry Inc owned a large piece of land. It subdivided that property into ten equal parts and sold three of them, as a single unit, to Cheshire Ltd. (Each of the three parts was individually described.) The transfer documents were immediately registered. Although Cheshire had initially intended to construct a number of warehouses on its new property, it soon developed economic difficulties. Since it no longer has any use for the property, Cheshire recently sold it to the Burns Corp. Shortly after that sale closed, Burns began to survey the land with a view to building a shopping mall. When it did so, however, Megarry's lawyer sent a letter stating that her client still owned part of the property that Burns was in the process of developing. After some investigation, the parties agree that Cheshire accidentally registered itself as owner of four parcels, rather than three. That mistake was overlooked, both at the time of the original sale and at the time of the recent resale by Cheshire to Burns. Who owns the disputed fourth section of the property? Do you require additional information to answer that question?

2. Ivan Perez owned Harvard Place, which he operated as an apartment complex for many years. That property is located in a jurisdiction that is governed by a registry system. Two years ago, Ivan decided to switch his focus from the rental market to condominiums. To finance his new venture, he borrowed $2 000 000 from Elsa Kamaguchi and gave a mortgage over Harvard Place as security. Elsa promptly registered her interest. Several months later, Ivan notified his tenants of his intention to develop his property into a condominium complex. Most of the tenants gradually left the premises, and as they did, Ivan sold their units to individual purchasers. Some tenants, however, remained, including Nelson Wolodko. He arranged with Ivan to terminate his lease and to purchase his old apartment as a condominium unit. As a result of an oversight, however, Nelson did not register his interest.

A short time later, the economy went into decline, and Ivan found that he was unable to repay his loan. Elsa claims that she has at least two options. (1) She has informed Nelson that she may seek a court order for the sale of premises. He insists, however, that he is immune to a sale, either because he owns his unit or because he occupies it as a tenant under a lease. (2) Elsa has informed Ivan that she may sue him for repayment of the loan. He insists, however, that he is generally immune to such an action because he has sold most of the units to people like Nelson. He also insists that, as a general rule, a mortgagor cannot be sued on a covenant. Discuss Elsa's likelihood of success under each option.

3. Darren Munt is an unsophisticated man who has spent most of his adult life working as a custodian in an elementary school. Recently, he decided to use the money that he had inherited from his father to

create a company that would sell books and videos over the Internet. Because he had no experience in that field, he visited Jenny Schmidt, the lawyer who had handled his father's estate. Jenny agreed to help Darren in exchange for a hefty fee. Several weeks later, she informed him that she had found a property with a building that would be suitable for a warehouse. They briefly toured the premises together. Darren was excited about the prospect, but expressed concern "about all of the little details." Jenny assured him that she had extensive experience in real estate matters and promised that, for a price, she would "do all of the legwork."

Jenny contacted the owner of the property. Two months later, the deal closed, and Darren acquired the fee simple to the premises. Shortly after he took possession, however, he became aware of a number of problems. (1) His neighbour complained that the warehouse, which had been built only three years earlier, was located partially on its land. (2) As a result of discussions with other people in the business, Darren realized that he had grossly overpaid for the property. (3) He discovered that the building's foundations were cracked and that its roof was in serious danger of collapse. (4) He was notified by government officials that a large pool of blood was buried only several metres underground on a part of the property that was adjacent to a river. The government explained that the land had previously been used as a slaughterhouse. Fearing that the water supply might become contaminated, the government has demanded a cleanup. (5) Several ex-employees of the slaughterhouse informed Darren that they had been injured on the job as a result of the previous owner's carelessness. They also informed him that they had successfully sued the former owner, and that they had filed writs of execution against the property two days before Darren's sale had closed. (6) And finally, Darren soon became aware that while he might be able to store merchandise in the warehouse, he could not process Internet orders from the same premises. Although he had not noticed them when he briefly visited the property with Jenny, and although they had not been registered against title, power lines had been installed directly overhead by a utility company. Those lines cause electrical interference with computer equipment.

Discuss Darren's situation from a risk management perspective. Is there any obvious solution to his various problems? Explain your answer.

4. Daniel Fossum entered into an agreement of purchase and sale with Visual Developments Inc. Fossum found the property unusually attractive for a number of reasons: (i) it was located on Whyte Avenue, in a historic part of Edmonton, where land seldom is offered for sale, (ii) it was situated across a narrow lane from another property that he already owned, (iii) it could accommodate an art gallery that he wanted to open, and (iv) it contained on-site parking and a rentable basement suite, both of which are rare in the area. Shortly before closing, however, Visual

had a change of heart. It has offered to pay damages, but it refuses to complete the sale. Fossum has sued Visual for breach of contract, claiming that he is entitled to specific performance. In response, Visual argues that the Supreme Court of Canada no longer allows that remedy to be awarded in cases involving commercial property. Which party is correct? Can Fossum compel Visual to transfer the property to him? Explain your answer.

5. Bamidele Diop entered into an agreement of purchase and sale with Elton Singh. Under the terms of that contract, she immediately paid $50 000 and promised to pay the remainder of the $500 000 price within six months. In exchange, Elton promised to transfer title to the property, known as White Oaks Landing, to Bamidele within three months. Create additional facts that would subsequently lead to the enforcement of (a) a purchaser's lien, and, alternatively, (b) a vendor's lien. Explain the nature and effect of each type of lien.

6. As a result of a recent illness, Pierrette Dumont was forced to borrow money from her bank to meet a number of outstanding bills. When she initially negotiated the loan with the bank manager, she agreed to grant a mortgage over her home as security. However, before actually proceeding with that transaction, Pierrette discussed the matter with her brother, Gaston. She became alarmed when he suggested that the mortgage would require her to immediately transfer the ownership in her home to the bank. The house had been in their family for generations and had great spiritual significance for both of them. Pierrette agreed with Gaston that it would be catastrophic if they ever lost possession of it. Are their concerns well founded? What additional piece of information do you require before fully answering that question?

7. Dominion Instruments Inc purchased an office complex from Premium Holdings Ltd for $1 000 000. Under the terms of that agreement, Dominion paid $400 000 immediately and gave a mortgage under which it promised to pay the remaining amount, with interest, in a lump sum five years after the date of closing. Although the time for payment has now arrived, Dominion has offered only $300 000 to Premium, along with a renewed promise to pay the outstanding amount within one year. Dominion has explained that its financial position is weaker than expected due to a trade dispute with the United States regarding government subsidies on the manufacture of musical instruments. However, it has also demonstrated that the situation will almost certainly be rectified within 12 months. Premium, however, insists that it is entitled to obtain clear title to the property by foreclosing at once. There is, therefore, a tension between the parties' interests. Discuss that tension by tracing the historical development of the rules regarding foreclosure and redemption.

8. Goldendale is a piece of land that is located in a jurisdiction that operates under a registry system. Zeljana purchased that property several years ago for a price

of $300 000. She financed the purchase by borrowing $200 000 from the First National Bank and by giving a mortgage over Goldendale as security for her debt. The bank promptly registered its interest. Zeljana recently sold Goldendale to Arturo for $400 000. After a quick search at the registry office, Arturo was satisfied that Zeljana owned the property, and he paid the full price. Shortly after he took possession of Goldendale, however, Arturo received a letter from First National stating (i) that Zeljana had defaulted on her mortgage by failing to repay the loan, and (ii) that it intended to foreclose on Goldendale. Arturo also received a letter from the local municipality stating (i) that Zeljana had failed to pay her property taxes for many years, and (ii) that it intended to seize and sell Goldendale in order to have that debt satisfied. Arturo explains that he never knew about the mortgage or the tax arrears, says he cannot in fairness be held responsible for Zeljana's debts, and insists that no one—not even the government—can take Goldendale from him. Is he right about all of that? Explain Arturo's rights and obligations.

9. The Acme Food Company borrowed $500 000 from the Imperial Bank on the strength of a mortgage over Sunnydale, its farm. Acme quickly defaulted on the loan and has indicated that there is little likelihood that it will ever repay the debt. To make matters worse, Sunnydale has recently been the subject of public concern. Although nothing has yet been proven, there are widespread allegations that the site is contaminated by toxic waste. For the foreseeable future, the government has prohibited human consumption of anything grown on Sunnydale. It has, however, stated that the farm's produce can be used for animal feed. Nevertheless, Acme has abandoned the property. Not surprisingly, the value of the land has dropped from $750 000 to $350 000. What remedy (or remedies) should the bank pursue? Explain your answer.

10. The Newton Widget Company owned two properties, each of which contained a factory. After recognizing the need to modernize its operations, it requested a loan of $500 000 from the Bank of the Rockies. The bank agreed, but insisted on taking a mortgage over both properties as security. Even with the loan, Newton found it very difficult to afford the computerized equipment that it intended to purchase. It therefore decided to cut back on other expenses. It accordingly stopped paying its property taxes and cancelled the insurance contract that previously provided compensation for any loss or damage that occurred to its land, buildings, or equipment. In an effort to streamline its production of widgets, it also levelled one of its factories, which was valuable but in need of repair and costly to maintain. It then consolidated all of its operations into the single factory. To this point, Newton has made mortgage payments as required under the par-

ties' agreement. The bank nevertheless feels aggrieved. Why? Has Newton done anything wrong? Explain your answer.

11. Ahmad Vaughan borrowed $50 000 from Sarah Jamal. The parties' agreement required Ahmad to repay the loan in monthly instalments of $1000. As security, Sarah took a mortgage over Ahmad's nightclub, which was worth $200 000. Unfortunately, due to the unusual nature of his business dealings, Ahmad frequently experienced tremendous fluctuations in his monthly income. What would be the likely outcome if, three months into the agreement, Ahmad received a large amount of money and attempted to repay the entire outstanding balance immediately? What if, instead, Ahmad suffered an economic setback and was unable to pay three consecutive instalments? If Sarah did not want to use her security to enforce repayment, is there any way that she could nevertheless sue Ahmad for immediate repayment of the entire outstanding balance? Explain your answer.

12. Srijan owned a large piece of land, called Greyland, in an area that he believed would soon be rezoned to allow for industrial developments. In preparation for a business venture that he planned to launch, he borrowed $1 000 000 from the Bank of London, and in exchange granted a first mortgage over Greyland. At that time, Greyland had a market value of $1 700 000. Unfortunately, the economy soon went into recession and Srijan's financial situation took a turn for the worse. In an attempt to keep his business alive, he borrowed $300 000 from the Bank of Ottawa, and in exchange granted a second mortgage over Greyland. As the recession grew deeper, however, Srijan found it impossible to repay either of his loans. The Bank of London then foreclosed on the land. At the time of foreclosure, it seemed like all three parties were losers. Srijan lost his property, the Bank of Ottawa lost its security, and the market value of the land that the Bank of London obtained through foreclosure had fallen to $900 000. Within a couple of years, however, the recession had passed and property values had skyrocketed. Consequently, the Bank of London was eventually able to sell Greyland to an unrelated corporation for $2 000 000. Srijan and the Bank of Ottawa now feel cheated. They note that the Bank of London received $2 000 000 even though it only lost $1 000 000 on its loan. Their lawyers argue that it would be fairer to split the $2 000 000 three ways: (i) $1 000 000 to the Bank of London, (ii) $300 000 to the Bank of Ottawa, and (iii) $700 000 to Srijan. That approach would put each of the parties back into their original positions. Will a court agree with that argument? Explain your answer. As you do so, think about the risks that each of the parties accepted by entering into the mortgage agreements.

WEBLINKS

Duhaime Law: Canadian Real Estate Law Centre   www. duhaime.org/Real-estate

This page contains links to a variety of websites dealing with real estate transactions.

Real Estate Institute of Canada   www.reic.ca

REIC offers educational programs on a variety of commercial, legal, and ethical topics and on issues related to real estate transactions, online articles, and links to other information resources.

Arvic Search Services   www.arvic.com/library/Buychecklist.asp

This site includes a checklist of the items business people should consider when purchasing an existing business, including real estate, leases, insurance, and other legal issues.

Teranet   www.teranet.ca/products/polaris/automationconversion.html

This website explains how land registration in Ontario is being converted from a paper-based land registry system to an electronic land titles system.

What Should I Know About Land Titles?   www.snb.cae/ 4000/4106e.asp

The four Atlantic provinces, as well as parts of Manitoba and Ontario, use both a registry system and a land titles system. This document, from New Brunswick, explains the procedure for transferring a piece of land from the former to the latter.

ADDITIONAL RESOURCES FOR CHAPTER 16 ON THE COMPANION WEBSITE

(www.pearsoned.ca/mcinnes)

In addition to self-test multiple-choice, true-false, and short essay questions (all with immediate feedback), three additional Cases and Problems (with suggested answers), and links to useful Web destinations, the Companion Website provides the following resources for Chapter 16:

- Appendix 16A—Sample Agreement for Purchase and Sale of Land (located in British Columbia)

Provincial Material

- **British Columbia:** Builders' Lien, Conveyance of Land, Land Title and Survey Authority, Power of Attorney, Real Estate Agents, Fixtures, Cost of Borrowing, Credit Reporting, Debt Settlement, Lien
- **Alberta:** Foreclosure, Land Titles System, Real Estate Agents
- **Manitoba and Saskatchewan:** Registry System in Manitoba, Land Titles System (Provincial Information), Agreement of Purchase and Sale, Judicial Sale
- **Ontario:** Charge, Discharge, Electronic Registration, Foreclosure, Judicial Sale, *Land Registration Reform Act*, *Mortgages Act*, Personal Covenant, Power of Sale

17 Personal Property: Bailment and Insurance

OBJECTIVES

After completing this chapter, you should be able to:

1. Distinguish between real property and personal property, and between tangible property and intangible property.

2. Describe four ways in which personal property rights can be acquired and four ways in which they can be brought to an end.

3. Define the term "bailment," and list the three elements of a bailment.

4. Explain the nature of a lien and a right of sale.

5. Explain five factors that a judge will consider in determining how a reasonable person would have acted in a bailment.

6. Describe the scope of liability for a common carrier, distinguish between the standard of reasonable care and the standard of insurer, and outline three sets of defences that may be available to a common carrier.

7. Describe the process of sub-bailment.

8. Distinguish between third-party insurance and first-party insurance by giving an example of each.

9. Explain the concept of indemnification, and explain how it is related to the ideas of an insurable interest, excessive insurance, and insufficient insurance.

10. Describe the process of subrogation.

real property is immoveable

personal property is moveable

Having looked at *real property* in the last two chapters, we can now turn to *personal property*. Although complications occasionally arise, the basic distinction is this: **Real property** is immoveable, and **personal property** is moveable. You cannot carry a piece of land around with you, but you can take a cat or a car from one place to the next. Another distinction is that real property is usually permanent, whereas personal property tends to be transitory. Different owners will come and go, but a particular piece of land will always exist (unless, for instance, it falls into the ocean following an earthquake). In contrast, cats and cars come into the world through birth and manufacture, and eventually pass away through death and destruction. A third distinction is beginning to disappear. Historically, wealth was concentrated in real property. Position and power in society depended upon the ownership of land. Increasingly, however, wealth is held in other forms of property. The dot-com billionaires are proof of that.

tangible property is a thing that can be touched

intangible property is a thing that cannot be touched

The general concept of personal property can be broken down into several other categories. The most important distinction is between *tangible* and *intangible* property. **Tangible property** is a thing that can be touched. You can, for example, pick up your cat and sit in your car. Such things are sometimes called *goods* or *chattels*.[1] **Intangible property** is a thing that cannot be touched. For instance, while you can physically hold a cheque, your real concern, as we saw in Chapter 14, is with the rights that that piece of paper represents. You cannot put your hands around those rights. At most, you can require the debtor to fulfill an obligation.[2] As we will see in Chapter 18, much of our new economy consists of a special type of intangible property known as intellectual property, which includes copyrights, patents, and trademarks.

ACQUIRING PERSONAL PROPERTY RIGHTS

Personal property rights are usually acquired through the *intention* of one or more people. For instance, you probably bought this text. The bookseller intended to transfer ownership in exchange for a payment of money. The same sort of process occurs when you rent something, like a moving van. Your rights once again arise from a contractual arrangement. The only major difference between purchasing and renting is that you receive a smaller package of rights when you rent. You cannot keep the vehicle indefinitely. You must return it at the end of the agreed period.

Property rights are not always acquired through contract. Sometimes you can get something for nothing. Assuming that the other person intends to give, and that you intend to receive, you can become the owner of a gift once it is delivered to you. Going further, you may be able to acquire property rights even if you act alone. There is some truth in the old saying that "possession is nine-tenths of the law." Sometimes, things have no owner at all. That is true, for instance, of a fox that is running wild or an intentionally abandoned bicycle by the side of the road. In that situation, you can acquire ownership of the thing by taking possession of it with the intention of controlling it for yourself.[3] There is also some truth in the old saying "finders keepers," but not "losers weepers."

[1.] The word "chattel" comes from the same source as the word "cattle." The root word first referred to moveable wealth generally, and then to livestock specifically. The overlap is understandable. Domesticated animals were once a primary form of wealth.

[2.] For that reason, lawyers refer to intangible property as *choses in action*. A chose in action is a "chose" (the French word for "thing") that can only be enforced through legal action. A piece of tangible property is a *chose in possession*, because it is a thing that can be possessed.

[3.] *Pierson v Post* 3 Cai 175 (NY SC 1805).

Suppose you find property that someone else lost. By intentionally taking control of that thing, you will acquire rights that are effective against everyone *except* the true owner.[4] Consequently, if I take that property from you, you can sue me in tort (as explained in Chapter 4) even if it is clear that you are not the true owner.[5] In the business world, however, a finder's rights may depend upon the circumstances. Although the law is rather unclear, it appears that an occupier is entitled to things that are found in the private, but not the public, parts of its premises.[6] Case Brief 17.1 discusses the leading decision.

CASE BRIEF 17.1

Parker v British Airways Board [1982] 2 WLR 503 (CA)

Alan Parker found a gold bracelet in the executive lounge at Heathrow Airport in London. He turned the bracelet over to the British Airways Board, which leased the airport, but made it clear that he wanted it back if the true owner did not come forward. The owner never appeared, and the board sold the jewellery for £850. Instead of paying that money to Parker, however, it kept it on the basis that it was entitled to anything found on its premises. Parker was understandably upset and sued.

The court ordered the board to pay the money to Parker. The judge agreed that an occupier is entitled to personal property *if* it is found in an area over which the occupier had a "manifest intention" to exercise control. That might be true, for instance, if Parker had discovered the bracelet under a desk in an office. On the facts, however, the item was discovered on the floor of a publicly accessible waiting area.

Some rights can be acquired through an act of creation. An author enjoys copyright as a result of writing a new book. And for somewhat different reasons, the owner of a cow acquires rights to any calves that are born. As both of those examples illustrate, property and property rights sometimes arise when none previously existed.

LOSING PERSONAL PROPERTY RIGHTS

Personal property rights do not last forever. For example, you will lose all of your rights to this book if you sell it to someone else. And if you rent it to a classmate for a term, you will no longer enjoy the right to immediate possession (but you will gain a right to a payment). More dramatically, since you cannot own something that does not exist, your rights will be lost if this book is destroyed in a fire. And while we have already seen that your rights will continue to exist even if this book is *lost*, the situation will be different if you *abandon* the text with an intention of giving up control.

Rights can also disappear if your personal property becomes attached to, or mixed with, land or other chattels. Although there are several possibilities, we will focus on the most common situation, which involves *fixtures*.[7] A **fixture**

a fixture is a chattel that has been sufficiently affixed, or attached, to land

---

[4.] Although a finder acquires substantial rights, it may also incur some obligations. A finder may be required to make a reasonable effort to locate the true owner and to preserve the goods.

[5.] *Armory v Delamirie* (1722) 93 ER 664 (KB).

[6.] There are other limitations. You cannot, for instance, acquire property rights in something that you discover while trespassing on another's land.

[7.] Similar rules apply when two chattels are joined together. For example, I may apply paint to your boat or tires to your car; my stallion may impregnate your mare and produce a foal; my grapes may become mixed with your grapes in a single barrel of wine; and my sheep may become mingled within your flock. Although the precise rules depend upon the situation, the courts will always try to strike a fair balance between our competing interests.

is a chattel that has been sufficiently affixed, or attached, to land or to a building.[8] The important point is that once a chattel becomes a fixture, it belongs to the owner of the land. Suppose you bought a dishwasher to use in your apartment. Although the decisions are frustratingly inconsistent, a court would be influenced by the following factors in deciding whether the machine became a fixture.

- **Degree of attachment:** A chattel is more likely to be considered a fixture if it is attached to a building rather then merely sitting under its own weight. Consequently, if you simply wheeled a dishwasher into the corner of the kitchen, it would presumably remain yours. However, if you installed it under the kitchen counter with screws and plumbing, it might be a fixture and therefore belong to your landlord.

- **Purpose of attachment:** A court would be even more concerned with the objective intention served by placing the dishwasher in the apartment. The key issue is whether a reasonable person would believe that the dishwasher became part of the building. If it was installed to enhance the value of the apartment, then it is probably a fixture. However, if it was merely done to make better use of the dishwasher itself, then it is less likely to be a fixture.

- **Tenants' fixtures:** There are special rules that would apply because your apartment was rented. The courts are concerned that tenants might unfairly lose ownership over things that they add to their premises. Consequently, even if the dishwasher did become the landlord's fixture, you could turn it back into your chattel if you removed it, within a reasonable time after the end of the lease, and without doing irreparable damage to the apartment. The same rule applies to trade fixtures. For instance, you probably could remove shelves and signs that you installed in a warehouse that you rented for storage.[9]

Concept Summary 17.1 reviews some of the ways in which ownership in personal property may be acquired or lost.

CONCEPT SUMMARY 17.1

Acquiring and Losing Ownership of Personal Property

Acquiring Personal Property	Losing Personal Property
purchase through contract with previous owner	*sale* through contract to new owner
gift received from previous owner	*gift* through intention and delivery to new owner
first possession of things that were never owned or that were abandoned	*abandonment* with intention to give up rights
finding of lost property (good against everyone *except* true owner)	*fixture* of chattel to land or building (subject to right of tenant's fixtures)
creation of new property	

[8] A building is usually a fixture itself because it is attached to land. An interesting issue sometimes arises with mobile homes.

[9] Since the issue of fixtures is almost always addressed in a lease, the parties can generally create their own terms. The basic rules discussed in the text, however, are usually followed.

BAILMENT

Many things can be done with personal property. We discussed a number of examples earlier in this text. For instance, contractual rights can be assigned, goods can be sold, and cheques can be negotiated. Another important type of arrangement, known as a **bailment**, occurs when one person temporarily gives up possession of property with the expectation of getting it back.[10] The person who delivers the property is the **bailor**. The person who receives it is the **bailee**.

A bailment may arise in a variety of ways. A *consignment* provides a good example. A **consignment** occurs when an owner gives property to another person for the purpose of selling it. The owner is called the *consignor* and the person making the sale is called the *consignee*. When the consignee sells the property on behalf of the consignor to a purchaser, ownership passes directly from the consignor to the purchaser. The consignee only ever had control and possession of the property for the purpose of making the sale—it was never the owner. Other examples of bailment include:

- renting a circular saw from a hardware store
- shipping furniture with a moving company
- delivering a machine to a shop for repairs
- placing equipment in a storage unit
- leasing a vehicle from a dealership
- borrowing a book from a library
- sending a package by courier
- lending a lawnmower to a neighbour

Those illustrations cover a lot of ground. Some arise in a business context, others more informally. Some involve a payment of money, others do not. They are all considered bailments, however, because they all satisfy the same requirements:

- one person voluntarily delivers property to another
- for a particular purpose
- with the intention that the property will be returned or disposed of as directed

Although the second and third requirements are usually straightforward, the first element occasionally causes problems. As a general rule, a bailment exists only if one person intends to deliver control and possession of property to another person.[11] It is, however, sometimes difficult to distinguish between a bailment and a *licence*. A **licence** is simply permission to do something that would otherwise be wrongful. The need to draw that distinction may arise if, for instance, you park your car on my parking lot.[12] If we have merely created a licence, then you are entitled to park on my land, but you have not given me

a bailment occurs when one person temporarily gives up possession of property with the expectation of getting it back

the bailor is the person who delivers property

the bailee is the person who receives property

a consignment occurs when an owner gives property to another person for the purpose of selling it

a licence is permission to do something that would otherwise be wrongful

---

10. The word "bailment" comes from the French word *bailler*, which means "to deliver."

11. That requirement is sometimes relaxed. For instance, a finder is often classified as a *quasi-bailee* (that is, *sort of like* a bailee) even though the person who lost the property did not voluntarily deliver possession and control of the goods. Likewise, if you leave your jacket in a store, the proprietors may be considered to be a type of bailee, at least if they pick it up with the intention of taking control of it.

12. Although the parking cases are the most common, there are many other examples. The same issue may arise, for instance, if you hang your coat in my cloak room as you enter my restaurant.

control and possession of your car. I therefore am not obliged to protect your vehicle. If, in contrast, I did receive control and possession of your car under a bailment, then I will have some obligation to take care of your vehicle. The distinction between a licence and a bailment is therefore critically important in terms of risk management.

In deciding whether a relationship is a bailment or a licence, it is necessary to ask how a reasonable person would view the parties' intentions. A bailment will exist if, according to the reasonable person, the parties intended for possession and control of the chattel to be substantially handed over. Otherwise, there is only a licence. Following our earlier example, Concept Summary 17.2 reviews several factors that a court would consider in deciding whether a parking lot involves a bailment or a licence. (Notice in particular that the mere payment of money by a car owner does not necessarily create a bailment.)

CONCEPT SUMMARY 17.2

Parked Car—Bailment or Licence?

- Did the car owner pay a substantial amount of money to an attendant (suggesting a bailment) or merely put a few coins into a machine (suggesting a licence)?
- Was the parking lot self-serve (suggesting a licence) or were there attendants on duty (suggesting a bailment)?
- Did the car owner keep the keys (suggesting a licence) or hand them over to attendants (suggesting a bailment)?
- If attendants collected the keys, did they merely put them in a safe place (suggesting a licence) or did they use them to drive the car (suggesting a bailment)?
- Did the car owner choose the specific parking spot (suggesting a licence) or was that decision made by attendants (suggesting a bailment)?
- Was the parking lot simply an open space (suggesting a licence) or was it enclosed with a controlled entrance and exit (suggesting a bailment)?
- Had the parking lot previously dealt with the car owner in such a way as to imply that it would (suggesting a bailment) or would not (suggesting a licence) assume substantial possession and control of the vehicle?
- Was there a sign or a ticket stub indicating that cars were left at the owners' risk (suggesting a licence) or would the reasonable person believe that the parking lot assumed some responsibility (suggesting a bailment)?

Business Decision 17.1 explores the difference between a bailment and a licence.

BUSINESS DECISION 17.1

Parking Lot: Bailment or Licence?[13]

You own and operate a restaurant. You also own and operate a nearby parking lot. On most nights, when business is reasonably relaxed, you simply allow customers of your restaurant to use that parking lot free of charge. But on special occasions, when the restaurant is very busy, you hire three or four attendants to maintain order in the parking lot. While some customers insist upon parking themselves, most are happy to hand over their keys, to allow the attendants to deal with parking, and to collect their vehicles at the end of the night. In either event, there is no charge for parking.

That system has generally worked well. Recently, however, you have been sued by Martin Miller. Miller was a

(continued)

---

13. *Martin v Town 'n' Country Delicatessen Ltd* (1963) 42 DLR (2d) 449 (Man CA).

(continued)

customer of your restaurant during a particularly busy evening last winter. He was happy to accept an attendant's offer to park his vehicle, but very upset at the end of the night when his car could not be found. As the police later discovered, Miller's car had been stolen, taken on a joy ride, and crashed into a tree. After recovering his car, Miller had to spend $5000 repairing damage that the thief had caused. Since the thief cannot be identified, Miller has sued your restaurant. He claims that a bailment was created when the attendant offered to park his car, and that there was a breach of that bailment relationship when the restaurant failed to reasonably protect his vehicle. You have argued in response that Miller simply enjoyed a licence to park his car on your property, and that you therefore were not obligated to guard his vehicle.

Questions for Discussion

1. Is a court more likely to find a bailment or a licence? Explain your answer.

2. What could you have done to clearly prevent a bailment from arising?

3. If the court finds that there was a bailment relationship between your restaurant and Miller, will you continue to do business the same way in the future? If not, what changes will you make?

Liability of Bailors

Most bailments occur without incident. The bailor delivers the property to the bailee, it is held for the intended purpose, and then returned in good condition. Exceptionally, however, difficulties arise on one side or the other. We consider the bailor's liability in this section and the bailee's in the next.

Consider a situation involving a lease. Suppose you are in the business of renting heavy machinery to construction firms. If you *sold* the same equipment, your transaction would be caught by the *Sale of Goods Act*, and you might be required, among other things, to ensure that it was fit for its intended purpose.[14] A lease, however, is not a sale. It is a bailment because you expect that the property will be returned to you at the end of the transaction. Nevertheless, the law requires you, as a bailor who is receiving consideration for the use of your property, to use reasonable care in providing appropriate machines.[15] Consequently, if a backhoe collapses and injures a worker, you might be held liable if you knew, or should have known, of the defect that caused the accident. You might also be required to provide a special warning regarding any unusual dangers, unless the bailee was already familiar with the type of equipment it was renting.

The other major basis of liability arises from a bailor's failure to pay a charge. Suppose you deliver your car to a garage for repairs or leave your furniture in a storage unit. You are expected to pay for the benefit that you receive from the mechanic or from the warehouse. To ensure that you do so, the bailee

---

[14.] We discussed the *Sale of Goods Act* in Chapter 13.

[15.] The lease itself can impose additional obligations upon the bailor or reduce the obligations that are normally imposed by the law.

a lien is the bailee's right to retain possession of property until the bailor pays a debt

a right of sale allows a bailee to sell the bailor's property to obtain payment of the bailor's debt

is entitled to exercise a *lien* over your property.[16] A **lien** is the bailee's right to retain possession of the property until the bailor pays a debt. Note that the bailee is only entitled to *retain* your property. If you somehow honestly recover your goods, the lien usually disappears. If a lien is exercised, and if you do not respond to it in a timely manner, the bailee can also exercise a statutory *right of sale*. Although the exact requirements vary between jurisdictions, a **right of sale** allows a bailee to sell the bailor's property to obtain payment of the bailor's debt. If the sale proceeds are larger than the debt, the bailor is entitled to the extra money.[17]

Liability of Bailees

A bailee's primary obligation is to return the property, in good condition, to the bailor at the end of the arrangement. A bailment, however, exposes the bailor to considerable risk. Suppose you deliver your truck to me. The vehicle might become lost, damaged, or destroyed. Furthermore, those events may occur while I am in possession. Since you would have little way of knowing exactly what happened to your truck, you might find it difficult to satisfy the usual requirements of, say, the tort of negligence.[18] The general rule in private law requires the plaintiff to prove that the defendant wrongfully caused a loss. But in our situation, I am the only one with access to all of the facts. The courts have therefore developed a special rule in this situation. If the bailor proves that goods were lost or damaged during a bailment, then the *burden of proof shifts* to the bailee. At that point, I would be required to prove that I was not to blame. If I could not do so, I would be held liable, even though you did not actually show that I was responsible for your loss. Although that rule provides a great benefit to the bailor, it is available only if the court is satisfied that the loss occurred during the bailment and that a shift in the burden of proof would not be unfair to the bailee. Consider the issue in You Be the Judge 17.1.

---

[16] Every province and territory has legislation that provides such rights to people who warehouse or store goods: *Warehouseman's Lien Act*, RSA 2000, c W-2, s 3 (Alta); *Warehouse Lien Act*, RSBC 1996, c 480, s 2 (BC); *Warehousemen's Lien Act*, CCSM c W20, s 2 (Man); *Warehouseman's Lien Act*, RSNB 1973, c W-4, s 2 (NB); *Warehousers' Lien Act*, RSNL 1990, c W-2, s 3 (Nfld); *Warehouse Keepers Lien Act*, RSNWT 1988, c W-2, s 2 (NWT); *Warehousemen's Lien Act*, RSNS 1989, c 499, s 3 (NS); *Warehouse Keepers Lien Act*, RSNWT 1988, c W-2, s 2 (Nun); *Repair and Storage Liens Act*, RSO 1990, c R.25, s 4(1) (Ont); *Warehousemen's Lien Act*, RSPEI 1988, c W-1, s 2 (PEI); *Warehouse Keepers Lien Act*, RSY 2002, c 226, s 2 (Yuk). Similar rights are given to people who repair or improve goods. However, the scope of mechanic's lien legislation varies between jurisdictions. See *eg Possessory Liens Act*, RSA 2000, c P-19, s 2 (Alta); *Repairers' Lien Act*, RSBC 1996, c 404, s 2(1) (BC); *Repair Shops Act*, CCSM c R90, s 1 (Man); *Liens on Goods and Chattels Act*, RSNB 1973, c L-6, s 2 (NB); *Mechanics' Lien Act*, RSNL 1990, c M-3, s 6(1) (Nfld); *Garagekeepers' Lien Act*, RSNWT 1988, c G-1, s 2(1) (NWT); *Mechanics' Lien Act*, RSNS 1989, c 277, s 6(1) (NS); *Garagekeepers' Lien Act*, RSNWT 1988, c G-1, s 2(1)(Nun); *Repair and Storage Liens Act*, RSO 1990, c R.25, s 3(1) (Ont); *Mechanics' Lien Act*, RSPEI 1988, c M-4, s 2 (PEI); *Garage Keepers Lien Act*, RSY 2002, c 99, s 2(1) (Yuk). A number of other statutes also confer rights on more specific types of people, such as threshers and woodsmen.

[17] Note that statutory liens and rights of sale are generally limited to bailees who repair and store property. For instance, while common carriers have the ability to exercise a common law lien, they do not have a right of sale.

[18] We discussed the tort of negligence in Chapter 6.

YOU BE THE JUDGE 17.1

Shifting the Burden of Proof[19]

Wong Aviation Ltd rented a Cessna airplane to Douglas Taylor one morning in late October. The weather was cold, visibility was limited, and the air was turbulent. Taylor took off with the intention of flying the plane in a tight circle around the Toronto Island Airport. Unfortunately, he and the aircraft disappeared without a trace. Although there is no positive evidence whatsoever regarding the disappearance, the evidence indicates that, given the weather conditions, it would have been possible for Taylor to lose control of the plane even if he did not act negligently.

Wong Aviation has sued Taylor's estate for $250 000, the value of the Cessna. Wong admits that it cannot succeed in a simple claim in negligence because it has no basis for positively proving, on a balance of probabilities, that Taylor carelessly caused the loss. Therefore it has based its action on the contract of bailment that was created when Taylor rented the plane. In doing so, Wong believes that it can shift the burden of proof. More specifically, it argues that since it has established that the property was lost during the bailment, to avoid liability, the defendant must prove that the loss was *not* caused by Taylor's lack of care. The defendant could not discharge that burden—no one has any idea what happened to Taylor and the aircraft.

Questions for Discussion

1. Under what conditions is the burden generally shifted in the context of a bailment?

2. Are those conditions satisfied in this case?

3. Would it be fair to shift the burden in any event?

Note that even if the burden of proof does shift, the bailee is not generally required to *guarantee* the safety of the bailor's property.[20] Liability will arise only from a failure to take reasonable care. But how much care must be used to avoid liability? Although the courts traditionally applied different standards of care to different types of bailments, they have moved toward a situation in which most bailees simply have to act as a reasonable person would act in similar circumstances.[21] Depending upon the circumstances, a reasonable person might exercise more or less caution and care. Several factors are especially important.[22]

- **Contract, custom, and statute:** If a bailment is contained within a contract, the parties are generally free to agree upon the level of care that the bailee must use. The court may also formulate the standard of care to reflect a practice that is customarily used in a certain type of business. Diamond merchants, for instance, use greater care than people who deal in bricks. Similarly, the standard may be affected by legislation.

- **Benefit of the bailment:** Greater care must be used if a bailment is entirely for the benefit of the bailee. That would be the case if I borrowed

---

19. *Taylor Estate v Wong Aviation Ltd* (1969) 3 DLR (3d) 55 (SCC).

20. We will see an exception that applies to common carriers. Furthermore, the defence of reasonable care is not available in a case of *deviance*, where the bailee dealt with the bailor's property in an unauthorized way. For instance, if you left your furniture in my storage facilities while you were abroad for a year, I might, without your permission, let my brother use it for a few months. If so, I could be held liable even if I was not directly at fault for the fact that the goods were lost or damaged: *England v Heimbecker* (1977) 78 DLR (3d) 177 (Sask Dist Ct).

21. That is a general trend in the law. We saw a similar development for the tort of occupiers' liability in Chapter 5.

22. While it is important to know which factors affect the content of the standard of care, you should not become too caught up in the exercise. The distinctions between situations are even harder to apply than they are to describe. At the end of the day, a judge usually adopts a common sense approach to all of the facts.

a truck from you, as a friend, because I was moving to a new apartment. In contrast, a lower level of care may be acceptable if a bailment is entirely for the benefit of the bailor. Perhaps I had possession of your vehicle simply because I allowed you, as a favour, to park it in my garage while you were on vacation.

- **Gratuity or reward:** A bailee's burden also depends upon whether it was *gratuitous* (free of charge) or for *reward* (for payment). If I was using your truck to move my furniture, I would have to exercise more care if I did not pay for that privilege. After all, I was getting something for nothing. However, if I rented the truck from you, a court might be more lenient, since the transaction benefitted you too.

- **Value and nature of the property:** A reasonable person's behaviour is influenced by the nature and value of the property. I would be expected to behave more cautiously if the truck that I borrowed from you was a fragile and priceless antique rather than a sturdy but well-used pick-up.

- **Bailee's expertise:** I might be expected to exercise greater care if I claimed to have special experience or training in handling the property. For instance, the standard would be higher if you stored your truck in my commercial parking complex rather than the garage attached to my house.

The expectation under the general standard of care can be quite demanding, especially if there is a gratuitous bailment entirely for the bailee's benefit. In exceptional circumstances, however, the bar is set even higher: The bailee is treated as an *insurer*. In other words, the bailee can be held liable even if it was *not* careless. The bailor is entitled to compensation simply because its property has been lost or damaged. We will consider the most important example in the business context: *common carriers*.[23]

Common Carriers

a **common carrier** is a company that offers to deliver any goods for any person in exchange for a standard price

A **common carrier** is a company that offers to deliver any goods for any person in exchange for a standard price (assuming that it has available space). That definition can apply to companies that transport by trains, trucks, ships, or airplanes. Notice, however, that a company must do more than commonly carry goods for money. It must also offer its services without reserving the right to refuse to deliver some goods while taking others. Railways, for instance, are often common carriers. In contrast, a moving company is a *private carrier*, rather than a common carrier, if its owner frequently turns away work that involves particularly heavy lifting. So is an airline that reserves the right to refuse some sorts of goods.

A private carrier is liable only if it fails to exercise the level of care that is reasonably expected from someone in its line of work. A different rule applies to common carriers, for largely historical reasons. In ancient times, unscrupulous carriers often agreed to transport goods, but then delivered the property to

[23.] A similar set of rules applies to innkeepers, who are people who offer food and lodging to the public without reserving a general right to turn away travellers: *Innkeepers Act*, RSA 2000, c I-2 (Alta); *Hotel Keepers Act*, RSBC 1996, c 206 (BC); *Hotel Keepers Act*, CCSM, c H150 (Man); *Innkeepers Act*, RSNB 1973, c I-10 (NB); *Innkeepers* Act, RSNL 1990, c I-7 (Nfld); *Hotel Keepers Act*, RSNWT 1988, c H-5 (NWT); *Tourist Accommodations Act*, SNS 1994–95, c 9 (NS); *Hotel Keepers Act*, RSNWT 1988, c H-5 (Nun); *Innkeepers Act*, RSO 1990, c I.7 (Ont); *Tourism Industry Act*, RSPEI 1988, c T-3.3 (PEI); *Hotel Keepers Act*, RSS 1978, c H-11 (Sask); *Hotel and Tourist Establishments Act*, RSY 2002, c 113 (Yuk).

highwaymen in exchange for a share of the loot. A *shipper* (a person who shipped the property) usually found it difficult to prove carelessness because it had no way of knowing exactly what happened. The loss occurred while the goods were out of its possession. To remedy that problem, the courts held that a common carrier was generally liable for any loss or damage, even if it was not personally at fault. The shipper merely had to prove that (i) the carrier was a common carrier, (ii) the property was given to the carrier in one condition, and (iii) the property either was not properly delivered to its destination or was delivered to its destination in worse condition.

That basic rule is still applied. Furthermore, a common carrier has very few defences.

- **War and act of God:** A carrier is not liable if goods are harmed as a result of war or an **act of God**, which is a natural catastrophe, such as an earthquake or flood. In either event, however, the carrier may be held responsible if it carelessly exposed the shipper's property to danger. A trucker, for example, might damage goods as a result of unreasonably driving under treacherous weather conditions.

  an act of God is a natural catastrophe

- **Inherent vice and shipper's fault:** The shipper's goods may have suffered damage as a result of an **inherent vice**, which is a defect in the goods themselves. For instance, cattle may die in transit because they were already diseased when they were brought on board. Similarly, the carrier is not responsible for loss or damage that is the shipper's fault. The person sending the property might, for example, improperly pack crystal bowls or fail to label their container as "fragile."

  an inherent vice is a defect in goods themselves

- **Exclusion clause:** By far the most important defence arises from the use of *exclusion clauses*. As we discussed in Chapters 9 and 12, an **exclusion clause** is a contractual term that protects one party from liability. Common carriers typically use standard form agreements that contain provisions along the following lines: "The carrier's liability is limited to $50 per package for any damage howsoever caused," or "The carrier shall only be liable for damage caused by negligence."[24] As usual, judges interpret such clauses narrowly and insist that they be sufficiently drawn to a shipper's attention before a contract is created. Furthermore, in the present context, exclusion clauses must be approved by the Canadian Transport Commission to ensure that customers are treated fairly. Within those limitations, however, exclusion clauses provide an important mechanism for risk management for both parties. The carrier is relieved of responsibility, and the shipper is alerted to the fact that it should purchase property insurance.

  an exclusion clause is a contractual term that protects one party from liability

Sub-Bailment

We need to briefly consider the concept of *sub-bailment*. As the name suggests, a **sub-bailment** occurs when property that is already held under a bailment is transferred into a further bailment. Suppose you deliver property to me, and that I then deliver it to someone else. You are called the *original bailor*. I am called the *bailee/bailor* (because I am the bailee under the original bailment, but the bailor under the sub-bailment). And the third party is called the *sub-bailee*. That sort of arrangement arises quite often in the business world. Three simple examples will illustrate the point.

a sub-bailment occurs when property that is already held under a bailment is transferred into a further bailment

---

24. In the second situation, since the burden of proving the defence is on the common carrier, it would have to prove that it had not been careless.

- I own a general repair shop. You deliver a television to me with instructions to fix the picture tube. Because I do not have the proper equipment to deal with that problem, I deliver the television to another company, with instructions that is should be returned to me once the job is done.

- I own a trucking company. You deliver a load of kitchen fixtures to me for shipment from Vancouver to Charlottetown. When I arrive at the east coast of New Brunswick, I learn that the Confederation Bridge, which links Prince Edward Island to the mainland, is closed for repairs. I therefore deliver the goods to a local ferry company for the last leg of the journey across the water.

- You manufacture heavy machinery. I operate a local construction supply company. My stock includes several vehicles that I have leased from you, including a bulldozer. As part of my business, I sublease that bulldozer to a construction firm for use on a particular project.

Figure 17.1 illustrates the process of sub-bailment.

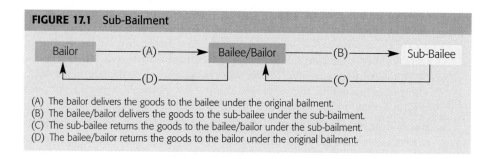

FIGURE 17.1   Sub-Bailment

(A) The bailor delivers the goods to the bailee under the original bailment.
(B) The bailee/bailor delivers the goods to the sub-bailee under the sub-bailment.
(C) The sub-bailee returns the goods to the bailee/bailor under the sub-bailment.
(D) The bailee/bailor returns the goods to the bailor under the original bailment.

A bailee is allowed to place the property into a sub-bailment only with the bailor's consent. A bailment contract may expressly state that the bailee is entitled to deliver the goods to a third party. However, the courts also often recognize implied consent from the circumstances. It is common for a court to assume that a person who delivers an automobile to a mechanic for repairs, or a package to a carrier for shipment, agrees to allow the bailee to transfer the property to a third party to complete the task if necessary. If a bailee places property into a sub-bailment without the bailor's permission, it can be held responsible for any resulting loss. It may even be held liable for the tort of conversion if its conduct seriously interferes with the bailor's ownership.[25]

The most important issue concerning sub-bailment arises if property is lost or damaged while it is in the sub-bailee's possession. As a general rule, that party is expected to use reasonable care in dealing with the goods. There are two possible actions if it fails to do so.

- A claim may be brought by the bailee/bailor, even though that party did not own the property and merely enjoyed a right of possession under the original bailment. If that claim is successful, then the bailee/bailor normally receives the damages from the sub-bailee on behalf of the original bailor.

[25.] The tort of conversion was discussed in Chapter 4.

■ The original bailor may also be entitled to sue the sub-bailee. That is true only if (i) the original bailor expressly or implicitly agreed to the sub-bailment, and (ii) the sub-bailee knew, or ought to have known, that it received possession of goods that were already held under a bailment.[26]

The situation can become quite complicated if property passes through a series of bailments and sub-bailments, especially if some of those arrangements involve exclusion clauses. Case Brief 17.2 provides a useful summary of the entire area.

CASE BRIEF 17.2

Punch v Savoy's Jewellers Ltd (1986) 26 DLR (4th) 546 (Ont CA)

Lenore Punch, who lived in Sault Ste Marie, received a ring from her aunt as a gift. It was a family heirloom that was worth more than $11 000. Because the ring was in need of repair, Ms Punch took it to a local shop, Savoy's Jewellers. Savoy realized that it could not perform the repairs itself and consequently sent the ring, by registered mail, to Harry Walker Jewellery in Toronto. In doing so, however, it purchased only $100 worth of insurance on the ring.

Harry Walker fixed the ring and was prepared to return it to Savoy. Due to a postal strike, however, it obtained permission from Savoy (but not from Ms Punch) to send the ring by CN Railway's courier service rather than by registered mail. A driver for CN collected the ring, and an employee for Harry Walker signed a shipping form that contained a provision that limited CN's liability for any loss to $100. Unfortunately, the ring disappeared. Although the exact cause of the loss was unknown, CN freely admitted that its driver may have stolen the property. (Oddly, CN never bothered to discuss the matter with its employee.)

Ms Punch relied on the bailment relationship and sued Savoy, Harry Walker, and CN. The Ontario Court of Appeal first held that she had implicitly consented to Savoy's sub-bailment to Harry Walker, and to Harry Walker's sub-sub-bailment to CN. Although Ms Punch had not discussed the matter with Savoy at the outset, she presumably knew that a sub-bailment was possible and she did not object. Furthermore, she admitted that if she had been asked, she would have consented. And finally, the evidence indicated that Savoy's use of a sub-bailment was common in the jewellery business.

Next, the court stated that since the ring disappeared while it was held on bailment, the burden of proof shifted

from Ms Punch. Each defendant consequently could be held liable unless it established that its carelessness had *not* caused the loss. None of the defendants were able to do so. Indeed, the evidence pointed in the opposite direction. Savoy carelessly failed to purchase adequate insurance coverage for the ring. It should have been more cautious, especially since it agreed to allow Harry Walker to return the ring by way of a courier service with which it had no experience. Harry Walker was also careless. It should have explored the possibility of obtaining better insurance coverage. And CN was careless because it allowed the ring to disappear while in its possession, probably through theft by its own employee.

Finally, the court held that the exclusion clause contained in CN's shipping document might be effective against Harry Walker, but not against Savoy or Punch. The exclusion clause was contained in a contract. And as we saw in Chapter 8, contractual terms can generally only be enforced between contractual parties—in this case, CN and Harry Walker. An exception may be created if a bailor agrees to be bound by a term. On the facts of this case, however, neither Savoy (as the bailor/bailee) nor Ms Punch (as the original bailor) even knew about the exclusion clause.

The defendants were therefore all liable to Ms Punch. She was entitled to recover from any or all of them up to the full value of her ring. (She could not, of course, recover complete compensation three times over.) Between themselves, the defendants were equally liable. CN tried to limit its liability with regard to Harry Walker, but the Court of Appeal narrowly interpreted the exclusion clause and found that it was ineffective because it did not cover losses created through theft.

[26.] Even if the bailor did not initially consent to the sub-bailment, it can subsequently *ratify* that arrangement. In other words, it can later adopt the bailee/bailor's act of placing the property into a sub-bailment as having been performed on its behalf.

PERSONAL PROPERTY, RISK MANAGEMENT, AND INSURANCE

Personal property raises interesting risk management issues. In one sense, property rights are very strong. They usually exist until their owner intentionally disposes of them.

- If you lose your property, you can recover it from me even though, as a finder, I acquired rights against everyone else in the world.

- If a thief steals your goods and sells them to me, I may be liable for the tort of conversion even if I acted in the reasonable belief that the thief was the true owner.[27] As a general rule, people cannot give more than they actually have.[28] I could not buy from the thief something that still belonged to you.

In a number of other respects, however, personal property rights are quite fragile.

- Even if I found your goods, you cannot sue me unless you know that I have your property. However, personal property is easily moved from one place to another. And while there are registration systems for keeping track of some chattels (such as vehicles), it is often impossible to locate goods that have gone missing.

- Personal property may be damaged innocently or in a way that does not support a valuable cause of action. Your computer may be ruined by an electrical storm that causes a power surge, or it may be crushed by a common carrier under a shipping contract that contains an effective exclusion clause.

Those sorts of concerns create the need for risk management. Some strategies are *proactive* because they reduce the risk of loss in the first place. For instance, security systems can prevent thefts, and training programs can help employees avoid accidents. Perhaps the most important form of risk management, however, is *insurance*.

In Chapter 3, we discussed the need for *liability insurance*, which involves an insurance company's contractual promise to pay damages on behalf of a person who incurs liability. In exchange for that promise, the insured party pays a price, called a *premium*. Since an employer may be vicariously liable for an employee's torts, liability insurance is often a matter of survival. Few businesses have sufficient assets to pay for all of the damage that they may cause in the course of their operations.[29] In this chapter, we look at another significant form of insurance: *property insurance*. **Property insurance** is a contract in which an insurance company, in exchange for a premium, promises to pay money if

property insurance is a contract in which an insurance company, in exchange for a premium, promises to pay money if property is lost, damaged, or destroyed

---

27. See Ethical Perspective 4.1.

28. The rule of *nemo dat quod non habet* (or *nemo dat* for short) is subject to several exceptions. The most important occurs if value is given in exchange for *money* rather than *goods*. Suppose a thief stole $5000 in cash from you. If I bought that money from the thief by selling a car to him, I can obtain ownership of the money. That exception is based on the need for cash to pass freely through the commercial world.

29. A business with sufficient assets may self-insure. Most businesses purchase insurance coverage year after year, even if they seldom incur liabilities. As an alternative, however, some businesses save the money that they would have used to purchase insurance, and use it instead to satisfy the liabilities that do occasionally arise.

property is lost, damaged, or destroyed.[30] The basic difference between the two types of insurance is reflected in the fact that liability insurance is often called *third-party coverage*, whereas property insurance is often called *first-party coverage*.

- **Third-party coverage:** Liability insurance provides third-party coverage because, in one sense, it is aimed at providing compensation to someone outside of the insurance contract.[31] The insurance company's obligation is triggered only if the insured party is accused of wrongfully inflicting a loss upon someone else.
- **First-party coverage:** Property insurance provides first-party coverage because it does not require the involvement of an outsider. The insurance company's obligation to pay is triggered by a loss to the insured party itself.

Figure 17.2 illustrates the difference between third-party and first-party insurance.

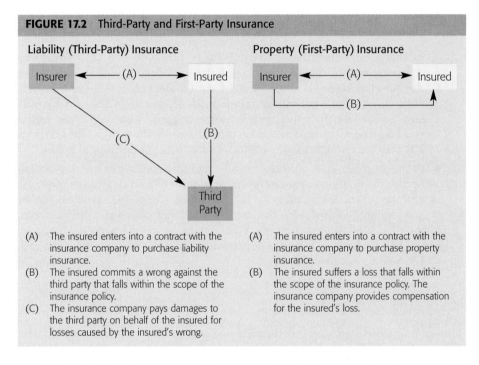

FIGURE 17.2   Third-Party and First-Party Insurance

Liability (Third-Party) Insurance

Property (First-Party) Insurance

(A) The insured enters into a contract with the insurance company to purchase liability insurance.
(B) The insured commits a wrong against the third party that falls within the scope of the insurance policy.
(C) The insurance company pays damages to the third party on behalf of the insured for losses caused by the insured's wrong.

(A) The insured enters into a contract with the insurance company to purchase property insurance.
(B) The insured suffers a loss that falls within the scope of the insurance policy. The insurance company provides compensation for the insured's loss.

Although the rules are complex, we can briefly summarize the essential points that arise in connection with property insurance.

---

[30] Although insurance is a type of contract, it is governed by special rules. Most significantly, while you generally are not required to volunteer information when you negotiate an agreement, the situation is different when you purchase insurance. Insurance is a contract of *utmost good faith*. You are therefore required to voluntarily disclose any facts that might affect the risks for which you are seeking coverage. If you fail to do so, your contract may be void.

[31] That statement is not strictly accurate. Liability insurance is actually intended to protect the insured party against the risk of being held liable to a third party. The important point, however, is that such coverage necessarily requires the involvement of a third party. Furthermore, a practical effect of liability insurance is that the third party is much more likely to receive compensation. The insurance company usually has enough money to pay damages even if the insured party does not.

Scope of Coverage

First, as a matter of risk management, it is critical to understand the scope of coverage that is provided by an insurance policy. You only get what you pay for.[32] Most insurance contracts are based on standard form agreements (as discussed in Chapter 9) that cover common events, like fires, floods, storms, and thefts. That basic coverage, however, is subject to restrictions. Standard fire insurance, for instance, may not cover accidents that arise from the storage of explosives or from riots. As a general rule, you can obtain extra protection for those events, but you will have to pay higher premiums.

Indemnification

Second, property insurance is never profitable. At most, it provides **indemnification**, which is reimbursement for a loss that has occurred. And it seldom offers even that much relief.

- There are different ways of calculating the loss that occurs when property is lost, damaged, or destroyed. Suppose a piece of equipment in your factory is badly damaged in a fire. Your policy may entitle you to replace it with a new machine. It is more likely, however, that your insurance company is merely obligated to pay the value that your equipment had the moment before it was destroyed. And if your equipment had been in use for some time before the accident, its *depreciated value* would probably be far less than the cost of a replacement.[33] Consequently, unless you can find a suitable second-hand substitute, the policy will not actually provide enough money to make your factory operational again.

- Property insurance policies usually include *deductibles*. A **deductible** occurs when the insurance company is not required to provide indemnification for the initial part of a loss. A common example involves cracked automobile windshields. The driver usually agrees to pay, for instance, the first $250 toward a repair. You can always ask for a policy that does not have a deductible and that provides full replacement cost. But again, you will pay accordingly.

Insurable Interest

You cannot obtain property insurance unless you have an *insurable interest*. That requirement is needed to avoid "moral hazards." Suppose you could buy coverage over my car. You would have an incentive to destroy my vehicle. Even though you would not actually suffer a loss (since the car belongs to me), you would be entitled to a payment under the insurance policy. The law therefore prevents you from obtaining insurance unless you have an *insurable interest*. An

insurable interest exists if you benefit from the existence of the property and would be worse off if it were damaged. Consistent with the goal of indemnifi-

---

[32.] And sometimes not even that much. In an effort to save money, unscrupulous insurance companies occasionally refuse to pay for losses that fall within the policies that they have sold. In doing so, they commit a breach of contract. To discourage that practice, a court may award punitive damages, as well as compensatory damages, against an insurance company: *Whiten v Pilot Insurance Co* (2002) 209 DLR (4th) 257 (SCC) ($1 000 000 in punitive damages).

[33.] Insurance policies also often give the insurer the option of paying to repair, rather than replace, damaged property. An insurance company will choose the cheaper alternative.

cation, you can be protected only from a loss that you could actually suffer. However, you do not necessarily have to *own* the property in question. The Supreme Court of Canada has held, for instance, that you can have an insurable interest in a corporation's property if you own a substantial number of shares in that company. Any loss to the business would also be harmful to you.[34]

Excessive and Insufficient Insurance

Since property insurance is limited to indemnification, it is important to avoid excessive insurance. There is nothing to be gained from purchasing the same coverage from two insurers. Suppose you insured the full value of your building, worth $500 000, against the risk of fire with both Insurance Company A and Insurance Company B. Even if your building were entirely destroyed by fire, you would be able to collect only $500 000, not $1 000 000. The premium that you paid to one of the companies therefore would be a waste of money. That extra payment would simply provide a benefit to the insurers. The doctrine of **contribution** states that if two parties are equally liable, they share the loss between themselves. Consequently, if you recovered $500 000 from Company A, it could demand $250 000 from Company B. In effect, the companies would enjoy a bargain at your expense. Each would be liable for only $250 000 even though it had charged you for $500 000 in coverage.

the doctrine of **contribution** states that if two parties are equally liable, they share the loss among themselves

Just as it is important to avoid *excessive* coverage, it is also important to avoid *insufficient* coverage. That proposition is especially important in one context. To encourage you to buy as much coverage as possible, insurance companies often put *co-insurance clauses* into their policies. A **co-insurance clause** states that, if you do not maintain a certain level of coverage, you may be held partially responsible if you suffer a loss of a *lesser* extent. We can demonstrate that difficult rule by using a simple example. Suppose you buy only $6000 worth of insurance, even though your equipment is worth $10 000. The policy contains a co-insurance clause that requires coverage for at least 80 percent of the value of your machine.

a **co-insurance clause** states that if an insured party does not maintain a certain level of coverage, it may be held partially responsible in the event of an accident

- If an accident occurs, and the damage to your machine is worth *at least* 80 percent of its value (say, $9000), you will be entitled to receive $6000, which is the full extent of the benefit that you bought.

- However, if an accident occurs and the damage to your machine is worth *less than* 80 percent of its value (say $4000) then you will be a co-insurer to the extent that you did not buy enough coverage. Since you bought only 75 percent of the protection required under the co-insurance clause (that is, $6000 coverage rather than $8000 coverage), you can recover only 75 percent of your loss (that is, $3000 of the $4000 loss). Figure 17.3 shows the relevant calculation.

FIGURE 17.3   Co-Insurance

$$\frac{\text{amount of coverage purchased}}{\text{minimum coverage required under co-insurance clause}} \times \begin{array}{c}\text{actual} \\ \text{loss}\end{array} = \begin{array}{c}\text{insurer's} \\ \text{liability}\end{array}$$

$$\frac{\$6000}{\$10\,000 \times 80\% \ (= \$8000)} \times \$4000 = \$3000$$

[34.] *Kosmopoulos v Constitution Insurance Co* (1987) 34 DLR (4th) 208 (SCC).

Subrogation

There is one more point to make in connection with indemnification. So far, we have ignored the possibility that the property protected under a policy may be *wrongfully* damaged by a third party. Suppose I destroy your factory by carelessly starting a fire. Generally speaking, the rights that you enjoy under your policy are not affected by the fact that I committed a tort against you. You will still receive compensation from your insurance company. But because your policy limits you to indemnification, you *cannot* also sue me in tort. If you did, you might recover twice for the same loss—once from me and once from the insurer. That is not to say, however, that I will not have to pay for my wrong. The terms of your policy will entitle your insurance company to *subrogation*. The doctrine of **subrogation** allows your insurance company to stand in your shoes and acquire the rights that you have against me. Consequently, after indemnifying you, your insurance company will, at its own cost, bring an action against me for negligently burning down your factory. Figure 17.4 illustrates the process of subrogation.

subrogation allows an insurance company to stand in the insured party's place and acquire any rights that it may have against a third party

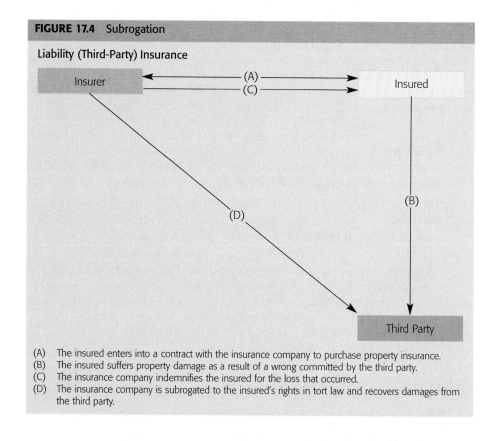

FIGURE 17.4   Subrogation

Liability (Third-Party) Insurance

(A)   The insured enters into a contract with the insurance company to purchase property insurance.
(B)   The insured suffers property damage as a result of a wrong committed by the third party.
(C)   The insurance company indemnifies the insured for the loss that occurred.
(D)   The insurance company is subrogated to the insured's rights in tort law and recovers damages from the third party.

Are the effects of the doctrine of subrogation fair? Consider Ethical Perspective 17.1.

ETHICAL PERSPECTIVE 17.1

Subrogation

Questions for Discussion

Answer these questions on the basis of the preceding example of subrogation.

1. Would it be unfair if you were entitled to both claim indemnification from the insurer and sue me for damages in tort? If you could have obtained damages from me if you had not purchased a policy, then why did you pay the premium to the insurance company? Was the policy really a benefit to you? Explain your answer.

2. Assume that (i) you paid $10 000 in premiums, (ii) you received $100 000 in indemnification, and (iii) your insurer recovered $100 000 in damages from me as a result of being subrogated to your rights in tort. Is it fair that the insurance company can retain the money that you paid in premiums even though it did not eventually suffer any loss in return? Explain your answer.

Other Forms of Business Insurance

Before leaving this topic, it is important to note that there are many types of insurance policies in addition to the ones that we have discussed. Some are especially important to the issue of risk management in the business world. In determining which are appropriate for a particular business, you should consult an insurance broker.

- Although property insurance may allow a business to replace or repair equipment and facilities that have been lost, damaged, or destroyed, there will usually be a delay before operations return to normal after an accident. And that delay may be very costly. Consequently, **business interruption insurance** is quite common. As the name suggests, it provides coverage for losses created by downtime. It can include, for instance, compensation for lost profits, wasted expenditures, and relocation expenses.

  business interruption insurance provides coverage for losses incurred as a result of downtime

- A similar issue arises as a result of computer saboteurs. The release of a single virus can easily cost the global economy billions of dollars as websites crash and hard drives are erased. Although the insurance industry is still coming to terms with that problem, it is possible for a business to purchase **hacker insurance**. Because of the potential size of the losses, however, coverage tends to be expensive and therefore is often practical only for enterprises like eBay and Amazon that rely heavily upon the Internet.

  hacker insurance provides protection from the economic consequences of computer saboteurs

- A business may suffer a substantial economic loss if an important member of its organization dies or becomes incapacitated. Although that person will be missed, a company may find it easier to adjust to the loss if it has access to funds with which it can hire and train a replacement. **Key person insurance** provides such a fund.

  key person insurance provides protection against the loss of important members of a business

- Many businesses also help to arrange **life, health, and disability insurance** for employees and their families. Typically, the employer and the employee reach an agreement in which both contribute to the cost of the premium. The employer's portion is part of the employee's total remuneration package. Such arrangements are advantageous to employees because, while they could individually purchase insurance for themselves, the costs of group coverage are substantially lower.[35]

  life, health, and disability insurance provides protection for employees in the event of health problems

---

35. An injured employee may also be entitled to benefits under workers compensation schemes: Chapter 3 and Chapter 26.

a **fidelity bond** provides coverage when an employee steals money, equipment, or other assets from a business or one of its clients

a **surety bond** is used to assure a client that it will be financially protected if a job is not performed as promised

■ *Bonds* are used to provide comfort in some business contexts. A **fidelity bond** provides coverage when an employee steals money, equipment, or other assets from a business or one of its clients. First-party fidelity covers the company's own property. Third-party fidelity covers property belonging to a client. A **surety bond** is used to assure a client that it will be financially protected if a job is not performed as promised. For instance, you may be concerned about a construction company's ability to complete a new building on time. If so, you might insist upon a surety bond that would allow you to receive compensation from an insurance company if the project is delayed.

CHAPTER SUMMARY

Broadly speaking, there are two types of property: real property and personal property. Personal property is either tangible or intangible. Personal property rights can be acquired in various ways: contract, gift, finding, and creation. They can also be lost in various ways: contract, destruction, abandonment, and fixture.

A bailment occurs when one person temporarily gives up possession of property with the expectation of getting it back. The person who delivers the property is the bailor, and the person who receives it is the bailee. Bailments arise in many circumstances, including leases for personal property.

A bailor may be liable for delivering goods that are not fit for the bailee's purpose. A bailor may also be liable to pay a price in exchange for the benefit of the bailment. If it fails to do so, the bailee may be entitled to exercise a lien and a right of sale.

A bailee's primary obligation is to return the property to the bailor in good condition. If the bailee fails to do so, the burden of proof may shift, and the bailee may be held liable unless it proves that it was not carelessly responsible for the loss or damage to the bailor's property. In rare circumstances, the standard of care is higher, and the bailee is treated as an insurer of the bailor's goods. That rule applies to common carriers.

A sub-bailment occurs when property that is already held under a bailment is transferred into a further bailment. In that situation, the sub-bailee may be held liable if the property is lost or damaged.

Insurance is one of the most important forms of risk management in business. Liability insurance, which we examined in Chapter 3, is sometimes called third-party insurance because, in one sense, it is aimed at providing compensation to someone outside of the insurance contract. Property insurance, on the other hand, is sometimes called first-party insurance because it does not require the involvement of an outsider and because the insurance company's obligation to pay is triggered by a loss to the insured party itself.

Basic property insurance policies are usually limited in scope. Furthermore, insurance merely provides indemnification for a loss. There are different ways in which to calculate losses for the purpose of insurance. Insurance benefits are often subject to deductibles.

Insurance is available only to a person who has an insurable interest in property. An insurable interest exists if a person benefits from the property and would be worse off if it were damaged or lost.

Businesses should avoid obtaining excessive insurance and insufficient insurance. Excessive insurance often provides a benefit to the insurance companies as a result of the doctrine of contribution. Insufficient insurance often gives rise to the problem of co-insurance.

The process of subrogation allows an insurance company to stand in the insured party's place and acquire any rights that the insured may have against a third party.

Besides liability insurance and property insurance, a business may wish to purchase other types of insurance, including business interruption insurance; hacker insurance; key person insurance; life, health, and disability insurance; fidelity bonds; and surety bonds.

REVIEW QUESTIONS

1. What is the difference between real property and personal property?

2. There are different ways of classifying personal property. Use examples to explain the difference between tangible and intangible property, and between choses in possession and choses in action.

3. List four ways in which personal property rights can be acquired.

4. "Finders keepers, losers weepers." Explain the extent to which the law adopts that phrase. Against whom does the finder of property have rights?

5. "You are always entitled to keep property that you find on someone else's premises." Explain the extent to which that statement is correct.

6. List four ways in which personal property rights can be lost.

7. What is a fixture? To whom does a fixture belong? Explain the factors that will influence a court's decision as to whether a chattel has become a fixture.

8. Define the term "bailment," and list the three elements of a bailment. Which party is the bailor, and which party is the bailee?

9. Using examples, describe situations in which leaving a car in a parking lot creates a bailment or a licence. In practical terms, what is the most important difference between a bailment and a licence?

10. "Since the bailor is simply delivering possession of goods to the bailee, the bailor never has an obligation with respect to the quality of the property." Is that statement true? Illustrate your answer with an example.

11. Explain when and how a bailee can use a lien or a right of sale to recover payment from a bailor.

12. Why does the law sometimes shift the burden of proof when the bailor complains that property has not been returned in a timely manner or in good condition? Briefly describe the situation in which the burden of proof will shift.

13. List and briefly explain five factors that will influence the judge's determination as to whether the bailee acted as a reasonable person would have acted in similar circumstances.

14. Define the phrase "common carrier." Is every business that transports goods for a price a common carrier? Explain your answer.

15. "A common carrier is an insurer of bailed goods." What does that statement mean? Will a common carrier always be held responsible if goods are lost or damaged while in its possession? List three types of defences that a common carrier can use against a bailor. In practical terms, which type of defence is the most significant? Explain your answer.

16. Explain the process of sub-bailment and identify the parties that are involved in that process. Is a bailee always entitled to place goods into a sub-bailment?

17. To whom can a sub-bailee be held liable for losing or damaging goods held on a sub-bailment? Outline the situations in which a sub-bailee can use the protection of an exclusion clause.

18. Use examples to explain the difference between third-party insurance and first-party insurance.

19. Define the term "indemnification." Explain how the concept of indemnification affects the ideas of (i) an insurable interest, (ii) excessive insurance and insufficient insurance, and (iii) contribution and co-insurance.

20. Explain the process of subrogation.

CASES AND PROBLEMS

1. Oliver Copperfield worked as a freelance chimney cleaner. In the course of completing a job, he found a diamond ring hidden in a small crevice that was within arm's reach of the fireplace. He took the ring to Felix Lechat, a jeweller, explained the situation, and asked for an appraisal. Felix immediately offered to buy the ring for $100. Oliver refused and indicated that he would return later in the day for the ring and the appraisal. Upon Oliver's return, however, Felix merely handed back the ring—without the diamond. When Oliver protested, Felix said, "You're no better than I am. You found the ring and took it. And now I found the ring and took it. Just deal with it." Who is entitled to the diamond?

Explain the relationship between the parties.

2. The Lazy Lion Restaurant was owned and operated by Leon Lowe. Although the property upon which the restaurant was located was owned by Lowe, it was also subject to a mortgage in favour of Ursula Aust. Likewise, although Lowe owned most of the equipment that was located within the restaurant, the main oven was subject to a conditional sales agreement that Lowe had created with Jeremy Froelich. (Froelich did not register that agreement under any personal property security legislation, as discussed in Chapter 23.) That conditional sales agreement stated that while Lowe was immediately entitled to possession and use of the oven, Froelich

retained ownership until the purchase price was paid in full. The agreement also stated that if Lowe failed to make a monthly payment, Froelich was entitled to re-acquire possession of the oven and to sue for damages. For reasons of safety and efficiency, Lowe had the oven bolted to the floor and actually incorporated into the adjacent wall. Exhaust shafts and electrical cords that were attached to the oven were similarly firmly built into the surrounding area.

The Lazy Lion unfortunately failed within two months of opening. That created a number of difficulties. On a personal level, Lowe was financially ruined. As a result, he was unable to meet his monthly payment requirements under the conditional sales agreement with Froelich. And for the same reason, he defaulted on his mortgage payments to Aust. Before Froelich was able to take any action, Aust began proceedings to exercise her right of foreclosure under the mortgage and to acquire ownership of the property (as explained in Chapter 16). A dispute consequently has arisen between Froelich and Aust. Aust claims that she is entitled to the entire mortgaged property, including the oven. Froelich claims that he continues to own the oven under the terms of the conditional sales contract and that he consequently is entitled to re-acquire possession of it. Who is right? Explain your answer.

3. Helen Cottee visited Franklin's Hardware Store and purchased a number of items. Because of the size and weight of those items, a store clerk provided Helen with a shopping cart to allow her to more easily transport the goods from the store to her car. While she was pushing the cart across the parking lot, however, one of its wheels fell off. The cart collapsed on Helen and caused extensive injuries. Helen brought an action against Franklin's seeking compensation for the accident. Will she succeed? Explain your answer.

4. Shortly before taking a three-year position as a nurse in Saudi Arabia, Noreen Rabby moved her furniture and personal belongings into a storage unit that she rented from Newtown Security Inc. The agreed price was $200 per month. For the next three years, Noreen purchased money orders on a monthly basis and sent them to the address that she had copied into her phone book before she left Canada. Unfortunately, Noreen had written that address incorrectly, so none of the cheques ever reached Newtown. Furthermore, for reasons that neither party can explain, her letters were never returned to her and the money orders have simply disappeared. And finally, Noreen had forgotten to give her address in Saudi Arabia to Newtown, so that the company had no way of contacting her in her absence. When Noreen returned from Saudi Arabia at the end of her job posting, she was surprised to learn that Newtown, acting under statutory authority, had sold her belongings to cover the rental payments that were never received. She is also very angry that the storage company insists on retaining all of that money, even though the proceeds from that sale exceeded her indebtedness by $2500. Newtown believes that it is entitled to the extra money on the grounds that it became the owner of the goods when Noreen failed to meet her obligations under the contract. Who is entitled to the $2500? Explain your answer.

5. Babe Ruth hit 60 home runs in 1927. Roger Maris hit 61 in 1961. Mark McGwire hit 70 in 1998. But in 2001, Barry Bonds surpassed them all. He wrote his name into the baseball record book with 73. His final home run that season also went into the law books. The game was held on October 7 at Pac-Bell Park in San Francisco. In anticipation of catching the record-setting ball, fans crowded into the outfield stands. Among them were Alex Popov and Patrick Hayashi. In the bottom of the first inning, Bonds connected with a knuckleball and sent it over the right field wall. The video evidence clearly shows the ball starting to enter the upper portion of Popov's outstretched baseball glove. Popov did not, however, have a chance to complete the catch. He was immediately swallowed up by the crowd and tackled to the ground. A mob descended on Popov with the obvious intention of seizing control of the ball. In the commotion, several other fans, including Hayashi, were knocked to the ground. A short time later, Hayashi crawled from the melee, stood up with the ball in his hand and was quickly whisked away by security personnel. A dispute then arose regarding ownership of the record-setting ball. There is no suggestion that Hayashi had participated in any of the violence. Popov did insist, however, that he had already acquired ownership of the ball by the time that Hayashi grabbed it off the ground. He also insisted that Hayashi therefore committed the tort of conversion (discussed in Chapter 4) when he took possession of the ball. The motivation for the lawsuit was, of course, profit. Although a baseball is normally worth only a few dollars, collectors are willing to pay a fortune for historical memorabilia. (For instance, the ball that Mark McGwire had hit to set the record in 1998 was purchased for US $3 200 000.) Who owned the ball? Hayashi? Popov? Or perhaps the party (Major League Baseball) that had purchased the ball in the first place? Explain your answer.

6. Occidental & Atlantic (OA) is a shipping company that offers to deliver goods for anyone anywhere in the world. Mediterranean Imports Ltd wished to have $500 000 worth of silk sent from a port in northeast Italy to Halifax. It entered into a contract with OA that included the following provisions.

(d) The carrier shall use whichever route is the most appropriate in the circumstances.

(g) The carrier's liability for loss or damage due to fire, storm, or act of God shall be limited to $500 per shipment.

(q) Any disputes arising between the parties shall be resolved under the laws of Canada.

Shortly before the journey began, an armed conflict erupted in a region of the Balkans, which lie to the east of Italy. Although carriers regularly passed through the affected area when transporting goods from northeastern Italy to North America, most carriers chose to adopt alternative routes during the course of the conflict. The captain of OA's vessel, however, realized that any deviation from the standard course would be costly and therefore decided to proceed as usual. Unfortunately, the entire cargo of silk was lost when OA's ship was caught in a crossfire and sank. Mediterranean Imports did not purchase first-party insurance for its property and therefore is anxious to recover compensation from OA. Is it entitled to do so? Explain your answer.

7. Miles Sivad, a wealthy music producer, owned a large number of expensive paintings and *objets d'art*. As a favour, he agreed to loan several paintings to a business colleague, Gilmore Green. He also gave Gilmore permission to lend the same paintings to other people on a short-term basis. Several weeks later, Bess Porgy, who believed that Gilmore owned the paintings in question, asked him if she could borrow one to spruce up her home for a party that she had planned. Gilmore agreed and Bess hung *Sketches of Spain* in her living room. At the party, the painting was stolen by one of several uninvited and untrustworthy guests. Gilmore sued Bess for failing to use reasonable care to safeguard *Sketches of Spain* while it was in her possession. The trial judge agreed with the claim and ordered Bess to pay to Gilmore $250 000, which was the value of the painting. It was only after the trial that Miles learned what had happened. His anger over the theft was exceeded only by his anger over the fact that Gilmore refused to hand over the $250 000 that he had received as damages from Bess. Was Gilmore actually entitled to recover that money from Bess? If so, was he obligated to transfer it over to Miles? Explain your answer.

8. Brenna Corp wanted to ship $25 000 worth of office supplies from Kamloops to Moncton. For that purpose, it contacted Hanjin Transport Inc, a general moving company. Although Hanjin reserved a general right to refuse certain types of goods, it agreed to deliver Brenna's property as requested. The parties entered into a contract that contained the following provision: "The carrier is entitled to subcontract on any terms for the handling of the goods." Hanjin used its own truck to take the office supplies from British Columbia to Manitoba. Once it arrived in Winnipeg, however, it paid Pilgrim Container Ltd, a reputable shipper, to complete the journey to New Brunswick. Pilgrim was informed that the goods belonged to Brenna. The contract between Hanjin and Pilgrim therefore contained the following provision: "Pilgrim's liability to any party with an interest in the goods shall be limited to $500." Somewhere east of Thunder Bay, the driver of Pilgrim's truck fell asleep at the wheel and drove into a lake. Although he emerged unhurt, his entire cargo, including Brenna's office supplies, was totally ruined. Discuss Brenna's rights against Hanjin and Pilgrim.

9. Western Paper Inc's warehouse was located next to Thames Explosives Ltd's factory. As a result of a careless manufacturing process, a fire erupted in Thames' premises and soon spread next door. By the time the blaze was contained by the local fire department, $100 000 worth of Western's product had been destroyed. Western had purchased from Fortress Insurance first-party coverage that entitled it to compensation for losses attributable to fire. Thames had purchased from Sentinel Insurance third-party coverage that entitled it to complete protection from losses that it carelessly inflicted as a result of careless manufacturing processes. Explain how the insurance policies will apply in this case. Who will ultimately pay for the loss created by Thames and sustained by Western? Explain your answer.

10. Horst and Jurgen Romani grew up in Europe. As an adult, Horst immigrated to Vancouver. Jurgen remained behind and, while in France, developed an idea for a perfume company. He then began to purchase the necessary supplies and equipment. As his project neared fruition, he asked his brother to join him in the venture. Although Horst was initially skeptical, he was eventually persuaded and agreed to meet the expenses associated with transporting Jurgen and his materials from France to Canada. Horst also gave his brother $11 000 to purchase additional materials. Once they were reunited in British Columbia, the pair informally agreed that they would create a company named Roma France Ltd to manufacture and distribute perfume in this country. They did not, however, actually go through the process of incorporation. Furthermore, while all of the property was stored in Horst's basement, it still belonged to Jurgen. Horst nevertheless purchased a fire insurance policy for it. In fact, a fire did occur and destroyed all of the equipment and supplies that the brothers had intended to use in their business. The insurance company, however, has refused to honour the policy on the grounds that the property in question belonged to Jurgen, with the result that Horst did not have an insurable interest in it. Is the insurer's argument persuasive? Explain your answer.

11. Nocturna Mattress Ltd kept a large inventory of beds in its warehouse. As a matter of internal management, it tried to keep about $60 000 worth of stock on hand at all times. It purchased property insurance from Citadel Insurance. That policy contained a co-insurance clause that called for the insured to hold 80 percent coverage. Nocturna nevertheless chose to pay for only $30 000 worth of coverage. As a result of a cycle of heavy snowfall and warm weather, Nocturna's warehouse was flooded, and much of its inventory sustained irreparable water damage. It therefore has made a claim under its policy with Citadel. How much will Nocturna

receive if (1) the total loss was valued at $50 000, (2) the total loss was valued at $40 000, (3) the total loss was valued at $30 000 and the policy also contained a $5000 deductible? Explain your answers.

12. Skynet Industries is one of several private corporations that manufacture components for the military. As such, it frequently is subject to various forms of protests from a number of interest groups. Although it employs almost 100 people, its chief engineer and CEO, Dyson Bennett, is the moving force behind the company. He is also primarily responsible for its most profitable branch: cyborg intelligence research. To protect its equipment and plant, Skynet purchased full coverage for any loss or damage that any of its property sustained from any cause. Given the unusually broad scope of that policy and the economic value of Skynet's assets, the annual premiums are very expensive.

   As part of a controlled, in-house testing program, Skynet recently detonated a small incendiary device at its plant. Although the explosion proceeded as planned, the plant was substantially destroyed by a fire that followed. That fire should have been automatically extinguished by the company's state-of-

the-art sprinkler system. It appears, however, that the system had been disabled by an unidentified protestor who had managed to break the security code for Skynet's main computer. Skynet consequently lost virtually all of its stock and equipment. Much more significantly, however, Dyson Bennett suffered severe burns while escaping from the building. Although he survived the incident, the medical evidence indicates that his injuries will prevent him from ever resuming his previous role with the company. And finally, while its financial position is strong enough to see the company through the disaster, Skynet has incurred substantial costs in temporarily relocating its operation to a new site while its own facilities are rebuilt. Among those costs is the loss of a large contract that it otherwise would have received from the Canadian military for the development of a new laser-directed missile-launching system.

   On the basis of the information that has been provided, does Skynet have sufficient insurance to compensate it against all of its losses? If not, suggest alternative forms of insurance that it should have bought.

WEBLINKS

Bailment

Sub-License and Bailment Agreement www.jurisint.org/pub/02/en/doc/404.htm

This document consists of a model licensing agreement between two corporations.

Repairer's Liens and Warehouse Liens in British Columbia www.singleton.com/publications/business/RepairersLiens.pdf

This document explains the laws that allow a lien to be exercised by a business that has repaired or warehoused goods. Although the author focuses on British Columbia, the laws are similar in other jurisdictions.

Warehouseman's Terms and Conditions www.theexpressgroup.ca/pdf/Warehousemans%20T&C.pdf

This documents provides a model of a contract for the storage of goods.

Insurance

Insurance-Canada.ca www.insurance-canada.ca

This website provides consumers and insurance professionals with information on insurance-related topics, including general information about the importance of insurance as a risk management tool and specific information on types of insurance.

Insurance Bureau of Canada www.ibc.ca

The IBC identifies and monitors policy issues affecting the insurance industry. Its site provides numerous links to industry-related publications and resources.

Risk and Insurance Management Society Inc www.rims.org

RIMS, a not-for-profit organization dedicated to advancing the practice of risk management, offers online articles and links to other risk management resources.

Export Development Canada www.edc-see.ca

The EDC is a department of the federal government that provides a wide range of risk management services, including insurance and financing, to Canadian exporters and their customers around the world.

Small Business Insurance: What You Need and Why You Need It www.cbsc.org/servlet/ContentServer?cid=1104766631277&pagename=CBSC_AB%2FCBSC_WebPage%2FAB_WebPage_Template&c=CBSC_WebPage

This website, belonging to the federal government, explains the importance of different types of insurance for small businesses.

Modern High Seas Piracy www.cargolaw.com/presentations_pirates.html

This website contains links to information regarding modern piracy, which costs businesses enormous amounts of money each year.

ADDITIONAL RESOURCES FOR CHAPTER 17 ON THE COMPANION WEBSITE

(www.pearsoned.ca/mcinnes)

In addition to self-test multiple-choice, true-false, and short essay questions (all with immediate feedback), three additional Cases and Problems (with suggested answers), and links to useful Web destinations, the Companion Website provides the following resources for Chapter 17:

Provincial Material

- **British Columbia:** Fixtures, Lien, Warehouse Lien, Repairers' Lien, Hotel Keepers, Insurance Legislation, Fraudulent Transfer of Property, *Creditor Assistance Act*
- **Alberta:** Common Carriers, Enduring Power of Attorney, Innkeepers' Liability, Personal Directives
- **Manitoba and Saskatchewan:** Hotel Keepers, Common Carriers, Insurable Interest (On Lives)
- **Ontario:** Common Carriers, *Consumer Protection Act 2002*, Pawnbrokers, Repair and Storage Liens, Warehousing, Innkeepers' Liability, Good Faith, Insurance Legislation, Subrogation

18 Knowledge-Based Businesses and Intellectual Property

CHAPTER OVERVIEW

OBJECTIVES

After completing this chapter, you should be able to:

1. Describe the nature of the new economy.

2. Demonstrate how the new economy is based on the commodification of information.

3. Distinguish between internal and external information-based assets.

4. Identify legal risks associated with the creation and use of information-based assets.

5. Determine whether a particular creation is protected under copyright legislation.

6. Outline the protection offered under trademark law, and determine whether an action for passing off may succeed.

7. Discuss the patentability of inventions, and identify possible grounds of infringement.

8. Explain how intellectual property law protects industrial designs.

9. Discuss trade secrets as a means of protecting information-based assets

10. Describe the nature of confidential information and the remedies available when confidentiality is breached.

Many believe that the power of high technology has ushered in a kind of industrial revolution, an economic shift that is transforming the way we do business. When they talk about the **new economy**, they are talking about a "world in which communications technology creates global competition—not just for running shoes and laptop computers, but also for bank loans and other services that cannot be packed into a crate and shipped. A world in which innovation is more important than mass production. A world in which investment buys new concepts or the means to create them, rather than new machines. A world in which rapid change is a constant. A world at least as different from what came before it as the industrial age was from its agricultural predecessor. A world so different its emergence can only be described as a revolution."[1] In addition to the material discussed in this chapter, Chapter 19 covers a number of these themes.

> in the new economy, investment buys new concepts or the means to create them rather than new machines

In this chapter, we investigate the legal aspects of knowledge-based businesses. We begin with an examination of information as a commodity. We then investigate the central legal mechanisms by which such assets can be controlled and exploited for profit—intellectual property laws.

INFORMATION AS A COMMODITY

The Nature of Information

Before the invention of Gutenberg's printing press, the reproduction of books took considerable time, energy, labour, and natural resources. The printing press enabled rapid and efficient mass-reproduction of books. However, the significance of this invention goes beyond these features. The printing press made it possible for information to be *universally possessed*. The possibility of universal possession is what distinguishes information from tangible commodities. **Universal possession** is possible when a good is available to many people at the same time in such a way that one person's possession and enjoyment of it does not diminish another's.

> universal possession is possible when a good is available to many people at the same time in such a way that one person's possession and enjoyment of it does not diminish another's

Exclusive possession characterizes an individual's ability to exercise power over a thing to the exclusion of all others. Exclusive possession is possible in the case of tangible goods because they occupy space and can therefore remain in the sole control of those who possess them. Running shoes, laptop computers, and other forms of tangible property are capable of *exclusive possession*. I can keep you from wearing my sneakers by tying them to my feet. I can stop you from using my laptop computer by locking it in my office. But I cannot easily prevent you from possessing information. Information can be replicated by word of mouth. Innovations like Gutenberg's printing press, the photocopier, and digital technologies further enhance the possibility of the universal possession of information. Put another way, recent developments in information technology increase the difficulty of establishing and maintaining exclusive possession over information and ideas.

> exclusive possession characterizes an individual's exercise of power over a thing at their pleasure to the exclusion of all others

Economics of Information

When the creator of an idea has the sole aim of spreading information, the possibility of universal possession of information is a benefit. However, many creators of ideas have additional motives. As the saying goes, "Information

---

[1.] J Browning & S Reiss *Encyclopaedia of the New Economy* (2002).

wants to be free. It also wants to be expensive."[2] For example, why would the creators of books—whose livelihoods depend on the number of copies sold—spend years writing, while passing up other financial opportunities, if they knew that anyone could easily reproduce their book without their permission, without cost or sanction? There is far less incentive for creators of ideas to toil in their creation if those ideas, once developed, can be universally possessed with no compensation to them.

Running shoes and laptops are commodities—they are bought and sold. My incentive to make shoes or laptops depends largely on the *natural scarcity* of those items. **Natural scarcity** occurs when the supply of a natural resource is inadequate. Because natural resources are finite, the market value of those resources usually increases when supplies become inadequate. Consider what would happen if natural resources were not finite. Suppose I could buy running shoes and laptops from you and then use nanotechnology to miraculously reproduce them in great numbers at no additional cost to me. That would allow me to affect your ability to sell them, since I could decide to give the newly created supply away for next to nothing to all of your potential customers. If natural resources were capable of universal possession in this way, there would be very little incentive for you to make the products. The phenomenon of natural scarcity is what allows shoe and computer makers to make a living.

Our ability to reproduce, distribute, and universally possess information at virtually no cost means that its supply is not finite. Therefore, information is not as easily bought and sold as running shoes and computers. To create a market for information, an *artificial scarcity* must be introduced. **Artificial scarcity** makes the supply of an informational resource inadequate, by making the information incapable of universal possession. Knowledge-based businesses depend upon the creation of an artificial scarcity to increase the value of their information-based assets. This type of scarcity is brought about through the law of intellectual property.

> natural scarcity occurs when the supply of a natural resource is inadequate

> artificial scarcity makes the supply of an informational resource inadequate

Information-Based Assets

One aim of a business is to generate assets. A knowledge-based business generates information-based assets. Sometimes referred to as *invisible capital*, these assets are distinguished from bricks and mortar or other more traditional forms of business capital.[3] The invisible capital of a business is like the three parts of a cake.

> human capital is the special talents and expertise of those employed by the business

- The bottom layer of the business is its *human capital*. **Human capital** is the special talents and expertise of those employed by the business. Bill Gates has said that the majority of Microsoft's assets walk out of the building at the end of the working day and, hopefully, return the next morning.

> internal information-based assets include business concepts, models, information systems, as well as any inventions or content created by the business

- The upper layer is the *internal information-based assets* of a business. **Internal information-based assets** include the business plan and other business concepts, models, and information systems, as well as any inventions or content created by those involved in the business. It also includes its customer lists, data administration, and processing systems.

> external information-based assets include the image and reputation of the business

- The icing is the *external information-based assets* of the business. **External information-based assets** include the image and reputation of the business, its brand recognition, and the relationships it has developed with suppliers and customers.

---

[2] S Brand *The Media Lab: Inventing the Future at MIT* (1988).

[3] L Downes "Invisible Capital" *The Industry Standard* (July, 10 2000).

Chapter 19 considers other aspects of information-based assets. This chapter focuses on the process by which businesses can protect such assets in a world where exclusive possession is no longer possible or desirable. That process is the law of intellectual property.

INTELLECTUAL PROPERTY

Intellectual property law aims to protect products of the mind. Although it does this to provide incentives to creators, intellectual property recognizes that creators should not be able to monopolize their ideas indefinitely. To allow a monopoly of ideas would grind human progress to a halt. Creators must be able to build on the creative works and ideas of those who came before them. In 1676, for example, Sir Isaac Newton famously acknowledged his debt to Robert Hooke, who came before him: "If I have seen further it is by standing on ye shoulders of Giants." Consequently, **intellectual property law** is a set of rules that aims to balance the rights of a creator against the public interest. The tension between these interests is readily apparent when a court is asked to establish a new legal precedent. Consider the decision in Case Brief 18.1.

intellectual property law is a set of rules that aims to balance the rights of a creator against the public interest

CASE BRIEF 18.1

Théberge v Galérie d'Art du Petit Champlain (2002) 210 DLR (4th) 385 (SCC)

Claude Théberge, an internationally-known Quebec painter, sued a gallery for making an illegal copy of his work. The gallery had purchased a poster from Théberge and, using sophisticated technology, literally lifted the ink right off the poster and transferred it to canvas. No copies of the work were made, and the poster was blank once the process was complete.

The Supreme Court of Canada held that, because no copy had been made in the transfer process, there was no infringement of copyright. In reaching its decision the court emphasized the importance of balance in copyright law, noting the danger to our society if the balance in copyright tilts too

far toward copyright owners: "[E]xcessive control by holders of copyrights and other forms of intellectual property may unduly limit the ability of the public domain to incorporate and embellish creative innovation in the long-term interests of society as a whole, or create practical obstacles to proper utilization."

The *Théberge* case marked the first time our Supreme Court placed such significant emphasis on user rights, the public interest, and balance in intellectual property law. The court seemed to affirm the principle that stronger intellectual property protection does not necessarily create greater incentives for the creation of original works and may, in fact, be contrary to the long-term interests of society.

The tension between the public interest and private rights, the idea that information wants to be both free and expensive, is a recurring theme of intellectual property law.

There are five main types of intellectual property law that are reviewed in this chapter: copyright, trademarks, patents, industrial designs, and trade secrets (sometimes called confidential information). Two additional, and more narrow, categories—integrated circuit topography and plant breeders' rights— are not discussed here.

Copyright

Copyright is the law of authorship. It rewards and protects an author's creative efforts by giving the author an exclusive right to publish or otherwise control the distribution of a work. Many people are under the mistaken impression that

copyright is the law of authorship

a copyright must be registered in order to be enforceable. In fact, although copyrights can be registered, copyright protection arises automatically upon the creation of an original work in a fixed medium. To protect the creative process, the law prohibits others from copying an author's work for a specified period of time, whether or not the author registers the copyright. Unless ownership of the copyright is somehow transferred to another person, only the author is permitted to produce or reproduce a work, and only the author can authorize others to do the same.

Forms of Expression That Are Protected

Another common misconception is that copyright protects ideas. Copyright law does not protect ideas, but rather the manner in which ideas are expressed. There are several ways in which an author can express an idea. The *Copyright Act* refers specifically to seven forms of expression that are protected.[4] Figure 18.1 provides examples of each.

FIGURE 18.1 Seven Forms of Expression Protected by Copyright	
	Examples of Copyright Material
literary works	stories, textbooks, instruction manuals, compilations, translations, computer programs
dramatic works	films, videos, screenplays, choreography, scenic arrangements, recitals
musical works	compositions, melodies, harmonies, sheet music
artistic works	paintings, drawings, photos, sculptures, engravings, maps, charts
performances	acting, dancing, singing, drumming
sound recordings	records, cassettes, compact discs
communication signals	broadcast signals

Source: Industry Canada *A Guide to Copyrights* (2000) at 3.

Some forms of expression are not protected by copyright. Slogans, short phrases, titles, names, and factual information are not generally subject to copyright law. Factual information is considered to be part of the public domain. Where a business report or magazine article contains factual information, it is the expression of the information that is subject to protection, not the facts themselves. Copyright does not apply to basic ideas.

Requirements for Copyright Protection

For a work to enjoy copyright protection in Canada, it must meet three requirements.

[4.] *Copyright Act*, RSC 1985, c C-42 (Can).

- The work must be *original*.
- The work must be *fixed*.
- The work must be *connected to Canada* (or to a World Trade Organization, Berne, Rome, or Universal Copyright Convention member state).

Originality Do not confuse the requirement of originality with the patent concept of novelty. The notion of an **original work** means that the work originated from the author, involved the exercise of the author's skill and judgment, and was not copied from any other source. After all, you cannot obtain a copyright for work that belongs to someone else. Note that the originality requirement has a low threshold. Business Decision 18.1 illustrates the meaning of originality.[5]

an **original work** is work that is not copied from any other source

BUSINESS DECISION 18.1

The Low Threshold of Originality

Mark and Jenny had been scheming for some time about starting up a business that would capitalize on student laziness on campus. Sitting in the half-empty lecture theatre of their mega-class, they realized that there was a market for class lecture notes. Therefore, they ran an ad in the student newspaper calling for dean's honour roll students enrolled in mega-classes to apply to be paid note-takers for their company, Campus Notes. Mark and Jenny met with a large group of applicants and explained that they would pay successful applicants a fixed fee in exchange for a copy of their class notes and permission to distribute them to Campus Notes customers. The note-takers were told that the best way to prepare the notes was not to transcribe the lecture word for word, but to organize the materials in a way that made sense, with many headings and subheadings, and with additional illustrations and examples.

Business boomed until the day that Campus Notes received a letter from several professors threatening to sue them for breach of copyright. In essence, the professors claimed that they held copyright in their lectures and that the lecture notes provided by the honour roll students were *not* original works.

Question for Discussion

1. Could Mark and Jenny claim that the lecture notes provided by their note-takers are original works?

Fixation Although the Act does not expressly stipulate this, copyright is usually restricted to the expression of a work in a fixed medium. For example, a choreograph must have its scenic arrangement fixed, usually in writing. Likewise, a broadcast must be recorded on tape or some other medium while being transmitted. There is a similar requirement for computer programs. The aim of such requirements is to add certainty to the law. Ensuring that an author is capable of identifying the work and demonstrating that it persists in some medium will ultimately prevent improper claims that spontaneous activity, including oral conversations, enjoy copyright protection.[6]

Connection with Canada (or a treaty country) A work is subject to Canadian copyright law only if it has some connection to Canada. All work created in Canada is protected. However, work created outside of Canada by a Canadian national or an ordinary resident of Canada is also protected. Due to

---

[5.] See also *Ladbroke (Football) Ltd v Williams Hill (Football) Ltd* [1964] 1 All ER 465 (HL).

[6.] See *Gould Estate v Stoddart Publishing Co* (1996) 30 OR 520 (Gen Div); *Canadian Admiral Corp v Rediffusion Inc* [1954] Ex CR 382.

a number of international treaties, copyright eligibility extends even further. Any author of an original work who is a citizen of, or ordinarily resident in, a country that is subject to the Berne Copyright Convention, the Rome Convention, the Universal Copyright Convention, or the World Trade Organization is protected by Canadian copyright law regardless of where the work was created. This is an important point for managers in knowledge-based businesses, who must take care to minimize the risk of their employees copying foreign material under the mistaken impression that it is not subject to Canadian law.

Copyright Ownership

Our discussion of copyright has focused on the perspective of the author. Generally, the author of a work is the copyright owner. Recall that the copyright owner has the legal power to prevent others from copying the work. Some authors and artists are interested in exploiting such power for monetary gains, but others are not. Those who, for any reason, are not interested in monetary gains can use their legal power to prevent others from gaining access to their work. For example, the American author JD Salinger once used the law of copyright to block the publication of his private letters.[7] Salinger also exploited the power of copyright law in the usual manner by transferring aspects of the copyright he owned to a book publisher in exchange for *royalties*. **Royalties** are the monetary compensation given to an author in exchange for the use of their copyrighted materials. Royalties are usually expressed as a percentage of the publisher's receipts from the sales associated with the copyrighted material. Some publishers even offer an author an incentive to write by way of an *advance on royalties*. An **advance on royalties** is an interest-free amount that is paid to the author before the completion of a work and that is later deducted from the sum of royalties.

Knowledge-based businesses can adopt many other ownership schemes. To understand the various business possibilities, you need to know the bundle of rights that the copyright owner can exploit. Figure 18.2 summarizes these rights.

royalties are monetary compensation given to an author in exchange for the use of their intellectual property

an advance on royalties is an interest-free incentive that is paid to the author before the completion of a work and is later deducted from the sum of royalties

---

FIGURE 18.2   **The Bundle of Rights Held by the Copyright Owner**

the right to *produce, reproduce, perform,* or *publish* a work

the right to *translate* a work

the right to *convert* a dramatic work into a novel, non-dramatic work, or sound recording

the right to *convert* a novel into a dramatic work through public performance or by sound recording

the right to *convert* a non-dramatic or artistic work into a dramatic work through public performance

(continued)

[7.] *Salinger v Random House Inc* 811 F2d 90 (2d Cir 1976).

FIGURE 18.2 *(continued)*

the right to *communicate* a work by telecommunication

the right to *reproduce, adapt,* or *present* a work by film or photograph

the right to *present* an artistic work at a public exhibition (works created after June 7, 1988)

the right to *create* a sound recording of a musical work

the right to *license* computer software

the right to *reproduce* any performance that has been fixed

the right to *fix* any performance that has not yet been fixed

the right to *reproduce, license,* or *publish* sound recordings

the right to *fix* or *reproduce* broadcast signals

the right to *authorize* another broadcaster to simultaneously retransmit the signal

Source: Industry Canada *A Guide to Copyrights* (2000) at 3–4.

Copyright can be unbundled into several discrete rights, many of which can be bought, sold, licensed, or given away. This gives those engaged in knowledge-based businesses a multitude of business opportunities.

The author of a work is *generally* the first copyright owner. However, an important exception occurs in the employment context. Generally, the copyright in a work created by an employee in the course of employment is owned by the employer. For example, copyright in a government brochure developed by a public servant belongs not to the brochure's creator but to the Crown. Note that the rule does not generally cover independent contractors. In order to obtain ownership, knowledge-based businesses that engage independent contractors to generate information-based assets should expressly provide that copyright is held by the business and not the contractor.

Duration of the Copyright

Copyrights do not last forever. Unlike property in tangible objects—which continues to exist until such objects are given away, sold, used up, or ruined—the bundle of rights inherent in copyright *always* comes to an end. When it does, the work is said to belong to the *public domain*. **Public domain** is the realm of works that belong to the community at large and that can be used by anyone. For example, the works of Shakespeare are in the public domain; the song "Happy Birthday" is not.[8] In Canada, the duration of copyright generally lasts for the life of the author and then for 50 years following the end of the calendar year in which the author dies.

public domain is the realm of works that belong to the community at large and that can be used by anyone

---

[8.] L Shrieves "Restaurants wish customers a happy birthday" *Knight-Ridder Tribune* (March 6, 2001).

Moral Rights

In addition to the bundle of rights that constitute copyright, the creation of an original work also gives rise to a separate package of *moral rights*, which are legally enforceable.[9] Moral rights are considered to be so important that they cannot be bought or sold—they are retained by the author even if ownership in a copyright is subsequently transferred to someone else. **Moral rights** include (i) the right of attribution, (ii) the right of integrity over a work, and (iii) the right to be associated (or not associated) with a work.

The right of attribution allows an author to ensure that their name is attached to the work. It also allows an author to remain anonymous or to work under a pseudonym. In either case, the attribution right prevents others, even if they own the copyright, from using the work and claiming it as their own.

The right of integrity provides an author with a further degree of control over the work after it is sold. It allows an author to prevent others from distorting, mutilating, or otherwise modifying the work where doing so would prejudice the author's honour or reputation. A famous Canadian artist exercised that right by forcing a shopping mall to remove Christmas decorations from his sculptures.[10] Note that the right of integrity in a work is not always easy to enforce. Often what one party sees as the distortion or modification of a work is perceived as free speech by another, or as an exercise of a right in the tangible property. Although the distortion of a work is sometimes grounds for a lawsuit, the courts will not always view the total destruction of a work as prejudicing the author's reputation.

The fact that an author retains moral rights in a work even after it is sold is offset by the fact that moral rights can be waived by the author. This is an important consideration for knowledge-based businesses that buy and sell copyrighted content. From a risk management perspective, a business should consider whether to include a contractual condition requiring an author to waive their moral rights. In some circumstances, this will provide the business with a greater ability to control the content that it has purchased with no strings attached.

> moral rights include the right of attribution, the right of integrity over a work, and the right to be associated (or not associated) with a work

Copyright Infringement

Since the copyright owner controls the work, any use of it without the owner's permission is a **copyright infringement**. If you publish, perform, or otherwise copy my work without authorization, you are probably infringing my copyright. However, this is not always the case. Sometimes, an act done in private is not considered an infringement. Since copyright includes a right of public performance, the law permits you to engage in a private performance of my material without running afoul of the law. For example, you are legally permitted to sing "Happy Birthday" in your basement at your son's birthday party. The same would not be true if his birthday party is being broadcast on national television. Unless you pay a licensing fee to perform the song in public, you are infringing copyright.

The digital networked world in which we live poses unique opportunities and challenges for copyright owners. On one hand, digital works can be distributed by copyright owners to millions of people on the Internet or on peer-to-peer networks at minimal cost. On the other hand, digital technologies have

> copyright infringement includes any use of an original work without the owner's permission

---

[9.] The name derives from the French *droits moraux*, which is better understood as a "personal right."

[10.] *Snow v Eaton Centre Ltd* (1982) 70 CPR (2d) 105 (Ont HCJ).

made it easier for individuals to infringe copyright works and to share the infringing copies with millions of other people through a simple click of a mouse. Even if copyright laws clearly applied to prohibit such online activities, enforcement is still a problem in a global networked world. The phenomenon of peer-to-peer file-sharing, for example, is discussed in Chapter 19, along with *BMG Canada v. Doe*, a legal case involving music downloading in Canada.

The Canadian government is in the process of considering amendments to copyright law to address perceived problems posed by digital technologies. These changes would, for example, make peer-to-peer file-sharing illegal, at least as we know it now. The changes would also provide legal remedies for copyright owners who use technological protections to safeguard their works against infringement. The law would make it illegal for people to break these technological locks on copyright works.[11]

 E T H I C A L   P E R S P E C T I V E   1 8 . 1

Creative Commons Canada

There recently has been a significant increase in alternative copyright licensing tools. One such tool is Creative Commons Canada. Creative Commons Canada operates a website that offers artists six options for constructing and attaching copyright licences to their works. Creators can, for example, choose to permit others to copy, modify, and share their works, provided that credit is given to the artists and the works are not put to commercial use.

A company has recently started a new record label. Many of its artists have expressed an interest in Creative Commons Canada. The company is anxious to know how those new copyright licensing tools might affect its business. Visit Creative Commons Canada's website at **http://creativecommons.ca** and answer the following questions.

Questions for Discussion

1. Are there any moral aspects to the decision whether to reserve only some rights, rather than all rights? Would the decision to reserve only some rights always be disadvantageous from a business perspective?

2. Does the issue of moral rights come into play? Explain why or why not.

3. The record label is concerned that none of the licences would meet its business needs. Is this true? Explain why or why not.

4. Recommend one of the six Creative Commons Canada licences for the record label to consider, and explain why it might be a good fit for its digital repository.

The law of copyright protects not merely whole works but also substantial parts of a work. The notion of a *substantial part* is as much a qualitative judgment as it is a quantitative one. The general principle is that copyright owners cannot protect every particle of a work, where the taking of that piece would not undermine the overall value of the work. For example, borrowing 60 lines of code in a software routine that consists of 14 000 lines was held not to infringe copyright.[12] On the other hand, taking just a few bars from the refrain of a pop song may be substantial. Courts consider a number of factors, including (i) whether the part taken is distinctive, (ii) whether the taking would significantly impair the incentive for similarly placed authors, (iii) whether the author's ability to exploit the copyright has been substantially affected,

---

[11] Details of the government's proposed amendments in Bill C-60 can be found at
<http://strategis.ic.gc.ca/epic/internet/incrp-prda.nsf/en/rp01145e.html>.

[12] *Delrina Corp v Triolet Systems Inc* (1993) 47 CPR (3d) 1 (Ont Gen Div), affd (2002) 17 CPR (4th) 289 (Ont. CA). This decision was not based merely on the actual percentage copied but also on the fact that "their extent was so slight, and their effect so small, as to render the taking perfectly immaterial."

(iv) whether the taker is unjustly enriched at the author's expense, and (v) whether the two works compete in the same market.[13] Figure 18.3 outlines examples of copyright infringement.

FIGURE 18.3 Examples of Copyright Infringement	
Infringement	Not Infringement
reprinting an article without the copyright owner's permission	quoting a few lines of the article in a research paper (fair dealing)
playing records at a dance without the copyright owners' permission	playing records at home
giving a public performance of a modern play without permission	giving a public performance of a play by Shakespeare (no copyright exists—public domain)
photocopying articles for a class of students without permission	obtaining permission from the author and paying a fee to them (if requested) to use an article
taping your favourite band at a music concert without permission	borrowing a musical tape from a friend to copy onto a blank tape for private use (a royalty payment to the owner of the song rights was paid when the blank tape was purchased)

Source: Industry Canada *A Guide to Copyrights* (2000) at 6.

Licensing Schemes

A number of licensing schemes have been developed to both (i) allow people to use copyrighted material without having to seek permission, and (ii) provide compensation to the copyright owner for use of the material. For example, it is now permissible in Canada to make a copy of a musical recording for private use without seeking authorization (such as copying a recently purchased CD onto cassette to listen to in your car). This is made possible by a blank audio recording media levy. Instead of trying to stop private copying, a compensation scheme transfers a percentage of revenue from the sale of blank recordable media back to the copyright owners through *copyright collectives*. **Copyright collectives** are organizations that administer certain rights granted by the copyright system on behalf of copyright owners, who are members of the collective. In the case of the audio recording media levy, the Canadian Private Copying Collective is responsible for collecting the levy. The monies collected are ultimately redistributed to performing artists, composers and lyricists, music publishers, and record companies through their own collectives, such as the Society of Composers, Authors and Music Publishers of Canada (SOCAN).

copyright collectives are organizations that administer certain rights granted by the copyright system on behalf of copyright owners who are members of the collective

---

[13.] D Vaver *Copyright Law* (2000), Chapter 5, Section A.9: Substantial Infringement, p. 143.

The Right to Use Another's Works

Intellectual property aims to balance the rights of copyright owners against the public interest. Therefore, copyright law provides a number of broad exemptions. For example, music may be performed without permission or licence at an event held for an educational or charitable purpose, or any activity incidental to it.[14] Likewise, what might otherwise amount to a copyright infringement is often excused where a person has good cause to deal with the material as a matter of public interest.

The most well-known exemption, and the one that is most important to knowledge-based businesses, is *fair dealing*. **Fair dealing** involves the legitimate use of a work for private study, research, criticism, review, or news reporting. For it to be considered fair, the person dealing with the work must provide proper attribution to the source and the author. Drawing a bright line between fair dealing and infringement is not, however, always possible. Often, the issue must ultimately be determined by a court. Case Brief 18.2 provides an illustration.

fair dealing involves the legitimate use of a work for private study, research, criticism, review, or news reporting

CASE BRIEF 18.2

CCH Canadian Ltd v Law Society of Upper Canada (2004) 236 DLR (4th) 395 (SCC)

In March 2004, the Supreme Court of Canada issued a significant ruling regarding originality, fair dealing for research, and liability for authorizing copyright infringement. The Law Society of Upper Canada (LSUC) operated a legal library. The library offered a "custom photocopy service" whereby the library would copy materials and deliver them to patrons in person, by mail, or by fax. The LSUC also provided and maintained self-service photocopiers in its library. It posted a notice near the copiers which stated that LSUC was not responsible for any infringement of copyright.

The plaintiff, CCH, was a publisher of legal materials, including court decisions with "headnotes." Headnotes typically consist of keywords and a short summary of a court decision. Like many other legal publishers, CCH created original headnotes, which it placed at the beginning of the reported court decisions. CCH claimed that LSUC was infringing copyright by copying the headnotes, along with the court decisions, and faxing them to patrons. CCH also claimed that, by providing self-service photocopiers, LSUC was liable for authorizing its patrons' infringement of copyright.

The first issue for the court to decide was whether the headnotes were "original" works. On this issue, the court held that a work must originate with the author and be the product of an author's exercise of skill and judgment. The author's efforts in this regard must not be so trivial as to be a purely mechanical exercise. The court noted that artistic creativity is

not necessarily required for a work to be original. On this basis, it found that headnotes are "original" works.

With respect to CCH's infringement claims, the court found in favour of LSUC. The court held that LSUC was not infringing copyright by copying and sending materials to its patrons. The court adopted a large and liberal interpretation of fair dealing for "research." The court held that "research" is not limited to non-commercial or private contexts, and that LSUC was engaged in fair dealing for the purpose of the "research" of its patrons. Although the LSUC was not engaged in its own research, its activities were carried out for the sole purpose of research and were a necessary and integral part of the research of its patrons.

The court also held that LSUC did not authorize copyright infringement by maintaining self-service photocopiers in its library: "[A] person does not authorize copyright infringement by authorizing the mere use of equipment (such as photocopiers) that could be used to infringe copyright. In fact, courts should presume that a person who authorizes an activity does so only so far as it is in accordance with the law." The court went on to add that "even if there were evidence of the photocopiers having been used to infringe copyright, [LSUC] lacks sufficient control over [its] patrons to permit the conclusion that it sanctioned, approved or countenanced the infringement."

---

14. *CAPAC v Kiwanis Club of West Toronto* [1953] 2 SCR 111.

Trademarks

Copyright is meant to protect the internal information-based assets of a business. Trademarks, on the other hand, protect external information-based assets, such as the image and reputation of the business, its brand recognition, and the goodwill that it has developed.

Why Trademark Law Is Important

The success of a business frequently depends on how the public perceives its products or services. The fact that a business may offer the best product or the finest service is often irrelevant. If your competitor has a stronger market presence, and its products or services are more easily distinguished from the rest, your business could be in trouble. It is well known that consumers are inclined to choose products or services with familiar names or symbols, especially where those names and symbols are trusted as reliable. In fact, the design, marketing, and protection of trade names, trademarks, logos, and package designs are often as important to a business as the products or services they represent.

a **trademark** is a word or words, symbol, or design that is used to distinguish one person's goods or services from another's in the marketplace

Trademark law is meant to protect businesses that invest in brands and similar forms of corporate identification. A **trademark** is a word or words, symbol, or design that is used to distinguish one person's goods or services from another's in the marketplace. Like other forms of intellectual property, trademarks can be sold, licensed, or otherwise exploited for profit. This is a fundamental premise of franchising and other business structures. In fact, obtaining a trademark is a prerequisite to franchising a business. But trademark law does not entitle the owner or licensee of the mark to exclusive use in the same way that copyright and patent do. For example, the law cannot stop me from using the word "Coke" in this sentence. But the law does prevent me from adopting a similar mark or name for use in association with my own products. If I were to do so—even inadvertently—I could be liable.

Passing Off

passing off occurs when one person represents its business, goods, or services as someone else's through a confusingly similar mark or name

A business is not required to register its trademarks. By using its name or mark for a certain length of time, the business will be able to establish ownership at common law. However, businesses must be extremely careful not to use a name or mark that is already in use by another business. Representing your business, goods, or services as someone else's through a confusingly similar mark or name could give rise to the common law tort of **passing off**. To succeed under this cause of action, the business claiming that its mark or name has been illegitimately used must prove three things: (i) that the business had established a reputation or goodwill in its name, mark, or logo, (ii) that the impostor represented itself in a manner that resulted in a misrepresentation or confusion between the two enterprises, and (iii) that the established business suffered or is likely to suffer harm. Is there passing off in You Be the Judge 18.1?

YOU BE THE JUDGE 18.1

Trademark and Passing Off[15]

After conducting thorough market research of its candy competitors, the maker of *Smarties* discovers a small candy maker merchandising a very similar product, called *Smoothies*. Although the smaller company uses noticeably superior chocolate (hence its choice of name), the candy-coated shells are identical in colour, though slightly smaller in size, and the packaging appears quite similar to the untrained eye. The maker of *Smarties* sues. The Smoothies people reply with the argument that the two names look and sound completely different and their dictionary meanings are entirely unrelated.

Questions for Discussion

1. Do you think that the general public might be confused between the two candies? Why?

2. Must the trade names look or sound alike to cause confusion in the marketplace? Provide examples to support your position.

In the Internet context, Canadian courts have held that the mere registration of a domain name can be a misrepresentation to the public for the purposes of the second element of a passing-off action.[16] Disputes involving domain names are discussed in detail in Chapter 19.

Registering a Trademark

Businesses do not usually leave matters to the common law doctrine of passing off. They usually register their names and marks as early as possible.[17] As with copyright registration, trademark registration is not absolute proof of ownership, but it does provide the registrant with certain advantages. In the case of a dispute, the fact that a trademark has been registered will shift the onus of proving ownership in the use of the mark to the challenger. Since businesses often engage in lengthy and expensive fights over the use of names and marks, a prudent risk manager will register, in Canada and other countries where the company does business, all variations on the names and marks used to represent its goods and services in the marketplace. By registering the name or mark, your company is protected across Canada for 15 years (and the trademark can be renewed indefinitely). The scope of protection for an unregistered mark is much narrower. The doctrine of passing off protects such marks, but only in the geographic area where the company has established a reputation. Outside of that geographic area, other companies are generally free to use the same mark.

Three basic categories of marks can be registered: *ordinary marks*, *certification marks*, and *distinguishing guises*.

- **Ordinary marks** are words, symbols, or designs that distinguish the goods or services of your business. Sometimes, the words are names (for example, Tom's House of Pizza® in Figure 18.4) and other times slogans (for example, "Pizza Made to Perfection"™).

> ordinary marks are words or symbols that distinguish the goods or services of your business

---

15. *Rowntree Co v Paulin Chambers Co* [1968] SCR 134.

16. *Law Society of British Columbia v Canada Domain Name Exchange Corp* (2002) 4 BCLR (4th) 373 (BSC).

17. See *Canada (Procureur général) v Effigi Inc* (2005) 41 CPR (4th) 1 (FCCA), which held that where two confusing trademark applications are pending, the one filed first will proceed and the other party (even if it has prior use of the mark in the market) must oppose the application.

FIGURE 18.4   Tom's House of Pizza

certification marks identify
goods or services that meet a
standard set by a governing
organization

distinguishing guises identify
the unique shape of a product
or its package

■ **Certification marks** identify goods or services that meet a standard set
by a governing organization (for example, "Recognized by the Canadian
Dental Association").

■ **Distinguishing guises** identify the unique shape of a product or its
package.

Canada's *Trade-Mark Act* does not specifically require or prohibit the use of
symbols such as ® (registered trademark) or ™ (unregistered trademark).[18]
Still, businesses ought to use these symbols appropriately, especially if that use
might find its way into another jurisdiction. A misleading use of the mark may
not be prohibited in Canada (such as using the label ® on an unregistered
mark), but it is prohibited in other jurisdictions, including the United States.

Trademark Infringement

A successful registration gives the owner a number of rights. Trademark law is
meant to protect the owner against infringements of those rights.

a knock-off is an item for sale
that looks like a product made
by the trademark holder and is
represented by a similar mark
but is usually of inferior quality

■ The first and most obvious kind of infringement occurs when an exact
imitation of the trademark is used without permission. A typical example is the *knock-off*. A **knock-off** is an item for sale that looks very much
like a product made by the trademark holder and that is represented by
a similar mark. It is usually of inferior quality.

■ A second kind of infringement occurs not through imitation, but when
some other mark has the effect of confusing consumers. Often such
infringements involve similar words, phrases, or symbols.

trademark dilution occurs
when a mark that is used in a
non-confusing manner has the
effect of tarnishing another
trademark's image or somehow
diminishing the value of its
goodwill

■ A third kind of infringement is known as *trademark dilution*. **Trademark
dilution** occurs when a mark that is used in a non-confusing manner has
the effect of tarnishing another trademark's image or somehow diminishing the value of its goodwill. According to the owner of the trademark for

---

[18.] *Trade-marks Act*, RSC 1985, c T-13 (Can).

Perrier mineral water, this occurred when a Canadian company started selling a bottled water product known as Pierre Eh!. The court agreed.[19]

- A fourth kind of infringement occurs when a foreign party imports an authentically branded product (*not* a knock-off) into Canada as though it were the authorized Canadian distributor. Where the Canadian distributor holds a registered trademark for the product in Canada, the foreign party will usually have to seek permission to import the product even if it holds the trademark in other jurisdictions.

Trademark infringement gives rise to a number of legal remedies.

- Typically, the trademark holder will claim that the illegitimate use of the trademark injured its reputation and diminished the value of its goodwill. When such a claim can be made out, the trademark holder is entitled to *damages*. This remedy will be applied in the same manner as it is in tort law.[20]

- Sometimes the trademark holder does not suffer damages, but claims that the trademark infringer has been unjustly enriched through the illegitimate use of the mark. If a profit has been earned as a result of the infringement, the court may order an *accounting of profits*, requiring the infringer to transfer profits made through the use of the mark to the trademark holder.[21]

- One of the more common and important remedies sought by trademark holders is an *injunction*. When an injunction is appropriate, the court will make an order restraining the infringer from continuing to do business in a manner that involves the illegitimate use of the mark.[22]

- Sometimes the infringing party is ordered to *deliver up* the infringing materials—turn over goods bearing the mark to the trademark holder or to otherwise dispose of them.

Patents

Many inventors believe that the chief value of a *patent* is that it gives them the time needed to develop and market their ideas. A **patent** grants a monopoly, allowing the inventor to exclude others from making, using, or selling the invention for a period of 20 years from the date of application.

patents grant a monopoly to inventors, allowing them to exclude others from making, using or selling their inventions for a period of 20 years from the date of application

Why the Patent System Is Crucial to Knowledge-Based Businesses

From the inventor's perspective, patents provide an incentive for research and development. With patent protection, inventors can be confident that the time and money spent on creating new products will not be undermined by speedy copy-cat manufacturers trying to take advantage of inventions. Patents allow inventors to profit by having the exclusive right to sell or license their inventions for a limited time. In the knowledge-based economy, inventors can also use their inventions as assets when trying to arrange corporate financing.

---

19. *Source Perrier SA v Fira-Less Marketing Co* [1983] 2 FC 18 (FCTD).

20. Tort damages were discussed in Chapter 3.

21. The account of profits was discussed in Chapter 12.

22. Injunctions were discussed in Chapters 3 and 12.

The *patent system* is also crucial to business and to the broader public interest. Because a clear description of the invention must be filed with the Patent Office (a division within the Canadian Intellectual Property Office) before a patent is granted, the patent system plays a pivotal role in the way that information and knowledge are shared. The Patent Office (and its website) is a critical resource not only for other inventors but also for businesses, researchers, academics, journalists, and others interested in keeping up with technological development. Given the breath-taking pace of innovation, knowledge-based businesses must regularly monitor the state of the art. Failing to do so may result in a waste of time and money. According to recent statistics, roughly 10 percent of all research and development in Canada results in duplicating patented technologies.[23] Businesses should therefore develop the habit of searching patent literature before developing new technologies.

Patentability

Not just any idea can be patented. Patent law protects inventions, which are defined in the *Patent Act* as an "art, process, machine, manufacture or composition of matter."[24] The Act also allows patents for new and useful "improvements" of existing inventions. In fact, 90 percent of patents granted in Canada are for such improvements.[25] Note that "useful" here does not mean that the invention must achieve some public benefit. It has always been thought that it is up to the market, not the Patent Office, to determine what inventions are useful.[26] Given that definition, a patentable invention may come in a number of forms, as Figure 18.5 shows.

FIGURE 18.5   Forms of Patentable Inventions

Form	Example
product	a knife
composition	chemicals that remove rust from knife blades
apparatus	a machine that makes knife handles
process	a method of assembling knives

Source: Industry Canada *A Guide to Patents* (2000) at 3.

Think of a patent as the *embodiment of an idea*. Just as one cannot copyright an idea (only its expression), one cannot patent a newly discovered natural law, scientific principle, or abstract theory. Other matters are unpatentable on the basis of public policy. For example, one cannot patent a medical treatment, although one can patent a drug used for the treatment of a disease. It is also said that computer programs and business methods are generally unpatentable, but recently, they have been allowed patents through indirect means.

[23.] Industry Canada *A Guide to Patents* (2000) at 15.

[24.] *Patent Act*, RSC 1985, c P-4 (Can); D Vaver *Intellectual Property* (1997) at 119.

[25.] Industry Canada *A Guide to Patents* (2000) at 3.

[26.] For example, patents continue to be granted for other lethal weapons. This approach was reinforced by Parliament in 1994 when it removed the requirement that inventions have *no illicit object in view*: *Patent Act*, RSC 1985 c P-4, s 27(3(Can)).

Computer software patents have become highly profitable assets for software makers, particularly when the patented product is in broad use or is needed as a component for other software companies to build upon. The importance of software patents is demonstrated in the tremendous increase in patent litigation involving software, particularly in the United States. However, software patents have generated a great deal of controversy because of their potential to lock down areas of technological development and obstruct software innovation. In Canada, the official position of the Patent Office is that computer programs are not themselves patentable *per se* because they are considered to be a mere scientific principle or abstract theorem. The presence of a computer program in an invention will not add or subtract from patentability. However, inventions incorporating a computer program can be patented where the subject matter is patentable and the computer program has been integrated with it, even where, for example, the hardware element of the invention is relatively minor.[27]

A patent is available only if it can be demonstrated that the proposed invention is:

- novel
- ingenious (non-obvious)
- useful

Novelty   The **novelty** criterion does not mean that an inventor must prove that no one else has ever come up with the idea or built a similar product. It is enough to satisfy the *non-disclosure requirement*. One must be able to show that the invention had not previously been disclosed and become known, or otherwise made available, to the public. Understanding the novelty requirement as a public disclosure issue is very important to knowledge-based businesses. Even if your invention is novel in the sense that it was the first of its kind in the world, if you allow your invention to become available to the public before your patent application, this could jeopardize its patentability.[28] Typical examples of such disclosures are (i) delivering a presentation about the invention at a conference or trade show, (ii) displaying the invention in a public place, or (iii) showing the invention to someone without requiring confidentiality.

The novelty rule makes it crucial for business managers to institute safeguards against premature disclosure of products under development. Although some legal mechanisms exist to protect *trade secrets*, prudent managers prevent the risk of untimely disclosure through confidentiality clauses in employment contracts, and by developing and distributing company policy on trade secrets.

It is also important for businesses to file a patent application as soon as the essential elements of the invention are complete. As a result of recent changes to the Act, if your business is working on a new invention, but a speedier competitor files it at the Patent Office before you do, your invention will not be seen as novel—even if you invented it first. This system has become known as a *first-to-file* (as opposed to a *first-to-invent*) system. This creates an incentive for businesses to file early and repeatedly in order to protect the core of their invention as it is developed. However, a business should be careful not to file a patent too

novelty depends upon a non-disclosure requirement

---

27. *Re Motorola Inc. Patent Application No 2 085 228* (1998) 86 CPR (3d) 71 (P.A.B.).

28. In Canada, and some other jurisdictions, there is a one-year grace period before filing during which a business can disclose: *Patent Act*, RSC 1985, c P-14, s 28(1) (Can). However, disclosure before filing can prevent patentability in other countries.

early. Filing too early can mean that others will try to patent a similar invention before you have obtained an adequate scope of patent protection for your invention.

Ingenuity   The second requirement is that the invention or improvement must be *ingenious*. **Ingenuity** means that the item for which a patent is sought would not have been immediately obvious to people fluent in similar technologies. It must be capable of provoking a "Why didn't I think of that!" reaction from other designers in the field. Note that the ingenuity requirement does not entail complexity. Simple ideas can be non-obvious. After all, someone invented the spoon straw. The spoon straw shown in Figure 18.6 illustrates the difference between ingenuity and complexity. At the same time, the simplicity of such an invention highlights the problem of hindsight. It is a feature of many great inventions that they appear obvious after their discovery. Inventors seeking patents must therefore think very carefully about how to present their work as a non-obvious improvement of the current state of the art.

ingenuity means that the item for which a patent is sought would not have been obvious to people fluent in similar technologies

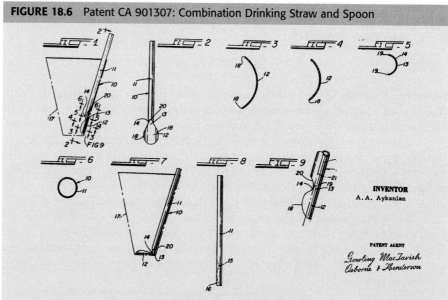

FIGURE 18.6   Patent CA 901307: Combination Drinking Straw and Spoon

Patent CA 901307: Combination Drinking Straw and Spoon

Not all patents stem from complex ideas. Indeed many of the most ingenious inventions result from a relatively unsophisticated leap of logic that was non-obvious at the time of conception. The Spoon-Straw illustrates how two simple yet effective snips of plastic can result in significant utility. Once the market need was determined, the inventor quickly assembled this drawing on a plane ride home from a meeting with the Coca-Cola corporation.

Reproduced by permission of Ardashus A. Aykanian.

Utility   The very definition of an invention implies that it serves some practical purpose. Product development merely for the sake of scientific curiosity is insufficient. If the product has no useful function or if it simply does not work, it cannot be patented. For example, if a manufacturing process has the effect of ruining the very items it is said to produce, it will be unpatentable.[29] The utility requirement does not, however, preclude the patenting of a wasteful, unsafe,

---

[29.] *TRW Inc v Walbar of Canada Inc* (1991) 39 CPR (3d) 176 (FC CA).

primitive, or commercially useless product.[30] As we have seen, it is up to the market and not the Patent Office to determine the value of the invention.

Exploiting a Patent

Patents can be exploited by their owners or licensees. However, it is important to note that, unlike copyright, there is no provision in the *Patent Act* which provides that an employer will own inventions patented by employees in the course of employment. Patent ownership clauses are therefore criticallly important in the employment context.

Once a patent is obtained, its owner must engage in a series of business decisions. What is the best means of profiting from this asset? There are usually several options.

- In some cases, the patent owner will choose to develop and market the product. By doing so, the owner retains full control over the invention. This choice allows the owner to select the image and branding of the product, its availability in the marketplace, pricing, profit margins, and so on. Retaining full control of the products also means assuming all of the risks. Even after years of research and development during the patenting process, it is possible to miscalculate what will happen in the market.

- If the owner of a patent is unable or unwilling to assume the risk, another option is to license the patent. Licences permit other businesses to bring the product to the market in exchange for royalties. Licensing schemes also allow smaller businesses with information-based assets to create capital without large investments or expenditures. They can be granted in any jurisdiction where a patent is held.

- The owner may choose to sell the patent outright. Although this usually requires assigning all rights as inventor, the owner receives in return a lump sum without incurring any risk in the marketplace. That may be important. An inventory of information-based assets, including a "patent portfolio," can be leveraged to raise capital for a growing company with few tangible assets. Sometimes, however, it is difficult to know how to determine the value of the patent, especially when the product has not yet been to market.

Patent Infringement

A successful patent registration gives the registrant a number of rights, most notably, the exclusive right of "making, constructing and using the invention and selling it to others to be used."[31] Although these rights are generally given a wide range of application, there are limits. As we have seen, the patent system aims to balance private rights with the public interest. Even if you hold a patent, you cannot prevent me from building an exact replica of your machine for my own private research, as long as I am not exploiting your invention for profit. However, most companies in the business of improving existing inventions usually enter into mutually beneficial agreements with the original patent holder, rather than working secretly on them without the patent holder's knowledge and consent.

[30.] D Vaver *Intellectual Property* (1997) at 138.

[31.] *Patent Act*, RSC 1985, c P-14, s 42 (Can).

Patent litigation has been on the rise in recent years, particularly in the United States. Because the US market is often the most important market for Canadian companies, having a US patent and avoiding infringing the US patents of other companies can become key risk management issues for Canadian businesses. Infringing a patent can result in millions of dollars in damages, even in cases that settle, and may in some cases threaten the very survival of a business.

Similar to copyright and trademark, patent infringement gives rise to a number of legal remedies.

- Typically, the patent holder will claim that the illegitimate use or sale results in damages. Again, this remedy will be applied in the same manner as it is in tort law. Damages might be calculated in part on the basis of the royalty that the infringer would have had to pay to the patent holder for use of the invention.

- Sometimes, the patent holder does not suffer damages directly but claims that the infringer has been unjustly enriched through the illegitimate use of the patented object or process. If there has been a profit as a result of the infringement, the court may order an accounting of profits, requiring the infringer to transfer profits made through the use of the patent to the patent holder.

- Another common remedy is injunctive relief. When an injunction is successfully sought, the court will order the infringer to stop doing business in a way that interferes with the patent holder's rights.

The Right to Use Another's Patent

I have a right to use your patented invention for experimental purposes and other non-commercial uses. Like the fair dealings doctrine in copyright law, the lines are not always clear, and litigation is often required to balance private rights against the public interest. Similarly, although it is usually an infringement to make or construct a patented item, users have the right to repair and, in some cases, modify them. Although excessive modification might approach reconstruction, there is a public interest in permitting repairs if they conserve resources. There are other circumstances in which users have the right to use a patented product. For example, to obtain governmental approval, a patented product may be used when necessary for public health or safety reasons.

Industrial Designs

Although the traditional forms of intellectual property are copyright, trademark, and patents, Canada protects other forms of intellectual property, including *industrial designs*.

industrial design is the features of shape, configuration, pattern, or ornament applied to a finished article

The success of a manufactured product often depends not only on its usefulness but also on its visual appeal. Because a distinctive product can be considered an intellectual asset, some manufacturers invest time and effort in the look of their product. An **industrial design** consists of the features of shape, configuration, pattern, or ornament applied to a finished article. Because the *Industrial Design Act* seeks to protect only the visual appeal of an object, you will not be permitted to register designs that are purely functional in nature, or designs that have no fixed appearance or that are not clearly visible, such as those hidden from view.[32] Nor can you register the use of particular materials or

32. *Industrial Design Act*, RSC 1985, c I-89 (Can).

colours. Although the use of particular materials or colours can certainly enhance the visual appeal of an object, no one is entitled to a monopoly on these alone. In some cases, however, a unique pattern that is created through the arrangement of certain contrasting tones will qualify.

Unlike copyright and trademark, an industrial design is protected only if it is registered. The *Industrial Design Act* protects registered original designs for up to 10 years by preventing others from making, importing for trade or business, renting, or selling the design. Once the 10-year term has expired, the design falls into the public domain, and anyone is free to make, rent, import, or sell it. It is useful to mark all registered designs with the proprietor's name and a "D" in a circle. Doing so will entitle the registrant to seek monetary damage awards from anyone who infringes the design. A failure to mark the design will limit the remedy to an injunction, that forbids the offending party from continuing use of the design. Registrants must enforce their rights within three years of the alleged infringement.

As with other forms of intellectual property, businesses can commercially exploit industrial designs in several ways. Design rights can be assigned to others in exchange for cash, merchandise, or credit. They can also be licensed. The advantage of licensing the design is that ownership of the design is retained. As well, an entrepreneurial designer may, for example, license the design to a number of parties (i) by geographic region to give the licensee exclusive rights to market the design within that region, or (ii) across Canada but for different periods of time.

TRADE SECRETS AND CONFIDENTIAL INFORMATION

Businesses should use intellectual property laws to protect their information-based assets. However, they should also know that there are other ways of legally protecting and exploiting business-related information.

Although potentially risky, the easiest means of protection is a *trade secret*. One creates a **trade secret** simply by taking steps to keep an information-based asset secret. A famous example of a trade secret is the formula for Coke. Keeping something secret can often involve exacting promises of secrecy from employees and independent contractors in their employment contracts and contracts for services. It can also involve establishing strict information access controls within an organization. For example, where a formula or process is intended to be kept secret, an organization could help maintain secrecy by permitting employees to know only small portions of the information relevant to their work functions, without any ability to access the whole picture. Not surprisingly, this strategy creates certain risks.

a trade secret uses legal rules to keep an information-based asset a secret until it is sold

- Even if you create such obligations contractually, it is possible for your employees and independent contractors (or anyone they might tell) to register your trade secret as though it were their own intellectual property. Despite your ability to prove that those information-based assets belong to you, you will still be forced to spend time and energy fighting to get back what was yours, and you may be forced to reveal the information in the process.

- Even if you effectively protect your trade secrets by way of contracts with your employees, your secrets may be vulnerable after an employee quits or is terminated, and your remedies may be purely contractual.

Although you can protect your secrets by way of contractual restrictions that continue to apply after an employee leaves your business, disgruntled employees may nevertheless disclose your trade secrets to others.

■ Even if your employees and independent contractors are completely trustworthy, protecting information-based assets exclusively by way of trade secrets runs the risk that someone else might independently discover the trade secret. If that happens, there is nothing to prevent that person from registering it as intellectual property or otherwise making it available to the public.

Although it can be risky to use trade secrets as the *sole* means of protecting information-based assets, trade secrets do have advantages. For example, in contrast to patents and copyrights, trade secrets do not involve a public disclosure of ideas, nor are they limited by a term. Businesses can exploit trade secrets indefinitely, so long as the information is still secret. This principle of trade secrets has allowed Coke to exploit its secret beverage formula for decades.

Another way to protect business-related information is to ensure that it is *confidential information*. The advantage of being able to prove that someone has used or disclosed your confidential information is that you can sue for *breach of confidence*. A **breach of confidence** occurs when a person who has been entrusted with confidential information uses that information improperly. The plaintiff must prove (i) that the information was of a confidential nature, (ii) that it was disclosed to the defendant in circumstances giving rise to an obligation of confidence, and (iii) that there was a misuse or unauthorized use of the information.[33]

The courts recognize that information may be confidential for a variety of reasons. Very often, however, it is difficult to decide whether knowledge acquired in the course of employment is confidential or merely common industry know-how. This is particularly difficult in the information technology industry, where it is hard to draw lines between confidential proprietary information and general industry knowledge. This problem is compounded by the fact that the information technology sector is rapidly evolving. Thus, without any breach of confidence, what was one company's trade secret or confidential information yesterday can be general industry knowledge in a matter of days or weeks. In situations of doubt, an employer should consider inserting a detailed confidentiality provision into an employee's contract. Such a clause should apply during the tenure of employment and after the employee leaves the business.

Customer lists are typically considered confidential information and should be protected by contract. Even in the absence of a contract, employees are normally prohibited from using or disclosing customer lists or other confidential information after they leave their employment. However, some courts have drawn a distinction between the actual taking of a list and merely recalling customer names through the use of a phone book or other means. Subject to a contract or a fiduciary duty, employees are often permitted to compete with their former employer by recalling customer names from memory and then soliciting the business of those customers.[34]

To prove that information is confidential in nature, one must be able to demonstrate that the information was not generally known to a substantial

breach of confidence occurs when a person who has been entrusted with confidential information uses that information improperly

---

[33] *Lac Minerals Ltd v International Corona Resources Ltd* (1989) 61 DLR (4th) 14 (SCC).

[34] *Valley First Financial Services Ltd v Trach* (2004) 30 BCLR (4th) 33 (CA).

number of people. There is no specific test to determine whether information is known to a substantial number of people. A judge will consider all of the facts to determine whether information can still be considered confidential despite some degree of disclosure. In some cases, an idea, formula, or process may be confidential, even if parts of it are generally known to a substantial number of people, as long as it is original as a whole. The confidentiality requirement, it is most easily met by telling all recipients of the information that it is secret and must not be disclosed. However, it is usually sufficient if the information is disclosed under circumstances that imply confidence. The final requirement entails proof that there has been a misuse of the information. Even if the claimant has not suffered any financial loss, the court may award relief simply because a secret was disclosed against that person's wishes.[35]

As in the case of intellectual property, the cause of action for breach of confidence supports a broad range of remedies, including injunctions, delivering-up, an account of profits, and compensatory damages.

CONCEPT SUMMARY 18.1

Differentiating Between the Five Main Types of Intellectual Property

	Copyright	Trademarks	Patents	Trade Secrets	Industrial Designs
Basis	Statutory	Statutory and common law (passing off)	Statutory	Common law	Statutory
Registration	Not mandatory but beneficial	Not mandatory but beneficial	Mandatory	Registration not possible	Mandatory
What it protects	Original forms of expression (*eg* dramatic, literary, software, musical)	Marks used in association with particular businesses, wares, and services	Useful, non-obvious and novel inventions	Secret information	Features, such as shape and pattern, that appeal to the eye as applied to a finished article
Term of protection	Generally life of the author plus 50 years	Renewable in perpetuity, unless mark is not used and then it is expunged	Maximum of 20 years from the date of filing application	Indefinite, so long as secrecy is maintained	Maximum of 10 years from the date of registration

---

35. *Cadbury Schweppes Inc v FBI Foods Ltd* (1999) 167 DLR (4th) 577 (SCC).

Chapter Summary

Information is distinguished from tangible commodities because it can be inexpensively reproduced and distributed, and universally possessed. Until recently, most businesses have on selling tangible commodities that become exclusively possessed by their customers. Traditionally, the value of tangible goods and services was determined in the market according to their natural scarcity. Information-based assets, however, require an artificial scarcity. This is achieved through intellectual property law.

Knowledge-based businesses use human capital to create internal information-based assets such as business plans, inventions, customer lists, data processing systems, and other tools that play an important role in the new economy. This invisible capital in turn generates the external information-based assets of a business—its brand recognition, goodwill, and reputation.

Intellectual property law seeks to balance private rights and the public interest through an incentive system for creators and entrepreneurs, by granting time-limited monopolies on various intellectual constructs, their expression, and their functionality. In addition to moral rights, authors are awarded copyright in their works, that allows them to prevent unauthorized copying and distribution. Exceptions are carved out for fair dealing and works that have fallen into the public domain. A copyright may be bought, sold, licensed, or given away. Moral rights may not be sold, but they may be indefinitely waived. To qualify for protection, a work must be original, in fixed form, and created in a copyright convention member state.

The law of trademarks is especially important to a business since its success often depends on how consumers perceive its particular products and services. Trademark owners are protected against competitors who try to confuse consumers through an illegitimate use of the mark, thereby diluting its value. Businesses are encouraged to register trademarks to increase the geographic range of their trademark. Unlike copyrights, registered trademarks do not automatically apply to countries that have intellectual property agreements with Canada.

The granting of a patent for an invention allows the inventor to exclude others from making, using, or selling the invention for a period of 20 years. Unlike trademarks, patents cannot be renewed. The patent system plays an important role in encouraging innovation, while ensuring the sharing of information and knowledge between businesses. Patent law protects original inventions and improvements to already existing inventions. Much like the fair dealing doctrine in copyright law, the public retains the right to use patented inventions for experimental and non-commercial purposes.

Industrial design law protects the distinctive visual appeal of manufactured articles. Original designs are protected for up to 10 years by preventing others from making, importing for trade or business, renting, or selling the design. After 10 years, the design falls into the public domain. Like the patent system, priority is based on the timing of registration, regardless of who came up with the design first. In the case of infringement, failure to register an industrial design limits its proprietor to an injunction rather than monetary damages.

Businesses can further protect their information by using trade secrets and confidential information practices and contracts. In determining the confidentiality of the information, courts will consider the degree to which the information had been disclosed to the public and the extent of the alleged infringer's duty of confidentiality.

Review Questions

1. Distinguish between "exclusive possession" and "universal possession," and give an example of each.

2. How does the scarcity of an asset affect its value? How can a prudent business manager increase the value of information-based assets?

3. Distinguish between internal and external information-based assets, and give an example of each.

4. Describe four ways a business can generate and capitalize on information-based assets.

5. What are the role and purpose of intellectual property law?

6. Does copyright law protect ideas? Explain your answer.

7. What are the requirements for copyright protection? Explain each requirement, and provide an example.

8. Who owns the copyright in a work created in the course of employment? How might a prudent business manager ensure that the employer is recognized as the copyright holder?

9. Explain the concept of "moral rights." How can a prudent business manager ensure that these rights will not conflict with copyrights held by the business?

10. Must a copyright be registered to be enforceable? Explain your answer.

11. List three kinds of trademark, and give an example of each.

12. Describe three types of trademark infringement.

13. What is "passing off"? How is it relevant to trademark law?

14. Outline the elements that must be proved to succeed under an action for passing off.

15. What legal remedies are available for trademark holders in a judicial finding of trademark infringement by another party?

16. Why should a business manager thoroughly search patent literature before developing new technologies?

17. Can any idea be patented? Explain your answer.

18. Outline three ways a patent owner can exploit the patent for financial gain. Briefly discuss the advantages and disadvantages of each option.

19. Explain the purpose of the protection afforded to industrial designs. Is registration required? Explain your answer.

20. Other than intellectual property laws like trademarks, copyright, patents, and industrial designs, name two means by which businesses can protect business-related information? Outline the elements needed to succeed in an action for breach of confidence.

CASES AND PROBLEMS

1. The Beautiful Boy Modelling School hired Keith to prepare commercial artwork for its company materials. Upon completion of the work, Keith invoiced the school for $1600 and was promptly paid. Later, when he realized that the modelling school was using the artwork more extensively than he was originally led to believe, Keith sued the school and its president, Dan, for copyright infringement. Dan, who was not only beautiful but was also a lawyer, argued that Keith's allegation of copyright infringement fails because his contract did not contain any limitations on the use of the work by the modelling school. Moreover, Dan argued that common business practices establish that in the case of work for hire, the commercial artist assigns all copyrights to the employer unless explicit restrictions are included as part of the terms of employment. What factors can the courts consider in determining whether Dan has infringed Keith's copyright? How could Dan, as a prudent business manager, have avoided this situation?

2. Talia sold her famous sculpture, *Angst of a Bicycle Tire*, to the owners of a new downtown shopping mall for a substantial price. The owners installed the sculpture in the foyer of the mall to the delight of both Talia and mall patrons. Years later, the mall owners allowed one of its tenants to use the sculpture to promote a bicycle tire sale. As part of the promotion, some of the sculpture's tires were adorned with the tenant's corporate logo as well as details of the sale. Talia, who was not consulted, was outraged. She sued, calling for the restoration of her sculpture to its original form. On what basis, if any, have the mall owners infringed Talia's intellectual property rights? How could the mall owners have avoided this situation altogether? Explain your reasoning.

3. Janet, always an enterprising young person, decided to start up a business after graduating. Her first product was an abridged version of government reports with which she was well acquainted through her course work and independent study. After a tip from an anonymous caller, the government sought a court order prohibiting Janet from continuing to make such abridged reports available for sale on the basis of copyright infringement. In her defence, Janet says that although she copied large portions of the original report, her abridged report constitutes fair dealing. Discuss Janet's legal argument. As a prudent business manager, how could Janet have better protected her product against infringement claims?

4. The Cameron Library for the Intellectually Gifted (the Cameron Library) has one of the most comprehensive libraries of rare books in Canada. It has a public facility in Vancouver where it permits patrons to review rare books in the library. Although the Cameron Library does not permit patrons to sign out the priceless works, it does provide a self-serve photocopier and digital scanner which patrons can use to copy materials. Upon request, the Library will also scan and e-mail materials to individual patrons outside the Vancouver area. This service is called the E-mail Service. The Cameron Library has a policy which states that copying in the Library and copying for the E-mail Service is permitted for research purposes. Recently, however, Dr Allworth, the author and owner of copyright in a book at the Cameron Library, discovered that his book had been copied by patrons in the Library. He also learned that the Library has scanned and emailed a portion of his book under the E-mail Service. He immediately commenced an action for copyright infringement against the Library. You work at the Cameron Library and have been asked to provide an opinion as to whether it has committed a copyright infringement through its E-mail Service.

5. With reference to the facts described in the previous problem, explain whether the Cameron Library would be liable for the patrons' use of the self-service copiers and scanners to infringe Dr Allworth's copyright.

6. Mangecakes International has decided to bring a passing-off action against competitor Liz Kalmanson Desserts Ltd. Mangecakes is seeking to prevent Liz from selling a cream-filled chocolate biscuit that is

similar in size, shape, and ingredients to its celebrated Mangecake. Liz markets her biscuits under the name Choco Liz. Both versions of the biscuits are sold in clear plastic wrapping and display their trademarked logos on the bottom of the packaging. Although Liz primarily sells her biscuits to caterers, they are also available for public purchase in several of the gourmet food shops that also sell Mangecakes. You are a senior manager at Mangecakes charged with stopping Liz before it is too late for the Mangecake empire. Outline the elements you must establish for a successful passing-off action and briefly make your case.

7. Greenberg Intelligent Agent Technologies, a recent start-up business, has just released its first product offering: a software bot capable of storing, indexing, and searching voice-mail messages. The bot is being marketed under the mark MAK2112. You have been retained to advise the company on intellectual property concerns associated with its products. Briefly explain the importance of trademark protection. Would the mark more likely qualify as an ordinary mark or as a certification mark? What are the advantages of trademark registration?

8. Backside Health Corp, the manufacturer and retailer of a very successful home-exercise device called Buns of Fury, is distressed by the emergence of a competitor marketing a strikingly similar product named Ferocious Buttocks. The Ferocious Buttocks machine is sold at a lower price due to the substandard materials used in its construction. Backside Health wants to sue the competitor on the basis of trademark infringement. How should they characterize the alleged infringement? What remedies may be available? Briefly outline each remedy and discuss which are preferred.

9. Depass Industries has contracted your intellectual property consulting firm for assistance in patenting its latest discovery. The company claims to have invented a way to prevent ice cream from leaking out of the bottom of waffle sugar cones, a problem that has plagued both the industry and consumers for years. The Depass process involves inserting a small amount of heated caramel syrup into each cone just before adding ice cream. The caramel must be heated to 48°C and added at 1 ml of syrup per 18 cm^2 of cone surface area. By doing so, the caramel collects at the bottom of the cone and hardens, forming an impermeable layer. The process, while seemingly unique, is subject to opposition as to its patentability. Does Depass's discovery seem to be a patentable form of invention? What requirements must the process meet to be patentable? Explain each. Briefly discuss how Depass might wish to exploit the patent, should it be awarded.

10. Belson Sisters Inc, once a harmonious and profitable company, has recently dissolved into two separate companies, each run by one of the sisters. The former company was in the business of manufacturing token-dispensing machines for use in video arcades and amusement centres. The younger sister, Jordan, was granted the company's prized international patent for the dispensing method in the break-up and now wants to sue her older sister, Marcia, for patent infringement. Whereas the old method involved counting each token, Marcia has developed a new process in which the tokens are dispensed by weight. Marcia's invention has not yet been awarded a Canadian patent. Jordan wants to "put Marcia out of business." What legal remedies would be available to Jordan if she is successful in making out her case against her older, wiser, and sneakier sister?

11. Louis Saint Chicken has sued its closest competitor, Bistro Poultry, for misappropriation of trade secrets, and a former employee, Nicolette Lemar, for breach of confidence with regard to its secret dipping sauce. Nicolette, who worked for Louis as a supervisor in its sauce laboratory for the last seven years, was recently recruited as the vice-president in charge of research and development at Bistro. Subsequently, Bistro began to produce and sell a garlic chicken wing sauce suspiciously similar to Louis's own world-famous dipping sauce. Louis alleges that, during the course of her employment, Nicolette was exposed to trade secrets with respect to its formula for its chicken wing sauce. There was no contractual clause barring Nicolette from disclosing the ingredients of the sauce, nor from undertaking future employment within the industry. What must Louis prove to succeed in its claim against Nicolette? How can Louis Saint Chicken better protect itself against the occurrence of a similar incident in the future?

12. Wotherspoon World Industries (WWI) is one of Canada's largest stock photography businesses. WWI supplies cutting edge digital photographs to advertisers, magazines, newspapers, journals, book publishers, businesses, and governments across Canada. WWI typically retains copyright in its photographs and grants each entity a non-exclusive licence for specific uses of the images. WWI employs a number of salespeople who have access to WWI's detailed and comprehensive customer list. WWI guards this secret customer list very closely. However, WWI does not have a confidentiality clause in its contracts with its salespeople. WWI believes that it can build better trust and loyalty of its salespeople by not using formal contracts. Recently, WWI learned that one of its former salespeople had opened a business in direct competition with WWI and that the salesperson was soliciting the business of all WWI's customers. When WWI checked its electronic records, it learned that the former salesperson had viewed and printed a copy of WWI's customer list the day before he quit. WWI believes that the salesperson took a copy of the confidential customer list. What must WWI show in order to succeed in a claim against the former salesperson? Does it make a difference if the salesperson did not actually take a copy of the customer list but instead merely recalled customers and contacts from memory?

WEBLINKS

Creative Commons Canada http://creativecommons.ca

Creative Commons is a non-profit organization that allows creators to share their works with others, and to use the works of others that have been issued under a Creative Commons licence. Creative Commons has a worldwide presence, including in Canada. The Creative Commons website at **www.creativecommons.org** contains information about the organization, including short animated movies that explain the history and concepts behind Creative Commons.

Intellectual Property Policy Directorate—Industry Canada http://strategis.ic.gc.ca/SSG/ip00001e.html

This directorate is responsible for reviewing and modernizing federal intellectual property laws. Its website provides news, research papers, laws and regulations, treaties, and links related to intellectual property.

Canadian Intellectual Property Laws and Regulations—Industry Canada http://strategis.ic.gc.ca/epic/internet/inippd-dppi.nsf/en/h_ip00007e.html

This site provides links to Canadian legislation regulating patents, copyright, trademarks, and industrial design.

Canadian Intellectual Property Office (CIPO/OPIC)
http://strategis.ic.gc.ca/sc_mrksv/cipo/welcome/welcom-e.html

CIPO was created to administer the intellectual property system in Canada and provide information on intellectual property. Its website links to the web pages of each subsection of intellectual property law.

World Intellectual Property Organization (WIPO)
www. wipo.org/index.html

This website provides information on intellectual property, WIPO activities and services, and links to treaties, decisions, and publications.

International Intellectual Property Treaties http://strategis.ic.gc.ca/epic/internet/inippd-dppi.nsf/en/h_ip00008e.html

This Industry Canada web page provides basic information on the international intellectual property treaties that Canada has signed and links to their full text.

Intellectual Property Institute of Canada (IPIC)
www.ipic.ca

IPIC is a professional organization concerned with patents, trademarks, copyright, and industrial design. It maintains a list of intellectual property agents and lawyers.

Copyright Board of Canada www.cb-cda.gc.ca

This site provides information on public hearings, recent decisions of the board, links to copyright collectives, and general information on copyright.

Society of Composers, Authors and Music Publishers of Canada (SOCAN) www.socan.ca

SOCAN collects and administers tariffs for music copyrights. Its website provides information on events, news, and other resources for music consumers, creators and publishers.

Recording Industry Association of America (RIAA)
www.riaa.org

RIAA represents the joint interests of many American film and music studios. Its site provides information on industry news, copyright, freedom of speech, licensing and royalties, piracy, audio technologies, and the interaction of music and the Internet.

US Copyright Office http://lcweb.loc.gov/copyright

This US government website provides a wealth of US copyright information, publications, legislation, announcements, and a searchable registration database.

Canadian Trade-Marks Database http://strategis.ic.gc.ca/cipo/trademarks/search/tmSearch.do

This online trademarks database allows you to search by trademark, status, application number, and registration number.

Canadian Trade-marks Journal http://napoleon.ic.gc.ca/cipo/tradejournal.nsf/$$ViewTemplate+for+TMJournal+English?OpenForm

This CIPO Web page archives the *Canadian Trade-marks Journal*, which operates under the authority of the *Trademark Act* and publishes applications for trademarks for public comment and opposition.

Canadian Patent Database http://patents1.ic.gc.ca/intro-e.html

This online searchable database lets you search, retrieve, and inspect over 1 500 000 Canadian patent documents.

US Patent and Trademark Office (USPTO) www.uspto.gov

This US Department of Commerce site allows users to search patents and trademarks, order copies, apply for patents, register trademarks, pay fees, and monitor file progress.

PATSCAN—Patent and Trademark Searching www.library.ubc.ca/patscan/welcome.html

This site provides patent and trademark searches for university and industry, intellectual property resources, and database access.

ADDITIONAL RESOURCES FOR CHAPTER 18 ON THE COMPANION WEBSITE

(www.pearsoned.ca/mcinnes)

In addition to self-test multiple-choice, true-false, and short essay questions (all with immediate feedback), three additional Cases and Problems (with suggested answers), and links to useful Web destinations, the Companion Website provides the following resources for Chapter 18:

- Business Decision 18W—Unbundling Copyright

Provincial Material

- **British Columbia:** Business Name
- **Alberta:** Trade Name/Trademark
- **Ontario:** Business Names

19 Electronic Commerce

CHAPTER OVERVIEW

OBJECTIVES

After completing this chapter, you should be able to:

1. Outline the general strategies adopted in electronic commerce legislation to ensure business certainty in the online environment.

2. Define functional equivalence and its role in electronic commerce legislation.

3. State the elements required to ensure successful contract formation in electronic commerce.

4. Discuss the contractual issues that are specific to automated electronic commerce and the legislative method for correcting keystroke errors.

5. Explain the importance of authentication in online business transactions.

6. Outline the business problems arising from the domain name system.

7. Discuss the jurisdictional implications of transacting in a global medium and explain how to minimize exposure to liability online.

8. Describe how an online business can shield itself from intermediary liability.

9. Describe how an organization can minimize the costs and risks of privacy violations while engaged in the collection, use, or disclosure of personal information.

10. Explain how consumer protection principles can be used to promote the reputation of a business, generate goodwill, and build trusting relationships.

electronic commerce refers to technology-mediated transactions

More and more, businesses of all types and sizes are distributing their products through various technological channels using *electronic commerce*. **Electronic commerce** refers to technology-mediated business transactions. These take place across a network and usually involve the transportation of goods, services, or information—either physically or digitally—from one place to another. It is tempting to think of the Internet when one thinks of electronic commerce, but the definition is actually much broader. It also includes, for instance, a transaction that occurs between a customer and an automated bank machine.

Electronic commerce has a number of benefits. Once a system is in place, transactions become easy and affordable. Technology allows a business to reach more customers, in more places. It allows contracts to be performed more quickly. And it can reduce the expenses associated with marketing products and creating contracts. However, electronic commerce also has its costs. One such cost is uncertainty. Uncertainty causes some businesses and consumers to avoid participating in electronic commerce.

The law is a significant source of uncertainty in electronic commerce. Generally speaking, law applies to electronic commerce in the same way it applies to other business contexts. However, the basic rules of commercial law were developed many years ago, when people usually dealt face to face. Not surprisingly, existing law does not easily accommodate every aspect of the transactions that are conducted over a network. For example, unsolicited commercial e-mail—called *spam*—has caused widespread damage to businesses and individuals alike, sometimes because of wasted time and resources spent reading and filtering through spam messages, sometimes because of viruses or worms that do damage to computers and other business assets. The law in this area has struggled to address the problem. Criminal law, contract law, privacy law, tort law, and trespass law have been invoked to attempt to address spam, and other countries have created entirely new laws to address spam.[1]

As a matter of risk management, a business that is involved in electronic commerce must be aware of potential problems. This chapter examines how the law has responded to technological changes in the business world. We begin with a survey of recent legislation that regulates electronic commerce. We then discuss how businesses can create enforceable electronic contracts and how they can address jurisdiction issues in electronic commerce. Because jurisdiction may be the single biggest problem encountered in electronic commerce, businesses must understand and address it. We also explore some specific issues that can arise in electronic commerce, including strategies regarding domain names, liability issues for Internet-related services, and the significance of peer-to-peer (P2P) file sharing. We conclude with an outline of business obligations and approaches to privacy and consumer protection laws.

ELECTRONIC COMMERCE LEGISLATION

A defining feature of electronic commerce is that it is global—it allows business to be done around the world. It is therefore desirable to have consistent laws from place to place. If every jurisdiction had a different set of rules, it would be

---

[1.] Canada formed a task force which in May 2005 made recommendations to the government regarding ways to deal with spam. See the Task Force on Spam website at <http://e-com.ic.gc.ca/epic/internet/inecic-ceac.nsf/en/h_gv00248e.html>.

impossible to achieve certainty in the electronic business world. As a result, the United Nations Commission on International Trade Law (UNCITRAL) encouraged countries to create uniform legislation based on a single model—the *United Nations Model Law on Electronic Commerce*.[2] The model law is not really a law. It does not create rights, powers, obligations, or immunities. It merely provides a *model* for the creation of a consistent set of laws. Ultimately, it is up to each government to decide how much of the model to adopt. Its goal is to remove barriers that technology may impose upon the creation of traditional commercial relationships.

Canada's *Uniform Electronic Commerce Act*

Because our Constitution states that commerce is generally a provincial matter, electronic commerce legislation has been enacted on a province-by-province basis. Still, the co-ordination of these rules was inspired on a national level. The strategy was similar to the international approach. A special working group of the Uniform Law Conference of Canada created its own model law—the *Uniform Electronic Commerce Act* (*UECA*).[3] Like UNCITRAL's model law, *UECA* has no legal force, but it has formed the basis for most electronic commerce laws in Canada. Some provinces have adopted all of it; others have adopted specific parts. Following this review of *UECA*, we will briefly describe how some provinces have adopted provisions different from *UECA*. However, because of the similarity between the key provisions of *UECA* and the actual laws adopted in each province, we will first examine *UECA*'s most important provisions in detail. In particular, we will consider:[4]

- its *scope*
- the role of *consent*
- the notion of a *functional equivalent*
- the rules pertaining to *electronic contracts*
- the rules pertaining to *sending and receiving electronic documents*
- the treatment of *government documents*

Scope

UECA has a broad scope. Rather than listing all of the transactions to which it applies, it lists those to which it does *not* apply. For instance, it follows UNCITRAL's model law by specifically excluding wills and dealings in land. Those sorts of arrangements are still governed by traditional legal rules. The list of exclusions differs, however, between jurisdictions. To manage risk, it is therefore important for a business involved with electronic commerce to know which exclusions apply in every jurisdiction in which it does business.

---

[2] The United Nations Model Law on Electronic Commerce: <www.uncitral.org/uncitral/en/uncitral_texts/electronic_commerce/1996Model.html>.

[3] The *Uniform Electronic Commerce Act* (*UECA*): <www.ulcc.ca/en/us/index.cfm?sec=1_&sub=1u1>.

[4] J Gregory "The *Uniform Electronic Commerce Act*," *Lex Electronica* 6(1) printemps 2000: <www.lex-electronica.org/articles/v6-1/gregory.htm>.

Consent

UECA does *not* require a business to use or accept electronic documents. Parties to a particular transaction may agree that they will not use or accept electronic documents. It is meant only to facilitate electronic commerce for those people who *choose* to engage in it. It is important to realize, however, that your consent may be express or implied. The courts may decide that you consented to use *UECA* if you behave in a way that supports that inference.

Functional Equivalence

As we saw in Chapters 10 and 16, some types of contract traditionally were enforceable only if they were in writing. That is still true. *UECA*, however, recognizes that the writing requirement can sometimes be satisfied through *functional equivalence*. **Functional equivalence** identifies the essential purpose of a traditional rule and indicates how that purpose can be accomplished electronically.

functional equivalence identifies the essential purpose of a traditional rule and indicates how that purpose can be accomplished electronically

For example, some statutes that regulate the enforcement of contractual terms require certain documents to be signed. That signature is intended to demonstrate the signer's willingness to be bound by the terms. However, that same purpose may be achieved through the click of a mouse. For instance, a dialogue box may appear on a computer screen that contains a box that says, "I accept these terms." Clicking on that box may be the functional equivalent of signing a document.[5]

Electronic Contracts

UECA does more than permit functional equivalents. It even allows transactions to be achieved, without human intervention, by computer programs. For instance, contracts may be created by shopping bots and other automated electronic devices.

Sending and Receiving Electronic Documents

UECA also facilitates electronic commerce by removing uncertainty about *where* and *when* a message is sent or received.

A message is deemed to be sent from the sender's place of business and received at the recipient's place of business.[6] Suppose your place of business is in Alberta, but you send a message through your Internet server in Manitoba, while you are travelling in the Yukon. It can plausibly be said that your message was sent from any one of three places. *UECA* therefore eliminates the uncertainty and promotes commerce by consistently choosing one of those possibilities.

UECA also contains clear rules that determine *when* a message is *sent* or *received*. A message is deemed to be *sent* when it leaves the sender's control. Consequently, once you push a button and can no longer stop the message from being sent, that message is considered sent, even if it is never received. A message is deemed *received* when it reaches an information system in the control of the person to whom it is sent. That rule can be tough on recipients because they can be held responsible for messages even if they never actually read them.

[5.] There are many other examples. The essential function of writing is memory, which can also be satisfied by electronic information, as long as it is accessible for future reference. See Case Brief 19.1 (on p. 441).

[6.] The rules are more complicated if a company has several places of business or no place of business.

However, a recipient can claim that a particular message was never received by proving, for instance, that it could not be downloaded from the server. The best way for a business to avoid disputes about the transmission of its messages is to either require acknowledgment that communications have been received or invoke a system of automated confirmation.

Note that *UECA*'s provisions do not change the common law rules regarding the communication of acceptance. As we saw in Chapter 7, contractual acceptance must be communicated to be effective. Furthermore, the time and the place of the acceptance depend upon the *medium of communication*. *UECA* has avoided the issue of instantaneous versus non-instantaneous communication, recognizing that the decision about whether to treat a particular electronic transmission as similar to a phone call or first-class mail depends upon the circumstances and must be determined on a case-by-case basis.

The rules eliminating uncertainty about where and when a message is sent or received are merely default rules. In other words, parties can choose, by mutual consent, to adopt their own rules that are different from *UECA*.

Government Documents

Governments electronically exchange an enormous amount of information with businesses and citizens. They will do so even more as Canada's *Government Online*, and similar provincial initiatives, are fully implemented. *UECA* therefore contains a number of provisions regarding electronic documents that are sent to government.[7] Some provisions protect governments from being swamped by electronic documents that arrive in various incompatible formats. A government can, for instance, specify the formats that it is willing to accept.[8]

Provincial Electronic Commerce Legislation

UECA is a model for provincial electronic commerce legislation.[9] Many provinces have adopted that model entirely or with minor variations.[10] Others have attempted to overcome the same problems by other means. Although it is impossible to provide a detailed comparison of each jurisdiction's approach, we can mention a few important differences.

The most substantial differences occur in New Brunswick and Quebec. For example, unlike most of its counterparts, the New Brunswick legislation does not regulate the process of offer and acceptance. And the Quebec legislation is much more extensive than its counterparts. It contains, for example, a number of detailed provisions regarding the consultation and transmission of documents

---

[7.] For the purposes of *UECA*, the term "government" does not include Crown corporations, but it may include municipalities, if the provincial or territorial legislature so decides.

[8.] Some jurisdictions, including Ontario, Nova Scotia, and the Yukon have adopted those provisions. Others, including British Columbia and New Brunswick, have not.

[9.] Bill 21, *Electronic Transactions Act*, 1st Sess 25th Parl, Alberta, 2001 (Alta); *Electronic Transactions Act*, SBC 2001, c 10 (BC); *Electronic Commerce and Information Act*, CCSM, c E55 (Man), amending *Manitoba Evidence Act*, CCSM c E150 (Man) and amending *Consumer Protection Act*, CCSM, C200 (Man); Bill 70, *Electronic Transactions Act*, 3d Sess, 54th Parl, New Brunswick, 2001 (NB); *Electronic Commerce Act*, SNS 2000, c 26 (NS); *Electronic Commerce Act*, SO 2000, c 17 (Ont); *Electronic Commerce Act*, SPEI 2001, c 31 (PEI); *Act to Establish a Legal Framework for Information Technology*, SQ 2001, c 32 (Que); *Electronic Information and Documents Act*, SS 2000, c E-722 (Sask); *Electronic Commerce Act*, SY 2000, c 10 (Yuk).

[10.] That is true of Alberta, British Columbia, Manitoba, Nova Scotia, Ontario, Prince Edward Island, Saskatchewan, and the Yukon.

that have legal implications for third parties, like online service providers. As a matter of risk management, businesses that are not confined to a single province or territory should consult the relevant legislation to avoid difficulties.

CONTRACTING ONLINE

It is important to note that, for the most part, contract law applies to electronic commerce exactly as it applies to traditional commerce. Although *UECA* and the statutes that it inspired remove many sources of uncertainty about electronic commerce, including the application of contract law to electronic commerce, a number of difficulties remain. In this section we will look at three issues:

- contract formation
- automated electronic commerce
- authentication and security

Contract Formation

The fact that commerce is conducted electronically creates certain problems for traditional rules governing the formation of contract. Some pertain to *shrink-wraps*, *click-wraps*, and *web-wraps* (or *browse-wraps*), while others pertain to the basic process of *offer and acceptance*.

Shrink-Wraps, Click-Wraps, and Web-Wraps

A *shrink-wrap licence* occurs in the context of mass-marketed software. The software is placed in a package that is wrapped in clear plastic wrap. Underneath the wrapping is a card, which states the rules that are attached to the use of the software. That card also informs consumers that, by removing the wrapper, they are agreeing to abide by those rules—they can use the software, but they must honour the terms of the *licence* that has been created. In general terms, a licence is a form of contract that grants permission to use a product in particular ways. In this case, the licence allows the customer to use the manufacturer's software on specific terms. Licences are used in the software industry and in electronic commerce where a business wishes to retain a degree of control over the use of its products. For example, software licences often prohibit the user from making copies or reselling the product.

The same basic process can be used for online commerce. A *click-wrap licence* is created when a person agrees to accept the terms of an online contract by clicking a mouse or touching an icon that says, "I accept." A **click-wrap licence** is a licensing agreement triggered by the click of a mouse. A *web-wrap licence* is similar, but more specific. A **web-wrap licence** is triggered by some form of online interaction. For example, while viewing a document online, you try to download or install software, or order goods or services. A window pops up that (i) contains the terms of a contract, (ii) asks you to read those terms, and (iii) tells you to click on one box to accept those terms or on another to reject them. If you click on the first box, you may be bound by a contract. Canadian courts have said that, when properly constructed, such agreements are "afforded the same sanctity that must be given to any agreement in writing."[11] Case Brief 19.1 illustrates this.

a **click-wrap licence** is a licensing agreement triggered by the click of a mouse

a **web-wrap licence** is triggered by some form of online interaction

---

[11.] *Rudder v Microsoft* (1999) 47 CCLT (2d) 168 at para 17 (Ont SCJ).

CASE BRIEF 19.1

Rudder v Microsoft (1999) 47 CCLT (2d) 168 (Ont SCJ)

Microsoft Network (MSN) provides online information services to members of its network. The plaintiffs were two Canadian law students who had entered into an online contract to receive MSN's services. They started a lawsuit in Ontario against MSN when they believed that they had been improperly charged for certain services.

MSN pointed to a provision in the online contract that it had created with the plaintiffs. That provision required any disputes to be resolved through the courts in the State of Washington. MSN therefore said that the case could not be heard in Canada. In response, the plaintiffs argued that they had not noticed the "forum selection clause" and argued that the clause should be treated as "fine print," since only a portion of the agreement was on screen at any given time.[12]

The court held that the plaintiffs had agreed to obey the terms of the online contract when they clicked on the button that said, "I agree." The court then rejected the argument that any terms not wholly in view must be understood as fine print. Such a claim, it held, was no different from saying that only the terms and conditions that appear on the signature page of a printed document should apply. The court also said that ignorance of the relevant term was no excuse since MSN's agreement required potential members to view its terms on two occasions and signify acceptance on each occasion. In fact, the second display of the terms advised users that, "If you click 'I agree' without reading the membership agreement, you are still agreeing to be bound by all of the terms. . . without limitation."

The court in *Rudder v Microsoft* stressed the fact that click-wrap and web-wrap agreements are similar to traditional contracts in one important way—the terms of a contract are effective only if they are sufficiently brought to the parties' attention.[13] The boundaries of this concept were tested in a more recent case. In *Kanitz v Rogers Cable Inc*, an Ontario court had to decide whether unilateral changes to the terms of a contract were valid when they were merely posted on a website. The court held that the changes to the contract were valid because the original contract stated that the defendant could make changes if it sent customers a notice by e-mail or postal mail, or if it posted the changes on its website. Although the court noted that the defendant could have done more to notify its customers of the changes to the contract, the defendant's posting of the changes on its website was found to be sufficient, given the wording of the original contract.[14]

The decision in *Kanitz v Rogers Cable Inc* suggests that businesses may be able to make binding changes to a contract if they reserve the right to do so and fulfill any notice requirements set out in the contract. In order to manage risk, however, businesses should strive to make contractual terms and changes to such terms as conspicuous as possible. If terms are hidden in a remote hyperlink or camouflaged in small fonts or footnotes, they may not be effective.

Offer and Acceptance

Online contracts also create challenges for the traditional rules regarding offer and acceptance. For instance, if a website proposes a contract, does it create an *offer* or merely an *invitation to treat*? As we saw in Chapter 7, if an offer is made to the world at large, it may be accepted by many people. The offeror may therefore be required to fulfill many contracts, even if it really wanted to create only one. As a matter of risk management, you should design your website so that it

---

[12.] In Chapter 9, we considered how courts deal with the "fine print" terms in standard form agreements.

[13.] That was traditionally true in the "ticket cases," which were discussed in Chapter 9.

[14.] *Kanitz v Rogers Cable Inc* (2002) 58 OR (3d) 299 (SCJ).

merely extends an invitation to treat. You could, for example, require potential customers to place their orders as offers, which you are entitled to accept or reject. Your website should also clearly state that you reserve the right to accept or reject all offers made.

Electronic commerce also raises issues about the communication of acceptance. Chapter 7 explained how the traditional common law rule depends upon whether the communication is instantaneous (like a telephone call) or non-instantaneous (like a letter). Most jurisdictions in Canada do *not* specify whether particular forms of communication are instantaneous or non-instantaneous. Businesses should prepare for the possibility that an e-mail may be lost or delayed in cyberspace. The safest route is to use various means of communication. For example, if an e-mail message is important, it might be backed up by a fax, regular letter, or telephone call. While electronic commerce is generally intended to avoid that inconvenience, it is still sometimes better to have a back-up plan. In some situations, the extra effort may avoid the time and expense of litigation. Admittedly, however, such safety mechanisms may become impossible as transactions become completely automated.

Automated Electronic Commerce

The cornerstone of traditional contract theory, the notion of *consensus ad idem* (a "meeting of the minds") becomes more difficult to apply in electronic commerce. Electronic commerce transactions may not be created and performed exclusively by humans. Many transactions are initiated and completed by computer software programs and do not easily fit within traditional notions of contract. In fact, part of the point of developing technologies that automate electronic commerce is to allow transactions to take place without any need for humans to review or even be aware of particular transactions. As demonstrated by Case Brief 19.2, a business must take care in the way that it designs and implements automated services.

CASE BRIEF 19.2

Zhu v Merrill Lynch HSBC 2002 BCPC 0535 (BC PC)

Zhu was a stock trader who used Merrill Lynch's NetTrader automated online stock trading system to buy and sell stocks. Immediately after selling stocks on one occasion, Zhu attempted to cancel the sale. He received an automated confirmation that some stocks had already been sold but that the sale of the remaining stocks was cancelled. In fact, the remaining stocks had also been sold. Zhu did not know this and sold the remaining stocks through another transaction. This meant that Zhu had sold the same stocks twice. Zhu had to buy back the stocks under the second transaction. However, by the time he was required to do that, the price of the stock had increased, causing him a loss of nearly $10 000. Merrill Lynch argued that the cancellation notice did not indicate that the cancellation was successful and that Zhu should have called to confirm that the cancellation was complete before making further sales.

The court held that Zhu was entitled to rely on the online prompts: "Surely common sense dictates that 'cancelled' means 'cancelled' and [Zhu] is entitled to treat that as a confirmation that his cancellation has been completed. It strikes me that [Merrill Lynch's] system could easily have issued a prompt saying 'cancellation pending' or 'please wait until advised that cancellation is completed before placing another order.'" Because of the high risk of loss of investment funds, the court also held that Merrill Lynch owed its customers a higher duty of care and performance in providing the automated online service. This decision suggests that businesses providing online services should design their systems and automated notices in a way that consumers can readily understand. This is particularly important for services where there is a high risk of loss to customers.

Most Canadian electronic commerce statutes allow contracts to be created by automated electronic devices.[15] However, it may be dangerous to rely on such systems. Most of the statutes also say that transactions are unenforceable when purchasers make a *keystroke error* when dealing with an automated system. A **keystroke error** occurs when a person mistakenly hits a wrong button or key. For instance, you may order 1000 items instead of 100, or you may hit the "I agree" button instead of the "I decline" button. An automated system normally cannot recognize subsequent messages that you send in an attempt to correct a mistake. It will simply fill your order as originally received. The legislation may allow you to escape the consequences of your error in certain circumstances. Basically, you must prove that (i) the automated system did not provide an opportunity to prevent or correct the error, (ii) you notified the other party of the error as soon as possible, (iii) you took reasonable steps to return any benefit that you received under the transaction, and (iv) you have not received any other material benefit from the transaction. An online business can avoid those sorts of situations by creating an automated mechanism to correct such errors. The simplest tactic is to require the purchaser to confirm the order by repeating the important steps (for instance, by retyping the number of items that the purchaser wants to receive).

> a **keystroke error** occurs when a person mistakenly hits wrong buttons or keys

Authentication

In our earlier discussion of functional equivalents, we saw that a signature can serve the important goal of demonstrating a person's willingness to be bound to a contract. But a signature can also provide an *authenticating function*. An **authenticating function** identifies the signatory and ties that person to the document. In many situations, contractual parties are not concerned about each other's identity. If you buy a bowl of matzo ball soup from my deli, I do not care who you are, and you do not care who I am. However, a party's identity is often important, especially in electronic commerce. Suppose we create a contract online that requires you to pay $10 000 and that requires me to deliver an Internet server. Without some form of authentication, either you will have to pay and trust me to send the server, or I will have to send the server and trust you to pay. Although people often do business on the basis of trust, it can be a dangerous practice, especially among strangers. Risk management therefore suggests the need for authentication. At least one of us has to be satisfied that the other can be trusted. *Electronic signatures* can be used for that purpose.

> an **authenticating function** identifies the signatory and ties that person to the document

Electronic Signatures

An **electronic signature** is electronic information that people can use to identify themselves. The process in which a person uses an electronic signature usually involves two components: a trusted third party known as a *certification authority* and technology known as *public key cryptography*. A discussion of public key cryptography technology is largely a technical matter beyond the scope of this chapter. We will, however, review the role of certification authorities below.

> an **electronic signature** is electronic information that people can use to identify themselves

Certification Authorities   An electronic signature is reliable if it is used in conjunction with a *trusted third party*. A **trusted third party** is a person or other entity whom both contractual parties can trust. That trusted third party therefore uses a *digital certificate* to verify the identity of the person who provided the

> a **trusted third party** is a person whom both contractual parties can trust

---

[15.] *UECA* s21 states: "A contract may be formed by the interaction of an electronic agent and a natural person or by the interaction of electronic agents."

a digital certificate is an electronic document that authenticates the identity of a particular person

electronic signature. **A digital certificate** is an electronic document that authenticates the identity of a particular person. In many ways, it is like an electronic credit card—it is used to establish your credentials when doing business online. A trusted third party who provides that sort of certificate is known as a *certification authority*. There are a number of businesses in Canada and around the world that provide certification authority services.

Note that a certification authority need not be limited to verifying a person's identity for electronic signatures in online contracts. Digital certificates can also be used to certify a person's age, whether that person holds a licence to use certain online services, whether a person's level of security clearance authorizes access to an information system, and so on.

The Canadian government has recognized the importance of electronic signatures and authentication in Canada. In May 2004, it released a draft of the *Secure Electronic Signature Regulations*[16] and the *Principles for Electronic Authentication*.[17] The former rules contain technical requirements for electronic signatures and permit the government to verify which certification authorities have the power to issue trustworthy certificates for certain purposes. On the other hand, the stated purpose of the *Principles for Electronic Authentication* is "to provide guidance [as benchmarks] for the development, implementation and use of authentication products and services in Canada."

Information Security

Security measures are crucial to the success of electronic commerce. Online intruders can steal information-based assets, dilute corporate brands, cause critical infrastructure failures, service breaks and system failures, and scare away customers. Security protects corporate assets from external threats. Information security can be used to protect your business against the threat of things like tampering, interception, worms, viruses, and logic bombs. **Information security** is a combination of communications security and computer security. **Communications security** protects information while it is transmitted from one system to another. **Computer security** protects information within a computer system.

information security is a combination of communications security and computer security

communications security protects information while it is transmitted from one system to another

computer security protects information within a computer system

Hardware and software are not the only means of protection. A comprehensive information security system must include other forms of control, including strict workplace policies and personnel security. For example, different employees might enjoy different levels of access to sensitive business information. Businesses can also protect themselves by using the law as a deterrent, by informing those with access to information systems that they will be punished (perhaps by the loss of Internet privileges or even summary dismissal) if they engage in illegal activities like online gambling, possessing child pornography, sexual harassment, and fraud.

Businesses should also publicize the fact that the *Criminal Code of Canada* contains a number of provisions designed to prevent security breaches.[18]

- Section 342.1 prohibits the *unauthorized use of a computer*, including theft of computer services, breaches of privacy, and trafficking in computer passwords.

---

[16] *Secure Electronic Signature Regulations*: <http://canadagazette.gc.ca/partl/2004/20040508/htmil/regle6-e.html>.

[17] *Principles for Electronic Authentication*: <http://e-com.ic.gc.ca/epic/internet/inecicceac.nsf/en/h_gv00240e.html>.

[18] *Criminal Code*, RSC 1985, c C-46 (Can).

- Section 430 (1.1) prohibits *computer mischief* that (i) destroys or alters data, (ii) renders data meaningless, useless, or ineffective, (iii) obstructs, interrupts, or interferes with the lawful use of data, or (iv) obstructs, interrupts, or interferes with any person in the lawful use of data or denies access to data to any person who is entitled to access thereto.

- Sections 183 and 184 prohibit the *interception of private communications*. The definition of "private communications" is quite broad, and includes any telecommunication made in Canada or intended to be received in Canada. Business managers charged with information security will be relieved to know that an exception exists where it is reasonable to expect that the communication may be intercepted, as in the employment context.

Businesses can use contract law to protect themselves against some security risks. As we saw in Chapter 18, they can adopt confidentiality agreements. Likewise, they should create and publicize an Internet use policy that will be enforced against all company employees. That policy should include provisions governing (i) the use, disclosure, and return of confidential information, (ii) the use of the Internet, and (iii) permission to monitor employee communications. Businesses can also reduce some security risks by outsourcing to security providers, including certification authorities. The security provider or its insurer will likely assume some of the risk of maintaining security.

JURISDICTION IN ELECTRONIC COMMERCE

Problems cannot always be avoided, and disputes cannot always be settled. Litigation may be inevitable, especially if a business is engaged in global e-commerce. In that situation, it may not be enough to comply with local laws. Website owners and operators must also consider the possibility of being dragged into court in some remote place. They must factor that possibility into the cost of doing business. And while it is expensive to ensure compliance in foreign legal systems, it is sometimes even more expensive to become embroiled in a faraway legal battle. Before considering compliance issues and the kinds of liability that might result from an electronic transaction, we need to first examine the question of *jurisdiction*. **Jurisdiction**, in this context, refers to the ability of a court from a particular place to hear a case. Although the issue of jurisdiction can arise in any kind of case, it is particularly important in electronic commerce. Suppose you have a company in British Columbia with a registered trademark. You discover that a dot-com company in Saskatchewan that sells goods to people in Germany has improperly used your trademark on its website. That website is hosted by a server that is located in France. Where can you sue? British Columbia? Saskatchewan? France? Germany? At least three tests can be used to answer that question:

- a real and substantial connection test
- a passive versus active test
- an effects-based test

In Canada, the courts usually use a **real and substantial connection test**. They ask whether the plaintiff's cause of action and the effects of the defendant's

jurisdiction refers to the ability of a court from a particular place to hear a case

a real and substantial connection test asks whether the plaintiff's cause of action and the effects of the defendant's conduct are sufficiently linked to the place in which the plaintiff wants to sue

conduct are sufficiently linked to the place in which the plaintiff wants to sue.[19] Unfortunately, the courts are not yet sure how to apply that test in an e-commerce context.[20] Early cases in the US likened the Internet to a continuous advertisement.[21] On that basis, they said that information posted on a given website is directed to *every* place capable of accessing the site. Early decisions in Canada followed suit. For example, in *Alteen v Informix*, the defendant, an American manufacturer of information management hardware, allegedly issued untrue and misleading statements that led to an inflated stock price.[22] When Newfoundland shareholders tried to sue, Informix argued that the Newfoundland court had no jurisdiction. Informix argued that it had no real and substantial connection to Canada because it (i) did not trade shares on a Canadian stock exchange, (ii) never made press releases in Canada, and (iii) had no direct contacts with the plaintiffs. Still, the court held that the mere availability of the misleading statements on the Internet was sufficient to assert jurisdiction. Note that the stunning effect of this approach is to potentially make *every* business liable in *every* jurisdiction where the material is accessible.

Online business activity can take many forms, and the analogy between a website and a continuous advertisement is not always appropriate. Consequently, some courts now examine the online interaction to determine (i) the level of interactivity between the parties, and (ii) the commercial nature of the exchange of information that occurs on the website.[23] Under this **passive versus active test**, a court looks at the way in which each party does business online. Is it merely posting information, or does it require customers to interact through the exchange of information online? Does its website send e-mail to particular places? Does it encourage customers from foreign places to call by providing a local or toll-free number? The more interactive a website is in a particular country, the more likely that a court in that country has jurisdiction to hear a case. There is an important point for risk management. If a company does not want to be involved in litigation in a particular place, it should avoid interacting online with people in that place. This issue is highlighted in You Be the Judge 19.1.

the passive versus active test requires a court to look at the way in which the parties do business online.

YOU BE THE JUDGE 19.1

Dow Jones & Company Inc v Gutnick (2002) 210 CLR 575 (HCA)

Joseph Gutnick was a resident of the State of Victoria in Australia. In October 2000, *Barron's* magazine, and its website *Barron's Online*, published a story about Mr Gutnick entitled "Unholy Gains." Among other things, the article implied that Mr Gutnick had engaged in money laundering. Mr Gutnick sued

Dow Jones & Company Inc (the company that owned *Barron's*) in the Supreme Court of Victoria for defamation.

Dow Jones applied to the court to have the action set aside. Dow Jones claimed that the publication of the article had taken place in New Jersey because its servers containing

(continued)

---

19. *Tolofson v Jensen* (1994) 120 DLR (4th) 289 (SCC); *Morguard Investments Ltd v De Savoye* (1990) 76 DLR (4th) 256 (SCC); *Beals v Saldanha* (2003) 234 DLR (4th) 1 (SCC).

20. The Supreme Court of Canada recently said that relevant connecting factors in the *real and substantial connection test* include the locations of the content provider, the host server, the intermediaries, and the end user: *Society of Composers, Authors and Music Publishers of Canada v Canadian Association of Internet Providers* (2004) 240 DLR (4th) 193 (SCC).

21. *Inset Systems Inc v Instruction Set Inc* 937 F Supp 161 (D Conn 1996).

22. *Alteen v Informix* (1998) 164 Nfld & PEIR 301 (Nfld SC TD).

23. *Zippo Manufacturing Co v Zippo Dot Com Inc* 952 F Supp 1119 (WD Pa 1997); *Braintech Inc v Kostiuk* (1999) 171 DLR (4th) 46 (Ont CA).

(continued)

the article were located in that state. In response, Mr Gutnick argued that the publication took place in Australia because the article could be downloaded there and because Australia was the place where he experienced harm to his reputation.

The High Court rejected Dow Jones' arguments and held that, for the purpose of defamation, publication takes place on the Internet when an article is downloaded and read. The court stated that publication does not take place when an article is loaded onto a server. For the purpose of determining jurisdiction, the court stated that "[t]he most important event so far as defamation is concerned is the infliction of the damage, and that occurs at the place (or the places) where the defamation is comprehended."

Questions for Discussion

1. Do you agree with the decision of the Australian High Court? Why or why not?

2. What are some possible global ramifications of this decision? Should a person be able to sue in each jurisdiction where he or she suffers harm?

3. If your managerial duties included overseeing a website that publishes online content, what changes might you make to the availability of your site in foreign jurisdictions?

Several courts have moved away from a test that examines the specific characteristics, or the *potential impact*, of a particular website. Instead, they have adopted a broader **effects-based approach** that focuses on the *actual impact* that a website has in the place where jurisdiction is being sought. This type of approach was adopted in *Dow Jones & Company Inc v Gutnick* (discussed in You Be the Judge 19.1) and has more recently been followed in Canadian courts.[24] To the extent that the courts are tempted to look at *where* the harm is done rather than *how* it is done, it will be very difficult for businesses to insulate themselves from possible liability in remote jurisdictions.

an **effects-based approach** focuses on the actual impact that a website has in the place where jurisdiction is being sought

One way a business can protect itself from liability in specific jurisdictions is to avoid *targeting a location*.[25] **Targeting a location** means specifically choosing to create relationships with people within that location. A business that targets individuals or corporations within a particular place is more likely to have the courts in that place take jurisdiction.

targeting a location means specifically choosing to create relationships with people within that location

CONCEPT SUMMARY 19.1

Managing and Minimizing Internet Jurisdiction Risks

- Assess, minimize, and eliminate any connections your business might have with jurisdictions in which it does not wish to face potential liability. These connections might include physical assets, bank accounts, country code domain names, host servers, and intermediaries.

- Insert a jurisdiction clause into contracts that requires any disputes arising from the agreement to be heard by the courts in a specified place in accordance with the laws of that place. As we saw in our investigation of click-wrap and web-wrap contracts, such a clause will only be effective if adequate notice is given and if the other party is capable of agreeing to it.

- Use geo-location targeting technologies. Such technologies allow a company to manage the legal risks of e-commerce by restricting the geographical area in which it does business. For example, for legal or business reasons, a website based in Canada might wish to sell goods to customers in Canada and the United States, but not European countries. Geo-location technologies can help achieve this end, thereby minimizing the possibility of legal liability in non-targeted countries.

---

24. *Bangoura v Washington Post* (2004) 235 DLR (4th) 564 (Ont SCJ).

25. M Geist "Is There a There There? Toward Greater Certainty for Internet Jurisdiction" (2001) *Berkeley Tech LJ* 1345.

DOMAIN NAMES

a **domain name** locates the website(s) of an organization or other entity on the Internet

We have examined the core contractual aspects of electronic commerce. Now we will investigate other legal issues that can arise as a business migrates to the online terrain. Although a key benefit of electronic commerce is that geography becomes less important, the marketing slogan—location, location, location—is still relevant online. Perhaps the most important real estate in cyberspace is the *domain name*. A **domain name** locates an organization's website(s) on the Internet. For example, by entering www.pearsoned.ca into an Internet browser or search engine, you will locate the website of the company Pearson Education Canada, the publisher of this book.[26] Because of the enormous number of domains on the Internet, several national and international organizations regulate their acquisition and use.[27]

a **cybersquatter** purchases a potentially valuable domain name with the intention of later selling it to the highest bidder

In the world of real estate, a person may buy a piece of land with a view to reselling it at a profit. The same sort of activity can happen on the Internet. A **cybersquatter** purchases a potentially valuable domain name with the intention of later selling it to the highest bidder. For example, some cybersquatters reserve domain names for common English words (like drugstore.com or furniture.com) in the hope of reselling them to companies that are interested in dealing with the relevant products online. Domain names are typically registered on a first-come, first-served basis. The first person to register it becomes the owner and has the right to resell it. Problems arise, however, when a domain is not merely a common word but rather a name in which someone else asserts some sort of proprietary interest. Although the regulating authorities have received complaints about thousands of domain names, the disputes usually fall into three groups.

- A person may innocently, or with some justification, register a domain name that is later disputed. For example, if your newborn nephew is named Ed Pearson, you might register the domain www.pearsoned.ca and post pictures of him at that address. You may receive a complaint from Pearson Education Canada, which holds a proprietary interest in that name.

- A person may register a domain name that resembles a trademark to which both parties claim a commercial right. For example, if you hold the US trademark Pearson International, you may register www.pearson international.ca. If so, you may receive a complaint from the Greater Toronto Airport Authority, which believes that, as operator of Pearson International Airport and holder of a similar registered Canadian mark, it has a stronger claim to that domain name.

- A person may register a domain name in which it has no commercial rights. For example, you might try to be the first to register www.pearsoned.ca, either to prevent Pearson Education Canada from using it, to sell it to Pearson at a price far exceeding its cost, or to offer it for sale to Pearson's competitors.

In some circumstances, a business may wish to commence trademark infringement or passing-off litigation against the offending party. However, litigation may require a considerable investment of time and money. That is especially true if the case involves a jurisdiction issue because the cybersquatter

---

26. Like many other international companies, Pearson Education has registered several other domain names, such as <www.pearsoneducation.com>.

27. For instance, dot-ca (as in <www.pearsoned.ca>) is administered by the Canadian Internet Registry Authority (CIRA).

lives in some distant part of the world. These costs may be out of proportion to the value of the domain name.

As a result of these issues, the bodies that regulate domain names have adopted procedures for resolving disputes through online arbitration.[28] As we discussed in Chapter 2, arbitration is a form of alternative dispute resolution (or ADR) that allows the parties to settle their argument without the involvement of a court. In the domain name context, arbitration can resolve disputes far more quickly and cost-effectively than court systems. Domain name arbitrators require less evidence and generally do not allow evidence to be tested. There is, however, a significant disadvantage to domain name arbitration. The only remedy typically available is transfer of the domain name from the cybersquatter to the business. Damages and legal costs are not available (as they are in court proceedings). Cybersquatters may therefore operate with relatively little to fear from domain name arbitration.

A business with a domain claim may therefore need to choose between arbitration and litigation. In doing so, it should consider a number of risk management factors. The first factor to consider is whether arbitration is appropriate at all. Domain name dispute arbitration is typically designed only to handle a narrow category of cases—clear cases of bad faith cybersquatting. Disputes between two companies with competing trademark rights to a name will normally not be suited for resolution by online arbitration.

If both litigation and arbitration are options, then the claimant will need to consider a number of factors including (i) the strength of the trademark, (ii) the evidence available about the cybersquatter, (iii) the urgency of resolving the dispute, (iv) the acceptable costs of resolution, and (iv) the ultimate objectives (such as whether the business merely wants a transfer of the domain name or whether it also wants money damages for trademark infringement). Generally speaking, arbitration can be an efficient and low-risk way to resolve a domain name dispute where a strong case can be made out on paper. If credibility is an issue, evidence against a cybersquatter is lacking, or a claimant wants an award of money damages for trademark infringement, then litigation in court may be preferable.

BUSINESS DECISION 19.1

Parody Websites[29]

Ken Harvey was a speculator in domain names who lived in Newfoundland. Upon registering walmartcanadasucks.com and a number of similar domains, Ken created and uploaded a Web page stating that, "This is a freedom of information site set up for dissatisfied Wal-Mart Canada customers." The site exhorted visitors to "Spill Your Guts" with a "horror story relating to your dealings with Wal-Mart Canada." Wal-Mart responded by filing a complaint to a dispute-resolution provider, indicating that the domains were registered in bad faith. According to Wal-Mart, Ken's free speech argument was merely a cybersquatter's convenient and transparent dodge. On that basis, Wal-Mart sought to have control of the domain name walmartcanadasucks.com.

The dispute resolution provider held that Ken's conduct, even if distasteful, should not result in an unwarranted expansion of the domain name dispute process. According to the arbitrator, the dispute resolution process is meant to protect against bad faith domain name registrations, not provide a general remedy for all misconduct involving domain names.

(continued)

[28.] Arbitration was discussed in Chapter 2. In some instances, a party can appeal the arbitrator's decision to a court. The rules for resolving a dispute regarding a dot-ca can be found at <www.cira.ca/en/cat_Dpr.html>.

[29.] *Wal-Mart Stores Inc v <walmartcanadasucks.com> and Kenneth J Harvey*, WIPO Arbitration and Mediation Center, Case No D2000-1104.

(continued)

Having held that the walmartcanadasucks.com domain name is not identical or confusingly similar to Wal-Mart's trademarked name, the arbitrator decided that Ken did not register the domain name in bad faith. In fact, the arbitrator ruled that Ken had "a legitimate interest in respect of the domain name, to use it as a foundation for criticism of the complainant." On this basis, the request to transfer the domain name to Wal-Mart was refused.

Questions for Discussion

1. Should consumers be allowed to say whatever they want about a business, even if what they say is harmful and results in a loss of profits?
2. If you were the Wal-Mart executive charged with handling the matter, how might you have avoided arbitration?

As a matter of risk management, the best strategy is to avoid domain name difficulties altogether. While that is not always possible, businesses can take steps to minimize the potential for domain name disputes. For instance, as a component part of its overall intellectual property strategy, a business should register trademarks and business names as domain names as early as possible to avoid being held hostage by a cybersquatter. This might include registering domain names that correspond to company names, brand names, slogans, and product names. While dot-com, dot-net, and dot-org domain names tend to be the most popular domain names, a business should also consider the various country-code domain names that it might wish to register, including dot-ca, dot-uk, and dot-us. Note that a registered trademark will not guarantee your business a proprietary interest in a particular domain name.

CONCEPT SUMMARY 19.2

Business Strategy Regarding Domain Names

- Avoid disputes by registering key trademarks, product names, and business names as domain names before someone else does (for example, register key domain names *prior* to the launch of the relevant business or product if possible).
- Consider registering generic domains (such as dot-com), and country code domains (such as dot-ca) for the countries you do business in.
- If a dispute arises regarding a domain name, consider whether arbitration under a dispute resolution policy is an option.
- When deciding whether to pursue arbitration or litigation, consider factors such as the strength of the trademark, the evidence available about the cybersquatter, the urgency of resolving the dispute, the cost you are willing to incur, and your objectives.

LIABILITY OF ONLINE INTERMEDIARIES

For the most part, the threat of liability in electronic commerce is much the same as it has always been. The elements of defamation, for instance, are identical whether the tort is committed in person or over the Internet. As discussed above and demonstrated by You Be the Judge 19.1, however, the Internet does pose unique jurisdictional problems in the area of online defamation. It may also affect the damages that result from the tort because defamatory material in digital form may be accessed, copied, and distributed widely, with the possible effect of increasing the harm suffered. And finally, beyond posing challenges for existing law, electronic commerce may also generate new forms of liability for certain kinds of online businesses, because of the role that *online intermediaries* play in various online relationships.

An **online intermediary** is a party that enables or facilitates an online transaction between others. Think about all the things that need to happen before you can sell to me stuff that is advertised on your website. First, someone has to agree to host your website. Second, unless I am fortunate enough to own an Internet server, someone needs to provide me with access to the Internet. I also need an e-mail account. So do you. Someone is probably in the business of storing or managing most of that data. There are, then, many kinds of businesses that *intermediate* our transaction. They are all considered online intermediaries. In fact, you might even be one. If your business provides employees with access to the Internet or e-mail, then you are an online intermediary in any of their transactions. Other online intermediaries might include courier companies or financial intermediaries like banks or credit card companies. Here, we will focus on two different kinds of online intermediaries:

an online intermediary is a party that enables or facilitates an online transaction between others

- Internet service providers
- online service providers

Internet Service Providers

An **Internet service provider**, sometimes called an *ISP* or an *Internet access provider*, provides others with access to the Internet. Suppose you start a business that provides Internet access for a flat fee. What happens if one of your customers uses your service to defame someone, download obscene materials, or breach copyright? As an intermediary, can you be held accountable? Generally speaking, the law says "no." Internet access providers, like phone companies, are usually given special treatment, because they are in the business of supplying the pipeline, not monitoring its flow. That is not to say that an access provider is immune from all forms of liability. Suppose you are an Internet access provider, and your standard contract absolutely guarantees customers uninterrupted service. One day, your service will go down. When it does, you will be liable for breach of contract. You could have avoided liability if you had anticipated service interruptions and provided for them in your standard contract. Or, suppose you do not provide access for a fee, but for free to your employees. It is possible that they might do things online that attract liability to you as the access provider.[30]

an Internet service provider provides others with access to the Internet

Online Service Providers

Intermediary liability becomes much more difficult to determine in the context of *online service providers*. An **online service provider** offers goods or services, beyond mere Internet access, in exchange for something of value. Electronic commerce examples include e-mail suppliers, bulletin board operators, auction hosts, anonymous remailers, and commercial websites. Many ISPs act as both an ISP and an online service provider.

an online service provider offers goods or services, beyond mere Internet access, in exchange for something of value

---

[30.] For example, an employee may download obscene materials in the workplace. By allowing the employee to create a hostile work environment, the employer may be held liable under human rights legislation, especially if the employer adopted a policy of monitoring employee conduct online but failed to enforce the policy.

An online service provider usually enters into a contract with its subscriber. As usual, it can be held liable to that person if it breaches the agreement. It can, of course, manage that risk by inserting an exclusion clause into the contract. Significantly, however, that strategy cannot protect an online service provider from liability to a third party. Since that party is not part of any contract and is therefore not bound by any exclusion clause, it may sue the service provider *as an intermediary*.[31] For example, when a customer uses Yahoo! or AOL Canada to distribute a defamatory statement, the victim of that tort may sue both the customer and the online service provider. The victim may also sue the service provider for failing to reveal the true identity of the customer if that statement was posted under a false name. It is important to recognize, however, that you do not have to be an Internet giant to expose your business to these kinds of lawsuits. Risk managers will want to shield their online businesses against liability for (i) publishing defamatory remarks, (ii) distributing materials that infringe copyright, (iii) disclosing personal information, (iv) infringing trademarks, (v) participating in computer mischief, and (vi) possessing or distributing child pornography, to name a few.

CASE BRIEF 19.3

Society of Composers, Authors and Music Publishers of Canada v Canadian Association of Internet Providers (2004) 240 DLR (4th) 193 (SCC)

The Society of Composers, Authors and Music Publishers of Canada (SOCAN) is a collective society which administers Canadian copyright in music for Canadian and foreign copyright owners. SOCAN collects royalties from radio stations that play copyright songs that SOCAN is responsible for administering. In this case, SOCAN tried to collect royalties from Canadian Internet service providers on the basis that ISPs infringe the right of copyright owners to communicate their works to the public and to authorize such communication.

The Canadian Association of Internet Providers (CAIP) opposed SOCAN's attempt to collect royalties from ISPs. CAIP argued that ISPs do not communicate copyright works or authorize such communication. According to CAIP, ISPs are merely conduits for communications and do not regulate the content of communications passing over their networks.

The Supreme Court of Canada held that ISPs are not liable to pay SOCAN royalties when they merely function as content-neutral conduits. That is true when ISPs do not have knowledge of the infringing content and when, from a technical and economic standpoint, they cannot practically monitor the vast amount of content passing over their networks. "Caching" (the temporary storage) of content by an ISP is a conduit function because it is content-neutral and it is motivated by the need to deliver faster and more economical Internet access service. The court did not, however, rule out the possibility that ISPs might have to pay royalties when they act as more than mere conduits.

Finally, the court held that an ISP does not "authorize" an infringement merely because it knows that a user *might* use an ISP's facilities to commit infringement.

In the United States and within the European Union, specific legislation has been passed to shield Internet service providers from liability in some circumstances.[32] Unfortunately, very few Canadian law makers have squarely addressed

---

[31] We discussed exclusion clauses and privity of contract in Chapter 8.

[32] In the United States, the *Digital Millenium Copyright Act of 1998*, Pub L No 105-304, 112 Stat 2860 provides a safe harbour from liability where an ISP complies with a notice and take-down system. In the United Kingdom, a restricted immunity from liability is stipulated in the *Defamation Act, 1996* (UK) 1996, c 31, s.1. Applying this provision to the online environment, a service provider who (i) is not an author, editor, or publisher, (ii) takes reasonable care, and (iii) does not know, or have reason to believe, that what they did contributed to, or caused the publication of, a defamatory statement, will be protected from liability for defamation. The European Union's *E-Commerce Directive 2000/31 of the European Parliament and of the Council of June 8, 2000 on certain legal aspects of information society services, in particular electronic commerce, in the Internal Market (Directive on electronic commerce)*, [2000] OJL178/1 provides that intermediaries are not liable where their actions are limited to "the technical process of operating and giving access to a communication network over which information made available by third parties is transmitted or temporarily stored."

these issues. Canadian businesses are therefore often in the precarious position of relying on the courts to correctly interpret and apply the *SOCAN* decision.[33] One province that has legislatively intervened is Quebec. According to section 27 of its *Act to Establish a Legal Framework for Information Technology*, service providers acting as intermediaries are not required to monitor the information communicated on their networks or in the documents stored on them, nor are they required to report communications or documents that may be used for illegal activities.[34] Even if a service provider chooses to monitor or report, its decision to do so will not automatically result in intermediary liability if illegal content is later found on its site. Section 36 of the Act states that service providers acting as intermediaries are not generally responsible for the illegal acts of service users. However, it also states that a service provider *may* incur liability if it *participates* in acts performed by service users.[35]

What about online service providers in other provinces? How can you shield your business from intermediary liability?

- You should have a clear contract with each user, possibly through a click-wrap agreement. Each user should be required to clearly consent to the *terms of service* that are contained in that contract. And those terms should allow you to claim *indemnification* from a user if you are ever held liable for something that they posted.[36]

- Those *terms of service* should clearly explain, with examples, which uses are acceptable and which are unacceptable. While you should not commit yourself to monitoring content, you should reserve the right to remove content where the content is in violation of your terms of service or where you wish to remove it for other reasons at your discretion.

- You should, whenever possible, set up your business so that you can demonstrate that it merely acts as a conduit or pipeline for the materials that pass through the system.

- If you are sued, you should try to convince the court that while the legislation in Quebec, the US, and the European Union are not binding in other places, they are based on policies that should be adopted. The Supreme Court of Canada's decision in *SOCAN v CAIP* may also be helpful.

P2P FILE-SHARING

Peer-to-peer (P2P) file-sharing systems are among the most popular and controversial online applications in use today. These systems allow individuals to search for and share files of all kinds over a distributed network. Although Napster was the first widely used P2P system, newer, more sophisticated technologies are now in widespread use, including BitTorrent, Morpheus, and eDonkey. P2P technologies continue to evolve rapidly and are being used by millions of people to share an extraordinary number of files (especially music files) online.

[33.] There is, however, a recent indication that the federal government intends to act in this area. See Bill C-60, *An Act to Amend the Copyright Act*, introduced in June 2005.

[34.] *Act to Establish a Legal Framework for Information Technology* (Que), SQ 2001, c 32.

[35.] For example, liability may be imposed if the service provider (i) sends a document, (ii) selects or alters the information in a document, (iii) determines who transmits, receives, or has access to a document, or (iv) stores a document longer than is necessary for its transmission.

[36.] Indemnification would require the user to compensate you for any losses that you suffered (for example, by being successfully sued as an intermediary by a third party).

Some copyright owners claim that P2P systems are being used to infringe their copyrights on a mass scale. Their reaction to P2P has been multi-faceted. For example, some copyright owners have launched and sanctioned music download services of their own. Some have sued P2P users and the companies that make P2P software. Ethical Perspective 19.1 describes one such example in Canada. In the United States, legislation (such as the *INDUCE Act*) that would effectively ban P2P software has been introduced in Congress.[37]

ETHICAL PERSPECTIVE 19.1

BMG Canada Inc v John Doe (2004) 239 DLR (4th) 726 (FC TD), affd (2005) 39 CPR (4th) 97 (FC CA)

The Canadian Recording Industry Association (CRIA) brought an action in Federal Court against 29 unnamed individuals, alleging that they had illegally shared hundreds of music files on P2P systems. Though the 29 individuals could not be identified by their legal names, CRIA claimed that it was able to determine their P2P pseudonyms (such as Geekboy@KaZaA.com) and their internet protocol (IP) addresses (a unique number associated with their computers). Because CRIA was not able to determine the actual identities of the individuals it was targeting, it asked the court to order five Internet service providers (ISPs) to reveal the legal names associated with the P2P pseudonyms using P2P to download songs. CRIA claimed that it had linked the P2P pseudonyms to IP addresses at particular times and that the ISPs would have records linking the legal names to the associated IP addresses.

Citing concerns about online privacy, doubts about whether P2P file-sharing even amounted to copyright infringement under Canadian law, and weaknesses in CRIA's evidence, the court refused to order the ISPs to reveal the names of their subscribers to CRIA.[38] For example, the court stated that "[t]here is no evidence explaining how the pseudonym 'Geekboy@KaZaA' was linked to IP address 24.84.179.98 in the first place. Without any evidence at all as to how IP address 24.84.179.98 has been traced to Geekboy@KaZaA, and without being satisfied that such evidence is reliable, it would be irresponsible for the Court to order the disclosure of the name of the account holder of IP address 24.84.179.98 and expose this individual to a lawsuit by the plaintiffs."

Questions for Discussion

1. Do you agree with the decision of the Federal Court refusing to order ISPs to reveal the names of their customers? Why or why not? Under what circumstances should ISPs be required to disclose the names of their subscribers?

2. Assuming that sharing copyrighted music on P2P networks is illegal, why do you think that so many people are using P2P for that purpose? Has the law fallen out of step with socially acceptable behaviour when it comes to P2P?

3. What do you think of the morality of CRIA's strategy of suing individual users? If you were a decision maker at CRIA, would you take the same approach to perceived problems regarding P2P networks? What other options might you consider?

Copyright issues aside, the P2P phenomenon illustrates how technology may challenge existing business models. P2P systems allow users to sample music for free and to download only those songs that they actually want. These systems threaten traditional distribution channels within the recording industry. Until recently, the music industry focused on the album format. Because it delivered songs in pre-arranged packages, the album format often forced users to buy some songs that they did not want. In those situations, the choice between album formats and P2P systems is obvious from a consumer perspective. Consequently, unless they are prepared to lose profits, and perhaps even their place in the market, traditional music companies will need to adapt and evolve alongside emerging technologies.

---

[37] US, Bill S 2560, *Inducing Infringements of Copyright Act of 2004*, 108th Cong, 2004.

[38] K Damsell "Uploaders not 'pirates,' court told" *Globeandmail.com* (15 March 2004).

ONLINE PRIVACY

The growth in e-commerce has caused increased concern about privacy. Many online businesses have technology that allows them to record, store, and process personal information about their customers. Consumers very often give up those details without consent and, indeed, without even knowing it. The law has therefore begun to provide additional protection. Businesses need to carefully consider their obligations under those laws. By limiting the types of information that it collects from its customers, a company may be able to minimize its exposure to liability and reduce compliance costs.

The *Personal Information Protection and Electronic Documents Act* (*PIPEDA*) is Canada's legislative attempt at regulating the collection, use, and disclosure of "personal information" in the private sector. *PIPEDA* defines "personal information" as information about an identifiable individual, but does not include the name, title, business address, or telephone number of an employee in an organization. In the online context, information collected through the use of "cookies" on a website can constitute personal information.[39]

PIPEDA generally applies when (i) an organization collects, uses, or discloses personal information in the course of commercial activity, and (ii) an organization collects, uses, or discloses personal information about an employee in connection with some activity of the federal government. The Act does not apply, however, in those provinces that have enacted similar legislation. To date, only British Columbia, Alberta, and Quebec have done so.[40]

In one form or another, *PIPEDA* and the provincial equivalent privacy laws require organizations to comply with 10 legal obligations:

1. **Accountability:** An organization is responsible for personal information under its control. It must name a person who can be held accountable for the organization's compliance with the obligations in this list.

2. **Identifying purposes:** Before collecting personal information, an organization must state its reason for doing so.

3. **Consent:** An organization should generally obtain informed consent from a person before collecting personal information. That requirement does not apply, however, where it would be inappropriate.

4. **Limiting collection:** An organization must act fairly and lawfully when collecting personal information, and it must not collect more information that it needs for its stated purpose.

5. **Limiting use, disclosure, and retention:** Unless it either has the person's consent or is under a legal obligation to act differently, an organization can use personal information only for its stated purpose. An organization should not retain personal information any longer than necessary.

6. **Accuracy:** An organization should take all reasonable steps to ensure that its information is accurate and up to date.

[39.] Privacy Commissioner of Canada *PIPEDA* Case Summary #162, *Customer complains about airline's use of "cookies" on its Web site* (2003). The Privacy Commissioner of Canada defines "cookies" as "small text files that are placed on your computer's hard drive when you visit websites. Cookies collect and store information about you based on your browsing patterns and information you provide." See <www.privcom.gc.ca/cf-dc/2003/cf-dc_030416_7_e.asp>.

[40.] *Personal Information Protection Act*, SBC 2003, c 63 (BC); *Personal Information Protection Act*, SA 2003, c P-6.5 (Alta); *Act Respecting the Protection of Personal Information in the Private Sector*; RSQ, c P-39.1 (Que). The fact that businesses are subject to either the federal *PIPEDA* or a provincial equivalent may raise a question of constitutional authority. We discussed the division of powers between the two levels of government in Chapter 1.

7. **Safeguards:** Personal information must be protected by safeguards that are appropriate to the circumstances.

8. **Openness:** An organization must be prepared to provide individuals with details about its personal information policies and practices.

9. **Individual access:** Upon request, an organization must provide each individual with access to information that has been collected about him or her. The individual has the right to challenge the accuracy and completeness of that information, and the right to have errors or omissions rectified.

10. **Challenging compliance:** An individual has the right to direct complaints and concerns arising under these rules to the person whom the organization has made accountable.

As a result of interpreting the legislation, judges have begun to provide businesses with guidance on how to meet their obligations under *PIPEDA*. When presented with a potential problem, an organization should ask itself the following questions.

- Is the collection, use, or disclosure of personal information necessary to meet a specific organizational need?

- Is the collection, use, or disclosure of personal information likely to be effective in meeting that need?

- Is the loss of privacy proportional to the benefit gained?

- Is there a less privacy-invasive way of achieving the same end?

The Federal Court applied that framework in *Eastmond v Canadian Pacific Railway*.[41] CPR installed video surveillance equipment in an effort to deter theft and vandalism on its property. The court received a complaint that, in doing so, CPR had violated *PIPEDA*. The court disagreed. It said that (i) CPR had a specific need to investigate and deter trespassers and vandalism, (ii) the video surveillance was likely to meet that need, (iii) because the area in question was outdoors, where people have a reduced expectation of privacy, the loss of privacy was minimal and proportional to the benefits of surveillance, and (iv) because other strategies for dealing with theft and vandalism were considerably more expensive, there was no other *effective* solution that involved less invasion of privacy.

[41.] *Eastmond v Canadian Pacific Railway* (2004) 16 Admin LR (4th) 275 (FCTD). See also *Englander v Telus Communications* (2004) 247 DLR (4th) 275 (FC CA).

CONCEPT SUMMARY 19.3

Strategies for Minimizing Privacy Compliance Risks and Costs

- Gain a clear understanding of how your business and your technology might collect, use, or disclose personal information. Talk to your information technology staff and involve them in your privacy compliance plans.

- Appoint a person or team of people to be responsible for privacy issues. Ensure that all of your employees receive adequate training in privacy.

- Consider strategies for limiting, as much as possible, the collection of personal information—especially information of a sensitive nature.

- Before dealing with personal information, always ask how a reasonable person would view the situation.

- Ask the following questions before dealing with personal information:
  (i)   Is it necessary to meet a specific need?
  (ii) Is it likely to be effective in meeting that need?
  (iii) Is the loss of privacy proportional to the benefit gained?
  (iv) Is there a less privacy-invasive way of achieving the same end?

- Whenever possible, obtain consent before dealing in personal information. And, of course, always comply with the consent requirements under *PIPEDA* and similar statutes.

ONLINE CONSUMER PROTECTION

We end this chapter with a brief look at consumer protection principles in the e-commerce environment. Consumer protection principles are important to individuals as consumers, but they are also important to businesses. By adopting them, along with the privacy practices described above, a business can enhance its reputation, strengthen consumer confidence, and ultimately increase sales. This is particularly important in electronic commerce, where consumer confidence remains relatively low.

Although some provinces have amended existing consumer protection legislation in light of electronic commerce, full-scale law reform has not yet occurred. Industry Canada (a branch of the federal government) has promoted a code of practice in its *Canadian Code of Practice for Consumer Protection in Electronic Commerce*.[42] Although the Code is not law, its provisions reflect a number of the legal obligations described throughout this chapter. The Code contains suggestions for ethical and effective business practices that are intended to supplement the laws that already protect consumers. Compliance with the Code will likely minimize legal risks in a number of areas. In 2004, the Code was endorsed by federal, provincial, and territorial ministers responsible for consumer affairs. The Code is now open for endorsement by private sector organizations and consumer organizations. We summarize here the provisions of the Code.

1. **Information provision.**

   Consumers should be provided with clear and sufficient information to make informed choices about whether and how to make a purchase. Online businesses should avoid jargon and use plain language whenever possible. They should clearly distinguish marketing and promotional material from

---

[42.] Industry Canada *Canadian Code of Practice for Consumer Protection in Electronic Commerce* (2004). This document is itself based on the OECD Council *Recommendation of the OECD Council Concerning Guidelines for Consumer Protection in the Context of Electronic Commerce* (1999). It is excerpted from CSA Standard *Model Code for the Protection of Personal Information* (1999).

the terms and conditions of sale. They should disclose the legal identity of their business, their business address, and any geographic limitations on where a product or service is for sale. They should fairly and accurately describe their goods. They should set out a complaints procedure and provide consumers with their own record of the transaction.

2. **Language.**

   When an online business offers products or services in a given language, it shall use that language to provide all of its material information about itself, its policies, its product or service, and the terms of the transaction. When information or support is not available in that language, that fact shall be stated by the vendor in the language in which the transaction was conducted.

3. **Contract formation and fulfillment.**

   Vendors should take reasonable steps to ensure that the consumer's agreement to contract is fully informed and intentional. The consumers should be provided with an opportunity to correct or cancel the order before it is accepted and filled. A vendor who cannot deliver a product within the time frame originally specified shall promptly notify the consumer and give them the option of cancelling the order at no charge, except where unreasonable.

4. **Online privacy.**

   An online business should set up its data collection system with a view to respecting and protecting its customers' privacy in compliance with the CSA *International Model Code*.

5. **Security of payment and personal information.**

   Vendors and intermediaries should take reasonable steps to ensure that transactions in which they are involved are secure. An online business should use the technology and procedures that are discussed in this chapter, and that are consistent with industry standards in order to safeguard payment and personal information that is collected as a result of a transaction.

6. **Complaint handling and dispute resolution.**

   Consumers should have access to fair, timely, effective, and affordable means of resolving problems with any transaction. An online business should have resources for handling consumer complaints efficiently and effectively. Vendors should offer an internal complaints-handling process that is easily accessible, available to consumers free of charge, easy to use, acknowledges complaints within seven business days, endeavours to resolve or address complaints within 45 days, and records and monitors complaints.

7. **Unsolicited e-mail.**

   Vendors should not send unsolicited e-mail to consumers without consent. If a vendor has more than a passing relationship with a consumer, consent may not be required. In any marketing e-mail, vendors shall provide a return address and a simple way for consumers to indicate that they do not wish to receive such messages. Online businesses should avoid spamming or sending unsolicited e-mails to a large number of people. Not only is spam bad Internet etiquette, or "netiquette," it also exposes a business to the risk of being associated with products that are worthless, deceptive, or fraudulent. Many of the online scams that we discussed above are perpetrated through unsolicited mass e-mail. Why risk your business reputation when there are more sophisticated and successful means of advertising?

8. **Communications with children.**

Vendors have a social responsibility to determine whether they are communicating with a child in any given transaction. Vendors should not exploit children's lack of experience or sense of loyalty, and they should not exert pressure on children to urge their parents to purchase products or services. Vendors should take reasonable steps to avoid monetary transactions with children and should not collect personal information from children except where express parental consent has been obtained.

Chapter Summary

Electronic commerce refers to technology-mediated business transactions. Although e-commerce has facilitated the development of the knowledge-based economy, its success will ultimately depend on eliminating various legal uncertainties and impediments.

Electronic commerce legislation tries to facilitate online transactions by removing commercial uncertainty and other impediments. The co-ordination of model laws at both the international and national level has facilitated the global implementation of uniform laws at the provincial level. Canada's model law, the *Uniform Electronic Commerce Act*, sets out a framework for inferring consent to participate in electronic transactions, the functional equivalents of paper-based requirements, the proper treatment of government documents, and a clarification of the rules of contract formation in the online setting (including the timing requirements for sending and receiving electronic documents). Although the adoption of electronic commerce in various Canadian jurisdictions differs in detail, many provinces and territories have maintained fidelity to much of the approach taken in *UECA*.

Online contracts, such as click-wrap and web-wrap agreements, have been recognized as enforceable provided the basic requirements of contract formation are adequately met. To ensure that an agreement is enforceable, managers charged with Web development should design online transactions with the requirements of electronic commerce legislation in mind. They should also ensure that the design of those transactions provides reasonable notice of the terms and conditions, and, if necessary and desirable, reserves the right to make modifications to contractual terms and to post them to a website. Automated electronic commerce promises to dispense with the need for human supervision in the contract-formation process. Although most provincial legislation contemplates a method for rectifying keystroke errors, managers should incorporate safety mechanisms into their electronic contracts to protect their businesses against liability for computer-generated errors.

Electronic signatures and related technologies promise to fortify the flimsy foundation of trust resulting from global online interaction. Information systems such as these can be used to authenticate transactions, ensure their integrity, and enhance online security. Technological measures are not, however, the sole means of ensuring information security. Business managers must also consider legal measures, including the adoption and enforcement of terms of service agreements and other strictly enforced corporate policies. A careful approach to information security will ultimately prove fundamental to the success of electronic commerce.

Although one key benefit of electronic commerce is that geography becomes less important, location is still relevant online. Domain names provide the virtual storefronts necessary for electronic commerce. Mimicking traditional real estate speculation, some individuals and companies are in the business of cybersquatting. Domain name registration authorities have developed uniform dispute resolution procedures to help resolve complaints brought by those claiming a proprietary interest in a particular domain name. For a fee, dispute resolution professionals will mediate and, if necessary, arbitrate disputes through various electronic media, thus decreasing the time and expense associated with traditional litigation.

The global reach of electronic commerce means that compliance with local laws is no longer sufficient protection from legal risk. Website owners and operators must consider the possibility that they may be dragged into a court battle in some remote jurisdiction. In resolving these disputes, Canadian courts consider whether there is a real and substantial connection between the cause of action, its effects, and the location in which the action has been commenced. Other considerations include the passivity or interactivity of the website and the actual effects of the alleged transgression in the location where jurisdiction has been sought. Targeting strategies, including the use of technological measures, will reduce the risk of being sued successfully in a foreign jurisdiction. The question of liability for online intermediaries is not perfectly settled. Early decisions have held that service providers who exercise no editorial control over their sites are immune from liability, whereas service providers who exercise even a low level of control might be held liable. Concerned that this approach provides a clear disincentive for service providers to read and remove illegal content from their websites, some jurisdictions have enacted legislation that provides a more balanced approach, extending further protection to online intermediaries under certain circumstances. The prospect of enhanced liability has led many Internet access and online service providers to insist on exclusion clauses in their terms of service. Prudent online intermediaries have also sought to implement practices to shield themselves from liability by demonstrating that they operate as mere conduits of electronic communication.

P2P file-sharing continues to be one of the most hotly contested areas of online activity. There are lessons to be learned for the way that law and business react to new technologies.

Privacy has taken on a great significance in electronic commerce. Technology increasingly enables the collection, use, and disclosure of vast amounts of personal information. *PIPEDA*, as well as the enactment of privacy laws in certain provinces, will require some businesses to ensure that adequate steps have been taken in order to minimize their risks and costs of compliance associated with the collection, use, and disclosure of personal information.

Full-scale law reform in the consumer protection area has not yet occurred. The most substantial development is a Code promoted by Industry Canada. Since the Code is not law, any action taken by the Competition Bureau is merely educational in nature. Still, these guidelines offer insight to businesses and consumers about the shortcomings of conducting business online in a manner that does not ensure the development of trusting relationships with customers and clients.

REVIEW QUESTIONS

1. In what sense is the law a source of uncertainty in the electronic commerce marketplace?

2. What are four potential benefits that electronic commerce offers to businesses willing to implement the use of information technologies?

3. What is the role and purpose of Canada's *Uniform Electronic Commerce Act*?

4. How is Canada's *UECA* enforced in each province and territory?

5. What are the relevant rules about sending and receiving electronic documents? As a risk manager, what steps can you take to avoid related disputes?

6. Given that electronic commerce legislation is provincially enacted, discuss several issues that a business manager should consider when engaged in interprovincial commerce.

7. Explain the difficulties associated with the formation of contracts online. What lesson can business managers learn from the case of *Rudder v Microsoft*?

8. Does *Kanitz v Rogers Cable* suggest a different lesson from *Rudder v Microsoft*?

9. How can information about products or services be designed to ensure that it is considered an invitation to treat? Why should a Web designer seek to do so?

10. Explain the complexities associated with automated electronic commerce. How can a business safeguard against the undesirable consequences of keystroke errors?

11. Why are the services of trusted third parties crucial to electronic commerce?

12. Distinguish between *communications* security and *computer* security, and provide an example of each.

13. What steps can a business take to avoid targeting a particular jurisdiction?

14. Name and discuss the variables that a court may consider in deciding if a specific online interaction falls under its jurisdiction.

15. What is cybersquatting? Is it ever legally permissible?

16. Describe three typical disputes arising from the domain name registration system, and provide an example of each. How can business managers avoid domain name disputes?

17. Distinguish between Internet access providers and online service providers, and give an example of each. In which role is an online intermediary most likely to attract potential liability? Why?

18. As an online service provider in the province of Newfoundland and Labrador, describe how you can shield yourself from possible liability as an online intermediary.

19. Name one way that an online business can minimize its privacy compliance risks and costs.

20. Describe how a business can incorporate consumer protection principles into its online contracting practices.

CASES AND PROBLEMS

1. You are the general manager of a company that does business exclusively in Saskatchewan. With the aim of increasing efficiency and cutting costs, you are contemplating a change in corporate software that would enable filing all necessary government documents in electronic form. However, you are uncertain whether the provincial government will be obligated to accept documents in that form. Before paying a lawyer, you have decided to review the relevant legislation yourself to see if there is a clear answer. Using the legislation set out below, decide whether your company should switch to an electronic format. Can your provincial government force you to file solely by electronic means?

The *Uniform Electronic Commerce Act* contains these clauses concerning the filing of electronic forms with the government:

6. (1) Nothing in this Act requires a person to use or accept information in electronic form, but a person's consent to do so may be inferred from the person's conduct.

(2) Despite subsection (1), the consent of the Government to accept information in electronic form may not be inferred by its conduct but must be expressed by communication accessible to the public or to those likely to communicate with it for particular purposes.

9. A requirement under law for a person to provide information to another person in a specified non-electronic form is satisfied by the provision of the information in an electronic document,

(a) if the information is provided in the same or substantially the same form and the electronic document is accessible by the other person and capable of being retained by the other person so as to be usable for subsequent reference, and

(b) where the information is to be provided to the Government, if
 (i) the Government or the part of Government to which the information is to be provided has consented to accept electronic documents in satisfaction of the requirement; and
 (ii) the electronic document meets the information technology standards and acknowledgment rules, if any, established by the Government or part of Government, as the case may be.

Saskatchewan's *Electronic Information and Document Act* does not contain sections corresponding to 6(2) or 9(b) as do many of the other provinces. Instead it contains the following clause:

28.(1) A person may file a document or information in an electronic format with the appropriate department pursuant to a designated Act, but only if:

(a) the document or information is of a class that is prescribed in the regulations made pursuant to the designated Act as a document or information that may be filed electronically;

(b) the electronic format used is a format that is prescribed in the regulations made pursuant to the designated Act;

(c) the document or information is recorded on a system of electronic data storage that, in the option of the person responsible for the maintenance of the document or information to be filed, can be read by the computer or other equipment used in the information filing system; and

(d) the person filing the document or information is, or is a member of a class of persons that is, authorized to file the document or information in an electronic format by:
 (i) a person who has the power to grant that authorization pursuant to the designated Act; or
 (ii) if there is no person who has the power to grant that authorization pursuant to the designated Act, the member of the Executive Council to whom for the time being the administration of the designated Act is assigned.

2. You are the information manager of an electronic mailing service, BadNews.ca. Your primary customers are collections agencies. BadNews.ca assists these agencies by locating debtors and delivering legal notices to them before the repossession of their assets. You were taking the position that simply sending an e-mail message would fulfill the written notice requirements set out in the provincial legislation that regulates the collection of debts. Recently, however, you discovered that the law requires such notices to not merely be sent but to actually be received. You have been asked to determine the effect that the *UECA* will have on your company's business practices. Prepare a brief memo explaining the rules governing the sending and receiving of electronic messages. Make sure that your memo provides some advice indicating the best way to avoid disputes with intended recipients.

3. Unlike most of your friends in business, you are quite familiar with encryption technologies and have been using them for a few years. Recently, you have done further research on the use of trusted

third parties in electronic commerce. In so doing, it has come to your attention that it is possible for a hacker to forge a pair of encryption keys, using them to deceive you into thinking that you have authenticated the sender's identity when in fact you have not. Recognizing this possibility, you have decided to write a memo to the senior vice-president of your company explaining what a certification authority is and why your company should consider using one. Draft the memo.

4. Your company is drawing up a terms of service agreement for your employees. One paragraph states:

> The computer network and connected devices are the property of the employer. The employer retains ownership and associated rights of all files, documents, and communications received, created, or stored by employees. The computer system is to be used for business purposes only. The e-mail system must not be used to transmit, view, or store obscene, defamatory, discriminatory, pornographic, threatening, sexually explicit, harassing, or any other offensive material. The e-mail system must not be used to duplicate or transmit copyright-protected material without the appropriate permission. At no time should confidential or trade secrets be transmitted over the Internet. The employer reserves the right to monitor e-mail communication and Internet browsing, and to make use of keystroke technologies at any time without notice. The employer retains the right to disclose an employee's personal information, e-mail communication, and Internet browsing history upon request and without notice. Violation of this policy will result in employee discipline. By using the employer's communication facilities, the employee acknowledges and consents to the above terms and conditions of usage.

Review this agreement. As a manager who is concerned about information security and intermediary liability, what is your opinion on its merits and shortcomings? What changes might be made to improve it?

5. Marcus is an employee of Scroll Networks. Alone at the office late one night with a pounding headache, deep concerns about meeting a deadline, and the knowledge that he was nowhere near finishing the assigned corporate memo, Marcus happened upon an idea. He decided that he would simulate a lightning strike on his company-issued laptop by stripping the Ethernet wire and inserting it into the 100 volt AC electrical wall outlet. Much to his surprise, he destroyed not only his laptop but also a cluster of workstations in the office. Although he stuck to his game plan, claiming that the office was struck by

lightning, the hidden surveillance camera revealed otherwise. You are in charge of information security at Scroll Networks. What possible courses of action does the company have against Marcus? Assuming that you want to use the law as a means to educate employees at Scroll Networks and deter future information security breaches, which course of action will you choose, and why?

6. You are the owner of a small digital content provider based in Brandon, Manitoba. Your content is marketed under your Canadian registered trademark, dFOX. As well, you are the registered owner of the dFOX.com and dFOX.ca domain names. It has come to your attention that a US software company is advertising its newest voice-mailbot under the name dFOX on its website, codeworks.com. Code Works does not have a registered trademark for the dFOX product in the US or anywhere else. The Code Works site is targeted to Americans and explicitly warns that its voice-mailbot software may only work with US telecommunications hardware. The site has a US-only 1-888 number, but allows transactions to be completed online from anywhere in the world. The terms and conditions say that the warranty for the product is valid only for sales in the US. You decide to write a demand letter to Code Works, insisting that they cease using your trademark immediately. In the letter, you indicate that, for the past several weeks, customers confused by Code Work's use of your mark have flooded your Web server, causing e-mail transmission problems and irreparable damage to some of your corporate hardware. Code Works ignores your demand and continues to market dFOX voice-mailbots on its website. You decide to go to a Manitoba court to seek a remedy for trademark infringement and economic loss. Outline the jurisdictional issues and tests you will be facing. What will your argument be? What can you expect Code Works to argue? As a risk manager, how can you seek to avoid legal liabilities in foreign jurisdictions?

7. As the information manager of the XACTO Standard Weights and Measurements Corp, you have received an e-mail from a party identified as koko_k@pobox.com. The e-mail asks whether you are interested in purchasing the rights to the domain name www.xacto.ca. After entering the URL into your web browser, you determine that the site is not currently in use. You then consult CIRA's website and ascertain that the domain name was registered to a party named Koko Kerasic of Edmonton, Alberta only one week ago. Somewhat curious, you decide to respond to the koko_k e-mail, inquiring about the price. A reply to your e-mail comes only moments later demanding $75 000. As the person charged with overseeing your firm's intellectual property enforcement, you are deeply concerned about securing that domain name.

You seek preliminary advice from your lawyer, Erik, who asks whether your company owns the Canadian trademark for XACTO. Your answer is "yes." Erik then does a business search in Alberta to determine whether Koko has registered a business operating under the name XACTO. No such business name is registered. Upon further investigation, it turns out that Koko is an industrious 19-year-old high-school student who heard about cybersquatting in an ICQ chat room. Erik indicates that this matter must be resolved in accordance with the CIRA dispute resolution policy and quotes his fee for representing you in the matter. Given that your company is a financially-strapped start-up, you decide to handle the matter without representation. You point your Internet browser to www.cira.ca and review the CIRA *Domain Name Dispute Resolution Policy*. What position will you take when making XACTO's submissions to the CIRA dispute resolution provider? What argument can you expect from Koko or her parents? How is the matter likely to be resolved?

8. You work for a video game development company, CuddleTech, that has just started selling a major new game—an extreme mountain bike game called CuddleBike. Having a Web presence is a key component of the launch, as well as the ongoing promotion and sale of the product. Although sales of the game will be international, your main market for the game is in Canada and the United Kingdom.

   You are responsible for the launch of the new game, particularly in relation to the Web presence. You have arranged for CuddleBike trademark applications to be filed and your lawyer has advised you that there are no similar trademarks or business names registered in Canada. However, when you begin to looking into registering domain names, you discover that a person named Eddy had registered the domain name www.cuddlebike.com just a few days earlier. You write to Eddy by e-mail and ask him to contact you regarding the domain name. The next day, Eddy contacts you by telephone. During your conversation, he tells you that he knows a girl named Nicolle who works at CuddleTech. Eddy tells you that Nicolle mentioned the CuddleBike game to him at a party before the launch of the game. He tells you that he planned to use the domain name to develop a fan site for the game after it was released. When you ask whether he would be willing to sell the domain to CuddleTech, he says he would sell it for $200 000. He then tells you that if CuddleTech doesn't want to buy it, he will sell it to a competitor of CuddleTech. In light of these statements, you question Eddy about his true motives in registering the domain name. He says that he will deny ever offering to sell the domain for $200 000 or to a competitor. You do not have a recording of the call.

   Briefly indicate what domains you might register for CuddleTech's new game. With respect to the www.cuddlebike.com domain name, do you think that online arbitration could be an appropriate option for CuddleTech to resolve the dispute with Eddy? Assuming that arbitration could be appropriate, do you think CuddleTech should pursue litigation or arbitration? Support your answer by

describing the factors that you would consider in making your decision.

9. Using the facts in the previous case problem, describe how the matter might be resolved under the Uniform Domain Name Dispute Resolution Policy (UDRP). The UDRP can be accessed at www.icann.org/udrp/udrp-policy-24oct99.htm.

10. You have decided to go into business as an online intermediary. Among other things, you maintain an online discussion board dedicated to financial issues and publicly-traded companies. At times—especially when stock prices drop—conversation on the discussion boards heats up, and people start to point fingers. Sometimes inflammatory and demeaning remarks are made. To maintain community standards and keep the peace online, you have on occasion directed your Web master to remove certain remarks that you believe to be defamatory. Sometimes, the decision to remove such remarks results from your own random monitoring of the discussions. Other times, the decision results from requests or demands made by discussion board participants.

    Today, you received a statement of claim alleging that you are liable for defamatory statements posted on your discussion board. The claim, filed by a large corporation and its CEO, is seeking millions of dollars in damages. This is the first that you have heard of any disparaging remarks made about that company. Although you have a policy to remove postings when asked, neither the corporation nor its CEO made any such request, and no one on your staff had noticed the remarks. Needless to say you are very concerned. You immediately check the discussion group and, sure enough, six false, disparaging remarks had been posted. After checking various financial records, you see that the complaining company's stock prices plunged substantially the day after the remarks were made and have not since recovered. Is there any chance that the company might actually succeed against you? Explain why. How might a different approach to website management have reduced exposure to liability?

11. Marie-Sophie is the owner of *Tixe*—one of Canada's most exclusive online luxury stores for women. Paul is the Vice-President in charge of Online Security and you have been retained to provide legal advice. In the past six months, *Tixe* has been attacked by hackers on two occasions. There had never been attacks before. While the hacking attacks diverted some staff and technology resources for a short time, the *Tixe* online operations were not affected and no business was lost. However, Marie-Sophie is very concerned about the attacks and has instructed Paul to ensure that the situation does not reoccur.

    You know that there are vulnerabilities in *Tixe's* online ordering system which likely contributed to the fact that the attacks were not stopped at an earlier stage. You also know that although those vulnerabilities could be fixed and would stop the hackers, it would be expensive to do so and it might slow down overall system performance. But Paul thinks he has a better solution; he wants to catch the hackers in the act. To do so, he wants to install a key-logging program on the computer of every user who visits the *Tixe*, website. This program would be invisible to all but the most sophisticated computer users and it would keep track of every key a user types on their computer. That information would be relayed back to *Tixe* where Paul could monitor it for suspicious patterns or activities. Paul thinks this is a real win–win solution because the hackers would be caught and *Tixe* could also use the information it gathers for marketing or other purposes. Your job is to advise Paul about whether his proposed solution is acceptable for the company from a legal perspective in light of *Tixe's* obligations under *PIPEDA*. If you do think that there are problems with his system from a pri-

vacy perspective, how might those problems be addressed?

12. The proliferation of electronic commerce has left consumer protection legislation slow to catch up. This has spurred Industry Canada to announce a policy that includes updated consumer protection principles tailored to the online environment. One of those principles is that "[v]endors should not transmit commercial e-mail without the consent of consumers, or unless a vendor has an existing relationship with a consumer." If followed, would this principle always provide more protection to consumers? As a Canadian corporation, is your business required to adopt this policy? What are the likely business consequences of adopting it and the other principles announced by Industry Canada? What are the likely business consequences of ignoring them? Develop an appropriate e-mail business practice policy statement for your company.

WEBLINKS

Intellectual Capital—Industry Canada http://strategis.ic.gc.ca/SSG/pi00004e.html

This website provides information on current developments and intellectual capital through links to journal articles, research papers, and interviews.

Electronic Commerce http://canada.justice.gc.ca/en/ps/ec

The Department of Justice site addresses proposed statutes on electronic commerce and provides links to news releases, consultation papers and reports, and other resources.

Electronic Commerce Task Force http://e-com.ic.gc.ca/english/strat/641.html

This Industry Canada site offers information for companies involved in electronic commerce on marketplace rules—legal and commercial frameworks, financial issues and taxation, and intellectual property protection.

Privacy Commissioner of Canada www.privcom.gc.ca/legislation/index_e.asp

This site provides links to Canadian privacy legislation, privacy guides, reference materials, and other privacy-related sites.

The Validity and Enforceability of Web-Wrap Agreements www.law.ualberta.ca/alri/ulc/current/ewebwrap.htm

This article examines the enforceability of online contracts with respect to traditional standard form contracts and fundamental contractual requirements.

UNCITRAL Model Law on Electronic Signatures www.uncitral.org/english/workinggroups/wg_ec/wp-88e.pdf

This document contains a draft guide to the UNCITRAL Model Law on Electronic Signatures and provides insight into the principles of electronic signatures.

Canadian Internet Registration Authority www.cira.ca

Operating as the authority for the registration of .ca domain names, this site also provides access to its official dispute resolution policy and rules.

Internet Corporation for Assigned Names and Numbers www.icann.org

An internationally operated non-profit organization responsible for managing the generic and country code domain name systems. Its dispute resolution policy—the UDRP—and cases decided under that policy can be viewed on its site.

ADDITIONAL RESOURCES FOR CHAPTER 19 ON THE COMPANION WEBSITE

(www.pearsoned.ca/mcinnes)

In addition to self-test multiple-choice, true-false, and short essay questions (all with immediate feedback), three additional Cases and Problems (with suggested answers), and links to useful Web destinations, the Companion Website provides the following resources for Chapter 19:

- Business Decision 19W—Respecting Consumer Protection

Provincial Material

- **British Columbia:** Privacy Rights, Consumer Protection Legislation, Electronic Transactions
- **Alberta:** Electronic Transactions
- **Manitoba and Saskatchewan:** Online Privacy (Health Information), Internet Agreement Legislation
- **Ontario:** E-commerce Legislation, Privacy Legislation, Amending E-contracts

Art in Motion: Counterfeiting from Canada to China

Art in Motion is a Canadian success story. Twenty years ago, Garry Peters operated a small business out of his home in Coquitlam, British Columbia. He worked together with a few local artists to design, produce, and frame fine art. He continues to do much the same thing today—but on a much larger scale. While he still works with local artists, he also commissions art from more than one hundred artists around the world. And instead of packaging the pieces himself, he employs more than five hundred employees and operates out of a 12 000-square-metre facility in Coquitlam. From humble origins, Art in Motion now sells millions of dollars worth of fine art to purchasers in over 70 countries.

Art in Motion's future success is not, however, a sure thing. In fact, the company's very existence is threatened by every artist's worst nightmare: counterfeiters. While on a business trip to China, Garry Peters discovered that many of his company's products were being peddled on the black market. But it was only after digging deeper that he began to appreciate the enormity of the problem. Dozens of Chinese companies have sold several hundred thousand counterfeit pictures worth more than a billion dollars. Garry Peters calls that "out and out theft."

The success of the counterfeit operations is easy to understand. Art in Motion devotes a large part of its budget to the commission, design, and creation of art work. The artists are the heart of the company and they are paid accordingly. In contrast, counterfeiters require nothing more than high-quality copying machines. And because they face far lower production costs, they are able to sell their pieces at much lower prices.

Although he has been able to shut down a few of the counterfeit operations, Garry Peters realizes that the situation is getting worse. If the counterfeiters earned one billion dollars last year, they may earn twice that much next year. Peters also knows that every dollar gained by the black market is a dollar lost to legitimate operations like his own. Consequently, there is a danger that, unless the problem is solved, Art in Motion will be driven out of business. If that happens, a lot of people will suffer. Garry Peters will lose his company. Hundreds of employees will lose their jobs. Artists will lose an important source of income. And ultimately, consumers will lose access to high-quality art. After all, artists will not be willing to create new works unless they have some assurance that the profits will go to themselves, rather than to counterfeiters.

Garry Peters doubts that those problems can be entirely solved simply through the enforcement of international copyright laws. The real solution, he believes, lies closer to home. Chinese counterfeiters are successful only because purchasers—especially those in North America, who form the biggest part of the world market—are willing to buy rip-off reproductions. Consumers must there-fore be made to recognize the consequences of their actions. They must realize that the money that they save by buying black market art comes straight out of the pockets of the people who created the images in the first place.

Questions to Consider

Some of the difficulties facing Garry Peters arise from the fact that the counterfeiters were operating in China. To a large extent, however, the laws protecting artists are much the same all over the world. The following questions can therefore be answered on the basis of Canadian law.

1. Use the concepts of *natural scarcity* and *artificial scarcity* to explain the basic problem facing Art in Motion.

2. Art in Motion is unhappy because counterfeiters are making reproductions of *new* images. Would the situation be any different if Art in Motion were dealing with *very old* pieces of art, like Leonardo da Vinci's *Mona Lisa*, which was created 500 years ago?

3. Art in Motion sells reproductions of images that it receives from artists. In terms of copyright, does it matter whether those artists are classified as *employees* of the company, as opposed to *independent contractors*?

4. To what extent is the protection of artists' rights a matter of *morality*, rather than *law*? How effective is the law at preventing copyright violations? Have you ever broken the copyright laws?

Video Resource: "Chinese Counterfeiters: Art, Lies and Videotape" *Venture* # 906 (21 December 2003).

Additional Resources

Art in Motion www.artinmotion.com
This is the website for Art in Motion, the Canadian company at the heart of the story.

Art Copyright Coalition www.artcc.org/board.html
This website belongs to the Art Copyright Coalition. Garry Peters, the founder of Art in Motion, is also the ACC's board of directors. The purpose of the organization is to protect copyright holders and to educate the public about the nature and effects of copyright in fine art.

Copyright Act http://laws.justice.gc.ca/en/C-42
This website contains a complete copy of Canada's *Copyright Act*, which determines the rights and obligations that arise when an artist creates a painting.

Study Page: *Mona Lisa* in Book Cover Art www.studiolo.org/Mona/MONA39Th.htm
This website provides several examples of how the *Mona Lisa* has been reproduced in popular culture.

Mona Lisa Images for the Modern World http://desktop
pub.about.com/gi/dynamic/offsite.htm?site=http://www.studiolo.org/
Mona/MONALIST.htm
This website contains provides an entertaining demonstration of
the various ways in which Leonardo da Vinci's *Mona Lisa* has
been exploited in popular culture and commerce.

Tim's Journal: Public Domain http://torque.oncloud8.com/archives/
cat_public_domain.html
This website provides a brief explanation of the extent to which
old images may be within the public domain and therefore open
to exploitation.

20 Agency and Other Methods of Carrying on Business

CHAPTER OVERVIEW

OBJECTIVES

After completing this chapter, you should be able to:

1. Identify four ways in which an agency relationship can be created.

2. Distinguish between the actual authority and apparent authority of agents to enter into contracts on behalf of their principals.

3. Identify three situations in which an agent's fiduciary duty to act in the best interests of a principal may limit the agent's business opportunities.

4. Describe one situation in which a principal will be bound by a contract entered into by an agent without any authority from the principal.

5. List five events that will terminate an agency relationship.

6. Explain the circumstances in which a principal may be liable for the torts of its agent.

7. Describe practical and legal strategies that a principal can use to manage the risk that its agent will bind it to unauthorized obligations.

8. List four methods of carrying on business in which questions may arise as to whether a person is an agent.

9. Explain how franchises can reduce the business risk for franchisees.

10. Identify the risks for franchisees in entering into franchise agreements, and explain how the franchise laws in various jurisdictions address them.

In business, one person often represents another for a specific purpose. Stockbrokers are independent business people, but they represent you to execute your purchases and sales of shares. A manager employed by a car dealership represents the dealership when negotiating the terms under which the dealership will sell you a new car. In each case, the person acting on behalf of someone else is called an **agent**. The person being represented is called the **principal**.

Sometimes, the agent has authority to bind the principal to a contract. In the car dealership example, the manager has authority to agree to the terms on which the dealership will sell you the car. Often, however, a question will arise as to whether the manager has acted within the authority the dealership has granted. If the dealership has not authorized the manager to give you a price reduction of more than 10 percent, it will not want to be bound to sell you the car if the manager does so. On the other hand, as the person negotiating the contract with the agent, you will want to be able to rely on the agent having authority to bind the dealership to give you the discount. The legal rules of agency govern the circumstances in which an agent's actions bind the principal. As a result, these rules have a significant impact on the risks for principals and third parties when they deal through agents and define the risk management strategies available to each. The rules regarding an agent's authority to contract are one of the important subjects of this chapter.

Agents do not always have authority to enter into legal obligations on the principal's behalf. They may merely represent the principal's interests. If you are selling your house, for example, your real estate agent will not usually have the authority to commit you to selling for a particular price, but will be responsible for finding prospective purchasers and assisting with the sale process. Even in these situations, however, agents are subject to legal standards of behaviour that are designed to protect principals from the risks to which their agents may subject them. Principals have a much more limited set of obligations to their agents. In this chapter, we discuss these basic standards of behaviour.

In some settings, these general legal standards of behaviour for agents have been found to be insufficient to protect people dealing with agents. As a result, some agency relationships are governed by special statutes. For example, legislation addresses the risks that stockbrokers may not have sufficient assets to pay claims against them by their clients. This chapter provides a basic overview of some of these statutory regimes.

We will also look at *franchises*. A **franchise** is a common business method that allows entrepreneurs to start their own business using the franchisor's established name and business concept, substantially reducing the risks associated with a new business. It is less risky to set up a McDonald's franchise than it is to set up an independent fast-food restaurant specializing in hamburgers. An important trade-off for that risk reduction, however, is that franchisors insist on a high degree of control over the franchisee's operations to ensure the quality of the products and services. Franchisors also charge substantial fees for the right to operate the franchise. Like agency, franchising is a way for the franchisor to carry on its business through someone else. Legally, however, the franchisor and franchisee are separate businesses. No agency relationship is present. We discuss the characteristics of franchising and the legal rules governing the franchise relationship in the last section of this chapter.

Agency relationships arise in some other kinds of business organizations, including partnerships and corporations. These relationships are discussed in detail in Chapters 21 and 22.

> an **agent** is a person who represents someone else for some specific purpose

> a **principal** is a person whom an agent represents for some specific purpose

> a **franchise** allows entrepreneurs to start their own business using the franchisor's established name and business concept

BASIC RULES OF AGENCY

Creation

There are several ways to create an agency relationship. One of the most common is by express agreement. The principal and the agent enter into a contract that sets out the terms of the appointment of the agent, including the scope of the agent's authority and the agent's remuneration. In those provinces where the *Statute of Frauds* is still in force, the contract must be in writing if the relationship is to last longer than one year.[1] As well, the agreement must be in writing if the agent is going to have the authority to sign cheques on behalf of the principal.[2] The listing agreement that you sign with a real estate agent is an example of an agency relationship that is created by express agreement.[3] What is commonly called a *commercial representation agreement* is also a kind of express agency. **A commercial representation agreement** occurs when a manufacturer of goods, such as sportswear, agrees to allow someone to enter into contracts with retail sporting goods stores on behalf of the manufacturer to sell its clothes. Figure 20.1 illustrates the creation of agency.

a commercial representation agreement occurs when a manufacturer of goods agrees to allow someone to enter into contracts with customers to sell its goods

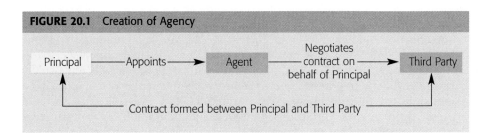

FIGURE 20.1   Creation of Agency

Principal ——Appoints——▶ Agent ——Negotiates contract on behalf of Principal——▶ Third Party

Contract formed between Principal and Third Party

Many other business relationships created by express agreement may have the effect of making someone your agent, even if they are not referred to by that name. If you authorize a lawyer to act on your behalf in closing a real estate transaction, the lawyer is acting as your agent.

In Chapter 22, we will discuss agency and corporations. Corporations and other forms of business organizations can act only through human beings. Individuals acting on behalf of a corporation are acting as its agents. The directors and officers of a corporation as well as its salespeople, purchasing clerks, and other employees may all be given authority to act as agents of the corporation for particular purposes. An employee of a corporation can receive express authority to act on behalf of the employee's corporate employer (i) under the terms of an employment contract, (ii) through a resolution of a corporation's board of directors, or (iii) by virtue of being appointed to a particular position, like sales manager, so long as the person is properly appointed. In all these situations, a principal has given an agent **actual authority** to act on its behalf. Actual authority can also be granted less formally, such as through an oral delegation of authority.

actual authority exists when the principal actually authorizes the agent to act on its behalf

---

[1.] Provincial writing requirements are discussed in Chapter 10.

[2.] *Bills of Exchange Act*, RSC 1985, c B-4 (Can). Cheques are discussed in Chapter 14.

[3.] In some provinces, listing agreements with real estate agents must be in writing: *eg Real Estate Act*, RSA 2000, c R-5, s 1 (Alta); *Real Estate Trading Act*, SNS 1996, c 28, s 26 (NS); *Real Estate and Business Brokers Act*, RSO 1990, c R.4, s 23 (Ont).

An agency relationship can arise without the principal's express agreement. An agency relationship exists when a principal represents, or holds out, someone as its agent in discussions with a third party. That person will have the authority to deal with the third party in the ways suggested by the principal's actions, even if that person was never properly appointed by the principal as an agent. This is called **apparent authority**. We will discuss the scope of apparent authority below.

apparent authority occurs when the principal creates the reasonable impression that the agent is authorized

Finally, agency can arise as a matter of law. We will discuss partnerships in Chapter 21. Under partnership law, each partner is an agent of the partnership and can bind the partnership to obligations that arise in connection with carrying on the business of the partnership in the usual way.

Ratification

Even if an agency relationship does not exist, an agent can still enter into an agreement that ultimately binds a principal in limited circumstances. Suppose that Gary, someone with no authority to act on your behalf, purports to enter into a contract to buy a fax machine for you from a third party, telling the third party that he is your agent. Perhaps Gary knows that you wanted to buy a fax machine and hopes that you will reward him if he negotiates a good price for you. Since Gary has no authority to act for you, the contract he has negotiated is not binding on you. However, you could agree to **ratify** the contract—you could choose to accept the contractual obligation. If you do so, the contract will become binding upon you. It will be as if you had given Gary authority to act on your behalf at the outset.

a contract is **ratified** when someone accepts a contract that was negotiated on their behalf but without their authority

For ratification to be effective, it must meet these requirements.

- It must be clear. Ratification can, however, be either *express or implied* from behaviour. In the previous example, your ratification of the contract would be implied if you took delivery of the fax machine and used it.[4]

- It must occur within a *reasonable time* after the creation of the contract. What is reasonable depends on the facts. If someone without your authority purported to act on your behalf to enter into a fire insurance contract on a building that you owned, you could not wait and ratify it after the building burned down.[5]

- The principal must accept the *whole contract* or none of it. For example, if you had developed some software and someone purported to license the software to a third party on your behalf, you could not accept the royalties under the licence without also accepting the support and maintenance obligations in the licence.

- The principal must have been *identified* by the agent. An agent cannot make a contract, either on its own behalf or on behalf of some person the agent has not yet identified, and then try to find someone to ratify it.

- The principal must have had the legal *capacity* to enter into the contract both at the time the agent created the contract and at the time of ratification.

4. *Findlay v Butler* (1977) 19 NBR (2d) 473 (QB); *Canada Trust Co v Gordon* [1978] 5 WWR 268 (Sask QB).

5. *Portavon Cinema Co Ltd v Price and Century Insurance Co Ltd* [1939] 4 All ER 601 (KB).

What happens if an agent without authority purports to enter into a contract on behalf of a principal but the principal does not ratify it?[6] In that situation, the agent is not personally liable to the third party under the contract *unless* the third party and the agent intended the contract to be binding on the agent personally.

Pre-Incorporation Contracts Special ratification rules apply when a person purports to enter into a contract with a third party on behalf of a corporation that does not yet exist. A **pre-incorporation contract** might be used, for example, if there has not been time to set up the corporation before the agent started negotiating the contract with the third party.

a pre-incorporation contract is a contract created by an agent on behalf of a corporation that does not yet exist

Under most Canadian corporate statutes, a person who enters into a pre-incorporation contract with a third party is personally bound to perform the contract and is entitled to its benefits.[7] But if a corporation does come into existence and adopts the contract, the agent drops out, and the corporation acquires those rights and liabilities. Those rules may, however, be varied.

- The third party and the agent can agree that the agent will not be bound by the agreement in any event.
- The third party can ask a court to impose liability on *both* the agent and the corporation, even if the corporation adopts the agreement. The third party might do so if the corporation was financially unable to perform the agreement.

Those rules allocate the risk that the corporation will not be created or adopt the contract. The third party bears that risk only if it agrees to release the agent from liability in these situations. Otherwise, the agent bears the risk. This scheme reflects the fact that the agent is usually in the best position to ensure that the corporation is created and adopts the agreement with the third party. The rules regarding pre-incorporation contracts are set out in Concept Summary 20.1.

CONCEPT SUMMARY 20.1

Allocation of Liability under Pre-Incorporation Contracts

	Agent Is Liable?	Corporation Is Liable?
Before corporation comes into existence	Yes Unless parties agree that agent will *not* be liable	No
After corporation comes into existence	Yes Unless corporation adopts contract *or* parties agree that agent will *not* be liable	No Unless corporation adopts contract
A court may order that the agent or the corporation or both be liable.		

[6.] If an agency relationship never arises in a technical legal sense, there may never really be an "agent" or "principal." These terms nevertheless are used here for convenience.

[7.] *Eg Business Corporations Act*, RSA 2000, c B-9, s 15 (*ABCA*) (Alta); *Canada Business Corporations Act*, RSC 1985, c C-44, s 14 (*CBCA*) (Can); *Business Corporations Act*, SNB 1981, c B-9.1, s 12 (*NBBCA*) (NB); *Business Corporations Act*, RSO 1990, c B.16, s 21 (*OBCA*) (Ont).

When Is the Principal Liable?
The Scope of an Agent's Authority

Most disputes about agency relate to the scope of the agent's authority. Did the agent have authority to enter into the agreement that the third party is trying to enforce against the principal? The rules regarding when a principal is liable in contract balance the interests of the principal with the interests of third parties seeking to enter into contracts with it.

- On the one hand, a principal does not want to be bound by an agent who purports to act on its behalf but who, in fact, was not authorized to do so.

- On the other hand, a third party that enters into a contract with an agent on behalf of a principal does not want to spend much time or money deciding whether the principal has actually given authority to that person. It wants to rely on commonly accepted indicators of authority, such as a letter of introduction from a corporation's president on the corporation's letterhead.

In large transactions, the parties will do a significant amount of investigation to satisfy themselves that the person executing a contract on behalf of a business has authority to do so. These investigations will be backed up by documentation, such as certified copies of resolutions of a corporation's board of directors authorizing certain people to enter into the transaction, and lawyers' opinions regarding authority. In most situations, however, the size of the transaction simply does not justify incurring the costs associated with that degree of certainty.

As we saw above, an agent may have received *actual authority* from the principal to enter into commitments on its behalf. If an agent is appointed under the express terms of a contract, such as an employment contract, the employee's actual authority is usually spelled out in the contract. Actual authority can also arise in other ways. However the agent acquires actual authority, the principal is bound by any obligation that the agent creates within the scope of that authority. That is true whether or not the third party knows the exact scope of the agent's actual authority.[8]

A third party usually does not know—and has no easy way of finding out—the extent of an agent's actual authority. That information is often contained in a contract or other document to which the third party does not have access, such as internal corporate records. The third party may only be aware of common indications of authority, such as a name tag that identifies a person as a "sales manager." The law increases the likelihood that the third party will be able to enforce a contract negotiated by someone with such indications of authority. In these situations, the third party may rely on words or conduct by the principal that indicate that the agent has authority. As discussed above, when the principal creates the reasonable impression that the agent is authorized, that gives the agent *apparent authority*. The principal is liable to the third party under any contract that the agent created within the scope of that apparent authority.[9]

[8.] *Freeman & Lockyer v Buckhurst Park Properties (Mangal) Ltd* [1964] 1 All ER 630 (CA).

[9.] That form of authority is sometimes described as "ostensible authority," "agency by estoppel," or "agency by holding out." Estoppel is discussed in Chapter 8. Holding out in the context of partnerships is discussed in Chapter 21.

Apparent authority is not necessarily connected with actual authority. In practice, however, they often overlap. Suppose you are the office manager of a business that is being conducted through a corporation. You want to buy a photocopier for that business. You may have actual authority to do so under the terms of your employment contract with the corporation. You may also have apparent authority because the corporation's president wrote a letter to the photocopier supplier saying that you were authorized to buy the photocopier. Nevertheless, one form of authority can exist without the other. That would be true, for instance, if the president's letter were inaccurate because your employment contract said that only the vice-president was authorized to buy office equipment. In such a case, you would have apparent, but not actual, authority. It is impossible to list every form of behaviour that can create apparent authority. Significantly, only the principal's conduct—not the agent's—is relevant. When the principal actually tells the third party that the agent is authorized to contract, apparent authority will be established. But less direct forms of communication may also be enough for a third party to reasonably believe that an agent has authority. For example, hiring a lawyer to defend a lawsuit may give that lawyer apparent authority to settle the claim on your behalf. If the lawyer does so, you may be bound by the settlement agreement, even if you never gave the lawyer actual authority to settle.[10] You could, however, sue your lawyer for exceeding the scope of the authority that you did give.[11]

In each case, the court asks if it was reasonable for the third party to believe that the agent had authority. As our examples suggest, the answer to that question largely depends on two factors:

- the nature and content of the principal's communication to the third party
- the circumstances in which that communication occurs, including the kind of business that is involved

It may be enough if a business allows a person to act with certain authority. Putting someone in a particular position constitutes a representation that the person has the usual authority for that position. This kind of apparent authority is referred to as **usual authority**.[12] What is usual is determined by reference to the authority of agents in similar positions in similar businesses. Agents with titles like vice-president, treasurer, and secretary, however, may have widely varying degrees of authority in different industries and even within industries. For a third party to rely on apparent authority, the person who makes the representation creating it must have authority to do so, such as a senior officer.

A principal will be bound by contracts within the agent's apparent authority only if the third party relied on that appearance of authority. As a practical matter, that is seldom hard to prove. The third party cannot enforce a contract if it knew, or should have known, that the agent did not have authority.[13] Case Brief 20.1 illustrates how apparent authority can arise without any express representation by the principal.

usual authority allows a person appointed to a particular position to exercise the authority usually associated with that position

---

[10] *Sign-O-Lite v Bugeja* [1994] OJ No 1381 (Gen Div).

[11] As your agent, the lawyer has a duty to follow your instructions and has a fiduciary duty to you. Both of those duties would be breached if the lawyer agreed to the settlement without your consent.

[12] *Freeman & Lockyer v Buckhurst Park Properties (Mangal) Ltd* [1964] 2 QB 480 (CA). Certain special rules applicable to agents of corporations are discussed in Chapter 22.

[13] *Hazelwood v West Coast Securities Ltd* (1975) 49 DLR (3d) 46 (BC SC), aff'd (1976) 68 DLR (3d) 172 (CA).

CASE BRIEF 20.1

Spiro v Lintern [1973] 3 All ER 319 (CA)

John owned a house. He directed his wife, Iris, to list the property with a real estate agent, but did not give her authority to sell the house. Iris entered into a contract to sell the house to Lintern. John was aware of what his wife had done but did nothing about it. He even permitted Lintern to come to the house with his architect to plan some repairs. At the time of the contract, Lintern had no idea that Iris was not the owner of the house. John refused to sell, arguing that Iris had no authority to sell his house. The court held that, by allowing Iris to act as she had, John had given her apparent authority to sell the house.

CONCEPT SUMMARY 20.2

When a Principal Is Bound by the Acts of an Agent

- Agent acts within the scope of the actual authority given by the principal to the agent created
  - by express delegation to the agent
  - by appointing the agent to a position with that authority
  - by implication from the circumstances
- Agent acts within scope of apparent authority created by principal's representation to a third party, which may consist of
  - the principal's statement or conduct
  - the principal acquiescing to the agent acting with that authority
  - the principal appointing the agent to a position that would usually have that authority
- Partner acts within the normal course of the partnership business.
- Agent enters into a contract on behalf of an identified principal but without the principal's authority, and the principal subsequently ratifies the contract.
- Agent enters into a pre-incorporation contract, and the corporation adopts the contract after it comes into existence.

When Is the Agent Liable?

An agent is normally not liable personally because it is usually clear that it was contracting on behalf of an identified principal. However, the agent and the third party may agree otherwise. And even if the contract does not expressly provide for liability, a court may decide that the parties implicitly intended the agent to be liable. The agent can also be held personally liable if it presented itself to the third party as the principal.[14] That can happen if the agent fails to disclose that it was acting on behalf of a principal. If the third party later discovers that the person it dealt with was only an agent, and if that agent had authority to act on behalf of the **undisclosed principal**, the third party can hold either the agent or the principal liable.[15] Therefore, to avoid the risk of personal liability, an agent should clearly explain its own role, and disclose the existence of the principal to the third party.

an undisclosed principal exists when the agent purports to contract without disclosing that it is acting on behalf of a principal

---

[14.] The agent will be liable only if there is clear evidence that the parties intended the agent to be liable: *Petro-Partners v Eastside Management 94 Inc* [1999] OJ No 2269 (CA).

[15.] The undisclosed principal can also enforce the contract against the third party.

Suppose an agent purports to contract on behalf of a principal, but does not actually have authority to do so. The agent is not personally liable under that agreement unless it and the third party specifically agreed that it would be. The agent nevertheless may be responsible for any loss that the third party suffers as a result of the transaction. An agent that knew it was not authorized to act on the principal's behalf may be liable for fraud or deceit.[16] And even if the agent did not act fraudulently, it may be liable to the third party for a *breach of warranty of authority*. **A breach of warranty of authority** occurs when an agent incorrectly indicates that it is authorized to act for a principal. That liability arises even if the agent honestly, but mistakenly, thought that it had the principal's authority.[17]

a breach of warranty of authority occurs when an agent indicates that it is authorized to act for a principal when it is not

The Agent's Duty to the Principal

When an agent is appointed by contract, its responsibilities may be set out in some detail. It must comply with those duties and follow any instructions given by the principal. The agent can be held responsible for failing to do so. In one case, a principal appointed an agent to insure a ship. The agent failed to do so. When the ship was lost, the agent was liable to the principal for the loss that the insurance would have covered.[18] Furthermore, an agent may have duties that are not mentioned in the contract, but that arises from the circumstances. For example, an agent that receives goods to sell may have the duty to insure them while they are in its possession.

In general, an agent's obligations cannot be delegated to anyone else—they are personal obligations. That rule recognizes that a principal often puts great trust in the judgment and skill of its agent. There are important practical exceptions to this general rule. For instance, if a law firm or a large business enterprise is appointed as an agent, responsibility necessarily is delegated to someone within that organization.

Because an agency relationship exposes the principal to the risk of being held liable in unwanted ways, the common law also imposes two other types of duties on agents:

- a fiduciary duty
- a duty of care

Both duties reduce the principal's risk.

Fiduciary Duty

a fiduciary duty requires an agent to act in good faith and in the best interests of the principal

Agents have a **fiduciary duty** to act in good faith and in the best interests of their principals, in most circumstances.[19] While the precise content of that duty depends on the facts, one of its key requirements is that agents avoid situations in which their personal interests conflict with the best interests of their principals. For instance, if you were appointed to negotiate a contract for the sale of your principal's land, you could not buy that property yourself. There would be

---

[16] *Doiron v Devon Capital* (2003) 38 BLR (3d) 82 (Alta CA); *Keddie v Canada Life Assurance Co* (1999) 179 DLR (4th) 1 (BC CA). The tort of deceit was discussed in Chapter 5.

[17] *Yonge v Toynbee* [1910] 1 KB 215 (CA).

[18] *Turpin v Bilton* (1843) 134 ER 641 (CP).

[19] *R v Kelly* (1992) 92 DLR (4th) 643 (SCC). We discuss the fiduciary duty that partners in a partnership owe each other in Chapter 21 and the fiduciary duty that directors and officers owe to a corporation in Chapter 22.

an obvious conflict of interest. You would be acting for the principal as the seller *and* for yourself as the buyer.[20] You would be tempted to favour your own interests over the principal's.

A conflict of interest would also arise if, without your principal's knowledge, you arranged for the property to be sold to someone with whom you have a relationship.[21] Suppose I agreed to pay you $5000 if you found a suitable piece of land for me. You then arranged for me to buy your principal's property for $200 000. You have breached your fiduciary duty. Your desire to obtain $5000 from me may have interfered with your obligation to find the best deal possible for your principal. You would have to pay the $5000 finder's fee over to your principal.[22] It would not matter if $200 000 was an entirely fair price for the land—the fiduciary duty may be breached even if the principal did not suffer any loss. That rule is imposed because of the need to ensure that agents never have any incentive to act in their own interests at the expense of their principals. You would be entitled to keep the $5000 that you received from me only if you had explained the entire situation to your principal, who then allowed the sale to be completed.

The fiduciary duty involves several other obligations.

- An agent must disclose to the principal any information that may be relevant to the principal's interests.[23] For example, if you are appointed to buy cars, you must reveal any bargains that you find.

- An agent cannot personally profit from the unauthorized use of information or opportunities that arose as a result of the agency relationship.

- An agent cannot compete with the principal. Consequently, if you are appointed to sell goods for your principal, you cannot also sell the same kind of goods for yourself or for the principal's competitor.

An agent's fiduciary duty may, however, be displaced by the principal's instructions. If your principal specifically tells you to act in a certain way, you must do so, even if you think some other course of action would be in the principal's best interests.[24] Also, in some cases, the nature of the relationship between the agent and the principal may mean that no fiduciary duty arises.[25]

Duty of Care

Every agent owes its principal a *duty of care*. The **duty of care** requires an agent to take reasonable care in the performance of its responsibilities. The precise content of that duty depends upon the circumstances and on what the agent agreed to do.[26] If that duty is breached, the agent generally must compensate the principal for any loss that it suffers. The principal may be denied recovery, however, if it knew that the agent was incompetent or unqualified.[27]

the duty of care requires an agent to take reasonable care in the performance of the agency responsibilities

---

[20] *Aaron Acceptance Corp v Adam* (1987) 37 DLR (4th) 133 (BC CA).

[21] *Andrews v Ramsay* [1903] 2 KB 635.

[22] *Raso v Dionigi* (1993) 100 DLR (4th) 459 (Ont CA).

[23] *McCullough v Tenaglia* (1998) 40 BLR (2d) 222 (Ont Gen Div).

[24] *Bertram v Godfray* (1830) 12 ER 364 (PC); *Volkers v Midland Doherty Ltd* (1995) 17 DLR (4th) 343 (BC CA).

[25] *Hunt v TD Securities Inc* (2003) 66 OR (3d) 481 (CA).

[26] *Tonks v Aetna Life Assurance Co of Canada* (1992) 98 DLR (4th) 582 (Ont Gen Div).

[27] *Hillcrest General Leasing Ltd v Guelph Investments Ltd* (1971) 13 DLR (3d) 517 (Ont Co Ct) (negligence in selecting sub-agent).

Case Brief 20.2 illustrates how an agent must understand the scope of its obligations, ensure that it is able to fulfill those obligations, and alert its principal to any deficiency in its skills.

CASE BRIEF 20.2

Fine's Flowers Ltd v General Accident Assurance Co of Canada (1977) 81 DLR (3d) 139 (Ont CA)

Fine's Flowers Ltd appointed an insurance agent to obtain "full coverage" for its garden business. The agent obtained insurance against a number of business risks—but not damage to plants caused by freezing as a result of a heating system failing. Unfortunately, that is exactly what happened. Fine's sued the agent for breach of contract and negligence.

The Court of Appeal held that the agent's undertaking to obtain "full coverage" created an obligation to ensure that Fine's was insured against all foreseeable and normal risks. The agent was liable for failing to fulfill its contractual duty to obtain adequate insurance and for breaching its duty of care to Fine's by failing to warn it about the gap in coverage.[28]

The Principal's Duty to the Agent

Like an agent, a principal must fulfill any obligation that is set out in the agency contract. Furthermore, a principal generally must satisfy certain obligations that are imposed by law.

- Unless the parties agreed that the agent would work for free, the principal must pay reasonable remuneration for the agent's services.[29]
- A principal has an implied obligation to indemnify the agent for liabilities and expenses that are reasonably incurred in connection with the agency relationship. Suppose you are asked to obtain insurance for your principal. You do so and pay the first premium on the principal's behalf. The principal must reimburse you for that expense. A principal is not, however, under any obligation if an agent acts illegally or in breach of the agency agreement.[30]

Termination

There are several ways to terminate an agency relationship.

- Either party gives the other notice of termination.
- The relationship ends in accordance with the agency contract.
- The agent is appointed for a specific project or a particular period, and the project is completed or the period expires.
- Performance of the agency becomes impossible.
- The principal loses the capacity to contract as a result of death, insanity, or bankruptcy.[31]

[28.] Fine's could not recover compensation for the same loss twice. It was required to elect between damages for breach of contract and damages for breach of fiduciary duty.

[29.] *Banfield, McFarlane, Evan Real Estate Ltd v Hoffer* [1977] 4 WWR 465 (Man CA).

[30.] *Duncan v Hill* (1873) LR 8 Ex 242, cited in GHL Fridman *Law of Agency* 7th ed (1997) at 202.

[31.] Capacity to contract is discussed in Chapter 10. The agency relationship is also terminated if the agent dies or becomes insane.

That last ground can create practical difficulties if the agent is unaware that the principal has lost capacity. Since the principal cannot be liable for obligations that arise after the incapacity occurs, the third party may try to hold the agent personally responsible. In some circumstances, the agent may be liable for breach of warranty of authority.

Because an agency may be terminated by notice from either party, the relationship can be very fragile. For that reason, agency agreements often require a reasonable notice period before termination. Furthermore, if an agent is an employee, the law states that the agency–employment relationship can be terminated only for just cause, or with either reasonable notice or compensation in lieu of notice.[32] Consequently, the precise nature of the parties' relationship will determine the rules that apply on termination.

Risk Management Issues

Before concluding our general discussion of agency, it is appropriate to highlight the issue of risk management in regard to liabilities in both contract and tort.

Contracts

A principal is liable for contracts created on its behalf by an agent with either actual or apparent authority. The principal's risk of being bound to unwanted contracts is more easily managed with respect to *actual authority*. The principal can use an agency agreement to clearly state what the agent is and is not authorized to do. That document should be carefully drafted to ensure that it is broad enough to allow the agent to do a proper job, but not so broad as to permit the agent to create unintended liabilities.

Risks associated with *apparent authority* can also be managed, but not as easily. To avoid giving an agent apparent authority to enter into unwanted obligations, the principal must carefully monitor how it communicates, directly and indirectly, with third parties.[33] The principal must also realize that apparent authority may exist even after the actual agency relationship has come to an end. If a third party dealt with the agent before the agency relationship was terminated, it may continue doing so afterwards. And if that third party was unaware of the termination, it may be able to enforce any new agreements against the principal. To avoid that possibility, the principal should notify all of its customers whenever it terminates an agent's authority.[34]

Torts

If an agent commits a tort, the principal is vicariously liable to the victim if (i) the agent was an employee, and (ii) the tort was committed within the course of employment.[35] The basic rules for vicarious liability were discussed in Chapter 3. In Chapter 26, we will discuss the rules that determine when a person is, in law, an employee.

---

[32] The characteristics of the employment relationship are discussed in Chapter 26. The question of when an agent should be considered an employee was considered in *Renmar Sales Agency Inc v 806897 Ontario Inc* [1999] OJ No 3956 (SCJ).

[33] When the agent acts outside the actual authority given by the principal, but in circumstances in which the third party can rely on apparent authority, the third party can hold the principal liable, but the principal may also be able to sue the agent for breach of the agency agreement.

[34] This issue of managing the risk of liability after the departure of a partner is discussed in Chapter 21.

[35] If the principal is forced to pay compensation to the victim, it is generally entitled to recover that amount from the agent-employee. Often, however, the principal does not exercise that right.

A principal may be liable even if an agent was not an employee. In general, if the agent is acting within the scope of its actual or apparent authority, the principal is liable for the agent's fraud or negligent misrepresentation.[36]

As we have seen, a principal is exposed to substantial risks whenever it uses an agent. Often, the best strategy for avoiding such risks is to carefully select, train, supervise, and monitor agents. You Be the Judge 20.1 illustrates the importance of that strategy. Ethical Perspective 20.1 addresses the appropriateness of using criminal penalties as a way of reducing the risk that agents will not fulfill their duties to their principals.

YOU BE THE JUDGE 20.1

Authority of Insurance Broker[37]

Horne carried on business as an insurance broker on behalf of several insurance companies, including Canada Life. Under his contract with Canada Life, he was authorized to solicit customers for life insurance and various other products, but he was not authorized to incur any liability for Canada Life without prior approval from the company.

In 1990, Horne met Keddie, who was seeking to make an investment. He told her that he was a Canada Life broker operating under the name Royal Pacific Consulting. On Horne's advice, Keddie purchased a $375 000 Canada Life annuity contract. Horne subsequently gave Keddie a folder containing information about the annuity. The folder had a picture of the Canada Life building in Toronto on the front, and the name and address of Canada Life on the back.

In 1992, Keddie was interested in making another investment. Horne convinced her that she should purchase another Canada Life annuity. Keddie gave Horne a cheque for $300 000 payable to Royal Pacific Consulting. Horne invested $105 000 in an annuity offered by another financial institution and kept the remaining $195 000 for himself. Horne later gave Keddie a folder, similar to the first one, that con-

tained information about the annuity inside. However, whereas the earlier policy simply referred to "Canada Life," the new policy statement referred to "Royal Pacific Group Representing the Canada Life/NN Financial Group."

There was no evidence as to how Horne got the folders. There was, however, evidence that he had been provided with a large quantity of material from Canada Life, including application forms and brochures. The only information that Keddie had about Horne's relationship to Canada Life was based on what he had told her.

When Horne eventually stopped making payments to her, Keddie successfully sued him for fraud. Unfortunately, Horne no longer had any assets and therefore could not satisfy that judgment. Keddie then sued Canada Life, alleging that Horne was Canada Life's agent and Canada Life was liable for his fraud.

Question for Discussion

1. Should Keddie succeed against Canada Life?

ETHICAL PERSPECTIVE 20.1

Agent's Criminal Liability[38]

Over a two-year period, almost three dozen investors purchased shares in two companies on the advice of Hudec. The majority of the investors received no information about the companies and relied exclusively on Hudec's advice. Hudec continued to play a role in advising the investors from time to

time as to the status of their investments. He later admitted that one company had given him $43 000 and the other 79 000 shares in return for directing his clients to them. He also later admitted that he did not tell any of the investors that he had received benefits from those companies.

(continued)

---

[36]. When an agent has made a misrepresentation, the third party may be able to rescind the contract, even when the principal did not authorize, or even forbade, the misrepresentation: *Betker v Williams* [1992] 2 WWR 534 (BC CA).

[37]. *Keddie v Canada Life Assurance Co* [1999] BCJ No 2165 (CA); *Doiron v Devon Capital* (2003) 38 BLR (3d) 82 (Alta CA).

[38]. *R v Hudec* [1992] OJ No 2992 (HCJ). The relevant provision of the *Criminal Code*, RSC 1985, c C-46 (Can), is s 426.

(continued)

Hudec was found guilty under the *Criminal Code* for accepting commissions without his clients' knowledge and consent. He realized that he was an agent for his clients. The court found that they were entitled to know that he was receiving benefits from the companies in question. If they had known, they might have invested elsewhere.

2. Should liability depend on whether the investors lose their investments?

3. Why would civil liability to compensate for any investor losses not be sufficient?

Questions for Discussion

1. Is it appropriate for agents to be held criminally liable in these circumstances?

BUSINESS RELATIONSHIPS IN WHICH AGENCY ISSUES ARISE

Agency arises in a variety of business arrangements. We will look at partnerships in Chapter 21 and corporations in Chapter 22. In this section, we will consider several other situations that can involve agency relationships:

- joint ventures and strategic alliances
- distributorships
- agents governed by special statutes

Joint Ventures and Strategic Alliances

A *joint venture* is not a distinct form of business organization, nor is it a relationship that has a precise legal meaning. A **joint venture** is simply any legal arrangement in which two or more parties combine their resources for a limited purpose, or a limited time, or both. For instance, a small exploration company may own the rights to mine gold from a certain area, but not have the financial resources needed to actually build the mine. It could enter into a joint venture with a larger mining company that does have sufficient resources. That joint venture could operate through a corporation in which each party has an investment as a shareholder, or through a partnership in which each party is a partner. Alternatively, the parties could regulate their relationship entirely through a contract.

Strategic alliances are even more broadly defined. A **strategic alliance** refers to any arrangement in which two or more parties agree to co-operate for some purpose. That arrangement can be legal or informal. It can involve greater or lesser degrees of co-operation. A joint venture or partnership may be referred to as a strategic alliance. That term may also be used, for example, to describe an arrangement in which the parties (i) conduct a research project together, (ii) jointly market products, or (iii) share information.

If a joint venture or strategic alliance is purely contractual, the participants are not automatically agents for each other.[39] They may, however, agree to set

> a joint venture is a legal arrangement in which two or more parties combine their resources for a limited purpose, a limited time, or both

> a strategic alliance is any arrangement in which two or more parties agree to co-operate for some purpose

---

[39.] *Canadian Mortgage and Housing Corporation v Graham* (1973) 43 DLR (3d) 686 (NS SC TD) is one case in which one contractual joint venturer was held responsible for the obligations of the other.

up an agency relationship. Joint venturers often agree that each will have authority to create obligations for both in connection with the joint venture business. When that is done, the precise scope of the agency relationship should be clearly stated in the joint venture agreement. Even if no *actual authority* is given in the joint venture agreement, one party's actions may, in the circumstances, provide the other with apparent authority. A third party may be entitled to rely on that appearance of authority.

Distributorships

a **distributorship** exists when one business contractually agrees to sell another's product

A **distributorship** exists when one business contracts to sell another's product. In addition to selling the basic product, a distributor may also perform some of the responsibilities that would normally fall upon the manufacturer or supplier. The distributor may, for example, provide warranty service.

A distributorship does not normally involve an agency relationship. The parties can agree that the distributor acts on behalf of the supplier when it deals with customers. Usually, however, the distributor buys the supplier's products and then resells them on its own behalf. In fact, most distributorship agreements expressly state that the distributor is *not* an agent and has no authority to bind the supplier. Suppliers do not want to be exposed to the risk of unwanted obligations negotiated by the distributor. For that reason, suppliers must be concerned about creating *apparent authority*. If a distributor is made to look like an agent, a customer may acquire rights against the supplier, regardless of what the distributorship agreement says.

Agents Governed by Special Statutes

Some kinds of agents are governed by special statutes that are intended to protect the people with whom they deal. For example, lawyers, real estate agents, insurance agents, stockbrokers, and travel agents are subject to rules that complement the basic common law rules that we have discussed.

For example, to work as a real estate agent, a person must be either licensed or employed by a licensed agent under provincial legislation.[40] Licensing bodies try to ensure that agents meet certain standards for competence, honesty, integrity, and financial responsibility. They enforce specific rules relating to trading (including prohibiting agents from supplying false information), handling clients' money, advertising, and disclosure regarding any personal interest that an agent may have in the transaction. For instance, real estate agents are required to tell the principal about any compensation they will receive from another party to the transaction. Typically, licensing bodies have the power to suspend or revoke licences when the required standards are not met.

Regulatory schemes often have a complaints process. Anyone concerned about the actions of a real estate agent can file a complaint with the licensing body, which has the power to inspect the agent's premises and records. If it discovers wrongdoing, it may subject the agent to disciplinary proceedings, which can lead to the suspension or revocation of the agent's licence, or even criminal charges.

[40.] In Ontario, for example, licensing is under the *Real Estate and Business Brokers Act*, RSO 1990, c R.4. Since 1997, it has been administered by the Real Estate Council of Ontario, a non-profit body created by statute. Real estate agents in Alberta are regulated under the *Real Estate Act*, RSA 2000, c R-5, and in Nova Scotia under the *Real Estate Trading Act*, SNS 1996, c 28.

Similar schemes apply to insurance agents and travel agents.[41] Stockbrokers are governed by a more comprehensive scheme of regulation, which includes standards for internal controls, insurance, and sufficient capital to ensure that brokerage firms are solvent.[42] The Canadian Investor Protection Fund covers customers' losses of securities and cash balances resulting from the insolvency of a brokerage firm.

FRANCHISING

A **franchise** is a purely contractual relationship under which the franchisor gives the franchisee the right to operate its "system" in return for a set of fees. The franchise agreement:

- includes a licence that allows the franchisee to use the franchisor's trademark[43]
- requires the franchisor to assist in the operation of the franchised business (by providing training, uniforms, and so on)
- requires the franchisee to maintain certain standards and follow certain rules
- requires the franchisee to pay fees based, in part, on the volume of sales

While we often think of franchises in the fast-food context, they are common in many other areas, like retailing.

a franchise is a purely contractual relationship under which the franchisor gives the franchisee the right to operate its "system" in return for a set of fees

Advantages and Disadvantages for the Franchisor

Franchising offers both pros and cons for the franchisor. On the positive side, franchising provides a way of expanding operations without the need to provide all of the investment capital or take all of the risks. On the negative side, the franchisor must share the profits with its franchisees. It also bears the risk that its reputation may be damaged by a shoddy franchisee.

A franchise could be set up as an agency relationship, whereby the franchisee conducts business on behalf of the franchisor. In practice, however, agency relationships are not used because they would expose the franchisor to the risk of liability in connection with every franchised outlet. That is a risk that franchisors want to avoid.

Advantages and Disadvantages for the Franchisee

Franchising has several advantages from the franchisee's perspective.

- Franchising reduces many of the risks that are associated with starting a business. The franchisor may provide an established reputation in the marketplace, a proven business concept, and assistance in the form of staff training, operational advice, and low-cost supplies.
- A franchisor may provide advice on the best location. It may even rent that location to the franchisee.

[41.] *Eg Registered Insurance Brokers Act*, RSO 1990, c R.19 (Ont); *Travel Agents Act*, RSBC 1996, c 459 (BC); *Travel Industry Act*, RSO 1990, c T.19 (Ont).

[42.] *Eg Securities Act*, RSBC 1996, c 418 (BC); *Securities Act*, RSO 1990, c S.5 (Ont).

[43.] A licence gives permission to act in a way that would otherwise be prohibited.

- A franchisor may provide advertising for the benefit of all its franchisees.

There are also important disadvantages.

- To ensure that every outlet operates under the same standards for quality and service, the franchisor imposes restrictions on the franchisee's ability to do business. Those restrictions are sometimes quite onerous.
- The franchisee may be left with little profit after paying the franchise fees.
- Franchise agreements tend to be very long and complex. Potential franchisees may find them difficult to understand.
- Potential franchisees may find it difficult to obtain information about the actual operation of the business. That is especially true if the franchise business is new and unproven. Sometimes, the franchisor is the only source of information—and that party may not be entirely reliable.

Legal Rules Governing Franchise Relationships

A franchisor has certain advantages over a potential franchisee during negotiations. The franchisor knows its business better than the franchisee. The franchisor is also intimately familiar with the rights and obligations that are set out in the franchise agreement. Furthermore, some potential franchisees have little previous business experience. Together, those factors increase the risk that franchisees will make a bad bargain.

Even if a franchisee identifies a potential concern regarding a proposed franchise agreement, the franchisor is not likely to be flexible. Usually, a franchisor will strongly resist any attempt to modify its standard form agreement because it wants to ensure that all of its franchisees receive the same deal. Preferential treatment for one franchisee will encourage others to seek the same. For that reason, franchises are often offered on a take-it-or-leave-it basis.

The common law rules of contract that we discussed in Chapters 9 and 10 provide some protection for franchisees. For instance, if a franchisee is induced to enter into a franchising agreement on the basis of a franchisor's misrepresentation regarding an outlet's profitability, that contract may be set aside.[44] The same relief may be available if an agreement is unconscionable. The franchisor does not, however, have a general duty to disclose all information that might affect a franchisee's decision.

Because the common law protections are often inadequate, Alberta and Ontario have enacted legislation that imposes obligations on franchisors for the protection of current and prospective franchisees.[45] These are the key elements of the law in those provinces.

- Franchisors have a minimum obligation to deal fairly with franchisees and prospective franchisees. Franchisors must act in good faith and in accordance with reasonable commercial standards.

[44.] A franchisor was implicated in a misrepresentation in *Country Style Food Services Inc v 1304271* [2005] OJ No 2730 (CA). The relationship between a franchisor and a franchisee has been held not to give rise to a fiduciary relationship: *Jirna v Mr Donut* (1973) 40 DLR (3d) 303 (SCC), affg (1971) 40 DLR (3d) 303 (Ont CA).

[45.] *Franchises Act*, RSA 2000, c F-23 (Alta); *Arthur Wishart Act (Franchise Disclosure), 2000*, SO 2000, c 3 (Ont). Prince Edward Island passed similar legislation in June 2005 that will come into force on a date to be proclaimed: *Franchises Act*, SPEI 2005, c 36.

■ Franchisors must provide extensive disclosure to prospective franchisees regarding the risks associated with the franchise business.

■ Any franchisee who signs a franchise agreement has a right to withdraw from the agreement within 60 days of signing, or within two years if the required disclosure documents were never provided.

■ Franchisees have the right to damages for any misrepresentation in disclosure documents.

■ Franchisees have the right to organize themselves to deal collectively with the franchisor.

Business Decision 20.1 asks you to decide how best to structure a business relationship.

BUSINESS DECISION 20.1

Method of Carrying on Business

You are a new manufacturer of tennis rackets and you are looking for someone to help you sell your product in Alberta. Jordan has worked for several years as a distributor of in-line skates in Alberta and sells to many of the same retailers that you would like as customers. You want to enter into some kind relationship with Jordan to help you sell to those retailers.

Questions for Discussion

1. What are the options for structuring your relationship with Jordan?
2. What are the advantages and disadvantages of each?

CHAPTER SUMMARY

In an agency relationship, an agent represents a principal for some specific purpose. That purpose may include the creation of contracts. Agency relationships themselves are often created by a contract between the principal and the agent. They exist as a matter of law in partnerships. Agency can also be created by the principal holding out, or representing a person as having the authority of an agent.

Even if a person is not an agent when an obligation is purportedly created on behalf of a principal, that obligation can become binding on the principal if the principal ratifies it. A special rule applies to pre-incorporation contracts. In most provinces, an agent is personally liable under contracts it enters into on behalf of a corporation before it is incorporated. Afterwards, the corporation can adopt the contract. If it does, the contract becomes binding on the corporation, and the agent ceases to be personally responsible.

The principal is liable for a contract entered into by an agent on its behalf if it gave the agent either actual authority or apparent authority to contract. An agent is not normally personally liable for contracts entered into on behalf of a principal unless the agent and third party otherwise agreed. If an agent purports to enter into a contract on behalf of a principal and has no authority to do so, the agent may be liable to the third party for breach of warranty of authority.

An agent is required to fulfill any obligations created under the agency agreement. An agent also has a fiduciary duty to act in the principal's best interests in most cases, and a duty of care to act reasonably when performing the agency obligations. A principal must comply with the obligations specified in the agency agreement. In the absence of an express provision to the contrary, a principal must pay reasonable remuneration and indemnify the agent for any reasonable expenses.

An agency relationship can be terminated in several ways. If the agent is an employee, statutory and common law rules regarding notice must be observed.

An agency relationship can exist in the context of some methods for carrying on business, such as a contractual joint venture or a strategic alliance. Generally, distributorships and franchises are not agencies. Some agency businesses are subject to special regulatory schemes designed to protect the public and consumers.

Franchises are contractual relationships under which the franchisor gives the franchisee the right to operate its business system in return for fees. Franchises have advantages and disadvantages for both franchisors and franchisees. Alberta and Ontario have special statutes to protect franchisees.

REVIEW QUESTIONS

1. Why would you appoint an agent to act on your behalf? What are the risks in using an agent?

2. Can a contract negotiated by an agent on behalf of an identified principal, but without the principal's knowledge or consent, be binding on the principal? Can it be binding on the agent?

3. The president of a corporation you are dealing with tells you that Alton has authority to sell you one of the corporation's cars. You find out that the president was mistaken because Alton's employment contract says that he does not have this authority. Can you rely on the president's statement to enforce a contract with the corporation that you negotiated with Alton?

4. If you were a third party negotiating a contract with an employee of a corporation, would you be concerned about the authority of that person to commit the corporation to the contract?

5. If you were a real estate agent acting for someone trying to sell a house, could you buy that house for yourself? How could you deal with that situation in a way that would allow you to buy the house and fulfill your duties as an agent?

6. If you appointed an agent to buy a car for you at a car auction, what concerns would you have about the unauthorized actions of the agent, such as agreeing to a higher price than you were prepared to pay? How would you deal with those concerns?

7. Can you enter into a contract on behalf of a corporation that has not yet been incorporated? Who would be responsible for performing the contract if you did?

8. Explain the situations in which a principal can be held liable for torts committed by its agent. Is there anything that the principal can do to reduce those risks?

9. Are the parties to a contractual joint venture, strategic alliance, distributorship, or franchise agreement in an agency relationship?

10. You negotiated a contract with an agent, but later found out that the agent had no authority to contract on behalf of the principal. Assuming that the principal is not liable, do you have any recourse against the agent?

11. Jane appointed you to act as her agent to negotiate the purchase of some cattle. Before you signed the purchase contract, Jane died. What effect, if any, does her death have on your authority as agent?

12. You contracted with Lana to act as your agent in purchasing lumber. That contract does not say that she is entitled to be paid. Are you required to pay her? Are you required to pay her expenses for travelling to visit lumber producers to acquire lumber for you?

13. Allan has appointed you as an agent to sell his line of ski jackets to retailers. Another manufacturer asks you to carry its line of ski jackets as well. Can you agree to carry the other line?

14. At 9:00 a.m., you instruct your stockbroker to buy 1000 shares of Bolt Networks Inc as soon as possible at the current market price of $10. The stockbroker forgets to place your order until the next day when the price has gone up to $15. Do you have any claim against the agent?

15. Is there a difference between a strategic alliance and a joint venture?

16. You bought a piece of commercial real estate with the help of your agent. You now believe that the agent misled you regarding the zoning of that property. What could you do about it?

17. Why might you consider a franchise rather than starting a new business from scratch?

18. If you were negotiating with a franchisor in Manitoba, would you have any concerns about revenue estimates shown to you by the franchisor to encourage you to agree to become a franchisee? Would your concerns be different if you were in Ontario?

19. If you had appointed the operator of a marina as an agent to sell your boat for you, what would you have to do to terminate that agency relationship?

20. You have entered into a contract with Azam to supply your business with stationery. You have known Azam for a long time and trust him to be a reliable supplier. A few days later, Azam discloses that he was acting as an agent for a paper manufacturer that you have never heard of. Can you enforce the contract against the paper manufacturer or Azam?

CASES AND PROBLEMS

1. Jensen entered into a contract to buy a mobile home from South Trail Mobile Ltd. The contract provided that all sales had to have the approval of the president of South Trail. When Jensen asked about this approval, Hiram, the salesman with whom Jensen was dealing, said that it had been obtained as required. In fact, the president had not approved the contract. Can Jensen enforce the sale contract against South Trail?

2. Tatiana was looking for a BMW to lease. She went to Reston Sales and Leasing Inc and met with Joe Reston, the manager and sole owner. After some discussion, Reston said he could arrange for a two-year lease on the car that Tatiana wanted from Corporate Leasing Inc. Though nothing in Tatiana's dealings with Reston had indicated that he was acting for Corporate Leasing, Tatiana said that if the terms were acceptable to her, she would contract with Corporate Leasing. Reston telephoned Corporate Leasing and, after Corporate Leasing did a credit check on Tatiana, it faxed Reston a lease agreement. Tatiana signed the agreement that provided for a fixed lease term of two years with no right to cancel before the end of the term. After signing the agreement, she asked Reston if she could have the right to cancel the agreement on written notice from her. Reston said she could and confirmed this in writing. After six months, Tatiana lost her job and wrote to Corporate Leasing cancelling the lease. Corporate Leasing says that cancellation is not permitted under the terms of the lease. Can Tatiana cancel the lease?

3. Jennifer is an agent of MB Forest Products Inc. Under her agency contract, she has authority to buy raw logs from independent logging companies. While Jennifer is visiting some logging companies in the interior of British Columbia, MB goes bankrupt. Jennifer later signs a contract with ForCan Logging Ltd on behalf of MB for the purchase of 1000 logs. The contract is at a very favourable price for ForCan. Can they enforce the contract against MB? Do they have any rights against Jennifer?

4. Martina was interested in running a pizza business in Toronto, but had no business experience. She approached Mr Pizza, a franchisor that was advertising for new franchisees in the newspaper. The franchisor showed her some financial statements for a Mr Pizza location in Toronto, which suggested profits of over $1 000 000 a year. Mr Pizza told Martina that the location could be hers for $100 000. Martina was very interested. Mr Pizza asked her to sign a 75-page agreement. When she suggested getting some legal advice, Mr Pizza discouraged her by saying, "Why share your future profits with lawyers?" Martina signed the agreement and began carrying on the business. She worked 15-hour days for six months and took home only $25 000. The

basic business is profitable, but what she can take out of the business is limited by the fees she has to pay: advertising fees, royalties for use of the trade mark, fees for training employees, fees for uniforms, and fees to have the premises inspected each month. Martina wants out. Her agreement, however, provides for a two-year term. Is there anything that she can do? Would your answer be different if Martina's pizza restaurant was in Halifax?

5. Geomedia Inc helps retailers promote sales by arranging to distribute advertising flyers to consumers, usually in the form of newspaper inserts. Red Rose Inc sells arts and crafts supplies across Canada. In the past, it managed its own advertising by contracting with the *Regina Post*, to distribute its flyers. Recently, Red Rose hired Geomedia to act as its agent to distribute flyers. It then faxed an announcement to the *Regina Post* that said, "From this point forward, Geomedia will be managing all media distribution for Red Rose." The *Regina Post* interpreted that fax to mean that it would be contracting with Geomedia rather than Red Rose.

   The *Regina Post* subsequently received several orders from Geomedia that involved advertisements for Red Rose. Those orders, printed on Geomedia letterhead, said: "Please bill Red Rose care of Geomedia." The *Post* published those ads, but has not been paid. To make matters worse, Red Rose has gone bankrupt. Is the *Post* entitled to receive payment from Geomedia?

6. Koh Corporation agreed to provide cleaning services for one year to Mid-Town Management Inc, which operates several large office cleaning buildings in Saskatoon. The contract price was much cheaper than what other cleaning services were offering. In its dealings with Mid-Town, Koh always made clear that it was acting on behalf of a principal in contracting to provide the services, though it never identified who that principal was. In fact, Koh was acting on behalf of Down-Town Realty Inc, a competitor of Mid-Town's. After six months, Koh stopped providing the services. Is Koh liable to Mid-Town for breach of contract?

7. Orlof was interested in buying real estate from Danilova. He signed an agreement to purchase the property "on behalf of a corporation to be incorporated." Orlof then instructed his lawyers to prepare the necessary documents to complete the transaction. To close the transaction, a lawyer in the firm decided to use a corporation that had already been incorporated (a "shelf corporation") by another partner in the law firm. She drafted a transfer of the one issued share from the partner to Orlof, a shareholder's resolution appointing Orlof as the sole director, a director's resolution authorizing the transaction, a legal opinion, and some other documents in the name of the shelf corporation. She then

sent that package to Danilova's lawyer for comments, together with a cover letter indicating that the shelf corporation would complete the purchase. When the date came to close the transaction, Orlof decided that the price was too high. He therefore refused to take a transfer of the share, to sign the resolutions, or to pay Danilova.

The law firm later transferred the partner's share in the shelf corporation to another client, who began to carry on a profitable business through the shelf corporation. Danilova sued the shelf corporation. She alleged that the agreement to buy her property was a pre-incorporation contract that had been adopted by the corporation based on the sending of the draft documents by Orlof's lawyers to Danilova's lawyers. Will Danilova succeed? What would you do if you were the client who was now carrying on business using the shelf corporation?

8. Trusty Resources Ltd is a producer of natural gas. Trusty entered into a contract with Power Marketing Inc to find a natural gas purchaser that would commit to a long-term purchase agreement. Trusty entered into a 15-year supply agreement with Clean Energy Inc, a purchaser found by Power. The agreement provided that Trusty would pay Power a fee for each unit of gas purchased under the contract. For five years, Clean purchased gas under the contract and Trusty paid Power the agreed fee. After five years, Clean wanted out of the agreement because the price that it had to pay under the agreement was too high. Trusty agreed to terminate the contract at the end of the sixth year. Halfway through the sixth year, Clean and Trusty agreed that Clean would no longer be obliged to purchase gas under the contract in return for a payment to Trusty of $100 000. Does Trusty have any liability to Power for the fees that would have been paid if the contract had continued for the full 15-year term? Until the end of the sixth year?

9. Porter entered into a contract with Hip Sports Inc under which Hip agreed to sell Porter's basketball shoes. Hip was authorized to enter into contracts to sell the shoes on Porter's behalf and Porter agreed to pay (i) a commission of 10 percent of the sale price of the shoes, and (ii) all of Hip's advertising expenses. Hip represented several other lines of products.

Hip planned to advertise Porter's shoes through a flyer campaign. The going rate for that service was $5000. However, Hip was able to negotiate a discount of $1000 because it did a high volume of business with the flyer producer. Hip saw no reason to pass that benefit on to Porter since it was granted on the basis of *all* of the business that Hip did with the flyer company—for Porter and for other customers. Hip therefore charged Porter the full $5000. Is Hip liable to give Porter the benefit of the discount?

10. Goran and Basil were partners in a partnership named GB Computer Leasing. GB carried on a business of leasing personal computers and related equipment from a retail store. It was an express term of the partnership agreement that neither Goran nor Basil would enter into contracts to buy personal computers without the consent of the other. Goran bought 20 computers from Ellen. Ellen agreed to defer payment for one month. Basil has discovered the transaction and refuses to approve it. Can Ellen enforce the contract against the partnership? If not, does she have any action against Goran?

11. Sharif owned 10 percent of the shares of Orca Environmental Consulting Inc. Jenna, the lawyer for Orca, approached Sharif, telling him that she represented "a group of investors" who were interested in purchasing Sharif's shares. Jenna made an offer, accompanied by a deposit, and Sharif accepted it. There was no "group of investors." Jenna had thought that she would be able to put together a group after she had negotiated the purchase from Sharif. She could not do so and the purchase was never completed. Is Jenna personally liable for failing to purchase Sharif's shares? What is the legal basis of liability?

12. Able has acted as an agent for Solon Corp for several years. Solon was in the business of selling security services. Able's contract required him to seek customers for Solon's services. In the course of working with Solon, Able learned a great deal about the security business and the sophisticated software that Solon uses. Able wants to use this knowledge to start up his own security service business. Can he do so?

WEBLINKS

Agency

Insurance Canada   www.insurance-canada.ca/index.php

This site contains extensive information on insurance and insurance agents and brokers for both consumers and insurance professionals, including a very useful glossary of insurance terms and pages on becoming an insurance agent or broker.

Canadian Real Estate Association   www.crea.ca/index.htm

This is the site of the Canadian real estate industry trade association, representing more than 76 000 real estate brokers/agents and salespeople working through more than 100 real estate boards, 10 provincial associations, and one territorial association. The site contains information on the codes of ethics and standards of business practices applicable to real estate agents and on the services a real estate agent can provide.

Franchising

Canadian Franchise Association   www.cfa.ca

The CFA site contains a wealth of information for people interested in franchising, including the association's code of ethics and its disclosure rules, links to its magazine and publications, and an overview of the franchising legislation in Alberta and Ontario.

Canadian Franchise   www.canadianfranchise.com

This site contains general information on franchising, including a glossary of franchising terms, tips on entering franchise relationships, and a searchable database of franchising opportunities.

Osler Hoskin Harcourt: Franchise Law Briefing
www.osler.com/index.asp?navid=1072&csid=132&fid3=1216

This law firm site provides information on current issues in franchising, such as Ontario legislation that protects franchisees, and a detailed discussion of terms in franchise agreements.

Royal Bank Information on Franchising   www.royalbank.com/franchise/five_pt_guide.html

This site provides a brief practical guide to what to consider before entering into a franchise. It has links to a more comprehensive guide to franchising that explains the nature of the relationship, the key provisions of a franchise agreement, and how to finance an investment in a franchise.

ADDITIONAL RESOURCES FOR CHAPTER 20 ON THE COMPANION WEBSITE

(www.pearsoned.ca/mcinnes)

In addition to self-test multiple-choice, true-false, and short essay questions (all with immediate feedback), three additional Cases and Problems (with suggested answers), and links to useful Web destinations, the Companion Website provides the following resources for Chapter 20:

- Business Decision 20W—When Is the Government Liable as Principal?

Provincial Material

- **British Columbia:** Power of Attorney, Real Estate Agents, Collection Agents, Travel Agents
- **Alberta:** Franchises, Liability for Agent's Tortious Conduct, Agency by Necessity
- **Manitoba and Saskatchewan:** Pre-Incorporation Contracts, Real Estate Agency Rules
- **Ontario:** Agency by Necessity, Fiduciary Duty, Franchising Legislation, Powers of Attorney, Real Estate Agents

21 Basic Forms of Business Organizations

OBJECTIVES

After completing this chapter you should be able to:

1. Identify four basic forms of business organization.

2. Explain how a sole proprietorship is created and how it operates.

3. Identify the factors that determine when a partnership comes into existence.

4. Describe strategies for minimizing the risk of being a partner.

5. Identify the key elements of a partnership agreement.

6. Distinguish between general and limited partnerships.

7. Describe the process of incorporating and organizing a corporation.

8. Describe the implications of the separate legal existence of the corporation.

9. Explain the division of power among the shareholders, the directors, and the officers to manage and control the corporation.

10. Identify three basic characteristics of shares of a corporation.

Doing business has risks. A manufacturer, for example, faces the risk that no one will buy its products, or that its products will hurt someone. But who bears those risks? The answer depends upon the type of organization that is carrying on the business. We will focus on four possibilities:

- sole proprietorship
- general partnership
- limited partnership
- corporation

In each type of organization, the law strikes a different balance between the interests of the people who have a stake in the operation of the business (identified in Figure 21.1). Significantly, the law determines the extent to which entrepreneurs benefit when their businesses prosper and are responsible for losses when they do not. By affecting the risk to entrepreneurs in this way, the law influences incentives for entrepreneurs to start and maintain businesses.

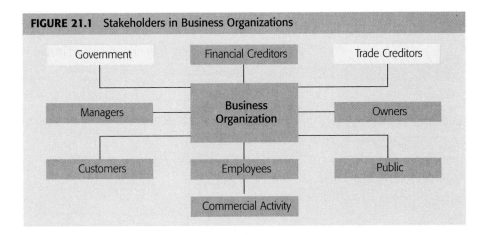

FIGURE 21.1   Stakeholders in Business Organizations

The law governing business organizations also provides a structure for the *operation* of businesses, focusing on the relationship that owners and managers have with the business and with each other. It deals with the rights and obligations of owners to manage the business themselves and to monitor and control others who manage on their behalf. When management acts in a manner contrary to the best interests of the business, it provides remedies to business owners.

The law of business organizations also addresses the responsibilities that owners and managers have to other stakeholder groups—but only to a limited extent. For the most part, other types of laws govern the relationships between the business and other stakeholders. These are discussed in other chapters of this book.[1]

[1.] The rights and obligations of employers and employees are discussed in Chapters 26 and 27. The relationships between a business and its trade creditors (like suppliers of goods and services), financial creditors (like banks), and customers are examined in chapters of this book dealing with contract, tort, property, commercial, and criminal law. Businesses are subject to various forms of direct regulation to protect the public interest, as discussed in Chapter 25.

SOLE PROPRIETORSHIPS

The *sole proprietorship* is the simplest form of business organization. **A sole proprietorship** comes into existence when a person starts to carry on business on their own, without taking steps to adopt another form of organization, such as a corporation. If you agree to cut your neighbour's grass for money each week, you are carrying on business as a sole proprietor.

As a sole proprietor, you could enter into a contract to *employ* someone else to cut your neighbour's grass, but you remain the sole owner of the business and the only person responsible for its obligations. Both legally and practically, there is no separation between the sole proprietorship business organization and the individual who is the sole proprietor. As the sole proprietor, you cannot be an employee of the business because you cannot contract with yourself.

In this form of organization, the sole proprietor gets all of the benefits, and all of the burdens, of the business. This has several important implications in terms of the relationships between the business and its other stakeholders.

- The sole proprietor is exclusively responsible for performing all contracts entered into in the course of the business, including contracts with customers, suppliers, employees, and lenders.

- The sole proprietor is exclusively responsible for all torts committed personally in connection with the business. That person is also vicariously liable for all torts committed by employees in the course of their employment. As we saw in Chapter 3, vicarious liability occurs when an employer is held liable for a tort that was committed by an employee.

- For income tax purposes, the income or loss from the sole proprietorship is included with the income or loss from other sources in calculating the sole proprietor's personal tax liability.

The main advantage of a sole proprietorship is that it is simple and easy to set up. It is equally easy to dissolve: The sole proprietor simply stops carrying on the business. Just because you stop carrying on business, however, does not mean that you cease to be liable for the obligations that arose in connection with the business while it was being carried on.

The main disadvantage of a sole proprietorship is *unlimited personal liability*. **Unlimited personal liability** means that third parties may take all of the sole proprietor's personal assets—not just those of the business—to satisfy the business's obligations. As the scale of the business and the related liabilities increase, this exposure to personal liability becomes an increasingly important disincentive to using a sole proprietorship. Suppose your grass-cutting business was wildly successful and you had entered into contracts to cut 1000 lawns each week and hired 100 students to do the work. As a sole proprietor, you would be personally responsible for all the work and to each employee. If one of your customers was not happy with the work and demanded a refund, or if an employee whom you fired sued you for wrongful dismissal, the liability would be yours alone. While you could try to manage the liability risk through contracts and insurance, incorporation is often a less expensive and more effective strategy.

Another problem with sole proprietorships is raising money. Every business needs investment to grow. Since it is not possible to divide up ownership of the sole proprietorship, the only method of financing is for the sole proprietor to borrow money directly. An advantage of other forms of business is that they permit a wider range of financing possibilities. Consequently, sole proprietorships are used only for relatively small businesses.

a sole proprietorship exists when a person carries on business without adopting any other form of business organization

unlimited personal liability means that all of the sole proprietor's personal assets may be taken by third parties to satisfy the business's obligations

Legal Requirements for Sole Proprietorships

There are a few rules for carrying on a sole proprietorship. The name of a sole proprietorship must be registered if that name is something other than, or more than, the proprietor's personal name. For example, Amman Malik does not have to register if he carries on a grass-cutting business under his own name. But he does have to register if he uses the name "Malik's Gardening Services" or "Superior Gardening Services." Registration must be completed in every province or territory in which the sole proprietorship carries on business.[2] Note that registration does not create any ownership interest in the business name. This interest may be protected, however, under provincial passing-off laws and federal trademarks legislation, which are discussed in Chapter 18.

A second rule, which applies to all forms of business organization including sole proprietorships, is that a *business licence* is required for some types of activities. A **business licence** is government permission to operate a certain kind of business. For example, most municipalities require the proprietors of taxi-driving businesses and restaurants to obtain a licence. Provincial governments have enacted licensing requirements for many types of businesses, including real estate agents, car dealers, and securities dealers.

a business licence is government permission to operate a certain kind of business

GENERAL PARTNERSHIPS

Where people pool their resources, knowledge, or skills, they may carry on business as a *general partnership* (or, more simply, a *partnership*). A **general partnership** is a form of business organization that comes into existence when two or more people carry on business together with a view to a profit. Partnership arises automatically by operation of law. Its creation does not require any formalities, although it may have to register the partnership name and obtain a business licence. For example, you and I agree to develop a business together: I agree to buy a lawnmower, and you agree to cut lawns with it. The profits are split between us. We have created a partnership.

a general partnership is a form of business organization that comes into existence when two or more persons carry on business together with a view to a profit

Characteristics of General Partnerships

Like sole proprietors, partners carry on business on their own behalf. Although the business can do some things in the name of the partnership, such as hold title to land or be sued, the partnership is not legally separate from the partners. That fact has several consequences.

- A partner cannot be employed by the partnership.
- All benefits of the partnership business accrue directly to the partners.
- All partners, even those who did not consent to a particular obligation, are personally liable for all of the obligations of the business, including torts committed by a partner or an employee of the partnership.

If a partnership is liable for an obligation, each partner is liable to the full extent of the obligation. *All* of a partner's *personal* assets—not just those that the partner committed to the business—may be seized to satisfy a partnership debt.

[2.] This is the requirement in most provinces: for example, *Business Names Act*, RSO 1990, c B.17, s 2(2) (Ont).

The nature of a partnership means that its creditworthiness is partially based on the creditworthiness of the individual partners. For example, assume that Eli and Taylor are partners in a restaurant business. The partnership has asked you to supply $200 000 worth of restaurant equipment today but wait 90 days for payment. Suppose you provide the equipment but are not paid on time. If the business's assets are worth only $100 000, you could get a judgment against the partnership and seize those assets *and* then seek to recover the remaining money from Taylor and Eli personally. You could collect $50 000 from each, or $100 000 from either.[3] When you contract with a partnership, you should consider the assets that are held by the business *and* by the partners personally.

To determine the liability of partners for income tax, the income (or loss) of the partnership is calculated by adding up all revenues of the partnership business and deducting all expenses. A share of the income (or loss) is allocated to each partner according to the partner's entitlement to share in the profits of the business. The partner's share of any business income must be included in their personal income, even if those profits were re-invested in the business and were not actually paid to the partner.

Partnership Property

Partnership property is all property acquired on behalf of the partnership or for the partnership business. If property is bought with partnership money, it is considered to have been bought on behalf of the partnership. Once property becomes partnership property, it must be held and used exclusively for the partnership and in accordance with the terms of the partnership agreement. Suppose you bought a car for use in the partnership business. It would become partnership property. Even if you had paid for it out of your own pocket and were the registered owner, you could not convert it back to your personal use without the consent of the other partners.

> **partnership property** is all property acquired on behalf of the partnership or for the partnership business

Partnership Legislation and Partnership Agreements

The courts in England developed the law of partnerships and it was codified in the English *Partnerships Act* of 1890. All provinces, other than Quebec, have partnership legislation based on that English statute.[4] These short acts often do not provide a satisfactory set of rules for organizing a partnership today. For that reason, partners often use a contract, called a **partnership agreement**, to supplement or modify the rules governing their relationship. Issues concerning the operation of a partnership are usually resolved on the basis of both the legislation and the partnership agreement.

> **a partnership agreement** is a contract between partners regarding the operation of the partnership

Creating a Partnership

A partnership comes into being when two or more persons carry on business together with a view to profit.[5] Sometimes, it is unclear if that relationship actually exists. It is then necessary to consider a number of factors. The most important is the sharing of *profits*. The focus on profit sharing is directly related

---

[3.] If you choose the second option and collect $100 000 from Eli, he can recover $50 000 from Taylor, unless they had some other arrangement between them.

[4.] *Eg Partnership Act*, RSBC 1996, c 348 (*BCPA*) (BC); *Partnership Act*, RSNS 1989, c 334 (*NSPA*) (NS); *Partnerships Act*, RSO 1990, c P.5 (*OPA*) (Ont).

[5.] *BCPA* s 2; *NSPA* s 4; *OPA* s 2.

to the basic requirement that partners must *carry on business together*. Someone who is simply compensated out of revenues only has a stake in how much the business can sell. In contrast, someone who is sharing profits must be concerned with the entire business operation, including the management of expenses. People are more likely to be found to be carrying on business together if they have a financial stake in the management of the business.

However, a partnership does not *necessarily* exist simply because the parties created a profit-sharing arrangement. They may do so *without* carrying on business together, such as in the following situations.

- A loan is to be repaid out of the profits of the borrower's business.
- An employee's remuneration varies with the employer's profits, such as in a profit-sharing scheme.
- The purchaser of a business agrees to pay some of the business's profits to the seller as part of the purchase price.

Since profit sharing is not conclusive, it is often difficult to determine if a partnership exists.

- The idea of carrying on business together usually suggests the existence of an enduring relationship, but even that factor may be inconclusive. There is probably no partnership if two competitors simply co-operate on an isolated transaction, as when a pair of software companies split the cost of a particular research project. The courts have held, however, that a partnership *may* arise even in relation to a single, time-limited activity.[6]
- A partnership is less likely to be found to exist if the people involved are merely passive investors, such as where they simply jointly own an apartment building and collect rent.[7] The situation may be different, however, if co-ownership of real estate is combined with active participation in its management and a sharing of profits.[8]

In the final analysis, to determine if a partnership exists, a court will look at a number of factors:

- sharing profits
- sharing responsibility for losses, including guaranteeing partnership debts
- jointly owning property
- jointly controlling the business
- participating in management, including having signing authority for contracts and bank accounts, and enjoying access to information regarding the business
- stating an intention to form a partnership in a contract
- filing certain government documents, such as registration under business names legislation as a partnership

---

[6.] *Spire Freezers Ltd v The Queen* (2001) 196 DLR (4th) 210 (SCC).

[7.] *AE Lepage Ltd v Kamex Developments Ltd* (1977) 16 OR (2d) 193 (CA). See also *Hickman Motors Ltd v The Queen* (1997) 148 DLR (4th) 1 (SCC); *Spire Freezers Ltd v The Queen* (2001) 196 DLR (4th) 210 (SCC).

[8.] *Volzkhe Construction v Westlock Foods Ltd* (1986) 70 AR 300 (CA).

- holding oneself out as a partner
- using a firm name, perhaps in advertising
- establishing a separate address for the business

Every partnership needs money to set up business and to cover ongoing operating expenses, such as salaries and rent. Extra money may also be needed from time to time to buy new equipment or expand operations. Money can be raised from the partners or borrowed from a third party, such as a bank. The amount contributed by the partners is called the **capital**. The contribution of capital (in the form of money, property, or services) by a number of parties is indicative of a partnership between them.

> **capital** refers to assets that the partners contribute to the business

You Be the Judge 21.1 discusses the question of the existence of a partnership.

YOU BE THE JUDGE 21.1

Is There a Partnership?[9]

Groscki and Durocher were chartered accountants. Groscki ran a business giving tax advice and providing accounting services, which he operated out of premises that he owned. In 1989, he entered into an agreement with Durocher under which Durocher agreed to review financial statements and prepare tax returns for Groscki's clients for $20 an hour plus $913 a month. They agreed that Durocher would not be classified as an employee. That allowed Durocher to deduct certain expenses in connection with his work for income tax purposes. Over time, Durocher assumed more responsibility for managing the business and supervising the staff. Groscki increasingly worked on other business ventures. In 1993, the name on the business letterhead and its sign was changed to say "Groscki and Durocher." Nevertheless, Durocher was never given signing authority for the business bank account and did not have access to the financial records of the business. In 1993, Durocher loaned $25 000 to Groscki for the business. In 1994, Durocher terminated his relationship with Groscki. Durocher argued that some of the firm's business belonged to him because he was a partner.

Questions for Discussion

1. What factors support the conclusion that the relationship between Groscki and Durocher was a partnership?
2. What factors suggest that it was not a partnership?
3. Which conclusion do you favour? Why?

Risk and Liability in General Partnerships

Business people need to know whether they are members of a partnership, primarily due to the risk of unlimited personal liability. An entrepreneur may be willing to accept that risk, either because it can be managed or because it is outweighed by the benefits of a partnership, such as the ability to deduct partnership losses for personal tax purposes. However, other people who are involved with a business, such as lenders, may want to avoid the risk of unlimited liability. For that sort of person, being found to be a partner may have unanticipated and disastrous financial consequences.

Managing the Risk of Becoming a Partner

As a matter of risk management, before entering a proposed relationship, you should examine it carefully to determine if you would be entering into a partnership. If you have any concerns that you may get caught in a partnership,

---

[9.] *Groscki v Durocher* [1999] OJ No 2052 (SCJ), affd [2001] OJ No 39 (CA).

seek advice from a lawyer. In negotiating the terms of the relationship, you may insist on a contract with the other parties that expressly excludes a partnership.[10] You can also negotiate to restructure the business organization so that it is a not a partnership. If the matter is in doubt, you should insist upon sufficient compensation to reflect the risks that you are facing. Finally, as we will discuss, you can take steps to minimize the consequences if you actually are found to be a partner.

How Liabilities of a Partnership Arise

Provincial partnership statutes determine when a partnership incurs liabilities.[11] The basic principle is that each partner is an agent of the partnership. Therefore, each partner, when acting in the usual course of the partnership business, binds the partnership. That is the principle of **mutual agency**. An exception exists only if a partner did not have authority to act in a particular way (perhaps because of a restriction in the partnership agreement) *and* the outside party knew that that partner lacked authority.

> **mutual agency** means that each partner, when acting in the usual course of partnership business, binds the partnership

The principle of mutual agency effectively places the risk of unauthorized behaviour by a partner on all of the partners. Partners are also liable for torts, such as negligence, that their fellow partners commit in the ordinary course of the partnership business. Given the unlimited personal liability of each partner, these liability risks are significant.

Managing Liability Risk If You Are a Partner

There are several legal and practical strategies for managing the risks associated with being a partner.

> the **fiduciary duty** requires a partner to act in the best interests of the partnership

First, each partner owes a **fiduciary duty** to the others.[12] That duty reduces the risk of unwanted liability. It requires each partner to act honestly and in good faith with a view to the best interests of the partnership. Partners must never put their personal interests ahead of those of the partnership. For instance, a partner cannot sell a piece of property to the partnership for an unfairly high price. A partner is also prohibited from competing with the partnership or using the name, property, or business reputation of the partnership to obtain a personal benefit. A partner who breaches the fiduciary duty must pay any resulting profits to the partnership.[13]

Second, the partnership agreement can be used to manage the risk of liability. Each partner can be given limited authority and can be subject to formal control and monitoring mechanisms.[14] For instance, restrictions can be placed

---

[10.] Partnership status cannot be avoided, however, by a simple document to that effect: *Lansing Building Supply Ltd v Ierullo* (1990) 71 OR (2d) 173 (Dist Ct). A court will consider how the parties actually acted under their agreement.

[11.] *Eg OPA* ss 6–19.

[12.] *BCPA* s 22 (1). Although there is no general expression of the duty in the *OPA* or some other partnership statutes, it is well established that the fiduciary duty is a guiding principle of partnership law: *Hitchcock v Sykes* (1914) 23 DLR 518 (SCC).

[13.] These obligations are specifically addressed in provincial partnership statutes: *BCPA* ss 32, 33; *NSPA* ss 32, 33; and *OPA* ss 29, 30.

[14.] A partner may seek to minimize the risk associated with liability as a partner by holding the partnership interest in a corporation. A partner may also consider the scope for limiting liability of the partnership to those with whom the business has a contractual relationship by trying to negotiate protections in the contract. Alternatively, insurance may be a good mechanism for dealing with some risks. If some partners pay more than their share of a partnership debt, they can claim reimbursement from the other partners. That right, provided for in partnership statutes, is also a form of indemnification.

on who can write cheques or sign contracts. Note that these mechanisms do not prevent liability to a third party. When a partner fails to follow the rules and creates a liability, the firm will usually still be liable. These mechanisms are designed to reduce the risk that the liability will be created. When a liability is created in breach of the partnership agreement, the partnership agreement may require the offending partner to compensate the others for the amounts that they must pay to the third party. That is called a *right to indemnification*.

Third, partners can take practical steps to reduce the risk of partnership liability. Some partnerships involve only a small number of people who know each other very well. There is a natural relationship of trust and confidence. Furthermore, since each partner may be involved in the business on a daily basis, opportunities for informal monitoring exist. In that situation, there is relatively little likelihood of unauthorized activity. Those protections break down, however, as a partnership grows. The business becomes larger and more impersonal. In large law and accounting firms, for example, few partners are actively involved in all aspects of the business. Formal monitoring mechanisms therefore must be established under increasingly elaborate partnership agreements.

The lack of informal protections in large partnerships, coupled with an explosion in the number and size of professional liability claims, has encouraged professionals to lobby governments to change the law. That tactic has worked in all provinces, other than Newfoundland and Labrador. Certain professional partnerships, such as lawyers and accountants, can agree to become **limited liability partnerships**. Under this special form of general partnership, individual partners are not personally liable for the professional negligence of their partners if certain requirements are met.[15] Most large law and accounting firms have now become limited liability partnerships. All partners remain personally liable for obligations other than negligence, and the limited liability partnership is the same as a general partnership in all other respects.

> in a **limited liability partnership**, individual partners are not personally liable for the professional negligence of their partners if certain requirements are met

Managing Liability Risk When You Are Not a Partner

You generally are *not* liable for partnership liabilities that arose before you joined, or after you left, the firm. However, you *may* be liable for a partnership obligation, if you **hold yourself out** as a partner or allow someone else to do so.[16] Suppose you allow your name to be associated with a partnership even though you are not a partner. Thinking you are a partner, a bank lends money to the partnership because it knows that you are personally creditworthy. The bank can seek repayment from you if it relied on your *apparent* membership in the firm when deciding to make the loan.[17] You are also at risk if, for instance, you allow your name to appear on the partnership's letterhead, invoices, or business sign. Significantly, however, you cannot be held liable unless you actually *hold yourself out* as a partner or *know* that your name was being associated with the partnership and do nothing about it.[18]

> **holding out** occurs when you represent yourself as a partner or allow someone else to do so

---

[15.] *Eg Limited Liability Partnerships Act*, SO 1998, c 2 (Ont.); *Partnership Act* RSA 2000, c P-3 (Alta); *Partnerships Amendment Act, 2004*, SBC 2004, c 38 (BC). Ontario recently passed a law allowing small partnerships to incorporate for tax purposes. Full corporate limited liability, however, is not granted: *Balanced Budgets for Brighter Futures Act, 2000*, SO 2000, c 42. Some other provinces have similar laws.

[16.] *BCPA* s 16; *NSPA* s 17; *OPA* s 15.

[17.] *Bet-Mur Investments Ltd v Spring* (1994) 20 OR (3d) 417 (Gen Div).

[18.] You cannot be held liable simply because you carelessly failed to realize that your name was being associated with the firm: *Tower Cabinet Co v Ingram* [1949] 1 All ER 1033 (DC).

The issue of holding out often arises when a partner leaves a firm. In most cases, you want to avoid responsibility for any debts that arise *after* that time. There are two groups of clients that should concern you.

- Clients who dealt with the firm *prior* to your departure. These clients may honestly continue to rely on your creditworthiness when dealing with the firm. You will continue to be liable to them until they learn of your departure.

- Clients who deal with the firm for the first time after your departure, or who never knew that you were a member of the firm. These clients cannot hold you liable unless you were held out to be a partner when they did business with the partnership.[19]

To manage those risks, you should ensure that clients who dealt with the firm before you left receive actual notice of your departure. You should also ensure that your name is deleted from the partnership registration filed with the provincial government. A notice published in a local paper may also be desirable, especially if the nature of the firm's business makes notice to each client impractical. You should only allow the firm to continue using your name if the partnership agrees to indemnify you for any liabilities that you might incur as a result.

Internal Organization of the Partnership

Since partnerships involve more than one person, they need rules to settle basic issues, such as what each partner will do for the business, and how responsibility will be shared if something goes wrong. The partnership legislation in each jurisdiction provides a kind of standard form agreement that applies unless the partners agree to something else. These **default rules** give partners great flexibility to customize structure to fit their particular needs.

default rules for the internal organization of a partnership in partnership statutes apply unless the partners agree to some other arrangement

The default rules governing partners' relations presume that all partners are *equal*, in terms of their financial interest *and* their rights to participate in management. In practice, however, that is hardly ever the case. Partners typically make unequal contributions of capital and services to the business, and their respective shares in the profits reflect those unequal contributions. Also, except in the smallest partnerships, partners generally delegate certain management functions to particular partners or committees. It is too cumbersome to have a firm run by many individuals.

In most cases, there is a significant difference between the statutory default rules and the parties' expectations. It is important to know what the default rules are, if only so that they can be altered by the partnership agreement. These are the most important default rules.[20]

- Each partner shares equally both in the capital of the partnership and in any partnership profits. They must also contribute equally to any losses incurred.

- Each partner is entitled to be indemnified for payments that they make in the ordinary course of the partnership business.

- A partner generally is not entitled to interest on capital that they contributed.

[19.] *BCPA* s 39; *NSPA* s 39; *OPA* s 36. In Ontario, publishing notice in the *Ontario Gazette* is sufficient to avoid liability to new clients of the firm.

[20.] This is the basic framework of default rules in *BCPA* ss 21–34, *NSPA* ss 22–34, and *OPA* ss 20–31. These rules vary slightly from one province to another.

- Each partner has a right to participate in the management of the partnership business.
- Decisions about ordinary matters connected with the partnership business may be decided by a majority of the partners, but unanimous consent is required for admission of a new partner, expulsion of a partner, or any change in the nature of the partnership business.
- Each partner has equal access to the partnership books.
- Any variation of the default rules requires unanimous consent.

Dissolution of Partnerships

Dissolution is the termination of the partnership relationship. Partnerships can be dissolved easily. Any partner may terminate the partnership by giving notice to the others. Partnerships may also be dissolved if a partner dies or becomes insolvent.[21] If you set up a partnership for a specific purpose or for a limited time, such as to operate a painting business for one summer, it dissolves upon the achievement of that purpose or the expiry of that time.[22]

> dissolution is the termination of the partnership relationship

Partnership legislation provides a basic process to deal with the claims that arise upon dissolution.

- First, debts and liabilities to persons who are not partners are paid.
- Second, debts to partners (other than advances of capital) are paid.
- Third, invested capital is returned to the partners.
- Fourth, if anything is left, it is paid out to the partners according to their respective rights to the profits. The statutory scheme with respect to what the partners are entitled to on dissolution may be modified or fleshed out in an agreement.[23]

Concept Summary 21.1 identifies some of the most important issues to be considered in drafting a partnership agreement in light of the dissolution and other default rules in partnership statutes.

CONCEPT SUMMARY 21.1

Key Issues to Address in a Partnership Agreement

Issue	Content
Name	What is the name of the partnership? Who will be entitled to use it if the partnership breaks up?
Membership of partnership	What criteria will be used for admission and expulsion? What process will be required to admit or expel a member?
Capitalization	What will be the capital contributions of the partners now and in the future?
Profits	How will the profits be shared between the partners? On what basis will they be paid?
Management	How will the partnership make decisions? What monitoring and control procedures will be put in place to guard against unauthorized liability and negligence? How will disputes be resolved?
Dissolution	What limits will be placed on the right of dissolution? Will death, insolvency, or resignation of a partner terminate the partnership for all partners? How will assets be distributed on dissolution?

[21.] *BCPA* ss 29, 36(1); *NSPA* ss 29, 36(1); *OPA* ss 26, 33.

[22.] *BCPA* s 30; *NSPA* s 30; *OPA* s 27.

[23.] *BCPA* s 47; *NSPA* s 47; *OPA* s 44.

Business Decision 21.1 asks you to consider whether a partnership is an appropriate form of business organization in a specific situation.

BUSINESS DECISION 21.1

Creation of a Partnership

Melvin and Erin have known each other since childhood, and trust and respect each other. They have an idea for a new business—Ramps R Us. They have noticed that many businesses around Saint John (where they live) do not have adequate access for people in wheelchairs. They believe that they could make money by supplying low-cost ramps to businesses. Melvin has experience with metal fabrication, and Erin has worked for several years in retail marketing. Their plan is that Erin will get orders from local businesses, and that Melvin will construct and install the ramps. To get started, they need $100 000 for the metal-fabricating equipment, rent, and initial marketing expenses.

Melvin has a new car, owns his house, and has $50 000 in savings, which he is willing to contribute to the business. He is the sole supporter of two small children. He also currently operates as a sole proprietor under the name of Mel's

Metal. Mel's Metal has made a few wheelchair ramps in the past. Mel intends to continue working full time at Mel's Metal, at least initially. He will work in the new business at nights and on weekends.

Erin is single and has no dependants. She has no cash and no source of income at the moment. She also has substantial outstanding debts to various financial institutions.

Erin wants to be able to make commitments to prospective customers without having to consult Melvin. Even though Melvin trusts Erin and will be busy with his work at Mel's Metal, he does not want Erin to be able to bind the business without his consent.

Question for Discussion

1. What are the advantages and disadvantages of using a partnership to carry on this business?

LIMITED PARTNERSHIPS

All jurisdictions in Canada recognize a special form of partnership called a limited partnership.[24] There are three essential distinctions between limited partnerships and general partnerships.

*a **limited partnership** is a partnership in which the personal liability of at least one partner is limited to the amount of the partner's investment in the business*

- First, in general partnerships, all partners have unlimited personal liability. But in **limited partnerships**, at least one of the partners, called a *general partner*, has unlimited liability, while at least one other, called a *limited partner*, has liability limited to the amount of their investment. Suppose you invested $5000 in a limited partnership as a limited partner. The partnership is sued by an unpaid creditor. All of the partnership assets *and* the personal assets of the general partner can be used to satisfy that debt. Your liability, however, is limited to the amount of your investment—$5000.

- Second, limited partnerships come into existence only when a partnership declaration is filed with the appropriate government authority. A general partnership comes into existence as soon as the partners start carrying on business together with a view to a profit.

- Third, limited partners can be agents or employees of the limited partnership. They will, however, lose their limited liability if they participate in controlling the business or if they allow their names to be used in the firm name (but not if they merely provide management advice). In practice, it is often difficult to know when advice ends and control begins.

---

24. *Eg BCPA*, Part 2; *Limited Partnerships Act*, RSNS 1989, c 259 (NS); and *Limited Partnerships Act*, RSO 1990, c L.16 (Ont).

For instance, in many limited partnerships, the general partner is a corporation. Someone may be both a limited partner in the partnership and a senior employee of the corporation. That person may manage the limited partnership, but in the capacity of an employee of the corporation. Since that limited partner is not in control of the business in a *personal* capacity, they may still have limited liability.[25]

Apart from these distinctions, most of the rules applicable to general partnerships apply to limited partnerships. Limited partnerships are usually attractive to passive investors who want to be treated as partners so they can deduct any partnership losses against their other income for tax purposes. Otherwise, they want their liability limited.

CORPORATIONS

The corporation is the most common form of business organization. It is used for all types and sizes of businesses, from one-person operations to large multinationals. In this chapter, we will introduce the basic characteristics of the corporation and the process of incorporation. We will restrict our discussion to general business corporations and exclude publicly owned entities and specialized corporations, like banks and charities, that are governed under their own legislation. In Chapter 22, we will consider the legal rules for corporate governance.

Incorporation Process

Unlike sole proprietorships and general partnerships, corporations do not come into existence simply because one or more people start doing business. A corporation is created only when certain documents are filed with the appropriate government office under either the federal *Canada Business Corporations Act* (*CBCA*) or one of its provincial or territorial counterparts.[26] Once incorporated, the company is governed by the laws of the jurisdiction where incorporation occurred. The corporate laws in Alberta, Manitoba, Newfoundland, New Brunswick, Ontario, and Saskatchewan follow the federal model.[27] Though the structure of the corporate law rules in Prince Edward Island, Quebec, British Columbia, and Nova Scotia are somewhat different from the *CBCA*, the effect is similar in most respects.[28] Under the *CBCA* and the provincial Acts that follow it, incorporation requires the filing of:

- articles of incorporation
- a name search report on the proposed name of the corporation
- the fee

---

[25] *Nordile Holdings Ltd v Breckenridge* (1992) 66 BCLR (2d) 183 (CA). The circumstances in which a limited partner loses limited liability are more restricted under the Manitoba *Partnerships Act*, RSM 1987, c P30, s 63.

[26] *Canada Business Corporations Act*, RSC 1985, c C-44 (Can).

[27] *Business Corporations Act*, RSA 2000, c B-9 (Alta); *Corporations Act*, RSM 1987, c C225 (Man); *Business Corporations Act*, SNB 1981, c B-9.1 (NB); *Corporations Act*, RSNL 1990, c. C-36 (Nfld & Lab); *Business Corporations Act*, RSO 1990, c B.16 (Ont); *The Business Corporations Act*, RSS 1978, c B-10 (Sask).

[28] *Business Corporations Act*, SBC 2002, c 57 (*BCBCA*) (BC); *Companies Act*, RSNS 1989, c 81, (*NSCA*) (NS); *Companies Act*, RSPEI 1988, c C-14 (*PEICA*) (PEI); *Companies Act*, RSQ, c C-38 (*QCA*) (Que). The basic architecture of these statutes differs from statues modelled on the *CBCA*.

the **articles of incorporation** define the corporation's basic characteristics

The **articles of incorporation** set out the fundamental characteristics of the corporation—its name, the class and number of shares authorized to be issued, the number of directors, any restrictions on transferring shares, and any restrictions on the business that the corporation may conduct.[29] Once the required documents are properly filed along with the fee, the responsible official issues a certificate, which is then attached to the articles. That official document certifies that the corporation was incorporated on the date of the certificate.

The actual process of filing the requisite documents and receiving a certificate of incorporation is straightforward. Incorporation kits even permit do-it-yourself incorporations. However, since tax planning and other issues can arise in connection with incorporation, it is often wise to seek professional advice.

Upon incorporation, the company can start doing business. The business may be entirely new, or an existing business may be transferred to it. Several more steps are required, however, before the corporation is fully organized. First, the directors named in the incorporating documents must have a meeting and pass a resolution to issue shares to the shareholders. At that meeting, the directors usually adopt arrangements for carrying on the formal legal business of the corporation. The directors decide, among other things:

- the notice to be given for meetings of directors and shareholders
- what constitutes a quorum for meetings
- who can sign contracts on behalf of the corporation
- what officers the corporation will have

a **general bylaw** sets out the arrangements for carrying on the legal business of the corporation

Those arrangements are usually set out in a **general bylaw**.[30] To take effect, a bylaw must be passed by the directors, but it only continues in effect if it is passed by the shareholders at their next meeting.

If a corporation has few shareholders, the final organizational step is usually the creation of a *shareholders' agreement*. Corporate statutes set default rules for the rights and obligations of shareholders in a corporation. A **shareholders' agreement** is a contract between shareholders that customizes their relationship by providing rules that are better suited to their particular needs. Shareholders' agreements are discussed in Chapter 22.

a **shareholders' agreement** is a contract between shareholders that customizes their relationship

a **minute book** is a book in which corporate records are kept

The corporation must maintain the articles of incorporation, bylaws, shareholders' resolutions, and any shareholders' agreement at its registered office, usually in a **minute book**. Shareholders and creditors must be given access to those documents. Articles, as well as any other documents (such as annual information filings) that are filed with a government agency, are maintained by the agency in a publicly accessible record.

A corporation does not have to register under provincial business names legislation unless it uses something other than its corporate name. However, it may require a business licence. Also, if a corporation wants to conduct business outside of the province or territory where it incorporated, it may need permission from the government of the jurisdiction where it wants to operate. Corporations incorporated under the *CBCA*, however, have a right to carry on business throughout Canada.

---

[29] The equivalent of articles under the *NSCA* is the memorandum of association; under the new *BCBCA* it is the notice of articles, combined with some elements of the articles and an incorporation agreement; under the *PEICA* it is the letters patent.

[30] Many of the provisions contained in a by-law are included in the articles under the *BCBCA* and the *NSCA*.

Characteristics of Corporations

Separate Legal Existence

Unlike a sole proprietorship or a partnership, a corporation has a *separate legal existence*. The corporation *itself* carries on business, owns property, possesses rights, and incurs liabilities (including liability for crimes and torts). In most ways, a corporation has the same rights, powers, and privileges as a natural person. Shareholders have a bundle of rights in relation to the corporation through their ownership of shares. Shareholders do not, however, own the business that is carried on by the corporation, or the property belonging to it. This contrasts with sole proprietors and partners, who carry on the business, own the property of the business, possess its rights, and are responsible for its liabilities directly.

Separate legal existence has three important implications.

- First, a shareholder can be an employee or a creditor of the corporation.[31] The shareholder and the corporation are two distinct entities.

- Second, for the same reason, the corporation is unaffected if a shareholder dies or withdraws from the business.

- Third, the corporation is treated separately for income tax purposes. Income or losses that are generated through the business are attributed to the corporation and taxed at the corporate level. Shareholders are taxed only when they personally receive something from the corporation, such as a *dividend*. A **dividend** is a payment of cash or property by the corporation to shareholders, which is authorized by the directors. The payment of dividends is one way that shareholders receive a return on their investment in the corporation. Concept Summary 21.2 summarizes the taxation of the main forms of business organization discussed in this chapter.

> a dividend is a payment by the corporation to shareholders of cash or property which is authorized by the directors

---

CONCEPT SUMMARY 21.2

Taxation of Business Organizations

Sole Proprietorship	Partnership	Corporation
Income (or loss) from business added to (or deducted from) individual sole proprietor's taxable income	Income (or loss) from business calculated for partnership but added to (or deducted from) individual partner's taxable income • in proportion to partner's entitlement to profits • whether or not cash distributed to partner	Income (or loss) from business added to (or deducted from) corporation's taxable income • shareholders only pay tax on any distribution actually received from corporation (*eg* dividends)

It is often said that shareholders have **limited liability** for the obligations of the corporation. Strictly speaking, however, shareholders have *no direct liability* for a corporation's obligations. To obtain shares, shareholders provide the corporation with money, property, or services. Shareholders are said to have limited liability because their maximum loss in connection with the business is limited to the value of what they transfer to the corporation in return for their

> limited liability means that shareholders cannot lose more than they invest in the corporation in return for their shares

---

[31.] *Salomon v Salomon & Co* [1897] AC 22 (HL).

shares. Creditors, employees, and other claimants against the corporation can demand to be paid out of the corporation's assets. But once the corporation's assets are exhausted, the creditors cannot claim against the shareholders personally. In the worst case, if all the assets of the corporation are taken by creditors, then the shareholder's shares may be worth nothing. They will have lost all their investment—but nothing more. Limiting the risk for shareholders in this way—a key characteristic of the corporation—is intended to encourage entrepreneurship and shareholder investment.

Limited liability effectively shifts the risk of loss from the shareholders to the creditors and other stakeholders of a corporation. Creditors can recover what is owed them only from the assets owned by the corporation. If a corporation has few assets, other parties may refuse to lend money to it unless a creditworthy shareholder provides a *personal guarantee* for the corporation's debt. If a shareholder gives such a guarantee and the corporation defaults, the shareholder is personally liable for the corporation's obligation.[32]

piercing the corporate veil occurs when a court refuses to give effect to the separate legal existence of the corporation and imposes personal liability on a shareholder

While the courts generally adhere to the concept of limited liability, they sometimes disregard the separate existence of the corporation in relation to a specific claim. In other words, they **pierce the corporate veil**.[33] For instance, a judge may permit a creditor of a corporation to claim directly against a controlling shareholder if the corporation has insufficient assets to satisfy the creditor's claim. Disregarding the corporation in this way does not destroy its separate existence for all purposes, but only for the *limited purpose* of granting relief to the creditor directly against the shareholder.

It is very difficult to predict when a court will pierce the corporate veil, although usually there must be some kind of serious wrongdoing or unfairness or both. When a business has been incorporated to do something (or facilitate the doing of something) that would be illegal or improper for the individual shareholders to do personally, the courts have disregarded the separate existence of the corporation. That occurs when a corporation was used to commit a fraud, as in Case Brief 21.1. Ethical Perspective 21.1 (on page 507) presents a case in which the arguments for piercing the corporate veil are not as clear.

CASE BRIEF 21.1

Big Bend Hotel Ltd v Security Mutual Casualty Co (1979) 19 BCLR 102 (SC)

Kumar operated a hotel that was destroyed in a fire. Due to suspicious circumstances surrounding the fire, his fire insurance was cancelled. Kumar decided to acquire another hotel but knew that he would be turned down for fire insurance. He therefore incorporated Big Bend Hotel Ltd and had it acquire the hotel and apply for the insurance. The hotel burnt down. The insurance company refused to pay. The corporation sued for payment of the insurance proceeds.[34]

The court denied the corporation's claim. It held that the insurance company would not have issued the policy to Kumar. Even though the corporation was a distinct legal person from Kumar, it was being used solely to disguise the real person behind the corporation. The insurance company should be able to disregard the separate personality of the corporation and treat the policy as if it had been applied for by Kumar directly. On that basis, the insurance company did not have to pay because Kumar had fraudulently failed to disclose the prior fire loss.

---

[32] Chapter 22 discusses how shareholders may incur liability as directors and officers when they act in that capacity; Chapter 23 discusses guarantees.

[33] *Littlewoods Mail Order Stores Ltd v Inland Revenue Commissioners* [1969] 3 All ER 855 (HL).

[34] Property insurance was discussed in Chapter 17.

ETHICAL PERSPECTIVE 21.1

Limited Liability[35]

Carleton operated a taxi business using a number of separate corporations, each of which owned two cabs. Carleton owned all the shares of each corporation and managed the corporation's business. Each corporation maintained the minimum amount of third-party liability insurance coverage required by law—$10 000. Walkovszky was hit by a taxicab owned by one of Carleton's corporations and suffered serious injuries. She sued the corporation that owned the car and was awarded compensatory damages in an amount that far exceeded $10 000. However, because the defendant corporation had no assets other than the cars, which were not worth much, she could not actually collect much more than the $10 000 that was available under the corporation's insurance policy.

Questions for Discussion

1. Is it appropriate for a person to carry on a taxi business though a corporation with assets that are insufficient to meet the reasonably foreseeable liabilities resulting from car accidents?

2. Should the court disregard the separate legal existence of the corporation and hold Carleton personally liable?

Separation of Ownership and Management

There is a legal distinction between managers of a corporation—the directors and officers—and the shareholders. By a majority vote, the shareholders elect a **board of directors** to manage the corporation. Those directors then delegate the responsibility for managing the corporation to the **officers** that they appoint. It is the directors who have the authority to monitor and supervise the officers' management of the corporation's business. Shareholders do not participate, as shareholders, in management. Unlike partners, they are not agents of the firm. In many corporations, especially small ones, however, these legally distinct roles are played by the same people: The shareholders are also the directors and officers. But in larger businesses, directors and officers are unlikely to hold all of the shares of a corporation. Very large corporations, like Bell Canada Enterprises Inc, have thousands of shareholders, including the officers and directors. The separation of ownership and management creates a number of issues regarding internal relationships in the corporation that are discussed in Chapter 22, including how shareholders can ensure that management acts in their interests.

a board of directors consists of the individuals whom shareholders elect to manage the corporation

officers are the people to whom the board of directors delegates responsibility for managing the corporation

Corporate Finance

Corporations are financed in two basic ways:

- **equity**—the shareholders' investment in the corporation
- **debt**—loans that have been made to the corporation by shareholders, commercial lenders, or other creditors

There is a basic difference between equity and debt. Debt is a claim for a *fixed amount*. The **shares** issued in connection with an equity investment represent a claim to the *residual value* of the corporation after the claims of all creditors have been paid. The value of that residual claim is a function of the value of the corporation's business. Valuing a business is complex and imprecise

equity is what the shareholders have invested in the corporation in return for shares

debt consists of loans that have been made to the corporation

shares represent a claim on the residual assets of the corporation after the claims of all creditors have been paid

35. *Walkovszky v Carleton* 223 NE 2d 6 (NY CA 1966).

because it depends on numerous factors that change over time. The value of a business depends, in part, on the value of the tangible assets owned by the business, which may be difficult to assess. Increasingly, it also depends on intangible assets, which are even harder to value. How much is Microsoft's copyright in Windows worth? The value of a business is also affected by the corporation's plans for it. Most businesses are worth more as a **going concern**, that is, as an operating unit, than as a collection of assets that will be sold piecemeal. The expected future growth of a business is also a significant factor. Because businesses are hard to value, the residual claim that shares represent is also difficult to value. Shares are attractive because their value increases with the value of the business. Unlike debt, there is no limit on what they may be worth; nor, however, is there any guarantee that they will have any value at all.

the going concern value represents the value of a corporation as an operating unit

There is another critical difference between debt and equity. If a debt obligation is not repaid, there is a breach of contract. The creditor can sue for damages and even force the corporation into bankruptcy. But if an obligation to a shareholder, such as a dividend payment, is not met, the shareholder cannot put the corporation into bankruptcy. In fact, there may not be any remedy at all, as discussed in Chapter 22. Since shareholder rights are not as easily enforced as debt-holder rights, and because the value of shares depends on the residual value of the corporation, shares are much riskier than debt.

A corporation can have different classes of shares with different characteristics. Every corporation must have shares that provide at least three basic rights:

- to vote for the election of directors
- to receive dividends when declared by the board of directors
- to receive the property that remains after a corporation has been dissolved and all prior claims have been satisfied

These basic rights do not have to be attached to any *single* class of shares—they can be allocated to different classes, so long as all shareholders in a particular class have the same rights. In practice, most corporations have one class of shares, called **common shares**, that includes all three basic rights. A corporation may also have *preferred shares*. Usually **preferred shares** are entitled to receive fixed dividends on a regular basis. Those shares enjoy two kinds of preferences: (i) dividends must be paid on preferred shares before they are paid on common shares, and (ii) on dissolution, the investment in preferred shares is repaid before the investment in common shares. Preferred shares are therefore less risky than common shares. On the other hand, they usually have no voting rights and no claim to the residual value of the corporation after the amount invested has been repaid.

common shares usually carry three basic rights

preferred shares usually are entitled to receive fixed dividends on a regular basis and a return of the amount invested before any payments are made to common shares

A wide range of names and characteristics can be given to shares. The specific bundle of rights that shareholders have is set out in the articles and is designed to create shares that will be attractive to prospective shareholders. The flexibility of equity financing is a significant advantage of the corporation.

CHAPTER SUMMARY

The sole proprietorship is the simplest form of business organization. It comes into existence whenever a person begins carrying on a business. A sole proprietor has unlimited personal liability for the obligations of the business and is solely entitled to its benefits. Sole proprietorships (and other forms of business organization) may have to register under provincial business names legislation, and obtain a business licence.

A partnership comes into existence when two or more people start to carry on business together with a view to a profit. Partnerships are governed by special statutes in each province that provide (i) default rules governing the relations of partners to each other, and (ii) mandatory rules governing the relationship of the partnership to outsiders. Partners are personally responsible for the obligations of the business and are entitled to the benefits from it. Each partner is considered the agent of the partnership capable of creating partnership obligations within the usual course of its business.

The risks associated with unlimited personal liability, and the ability of all partners to bind the partnership, are addressed legally by the fiduciary duty owed by each partner to the partnership and by provisions in partnership agreements. In smaller partnerships, those legal protections are supplemented by informal monitoring of each partner by the other partners who work in the business. A limited partnership is a special form of partnership in which at least one partner's liability is limited to the amount it invested in the partnership.

A corporation is formed when certain documents are filed with the appropriate government authority. A corporation is legally separate from its shareholders and managers. The corporation alone is responsible for the obligations of the business that it carries on and is solely entitled to the benefits from the business. Shareholders have a financial interest in the corporation represented by their shares. They elect directors who have responsibility for managing the business and affairs of the corporation. Directors usually delegate some of their management responsibility to officers.

A corporation can be financed in two ways. Equity is what the shareholders have invested in the corporation in return for shares. Debt consists of loans that have been made to the corporation. Shares represent a claim to the residual value of the corporation after all others with claims against the corporation are paid. Because they rank last, shares are a riskier investment than debt.

REVIEW QUESTIONS

1. What is the main purpose of business organizations law?

2. What do you have to do to create a sole proprietorship?

3. Who is responsible for the obligations of a business that is carried on by a sole proprietor? What does this mean in practice for sole proprietors?

4. Can a person who is a sole proprietor also be an employee of the sole proprietorship? Explain your answer.

5. What are the major limitations of the sole proprietorship?

6. Is a partnership a separate legal entity? Are there some circumstances in which it is treated like a separate entity?

7. What are the criteria for the creation of a partnership?

8. Identify three situations in which sharing of profits does not result in the creation of a partnership.

9. If you were entering a business relationship and did not want to be a partner, what could you do?

10. What is mutual agency? What are the implications of mutual agency in terms of the risks that individual partners face?

11. If you are a partner, how do you protect yourself against the risk of other partners creating unauthorized obligations for the firm?

12. What is a limited liability partnership, and how is it different from a limited partnership?

13. How can you avoid being held liable for obligations that a partnership incurs after you have left that partnership?

14. What kinds of rules does provincial partnership legislation provide for the internal organization of partnerships? How are these rules addressed in a partnership agreement?

15. How is a corporation created? Why would you need a lawyer to advise you on creating a corporation?

16. What key documents define the characteristics of a corporation?

17. What does organizing a corporation involve?

18. "A corporation is a separate legal entity." What does that statement mean?

19. Does limited liability always protect a shareholder?

20. What are the differences between debt and equity from an investor's point of view? From the corporation's point of view?

CASES AND PROBLEMS

1. Oren and Jenna carry on their business of buying and selling real estate as a partnership. Each is entitled to 50 percent of the profits from the business. Oren bought and sold a parcel of real estate without Jenna's permission or knowledge. Oren took all $100 000 of the profits from the sale himself. Is there a legal basis for Jenna to claim compensation from Oren? If so, how much is she entitled to receive?

2. Carol carried on a consulting business as a sole proprietorship. She met Steven Stevenson at a conference. Steven told Carol that he was a "senior litigator and partner" in a mid-sized Saskatoon law firm and gave her a business card that set out his name and the name "Steven, Smith, Jones and Khan, Barristers and Solicitors." Carol did work for Steven and billed him $20 000. While providing the services the respondent received letters from Steven on a letterhead bearing, at the top, the same firm name as the business card and the full names of Steven, Smith, Jones and Khan at the bottom. Steven did not pay. Carol sued Steven along with Smith, Jones and Khan. Assuming that Steven and the three other individuals named on the letterhead were not partners, will Carol succeed in holding them liable for her account? What else would you need to know to answer the question?

3. You are the president of a large steel manufacturer, and all of your corporation's legal work is done by one of the largest law firms in the country, Osman & Co. Your company regularly relies on opinions from Osman & Co in making million-dollar business decisions. You have never worried about receiving bad advice from the firm because, if the firm was negligent and gave the wrong advice, the firm's insurance and the assets of all its rich partners would be available to satisfy any judgment in your favour. Today, you receive in the mail an announcement that Osman & Co is becoming a limited liability partnership. Would you have any concerns about this change and, if so, what might you do about it?

4. John and Rita are partners in a marketing firm. Under the terms of the partnership agreement, John and Rita each contributed $15 000 to the capital of the partnership and each is entitled to receive 50 percent of the business profits. Recently, the firm has been experiencing financial difficulty. John and Rita have therefore decided to dissolve the partnership. John and Rita are concerned that the partnership may not be able to pay off all of its debts and liabilities. The partnership owes $5000 to its landlord and has a bank loan of $10 000. As well, John has loaned $7000 to the partnership. They cannot decide which debts to pay off first, but believe that they are entitled to be paid first since they contributed the most to the partnership and have the most to lose. Can John and Rita pay themselves first? Assuming that the assets of the partnership are $30 000, how would they be distributed?

5. Bobby was one of several limited partners in a limited partnership called Typecast Limited Partnership, as well as the sole shareholder and president of a corporation named Live Life Magazine Inc, which was the general partner of Typecast. In his capacity as president of Live Life, he acted as the manager of the limited partnership. On behalf of the limited partnership, Bobby negotiated a contract with Gold Dust Graphics Ltd to supply printing services worth $50 000. Gold Dust paid the $50 000 to Typecast, but the limited partnership failed to perform the services. Gold Dust sued the limited partnership and got a judgment for $50 000, only to discover that neither Typecast nor the general partner, Live Life, has any assets. Can Gold Dust seek to recover its $50 000 from Bobby?

6. In 1995, Pan and Vladimir set up a mechanical contracting business in rented premises in Toronto, operating under the name Lakeside Contracting. Vladimir contributed tools and a truck to the business, while Pan contributed no assets. Vladimir was the only one with signing authority on the Lakeside Contracting bank account. In 2000, Vladimir bought the premises in which the business operated. From the start of the business, Pan and Vladimir worked side by side in serving the customers of the business, performing essentially the same functions and sharing management responsibilities. Pan was paid $500 per week by Vladimir, though often he received more out of cash payments made by customers of the business. Vladimir paid himself varying amounts, from time to time, out of the Lakeside Contracting bank account and from cash received by the business. In 2005, Pan sought a declaration that he and Vladimir were partners and that half the assets of the business were his. Is Pan a partner and entitled to one half of the assets of the business? What else would you need to know to help you to answer the question?

7. For over five years, Rick was the CEO of JB Guitars Inc, a corporation operating a chain of retail guitar stores. He had gained tremendous practical experience and decided to start his own business selling guitars. However, he had entered into an agreement with JB Guitars when he first started working there, under which he promised that he would not carry on a competing business for two years after he ended his employment with JB Guitars. To avoid breaching that contract, Rick incorporated a corporation named Generation X Guitars Inc to carry on the business. He is the sole shareholder, director, and president. Rick's old employer claims that the new corporation is just a way of getting around the non-competition agreement and sued for a court order prohibiting Generation X Guitars from carrying a business competing with JB Guitars. Will JB Guitars be successful?

8. Dimitri operated a small dry-cleaning business as a sole proprietorship. His accountant recommended that he transfer the business to a corporation—in which Dimitri would be the sole shareholder, officer, and director—to limit his liability. Dimitri did set up the corporation and transferred his business to it. Subsequently, when he renewed his fire insurance on the business assets, however, he did not name the corporation as the owner of the assets and the person to be compensated in the event of fire. Instead, he named himself. Later, a fire destroyed all the assets of the business. The insurance company refused to pay on the basis that under the terms of the policy only a person with an insurable interest in the property could validly obtain insurance. A person has an insurable interest in property if they would be hurt as a consequence of the property's loss or damage. The insurance company said that since the corporation owned the property, only it had an insurable interest. Is Dimitri entitled to claim compensation under the insurance policy?

9. Seth and Marta have decided to start a travel agency business using a corporation. Seth will make only a small initial financial investment in the corporation, but will manage the business on a daily basis. Since the business will succeed or fail on his efforts, he wants to have his returns from the business depend entirely on how the business is doing. Marta works for the public service and is the sole support for her family of three. She recently sold her house and has $150 000, which she wants to invest in the business. Marta is not interested in working in the business and is content to have Seth manage it on his own. Her only concern is that she wants to receive a fixed annual return of 10 percent on her investment. What kind of shares would Seth and Marta each want?

10. Alice has been carrying on a sporting goods business in Ottawa as a sole proprietorship under the name A-Sport since 1999. By the spring of 2004, she was unable to cover the substantial costs associated with the business. By September 2004, she had sold many of her personal assets, including her house, to pay the business's expenses. Alice is very worried that she will lose the business and not be able to support her daughter, since she is a single mother and has no other source of income.

In September 2004, Alice met Mario at a trade show in Monalso as a sole proprietorship. The key to his success has been a combination of innovative inventory management techniques and the use of aggressive television advertising. Mario is married with three children.

Alice and Mario talk about the possibility of carrying on the A-Sport business in Ottawa together in some way. Mario has $100 000 available to invest in Alice's business and has substantial other assets, including three store premises and a warehouse in Toronto. They agree on the following.

- Alice will contribute all of her interest in the A-Sport business.

- Mario will contribute $100 000 in cash.

- Alice will manage the A-Sport stores on a day-to-day basis, while Mario will be responsible for marketing and inventory management. Mario will continue to spend most of his time in Toronto looking after his business there.

- All major decisions for the business will require the agreement of both Mario and Alice.

What issues should Alice and Mario address before going into business as a partnership?

11. Based on the facts in Problem 10, how would these issues be addressed differently if Alice and Mario were to set up a corporation to accomplish their business objectives?

12. Peter and Sarah were both accountants carrying on business as sole proprietors. They decided to enter into an arrangement that would reduce their expenses.

- They rented premises consisting of three offices and a reception area, out of which they would both practice. Each signed the lease as a tenant.

- They hired a secretary to work for both of them.

- They will each contribute equally to the office expenses.

- Apart from those shared expenses, all expenses are the responsibility of the person incurring them.

- All decisions regarding the management of the office (such as the secretary's rate of pay) require the consent of both Peter and Sarah.

- Each will bill and be exclusively entitled to the fees received in return for their own work.

Is this a partnership? To be certain, what other information would you need?

WEBLINKS

Business Organizations

Industry Canada—Corporations Directorate
http://strategis.ic.gc.ca/sc_mrksv/corpdir/engdoc/homepage.html

This website offers information on incorporation under the federal *Canada Business Corporations Act* (*CBCA*), including such important issues as how to choose a corporate name. It also allows you to conduct the entire *CBCA* incorporation process online.

Manitoba Companies Office   www.gov.mb.ca/cca/comp_off/index.html

This website is similar to other sites maintained by many provincial and territorial governments that offer information on the process of incorporation under provincial law. This site also enables searches for corporate, partnership, and sole proprietorship names in use in Manitoba.

Canadalegal.com   www.canadalegal.com/gosite.asp?s=4557

On this site is a detailed discussion on how to choose the right form of business organization, including both legal and business issues, such as selecting a corporate name and registering a sole proprietorship, partnership, or corporation.

National Library of Canada   www.collectionscanada.ca/caninfo/ep034.htm

This site provides links to sites containing all federal and provincial laws (except the laws of Prince Edward Island and Newfoundland and Labrador). By visiting the sites for each jurisdiction, you can find their statutes on partnerships, limited partnerships, and corporations.

ADDITIONAL RESOURCES FOR CHAPTER 21 ON THE COMPANION WEBSITE

(www.pearsoned.ca/mcinnes)

In addition to self-test multiple-choice, true-false, and short essay questions (all with immediate feedback), three additional Cases and Problems (with suggested answers), and links to useful Web destinations, the Companion Website provides the following resources for Chapter 21:

- Business Decision 21W—Partnership Tax Losses and the Creation of a Partnership

Provincial Material

- **British Columbia:** Sole Proprietorships, Partnerships, Limited Partnership, Limited Liability Partnership, Business Corporations, Incorporation, Societies and Associations, Business Name, Corporate Name Registration

- **Alberta:** *Business Corporations Act*, Incorporation, Limited Liability Partnerships, Limited Partnerships, Partnership in Alberta, Pre-Incorporation Contracts, Income Trusts, Other Incorporated Bodies, Professional Corporations, Taxation of Corporations, Unlimited Liability Corporations

- **Manitoba and Saskatchewan:** Legal Requirements of the Sole Proprietorship (Government Regulations), Limited Liability Partnerships, Limited Partnerships, Non-Share Capital Corporations, Incorporation Process

- **Ontario:** Articles of Incorporation, Business Names, Fiduciary Duty, Limited Liability Partnerships, Limited Partnerships, Multi-disciplinary Partnerships, Not for Profit Corporations, Ontario Corporations, Partnership Agreements, Professional Corporations, Prospectus, Reporting Issuers, Registration of Partnership, Securities Legislation

22 Legal Rules for Corporate Governance

CHAPTER OVERVIEW

OBJECTIVES

After completing this chapter you should be able to:

1. Describe the basic allocation of power and responsibility in the corporation among directors, officers, and shareholders.

2. Explain how the allocation of power contemplated in corporate law does not always operate in practice.

3. Identify four common situations in which the personal interests of directors and officers may be in conflict with the best interests of the corporation.

4. Explain the legal standard of care that management must observe when making business judgments.

5. Determine what the fiduciary duty, the duty of care, and the oppression remedy require of management in specific situations.

6. Describe one of the few corporate law rules that are designed to protect creditors.

7. Outline five legal strategies available to shareholders for ensuring that management is accountable to them.

8. Explain when a corporation will be liable for torts and crimes due to the actions of people working on its behalf.

9. Identify whether a corporation's employee has authority to enter into a contract on behalf of the corporation.

10. Identify the liability risks associated with being a director or officer and some strategies that can be used to avoid these risks.

The rules for how corporations are governed in Canada have a fundamental impact on how they are structured. Rules defining when someone can bind a corporation to a contract, for example, affect how corporations organize their contract approval process to ensure that contracts are not entered into unless they are properly authorized. Corporate governance rules also affect incentives for investors to invest in businesses, and for managers to work for businesses. One key issue is how management is made accountable to investors. Without sufficient accountability, shareholders will not invest. However, accountability obligations must not be so great that they interfere with management's ability to do its job or discourage capable people from becoming managers.

In this chapter, we discuss the basic legal rules for corporate governance in Canada. We begin by laying out the distribution of power and responsibility among directors, officers, and shareholders as set out in the *Canada Business Corporations Act* (*CBCA*) and most other corporate statutes in Canada.[1] Next, we look at the standards for management behaviour that are imposed by corporate statutes to ensure management accountability to shareholders. Those standards include the fiduciary duty and duty of care. We also look at the procedures that shareholders can use to enforce those standards.

Management also has responsibilities to non-shareholder stakeholders, such as employees, creditors, and the public. In this chapter, we look at situations in which corporations become liable in contract, tort, and criminal law, and the implications that these liability rules have for corporate organization. Another important aspect of the governance scheme are the regulatory statutes designed to protect the public, many of which impose personal liability on corporate managers. Statutes that impose fines on directors for environmental damage caused by corporate activities are one example. Environmental and other forms of regulation are discussed in Chapter 25.

MANAGEMENT AND CONTROL OF THE CORPORATION

Power and responsibility in the corporation belong to different groups of people.

shareholders are the residual claimants to the assets of the corporation and elect the directors

- **Shareholders** are entitled to the assets of the corporation remaining after all the creditors are paid on its dissolution. Their only powers are to vote for the election of directors, to appoint the auditor, and to vote on proposals made to them. As shareholders, they do not participate in managing the ordinary business of the corporation.

directors are responsible for managing or supervising the management of the business of the corporation and its internal affairs

- **Directors** are responsible for managing or supervising the management of the business of the corporation and its internal affairs, including issuing shares, declaring dividends, and calling shareholder meetings.

officers are appointed by the directors of a corporation and exercise management powers delegated to them by the directors

- **Officers** are appointed by directors and exercise substantial management powers delegated to them by the directors.

[1.] *Canada Business Corporations Act*, RSC 1985, c C-44 (*CBCA*) (Can); *Business Corporations Act*, RSA 2000, c B-9 (*ABCA*) (Alta); *Corporations Act*, RSM 1987, c C225 (*MBCA*) (Man); *Business Corporations Act*, SNB 1981, c B-9.1 (*NBBCA*) (NB); *Corporations Act*, RSNL 1990, c C-36 (*NCA*) (Nfld & Lab); *Business Corporations Act*, RSO 1990, c B.16 (*OBCA*) (Ont); *Business Corporations Act*, RSS 1978, c B-10 (*SBCA*) (Sask). In subsequent notes, references will be made to illustrative provisions, rather than to all statutes. As noted in Chapter 21, corporate statutes in British Columbia, Quebec, Nova Scotia, and Prince Edward Island are based on different models. Nevertheless, most of the discussion in this chapter is equally applicable to corporations incorporated in those jurisdictions.

Figure 22.1 lays out the relationships among these three groups of people.

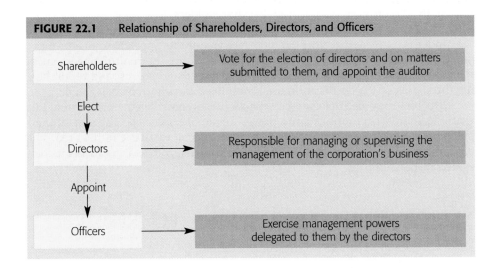

FIGURE 22.1   Relationship of Shareholders, Directors, and Officers

Shareholders → Vote for the election of directors and on matters submitted to them, and appoint the auditor

Elect

Directors → Responsible for managing or supervising the management of the corporation's business

Appoint

Officers → Exercise management powers delegated to them by the directors

HOW DIRECTORS AND OFFICERS EXERCISE POWER

Directors

Under the *CBCA*, the first directors of a corporation are those named in the articles of incorporation. These directors hold office until the first meeting of shareholders, which must be held within 18 months of incorporation.[2] At that meeting and others at which an election is required, shareholders must, by simple majority vote, elect directors. Some corporate statutes impose Canadian residency requirements for some proportion of directors. Under the *CBCA*, it is 25 percent for most corporations.[3]

Directors exercise their power collectively, primarily at meetings. However, a written resolution signed by all directors is as effective as a resolution passed at a meeting. As Chapter 21 explained, the corporation's bylaws typically contain its rules for calling and conducting meetings, such as the necessary quorum and who is the chair. Corporate statutes provide some default rules if the corporation has not set its own.

Officers

Nothing in Canadian corporate legislation addresses what officers a corporation should have or what they are to do. Most corporations have officers called chief executive officer (CEO), president, and secretary. A common corporate structure gives the CEO overall responsibility for running the corporation's business, while the day-to-day operations are delegated to others who report to the CEO. Directors can be officers, but they need not be.

---

[2] *CBCA* s 133; *OBCA* s 119.

[3] *CBCA* s 105(3). In some provinces, such as Ontario, a majority of directors must be Canadian residents (*OBCA* s 123).

Corporate statutes give directors the power to designate offices, like president, and to specify the duties of those offices. Usually this is done in a bylaw passed by directors and approved by shareholders just after incorporation. After setting up the offices, the directors appoint people to fill them.

Under the *CBCA*, directors can delegate any of their powers to one or more officers, except for certain key powers relating to the internal management of the corporation. Issuing shares, declaring dividends on shares, and repurchasing the shares of the corporation are functions that cannot be delegated.[4]

Directors may also delegate power to a person outside the corporation. For example, many corporations grant power to manage some specific area of their business to a management company that has special expertise in the area. The directors remain responsible for supervising the delegate as it performs its delegated responsibilities.

MANAGEMENT'S DUTIES TO THE CORPORATION

Fiduciary Duty

the fiduciary duty is the duty of officers and directors to act honestly and in good faith with a view to the best interests of the corporation

The **fiduciary duty** is the most important legal standard of behaviour for officers and directors. Section 122(1)(a) of the *CBCA* defines this duty.

> Each director and officer in exercising his powers and discharging his duties shall. . . act honestly and in good faith with a view to the best interests of the corporation. . . .

What the fiduciary duty requires in specific situations can be elusive. The duty to act honestly is straightforward: Directors and officers cannot defraud the corporation, such as by stealing corporate assets. Beyond honesty, directors and officers must try to do what is best for the corporation and must not put their personal interests ahead of the interests of the corporation.

The fiduciary duty is owed to the corporation, not to the shareholders or to employees, customers, suppliers, creditors, the public, or any other corporate stakeholder. It is often difficult, however, to define what the interests of the corporation are. For example, is it in the corporation's best interests to pay high wages or to keep wages as low as possible? While high wages may lead to happy, productive workers, it may reduce cash flow available to pay off creditors. Does the obligation of management to act in the best interests of the corporation require it to try to accommodate the divergent interests of employees and creditors?

The courts have avoided this problem by treating the interests of the corporation as defined by the interests of shareholders: Whatever maximizes the value of shareholders' investment in the corporation's shares is in the best interests of the corporation. No corporation will maximize share value if it completely ignores the interests of its employees, customers, creditors, and other stakeholders, but management is not permitted to favour the interests of other stakeholders at the expense of share value.

Managers must be particularly concerned about their fiduciary duty when their personal interests and their duty to the corporation conflict. We will discuss the most common situations in which such conflicts may arise.

---

4. *ABCA* s 110; *CBCA* s 115(3); *OBCA* s 127(3).

Transacting with the Corporation

A conflict of interest arises when a director or officer contracts with the corporation. Suppose you have an opportunity to sell goods to a corporation of which you are a director. As the seller, you want to negotiate the highest possible price for your goods. However, the corporation's interest is precisely the opposite. It wants to get the goods for the lowest possible price. If, as a director, you are responsible for negotiating the contract on behalf of the corporation, you have a serious conflict of interest. Your duty binds you to do whatever is in your power to get the lowest price for the corporation. At the same time, your personal interest is in selling for the highest price. Even if you are not directly involved in the negotiations on behalf of the corporation, as a director, you may be in a position to influence the corporation's decision making either directly, as a member of the board if the contract must be approved by the board, or indirectly, by virtue of your relationship with the corporation and its personnel. A conflict still exists and may result in an unfavourable transaction for the corporation.

Historically, because of the inevitable conflict between duty and personal interest, a fiduciary was prohibited from participating personally in any transaction with the corporation. This creates a practical problem where the best price or the only source of supply is a director or officer or a business related to a director or officer. This problem often arises in transactions between corporations with common ownership that do business with each other. Consider two corporations under common ownership where one supplies the raw materials that the other uses in its business.

The solution to this problem in the *CBCA* and most other Canadian statutes is to permit a transaction between the corporation and a director or officer (or a business related to them) *if procedural safeguards are observed*. The director or officer must give adequate notice of the interest and may not vote on the approval of the contract by the board of directors. As well, the contract must be fair and reasonable to the corporation. In practice, notice regarding the interest should be recorded in the minutes of the board meeting at which the contract is approved. Compliance with these requirements is the only way to avoid a fiduciary breach. If this scheme is not complied with, the corporation may refuse to complete the transaction.[5]

Taking Corporate Opportunities

A conflict between personal interest and fiduciary duty arises when the fiduciary considers taking advantage of some project or opportunity in which the corporation has an interest. This situation often arises because a principal task of management is to choose the projects the corporation should invest in—acquiring an asset, establishing a business, or signing a contract. If fiduciaries were permitted to personally invest in projects, there is a risk that they would take for themselves valuable investment opportunities that they should have tried to obtain for the corporation. The fiduciary duty prohibits fiduciaries from allowing their personal interest to conflict with their duty to the corporation and taking an opportunity belonging to the corporation. If they do, any personal profit from the opportunity must be paid over to the corporation. This obligation is intended to eliminate any incentive for the fiduciary to take the opportunity in the first place.

[5.] *CBCA* s 120; *OBCA* s 132.

When does the opportunity belong to the corporation, so that the fiduciary should be prohibited from taking it? Case Brief 22.1 illustrates how to deal with this question.

CASE BRIEF 22.1

Canadian Air Services Ltd v O'Malley (1974) 40 DLR (3d) 371 (SCC)

Canadian Air Services Ltd (Canaero) was in the business of mapping and geographic exploration. O'Malley, the president, was assigned to Guyana to obtain a contract for mapping that country. After working on this project for some time, he resigned from Canaero and incorporated his own business, Terra Surveys Ltd, to perform work similar to what he was doing for Canaero. The government of Guyana asked for bids to map the country and accepted Terra's bid over Canaero's. Canaero sued O'Malley, alleging that he had breached his fiduciary duty to Canaero by taking the benefit of an opportunity belonging to the corporation.

The Supreme Court of Canada held that O'Malley did breach his duty. The court cited several factors that showed that the opportunity to map Guyana belonged to Canaero.

- **Specific nature of opportunity:** It was a specific opportunity that the corporation had been actively pursuing,

rather than one that was simply in the same area as the corporation's business.

- **Maturity of opportunity:** It was also a mature opportunity in the sense that Canaero had done extensive work in preparing for it. It was substantially the same opportunity that Canaero had been working on through O'Malley, although the ultimate contract was different in some respects.

The court also decided that O'Malley's close relationship to the opportunity while at Canaero supported a conclusion that he should be prohibited from taking it. O'Malley learned all about the opportunity through his position, did the preparatory work relating to the opportunity, and negotiated for it on behalf of Canaero.

Whether a breach of fiduciary duty will be found in any case depends on several factors. In addition to the ones cited in *Canadian Air Services*, the courts have said that these factors indicate that the opportunity belonged to the corporation.

- **Significance of opportunity:** The opportunity would have represented a major component of the corporation's business if acquired or was a unique opportunity rather than merely one of many considered by the corporation.
- **Private opportunity:** The opportunity was not publicly advertised or otherwise widely known, but was one to which the fiduciary only had access by virtue of the fiduciary's position in the corporation.
- **Rejection:** The opportunity had not been rejected by the corporation before the fiduciary acquired it.[6]

Competition by Directors and Officers

In general, it is not a breach of fiduciary duty to terminate one's relationship with a corporation and go into competition with it. Otherwise, the fiduciary duty might become an unreasonable restraint on a person's ability to earn a living. However, a fiduciary may not compete with the corporation while remaining in a fiduciary relationship with it. As Case Brief 22.1 showed, a fiduciary

---

[6.] *Peso Silver Mines Ltd v Cropper* (1965) 56 DLR (2d) 117 (BC CA), affd 58 DLR (2d) 1 (SCC). In this case, a rejection by the board of an opportunity was held to be sufficient to allow a board member to take the opportunity himself.

cannot quit to take an opportunity developed by the fiduciary while working for the corporation. Any competing fiduciary will be forced to pay over all profits from the competing business to the corporation.[7]

Duty of Care

The second important legal standard of behaviour for management is the **duty of care**, which the *CBCA* defines in these terms:[8]

> Every director and officer of a corporation in exercising his powers and discharging his duties shall. . . exercise the care, diligence and skill that a reasonably prudent person would exercise in comparable circumstances.[9]

the duty of care requires every director and officer to exercise the care, diligence, and skill that a reasonably prudent person would exercise in comparable circumstances

The degree of care required by this standard depends upon the facts of each case. In all cases, however, directors must have at least a basic understanding of the business. A director who does not have this minimal level of understanding should acquire it or resign.[10]

In addition to a basic level of competence, the duty of care requires some monitoring of the business by directors. The duty does not require a detailed inspection of the daily activities of the corporation; however, directors must keep informed about the corporation's policies and its business as well as regularly attending board meetings.

The reference to a person "in comparable circumstances" means that the duty has a subjective element. If you have significant knowledge or experience, you have to meet a higher standard of care.[11] The standard of care also depends upon a person's position. For example, all **public corporations**, which are large corporations that have issued shares to members of the public, must have an audit committee to review the financial statements and the financial reporting process. Directors who serve on this committee have more opportunity to examine the financial affairs of the corporation than other directors. Therefore, more is expected of them in terms of monitoring these affairs and warning other directors about problems.

public corporations have issued their shares to the public

Being removed from some aspect of the corporation's business, however, does not relieve directors of their duty. For example, only one director, say a chartered accountant who is also the chief financial officer, may be responsible for dealing with the financial side of a corporation's business. However, the other directors are still required to comply with a standard of care in relation to financial matters. If another director learns that the corporation failed to properly withhold income tax from employee wage payments and remit the tax to the Canada Revenue Agency, that director must do everything reasonably possible to ensure that the corporation puts in place procedures to prevent a recurrence. This might include requesting a board meeting to discuss the problem, inquiring into the problem, designing a solution, and monitoring to ensure that the solution is put into effect.[12]

---

7. *Bendix Home Systems Ltd v Clayton* (1977) 33 CPR (2d) 230 (Ont HCJ).

8. *CBCA* s 122(1)(b). Provincial statutes, other than those in Nova Scotia and Prince Edward Island, also impose a duty of care: for example, British Columbia's *Business Corporations Act*, SBC 2002, c 57, s 142(1)(b) (*BCBCA*) (BC), and *OBCA* s 134(1)(b).

9. In Chapter 6, we discussed the duty of care (and standard of care) that applies under the tort of negligence.

10. *Peoples Department Stores (Trustee of) v Wise* (2004) 244 DLR (4th) 564 (SCC).

11. *Re Standard Trustco Ltd* (1992) 6 BLR (2d) 241 (Ont SC).

12. *Fraser v MNR* [1987] DTC 250 (TCC).

The courts have been reluctant to find a breach of the duty of care when this involves second-guessing management on issues of general business judgment, such as whether a particular deal was the best one for the corporation. They have acknowledged their lack of business expertise. Courts often say that they do not want to set the standard for the duty of care so high that it inhibits business people from doing their jobs or discourages people from becoming directors and officers at all. As a result, business decisions are presumed not to be a breach of duty in the absence of fraud, illegality, or conflict of interest on the part of the decision maker. The duty of care still requires that the process for making the decision is reasonable in the circumstances. For example, managers must try to ensure that decisions are based on adequate information and advice. The approach taken by courts to business decisions is sometimes referred to as the **business judgment rule**.[13]

the business judgment rule is a presumption that, in making business decisions, directors and officers are not in breach of their duty in the absence of fraud, illegality, or conflict of interest

Especially in large corporations, officers and directors must rely on the advice of experts. Directors and officers are not liable for breach of their duty of care if they rely on financial statements or reports of lawyers, accountants, and other professionals.[14]

Protection for Creditors

Directors and officers have no duty to protect the interests of creditors of the corporation.[15] For the most part, creditors are left to protect themselves by contract, as Chapter 23 explains. There are, however, some corporate law provisions that benefit creditors. Corporate law tries to ensure that the corporation's money and assets are not distributed to shareholders, directors, officers, or employees, if that would threaten the corporation's ability to pay its creditors.

Directors cannot authorize either the payment of a dividend to a shareholder or the corporation's purchase of a shareholder's shares if there are reasonable grounds for believing that (i) the corporation could not pay its liabilities to its creditors as they become due, or (ii) the realizable value of the remaining assets (after the payment) would be less that the total amount owed to creditors plus the total of all shareholder investments.[16] Directors are personally liable if they authorize such payments. Under some corporate statutes, the directors are also liable to the corporation if they authorize the corporation to lend money or provide other financial assistance to directors, officers, shareholders, or employees of the corporation when either of these tests is not met.[17]

Even though the main purpose of these provisions is to protect creditors, they are not enforceable directly by creditors. The directors' obligation not to authorize payments if the tests are not met, and to compensate the corporation if they do, is owed to the corporation. Only the corporation can enforce those obligations.

[13.] The business judgment rule has been endorsed by Ontario courts: *eg Pente Investments Management v Schneider Corp* (1998) 42 OR (3d) 177 (CA).

[14.] *BCBCA* s 157; *CBCA* s 123(4); *OBCA* s 135(4). This defence is not available under the *NCA*.

[15.] *Peoples Department Stores (Trustee of) v Wise* (2004) 244 DLR (4th) 564 (SCC).

[16.] *CBCA* ss 34, 35, 36, 42, 118; *OBCA* ss 30, 31, 32, 38, 130.

[17.] The *CBCA* does not impose this restriction. The fiduciary duty would nevertheless prevent giving assistance when the corporation would be prejudiced. Directors are also liable to employees for up to six months' unpaid wages if the corporation is either bankrupt or in liquidation proceedings, or the corporation has been successfully sued for the debt and the judgment has been unpaid for six months: *ABCA* s 119; *CBCA* s 119; *OBCA* s 131.

HOW SHAREHOLDERS EXERCISE POWER

For most purposes, shareholders must act collectively. This usually takes place at meetings during which shareholders have an opportunity to question and criticize management, as well as to discuss and vote on proposals made to them. Directors are responsible for calling meetings but, under most corporate statutes in Canada, a group of shareholders holding at least five percent of voting shares may require the directors to call a meeting.[18] Directors are obligated to call *annual meetings* at least every 15 months. At an **annual meeting** (i) directors are elected, (ii) the auditor is appointed for the coming year, and (iii) financial statements for the past year are discussed. Directors must ensure that shareholders receive advance notice of the meeting, along with information regarding these three items and any other business.

> at an **annual meeting**, shareholders elect directors, appoint an auditor, and review the annual financial statements

Only a small percentage of shareholders of public corporations attend shareholders' meetings in person. Shareholders can participate without attending by appointing a *proxy*, who need not be a shareholder, to represent them at the meeting and vote their shares. The **proxy**, or **proxy holder**, has all the powers of the shareholder at the meeting, but must vote in accordance with any direction given by the shareholder.

> a **proxy**, or **proxy holder**, is a person designated by a shareholder to vote at the shareholders' meeting

For all public corporations, management must send the shareholders a form of proxy allowing them to appoint a proxy.[19] The form is sent along with a **management proxy circular**, a document that contains information regarding the proxy, the business to be dealt with at the meeting, and certain other information. The information provided by the circular enhances shareholder participation.

> a **management proxy circular** is a document sent to the shareholders that contains management proposals and other information related to shareholder meetings

Shareholders who disagree with management proposals may try to encourage their fellow shareholders to vote against them. Such **dissident shareholders** are entitled to obtain a list of shareholders and their addresses from the corporation and use it to contact other shareholders to influence their voting.[20] Dissident shareholders must send out a **dissidents' circular** with information on the identity of the dissidents, their relationship to the corporation, and their interest in the proposal.[21] Dissidents' circulars are relatively rare in the Canadian marketplace. The costs of complying with the disclosure requirements are often too high.

> **dissident shareholders** disagree with management proposals and seek to solicit the votes of their fellow shareholders to defeat management

At the meeting, voting is usually by a show of hands, but any shareholder may require that each vote be recorded on a ballot that is collected and counted.[22] Approval is usually by an ordinary majority vote.

> a **dissidents' circular** is a document sent to all shareholders by any shareholder who seeks the votes of other shareholders against management

Shareholders' Access to Information

All shareholders have access to certain information to enhance their ability to monitor management and to exercise their rights as shareholders. A corporation must maintain these records and allow shareholders access to them:[23]

---

18. *ABCA* s 131; *BCBCA* s 167; *CBCA* s 143.

19. *Eg OBCA* s 112. All corporations with more than 50 shareholders incorporated under the *CBCA* must meet this requirement (*CBCA* s 150). Under the *ABCA* the threshold is 15 shareholders (*ABCA* s 150).

20. *ABCA* s 21(3), (9); *CBCA* s 21(3), (9); *OBCA* ss 145, 146.

21. *OBCA* s 144; RRO 1990, Reg 62, ss 33–36; *CBCA* s 150(b); *CBCA Regulations*, SOR/2001-512, ss 61–64.

22. *ABCA* s 140; *CBCA* s 141.

23. *ABCA* ss 20, 20.1, 21; *CBCA* ss 20(1), 21; *OBCA* ss 145, 146.

- articles
- bylaws
- minutes of meetings of shareholders
- a share register showing the owners of all shares

Shareholders as well as creditors may examine and copy these during business hours. They have no right to inspect minutes of directors' meetings.

The most important information shareholders receive are the annual financial statements of the corporation. For public corporations, these are usually contained in an annual report. Annual statements must be audited by an independent firm of accountants that determines whether the statements created by management were prepared in accordance with generally accepted accounting principles and fairly present the financial results of the corporation for the year. The auditor bases its opinion on an evaluation of the financial records of the corporation. Shareholders may unanimously agree to dispense with the audit requirement. This is commonly done in small corporations where all the shareholders are closely involved in its business and do not consider the protection of an independent assessment of the corporation's financial statements to be worth the expense.

Shareholders' Agreements

If a corporation has few shareholders, they often use a shareholders' agreement to create an arrangement for governing the corporation that is different from the arrangement that occurs under the statute. They may:

- change shareholder voting entitlements
- change shareholder approval requirements
- create rules for share transfers

Voting and Management

Shareholders may want to allocate decision-making power between themselves in a way that is different from the allocation that would result from the number of shares each holds. Suppose Ellen, Ranjan, and Phillipe decide to set up a corporation to carry on a business of distributing computer software. Phillipe will contribute the $100 000 needed to set up the business and will be the sales manager. Ranjan will contribute $12 500 and will be responsible for the financial side of the business. Ellen will contribute some software she has developed. Because of his large financial contribution, Phillipe will get 80 percent of the shares, while Ranjan and Ellen will get 10 percent each. If each share has one vote, Phillipe would have enough votes to determine who will be on the board. He does not have to include Ellen or Ranjan. But what if Phillipe, Ellen, and Ranjan consider themselves to be in a relationship in which each should have an equal say and each wants to be on the board?

They could address this in a shareholders' agreement. All three could agree that they will vote their shares to elect all three of them as directors. Ranjan, Ellen, and Phillipe may also agree that all shareholder decisions must be approved by shareholders unanimously.

The *CBCA* and statutes modelled on it permit all the shareholders of a corporation to agree to alter the allocation of power between directors and shareholders. Such **unanimous shareholders' agreements** may "restrict, in whole or in part, the powers of the directors to manage the business and affairs of the

a unanimous shareholders' agreement is an agreement of all shareholders to transfer some or all of the directors' powers to themselves

corporation." Shareholders who are party to such an agreement have all the rights and powers, as well as the duties and liabilities, of a director to the extent of the restriction. The directors are relieved of their duties and liabilities to the same extent. This allows a small corporation to organize its structure to reflect the fact that it is the shareholders who are running the business by giving them management powers.[24]

Share Transfer

In small corporations, share transfer is a problem. Typically, the business is tied up with the individuals who are the shareholders. To continue with our example: Ellen would probably have difficulty selling her shares if she leaves the business, because the business would have trouble operating without her expertise. Another problem with finding a buyer for an interest in a small corporation is that such interests are inherently hard to value. There is no market like the Toronto Stock Exchange to establish prices.

Share transfers are also difficult for non-financial reasons. Shareholders do not want other shareholders to be able to sell their shares to just anyone. They want some restrictions on share transfer so that they can control who becomes involved in the business as a shareholder. At the same time, all shareholders want minimal restrictions on their ability to sell their own shares, given the financial difficulties of selling them.

It is therefore common to deal with share transfers in a shareholders' agreement by prohibiting transfers except in accordance with specified procedures. A common situation in which transfers are permitted is upon compliance with a **right of first refusal**. If Ellen wanted to sell her shares, a right of first refusal would require her to offer them first to the other shareholders at a price set by her. Ranjan and Phillipe would then have a limited time to purchase Ellen's shares, usually in proportion to their existing share holdings. If they do not purchase her shares, Ellen may offer them for sale to someone else at the *same price* for a limited time. The requirement to sell at the same price discourages Ellen from setting an unreasonably high price for her shares in the first place.

> right of first refusal is the right for shareholders to be offered shares that a shareholder wants to sell first before they are offered to non-shareholders

In a corporation with just two shareholders, the shareholder agreement may contain a *shotgun buy-sell* provision. A **shotgun buy-sell** is a share transfer mechanism that forces one shareholder to buy out the other. If Marsha offers all of her shares to John at a price she specifies, John must then either (i) buy all of Marsha's shares, or (ii) sell all of his shares to her at the same price. Either way, one of them ends up with all the shares in the corporation. This drastic mechanism can be used to break a deadlock between shareholders.

> a shotgun buy-sell is a share transfer mechanism that forces one shareholder to buy out the other

SHAREHOLDER REMEDIES

The directors are responsible for making the corporation pursue relief for injuries or losses it suffers. Nevertheless, shareholders may seek a court's permission to pursue relief on the corporation's behalf for breach of fiduciary duty or any other wrong done to the corporation. The action commenced by the shareholder is called a **derivative action**.[25] Shareholders also have remedies to obtain relief directly against management and the corporation when management fails to act in their interests.

> a derivative action is an action commenced by a shareholder on behalf of a corporation to seek relief for a wrong done to the corporation

---

[24.] *ABCA* s 146(2); *CBCA* s 146(2); *OBCA* s 108. There are many unresolved issues with respect to how a corporation that is subject to a unanimous shareholders' agreement will function. For example, would it still need to have directors if the shareholders have removed all of their powers?

[25.] *CBCA* s 239; *OBCA* s 246; *NBBCA* s 164.

Dissent and Appraisal Rights

The shareholders may approve, by a two-thirds majority vote, certain fundamental changes to the corporation, such as (i) specific major amendments to the articles, (ii) amalgamation with another corporation, or (iii) the sale, lease, or exchange of all, or substantially all, of the assets of a corporation outside of the ordinary course of business. Shareholders who vote against such changes are entitled to have their shares bought by the corporation for their fair value.[26] This **dissent and appraisal right** allows a change approved by most shareholders to go ahead, while permitting those who strongly disagree to exit the corporation. If many shareholders exercise their rights, however, implementing the change can become very expensive for the corporation. The corporation could decide not to go ahead with the change even though it received the necessary shareholder approval in such a case.

the dissent and appraisal right entitles shareholders who dissent from certain fundamental changes to have the corporation buy their shares

Oppression

When actions by the directors or the corporation have oppressed or unfairly disregarded or prejudiced their interests, shareholders may claim relief under the **oppression remedy**.[27] The courts have interpreted their authority to provide this relief broadly. In general, relief is available when the *reasonable expectations* of shareholders about management behaviour have not been met. Relief can include anything the court decides is necessary to remedy the problem, including ordering the corporation to buy the oppressed shareholder's shares. These are examples of behaviour that the courts have found oppressive:[28]

the oppression remedy allows a shareholder to claim compensation for a loss that was caused by an act or omission by the corporation or its directors, which oppresses the interests of the shareholder

- approval of a transaction lacking a valid corporate purpose that is prejudicial to a particular shareholder
- failure by the corporation and its controlling shareholder to ensure that a transaction between them was on terms that were comparable to the terms that would have been negotiated by parties who were not related to each other
- discrimination against shareholders that benefits the majority shareholder to the exclusion or the detriment of minority shareholders
- lack of adequate and appropriate disclosure of information to minority shareholders
- planning to eliminate minority shareholders[29]

Other Shareholder Remedies

Shareholders may seek other remedies, such as a court order that directs compliance with the governing statute or the rectification of corporate records that contain errors. On an application by a shareholder, a court may even direct that the assets of the corporation be sold, its creditors paid off, and any surplus distributed to the shareholders. This extreme remedy is called **liquidation and dissolution**, or **winding up**. It may be ordered when it is just and equitable to

under a liquidation and dissolution, or winding up, the corporation's assets are sold, its creditors paid off, the remaining money distributed to the shareholders, and the corporation's existence terminated

---

26. *BCBCA* ss 237–247; *CBCA* s 190; *NBBCA* s 131; *NCA* ss 300–301.

27. Eg *BCBCA* s 227; *CBCA* s 241; *NBBCA* s 166.

28. *Arthur v Signum Communications Ltd* [1991] OJ No 86 (Gen Div), affd [1993] OJ No 1928 (Div Ct).

29. Creditors and anyone else may seek permission from a court to bring an oppression action.

end the corporation's existence. For example, a court may order the winding up of a corporation with two shareholders who cannot agree on how the corporation should carry on business.[30]

Business Decision 22.1 looks at the application in practice of the legal rules for corporate governance.

BUSINESS DECISION 22.1

Corporate Governance in Practice

Corporations vary in size. At one extreme, a corporation may have only a single shareholder, who is also the sole director and officer. At the other, a large public corporation may have thousands of shareholders spread out around the world and more than 20 directors, some of whom work as managers in the corporation. The operation of corporate governance rules varies significantly depending on where a corporation is on this continuum.

If one person is the sole shareholder, director, and officer, the allocation of rights and responsibilities contemplated in corporate statutes is a mere formality and generally irrelevant. Even if the sole shareholder elects other directors, it will be the shareholder who ultimately makes management decisions. If there are a few shareholders, usually they will also be the managers. The legal arrangements for management are likely to be set out in a shareholders' agreement and may be quite different from what the corporate statute provides.

As the number of shareholders increases, not all of them will be involved in management. In this situation, managers may be tempted to act in a way that benefits themselves at the expense of the corporation. If they pay themselves excessive salaries or other perquisites, they receive 100 percent of the benefit. While these kinds of actions may reduce the value of the corporation's shares, including those held by management, the loss experienced by management will be much less than the benefit to them. Furthermore, as the size of a corporation increases, it becomes more difficult for shareholders to detect and prevent managerial abuses. Managers therefore have even more incentive to misbehave.

In a large corporation, shareholders are at a disadvantage partly because they do not have enough information to understand and evaluate management's performance. Even if some are willing and able to gather sufficient information and analyze it, they may find it difficult and expensive to mobilize many other shareholders, who are spread around the country or the world. The relatively small financial stake of most individual shareholders will discourage them from incurring these costs. As a result, shareholders' legal rights to vote and pursue shareholder remedies may not be very useful.

Another problem with the legal corporate governance scheme is that it is designed to ensure only that the *board of directors* is accountable to shareholders. Little attention is paid to the accountability of *officers*, who run corporations in practice. In large public corporations, the board of directors tends to be dominated by the full-time professional managers of the corporation.

In the wake of the corporate scandals in the United States, including the bankruptcy of Enron, the rules for corporate governance in both Canada and the United States have been changed to require the adoption of certain governance best practices that are designed to improve the accountability of management to shareholders. These include additional requirements (i) for boards to be independent of management so they can exercise more effective oversight of management's activities, and (ii) for chief executive officers to certify the accuracy of financial statements. Some of these new requirements are backed up by criminal penalties. Recently, many business leaders have complained that the new requirements are too costly and onerous.[31]

Question for Discussion

1. Can good corporate governance be mandated by law or would it be better to leave it up to the marketplace?

[30.] Liquidation and dissolution may be ordered in other circumstances: *CBCA* ss 213, 214; *OBCA* s 207.

[31.] More details regarding recent changes to corporate governance rules can be found on the Companion Website for this book on the Updates and Other Resources page at <http://wps.prenhall.com/ca_ph_mcinnes_buslaw_1>.

CORPORATE LIABILITY

The rules governing a corporation's liability for contracts, crimes, and torts determine how a corporation is legally affected by the behaviour of people acting on its behalf. Those rules influence how the corporation organizes itself to participate in the marketplace. The rules that determine when a corporation is liable in tort, for example, determine how a corporation supervises its employees in their interaction with customers to minimize the risk of liability.

Liability in Contract

A corporation only becomes liable to perform contracts as a result of actions by **agents**, who act on its behalf. Salespeople, purchasing clerks, directors, and officers may all be considered agents of the corporation for specific purposes. As discussed in Chapter 20, an agent can only bind a corporation if the corporation has given the agent one of these types of authority:

> an **agent** of a corporation is a person who is authorized to act on behalf of the corporation

- **Actual authority**: The agent is authorized by the corporation to enter into the obligation in question.

> **actual authority** is authority that is actually given to an agent by a corporation

- **Apparent (or ostensible) authority**: The corporation represents that the agent has authority to bind the corporation to the obligation in question. For a third party to rely on apparent authority, the representation must have induced the third party to enter into the disputed contract with the corporation.[32]

> **apparent, or ostensible, authority** is created by a representation on behalf of the corporation that an agent has authority to bind the corporation

Many corporations are complex organizations that use many types of agents with many types of authority. Often it is difficult for people seeking to contract with a corporation to determine whether the people they are dealing with are actually authorized to act on the corporation's behalf. Consequently, most corporate statutes prevent corporations from avoiding liability by relying on internal corporate restrictions. The risk of unauthorized conduct falls upon the corporation. The **indoor management rule** states that a corporation cannot rely on certain kinds of defects in the authority of an agent who purports to act on its behalf in entering into a contract with a third party. Those defects may (i) restrict the authority of the agent to bind the corporation, or (ii) require some procedure to be followed before a contract can be created. More specifically, a corporation cannot rely on any provision in its articles or bylaws, or in any unanimous shareholder agreement, that creates a defect in the agent's authority. As well, a corporation cannot claim that a person held out by a corporation as an officer, director, or agent has not been duly appointed or does not have the authority that a person in that position usually has in the business of the corporation.[33]

> the **indoor management rule** states that a corporation cannot rely on certain kinds of defects in the authority of an agent who purports to act on its behalf in entering into a contract with a third party

However, a third party cannot enforce a contract if it knew that there was a defect in the agent's authority, or if it should have known of that defect. Suppose you are a customer of a shoe manufacturer. The corporation's sales representative purports to sell you $1 000 000 worth of inventory. If you know that sales representatives are not allowed enter into contracts for more than $500 000, the sale contract would be unenforceable.

[32.] *Freeman & Lockyer v Buckhurst Park Properties (Mangal) Ltd* [1964] 2 QB 480 (CA).

[33.] *CBCA* s 18; *OBCA* s 19; *NBBCA* s 15.

Liability for Crimes

The consequences of imposing criminal liability on corporations are different from those of imposing criminal liability on individuals, because corporations have "no soul to damn; no body to kick."[34] Corporations will be concerned about the effect of a criminal conviction on their reputation, but the threat of a conviction may not deter them from misbehaving to the same extent. Also, criminal penalties are problematic when a corporation is the offender. Imprisonment of the corporation itself (as distinct from its officers and directors) is impossible. If a fine is imposed on a corporation, its shareholders and all those with financial claims against the corporation, including employees, may suffer. Despite those distinctive characteristics of criminal punishment for corporations, they can be held criminally responsible. The practical issue is how to determine when a corporation has committed a crime.

There are three broad categories of offences, each with different rules about what is required for corporate liability.

- **Absolute liability** offences are committed whenever the accused engages in prohibited behaviour. Corporate liability arises when a person commits the prohibited act on behalf of the corporation. The acts of employees in the course of their employment will satisfy this test.[35] If an employee drove a company truck that did not meet mandatory safety standards, for example, the corporation could be held liable.

  *an **absolute liability** offence occurs upon the commission of an act prohibited by law*

- A **strict liability** offence occurs when a person, acting on behalf of the corporation, commits a prohibited act. Unlike an absolute liability offence, however, the *defence of due diligence* is available for a strict liability offence. That means that liability does not arise if the accused acted reasonably in the circumstances. A corporation can rely on that defence if the person with managerial responsibility for the relevant area of the corporation's affairs used due diligence. That person is described as the **directing mind** of the corporation. The care exercised by that person is considered to be the care exercised by the corporation itself.[36] If a due diligence defence was available to the corporation in the trucking example above, and if the corporation's trucking manager had exercised the required level of care to ensure that the truck met the safety standards, the corporation would not be liable. As Chapter 25 explains, absolute and strict liability offences usually form part of a regulatory scheme, such as those protecting public health, safety, and the environment.

  *a **strict liability** offence occurs upon the commission of an act prohibited by law unless the accused acted reasonably in the circumstances*

  *the **directing mind** is the person who has responsibility to manage the business of the corporation in the area in which the offence occurred*

- Most criminal offences, such as fraud, are committed only if the accused had some degree of knowledge or intention, referred to as **mens rea** (or "guilty mind"), when it performed a prohibited act. Under the traditional common law rules, a corporation may be liable under this category of offence if the person who had the *mens rea* while committing the crime was also the directing mind of the corporation. The

  *a **mens rea** offence arises upon the commission of an act prohibited by law by a person who had some degree of knowledge or intention*

[34.] Lord Thurlow, quoted by G Williams *Criminal Law: the General Part* 2d ed (1961) at 856.

[35.] Convicting a corporation of an absolute liability offence punishable by imprisonment may be contrary to the freedom from being deprived of life, liberty, and security of the person under s 7 of the *Canadian Charter of Rights and Freedoms*. Corporations cannot be convicted under a law which would be unconstitutional if applied to individuals: *R v Big M Drug Mart* (1985) 18 DLR (4th) 321 (SCC). We discussed the *Charter* in Chapter 1.

[36.] *R v Sault Ste Marie* (1978) 85 DLR (3d) 161 (SCC).

person who was the directing mind can be held *individually* responsible as well.

Recent amendments to the *Criminal Code* have broadened the category of people whose actions can trigger corporate liability. The category now extends to any senior officer, meaning any person who either plays an important role in setting the corporation's policies or is responsible for managing an important aspect of the corporation's activities.[37]

A corporation may have many senior officers. Each person responsible for a discrete aspect of the corporation's business—whether that aspect is defined functionally, geographically, or otherwise—may incur criminal liability for the corporation. It is not only the president or the board of directors who may do so. In *Waterloo Mercury Sales*, liability was imposed on a corporation operating a car dealership because the used car sales manager fraudulently had odometers on used cars turned back.[38] In this case, the employee with *mens rea* was given—expressly, implicitly, or practically—the authority to *design and supervise* the performance of corporate policy relating to used cars. Before the amendments to the *Criminal Code*, corporate liability was not triggered if the crime was committed by a person who had authority only to *carry out* policies that someone else in the corporation created.[39] As a result of the new amendments, however, liability may be imposed even if the manager who acted did not have authority to set policy.

The recent amendments also make clear that corporate liability can arise where the actions constituting the crime were innocently committed by employees or other lower level representatives of the corporation, so long as a senior officer had the required guilty mind. If a senior officer directed employees to deal in stolen goods, the corporation would be liable, even though the employees had no knowledge that the goods were stolen. A corporation can also be held liable if a senior officer knew employees were going to commit a crime but failed to take all reasonable measures to stop them.[40]

Note that a corporation will not necessarily escape liability merely because it had a policy *against* the behaviour that constituted the crime. In *Waterloo Mercury Sales*, the dealership had a policy against turning back odometers. The court still imposed liability. The lesson is clear. In some situations, the best that a corporation can do by way of risk management is to adopt clear policies *and* hire responsible people to carry them out.

Liability in Tort

A corporation may be liable in tort in two ways. It may be directly liable when a person who is the directing mind and will of the corporation itself has committed the tort. Alternatively, it may be vicariously liable for acts of employees in the course of their employment, as discussed in Chapter 3.

[37.] *An Act to Amend the Criminal Code (criminal liability of organizations)*, SC 2003, c 21, s 2.

[38.] *R v Waterloo Mercury Sales Ltd* (1974) 49 DLR (3d) 131 (Alta Dist Ct).

[39.] *R v Safety-Kleen Canada Inc* (1997) 145 DLR (4th) 276 (Ont CA).

[40.] *An Act to Amend the Criminal Code (criminal liability of organizations)*, SC 2003, c 21, s 22.2. The *Criminal Code* amendments expand the scope of corporate liability in other ways as well, and address the liability of non-corporate forms of organizations including partnerships.

PERSONAL LIABILITIES OF DIRECTORS AND OFFICERS

Directors and officers are subject to a wide range of potential liabilities. Governments have imposed personal liability, including fines and imprisonment, as a way of encouraging corporations to comply with laws relating to unpaid income taxes, environmental protection, and other regulatory schemes. Some of these laws are discussed in Chapter 25. Furthermore, directors and officers are increasingly being held personally responsible for torts, such as the tort of inducing breach of contract, which was discussed in Chapter 5.

Exposure to these liabilities creates a strong disincentive to becoming a director or officer of a corporation. To offset these risks, a corporation can reimburse directors and officers for any expenses that they *reasonably* incur in connection with the defence of any civil, criminal, or administrative proceeding that is connected to their position within the corporation. This reimbursement, called an **indemnity**, is mandatory if the directors or officers:

- were not found to have committed any fault
- complied with their fiduciary duty to act honestly, in good faith, and with a view to the best interests of the corporation
- had reasonable grounds for believing their conduct was lawful[41]

indemnity is compensation paid by a corporation to a director or officer for costs incurred in connection with performing their duties

Even when a director or officer does not meet the first criterion, a corporation may still provide indemnification if the other two criteria are met. Indemnification may include amounts not directly relating to the defence, such as money paid to settle an action or satisfy a judgment. You Be the Judge 22.1 asks you to apply these rules regarding indemnification.

YOU BE THE JUDGE 22.1

Consolidated Enfield Corporation v Blair (1995) 128 DLR (4th) 73 (SCC)

Blair was the president and a director of Consolidated Enfield Corporation. At Enfield's annual meeting, a slate of nominees proposed by management, and including Blair, stood for election. Canadian Express Ltd, a major shareholder, nominated a candidate for director to replace Blair. Canadian Express had enough votes to ensure that its candidate would be elected. After the votes on the election of directors were cast, a lawyer advised Blair that he, as chair, had to make a ruling on the results of the vote, even though his own election was at stake, and that the votes cast by Canadian Express against Blair were invalid. He took the advice and ruled (i) that the votes cast for the Canadian Express nominee were invalid, and (ii) that the

management slate was elected. In subsequent legal proceedings, a court ruled that the votes cast in favour of the Canadian Express nominee were valid, and so Blair had not been re-elected. Blair claimed indemnification from Enfield for his legal costs in connection with these proceedings.

Questions for Discussion

1. Should Blair be entitled to indemnification in these circumstances?

2. What arguments may be made for and against indemnification?

---

41. *ABCA* s 124; *CBCA* s 124; *OBCA* s 136.

Indemnification commitments are only as good as the ability of the indemnifier to pay. If there is a risk that an indemnifying corporation may not have enough money to pay, a director or officer may seek a guarantee, perhaps from a shareholder, to provide greater security. It has become common for directors and officers to ask their corporations to pay for insurance against their personal liability.

Ethical Perspective 22.1 asks you to think about when a corporation should pay an indemnity. Business Decision 22.2 requires you to consider what protection an indemnity provides and what other strategies you could use as a director to protect yourself. Concept Summary 22.1 (on page 531) identifies sources of corporate liability and strategies for risk management.

ETHICAL PERSPECTIVE 22.1

Indemnification for Liabilities under Regulatory Statutes

Governments have tried to strengthen environmental and other regulatory schemes by imposing liability on directors and officers. This has raised questions about when indemnification and insurance to cover these liabilities should be available. On the one hand, with the range and seriousness of potential liability increasing, indemnities and insurance become more important as a way of ensuring that competent people are willing to become officers and directors. On the other hand, the intended effect of imposing liability on directors and officers is to discourage businesses from acting illegally. But if directors and officers are insulated from this liability by indemnification and insurance, the effectiveness of the legislative scheme is reduced. In a recent case, several officers were convicted of the offence of failing to take all reasonable care to prevent the corporation from permitting the unlawful discharge of wastes. The judge ordered the officers to pay fines.[42]

Question for Discussion

1. Should the corporation indemnify the officers by paying their fines for them?

BUSINESS DECISION 22.2

Joining a Board of Directors

You run an environmental consulting business, and your major client is Medex Inc, which has carried on a business of collecting and disposing of medical waste in Ottawa and eastern Ontario since 1990. Jamal is the majority shareholder, CEO, and chair of the board of directors of Medex. He has asked you to join the board as its fifth member and to go on the environmental compliance committee, which the board intends to set up.[43]

Questions for Discussion

1. What concerns would you have about accepting this offer?

2. Are there any strategies that you could adopt to minimize these risks?

---

[42] *R v Bata Industries* (1995) 127 DLR (4th) 438 (Ont CA).

[43] *Stuart v MNR* [1995] 2 CTC 2458 (TCC).

CONCEPT SUMMARY 22.1

Corporate Liability and Risk Management

Sources of Personal Liability for Directors and Officers	Strategies Available to Manage Liability Risk
General standards of behaviour • fiduciary duty • duty of care • oppression remedy	Diligence • regularly attending board meetings • keeping informed and acting when put on notice • conducting risk assessment • establishing compliance policy and monitoring systems, including timely reporting and education • seeking advice • being sensitive to conflicts of interest
Examples of specific liability risks • environmental offences • failure to remit employee withholdings • authorizing dividends, share buy-backs, or financial assistance to employees and other insiders when solvency and other financial tests not met • up to six months of unpaid employee wages • liability under many other statutes	Indemnification
	Insurance
	Resignation

CHAPTER SUMMARY

Under Canadian corporate statutes, directors are responsible for managing the business of the corporation or supervising its management. Officers are appointed by the directors and exercise powers delegated to them. Directors and officers are subject to a fiduciary duty to act honestly and in the best interests of the corporation. Fiduciaries may not (i) be involved personally in transactions with the corporation unless certain safeguards in the corporate statute are observed, (ii) personally take opportunities belonging to the corporation, or (iii) compete with the corporation. Directors and officers also have a duty to exercise the care, diligence, and skill that a reasonably prudent person would exercise in comparable circumstances. Shareholders are the residual claimants to the assets of the corporation, but their only power is to vote for the election of directors, on proposals made to them, and on the appointment of an auditor.

Corporate law requires that shareholders have access to certain information to allow them to monitor management and exercise their rights as shareholders. Shareholders may enter agreements to exercise their powers differently from those provided in governing corporate law and to create rules to govern share transfers. When shareholder agreements are unanimous, they may transfer some or all of the directors' powers and responsibilities to the shareholders. Shareholders have several remedies to seek relief from the actions of the corporation and management, including the dissent and appraisal right and the oppression remedy. The legal scheme for corporate governance may be ineffective in public corporations because of the practical inability of shareholders to take advantage of the accountability mechanisms provided for and the failure of these mechanisms to impose direct accountability on officers.

Corporations are liable for contracts made by persons with actual or apparent authority to contract on their behalf. A corporation is liable for crimes and torts committed by a person who is the directing mind of the corporation, and in some other circumstances. Directors and officers are subject to a wide number of statutory liabilities but, if they have discharged their fiduciary duty, they may be indemnified for liabilities incurred in connection with fulfilling their responsibilities.

REVIEW QUESTIONS

1. Are directors always responsible for managing the business of a corporation?

2. How does a corporation get its first directors? Its next directors?

3. Are there restrictions on the directors' ability to delegate management responsibility to officers or to people outside the corporation? Why would the directors give someone outside the corporation management responsibility for some of its business?

4. What is the fiduciary duty, and how is it "owed to the corporation"?

5. Is a director of a corporation allowed to be involved personally in a transaction with the corporation? If so, when?

6. How do you determine whether a fiduciary can pursue an opportunity?

7. To what extent does the fiduciary duty of corporate officers continue after they leave their positions with the corporation?

8. What are the basic elements of the duty of care that directors and officers have?

9. What is the significance of a person's position and personal characteristics in determining what the duty of care requires?

10. Explain how the duty of care applies to business judgments made by directors and officers.

11. How does corporate law try to facilitate shareholders' exercise of their rights?

12. Assume a corporation had two shareholders holding 10 percent and 90 percent of the corporation's common shares. Both shareholders wanted an equal say in any major decision about the corporation's business. Do these shareholders need a shareholders' agreement? If so, what would be its main provisions?

13. What is the "dissent and appraisal" remedy? What impact does it have on corporate governance?

14. Why is the oppression remedy more useful to shareholders than the derivative action?

15. Why do the legal mechanisms by which shareholders keep directors accountable to them not work very well in large corporations?

16. What must a person dealing with a corporation establish to enforce a contract with it?

17. Who is the "directing mind" of the corporation? What is the significance of this concept in relation to corporate liability for crimes? For torts?

18. How can corporations reduce the risk of being found liable for the criminal activities of their employees?

19. What limits are there on the ability of a corporation to indemnify its directors for costs incurred in defending an action to which they were made a party only because they were directors?

20. How can directors and officers minimize their risk of liability for actions in the course of fulfilling their roles in the corporation?

CASES AND PROBLEMS

1. Carl owns 51 percent of the shares of Probex Inc, a successful building supplies business. At the last shareholders' meeting, Carl elected Morris, Ellen, and himself as the directors of the company. Morris, Ellen, and Carl appointed Carl as the CEO and president of the company. The corporation's business has been slow this year. Both Morris and Ellen believe that the current slowdown of the business is a direct result of Carl neglecting his duty to oversee the day-to-day operations of the business.

   By outvoting Carl at the next directors' meeting, Morris and Ellen replace Carl as CEO and president with Philip. Carl is furious and tells Morris and Ellen that since he owns 51 percent of the company, they had no right to replace him, especially since he elected them. Carl further advises them that, given his authority as the controlling shareholder, he is reclaiming his position as CEO and president of Probex. Is Carl entitled to be the CEO and president of the corporation? What can he do to ensure that he is appointed to these offices?

2. Claire, Stephan and Gopa decided to go into business together to provide consulting services. Each invested $100 000 in return for one-third of the shares in a corporation. There was an oral understanding, but no written contract, that:

   - Gopa would not be involved in the day-to-day decision making related to the business,

   - Claire and Stephan would be elected as the directors and appointed as the president and vice-president of the corporation, and

   - all major decisions of the corporation, including selling the business, would require the consent of all shareholders.

   For several years, the business operated on this basis, but in 2005, Claire and Stephan decided to sell the assets of the business. They called a shareholders' meeting to vote on the sale. Gopa did not agree but she was outvoted at the shareholders' meeting. Now that the sale has been approved, is there anything Gopa can do about it?

3. Crook was employed as the scrap manager for Canada Labs Inc. In that capacity, Crook regularly sold waste gold generated by the experimental work conducted by Canlab to Golden Corona Mines Inc for recycling. Corona also sold gold, although Canlab had never been one of its customers.

   Crook devised a scheme to make himself wealthy. One day, he sent a purchase order on a Canlab order form to Corona for $1 000 000 in gold. Because Corona had not sold gold to Canlab in the past, it called Smith, the manager of purchasing for Canlab, to ask if the gold order from Crook was authorized. Smith, who was responsible for all purchases made by Canlab, said she would check into it. She called Crook, and he convinced her that the gold was needed for a particular set of experiments. Smith was too busy to inquire further and forgot to call Corona back. Corona called Smith several more times, but Smith did not call back. In frustration, after five days, Corona called Crook who, of course, confirmed that Corona should send the gold.

   Corona did send the gold to Canlab. It was received by Crook, who then skipped the country and took the gold with him. Corona sued Canlab for payment for the gold. On what basis could Canlab be liable to pay for the gold? Are any defences available to Canlab?

4. Sarah, a shareholder in Corporation X, wanted to sell her shares. She asked Peter, the chair of the board of directors, if he knew of anyone who wanted to buy shares of Corporation X. Peter said he would buy them for $10 per share. Peter did not tell Sarah that the corporation was having discussions with Tony, who was interested in buying all the shares of the corporation for $15 per share. Should Peter have told Sarah about these discussions?

5. Xena was the original shareholder and sole director of Aberdeen Consulting Ltd. She held 10 shares. The corporation had been profitable, but it needed more capital to engage in new business projects. To raise capital, Aberdeen issued 20 shares to Raju for $1000 per share.

   Upon reviewing the corporation's financial statements, Raju discovers that the corporation has a consulting contract with a company controlled by Xena. The contract fees are much higher than the usual market rate for consulting services and have substantially reduced the profits of the business. Raju decided that, at the next shareholders' meeting when Xena's term expires, he would elect himself as director, terminate the contract, and put the business of the corporation on a much stronger financial footing. Upon hearing of this plan, Xena issued herself an additional 20 shares. At the shareholders' meeting, much to Raju's surprise, Xena outvoted him, re-electing herself as director. Raju is outraged and certain that something must be done to remedy this terrible situation.

   Is there anything Raju can do?

6. Marilyn was the founder, majority shareholder, president, and a director of Escada Cosmetics Ltd. Since its incorporation in 1984, the company has been successful due to Marilyn's hard work. However, after 20 years, she was ready to play a reduced role. Marilyn believed that her daughter, Chloe, would make an excellent new manager. At Marilyn's suggestion and urging, the board appointed Chloe as director and president in July 2004.

   Things went well at first, but managing the business soon became too much for Chloe, who did not have any knowledge of or experience with the day-to-day operations. Consequently, Escada began to do poorly, and by the end of October 2004, its profits had disappeared. Despite its weak financial position, in November 2004, the board of directors of Escada paid a $1 000 000 dividend to Marilyn to help her buy a home in California.

   Full Moon Financial Group, a minority shareholder of Escada, is worried about its investment, which it made in August 2004 before the desperate financial condition of Escada was known. What options does Full Moon have for protecting its investment?

7. Florence Industries Ltd, based in Alberta, manufactures household cleaning products. Its president, Ebenezer, entered into negotiations with Second Class Disposal Services Inc for a service contract. Second Class promised Ebenezer that their disposal services, which were much less expensive than what other disposal businesses were offering, met all legal requirements. Ebenezer was satisfied by their assurances and signed the contract without further investigating Second Class or its track record.

   Three months into the contract, Ebenezer was accused of authorizing the disposal of industrial waste into the Bow River, contrary to the Alberta *Water Resources Act*. This statute provides that an accused who exercised reasonable care to prevent the corporation from disposing of the waste can avoid liability.

   Assuming that industrial waste was dumped into the Bow River on behalf of Florence Industries by Second Class, discuss whether the president *or* Florence Industries can be held liable under the *Act*.

8. New Technology Co is a public company whose shares are widely held and listed on the Toronto Stock Exchange. In the last year, the corporation's business has struggled, and its share price has fallen from an all-time high of $150 to $15. Over the same period, its competitors have done well, and their shares have increased in value. This month, it was announced that the board of directors had decided that the president should be given a $10 000 000 bonus. Assume that you bought 1000 shares at the peak of the market for $150 000 and that your shares are now worth only $15 000. You are very angry that, while the shareholders are suffering, the president is getting this enormous bonus. What can you do?

9. FaxCo Inc is a distributor of fax machines. The corporation has ten shareholders, including Frances and her two sons, who together hold 60 percent of the shares and are also the directors of the corporation. The sons run the business. Frances has no

experience in business and is not involved in any way. She pays no attention to what is going on, although she regularly attends board meetings. In 2004, the sons started taking large amounts of money out of the business in the form of loans to themselves.

When the financial statements for the year were prepared, they showed that shareholder loans had ballooned from nil to $1 000 000 in a year, when revenues of the business had been only $2 000 000 over the same period. The board of directors approved the statements. Frances was at the meeting but did not look at the statements. Within two months, the corporation was not paying its debts, and one of its creditors obtained a court order appointing a receiver to take control of the business. The receiver discovered the loans to the sons. The sons, themselves, are now insolvent. Frances, however, has substantial personal assets. Is there any way that the receiver, acting on behalf of the corporation, can seek relief against Frances?

10. Katrina, Charlie and Madeleine are interested in opening a retail sporting goods business. They propose to set up a corporation to carry on the business. Katrina has a building that she proposes to transfer into the corporation in return for 75% of the shares of the corporation. Charlie has agreed to contribute $30 000 in cash for 15% of the shares and Madeleine will contribute $20 000 in cash for the remaining 10%. Each will play an active role in the business: Katrina and Charlie will work as sales people and Madeleine will deal with the finances, inventory management, and marketing. They agree that each should be named a director of the corporation in the articles. Do you see any problem with this proposed arrangement? How would it be put in place?

11. Simone is a director of Pace Computers Ltd. She is also the sole shareholder and director of Simtronics Supply Inc, which sells parts for personal computers. At a Pace board meeting, Simone suggests that Pace could get its parts inventory for less money from Simtronics than from its current supplier. Is there anything preventing Pace from entering into a supply contract with Simtronics? Should Simone take any steps to ensure that no legal problems arise?

12. Blaine Manufacturing Inc produces disposable coffee cups and has annual revenues of approximately $10 000 000. The President of Blaine proposed to the board of directors that the corporation buy all of the shares of London Properties Ltd for $25 000 000. He told the board that London Properties owns some attractive commercial real estate that it will be able to sell for huge profits. After a 10-minute presentation from the President, the board approved the transaction unanimously. No information was provided to the board in advance of the meeting. Within a few months, the market for commercial real estate crashed and London Properties could not sell its real estate. Payments on the substantial loan that Blaine took out in order to buy the property have meant that dividend payments have been suspended. If you were a minority shareholder of Blaine, is there anything you could do about this situation?

WEBLINKS

Industry Canada http://strategis.ic.gc.ca/epic/internet/ incilp-pdci.nsf/en/h_cl00730e.html

This site provides a set of detailed recommendations for improving corporate governance rules in the *Canada Business Corporations Act* and links to other information on corporate governance.

Osler Hoskin Harcourt www.osler.com/index.asp?navid= 1086&csid=3029&lang=1

This law firm's website provides an excellent overview of legal corporate governance issues for business people in an online publication, *Directors' Duties*, that contains information on a wide range of directors' responsibilities, statutory liabilities, and risk management.

PricewaterhouseCoopers www.pwcglobal.com/ca/eng/ ins-sol/spec-int/ipo-cgf.html

This accounting firm's website provides useful guidance on organizing a corporation in anticipation of becoming a public corporation.

Additional Resources for Chapter 22 on the Companion Website

(www.pearsoned.ca/mcinnes)

In addition to self-test multiple-choice, true-false, and short essay questions (all with immediate feedback), three additional Cases and Problems (with suggested answers), and links to useful Web destinations, the Companion Website provides the following resources for Chapter 22:

■ Business Decision 22W—Fiduciary Duties and Hostile Takeover Bids

Provincial Material

■ **British Columbia:** Liability of Management, Liability of Shareholders, Shareholder Remedies, Derivative Actions, Corporate Dissolution, Oppression Remedy

■ **Alberta:** Directors' Liability, Corporate Management, Shareholders' Remedies

■ **Manitoba and Saskatchewan:** Personal Liabilities of Directors and Officers

■ **Ontario:** Business Judgment Rule, Conflict of Interest, Corporate Governance, Directors' Liability, Directors' Duties, Disclosure, Insider Trading, Legislation Imposing Directors' Liability, Oppression Remedy, Sarbanes Oxley, Secondary Market Liability, Code of Conduct

23 Secured Transactions

CHAPTER OVERVIEW

OBJECTIVES

After completing this chapter, you should be able to:

1. Explain why financial institutions and other creditors seek security for the performance of obligations owed to them.

2. Describe three types of transactions in which a creditor gets a right to seize a debtor's property if the debtor fails to perform its obligations to the creditor.

3. Explain how a lease can be used to finance the acquisition of an asset.

4. Identify problems that secured creditors may encounter in trying to reduce the risk of a bad debt.

5. Describe the advantages of the current rules protecting security interests for creditors.

6. Explain how a supplier of goods can ensure that its claim for payment from the buyer can be secured most effectively.

7. List three steps followed by secured creditors to enforce their rights against the personal property of debtors.

8. Describe the obligations of a creditor that seizes a debtor's property.

9. Outline the risks for a person acquiring personal property from someone who has previously given security interests in the property to a creditor, and explain how to manage them.

10. Identify four situations in which one person's guarantee of another's credit obligation becomes unenforceable.

We all rely on credit, at least some of the time. If you promise to pay later to get something now, you are a *debtor*, the person who owes the credit obligation. The person who allows time to pass before requiring you to pay is the *creditor*. If you buy furniture and do not have to pay for it until next year, you are a debtor who owes a credit obligation to the furniture store. A creditor has two main ways of reducing the risk of non-payment:

- security interests
- guarantees

A **security interest** allows a creditor to seize some of a debtor's personal property if a debt is not repaid, usually without the delay and expense of going to court. Suppose you want to borrow money from a bank to buy a new delivery truck. The bank will base its decision to accept or reject your loan application largely on your ability to repay the loan. But what if, after examining your income and expenses, the bank still has concerns about your ability to make the payments? The bank would be more willing to give you credit if it received your permission to seize and sell your assets if you failed to repay the loan. In other words, you might offer to create a security interest by using your personal property as *collateral*. **Collateral** is personal property that is subject to a security interest.

> a **security interest** allows a creditor to seize a debtor's personal property if a debt is not repaid

A security interest gives the bank advantages over an ordinary creditor. If the bank has a security interest, it is entitled to seize the collateral. If the bank did not have a security interest, it would have to sue you successfully for the unpaid debt and then get an order to seize your property. Even if its lawsuit was successful, the bank would not be able to get such an order if the property was already subject to a security interest held by another creditor.

> **collateral** is property that is subject to a security interest

A security interest can be given over any type of *personal property* to any type of creditor. Personal property, as discussed in Chapters 17 and 18, includes both *tangible* property (assets that can be touched) like cars, and *intangible* property (assets that cannot be touched) like corporate shares, life insurance policies, some kinds of licences, and intellectual property. In this chapter, we will discuss the creation, registration, and enforcement of security interests in personal property. We will not discuss security interests in *real property*, such as mortgages, which we examined in Chapter 16.

Even with a security interest, a bank may not be willing to lend you money unless you provide a *guarantee*. A **guarantee** is a contractual promise by a third party, called a *guarantor*, to satisfy the principal debtor's obligation if that debtor fails to do so. Suppose you persuade a friend to act as the guarantor of your loan. If you fail to repay that loan, the bank can demand payment from your friend. In some situations, however, the law recognizes that the debtor and the creditor may act in ways that unfairly hurt the guarantor. For instance, if the debtor agrees to pay a higher rate of interest on the debt, the guarantor's potential liability is increased. If that occurs after the guarantee is signed and without the guarantor's consent, the law may release the guarantor from liability. Our discussion of guarantees will focus on the situations in which guarantors are relieved of their obligations.

> a **guarantee** is a contractual promise by a third party to satisfy the principal debtor's obligation if the debtor fails to do so

PROVINCIAL PERSONAL PROPERTY SECURITY LAWS

secured creditors, or **secured parties**, are people who extend credit to a debtor and who receive a security interest from the debtor

Personal property security legislation (PPS legislation) in each province provides legal rules relating to security interests.[1] The main purpose of those laws is to make it easier for **secured creditors**, or **secured parties**, like the bank in our example, to acquire enforceable security interests. PPS legislation creates a system that allows a secured creditor to register its security interest. Registration generally gives that creditor priority over (i) all unregistered interests in the same collateral, and (ii) any interest in the collateral registered later. Once registered, the secured creditor's interest is listed in a publicly accessible database. Anyone thinking of extending credit to the same debtor can find out whether that person has already given a security interest over its assets.

HOW SECURITY INTERESTS ARE CREATED

Conditional Sales

a conditional sale occurs when the seller retains ownership of the goods to secure payment of the purchase price by the buyer

In the commercial world, a buyer is often allowed to postpone paying at least part of the purchase price. As security for that debt, the seller may retain an interest, usually in the form of ownership, in the goods that are being sold. The buyer gets *possession* of the goods immediately, but it does not *own* them until it pays the full price. This arrangement is called a **conditional sale**.

Conditional sales are very common in consumer transactions where a person buys furniture or other household items, but defers payment until some time in the future. They are also quite common if two businesses have an ongoing relationship for the purchase of goods. For instance, a manufacturer may retain a security interest in the equipment that it supplies to a distributor. In each case, the security interest is taken to secure the payment of the purchase price. If the buyer defaults, the seller can take back the goods. Usually, the buyer is responsible for any damage to the goods. Sometimes, the buyer may be required to buy insurance to cover the goods while payment is pending. The seller may require that it be named as the beneficiary under that insurance policy.

Special Cases

There are two kinds of transactions that are similar to conditional sales and are often used to create security interests:

- consignment
- lease

[1.] *Eg Personal Property Security Act*, RSA 2000, c P-7 (*APPSA*) (Alta); *Personal Property Security Act*, RSBC 1996, c 359 (*BCPPSA*) (BC); *Personal Property Security Act*, SM 1993, c 14 (*MPPSA*) (Man); *Personal Property Security Act*, SNB 1993, c P-7.1 (*NBPPSA*) (NB); *Personal Property Security Act*, SNL 1998, c P-7.1 (*NLPPSA*) (Nfld & Lab); *Personal Property Security Act*, SNS 1995–96, c 13 (*NSPPSA*) (NS); *Personal Property Security Act*, RSO 1990, c P.10 (*OPPSA*) (Ont); *Personal Property Security Act*, SPEI 1997, c 33 (*PEIPPSA*) (PEI); *Personal Property Security Act*, SS 1993, c P-6.2 (*SPPSA*) (Sask). Quebec's *Civil Code* also provides for security interests but its rules remain distinct. Our discussion is based on the rules in the other provinces.

A **consignment** occurs when the owner of goods transfers possession, but not ownership, to someone else. The owner is called the **consignor**. The person who receives possession of the goods is called the **consignee**. There are many business reasons for creating a consignment.

a consignment occurs when the owner of goods transfers possession, but not ownership, to someone else

- The consignee may be examining the goods for possible purchase.
- The consignee may have agreed to try to sell the goods on the consignor's behalf. This is what we usually mean when we say goods are held by someone "on consignment." A children's used-clothing store may take clothes on consignment from a parent, offer them for sale, and then pay the parent a percentage of the purchase price if the clothes are sold.

the consignor is the owner of the goods

the consignee is the person who receives possession of the goods, but not ownership

In a true consignment, the consignee is not bound to pay for the goods until it does something, such as selling them to a third party. However, the term "consignment" is also sometimes used to refer to a situation in which the "consignee" has already agreed to pay for the goods and the "consignor" holds onto ownership to secure full payment of the price. In effect, that situation involves a conditional sale, not a true consignment. Retention of ownership under the consignment is a form of security interest.[2]

A lease can also operate like a conditional sale and as an alternative to a secured loan. Suppose you want to buy a truck for $50 000. You could arrange to buy the truck from the seller. To finance that purchase, the seller might agree to a conditional sale in which it gave you time to pay but retained ownership of the truck until you had paid the full price, plus interest in 60 blended monthly installments of, say, $1000. Alternatively, you could borrow $50 000 from a bank, agreeing to repay that amount, plus interest, in 60 blended monthly installments of $1000. As security for those monthly installments, you could give the bank an interest in the truck.

You could also acquire the truck in a financing transaction set up as a lease. Under a **lease**, the lessor retains ownership of an asset, but gives possession of it to the lessee for a period of time in return for the lessee's promise to make regular payments. When used for financing, the lessor's ownership of the leased asset is a security interest. Its purpose is to secure the lessee's obligation to make payment. To acquire the truck in a lease financing transaction, you could enter into an arrangement with a lessor, who would buy the truck that interests you. The lessor would then agree to lease that vehicle to you for 60 months in exchange for your promise to make monthly payments of $1000. The lessor would also give you an option to purchase the truck at the end of the 60 months for the price of $1.

a lease is a relationship where the lessor retains ownership of an asset, but gives possession of it to the lessee for a period of time in return for the lessee's promise to make regular payments

With the bank financing, you get ownership of the truck at the outset, which you use as collateral for the bank loan. The bank makes its decision to lend the money to you based on two factors: (i) its assessment of your ability to make the loan payments, and (ii) its assessment of its own ability to acquire and sell the truck if you fail to make the payments.

In the lease financing and the conditional sale, you do not get ownership of the truck at the outset. The lessor or the seller owns the truck. You do get the right to possess and use the vehicle. In a conditional sale, you receive ownership when you have made all the payments. Under the lease, you have an option to obtain ownership after making all of the payments. Like the bank, the lessor and the conditional seller will make their decisions to enter into a transaction

---

[2.] In *Re Stephanian's Carpets Ltd* (1980) 1 **PPSAC** 119 (Ont SC), it was held that if a consignee has an unrestricted right to return the goods under the consignment, the consignor does not have a security interest.

with you based on two factors: their assessment of (i) your ability to make the monthly payments, and (ii) their own ability to acquire and sell the truck if you fail to make those payments.

This example has shown how a lease of an asset can be structured to have the same financial characteristics as a conditional sale or a secured bank loan to fund the purchase of the asset:

■ The same amount of credit is extended to you in each transaction—$50 000 (the price of the truck).

■ You are obligated to repay the price of the truck *plus* some interest. Consequently, while the truck only costs $50 000, you must make 60 monthly payments of $1000 each.

■ You give up an interest in the vehicle to secure your payments.

■ You will own the truck at the end of the arrangement. The only distinctive characteristic of the lease financing is that you must actually exercise your option to buy the vehicle for $1. Of course, it would be economically irrational for you *not* to exercise that option unless the truck was so badly damaged that it was worth less than $1.[3]

Granting a Security Interest in Specific Assets

In a lending transaction, the debtor often agrees to provide the creditor with ownership, or some other form of security interest, in a specific piece of personal property. In our example of the bank financing model, you gave the bank an interest in your truck. From the creditor's perspective, that arrangement is attractive because it is easy to determine the value of the collateral, and it is relatively easy to enforce the security interest. The bank knew that the collateral was worth $50 000, and to enforce its rights, it simply had to seize the vehicle if you failed to repay the loan. When the debtor transfers title in a specific asset to a secured party, the transaction is sometimes called a **chattel mortgage**.[4]

a **chattel mortgage** is a transaction in which a debtor gives a creditor title to some specific personal property to secure the performance of an obligation it owes to the creditor

Granting a Security Interest in All the Debtor's Assets

A creditor may not be satisfied with security over specific pieces of personal property. For example, if you are trying to buy a business, the bank may not lend you the purchase price unless you are willing to enter into a **general security agreement**, which provides the bank with a security interest in *all* your assets. A bank often requires a general security agreement because it ensures that the bank has a claim to whatever assets the debtor has. Since it is not in either party's interest to freeze operations, however, the debtor typically will be given permission to carry on business as usual, including selling inventory and replacing worn-out equipment.

a **general security agreement** provides a creditor with a security interest in *all* of the debtor's assets

---

[3] In practice, option prices are usually more than $1. Even when the option price is substantial, however, a lease transaction may be functionally equivalent to a conditional sale or a bank-financed purchase if the price is at, or less than, the market value of the leased goods at the end of the lease term.

[4] In Chapter 17, we considered the source of the word "chattel" and examined rules regarding the acquisition and loss of chattels.

Assignment of Accounts Receivable

Most businesses sell at least some of their products on credit. For instance, customers may be given 30 or 60 days to pay for goods or services they have bought. The amounts that a business is entitled to collect from its customers are its **accounts receivable**. Those accounts usually represent a substantial asset, which can be used as security if the business wants to borrow money. The business can give the bank an **assignment of accounts receivable**, which would allow the bank to collect the debts (or "book debts") owing to the business if the loan is not repaid.

accounts receivable are the amounts that a business is entitled to collect from its customers

When a debtor makes an assignment of accounts receivable, the creditor does not usually collect money that is owing to the debtor. In most cases, the debtor is allowed to collect its own accounts receivable and to carry on business as usual. The creditor steps in and demands payment from the debtor's customers only if the debtor fails to fulfill its obligations to the creditor.[5] Figure 23.1 illustrates the process of assigning accounts receivable as security.

an assignment of accounts receivable allows a creditor to collect money owing to a debtor if the debtor does not fulfill its obligations

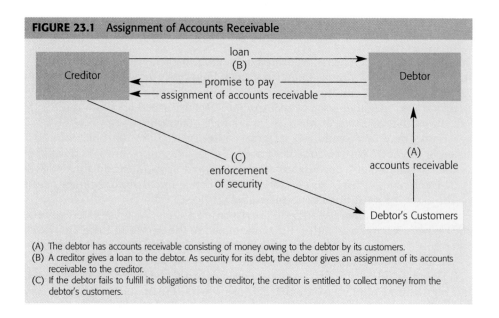

FIGURE 23.1 Assignment of Accounts Receivable

(A) The debtor has accounts receivable consisting of money owing to the debtor by its customers.
(B) A creditor gives a loan to the debtor. As security for its debt, the debtor gives an assignment of its accounts receivable to the creditor.
(C) If the debtor fails to fulfill its obligations to the creditor, the creditor is entitled to collect money from the debtor's customers.

After-Acquired Property

To get maximum protection, banks and other financial institutions often take security over *all* of the debtor's assets in a general security agreement. The security interest in such an agreement typically covers assets that the debtor acquires *after* the security agreement becomes effective. Provincial PPS legislation permits such security interests in after-acquired property.

Before the PPS legislation was created, creditors often used a *floating charge* to take security in after-acquired property. A **floating charge** is a security interest that *hovers* above the debtor's assets until some event causes the charge to become *fixed* or *crystallized* on those assets. The contract that creates that interest usually states that the charge hovers over *all* of the debtor's property, both present and future. It also usually states that the charge

a floating charge is a security interest that *hovers* above the debtor's assets until some event causes the charge to become *fixed* or *crystallized* on those assets

---

[5.] We discussed assignments of accounts receivable in Chapter 8.

descends and becomes fixed if the debtor misses a payment and is provided with notice of default by the creditor. Until then, the debtor can carry on business, including buying and selling assets, without regard to the floating charge. However, once the relevant event occurs, the debtor can only sell its assets *subject to the creditor's charge*. That means that a purchaser of the debtor's assets does not own them outright—the creditor's interest continues to exist in them. Many of the cases on floating charges dealt with the difficult task of determining precisely when the charge crystallized.

Floating charges are not often used any more because the PPS legislation allows a creditor to take a similar but more effective sort of security interest. A secured party's interest can attach to all of the debtor's current and after-acquired property as soon as the property is acquired by the debtor without any requirement for crystallization. With some exceptions, that interest continues to exist even if the debtor disposes of its property to a third party. In practice, security agreements that deal with after-acquired property under the PPS legislation usually allow the debtor to deal with its assets free of the secured party's interest to the extent necessary to carry on its business.[6]

Special Security Interests of Banks

In Canada, banks can be incorporated only under the federal *Bank Act*.[7] Section 427 of the Act allows banks to take a special kind of security in certain types of assets, which other creditors cannot take. Banks may take section 427 interests *in addition* to the other sorts of security interests described above, and often do take more that one type of security for a single obligation.

Banks may take section 427 security interests only in the types of assets listed in the Act. These include the goods (usually inventory, but not always) of retailers, wholesalers, and manufacturers, as well as mining and forest products. Banks cannot take this special kind of interest in either consumers' assets or the assets of most businesses providing services.

Under the Act, there is a special registration system for these interests. For the registration to be effective, the bank must get the debtor to file a "notice of intention" to give security to the bank at the branch of the Bank of Canada closest to the debtor's place of business.

The main advantage of a section 427 security interest for banks is that a single registration applies to all the debtor's assets, no matter where they are located. In contrast, the PPS legislation of a province is effective only with respect to assets in that province. Consequently, a section 427 security interest is less burdensome to register if the debtor has assets in several provinces. Another advantage of section 427 interests is that they will prevail over most other forms of security interests in the same collateral.[8]

Concept Summary 23.1 reviews the common ways in which security interests are created.

---

[6] *Eg Re Credit Suisse Canada and 1133 Yonge Street Holdings Limited* (1998) 41 OR (3d) 632 (CA).

[7] *Bank Act*, SC 1991, c 46 (Can).

[8] The precise relationship between interests created under the federal *Bank Act* and provincial PPS legislation is not clear, as discussed below.

CONCEPT SUMMARY 23.1

Common Ways Security Interests Are Created

Conditional sale	The seller of goods retains title, or some other form of security interest, to secure future payment of the purchase price by the buyer.
Granting a security interest in a specific asset	The debtor gives a security interest in some of its personal property to a creditor to secure performance of an obligation owed by the debtor (chattel mortgage).
Assignment of accounts receivable	A person (the *assignor*) who is owed a debt (the *account receivable*) assigns it to someone else (such as a bank) to secure performance of an obligation owed by the assignor to the bank.
Granting a security interest in all the debtor's assets, including after-acquired property	The debtor gives a security interest in all of its personal property, including all property acquired by the debtor *after* the date that the security agreement is created, to a creditor to secure performance of an obligation owed by the debtor (a general security agreement).
Special security interests created under the *Bank Act*	The debtor gives a bank a security interest in certain types of property described in the Act. A single registration protects this interest in the debtor's assets wherever they are in Canada.

PROVINCIAL PERSONAL PROPERTY SECURITY LEGISLATION

Each method of creating a security interest that we have discussed has the same function: to give the creditor an interest in the debtor's property to secure the debtor's performance of an obligation. Historically, each type was governed by special legislation or common law rules. They carried different remedies and enforcement procedures. Different types of security interests had to be registered at different places. That situation was inconvenient for a business considering extending credit, for at least two reasons.

- Even within a single province, a potential creditor who wanted to know whether a debtor had already given a security interest in a particular asset to another creditor had to search separate registries for each type of registered interest.

- Since most of the relevant laws were provincial, a secured party had to search separately in every province where the debtor had assets that it offered as security.

It is still necessary for secured parties to search in every province where the debtor has assets. And in some cases, it may be difficult to tell which provincial laws apply, such as when a truck that is collateral moves between provinces. Within each province, however, PPS legislation now integrates the sometimes conflicting common law and statutory rules for security interests. The details of the provincial systems differ. But *most* security interests are now governed by a single legislative scheme. We will discuss the general rules, as well as some of the exceptions.

The unified approach under PPS legislation allows creditors to assess and manage risks more easily and accurately. It provides a simple and inexpensive system for secured parties to register their interests. Provincial registers can be searched to determine what security interests a debtor has granted, and PPS

priority is the ranking of a secured creditor's right to enforce its claim against a piece of collateral compared to the claims of other secured creditors in the same collateral

legislation establishes a clear set of rules for determining the **priority**, or ranking, of competing claims to the same collateral. Provincial legislation also provides a single system of default rights that applies to almost all types of security interests. In all these ways, the PPS legislation provides greater certainty for creditors.

Scope of Application

Most provincial PPS legislation applies to all agreements between a debtor and a secured party that create a security interest in personal property.[9] A security interest is defined simply as an interest in personal property that secures the payment or performance of an obligation. This functional definition was intended to catch all kinds of security interests that arise by agreement, regardless of their form. It includes, for instance, conditional sales, assignments of accounts receivable, and general security agreements.

Leases

One difficult, but important, issue is how to determine if a lease transaction creates a security interest. As discussed earlier, a lease of goods can be used as a substitute for a secured loan to finance the acquisition of the goods. Whether the lessor's title functions as a security interest depends upon the terms of the lease and circumstances of the transaction. Some jurisdictions have tried to avoid the problem of determining when a lease creates a security interest by providing that any lease that has a term of over one year is caught by the PPS legislation.[10] In Ontario, however, it is still necessary to analyze each transaction to see if the lease, in substance, creates a security interest.

If a lease is subject to the provincial PPS legislation, the priority of the lessor's security interest is determined by the legislation. If a lease is not subject to the PPS legislation, the lessor's ownership of the leased assets typically gives it a claim ranking ahead of all other creditors of the lessee, including those who have registered under the legislation. This is always the lessor's preferred result.

Exceptions

The rules in provincial PPS legislation do not apply to all forms of interests in personal property.[11] Rights created by statute, rather than agreement, are not caught. These are the most important statutory rights.

the **right of distress**, or **distraint**, allows a landlord to seize property that is on the rented premises and belongs to the tenant, sell it, and use the sale proceeds to pay the outstanding rent

- A landlord under a commercial lease usually enjoys the *right of distress*, or *distraint*, if the tenant has not paid rent (as discussed in Chapter 15). The **right of distress**, or **distraint**, allows a landlord to seize property that is on the rented premises and belongs to the tenant, sell it, and use the sale proceeds to pay the outstanding rent. That right normally cannot be used against non-commercial tenants.

under a **deemed trust**, some assets of a business are deemed as a matter of law to be held for the benefit of the government and cannot be used for the business

- *Deemed trusts* that are created under some statutes for the benefit of the government are exempt from the application of provincial PPS legislation. Under a **deemed trust**, some assets of a business are deemed as a matter of law to be held for the benefit of the government and cannot be used for the business. The most important deemed trust is the provision

---

[9.] *Eg BCPPSA* s 2(1); *NBPPSA* s 3(1); *OPPSA* s 2.

[10.] *Eg BCPPSA* s 3(b)(c); *NBPPSA* s 3(2); *NSPPSA* s 4(2).

[11.] Exceptions are provided for in PPS legislation: *eg BCPPSA* s 4; *NBPPSA* s 4; *OPPSA* s 4.

of the *Income Tax Act* that states that tax deductions from employee wages by employers are deemed to be held in trust for the government. As a result, the government beneficially owns the funds, which must be remitted to the Canada Revenue Agency.[12]

- *Liens* for people who provide repair or storage services are usually excluded from the PPS legislation. A person who is in possession of personal property for the purpose of either repairing or storing it can retain the property until the owner pays the price of the repairs or storage. For instance, a mechanic who fixes your car can keep the vehicle until you pay the repair bill. The mechanic's right against your car is like a security interest since it is used to reduce the risk that the bill will not be paid. It is different from a security interest, however, because it arises without you, as the debtor, consenting. That right, called a **lien**, usually exists only if the person providing the goods or services is in possession of the property. In some situations, however, a non-possessory lien may be available.[13]

a lien allows a person who has not been paid to retain possession of goods that the person has repaired or stored

These exceptions mean that the specified creditors do not have to register under the PPS legislation, and, in most cases, they have priority over ordinary security interests that are subject to the legislation.

The interests of banks under section 427 of the *Bank Act* represent a sort of hybrid. In Ontario, the courts have said that a bank may register these interests under PPS legislation and take advantage of whatever rights registration may provide in terms of priority over other creditors. Banks do not have to register, however. They may choose to register only under the special system set up under the *Bank Act* and enforce their rights under that statute.[14] In some other provinces, PPS legislation provides that it does not apply to section 427 interests. Although no case has decided the issue, rights under the *Bank Act* likely rank ahead of rights subject to PPS legislation.

Protecting Security Interests under PPS Legislation

As we saw in Chapter 8, contracts usually can be enforced only against those who are parties to them. That rule of *privity* generally applies to contracts that create security interests. Under provincial PPS legislation, however, a security agreement may be effective against third parties, such as other secured parties, if the security interest meets the requirements for **attachment** in the PPS legislation.

attachment allows a security interest to be enforced against third parties

Attachment

Attachment occurs when three requirements are met:

- The debtor signs a written security agreement containing a description of the collateral, or the secured party gets possession of collateral.

[12.] *Income Tax Act*, RSC 1985 (5th Supp), c 1, s 227(4) and (4.1) (Can). The equitable concept of the trust was discussed in Chapter 1.

[13.] *Repair and Storage Liens Act*, RSO 1990, c R.25, Part II (Ont). Even though they are not generally subject to PPS legislation, the statutes in some provinces state that repair and storage liens prevail over interests that are subject to the legislation: *eg OPPSA* s 31. As well, the Ontario *Repair and Storage Liens Act* sets out certain requirements for a lien and creates some exceptions to its priority: ss 7(3), 16(1)(c) and (d). Repairers and storers may register their liens under the Ontario PPS legislation. Liens were discussed in Chapter 17.

[14.] *Re Bank of Nova Scotia and International Harvester Credit Corp of Can Ltd* (1990) 73 DLR (4th) 385 (Ont CA); *Royal Bank of Canada v Sparrow Electric Corp* (1997) 143 DLR (4th) 385 (SCC).

- The secured party gives some value, such as a loan, to the debtor.
- The debtor has some rights in the collateral.[15]

Perfection

To fully protect the priority of its claims to a debtor's assets, a secured party must *perfect* its security interest. **Perfection** usually occurs when a security interest has attached, and the secured party has registered under the PPS legislation. It is also possible, though less common, for a secured party to perfect its security interest by taking possession of the collateral.[16]

To perfect by registration, the secured party must file a **financing statement** with the registrar responsible for administering the PPS legislation in that province. The registrar will note the time and date of registration. That information is used to determine the priority of the secured party's interest in relation to any other security interest under the PPS legislation. A security interest perfected by registration has priority over all *subsequently* registered security interests in the same collateral, but not over *previously* registered security interests. Registration also ensures that the existence of a security interest is disclosed to people who search the register, including other potential creditors. Registration continues for a period chosen by the registering secured party. Registration fees increase with the duration of the registration.[17]

The financing statement identifies the debtor, the secured party, and the general nature of the security interest. Paper financing statements are scanned and stored in an electronic database. Financing statements can also be filed directly in electronic form. This *notice filing system* has several advantages over older systems that required the security documents themselves to be filed.

- It is easier to file, store, and search electronic records.
- The specific terms of the security agreement remain confidential, known only to the debtor and the secured party.
- A single financing statement can relate to more than one security interest given by a debtor to a secured party. For instance, a creditor who takes an interest in a debtor's inventory and accounts receivable in separate security agreements can perfect both interests by filing a single financing statement.
- A secured party can register before the security agreement is created.

Business Decision 23.1 (on the next page) illustrates the benefits of that last feature of the notice filing system.

Priorities under PPS Legislation

A great advantage of PPS legislation is that it provides a system for determining who prevails when more than one secured party claims an interest in the same collateral. The relative priority of claims is often critically important. A debtor in default on its credit obligations usually does not have enough assets to pay off all its creditors.

[15.] *Eg BCPPSA* s 12; *OPPSA* s 11(2).

[16.] Under the *OPPSA*, perfection is possible through registration (s 23) or possession (s 22).

[17.] In Ontario, a registration for up to 25 years can be obtained for $8 per year.

BUSINESS DECISION 23.1

Registration Before Attachment

Lenders generally file a financing statement to register their security interest *before* closing the financing transaction. This is a typical example.

Keeshon Construction Ltd and the Royal Bank discussed a loan from the bank to Keeshon of $1 000 000. The loan was to be secured on all of Keeshon's assets. They arranged that the loan and security agreements would be signed and the money advanced on September 19, 2004.

In anticipation of the loan, the bank registered a financing statement against Keeshon on September 15. Four days later, as anticipated, the parties signed the loan and security agreements, and the bank gave Keeshon a cheque for $1 000 000.

The bank's security interest attached in all of Keeshon's assets as soon as the security agreement was signed and value was given by the bank on September 19. Perfection occurred at the same time because the financing statement relating to the interest had already been filed. For perfection to occur, there must be attachment plus a registration, but the order in which the two requirements are met does not matter.

Question for Discussion

1. Why would the bank want to register its interest as soon as possible?

All security interests subject to provincial PPS legislation are treated the same way regardless of their form. It does not matter, for example, whether one security interest consists of ownership of a piece of collateral retained by a conditional seller and another is a security interest of a bank in the same collateral under a general security agreement. The basic rule is that the first to register has the best claim. It makes no difference if a subsequently registered secured party knew about another secured party's interest that was registered earlier or that attachment occurred after registration.[18] In Business Decision 23.1, the relevant date for determining the bank's priority in any contest with another secured party is the date of its registration, September 15, 2004, even though perfection did not occur until September 19. If another secured creditor had obtained and perfected by registration a security interest in Keeshon's assets on September 18, it would still rank behind the bank.

An **unperfected security interest**, meaning simply a security interest that has not been perfected, is subordinate to:

an unperfected security interest is a security interest that has not been perfected

- any perfected interest
- other unperfected interests that attached earlier
- any lien created under any law
- any creditor who has both successfully obtained a judgment against the debtor and taken steps to enforce it by seizing the debtor's property[19]

Unperfected interests are also ineffective against anyone who represents the debtor's creditors, such as a trustee in bankruptcy.[20] Secured creditors of a bankrupt debtor can enforce perfected security interests against the trustee. An unperfected security interest, however, is treated as an unsecured debt. A creditor with an unsecured debt is entitled only to share in whatever assets are left *after* the creditors with perfected security interests enforce their rights to the

---

[18.] *Robert Simpson Co v Shadlock* (1981) 119 DLR (3d) 417 (Ont HCJ). The rules are different where the secured party has perfected by taking possession of the collateral. In that case, the first to take possession or register prevails: *BCPPSA* s 30; *NBPPSA* s 30; *OPPSA* s 30.

[19.] *Eg OPPSA* s 20(1)(a); *SPPSA* s 20(1)(a)(b).

[20.] *Eg OPPSA* s 20(1)(b); *SPPSA* s 20(1)(d).

debtor's collateral. Each unsecured creditor will receive a share of the debtor's remaining assets equal to the proportion that the debt owed to that creditor represents of the debtor's total unsecured debt. For example, assume that a debtor's obligations exceed its assets by a 10:1 ratio. It owes $1 000 000, but it has assets worth only $100 000 and there are no creditors with perfected security interests. If you, as an unsecured creditor, are owed $50 000, you will receive only $5000. If you were the only secured creditor with a perfected security interest, you would be entitled to seize $50 000 of the debtor's remaining assets, forcing the unsecured creditors to share the remaining $50 000. As a matter of risk management, you should have perfected your interest.

Purchase Money Security Interests

Banks and other financial institutions generally take security interests in *all* of the debtor's property, including property acquired after the loan is made and the security agreement is created.[21] Such security interests in after-acquired property can be troublesome to a debtor who wants to acquire new assets on credit.

Suppose a farm equipment distributor takes a bank loan, giving a security interest in all of its assets, both present and future. The bank files a financing statement to register its security interest under the PPS legislation. The distributor now wants to purchase more inventory from a manufacturer. Since it has little money, it wants to buy on credit. There may be a problem. The manufacturer may not agree to sell on credit unless it can take an effective form of security. However, all of the distributor's assets, including any subsequently acquired from the manufacturer, are *already* subject to the bank's perfected security interest. That means that the manufacturer's security interest would necessarily rank second at best. The first priority of the bank's security interest in after-acquired property may jeopardize the distributor's ability to acquire new assets for the business.

Because this is a frequent problem, PPS legislation provides a special priority rule that applies in such circumstances. When a security interest in collateral is taken by a seller of personal property to secure payment of the purchase price, the seller's security interest can be given priority over all other security interests in the same collateral given by the debtor. This is called a **purchase money security interest (PMSI)**. A PMSI can also be acquired by a lender, such as a bank, if (i) it lends money to the debtor to acquire an asset, (ii) the debtor actually uses that money to acquire that asset, and (iii) the debtor uses that asset as collateral for the loan.[22]

In either case, to obtain the PMSI super priority, the secured party must register its interest within 10 days of the debtor getting possession of the collateral. Suppose you want to buy a car on credit from a car dealer, but you have already given your bank a security interest in all of your property, including after-acquired property. The car dealer could get a PMSI in the car and rank ahead of the bank if it registered its financing statement to perfect its security interest within 10 days of your getting possession of the car.[23]

a purchase money security interest (PMSI) is a security interest in a particular asset given by a debtor to a secured party that either sells that asset to the debtor or finances the debtor's acquisition of that asset

---

[21.] Security interests in after-acquired property are expressly permitted in *OPPSA* s 12. After-acquired property clauses for the benefit of conditional sellers are not enforceable against consumers: *BCPPSA* s 13(2)(b); *OPPSA* s 12(2)(b); see also *Consumer Protection Act, 2002*, SO 2002, c 30, s 24 (Ont).

[22.] PMSIs are defined in *OPPSA* s and their super priority is granted in *OPPSA* 33. It is possible for creditors to enter into an agreement to fix the priority of their security interests in a way that is different from what the PPS legislation would provide. Where a secured party agrees to a lower priority, the agreement is called a "subordination agreement."

[23.] *Eg BCPPSA* s 34; *NBPPSA* s 33; *OPPSA* s 33.

Special rules apply to PMSIs in **inventory**, those goods held for sale or lease by the debtor. They must be registered *before* the debtor gets possession of the collateral, and notice must be given to any secured party who previously filed a financing statement indicating an interest in inventory. Case Brief 23.1 illustrates these rules.

inventory consists of goods held for sale or lease

CASE BRIEF 23.1

Clark Equipment of Canada Ltd v Bank of Montreal (1984) 4 PPSAC 38 (Man CA)

In 1977, the Bank of Montreal made a loan to Maneco Equipment Ltd. As security for the loan, the bank obtained a security interest in all property currently owned or acquired in the future by Maneco. It registered its interest in 1977 by filing a financing statement.

In 1978, Clark Equipment of Canada Ltd entered into an agreement to finance the acquisition of Clark equipment by Maneco, whose business was selling and leasing Clark equipment. On September 7, 1978, Clark gave notice to the bank that it would have a PMSI in the equipment that Maneco would acquire from Clark. Clark filed a financing statement in relation to this interest on September 20, 1978. Subsequently,

in 1979, 1980, and 1981, Maneco acquired three pieces of equipment from Clark, but did not pay for them.

In June 1981, Maneco defaulted on its loan, and the bank seized the equipment. Clark claimed that it had first claim to the equipment because it had a PMSI that ranked ahead of the bank's previously registered security interest.

The court held that the requirements for a PMSI had been met: (i) Clark's interest had been perfected by registration before Maneco got possession of the collateral, and (ii) Clark gave notice to the bank of its PMSI claim in Maneco's inventory. Clark was therefore entitled to recover the equipment.

Security Interests When Collateral Is Transferred

One key protection for secured parties in **PPS** legislation is that a security interest in personal property may continue to exist even when the property is transferred by the debtor to someone else.[24] This means that the buyer of the property has to respect the secured party's interest, even if it did not know about the interest. If the debtor defaults, the property could be seized from the buyer. While the buyer will be able to sue the seller for what it paid plus any damages it suffers, that action may not be very useful. If the secured party has been driven to actually enforcing a security interest, the debtor presumably has little money.

Buyers will want to avoid this kind of risk. For each sale, a buyer could search the register maintained under **PPS** legislation to make sure that the seller had not granted a security interest in the goods. However, that strategy would be expensive and time consuming, and it would not disclose unregistered interests. If that were the only strategy for avoiding risk, many commercial transactions would be discouraged. Consider the problem of having to do a search every time you bought something at a store. Because of that difficulty, the **PPS** legislation contains exceptions to the general rule that a secured creditor's security interest in collateral follows the collateral into the buyer's hands.[25] An exception arises if

---

24. *Eg OPPSA* s 25(1)(a); *SPPSA* s 28(1)(a). Provincial **PPS** legislation also requires that secured parties make a new filing, called a *financing change statement*, within a specified time after they find out about the transfer. That document, which names the buyer, is needed to maintain the perfection of the secured party's interest: *eg OPPSA* s 48.

25. *Eg OPPSA* ss 25(1)(a), 28; *SPPSA* ss 28(1)(a), 30.

- the secured party has permitted the debtor to sell or otherwise deal with the collateral, or
- the debtor sells the collateral in the ordinary course of the debtor's business

In either of those situations, the buyer receives the collateral free of any security interest given by the seller, even if the security interest is perfected and the buyer knows it. The only time that the buyer is not protected is when (i) the sale was a breach of the security agreement between the seller and a secured party, and (ii) the buyer knew it.

The first exception is hard to rely on because a buyer seldom knows the content of a security agreement that exists between the seller-debtor and that party's creditor. Consequently, the key question from the buyer's perspective is usually whether the sale occurred in the ordinary course of the seller-debtor's business. A buyer who is in doubt on that question should search the register that is maintained under the PPS legislation.

A buyer does not have to worry about unperfected security interests. PPS legislation provides that unperfected interests are not effective against a buyer who had no knowledge of the interest.[26] This is another good reason for secured parties to register their interests.

Concept Summary 23.2 reviews the priorities rules under PPS legislation.

CONCEPT SUMMARY 23.2

Priority of Security Interests in an Asset under PPS Legislation

1. Purchase money security interest in the asset*	Rights of certain creditors with claims outside the scope of PPS legislation (*eg* landlord's distress rights) have priority over security interests subject to PPS legislation
2. Perfected security interests in the asset ranked in order of the time of registration*	
3. Unperfected security interests in the asset ranked in order of the time of attachment* BUT subordinate to claims by • trustee in bankruptcy or other representative of creditors • creditor with a judgment • buyers of the asset without knowledge of security interest *None of these interests are enforceable against a person who acquires the asset in a manner permitted under the security agreement or in the ordinary course of the seller's business (unless sale was a breach of the security agreement and the person knew it)	

Enforcement of Security Interests

In this section, we discuss the enforcement of security interests by secured parties, including the rules protecting the interests of debtors.

[26.] *Eg OPPSA* s 20(1)(c); *SPPSA* s 20(1)(d).

Default by the Debtor

A secured party can take possession of the collateral when the debtor has defaulted on its obligations. A **default** occurs when

- the debtor fails to pay or to perform any other obligation secured under the security agreement, or
- an event occurs that is defined as a default in the security agreement

Security agreements often define default to include a failure to

- maintain the collateral in good working order
- maintain insurance on the collateral

A security agreement may give the debtor a period, such as 30 days, to remedy the default. The creditor cannot take steps toward enforcement until that period expires.

default occurs if either the debtor fails to pay or perform any other obligation secured under the security agreement, or an event occurs that is defined as a default in the security agreement

Taking Possession

The secured party's first step when a debtor defaults is to take possession of the collateral. Possession may not be taken by force.[27] If the debtor resists, the secured party must seek a court order for possession. Once a secured party has taken possession of collateral, it has an obligation to take reasonable care of it.[28]

To take possession of the collateral, the secured party must give reasonable notice to the debtor.[29] What is reasonable varies from no notice at all to a few days. No notice would be appropriate if, for example, the debtor had no prospect of paying, and the collateral was at risk. Imagine, for example, that the collateral consisted of a truckload of ripe peaches. If collateral consists of accounts receivable, the secured party can simply give notice to the person obligated to make payment to the debtor that all future payments should be made directly to the secured party.[30]

Disposition of Collateral

Once the secured party has obtained possession of the collateral, it usually wants to sell it and apply the proceeds of the sale toward the outstanding debt. There are few legal rules regarding such sales. The secured party may advertise the sale to the public or enter into a private agreement with a buyer. It must give at least 15 days notice of the sale to the debtor and others with an interest in it.[31] Alternatively, the secured party may also decide to lease the collateral to someone or do something else. Whatever it decides to do, the secured party must act in a manner that is commercially reasonable.[32]

---

[27] *R v Doucette* (1960) 25 DLR (2d) 380 (Ont CA). Any method permitted by law may be used: *OPPSA* s 62(a). A conditional seller may not take possession of the property sold if the buyer is a consumer who has paid at least two-thirds of the purchase price: *Consumer Protection Act, 2002*, SO 2002, c 30, s 21 (Ont); *BCPPSA* s 58(3).

[28] *Eg BCPPSA* s 17; *NBPPSA* s 17; *OPPSA* s 17.

[29] *Ronald Elwyn Lister Ltd v Dunlop Canada Ltd* (1982) 135 DLR (3d) 1 (SCC). There are special notice requirements when a secured party intends to enforce its security interest against an insolvent debtor provided for in the *Bankruptcy and Insolvency Act*, RSC 1985, c B-3, amended SC 1992, c 27 (Can). See Chapter 24.

[30] *Eg BCPPSA* s 61; *NBPPSA* s 61; *OPPSA* s 61.

[31] *Eg OPPSA* s 63(4), (5), (6), (7).

[32] *Eg OPPSA* s 63(2); *SPPSA* s 59(2), (3).

What is commercially reasonable depends upon the circumstances. In general, the secured party must take reasonable care to ensure that it obtains the fair value of the collateral and does not act negligently. In some cases, the secured party will be obliged to either advertise the sale to ensure that a competitive bidding process takes place or obtain a professional valuation to ensure that the collateral is not sold for less than its worth.

The requirement for the secured party to act in a commercially reasonable manner provides important protection for the debtor. The secured party is interested only in recovering what it is owed, plus any expenses that it incurred as a result of enforcing its rights. Since the secured party cannot keep any excess money, it might be tempted to quickly sell the collateral for less than it is worth. Consider the case in You Be the Judge 23.1.

YOU BE THE JUDGE 23.1

Commercial Reasonableness and the Disposition of Collateral[33]

Copp and Piccininni carried on a dental practice together through a management corporation. For that practice, the corporation leased equipment from Medi-dent Services Ltd under a number of long-term leases. Copp and Piccininni got into a fundamental disagreement about how to run the practice. Everything stopped, including the payments to Medi-dent. Eventually, Medi-dent seized the equipment. At that time, Medi-dent was owed $31 000 under the leases.

On April 18, 1990, Medi-dent gave a notice to the corporation, as well as to Piccininni and Copp, that it would sell the equipment at a public or private sale after May 14 if the full amount of the indebtedness was not paid before that date. Piccininni contacted Medi-dent immediately after the seizure and offered to buy the equipment himself for

$31 000. Medi-dent readily agreed since that was a simple and inexpensive way to get its money out. The sale was concluded on May 15.

Copp subsequently challenged the sale on the basis that it was not commercially reasonable. Copp argued that Medi-dent had not had a valuation done, nor had it tried to sell the equipment through a competitive bidding process. He also produced evidence that the equipment had a fair market value of at least $79 000.

Questions for Discussion

1. Did Medi-dent act in a commercially reasonable manner?
2. What should Medi-dent have done?

When a secured party sells the collateral, it can keep from the proceeds (i) any reasonable expenses it incurred while seizing and disposing of the collateral, and (ii) the amount it is owed on the debt. Any amount left over must be paid to the debtor. If there are other secured parties, proceeds may have to be paid to them rather than the debtor, in accordance with the priorities scheme in the provincial PPS legislation. If the secured party does not recover all that it is owed, the debtor remains liable for any deficiency.

When a Secured Party Can Keep the Collateral

Sometimes, a secured party will decide to keep the collateral after it has taken possession. Suppose the secured party runs an electrical contracting business. It sold some extra wiring it had on hand to another electrical contractor on credit and took a security interest in the wiring to secure the payment of the purchase price. If the buyer defaulted and the seller took possession of the wiring, the seller might want to keep the wiring to use in its own business.

[33.] *Copp v Medi-dent Services Ltd* (1991) 3 OR (3d) 570 (Gen Div).

Under PPS legislation, if the seller decides to keep the wiring, it gives up any claim it has against the buyer for payment of the price. The seller therefore would have to be satisfied that the goods are worth at least the amount of the buyer's obligation before it decided to keep the collateral. Before the seller can do so, however, it must give notice to the buyer and to any other secured party with a security interest in the collateral. If anyone objects to the seller keeping the collateral, it has to be sold. Objections most commonly arise when the collateral is worth more than the debt owed to the secured party.[34]

When a Debtor Can Get the Collateral Back

The Ontario *PPSA* permits a debtor to **redeem collateral**—recover it back from a secured creditor who has seized it—only if the debtor has (i) fulfilled all the secured obligations, and (ii) paid all of the secured party's reasonable expenses.[35] In Ontario, a debtor does not have any right to cure a default and put the credit obligation back into good standing by making only its missed payments. Unless the secured party agrees, the debtor must redeem the collateral before the debtor can get it back. Secured parties who rank behind the secured party in possession of the collateral can also redeem it.

In other provinces, the debtor can redeem the collateral but can also get the collateral back by making the missed payments plus paying the secured party's expenses.[36] This is called **reinstating the collateral**.

Concept Summary 23.3 reviews the rules for enforcing security interests.

> **redeeming collateral** means recovering the collateral from a secured creditor, who has seized it, by fulfilling all obligations owed to the secured party and paying any expenses it has incurred

> **reinstating the collateral** means the debtor gets the collateral back from a secured party that has seized it by making the missed payments plus paying the secured party's expenses

---

CONCEPT SUMMARY 23.3

Steps in Enforcing a Security Interest

1.	Debtor defaults.
2.	Secured party takes possession of collateral.
3.	Secured party retains collateral in full satisfaction of the debtor's obligation, *or*
	Secured party disposes of collateral and applies proceeds to debtor's debt, *or*
	Debtor gets collateral back by (i) redeeming it, meaning paying all outstanding amounts owed to the secured party, *or* (ii) in some provinces, reinstating it, meaning paying amounts owing at the time of default. To reinstate or redeem, the debtor must also pay the expenses of the secured party.
4.	Debtor remains liable for any deficiency, and any surplus is distributed in accordance with scheme of priority in the relevant PPS legislation.

GUARANTEES

A creditor can reduce the risk of non-payment by taking security. A creditor can also reduce that risk by obtaining a *guarantee*, a contractual promise by a third party, called a *guarantor*, to satisfy the principal debtor's obligation if the debtor

---

34. *Eg OPPSA* s 65(2)–(7).

35. If collateral is consumer goods, the debtor has a right to reinstate the debt in Ontario: *OPPSA* s 66(2), (3).

36. *Eg SPPSA* s 62, applied in *Bank of Nova Scotia v Sherstobitov* (1987) 64 Sask R 293 (QB); *MPPSA* s 62.

fails to do so. For example, if you were going to borrow money to buy a car, the bank might ask your parents to sign a guarantee of your obligation to make the loan payments. Your parents' guarantee would mean that if you failed to pay, the bank could demand payment from them.[37] A bank may also ask for a guarantee if the borrower is a corporation with few assets or is starting a new business. A guarantee from a shareholder with substantial personal assets may convince the bank to make the loan. The obligation under a guarantee is typically independent of the debtor's obligation, meaning that, after the debtor has defaulted, it is not necessary for the creditor to take steps against the debtor to enforce the debtor's obligation before making demand on the guarantor for performance. Figure 23.2 illustrates how a guarantee works.

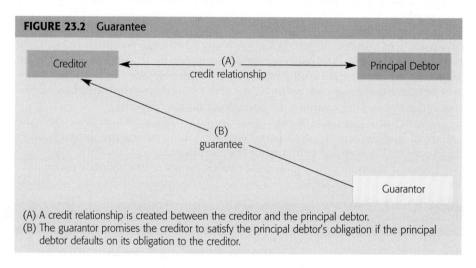

FIGURE 23.2 Guarantee

(A) A credit relationship is created between the creditor and the principal debtor.
(B) The guarantor promises the creditor to satisfy the principal debtor's obligation if the principal debtor defaults on its obligation to the creditor.

A guarantor may be relieved of liability if the guarantor's risk is increased without the guarantor's consent. That may occur in four situations.

- The contract between the creditor and principal debtor may be modified, without the consent of the guarantor, in a way that is prejudicial to the guarantor.[38] This commonly occurs when the creditor and the debtor agree to increase the size of the loan or the rate of interest to be paid by the debtor. In either event, the guarantor's exposure is increased.
- The creditor may breach its contract with the principal debtor in a way that affects the guarantor's risk. Suppose a loan agreement stated that the debtor's failure to send the creditor annual financial statements was a default, but also that the creditor could take no action on the default for 30 days. If the creditor initiated enforcement proceedings when the statements were only one day late, and refused to accept the statements on the following day in breach of its obligations, the guarantor would be released. The creditor's action eliminated the debtor's right to cure the default.
- The creditor may do something that decreases the value of the collateral that the principal debtor gave as security. In this case, the guarantor's obligation is reduced to the extent that the creditor diminished the value of the collateral. Suppose the security was a shipment of pork bellies.

[37.] There are many business situations in which guarantees may be sought and given, but the rules in each case are always the same rules as described in this section.
[38.] *Reid v Royal Trust Corp of Canada* (1985) 20 DLR (4th) 223 (PEI CA).

The bank took possession, but then let the goods sit for an unreasonable time. The pork became rancid and unsellable.[39]

■ The creditor may breach the contract of guarantee. This might occur if, for instance, the contract required the creditor to notify the guarantor before demanding payment, but the creditor failed to do so.

In general, the guarantor can resist enforcement of the guarantee by using any defence that the principal debtor could use against the creditor. Suppose the creditor sold a television to your brother, and you signed a guarantee of your brother's obligation to pay the purchase price. If the television did not work, and your brother was entitled to refuse to pay the price, you could also refuse to make payment under the guarantee. Often, however, the contract that creates the guarantee will require the guarantor to waive those defences, as well as the grounds that we examined in the previous paragraph that would relieve the guarantor of responsibility.[40] If a guarantor pays off the debt owed to the creditor, it can seek payment from the principal debtor.

A guarantee is often a significant obligation from which the guarantor may get little direct personal benefit.[41] The courts have held that a guarantee will not be enforceable if the guarantor does not understand the nature of the obligations that have been created. This is why guarantees must be in writing to be enforceable in every province except Manitoba.[42] Likewise, in some situations, courts have insisted that guarantors receive independent legal advice regarding the obligations that they are assuming, especially if they are in a vulnerable position and if the guarantee exposes them to great risk.[43] Ethical Perspective 23.1 illustrates this issue.

ETHICAL PERSPECTIVE 23.1

Informed Consent of Guarantor

Aline carries on a trucking business and is negotiating a loan of $100 000 from her bank. The bank is concerned that Aline will not be able to make her payments and asks her for security. Aline says that she does not have any collateral. However, she also says that she lives with her grandmother, who has a portfolio of stock worth about $500 000. The bank suggests that if Aline could get her grandmother to guarantee Aline's debt and give a security interest in the stock portfolio to secure her obligation under the guarantee, it would make the loan.

Aline comes back to the bank several days later with her grandmother. When the banker tries to explain what she is committing herself to, the grandmother says she does not want to be worried about the details, but just wants to help her granddaughter. The grandmother signs a guarantee and a security agreement that gives the bank a security interest in her stock portfolio. She does so without reading or receiving any explanation of either document.

Question for Discussion

1. Should the bank worry that the grandmother may not have fully appreciated the nature of the legal obligations to which she was committing herself? What difference would it make if the grandmother's sole source of income is what she receives from her stock portfolio?

---

[39] *Bank of Montreal v Korico Enterprises Ltd* (2000) 190 DLR (4th) 706 (Ont CA).

[40] These sorts of waivers are interpreted strictly against the creditor: *Bank of Montreal v Korico Enterprises Ltd* (2000) 190 DLR (4th) 706 (Ont CA).

[41] Typically, the consideration received by the guarantor for giving the guarantee is the granting of credit to the principal debtor.

[42] In Alberta, a guarantee must be acknowledged before a notary public to be enforceable: *Guarantees Acknowledgement Act*, RSA 2000, c G-11.

[43] *Bertolo v Bank of Montreal* (1986) 33 DLR (4th) 610 (Ont CA).

Business Decision 23.2 asks you to apply your knowledge of secured transactions and guarantees in a practical context.

BUSINESS DECISION 23.2

Setting up a Distributorship

Meena Inc is setting up a national chain of distributors for its tractors. Meena knows that most of its distributors will not have enough cash on hand to pay for the tractors when they are delivered. Therefore, it will not receive payment on any particular tractor until the tractor is actually sold by the distributor to a customer.

Question for Discussion

1. How should Meena protect itself in its distributorship agreements against the risk of non-payment?

CHAPTER SUMMARY

In credit transactions there is a risk that the creditor may not receive payment from the debtor. To reduce that risk, a creditor may take a security interest in the debtor's personal property. A security interest allows the creditor to seize and sell the collateral if the debtor does not fulfill its obligations.

Security interests are created by agreement between the debtor and a creditor in three main ways: (i) conditional sales, including some leases and consignments, (ii) security interests in specific assets, including accounts receivable and after-acquired property, and (iii) special security interests created under the *Bank Act*.

Each province has personal property security (PPS) legislation that creates rules for the creation, registration, priority, and enforcement of security interests in personal property. These rules make it more likely that secured creditors will be able to obtain and enforce their security interests in a cost-effective way. PPS legislation applies to every transaction that creates a security interest, subject to some exceptions. These include statutory rights like landlords' distraint rights and deemed trusts in favour of the Canada Revenue Agency. Under PPS legislation, secured parties may perfect their interests in collateral if they have attached by registering a financing statement or taking possession of the collateral. PPS legislation creates a scheme of priorities. For registered security interests, priority is determined by the date of registration. An

important exception to this rule is the super priority given to secured parties who supply goods to the debtor or directly finance their acquisition by the debtor. These purchase money security interests, or PMSIs, have priority over all other security interests created by the debtor in the goods if certain requirements are met. Security interests usually follow the collateral into the hands of anyone who buys it from the debtor. To protect buyers, a security interest does not follow the collateral when (i) the sale is in the ordinary course of business, (ii) the sale was permitted by the secured party, or (iii) the secured party's interest was unperfected, and the buyer was unaware of it.

Three steps are followed in the enforcement of a security interest by a secured party following default by a debtor: (i) secured party takes possession of collateral, (ii) secured party retains collateral or disposes of it, or debtor redeems it, and (iii) after disposition, any surplus is distributed in accordance with scheme of priority in PPS legislation. The debtor remains liable for any deficiency.

Creditors can also reduce the risk of non-payment or non-performance by acquiring a guarantee from someone other than the principal debtor. Guarantors are released from liability when the creditor or the principal debtor acts in certain ways that prejudice the guarantor's position without the guarantor's consent.

Review Questions

1. What is a security interest?

2. Why would a creditor be interested in obtaining a security interest?

3. Identify two ways that a creditor can obtain a security interest in property that a debtor does not possess when the security agreement is created. Which is better from the creditor's point of view?

4. When is a consignment the same as a conditional sale?

5. When should a lease be treated as a transaction creating a security interest? When is it subject to provincial PPS legislation?

6. From a creditor's perspective, explain one advantage of taking a security interest in accounts receivable rather than other assets.

7. Why is the security that banks may take under s 427 of the *Bank Act* different from other types of security interests?

8. Why is PPS legislation an improvement over the previous legal process for creditors?

9. What kinds of property can be used as security under provincial PPS legislation?

10. What types of interests are not subject to PPS legislation? What problems does this pose for secured parties?

11. What are the differences between security interests created by contract and similar entitlements arising under statutes?

12. What advantage does a secured party obtain by perfecting its security interest? When should a secured party perfect?

13. What must happen before a secured party can seize collateral?

14. When does a creditor's obligation to act in a commercially reasonable manner arise, and what does it require?

15. If a manufacturer wanted to sell its product on credit to a dealer who had already given a security interest in all of its current and future property to a bank, could the manufacturer obtain a security interest in the product it supplied that would rank ahead of the bank's?

16. If a secured party has perfected its security interest by filing a financing statement under the appropriate PPS legislation, can anyone else's interest have priority over it?

17. What rights does a debtor have once the secured party has taken possession of the collateral following a default?

18. If you were buying a boat from a friend, would you have any concerns about whether your friend had given a security interest in the boat to a creditor? If so, what would you do about it?

19. When is a guarantor relieved of its obligations?

20. When the debtor defaults on an obligation and a guarantor is required to pay, does the guarantor have any rights against the debtor?

Cases and Problems

1. Tornado Tyres Inc borrowed $1 000 000 from National Bank. As security for its loan, Tornado gave National a security interest in all personal property that it owned at the time that it entered into the security agreement or acquired later. National registered a financing statement relating to its interest on January 1, 2004. In June 2005, Tornado ran into financial difficulty and failed to remit to the Canada Revenue Agency $50 000 that it had withheld from employee wages for income tax. Tornado also stopped making its loan payments to National.

   Acting under its security agreement, National seized all of Tornado's assets, including the $50 000 that was in Tornado's bank account at National. National has checked and there are no other security interests registered under the PPS legislation. Is there any reason that National should not apply the $50 000 against the liability of Tornado under the loan? Would it make any difference to your answer if National had never properly registered its interest under the PPS legislation?

2. RevCo Inc is the exclusive Ontario distributor of Automated Teller Machines (ATMs) for E-Cash Ltd. In January 2002, RevCo entered into a general security agreement with A-Bank covering all the assets that it owned at the time or later acquired, including inventory, to secure a line of credit from the bank. A-Bank properly registered a financing statement that same month, indicating an interest in inventory and equipment. E-Cash supplied 10 ATMs to RevCo in January 2004 and has not been paid. Before supplying the ATMs, E-Cash and RevCo had entered into an agreement that provided that the ATMs were only given to RevCo on consignment and that RevCo was not obliged to pay the wholesale price to E-Cash unless it sold the ATMs. E-Cash registered a financing statement against RevCo in February 2004, indicating a security interest in inventory.

RevCo has become insolvent. A-Bank is owed $200 000 under RevCo's line of credit, and a dispute has arisen with E-Cash as to who is entitled to the 10 ATMs supplied by E-Cash. Who is entitled to the ATMs, and why?

3. In June 2004, Cory leased a truck from Superior Leasing Inc for the snow-plowing business he carried on in Toronto. The lease allowed Cory to use the truck for three years with an option to purchase the truck at the end of the term for a fixed price of $7000. The option price was based on an estimate of the wholesale value of the truck at the end of the lease period. If Cory chose not to exercise the option, the truck would be sold at an auction and any surplus over the option price would be paid to Cory. If the truck sold for less than the option price, Cory would have to pay the difference. Superior did not file a financing statement in relation to its interest in the truck. Cory had also borrowed $40 000 from the Bank of Toronto and had given the bank a security interest in all his property. The bank properly registered a financing statement relating to this interest on January 1, 2005.

Who is entitled to the truck if Cory defaults on his payments to both the bank and Superior? Would it make any difference if this transaction and all the parties were in British Columbia?

4. Erin bought a new car from Davis Motors Inc for $20 000. Under the terms of the purchase, Erin paid $5000 down and agreed to pay the balance in regular monthly instalments. To secure her obligation, Erin gave Davis a security interest in the car. Erin defaulted on the payments when she had just $3000 left to pay. Acting under its security agreement, Davis repossessed the car. The manager of Davis liked Erin's car and offered to buy it from Davis for $7500. Davis agreed. When Davis received the money from the manager, it applied $3000 to the loan and paid the balance of $4500 to Erin. Erin is unhappy because she recently saw an identical car advertised for $10 000.

Is there any basis upon which Erin could complain about what Davis has done?

5. Samra had agreed to guarantee a loan of $50 000 that her brother, Amman, had received from the Bank of Vancouver. Amman had entered into an agreement with the bank giving it a security interest in all his personal property, which included several vehicles and some jewellery. After Amman had paid back $25 000, he approached the bank asking for permission to sell one of his rings to a friend for $5000. He convinced the bank that his remaining personal property would be more than enough to cover the amount of the debt still unpaid. The bank agreed. Amman and the bank signed an agreement releasing the bank's security interest in the ring, and Amman sold it.

Two years later, Amman defaulted on his loan. Under the terms of the loan, the whole amount of the debt outstanding at the time of default, $5000, became due on default. The first thing that the bank did was to ask Samra to pay the full amount of the debt under her guarantee. Does Samra have to pay?

6. Goldie bought a new refrigerator from Cool Refrigerators Ltd, a retail appliance dealer, under a conditional sales agreement. In the contract, Goldie was given the right to possession of the refrigerator in return for promising to make six equal monthly payments of $150. Cool was to retain ownership of the refrigerator until the full price was paid. The contract also stated that if Goldie failed to make a payment, the total of all the outstanding payments became immediately due upon notice from Cool. Moreover, Cool was entitled to take possession of the refrigerator. Goldie has failed to make any payments since the initial instalment. What can Cool do? Describe all the steps that Cool would have to take to enforce its interest.

7. Jean operates a moving business as a sole proprietorship in Ontario. In order to finance the business, Jean negotiated a line of credit with M-Bank on January 1, 2005. The line of credit is secured against all of the assets of the business, including all property that Jean acquires after January 1, 2005. M-Bank registered its security interest by filing a financing statement under the Ontario PPS legislation on January 5, 2005. On March 1, 2005, Jean bought a truck. The seller, Metro Auto Inc, agreed to accept payment over three years and obtained a security interest in the truck from Jean. Metro filed a financing statement under the Ontario PPS legislation on March 3, 2005. Jean went into default on his obligations to M-Bank and Metro. Both creditors claim the truck. Whose claim has first priority?

8. Roma is going to buy a used tractor from a farmer. How can she protect herself from the risk that there are security interests in the tractor that would be enforceable against her?

9. Iaasic is interested in buying a computer from Electronic Gadgets Inc, but he does not have enough money to afford the purchase. His friend Ophelia agrees to lend him the money to buy the computer, but she is concerned that she may not get repaid. Iaasic is already in debt to his bank and has given a security interest in all of his assets, present and future, to the bank to secure his obligation to repay the loan. What can Ophelia do to protect her interests?

10. Giovanni has a line of credit with Imperial Bank in Vancouver. The line of credit is secured on all of the assets that Giovanni has or later acquires. The Bank filed a financing statement to register its security interest under the British Columbia PPS legislation on March 1, 2005. In June 2005, Giovanni bought a 1999 boat from West-End Marina under a conditional sales contract for $15 000. That contract provided that Giovanni would make regular monthly payments for five years. West-End retained ownership of the boat as security for Giovanni's obligations to make the payments. West-End assigned its interest in the boat and the conditional sales contract to Springliner Finance Corp.

At the end of three years and after he had paid $11 000, Giovanni defaulted on his payments under the conditional sales agreement. What should Springliner do? Is there anything that Springliner could have done to better protect its interests?

11. On June 30, 2005, Pierre bought a car from a local car dealership in Toronto, paying with money from a line of credit that he has with NRG Bank. When he negotiated the line of credit, he gave NRG Bank a security interest in all assets that he owned at the time or acquired afterwards. NRG filed a financing statement to register its security interest under the Ontario PPS legislation on April 1, 2005. In May 2005, Pierre had an accident with the car and took it to Sydney Auto Repair Inc to have it repaired. The bill came to $10 000. Pierre could not pay the full amount. Initially, Sydney refused to give Pierre back the car until he paid the entire bill. After some discussion, Sydney agreed to let Pierre have the car if he paid $5000 when he picked up the car and the balance of $5000 within 30 days. At the end of 30 days, Pierre did not pay. He was also in default

under his line of credit. NRG seized the car. Sydney claims that it is entitled to the car. Whose claim on the car has the higher priority?

12. Global Realty Inc owned an office building. It leased the fourth floor to Jensen Corp for two years beginning January 1, 2005. Sarah Jensen, the president and sole shareholder of Jensen Corp, gave Global a personal guarantee of all of Jensen Corp's obligations under the lease. By June 2005, Jensen Corp was having difficulty with its obligations and wanted to sublet part of the fourth floor. The lease permitted Jensen Corp to sublet so long as the landlord, Global, consented. The lease also provided that Global's consent could not be unreasonably withheld. Jensen Corp found five different possible tenants, but Global would not consent to any of them. Global did not give any reason for its refusal. Eventually, Jensen Corp defaulted on its lease payments and Global demanded payment from Sarah Jensen under her guarantee. Is Sarah Jensen obliged to pay?

WEBLINKS

Nova Scotia Personal Property Registry www.gov.ns.ca/snsmr/property/default.asp?mn=282.46.82

This site is typical of the Web-based registers maintained by each provincial and territorial government of filings under its personal property security legislation. Most permit secured parties to register their security interests online and to search for registrations against a particular debtor, as well as providing general information regarding the personal property security legislation in that province.

PPSA.Net www.ppsa.net/body.htm

This website provides links to the text of all personal property security legislation in each Canadian jurisdiction.

National Law Center for Inter-American Trade www.natlaw.com/pubs/overview.htm

This site provides an excellent overview of the personal property security system in Canada by a leading academic, Ron Cuming, who also comments on the effectiveness of the system.

Canada Legal.com www.canadalegal.com/gosite.asp?s=2478

This site highlights the practical risks for lenders created by the law of guarantees based on a recent decision of the Supreme Court of Canada.

ADDITIONAL RESOURCES FOR CHAPTER 23 ON THE COMPANION WEBSITE

(www.pearsoned.ca/mcinnes)

In addition to self-test multiple-choice, true-false, and short essay questions (all with immediate feedback), three additional Cases and Problems (with suggested answers), and links to useful Web destinations, the Companion Website provides the following resources for Chapter 23:

- Business Decision 23W—Enforcing Security Interests in Software

Provincial Material

- **British Columbia:** Enforcement of Security Interests, *Personal Property Security Act (PPSA)*, Perfection and Priority of Security Interests, Personal Property Registry
- **Alberta:** *Builders Lien Act*, Debt Collections, Garnishment, Guarantees, Liens, Loan Transactions, Personal Money Security Interest, Personal Property Registry, *Personal Property Security Act*, Seizure
- **Manitoba and Saskatchewan:** Provincial Personal Property Security Legislation
- **Ontario:** Attachment, Financing Statement, Personal Property, *Personal Property Security Act*, Purchase Money Security Interest, Registration, Security Interest, Sale of Collateral

24 Dealing with Bankruptcy and Insolvency

OBJECTIVES

After completing this chapter, you should be able to:

1. Distinguish between bankruptcy and insolvency.

2. Explain how bankruptcy differs from creditor–debtor action.

3. Describe three ways in which bankruptcy in a consumer context differs from bankruptcy in a corporate context.

4. Identify four individuals involved in a bankruptcy and the roles they play.

5. Distinguish between an assignment, a petition, and a proposal.

6. Specify three categories of creditors, and describe the rights and responsibilities of each in bankruptcy.

7. Explain the principle of creditor equality.

8. Describe what exempt creditors are, and name two categories of exempt creditors.

9. Distinguish between settlements and preferences, and explain how each is treated in bankruptcy.

10. Describe three types of proposals, and explain the advantages of each.

This book has discussed various situations in which a business is created or acquired. Generally speaking, those are the "good times." They are the times of planning, projection, and expansion, when things are going well and the assumption is that they will continue to do so. It would be great to think that doing business is always so rewarding. Unfortunately, an unavoidable part of any business venture—as we stress throughout this book—is risk. In this chapter we focus on the risk of business failure.

Business people work in the real world, where success can be difficult. Cash is often in short supply. Liabilities may exceed assets. Even the future of operations can be in doubt. Recent statistics indicate that more than 80 percent of small businesses in Canada fail during the first five years of operation.[1] The liquidation of several well-established companies during the past decade reminds us that big business is not immune from the risk of failure either. It is therefore prudent to know something about the law relating to business distress and failure.

Canadian law provides for several formal methods of dealing with a business's failure. For the most part, those methods are borrowed from the common law of bankruptcy that was developed by English courts starting around 1500.

■ The traditional model focuses on people who are *bankrupt*. A person may be **bankrupt** when their debts exceed their liabilities, and they cannot meet their debts as they come due. In that case, the bankrupt's assets are *liquidated*. **Liquidation** is the sale of assets so that they assume the "liquid" form of money and can be distributed to the bankrupt's creditors. Once that distribution has occurred, the law prohibits new claims from being launched against the bankrupt for any pre-existing debt. Instead, the bankrupt is financially disabled for a time and will eventually be either *discharged* or *wound up*. **Discharge** is the release of a debtor from the status of a bankrupt. **Winding up** involves the termination of an business's affairs so that it ceases to operate.

■ Another, more modern, method of dealing with financial distress is for the debtor to make a *proposal* to creditors to re-establish its financial affairs. A **proposal** is a contract between a debtor and its creditors providing for a rearrangement of debts outside of formal bankruptcy. If the proposal is successful, the debtor continues to operate. If not, the debtor is placed into bankruptcy.

Bankruptcy law tries to reconcile financial failure with real business behaviour. Debtors work hard to prevent bankruptcy, as do creditors, who sustain significant non-monetary costs in pursuing debtors. The aggravation and expense of collecting overdue debts can cause creditors to hesitate before strictly enforcing their right to payment. Creditors may also hesitate for fear of suffering intangible losses during the bankruptcy process, particularly the loss of business synergies, established relationships, and accrued **goodwill**—a favourable and valuable public reputation. A creditor that acts too quickly and too harshly can be viewed poorly in the business community.

For all of the above reasons, creditors are frequently patient when dealing with debtors. They know that there are hidden costs to putting a debtor in bankruptcy involuntarily. They also know that they often stand to gain more by adopting a flexible attitude. The legal regime regulating financial distress and failure in Canada therefore encourages debtors and creditors to work out their differences co-operatively.

---

[1] F Zaid *Canadian Franchise Guide* (1983) at 1–401.

Margin glossary:

a person may be **bankrupt** when their debts exceed their liabilities, and they cannot meet their debts as they come due

liquidation is the sale of assets so that they assume the "liquid" form of money and can be distributed to the bankrupt's creditors

discharge is the release of a debtor from bankruptcy status

winding up terminates a business's affairs so that it ceases to operate

a **proposal** is a contract between a debtor and creditors providing for a rearrangement of debts outside of formal bankruptcy

goodwill is a business's favourable and valuable public reputation

Canadian law is also shaped by a number of other considerations. Historically, one of the main purposes of bankruptcy was to reinforce the stigma of financial failure in order to encourage careful business behaviour. In England, for example, it used to be common for bankrupts to spend time in prison. Some of these legal and social restrictions still exist in Canada. However, the main focus of the law today is rehabilitation.[2] If the bankrupt is a legal person (such as a corporation), it can seek extra time to rearrange its affairs and repay its debts. If the bankrupt is a natural person (that is, an individual), they can seek a prompt discharge and return to being a productive member of society. The forgiveness now embodied in the law is a contemporary recognition of the fact that some risk taking is necessary for economic growth.

None of this should suggest that we approve of bankruptcy. There remain serious problems for those who are unfortunate enough to enter it, the most serious of which is that corporate and consumer bankrupts will usually find it difficult to re-establish their credit. But we do not suggest that bankruptcy marks the end of a promising career, as it often did in the past. We now view bankruptcy as necessary for achieving social purposes. Just as the risks of doing certain types of business have grown, so too have the potential consequences. With this development has come a new appreciation of the the need to see business failures in context.

Well-developed bankruptcy laws also help to reduce uncertainty in the business world. They give creditors some idea of the risks that arise when they extend credit. They also provide debtors with several alternatives for rehabilitation. To parties on both sides of the credit transaction, they offer a preview of what will happen in the event of financial failure and, to that extent, they promote predictability in what is often a very difficult and emotional experience. Bankruptcy laws are therefore an essential tool in risk management.

REGULATION OF BANKRUPTCY

Canada's Constitution assigns the power to enact bankruptcy legislation to the federal government.[3] The current federal act, the *Bankruptcy and Insolvency Act* (*BIA*), provides a framework to administer the bankruptcy process, various forms of proceeding in bankruptcy (assignments and petitions), non-bankruptcy alternatives (proposals), detailed regulations concerning the debtor's property, the administration of estates, the duties of a bankrupt, and miscellaneous matters.[4]

Broadly speaking, the Act aims to:

- provide for an equitable distribution of the bankrupt's assets to creditors in accordance with a generally recognized scheme
- limit the possibility of discharging or eliminating certain debts, such as family support obligations and student loans, that are considered socially important
- punish debtors for engaging in behaviour that undermines the principles of creditor equality and debtor rehabilitation, such as fraudulent pre-bankruptcy transfers and repeated financial failure

---

[2.] In many provinces, for example, an undischarged bankrupt cannot act as a chartered accountant or a corporate director: *Business Corporations Act*, RSO 1990, c B.16, s 118(1) (Ont); *Canada Trustco Mortgage Co v Sugarman* (1999) 7 CBR (4th) 113 (Ont Gen Div).

[3.] The division of legislative authority between the federal and provincial governments was discussed in Chapter 1.

[4.] *Bankruptcy and Insolvency Act*, RSC 1985, c B-3 (Can).

- promote confidence and certainty in the credit system
- provide for the rehabilitation of debtors
- promote uniformity of laws in a field of importance to Canadian business

There are some important exceptions and qualifications to the Act's coverage. It does not apply to banks, insurance companies, trust companies, and railways—key economic institutions that are dealt with under separate statutes. In addition, farmers and fishermen cannot be placed into bankruptcy. That reflects a policy decision based on the highly volatile nature of the farming and fishing industries.

The Act is by far the most commonly looked-to statute concerning financial distress and failure in Canada, but it is not the only one. The federal *Companies' Creditors Arrangement Act* (*CCAA*) allows a debtor to seek a *stay*, or *bar*, of all claims pending the acceptance of a reorganization plan.[5] A **stay** is a court-ordered suspension of legal proceedings. And the federal *Winding-Up and Restructuring Act* applies to the liquidation of federally incorporated entities, banks, and insurance companies.[6] Later in this chapter, we will discuss how those statutes interact with the *BIA*.

A number of provincial statutes apply to debtor-creditor relations by virtue of provincial jurisdiction over property and civil rights. These may be invoked with certain advantages, but in case of conflict, the *BIA* prevails.[7] For instance, an early version of the Ontario *Employment Standards Act* purported to give priority to unpaid wages over all other claims. The applicable section of the Act was held to be inapplicable in the event of a bankruptcy because it directly conflicted with the *BIA*, which subordinates wage claims to the claims of secured creditors.[8] The priority that the federal bankruptcy law provides is sometimes an important bargaining tool for debtors who are seeking to manage their exposure to risk.

a stay is a court-ordered suspension of legal proceedings

CORPORATE AND CONSUMER BANKRUPTCY

About 92 500 Canadians enter bankruptcy annually. Of these, about 91 percent are consumers and 9 percent are corporations. In 2004, total corporate liabilities amounted to $3.054 billion, or $375 856 per bankrupt, while total consumer liabilities were $4.75 billion, or $56 313 per bankrupt.[9]

[5.] *Companies Creditors' Arrangement Act*, RSC 1985, c C-36 (Can).

[6.] *Winding-Up and Restructuring Act*, RSC 1985, c W-11 (Can).

[7.] Federal jurisdiction over bankruptcy differs from provincial debtor–creditor legislation in at least three ways. First, bankruptcy law is federal law and is uniform across Canada. Most debtor–creditor statutes are provincial in scope and vary between jurisdictions. Second, provincial debtor–creditor legislation focuses on individual action by creditors. Bankruptcy is a form of court-supervised class action against the debtor. In bankruptcy, all claims are consolidated, prioritized, and satisfied. Third, the possibility for debtor relief and a "fresh start" is greater under bankruptcy than under creditor–debtor statutes, since the operation of a stay on further proceedings against the debtor are prohibited in bankruptcy. No such stay operates once an individual creditor–debtor action begins. Provincial statutes with application in financial recovery include provincial fraudulent conveyances, business corporations, and personal property security legislation.

[8.] *Re Lewis Department Stores Ltd* (1972) 17 CBR (NS) 113 (Ont Reg).

[9.] Office of the Superintendent of Bankruptcy Canada *Annual Statistical Report for the 2004 Calendar Year* (2004) at 4–5. There were also some 18 386 proposals filed in 2004 with liabilities of $3.247 billion.

The marked difference in the size and scope of bankrupts in each category suggests that there should be different rules for each type of bankruptcy proceeding. Two differences are especially important.

■ Under federal law, corporations may make proposals with their creditors to settle their obligations. Creditors must vote upon these proposals, which require the approval of a majority in each class of creditors who represent at least two-thirds of the value of the assets in each class. Consumers can make a simplified form of proposal that only needs to be approved by a bare majority of creditors.

■ Corporate debtors are rarely discharged from bankruptcy unless they pay all of their debts. However, first-time consumer debtors who demonstrate responsible behaviour are usually discharged within nine months.

Despite the differences, there are fewer explicit distinctions between corporate and consumer bankruptcy than might be expected.[10] This chapter focuses on corporate bankruptcy. Nevertheless, because consumer bankruptcies have become increasingly common, they are an important source of law and we will consider them from time to time.

BANKRUPTCY

Bankruptcy and Insolvency

English law concerning financial distress and failure originated in the courts of equity. As we saw in Chapter 1, equity was a separate system of rules that arose during the late Middle Ages, and was intended to soften the harsh results that were occasionally produced by the older, more rigid system of common law. The courts of equity had their own judges and procedures, and they devised their own solutions to deal with legal problems that the common law was incapable of handling effectively.

At common law, a debtor could be sued by creditors for non-payment. However, news of a single suit often triggered a legal stampede among creditors, who were all trying to claim the same assets. Furthermore, once all the claims came before the court together, there was no way to determine which claims were valid and which creditors should rank ahead of others.

The equity court's response was to halt all claims against the debtor, pool the remaining assets, and provide for their liquidation and distribution to the creditors. The net effect was a kind of "time out" for the bankrupt. Once the proceeds of the liquidation were distributed, no further claims could be brought against the bankrupt for debts previously incurred.

Equity's approach might appear unjust, particularly for creditors, who often received far less than the face value of their loans. However, equity's innovation also had several advantages.

■ First, a single proceeding prevented the "race to the bank." All creditors were treated on the same basis by a single judge, who heard all of the evidence of the debtor's various debts.

[10.] *BIA* s 66.11 defines a "consumer debtor" as an insolvent natural person whose total debts, excluding those secured by their principal residence, do not exceed $75 000.

- Second, because the debtor was exposed to only one set of legal proceedings, their assets were not depleted by the need to hire lawyers for a variety of claims. Money that would have gone to the debtor's lawyers went to creditors instead.

- Third, the bankrupt was given a fresh start. Although the stigma of bankruptcy was harsh, the bankrupt's rehabilitation could begin as soon as they were discharged.

Over time some of those procedures changed, but on the whole they still apply in Canada today. Similarly, the law and language of financial distress retain many features that were originally developed in England. Two concepts that are particularly important to understand are *bankruptcy* and *insolvency*.

Almost every person is at some point unable to pay some financial obligation. Bankruptcy is a different matter. Canadian law formally defines **bankruptcy** as a situation in which someone is at least $1000 in debt and has committed an "act of bankruptcy." That act of bankruptcy usually involves failing to meet liabilities as they come due.[11] Simply meeting the definition is not sufficient, however. Before a person actually becomes legally bankrupt, the situation has to be serious, and a court must decide that a bankruptcy has occurred.

Insolvency is an inability to meet financial obligations as they become due. That definition is close to the one for bankruptcy, but it is distinct. Many businesses operate in, or near, a state of insolvency due to ordinary lags in payment and the general acceptability of assuming a certain level of debt in modern business.

The central distinction between bankruptcy and insolvency is one of degree: A bankrupt is less likely to be able to pay debts over a longer period than an insolvent. Under Canadian law, all bankrupts must be insolvent, but as we have seen, not all insolvents will be bankrupt. Insolvency constitutes the threshold of bankruptcy. Most creditors are prepared to wait well beyond mere insolvency to begin bankruptcy proceedings. They adopt that attitude in order to maintain business relationships, preserve assets, and avoid the expense of legal action.

Petition and Assignment

Bankruptcy and insolvency involve different procedures. The power of the courts in equity was originally discretionary—that is, it was exercised only when a judge thought it was necessary and appropriate.[12] Creditors therefore had to **petition**, or request, the court to place an individual or corporation into bankruptcy. The court could allow or dismiss the petition as it saw fit. If the court decided to allow the petition, it would usually issue a *receiving order* for the debtor's property. A **receiving order** is a command to the debtor to release all of its assets to the court or to a court-appointed agent, usually a trustee in bankruptcy. The law later developed to allow a person or corporation to voluntarily **assign**, or place, itself in bankruptcy. In modern Canadian law, a person is bankrupt if they (i) meet the requirements for bankruptcy, and (ii) have either been subject to a receiving order or voluntarily been assigned into bankruptcy. Figure 24.1 illustrates the methods of entering bankruptcy.

in Canadian law **bankruptcy** is a situation in which someone is at least $1000 in debt and has committed an "act of bankruptcy"

insolvency is an inability to meet financial obligations as they become due

a **petition** is a request by creditors to a court to place an individual or corporation into bankruptcy

a **receiving order** is a command to the debtor to release all of its assets to the court or to a court-appointed agent, usually a trustee in bankruptcy

an **assignment** is a procedure by which a debtor voluntarily assigns itself into bankruptcy

---

11. *BIA* s 42 sets out nine other possible "acts of bankruptcy," including the making of an assignment, a fraudulent conveyance or preference, a debtor's departure from Canada, the disposition of assets, a declaration of insolvency, a declaration of a moratorium on debt payments, and a bankrupt's default on a proposal.

12. This is unlike the common law, where the law was applied mandatorily. As we saw in Chapter 1, however, common law and equity were combined into a single court system during the nineteenth century.

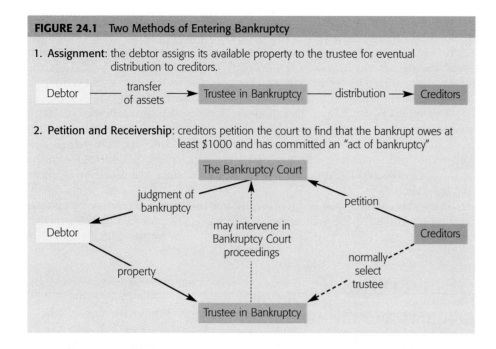

FIGURE 24.1   Two Methods of Entering Bankruptcy

We will examine the procedures for petitions and assignments later. Case Brief 24.1 deals with one aspect of bankruptcy procedure—commencement of proceedings in the debtor's locality.

CASE BRIEF 24.1

Re Malartic Hygrade Gold Mines Ltd (1966) 10 CBR (NS) 34 (Ont SCJ)

In Canada, bankruptcy proceedings must be started in the debtor's "locality." That requirement occasionally causes problems, because the debtor's locality may appear to be in several places. These include the places where the debtor is physically located, where the debtor carries on business, where the majority of their assets are situated, or where their creditors reside. The *BIA* focuses on the place where the debtor carries on business, where they reside, or sometimes where the greater part of the bankrupt's property is located.

Malartic Hygrade Gold Mines Ltd carried on a substantial amount of business prospecting for gold in northern Quebec.

It had creditors there and was making plans to expand operations in that province. However, the head office of the company was in Ontario, the company was incorporated in Ontario, the company's books were located in Ontario, and the company's share register was in Ontario.

The court decided that in all of the circumstances, Ontario was the debtor's locality. Although some later cases have decided differently, that decision illustrates the importance of the *legal* presence of a debtor when other factors are conflicting or inconclusive.

Insolvency is a less definite status than bankruptcy. It is also subject to several statutes related to creditor–debtor relations and fraudulent conveyances. Those statutes recognize that the payment of money is often a hotly disputed issue.

Proposals

Canadian law has recently encouraged greater co-operation between debtors and creditors by allowing for *proposals* as an alternative to assignment or

a **proposal** is a court-approved contract between a debtor and creditors that gives the debtor time to adjust its financial affairs while business operations continue

petition in bankruptcy. A **proposal** is a court-approved contract between a debtor and creditors that gives the debtor time to adjust its financial affairs while business operations continue. The great advantage of a proposal is that it keeps the debtor *out of formal bankruptcy*. That, in turn, usually permits the debtor to safeguard its credit rating and to preserve its intangible assets, including its business relationships, reputation, and goodwill.

A proposal is voted upon by creditors. If successful, the proposal binds *all* creditors covered under the plan and allows the debtor to proceed with business. In exchange, the debtor often agrees (i) to repayment at a higher rate of interest in future, (ii) to restructure its operations, (iii) to heightened scrutiny of its affairs by creditor representatives, or (iv) to some combination of these and other options.

Proposals can be made by an insolvent person, by a bankrupt, or by various bankruptcy officials. We will examine proposals in more detail later in this chapter.

CREDITORS

Creditors and the Market for Credit

Until now, this chapter has focused on debtors. After all, they are the ones upon whom the law of bankruptcy focuses. For every debtor, however, there are also creditors. Business people should be aware that they will probably enjoy the status of both debtor *and* creditor at some point in the court of normal business operations. It is therefore useful to understand how the *BIA* regulates creditors.

Bankruptcy occurs because a debtor cannot pay its debts. By definition, therefore, bankruptcy protection involves *discounting*, or reducing, claims. For instance, if there is only a 50 percent chance that you will repay $2000 that you borrowed from me, my rights under that loan may be worth only $1000. That is something that professional creditors, like banks, know *before* they extend credit. For that reason, the interest rate on a bank loan reflects the bank's best guess as to (i) whether a debtor will be able to repay a loan, and (ii) the amount that it will actually be able to recover if the debtor defaults under the loan.

a **secured creditor** is a creditor whose interest is directly linked to a particular asset

The *BIA* reflects and influences that situation. Under it, creditors may be *secured*, *preferred*, or *unsecured*. As we saw in Chapter 23, a **secured creditor** is a creditor whose interest is directly linked to a particular asset, such as a tractor or an assignment of the debtor's accounts receivable. The creditor is "secure" in the sense that there are definite assets that it can look to for payment in the event of a bankruptcy. For this reason, creditors will often be willing to make secured loans even in situations of advanced financial distress. Secured credit represents the highest degree of protection and (at least initially) it is privileged under the *BIA*. That privilege exempts the creditor from the *stay* that is placed upon disposition of the debtor's assets.[13] (As previously explained, a stay is a court order that stops, or suspends, legal proceeedings.) The secured creditor can therefore retrieve the secured asset for itself immediately. This is a critical advantage. Lower-ranked creditors can wait years for their *pro rata* share to be paid, or they may not be paid at all. Secured creditors enjoy another form of protection as well. If the property that the debtor gave as security has lost value, the secured creditor can take that asset and then sue for the balance as an unsecured creditor.

[13.] *BIA* s 244(1) allows a secured creditor to enforce its security against a debtor 10 days after giving notice of intent to enforce.

The *BIA* divides unsecured creditors into two categories. A **preferred creditor** is a creditor that is preferred in relation to all other unsecured creditors, generally by operation of law. Those who are owed unpaid wages and taxes normally fall into this category. So too do those bearing the administrative costs of carrying out the bankruptcy. They are "preferred" because society deems them to be important enough to enjoy priority over other unsecured creditors.

Finally, there is the residual category of **unsecured creditors**. This is normally the largest class of creditor. Ordinary suppliers of goods and services, small lenders, and other creditors will be grouped together and paid out of whatever is left over after the other priority claims are satisfied. Depending on the size of the bankrupt's estate, there is frequently little or nothing remaining. Unsecured creditors must therefore take this risk into account when deciding whether to lend.

a preferred creditor is a creditor that is preferred in relation to all other unsecured creditors, generally by operation of law

unsecured creditors are creditors that are neither secured nor preferred

CONCEPT SUMMARY 24.1

Classes of Creditors

Secured		Creditors whose interests are "secured" by some specific asset of the debtor, such as a piece of equipment, inventory, or accounts receivable. If the debtor defaults on the loan, the creditor is in a position to claim the asset and, depending on its value, claim for the balance of the debt owing as an unsecured creditor.
Unsecured	Preferred	Creditors who are "preferred" in relation to other general creditors by operation of law. For instance, creditors who are owed wages, taxes, rent, and support payments fall into this category, as do those bearing the administrative costs incurred in carrying out the bankruptcy.
	General unsecured	The residual class of creditor, paid after all other claims are satisfied.

Creditor Equality

One key point concerning creditors is the principle of creditor equality. This has two aspects.

- **Stay:** All unsecured creditors are subject to a *stay* on court proceedings against the debtor, once bankruptcy is formally determined. This means that they cannot bring independent actions against the bankrupt for their pre-existing debts. It also means that any proceedings that they previously began are stayed in favour of the bankruptcy action. The stay guarantees procedural equality among creditors.

- **Pro rata sharing:** In the event of a bankruptcy, all creditors in the same class recover on a *pro rata* basis. Suppose the debtor has assets of $100 000, but owes $600 000 to unsecured creditor A and $400 000 to unsecured creditor B. A will get $60 000 and B will get $40 000. Sometimes, a creditor may try to "jump the queue" and receive a higher rate of recovery, either through a pre-bankruptcy transfer or other voidable *preference*. A **preference** is the payment to one creditor of a larger amount than they would be entitled to receive in a *pro rata* distribution. Improper transfers to a creditor can be cancelled or even punished by the bankruptcy court. For instance, the court may subordinate the guilty creditor to all other creditors and therefore substantially lessen its chances of recovery.

a preference is the payment to one creditor of a larger amount than they would be entitled to receive on a *pro rata* distribution

Proof of Claim

To be officially recognized in the bankruptcy process, each creditor must prove its claim before a bankruptcy official. The claim process is designed to identify the pool of potential claimants, to eliminate ineligible claims, and to streamline the bankruptcy process. Unsecured creditors must, by a certain date, submit a *proof of claim* setting out the amount at issue, how it arose, and whether the bankrupt has any counterclaim against the creditor.[14] Failure to do this usually voids a claim.

OFFICIALS

A number of officials play a role in the bankruptcy process. Since bankruptcy procedures arose in the courts of equity and remain to some extent distinct from ordinary court procedures, it is important to know who these people are and what they do. Figure 24.2 provides an overview.

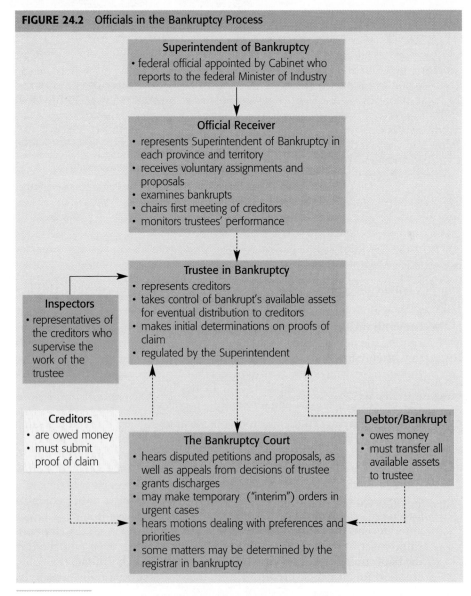

FIGURE 24.2 Officials in the Bankruptcy Process

Superintendent of Bankruptcy
• federal official appointed by Cabinet who reports to the federal Minister of Industry

Official Receiver
• represents Superintendent of Bankruptcy in each province and territory
• receives voluntary assignments and proposals
• examines bankrupts
• chairs first meeting of creditors
• monitors trustees' performance

Inspectors
• representatives of the creditors who supervise the work of the trustee

Trustee in Bankruptcy
• represents creditors
• takes control of bankrupt's available assets for eventual distribution to creditors
• makes initial determinations on proofs of claim
• regulated by the Superintendent

Creditors
• are owed money
• must submit proof of claim

Debtor/Bankrupt
• owes money
• must transfer all available assets to trustee

The Bankruptcy Court
• hears disputed petitions and proposals, as well as appeals from decisions of trustee
• grants discharges
• may make temporary ("interim") orders in urgent cases
• hears motions dealing with preferences and priorities
• some matters may be determined by the registrar in bankruptcy

---

[14.] A counterclaim occurs when the debtor sues the creditor, usually to offset the amount owing under the original debt. Counterclaims were discussed in Chapter 2.

Superintendent of Bankruptcy and Official Receivers

The chief administrative official in bankruptcy in Canada is the *Superintendent of Bankruptcy*, a Cabinet appointee who reports to the federal Minister of Industry. The Superintendent has wide powers to inspect and investigate bankrupts' estates, to regulate and examine the work of trustees in bankruptcy, and to intervene in bankruptcy court proceedings across Canada.

The Superintendent is represented in each province and territory by an *Official Receiver*, whose office "receives" a copy of receiving orders and other bankruptcy documents from the Bankruptcy Court. An Official Receiver's tasks include receiving voluntary assignments and proposals, examining bankrupts, chairing first meetings of creditors, and generally monitoring trustees' performance.

Trustee in Bankruptcy

Creditors in a bankruptcy are usually represented by a *trustee*, whom the debtor arranges to administer its assets after preliminary selection by the creditors. The trustee is professionally licensed by the Superintendent and assumes control of the debtor's assets once appointed by a court (in the case of a receiving order) or by the Official Receiver (in the case of an assignment). As we saw in Chapter 1 and Chapter 8, a trustee is someone who has possession of property for the benefit of someone else. In the bankruptcy context, a trustee becomes the legal owner of the bankrupt's property. The trustee takes possession of the bankrupt's assets, prepares essential documents in connection with the bankruptcy, reports on the bankrupt's affairs, adjudicates on creditor's proofs of claim, and then liquidates the assets and distributes the proceeds. The trustee is entitled to be paid for that work.

Bankruptcy Court

The law of bankruptcy was originally created in the courts of equity, which were separate from the courts of common law. Today, while most provinces continue to call a court a "bankruptcy court" when it hears a bankruptcy case, there is no formally separate system of courts for that purpose. Most bankruptcy courts are staffed by regular judges appointed for their competence in bankruptcy and commercial matters. The judges hear appeals from the registrar, disputed petitions and proposals, applications for discharge from bankruptcy, and certain motions dealing with preferences and priorities.

Registrar in Bankruptcy

The *Registrar in Bankruptcy* is like a deputy judge, with the power to hear unopposed petitions and proposals, grant discharges, make interim orders in cases of urgency, hear proofs of claim and appeals from decisions of a trustee, and deal with various administrative questions related to the trustee's administration of a bankrupt's estate.

Inspectors

Under the *BIA*, the creditors have the right to appoint a maximum of five *inspectors* to supervise the trustee in managing the bankrupt's estate. In practice, the inspectors are usually the representatives of the largest creditors, but they undertake their role as fiduciaries for all of the creditors.[15] Their decisions may be reviewed by the Bankruptcy Court if fraud or partiality is shown.

[15.] The concept of fiduciary duties was discussed in Chapter 22. It is essentially a duty of utmost loyalty.

THE PROCESS OF BANKRUPTCY

A number of important tactical considerations arise *before* bankruptcy proceedings begin. They are largely informal and do not appear in the *BIA*, but they are critical to the task of risk management. Debtors must choose whether they want to leverage their existing assets to keep operations going or use the threat of assignment to play for time. For instance, a debtor may be so important in the community that financial institutions feel unable to "pull the plug," at least immediately. Likewise, creditors must decide whether to petition immediately or to keep the debtor afloat. Personal relationships and the hope of a turn-around may argue against quick creditor action. The outcome of strategic thinking usually dictates which procedure is used.

As we saw in an earlier section, bankruptcy has two basic requirements: (i) the debtor must owe at least $1000, and (ii) the debtor must have committed an act of bankruptcy—usually a failure to pay debts as they come due. If those requirements are met, bankruptcy can be triggered in two ways:

- voluntary assignment
- involuntary petition

Assignment

Even before creditors have decided to take court action, the debtor may realize that its financial situation is dire. In such a case, assignment may be appropriate. Assignment is the most commonly used bankruptcy procedure in Canada. The debtor voluntarily assigns its property to a trustee for the benefit of its creditors. In doing so the assignee commits an "act of bankruptcy" under the *BIA*. If the debtor is a corporation, the directors must call a meeting so that the corporation can assign itself into bankruptcy.

In assignment, the debtor completes a preliminary statement of affairs that sets out a list of debts and creditors. After taking possession of the bankrupt's property, the trustee meets with the debtor to prepare a long-form statement of affairs and a notice of the first meeting of creditors. At that meeting, the trustee advises creditors on how it intends to liquidate the assets and distribute the proceeds. Individual debtors can apply for an automatic discharge from bankruptcy within nine months (i) if there is no creditor opposition, and (ii) if the debtor attends mandatory counselling sessions. If the bankruptcy is the bankrupt's second, or if it is opposed, discharge can take a year or more. Corporate debtors are rarely discharged unless they have repaid all of their debts, which is uncommon.

Petition and Receivership

A petition for a receiving order is less attractive than an assignment. It is the creditors' attempt to force the debtor into bankruptcy. Not surprisingly, the debtor often resists that process. As a result, petitions are often contrary to the spirit of co-operation that should characterize the effort to resolve the debtor's financial difficulties.

A petition normally begins with clear evidence that the debtor is insolvent and can no longer pay their debts. Where one creditor is acting alone, it must prove that it is owed at least $1000 before it can start proceedings. Furthermore, it must prove that the debtor committed an act of bankruptcy within the past six months. As a result, a petitioning creditor often makes a fresh demand for payment to ensure that the evidence in support of the petition is timely. The creditor also needs evidence from other creditors that the debtor has ceased to meet its liabilities "generally," and therefore will *examine* other creditors for that purpose. Because that examination is informal, being outside or prior to a court action, there is no guarantee that the other creditors will co-operate.

Submitting a Petition

A petition can be submitted by one creditor acting individually or by several creditors acting together. In either event, once submitted, it becomes a *class action* in the name of all the creditors. A **class action** is legal action taken by one or several people on behalf of a group that is too large to bring before the court.[16] The legal action is therefore consolidated into one claim or a group of claims with common legal elements. A petition in bankruptcy will include an *affidavit*, a voluntary written statement made under oath, that supports the statements made in the petition, as well as a notice that sets the date for hearing of the matter before the registrar or a bankruptcy judge.

> a class action is legal action taken by one or several people on behalf of a group that is too large to bring before the court

An undisputed petition may be heard by the registrar who, after examining the documents, may grant the receiving order if satisfied that the requirements of the *BIA* have been met. Disputed petitions are heard by a bankruptcy judge. The main issues before the judge are usually whether the debtor has committed the alleged act of bankruptcy, and whether the debts claimed by the petitioning creditors are valid.

After filing the petition, creditors should not contact the debtor's customers for any reason that is related to the debtor's financial condition. Contact may hurt the business reputation of the debtor and may provide grounds for an action in interference by the trustee.[17]

Creditors should also realize that if they start proceedings too quickly, they may be held liable for any losses that the debtor suffers as a result. That situation is examined in You Be the Judge 24.1.

YOU BE THE JUDGE 24.1

Demanding a "Demand" Loan—Can a Debt Be Called Too Soon?[18]

In today's economy it is common for financing to be fluid. Financial institutions often make "demand loans," which allow them to call the money back at almost any time. Can they actually exercise that right at any time, even if it forces the debtor into bankruptcy?

Joe Murano was a successful entrepreneur in the video store business. In 1989, he bought four video stores with the assistance of a loan from a bank. In March 1991, Murano was in the midst of expansion plans for the venture when the bank demanded immediate repayment of all the loans. In addition, the bank appointed a receiver, who took possession of the stores two hours after written demands were delivered. The bank also informed other bankers, lenders, business associates, and suppliers that it was appointing a receiver because of Murano's allegedly dishonest conduct. As a result, Murano lost other business opportunities.

Questions for Discussion

1. Does a "demand loan" imply that a bank may call a loan at virtually any time? What criteria could be used to evaluate such a demand?

2. How much damage should a creditor be responsible for? What if a creditor let other creditors know that the debtor is having trouble, resulting in the debtor suffering further losses, even though the information later turns out to be false? Should a creditor be liable for that additional behaviour as well?

[16.] Class actions were discussed in Chapter 2.

[17.] *Re Velvet Touch Furniture Stripping Ltd* (1980) 34 CBR (NS) 32 (Ont SCJ).

[18.] *Murano v Bank of Montreal* (1995) 31 CBR (3d) 1 (Ont Gen Div).

The Receiving Order

If a petition is unopposed, it is handled by the registrar. If a petition is contested it must be resolved by a judge. The receiving order is in a standard form that is set out in the *BIA* and it is often accompanied by a notice directing the bankrupt, or their representative, to make themselves available to be examined by the trustee.

The receiving order allows the trustee to take control of almost all of the debtor's property. The trustee therefore must (i) receive the keys, passwords, and operating instruments of the bankrupt, (ii) take possession of the bankrupt's assets, and (iii) notify insurers, banks, sheriffs, and landlords about the change in management. The trustee must also tell the Official Receiver which of the bankrupt's officers will answer questions and perform the obligations that are imposed upon the bankrupt by the *BIA*. That officer is usually the person who oversaw the bankrupt party's day-to-day operations before the bankruptcy occurred.

The Official Receiver examines or questions the bankrupt's officer about the causes of the bankruptcy, the whereabouts of creditors, and the status of debts. That information is written into a *statement of account*, which the trustee uses to plan and perform the liquidation of the bankrupt's assets.

Distribution of Assets

Once the trustee has taken possession of the bankrupt's property, several issues arise.

Undischarged Debt

Most of the bankrupt's debts are *released* once the bankrupt is discharged. That means that the debtor does not have to pay them. There is, however, a class of debts that are non-dischargeable. These are debts that, for policy reasons, the debtor should not be able to walk away from. Debts in this category include fines, spousal and child support orders, judgments against the debtor for assault and misrepresentation, and student loans made under federal or provincial statutes. Ethical Perspective 24.1 discusses the dischargeability of student loans.

ETHICAL PERSPECTIVE 24.1

Discharging Student Loans in Bankruptcy—Think Again[19]

Like cars and laptop computers, loans have become an increasingly common part of student life. Many students need loans to complete their studies. Many students also want to know if they can discharge—get rid of—their student loans by entering bankruptcy.

Until October 1997, student loans were fully dischargeable. Soaring student bankruptcy rates, however, forced the federal government to rethink the law. In June 1998, the *BIA* was amended, making student loans *nondischargeable for 10 years* after full- or part-time studies cease. However, the *BIA* provides that a bankrupt can be discharged from such debt if the court is satisfied (i) that the person acted in good faith, and (ii) that they will continue to experience financial difficulties that will likely prevent repayment.

The current law reflects the fact that while bankruptcy is an opportunity to "clean the slate," it is rarely a cure-all. In many cases, student loans still remain payable. Bankruptcy normally has a serious effect on a person's credit rating, and it may be some time before they can apply for fresh credit without a guarantor.

Question for Discussion

1. Why should students not be able to discharge their student loans in bankruptcy?

---

[19] *Re Minto* (1999) 14 CBR (4th) 235 (Sask QB).

Exempt Property

Generally speaking, all of the bankrupt's assets are available for distribution to the creditors. However, individual consumers who enter bankruptcy are entitled to certain *exemptions* that ensure they do not become destitute. Individuals are allowed to keep:

- tools of the trade up to $2000
- necessary clothing up to $1000
- household furniture and utensils up to $2000
- insurance proceeds
- statutory pension benefits
- damages for pain and suffering

Since both federal and provincial governments have the power to designate exempt property, the entitlements vary slightly between jurisdictions.[20] In addition, bankrupts are entitled to keep wages that they earn during bankruptcy, but only to a maximum set by the Official Receiver.[21] Corporate bankrupts are not entitled to exempt property.

Exempt Creditors

Some creditors are partly or entirely exempt from the restrictions on recovery under the *BIA*. The most important of these are secured creditors, who are entitled to full repayment. The *BIA* allows secured creditors to deal with their security as if the bankruptcy never happened. And if they enforce their security, for example, by seizing a particular asset, they can claim as ordinary unsecured creditors for any *deficiency*.

Suppose Nancy borrowed $250 000 from Mark and used a dump truck to secure the loan. Nancy has now defaulted on the loan and, indeed, she has gone into bankruptcy. Three points are important.

- **Enforcing the security:** Mark can enforce his security in one of two ways. As we saw in Chapter 23, he may be entitled to simply seize and retain the dump truck. However, that option may create difficulties. For instance, he may insist that the vehicle is worth only $200 000, leaving a deficiency of $50 000. Nancy's trustee in bankruptcy, in contrast, may claim that the truck is worth $220 000, leaving a deficiency of only $30 000. If the parties cannot eventually agree, the court may order the truck to be sold.[22] Indeed, to avoid such complications, creditors often proceed directly to a sale of the collateral.[23]

- **Suing for the deficiency:** Whether or not the truck is sold, Mark is entitled to register a proof of claim as an ordinary unsecured creditor for the deficiency. While he is entitled to the full value of his security, he will not fully recover the deficiency. Nancy clearly has too many debts and too little money, and Mark will have to share her inadequate assets with her

---

[20] *BIA* s 67(1)(b).

[21] The amount is calculated by a formula. In general, a family of four receiving a monthly income of $3500 would be required to contribute approximately $140 monthly to the trustee for distribution to creditors. Those payments stop when the bankrupt is discharged: <http://strategis.ic.gc.ca/epic/internet/inbsf-osb.nsf/en/br01055e.html#appendixA>.

[22] *BIA* ss 127–35.

[23] Mark might also proceed directly to sale simply because he does not have any need for a dump truck.

other creditors. Generally, he will have taken this risk into account before setting the terms of the loan agreement with her.

- **Limiting recovery:** Mark cannot, in any event, recover *more than* the value of Nancy's debt to him. If, for instance, she owed $250 000, but the truck was sold for $275 000, he would have to pay the extra $25 000 to her trustee in bankruptcy.

In situations involving a *proposal*, landlords can also become exempt creditors. Insolvency often triggers the breach of a lease, and the landlord therefore becomes a significant creditor of the tenant. Under normal contractual rules, the landlord may be entitled to claim the value of the full rent until the end of the lease if no other tenant can be found. The *BIA* modifies that rule, however, by offering two options to an insolvent *commercial* tenant.

- The first option allows the insolvent tenant to pay the landlord for its actual loss.

- The second option allows the insolvent tenant to pay the landlord the lesser of (i) three years' rent, or (ii) 100 percent of the rent that would have been paid in the first year after the lease was prematurely terminated, plus 15 percent of the rent for the remainder of the term.

Those rules recognize that rental markets are often flexible and that landlords with insolvent tenants might try to "double-dip" when substitute tenants are otherwise available.[24]

Settlements and Preferences

The period leading up to bankruptcy can be hotly contested. Debtors and creditors may both be tempted to engage in questionable behaviour. Debtors may try to transfer assets to related companies, friends, or relatives in the hope that these can somehow escape distribution. Such transfers are known as **settlements** if they are made for free or for nominal payment. Likewise, debtors may attempt to **prefer**, or favour, some creditors over others by paying certain debts in advance of assignment or petition.

That sort of behaviour undermines the equality of creditors and decreases the assets available for distribution. Courts therefore developed rules for settlements and preferences that (i) allowed creditors to void improper transfers by debtors, and (ii) allowed trustees in bankruptcy to reclaim assets. Those historical doctrines are now contained in the *BIA*.

- **Void settlement:** Any settlement made within a one-year period before bankruptcy is void.[25]

- **Void preference:** A transfer made to a creditor 90 days before bankruptcy is void if the aim of the transfer was to prefer that creditor over others.[26] In the case of a non-arm's length transaction between related parties, such as a husband and wife or affiliated companies, the avoidance period is one year.[27]

a **settlement** is the transfer of property that is made for free or for nominal consideration

to **prefer** a creditor means to satisfy their claims in a larger amount than is permissible under bankruptcy law

24. *BIA* s 65.2.

25. *BIA* s 91(1).

26. *BIA* s 95(1).

27. *BIA* s 96.

Director Liability

When a limited company goes bankrupt and does not have enough money to pay its creditors, its directors are usually not liable for the deficiency. Nor, under Canadian law, do they owe a fiduciary duty to creditors.[28] However, a bankrupt company's directors may be liable if they have given personal guarantees for the company's debts or if a statute imposes liability upon them. For instance, the *Ontario Business Corporations Act* imposes liability on the directors of a corporation for:

- debts reflecting six months' wages for employees
- debts reflecting twelve months' vacation pay for employees
- debts reflecting wages or vacation pay arising under a collective agreement with a union[29]

To cover such liability, most directors today maintain insurance. Business Decision 24.1 describes some of the issues that arise when companies offer director protection themselves.

BUSINESS DECISION 24.1

Director Protection: A "Feast amid Famine"?[30]

In recent years there has been a trend toward "super" protection of corporate directors and officers as a debtor corporation's condition deteriorates. This protection often takes the form of promises by the corporation to indemnify directors and officers in ways that otherwise go beyond corporate law. For example, individuals can be offered very large fees enjoying super-priority status for themselves and their lawyers in the event of a bankruptcy or court-ordered protection. Such promises often use the corporation's precious cash flow at a critical time in business operations.

The traditional justification for this kind of behaviour is that officers and directors are thought to "know the company best." Consequently, they should be in a superior position to steer it clear of difficulty. The problem with this justification, however, is that it is not universally true. Existing officers and directors may have insider knowledge that helps to avoid trouble, but then again, they may be the source of much trouble as well. Furthermore, as society becomes more sensitive to managerial privilege and wrongdoing, it seems unjust to allow one class of people to effectively escape responsibility for their actions.

Canadian corporate law has provisions that prohibit corporations from indemnifying directors or maintaining insurance to cover situations where liability relates to the failure to act honestly and in good faith. In addition, the trend toward "super" protection has generated something of a counter-trend among shareholders, corporate governance advocates, and academics who want to see greater restrictions on the kinds of benefits that can be extended by a corporation to its directors and officers in situations of business distress.

Questions for Discussion

1. What arguments could you make to support enhanced corporate director and officer protection in bankruptcy? Against?

2. Where could you contest a company's decision to award director or officer protection?

3. Do you think governments have a role in defining what the level of director protection should be?

---

[28] This point was clarified recently by the Supreme Court of Canada in *Re People's Department Stores Inc.*, [2004] 3 SCR 461, where the court held that while corporate directors owe a duty of care to creditors, that duty does not rise to the level of a fiduciary duty.

[29] *Business Corporations Act*, RSO 1990, c B.16 (Ont). For the directors to be held liable under the statute, the employee must sue them while they are directors or within six months of their resignation. In the case of a debt, directors may be held liable for six months after the debt is incurred.

[30] *Re Air Canada* (2003) 42 CBR (4th) 173 (Ont SCJ).

PROPOSALS

a proposal is a court-approved contract between a debtor and creditors that gives the debtor time to adjust its financial affairs while business operations continue

A **proposal** is a court-approved contract between a debtor and its creditors that gives the debtor time to adjust its financial affairs while business operations continue. The following are some of the most important kinds of proposals.

- A *composition* is an agreement between a debtor and its creditors under which the creditors agree to accept, in satisfaction of their claims, less than the amount that is owing to them.

- An *extension of time* prolongs the time available for repayment. That may happen alone or together with a composition.

- A *scheme of arrangement* is a situation where the debtor's assets are vested in, or controlled by, a trustee for the benefit of creditors while the proposal is being performed.

- Under a *liquidation proposal*, the debtor agrees to sell assets and distribute the proceeds. The benefit of that procedure is that the debtor *itself* can assist in the recovery of receivables, such as payments from its *own* debtors. Under a normal bankruptcy, that job is performed by the trustee.

- A *share exchange* occurs when the debtor offers to exchange shares in a company for outstanding debt. That procedure is sometimes called a "debt–equity swap."

The first possibility may seem strange. Why would a creditor ever accept less than the full value of a debt? The answer is that the alternatives may be even less attractive. If the creditor enforces its rights to the letter, it will have to spend much time and expense in litigation. In addition, in doing so the creditor may scare away customers, making the debtor's business conditions even more difficult. Believe it or not, creditors' reputations are also important. They are often in the business of lending, and if anything goes wrong, a debtor would rather deal with Bank A, which has a reputation for fairness and flexibility, than Bank B, which has a reputation for squeezing debtors as hard as possible.

A proposal is, in some sense, an attempt to give the debtor another chance. Normally, the hope is that the debtor, by continuing to operate, will at least be able to pay off its immediate debts. The real benefit is time. Temporarily removing the pressure of repayment may allow the debtor to return to profitability in future.

Form and Requirements

A proposal can be made by a bankrupt, an insolvent person, a liquidator or a receiver, or a trustee in bankruptcy. Usually, the debtor drafts a plan that takes into account the general business conditions and the wishes of its creditors.[31] The debtor has a strong incentive to be realistic, given that a proposal is less likely than either an assignment or a receiving order to hurt its credit rating or attract the stigma of bankruptcy. Creditors may also be encouraged to participate since the proposal will be externally verified both (i) by a trustee, who provides an independent opinion on a draft, and (ii) by creditors, many of whom will later vote on it.

[31.] Before the court approves a proposal, it must be satisfied that the terms are reasonable. Therefore, the proposal should have a reasonable chance of success: *Re McNamara and McNamara* (1984) 53 CBR (NS) 240 (Ont SCJ).

The proposal itself is made to creditors, who are categorized in classes according to their common interests. There may be, for example, a class of unsecured creditors with claims under $1000 and another with claims above that amount. The *BIA* is formally silent as to how classes are to be defined with respect to preferred and unsecured creditors. However, if the proposed classification is unfair, creditors will likely object, and the matter may be brought to court. Indeed, the debtor has the option of applying directly to the court for a determination of the appropriate classes.

The *BIA* does *not* require secured creditors to be dealt with under a proposal. The debtor may deal with them separately, as long as the debts owed to those creditors are *fully satisfied*. However, when secured creditors are included in a proposal, they must be placed in the same class if they are secured against the same assets. Again, it is possible for the debtor to apply to court for a determination as to the appropriate class or classes of secured creditor.

Besides dividing creditors into classes, proposals must meet other requirements. If secured creditors have given notice that they intend to enforce their securities, the proposal should provide that their claims are paid according to the terms of the security. In addition, the proposal must ensure that the ranking of creditors is respected. Consequently, secured creditors must recover fully before general unsecured creditors.

Preparation and Voting

A debtor often does not file a proposal immediately. Rather, it files a notice of intent with the Official Registrar to provide a proposal and then consults with its creditors. Depending upon the outcome of those consultations, it may then file a formal proposal with the Official Registrar at a later date. It generally must do so within 30 days, but the Bankruptcy Court can extend that time by periods of 45 days. The court cannot, however, grant more than five months of extensions on the original 30-day period.

Once the proposal is submitted, it must be considered by a meeting of creditors within 21 days. The trustee then calls a meeting of creditors to consider and vote on the proposal. The court may, at any time before the first meeting of creditors, declare that the proposal has been refused by creditors if it is satisfied that the debtor is not acting in good faith or that there is little real chance that the proposal will be accepted.[32]

For the proposal to be formally approved, it must receive the support of at least half of the creditors in each class, who hold at least two-thirds of the face value of the debtor's assets in that class. Once the proposal is approved, it binds all creditors that are covered by its terms, including those who may have voted against it. A court must then approve the proposal within 15 days.

If the creditors do not vote in favour of the proposal, the debtor is automatically deemed to be bankrupt. The Official Receiver steps forward and conducts the first meeting of creditors. Alternately, it is possible for the trustee to use *voting letters* deposited by the creditors and vote in favour of the proposal, or to call a second meeting to consider a revised or reformulated plan. **Voting letters** are letters that creditors use to vote on a proposal even though they did not attend the meeting.

voting letters are letters that creditors use to vote on a proposal even though they did not attend the meeting of creditors

---

32. *BIA* s 50(12).

OTHER STATUTES DEALING WITH FINANCIAL DISTRESS AND FAILURE

The *BIA* is not the only statute that deals with financial distress and failure. There are some provincial statutes that regulate general debtor–creditor relations, such as fraudulent conveyances, business corporations, and personal property security acts. Some may provide more favourable options for debtors or creditors than an assignment, receivership, or proposal under the *BIA*. In the relevant circumstances, they should be carefully considered.[33]

One important alternative is the *Companies' Creditors Arrangement Act* (*CCAA*), which applies to corporations that have issued *debentures* in series. **Debentures** are promissory notes or bonds backed by the general credit of a corporation.[34] They are usually not secured by any specific property. An insolvent company that meets the requirements can apply to a court for protection while assembling a plan of reorganization—but only if its total outstanding debts exceed $5 000 000.

The benefit of applying under the *CCAA* is that action by *all* creditors, including secured creditors, is stayed. That is a significant advantage over the *BIA*, and most major companies in Canada have issued debentures in series or deeds of trust to take advantage of the option.

Unfortunately, the relationship between the *BIA* and the *CCAA* is somewhat unclear. It appears that an insolvent corporate debtor with debentures can take advantage of protection under either Act, or possibly both. However, the law remains vague on this point.

The *Winding-Up Act* (*WUA*) applies to the default of federally incorporated companies, banks, and insurance companies, as well as some insolvent provincial companies. Its application is mandatory for banks and insurance companies, but it is an alternative to *BIA* procedures for all other covered entities. The *WUA* differs substantially from the *BIA* in both substance and technique. Under the *WUA*, for instance, proceedings may be commenced if the debtor is merely insolvent, whereas the *BIA* requires a bankruptcy. If proceedings have been commenced under the *BIA*, they preclude application of the *WUA*. Due to its limited application, the *WUA* has been rarely used in recent years.

Business Decision 24.2 deals with one important aspect of the *Companies' Creditors Arrangement Act*.

debentures are promissory notes or bonds backed by the general credit of a corporation

---

[33] *Eg* many provincial statutes allow a creditor to claim priority for both a debt *and* the costs associated with recovering that money through execution proceedings by the sheriff. Creditors in bankruptcy are governed by *BIA*-set priorities and normally recoup only a small percentage of their court costs: *Royal Bank v R* (1981) 40 CBR (NS) 27 (Ont Div Ct).

[34] Promissory notes were discussed in Chapter 14.

BUSINESS DECISION 24.2

Insolvency and the CCAA[35]

One requirement of seeking protection under the *Companies' Creditors Arrangement Act* (*CCAA*) is insolvency. There is, however, a tendency to ignore that issue. Everyone with an interest in the case—the debtor, creditors, suppliers, and even employees—may agree that the debtor's financial position is dire. Consequently, courts sometimes gloss over the technical question of insolvency. Still, the law is the law, and this raises the question whether a business must be completely "broke" before it can take advantage of *CCAA* status.

In a recent case, *Re Stelco*, the judge appeared to open the door to a more liberal "reasonable foreseeability" test for insolvency under the *CCAA*. The judge held that the law does not require a debtor to meet the exact definition of insolvency in all cases. Instead, a financially troubled corporation can be insolvent for *CCAA* purposes if it reasonably expects to run out of liquidity within a certain amount of time. The judge based his decision on the idea that as the financial condition of the debtor grows worse, it often becomes increasingly difficult for the debtor to assemble a survival package.

While this interpretation has not yet been adopted by every Canadian court, it appears to be the start of a trend toward recognizing that businesses do not need to be on their "last legs" in order to take advantage of *CCAA* restructuring. The decision is also consistent with international trends. In the United States and elsewhere, similar laws only require that a company demonstrate "financial distress" in order to qualify for restructuring protection. The decision should help companies to manage their financial risks in a more proactive way.

Questions for Discussion

1. Explain the idea behind court-authorized restructuring. What problems does it avoid?

2. What are three advantages of a more liberal approach to corporate restructuring under the *CCAA*? What are three disadvantages?

---

35. *Re Stelco Inc* (2004) 48 CBR (4th) 299 (Ont SCJ).

Chapter Summary

A key aspect of risk management is planning for the possibility of business failure. In Canada, bankruptcy law is designed to provide several means for resolving business failure and gives debtors and creditors options to choose from. In this respect, it is an important tool in risk management.

The main Canadian statute relating to bankruptcy and insolvency is the *Bankruptcy and Insolvency Act* (*BIA*). It provides two principal procedures in bankruptcy: assignment or petition. An assignment is a voluntary act by the debtor placing itself in bankruptcy. A petition is a request by creditors to the court to place the debtor in bankruptcy. In both cases, the value of formal bankruptcy status is to provide a stay of action and a limit on recovery against the debtor. In exchange, creditors are paid in priority to the extent that the assets permit.

The *BIA* also provides for a third procedure outside bankruptcy in the form of a proposal. A proposal involves an understanding between the debtor and creditors in which the parties agree to compromise or rearrange debts. A proposal must be approved by at least half of the credi-

tors in each class, constituting at least two-thirds of the value of the assets represented by that class. A proposal offers significant advantages to a debtor, given that a proposal is less likely than either assignment or a receiving order to impair its credit rating or stigmatize it as a bankrupt.

Each procedure has its own advantages. The ultimate choice of procedure is dictated by the appreciation of risk, including prospects for the debtor, the relationship between the parties, and general economic conditions. In some situations, common sense calls for an assignment, rather than the drawn-out struggle of a petition. In others, the debtor may be wiser to recognize financial reality and make a proposal or agree to a petition. Creditors should be careful about acting too quickly, as Canadian courts have found creditors liable for rash behaviour that destroys a debtor's business.

Canadian law relating to bankruptcy and insolvency attempts to strike a balance between the orderly repayment of debts, the rehabilitation of debtors, and economic growth. It is a realistic response to an unfortunate event.

REVIEW QUESTIONS

1. What is meant by the terms "insolvency" and "bankruptcy"? How do they differ?

2. What is an act of bankruptcy? How is it related to insolvency?

3. What are the purposes of bankruptcy law? How does bankruptcy help the debtor? Creditors? Society?

4. How does bankruptcy differ from an individual debtor–creditor action? What problems in the common law did the development of bankruptcy overcome?

5. How does the law differ between commercial and consumer bankruptcies? Is the recent rise in the rate of consumer bankruptcy in Canada a good thing? Why?

6. Explain who is responsible for bankruptcy legislation in Canada, and why.

7. Distinguish between an assignment in bankruptcy and a petition. What are some of the advantages of an assignment? What is the priority between assignment and petition?

8. What are some of the advantages of a proposal? What majority is necessary for approval of a proposal? Who approves it?

9. Describe several important types of proposal. On what does the type or timing ultimately depend?

10. Against whom does the "stay" operate in bankruptcy? What does it stay?

11. Explain the distinction between a secured and an unsecured creditor. What is the relationship between categories of creditor and the market for credit?

12. What is a proof of claim? Why is it necessary, and who submits it? What happens if it is not submitted?

13. Describe the role of the trustee. Who does the trustee represent? Who regulates the trustee?

14. What is a discharge from bankruptcy? What debts are non-dischargeable? Why?

15. What is "exempt property" under the *BIA*, and what is its purpose? Who is responsible for defining what property is permissibly exempt under the law?

16. Explain the concept of a reviewable transaction. How long a period may be reviewed? Is the interval of review a period pre-bankruptcy or post-bankruptcy?

17. Can student loans accrued as a result of a federal or provincial education loan program be discharged in bankruptcy? Why?

18. What are two aspects of the doctrine of creditor equality?

19. Who can take advantage of an arrangement under the *CCAA*? Explain why action under the *CCAA* is occasionally preferred to action under the *BIA*. How do the two statutes interact?

20. Which types of enterprises are exempt from bankruptcy? What are the policy reasons for their exemption from the *BIA*?

CASES AND PROBLEMS

1. Elaine runs the Five Brothers restaurant in Niagara Falls. She has given the bank a general security interest on the property in exchange for a loan of $200 000. The restaurant is not successful and, due to a recent decline in tourism, has a fair market value of only $150 000. If Elaine decides to seek an assignment, what can the bank do to recoup its loan?

2. Bengt Norsson lives in Calgary. He works as a carpenter and drives into work at various sites everyday. Unfortunately, he does not really like his job and gambles on the side. Bengt lost thousands of dollars recently and is contemplating an assignment in bankruptcy. One of his principal concerns is whether an assignment would require him to give up his tools of the trade, without which he cannot work. Would he be able to keep them?

3. Ernie goes into bankruptcy, taking with him the dotcom online software company that he built from scratch. A trustee is appointed and starts running the business. He employs Ernie on a contingency basis to help an accountant prepare the business's income tax returns. Before discharge, Ernie also provides other services to ensure that the business continues to operate, with the happy result that it is sold for a higher amount than it would be otherwise. Ernie wants to know if he can claim wages from the trustee or if his efforts simply become part of the bankrupt's estate.

4. Belinda and Joe previously lived together. After a disagreement, she and her daughter, Marianna, moved out 18 months ago. She had received an alimony order from a British Columbia court against Joe, who is required to pay $1200 a month to her for support. Joe sends cheques for seven months and then stops making payments. When Belinda calls, Joe tells her that he is "between a rock and a hard place." Can Belinda petition Joe into bankruptcy?

5. Kerry's Bagels Inc is a bakery company owned and operated by Paul Kerry in Victoria, British Columbia. Bagels were a popular item in the late 1990s but recently the trend has been toward wraps and Italian-style sandwiches, and Paul's sales have consequently fallen off. In June 2003, Paul found that he was unable to fund his payroll of 12 employees due to continuing financial difficulties. At the same time, however, he arranged for funds to be paid to himself in settlement of his own wages as president of the company. On September 10, 2003, less than a month after paying the funds to himself, Paul decided he had had enough and gave notice that he intended to make a proposal concerning the affairs of Kerry's Bagels Inc. The trustee of the proposal has now come forward and wants to know whether the wage payment made to Paul could be challenged under the BIA as a preference.

6. Maria owes Karen $50 000. She has failed to repay that money for some time and has always been very secretive. As a result, Karen has difficulty locating Maria's creditors and begins to wonder if she alone can petition Maria into bankruptcy. After all, she remembers something about the need for evidence from multiple creditors to petition. Could Karen petition Maria into bankruptcy?

7. NorthStar is a pharmaceutical company in Montreal. It specializes in fertility drugs and HIV resistance products. Due to the heavy demand for its products, it seeks to expand production. To finance the expansion NorthStar takes out a loan from Bank X, which is secured against a building and new pieces of equipment it purchases with the loan. Shortly thereafter, however, NorthStar stumbles when competitors introduce a number of new drugs that eat into its most lucrative markets. As a result, the company is forced to assign itself in bankruptcy. Bank X then seeks to realize on its security. It claims the building and equipment and now wants to know whether it can operate them itself.

8. Tony has owned a hardware store on the west island of Montreal for the last 15 years. Business has been only so-so, and in an effort to generate publicity, he decides to give hardware kits worth $200 each to five local charities, which plan to use them as raffle prizes at various events in the coming year. A month later, Tony realizes that the business is no good and decides to make a voluntary assignment. Can the trustee seek a return of the hardware kits? What about a new colour television that Tony gave to his wife as a present for her birthday the year before?

9. Janetti Inc, a Montreal sweater manufacturer, concludes a security agreement with Bank Y in which it gives the bank a general security over all of Janetti's accounts receivable. This is in exchange for a loan of $1 million. Janetti then files for bankruptcy, and the bank gives notice that it seeks to realize on its security. Bank Y recovers only $300 000 from the accounts and wants to know if it can claim the balance of its loan in some way. What if, instead, it was able to recover $1.2 million?

10. Turner & Whitehead is an engineering firm in Vancouver that, after many years of successful operation, assigned itself into bankruptcy under the BIA. The Director of Employment Standards for the Province of British Columbia then brought a claim for severance pay owed to the terminated Turner & Whitehead employees. The Trustee in Bankruptcy disallowed the claim, holding in effect that BC employment standards legislation was ineffective when it conflicted with the BIA. Employees are not creditors, the Trustee reasoned, so they should not be able to collect. At the same time, it should be noted that the BIA is formally silent on claims for severance pay resulting from termination of employment caused by a bankruptcy. Is the Trustee correct?

11. Bluebird Finance of Saskatoon offered Rubina Naderi a $50 000 loan to start a dressmaking and tailoring business. The loan was to be secured by a security agreement that created a "floating charge" over all of Naderi's assets. The floating charge would only crystallize at the moment that Rubina was declared bankrupt. Rubina went into business in a Saskatoon mall and began making payments to repay the loan. However, her efforts were not enough. After several months she went out of business and assigned herself into bankruptcy. She wonders if Bluebird Finance remains a secured lender given that she owes it less than the full $50 000.

12. Joseph Inc, a retail fashion chain, contemplates making a proposal to its creditors. It is thinking about making the proposal to both secured and unsecured creditors in the form of an arrangement or debt–equity swap. Is it required to include secured creditors in its proposal?

WEBLINKS

Secured Transactions

Nova Scotia Personal Property Registry www.gov.ns.ca/snsmr/property/default.asp?mn=282.46.82

This site is representative of the Web-based registries maintained by most provincial and territorial governments under their PPS legislation. Most permit secured parties to register their security interests online and search for registrations against a particular debtor, and provide general information about the PPS legislation in that province.

PPSA.Net www.ppsa.net/body.htm

This website provides links to the text of all PPS legislation in each Canadian jurisdiction.

Uniform Law Conference www.law.ualberta.ca/alri/ulc/priority/ecomlaw.htm#l.%20%20%20COMMERCIAL%20LAW

This useful site discusses provincial PPS law in a broad commercial law context.

National Law Center for Inter-American Trade
www.natlaw.com/pubs/overview.htm

This site provides an excellent overview of the PPS system in Canada by a leading academic, Ron Cuming, who also comments on the effectiveness of the system.

Personal Property Security in Canada www.duhaime.org/Civil/ca-ppsa.aspx

This page provides a good general overview of PPS law in Canada, including Quebec. It provides a more detailed discussion of the rules in British Columbia.

Bankruptcy and Insolvency

The Office of the Superintendent of Bankruptcy
http://strategis.ic.gc.ca/epic/internet/inbsf-osb.nsf/en/home

This is the official website for the federally appointed Superintendent of Bankruptcy. The site offers information for creditors, debtors, and trustees, including monthly bankruptcy statistics and legislation related to bankruptcy. It also includes a downloadable version of *The Financial Guide for Post-Secondary Students*.

Bankruptcy Canada www.bankruptcycanada.com

Bankruptcycanada.com provides general information to individuals facing bankruptcy. This site is aimed at consumers who are contemplating assignment, the possibility of a petition, or a proposal to creditors under Canadian Law. It features information on financial self-assessment, credit reporting, and finding a trustee. It also includes some useful information for those who have taken out student loans and are facing financial distress.

The Bankruptcy and Insolvency Act http://laws.justice.gc.ca/en/B-3

This link takes you to the *Bankruptcy and Insolvency Act* on the Federal Department of Justice website. In the Act you can find a more detailed description of some of the concepts introduced in the chapter. Consider looking at the following sections: **Interpretation** provides the legislative interpretation of terms used in the BIA, **Part I** identifies Administrative Officials under the BIA and defines their roles, **Part II** defines Receiving Orders and the process of obtaining a receiving order, **Part III** defines proposals and sets out how a party makes a proposal, **Part IV** identifies what property of a bankrupt is available to creditors under bankruptcy proceedings.

Canadian Bankruptcy Law Centre www.duhaime.org/Bankruptcy

This site contains a list of Canadian bankruptcy and insolvency law articles on aspects of financial distress and failure, and links to other useful bankruptcy law sites.

Canada's Credit Doctor www.creditdoctor.ca/index.htm

This site is dedicated to helping people understand credit and how it affects their everyday lives, the work of credit-reporting agencies, and ways in which consumers can achieve and maintain a healthy credit rating.

Public Legal Education Association of Saskatchewan
www.plea.org/freepubs/freepubs.htm

This site has information about Canadian law and the law of Saskatchewan relating to debtor and creditor rights. It also has a useful section on farm financial difficulties.

MoneyProblems.ca www.moneyproblems.ca

This private service is dedicated to helping Canadians avoid bankruptcy, repair their credit, get loans, and plan for the future. It provides information on credit-card debt, credit-counselling services, and tax problems.

Legal.com Bankruptcy Page www.legal.com/bankruptcy

This site contains information on consumer bankruptcies in Canada and the US.

The International Association of Insolvency Regulators
www.insolvencyreg.org

The International Association of Insolvency Regulators comprises government officials from member nations that are responsible for insolvency legislation in their respective countries. The purpose of the Association is to facilitate regulation of bankruptcies across borders. Though each country has its own regulatory framework for bankruptcy, the Association promotes understanding of the issues, procedures, and practices of each member country.

Supreme Court of Canada Bankruptcy www.lexum.umontreal.ca/csc-scc/en/concept/ndx058002.html

Though Bankruptcy law is set out in the BIA, court decisions illustrate how the Act is to be applied. The cases listed on this site are decisions of the Supreme Court of Canada which pertain to issues discussed in this chapter, including property of the bankrupt, priorities in bankruptcy, and settlement.

Bankruptcy Court www.courts.ns.ca/bankruptcy/index_br.htm

As noted in the chapter, bankruptcy court is not a separate court within the court system. However, bankruptcy presents unique issues for the parties involved. As such, these issues are best settled by judges with competence in bankruptcy and commercial law. The website for the Nova Scotia Bankruptcy Court provides users with information unique to bankruptcy proceedings.

Personal Insolvency Services www.bdo.ca/en/services/personalbankruptcy/index.cfm

This is one of many websites that offer individuals or businesses guidance when facing bankruptcy. Many law firms and assurance companies offer services to help parties through a bankruptcy on both the debtor and creditor sides. (Note: This is not an endorsement of the services offered by this particular firm; the website is only an example of the services available to debtors and creditors.)

KPMG Personal Bankruptcy www.personalbankruptcy.com

This site contains information on personal bankruptcy in Canada, including a question-and-answer section and a bankruptcy forum.

Continuing Legal Education Society of British Columbia www.cle.bc.ca/CLE/Analysis/Collection/02-bankruptcy2

Compiled by the Continuing Legal Education Society of British Columbia, this article outlines the procedure for making a proposal under the BIA. The cases cited throughout the article clarify how the Act applies. The body of bankruptcy law comprises both bankruptcy legislation and court decisions.

Investopedia.com www.investopedia.com/articles/fundamental/04/021104.asp

Being able to avoid bankruptcy entirely is likely in the interest of a potential creditor. The link provided sets out the Altman Z test, one of the most widely used tests for predicting corporate bankruptcy, and explains how it is applied.

ADDITIONAL RESOURCES FOR CHAPTER 24 ON THE COMPANION WEBSITE

(www.pearsoned.ca/mcinnes)

In addition to self-test multiple-choice, true-false, and short essay questions (all with immediate feedback), three additional Cases and Problems (with suggested answers), and links to useful Web destinations, the Companion Website provides the following resources for Chapter 24:

- Business Decision 24W.1—Trustees and Environmental Liability
- Business Decision 24W.2—Selling Assets: A "Good Price" or Simply the "Best"?
- Business Decision 24W.3—International Bankruptcy
- Additional Weblinks on Bankruptcy

Provincial Material

- **British Columbia:** Fraudulent Transfer of Property, Corporate Dissolution
- **Alberta:** Bankruptcy and Insolvency, Fraudulent Conveyances, Fraudulent Preferences
- **Manitoba and Saskatchewan:** Exempt Property
- **Ontario:** Assignment and Preferences, Debt Collection Process, Construction Liens, Fraudulent Conveyances, Limitation Periods

25 Government Regulation of Business

OBJECTIVES

After completing this chapter, you should be able to:

1. Explain the importance to business regulation of the federal trade and commerce power and the provincial power over property and civil rights.

2. Describe the relevance of the *Canadian Charter of Rights and Freedoms* for business in Canada.

3. Identify the jurisdiction and relevance of the Federal Court of Canada.

4. Describe the difference between direct and indirect taxation.

5. Explain the distinction between conspiracies, mergers, and abuse of dominant position under the *Competition Act*.

6. Define a restrictive business transaction and give two examples.

7. Explain the difference between a reviewable matter and a criminal matter under the *Competition Act*.

8. Explain the role of the Agreement on Internal Trade.

9. Explain the legal framework for environmental regulation in Canada.

10. Identify one method for a person to commence action against anti-competitive conduct or environmental pollution in Canada.

Canada's federal and provincial governments are important regulators of business. They regulate when policy objectives or operating conditions make it necessary to do so. Their power is not, however, unlimited. In regulating business, they must respect the constitutional division of powers, basic considerations of fairness, and market requirements. Their success in doing so is vital to making Canada an attractive place to invest and work.

In this chapter, we examine government's regulation of business. Understanding how and what governments regulate is essential to properly managing business risks. Note that Canada's limited domestic market and harsh climate have traditionally made it necessary for governments to regulate business. These requirements have promoted a generally positive view of government, something very different from the view of government taken in the United States. While government is less of an active participant in the economy today than it has been in the past, it remains a significant facilitator of business behaviour.

Note, too, that business can be done through certain activities that are, strictly speaking, harmful if done in unrestricted ways. In other words, there must be some competitive conduct or some pollution permissible, or else business would grind to a halt. This trade-off dictates the adoption of a regulatory model of behaviour that allows certain activities to occur, and that adopts a more flexible approach to violations than is seen, for instance, in criminal law.

BUSINESS REGULATION

As we saw in Chapter 1, Canada's Constitution assigns responsibility over specific subjects of regulation, or "heads of power," to the federal and provincial governments. In the business context, for instance, the federal government is responsible for banking, currency and coinage, bankruptcy and insolvency, interprovincial transport, and trade and commerce. The provinces are responsible for property and civil rights, "local works and undertakings," and "all matters of a merely local or private nature in the province."

The original division of powers was created at the time of Confederation in 1867 and reflects the distribution thought appropriate then. It has since been amended to take into account new subjects that were not in existence at Canada's founding, such as aeronautics and the environment, and to clarify the original division in light of contemporary conditions.

The most important federal power related to business regulation is the express federal power over "trade and commerce." This power is exceptionally broad and it potentially conflicts with the provincial power concerning "property and civil rights."[1] Most "trade and commerce" is carried out by contracts, which lie at the heart of "property and civil rights." It therefore has been necessary for courts to define the boundary between the federal and provincial powers.

The leading authority on the division of powers is *Citizens Insurance Co v Parsons*.[2] In that case, the court examined the validity of an Ontario statute that

---

[1] The Canadian term "trade and commerce" may seem broader than its American counterpart under the US Constitution, the Commerce Clause, which provides that the US federal government shall have the power "to regulate commerce with foreign nations, and among the several States, and with the Indian tribes." Professor Hogg notes, however, that despite the broader Canadian language, the Canadian "trade and commerce" clause has been interpreted more narrowly than the Commerce Clause. As a result, the American Congress has more extensive powers than the Canadian Parliament over a wide range of business behaviour including competition law (antitrust), insurance, labour, marketing, securities, transportation, and communication: P Hogg *Constitutional Law of Canada* (1997) at 20–1.

[2] *Citizens Insurance Co v Parsons* (1881) 7 App Cas 96 (PC).

required certain conditions to be included in all fire insurance contracts written in that province. The insurance company argued that the Ontario law was an intrusion into the federal government's domain of regulation. In rejecting that argument, the court held that the Ontario statute was a valid exercise of the provincial power in relation to property and civil rights. The law did not infringe trade and commerce because that power did not encompass "the power to regulate by legislation the contracts of a particular business or trade, such as the business of fire insurance in a single province." Instead, the court said that the federal power extends to business activities of an interprovincial nature, including the "general regulation of trade affecting the whole dominion."

Later cases upheld *Citizens Insurance*, and it is now generally accepted that provincial governments have the power to regulate business dealings of a purely local nature. Over time, however, certain statements in *Citizens Insurance* about the extent of federal regulation over business activity have gained importance. In some cases, the federal power over trade and commerce has been held to support transactions that are completed *entirely within* a province, such as the local sale of domestically grown wheat or the marketing of farm products.[3] In other cases, it has not.[4] Nevertheless, the courts have clearly said that federal power can be exercised where there is a need for broad national standards, as is true of marketing boards and the regulation of competition.[5]

In comparison, provincial power over property and civil rights is local and specific. It involves the regulation of discrete business activities, including insurance, the professions and trades, labour relations, marketing, securities, property, debt adjustment, and consumer protection. Consequently, provincial power has been held to validly regulate land ownership and the sale of goods. Given their frequency, those types of transactions fall within the provincial jurisdiction over property and civil rights more often than they trigger the federal jurisdiction over trade and commerce.[6]

Concurrency and Paramountcy

concurrency refers to the idea of shared powers between levels of government

In addition to subjects of exclusive federal and provincial jurisdiction, the drafters of Canada's Constitution recognized certain shared, or **concurrent**, powers in relation to such matters as labour, business organization, and the environment. Here, the exact division of jurisdiction was not clear and has been only partly resolved through subsequent negotiations and legislative amendments.[7] Concurrent jurisdiction remains a source of contention in federal–provincial affairs.

[3.] *R v Klassen* (1959) 20 DLR (2d) 406 (Man CA); *Re Agricultural Products Marketing Act* (1978) 84 DLR (3d) 257 (SCC).

[4.] *Dominion Stores v The Queen* (1980) 106 DLR (3d) 581 (SCC); *Labatt Breweries v AG Canada* (1980) 52 CCC (2d) 433 (SCC).

[5.] *General Motors v City National Leasing* (1989) 58 DLR (4th) 255 (SCC).

[6.] P.Hogg *Constitutional Law of Canada* (1997) at 21–4.

[7.] Three provisions explicitly confer concurrent power. Section 92A(2) of the Constitution, added in 1982, gives provincial legislatures the power to make laws in relation to the export of natural resources. Section 94A, added in 1951 and amended in 1964, gives the federal government the power to regulate old age pensions and other associated benefits. Section 95 gives concurrent power over agriculture and immigration to both levels of government. Concurrency can also arise from the way in which the courts interpret the Constitution. The judicial doctrine of "double aspect" provides that many powers fall under both heads of power. For instance, a law concerning drunk driving has a criminal (federal) and a highway safety (provincial) aspect. And the "pith and substance" doctrine states that where a power is exercised under one head of power, it is valid, even though it may incidentally regulate some matter under the other head of power. See P Hogg, *Constitutional Law of Canada* (1997) at 40–1.

The breadth of both federal and provincial power in relation to business raises the possibility of conflict. Where no other interpretation is possible, the courts must decide which government's legislation will prevail. In most instances, the **doctrine of paramountcy**, which is based on the Constitution's division of powers, determines which law is pre-eminent. However, the fact that many business activities have an overlapping federal and provincial aspect means that there is often a need for federal–provincial co-ordination. Examples include securities and highway regulation. Case Brief 25.1 illustrates the operation of this doctrine.

the doctrine of paramountcy determines which law is pre-eminent based on the Constitution's division of powers

CASE BRIEF 25.1

Bank of Montreal v Hall (1990) 65 DLR (4th) 361 (SCC)

The constitutional principle of paramountcy determines which law prevails if there is an inconsistency between federal and provincial legislation. In *Bank of Montreal v Hall*, the issue was whether a procedure under the federal *Bank Act* for mortgage foreclosure overrode a provincial *Limitation of Civil Rights Act*. The Ontario statute required a creditor, before starting any foreclosure proceeding, to notify the debtor that there was one last chance to pay the debt. The federal law did not require such notice. The bank followed federal law, failed to serve the notice, and later found itself facing an argu-

ment that its foreclosure was invalid under provincial law.

The Supreme Court held that the bank was not required to comply with provincial law. The Ontario statute was inconsistent with federal legislation. In that situation, the conflict between federal and provincial law was direct. In other words, it would be impossible to comply with one set of laws without violating the other. The court observed that "there could be no clearer instance of a case where compliance with the federal statute necessarily entails defiance of its provincial counterpart."

THE *CANADIAN CHARTER OF RIGHTS AND FREEDOMS*

As we saw in Chapter 1, the *Canadian Charter of Rights and Freedoms* was added to Canada's Constitution in 1982 to protect fundamental democratic values. Those include the right to free speech, assembly, security of the person, and non-discrimination. The *Charter* applies to both natural and legal persons—individuals and corporate entities—in different degrees.

- The *Charter* does not protect private property.[9] That deliberate choice of the drafters reflects Canada's social democratic tradition. It stands in sharp contrast to the US Constitution and Bill of Rights, whose Fifth Amendment provides that "no person shall be deprived of life, liberty, *or property*, without due process of law."

- As we saw in Chapter 1, some *Charter* provisions apply to "everyone" or to "every individual." Those provisions are limited to natural persons (human beings) and do not extend to legal persons (such as corporations). For instance, section 15(1) of the *Charter* prohibits discrimination against individuals on certain grounds. Because a corporation is not, strictly speaking, an "individual," and because it has no race, national or ethnic origin, nor any colour, religion, sex, age, mental or physical disability, it does not enjoy protection under section 15(1).[10]

---

[9] *Home Orderly Services Ltd v Government of Manitoba* (1981) 32 DLR (4th) 755 (Man QB).

[10] *Milk Board v Clearview Dairy Farm Inc* (1987) 33 DLR (4th) 158 (BC CA).

- Some *Charter* provisions provide less protection to businesses than to individuals. For instance, advertising enjoys protection under section 2(b) as freedom of expression, but to a lesser extent than expression for purely political, religious, or social purposes. Likewise, businesses enjoy protection under section 8 against unreasonable search and seizure. In practice, however, they may enjoy less privacy than natural persons because of a distinction that is drawn between searches in the criminal and quasi-criminal context.[11]

THE FEDERAL COURT SYSTEM

In Chapter 1, we discussed the Canadian court system. One court that we briefly considered was the Federal Court of Canada. In the context of government regulation of business, that particular court plays a major role.

The Federal Court cannot hear a case unless three requirements are met:

- **Jurisdiction of the Federal Court:** First, the Federal court must have jurisdiction to hear the matter by virtue of the *Federal Court Act* or some other statute. The *Federal Court Act* refers to claims against the federal government, administrative remedies against federal agencies and tribunals, applications for judicial review, intellectual property, citizenship and immigration, maritime law, bills of exchange and promissory notes, and certain other matters. An example of a statute providing jurisdiction is the *Immigration Act*, which gives the Federal Court the exclusive competence to hear appeals of immigration rulings.

- **Jurisdiction of the federal government:** Second, the Federal Court cannot hear a case unless it involves an issue that falls within the federal government's jurisdiction. For example, a claim for damages arising out of a contract to build a marine terminal falls presumptively within the federal government's power to regulate shipping under the Constitution.

- **Application of federal law:** Third, the resolution of a case must *also* be based on an existing body of federal law. Consequently, the Federal Court has held that it did *not* have jurisdiction in the previous example because the claim for damages was simply a contractual matter that fell under the provincial government's power to regulate "property and civil rights."[12] The situation could have been different, however, if the dispute had concerned the operation of the terminal or its employees'

---

[11] Corporations are more likely to be charged with regulatory offences than criminal offences. Criminal matters require proof "beyond a reasonable doubt." The standard of proof is somewhat lower in the administrative and regulatory context. For instance, the Supreme Court of Canada has held that searches and seizures conducted by taxation authorities under the *Income Tax Act* to ensure the integrity of the tax system are permissible whether or not an inspector has reasonable grounds for believing that a particular taxpayer has breached the Act: *R v McKinlay Transport Ltd* (1990) 68 DLR (4th) 568 (SCC); *British Columbia (Securities Commission) v Branch* (1995) 123 DLR (4th) 462 (SCC).

[12] *Quebec North Shore Paper Co v CP Ltd* (1977) 71 DLR (3d) 111 (SCC).

hours of work. Shipping and labour law are existing categories of federal law.[13]

The Federal Court has two courts: the Trial Court and the Federal Court of Appeal. Federal Court judges sit in each province and territory. Appeals from the Trial Court may be taken to the Federal Court of Appeal. The Trial Court itself has jurisdiction to hear appeals from any "federal board, commission or other tribunal," except where appeal must be taken to the Federal Court of Appeal, as set out in section 28(1) of the *Federal Courts Act*.[14]

TAXATION

The drafters of Canada's first Constitution, set out to create a strongly centralized country. The federal government was therefore given the power to make laws for the purpose of raising of money "by any mode or system of taxation." This broad power was designed to allow the federal government to pay for big projects, like railways and harbours, that were vital to the development of the country as a whole. The provinces, in contrast, were given jurisdiction over more localized matters, such as the administration of justice, health care, and education, which were considered less costly. The provinces' taxation power was therefore restricted to the imposition of "direct" taxes and licence fees.

Since 1867, the growing complexity of Canadian society and demands on different levels of government have altered the way in which these powers are applied. The federal government remains responsible for imposing the largest portion of tax, but much of its take is now redistributed to the provinces to pay for expensive social programming (such as health care). In addition, the federal government is committed to a system of transfer payments that is designed to equalize conditions between rich and poor provinces. Those transfer payments do help to create reasonably consistent standards of living across the country. But because the federal government requires the provinces to satisfy certain conditions in order to receive their payments, the transfer system is a frequent source of tension within federal–provincial relations.

Today governments at all levels recognize the need to make Canada attractive to business people. They consequently have aimed to reduce business taxes to a level that is competitive with the tax burden in the United States, and they have introduced a number of other tax-related incentives that is designed to attract and retain research-intensive industries. These moves demonstrate how tax can be an important instrument of social policy. They also highlight how Canada's governments must work together to maintain a proper balance between revenue generation and international competitiveness.

[13.] Consider *ITO-Int'l Terminal Operators Ltd v Miida Electronics Inc* (1986) 28 DLR (4th) 641 (SCC). The dispute concerned the validity of a contractual clause between Mitsui and Miida that limited Mitsui's liability for negligence and purported to cover Mitsui's agents as well. The question for the Court was whether the issue of contractual limitation had a sufficient maritime connection and therefore fell within the broad head of "navigation and shipping" under s 91(10) of the Constitution. The Court held that it did. The Federal Court consequently had jurisdiction to hear the case.

[14.] The Federal Court of Appeal has jurisdiction to hear and determine applications for judicial review from 14 agencies, including the Canadian Radio-television and Telecommunications Commission, the Canadian International Trade Tribunal, and the Copyright Board of Canada.

Types of Taxation

Governments levy several types of taxes in Canada. The most important of these is income tax, which is levied both by the federal and provincial governments. In general, the federal government charges the highest percentage of income tax while the provinces charge a lesser percentage. For example, in 2004 the federal personal income tax had four basic rates:

- 16 percent on the first $35 000
- 22 percent on amounts above $35 000 up to $70 000
- 26 percent on amounts above $70 000 up to $113 804
- 29 percent on amounts over $113 804

Corporate income tax rates for small businesses were on average 26.12 percent on the first $75 000 and 22.12 percent on income above that amount.

Every province, except Alberta, Newfoundland and Labrador, New Brunswick, and Nova Scotia, has a provincial sales tax.[15] The amount of tax varies from province to province and item to item. In 1991, the federal government also introduced its own sales tax, the Goods and Services Tax (GST), which now stands at 7 percent and is applied on top of provincial sales taxes. Although the GST was initially criticized as a money grab by the federal government, it has arguably made the Canadian economy more competitive because it does not apply to exports.

In addition to income and sales taxes, Canadian governments also levy taxes on property, consumption, payroll, and corporate earnings through a variety of statutes. Property taxes are an important source of revenue for municipal government. Consumption taxes, also known as "excise" taxes, are levied on non-essential goods such as cigarettes, alcohol, and gasoline, often constituting a significant portion of the cost of these items. Payroll taxes are levied on most workers' salaries and are used to fund unemployment insurance, the Canada Pension Plan, and workers' compensation. Finally, corporations pay taxes on profits and capital gains. As mentioned, corporate income tax varies from province to province and can be significantly higher in some jurisdictions than others. Capital gains taxes are levied on the profit realized from the sale of an asset.

In recent years it has become common for employers to issue shares, or options to buy shares, to their employees. In Canada, such offers are considered a taxable benefit in the hands of the employee. The taxable amount is the difference between the fair market value of the shares and the amount the employee paid to acquire them. As a general rule, this amount is included in income when the shares are acquired (for instance, the tax on a stock option is triggered when the option is exercised).

However, in certain circumstances—in the case of options granted by Canadian-controlled private corporations and in the case of up to $100 000 worth of shares of publicly traded companies—taxation may be deferred until the employee sells the shares. In the case of stock options, Canadian law also allows employees to take a stock option deduction equal to 50 percent of the taxable amount where:

- the amount paid by the employee for the shares (the exercise price under the option) equals or exceeds the fair market value of the shares when the option was granted,

---

[15.] In three Atlantic provinces, however, the GST is combined with a provincial sales tax into a Harmonized Sales Tax (HST).

- the shares are common shares of the company, and
- the employee was dealing at arm's length with the company when the option was granted.

The first two conditions need not be met in the case of options granted by a Canadian-controlled private corporation, provided that the employee owns the shares for at least two years after the options are exercised. The objective of the deduction is to mirror the treatment of capital gains.

Direct and Indirect Taxation

Because the power to tax in Canada is based on specific grants of authority under the Constitution, lawmakers must pay attention to them when design-ing and implementing taxes. A key distinction is the difference between direct and indirect taxation. The distinction arises because the provinces are limited to direct taxation and licensing. A **direct tax** is one which is imposed on the very person who winds up paying it, whereas an **indirect tax** is paid by some-one who ultimately seeks reimbursement for the tax from someone else. For example, a direct tax is levied when a student buys a fast-food lunch subject to sales tax. The student, as consumer, will pay the tax. An indirect tax could be levied on the student in the course of the same transaction if another por-tion of the overall tax goes to pay for the fast-food franchisor's business tax. That is something that the vendor presumably passes on to its customers as an operating cost.

a **direct tax** is one paid by the person on whom it is imposed

an **indirect tax** is one paid by someone who seeks reimburse-ment for it

Although the distinction between direct and indirect taxation can appear artificial, it exists for good reason. The limitation to direct taxation and licensing is designed to ensure that provincial tax powers, like most provincial legislative powers, remain confined *within* the territory of a province. Indirect taxation is more likely to go beyond provincial borders because in the ordinary flow of com-merce it might ultimately be paid by consumers outside the jurisdiction.

Taxation and Federal–Provincial Relations

The limitation on direct taxation by the provinces has some significant impli-cations. First, it means that the federal government continues to receive the lion's share of national tax revenue. That gives the federal government consid-erable power in determining national policy. At the same time, however, the fed-eral government cannot fund activities that fall outside the scope of its legislative authority under the Constitution. Consequently, if the federal gov-ernment wants to create national standards in areas like health care, which fall under provincial authority, it must reach agreement with the provinces. This requirement allows provinces to have some voice in the design of national pro-gramming. Ongoing dialogue between levels of government is a vital part of Canadian federalism.

Second, the conditional nature of federal funding promotes a constant search for alternative sources of revenue by the provinces. One of these has been the growth of provincial sales taxes. The provincial power to tax appears to prohibit such taxation, since it would require an intermediary, such as a shopkeeper, to collect the tax, violating the directness requirement. An ingen-ious way around the limitation was identified in *Atlantic Smoke Shops v Conlon*.[16] The court was asked to rule on the constitutionality of a New

---

[16.] *Atlantic Smoke Shops v Canlon* [1943] AC 550.

Brunswick tobacco tax levied at the point of sale. The court held that the tax was within provincial jurisdiction because provincial law made all sellers of tobacco in New Brunswick agents of the provincial government. The decision eventually opened up the field of retail sales taxes to the provinces. Today all provinces apart from Alberta levy a general retail sales tax.

Income Tax Administration and Audits

The principal body of tax law in Canada is the federal *Income Tax Act*.[17] The Act is administered by the Canada Revenue Agency (CRA) and is designed to be the primary source of income tax in Canada. Most provinces other than Quebec levy their personal income tax on the basis of the federal act. Some provinces have enacted separate income tax statutes under which they collect provincial levies.

Each year, CRA receives tax returns from more than 23 million individual Canadians and registered trusts, and more than 1.5 million corporations. It also collects in excess of $300 billion. For most individuals who work as salaried employees, filing is simply a necessary formality. In the majority of cases, employers directly withhold tax from salaries throughout the year and remit it to the government, reducing the blow of the burden of the tax and the incentive for fraud. All filers of tax returns must report their total income, which is reduced by the total amount of deductions claimed. The total amount is further adjusted by the total of federal and provincial personal tax credits available.

The administration of the federal *Income Tax Act* inevitably gives rise to complex disputes that require specialized expertise for their resolution. The first step in the process is to object to the CRA's Notice of Assessment and to launch an administrative appeal. This involves discussions with the agency. If the administrative appeal fails, the dispute may be taken to the Tax Court of Canada, which applies an expedited procedure for cases involving limited amounts (usually between $12 000 and $24 000). The Tax Court uses its general procedures for cases involving larger amounts. Appeals from the Tax Court may be taken to the Federal Court of Appeal.

an **audit** is a detailed examination of the taxpayer's annual income and tax payable

the **field audit** is usually a detailed examination of books and records conducted by CRA representatives at the taxpayer's place of business

Every year a number of individuals and businesses are selected by the CRA for audits. An **audit** is a detailed examination of the taxpayer's annual income and tax payable. The *field audit* is the main tool in the Agency's audit program. The **field audit** is usually a detailed examination of books and records conducted by CRA representatives at the taxpayer's place of business. When the audit is completed, the auditor may propose to adjust the tax payable by reassessing the taxpayer's return. If the taxpayer disagrees, they can appeal in the usual manner.

COMPETITION

Competition is vital for the promotion of new ideas, products, and services. Canada's federal and provincial governments have the difficult job of legislating to promote a healthy degree of competition in today's fast-paced business environment.

[17.] *Income Tax Act*, RSC 1985, c 1 (5th Supp (Can)).

Competition and the Common Law

The common law allows actions in *contract* against arrangements that unreasonably restrain trade, including some franchise arrangements, partnerships, shareholdings, and non-compete clauses. Restraint of trade clauses are presumptively valid, but the courts scrutinize them carefully to ensure that they do not unduly restrict competition. Chapter 10 discussed contractual covenants in restraint of trade. Contractual actions are, however, available only between contracting parties.

As Chapter 5 explained, the common law also allows actions in *tort* for conspiracy and unlawful interference with trade. Those actions are, however, difficult to prove and rarely successful. They require the plaintiff to prove that the defendant deliberately inflicted a loss, by either (i) conspiring with another party to restrain trade, or (ii) inducing a breach of contract.

A Law of Competition

In 1889 Canada enacted the world's first anti-combines legislation. That statute focused on preventing large-scale mergers among businesses that sought to restrain trade. Later, as concern grew about the pervasive nature of anti-competitive conduct, the focus of legislative attention expanded to include monopolies, mergers, other anti-competitive practices, and consumer protection.

The main piece of federal legislation regulating competition today is the *Competition Act*.[18] It aims to restrict anti-competitive practices and stimulate competitive conduct. The Act contains key provisions relating to anti-competitive behaviour and issues like misleading advertising, abusive market practices, and consumer protection.

Enforcement

The *Competition Act* is administered by the Commissioner of Competition, who oversees the operation of the Competition Bureau in Ottawa. The Commissioner is responsible for enforcement of the Act and three other standard-setting statutes.[19] Violations of the Act are categorized as *civil*, *criminal*, or *dual* matters.

- **Civil matters:** Civil matters under the Act are also known as **reviewable matters**, because they are investigated or reviewed by the Commissioner. They may be referred to the Competition Tribunal, which is an administrative tribunal composed of judges and lay members. The tribunal has the power to impose a number of remedies aimed at stimulating competition. Those remedies include (i) the removal of customs duties on foreign goods, (ii) the dissolution of mergers, and (iii) orders requiring entities that are contemplating a merger to be "held separate." Appeals from the tribunal's orders can be taken to the Federal Court of Appeal. Matters that are currently reviewable include refusals to deal, consignment selling, exclusive dealing, tied sales, market restriction, delivered pricing, foreign refusals to supply, and specialization agreements.

reviewable matters involve civil claims under the *Competition Act*

---

[18] *Competition Act*, RSC 1985, c C-34 (Can).

[19] The bureau is also responsible for the *Consumer Packaging and Labelling Act*, RSC 1985, c C-38 (Can); the *Textile Labelling Act*, RSC 1985, c T-10 (Can); and the *Precious Metals Marking Act*, RSC 1985, c P-19 (Can). All those statutes deal with some aspect of consumer or industrial protection.

- **Criminal matters:** The Commissioner refers criminal matters to the Attorney General for prosecution in court. Matters that are currently categorized as criminal include conspiracy, bid-rigging, price discrimination and predation, promotional allowances, and resale price maintenance.

- **Dual matters:** A small category of dual criminal-civil matters exists in the area of deceptive marketing practices, such as misleading advertising, deceptive telemarketing, and multi-level marketing. The Commissioner decides whether the behaviour was committed intentionally or recklessly. If so, it can be referred to the Attorney General for prosecution. If criminal prosecution is not pursued, the Commissioner retains the option of reviewing the matter.

The enforcement mechanisms are reviewed in Concept Summary 25.1 and Figure 25.1 (on page 597).

CONCEPT SUMMARY 25.1

Criminal Offences and Civil Reviewable Matters under the *Competition Act*

Nature of Offence/Matter	Activity Prescribed
Civil matters	refusals to deal, consignment selling, exclusive dealing, tied sales, market restriction, delivered pricing, foreign refusals to supply, specialization agreements
Criminal offences	conspiracy, bid-rigging, price discrimination and predation, promotional allowances, resale price maintenance, deceptive notice of winning a prize
Dual matters	misleading advertising, deceptive telemarketing, multi-level marketing

The Competition Bureau generally tries to serve its functions through moral suasion and consent, and businesses normally comply after being asked to do so. The Commissioner enjoys broad discretion in enforcing the Act and may decide to resolve lesser matters by a written undertaking or promise of the defendant, or by recommending in a criminal matter that the Attorney General seek a consent order from the court. If the defendant does not co-operate or if there is evidence of a continuing violation, the bureau may (i) take coercive measures (such as a search or seizure), (ii) seek to review the matter before the tribunal, or (iii) refer the matter to the Attorney General for criminal prosecution.

Private Action under the Act

The ability to bring a private action against anti-competitive conduct under the Act is currently limited. Section 36 allows a civil action for damages if (i) a person has suffered damage because of anti-competitive behaviour, and (ii) the accused's conduct is either (i) being prosecuted as a criminal act or (ii) is in violation of a court or Competition Tribunal order. In addition, the *Competition Act* has been amended recently to provide for a private right of action in cases of refusals to deal, exclusive dealing, tied selling, and market restrictions. (Those concepts are examined further below.) In such cases the law requires that the complainant first obtain the tribunal's permission to take action by showing that it is directly and substantially affected by the behaviour in question. If successful before the tribunal, the complainant is only allowed to obtain a cease-and-desist order against the defendant, *not* damages. The complainant is,

FIGURE 25.1 *Enforcement under the Competition Act*

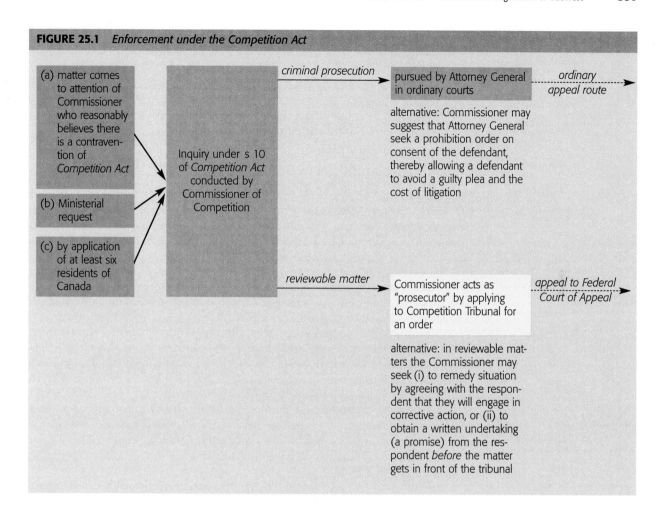

however, permitted to request reimbursement of its legal costs. Otherwise, the *Competition Act* does not currently allow a person to pursue private action in connection with a reviewable matter.

The *Competition Act*

Broadly speaking, matters under the Act fall within three categories.

- The first category consists of *co-ordinated conduct* or conduct relating to *pricing*. These activities are considered to be serious, either because they involve behaviour of more than one individual or because they distort prices, the very mechanism on which efficient markets depend. They are therefore criminalized.[20]
- The second category involves *deceptive marketing practices*. These consist of claims *about* goods and services and therefore are only indirectly

---

[20.] The federal government unveiled proposed amendments to the *Competition Act* at the end of 2004 that would decriminalize the following pricing practices: price discrimination, predatory pricing, and promotional allowances. In their place, the law would introduce a new, multi-million dollar administrative penalty for abuse of dominant position. Nevertheless, existing criminal prohibitions on price maintenance would remain. The government has not announced a timetable for bringing the proposed amendments into law.

about the actual products themselves. Consequently, they are regulatory offences under the Act and they may be prosecuted either as criminal or civil matters.

■ The third category consists of all other matters and generally involves issues of *supply*. These are considered to be lesser offences because consumers will usually have the option of buying a close substitute when supplies are limited. Such matters are reviewable.

Co-ordinated and Pricing Behaviour

Co-ordinated and pricing behaviour concerns conduct that is inconsistent with the spirit of free markets. Consequently, it is criminalized under the *Competition Act*. Section 45 of the Act, for instance, makes it a crime to conspire to "lessen competition unduly." However, proving a **conspiracy**—a joint action of more than one party—is difficult. While the prosecutor must prove that the defendants' conduct was intentional, most conspirators are careful to cover their tracks. In addition, the statute has been interpreted to require specific knowledge among the conspirators that their agreement would lessen competition. That high threshold is rarely met.[21]

conspiracy is the joint action of more than one party

Consumers often make allegations of conspiracy when gas stations uniformly raise their prices to the same level within a very short time. The *Competition Act*, does not, however, prohibit *conscious parallelism*. Gas stations (and other types of business) are entitled to raise their prices to the same level as their competitors, as long as those increases are voluntary and unforeseen.

Bid-rigging is related to conspiracy.[22] It is another form of collusion. **Bid-rigging** occurs when a person either agrees to not submit a bid in response to a call for tenders or submits a bid that is based on prior agreement. Bid-rigging is punishable by fine at the discretion of the court or imprisonment for up to five years.

bid-rigging occurs when a person either agrees to not submit a bid in response to a call for tenders or submits a bid that is based on a prior agreement

In addition to conspiracy and bid-rigging, the Act prohibits three other pricing practices: *price discrimination*, *predatory pricing*, and *price maintenance*.[23]

discriminatory pricing occurs when a business systematically sells the same goods or services to competing customers at different prices

■ **Discriminatory pricing** occurs when a business systematically sells the same goods or services to competing customers at different prices without a valid reason (such as a volume discount). For example, a seller might consistently provide more favourable credit terms to Buyer A than to Buyer B.

predatory pricing occurs when goods or services are sold below cost or at unreasonably low levels to drive a competitor out of business

■ **Predatory pricing** occurs when goods or services are sold below cost or at unreasonably low levels in an effort to drive a competitor out of business.

price maintenance involves an attempt to restrict the price at which a product is sold or resold

■ **Price maintenance** involves an attempt to restrict the price at which a product is sold or resold. For example, it may be an offence for a wholesaler to impose mandatory pricing guidelines that require retailers to resell a product at a specific price. A wholesaler can, however, *suggest* an appropriate retail price.

---

[21] As we saw in Chapter 5, it is also very difficult to prove the *tort* of conspiracy.

[22] *Competition Act*, s 47.

[23] *Competition Act*, s 50. Few important convictions have been secured under that section. The Competition Bureau's website lists recent convictions: <http://competition.ic.gc.ca>.

Misleading Advertising and Other Representational Offences

Misleading advertising occurs when the public receives an intentionally or carelessly deceptive message about a product or a business. Since misleading advertising depends on the customer's perception, it involves an element of individual judgment and responsibility. It is therefore considered to be less serious than collusive or price-related behaviour. As a result, it forms part of the small category of dual nature offences under the *Competition Act*, which can be either reviewed civilly or prosecuted criminally. It is not necessary to prove that any person was actually deceived or misled by the representation. However, in a prosecution, the court will look at both the literal meaning and the general impression of the words in question. If misleading advertising is prosecuted criminally, then the accused is entitled to plead the *defence of due diligence*. The **defence of due diligence** applies if the person responsible for the advertisement acted with reasonable care.

Deceptive telemarketing may also be an offence. **Telemarketing** involves the sale of goods or services over the telephone. Section 52.1 of the Act requires telemarketers to promptly and fairly identify themselves, describe their product, state their prices, explain the purpose of their call, and so on. That section also prohibits misrepresentations, telephone contests and lotteries, and some pricing schemes. Section 53 of the Act has also been introduced to prohibit deceptive notices of winning prizes. Unlike other representational offences, which are hybrid in nature, deceptive notification is strictly a criminal offence.

Multi-level marketing plans may be an offence under the Act. A **multi-level marketing plan** occurs when participants in a scheme are promised benefits in exchange for persuading other people to join the scheme. A classic example involves a pyramid. You may pay me for the right to participate in a sales scheme. In turn, you will receive payments from people whom you persuade to join the scheme. And they in turn will receive payments from the people whom they enlist. And so on. The people at the bottom of the pyramid suffer the loss. The Act therefore protects consumers from deceptive practices regarding the compensation they will receive, bonuses, inventory requirements, and product return policies.

Distribution Practices

The Act prohibits certain distribution practices that restrict *supply*. For instance, in some circumstances, the Competition Tribunal can order a supplier to sell a product to a particular customer who is willing to meet the usual trade terms and who cannot otherwise obtain the product. Certain other distribution practices, such as *exclusive dealing*, *tied selling*, and *market restriction*, are reviewable.

- **Exclusive dealing** occurs when, as a condition of supply, a supplier requires a customer to deal only, or primarily, in products designated by the supplier. Such arrangements often arise in franchising.
- **Tied selling** occurs when the purchase of one product is tied to the purchase of another in some way. That can include the actual purchase of another product, more favourable terms for certain purchases, or prohibitions on the use of products supplied by third parties. An example might be the requirement to buy a certain brand of industrial lubricant when buying a piece of machinery.

---

misleading advertising occurs when the public receives an intentionally or carelessly deceptive message about a product or a business

the defence of due diligence applies if the person responsible for the advertisement acted with reasonable care

telemarketing involves the sale of goods or services over the telephone

multi-level marketing plans occur when participants in a scheme are promised benefits in exchange for persuading other people to join the scheme

exclusive dealing occurs when, as a condition of supply, a supplier requires a customer to deal only, or primarily in, products designated by the supplier

tied selling occurs when the purchase of one product is tied the purchase of another in some way

market restrictions occur when a supplier restricts the people to whom the purchaser can resell a product

■ **Market restriction** occurs when a supplier restricts the people to whom the purchaser may resell a product. A violation may arise if a manufacturer prohibits retailers from selling its products beyond a given geographic region.

Abuse of Dominant Position

Most people realize that there are laws regarding monopolies. A monopoly is, however, only one kind of *abuse of dominant position*. **Abuse of dominant position** occurs anytime that competitive conduct results in an undue reduction of competition. That broader concept reflects the fact that the prohibited behaviour often is not a "monopoly" in fact. There may be more than one company that offers the same goods or services. Nevertheless, the government will still be concerned about companies that substantially control a particular type of business and that engage in behaviour which, if unchecked, will significantly lessen competition.

abuse of dominant position occurs when competitive conduct results in an undue reduction of competition

Section 78 of the Act lists several examples of abuse of dominant position. We look at three.

■ The *cutting of profit margins* occurs when a supplier lessens competition by directly selling goods in the market for a price that is lower than the one that it charges to retailers.

■ The *use of loss leaders* involves temporarily introducing "fighting brands" into the market at below normal cost in order to hurt or eliminate a competitor.

■ The *pre-emption of scarce facilities* involves withholding facilities or resources in an attempt to reduce competition.

A company accused of one of these practices may plead the defence of *superior competitive performance*. If so, the tribunal will have to decide whether the defendant's record in the marketplace is simply a reflection of better business practices.

A recent case involving alleged abuse of dominance began in mid-1997 with an investigation of the marketing and selling practices of HJ Heinz, a well-known manufacturer of baby food. The bureau was concerned about Heinz's practice of (i) making large, lump-sum payments to retailers that did not stock competitor brands, (ii) entering into multi-year contracts for exclusive supply with retailers, and (iii) providing discounts conditional on exclusive supply. In 2000, Heinz settled the matter with the Bureau by promising to stop such practices. More recently there was concern about the potential for re-emergence of monopolistic practices in Canada's airline industry following the acquisition of Canadian Airlines International by Air Canada in 2000.[24] Ethical Perspective 25.1 illustrates the problem of exclusive dealership.

[24.] Following the acquisition, the *Competition Act* was amended in July 2000 to provide the Commissioner of Competition and the Competition Tribunal with new powers to deal with potential abuses by Air Canada. Because of the subsequent entry of several low-cost carriers into the domestic airline market, however, the federal government has proposed withdrawing these provisions in new amendments to the Act introduced at the end of 2004. However, the government did not announce a timetable for bringing the proposed amendments into law.

ETHICAL PERSPECTIVE 25.1

Single Source Contracts: Private Choice in Public Places[25]

There has recently been increasing concern about "single-source," or exclusive dealership, agreements in shopping malls and on school campuses across Canada. Brands buy the right to be marketed in certain public (or *quasi*-public) facilities in a way that makes true free choice difficult. For instance, on some university campuses it is impossible to buy carbonated soft-drinks that are not manufactured by Coca-Cola.

Single-source marketing raises difficult issues. On the one hand, consumer groups are concerned about its impact on perceptions of choice and institutional freedom. On the other hand, marketers and facility managers argue that exclusive dealership arrangements provide important market data and valuable revenue for cash-strapped public institutions. They do acknowledge, however, that targeting key groups—like students—pays off handsomely for many years. Captive audiences are more likely to remember brands and to select them even when they are presented with alternative products.

From a legal perspective, single-source contracts are presumptively valid long-term supply contracts for goods or services. However, they are not immune from attack and they can be challenged under the *Competition Act*. But they usually avoid scrutiny because of the relatively small size of the market that is contained in a shopping mall, campus, or single workplace.

Question for Discussion

1. Are single-source contracts worthwhile? What alternatives could be proposed?

Mergers

A **merger** involves the combination of two or more business entities. There are three basic types.

- **Vertical merger:** Entities that merge mainly to combine businesses that are complementary, such as a quarry and a cement manufacturer, engage in *vertical merger*.

- **Horizontal merger:** Entities that merge mainly to combine businesses at the same stage of production, such as the acquisition of one car maker by another, engage in a *horizontal merger*.

- **Diversification merger:** Entities that combine with other entities having little or no relevance to their existing business engage in a *diversification merger*.

a merger involves the combination of two or more business organizations

Depending on the market, market dominance concerns are normally highest in a horizontal merger.

Section 91 of the Act defines a merger as the acquisition of "a significant interest in the whole or a part of the business of a competitor, supplier, customer or other person." A reviewable offence occurs "where a merger is likely to lessen competition substantially in a trade, industry or profession." The Competition Tribunal is given the power to dissolve the merger, dispose of assets, or take other necessary action.

The Competition Bureau has been required to review an increasing number of mergers, mainly due to the effects of globalization, deregulation, and resulting concentration in certain markets. The bureau engages in pre-merger review of (i) all transactions in Canada worth more than $50 million, and (ii) all transactions involving entities with combined annual revenues of more than $400

---

[25] *McDonalds Restaurants of Canada Ltd. v West Edmonton Mall Ltd.* [1994] AJ No 634 (QB)

million.[26] If entrepreneurs are uncertain about the anti-competitive effects of a proposed merger, they can seek an advance ruling from the bureau.

BUSINESS DECISION 25.1

Taking on the Agreement on Internal Trade[27]

Trade between Canada's provinces is sometimes problematic. Until recently, British Columbians could not buy beer brewed in the Maritimes, and Ontario construction workers still find it difficult to work legally in Quebec. These aspects of domestic competition reflect the strong local policies of an earlier era, as well as the traditionally weak federal power over trade and commerce. As a result, Canada is a less open economy than the US, where goods and services flow freely from state to state by virtue of the US Constitution's interstate Commerce Clause. In an attempt to do away with restrictions on inter-provincial trade, Canada's federal, provincial, and territorial governments signed the Agreement on Internal Trade (AIT) in 1995. The AIT promotes the free movement of goods, services, and people *within* Canada to make the country more competitive economically. It is based on six general principles that are designed to prevent governments from erecting new trade barriers and to reduce existing barriers: (i) non-discrimination, (ii) the right of entry and exit, (iii) no obstacles to internal trade, (iv) legitimate objectives to government legislation, (v) reconciliation of provincial standards, and (vi) transparency. Eleven specific business sectors are covered.[28] Negotiations are continuing with respect to other sectors.

The AIT also features a formal dispute settlement mechanism to deal with grievances. It is administered by the AIT Secretariat in Winnipeg. The dispute settlement system can be invoked both by governments *and* private businesses. That system has been criticized, however, because AIT rulings are *not* legally binding and cannot be enforced in court.

The system has also been criticized for its delays. Several early decisions under the AIT have yet to be implemented. These include decisions condemning a New Brunswick restriction on fluid milk distribution licences, a Quebec ban on the sale of coloured margarine, and a challenge by the Certified General Accountants Association of Canada (CGA) to force Ontario to allow CGA members to practise public accountancy in that province. The results have led some people to believe that trade *within* Canada is more restrictive than trade between Canada and other countries.

Questions for Discussion

1. If AIT decisions could be enforced in court, how could damages be calculated?

2. What sectors of a province's economy should continue to be protected from goods and services originating in other provinces?

[26.] The thresholds are set out in ss 109–110 of the *Competition Act*. In 2002–2003, the bureau performed 279 merger examinations. Of these, six involved a solution with agreed remedies and three involved consent orders: *Annual Report of the Commissioner of Competition 2002–2003* (2003) at 36. Bureau merger guidelines issued in September 2004 observe that "the Commissioner generally will not challenge a merger on the basis of a concern related to unilateral exercise of market power when the post-merger market share of the merged entity would be less than 35 percent." In addition, the Commissioner generally will not challenge a merger on the basis of a concern related to a co-ordinated exercise of market power when (i) the post-merger market share accounted for by the four largest firms in the market would be less than 65 percent, or (ii) the post-merger market share of the merged entity would be less than 10 percent. Mergers that give rise to market shares or concentration that exceed these thresholds are not necessarily anti-competitive. Under such circumstances, the bureau will examine various factors to determine whether a merger likely creates, maintains, or enhances market power: Competition Bureau *Merger Enforcement Guidelines* (September 2004) at 17–18.

[27.] See the AIT homepage at <www.intrasec.mb.ca>.

[28.] These are procurement, investment, labour mobility, consumer-related measures and standards, agricultural and food products, alcoholic beverages, natural resource processing, energy, communications, transportation, and environmental protection.

CONSUMER PROTECTION

The idea of a law of consumer protection is relatively new. In the past, most consumers knew their suppliers personally and could approach them directly about shortcomings, defects, and product safety. Actions arose in contract to resolve problems in quality and reasonable fitness, and in tort to cover cases of fraud.

More recently, federal and provincial governments have intervened to protect consumers through legislation in four key areas:

- misleading advertising
- product regulation
- regulation of business conduct
- disclosure of the true costs of credit

Unfortunately, those topics have not been covered in a consistent way. The applicable legislation often appears to be somewhat haphazard.

Deceptive Marketing Practices

One important source of consumer protection legislation is the *Competition Act*. In addition to conspiracy and pricing arrangements, misleading advertising, and distribution practices, the statute also prohibits a broad range of anti-competitive behaviour that is targeted at consumers. Those practices fall under the heading of *deceptive marketing practices*. **Deceptive marketing practices** are false representations that are made to promote a product or a business interest.

Many types of deceptive marketing practices are prohibited. For instance, goods cannot be offered for sale under a "bait and switch" or at a price for which they will not be realistically sold.[29] Likewise, products cannot be promoted on the basis of misleading testimonials or product testing results. Those offences are all reviewable matters under section 74 of the Act, and the Competition Tribunal will consider both the literal meaning of a representation and the general impression that it conveys. In the case of misleading advertising, however, the Commissioner has the option of either (i) applying to the tribunal for a remedy, or (ii) referring claims for prosecution by the Attorney General.

deceptive marketing practices are false representations that are made to promote a product or a business interest

Other Fair Practices Legislation

In addition to the *Competition Act*, a number of other federal statutes provide common standards for consumer products.

- The *Consumer Packaging and Labelling Act* requires products to be identified by their common name and their amount of content. Certain listed products, such as canned foods and milk, must be sold in standardized containers and bilingual labels must be provided.

- Under the *Textile Labelling Act*, each piece of clothing must bear a label that states the materials used and the place of origin. Most clothing also bears labels that contain suggestions for recommended care.

[29.] A store engages in a "bait and switch" when it advertises a product for a very low price, but tells customers who come to the store that while the advertised product is no longer available, a different, higher-priced alternative is in stock. The tactic relies on the fact that many people will buy the more expensive item, rather than waste the trip and go home empty handed.

- For hazardous products, such as lead-based paints, glues, and industrial chemicals, the *Hazardous Products Act* creates two schedules for goods that are prohibited from production in Canada, or that can only be produced and handled according to standards set out in regulations under the Act.

- The *Food and Drug Act* deals with many aspects of food and drugs, including their processing, storing, and labelling. The Act's provisions deal with sanitary conditions maintained by producers; measures designed to prevent food, cosmetic, and pharmaceutical adulteration; requirements for the listing of ingredients; and dating for products with limited shelf life.

- The *Motor Vehicle Safety Act* applies to motor vehicles made or imported into Canada. Its provisions deal with safety features and procedures in case of vehicle recall.

Some provincial statutes also protect consumers. In Chapter 13, we discussed terms that are implied into contracts by the *Sale of Goods Acts*. Some of those terms deal with issues like merchantability and fitness for purpose. Those provisions are mandatory and cannot be eliminated by contract.

The statutes that we have discussed all deal with goods. However, a growing section of our economy is is devoted to the provision of services. That makes regulation more difficult. In 2001, in response to a wave of complaints about bank branch closures and hidden costs in consumer credit, the federal government created the Financial Consumer Agency of Canada (FCAC) to protect and educate consumers of financial services.

Public Safety and Security

Recent concern about public safety and security in Canada has prompted the federal government to strengthen legislation dealing with corruption, money laundering, and terrorist financing. These activities have a direct impact on the way business is done in Canada and by Canadians abroad.

Under the *Criminal Code* it is now an offence to offer bribes to foreign public officials in the exercise of their functions. The aim of the legislation is to stop the corruption of government employees, particularly in developing countries where governance structures are often weak. The effect of those provisions is, however, limited by a number of factors. For instance, the Crown is required to prove that the accused acted with the intention of gaining a business advantage. Unfortunately, because much of the evidence will be located outside of Canada, that element of the crime will often be difficult to prove. Furthermore, the accused is entitled to argue that the transfer in question was a routine facilitation payment that was made in the ordinary course of business. The argument, if accepted, is a complete defence.

There are also indications of a general toughening of attitudes toward corruption internationally. In 2003, an Ontario-based consulting firm, Acres International, was found guilty by a court in the African nation of Lesotho of corruption relating to the construction of a water diversion project. That firm was subsequently banned from bidding on projects financed by the World Bank until 2007. Recently, other Canadian companies have been investigated for similar behaviour. These incidents are a reminder to Canadians that they must operate within the law whether they are doing business at home or abroad.[30]

Finally, following the events of September 11, 2001, the federal government has introduced new legislation designed to deal with the threat of money laundering and terrorist financing. These are described in greater detail on the Companion Website for this book.

ENVIRONMENTAL PROTECTION

Until recently, the environment was not the subject of popular concern. Today, of course, that has changed. There is growing apprehension about the state of the environment and the government's ability to protect it.

Businesses are now subject to environmental protection legislation. That legislation obviously creates a new form of legal risk. Businesses are, however, usually able to design their operations in an environmentally sensitive manner. And businesses that do adopt pro-active approaches to the environment not only avoid the threat of legal liability, but also benefit from enhanced public goodwill.

Common Law Approaches to Environmental Protection

The common law traditionally addressed environmental concerns through a variety of torts. We saw several possibilities in earlier chapters. For example, under the rule in *Rylands v Fletcher*, a business can be held strictly liable for non-natural use of land if something escapes from its property and causes injury. Common law actions for environmental damage are, however, affected by at least three drawbacks:

- They require court action and possibly protracted litigation. Environmental damage often requires a much quicker response.

- Common law actions are normally property-related. Consequently, people who do not have property cannot complain about damage that is being done to society's collective property ("the commons," as it is sometimes called).

- Common law tort liability requires proof that is often hard to obtain, particularly given the transitory nature of many types of pollution. Without obvious causation, liability can be hard to prove.

These defects led to the introduction of comprehensive environmental legislation in Canada in the early 1970s.

[30.] Canada has signed a number of international agreements against corruption including the OECD Convention on Combating Bribery of Foreign Public Officials in International Business Transactions and the Inter-American Convention Against Corruption. At the end of 2004, Canada was also helping to draft a new United Nations Convention Against Corruption. The UN Convention will better facilitate co-operation against corruption and improve information sharing and law enforcement co-operation.

Jurisdiction over the Environment

The original text of Canada's Constitution did not mention the environment as a single, comprehensive subject in the modern sense. Instead, the provinces were given jurisdiction over local matters such as forests, minerals, and fresh water, whereas the federal government was given jurisdiction over matters of inter-provincial concern, such as marine pollution. While that jurisdictional division continues, it is very difficult to apply it neatly in practice. Consequently, a great deal of environmental management in Canada involves consultation, co-operation, and agreement between levels of government.[31]

Federal Legislation

The most important piece of federal legislation over environmental matters is the *Canadian Environmental Protection Act* (*CEPA*).[32] *CEPA* contains environmental quality objectives, guidelines, and codes of practice. The Act is concerned mainly with systemic threats to the environment, including (i) nutrient-, marine-, and fuel-based pollution, (ii) the release of toxic substances and animate products of biotechnology, and (iii) control over the movement of hazardous waste. It also sets out standards for recycling, storing, and disposing of waste and other hazardous substances. The Act contains broad powers that allow the federal government to prosecute polluters and others who break environmental laws. Actions for environmental damage under *CEPA* can, however, be brought only by the federal environment ministry. Civil claims are limited to the torts of nuisance and possibly negligence, but only if the mandatory federal standards have not been met.

Once a court finds that *CEPA* has been violated, it may impose a number of remedies. A judge may, for instance, require a polluter to (i) stop polluting, (ii) cleanup a polluted site, or (iii) pay for the cost of an environmental cleanup performed by the government. A polluter may also be fined and, in exceptional cases, sent to prison. Corporate directors and officers can be held personally liable in this regard. *CEPA* is supported by a number of other federal statutes that govern specific environmental activities. For instance, the *Transportation of Dangerous Goods Act* deals with safety in the movement of hazardous materials, the *Canada Shipping Act* sets emission standards for ocean-going vessels, and the *Fisheries Act* regulates marine pollution.[33]

Provincial Legislation

Provincial environmental legislation varies between jurisdictions, but every province has at least one general law concerning the subject. These general statutes are supplemented by laws related to specific activities, such as the protection of water resources, environmental assessment, and pesticide use.[34]

[31.] Municipalities also have a substantial role to play in environmental protection through the passage of by-laws dealing with issues like zoning, garbage disposal, and water use. Municipalities will not, however, be discussed in this chapter.

[32.] *Canadian Environmental Protection Act*, 1999, SC 1999 c 33 (Can).

[33.] *Transportation of Dangerous Goods Act*, SC 1992, c 34 (Can); *Canada Shipping Act*, RSC 1985, c S-9 (Can); *Fisheries Act*, RSC 1985, c F-14 (Can).

[34.] *Eg* the *Environmental Protection Act*, RSO 1990, c E.19, which is supplemented by *Ontario Water Resources Act*, RSO 1990, c O40 (Ont), *Environmental Assessment Act*, RSO 1990, c E.18, and *Pesticides Act*, RSO 1990, c P.11 (Ont). A number of other laws with environment-related application also exist.

Several provinces and territories have also enacted environmental bills of rights to enshrine environmental protection as a fundamental value in society and to emphasize the public's role in environmental protection.[35]

The coverage of most provincial law is similar. In Ontario, for instance, the *Environmental Protection Act* covers motor and vehicle emissions, water, waste management, ozone depletion, and litter, packaging, and containers. Liability in each subject area arises on the basis of either *mens rea*, *strict*, or *absolute* liability offences.

- *Mens rea* offences require proof of a culpable act *and* a culpable *intent*. Successful prosecutions are rare because people seldom pollute on purpose.
- *Strict liability* offences are most common under environmental statutes. Guilt is based on proof of a culpable act. The accused can, however, escape liability by proving that it had acted with due diligence or reasonable care.
- *Absolute liability* offences are also based on proof of a culpable act, but the defendant is not allowed to avoid liability by proving due diligence. Such offences are rare.

Liability for environmental offences generally arises from one of four categories of activity. We use the Ontario *Environmental Protection Act* to illustrate.

- *Substantive offences* deal with actual pollution and improper waste disposal. Section 14 of the Act states that "no person shall discharge a contaminant or cause or permit the discharge of a contaminant into the natural environment that causes or is likely to cause an adverse effect."
- *Reporting offences* arise from the failure to notify the government that pollution has been released into the environment. If a business is convicted of polluting, its sentence may be reduced if it promptly reported the problem and co-operated in the investigation and cleanup.
- *Information offences* concern the failure to provide accurate and timely information to government inspectors and other officials. For instance, under section 184, it is an offence to hinder an inspector by concealing information or providing false information.
- *Regulatory offences* arise from the failure to obey government orders, directives, certificates, and other mandatory requirements. Section 186, for instance, makes it a regulatory offence to exceed the permissible discharge levels that are set out in a ministerial certificate of approval.

While those categories of environmental offences may seem clear and straightforward, the actual practice of environmental protection is often complicated. You Be the Judge 25.1 illustrates some of the difficulties.

[35.] *Eg* Yukon *Environment Act*, SY 1991, c 5 (Yuk) and Northwest Territories' *Environmental Rights Act*, RSNWT 1988, c 83 (NWT). Other legislation containing limited aspects of an environmental bill of rights include the Quebec *Environmental Quality Act*, LQ 2001, c Q-2 (Que) (which has included, since 1972, a substantive right to environmental quality), Alberta's *Environmental Protection and Enhancement Act*, RSA 2000; c E-12 (Alta), and Nova Scotia's *Environment Act*, SNS 1994–95, c 1 (NS).

YOU BE THE JUDGE 25.1

Species at Risk

Several hundred wild plant and animal species are currently at risk of disappearing in Canada. For this reason the federal government brought the *Species at Risk Act* (*SARA*) into full effect in June 2004. The Act makes it an offence to disturb species at risk that are designated under the Act. An immediate problem with the law is that it only applies to such species on federal land. This limitation applies even though plants and animals do not recognize human boundaries.

Consequently, the federal government has had to work with a wide range of stakeholders, including the provinces, farmers, ranchers, environmental organizations, and conservation groups, to promote species-at-risk protection. For their part, the provinces have promised to adopt and enforce their own species-at-risk legislation. Nevertheless, *SARA* Article 80 has provisions that act as a safety net by authorizing the federal government to protect species at risk where other legislation fails to do so.

Questions for Discussion

1. Do you think it would be best for a single level of government to be responsible for species at risk?

2. Given that the *Species at Risk Act* deals with irreplaceable biologic heritage, what kinds of penalties should be in place for people who violate it?

Corporate Exposure to Environmental Liability

Corporations are exposed to environmental liability in the course of day-to-day operations. It is important to understand how this liability arises, who is responsible, and what can be done to control the risk of liability.

Corporate exposure to environmental liability arises most often in one of three ways: (i) ownership of contaminants, (ii) acts of a corporation's "directing mind," or (iii) acts of a corporation's agents or employees.

Ownership Liability

Ownership liability arises from a corporation's legal relationship to contaminants. The extent of ownership liability has increased significantly under most provincial laws due to growing environmental awareness and legal responses to it. Canadian governments have decided to cast the net of responsibility far and wide, with potentially onerous results.[36] In Ontario, for example, the current regime imposes a type of "no-fault" liability on owners. A business that owns property is potentially liable for its conditions and cleanup even if (i) the business acted in a careful and responsible manner, (ii) the pollution was created by a previous owner or tenant, or (iii) the pollution migrated to the property from another site.[37]

The specific rules vary from province to province. Three general methods of limiting owner liability have, however, evolved.

---

[36] Canadian governments have not adopted American-style "Superfund" legislation to deal comprehensively with environmentally "hot" properties. Superfund laws were introduced by the US federal government in 1980 to impose liability for contaminated lands on responsible parties in the hope that this would help to clear the title and promote the redevelopment of environmentally questionable property. Under Superfund legislation, federal and state funds were established to pay for the clean-up of property, and statutory exemptions from liability were given to secured lenders and to parties meeting the definition of "innocent landowner."

[37] K van Rensburg "Brownfields Development—The Legal Liability Challenges" (2000) at <www.aboutremediation.com/PDFS/Brownfields%20Development%20-%20The%20 Legal%20Liability%20Challenges.pdf>.

- **Lender liability agreements:** It is often possible for lenders, but not existing owners, to negotiate lender liability agreements with some provincial environment ministries. These agreements permit lenders to investigate land, secure the borrower's property, and take other measures without necessarily attracting liability.

- **Comfort or no-action letters:** Officials may issue "comfort" or "no action" letters to help with the conveyance of property. While such documents may help in a given transaction, they lack uniformity.

- **Site condition records:** Some governments have begun to formally acknowledge site condition records that have been prepared by private consultants. These records describe the state of a piece of property at a given time. They may help to document the environmental conditions of a site, they but do not guarantee immunity from action in future.

Given the ever-increasing nature of ownership liability, the best way to manage risk is to purchase environmental insurance. A number of environmental insurance products are on the market to protect against compliance cost overruns or against the possibility of future environmental liability.[38]

Management Liability

Management liability refers to corporate responsibility for acts of the company's "directing mind." Under provincial law, anything that is done by someone who is the directing mind of a company is automatically attributed to the corporation and may attract liability. If the individual commits an environmental offence, so too does the corporation.

Identification of the corporation's "directing mind" depends on the situation and on the way in which a corporation manages itself. The directing mind normally consists of people who manage the business, including officers, directors, and others with management capacity. Whether a corporation has exercised due diligence depends on whether the directing mind acted reasonably in the circumstances. The standard of care is objective. A director's behaviour is judged against the behaviour of a reasonable director, not against the behaviour of an ordinary person.[39]

Liability for the Acts of Agents and Employees

A corporation can be held liable for environmental damage caused by its agents and employees in the course of their duties. Agents (as described in Chapter 20) and employees (as described in Chapter 26) are "the hands to do the work," rather than the corporation's directing mind.[40]

Due Diligence

Most environmental offences are based on strict liability. While responsibility is triggered simply by a prohibited act, the defendant can avoid liability by proving that it acted carefully and with due diligence. In many provinces, however, due diligence is not only a defence; it is also a specific duty under law. Section 194 of the Ontario *Environmental Protection Act*, for instance, states

---

[38.] Insurance was discussed in Chapter 1, Chapter 3, and Chapter 17.

[39.] Similarly, as we saw in Chapter 6, the standard of care under the tort of negligence (as well as several other torts) is objective.

[40.] *HL Bolton Engineering Co v TJ Graham & Sons Ltd* [1957] 1 QB 159 at 172.

that officers and directors of a company commit an offence if they fail to act with due diligence.

(1) Every director or officer of a corporation that engages in an activity that may result in the discharge of a contaminant into the natural environment. . . has a duty to take all reasonable care to prevent the corporation from causing or permitting such unlawful deposit, addition, emission or discharge.

(2) Every person who. . . fails to carry out that duty is guilty of an offence.

In one well-known case, criminal charges were brought against the president, a director, and a plant manager of Bata Shoes, a major Canadian footwear manufacturer.[41] Bata operated a plant that generated liquid waste, which was stored in drums and barrels on the plant site. Over time, many of the drums and barrels began to leak. The company was charged with allowing toxic waste to enter the environment. All three executives raised the defence of due diligence. Only the president invoked the defence successfully. He satisfied the court that he had taken all reasonable care to establish a pattern of environmental responsibility. The court also found that he was entitled to rely on the experienced on-site director to bring problems to his attention. The director and plant manager, in contrast, could not invoke the due diligence defence and therefore were convicted. The evidence showed that the director knew of the situation, but failed to take remedial steps. Likewise, the court held that the plant manager's bi-weekly visual survey of the site was insufficient to meet the requirement of reasonable care.

When will a business need a due diligence program? The answer depends upon the identification of a risk, which is a function of specific business conditions. For instance, chemical and pharmaceutical manufacturing usually involves greater environmental risks than babysitting or book selling. In any event, however, evolving attitudes and increased scope of liability mean that the risk is often greater than might be imagined. It is therefore wise to have an outsider—preferably a professional environmental consultant—conduct an environmental audit of an enterprise. The exercise should identify infractions of environmental laws and the risks associated with past and present operations. Nevertheless, as Case Brief 25.2 demonstrates, courts often find it difficult to formulate appropriate remedies in response to environmental infringements.

CASE BRIEF 25.2

R v Northwest Territories Power Corp [1990] NWTR 125 (SC)

The Northwest Territories Power Corporation was convicted of discharging waste harmful to fish. At trial, it was ordered to pay a $15 000 fine and to publish an apology to the people of the territory, which included the name and photograph of each corporate director. On appeal, the court held that the provisions of the *Fisheries Act*, under which the charges were brought, did not authorize a court to require the company to publish an apology. A court order requiring a public apology to be made when none had been offered was coercive and

could violate fundamental rights to "life, liberty and security of the person" contained in section 7 of the *Canadian Charter of Rights and Freedoms*.

The court also held that when a company—but not its directors—are convicted, it is inappropriate to "pierce the corporate veil" and to identify the people in control of the corporation.[42] It was therefore contrary to section 7 of the *Charter* to punish the directors by including their photographs in the forced apology.

---

41. *R v Bata Shoe Industries Ltd* (1992) 7 CELR (NS) 245 (Ont Prov Ct).

42. The difficult issue of "piercing the corporate veil" was discussed in Chapter 21.

CHAPTER SUMMARY

Government regulation of business in Canada arises from two principal powers. Federal regulation is derived mainly from federal jurisdiction over trade and commerce. Provincial regulation is derived mainly from power over property and civil rights. The distinction is often drawn in practice between matters needing national co-ordination versus matters of purely local concern. Federal and provincial powers can also overlap and the courts have developed techniques to determine which ones take priority. In addition, there are several fields of co-ordinate jurisdiction, such as transportation, natural resources, and the environment.

One concern of government is to ensure that there are sufficient funds for government operations. For that reason, the federal government has broad powers to tax. The provinces are more limited in their jurisdiction to tax, because they are restricted to direct taxation.

Another principal concern of government is to promote competition and protect consumers. For that reason, the *Competition Act* promotes choice by prohibiting a wide range of activities that decrease competition. That includes provisions against monopolies and conspiracies. It also requires the review of mergers. There is recognition that some mergers may be beneficial to Canadian society, particularly if they enhance exports. At the same time, however, government has taken steps to promote competition through provisions against bid-rigging, price maintenance, price discrimination, and market restrictions.

Consumer protection legislation exists in a number of different statutes. Legislation is necessary to supplement the traditionally weak power of consumers. The *Competition Act* contains provisions against misleading advertising, deceptive marketing, and telemarketing. Other laws attempt to protect consumers through the regulation of industrial or commercial activities like consumer packaging and labelling, food and drug safety, and the availability of basic services.

Environmental protection has also become an important issue today and is reflected in federal and provincial environmental protection statutes.

REVIEW QUESTIONS

1. Under what federal and provincial powers is business regulated in Canada?

2. How is a conflict between federal and provincial law resolved in Canada?

3. Name two business-related subjects under federal jurisdiction and two under provincial jurisdiction.

4. Can the *Canadian Charter of Rights and Freedoms* be invoked by businesses? If so, how?

5. What role does the Federal Court system play in the regulation of Canadian business? When will the Federal Court have jurisdiction?

6. Explain the difference between direct and indirect taxation.

7. Identify the common law actions that can be brought for anti-competitive behaviour, and explain why a purely common law approach to anti-competitive behaviour is insufficient.

8. Name the official responsible for overall promotion of competition in Canada and indicate what powers the Competition Bureau has to enforce competition.

9. What are four subjects within the Competition Bureau's authority? Describe a defining feature of each.

10. What is the status of private actions for anti-competitive behaviour under the *Competition Act*?

11. What is the distinction between a criminal matter and a reviewable matter under the *Competition Act*?

12. What are the elements of a conspiracy under the *Competition Act*? A merger? An abuse of dominant position?

13. What are "dual" offences under the *Competition Act*? What is due diligence?

14. Name three types of merger.

15. What are the quantitative and transaction-size thresholds for merger review? What percentage of market share by the merging entities will likely trigger review by the Bureau?

16. List two statutes concerned with consumer protection in Canada and explain how they protect the public.

17. Why was it necessary for the federal government, the provinces, and the territories to conclude an *Agreement on Internal Trade*? What is one major advantage of the accord? One deficiency?

18. Which level of government is responsible for environmental protection in Canada?

19. What is a "nuisance" at common law?

20. Name three ways that a business can incur environmental liability.

Cases and Problems

1. Manitoba decides to legislate hours of work, pay, and unionization requirements. These are to apply "all employees in the province of Manitoba." Marina Papadopoulos is the President and Chief Executive Officer of "Zeus.com," a small long-distance phone reseller whose main business is providing cheap long-distance service in the province. Several months after Zeus.com begins operations, Marina has hired several dozen people and one of her employees comes to her with a petition to unionize the company under provincial legislation. Marina contests the unionization petition in court because she claims that long-distance service providers are federally regulated. Will she be successful?

2. The federal government decides to enact national standards under the federal *Food and Drugs Act* for the composition of beer. According to federal standards, light beer has to contain no more than 2.5 percent alcohol. John Simpson Inc, a popular micro-brewery in Kingston, Ontario, violates this provision by retailing "John Simpson Lite" beer with an alcohol content of 4 percent. It decides to challenge the federal statute as being outside government powers over trade and commerce. You should note that most sectors of the food industry are highly concentrated, with large manufacturing suppliers advertising their products on national television and engaging in national distribution. It would be expensive and cumbersome for food manufacturers to have to comply with a variety of provincial regulations. There is also growing consumer concern about the use of genetically modified products in food and beverages. Would the national beer standard survive attack?

3. The federal government decides to ban tobacco advertising and other promotional events linked to the tobacco industry, such as sports events and entertainment sponsorships. The government claims that advertising increases tobacco consumption, particularly among young women. Could a cigarette manufacturer challenge the ban on the basis that it prohibits the exercise of a company's right to free speech?

4. Bigrow Inc imports saplings from the United States into Canada that—unknown to it—contain gypsy moth larvae. The gypsy moth is a pest that Canadian officials want to contain and eliminate. At a routine inspection of a shipment on Bigrow's premises, officials find larvae and order Bigrow management to destroy the saplings. When they refuse to do so, a federal inspector, accompanied by provincial officers, enters Bigrow's premises and supervises the destruction of the saplings. Bigrow wonders if it can invoke the *Canadian Charter of Rights and Freedoms* to bring an action against the federal government. In particular, it wonders if it can claim a violation of s 8 of the *Charter*, which provides that "Everyone has the right to be secure against unreasonable search or seizure."

5. Mondtel is a Canadian cellphone exporter. It has a sales force constantly at work around the world, but at present only does business in the major countries of Western Europe and Asia. Recently its wholly owned French subsidiary, Mondtel SA, was approached by a Senegalese intermediary, Youssou M'Bow, about bidding on a contract to supply all Senegalese civil servants with cellphones. This would involve at least 500 000 cellphones and would probably require Mondtel's long-term commitment to a presence in the Senegalese market, something which it does not currently have. M'Bow tells the vice-president of Mondtel SA in France that a "routine payment" of "approximately $200 000" would be needed to "convince" Senegalese government officials to choose any Mondtel bid. Could such a routine payment lead to Mondtel's prosecution in Canada?

6. Manitoba wants to tax the sale of liquor on all airline flights that fly through Manitoba airspace. It decides to take legal action to compel payment against a major airline carrier that actually has offices in Winnipeg and lands there, but it is hopeful that the court will approve application of the tax to all airlines flying through Manitoba airspace. What outcome is likely?

7. Several British Columbia municipalities decide to levy a tax on the extraction of gravel as part of legislation designed to regulate gravel and soil extraction for environmental purposes. The fees are calculated on the volume of gravel extracted and are usually passed on as a business cost. The authority to impose the fees is conferred by the *British Columbia Municipal Act* and is not linked to any regulatory purpose such as road repair or general highway maintenance. Similarly, the municipal bylaws that impose the fee make no reference to purpose. Would the fees be considered an indirect tax, and therefore outside the provincial jurisdiction to tax?

8. For a number of decades, the six manufacturers of microscopes in Canada operated under an informal agreement that involved little or no competition on pricing, but high competition in performance and service. The manufacturers in the arrangement often re-designed their products and generally maintained the technology of their products at world-class levels. The government now wants to know if it could prosecute those manufacturers, either individually for abuse of their dominant positions or jointly for conspiracy.

9. Nancy and Bob Brown ran a successful lock-smithing and security business in Perth, Ontario for 17 years. They were well-known and highly respected in the community. The Browns were thinking of retiring and decided to sell their com-

pany to Vladimir Markovic, who had just moved to Perth. As a term of the sale, the Browns signed a non-compete agreement with their old business that prohibited them from operating a similar business similar within 100 kilometres of Perth for 10 years. Once out of the business, however, the Browns incorporated a business and acted as a competitor to Markovic and their old company. Markovic then brought an action to enforce the terms of the non-compete agreement. He wants to know if the non-compete clause can be enforced.

10. Jim Tate was store manager at Buyco on the outskirts of Edmonton. Buyco was a general retailer that was in the habit of placing weekly advertisements in local newspapers. To "move" some high-tech toys sitting in a nearby warehouse, Tate decided to advertise a one-week fall sale. News of this sale went out in a flyer, but not in the newspaper itself. Nevertheless, there was a stampede into the store by customers when it opened on the first day of the sale. Later that day, the store had sold out. Many customers on subsequent days were disappointed. Tate offered them rain checks, but was later told by suppliers that they would not be able to get more product to Buyco until after the busy holiday season.

The Attorney General's office decided to prosecute Buyco and Tate under s 57(2) of the *Competition Act* for advertising high-tech toys at prices that they did not supply in reasonable quantities. What are the prospects of a successful conviction?

11. Storey's Landfill and Dump operated on the outskirts of Miramichi, New Brunswick. One side of the site was a river filled with fish; the other was an escarpment. The company had installed overflow pipes, ditches, a culvert system, and settling ponds to keep pollution from the landfill and dump from contaminating the water table underneath the property and the river. However, excessive rain caused a mudslide from the escarpment and into the river. That contaminated the water and caused hundreds of fish to die. Storey's was then charged with unlawfully permitting the release of a hazardous substance into the water under environmental legislation. It wants to know what standard will be followed to secure a prosecution.

12. Mr Zinger owned a farm near Bracebridge, Ontario, on which he raised tomato and cucumber crops. The Town of Bracebridge established a garbage dump near the farm where large amounts of garbage were dumped each weekday. Other methods of disposing of the garbage, such as burial, were available, but the Town chose to burn its garbage in the open air at the site, which caused offensive smells and smoke. The dump also attracted a large number of gulls, which attacked Zinger's tomato crop; the smoke also reduced his cucumber crop. Zinger wants to know what he can do about the situation.

WEBLINKS

Government Regulation of Business

Department of Justice Canada http://laws.justice.gc.ca/en

This is the principal website for obtaining the texts of Canada's laws, including the Constitution, major statutes, frequently accessed statutes and related statutory resources. The site also contains information on amendments and pending changes. It is a valuable first step in any assessment of laws relating to business activity in Canada.

Province of Ontario e-Laws www.e-laws.gov.on.ca/home_E.asp?lang=en

This website is run as a joint project by the Ontario Ministry of Consumer and Business Services and the Ontario Ministry of the Attorney General. It provides access to all Ontario legislation and has useful search functions, a frequently-asked-questions section, a glossary, as well as a section on pending bills.

The Federal Court and the Federal Court of Appeal www.fct-cf.gc.ca/index_e.html and http://www.fca-caf.gc.ca/index_e.shtml

These are the official website of the Federal Court of Canada and the Federal Court of Appeal. They provide information about the history of the courts, their jurisdiction, decisions, and procedures.

Taxation

The Canada Revenue Agency www.cra-arc.gc.ca/menu-e.html

The Canada Revenue Agency (CRA) administers tax laws for the Government of Canada and for most provinces and territories, and various social and economic benefit and incentive programs delivered through the tax system.

Tax Court of Canada www.tcc-cci.gc.ca

The Court has jurisdiction to hear appeals under a number of tax-related Acts of Parliament, including the *Income Tax Act*, the *Canada Pension Plan*, the *Petroleum and Gas Revenue Tax Act* and the *Unemployment Insurance Act*.

Competition

Competition Bureau of Canada http://competition.ic.gc.ca/epic/internet/incb-bc.nsf/en/Home

The Competition Bureau is responsible for administration and enforcement of the *Competition Act*, the *Consumer Packaging and Labelling Act*, the *Textile Labelling Act* and the *Precious Metals Marking Act*. Its role is to promote and maintain fair competition so that Canadians can benefit from lower prices, better product choice, and quality services.

Competition Bureau Law and Litigation
www.competitionbureau.gc.ca

This site includes summaries of judgments and orders issued by the courts. It also provides a table listing the penalties that have been imposed regarding international cartels.

Consumer Protection

Health Canada's Product Safety Programme www. hc-sc.gc.ca/cps-spc/index_e.html

Government, industry, and consumers share a responsibility for product safety. Consumer products that do not

fall under the mandate of any other federal department and are potently hazardous are tested by Health Canada's Product Safety Programme.

Consumer Connection http://strategis.ic.gc.ca/epic/internet/ inoca-bc.nsf/en/Home

The Office of Consumer Affairs is Industry Canada's window to consumers in the marketplace. It manages a number of online initiatives from this site that help consumers find the right information about the law regarding consumer protection.

Environmental Protection

The Green Lane www.ec.gc.ca/envhome.html

This is the main site for Environment Canada, including information on what the federal department does, its legislation, frequently-asked-questions, international relations, programs, services, organizations, and environmental work in the various regions of Canada.

ADDITIONAL RESOURCES FOR CHAPTER 25 ON THE COMPANION WEBSITE

(www.pearsoned.ca/mcinnes)

In addition to self-test multiple-choice, true-false, and short essay questions (all with immediate feedback), three additional Cases and Problems (with suggested answers), and links to useful Web destinations, the Companion Website provides the following resources for Chapter 25:

- You Be the Judge 25W—Can Mergers Be Efficient?
- Environmental Remedies
- Environmental Impact Assessments
- International Environmental Protection
- Additional Weblinks on Government Regulation of Business, Taxation, Competition, Consumer Protection, and Environmental Protection
- *Canadian Charter of Rights and Freedoms*

Provincial Material

- **British Columbia:** Credit Reporting, Debt Collection, Collection Agents, Consumer Protection Legislation, *Sale of Goods Act*, Dishonest Trade Practices, Cooling Off Period, British Columbia Environmental Legislation, Consumer Taxes, Cost of Borrowing, Credit Cards, *Creditor Assistance Act*, Direct Sales Contracts, Distance Sales Contracts
- **Alberta:** Environmental Legislation, Practices, Occupational Health and Safety
- **Manitoba and Saskatchewan:** Consumer Protection (Provincial Legislation), False Claims
- **Ontario:** Agreements to Share Power, *Consumer Protection Act*, 2002, Environmental Protection Legislation, Unfair Business Practices

A Century of Slag:
Who Pays for Cross-Border Pollution?

Water is essential to human life. It makes up between 60 to 70 percent of our bodies. We drink it and we bathe in it. We harvest food from lakes and oceans, and we irrigate our crops and gardens. And sometimes, we use water as a sewer system.

All of that is true of the Columbia River, one of North America's great waterways. The Columbia majestically winds its way for more than 2000 kilometres from southeast British Columbia, through Washington, and into the Pacific Ocean off the Oregon coast. The river has been at the centre of human activity in the Pacific Northwest for centuries. Long before Europeans arrived, it provided an important source of transportation, and a seemingly endless stock of salmon, to Aboriginal peoples. More recently, a series of dams has created a clean and relatively inexpensive supply of hydro-electric energy, at the same time that controlled flooding has turned desert into farmland. Since the late 1800s, the Columbia River has also played a vital role in the region's mining industry.

Teck Cominco is one of the world's largest mining companies. It conducts business throughout Australia, South America, and North America. Its operations in Trail, British Columbia, 18 kilometres north of the American border, are among its most valuable. Those facilities produce 5 percent of the world's zinc supply, directly employ 1500 people, and generate annual profits of approximately $200 000 000. They are, in other words, a substantial factor in the province's economy.

Unfortunately, mining is often a dirty business. Before it can be put to use, zinc has to be super-heated and reduced to a liquid form. That *smelting* process leaves behind a black, sand-like substance called *slag*, which frequently contains high levels of toxins. Although it stopped the practice in 1995, Teck Cominco had dumped enormous amounts of slag into the Columbia River for decades. By one estimate, the river received almost 20 000 000 tonnes of the stuff, the equivalent of one dump truck load every hour for sixty years.

Not surprisingly, people living along the Columbia River have become worried. Although the scientific evidence is in dispute, several studies have reported dangerously high levels of zinc, mercury, arsenic, lead, copper, and cadmium in the river- and lakebeds. Sediment in one area was found to contain 900 times the normal level of such pollutants. As a result, few people are willing to eat fish caught downstream from Trail. Worse yet, although the scientific evidence is again controversial, Teck Cominco's Trail operations have allegedly caused a marked increase in serious health risks, including cancer and colitis.

Tom Louis knows the situation well. He is a Native American from the Inchelium community in Washington State, just south of the Canadian border. The Columbia River has always been at the centre of his life. Until quite recently, he swam in it for recreation, fished in it for food, and built a house along its banks. His attitude changed, however, when scientists began to issue damning reports in the early 1990s. Now, as a first-time father at the age of 61, he is outraged and ashamed. "I have a daughter. And now she's five.. . . I can't take her down to the water. I have nothing to leave her."

The EPA, the American Environmental Protection Agency, agrees. It insists that Teck Cominco is responsible for potentially lethal contaminates that are found in the Columbia. It therefore asked the company to sign an agreement to clean up the river. Teck Cominco refused. It denies that slag is a health hazard. It says that, because it is a Canadian company operating in Canada, it is beyond the reach of an American regulatory agency like the EPA. And finally, it is reluctant to commit itself to a project that may cost hundreds of millions of dollars. The company did, however, offer to get involved on a much smaller scale, as long as the expense did not exceed $13 000 000. The EPA rejected that proposal as "substantively inadequate."

Typical of pollution cases, the Columbia River dispute is complicated in a number of respects. To begin with, it is difficult to determine the actual state of affairs. As previously mentioned, scientific opinion is split. Some studies support Teck Cominco, others side with the EPA. Furthermore, the issues go well beyond the immediate parties. Many people living near the river, on both sides of the border, are concerned about their personal well-being. At the same time, however, many of those same people are worried that their livelihoods will be lost if the EPA succeeds in having the area designated as a cleanup site. Tourism is one of the main sources of employment in the Columbia River basin, especially in the United States. Official recognition that the river is a toxic soup would have a devastating impact on the region's tourist industry.

The Province of British Columbia has been monitoring the dispute closely. Governments are, of course, often protective of companies that employ thousands of people and that substantially contribute to tax revenues. British Columbia's interest in the matter is, however, even closer than that. Teck Cominco denies responsibility on a number of grounds. But its primary argument is that, even if it has created an environmental hazard, it has always operated in compliance with government regulations. Consequently, some commentators have suggested that, if liability is imposed, it might be shared between the company and the province (or, more precisely, between the company and the province's taxpayers). From that perspective, it is perhaps unsurprising that British Columbia's environmental regulators have long said that the pollution from the Trail smelting plant becomes harmlessly diluted as it flows down river.

Questions to Consider

Although this Canadian Case Study appears at the end of the chapter on government regulation of business, it raises issues that cut across several areas of law. Consequently, some of the following questions allow you to revisit other chapters.

1. Pollution is often an international problem. In this case, the Columbia River carried slag from the Province of British Columbia to the State of Washington. So far, however, Teck Cominco has largely kept out of the Environmental Protection Agency's reach. Even the EPA admits that there is little, if any, precedent for directly imposing American law on a Canadian company for actions that occurred entirely in Canada. The explanation is simple. It is a basic principle of international law that a country generally cannot enforce its laws outside of its own borders. Does that mean that there is no way to prevent a company in one country from creating pollution that affects people in another jurisdiction? If not, identify several strategies for dealing with the problem of cross-border pollution.

2. Teck Cominco and the EPA have already attempted, without success, to resolve their dispute by agreement. They may, of course, try again. But even if they do get an agreement in place, other disputes may arise in the future. The parties may, for instance, disagree on the application of a formula that they created to determine the amount of money that the company is required to pay toward a cleanup operation. If so, disputes may also arise with respect to the enforcement of the contract. Which *laws* will govern those disputes: British Columbia's, Washington's, Oregon's, or those of some other jurisdiction? And which *courts* will resolve those disputes: British Columbia's, Washington's, Oregon's, or those of some other jurisdiction? Indeed, will the dispute even be heard in a regular court? Although those questions are not addressed in the current chapter, you will find answers in Chapter 28W, Doing Business in a Global Economy, which is located on the Companion Website.

3. Teck Cominco appears to have acted in accordance with the laws of British Columbia and Canada.

Unfortunately, that is not always true. Canadian corporations occasionally break domestic laws. The issue of corporate pollution is addressed in Canada by both federal and provincial (or territorial) legislation. Of course, a corporation is not a natural person and therefore does not feel the sting of punishment in the same way as a human being. It has "no soul to damn; no body to kick."[1] Does that mean that liability for polluting carries little actual threat? Or is it ever possible, in Canadian law, to impose responsibility on a corporation's human agents, such as its directors and employees? Before answering that question, you may want to re-read certain parts of Chapter 22, Legal Rules for Corporate Governance.

4. Most of the complaints about Teck Cominco's slag have come from the United States. Of course, Canadians living downstream from the company's Trail facilities may also be affected by the same pollution. Would it be possible for a Canadian citizen to successfully sue Teck Cominco in tort? Before answering that question, you may want to re-read certain parts of Chapter 5, Miscellaneous Torts Affecting Business.

[1] Lord Thurlow, quoted by G Williams *Criminal Law: The General Part* 2d ed (1961) at 856.

Video Resource: "Century of Slag" *The National* (15 December 2003).

Additional Resources

Century of Slag   **www.cbc.ca/news/background/environment/century ofslag.html**
This website contains a complete transcript of the video program.

Teck Cominco   **www.teckcominco.com/articles/roosevelt/index.htm**
This page within Teck Cominco's website provides links to information regarding the dispute between the company and the EPA.

Environmental Protection Agency: Cleanup News   **www.epa.gov/ Compliance/resources/newsletters/cleanup/cleanup15s.pdf**
This document briefly outlines the EPA's position with respect to pollution attributed to Teck Cominco's operations in Trail.

Business and Human Rights Resource Centre   **www.business-humanrights.org/Categories/Individualcompanies/T/TeckCominco**
This website, which is affiliated with Amnesty International, provides links to a number of documents dealing with the dispute between the EPA and Teck Cominco.

26 Individual Employment

CHAPTER OVERVIEW

OBJECTIVES

After completing this chapter, you should be able to:

1. Develop business strategies to ensure that pre-employment practices comply with employment legislation.

2. Distinguish between employees and independent contractors.

3. Explain the difference between non-competition and non-solicitation covenants.

4. Outline the circumstances in which a business is liable to third parties for the conduct of its employees and describe three ways in which a business can improve the supervision of its employees.

5. Identify five employer obligations imposed by employment standards legislation.

6. Discuss human rights in the workplace.

7. Explain the basic statutory measures designed to ensure safety in the workplace.

8. Distinguish between summary dismissal, wrongful dismissal, and constructive dismissal, and define just cause for dismissal as well as the notice periods that must be provided when dismissing an employee without cause.

9. Distinguish between severance packages and settlement packages, and explain the effect of a signed release.

10. Discuss the possible post-employment obligations of employees in the absence of contractual obligations.

In this chapter, we will consider the three main phases of the employment relationship. First, we will consider *pre-employment matters*, including recruiting, hiring, and the employment contract. Then we will examine *employer obligations* and *worker protection* mechanisms imposed by statute and see how the employment relationship is maintained. Finally, we will investigate issues that arise when the employment relationship breaks down, including the *termination of employment* and *post-employment practices*, such as severance, settlement packages, and ongoing obligations.

PRE-EMPLOYMENT MATTERS

Job Descriptions

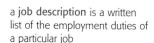

a **job description** is a written list of the employment duties of a particular job

Before hiring for a position, an employer should define its requirements in a *job description*. A **job description** is a written list of the employment duties of a particular job. A well-drafted job description makes it easy for an employer to find the right person for the job. When included in an advertisement for a position, a job description also saves considerable time and money by reducing the number of applicants. It also functions as a standard of measurement that can be used to discipline or, if necessary, dismiss an employee who is not living up to the employer's expectations. Although not technically a legal document, a job description that is poorly drafted is a liability. If the job description is too narrowly drafted, it can provide leeway for an employee to refuse certain tasks on the basis that they fall outside of their job. One way to manage this risk and achieve flexibility is to include a provision near the end of the job description that acknowledges that the job may include additional duties as assigned by the employer.

Advertising Positions

After they have drafted a proper job description, many employers advertise the position. Advertising not only allows employers to select from a broad and diverse applicant pool, but also provides the appearance of impartiality during the hiring process. However, there are risks associated with advertising. For instance, an advertisement may violate human rights legislation. Consider the example in Business Decision 26.1.

BUSINESS DECISION 26.1

Advertisements and Human Rights

Giuseppe's Pizza needs to hire someone to answer the phones and to take walk-in orders. Since Giuseppe regularly advertises in the local classified ads for delivery drivers, he decides to run his usual ad:

> Giuseppe's is now hiring. Good wages, flexible hours, and free pizza (while on the job). Call Giuseppe's today! Valid driver's licence required.

Although this ad may seem perfectly reasonable, it probably violates human rights legislation. Since the ad is for a phone attendant—not a driver—requiring a valid driver's licence may discriminate against certain people who might

otherwise apply for the job. For example, someone with a visual impairment might be perfectly well qualified for the job even though they may not be able to drive. By advertising a valid driver's licence as a requirement for the job, Giuseppe's has unintentionally discriminated against persons on the basis of physical disability.

Questions for Discussion

1. How could Giuseppe's Pizza have avoided that problem?

2. Would Giuseppe's Pizza lose anything if it re-wrote its advertisement to comply with human rights legislation?

Application Forms and Interviews

A successful advertisement will generate many job applications. To fill positions with appropriate people, employers need more information, often obtained through application forms and personal interviews. Many employers use an **employment application form**, which allows them to screen job candidates for the necessary qualifications. However, employers must be careful not to ask questions that are too invasive. Questions must relate to the applicant's ability to do the job. Unrelated questions may violate provincial human rights legislation or privacy legislation, as discussed later in this chapter. Figure 26.1 lists several kinds of information that may be sought in an application form or an interview, and, as a matter of risk management, suggests questions that should and should not be used.

an employment application form is a tool that allows employers to screen job candidates for the necessary qualifications

FIGURE 26.1 Managing Risk in Employment Applications and Personal Interview Questions

Information Sought	Do not ask:	Do ask:
Name	What is your Christian name?	What is your first name?
Emergency contact	Who should be contacted in case of an emergency? What is your relationship with this person?	Who should be contacted in case of an emergency?
Eligibility for work	What is your nationality?	Are you legally entitled to work in Canada?
Education	What schools did you attend?	What is the highest level of education you have attained?
Ability	Describe any disabilities you may have.	Are you able to perform the following duties? If not, what is the nature of accommodation that you require?
Availability	What religious holidays do you celebrate?	Are you available for shift work? If not, what accommodations are necessary?
Languages	What is your mother tongue?	What languages do you speak?
Mobility	Are you married?	Are you able to transfer to another city?
Associations	Do you have any memberships in clubs or other organizations?	Do you have any memberships in clubs or other organizations that do not reveal your gender, race, religion, ancestry, or place of origin?

Source: Rearranged and reprinted with permission from RS Echlin & CM Thomlinson *For Better or for Worse: A Practical Guide to Canadian Employment Law* (1996) at 14–20.

Statements Made during Hiring

When the employer has selected an applicant, the parties usually negotiate the terms of employment. Both sides need to be careful to avoid making false statements that could amount to misrepresentations, as discussed in Chapter 9. A misrepresentation by either party could allow the other to walk away from the employment contract with impunity. If a misstatement is negligent or fraudulent, it could even lead to a cause of action in tort or criminal law. Case Brief 26.1 illustrates the possible consequences of an employer's misrepresentation.

CASE BRIEF 26.1

Queen v Cognos Inc (1993) 99 DLR (4th) 626 (SCC)

Queen, an accountant, had a good job with decent pay, but was looking for something different. He saw an advertisement in a Calgary newspaper for a job with Cognos, a high-tech company. Queen applied for the job. During his interview, Queen was told that the position was a permanent one and that the successful applicant would play a lead role in developing a new accounting software program. The interviewer failed to mention that the entire project—including the budget for the lead position and the hiring of additional staff—was subject to further approval. Queen took the job. Soon after, Cognos decided to slash the funding allocated to the project. Consequently, no other staff were hired and, as a result,

Queen's job became much less significant. He was dismissed 18 months later. He then sued Cognos for negligent misrepresentation, claiming that he never would have agreed to leave his former position if Cognos had not inflated the significance of the project and Queen's role in it.

The Supreme Court of Canada agreed with Queen. It held that employers have a duty during employment interviews to exercise reasonable care and diligence when making representations about the nature of an employment opportunity. According to the Court, it is not enough that the interviewers be honest. They owe a further duty to make sure that their representations are accurate.

Nature of the Work Relationship

Our discussion has focused on the employment relationship. However, not all work- or service-related contracts are contracts of employment. Nor are all workers considered to be employees.

Employees

an **employee** is a person who contractually agrees to work under the control and direction of an employer

An **employee** is a person who contractually agrees to work under the control and direction of an employer. Employees are legally protected in some ways that other workers are not. For example, an employee is entitled by both statute and common law to reasonable notice before being dismissed. The failure to give such notice entitles the employee to sue. The same is not true for workers who lack employee status.

Independent Contractors and Consultants

an **independent contractor** is a person who contractually agrees to work but who is *not* controlled by another person in how they accomplish a task

One kind of worker who lacks the legal status of an employee is an *independent contractor*. An **independent contractor** contractually agrees to work but is *not* controlled by another person in how they accomplish a task. Independent contractors and consultants are not entitled to many of the rights that employees enjoy, including those discussed later in this chapter: reasonable notice of termination, statutory termination and severance pay, overtime pay, vacation pay, and statutory holiday pay.

Being an independent contractor involves a trade-off. Independent contractors and consultants do not owe the same loyalty as employees. Subject to the terms of their contracts, they have more freedom in deciding when to work, how to work, where to work, for whom to work, and so on. As communication and networking technologies continue to improve, employers are becoming more willing to relinquish control of those choices. This significantly reduces the costs generally associated with employee protection. It can also reduce the overall financial risk of employing a large number of employees. For example, independent contractors can be hired for specific or time-limited projects when the time and resources of the business permit, without taking on the responsibility of hiring a full employee.

Although employee and independent contractor contracts will often state explicitly whether the person is hired as an employee or not, it is sometimes difficult to distinguish between employees and independent contractors or consultants. One test asks how much control is asserted by the party paying for the work. The **control test** is based on four significant factors: (i) the employer's authority to select individuals for employment, (ii) the employer's ability to decide the payment scheme, (iii) the employer's ability to control and direct the type, manner, and timing of the work, and (iv) the employer's right to discipline the worker. The more control that can be exercised, the more likely the worker will be considered an employee.[1]

the **control test** may determine whether a worker is an employee or an independent contractor based on the degree of control exercised by the party paying for the work

Since highly skilled professional employees are not always subject to direct supervision, the degree of control is not always a determining factor. Therefore, courts have considered such other factors as (i) who owns the equipment used to perform the job, (ii) whether the worker had the chance to profit, and (iii) who risks any loss. Courts have also recently considered the overall role that the worker plays in the organization. The **organization test** attempts to determine whether the work is an integral part of the overall business.

the **organization test** attempts to determine whether a person's work is an integral part of the overall business

Given the variety of factors that judges take into account, it is difficult to ensure that a particular worker will be considered an independent contractor rather than an employee. Figure 26.2 gives a number of tips for companies that want to set up independent contractor relationships.

FIGURE 26.2 Risk Management Strategy: Ensuring an Independent Contractor Relationship

- Expressly state in the written contract that the party performing the services is not an employee and is not entitled to any of the statutory protections afforded to employees.
- Do not take any statutory deductions, such as income tax, employment insurance, Canada Pension Plan, or workers' compensation off the worker's pay.
- Do not provide vacation pay, statutory holiday pay, or overtime pay.
- Do not provide benefits such as health-care plans, stock options, or bonuses.
- Do not provide a company uniform, business cards, a company vehicle, company equipment (such as a computer, a desk, voice-mail or e-mail, or office space).
- Do not provide bookkeeping, invoicing, or secretarial services.
- Do not provide performance reviews or disciplinary measures. (This does not preclude a termination provision in the contract.)
- Expressly allow the worker to set their own work schedule.
- Expressly allow the worker to work for competitors or to generate income from other sources.
- Encourage the worker to set up a company, sole proprietorship, or a partnership with a GST number.

Source: Rearranged and reprinted with permission from RS Echlin & MJ MacKillop *Creative Solutions: Perspectives on Canadian Employment Law* (2000) at 17.

THE EMPLOYMENT CONTRACT

Once your business has decided which applicant it wants to hire as an employee, it typically will make an offer of employment to that person. The process (including issues like offer and acceptance), which leads to a binding employment contract, is governed by the same rules that apply for contracts generally, as discussed in Part 3.

[1.] RS Echlin & CM Thomlinson *For Better or for Worse: A Practical Guide To Canadian Employment Law* (1996) at 43–4.

The employment contract is an essential tool in the risk management strategy of any business. Employment contracts should normally be in writing to avoid disputes, and should clearly describe the obligations of the employee and employer. Any number of issues can be addressed in an employment contract, including terms of pay, salary, job description, and benefits. Employment contracts will often require the employee to agree to read and abide by all of the employer's policies and procedures. In addition to these important issues, which are discussed later in this chapter, there are at least two other key issues that should be specifically addressed in many employment contracts: *non-competition/non-solicitation* and *confidentiality*. Trade secrets and confidentiality obligations (discussed in Chapter 18) are particularly important for knowledge-based businesses. Here we focus on non-competition and non-solicitation clauses.

Non-Competition and Non-Solicitation

a **non-competition clause** is a form of restrictive covenant that prohibits or restricts an employee's ability to work for a competitor or to start a business that would compete with the employer

a **non-solicitation clause** is a form of restrictive covenant that prohibits the employee from soliciting the customers of the employer, but otherwise leaves the employee free to compete

Generally speaking, a **non-competition clause** is a form of restrictive covenant that prohibits or restricts an employee's ability to work for a competitor or to start a business that would compete with the employer. A **non-solicitation clause** is a form of restrictive covenant that prohibits the employee from soliciting the customers of the employer, but otherwise leaves the employee free to compete. These covenants typically continue to apply after the breakdown of the employment relationship, which is usually when they are most important. For example, a non-competition clause might prohibit the employee from working for a competing business within 100 kilometres of the employer's place of business for a period of five years after termination of the employment relationship.

In certain circumstances, courts will refuse to enforce non-competition, non-solicitation, or confidentiality clauses in an employment contract. Unreasonable covenants in restraint of trade, for example, can be contrary to public policy. If so, they may be illegal and unenforceable, as discussed in Chapter 10. This concern is particularly important in the employment context where restrictive covenants are construed more strictly against the employer. Given the risk that such terms may be found unenforceable, knowledge of the law and special care are required when crafting such clauses.

In the employment context, courts will consider three factors in deciding whether to enforce a restrictive covenant:[2]

- whether the employer has a *proprietary interest* worthy of protection
- whether the *temporal* and *geographic restrictions* are more broad than would reasonably be required to protect the employer's proprietary interest
- whether the covenant *restricts competition generally*, or merely bars solicitation of the former employer's clients

With respect to the first factor, an employer might have a proprietary interest in its trade connections with clients or customers. This can be particularly important where customers of a business are long-term or repeat customers with whom it is important for the business to maintain a close relationship. However, the general rule is that courts are reluctant to enforce a non-competition covenant where a mere non-solicitation covenant would have protected the employer's proprietary interest.

[2.] *Elsley v JG Collins Insurance Agencies Ltd* (1978) 83 DLR (3d) 1 (SCC).

Exceptions to the general rule will be made where the temporal and geographic limits in a non-competition covenant are reasonable. There are no hard and fast rules for deciding what is reasonable. The circumstances of each case must be taken into account. For example, a two-year non-competition clause might be reasonable in the insurance industry but not for high-tech employees—two years at "Internet time" might be unreasonable given how quickly technology is evolving and the need for workers to keep up-to-date in their area of work.

It is important to note that where an employer repudiates the employment contract by, for example, wrongfully dismissing the employee, the employer usually cannot enforce any restrictive covenants against the employee.

CONCEPT SUMMARY 26.1

Managing Risk Through the Use of Restrictive Covenants in an Employment Contract

- Know the law and draft your restrictive covenants with the legal requirements in mind.
- Define the proprietary interest you are trying to protect through the clause, for example, your trade connection with your clients.
- Consider whether to include non-competition, non-solicitation, and confidentiality clauses. Consider whether a non-solicitation clause would be sufficient to protect your interest, rather than a non-competition clause.
- When drafting a non-competition clause, bear in mind the circumstances of your industry and the employee, and draft the restriction to be reasonable, both temporally and geographically. Do not be overbroad.
- Be aware that if you repudiate the employment contract, you may not be able to enforce its restrictive covenants.

EMPLOYERS' OBLIGATIONS AND WORKER PROTECTION LEGISLATION

We now survey some of the more important obligations that employers owe to their employees and others: *third party liability*, *supervision*, and *statutory protection*.

Third-Party Liability

A worker's status is important to the company that commissioned the work if that person causes damage to a third party. As we saw in Chapter 4, the injured third party can sue not only the individual worker, but also the company. **Vicarious liability** occurs when an employer is held liable for an employee's tort. That doctrine is, however, subject to two important restrictions.

vicarious liability occurs when an employer is held liable for an employee's tort

- The doctrine does *not* apply to independent *contractors*.[3]
- The doctrine applies to an employee's torts *only if* the employee was acting in the course of employment.

To determine whether an employee was acting in the course of employment, a court will look at several factors. The location of the incident, the time

---

[3.] A company may be held liable for failing to exercise reasonable care when hiring an independent contractor. In that case, the company's liability is not based directly on the independent contractor's wrong, but rather on its own wrongful act in hiring an inappropriate worker. Therefore, it is not vicarious.

of day, and the fact that company equipment was involved are important considerations, but they are not always conclusive.[4] The fundamental issue is whether the harmful act occurred while the employee was carrying out assigned duties. You Be the Judge 26.1 focuses on that issue.

YOU BE THE JUDGE 26.1

Cole v California Entertainment Ltd [1989] BCJ No 2162 (BC CA)

Wayne Cole and some friends entered the Club California while wearing their matching red bomber jackets bearing the crest *Victoria Kick Boxing Club*. A doorman named Wolf explained the club's dress code and said that they would have to take off their jackets if they wanted to enter. The group exchanged words with Wolf and other staff members. The club owner then instructed the bouncers to clear the entrance. When the altercation moved outside, the club owner went back into his office and closed the door. Cole and his friends left the club along with the four bouncers and walked to a nearby parking lot. Wolf challenged one of Cole's friends to a fight. A brawl broke out. Eventually, Wolf went after Cole who, being a lot smaller, backed away and said he did not want to fight. But Wolf kept coming. He grabbed Cole by the front of his jacket and hurled him through the plate glass window of a nearby store, pulled him out, and threw him against a car parked in front of the store. Wolf kept punching until two people pulled him off Cole. Cole staggered across the street and collapsed. He was later taken to the hospital.

Questions for Discussion

1. Did the fight fall within the owner's instructions to clear the club's entrance?

2. Was Cole injured within the course of Wolf's employment?

Supervision

The risk of vicarious liability and other workplace hazards imposes certain responsibilities on employers to supervise their employees; however, even the most conscientious employer cannot stand guard around the clock. There are other ways in which employees can be controlled, including:

- employment policy manuals
- performance reviews
- promotion or probation

Employment Policy Manuals

*an **employment policy manual** explains the conduct that is expected of employees in the course of their employment*

The basis of a good employment relationship is communication. Employers can use an **employment policy manual** to explain the conduct expected of employees in the course of their employment. A carefully drafted policy manual also details the manner in which its policies will be implemented, applied, and enforced. Ethical Perspective 26.1 illustrates the legal importance of a policy manual.

Performance Reviews

*a **performance review** is an evaluation of an employee that provides feedback about the quality of their work*

Another way to direct the behaviour of employees is to conduct regular *performance reviews*. A **performance review** is an evaluation of an employee that

---

[4.] Some provinces (such as British Columbia) have legislation that makes the registered owner of a motor vehicle vicariously liable for the accidents of any authorized driver of the vehicle, whether an employee or not: *Motor Vehicle Act*, RSBC 1996, c 318, s 86 (BC). In such case, the fact that a company vehicle was used is determinative.

ETHICAL PERSPECTIVE 26.1

Smyth v Pillsbury Co 914 F Supp 92 (1996)

What began as a simple disagreement between Smyth and his work supervisor quickly turned into an online shouting match. Eventually, Smyth was dismissed from his employment for sending "inappropriate and unprofessional comments" over Pillsbury's internal e-mail system. Smyth then sued Pillsbury. He argued that the interception of his e-mails—many of which he had sent from his home computer—not only infringed his right to privacy but was also directly contrary to Pillsbury's employment policy manual. This manual assured its employees that "all e-mail communications would remain confidential and privileged" and that "e-mail communications could not be intercepted and used by [Pillsbury] against its employees as grounds for termination and reprimand."

In spite of the written policy, the court held that Pillsbury did not interfere with Smyth's right to privacy when it inter-cepted his e-mails and fired him on the basis of their content. According to the court, because Pillsbury owned the e-mail system and therefore did not invade any of Smyth's personal effects in the workplace, the interception of his communications was neither a substantial, nor a highly offensive, invasion of his privacy. The court concluded that the company's interest in preventing "inappropriate and unprofessional comments, or even illegal activity over its e-mail system, outweighs any privacy interest that Smyth might have had."

Questions for Discussion

1. Should the company be allowed to operate contrary to its written policy?

2. Can you suggest an alternative corporate e-mail policy?

---

provides feedback about the quality of their work. Most performance reviews are conducted in person. However, employers should have a standard written evaluation form to guide the process (i) to ensure that all employees are treated the same, and (ii) to provide a written record in case the employment relationship breaks down. If an employer has recorded a string of poor performance reviews in an employee's file, it is difficult for the employee to argue that they were wrongfully dismissed. It is also important to note that a properly conducted performance review can be used to identify and correct workplace problems in their infancy.

Promotion and Progressive Discipline

Employee behaviour can be directed through rewards and punishments. Employers should recognize employees who consistently perform well and consider them for promotion to higher positions. This both rewards productivity and sets a behavioural benchmark for other employees. A **promotion** usually entails new duties on the part of the employee, whether or not it includes a pay raise.

When an employee has received a number of poor performance reviews or is otherwise misbehaving in the workplace, the employer should consider a *progressive discipline program*. A **progressive discipline program** involves a series of disciplinary steps that may progress from verbal or written warnings, through degrees of suspension, to dismissal.[5] It is useful to explain such a program in the employment policy manual. Suspension is a drastic measure and must be used only in appropriate circumstances. However, when there is a plausible basis for commencing an investigation and the employer carries it out in good faith, courts have held that a brief period of suspension is a reasonable course of conduct.[6]

a promotion usually entails new duties on the part of the employee, whether or not it includes a pay raise

a progressive discipline program involves a series of disciplinary steps

---

[5.] Echlin & Thomlinson *For Better or for Worse* (1996) at 164–6.

[6.] *Pierce v Canada Trust Realtor* (1986) 11 CCEL 64 (Ont HCJ).

Statutory Protection

The employment relationship traditionally was governed exclusively by the law of contract. Today, however, workers are also protected by various statutory schemes. Much of the legislation falls under provincial jurisdiction and varies in detail among provinces.[7] Sophisticated employers usually hire human resource experts or employment law specialists to navigate the intricacies of these statutory measures. We will discuss five statutory regimes: *employment standards*, *human rights*, *employee privacy*, *occupational health and safety*, and *workers' compensation*.

Employment Standards

Employment standards legislation requires an employer to meet minimum obligations, which apply only to employees and not to independent contractors or consultants. An employer cannot generally contract out of the legislation's minimum obligations. If an employment contract fails to meet those requirements, the employer must nevertheless compensate the employee according to the legislation. Furthermore, the legislation establishes *minimum standards*. If an employment contract actually provides the employee with greater protection, the employer cannot use the statute to reduce those rights. We briefly consider minimum standards in connection with holidays; wages; work hours, overtime, and rest days; leaves; and vacations.

Holidays   Every jurisdiction requires employers to pay employees for specific public holidays. This does not mean that employees cannot work on these days, nor does it prevent an employer from requesting its employees to work, as long as they are adequately compensated for it. Some provinces, such as British Columbia, Manitoba, Nova Scotia, and Prince Edward Island, entitle employees to public holidays only if they have worked 15 or more days in the month preceding the public holiday. Other provinces, such as Newfoundland and Labrador, New Brunswick, and Ontario, allow certain kinds of employers, such as those in hospitals or the hotel and restaurant industry, to require their employees to work on public holidays. Usually, these employees are entitled to additional compensation for working on those days.

Wages   Every province has set a minimum wage. Minimum wage legislation ensures that an employee's pay increases in line with the cost of living. The minimum wage is determined on an hourly basis, but it also applies to employees who are compensated in other ways. In such cases, it is up to the employer to ensure that the statutory minimum is met. Some jurisdictions have set different minimums for different categories of employees. For example, Alberta has set a lower minimum for workers under 18 years of age. Quebec has a lower minimum for people who usually receive tips. And the Northwest Territories sets a higher minimum for those not living along a highway. The typical minimum wage varies substantially between provinces and is influenced by such factors as the level of industry, the cost of living, and the political beliefs of the government in power.

Work Hours, Overtime, and Rest   Every jurisdiction regulates the number of hours that an employee can be asked to work. In most jurisdictions, this

---

[7.] Federal legislation governs some employees, including those in federal government, transportation, shipping, radio, and banking. The division of legislative authority between the federal and provincial governments was discussed in Chapter 1.

varies from 40 to 48. An employee can refuse to work more than that without fear of disciplinary action. Employees who choose to work more are entitled to overtime pay. In most provinces, the minimum rate of pay for overtime is 1.5 times the employee's regular wages. In a few provinces, the minimum rate is 1.5 times the minimum wage. A minimum daily rest period is also imposed in most provinces. Employees are typically entitled to 30 minutes for every five-hour period worked.

Leaves   Many jurisdictions entitle employees to unpaid leaves of absence. In some jurisdictions, bereavement leave is available for employees who grieve the loss of a loved one—sometimes it is paid, sometimes not. Employees are also entitled to take time off to vote in elections. Every jurisdiction entitles women who have fulfilled a minimum service requirement to a leave of absence during and after pregnancy. Although most parental leaves are unpaid, many employers continue to offer benefits, which may include part pay. Other employers offer no benefits, leaving the pregnant employee to claim employment insurance. Women who take pregnancy leaves are entitled to return to their jobs after leave and do not lose seniority in their position. If it is impossible to reinstate the employee to her previous position, she must be provided with a comparable job with equivalent wages and benefits.

Vacations   Employees are entitled to paid vacation. In most jurisdictions, the length depends on years of service. Vacation allowance often begins to accrue from the first day of service, but employees are often required to work a full year before taking a paid vacation. The legislation usually provides a minimum of two weeks and sometimes allows employees to postpone vacations. Employees do not have a right to take vacations whenever they want—the employer may usually set the dates. As a practical matter, however, flexibility should be allowed, especially since most employees regard vacations as very important.

According to employment standards legislation, employers are usually required to keep accurate records as evidence that they have met the minimum statutory requirements. For example, employers must keep records of wages paid, hours worked, and vacations accrued. If a dispute arises and no accurate records have been kept, the employer risks having an employment standards referee defer to the recollection of the employee. If so, the employer may have to meet the statutory minimum for a second time if the employee's evidence is incorrect.

Human Rights

Both provincially and federally, special statutory provisions deal with human rights in the employment context. As we saw in connection with job advertising, such legislation is remedial in nature. Its main purpose is not to punish the employer, but to provide a remedy to the employee who has been discriminated against.

Discrimination, in this context, means treating someone differently on the basis of one of the grounds prohibited by human rights legislation, including race, ancestry, place of origin, colour, ethnic origin, sex, sexual orientation, disability, marital status, family status, and religion.[8]

discrimination is treating someone differently on the basis of a ground prohibited by human rights legislation

---

8. *Human Rights Code*, RSBC 1996, c 210, s 11 (BC). See also *Saskatchewan Human Rights Code*, SS 1979, c S-24.1, s 14 (Sask); *Human Rights, Citizenship and Multiculturalism Act*, RSA 2000, c H-14, s 8 (Alta); *Human Rights Code*, RSO 1990, c H.19, s 23 (Ont); *Human Rights Act*, RSNB 1973, c H-11, s 3(4) (NB); *Fair Practices Act*, RSNWT 1988 (Supp), c 11, s 3(3) (NWT).

direct discrimination occurs when an employer adopts a rule or practice that treats a person differently on the basis of one of the prohibited grounds

indirect discrimination occurs when an employer treats someone differently on the basis of some characteristic other than a prohibited ground, but in a way that adversely affects that person by virtue of a prohibited ground

BFOR, or a *bona fide* occupational requirement, justifies discrimination that would normally be prohibited

harassment involves any demeaning or offensive conduct connected to a prohibited ground of discrimination

sexual harassment involves unwelcome or objectionable sexual advances, or any sexual comment, gesture, or conduct that the offender knew (or should have known) was unwelcome

the **duty to accommodate** requires an employer to make adaptations to the workplace to meet the needs of an employee who would not otherwise be able to work there

It is possible for an employer to discriminate either *directly* or *indirectly*. **Direct discrimination** occurs when an employer adopts a rule or practice that treats a person differently on the basis of one of the prohibited grounds. For example, if an employer refuses to hire a woman because she may decide to get pregnant, this would be direct discrimination. **Indirect discrimination** occurs when an employer treats a person differently on the basis of some characteristic other than a prohibited ground, but in a way that adversely affects that person by virtue of a prohibited ground. For example, Giuseppe's Pizza refused to hire Aruna as a receptionist because she does not have a valid driver's licence. If Aruna does not have a licence because of some visual impairment, Giuseppe's Pizza is indirectly discriminating against her on the basis of a disability, which is a prohibited ground of discrimination.

An employer is not necessarily liable merely because it discriminated against an employee. Human rights legislation recognizes a number of defences. The nature of some jobs justifies discrimination that would normally be prohibited. The acronym for that sort of defence is **BFOR**, *bona fide* occupational requirement.[9] To defend against a claim of discrimination, an employer must be able to demonstrate that the allegedly discriminatory requirement was imposed in good faith and with the sincere belief that it was imposed in the interests of adequate performance of the job.[10] For example, requiring a candidate for a firefighting job to meet some minimum requirement of physical ability is justified if the employer believes that such a requirement is truly necessary to carry out the job duties safely and economically. If the job involves climbing a ladder while carrying a heavy object, then the requirement would be justified. It would not if the position were a desk job.

Harassment is a form of discrimination in the workplace. **Harassment** involves any demeaning or offensive conduct connected to a prohibited ground of discrimination. As with other forms of discrimination, harassment can occur even if the conduct was not intended to be demeaning or offensive. **Sexual harassment** involves unwelcome or objectionable sexual advances, or any sexual comment, gesture, or conduct that the offender knew (or should have known) was unwelcome. In many jurisdictions, including Manitoba, New Brunswick, Prince Edward Island, and the federal jurisdiction, employers have an obligation to take reasonable proactive steps to prevent sexual harassment. An employer that fails to do so is vicariously liable for the acts of its employees.

The *duty to accommodate* is often used to remedy some forms of discrimination under human rights legislation. The **duty to accommodate** requires an employer to make adaptations to the workplace to meet the needs of an employee who would not otherwise be able to work there. These include wheelchair access, braille signage, and ergonomic workstations. Note that the scope of an employer's duty to accommodate is not absolute, but is limited to situations where it would not cause *undue hardship* to the employer. Relevant factors include (i) the cost of the accommodation, (ii) the ease of its implementation, (iii) health and safety requirements, (iv) whether outside sources of funding are available to assist in making the accommodation, (v) whether the accommodation will disrupt a collective agreement, and (vi) whether the accommodation will affect the morale of other employees.[11] Safety risks to the public should be given significant weight when employers are

---

[9.] The wording in some provinces is "*bona fide* occupational qualification" (or BFOQ).

[10.] *Etobicoke (Borough) v Ontario (Human Rights Commission)* (1982) 132 DLR (3d) 14 at 19–20 (SCC).

[11.] Echlin & Thomlinson *For Better or for Worse* (1996) at 116.

analyzing undue hardship and the scope of their duty to accommodate. In this regard, employers are entitled to rely on their own observations regarding the employee, without the need to defer exclusively to medical experts.[12]

It is sometimes hard to know when there is a duty to accommodate, but it is generally up to employees to express their need to be accommodated.[13] They also have a duty to take reasonable steps to assist their employers in making those accommodations.[14] The employee is not entitled to a perfect solution—if the employer has made a reasonable adaptation to the workplace, it has discharged its duty to accommodate.

CONCEPT SUMMARY 26.2

Managing Risk in Association with Human Rights Law

- Know the relevant provincial and federal laws, and be proactive, not reactive, in meeting your obligations.
- Be clear about job requirements and the BFOR for each position in order to ensure that any discrimination can be justified.
- Adopt employment policies and procedures that reflect and comply with human rights legislation.
- Institute informal complaints procedures and appoint a person in the workplace to investigate potential human rights complaints in a neutral way.

Employee Privacy

In Chapter 19, we discussed privacy law in the context of online privacy, outlining the general requirements of privacy laws. However, a number of specific issues arise in the employment context. For example, Canada's federal private sector privacy law, the *Personal Information Protection and Electronic Documents Act* (*PIPEDA*), defines "personal information" as information about an identifiable individual, but does *not* include the name, title, business address or telephone number of an employee in an organization. Privacy laws do not regulate the collection, use, or disclosure of this kind of information.

Privacy laws in British Columbia and Alberta contain an employment-related exception not expressly found in *PIPEDA*.[15] In the case of the BC law, employers are permitted to collect, use, and disclose an employee's personal information without the employee's consent for purposes reasonably required to establish, manage, or terminate an employment relationship. The employer is, however, required to notify the employee of the purposes.

As another example of the overlap between privacy and employment, *PIPEDA*, and the laws in British Columbia and Alberta, all provide whistle-blower protections for employees. This protection prohibits an employer from dismissing, suspending, demoting, or disciplining an employee who in good faith reports the employer for violating privacy laws.

Employee privacy in the workplace is also a very important consideration in relation to surveillance of employees. Employers often have good reasons to

---

[12.] See *Oak Bay Marina Ltd v British Columbia (Human Rights Commission)* (2002) 217 DLR (4th) 747 (BC CA).

[13.] *Emrick Plastics v Ontario (Human Rights Commission)* (1992) 90 DLR (4th) 476 (Ont Div Ct).

[14.] *Central Okanagan School District No 23 v Renaud* (1992) 95 DLR (4th) 577 (SCC).

[15.] *Personal Information Protection Act*, SBC 2003, c 63, s 16; *Personal Information Protection Act*, SA 2003, c P-6.5, s 15.

use surveillance cameras or other monitoring devices. That sort of equipment can be used as a tool to prevent, deter, or investigate fraud or theft. Surveillance in the workplace can, however, also have an adverse effect on employee morale, particularly when it is targeted directly at employees rather than the business premises in general. Pervasive surveillance may make all employees—even those doing excellent work—feel like they are not trusted and it may, as a result, adversely affect their job performance. Surveillance in the workplace can also be illegal.

As discussed in Chapter 19, the Privacy Commissioner of Canada and the courts have developed a four-part test for determining whether surveillance complies with the requirements of *PIPEDA*: (i) is the surveillance necessary to meet a specific organizational need, (ii) is the surveillance likely to be effective in meeting that need, (iii) is the loss of privacy proportional to the benefit gained, and (iv) is there a less invasive way of achieving the same end?

Organizations considering surveillance measures in the workplace should bear in mind how they would answer each of these questions. For example, it might be difficult to justify a comprehensive camera surveillance system on the basis that it will prevent theft when the workplace has had virtually no incidents of theft. In such a case, there might be no specific need. And even if there were a need, it may not warrant comprehensive surveillance. Unless the threat of misconduct was particularly strong, the benefit to the employer would not be proportional to the employees' loss of privacy. Finally, even if the risk of theft were substantial, it might be possible for the employer to adopt less invasive ways of achieving the same end, for example, by providing employees with desk drawers that lock.

Occupational Health and Safety

Every employer must meet minimum standards for workplace health and safety. Health and safety legislation is aimed at preventing accidents, injuries, and industrial diseases. That is accomplished by reducing risks through educational and punitive measures. Many jurisdictions require the creation of workplace advisory groups composed of workers and managers. Employees have the right to refuse to work in unsafe conditions. The employer is then required to investigate the problem. An employee who is not satisfied with the investigation may take up the matter with the workplace advisory group and, ultimately, with the responsible governmental agency. In exceptional circumstances, an unsafe workplace may be shut down.

In most jurisdictions, a serious violation of occupational health and safety standards can be a crime. A violation of a health and safety inspector's order may also be criminal. Companies and individuals may, however, use the defence of *due diligence*. **Due diligence** occurs when the accused took every reasonable precaution to avoid violating the safety standard.

due diligence occurs when the accused took every reasonable precaution to avoid violating the safety standard

Workers' Compensation

While occupational health and safety legislation is aimed at preventing workplace injuries, workers' compensation schemes (which we discussed in Chapter 3) were created to redress injuries that do occur by financially compensating injured workers. Many workplace injuries may be addressed through tort actions. However, there are at least two difficulties with formal litigation. First, it is very expensive. Second, it operates on an all-or-nothing basis. If the defendant wrongfully caused the injury, the plaintiff receives full compensation. Otherwise, the plaintiff does not receive any relief. Workers' compensation schemes use a much simpler and less expensive procedure. Furthermore, they provide some compensation even if a worker cannot prove that someone else was at fault. In exchange for those benefits, the legislation generally prevents a person from suing in tort for workplace injuries.[16]

Workers' compensation schemes are funded through compulsory contributions by employers. The amount that an employer must contribute depends on the industry in which it is involved—more dangerous industries naturally carry higher rates.

Workers' compensation schemes provide benefits in several circumstances.

- A *partial disability* allows the worker to continue performing in some capacity. Compensation for partial injuries is based on the difference between the worker's pre-accident earning capacity and post-accident earning capacity.

- A *total incapacity* prevents the worker from performing in any capacity. Workers who suffer a total, though temporary, disability are paid a portion of their pre-accident earning capacity while they are unable to work.

- If a worker is *killed* in the course of employment, their dependants are entitled to compensation. For a spouse, some provinces provide periodic payments until the spouse remarries or reaches the age of 65. In other provinces, the spouse receives a lump sum payment equal to the amount that the worker would have received if they had been permanently injured rather than killed. The worker's children are also entitled to compensation until they reach the age of majority. In some provinces, dependent children are entitled to a further amount toward post-secondary education.

TERMINATION OF EMPLOYMENT

An employer's obligations do not last forever. They sometimes end abruptly—an employee may quit or be fired, or a company may cease to exist. We end this chapter by examining some issues that arise when the employment relationship breaks down. We will (i) look at an employer's right to dismiss employees who are in serious breach of their employment obligations, (ii) consider the rights of employees under the law of wrongful dismissal, (iii) examine the concept of constructive dismissal, and (iv) survey post-employment practices, such as restrictive covenants and confidentiality, severance packages and settlements, and post-employment obligations.

Summary Dismissal

Employees sometimes misbehave on the job. If they do not perform their duties properly, they may be in breach of their employment contracts. The usual contractual rule applies. If the employee commits a serious breach, the employer is entitled to terminate the contract. In the language of employment law, the employer is entitled to a self-help remedy known as *summary dismissal*. **Summary dismissal** occurs when an employer dismisses the employee and thereby terminates the employment relationship without notice. That remedy is

summary dismissal occurs when an employer dismisses the employee and thereby terminates the employment relationship without notice

---

16. Some provinces, including British Columbia, Manitoba, New Brunswick, and Ontario, provide exceptions, such as when an employer negligently maintains defective machinery or when the injury was caused by another employee.

just cause means that the employer was justified in firing the employee without notice

available only if the employer has *just cause*. **Just cause** means that the employer was justified in firing the employee without notice. It is limited to certain types of breach, including:

- absenteeism
- substance abuse
- incompetence and carelessness
- dishonesty and disobedience
- conflicts of interest
- criminal behaviour

Absenteeism

absenteeism is an unauthorized failure to report for work that is not the product of an illness

The employment contract requires the employee to regularly attend work during specified hours. If those hours are not expressly stated in the contract, the courts will imply a term that is in line with the employer's normal hours of business. Although the failure to report for work on a single occasion will not usually constitute grounds for dismissal, repeated *absenteeism* will.[17] **Absenteeism** is an unauthorized failure to report for work that is not the product of an illness. When absenteeism hurts its business interests, the employer is justified in terminating the employee.

Under some circumstances, a repeated pattern of lateness will also constitute grounds for dismissal. After recognizing a pattern of lateness, the employer must clearly warn the employee that such behaviour will not be tolerated. A similar tactic should be applied in dealing with employees who repeatedly leave work early or before the end of their shift. Before dismissing an employee on the basis of absenteeism or lateness, an employer should document a pattern of conduct as well as a series of warnings. The document should state that the employee did not have a legitimate reason for being absent or late.

Substance Abuse

Some employees have been known to come to work under the influence of alcohol or other drugs. This may be grounds for dismissal.

- First, courts consider whether the employee's job performance was impaired. The mere smell of alcohol on the breath of the employee is insufficient to warrant dismissal.
- Second, courts consider whether the employee's abuse of alcohol or other drugs threatened the safety of the workplace. It may be possible to dismiss a forklift operator who is drunk on the job, but perhaps not a typist who is inebriated at an office party.
- Third, courts consider whether the employer's business reputation has been harmed by the employee's conduct.
- Fourth, courts consider whether the employer had a policy in place that prohibited such conduct and if it was known, or ought to have been known, by the employee.

condonation occurs whenever an employer fails to reprimand the employee for their misconduct

Courts tend to be more lenient if it appears that the employer *condoned* the employee's conduct. **Condonation** occurs whenever an employer fails to repri-

---

[17.] *Bowie v Motorola Canada Ltd* (1991) 44 CCEL 307 (Ont Gen Div).

mand an employee for their misconduct. If a business maintains an extremely permissive attitude in the workplace, its *apparent* condonation may deprive it of the authority to dismiss a drunken employee. To avoid that risk, a business should implement and enforce a clearly worded policy that defines acceptable and unacceptable conduct.

Incompetence

Employers are often dissatisfied with workers' performance. That alone does not mean that an employee has breached their employment obligations. One situation where poor performance does justify dismissal occurs when an employee is *incompetent*. **Incompetent** employees lack basic skills or qualifications, or are otherwise unable to perform their assigned jobs. To prove incompetence, the employer must do more than show that a job could have been done better; it must prove that the employee fell below a standard of basic competence.

incompetent employees lack basic skills or qualifications, or are otherwise unable to perform their assigned jobs

A good risk manager will notify an employee that their work is substandard, and state that such shoddy performance will not be tolerated in the future. The employer should (i) clearly identify the problems with the employee's work, (ii) establish a review process to help the employee improve, and (iii) inform the employee that a continued substandard performance will result in termination.

Dishonesty and Disobedience

An employment relationship imposes a duty on the employee to be faithful and honest. When dishonesty causes the employer to lose trust and confidence in the employment relationship, it is grounds for dismissal. In fact, the nature of some jobs requires an even higher standard of honesty. Employees who hold positions of trust, such as senior managers in financial institutions, are generally obligated to act in the best interests of the business. Although honesty is usually required only when the employee is acting in the course of their employment, courts have sometimes allowed an employer to dismiss an employee for dishonest conduct outside of the course of employment.[18] However, not every act of dishonesty will justify dismissal. Employers must consider whether, on a balance of probabilities, the evidence indicates that the employee has been dishonest. If so, the employer must then consider whether the nature and degree of the dishonesty justifies dismissal. The test is whether the employee's dishonesty gives rise to a breakdown of the employment relationship.[19]

Two common forms of dishonesty are *employee fraud* and *employee theft*. **Employee fraud** occurs when an employee intentionally deceives the employer in a way that is detrimental to its interests. The employee can be dismissed if the nature of the fraud is incompatible with a continuing employment relationship. **Employee theft** occurs when an employee steals from the employer. The law implies a term in every contract that prohibits employee theft. Since loyalty and honesty are at the core of the employment relationship, a single incident of theft may justify termination.

employee fraud occurs when an employee intentionally deceives the employer in a way that is detrimental to its interests

employee theft occurs when an employee steals from the employer

Disobedience is also a ground for dismissal. **Disobedience** typically occurs when an employee repeatedly and deliberately defies a supervisor's clear instructions or refuses to perform without reasonable excuse. The employment

disobedience occurs when an employee repeatedly and deliberately defies a supervisor's clear instructions or refuses to perform without reasonable excuse

---

[18] *Marshall v Pacific Coast Savings Credit Union* (1992) 44 CCEL 261 (BC CA).

[19] *McKinley v BC Tel* (2001) 200 DLR (4th) 385 (SCC).

relationship is based on the idea that the employer controls and directs the work of its employees. A repeated failure to follow instructions not only results in unaccomplished tasks, it also undercuts the authority of the employer and generally lowers employee morale. Likewise, a repeated pattern of severe disrespect, or insulting behaviour directed at the employer or supervisors, may be grounds for dismissal.

Conflicts of Interest

a **conflict of interest** occurs when an employee acts in a way that conflicts with the employer's best interests

An employee is required to avoid a *conflict of interest*. A **conflict of interest** occurs when an employee acts in a way that conflicts with the employer's best interests. An employee cannot, for example, (i) carry on a business that competes with the employer, (ii) accept personal gifts or other advantages from a party who conducts business with the employer, (iii) have personal dealings with the employer's clients, customers, or suppliers, or (iv) provide confidential information acquired during the course of employment to a competitor in exchange for some benefit. An employee may argue that the conduct in question did not *actually* hurt the employer. The lack of harm may be irrelevant, however, especially if the employer imposed a policy that prohibited the conduct in question, or if it was expressly prohibited by the employment contract.[20]

Criminal Behaviour

In addition to dishonest acts such as fraud or theft, other criminal conduct during the course of employment can lead to dismissal. Typical examples are physical assault and property offences. When an employee commits a crime on the job, they may be dismissed as soon as charges have been laid—even before there has been a conviction. As a matter of risk management, however, the employer should not dismiss an employee until a thorough investigation shows that a crime has been committed. If it makes a false allegation, an employer may be liable for punitive damages.[21]

Concept Summary 26.3 reviews the grounds for summary dismissal.

CONCEPT SUMMARY 26.3

Grounds for Summary Dismissal

- absenteeism, lateness, and leaving work without permission
- substance abuse
- incompetence and carelessness
- dishonesty and disobedience
- conflicts of interest
- criminal behaviour

---

[20] *Ennis v Canadian Imperial Bank of Commerce* (1989) 13 CCEL 25 (BC SC).

[21] *Conrad v Household Financial Corp* (1992) 115 NSR (2d) 153 (SC TD), affd 45 CCEL 81 (SC AD).

Wrongful Dismissal

Reasonable Notice

Summary dismissal is an exception to the general rule. An employee may be summarily dismissed only in the sort of exceptional circumstances we have discussed. Normally, the common law and provincial employment standards legislation require an employer to provide an employee with some reasonable period of notice before terminating the employment relationship. The notice period gives the employee an opportunity to receive an income while looking for another job.

It is not always possible to provide reasonable notice. If the employer fails to do so, the employee is usually entitled to *money in lieu of notice*. Sometimes an employer will offer to pay that amount and ask the employee to leave immediately. Other times, the end is not so smooth. **Wrongful dismissal** occurs when an employee is dismissed without cause and without reasonable notice or money in lieu of notice. Although an employer generally cannot be forced to retain a particular employee, it may be held liable if it fires that person without cause and without reasonable notice. In that situation, the employee may sue to recover not only money owed in lieu of notice, but also damages for the loss of commissions, bonuses, or benefits.

wrongful dismissal occurs when an employee is dismissed without cause and without reasonable notice or money in lieu of notice

The "reasonable notice period" depends upon the circumstances. Employment standards legislation always states a minimum notice period. Most jurisdictions require at least two weeks' notice for employees who have been at a job for two years. Employees who have been at a job for 10 or more years are often statutorily entitled to four to eight weeks' notice, depending on the jurisdiction. Note that these are the minimums, and courts often require much longer notice periods. Judges sometimes try to determine the length of the notice period that the parties themselves would have set if they had addressed the issue when they created their contract.[22] Usually, however, the courts look at such factors as (i) the employee's age, (ii) the nature of the position held, (iii) the length of service, (iv) the salary level of the employee, and (v) the employee's likelihood of securing alternative employment. It is generally accepted, however, that the upper limit, even for the most senior executives, should not exceed 24 months.

Courts have recently begun to examine the behaviour of the employer around the time of dismissal. According to a majority of the Supreme Court of Canada, if an employee establishes that the employer engaged in *bad faith* conduct or unfair dealing in the course of dismissal, the resulting harm can be compensated by lengthening the usual notice period. These are sometimes called "Wallace damages," named after the case in which the rule was created.[23] According to the Court, **bad faith** includes "untruthful, misleading or unduly insensitive conduct on the part of the employer." A bad faith dismissal that causes humiliation, embarrassment, or damage to the employee's sense of self-worth exposes the employer to the risk of being held liable for more than the normal amount of money in lieu of notice.

bad faith includes untruthful, misleading or unduly insensitive conduct on the part of the employer

---

[22] *Lazarowicz v Orenda Engines Ltd* (1960) 26 DLR (2d) 433 (Ont CA).

[23] *Wallace v United Grain Growers Ltd* (1997) 152 DLR (4th) 1 at 33 (SCC). Iacobucci J justified the majority's extension of the notice period with this rationale:

"The point at which the employment relationship ruptures is the time when the employee is most vulnerable and hence most in need of protection. In recognition of this need, the law ought to encourage conduct that minimizes the damage and dislocation (both economic and personal) that result from dismissal. To ensure that employees receive adequate protection, employers ought to be held to an obligation of good faith and fair dealing in the manner of dismissal, breach of which will be compensated for by adding to the length of the notice period."

The Duty to Mitigate

Even when employees are wrongfully dismissed, they cannot simply do nothing while they sue their former employers for damages. Employees have a duty to mitigate their damages by promptly taking reasonable steps to minimize the losses flowing from their dismissal. Normally this means that they must make reasonable efforts to seek out new employment. They will not be compensated for damages that they could have avoided through reasonable efforts at mitigation. Nor will the employee be compensated for damages that they did avoid through mitigation. For example, if the employer should have given six months' notice, resulting in a payment of $40 000, and the employee was able to get another job and earn $10 000 within six months, then the former employer would only be required to pay $30 000.[24]

Wrongful Resignation

There is also an implied term in employment agreements that requires employees to give their employers reasonable notice before quitting. An employer is entitled to a reasonable amount of time in which to find a replacement, or mitigate the loss in some other way. This period is not necessarily the same as the period that an employer would be required to give if it wished to terminate the contract. However, industry norms may provide some guidance in determining how much notice an employee must give. Employees may be liable to their former employer for losses sustained as a result of a wrongful resignation.

Constructive Dismissal

An employer may try to avoid a notice period by making a situation so intolerable that the employee simply quits. The law responds to that tactic through the doctrine of *constructive dismissal*. **Constructive dismissal** occurs when an employer fundamentally changes the nature of a person's job. The three most common changes amounting to constructive dismissal are (i) a reduction in salary or benefits, (ii) a change in job status or responsibility, or (iii) change in geographical location. If constructive dismissal can be proved, the employee is treated as though they were dismissed without notice and consequently will be entitled to damages in lieu of notice.

constructive dismissal occurs when an employer fundamentally changes the nature of a person's job

Severance Packages and Settlements

Fortunately, most employment relationships do not end with the employer's complete disregard for the employee's welfare. Many employers offer a **severance package**, a lump-sum payment that is meant to cover everything that is due to the employee at the time of termination. It is called a "severance" package because it includes *severance pay*. **Severance pay** is the amount that is owed to a terminated employee under employment standards legislation. A severance package may also include (i) salary, commissions, or bonuses owing, (ii) benefits owing, (iii) contributions to Canada Pension Plan, (iv) contributions to registered retirement savings plans or private pension plans, (v) an automobile allowance, (vi) vacation pay and sick leave, (vii) stock options, (viii) employee discounts and staff loans, and (ix) reference letters.

a **severance package** is a lump sum payment meant to cover all items due to the employee at the time of termination

severance pay is the amount that is owed to a terminated employee under employment standards legislation

---

[24.] We discussed mitigation in Chapters 3 and 12.

Sometimes an employer and employee negotiate the items to be included in the package so that it includes more than is required by legislation. This is sometimes called a *settlement package*. A **settlement package** is what the employer gives to the employee to bring an employment dispute to an end. As a matter of risk management, the employer should deliver the settlement package only after the employee has signed a *release*. A **release** is the employee's written promise to release the employer from any possible legal claims that the employee might have against the employer. Like other contracts, a release is effective only if the employer provides new consideration—something more than what the employee was already owed under the employment contract and the employment standards legislation.

a **settlement package** is what the employer gives to the employee to bring an end to an employment dispute

a **release** is the employee's written promise to release the employer from any possible legal claims that the employee might have against the employer

Post-Employment Obligations

Generally speaking, the employer's obligations come to an end when the employment contract is terminated. However, there are two exceptions where ongoing obligations arise. First, the employment contract itself might provide for ongoing obligations. For example, an employer might agree to relocate an employee in the event of an unexpected termination of employment. Second, employers can incur ongoing obligations as part of a settlement package when resolving a dispute with an employee. For example, as part of a settlement, an employer might agree to make periodic payments for a specific time period.

The situation is quite different for employees. Earlier we discussed why an employer should ensure that an employment contract imposes non-competition, non-solicitation, and confidentiality obligations on an employee. Those obligations should be written to survive the termination of the employment relationship. That advice, unfortunately, is not always followed. A restrictive covenant may be unenforceable (because, for example, it is too broad); the employment contract may not contain an appropriate term; or the parties may have operated without a formal contract. In those situations, the employer must rely on the common law to establish a post-termination obligation against the employee.

Without an enforceable non-competition or non-solicitation clause, employees are entitled to solicit clients of their former employer and to compete, provided they do so in a fair manner. They are allowed to make arrangements for their new business while they are still employed. And while they cannot physically remove customer lists belonging to their employer, they can commit those lists to memory and later recall the customers' names with the help of a phone book.

In cases involving key or senior former employees, or in situations of manifest unfairness, courts may impose restrictive obligations on former employees. Key employees and senior employees usually owe fiduciary duties to their employer that survive termination of the employment relationship. This means that they may be restricted in their ability to compete for former clients. Situations of manifest unfairness may also justify restrictions, even for regular employees, and are usually quite obvious. Case Brief 26.2 provides an example.

CASE BRIEF 26.2

57134 Manitoba Ltd v Palmer (1989) 37 BCLR (2d) 50 (CA)

Palmer was an employee at 57134 Manitoba Ltd (the "Company"), based in Winnipeg. In 1972, Palmer was sent to Vancouver where he opened and operated a BC branch for the Company's operations. Although the Company retained control over Palmer, he was a trusted employee and had a good deal of responsibility over the BC branch. In 1979, the Company told Palmer that the BC branch would have to be scaled back to improve profitability. Palmer viewed this as a "bombshell" and immediately gave 30 days' notice of his resignation.

Before the 30 days were up, Palmer entered into the employment of another company in a similar business. During that time, he also:

- persuaded a junior employee of the Company to leave the Company and join Palmer's new employer
- persuaded an agent of the Company in Vancouver to terminate his agency

- carried out a systematic attack on the Company's business, including diverting three maturing orders to his new employer, and telling the junior employee to do the same
- copied the Company's customer cards, which included the name, address, and order history of each customer
- solicited the Company's customers by personally calling on them for orders for his new employer
- took and used the Company's price lists

These actions dealt a staggering blow to the business of the Company and resulted in more than 300 accounts being moved to Palmer's new employer. The court was invited to address the issue of fiduciary duty, but felt no need to do so. It held that—regardless of whether Palmer was a senior or key employee to whom fiduciary duties applied—he was required, as an employee, to compete with his former employer in a fair manner. The court further held that Palmer's activities were unfair by *any standard*.

CHAPTER SUMMARY

Before hiring an employee, an employer should draft a job description that accurately defines the duties attached to the position. Any advertisements should refer only to *bona fide* occupational requirements. When obtaining additional information from job applicants, employers must be careful to limit their questions to those relating to the applicant's ability to do the job. Both the employer and applicant should avoid misstatements during contract negotiations. The contract should be written.

Not all work- or service-related contracts are contracts of employment, nor are all workers employees. One way to test the nature of the work relationship is by determining how much control is asserted by the party paying for the work. Another test determines whether the work is an integral part of the overall business of the organization. Employment contracts are essential tools for risk management and should usually include non-competition or non-solicitation clauses. The risk of vicarious liability and other workplace hazards imposes responsibilities on employers to supervise their employees. Risk management requires employment policy manuals, performance reviews, and promotion or probation.

Statutory protection for workers includes (i) employment standards—which are concerned with holidays, wages, work hours, overtime and rest periods, leaves, and vacations, (ii) human rights—which are concerned with discrimination, harassment, and the duty to accommodate, (iii) privacy laws—which protect employees' privacy, (iv) occupational health and safety—which is concerned with the prevention of accidents, injuries, and industrial diseases through educational and punitive measures, and (v) workers' compensation—which is concerned with redressing workplace injuries through an accident compensation scheme that is funded by compulsory contributions from employers. Due to the complexity of employment law, many employers hire trained human resource personnel or employment law specialists.

An employer's obligations may end abruptly. Summary dismissal occurs when an employer dismisses an employee without providing notice. It is allowed when the employer can establish just cause. Just cause may exist if an employee is guilty of (i) absenteeism, (ii) substance abuse, (iii) incompetence and carelessness, (iv) dishonesty and disobedience, (v) a conflict of interest, or (vi) criminal behaviour. The best way for a business to avoid being perceived to condone employee misconduct is to implement and enforce a clearly worded policy that defines the limits of acceptable and unacceptable conduct.

The common law and provincial employment standards legislation generally require an employer to provide employees with some reasonable period of notice before terminating an employment relationship. Employees are also required to give reasonable notice before quitting. Wrongful dismissal may arise if an employee is dismissed without cause and without reasonable notice or money in lieu of notice. Employees are under a duty to mitigate their losses flowing from a wrongful dismissal. The notice period will be further extended by a court in the case of bad faith dismissal. Constructive dismissal may arise if an employer fundamentally changes the nature of a person's job to force that person to quit.

Some employers put together a severance package when terminating an employee. A severance package is meant to cover everything that is due to the employee at the time of termination. That package will include severance pay, which is the amount that is owed to a terminated employee under employment standards legislation. Some employers provide their employees with additional items in their severance packages. If an employer wants to end the relationship amicably, it may offer the employee a settlement package, which generally includes more than the statutory minimums and is negotiated in return for the employee's willingness to sign a release, which effectively terminates the employment relationship and any potential disputes arising from it.

Without an enforceable contractual non-competition or non-solicitation clause, employees are generally free to compete with their former employers and to solicit customers. However, they must not do so in a manner that is manifestly unfair.

REVIEW QUESTIONS

1. Why is it important to carefully draft a job description before advertising a position? Give an example that illustrates how a broadly drafted job description can be advantageous to both an employer and an employee.

2. Name an occupational requirement that might appear to be discriminatory. Give an example of how such a requirement might be justified as a *bona fide* occupational requirement.

3. What is the difference between an employee and an independent contractor? What are the benefits to an employer of hiring an independent contractor rather than an employee?

4. Compare the control and organizational tests for determining the nature of a work relationship.

5. Explain the ways that you can effectively manage risk through the use of enforceable restrictive covenants in an employment contract.

6. Provide four examples of basic workplace issues that an employment policy manual should address.

7. What is the value of giving employees regular performance reviews?

8. When is the suspension of an employee a reasonable course of conduct?

9. Name several statutory regimes that have been created to protect employees. Give an example of each.

10. How many hours make up a standard work week? Under what circumstances is an employee entitled to a leave of absence?

11. Distinguish between direct discrimination and indirect discrimination.

12. Explain a situation in which being unmarried would be justified as a BFOR.

13. Can harassment be found to have occurred even if the conduct in question was not intended to be demeaning or offensive? Why?

14. Give two examples of how a risk manager can help to prevent violations of human rights legislation.

15. Which factors should be considered in deciding if, and to what extent, an employer has a duty to accommodate an employee's special needs due to disability?

16. Explain the aim of health and safety legislation. How can an employer defend itself against a violation of health and safety standards?

17. List six forms of employee misconduct that are considered to be just cause for a summary dismissal.

18. What factors should employers consider in determining a reasonable notice period for dismissing an employee? Is there a cause of action that exists for employees who feel that they have not been provided with reasonable notice of dismissal?

19. Define "constructive dismissal." What are the three most common kinds of changes that amount to constructive dismissal? What are the legal implications of proving constructive dismissal?

20. Explain the post-employment obligations that an employee may be bound by, even in the absence of enforceable obligations in an employment contract.

CASES AND PROBLEMS

1. William Lee has been employed as a farmhand at Jean-Louis Mushroom Farms for four years. Following a decline in the value of mushrooms, Jean-Louis was forced to unilaterally alter the terms of William's pay. Jean-Louis also decided that it was necessary to abolish his custom of allowing employees to eat as many mushrooms as they desire while at work. He also reduced Jean-Louis's wages slightly to the current minimum wage. Despite the fact that it was only a minor reduction, William refuses to work for minimum wage and has brought an action for the balance of wages owing at his previous hourly rate. William is relying on his employment contract as well as past payment accounts, which prove his previous rate of pay. Discuss the factors that affect minimum pay rates. Is Jean-Louis justified in lowering William's wages if they continue to meet minimum wage requirements? Explain.

2. NumbersMagic Inc alleged that its bookkeeper, Chris Ginsberg, had stolen from it. The company made a claim against its insurer, Neverpay Insurance Ltd, to recover the loss. Neverpay refused the claim on the basis that the policy stated that:

   > In the event of loss and/or damages which can be attributed, even in part, to the acts of an employee, Neverpay Insurance will not be held responsible for compensating the company for said losses and/or damages.

   The issue is whether Chris was a company employee at the time of the thefts. The evidence indicates that he performed basic bookkeeping services for the company, worked regular hours out of the NumbersMagic offices, and was subject to the direct supervision of a company manager. Chris was not a member of a recognized professional association, and his duties were those normally associated with a bookkeeper, not a professional accountant. Consequently, Chris was paid on an hourly basis—he did not set fees depending upon the nature of services he performed. He had no shares in the company, nor any incentive-based remuneration. No deductions were made from his cheques, nor did he receive holiday pay or any other company benefits. Apply both the control test and the organization test to determine whether Neverpay Insurance will likely have to make a payment under the policy. Support your position.

3. Erica performed deliveries for Speed of Sound Delivery Service. She used her own vehicle. She had the luxury of choosing when she wanted to work but, while on shift, she was subject to tight control by a Speed of Sound dispatcher. That meant that she could not deliver for anyone else during her shifts. Erica was paid by commission. No deductions were made on her cheques. After four years of uninterrupted work for Speed of Sound, Erica was dismissed without notice or cause. Erica brought an action for damages. Erica feels that her dedicated work for Speed of Sound Corporation entitled her to money in lieu of two months' notice, which is the amount recently received by another employee who was dismissed without notice. Do you think Erica will be successful in her claim? How much notice, if any, was Erica entitled to? Support your position.

4. You are a manager at a factory that manufactures bike frames. You supervise workers at the factory by periodically walking around and observing productivity. However, you cannot be in all places at once. Therefore, in addition to your personal supervision, the employees are required to punch time-cards so you know when they come and go from the factory. Of course, you also keep detailed records about how many bike frames are produced by each employee at the factory. The factory has turned a reasonable profit every year under this system. Despite these measures and the relative success of the factory, Billy Buckston, the owner of the factory, has recently put pressure on you to boost profits. He wants you to increase the performance of the factory workers. He thinks that they are not working fast enough and suggests that you install web-cameras in the factory to manage employee productivity. These cameras would be linked to a computer in your office where you could watch over every worker in the factory at all times. Through the sound system installed in the factory, you would then be able to yell directions at any workers who were not working fast enough. Do you think Mr Buckston's idea would be justified in light of Canada's privacy laws? In particular, do you think the cameras would be effective in achieving Mr Buckston's goal of increasing productivity? Can you think of any other less privacy-invasive ways of trying to achieve the same goal?

5. WeBuildIt Construction Ltd hired Danele, an architect and construction manager, to build part of a tuna-canning plant. Danele was responsible for completing the project for a fixed sum. Her arrangement required her to employ workers and purchase materials, subject to the budgetary approval of WeBuildIt. The overall supervision of the workers remained under the direction of WeBuildIt's chief architect, Marty McPencil, who provided instruction to Danele and four other construction managers involved in the project. Following Marty's instructions, Danele designed and installed a giant metal tuna on the outside of the building. Ironically, on the opening day of the plant, the giant tuna fell and killed a fisherman who had just delivered his week's catch to the plant. The fisherman's wife is now seeking to recover damages from both Danele, who oversaw the installation of the giant tuna, and WeBuildIt Construction Ltd. Discuss the potential liability resulting from this situation.

6. Following the conclusion of his contract, Puneet is seeking to recover overtime pay for time worked in excess of a 48-hour week. The facts are as follows. His contract is silent as to the number of hours to be worked in consideration for stated remuneration. His tendered record of the exact number of hours worked, although detailed, is uncorroborated. He has already been paid well in excess of the minimum hourly rate for all recorded hours worked. He is not a farmer or an emergency worker of any kind. Puneet has approached you to represent him in this matter. What legal issues does this scenario raise? What type of employment legislation is relevant to the resolution of this dispute? Does Puneet have a legal basis upon which to make this claim?

7. The Bank of Acadia adopted a policy that requires employees to provide urine samples for drug testing. That policy applies to all employees, although it is mandatory only for some, including new employees. The stated purpose of the policy is "to maintain a safe, healthy, and productive workplace for the employees; to safeguard customers, bank, and employee funds; and to protect the bank's reputation." An employee who tests positive is required to attend treatment and rehabilitation counselling, which the bank pays for. If rehabilitation is unsuccessful, refused, or abandoned, the employee may be terminated from their employment. Concerned about the effect of such a policy on civil liberties, an activist group has filed a complaint with the Canadian Human Rights Commission, claiming that the bank is engaged in a practice of indirect discrimination. According to the group, the bank's policy has the effect of depriving drug-dependent people of their jobs. Do you think that the bank's policy constitutes direct or indirect discrimination? Are there *bona fide* occupational grounds for doing so? Explain your answer.

8. Sylvan was employed as the garage manager for Tough Lucy's Trucking Ltd for seven years. During that time, he reported directly to the owner, Lucy LaRue. Sylvan proved to be an exemplary manager. He was known for his charm and got along well with other employees. However, according to several witnesses, Lucy seemed to think that Sylvan was not getting along with one employee in particular, namely Lucy's 24-year-old nephew, whom she had hired to be the garage bookkeeper. Upon arriving to work one snowy January day, Sylvan was informed by Lucy that, due to financial difficulties, Lucy would take over as garage manager and Sylvan would be reassigned to drive a company manure truck. There is no evidence that the garage was anything but profitable. The change in Sylvan's position involved a considerable change in responsibility as well as a lower salary, longer working hours, and substantially smellier working conditions. Sylvan was flabbergasted and appealed to Lucy on the basis of their long and pleasant working relationship. Lucy told him he could take it or leave it. Sylvan refused, resigned, and commenced a lawsuit. What

is Sylvan's cause of action? What will he have to prove to win? Do you think that he will succeed? How might Lucy have otherwise achieved her purpose without risking a lawsuit?

9. Shortly after his high-school graduation, Sweyn agreed to help his older sister, Svetlana, and her husband construct their home. The first day, Sweyn wore tennis shoes instead of proper boots. Although the issue was raised by another person who was on the construction crew, nothing was done about it. Since Sweyn had been driven to the construction site by Svetlana, he had no way to acquire adequate footwear, and his sister did not offer to drive him home. In fact, she and the rest of the crew seemed eager to commence work immediately. After walking through wet cement for several hours, Sweyn's feet began to turn yellow. Everyone knew this, but no one told him to stop working. Svetlana's husband said that he could continue working and would be fine as long as he washed his feet off, which he did. However, Sweyn suffered severe burns to his feet. He was on crutches for several weeks and has had trouble walking ever since. Sweyn has sued Svetlana. He contends that, during the construction project, he was effectively her employee, and therefore she had breached her duty of care as an employer when she brought Sweyn onto the work site without providing him with proper work boots. Do you think that the minimal standards set out by occupational health and safety legislation apply in this case? Explain your position. What kind of evidence would Svetlana need to prove to invoke a defence of due diligence?

10. Lucia, the district sales manager of Sharky's Credit Union, extended credit to a customer contrary to company policy. Mike, Sharky's CEO, responded by personally reprimanding Lucia and suspending her scheduled pay increase. Slightly poorer, but still unable to control her corporate generosity, Lucia subsequently extended substantial additional credit to the same customer. Mike discovered this during his weekly review of the company's accounts and immediately dismissed Lucia without notice. According to Mike, Lucia had attempted to withhold reports from the company that would have revealed the extension of credit to this and other customers. Were Lucia's breaches of company policy just cause for her summary dismissal? Is it necessary for Mike to prove fraud to justify the dismissal?

11. For the past 10 years, Gurpreet has been employed as an investment analyst at one of Canada's largest financial institutions, BucksCorp. BucksCorp has always treated her very well. Gurpreet was recently offered a position at a competing financial institution, SkyBank. SkyBank offered Gurpreet a much higher salary and a better chance of promotion. However, SkyBank urgently needed to fill the position and told Gurpreet she would have to start the next day. Gurpreet checked her employment contract with BucksCorp. She found that it did not say anything about whether she had to give notice to quit her job at BucksCorp. Although she knew that

the industry norm was for someone at her level to give three weeks' notice, she nevertheless decided to move to SkyBank the next day. Discuss the possible repercussions of Gurpreet's decision not to give BucksCorp any notice when she quit.

12. Marc and Sarah were long-time managers at an Ontario company—SPM Tech—that sold and serviced large information technology systems to major corporations and government. They were very successful at their jobs from the time they started in 1985. In 1999, SPM Tech asked Marc and Sarah to move to Alberta to open a western branch of the company's operations. Because Marc and Sarah were such key and senior employees, and because they were trusted, they were given complete independence to run the western operation as they saw fit. Marc and Sarah landed a number of major clients and amassed an extensive list of potential clients and contacts. They built up the business of the western operations to a very significant level between 1999 and 2004.

In 2005, Marc and Sarah were due to be considered for a very significant pay raise according to the pay system in place at SPM Tech. They also expected a considerable bonus based on the success of the western operations. Believing that these payments would be forthcoming, Marc and Sarah decided to buy a house together. When SPM Tech did not give Marc or Sarah a raise or a bonus in 2005, Marc and Sarah were furious and panicked because they could not afford the extravagant house they had bought. Marc and Sarah gave two weeks' notice of their resignation. On the same day they gave notice, they made arrangements to begin a computer business of their own, whose services were identical to those of SPM Tech. They also copied customer lists, diverted SPM Tech clients to their new business, and persuaded other SPM Tech employees in Alberta to join them. Finally, they told all of SPM Tech's customers that SPM Tech had been engaged in fraud, was going out of business, and would no longer have a western operation. SPM Tech did not have an employment contract with Marc and Sarah. Discuss what a court might think of Marc and Sarah's actions.

WEBLINKS

General Information

Department of Human Resources and Skills Development: Services for Business   www.hrsdc.gc.ca/en/gateways/business/menu.shtml#hrm

This site offers a wide variety of resources, links, and information for businesses in the areas of collective bargaining, workplace equity, labour standards, and occupational health and safety, among many others.

Canadian Human Rights Commission   www.chrc-ccdp.ca/employers/default-en.asp

This site provides information for federally regulated employers regarding their legal obligations and the activities of the CHRC under the *Canadian Human Rights Act* and the *Employment Equity Act*.

Pre-Employment Matters

Application Forms and Interview Guide   www.gov.sk.ca/shrc/ pdfs/applicationforms-interviewguide.pdf

This site offers employers a guide to application forms and interviews that comply with the *Saskatchewan Human Rights Code*.

Employer's Obligations and Worker Protection Legislation

Nova Scotia Department of Environment and Labour— Labour Standards   www.gov.ns.ca/enla/labstand/lstcode

This website offers information related to the minimum employment standards and the complaint process under the *Nova Scotia Labour Standards Code*.

OHRC—Employment and Human Rights   www. ohrc.on.ca/english/publications/hr-at-work.shtml

This Ontario Human Rights Commission site provides information on human rights in the workplace, with links to the complaint process and related documents.

ADDITIONAL RESOURCES FOR CHAPTER 26 ON THE COMPANION WEBSITE

(www.pearsoned.ca/mcinnes)

In addition to self-test multiple-choice, true-false, and short essay questions (all with immediate feedback), three additional Cases and Problems (with suggested answers), and links to useful Web destinations, the Companion Website provides the following resources for Chapter 26:

- Business Decision 26W—Mandatory Vacation Dates

Provincial Material

- **British Columbia:** Discrimination in the Workplace, Harassment in the Workplace, Privacy Rights, *Employment Standards Act*, Workers' Compensation, Occupational Health and Safety, Child Employment, Leave of Absence, Minimum Wage, Termination and Layoff, Worker Pay

- **Alberta:** Conditions of Employment, Constructive Dismissal, Duty to Accommodate, Employment Standards, Summary Dismissal, Termination and Layoffs, Workers' Compensation, Wrongful Dismissal

- **Manitoba and Saskatchewan:** Vicarious Liability of Employees, Vicarious Liability & Motor Vehicles, Employment Standards (Minimum Standards in Legislation), Human Rights, Same-Sex Partners and Discrimination, Workers' Compensation, Reasonable Notice (Statutory Minimums)

- **Ontario:** Bad Faith, Discrimination, Duty to Accommodate, Employment Equity, Employment Standards, Human Rights, Mandatory Retirement, Occupational Health, Pay Equity, Workers' Compensation

27 Organized Labour

OBJECTIVES

After completing this chapter, you should be able to:

1. Distinguish between individual employment and organized labour.

2. Understand the nature and function of collective bargaining.

3. Explain the collective bargaining process and the manner in which bargaining rights are acquired.

4. Describe provisions typically contained in a collective agreement.

5. Discuss the nature and function of grievance arbitration.

6. Identify three typical employee grievances in the context of organized labour.

7. Describe several remedies typically awarded by labour arbitrators.

8. Distinguish between the jurisdiction of labour arbitrators and courts.

9. Summarize four aspects of industrial conflict, and identify the relationships between them.

10. Discuss the role played by labour relations boards in the resolution of industrial conflict.

Not all work relationships are *individual* relationships between workers and their employers. In fact, much of the Canadian labour force is organized and governed *collectively*. Therefore, we distinguish *employment law* from *labour law*. As we saw in Chapter 26, employment law is the system of rules that governs the relationship between individuals and their employers. **Labour law** is the system of rules that governs collective relations between management, trade unions, their members, and the institutions involved in such relations.[1] It is the collective nature of organized labour that distinguishes it from other kinds of employment.

In this chapter, we will the investigate the features of organized labour that distinguish it from individual employment and consider their impact on the legal aspects of doing business. We will then consider collective bargaining and examine the trade union, the instrument through which collective bargaining is achieved. We will discuss the aim of bargaining through unions: the establishment and maintenance of a collective agreement. We will look at the system of grievance arbitration that is used in connection with disputes under a collective agreement, and conclude with a survey of the legal treatment of such industrial conflicts as strikes, picketing, lockouts, and boycotts.

labour law the system of rules that governs collective relations between management, trade unions, their members, and the institutions in such relations

COLLECTIVE BARGAINING

Nature and Function of Collective Bargaining

The practice of collective bargaining took root primarily during the industrial revolution in Britain. Between the late eighteenth and mid-nineteenth centuries, large populations stopped farming, abandoned rural life and agrarian society, and began working in cities for employers in factories and other industrial settings. Workplace conditions in these new industrial settings were often appalling, and wages were low. Practically slaves, individual employees had little or no power against the captains of industry. Only by banding together were workers able to exert meaningful influence on their employers. Collective action has evolved into a number of contemporary workplace practices, which are discussed throughout this chapter.

While collective power can be used to escape intolerable working conditions, it can also be used to illegitimately intimidate and coerce employers (consider, for example, the plight of a ship's captain when its crew members engage in a mutiny). At one time, participating in organized labour was a crime in Canada. Eventually, the right to organize gained legal recognition, first in Britain in 1867, and not long after in the United States. In 1872, Canada adopted the *Trade Union Act*, which decriminalized collective bargaining. Workers could no longer be threatened with jail sentences simply for trying to improve working conditions. But even then, there were roadblocks. Workers who tried to organize unions were initially confronted with economic reprisals from their employers. Today, trade unions are recognized as a legitimate way of empowering individual workers and enforcing their collective rights.

Labour law aims to find an appropriate balance between slavery and mutiny by imposing a system of rules around *collective bargaining*. **Collective bargaining** is the process through which an employer and a *trade union* seek to negotiate a *collective agreement*. A **trade union** is an organization of employees

collective bargaining is the process through which an employer and a trade union seek to negotiate a collective agreement

a trade union is an organization of employees formed to regulate the relations between the employer and the collective of employees

---

[1.] HW Arthurs, DD Carter, J Fudge, HJ Glasbeek & G Trudeau *Labour Law and Industrial Relations in Canada* 4th ed (1993) at 32.

a **collective agreement** is a document containing the terms of employment, as well as the rights and duties of the employer, the trade union, and the employees

formed to regulate the relations between the employer and a collective of employees. A **collective agreement** is a document containing the terms of employment, as well as the rights and duties of the employer, the trade union, and the employees. In most jurisdictions, the collective agreement of any organized group of workers can be enforced only through an arbitration procedure that has been started by either the employer or the union.

Collective bargaining rights are based on legislation. Industries regulated by the federal jurisdiction are governed by the *Canada Labour Code*.[2] Other industries are regulated by similar provincial legislation, each of which establishes a statutory tribunal usually known as a *labour relations board*. A **labour relations board** administers labour relations legislation within a jurisdiction.

a **labour relations board** administers labour relations legislation within a jurisdiction

Not every worker is entitled to the benefits and protections of collective bargaining. Each jurisdiction defines which employees are eligible to bargain collectively. Most jurisdictions use the term "employee" in the context of organized labour almost the same way as in the context of individual employment. However, there are differences in its meaning. For example, a corporate manager is usually an employee in the context of employment law, but not in the context of collective bargaining.

There is no definitive test to determine who is a manager and who is an employee, but factors typically considered include (i) the nature of the organization, (ii) the person's position in the organizational structure, (iii) the extent of the person's authority over other workers, and (iv) the proportion of that person's work that is non-managerial.[3] Managers are not the only workers who are ineligible to bargain collectively. Other workers excluded from the collective bargaining process may include public employees like firefighters and police, as well as such professional employees as doctors, dentists, and lawyers.

Acquisition of Bargaining Rights

Just as some employees are ineligible to bargain collectively, some employee organizations are not qualified to take part in the collective bargaining process. For example, many employee associations that organize primarily for social or recreational purposes are not qualified to bargain collectively. In addition to being qualified, the organization must be recognized by the jurisdiction's labour relations board as an *appropriate bargaining unit*. An **appropriate bargaining unit** is a group of workers recognized by the labour relations board as having a common interest in the outcome of negotiations. It is important to distinguish the bargaining unit—the constituency of workers—from its *bargaining agent*. The **bargaining agent** is the trade union that is legally recognized as representing the interests of the bargaining unit.

an **appropriate bargaining unit** is a group of workers recognized by the labour relations board as having a common interest in the outcome of negotiations

a **bargaining agent** is a trade union that is legally recognized as representing the interests of a bargaining unit

voluntary recognition occurs when the employer agrees to recognize a trade union as the bargaining agent for its employees

A trade union can become recognized as a bargaining agent for a particular bargaining unit through *voluntary recognition* by the employer. **Voluntary recognition** occurs when the employer agrees to recognize a trade union as the bargaining agent for its employees. Voluntary recognition occurs more frequently in industries where job duration is temporary, such as the construction industry. The downside of voluntary recognition is that such arrangements are often challenged by employees who do not want to be represented by the bargaining agent agreed to by the employer.

[2.] *Canada Labour Code*, RSC 1985, c L-2.

[3.] HW Arthurs *et al Labour Law and Industrial Relations in Canada* 4th ed (1993) at 214.

The more common method of acquiring bargaining rights is through a *membership drive*. The aim of a **membership drive** is to persuade a majority of employees in an appropriate bargaining unit to become union members. In most provinces, a union that secures the required number of members automatically becomes a **certified bargaining agent** and thereby acquires exclusive bargaining rights on behalf of the bargaining unit. In Alberta and Nova Scotia, however, the employees must vote for a union to be certified, regardless of the success of a membership drive. In other jurisdictions, a vote is necessary if the membership drive fails to recruit a majority of employees. And in some jurisdictions, employees who do not want to be represented by a particular union may, under some circumstances, complain to the labour relations board.

a **membership drive** aims to persuade a majority of employees in an appropriate bargaining unit to become union members

a **certified bargaining agent** acquires exclusive bargaining rights on behalf of the bargaining unit

Collective Bargaining Process

Once a union has acquired the bargaining rights for an appropriate bargaining unit, it must negotiate with the employer to reach a collective agreement that protects the collective interests of the employees. A business that does not want its employees to organize, or that does not want to deal with the employees' chosen bargaining agent, may try to delay the creation of a collective agreement. That tactic sometimes threatens the very survival of the union as the bargaining agent.

Once a bargaining unit has selected and certified its bargaining agent, that union has the exclusive right to bargain on behalf of its members. Even if a collective agreement has not yet been created, other unions cannot attempt to bargain on behalf of the employees in that bargaining unit, even if some of those employees would prefer to be represented by another bargaining agent. Likewise, individual employees are prohibited from bargaining for themselves with their employer.[4]

One controversial obligation in the collective bargaining process is the *duty to bargain in good faith*. The **duty to bargain in good faith** imposes an obligation on both parties to make every reasonable effort to successfully negotiate a collective agreement. An employer or a union that intentionally tries to thwart the negotiation process violates that duty. Some people believe that either party should be entitled to negotiate as forcefully as it wants, and that the point of collective bargaining is to match the economic strength of the collective against that of the employer. Remember, however, that the aim of labour law is to strike a balance between slavery and mutiny. The duty to bargain in good faith is a reminder that the entire process will break down if both parties feel free to engage in tactics that are inherently destructive of the employer–employee relationship. The duty has therefore been interpreted by most labour relations boards as an obligation about the manner in which negotiations are conducted, not about the actual content of particular proposals. The duty to bargain in good faith includes (i) the duty to meet with the other party, (ii) the duty to engage in full and informed discussion, (iii) the duty to supply information, and (iv) the duty to complete negotiations.[5] Case Brief 27.1 illustrates a violation of this duty.

the **duty to bargain in good faith** imposes an obligation on both parties to make every reasonable effort to successfully negotiate a collective agreement

---

[4.] *Syndicat catholique des employés des magasins de Québec Inc v Cie Paquet Ltée* (1959) 18 DLR (2d) 346 (SCC).

[5.] HW Arthurs *et al Labour Law and Industrial Relations in Canada* 4th ed (1993) at 259–63.

Governing Counsel of the University of Toronto v Royal Conservatory of Music Faculty Association
[1985] 11 CLRBR (NS) 219

The University of Toronto was negotiating its first collective agreement with the union representing the Royal Conservatory. The University wanted to streamline its administration. It announced its desire to sever the Conservatory from the University entirely so that it could be dealt with as a separate, independent corporate entity. The Royal Conservatory's faculty association did not believe that such a move would be in its best interests. It asked the University management team for further negotiations. The University responded by saying that the request was an intrusion on its management rights, insisted that severance was non-negotiable, and refused to discuss the matter further. The union then filed a complaint with the labour relations board, claiming that the University had failed to bargain in good faith.

The labour relations board held that the University's outright refusal to discuss the issue of separation constituted a violation of its duty to bargain in good faith. Although the board made it clear that the University was not duty-bound to agree to the union's proposal, it did have a duty to hear and consider the union's proposal. The University's unwillingness to entertain the union's proposal, let alone respond to the union with an explanation of why it was opposed to the proposal, was in breach of the duty to engage in full and informed discussion.

COLLECTIVE AGREEMENTS

There are three essential requirements for any collective agreement.

- It must be in writing.
- It must be entered into by the employer and a trade union with a signature indicating the agreement of each party.
- It must contain provisions respecting the terms and conditions of employment.[6]

Although it is tempting to think of the collective agreement as a multi-party contract, there are several important differences between collective agreements and contracts. Collective agreements are enforceable not by common law but by labour legislation. Furthermore, labour legislation in most jurisdictions dictates the inclusion of particular statutory provisions that make the character of a collective agreement quite different from a common law contract. Some authors have suggested that the collective agreement is a kind of labour relations "constitution."[7] The following are some of the standard provisions.

Strike and Lockout Provisions

To promote industrial stability, most jurisdictions in Canada require collective agreements to prohibit strikes and lockouts while the collective agreement is binding. Consequently, some labour practices that would otherwise be legitimate are actually unlawful. Consider Business Decision 27.1.

[6.] G Adams *Canadian Labour Law* (1985) at 671.

[7.] HW Arthurs *et al Labour Law and Industrial Relations in Canada* 4th ed (1993) at 676.

BUSINESS DECISION 27.1

The Lockout Provision[8]

To cut costs and increase plant efficiency, Kerasic and Sons Meat Packing Ltd attempted to shorten its work week by one day to create a four-day work week. The International Brotherhood of Meat Packers filed a grievance on behalf of its employees, claiming that the attempt to alter the traditional work week was unlawful.

The labour relations board concluded that such an alteration was in breach of the mandatory provision in the collective agreement, which prohibited strikes or lockouts during a binding collective agreement. According to the board, the effect of changing to a four-day work week was to prevent workers from working on the fifth day, which is, in essence, an attempt to lock out workers on that day.

Questions for Discussion

1. Do you agree with the labour relations board?
2. How might management have achieved its desired result without causing a grievance?

Grievance Provisions

Since strikes and lockouts are prohibited during a collective agreement, most jurisdictions in Canada set out other mechanisms for resolving disputes about the interpretation, application, administration, or alleged violation of a collective agreement. The most common mechanism is the process of *grievance arbitration*. Some collective agreements have a very detailed grievance provision that sets out the entire procedure step-by-step. Others are completely silent on the issue. Labour relations boards sometimes amend arbitration provisions that are inadequate and, in some cases, impose a statutory "model arbitration" clause. Therefore, business managers who employ organized labour should include in their collective agreement a procedure they like (for example, a provision that requires arbitration decisions to be released within a specified period of time).

Union Security Clauses

Every jurisdiction permits the inclusion of a *union security clause*. A **union security clause** states how a union will be paid—whether by its membership or otherwise. Usually a union is remunerated through the payment of union dues. Unions typically adopt one of these three structures.

- First, the union might decide to operate as a *closed shop*. A **closed shop** is a requirement that management will not hire anyone who is not already a member of that union.
- A second approach is a *union shop*. A **union shop** requires a person to become a union member before starting their employment.
- A third approach, using the *Rand formula*, is the *dues shop*. A **dues shop**, sometimes called an agency shop, requires a person who is hired to pay union dues, but does not require that person to join the union.

In some jurisdictions, an employer is required to include a union security clause in a collective agreement if the union requests it. To ignore such a

a union security clause states how a union will be paid

a closed shop requires that management hire only people who are already union members

a union shop requires a person to become a union member before starting their employment

a dues shop, sometimes called an agency shop, requires a person who is hired to pay union dues, but does not require that person to join the union

---

[8.] *CE Lummus Canada Ltd* [1983] OLRB Rep Sept 1504.

request is considered to be a breach of the duty to bargain in good faith and is grounds for complaint to the labour relations board. Concept Summary 27.1 reviews these three approaches.

CONCEPT SUMMARY 27.1

Union Security: The Means by Which a Union Will Be Remunerated

Closed shop	Employers cannot hire a person unless they are already a union member in good standing.
Union shop	Employers cannot hire a person unless they promise to become a union member in good standing when starting employment.
Dues shop	Employers cannot hire a person unless they promise to pay union dues (though actual union membership is optional).

GRIEVANCE ARBITRATION

In order to understand the arbitration process, it is important to be aware of the four general categories of labour disputes that can arise: *recognition disputes*, *jurisdictional disputes*, *interest disputes*, and *rights disputes*.

Recognition disputes typically relate to the acquisition of bargaining rights and especially to the appropriateness of the bargaining unit. If a bargaining agent purports to represent a group of employees, the employer may dispute the bargaining agent's right to do so, for example, on grounds of the scope or terms of a voluntary recognition agreement.

Jurisdictional disputes can arise in a number of different ways. For example, there may be a dispute as to whether particular workers come under the jurisdiction of federal or provincial labour laws. This kind of situation can arise in areas like shipping, where many workers are under federal jurisdiction, but workers on the wharves, or in warehouses nearby, may be under provincial jurisdiction. There may also be a dispute as to whether an arbitrator or a labour board has jurisdiction to decide a particular substantive issue.

Interest disputes are not defined by the nature of the dispute, but rather by the nature of the process for resolving the dispute. In other words, under an interest dispute, a mediator or an arbitrator may hear presentations from the employer and the workers and then informally attempt to reach a resolution to the dispute through compromise. This is not strictly a legal process.

Rights disputes are traditional forms of disputes as to, for example, the respective rights and obligations of the parties under a collective agreement or labour laws. Unlike interest disputes, rights disputes are resolved through a stricter form of adjudication, including the arbitration process described in the next sections.

Arbitration Process

Most collective agreements contain an *internal* procedure for dealing with employee grievances. In addition, labour law provides an *external* method of resolving such disputes: *grievance arbitration*. **Grievance arbitration** is an external method of resolving labour disputes that cannot be resolved by the parties alone. Usually the process begins with the union notifying the employer of the dispute and their attempt to resolve it internally. If a settlement cannot be

grievance arbitration is an external method of resolving labour disputes that cannot be resolved by the parties alone

reached between the employee and management, the parties will engage in arbitration.

It is important to distinguish between (i) disputes brought before an arbitration panel, and (ii) disputes brought before the labour relations board. The labour relations board usually hears disputes about the violation of labour relations legislation. An arbitration panel or sole arbitrator hears and resolves disputes about the collective agreement. The role of arbitration is therefore to resolve a dispute between employee and management under an existing collective agreement.

The parties to a collective agreement are jointly responsible for appointing an arbitrator. If the matter can be resolved by a sole arbitrator, the parties must agree to that person's selection. If a panel of arbitrators is required, each party selects its own arbitrator to sit as a member on the panel, and then the parties jointly select a third member to chair the panel. The cost of the proceedings, including the expense of the arbitrators, is generally shared equally by both parties. Management and unions must therefore be careful to budget for these expenses.

If the collective agreement is insufficient to resolve the dispute, arbitrators look to outside sources, including (i) the traditional rules of interpretation, (ii) the labour legislation itself, and (iii) *arbitral jurisprudence*. **Arbitral jurisprudence** is the body of existing arbitration decisions. Although arbitrators do not strictly adhere to the doctrine of precedent (that is, follow decisions from earlier cases), previous arbitral decisions often play an important role in decision making.[9] Usually, an arbitrator follows a previous decision that is relevant unless they think it is wrong. Finally, an arbitrator may apply many of the principles of equity.

To determine whether the grievance is a proper subject for arbitration, some arbitrators allow the parties to make preliminary submissions before the formal hearing begins. An employer can make several arguments to try to end the grievance before the matter is formally heard. It may, for instance, argue that (i) the grievor is not a person covered under the collective agreement, (ii) the issue falls outside the scope of the collective agreement, or (iii) the submission of the grievance fell outside of the required time limits.[10]

arbitral jurisprudence is the body of existing arbitration decisions

Typical Grievances

Business people who will be operating in an organized labour environment need to know about the most typical grievances. We briefly consider three basic grounds of complaint: *discipline and discharge*, *seniority*, and *compensation*.

Discipline and Discharge

Like individual employment contracts, collective agreements often say how employee misconduct will be treated. One main difference is that disciplinary procedures are generally spelled out in the collective agreement. Disciplinary measures usually include suspensions, formal warnings, and sometimes demotion. Extreme misconduct leads to discharge. Another difference is that many collective agreements provide that the employer is allowed to discipline or discharge an employee only if there is just cause. Where such a provision exists, an arbitrator will interfere with the employer's handling of a disciplinary matter

---

[9.] The doctrine of precedent was discussed in Chapter 2.

[10.] HW Arthurs *et al Labour Law and Industrial Relations in Canada* 4th ed (1993) at 332.

only if the arbitrator believes that cause was lacking. Where a collective agreement does not contain such a provision, arbitrators will not usually interfere with an employer's decision to take action. For more leeway, business managers should therefore try to avoid a just cause provision.

It is sometimes difficult to tell whether an employer's particular conduct is of a disciplinary nature. *Demotion* is a typical example. **Demotion** occurs when an employer transfers an employee to a lower-rated job. Often employers demote employees due to their misconduct. In this context, demotion is a form of discipline and is subject to review if the collective agreement contains a just cause provision. What if an employee is demoted due to their incompetence? This is generally seen as a non-disciplinary demotion and is not subject to review by an arbitrator. Sometimes the line between disciplinary and non-disciplinary demotion is difficult to draw, as You Be the Judge 27.1 demonstrates.

demotion occurs when an employer transfers an employee to a lower-rated job

---

YOU BE THE JUDGE 27.1

Demotion[11]

Hilda had worked for a unionized bakery as a cashier for six months. Although she received some training from the bakery manager in handling cash, she made many errors on the deposit slips. Something seemed suspicious. Rather than warning Hilda about the possible consequences of continued errors, the bakery's management decided to see if she continued to mishandle cash. She did. Instead of making a fuss about it, the bakery's management simply demoted her to a packaging clerk. The bakery claimed that the demotion was non-disciplinary in nature and was purely a response to her inability to competently perform the job of cashier. Hilda felt that her demotion was disciplinary since the bakery's management had obviously formed the wrong impression about her and was suspicious that she was trying to steal cash. Consequently, Hilda decided to grieve the bakery's decision.

Questions for Discussion

1. If you were asked to arbitrate this dispute, how would you characterize the demotion?
2. What additional facts might you wish to know before deciding?

Seniority

seniority grants preferences to certain employees based on their accumulated length of service

A complaint that often arises in grievance arbitration is that an employer has acted without proper regard to an employee's *seniority*. The concept of seniority is central to virtually every collective agreement.[12] **Seniority** grants preferences to certain employees based on their accumulated length of service. Not only does seniority define who is eligible for certain monetary benefits, it also provides a way of determining which employee is entitled to job promotion and which employee is subject to a transfer or lay-off. Seniority provisions in collective agreements are usually one of two types: (i) *non-competitive clauses* and, (ii) *competitive clauses*.[13] **Non-competitive clauses** require seniority to be the determining factor, as long as the more senior person is competent. **Competitive clauses** require seniority to be the determining factor only when the skill and ability of the competing employees are relatively equal.

Many collective agreements contemplate *bumping*. **Bumping** occurs when a senior employee who is about to be laid off is allowed to invoke their senior-

non-competitive clauses require seniority to be the determining factor, as long as the more senior person is competent

competitive clauses require seniority to be the determining factor only when the skill and ability of the competing employees are relatively equal

bumping occurs when a senior employee who is about to be laid off is allowed to invoke their seniority and replace a more junior employee in a junior position

---

11. *SP Bakery Co and Teamsters Local 464* [1997] BCDLA 500.15.40.45-06 A-139/97.

12. DJM Brown & D Beatty, *Canadian Labour Arbitration* 3d ed (2000) 6:000.

13. HW Arthurs *et al*, *Labour Law and Industrial Relations in Canada* 4th ed (1993) at 343.

ity and replace an employee in a junior position. In many instances, this sets off a chain reaction. The junior person who was just bumped asserts their seniority against a still more junior person, and so on. Most collective agreements either explicitly or implicitly provide that an employee who has elected to bump into a lower position does not forfeit the right to return to their previous job if it is eventually recalled. Collective agreements that include bumping rights usually carry a minimum requirement that the senior person be capable of doing the junior person's job. However, if the junior position requires a specialized skill, the senior employee is usually entitled to the necessary training to learn that skill.

Business managers involved in negotiating a collective agreement should realize that employees may want to use the bumping procedure in reverse. **Bumping up** is an application of seniority rights in the context of promotion. Prudent business managers will not want a system of promotion that is based solely on seniority. To avoid that risk, management should negotiate an exclusive right to make appointments in a manner that applies seniority rights differently in promotions than in lay-offs.[14]

bumping up is an application of seniority rights in the context of promotion

Compensation

Compensation is a ground of complaint that often leads to grievance arbitration. Like the individual employment scenario, typical complaints involve (i) equal pay for equal work, (ii) unilateral change in wages, (iii) overtime pay, and (iv) entitlement to benefits. One issue that arises more often in the context of organized labour is *retroactive pay*. **Retroactive pay** is money that is owed by the employer to the employee as a result of a collective agreement that is deemed to come into effect some time before the date of its creation. The law generally presumes that wage increases apply retroactively. Although most employers are willing to comply with collective agreements for retroactive wages in the form of back-pay, disputes often arise about whether employees are also entitled to other benefits as of that date. Traditionally, arbitrators have drawn a distinction between monetary and non-monetary provisions.[15] Therefore, they usually require clear language that expressly includes benefits before awarding them retroactively.[16]

retroactive pay is money that is owed by the employer to the employee as a result of a collective agreement that is deemed to come into effect some time before the date of its creation

A business sometimes has to decide whether to offer back-pay to people who were employees at the time the collective agreement retroactively became effective, but ceased to be employees before the agreement was signed.

Arbitration Awards

Arbitrators often enjoy the ability to select from amongst a range of remedies. Three remedies are especially important.

- **Damages:** An arbitrator may award compensatory *damages* to a party that has suffered a loss. We examined the general rules of compensatory damages in Chapters 3 and 12. We also examined the issue in the employment context in Chapter 26.

[14.] DMJ Brown & DM Beatty *Canadian Labour Arbitration* 3d ed (2000) at 6:2340.

[15.] *Onesimus Community Resources* (1994) 39 LAC (4th) 289 (Thorne); *Sturgeon General Hospital* (1974) 6 LAC (2d) 360 (Taylor).

[16.] *Toronto Hospital* (1995) 49 LAC (4th) 1 (Thorne); *York Regional Board of Education* (1990) 11 LAC (4th) 345 (Marszewski).

a compliance order usually requires a specific obligation in the collective agreement to be fulfilled or a particular course of conduct to be brought to an end

- **Compliance order:** In appropriate circumstances, an arbitrator may grant a declaration of a party's rights by way of a *compliance order*. A **compliance order** usually requires a specific obligation in the collective agreement to be fulfilled or a particular course of conduct to be brought to an end.

- **Reinstatement:** An arbitrator may have the power to *reinstate* employees who were discharged without cause. Similarly, unless labour legislation or the collective agreement provides otherwise, arbitrators generally have the power to substitute a lesser penalty in the case of a suspension or discharge.[17]

rectification the process by which a contract is rewritten to better reflect the actual agreement contemplated by the parties

An arbitrator's authority to award remedies is, however, limited by both the labour legislation and the terms of the collective agreement. Consequently, if the parties want to allow arbitrators broad power in resolving grievances, they must consider this in negotiating the collective agreement. That is true, for example, with respect to the remedy of *rectification*. **Rectification** is the process by which a contract is rewritten to better reflect the actual agreement contemplated by the parties. According to the Supreme Court of Canada, arbitrators do not have the power to rectify a collective agreement unless that agreement expressly gives them the power to do so.[18]

Enforcement of Arbitration Awards

Although arbitrators have the power to order awards, they do not have the power to enforce them. Labour legislation in each jurisdiction therefore provides that arbitration orders are to be filed with the courts and enforced in the same way as a judicial order.

INDUSTRIAL CONFLICT

Disputes under a collective agreement are usually resolved through grievance arbitration. However, if the parties reach an impasse before establishing a collective agreement or after it is no longer in effect, one party may decide to use economic pressure to persuade the other to make the appropriate concessions. The most common practice used by employees is a *strike*, while employers often respond by *locking out* their employees. Strikes and lockouts sometimes lead to secondary activities, such as *picketing* and *boycotts*. We finish this chapter by briefly considering strikes, lockouts, picketing, and boycotts. We will discuss both lawful and unlawful industrial action.

Strikes

a strike is a cessation of work, resulting from a concerted activity, that has a common purpose to limit or restrict output

The term *strike* is not consistently defined across Canada. Most statutory definitions of a **strike** require that there be (i) a cessation of work, (ii) resulting from a concerted activity, (iii) that has a common purpose, (iv) designed to limit or restrict output. Some jurisdictions such as Alberta, Manitoba, and Nova Scotia require a fifth element: (v) the common purpose is to compel the employer to accept certain terms and conditions of employment.

[17.] *Heusis v New Brunswick Electric Power Commission* (1979) 98 DLR (3d) 622 (SCC).

[18.] *Port Arthur Shipbuilding Co v Arthurs* (1968) 70 DLR (2d) 283 (SCC).

Although employees who go on strike usually do so in a clear way, less obvious activities may also constitute a strike. Consider Case Brief 27.2.

CASE BRIEF 27.2

Re British Columbia Terminal Elevator Operators' Assn and Grain Workers' Union Local 333 (1994) 23 CLRBR (2d) 286 (Can LRB)

Due to a decline in shipping demand, the management of the Saskatchewan Wheat Pool decided that it had to temporarily stop operating its night shift. This resulted in a lay-off of 10 employees. In response to the lay-offs, other members of the Grain Workers' Union Local 333 were instructed to refuse to work overtime. According to the union, the refusal to work overtime was justified under the collective agreement, which expressly stated that overtime shifts were voluntary. Management, on the other hand, argued that the refusal

to work overtime was a concerted effort to stop working with the aim of limiting the Wheat Pool's output.

In determining whether the refusal to work overtime constituted an unlawful strike, the labour relations board held that a continued concerted refusal to work overtime would ultimately result in the employer's failure to fulfill its loading commitments. It therefore held that the refusal to work overtime was an unlawful form of strike. It ordered union members to cease and desist in their overtime refusal policy.

Although striking is a fundamental practice in the labour movement, neither the common law nor the Canadian *Charter of Rights and Freedoms* expressly identifies a general right to strike.[19] If there is a right to strike, it is limited to those circumstances in which striking is not otherwise prohibited under the governing labour legislation.

A strike is generally lawful if it is designed to gain economic objectives and if it starts after the statute's compulsory conciliation procedures have been exhausted. In contrast, a strike typically is unlawful if it (i) occurs while a collective agreement is in force, (ii) takes place during a statutory freeze period, (iii) begins before certain bargaining procedures have been exhausted, (iv) is designed to gain sympathy and bring pressure on a secondary employer, or (v) is undertaken for the purpose of a political protest.[20]

Most jurisdictions require union members to vote before striking. Usually, a strike is permitted only if a majority votes in favour of striking. It is usually necessary for the union to give notice of the vote to the employer and, in some cases, to the ministry of labour. Typical notice periods do not exceed 72 hours.

Although workers are sometimes free to strike, they may not have any guarantee that they will be able to return to their jobs afterwards.

- Some strikes put employers out of business permanently. When that occurs, there are no such jobs to return to.

- In other instances, some employees may lose their positions because their union could not negotiate positions for them under the new collective agreement.

- Even if a business can withstand the financial hardship of a strike, employees sometimes cannot. Although some unions provide strike pay to their members, some employees cannot afford to live on that lower amount and are therefore forced to look for other jobs.

[19.] As explained in Chapter 1, the *Charter* does not contain protection for economic or property rights.

[20.] HW Arthurs *et al, Labour Law and Industrial Relations in Canada* 4th ed (1993) at 276.

- Alternatively, rather than looking for a new job, some workers are willing to abandon the strike and return to their job.

In most jurisdictions, if an employee's position remains intact after a strike has ended, that employee has the right to be reinstated. But the right to reinstatement is not absolute. Employers have grounds to discharge an employee during a strike if the worker engaged in serious misconduct, such as sabotage against company property or violence on a picket line.

Lockouts

a lockout occurs when an employer closes the workplace, or refuses to continue to employ its workers, with the intention of compelling them to agree to certain conditions of employment

The flipside of an employee strike is an employer *lockout*. A **lockout** occurs when an employer closes the workplace, or refuses to continue to employ its workers, with the intention of compelling them to agree to certain conditions of employment. A number of high-profile lockout situations have occurred in major league sports, including the National Hockey League. Note that there is a subjective element to the definition of a lockout. For the business closure to be classified as a lockout, the employer must have intended to use it to compel its employees to agree to its terms. In some instances of industrial conflict, it is hard to tell what the employer's intentions are in shutting down operations. Industrial conflict often coincides with economic hardship for the business. The employer is free to make sound business decisions to suspend or cease operations altogether, and such decisions must be distinguished from closures designed to force concessions from a union. Consequently, if a business can show that its decision to shut down was irrevocable, it is better able to argue that it did not shut down with the intention of forcing an agreement.[21]

As is true of strikes, some lockouts are lawful, while others are not. The strategy of compelling workers to accept the employer's terms is completely legitimate if it is carried out within the statutory requirements that govern lockouts. If the lockout (i) begins only after the negotiation and conciliation procedures prescribed by statute have been exhausted, and (ii) does not involve any other unlawful activity, a business's management team can choose to shut down operations to achieve its bargaining position.

Picketing

picketing involves the presence of one or more persons, the communication of information, and the intention to secure a sympathetic response from some third party

Picketing is used as a response to a variety of situations including strikes, lockouts, and boycotts. **Picketing** involves:

- the presence of one or more people
- the communication of information
- the intention to secure a sympathetic response from some third party[22]

Well-meaning picketers try to distribute information in a peaceful way to convince customers, other companies, the employees of other companies, and even potential replacement workers to support their strike. Picketers often ask people not to cross picket lines. If successful, that tactic interferes with the

---

21. *Doral Construction Ltd* [1980] OLRB Rep Mar 310; *Westinghouse Canada Ltd* [1980] OLRB Rep Apr 577.

22. AWR Carrothers "Recent Developments in the Tort Law of Picketing" (1957) 35 *Can Bar Rev* 1005.

employer's ability to carry on business in spite of the strike. Unfortunately, while picketing is usually a peaceful communicative process, discussions between picketers and those nearby occasionally get emotionally charged and even violent.

Picketing is generally governed by the courts, because most issues that arise in a picketing dispute are based in either criminal or tort law. For example, under section 423 of the *Criminal Code*, it is a crime to surround or watch a workplace for the purpose of compelling a person to do, or refrain from doing, something lawful.[23] Similarly, picketing may violate the law of tort.[24] There are several possibilities. Since picketing is a form of communication, picketers must be careful with the message they are sending—false statements about an employer may be defamatory. When picketing behaviour leads to physical injury, picketers may be sued for either battery or negligence. Sometimes, when picketing interferes with another's property rights, picketers can be sued for the torts of nuisance or trespass. For this reason, many picketers are careful to picket on public property, where an employer has little recourse unless the picketers are actually blocking a public passage way.

Picketers expose themselves to additional liability when they engage in the practice of *secondary picketing*. **Secondary picketing** exerts pressure on a business indirectly by threatening or imposing sanctions against some third party. When picketers exert secondary pressure, they exceed the primary purpose of picketing, namely the peaceful communication of information about the strike. Picketing of this sort is prohibited by statute in some provinces.[25] As well, it sometimes gives rise to a cause of action in tort for *inducing breach of contract*.[26] When picketers intentionally induce a breach of contract, they wrongfully interfere with the economic relations between the employer and a third party. If the courts find that the aim of secondary picketing is not merely to communicate information but to induce a breach of contract, they may issue an order that brings the picketing to an end. Third-party businesses caught in the crossfire of an industrial conflict must often protect their own business interests, as Ethical Perspective 27.1 illustrates.

secondary picketing indirectly exerts pressure on a business by threatening or imposing sanctions against some third party

---

23. *Criminal Code*, RSC 1985, c C-46 (Can).

24. The torts mentioned in this paragraph were discussed in detail in Part 2 of this book.

25. In *RWDSU Local 558 v Pepsi-Cola Canada Beverages (West) Ltd* (2002) 208 DLR (4th) 385, the Supreme Court of Canada affirmed that (unless prohibited by statute) secondary picketing is generally lawful, as long as it does not involve tortious or criminal conduct. Asked to determine whether picketing the homes of Pepsi-Cola's management was unlawful, the Court applied the "wrongful action" approach, focusing on the character and effects of the activity rather than merely its location. The Court held that the conduct of union members amounted to disorderly conduct, accompanied by threats of harm, in an effort to make members of Pepsi's management refrain from doing what they had every right to do. Given its tortious nature, the conduct of the union members was held to be unlawful.

26. The tort of inducing breach of contract was discussed in Chapter 5.

ETHICAL PERSPECTIVE 27.1

Brett Pontiac Buick GMC Ltd v NABET Local 920 (1990) 94 NSR (2d) (SC AD)

During an industrial conflict, a radio station owned by CHUM FM locked out its employees, who were members of the National Association of Broadcast Employees and Technicians, Local 920. In response, the union members decided to picket in front of the business premises of one of CHUM's more important advertising clients, Brett Pontiac Buick. One day during the lockout, 15 picketers showed up at the dealership with union placards and positioned themselves in front of the driveway that provided customers with access to the premises. They began distributing pamphlets that referred to the dispute between the employer and the union, and concluded in bold print: "DON'T BUY FROM BRETT PONTIAC."

The owner of the dealership also received a letter that stated, "I have been advised that your Company continues to advertise on C-100 FM radio despite requests by illegally locked-out employees that you refrain from doing so. It is my intention to call upon the 2500 inside and outside postal workers in this area to boycott all companies who continue to support the Toronto-based CHUM radio in this illegal lockout, through their advertising. If I do not hear from you within the next seven days your Company will be included on the boycott list. I trust that you will decide to withdraw all ads until this labour dispute is settled."

The owner of Brett Pontiac did not take kindly to this letter, nor to several other attempts by the picketers to interfere with its business. Brett Pontiac applied for an injunction against the union to prevent it from interfering with its business operations.

Questions for Consideration

1. Have the union members exceeded the morally permissible bounds of free expression?

2. Can you think of a more ethical, though equally effective, strategy for the union members to achieve their goals?

Boycotts

a **boycott** occurs when people refuse to interact with a business, or to handle goods that are associated with that business, as support for a collective bargaining position

As the *Brett Pontiac* case illustrates, boycotts are often created by way of secondary picketing. A **boycott** occurs when people refuse to interact with a business, or to handle goods that are associated with that business, as support for a collective bargaining position. Although a boycott may involve picketing, it need not. Some boycotts are carried out through advertising or telephone campaigns. Regardless of the manner of the campaign, boycotts are economically dangerous. By definition, boycotts interfere with the interests of parties who are not directly involved in the industrial conflict. In some instances, businesses are forced to suffer financially even though they have absolutely nothing to do with the labour dispute. Not only are innocent third-party businesses affected by a boycott, such campaigns also cause harm to the employer—often even greater harm than would be caused by direct picketing.

The economic effect of strikes, lockouts, picketing, and boycotts has led to a response by both federal and provincial governments to temporarily revoke the right of some public sector groups to strike. In some instances, this has even led to wage control.[27] A number of jurisdictions have recently felt the need to invoke back-to-work legislation that forces workers to return to their jobs while their labour disputes are settled through compulsory arbitration. These rather drastic measures demonstrate governments' desire to keep the economy productive. Occasionally, when a large enough sector of organized labour is involved in an industrial dispute, there is a clash of wills. On such occasions, the matter is no longer merely a legal dispute between a business and its employees, but a political battle involving the public interest.

[27.] AWR Carrothers *Collective Bargaining in Canada* (1986) at 108–25.

CONCEPT SUMMARY 27.2

Managing Risk in Association with Industrial Conflict

- If your workers strike, consider your ability to argue that the strike is unlawful because, for example, the workers have not exhausted bargaining procedures, or because the purpose of the strike is political protest. Be aware of vote and notice requirements too.

- If you wish to lock out employees to achieve your bargaining position, ensure that you comply with statutory requirements.

- If your workers engage in picketing and ask other workers at your business not to cross the picket lines, consider whether you could argue that the other workers are engaging in an unlawful strike. Monitor pickets for any evidence that workers are engaged in criminal or tortious conduct. Watch for evidence of secondary picketing that may give rise to a cause of action against the workers in tort.

- Have a strategy in place for dealing with strikes, pickets, lockouts, and boycotts. For example, you can protect your business by training management staff to be able to perform a wide variety of tasks. This can be essential to the survival of your business in the event that unionized workers go on strike.

CHAPTER SUMMARY

Not all work relations are individual relationships. A substantial portion of Canadian industry is organized and governed collectively under labour legislation. Labour law is the system of rules that govern collective relations between management, trade unions, their members, and the institutions in such relations. The collective nature of organized labour distinguishes it from other kinds of work.

Labour law aims to find an appropriate balance between employer and employee objectives by imposing a system of rules on collective bargaining. Collective bargaining is the process by which an employer and a trade union seek to negotiate a collective agreement. A collective agreement is a document containing the terms of employment and the rights and duties of the employer, the trade union, and the employees. Not every worker is entitled to the benefits and protections of collective bargaining. Each jurisdiction defines those employees who are eligible to bargain as a collective and those who are not.

In addition to being eligible, employees who wish to bargain collectively must be recognized by the jurisdiction's labour relations board as an appropriate bargaining unit. Once recognized as such, the bargaining unit must choose a trade union to act as its bargaining agent. As soon as its bargaining agent has been selected and certified, that union has the exclusive right to bargain on behalf of its members. As its bargaining agent, the trade union must try to represent the interests of all of the employees in the bargaining unit. One of the more controversial obligations in the collective bargaining process is the duty to bargain in good faith. This duty imposes an obligation on both parties to make every reasonable effort to successfully negotiate a collective agreement.

Most businesses that employ organized labour put into place an internal procedure to deal with employee grievances. In addition to the internal grievance procedure that is usually stipulated in collective agreements, labour law provides an external method of resolving such disputes through a process known as grievance arbitration. Grievance arbitration is the final stage in the attempt to resolve an industrial dispute under an ongoing collective agreement. Typical grievances issues are discipline and discharge, seniority, and compensation. Disciplinary measures include suspensions, formal warnings, and demotion. The concept of seniority is central to almost every collective agreement. Not only does seniority define who is eligible for certain monetary benefits, it also provides a way for determining which employee is entitled to job promotion and which employee is subject to a transfer or lay-off. Typical complaints about compensation concern equal pay for equal work, a unilateral change in wages, overtime pay, entitlement to benefits, and retroactive pay.

The authority of an arbitrator to award remedies is limited in scope both by the labour legislation and by the terms of the collective agreement. Arbitrators usually have the power to award damages, issue compliance orders, and reinstate employees to their previous positions. Although arbitrators have the power to order such awards, they do not have the power to enforce them. The enforcement of arbitration awards is carried out by a court of competent jurisdiction.

When industrial disputes arise before or during the negotiation of a collective agreement, one party may decide to use economic pressure to convince the other party to make the appropriate concessions. The most common practice used by employees is a strike. Employers often respond in such situations by locking out their employees. Strikes and lockouts sometimes lead to secondary activities, such as picketing and boycotts. A strike or lockout is generally lawful if it is designed to gain economic objectives and if it is timely. Although workers are permitted to strike in certain circumstances, they do not always enjoy a guarantee that they will be able to return to their previous jobs afterwards. Under some conditions, an employer is permitted to shut down operations to convince employees to accept its bargaining position. In extreme cases, an industrial conflict may force a business to shut down operations permanently. Picketing is a mechanism used in response to a variety of situations including strikes, lockouts, and boycotts. Secondary picketing exerts pressure on a business indirectly by threatening or imposing sanctions against some third party. Boycotts interfere with the interests of parties who are not directly involved in the industrial conflict. Businesses that are the victim of secondary picketing and boycotts often have recourse in the courts.

Review Questions

1. Distinguish labour law from employment law. On what basis can organized labour be differentiated from other kinds of work?

2. Do all employees have collective bargaining rights? Does it matter what industry they are employed in? How are collective bargaining rights acquired?

3. Describe the test that is used to determine whether a person is a manager or an employee.

4. How does a trade union become recognized as the bargaining agent for a particular bargaining unit?

5. What is the first step when a union and management reach an impasse while negotiating a collective agreement?

6. What are the different elements of the duty to bargain in good faith? Why does labour law impose such a duty?

7. List the three essential requirements of an enforceable collective agreement. Are there other provisions that one of the parties can insist on including?

8. How does Canadian legislation differ from that in other countries in its treatment of strikes and lockouts?

9. Name and describe examples of three structures that a union might adopt in a workplace.

10. Failing an internal resolution, what can the two parties do to resolve an employee grievance? Outline the steps typically involved in this process.

11. Define "arbitral jurisprudence." How much deference must a labour arbitrator show to previous arbitration decisions?

12. Give three examples of disciplinary measures that an employer may take in the context of organized labour.

13. Describe the industrial practice known as "bumping." Distinguish between "bumping-up" and "bumping-down."

14. Provide examples of typical compensation complaints. How can managers prevent disputes over retroactive pay or benefits?

15. Do labour arbitrators and labour relations boards generally have remedial powers similar to those of judges? Be specific. Is it possible to expand or limit the authority of labour arbitrators? What about labour relations boards?

16. What factors should a panel of arbitrators consider when exercising its power to issue a "compliance order"?

17. List the four requirements common to most statutory definitions of a strike. What is a fifth requirement in some jurisdictions?

18. What is the defining feature of a lawful employer lockout? Why can this factor sometimes be difficult to isolate?

19. Outline the three elements that together define lawful picketing. In what venue is the resolution of picketing disputes generally achieved?

20. Define "secondary picketing" and "boycotts." Under what circumstances are these practices legal?

Cases and Problems

1. Local 54 has retained James Love to represent it in a grievance against Dilated Peoples Optical Inc. The union is grieving the employer's decision to exclude from the bargaining unit the position of dilation officer—which the employer decided to move from Edmonton to San Francisco. Dilated Peoples argued that dilation officers are excluded from the bargaining unit based on the collective agreement, which specifies that only staff "employed in the offices located in Edmonton" are to be included in the bargaining unit. Local 54 responded with the argument that the words used in the collective agreement were

meant to be descriptive, rather than limiting. Which interpretation do you think should prevail? Explain your reasoning.

2. Scrappy Aluminum Inc has asked the labour relations board to direct its employee union, Local 233, to sign a collective agreement. The terms of that agreement, set out in a memorandum of settlement, received the support of an overwhelming majority of union members in a recent vote. While Scrappy alleges that the agreement is all but signed, Local 233 holds a different view. It claims that the agreement has not yet been completed, in part due to a lack of understanding between the parties about a proposed employee dental plan. It seems that the majority of Local 233 members need orthodontic work, which is not explicitly included under "dental benefits." Therefore, despite the results of its recent member vote, Local 233 would like to see a further clarification of this issue before signing the collective agreement. Consequently, Local 233 insists that a collective agreement has not yet been reached. You have been called upon to decide the validity of Scrappy's request. In your opinion, did the parties achieve a collective agreement? Was Local 233's refusal to sign the collective agreement a violation of its duty to bargain in good faith? Support your position.

3. Employees at Rasta Pasta Ltd, represented by Local 111, have continued to work following the expiry of their collective agreement. Management at Rasta Pasta quickly drafted a short-term agreement to act as a bridge between the initial collective agreement and a future collective agreement to be negotiated by both parties. Both parties signed the short-term agreement. Although the issue was not specifically contemplated by either party in the agreement, Local 111 has recently tried to compel Rasta Pasta to continue certain payroll deductions in a manner set out in the initial collective agreement. Rasta Pasta's accountant has been consulted and has indicated that there are negative tax implications associated with continuing such deductions. As a member of Rasta Pasta's risk management team, you have been asked to determine how best to deal with this situation, given that the specific clause in question was not contemplated by either party when the short-term agreement was signed. Use your good judgment and sound risk management principles to generate a response that will satisfy Local 111. How might this problem have been prevented?

4. Local 393, a trade union representing employees of an Internet start-up company, is upset by a recent business decision made by the start-up. The plan is to transform many of the employees currently working in head office into teleworkers—requiring them to perform their jobs from home via the Internet. The employees are concerned because the collective agreement provides certain corporate benefits only to those employees who are "working at corporate headquarters." In adopting this cost-saving measure, the chief operating officer (COO) of the Internet start-up has relied on a labour relations board decision that defined "headquarters" as the main office, or centre of control, in any organization. The COO of the start-up agrees with the board that the main office is rightly considered the headquarters. The employees, however, argue that the Internet has decentralized the corporate structure in a way that makes the designation of headquarters meaningless; therefore, they are entitled to the benefits provided for in the collective agreement whether they are located in the corporate office tower or are connected to it through the Internet. Is the board bound to follow its previous decision? Create an argument on behalf of the employees indicating why it should not be bound to follow the previous decision. Explain your reasoning.

5. Mike Ladd was hired as a permanent express clerk for Dubb Express. After two years in that position, he was given the opportunity to move temporarily into the higher position of a "grade 2 dispatcher." After two years, he was given the position on a permanent basis. Two years later, Dubb Express merged with the Antipop Consortium, and Mike's grade 2 dispatcher position was temporarily eliminated. Rather than being laid off, Mike wanted to bump into a grade 1 dispatcher position. Upon making this request, Mike was told that, although he was at least two years more senior than either of the two grade 1 dispatchers, he was less qualified for that position than either of the people who occupied it. The job classification scheme in Dubb Express's collective agreement is determined by the employee's level of qualification, which is based solely on the employee's daily performance as a dispatcher. Qualification is measured as a ratio of the number of drivers that the employee is capable of supervising on a shift divided by the number of dispatching errors made during that shift. The collective agreement in place specifically gives Dubb Express the right to decide bumping requests on the basis of qualification. However, the collective agreement also contains a clause that recognizes various seniority rights, including "the right of a senior person to bump a more junior person." As a business manager at Dubb Express, you are asked to decide whether Mike should be allowed to bump one of the less senior dispatchers. Support your position. Does the concept of seniority include bumping-down when laid off?

6. Local 861 has brought a grievance against ESPO Broadcasting on behalf of one of its former employees, Addey Farberino. The grievance alleges that employees who had resigned during the term of the first collective agreement, but before ratification of a retroactive wage increase, were entitled to the wage increase recently issued by ESPO. The union alleges that it had proposed specific entitlement of retroactive pay to anyone who had been an employee under the first collective agreement, but that the proposal had somehow been dropped during the course of negotiations. The union claims that

it had allowed the specific proposal to be dropped because it had relied on a general presumption of retroactivity for wages and benefits. Nothing in the collective agreement explicitly contemplates this presumption. What position should management at ESPO take?

7. Khalil was transferred to a remote workplace contrary to the collective agreement between his union and his employer, Self Scientific Inc. Khalil filed a grievance. Although Self Scientific is prepared to reimburse Khalil for automobile and parking expenses, it argues that an arbitrator does not have the authority to provide any further remedies, and therefore is not in a position to order payment of salary in lieu of travel time. Does Self Scientific's argument have any merit? Is the arbitrator limited to remedies set out in the terms of a collective agreement?

8. Peter & Harvey Furs and Local 275 had previously entered into a collective agreement that explicitly prohibited strikes and lockouts before the end of the calendar year. However, on July 30, the union applied to the labour relations board to request a strike vote, referring to the labour legislation that stated: "Employers are prohibited from imposing conditions in contracts of employment which would restrain employees from exercising rights under this Act."

   Peter & Harvey has countered by seeking an order to prevent the strike vote by its employees. To support its position, it made reference to another section of the relevant legislation which provides that: "This section does not affect agreements between employer and union."

   Prepare an argument for the resolution of these two apparently contradictory provisions, first arguing on behalf of the employer and then on behalf of the union. Explain your reasoning in each case.

9. Randall's Motorcycle Shop employed the 208 members of LOCO 666. Until recently, every union member was employed on a full-time basis. Unfortunately, due to financial difficulties, Randall determined that he would have to unilaterally change the status of some employees to part-time to remain in business. In announcing his intention to the union, Randall stated that those employees with seniority would be given the opportunity to bump junior persons into the part-time positions. When they heard about these arrangements, several unruly junior employees refused to accept part-time status and threatened Randall with physical harm if he refused to reinstate everyone to a full-time position. Many of them also left work in the middle of their shift. Randall wants a declaration that those employees who left in mid-shift engaged in an illegal strike. In turn, the union is seeking a declaration that Randall had imposed an illegal lockout. Your business consulting firm has been called upon to mediate this dispute in an attempt to find a resolution without having to take matters before the labour relations board. You have wisely chosen to meet with each of the parties separately before making any recommendations. What will you say to each

party? How will you try to reach some sort of consensus?

10. You work as a senior manager at General Construction Company. You recently hired two members of the Plumbers Union, with whom your company has a collective agreement, to work on a construction project. After being hired, the plumbers were told that there was a picket line at the work site related to one of the other employers on the job. The two plumbers decided not to cross the picket line out of respect for the striking workers. Nothing in the collective agreement between the plumbers and your company authorized the plumbers to honour the picket lines established by other trade unions. Can you do anything to get the plumbers back to work?

11. Robots Inc has lawfully locked out its unionized factory workers after exhausting negotiation and conciliation procedures prescribed by the applicable labour relations statute. Despite the lockout, Robots Inc has been able to continue supplying machinery to large automotive manufacturers, largely through accumulated inventory. These car makers are the biggest customers of Robots Inc. The workers are furious that they have been locked out because they thought that their position during negotiations was quite reasonable. They are also getting desperate because they have been locked out for six months and are facing severe financial hardship. Picketing has not proven effective in getting media attention or in pressuring Robots Inc to come back to the negotiating table. The workers want to get their message out and want to get media attention to their plight. However, they want to do so in a lawful manner. What course of action would you suggest?

12. You are the manager of a giant movie theatre complex. Your projectionists are engaged in a lawful strike and are picketing regarding compensation issues. Projectionists have historically received high pay because of the danger of fire in the projection booth and because the projection equipment was sophisticated and required special training to operate. In recent years, however, projectionists' salaries have declined in light of the fact that modern projection booths are safe and projection equipment requires only the push of a button to operate. Fortunately, you planned for the possibility of a strike several years ago. You employed enough skilled managers that you could continue to operate your theatre with no disruption whatsoever. The projectionists have recently become very frustrated with the apparent ineffectiveness of their strike and picketing. In the past week, the picketers have been involved in three altercations with customers. One picketer punched and spit on a customer. That same picketer was caught circulating pamphlets which claimed that Mr Flick, the owner of the movie theatre, had once been convicted for using unsafe chemicals in popcorn to cause people to buy more of it. This statement was absolutely false. Explain what you might be able to do in this situation and in what forum you would seek to have the dispute resolved.

Weblinks

General Information

Department of Human Resources and Skills Development: Services for Business www. hrsdc.gc.ca/en/gateways/business/menu.shtml#hrm

This site offers a wide variety of resources, links, and information for businesses. Areas covered include collective bargaining, workplace equity, labour standards, and occupational health and safety, among many others.

Collective Bargaining

Office of Collective Bargaining Information www.gov.on.ca/LAB/english/lr/index.html

This office collects, analyzes, and distributes information on Ontario's collective bargaining relationships. Its site includes comprehensive information for small, medium, and large workplaces.

Collective Bargaining—Alberta Labour Relations www.gov.ab.ca/alrb/guide/4guidechap.htm

This page provides a guide to collective bargaining in accordance with applicable legislation. Topics include bargaining, strikes, lockouts, picketing, and dispute resolution measures.

Collective Agreements

Collective Agreements and Rates of Pay www.tbs-sct.gc.ca/pubs_pol/hrpubs/hr_941_e.html

This Treasury Board of Canada Secretariat site provides links to publications and policies governing the collective agreements and rates of pay for many group-specific agreements, and contains the adjustment appendix to PSAC collective agreements.

CIRB—Unlawful Strikes and Lockouts www.cirb-ccri.gc.ca/publications/info/01-06_e.asp

This information circular prepared by the Canada Industrial Relations Board provides information to employees, trade unions, and employers on unlawful strikes and lockouts to help them understand the board's processes.

Grievance Arbitration

Model Clause on Grievance Arbitration www.caut.ca/en/services/collectivebargaining/modelclauses/mc_grievarb.asp/URL

The CAUT-ACCPU provides a model clause dealing with arbitration in the collective bargaining process.

Collective Agreement Arbitration Bureau www.labour.gov.bc.ca/caab

This bureau, which provides personnel to resolve grievances between employers and trade unions during the term of a collective agreement, offers information on its site.

Industrial Conflict

LRB—Strikes, Lockouts, and Picketing www.lrb.bc.ca/bulletins/part5.htm

This bulletin from British Columbia's labour relations board provides information on strikes, lockouts, and picketing under the *Labour Relations Code*.

ADDITIONAL RESOURCES FOR CHAPTER 27 ON THE COMPANION WEBSITE

(www.pearsoned.ca/mcinnes)

In addition to self-test multiple-choice, true-false, and short essay questions (all with immediate feedback), three additional Cases and Problems (with suggested answers), and links to useful Web destinations, the Companion Website provides the following resources for Chapter 27:

- Business Decision 27W—Retroactive Pay to Former Employees

Provincial Material

- **British Columbia:** Essential Services, Union Certification and Decertification, Collective Bargaining, Unfair Labour Practices, Mediation and Arbitration, Strikes, Lockouts and Picketing
- **Alberta:** Labour Relations
- **Manitoba and Saskatchewan:** Labour Relations Boards
- **Ontario:** Public Sector and Essential Services, Labour Relations

Wal-Mart *v* The Unions

Wal-Mart is one of the most astonishing success stories in business history. Sam and Bud Walton opened their first store in Rogers, Arkansas, in 1962. A decade later, the company began to expand when it acquired 16 Mohr-Value stores throughout the United States. The empire has been growing ever since. In the United States alone, it controls over 3000 stores, directly employs 1.5 million people, and accounts for $8.90 out of every $100 that Americans spend on retail. No longer content to dominate the American market, the company has recently moved into Mexico, Puerto Rico, the United Kingdom, Brazil, Argentina, China, and South Korea. Wal-Mart came to Canada in 1994 when it bought up 122 Woolco stores. It currently operates more than 250 stores, with over 70 000 employees, across Canada. It plans to add another 30 outlets each year.

As a result of its continuous growth, Wal-Mart has become the world's largest corporation. In 2004, it boasted sales of $256 billion and profits of $8.9 billion. And while Sam and Bud Walton are no longer alive, their heirs include five of the thirteen richest people in the world, each worth about $18 billion.

Not everyone is impressed. Some people allege that Wal-Mart has built its fortune by exploiting its workers. The solution, they say, is unionization. They believe that if the company is required to deal with its employees collectively, rather than individually, then those employees will receive better treatment. That movement is especially strong in Canada. While only about 12 percent of the American work force was unionized in 2004, the figure in this country was closer to 29 percent. Union organizers hope that there is strength in those numbers.

Of course, as is often true in labour law, the situation is somewhat more complicated than it might first seem. Both sides are motivated by a variety of factors. Until very recently, Wal-Mart was almost entirely successful in keeping unions out of its stores. The company says that the explanation is perfectly innocent: Its employees do not want to be unionized. Since they already enjoy "open-door" access to management, they do not need union representatives to speak on their behalf. And because they already enjoy better treatment than their unionized counterparts at other stores, there is little chance that they would receive anything new in exchange for their payment of union dues. On a different level, however, Wal-Mart's reasons for resisting unionization may be somewhat more selfish. The company has prospered, at least in part, because it has always exercised complete control over its operations, and because it has always dealt directly with individual employees. Why would it now be willing to give up some of that control to a union? "If it ain't broke, don't fix it."

The situation on the other side of the table is similarly ambiguous. Union advocates undoubtedly believe that they can help improve working conditions at Wal-Mart. Their focus, however, is on the collective, rather than on the individual. They continually look for weak spots in Wal-Mart's defences, hoping that if they can unionize one store, the rest will follow. But of course, as in any war, casualties inevitably occur along the way. A recent episode provides a chilling illustration. The UFCW appeared to win an historic victory in August of 2004 when it was certified as the bargaining agent for employees at the Wal-Mart store in Jonquière, Quebec. The union eagerly began negotiating with the company in the expectation of creating a *collective agreement*. Within six months, however, Wal-Mart announced that it was impossible, given the union's demands, to create an agreement that would allow the store to be run "in an efficient and profitable manner." A short time later, Wal-Mart closed its Jonquière outlet and put two hundred people out of work. The UFCW rejected the company's official explanation for the closure. It saw the move instead as a threat to employees at other Wal-Mart stores: If you unionize, you will suffer.

As you will have gathered by now, the legal system plays a significant role in balancing the interests of the various parties: unions, corporations, employees, and consumers. For instance, the UFCW has been able to become the certified bargaining agent for workers at several Wal-Mart stores in Quebec (including the one in Jonquière) partially because the legislation in that province gives effect to *membership drives*.

A recent attempt to unionize employees at the Wal-Mart in Thompson, Manitoba, demonstrate how the laws in that province similarly support unionization, at least in some respects. In contrast to its counterpart in Quebec, the Manitoba Labour Relations Board will not automatically give effect to a membership drive unless at least 65 percent of employees have signed on. If that target is not met, the board will grant *certification* only if a majority of workers cast their votes in favour of unionization during a *secret ballot*. Unions do, however, enjoy some advantages during the process leading up to that vote. For instance, while representatives from UFCW were free to provide information to the workers at the Thompson Wal-Mart, the company and the store's managers had to remain virtually silent.

In the final analysis, that difference may not have mattered to the situation in Thompson. The employees voted 61–54 against unionization. In other circumstances, however, the law may play a decisive role. And it seems likely that those circumstances will eventually arise. The unions will never stop trying to unionize the world's largest company.

Questions to Consider

1. Unionization is often discussed as if unions, companies, and employees are the only interested parties. But, of course, the issue affects the broader community as well. While it is sometimes difficult to draw a meaningful distinction between an employee and a consumer (because the same person may be both), unionization may be favourable to one, but not the other. Discuss that proposition.

2. Wal-Mart avoided unionization in Jonquière by simply closing its store in that town. From the company's perspective, that would seem to be an easy solution. Does an employer always enjoy the option of walking away from the bargaining table whenever it disagrees with a bargaining agent's demands? Explain your answer.

3. It was easier for the UFCW to achieve certification in Jonquière than in Thompson, partly because Quebec's laws readily recognize the results of membership drives, whereas Manitoba's laws often require secret ballots. What are the advantages and disadvantages of membership drives and secret ballots?

Video Resource: "Wal-Mart Doc" *The National* (7 August 2003).

Additional Resources

CBC News: In-Depth Wal-Mart   www.cbc.ca/news/background/walmart
This page on the CBC's website provides a brief history of Wal-Mart, including highlights of the efforts to unionize the store's workers.

Wal-Mart Workers Canada   www.walmartworkerscanada.com
This website, which belongs to the UFCW rather than to Wal-Mart, provides news and opinions regarding the unionization drive.

Terry's Point: Wal-Mart Canada Sends a Message to the Unions   www.rightpoint.org/wal-mart.html
This website questions the extent to which unionization would benefit Wal-Mart employees, and comments on the advantages and disadvantages of membership drives and secret ballots.

MFL Labour Law   www.mfl.mb.ca/new/new2_lablaw.htm
This website, which belongs to the Manitoba Federation of Labour, suggests reasons why certification should be based on membership drives, rather than secret ballots.

Human Resources and Skills Development: Trade Union Application for Certification   www.hrsdc.gc.ca/asp/gateway.asp?hr=/en/lp/spila/clli/irlc/07trade_union_application_for_certification.shtml&hs=lzl
This website, belonging to the federal government, provides a summary of the certification rules that apply in the various jurisdictions across the country.

Wikipedia: Wal-Mart   **http://en.wikipedia.org/wiki/Wal-mart#History**
This page from the *Wikipedia Internet Encyclopedia* provides detailed information about Wal-Mart.

28W Doing Business in a Global Economy

CHAPTER 28W ON DOING BUSINESS IN A GLOBAL ECONOMY CAN BE FOUND ON THE COMPANION WEBSITE.

www.pearsoned.ca/mcinnes

Index